AEGEAN PREHISTORY · A REVIEW

AEGEAN PREHISTORY

A REVIEW

Edited by

TRACEY CULLEN

American Journal of Archaeology Supplement 1
Archaeological Institute of America
Boston

Publication of this volume was made possible in part
by the generous financial support of the Institute for Aegean Prehistory
and the Louise Taft Semple Fund of the University of Cincinnati.

© 2001 by the Archaeological Institute of America

Cover illustration: Treasury of Atreus at Mycenae, reproduced from H. Schliemann, *Mycenae:
A Narrative of Researches and Discoveries at Mycenae and Tiryns* (New York 1878) pl. 4.

♾ The paper in this book meets the guidelines for permanence and durability of the Committee
on Production Guidelines for Book Longevity of the Council on Library Resources.

Cover design by Peter Holm, Sterling Hill Productions
Set in ITC New Baskerville by Asterisk Typographics
Printed in the United States of America by Sheridan Books

10 09 08 07   5 4 3

Library of Congress Cataloging-in-Publication Data

Aegean prehistory : a review / Tracey Cullen, editor.
p. cm. — (American journal of archaeology. Supplement, ISSN 1532-5326 ; 1)
Includes bibliographical references and index.
ISBN 0-9609042-4-7 (cloth : alk. paper) — ISBN 0-9609042-5-5 (pbk. : alk. paper)
1. Civilization, Aegean. 2. Bronze age—Aegean Sea Region. 3. Aegean Sea
Region—Antiquities. I. Cullen, Tracey, 1950– II. Series.
DF220.A275 2001   939'.101—dc21   2001018817

Contents

Contributors

STELIOS ANDREOU   Department of Archaeology, Aristotle University of Thessaloniki

TRACEY CULLEN   American School of Classical Studies at Athens, Princeton

JACK L. DAVIS   Department of Classics, University of Cincinnati

MICHAEL FOTIADIS   Department of History and Archaeology, University of Ioannina

KOSTAS KOTSAKIS   Department of Archaeology, Aristotle University of Thessaloniki

PAUL REHAK   Department of Classical Studies, Duke University

CURTIS RUNNELS   Department of Archaeology, Boston University

JEREMY B. RUTTER   Department of Classics, Dartmouth College

CYNTHIA W. SHELMERDINE   Department of Classics, University of Texas at Austin

IOULIA TZONOU-HERBST   Department of Classics, University of Cincinnati

L. VANCE WATROUS   Department of Art History, State University of New York at Buffalo

AARON D. WOLPERT   Department of Classics, University of Cincinnati

JOHN G. YOUNGER   Department of Classical Studies, Duke University

Illustrations

Tables

Preface and Acknowledgments

With the accelerating pace of research and field-work in Aegean prehistory, it has become increasingly difficult to stay abreast of recent discoveries and scholarly trends. The seven critical overviews of Aegean prehistory reprinted here from the *American Journal of Archaeology*—each newly updated with an addendum—provide detailed syntheses of developments in the field over the past few decades. In contrast to the brief summaries that appear annually in the *Bulletin de correspondance hellénique* and *Archaeological Reports*, the review articles in this volume offer extensive discussion of current field projects, artifact and textual studies, and trends in archaeological thought and practice. The full documentation found in the footnotes bears witness to the diversity and sheer number of publications on Aegean prehistory that have appeared recently.

The authors present a wealth of evidence that is critical to understanding cultural change in the prehistoric Aegean. At the same time, they articulate and assess the history of scholarship, research problems, and controversies central to the study of different regions within this part of the Mediterranean. Viewed as a whole, the reviews constitute a snapshot of the discipline of Aegean prehistory at the end of the 20th century, clarifying questions of interest, research goals, and analytical procedures.

The review articles were originally published in *AJA* between 1992 and 1998, and are reprinted here in the order in which they appeared. The addenda updating the reviews were written in 1999 and, in most cases, modified in 2000. The series is intended to continue in *AJA*, but the first seven installments can stand alone as a unified summary of research into the prehistory of mainland Greece, Crete, and the Aegean islands, from the Palaeolithic to the end of the Bronze Age. The background and scope of the reviews are discussed in an introductory essay, in which the historical development and current status of the field of Aegean prehistory are also considered. The essay concludes with an appendix of relevant research tools, directed primarily at students and scholars who are not Aegean prehistorians themselves.

In the course of the seven years over which the reviews were first published, a degree of stylistic drift inevitably occurred in matters of terminology and capitalization. Each addendum has been edited in conformity with the primary article. Cross-references within the addenda are to page numbers in the present volume, not to the original *AJA* article. In addition to abbreviations specified at the beginning of each review article, standard *AJA* abbreviations are used, listed below on pages xv–xvii. References to classical literature employ the abbreviations found in *The Oxford Classical Dictionary*[3] (Oxford 1996).

The original publication of the Review of Aegean Prehistory series in *AJA* was supported by generous subventions from the Institute for Aegean Prehistory. The Louise Taft Semple Fund of the University of Cincinnati and the Institute for Aegean Prehistory provided partial funding for publication of this volume, which the authors and I gratefully acknowledge.

Many individuals have contributed substantially to the creation of *AJA*'s first supplementary volume. Fred S. Kleiner initiated and promoted the review series while he was Editor-in-Chief at *AJA*, and I owe a personal debt to Fred for many good years of collaboration. The current Editor-in-Chief, R. Bruce Hitchner, also enthusiastically supported the venture. Special thanks go to Mark Kurtz, Managing Editor at *AJA*, for coordinating efforts toward publication in innumerable ways. I am also grateful to Carol Stein, Eleni Hasaki, Marni Blake, and Kevin Mullen for their expert editorial assistance, and to Leslie Sanborn and her colleagues at Asterisk Typographics. Kay Banning gamely produced the index to the book under great pressures of scheduling, and Peter Holm designed the cover, transforming a vague idea into an elegant statement.

My sincere appreciation goes to the authors of the reviews, for their dedication to the concept of the series, and for their patience and good humor throughout the editorial process: Jack Davis (with Ioulia Tzonou-Herbst and Aaron Wolpert), Jerry Rutter, Vance Watrous, Curtis Runnels, Stelios Andreou, Mihalis Fotiadis, Kostas Kotsakis, Cynthia Shelmerdine, Paul Rehak, and John Younger. Many of them also read and commented on the introductory essay, for which I am especially grateful. My family offered generous support on many fronts, from editing the introduction to evaluating cover designs. Mehmet Rona also provided encouragement, and continues to be a source of inspiration and energy in my life. Finally, I thank Laurie Talalay for her help and advice at every stage of this book's production and, most importantly, for her incomparable friendship.

Tracey Cullen

Abbreviations

AA	Archäologischer Anzeiger
AAA	Αρχαιολογικά Ανάλεκτα εξ Αθηνών (Athens Annals of Archaeology)
AbhBerl	Abhandlungen der Deutschen Akademie der Wissenschaften zu Berlin
ActaArch	Acta archaeologica [Copenhagen]
ActaArchLov	Acta archaeologica Lovanensia
AfO	Archiv für Orientforschung
AIIN	Annali dell'Istituto italiano di numismatica
AJA	American Journal of Archaeology
AJP	American Journal of Philology
AM	Mitteilungen des Deutschen Archäologischen Instituts, Athenische Abteilung
AmerAnt	American Antiquity
AnatSt	Anatolian Studies
AntCl	L'Antiquité classique
AntCr	Antichità cretesi
AntJ	The Antiquaries Journal
AntK	Antike Kunst
AntW	Antike Welt. Zeitschrift für Archäologie und Kulturgeschichte
AnzWien	Anzeiger. Österreichische Akademie der Wissenschaften, Wien, Philologisch-historische Klasse
AR	Archaeological Reports (supplement to *JHS*)
ArchDelt	Αρχαιολογικόν Δελτίον
ArcheologiaWar	Archeologia. Rocznik Instytutu historii kultury materialnej Polskiej akademii nauk [Warsaw]
ArchEph	Αρχαιολογική Εφημερίς
ArchHom	F. Matz and H.G. Buchholz eds., *Archaeologia Homerica* (Göttingen 1967–)
ArchKorrBl	Archäologisches Korrespondenzblatt
ArchNews	Archaeological News
ArtB	The Art Bulletin
ASAtene	Annuario della Scuola archeologica di Atene e delle Missioni italiane in Oriente
BABesch	Bulletin antieke beschaving. Annual Papers on Classical Archaeology
BalkSt	Balkan Studies
BAR	British Archaeological Reports
BAR-IS	British Archaeological Reports, International Series
BASOR	Bulletin of the American Schools of Oriental Research
BCH	Bulletin de correspondance hellénique
BdA	Bollettino d'arte
BEFAR	Bibliothèque des Écoles françaises d'Athènes et de Rome
BerRGK	Bericht der Römisch-Germanischen Kommission
BIALond	Bulletin of the Institute of Archaeology of the University of London
BibO	Bibliotheca orientalis
BICS	Bulletin of the Institute of Classical Studies of the University of London
BMOP	British Museum Occasional Paper
BSA	Annual of the British School at Athens
CAH	Cambridge Ancient History

CAJ   Cambridge Archaeological Journal
CMS   Corpus der minoischen und mykenischen Siegel
CR   Classical Review
CRAI   Comptes rendus des séances de l'Académie des inscriptions et belles-lettres [Paris]
CretChron   Κρητικά Χρονικά
CurrAnthr   Current Anthropology
CW   Classical World
DialArch   Dialoghi di archeologia
DossPar   Histoire et archéologie. Les dossiers [Paris]
EchCl   Echos du monde classique. Classical Views
Ergon   Το Εργον της εν Αθήναις Αρχαιολογικής Εταιρείας
EtCret   Études crétoises
Franchthi   Excavations at Franchthi Cave, Greece (Bloomington 1987–)
GORILA   L. Godart and J.-P. Olivier, *Recueil des inscriptions en Linéaire A* (Paris 1976–1985)
GRBS   Greek, Roman, and Byzantine Studies
IEJ   Israel Exploration Journal
IJNA   International Journal of Nautical Archaeology and Underwater Exploration
ILN   The Illustrated London News
JAOS   Journal of the American Oriental Society
JAS   Journal of Archaeological Science
JdI   Jahrbuch des Deutschen Archäologischen Instituts
JEA   Journal of Egyptian Archaeology
JFA   Journal of Field Archaeology
JHS   Journal of Hellenic Studies
JIES   Journal of Indo-European Studies
JMA   Journal of Mediterranean Archaeology
JNES   Journal of Near Eastern Studies
JRGZM   Jahrbuch des Römisch-germanischen Zentralmuseums, Mainz
JSAH   Journal of the Society of Architectural Historians
MASCAJ   MASCA Journal. Museum Applied Science Center for Archaeology, University Museum,
               University of Pennsylvania
MeditArch   Mediterranean Archaeology. Australian and New Zealand Journal for the Archaeology of the
               Mediterranean World
MEFRA   Mélanges de l'École française de Rome, Antiquité
*MMR*²   M.P. Nilsson, *The Minoan-Mycenaean Religion*, 2nd ed. (Lund 1950)
MonAnt   Monumenti antichi
MüJb   Münchener Jahrbuch der bildenden Kunst
NatGeogRes   National Geographic Research
OA   Oriens antiquus
OJA   Oxford Journal of Archaeology
ÖJh   Jahreshefte des Österreichischen Archäologischen Instituts in Wien
OpArch   Opuscula archaeologica
OpAth   Opuscula atheniensia
OWAN   Old World Archaeology Newsletter
PCPS   Proceedings of the Cambridge Philological Society
PM   A. Evans, *The Palace of Minos* (London 1921–1935)

PN	C.W. Blegen and M. Rawson eds., *The Palace of Nestor* (Princeton 1966–1973)
PPS	Proceedings of the Prehistoric Society
Prakt	Πρακτικά της εν Αθήναις Αρχαιολογικής Εταιρείας
PraktAkAth	Πρακτικά της Ακαδημίας Αθηνών
PZ	Prähistorische Zeitschrift
RA	Revue archéologique
RAssyr	Revue d'assyriologie et d'archéologie orientale
RDAC	Report of the Department of Antiquities, Cyprus
REA	Revue des études anciennes
REG	Revue des études grecques
RendLinc	Atti dell'Accademia nazionale dei Lincei. Rendiconti
RendNap	Rendiconti dell'Accademia di archeologia, lettere e belle arti, Napoli
RivFil	Rivista di filologia e d'istruzione classica
RPhil	Revue de philologie, de littérature et d'histoire anciennes
RStLig	Rivista di studi liguri
SAOC	Studies in Ancient Oriental Civilizations
SIMA	Studies in Mediterranean Archaeology
SIMA-PB	Studies in Mediterranean Archaeology and Literature, Pocketbook
SkrAth	Skrifter utgivna av Svenska Institutet i Athen
SMEA	Studi micenei ed egeo-anatolici
SwCyprusExp	The Swedish Cyprus Expedition (Stockholm 1934–)
TUAS	Temple University Aegean Symposium
UgaritF	Ugarit-Forschungen. Internationales Jahrbuch für die Altertumskunde Syrien-Palästinas
WorldArch	World Archaeology
ZfA	Zeitschrift für Archäologie
ZfE	Zeitschrift für Ethnologie
ZivaAnt	Ziva antika. Antiquité vivante

Introduction:
Voices and Visions of Aegean Prehistory

TRACEY CULLEN

There stands the great hill of ruins, forming for realistic contemplation a phenomenon quite as unique as the "Sacred Ilios" for poetical feeling. . . . This excavation has opened for the studies of the archaeologist a completely new theatre—like a world by itself. Here begins an entirely new science. . . . And now the treasure-digger has become a scholar, who, with long and earnest study, has compared the facts of his experience, as well as the statements of historians and geographers, with the legendary traditions of poets and mythologers.

—Rudolf Virchow, 1881

With these remarks, Virchow introduces Heinrich Schliemann's *Ilios: The City and Country of the Trojans* and salutes the beginning of a new discipline—"a completely new theatre"—of Aegean prehistory.[1] Schliemann's excavations between 1870 and 1890, first at Troy and subsequently at Mycenae, Orchomenos, and Tiryns, brought to light a material reality behind the Homeric poems and established the existence of a preclassical culture that continues to fascinate us today. Although Schliemann's excavation methods have been compared to digging potatoes, and his character and motives assailed from several directions,[2] he stands as the nearly mythical ancestor of the field of Aegean prehistory. From its origins as the handmaiden of philology—a means by which to establish the veracity of Homeric texts—Aegean prehistory has developed over the 20th century into a distinctive area of archaeological research with a variety of theoretical and methodological concerns.

The past few decades, in particular, have seen a dramatic reorientation and expansion of goals and methods as well as a flood of new fieldwork in the Aegean. The effort to elucidate cultural processes in specific contexts and to evaluate critically the intellectual foundations and practices of the field has occupied many prehistorians. Interest in the sociopolitical and economic dimensions of past societies situated within a broad landscape has spurred a proliferation of intensive surface surveys. Excavations have continued apace as have studies of materials and texts, aided by a battery of scientific techniques. Our understanding of the earliest prehistory of the Aegean has advanced considerably and we more fully appreciate the complexities of social evolution and the legacy of interaction among Crete, the other islands, mainland Greece, and the wider Mediterranean world. The seven reviews of Aegean prehistory presented here convey the richness and diversity of current approaches to Aegean prehistory. At the same time, they offer a close look at the wealth of detail acquired about particular sites, sequences, and their articulation—details critical to building meaningful syntheses of local and regional change in the Aegean.

In the following pages, I briefly summarize the reviews, and then place them in historical context, tracing the evolution of Aegean prehistory from the 19th century to the present. The current status of the discipline is also assessed, with attention to political and academic constraints that affect research and fieldwork in the Aegean. Relevant research tools are noted in an appendix.

HISTORY AND SCOPE OF THE REVIEWS

The reviews of Aegean prehistory (RAP I–VII) collected in this volume were originally published in the *American Journal of Archaeology* between 1992 and 1998. The idea for the series was first conceived in 1991 by Fred S. Kleiner, Editor-in-Chief of *AJA* at that time, as part of an effort to expand the series of Newsletters in the journal. As he, Jeremy Rutter, and I discussed the idea, it immediately became apparent that the format of the *AJA* Newsletters, with their focus on recent bibliography, conferences, and discoveries in the field over the past year, was not well suited to presenting the work of Aegean prehistori-

---

[1] H. Schliemann, *Ilios: The City and Country of the Trojans* (London 1881) xiv, xvi.

[2] See, e.g., D.A. Traill, *Excavating Schliemann: Collected Papers on Schliemann* (Atlanta 1993); Traill, *Schliemann of Troy: Treasure and Deceit* (New York 1995); H. Duchêne, *Golden Treasures of Troy: The Dream of Heinrich Schliemann*, trans. J. Legatt (New York 1996); and S.H. Allen, *Finding the Walls*

---

of Troy: Frank Calvert and Heinrich Schliemann at Hisarlik (Berkeley 1999). Others, however, have long credited Schliemann with the beginning of modern archaeological field methods, e.g., C.W. Blegen, "Preclassical Greece," *Studies in the Arts and Architecture* (University of Pennsylvania Bicentennial Conference, Philadelphia 1941) 1–3.

ans. What was needed, we felt, were broader syntheses covering a larger segment of time and organized around questions central to research in a particular area. To oversee this project, a committee was formed of the prehistorians on the *AJA* Advisory Board: John Bennet, John Cherry, Jack Davis, Jeremy Rutter, and Joseph Shaw. As Associate Editor of *AJA*, I served as chair, and together we selected topics and invited colleagues to provide critical overviews of developments in prehistoric archaeology in the Aegean over roughly the past 20 years. The result was the series of reviews reprinted here.

The choice of topics (and authors) for the RAP series thus represents the consensus of a small group of Aegean prehistorians; others may have chosen differently. We decided to focus first on the prehistory of mainland Greece, Crete, and the other Aegean islands. Even within this restricted geographical range, many subjects of potential interest have not been covered, such as the Neolithic of central and southern Greece, although the appearance of recent syntheses and collected volumes on the Neolithic made the inclusion of this topic less urgent (see Appendix, p. 18).

The reviews are reprinted here in the order in which they appeared in *AJA*. Davis (1992) initiates the series with a review of research on the Aegean islands (excluding Crete and the Saronic Gulf islands). Rutter (1993) next provides an overview of recent work pertaining to the prepalatial Bronze Age of southern and central Greece. The third review (1994), by L. Vance Watrous, summarizes the archaeology of Crete from earliest prehistory through the Protopalatial period. Curtis Runnels (1995) outlines the history of scholarship on Stone Age Greece, looking particularly at current controversies concerning the Palaeolithic and Mesolithic. Stelios Andreou, Michael Fotiadis, and Kostas Kotsakis (1996) undertake a summary of the state of research on the prehistory of northern Greece, an area perhaps better known to European prehistorians than to most Aegeanists. The palatial Bronze Age of mainland Greece is the subject of the sixth review (1997), by Cynthia W. Shelmerdine. Paul Rehak and John G. Younger (1998) continue from where Watrous left off, surveying developments in Crete from the Neopalatial period to the end of the Bronze Age.

The review articles offer more than simple summaries of research. All are informed by the authors'

assessments of the relative importance of trends they detect in each area of study. Indeed, it is this aspect of the reviews that makes them a powerful research tool for the detailed exploration of Aegean themes. For every area, chronology is still in the process of being worked out, not as an end in itself but as a framework within which social, economic, and ideological change can be investigated. A detailed apparatus of footnotes is provided that not only highlights the immense number of publications that have appeared in Aegean prehistory over the past 20 years, but also serves as a point of departure for students and professionals wishing to learn more about a given subject. The authors themselves encourage further work by pinpointing questions and problems of interpretation that remain contentious and by noting current lacunae in exploration and data. The reviews by their nature are ephemeral: conclusions are provisional, intended to be challenged or modified as new finds and ways of looking at questions emerge.

Among those who urged us to reprint the reviews, many cited the lack of comprehensive or up-to-date syntheses suitable for use in the classroom as well as the convenience of a collected set of essays, particularly for those who do not subscribe to *AJA*. Reprinting the articles also gave the authors the opportunity to attach an addendum, in which they update bibliography, discuss recent findings, and address any critical responses to the original article that may have appeared.

The reviews were written primarily for an audience of Aegean prehistorians and graduate students. Colleagues in related disciplines may also find them useful, however, as may those who teach undergraduates, especially if supplemented with other syntheses such as Dickinson's *The Aegean Bronze Age* (see Appendix). Classic texts such as Vermeule's *Greece in the Bronze Age* (1964), Taylour's *The Mycenaeans* (1964), and Hood's *The Minoans* (1971) are understandably out of date now and, as Davis has noted, their continued use in classrooms has tended to fossilize migrationist and diffusionist models pervasive several decades ago.[3] The reviews presented here are more specialized syntheses than these volumes, intended to help scholars and students stay abreast of recent discoveries and intellectual trends in Aegean prehistory. The series is expected to continue in *AJA*, with three additional reviews commissioned at the present time of writing, on prehistoric western Ana-

---

[3] J.L. Davis, "An Aegean Prehistory Textbook for the 1990s?" *AJA* 99 (1995) 732, in a review of O. Dickinson's *The Aegean Bronze Age* (Cambridge 1994). Although Tay-

lour's volume was originally published in 1964, a subsequent edition (London 1983) was much revised.

tolia, the relations between western Europe and the prehistoric Aegean, and the rise of intensive surface survey in the Aegean.

OVERVIEW OF RAP I—VII

The reviews summarize research across a wide geographical and chronological expanse. Each author has approached his or her topic somewhat differently, as dictated by personal interests and also the nature of work carried out in the region or time period examined. The questions structuring research on the Palaeolithic of Thessaly or the Neolithic of Epirus, relatively new areas of research, are necessarily different from those pertaining to the fall of the Mycenaean palaces, about which scholars have written for a century. It is thus worthwhile to begin with the reviews themselves, looking particularly at the themes and questions selected by each author as important.

RAP I

Davis presents a summary of the recent groundswell of work on the Aegean islands, a region that, as he notes, had long been considered the backwater of Greek prehistory. As recently as 1964, only three settlements (Phylakopi, Thera, and Kastri) had been systematically excavated, in contrast to nearly 2,000 known (and often plundered) graves.[4] The cultural sequence at Phylakopi, excavated at the end of the 19th century, was generally taken to represent the Aegean islands as a whole. While Neolithic remains had been recognized on a few islands, none had been fully documented.

The picture today has changed radically. Many more sites and islands have been systematically explored, with the result that not only do we know much more about cultural sequences and regional variation in the Bronze Age, but the Neolithic has been better documented, and the first evidence for Middle Palaeolithic and Mesolithic occupation of the islands has appeared. While systematic work on individual islands is critical in building a firm relative chronology and refining our picture of local variation, Davis emphasizes a research agenda based on a wider Aegean perspective. The questions he frames concern issues of earliest colonization of the islands (the timing, conditions fostering settlement, and the role of exchange),[5]

the relationships between Crete and the other islands in the Middle Bronze Age and early Late Bronze Age, and the role of the islands within the Mycenaean empire. This broad perspective, looking not at a single site, island, or even group of islands, allows him to pose questions of wider significance: Why were the islands generally inhabited so much later than the adjacent mainland, despite their intermediary position between Anatolia and Greece and clear evidence for early visits? What was the nature of habitation in different regions of the Aegean? And, in terms of relations with Crete and Mycenaean Greece, how can we measure political control in artifactual variability?

Following a general discussion of such questions, Davis summarizes recent scholarship for the islands. In an addendum coauthored with Ioulia Tzonou-Herbst and Aaron Wolpert, he outlines the archaeology for previously unexplored islands (e.g., the northern Sporades), recent solutions to longstanding conundrums (e.g., the location of the Early Cycladic settlement at Chalandriani), and new evidence pushing back the earliest habitation of the islands. No longer can the Aegean islands be considered a marginal area for research.

RAP II

In the second review article, Rutter surveys the prepalatial Bronze Age of the southern and central Greek mainland. He prefaces his discussion with an overview of the rise of intensive surface survey in this area, which developed in response to increasing interest in reconstructing regional settlement systems. He advocates careful attention in regional studies to matters of environmental reconstruction, chronology, and site definition to ensure comparability of field results.

In turning to the archaeological record of the Early Bronze Age, Rutter isolates several problems around which current work revolves. Transitions between periods are not yet well understood: the boundary dividing the final phase of the Neolithic and Early Helladic I is blurred, and our understanding of the regional nature of EH I settlement and ceramics is only slowly coming into focus; the EH II–III transition, long thought on the basis of the Lerna sequence to represent an abrupt break occasioned by

---

[4] The antiquities market, especially in Cycladic figurines, is implicated in this widespread plunder: see D.W.J. Gill and C. Chippindale, "Material and Intellectual Consequences of Esteem for Cycladic Figures," *AJA* 97 (1993) 601–59.

[5] On which see, most recently, C. Broodbank, *An Island Archaeology of the Early Cyclades* (Cambridge 2000), in

which the author seeks to define a new framework for island archaeology. For a controversial critique of approaches to island biogeography in the Mediterranean, see P. Rainbird, "Islands out of Time: Towards a Critique of Island Archaeology," *JMA* 12 (1999) 226–29, and the responses that follow.

the arrival of a new population, has now been characterized elsewhere by continuity in several respects.[6] Cultural change is more profitably viewed as a complex and evolving process with different regional manifestations than as the outcome of a specific series of events. Other key issues include the function(s) of large structures similar to the House of the Tiles at Lerna, now known at sites across Greece; the dynamics of exchange networks; the unusual range and character of representational art in EH II; and the reasons for discontinuities in settlement patterns across regions.

For the Middle Helladic and early Mycenaean periods, Rutter outlines the ways in which recent work has forced revisions to our interpretation of the seemingly sudden wealth of the Shaft Graves. The emergence and nature of early Mycenaean social ranking remain the focus of inquiry, and the excavation of Kolonna on Aegina has contributed impressively to a more complex picture of Minoan-Mycenaean spheres of influence. Why was the pace of cultural change in the centuries prior to the Shaft Grave era apparently slower than on Crete or in the Cyclades? What are the mechanisms by which Minoan fashions in ceramics, metalwork, and possibly funerary architecture were transmitted? Questions such as these, together with a longstanding curiosity about the origins of the Mycenaean palaces and their connections with the Neopalatial centers on Crete, continue to structure investigation in this area of Greece.

RAP III

The early prehistory of Crete (through the Protopalatial period) is discussed by Watrous. After outlining the history of scholarship, he reviews theories concerning the earliest human presence on the island and Neolithic settlement. The focus of research on Early Minoan Crete has long been the nature and degree of complexity of social organization; scholars continue to disagree over whether or not social ranking is indicated at this early date. In his original review, Watrous concluded that current evidence did not support the inference of elites within EM II society, but he tempers this position in his addendum, reconsidering architectural evidence from Vasiliki

and citing recent findings from a surface survey near Gournia.

New research, especially the lower chronology proposed by Manning for the Early Bronze Age,[7] also caused Watrous to rethink some of his 1994 conclusions about EM III. In his addendum, he notes that as a result of the new chronology, EM III can be seen as a short period that corresponds roughly to the Egyptian First Intermediate period, and EM II appears to have lasted longer than previously believed. In a table superseding his earlier chronological scheme, Watrous (p. 222) distinguishes two periods of disruption: the first in EM IIB, primarily evident in mainland Greece and the Cyclades, and the second at the end of the third millennium (EM III), during which widespread drought and population loss are documented across the eastern Mediterranean.[8] The processes whereby palatial administration subsequently develops are central to research on Middle Minoan Crete and, in his review of recent fieldwork, Watrous focuses particularly on the impact of foreign trade and renewed contact with the Near East at that time.

A markedly different scenario thus emerges than that proposed by Renfrew and Branigan some 30 years ago. Rather than a rapid cultural development in EM I–II, followed by a gradual transition in EM III into the Protopalatial period, Watrous suggests a more modest development in EM I–IIA, followed by the abandonment of many sites during EM IIB and especially in EM III, and limited evidence for complex social hierarchy prior to the rise of urbanism in the Middle Minoan period. This revised interpretation, favoring revolutionary change over gradual sociopolitical evolution, is part of a long debate in Aegean prehistory on the origins of complex society on Crete.[9] The extent to which Watrous has modified his own views on Cretan cultural history over the past five years serves as a reminder of the provisional nature of these reviews.

RAP IV

Runnels next reviews the Stone Age of Greece from the Palaeolithic to the advent of the Neolithic,

---

[6] In this respect, an important recent addition to the literature is M.H. Wiencke, *The Architecture, Stratification, and Pottery of Lerna III* (*Lerna* IV, Princeton 2000).

[7] S. Manning, *The Absolute Chronology of the Aegean Early Bronze Age: Archaeology, History and Radiocarbon* (Monographs in Mediterranean Archaeology 1, Sheffield 1995).

[8] H. Nüzhet Dalfes, G. Kukla, and H. Weiss eds., *Third Millennium B.C. Climate Change and Old World Collapse* (Berlin 1997).

[9] The notion of revolutionary change in the rise of the

Minoan palaces was first advanced by J.F. Cherry in a series of articles: "Evolution, Revolution, and the Origins of Complex Society in Minoan Crete," in O. Krzyszkowska and L. Nixon eds., *Minoan Society* (Bristol 1983) 33–45; "The Emergence of the State in the Prehistoric Aegean," *PCPS* 30 (1984) 18–48; and "Polities and Palaces: Some Problems in Minoan State Formation," in C. Renfrew and J.F. Cherry eds., *Peer Polity Interaction and Socio-political Change* (Cambridge 1986) 19–45. For further bibliography on the subject, see infra ns. 28 and 30.

a period virtually unknown 40 years ago. Within the last decade, the earliest prehistory of Greece has assumed new importance within the larger arena of European prehistory as part of the debate over the emergence of modern humans. Runnels outlines the history of relevant research, and then presents evidence for a broad reconstruction of early habitation: Lower Palaeolithic fossil remains and stone tools mark the arrival of archaic *Homo sapiens* as early as 300,000 B.P.; around 100,000, Neanderthals or other archaic *Homo sapiens* moved into Greece from central and southeastern Europe; anatomically modern *Homo sapiens* may have come into contact with the resident Neanderthal population around 40,000 B.P., after which the Neanderthals disappear. From ca. 28,000 onward, modern humans appear to have been permanently established in Greece.

Runnels points out that the significant issues in the study of the earliest prehistory of Greece pertain to world prehistory as well (p. 230): "How do humans go about colonizing previously uninhabited areas? How have humans adapted to the changing climatic demands of the glacial and interglacial periods? How can the study of stone tools and biological remains from archaeological sites be used to understand the dynamics of human evolution?" Inasmuch as Greece was a probable point of entry for humans migrating from Africa to Europe, attention has focused on the timing of that entry and on the origins of modern humans. The Middle Palaeolithic is well represented in Greece, suggesting an early glacial migration of Neanderthals into the area. A number of puzzling issues are connected with the Upper Palaeolithic: an apparent drop in population, unexplained hiatuses in occupation, the rarity of open-air sites, and the uneven distribution of sites across Greece, although the last may also be a function of changes in sea level and patterns of reconnaissance.

The Mesolithic of Greece, documented at only a handful of sites, offers a picture of intensified exploitation of the landscape and sea in the early Holocene; mortuary rites at Franchthi Cave suggest changes in social and symbolic aspects of life at that time. Runnels reviews possible explanations for the rarity of Mesolithic sites and notes the difficulty this creates for our understanding of the origins of agriculture in the subsequent Neolithic. He suggests that Mesolithic culture was not an indigenous development but, like the succeeding Neolithic, resulted from migration from the Near East—a proposal certain to generate further discussion.[10]

RAP V

The fifth review, by Andreou, Fotiadis, and Kotsakis, is devoted to the Neolithic and Bronze Age of northern Greece. Neolithic Thessaly has been a target for research since the turn of the century, with special attention paid to the origins of agriculture, the establishment of long-term habitation sites (tells), and the rise of social complexity. The authors observe that the longstanding perception of Neolithic self-sufficiency and simplicity has been recently challenged by the discovery of extensive networks of exchange and specialized production. Surface surveys in Thessaly indicate a shift from dispersed settlements in the Neolithic to nucleated larger sites in the Bronze Age, accompanied by changes in socioeconomic organization. Mycenaean cultural traits are recognized within a different matrix from that of the palace societies of southern Greece, and current research aims to explicate the "particular political and ideological use of these traits, within and in opposition to a tradition of local political structures" (p. 281).

The authors characterize Macedonia as the "Other" of the Aegean, showing how the province has alternately been considered European or Aegean, proclaimed as key to the study of European prehistory, yet treated as a marginal area with its own peculiar history. The importance of the area was reinforced in the 1960s, when an interdisciplinary team established Nea Nikomedeia as the earliest Neolithic community then known in Europe. In assessing subsequent work, the authors note that distribution maps are filling with newly discovered sites, but analysis is hindered by the rarity of intensive surface surveys, particularly those that employ probabilistic sampling and geomorphological study. Investigation of large tell sites in Macedonia has focused on Late Bronze Age hierarchy, expressed, for example, in the capacity and centralization of agricultural storage and the internal arrangement of houses.

The authors also summarize cultural sequences and recent projects in Greek Thrace and Epirus, stressing the need for more intensive fieldwork in both areas. They conclude on a cautionary note concerning the earliest Neolithic in Greece. Although the consensus is that the Greek Neolithic is the result of colonization from the Near East, the authors insist that more fieldwork is critical to evaluate the apparent scarcity

---

[10] See the forthcoming volume edited by N. Galanidou and C. Perlès: *The Greek Mesolithic: Problems and Perspectives* (*BSA* Studies, London).

of settlement in the northern provinces during the Final Palaeolithic and Mesolithic. The paucity of very early Neolithic sites further compromises any secure inference about the nature of the transition to the Neolithic.[11] The authors' warning about overreaching the evidence in attempting explanatory syntheses of the major themes of Aegean prehistory is an important aspect of these reviews.

RAP VI

Shelmerdine, in her overview of the palatial Bronze Age of the southern and central Greek mainland, continues from the point where Rutter stopped. Her focus is Mycenaean culture in the 14th and 13th centuries, though she also discusses the destructions that occur at the end of LH IIIB and in LH IIIC. She takes a thematic approach rather than proceeding strictly chronologically or geographically. After summarizing recent work at palatial and other sites, she considers settlement patterns revealed by surface surveys, technological advances in archaeological methods, and ceramic studies with a regional focus.

As in other areas of Greece, the emphasis on the excavation of individual palaces or tombs is now giving way to increased interest in regional settlement patterns, with data best provided by intensive survey. Shelmerdine (p. 342) traces the shift in interest "from the Mycenaean king to his subjects, and from the center to its surroundings" to the 1960s and 1970s, when the Minnesota Messenia Expedition redefined the goals of archaeological fieldwork (see below). In drawing out the historical implications of survey data from different regions, she asks a number of questions: When are sites founded or abandoned? Where are new sites situated in relation to earlier ones and can we determine the function of those sites? How does the size of sites occupied continuously from the Middle to Late Bronze Age change through time, and how might such changes relate to the political landscape?

Shelmerdine, like Rutter, sees the central question occupying Mycenaean scholars as the rise of social complexity leading to the establishment of the palaces—"the transformation of scattered enclaves of power, characteristic of the Middle Helladic period, into the centralized states of LH IIIA–B" (p. 349). She incorporates the textual evidence of Linear B with other archaeological data in her discussion of the evolution of the state and Mycenaean

economic and political administration. Questions surrounding Mycenaean religion and cult practice have also received attention recently, particularly the location and nature of sacred spaces and the activities associated with worship. Assemblages formerly interpreted as signs of animal sacrifice might be better understood in the context of communal feasting, a suggestion supported by references in the Linear B texts to banquet supplies. Finally, in reviewing the theories accounting for the destruction or abandonment of the Mycenaean palaces, Shelmerdine notes that there is still little consensus among scholars, though current work strengthens the likelihood of widespread damage caused by earthquakes.

RAP VII

In the last article of the series to date, Rehak and Younger summarize work over the past 25 years on Neopalatial, Final Palatial, and Postpalatial Crete. They highlight a variety of problems, beginning with terminology and chronology. The major part of their review is devoted to the Neopalatial period, the foundations of which are traced back to the Protopalatial period in terms, for example, of hierarchies of settlement, use of communal tombs, and the emergence of monumental architecture. The authors survey recent architectural studies, noting that the current trend is to situate palaces, villas, and towns within wider regional settings. They go on to discuss new views on funerary customs, art (defined broadly), the so-called palatial prestige system, and the central role of Knossos within an extensive network of sites.

The authors detail the interrelationships, functions, and forms of Cretan Hieroglyphic, Linear A, and Linear B, and emphasize that the ways in which the palatial administration employed a sealing system to organize the storage, inventory, and distribution of goods are critical to understanding how the economy functioned. Turning to religion, they point out that, while we know a good deal about Minoan cult locations and equipment, we can say little about belief systems for the Neopalatial period. Linear B tablets augment the picture somewhat in the Final Palatial period (a term coined by the authors for LM II–LM IIIB early). Religion appears to have functioned in support of a political system in which the ruling class may have served, *inter alia*, as religious officials. Much recent work on religion has focused on separating Minoan and Mycenaean forms and prac-

---

[11] For the latest discussion, see A.J. Ammerman and P. Biagi eds., *The Widening Harvest: The Neolithic Transition in Europe* (Boston, forthcoming), the proceedings of the conference "The Neolithic Transition in Europe: Looking Back, Looking Forward," held in Venice, 29–31 October 1998.

tices. Rehak and Younger highlight aspects of performance connected with Minoan Neopalatial religion: open areas and courtyards could have accommodated large audiences, and most cult paraphernalia was portable for easy display.

Recent fieldwork has refined the early scenario of refugees hiding in the mountains during the Postpalatial period. While some sites are founded at high elevations during the period, sites at lower altitudes also thrive, and a complex picture of social and religious change is beginning to emerge. The authors conclude their survey with a call for further research into several areas: domestic architecture, jewelry as a social artifact, painted larnakes, and ceramic studies closely integrated with variables of architectural and demographic change. Finally, they argue, we should not let interest in abstract constructs blind us to the details of individual lives, either in our studies of the past or of contemporary Crete.

COMMON THREADS: A HISTORICAL PERSPECTIVE

The above outline of the seven reviews reveals much about modern archaeological practice. The shape of the field today is not a matter of chance, but is influenced by the particular history of the discipline's development. John Myres, writing about Aegean prehistory in the early part of this century, observed aptly that "the point where we stand now and survey the problem, backwards and forwards, is settled for us by our predecessors."[12] It is interesting in this respect to compare the questions on which the authors of RAP I–VII focus with those current a century ago. In 1899, David Hogarth framed the most pressing questions within the context of Hellenism,

the idealization of the classical Greek spirit as the cultural ancestor of Europe: "Whence originated this great early civilization of the Greek lands? And what in the end became of it? These are the questions that concern the world at large; for they bear in general on the mysterious origins of our civilization in Europe, and in particular on that seeming miracle of spontaneous growth, the art and culture of the Hellenes."[13]

The search for origins took on an added dimension for Greek archaeologists. Kotsakis and others have outlined the ways in which archaeology undertaken by Greeks in the 19th century operated within a nationalistic climate, serving to legitimate the new Greek state.[14] The claim to cultural continuity from prehistory not only to fifth-century Athens but on to the present was repeated often enough in the early 20th century until it seemed to become self-evident, hardly requiring archaeological proof. With the uncovering of the Minoan and Mycenaean civilizations, however, and the eventual discovery that Linear B was an early form of Greek, questions of origins, especially the "coming of the Greeks," fueled much research.

The spectacular early discoveries in the Aegean by Schliemann, Tsountas, Evans, Blegen, Wace, and others on Crete, the mainland, and in the Cyclades have been well chronicled and need not be repeated here.[15] From its inception Aegean prehistory revolved around regional cultures (or "civilizations"), but the concept of an archaeological culture was first defined systematically by Childe in a series of volumes published in the 1920s.[16] Similarities among artifacts were mapped and identified with essentialized cultural entities (e.g., Minoans, Mycenaeans, Trojans) assumed to represent distinct ethnic groups. External factors—migration, invasion, or diffusion—

[12] J.L. Myres, "The Cretan Labyrinth: A Retrospect of Aegean Research," *Journal of the Royal Anthropological Institute of Great Britain and Ireland* 63 (1933) 270.

[13] D.G. Hogarth, *Authority and Archaeology, Sacred and Profane: Essays on the Relation of Monuments to Biblical and Classical Literature* (New York 1899) 233.

[14] K. Kotsakis, "The Powerful Past: Theoretical Trends in Greek Archaeology," in I. Hodder ed., *Archaeological Theory in Europe: The Last Three Decades* (London 1991) 65–90. An extensive literature exists on the influence of nationalism on the development of Mediterranean archaeology. See, e.g., M. Herzfeld, *Ours Once More: Folklore, Ideology, and the Making of Modern Greece* (Austin 1982); P. Kitromilides, "'Imagined Communities' and the Origins of the National Question in the Balkans," *European History Quarterly* 19 (1989) 149–92; N.A. Silberman, *Between Past and Present: Archaeology, Ideology, and Nationalism in the Modern Middle East* (New York 1989); P.L. Kohl and C. Fawcett eds., *Nationalism, Politics, and the Practice of Archaeology* (Cambridge

1995); Y. Hamilakis and E. Yalouri, "Antiquities as Symbolic Capital in Modern Greek Society," *Antiquity* 70 (1996) 117–29; A.N. Karakasidou, *Fields of Wheat, Hills of Blood: Passages to Nationhood in Greek Macedonia, 1870–1990* (Chicago 1997); L. Meskell ed., *Archaeology under Fire: Nationalism, Politics, and Heritage in the Eastern Mediterranean and Middle East* (London 1998); and J.L. Davis, "Warriors for the Fatherland: National Consciousness and Archaeology in 'Barbarian' Epirus and 'Verdant' Ionia, 1912–22," *JMA* 13 (2000) 76–98.

[15] W.A. McDonald and C.G. Thomas, *Progress into the Past: The Rediscovery of Mycenaean Civilization*[2] (Bloomington 1990); J.L. Fitton, *The Discovery of the Greek Bronze Age* (Cambridge, Mass., 1996).

[16] V.G. Childe, *The Dawn of European Civilization* (London 1925); Childe, *The Most Ancient East: The Oriental Prelude to European Prehistory* (London 1928); and Childe, *The Danube in Prehistory* (Oxford 1929). See also J.L. Myres, "Neolithic and Bronze Age Cultures," *CAH* I (1923) 57–111.

were most often cited as explanations for artifactual discontinuities. The chronological focus of research in the Aegean through much of this century has been on the Bronze Age ("Homeric archaeology"), influenced strongly by the images and language of the epics.[17]

The Greek Neolithic has also been the subject of inquiry since Tsountas's excavations at Dimini and Sesklo beginning in 1901. As Runnels observes in RAP IV, the Neolithic of Greece assumed added significance within the wider European arena after Childe published his influential *The Danube in Prehistory* (1929), in which he outlined the origins of the Neolithic in the Near East, and the diffusion of the Neolithic way of life into Europe via the Balkans. Investigations of pre-Neolithic sites in Greece were limited to modest excavations by Markovits in the 1920s and Stampfuss in 1941; the implications of this work, as Runnels points out, were generally ignored until recently.

Carl Blegen, in an address in 1940 marking the bicentennial of the University of Pennsylvania, remarked that the "potent spell" cast by Aegean prehistory "is really a manifestation of that deep impulse by which the inquiring human mind is obsessed to probe into origins and causes."[18] He discounted the earlier vision of the miraculous flowering of Classical Greece, pointing instead to prehistoric antecedents and a long, gradual development. Meticulous documentation—building up chronological sequences and reconstructing cultural histories not only at the palaces and urban centers but also at rural sites—characterized prehistoric research in Greece in the decades leading up to the Second World War and beyond. Questions that had absorbed earlier excavators—the reality behind the Homeric poems; the origins and character of Mycenaean and Minoan civilizations and their interrelations; the relationship of preclassical cultures to Classical Greece; and the language, race, and origins of the earliest inhabitants of Greece—continued to be important and, indeed, their traces can be seen today in the RAP articles. The centrality of these themes often ensured a place for Aegean prehistory within departments of Classics in North American universities, as part of the larger discipline of classical archaeology (see below, Current Status of Aegean Prehistory).

After decades of reconstructing cultural histories, the 1960s represent a turning point in Aegean studies. Interdisciplinary projects such as the Minnesota Messenia Expedition (MME) and excavations at Nea Nikomedeia, Franchthi Cave (itself part of a larger regional project, the Argolid Exploration Project), Saliagos, and Sitagroi introduced a host of new questions and revolutionized the practice of Aegean archaeology. Led by William McDonald, MME has been called the first modern regional project in Greece.[19] Not since Schliemann brought architects, engineers, and scientists (including Virchow, quoted at the outset) to the Troad had an interdisciplinary team with such a broad range of expertise been assembled for a project in the Aegean. McDonald's focus was explicitly regional, as the subtitle of his final report—*Reconstructing a Bronze Age Regional Environment*—makes clear. The project encompassed surface survey, excavation, palaeoenvironmental research, archaeometric studies of artifacts and raw materials, ethnography, and analyses of economic and demographic texts (from the Mycenaean period to the present).

The many surface surveys cited throughout RAP I–VII trace their intellectual ancestry to McDonald's vision: they share his goal of exploring the interaction of humans and their environment through time; his commitment to presenting a balanced picture of settlement, with attention given to rural sites and everyday wares; and his emphasis on the economic potential of landscapes.[20] Fotiadis has de-

[17] As early as 1878, Charles Newton, Keeper of Greek and Roman Antiquities at the British Museum, skeptically assessed the close correlation of myth and prehistory proposed by Schliemann at Mycenae: "Dr. Schliemann's Discoveries at Mycenae," *Edinburgh Review* 1878, quoted in Fitton (supra n. 15) 42. Myres (supra n. 12) objected strongly to the implications underlying the use of terms such as Minyan or Achaean to describe archaeological cultures, observing wryly that Aegean prehistory "originated as a problem of literary criticism, and has never wholly or permanently dissociated itself from that origin." See also E. Vermeule, *Greece in the Bronze Age* (Chicago 1964) xi ("Homer has been rejected as evidence, with a pang. He is every Mycenaean scholar's passion.") and R. McNeal, "The Greeks in History and Prehistory," *Antiquity* 46 (1972) 25–26 ("For three generations now we have walked in the shadow of Heinrich Schliemann and dutifully followed where he wanted to lead").

[18] Blegen (supra n. 2) 6.

[19] W.A. McDonald and G.R. Rapp, Jr., *The Minnesota Messenia Expedition: Reconstructing a Bronze Age Regional Environment* (Minneapolis 1972); M. Fotiadis, "Modernity and the Past-Still-Present: Politics of Time in the Birth of Regional Archaeological Projects in Greece," *AJA* 99 (1995) 59.

[20] Similar themes and interdisciplinary approaches can also be seen in volumes such as P.N. Kardulias ed., *Beyond the Site: Regional Studies in the Aegean Area* (Lanham 1994); and P.N. Kardulias and M.T. Shutes eds., *Aegean Strategies: Studies of Culture and Environment on the European Fringe* (Lanham 1997). See also, e.g., C. Runnels, "Anthropogenic Soil Erosion in Prehistoric Greece: The Contribution of Regional Surveys to the Archaeology of Environmental Disruptions and Human Response," in G. Bawden ed., *Environmental Disruptions and the Archaeology of Human Response* (Albuquerque, forthcoming).

scribed the complex politics of time embodied by MME, in which the present is taken as a viable baseline from which to compare the past, leading to sophisticated ethnographic and ethnoarchaeological work but also generating a sharp, hierarchical distinction between researcher and researched.[21]

Jacobsen recently sketched the context of Aegean prehistory in the 1960s, when he first undertook work at Franchthi Cave in the Argolid.[22] While traditional concerns with chronology and cultural affinities still prevailed, a wide range of new questions and methods, primarily in the areas of palaeoenvironmental studies and palaeoeconomy, were being formulated, inspired by the work of Childe, Braidwood, Clark, Higgs, and less directly by the Anglo-American processualism of Binford and Clarke.[23] Jacobsen was one of the first in Aegean archaeology to recognize fully the potential of radiocarbon dating, eventually publishing a long series of calibrated dates that defined the sequence at Franchthi from the Palaeolithic through the Neolithic period.[24]

The radiocarbon revolution, as it is commonly called, and subsequent refinements by dendrochronology have had a profound impact on the study of Aegean prehistory. A major controversy over the past 20 years has centered on the date of the eruption of Thera. The conventional (low) chronology, established on the basis of artifactual correlations with the Near East and especially Egypt (with its secure historical timeline), has been seriously challenged by the composite picture resulting from scientific dating techniques (radiocarbon, dendrochronology, ice cores). Many scholars, including most of the RAP authors, are now convinced that the eruption occurred more than a century earlier than previously thought (1628/7 rather than 1500 B.C.). Good summaries of

the debate and bibliography can be found in Davis, Shelmerdine, and Rehak and Younger's reviews (RAP I, VI, and VII). As Manning has noted, the problem is not trivial, but has major ramifications for the chronologies of the eastern and central Mediterranean and for southeastern Europe, all of which are archaeologically entwined.[25] A sound chronological scaffolding is essential in identifying the sequence in which cultural factors change, an obvious prerequisite to uncovering causal links between them and understanding the nature of that change. Chronology-building has long been a primary focus of work in the Aegean, but with its recent refinements and the publication of numerous local sequences, questions of wider sociopolitical significance can now more plausibly be pursued.

The ability to correlate archaeological sequences with a calendrical chronology independent of cultural contacts enabled prehistorians to view innovations within a global context and to assess different rates of cultural change. It soon became apparent that innovations could occur independently in different regions and that change need not be explained solely in terms of diffusion from the Near East.[26] This realization in turn encouraged the search for indigenous factors underlying cultural change, well typified by Renfrew's highly influential *Emergence of Civilisation* (1972), in which he rejected the diffusionist assumptions of Oriental primacy and sought an explanation for the rise of Minoan palace society in terms of local antecedents. In proposing alternative models for the evolution of complex society in the Aegean, Renfrew conceptualized culture as an adaptive system of interconnected parts tending toward equilibrium. Borrowing from general systems theory, he posited that change occurs as a result of escalating feed-

---

[21] Fotiadis (supra n. 19) 59–78.

[22] T.W. Jacobsen, "Background of the Franchthi Project," in W.R. Farrand, *Depositional History of Franchthi Cave: Stratigraphy, Sedimentology, and Chronology* (Franchthi 12, Bloomington 2000) 1–10.

[23] Influential studies included V.G. Childe, *Piecing Together the Past: The Interpretation of Archaeological Data* (London 1956); Childe, *The Prehistory of European Society* (Harmondsworth 1958); R.J. Braidwood and B. Howe, *Prehistoric Investigations in Iraqi Kurdistan* (SAOC 31, Chicago 1960); J.G.D. Clark, *Prehistoric Europe: The Economic Basis* (London 1952); Clark, *Archaeology and Society* (London 1957); E.S. Higgs and C. Vita-Finzi, "The Climate, Environment, and Industries of Stone Age Greece, Part III," *PPS* 33 (1966) 1–29; S.R. Binford and L.R. Binford eds., *New Perspectives in Archeology* (Chicago 1968), especially L.R. Binford, "Post-Pleistocene Adaptations," 313–41; L.R. Binford, *An Archaeological Per-*

spective (London 1972); and D.L. Clarke, *Analytical Archaeology* (London 1968). For discussions of the influence of Childe's work on later archaeology, see, e.g., B.G. Trigger, *Gordon Childe: Revolutions in Archaeology* (London 1980); and A. Sherratt, "V. Gordon Childe: Archaeology and Intellectual History," *Past and Present* 125 (1989) 151–85. Indeed, Sherratt goes so far as to say (p. 185) that the writing of prehistory "is still a dialogue with the ghost of Childe."

[24] T.W. Jacobsen and W.R. Farrand, *Franchthi Cave and Paralia: Maps, Plans, and Sections* (Franchthi 1, Bloomington 1987) pl. 71.

[25] S.W. Manning, *A Test of Time: The Volcano of Thera and the Chronology and History of the Aegean and East Mediterranean in the Mid Second Millennium B.C.* (Oxford 1999) 5.

[26] C. Renfrew, *Before Civilization: The Radiocarbon Revolution and Prehistoric Europe* (Cambridge 1973).

back among cultural components, whereby innovation in one area of human activity spurs innovation in another.[27] Although aspects of Renfrew's argument have failed to hold up upon further investigation,[28] the boldness of his approach at that time—and the use of an anthropological model and cross-cultural evidence to define and tackle a longstanding sociopolitical problem in Aegean prehistory—introduced the New Archaeology to Greece and inspired a generation of prehistorians to rethink the idea of prehistory.

The emphasis on explaining processes of cultural change by reference to general principles of human behavior was an important part of processual archaeology of the 1960s and 1970s and is still embraced by many prehistorians working in Greece today. The rigorous framework of deductive reasoning and hypothesis-testing espoused by Binford and others encouraged many Aegean prehistorians to formulate problem-oriented research designs and to lay out assumptions and goals in a more explicit way than had been common before.[29] For example, following Ren-

frew's *Emergence,* competing models were proposed to explain the development of social complexity and the rise of the state in the Aegean.[30] Although all aspects of the cultural system were deemed amenable to archaeological analysis, most work centered on issues of subsistence, trade, settlement patterns, technology, and social organization, the issues most commonly recurring in the literature summarized in RAP I–VII.

Several of the RAP authors allude to the mark made on Aegean archaeology by anthropological archaeology. Watrous, for example, notes in RAP III that projects on Crete are now broader in scope and more rigorous in interpretation, employing a wide range of interdisciplinary methods and structured around new questions pertaining to demography, land use, and social and political organization. In part as a way to answer these questions, intensive surface surveys have been designed and carried out throughout the Aegean with increasing frequency over the past three decades, now recognized as standard and essential archaeological practice (see

[27] C. Renfrew, *The Emergence of Civilisation: The Cyclades and the Aegean in the Third Millennium B.C.* (London 1972).

[28] For criticisms or refinements of Renfrew's approach, see, e.g., C. Gamble, "Social Control and the Economy," in A. Sheridan and G. Bailey eds., *Economic Archaeology* (Oxford 1981) 215–29; C.N. Runnels and J.M. Hansen, "The Olive in the Prehistoric Aegean: The Evidence for Domestication in the Early Bronze Age," *OJA* 5 (1986) 299–308; Hansen, "Agriculture in the Prehistoric Aegean: Data versus Speculation," *AJA* 92 (1988) 39–52; P. Halstead, "On Redistribution and the Origin of Minoan-Mycenaean Palatial Economies," in E.B. French and K.A. Wardle eds., *Problems in Greek Prehistory* (Bristol 1988) 519–30; Halstead, "From Sharing to Hoarding: The Neolithic Foundations of Aegean Bronze Age Society," in R. Laffineur and W.-D. Niemeier eds., *Politeia: Society and State in the Aegean Bronze Age* (*Aegaeum* 12, Liège 1995) 11–21; and Y. Hamilakis, "Wine, Oil and the Dialectics of Power in Bronze Age Crete: A Review of the Evidence," *OJA* 15 (1996) 1–32. Disillusion with the application of general systems theory in archaeology also has undermined Renfrew's model; see, e.g., I. Hodder, "Theoretical Archaeology: A Reactionary View," in Hodder ed., *Symbolic and Structural Archaeology* (Cambridge 1982) 1–16.

[29] Early influential writings (from a long list) include works by Binford and Clarke (supra n. 23); P.J. Watson, S.A. LeBlanc, and C.L. Redman, *Explanation in Archeology: An Explicitly Scientific Approach* (New York 1971); M.P. Leone ed., *Contemporary Archaeology: A Guide to Theory and Contributions* (Carbondale, Ill., 1972); and K.V. Flannery ed., *The Early Mesoamerican Village* (New York 1976). For succinct assessments of the New Archaeology and its effect on classical archaeology, see G. Daniel and C. Renfrew, *The Idea of Prehistory* (Edinburgh 1988) 162–

69; S.L. Dyson, "A Classical Archaeologist's Response to the 'New Archaeology,'" *BASOR* 242 (1981) 7–13; and Dyson, "From New to New Age Archaeology: Archaeological Theory and Classical Archaeology—A 1990s Perspective," *AJA* 97 (1993) 197–98. See also B.G. Trigger, *A History of Archaeological Thought* (Cambridge 1989) 294–328.

[30] The bibliography on the origins of social complexity and the founding of the first palaces is vast. See, in addition to the works cited in notes 9 and 28, L.V. Watrous, "The Role of the Near East in the Rise of the Cretan Palaces," in R. Hägg and N. Marinatos eds., *The Function of the Minoan Palaces* (Stockholm 1987) 65–70; T.H. van Andel and C. Runnels, "An Essay on the 'Emergence of Civilization' in the Aegean World," *Antiquity* 62 (1988) 234–47; K. Branigan, "Social Transformations and the Rise of the State in Crete," in Laffineur and Niemeier (supra n. 28) 33–42; P. Halstead, "The North–South Divide: Regional Paths to Complexity in Prehistoric Greece" and S. Manning, "The Emergence of Divergence: Development and Decline on Bronze Age Crete and the Cyclades," in C. Mathers and S. Stoddart eds., *Development and Decline in the Mediterranean Bronze Age* (Sheffield 1994) 195–219 and 221–70, respectively; J.C. Wright, "From Chief to King in Mycenaean Greece," in P. Rehak ed., *The Role of the Ruler in the Prehistoric Aegean* (*Aegaeum* 11, Liège 1995) 63–80; and Manning, "Cultural Change in the Aegean c. 2200 B.C.," in Nüzhet Dalfes et al. (supra n. 8) 149–71. For additional bibliography and a summary of the different perspectives taken on this question, see J. Bennet and M. Galaty, "Ancient Greece: Recent Developments in Aegean Archaeology and Regional Studies," *Journal of Archaeological Research* 5 (1997) 84–87.

Rutter, RAP II). The rise of survey in the Aegean was also propelled by shrinking opportunities for foreign excavation (see below, Current Status of Aegean Prehistory).[31]

A few years ago, Snodgrass zealously declared that no development as far-reaching as surface survey has occurred in Aegean archaeology since the adoption of stratigraphic techniques of excavation at the beginning of the century.[32] Indeed, no one would deny the huge impact the rise of survey has had on the shape of Aegean prehistory and the formalization of regional units of study. A long tradition of earlier topographic reconnaissance existed in Greece, and calls for intensified survey go back many decades. Myres, for example, wrote in 1933 that "what is needed is not so much more extensive excavation, as regional survey supplemented with spade-reconnaissance."[33] The critical difference in intensive surface surveys characteristic of the 1980s and 1990s from earlier extensive surveys is the complete coverage by teams of fieldwalkers of a systematically selected sample of the landscape.[34] Davis notes that projects such as the Keos Survey, the Nemea Valley Archaeological Project, and the Pylos Regional Archaeological Project all espouse goals consistent with those of processual archaeology, in contrast, for example, to MME, whose purported ancestry included Schliemann's expeditions to Troy and the projects of Braidwood and Adams in the Middle East and Sanders in Mesoamerica.[35] Fotiadis has drawn attention to parallels between regional survey and the modern census, not only in the sorts of data collected but in their authoritative intensity, "untainted by the politics of local life." References to demography and adaptive exploitation of resources infuse interpretations at the regional level rather than, for example, a view of humans as active agents, "capable of political projects, of subverting structures of all kinds."[36]

Since the heyday of processualism in the 1970s and early 1980s, the realization that material culture is not a passive extension of ecological adaptation or social structure but is actively manipulated by people to disguise as well as reflect a social reality has spawned a diverse field of new approaches to prehistory, many emanating from Britain. Hallmarks of the postprocessualist world are fragmentation—approaches include neo-Marxism, contextualism, structuralism, landscape archaeology, phenomenology, feminist archaeologies, and the *Annales* school—and a move away from generalizing narratives to a concern with historical specificity, social diversity and conflict, individual agency, symbolism and systems of meaning, and multiple

[31] For comprehensive overviews of the development and promise of archaeological survey in the Mediterranean, see J.F. Cherry, "Frogs round the Pond: Perspectives on Current Archaeological Survey Projects in the Mediterranean Region," in D.R. Keller and D.W. Rupp eds., *Archaeological Survey in the Mediterranean Area* (*BAR-IS* 155, Oxford 1983) 375–416; Cherry, "Regional Survey in the Aegean: The 'New Wave' (and After)," in Kardulias (supra n. 20) 91–112; and Cherry, "Review of Aegean Prehistory VIII: The Impact of Archaeological Surveys and Regional Analysis on Aegean Prehistory, 1970–2000," *AJA* (in preparation). See also, most recently, J.L. Bintliff, M. Kuna, and N. Venclova eds., *The Future of Surface Artefact Survey in Europe* (Sheffield Archaeological Monographs 13, Sheffield 2000); and *The Archaeology of Mediterranean Landscapes*, an ambitious series of five volumes documenting the results of the Populus Project: J. Bintliff and K. Sbonias eds., *Reconstructing Past Population Trends in Mediterranean Europe (3000 B.C.–A.D. 1800)* (Oxford 1999); P. Leveau et al. eds., *Environmental Reconstruction in Mediterranean Landscape Archaeology* (Oxford 1999); M. Gillings, D. Mattingly, and J. van Dalen eds., *Geographical Information Systems and Landscape Archaeology* (Oxford 1999); M. Pasquinucci and F. Trément eds., *Non-destructive Techniques Applied to Landscape Archaeology* (Oxford 2000); and R. Francovich and H. Patterson eds., *Extracting Meaning from Ploughsoil Assemblages* (Oxford 2000).

[32] A. Snodgrass, "Response: The Archaeological Aspect," in I. Morris ed., *Classical Greece: Ancient Histories and Modern Archaeologies* (Cambridge 1994) 198.

[33] Myres (supra n. 12) 305. Blegen (supra n. 2) 12 made a similar plea in 1941.

[34] Cherry (supra n. 31) discusses the evolving conceptualization of surveys, adoption of a wide range of techniques from archaeological sciences, and the application of survey data to diverse questions such as the role of pastoralism in a region or the delineation of sacred landscapes.

[35] J.L. Davis, "Regional Studies in Greece: A *Vade Mecum?*" in Kardulias (supra n. 20) 397; see W.A. McDonald, "The Problems and the Program," in McDonald and Rapp (supra n. 19) 13–17; and also Fotiadis (supra n. 19) 67 for comments on the tactical shrewdness of MME's genealogy in the face of the extreme conservatism of classical archaeology in the 1960s. The more immediate ancestry of MME was a series of studies in Homeric geography: W.A. McDonald, "Where Did Nestor Live?" *AJA* 46 (1942) 538–45; R. Hope Simpson, "Identifying a Mycenaean State," *BSA* 52 (1957) 231–59; and Hope Simpson, "The Seven Cities Offered by Agamemnon to Achilles," *BSA* 61 (1966) 113–31. I thank John Cherry for reminding me of the twin ancestry of MME.

[36] M. Fotiadis, "Regions of the Imagination: Archaeologists, Local People, and the Archaeological Record in Fieldwork, Greece," *Journal of European Archaeology* 1:2 (1993) 163.

identities.[37] To a greater extent than in the past, archaeologists are looking at the ways in which interpretations are influenced by political and historical circumstances, personal biases, educational trends, financial constraints, class, and gender.[38] As noted earlier, the role of archaeology in advancing colonial and nationalist agendas has also been the subject of much recent work, some pertaining to the Aegean.[39] Globalism has promoted interest in broad spheres of past interaction, renewed attention to processes of diffusion and long-distance exchange, and application of concepts such as core, periphery, and peerpolity to archaeology.[40] Finally, the crippling effects of the antiquities market on archaeological knowledge have been addressed by a number of concerned scholars.[41]

RAP I–VII reflect the current concerns of Aegean prehistorians with a wide spectrum of issues: chronology, human origins, social and political change, artifactual discontinuities and transitions, settlement and land use, environmental constraints, subsistence and palaeoeconomy, the development of social complexity, technological innovations, the origins and function of writing, and the nature of interaction among polities—issues that might be broadly categorized as processualist or cultural historical. An explicitly regional perspective and a commitment to integrating multiple strands of evidence (e.g., artifactual,

---

[37] Ian Hodder has been at the forefront of postprocessualist thought in archaeology. See, e.g., I. Hodder, "Postprocessual Archaeology," *Advances in Archaeological Method and Theory* 8 (1985) 1–26; and Hodder, *The Archaeological Process: An Introduction* (Oxford 1999). Other relevant works include M. Shanks and C. Tilley, *Re-constructing Archaeology: Theory and Practice* (Cambridge 1987); Shanks and Tilley, *Social Theory and Archaeology* (Cambridge 1987); D. Miller and C. Tilley eds., *Ideology, Power and Prehistory* (Cambridge 1984); M. Spriggs ed., *Marxist Perspectives in Archaeology* (Cambridge 1984); I. Hodder ed., *The Archaeology of Contextual Meanings* (Cambridge 1987); C. Tilley, *A Phenomenology of Landscape: Places, Paths, and Monuments* (Oxford 1994); J.M. Gero and M.W. Conkey eds., *Engendering Archaeology: Women and Prehistory* (Oxford 1991); and A.B. Knapp ed., *Archaeology,* Annales, *and Ethnohistory* (Cambridge 1992).

For specific applications to southeast Europe and the eastern Mediterranean, see, e.g., I. Hodder, *The Domestication of Europe: Structure and Contingency in Neolithic Societies* (Oxford 1990); Hodder ed., *On the Surface: Çatalhöyük 1993–95* (British Institute of Archaeology at Ankara Monograph 22, Cambridge 1996); D. Kokkinidou and M. Nikolaidou, "Body Imagery in the Aegean Neolithic: Ideological Implications of Anthropomorphic Figurines" and L.A. Hitchcock, "Engendering Domination: A Structural and Contextual Analysis of Minoan Neopalatial Bronze Figurines," in J. Moore and E. Scott eds., *Invisible People and Processes: Writing Gender and Childhood into European Archaeology* (London 1997) 88–112 and 113–30, respectively; Kokkinidou and Nikolaidou, *Η αρχαιολογία και η κοινωνική ταυτότητα του φύλου: Προσεγγίσεις στην αιγαιακή προϊστορία* (Thessaloniki 1993); L.E. Talalay and T. Cullen, "Sexual Ambiguity in Plank Figures from Bronze Age Cyprus," in D. Bolger and N. Serwint eds., *Engendering Aphrodite: Women and Society in Ancient Cyprus* (Atlanta, forthcoming); Talalay, "A Feminist Boomerang: The Great Goddess of Greek Prehistory," *Gender and History* 6 (1994) 165–83; P. Rehak, "The Construction of Gender in Late Bronze Age Aegean Art," in M. Casey et al. eds., *Redefining Archaeology: Feminist Perspectives* (Canberra 1998) 191–98; Y. Hamilakis, "Eating the Dead: Mortuary Feasting and the Politics of Memory in the Aegean Bronze Age Societies," in K. Branigan ed., *Cemetery and Society in the Aegean Bronze Age* (Sheffield 1998) 115–32; L.A. Hitchcock, *Minoan Architecture: A Contextual Analysis* (SIMA-PB 155, Jonsered 2000); A.B. Knapp, "Ideational and Industrial Landscape

on Prehistoric Cyprus," in W. Ashmore and A.B. Knapp eds., *Archaeologies of Landscape: Contemporary Perspectives* (Oxford 1999) 229–52; A. Pilali-Papasteriou, "Social Evidence from the Interpretation of Middle Minoan Figurines," in I. Hodder ed., *The Meanings of Things: Material Culture and Symbolic Expression* (London 1989) 97–102; Pilali-Papasteriou, *Μινωικά πήλινα ανθρωπόμορφα ειδώλια της συλλογής Μεταξά* (Thessaloniki 1992); and M.L. Galaty and W.A. Parkinson eds., *Rethinking Mycenaean Palaces: New Interpretations of an Old Idea* (Los Angeles 1999).

[38] In this respect, several biographical studies are relevant: J. MacEnroe, "Sir Arthur Evans and Edwardian Archaeology," *Classical Bulletin* 71 (1995) 3–18, on the forces shaping Evans's idealization of the Minoans; J.A. MacGillivray, *Minotaur: Sir Arthur Evans and the Archaeology of the Minoan Myth* (New York 2000); N. Momigliano, "Evans, Mackenzie, and the History of the Palace at Knossos," *JHS* 116 (1996) 166–69; Momigliano, *Duncan Mackenzie: A Cautious Canny Highlander and the Palace of Minos at Knossos* (BICS Suppl. 72, London 1999); and M.J. Becker and P.P. Betancourt, *Richard Berry Seager: Pioneer Archaeologist and Proper Gentleman* (Philadelphia 1997). See also Fotiadis (supra n. 19); D. Frankel and J. Webb, "Gender Inequity and Archaeological Practice: A Cypriot Case Study," *JMA* 8 (1995) 93–112; J. Wiseman, "Archaeology in the Future: An Evolving Discipline," *AJA* 84 (1980) 279–85; Wiseman, "Conflicts in Archaeology: Education and Practice," *JFA* 10 (1983) 1–9; and further discussion below on the status of Aegean prehistory.

[39] Supra n. 14.

[40] For the use of world-systems models in archaeology, see, e.g., A. Sherratt, "What Would a Bronze-Age World System Look Like? Relations between Temperate Europe and the Mediterranean in Later Prehistory," *Journal of European Archaeology* 1:2 (1993) 1–57; G.J. Stein, "World-Systems Theory and Alternative Modes of Interaction in the Archaeology of Culture Contact," in J. Cusick ed., *Studies in Culture Contact: Interaction, Culture Change, and Archaeology* (Carbondale 1998) 220–55; and P.N. Kardulias, "Multiple Levels in the Aegean Bronze Age World-System," in Kardulias ed., *World-Systems Theory in Practice: Leadership, Production, and Exchange* (Lanham 1999) 179–201. For peerpolity models, see Renfrew and Cherry (supra n. 9).

[41] For the Aegean, see especially Gill and Chippindale (supra n. 4); C. Chippindale and D.W.J. Gill, "Cycladic Figures: Art versus Archaeology?" in K.W. Tubb ed., *Antiquities Trade or Betrayed: Legal, Ethical, and Conservation Issues* (Lon-

textual, geological, botanical) characterize much of the work summarized by the RAP authors.

Influence of the diverse theoretical approaches characteristic of the 1990s can also be detected in references to the social relations of production, the construction of Macedonia as the "Other" of the Aegean, the marginalization of certain topics of study (e.g., human origins), discussions of cognitive and ritual structures, consideration of the asymmetrical relations between the Near East and Crete in the Bronze Age, the call for more research into past gender roles and, in Rehak and Younger's phrase, "the lived life of individuals" rather than a preoccupation with expansive narratives and abstract social constructs. Cultures are no longer perceived as having sharply definable boundaries; indeed, the concept of discrete cultures recedes in the pages of these reviews, replaced by an abundance of specific contextual detail summoned to support social connections within a broad political and economic context and to address questions about individual and group actions, decisions, competition and emulation, and possible motivations. An appreciation that a problem may have more than one answer is apparent in many of the reviews, as well as a healthy skepticism toward overreaching the specifics of our data in the attempt to produce a grand synthesis.

At the close of the 19th century, the methods of prehistory were outlined by Hogarth as "seeking, examining, and ordering" material documents of the past as a way of countering "those rank growths of speculation that cumber the ground of prehistoric archaeology."[42] Cultural histories—seeking, examining, and ordering—are still the immediate goal of many prehistorians working in the Aegean today, undertaken less for the satisfaction of detailed description than as a step toward interpreting cultural process and historical diversity. Speculation continues to

flourish, a source of imagination and possibilities, but constrained by a "network of resistances"[43] provided by the archaeological and ethnographic record, and guided by a rigorous set of analytical constructs, if not yet an integrated theory.

CURRENT STATUS OF AEGEAN PREHISTORY

The origins and growth of Aegean prehistory as a distinct subdiscipline within classical archaeology have generally been addressed in the context of biography (individual excavators and their discoveries) or as an area of somewhat marginal concern in the wider focus on Hellenism and the so-called Great Tradition of classical studies in the West.[44] Valuable intellectual histories such as *The Idea of Prehistory*, by Daniel and Renfrew, and Trigger's *History of Archaeological Thought* seldom mention prehistory as practiced in the Aegean, and indeed Trigger relegates classical archaeology primarily to his chapter on antiquarianism. Dyson's recent volume *Ancient Marbles to American Shores* and earlier articles on the history and orientation of classical archaeology in the United States only tangentially incorporate the development of Aegean prehistory (notably in discussing the relatively substantial role played by women in fieldwork and in assessing the pioneering efforts of Blegen, McDonald, and Jacobsen, not only in their field projects but also for the impact of their interdisciplinary graduate programs). Nevertheless, much of Dyson's account of the emergence of classical archaeology and its evolution from amateur vocation to professional discipline is relevant to the growth of Aegean prehistory.[45] A few studies, mentioned above, have focused specifically on Aegean prehistory, situating it within the intellectual and historical context of changing politics, education, and ideologies,[46] and several of the RAP authors introduce their accounts with related comments (see especially Watrous, Run-

don 1995) 131–42; and, most recently, Chippindale and Gill, "Material Consequences of Contemporary Classical Collecting," *AJA* 104 (2000) 463–511. For the so-called Aidonia Treasure, see R. Elia, "Greece v. Ward: The Return of Mycenaean Artifacts," *International Journal of Cultural Property* 4:1 (1995) 119–28; and R.H. Howland ed., *Mycenaean Treasures of the Aegean Bronze Age Repatriated* (Washington, D.C., 1997). More generally, see R. Elia, "Popular Archaeology and the Antiquities Market: A Review Essay," *JFA* 18 (1991) 95–103; M.J. Lynott and A. Wylie eds., *Ethics in American Archaeology: Challenges for the 1990s* (Washington, D.C., 1995); K.D. Vitelli ed., *Archaeological Ethics* (Walnut Creek 1996), a collection of articles reprinted from *Archaeology* magazine; J. Dorfman, "Getting Their Hands Dirty? Archaeologists and the Looting Trade," *Lingua Franca* (May/June 1998) 28–36; and N. Brodie and J. Doole eds., *Illicit Antiquities: The Destruction of the World's Archaeological Heritage*

(Cambridge, forthcoming). Still a classic in the field is K.E. Meyer, *The Plundered Past* (New York 1973).

[42] Hogarth (supra n. 13) viii, x.

[43] A phrase first used by Shanks and Tilley in *Reconstructing Archaeology* (supra n. 37) 104.

[44] McDonald and Thomas (supra n. 15); Fitton (supra n. 15); I. Morris, "Archaeologies of Greece," in Morris (supra n. 32) 14–15; C. Renfrew, "The Great Tradition versus the Great Divide: Archaeology as Anthropology?" *AJA* 84 (1980) 287–98.

[45] Daniel and Renfrew (supra n. 29); Trigger (supra n. 29); S.L. Dyson, *Ancient Marbles to American Shores: Classical Archaeology in the United States* (Philadelphia 1998) 87–95, 175–79, 231–54.

[46] Fotiadis (supra ns. 19 and 36); Kotsakis (supra n. 14); and K. Kotsakis, "The Past Is Ours: Images of Greek Macedonia," in Meskell (supra n. 14) 44–67.

nels, and Andreou, Fotiadis, and Kotsakis, RAP III, IV, and V).

The establishment of foreign research institutes of archaeology in Mediterranean capitals in the 19th century provided a focus for Western excavations and study and a training ground for students. The American School of Classical Studies at Athens, for example, by controlling exclusive rights to fieldwork and strictly regulating admission and examination policies, has greatly influenced the direction of American classical archaeology, including Aegean prehistory. Davis has considered the institutional forces that perpetuate the gulf between classical archaeology and anthropological archaeology as practiced in North America, nevertheless citing many examples of anthropologically informed research in the Aegean, primarily drawn from prehistory.[47] As he points out, the location of most North American classical archaeology programs within Classics departments affects the training students receive and limits the ability of archaeologists to influence hiring decisions and professionally reproduce themselves.

In the United States, Aegean prehistorians may consider themselves social scientists but, grouped with classical archaeologists as humanists, they are rarely awarded funding by the National Science Foundation. The National Endowment for the Humanities, the traditional source of federal funding for Aegean archaeology, eliminated its independent archaeology program in 1996; support for archaeology in general has been radically reduced, and proposals for Aegean prehistoric research are now considered on an ad hoc basis together with collaborative projects in a range of fields. One devastating effect of this development has been to force prehistorians and others to rely once again on the generosity of wealthy patrons and their particular standards for worthwhile research.[48]

Partly as a result of these political and economic strictures, fewer large-scale field projects have been initiated by foreign teams in the Aegean in recent years, leading some to worry that students will not have ample opportunity to participate in fieldwork, especially excavation. The situation is particularly acute in Greece, where fieldwork permits per foreign school are strictly limited and bureaucratic complexities often overwhelm good intentions. Foreign schools with few or no excavations under their direct control must now seek to redefine their missions.[49] Kardulias has clearly described the clash between the foreign schools and the Greek Archaeological Service, the state agency under whose jurisdiction the protection of antiquities falls.[50] The Service is overburdened by a staggering number of salvage projects and often insufficient resources, leading to the haphazard curation of excavated materials and long delays in processing fieldwork applications from the foreign schools. Relations are further strained by a longstanding distrust of Westerners' motives in Greece, dating back to the early 19th century with Elgin's removal of sculptures from the Acropolis[51] and further exacerbated in the 20th century by American support of the military junta. In part because of difficulties in working in Greece, more archaeologists are turning to fieldwork in Cyprus, Turkey, and Albania.

Our understanding of the training, employment, research interests, and fieldwork experience of those who consider themselves Aegean prehistorians is based largely on the responses to a survey sent out in 1994 as part of an effort to compile the second edition of the *International Directory of Aegean Prehistorians* (*IDAP*).[52] A sample of 295 prehistorians was drawn from 25 countries, primarily the United States, Greece, Germany, and England. The majority work in Greece, and a small percentage conduct research in the Near East, Turkey, Italy, and Cyprus. Most teach at universities with graduate programs in departments of Archaeology, Prehistory, and Classics; fewer teach in Anthropology, History, or Art History departments. A sizable portion (58%) hold tenured or tenure-track positions. Statistics are not given on the relative numbers of men and women in tenured po-

[47] Davis (supra n. 35) 389–405; J.L. Davis, "Classical Archaeology and Anthropological Archaeology in North America: A Meeting of Minds at the Millennium?" in G. Feinman and T.D. Price eds., *Archaeology at the Millennium* (New York, forthcoming). I am grateful to Jack Davis for providing me with a copy of his forthcoming article. See also Renfrew (supra n. 44); A.M. Snodgrass, "The New Archaeology and the Classical Archaeologist," *AJA* 89 (1985) 31–37; and G. Gibbon, "Classical and Anthropological Archaeology: A Coming Rapprochement?" in N.C. Wilkie and W.D.E. Coulson eds., *Contributions to Aegean Archaeology: Studies in Honor of William A. McDonald* (Dubuque 1985) 283–94.

[48] Davis (supra n. 35) 394–95; Davis (supra n. 47); Dyson (supra n. 45) 283.

[49] My thanks to John Younger and Paul Rehak (personal communication) for stressing this point.

[50] P.N. Kardulias, "Archaeology in Modern Greece: Bureaucracy, Politics, and Science," in Kardulias (supra n. 20) 373–87.

[51] E.g., T. Vrettos, *The Elgin Affair: The Abduction of Antiquity's Greatest Treasures and the Passions It Aroused* (New York 1997).

[52] J.F. Cherry and J.L. Davis, "Aegean Prehistory in 1994: Results of the *IDAP* Survey Questionnaire," distributed with *Nestor* 21:8 (1994).

sitions for the worldwide sample, but among the 61 North American respondents in tenured or tenure-track positions, only a quarter (15) are women, though women make up half of the overall sample. Many other factors are considered in the survey, such as opportunities to teach prehistory, length of time to find an appointment, and general research interests (the study of economy, trade, and foreign contacts predominates).

Very similar trends can be seen in the results of a survey sent in 1996 to professional members of the Archaeological Institute of America (AIA).[53] Of the 135 respondents (all with a doctorate and most from North America) who indicate their specialty is Aegean prehistory, slightly more than half hold tenured or tenure-track positions. As in the *IDAP* survey, only a quarter of those positions are held by women, although 44% of the overall sample of respondents are women. In keeping with general trends in academe, men's salaries are much higher than those of women: while nearly three-quarters of the men who answered the question earned over $40,000 a year, only 36% of the female respondents could claim as much. Publishing rates also diverge: roughly equal proportions of men and women in the sample write journal articles, for example, but men on average published five articles over the five years preceding the survey, and women three.[54]

These figures should perhaps not come as a surprise if one considers the authorship of references cited in this introduction or, for that matter, the RAP authors themselves: one woman and nine men were invited to contribute to the series, most of whom are American and teach in research universities (in Classics, Classical Studies, or Archaeology departments) in the United States. Andreou, Fotiadis, and Kotsakis are Greek, holding professorships at Greek universities but educated in the United States and England. Wolpert and Tzonou-Herbst, the coauthors of Davis's addendum, are graduate students at an American university. Although women are visible in prominent po-

sitions within classical archaeology in North America (e.g., the current president and vice-president of the AIA), disparities in employment, publication rates, and in directing fieldwork are cause for concern.[55] More research into the sociopolitics of the discipline of Aegean prehistory, particularly from the European perspective, would be welcome.

Until relatively recently, classical archaeologists have tended to remain aloof from the theoretical and methodological debates current among anthropologically oriented British and American archaeologists—a distance deplored by many who would argue that a healthy discipline entails, in Clarke's famous phrase, "a loss of innocence," a self-critical perspective and an inquiry into the epistemology and sociopolitical circumstances that underlie archaeological interpretations.[56] In contrast, Aegean prehistory, characterized by Morris as "the soft underbelly of Hellenism,"[57] has by its marginal position in respect to classical studies and the Great Tradition been freer to absorb and contribute new and unconventional ideas, and also to adapt a wide range of scientific techniques to aid in the resolution of cultural questions.

An ambiguous status attaches to Aegean prehistory—at once holding a privileged position in its methodological sophistication and place in debates of world prehistory while at the same time marginalized within the wider discipline of classical archaeology, whose focus (and funding) is still primarily concerned with the historical era. Most museums in Greece reflect this divide; if they have a permanent exhibit of prehistoric artifacts, it is generally much more restricted than displays of classical art and highlights Minoan and Mycenaean art that is readily connected with Greek mythology or ancestry. Deeply embedded notions of the cultural superiority of Greeks of the Classical period have until recently tended to eclipse studies of earlier (and later) remains, especially of the earliest periods of Greek prehistory (see Runnels, RAP IV).

The schism that lies between the archaeology of

---

[53] T. Cullen, "Report on the AIA Survey of Professionals in Archaeology," *AIA Newsletter* 14:2 (1999) 6–7; T. Cullen and D. Keller, "Productivity in Archaeology: Report on the AIA Survey," *AIA Newsletter* 15:1 (1999) 6–7, 10.

[54] The sample of prehistorians who had published an article or book is small (n=91), but see Cullen and Keller (supra n. 53) 7 for comparable disparities in publishing rates among men and women in a larger sample of classical archaeologists (including prehistorians).

[55] See T. Cullen, "Contributions to Feminism in Archaeology," *AJA* 100 (1996) 412–13.

[56] D.L. Clarke, "Archaeology: The Loss of Innocence," *Antiquity* 47 (1973) 6–18. For the theoretical insulation of

classical archaeology, see, e.g., Morris (supra n. 44); S.L. Dyson, "The Role of Ideology and Institutions in Shaping Classical Archaeology in the Nineteenth and Twentieth Centuries," in A.L. Christenson ed., *Tracing Archaeology's Past: The Historiography of Archaeology* (Carbondale 1989) 127–35; Dyson, "Complacency and Crisis in Late Twentieth Century Classical Archaeology," in P. Culham and L. Edmunds eds., *Classics: A Discipline and Profession in Crisis?* (Lanham 1989) 211–20; Snodgrass (supra n. 47); Kotsakis (supra n. 14); and M. Shanks, *Classical Archaeology of Greece: Experiences of the Discipline* (London 1996).

[57] Morris (supra n. 44) 15.

historical Greece and the study of prehistory has long been recognized. A century ago, Hogarth distinguished between the Greater and Lesser Archaeology, the former including literary texts as a field of study and the latter restricted to "material remains." Prehistory—the Lesser Archaeology—"stops short of any possibility of truly reconstituting the past; for to that end the literary documents are all essential."[58] Historian David Lowenthal echoes these sentiments today: "From material remains alone we can merely speculate about past minds, hearts, and memories; only recorded words . . . reveal nuances of consciousness and intention, forethought and hindsight."[59] The notions that accessible meanings reside only in texts and that the historical record is more robust and hence superior to the archaeological have contributed to the divide between the study of text and material culture, and between history and archaeology. In the case of Aegean prehistory, recent scholarship on Late Bronze Age writing systems has focused on the integration of textual and archaeological evidence in order to provide a fully contextualized understanding of the political and economic administration of the palaces (see Shelmerdine and Rehak and Younger, RAP VI, VII).[60]

ENDNOTE

It is no coincidence that it was an Aegean prehistorian—Colin Renfrew—who in 1980 first entreated classical archaeologists to take notice of theoretical debates in anthropological archaeology, followed enthusiastically by Snodgrass and many others.[61] Dyson has written prolifically on the theoretical isolation of classical archaeology, quipping in 1981 that one "could probably fit most of the classical archaeologists really interested in the 'new archaeology' into a [telephone] booth without challenging the Guinness book of records, and talk about past interaction between the two groups could easily be accommodated within the length of a ten-cent call."[62] He hastened, however, to exclude "prehistorians who work in

the eastern Mediterranean," tacitly acknowledging that their inclusion would greatly exceed the capacity of his booth. Since that time, Aegean prehistorians have not only drawn upon advances in processual method and theory but have also contributed substantially to issues of international scope, from a multitude of perspectives.

Quoting William Pitt, Snodgrass once remarked that "youth is the season of credulity," going on to observe that "in Aegean Bronze Age archaeology, indeed, too much has been believed too readily, and repeated in a series of secondary treatments to the point where it acquired the status of an axiom."[63] The reviews of Aegean prehistory published here serve an invaluable purpose in calling our attention to the wealth of detail, gaps in knowledge, and leaps of faith underlying many of our reconstructions of the past. The scope of the discipline, however, is broader than one might infer from the review articles or this introduction, their primary focus being the prehistory of Greece. Aegean prehistorians routinely now address the archaeology of the wider Mediterranean, especially Anatolia, the Levant, Italy, the Balkans, and Egypt. This introduction is also skewed in its presentation of Aegean prehistory from a largely North American perspective, a reflection of my particular experience and training.

Although less conservative than its parent discipline, classical archaeology, Aegean prehistory as a whole is not characterized by radical experiment or theoretical forays, but remains a strongly empiricist enterprise. At the same time, a palpable sympathy for processualist goals can be traced throughout RAP I–VII. The optimism of 1970s positivism, however, has faded in the glare of postmodern doubts and the realization that more than one way of reading the past is valid. While rigorous and self-critical procedures are applauded, scientific objectivity is no longer held up by many prehistorians as an attainable goal, particularly as science itself is no longer viewed as a unified enterprise.[64] Efforts are made to

[58] Hogarth (supra n. 13) vii.

[59] D. Lowenthal, "Archaeology's Perilous Pleasures," *Archaeology* 53:2 (2000) 64.

[60] For efforts to bridge these divides, see D.B. Small ed., *Methods in the Mediterranean: Historical and Archaeological Views on Texts and Archaeology* (Leiden 1995); Morris (supra n. 32); and I. Morris, *Archaeology as Cultural History* (Oxford 2000). See also J. Bennet, "Knossos in Context: Comparative Perspectives on the Linear B Administration of LM I–III Crete," *AJA* 94 (1990) 193–211; I. Schoep, "Tablets and Territories? Reconstructing Late Minoan IB Political Geography through Undeciphered Documents," *AJA* 103 (1999) 201–21; J. Driessen and I. Schoep, "The Stylus

and the Sword: The Roles of Scribes and Warriors in the Conquest of Crete," in R. Laffineur ed., *Polemos: Le contexte guerrier en Égée à l'Âge du Bronze* (Aegaeum 19, Liège 1999) 389–401; and Bennet and Galaty (supra n. 30) 87–90 for a summary and additional bibliography.

[61] Renfrew (supra n. 44); Snodgrass (supra n. 47); Morris (supra n. 44); Davis (supra n. 47); and N. Spencer ed., *Time, Tradition, and Society in Greek Archaeology: Bridging the "Great Divide"* (London 1995).

[62] Dyson 1981 (supra n. 29) 7.

[63] Snodgrass (supra n. 47) 35.

[64] A. Wylie, "Questions of Evidence, Legitimacy, and the (Dis)unity of Science," *AmerAnt* 65 (2000) 227–37.

break down the boundaries between specializations, thus encouraging true collaborative research, and to resist dichotomies (e.g., science vs. humanism, history vs. anthropology) furthered by funding policies and academic structures.

Greater awareness of the complexity of archaeological interpretation and appreciation of archaeology as a political practice have fostered more explicit theorizing of data, at different scales of analysis, a long-term view complementing and drawing upon details of local context. In this respect, the reviews presented in the following chapters are witness to an openness and expansion of Aegean prehistory in many directions, a creative tension that surely signals a healthy discipline and provides a springboard into the new century.

AMERICAN SCHOOL OF CLASSICAL STUDIES
AT ATHENS
6–8 CHARLTON STREET
PRINCETON, NEW JERSEY 08540
TRACEY_CULLEN@ASCSA.ORG

Acknowledgments

My warmest thanks to several colleagues and friends for reading a preliminary draft of this introduction and making valuable comments: Jack Davis, Mihalis Fotiadis, Don Keller, Sandra Lucore, Paul Rehak, Curtis Runnels, Jerry Rutter, Vance Watrous, John Younger, and especially Laurie Talalay and John Cherry for extensive suggestions and bibliographical additions. I am also grateful to Mehmet Rona and my parents for their sound editorial direction and unflagging support.

Appendix
Research Tools for Aegean Prehistory

The following list is intended to serve as a useful starting point for students and scholars with other specialties who are interested in pursuing the study of Aegean prehistory. A remarkable variety of research tools now exists. With the virtual revolution in information technology has come a proliferation of electronic resources relevant to Aegean prehistory. Only a few major Web sites are cited here, but by way of linked files, one can easily find journal homepages, images, discussion lists, subject indexes, regional projects, museum exhibits, course materials, atlases, and more. The bibliography noted below is highly selective and relates to the geographical scope of RAP I–VII.

ELECTRONIC RESOURCES

ABZU: http://www-oi.uchicago.edu/OI/DEPT/RA/ABZU/ABZU.HTML. A guide to Internet resources in Near Eastern archaeology.

AegeaNet. A discussion list in Aegean prehistory. To subscribe, send the message "subscribe AegeaNet" to majordomo@duke.edu.

ARGOS: http://argos.evansville.edu. A search engine to limited areas in the ancient and medieval worlds.

Classics and Mediterranean Archaeology: http://classics.lsa.umich.edu/welcome.html. Site with links to a wide range of archaeological resources.

International Directory of Aegean Prehistorians[3]: http://classics.uc.edu/nestor/IDAP/isearch.lasso.

Kapatija: http://www.duke.edu/web/jyounger/Kapatija/. Provides links to Internet sites for the prehistoric and Classical Aegean.

Nestor: http://ucaswww.mcm.uc.edu/classics/nestor/nestor.html. A key source of bibliography relevant to Aegean prehistory. Searchable by author, title, or keyword. Also with many links to related Web sites.

Prehistoric Archaeology of the Aegean: http://devlab.dartmouth.edu/history/bronze_age/. A Web version of J. Rutter's Dartmouth College course on Aegean archaeology, with text, bibliography, and more than 500 illustrations.

BIBLIOGRAPHIES AND COMPILATIONS

B. Eder, *Staat, Herrschaft, Gesellschaft in frühgriechischer Zeit: Eine Bibliographie, 1978–1991/92* (*AnzWien* 611, Vienna 1994). Bibliography pertaining to kingship and society in the Late Bronze Age and Dark Age.

B. Feuer, *Mycenaean Civilization: A Research Guide* (Research Guides to Ancient Civilizations 5, New York 1996). An annotated bibliography organized by topic.

Corpus der minoischen und mykenischen Siegel.

Studies in Mycenaean Inscriptions and Dialect.

J. Chadwick et al., *Corpus of Mycenaean Inscriptions from Knossos.*

L. Godart and J.-P. Olivier, *Recueil des inscriptions en Linéaire A.*

ARCHAEOLOGICAL JOURNALS AND SERIES

For fieldwork in Greece, see *Αρχαιολογικόν Δελτίον, Το Εργον της εν Αθήναις Αρχαιολογικής Εταιρείας,* and *Πρακτικά της εν Αθήναις Αρχαιολογικής Εταιρείας.* Annual English and French summaries available in *Archaeological Reports* (published annually as a supplement to the *Journal of Hellenic Studies*) and the "Chronique des fouilles" section in the *Bulletin de correspondance hellénique*. Αμάλθεια, Κρητική Εστία, and Κρητικά Χρονικά publish reports on archaeological fieldwork in Crete.

Journals of the foreign schools in Greece include the *Annual of the British School at Athens, Annuario della Scuola archeologica di Atene e delle Missioni italiane in Oriente, Bulletin de correspondance hellénique, Hesperia: The Journal of the American School of Classical Studies at Athens,* and *Jahrbuch des Deutschen Archäologischen Instituts.*

Other journals featuring Aegean prehistory include the *American Journal of Archaeology, Antiquity, Cambridge Archaeological Journal, Journal of Archaeological Science, Journal of European Archaeology, Journal of Field Archaeology, Journal of Mediterranean Archaeology,* and the *Oxford Journal of Archaeology.* More specialized journals include *Aegean Archaeology* (Warsaw), *To Αρχαιολογικό Εργο στη Μακεδονία και Θράκη, Εγνατία, Kadmos,* and *Minos.*

Series that publish conference proceedings and monographs on Aegean topics include *Aegaeum: Annales d'archéologie égéenne de l'Université de Liège et UT-PASP, Sheffield Studies in Aegean Archaeology,* and *Studies in Mediterranean Archaeology.*

ATLASES

C.J. Gallis, Άτλας των προϊστορικών θέσεων της ανατολικής Θεσσαλίας (Larissa 1992).

J.W. Myers, E.E. Myers, and G. Cadogan eds., *The Aerial Atlas of Ancient Crete* (Berkeley 1992).

RECENT SYNTHESES

J. Bennet and M. Galaty, "Ancient Greece: Recent Developments in Aegean Archaeology and Regional Studies," *Journal of Archaeological Research* 5 (1997) 75–120.

C. Broodbank, *An Island Archaeology of the Early Cyclades* (Cambridge 2000).

O. Dickinson, *The Aegean Bronze Age* (Cambridge 1994).

C.N. Runnels and P. Murray, *Greece before History: An Archaeological Companion and Guide* (Stanford, forthcoming).

R. Treuil et al., *Les civilisations égéennes du Néolithique et de l'Âge du Bronze* (Paris 1989).

P.M. Warren, *The Aegean Civilisations*[2] (Oxford 1989).

GREEK PALAEOLITHIC, MESOLITHIC, AND NEOLITHIC

G.N. Bailey et al. eds., *The Palaeolithic Archaeology of Greece and Adjacent Areas* (*BSA* Studies 3, London 1999).

N. Galanidou and C. Perlès eds., *The Greek Mesolithic: Problems and Perspectives* (*BSA* Studies, London, forthcoming).

E. Alram-Stern, *Das Neolithikum in Griechenland, mit Ausnahme von Kreta und Zypern* (Die Ägäische Frühzeit, 2. Serie; Forschungsbericht 1975–1993 1, Vienna 1996).

A.J. Ammerman and P. Biagi eds., *The Widening Harvest: The Neolithic Transition in Europe* (Boston, forthcoming).

J.-P. Demoule and C. Perlès, "The Greek Neolithic: A New Review," *Journal of World Prehistory* 7 (1993) 355–416.

P. Halstead ed., *Neolithic Society in Greece* (Sheffield Studies in Aegean Archaeology 2, Sheffield 1999).

G.A. Papathanassopoulos ed., *Neolithic Culture in Greece* (Athens 1996).

C. Perlès, *The First Farming Communities in Europe: The Early Neolithic of Greece* (Cambridge World Archaeology, Cambridge, forthcoming).

BRONZE AGE CHRONOLOGY

S.W. Manning, *The Absolute Chronology of the Aegean Early Bronze Age: Archaeology, History and Radiocarbon* (Monographs in Mediterranean Archaeology 1, Sheffield 1995).

S.W. Manning, *A Test of Time: The Volcano of Thera and the Chronology and History of the Aegean and East Mediterranean in the Mid Second Millennium B.C.* (Oxford 1999).

P. Warren and V. Hankey, *Aegean Bronze Age Chronology* (Bristol 1989).

HISTORIOGRAPHIES

S.L. Dyson, *Ancient Marbles to American Shores: Classical Archaeology in the United States* (Philadelphia 1998).

J.L. Fitton, *The Discovery of the Greek Bronze Age* (Cambridge, Mass., 1996).

W.A. McDonald and C.G. Thomas, *Progress into the Past: The Rediscovery of Mycenaean Civilization*[2] (Bloomington 1990).

Review of Aegean Prehistory I:
The Islands of the Aegean

JACK L. DAVIS

INTRODUCTION

Not so long ago the islands of the Aegean (fig. 1) were considered by many to be the backwater of Greek prehistory.[1] Any synthesis of the field had perforce to base its conclusions almost exclusively upon data collected before the turn of the century. The entire prehistory of the islands received fewer than 16 pages of discussion in Emily Vermeule's *Greece in the Bronze Age* (Chicago 1964), almost all of this concerned with the art and graves of the Early Bronze Age Cyclades; other parts of the Aegean sea were generally mentioned only in passing. Vermeule had no choice but to write that for the Cyclades "only three village sites [Phylakopi on Melos, Kastri on Syros, and Thera] have been excavated in a manner one could call informative, in contrast to nearly two thousand known or suspected graves" (p. 47). Of these only Phylakopi also offered a deep stratigraphy covering all phases

of the Bronze Age, and it is no surprise that its sequence formed the basis for a tripartite Cycladic chronology, established parallel to Helladic and Minoan phases on the Greek mainland and Crete. The *existence* of a Neolithic in the islands, particularly on Keos, Saliagos, and Chios, had been demonstrated but in no instance had been fully documented.

A quarter century later, the situation has been altered drastically. Particularly in the last decade progress has been very rapid, hampering any attempt to produce a totally up-to-date synthesis of new data, as does the frequent appearance of important studies in new Greek periodicals of limited circulation. Indeed, publication has been so voluminous and diverse that it is difficult even for specialist Aegean prehistorians to stay abreast of new developments. The essential annual reviews of new work in Greece, published by successive directors of the British and French schools

---

[1] The publication of this review was made possible by a generous subvention from the Institute for Aegean Prehistory.

I am particularly grateful to those friends and colleagues who responded to requests for information concerning their recent research, and in particular to those who provided me with offprints, preprints, or photographs. The more specific contributions of several colleagues are acknowledged as appropriate later in this review. Here I should like to express my thanks to Robert Arnott, Robin Barber, Cyprian Broodbank, Tristan Carter, John Cherry, Christopher Chippindale, John Coleman, Michael Cosmopoulos, Tracey Cullen, Søren Dietz, Christos Doumas, Angelia Douzougli, Noel Gale, David Gill, David Hardy, Carol Hershenson, Donald Keller, Sandy MacGillivray, Sturt Manning, Lila Marangou, Mariza Marthari, Dimitris Matsas, Lyvia Morgan, Christine Morris, John Overbeck, Mehmet Özdoğan, Ernst Pernicka, Colin Renfrew, Efi Sakellaraki, Diamantis Sampson, Elizabeth Schofield, Zophia Stos-Gale, René Treuil, Sarah Vaughan, David Wilson, and Kostas Zachos. Tracey Cullen, Fred Kleiner, and Jerry Rutter conceived of this project and encouraged me to undertake it. Over the past year and a half I have at times regretted accepting the assignment, and in moments of panic have cursed them severally and collectively, but I am in the end thankful that they convinced me to do it. I am also grateful to Shari Stocker for help with the illustrations and proofreading, to Bill Parkinson for compiling references, and to John Bennet, Cyprian Broodbank, John Cherry, Mihalis Fotiadis, Donald Keller, Sandy MacGillivray, Sturt Manning, Curtis Runnels, Jerry Rutter, and David Wilson for their prompt comments on my penultimate draft.

The following special abbreviations are used in this paper:

AEMT	*Το Αρχαιολογικόν Εργον στη Μακεδονία και Θράκη.*
"Chronique"	"Chronique des fouilles," *BCH.*
Cycladica	L. Fitton ed., *Cycladica: Studies in Memory of N.P. Goulandris* (London 1984).
Cycladic Culture	L. Marangou ed., *Cycladic Culture: Naxos in the 3rd Millennium BC* (Athens 1990).
Dodecanese	S. Dietz ed., *Archaeology in the Dodecanese* (Copenhagen 1988).
Emporio	S. Hood, *Excavations in Chios 1938–1955: Prehistoric Emporio and Ayio Gala*, 1–2 (*BSA* Suppl. 15–16, London 1981–1982).
"First Colonization"	J.F. Cherry, "The First Colonization of the Mediterranean Islands: A Review of Recent Research," *JMA* 3 (1990) 145–221.
Gazetteer	R. Hope Simpson and O.T.P.K. Dickinson, *A Gazetteer of Aegean Civilisation in the Bronze Age* 1: *The Mainland and Islands* (*SIMA* 52, Göteborg 1979).
Greek Prehistory	E.B. French and K.A. Wardle eds., *Problems in Greek Prehistory* (Bristol 1988).
Karpathos, Saros and Kasos	M. Melas, *The Islands of Karpathos, Saros and Kasos in the Neolithic and Bronze Age* (*SIMA* 68, Göteborg 1985).
Kastro Tigani	R.C.S. Felsch, *Das Kastro Tigani: Die spätneolithische und chalkolithische Siedlung* (*Samos* II, Bonn 1988).

Originally published in *AJA* 96 (1992) 699–756.

in *Archaeological Reports* (*AR*) and in *BCH*'s "Chronique des fouilles" ("Chronique") are, of course, essential points of departure for both scholars and students, but can be patchy in their coverage and, in any case, are not intended to be synthetic.[2] The bible of Aegean prehistory, R. Hope Simpson and O.T.P.K. Dickinson's *A Gazetteer of Aegean Civilisation in the Bronze Age* 1: *The Mainland and Islands* (Göteborg 1979, completed 1977; hereafter, *Gazetteer*), is now nearly 15 years out of date, and in any case omitted coverage of the islands of the Aegean that lie north of Skyros and Chios.[3] Robin Barber's *The Cyclades in the Bronze Age* (Iowa City 1987) provides an excellent overview of the results of research in the southern Aegean, but publications relevant to Cycladic prehistory have been so prolific in the past six years that an update is also desirable.[4]

BEYOND THE CYCLADES TO A PAN-AEGEAN PERSPECTIVE

The decision to include virtually all islands of the Aegean (excluding only Crete and those of the Saronic Gulf) reflects trends in recent scholarship that have defined problems demanding a canvas much broader than that offered by the Cyclades alone.[5] Two examples of topics that require a pan-Aegean focus may suffice: the Neolithic colonization of the Aegean islands; and the Minoanization of the Aegean in the Middle Bronze Age and early part of the Late Bronze Age.

In the past decade there have been, for the first time, systematic attempts to describe initial settlement of the islands of the Aegean in terms of principles drawn from island biogeography.[6] The general idea

---

Les Cyclades	G. Rougemont ed., *Les Cyclades: Materiaux pour une étude de géographie historique* (Paris 1983).
Manika I–II	A. Sampson, *Μάνικα* I: *Μία πρωτοελλαδική πόλη στη Χαλκίδα* (Athens 1985); *Μάνικα* II: *Ο πρωτοελλαδικός οικισμός και το νεκροταφείο* (Athens 1988).
Minoan Influence	A.G. Papagiannopoulou, *The Influence of Middle Minoan Pottery on the Cyclades* (*SIMA-PB* 96, Göteborg 1991).
Minoan Thalassocracy	R. Hägg and N. Marinatos eds., *The Minoan Thalassocracy: Myth and Reality* (*SkrAth* 32, Stockholm 1984).
Neolithic and Protohelladic	A. Sampson, *Η Νεολιθική και η Πρωτοελλαδική I στην Εύβοια* (*Αρχείον Ευβοϊκών Μελετών, Παράρτημα του ΚΔ' Τόμου*, Athens 1981).
Neolithic Dodecanese	A. Sampson, *Η Νεολιθική περίοδος στα Δωδεκάνησα* (Athens 1987).
"Perspectives"	J.L. Davis, "Perspectives on the Prehistoric Cyclades: An Archaeological Introduction," in P. Getz-Preziosi, *Early Cycladic Art in North American Collections* (Richmond 1987) 4–45.
Prehistoric Cyclades	J.A. MacGillivray and R.L.N. Barber, *The Prehistoric Cyclades* (Edinburgh 1984).
Silber, Blei und Gold	G.A. Wagner and G. Weisgerber, *Silber, Blei und Gold auf Sifnos: Prähistorische und antike Metallproduction* (*Der Anschnitt*, Beiheft 3, Bochum 1985).
"Sources of Metals"	Z.A. Stos-Gale and C.F. Macdonald, "Sources of Metals and Trade in the Bronze Age Aegean," in N.H. Gale ed., *Bronze Age Trade in the Mediterranean* (*SIMA* 90, Jonsered 1991) 249–88.
TAW I	C. Doumas ed., *Thera and the Aegean World* I (London 1978).
TAW III	D.A. Hardy et al. eds., *Thera and the Aegean World* III.1: *Archaeology* (London 1990); 2: *Earth Sciences* (London 1990); 3: *Chronology* (London 1990).

[2] For an index to the sites described in *AR* between 1976 and 1986, see *AR* 33 (1987) 78–87. All references below to *AR* without further specification of title or author are to the annual reports, "Archaeology in Greece," compiled by H.W. Catling and, since *AR* 36 (1990), by E.B. French. References to "Chronique" are to "Chronique des fouilles," *BCH*, compiled by G. Touchais and, since *BCH* 114 (1989), by A. Pariente.

[3] The islands of the northern Aegean are included in D. Leekley and R. Noyes, *Archaeological Excavations in the Greek Islands* (Park Ridge, N.J. 1975), which is, however, further out of date than the *Gazetteer* and is not nearly so authoritative or exhaustive in its coverage.

[4] With reservations (see my review in *AJA* 93 [1989] 293–94), W. Ekschmitt, *Kunst und Kultur der Kykladen* I: *Neolitikum und Bronzezeit* (Mainz 1986) may also be recommended as a reasonably current review of Cycladic prehistory; the extensive illustrations, many in color, are particularly worthy. See also "Perspectives" for a recent brief overview of the Early Cycladic period.

[5] Islands of the Saronic Gulf include all those that currently belong to the administrative district of Peiraeus, including Spetses, Hydra, Kythera, and Antikythera. Covered in this review, in whole or part, are territories of the following Ephorates of Prehistoric and Classical Antiquities: 1st (Keos); 11th (Euboia and Skyros); 13th (northern Sporades); 18th (Thasos); 19th (Samothrace); 20th (Lesbos, Chios, Psara, and Limnos); 21st (Cyclades, Samos, and Ikaria, excluding Keos and Amorgos); and 22nd (Dodecanese and Amorgos). For a comprehensive description of the administrative districts that comprise the Greek Archaeological Service, see *AR* 36 (1990) 4. The order of presentation for yearly reports both in *AR* and in *ArchDelt* mirrors this administrative structure, and it will also be followed here.

[6] J.F. Cherry, "Pattern and Process in the Earliest Colonization of the Mediterranean Islands," *PPS* 47 (1981) 41–68, has considered these issues most extensively.

Fig. 1. Principal Aegean archaeological sites discussed in this review

of these studies is that geography has played a major role in determining the date, extent, and rate of settlement in the Aegean. Examination of the way in which both animal and plant species have come to inhabit island groups in other parts of the world suggested that certain patterns of colonization might also be recognizable in Greece. For example, it has been hypothesized that the distance of an island from adjacent mainland coasts, its absolute size, and the presence or absence of stepping stone islands between it and a mainland were important factors in determining the likelihood that the island will have been settled at a particular time in the past. This is not of course to suggest that social or political factors should be eliminated from the equation, but rather that biogeography can provide an initial investigative framework within which the importance of cultural determinants of settlement can be more explicitly defined.

Hand in glove with these analyses have come attempts to explain why extensive colonization of the Aegean islands occurred so long after settlement of adjacent mainlands. It has been realized for some years that the islands of the Aegean cannot have been inaccessible to potential human colonizers, inasmuch as obsidian from Melos was reaching the Greek mainland already in the later Palaeolithic and Mesolithic; finds are well documented in strata excavated at Franchthi Cave in the southern Argolid and are clearly Melian in origin.[7] The recognition that the Aegean was being navigated long before the introduction of agriculture to Greece has obvious and important repercussions for how the process by which agriculture was spread from the Near East to Greece is viewed: clearly an absence of evidence for settlement in the earlier phases of the Neolithic in the Greek islands no longer requires us to postulate the existence of a more northern route of migration for Neolithic immigrants, for which there has been precious little evidence. The Aegean sea of the later Palaeolithic was navigable and navigated.[8]

Of equal importance is the realization that inhabitants from the adjacent mainlands had the capability of establishing settlements in the Aegean islands long before they actually did so. Documentation in the future of any evidence for earlier transient activity is unlikely to make a great difference to present generalizations. While it is certainly true that some settlements of Palaeolithic and earlier Neolithic date may be lost to fluctuations in coastlines or may yet lie undetected, the fact remains that no clear evidence of a Palaeolithic presence has yet been recognized in the islands, at least not on any island that was then separated from an adjacent mainland by an appreciable gulf.

The evidence for earliest colonization of the Aegean islands has recently been updated.[9] Most of the islands of the Aegean appear to have been first inhabited during the EBA, although traces of Neolithic habitation are more plentiful today than even a year or so ago. A Neolithic presence has now been documented in the Cyclades (Keos, Naxos, Thera, Amorgos, Paros, Saliagos, and Siphnos), in the northern Sporades (Kyra Panayia and Youra), on Chios, Psara, Samos, in most of the Dodecanesian islands, and on Limnos, Lesbos, Samothrace, and Thasos. In all cases the earliest material yet recognized appears to be later in date than that from adjacent mainlands; in general, the final period of the Neolithic (FN) seems to have been the time of maximum expansion in settlement. The earliest well-documented Neolithic settlement is that of Ayios Petros on Kyra Panayia, situated near the eastern end of a string of islands that leads out into the Aegean from Thessaly, itself probably the most densely settled part of the Greek mainland during the Early and Middle Neolithic.[10] Certainly it

---

[7] See C. Perlès, *Les industries lithiques taillées de Franchthi (Argolide, Grèce)* 1: *Présentation générale et industries paléolithiques* (Franchthi 3, Bloomington 1987) 142–45; 2: *Les industries du Mésolithique et du Néolithique initial* (Franchthi 5, Bloomington 1990). For further discussion of Melos and Franchthi Cave, see now also C. Renfrew and A. Aspinall, "Aegean Obsidian and Franchthi Cave," in Perlès 1990, 257–70. These authors also note that postulated linkages between tunny fishing and collection of obsidian on Melos by mainlanders are not supported by the evidence from Franchthi Cave, since obsidian has been found there in levels earlier than those in which evidence for deep sea fishing first appears.

[8] Recent research in Thessaly has tended to support a hypothesis that agriculture was introduced to Greece from the Near East through migration, rather than through trade between Near Easterners and an existing Mesolithic Greek population. For a current review of the evidence, see J. Hansen, "The Introduction of Agriculture into Greece: The Near Eastern Evidence," *AJA* 96 (1992) 340–41 (abstract). See also J.M. Hansen, *The Palaeoethnobotany of Franchthi Cave* (Franchthi 7, Bloomington 1991) 174–81; C.N. Runnels, "Trade Models in the Study of Agricultural Origins and Dispersion," *JMA* 2 (1989) 149–55. On the scarcity of early Neolithic sites in Eastern Macedonia and Thrace, see C. Renfrew, "Sitagroi in European Prehistory," in C. Ren-

frew, M. Gimbutas, and E.S. Elster eds., *Excavations at Sitagroi: A Prehistoric Village in Northwest Greece* (Los Angeles 1986) 477–85; J.E. Coleman, "Greece and the Aegean," in R.W. Ehrich ed., *Chronologies in Old World Archaeology*[3] (Chicago, in press); and D. Grammenos, Νεολιθικές έρευνες στην κεντρική και ανατολική Μακεδονία (βιβλιοθήκη της εν Αθήναις Αρχαιολογικής Εταιρείας 117, Athens 1991) 29. Recent excavations and explorations in Turkish Thrace are of particular interest. At the site of Hoca Çeşme in 1990–1991 (phase IV), ceramics similar in character to those of central Anatolia, with parallels in Hacılar IX–VI, have been excavated. Preliminary notices of these results will appear in *Araştırma Sonuçları*, and *Germania*. See also M.J. Mellink, "Archaeology in Anatolia," *AJA* 96 (1992) 125; and M. Özdoğan, Y. Miyake, and N. Özbaşaran Dede, "An Interim Report on Excavations at Yarımburgaz and Toptepe in Eastern Thrace," *Anatolica* 17 (1991) 81–82.

[9] "First Colonization" 145–221.

[10] Palaeolithic finds have been reported from both Thasos and Euboia; both islands would then have been attached to adjacent mainlands. Palaeolithic finds have also been reported from various sites on Alonnisos, Kyra Panayia, and Skyros, all in the northern Sporades, but are not yet well documented; see "First Colonization" 167. Stretches of open sea between these islands and the mainland of Thessaly may also have been negligible.

cannot be doubted that Early Neolithic populations were capable of organizing and launching large-scale colonizations across open sea. The settlement of the island of Crete in the later eighth or earlier seventh millennium is an obvious example of a successful enterprise of that sort, one that "indicates an exogenous introduction of farming and farmers through a purposive, planned and comparatively long-range colonization." That island, like others of the Aegean, thus far lacks any clear evidence for pre-Neolithic activity.[11]

It is equally important that those conditions be determined that eventually *did* result in successful colonization of the Aegean islands and in extensive, widespread, and long-lived settlement. A Neolithic agricultural package of domesticated crops and animals would have offered potential colonists a better chance for long-term survival in areas where wild resources were restricted. But although a Neolithic way of life was an obvious precondition for the viability of long-term occupations on the tiny and resource-poor islands of the Aegean, it cannot have been the only factor in play. Indeed, there is a gap of some two to four millennia between the colonization of Crete and that of the Cyclades, northern Sporades, or the Dodecanese, despite the fact that some of these islands lie directly along potential lines of migration between Crete and Anatolia. Principles of island biogeography also suggest that the survival rate of settlements close to colonizing mainlands will be higher, since their populations will be able to look to the neighboring mainlands for support, whether for marriage partners, breeding stock, or, in crisis, even for seed grain.[12] The colonization of Crete should thus be seen as a purposeful effort to found a new settlement in an especially favorable island environment, and not as the result of a gradual expansion of population through the islands to its north and east.

Three general horizons of Neolithic colonization in the Cycladic islands have recently been defined: the first contemporary with the site on Saliagos, an islet that in the fifth millennium B.C. was situated on a

land bridge that joined Paros and Antiparos; the second contemporary with the fourth-millennium FN site of Kephala on Keos; and the third represented by the expansion of population at the transition between the Neolithic and EBA that resulted in the creation of the Early Cycladic culture.[13] Notional colonizations of the Cycladic islands have been modeled: one beginning from the Greek mainland (specifically from Attica and Euboia), and another starting from the Dodecanese and progressing via Ikaria and Astypalaia. On the basis of these models it has been suggested that in the Saliagos phase, it is most likely that colonists came to the Cyclades from the southeast Aegean alone, but that later colonists probably proceeded from both directions at once. In all cases, the survival of settlements on Naxos would have been especially favored by circumstances of natural geography. Indeed, only on Naxos have traces of all three phases of settlement been recognized and only on Naxos can a case for continuity in settlement throughout the Late Neolithic and Final Neolithic periods be made.

A clearer understanding of the factors that led to expansion of settlement into the islands of the Aegean will also require a careful examination of the character of societies in those areas likely to have provided colonists. Although a topic well beyond the scope of this review, it is worth noting that there appears to be a close correlation between an expansion of settlement on the island of Euboia and the establishment of settlements in many of the Cycladic islands during the Final Neolithic. In particular, the habitation of marginal parts of southern Euboia could be seen as part of a general movement of populations into marginal areas, the beginning of a trend that would lead to a prodigious expansion of settlement in the EBA.[14] Social, as well as geographical, problems would have been faced by early colonists in the Cyclades. Several of these have recently been examined in a study that seeks to explain the differential development of Crete and the Cyclades in the course of the EBA.[15] The role of exogamy in linking relatively tiny communities of

[11] C. Broodbank and T.F. Strasser, "Migrant Farmers and the Neolithic Colonization of Crete," *Antiquity* 65 (1991) 233–45.

[12] Broodbank and Strasser (supra n. 11) 238–39.

[13] See C. Broodbank, "Colonization and Culture in the Neolithic and Early Bronze Age Cyclades," *AJA* 96 (1992) 341 (abstract). I am extremely grateful to Cyprian Broodbank for a copy of the text of his paper as read, and for permission to summarize his argument here.

[14] On the relationship between settlement in southern Euboia and FN/EBA colonization of the Cyclades, see Keller and Cullen (infra n. 61).

[15] S.W. Manning, "The Emergence of Divergence: Development and Decline on Bronze Age Crete and the Cyclades," in C. Mathers and S. Stoddart, *Development and Decline in the Mediterranean Bronze Age* (in press). There has as yet, however, been no serious attempt to use ceramic characterization analyses to distinguish between a scenario in which items were produced on two different islands in the Neolithic within similar cultural traditions, and one in which items were traded between the same two islands. See J.E. Coleman's (supra n. 8) discussion of evidence for Neolithic trade in the Aegean. I am grateful to both authors for preprints of their forthcoming publications.

the islands is emphasized. Exogamy, it is suggested, also promoted a stylistic homogeneity in artifacts within the Aegean, of a sort recognizable already in the earliest Neolithic Saliagos culture of the Cyclades. By the second phase of the EBA, however, exchanged goods had come into the hands of specialist producers, partly because opportunities for the intensification of agricultural production were so limited, and the exchange of agricultural goods on a large scale infeasible.

It is clear that exchange played a crucial role in enabling permanent settlement in the islands of the Aegean, even if it is not yet possible to quantify the extent of this trade. In the EBA, the similarities in the formal characteristics of ceramics, marble vessels, figurines, and metal objects that typify the Early Cycladic culture are indicative of social and economic ties maintained among the settlements of the islands; these relationships may also be regarded as necessary adaptations that would have provided access to additional resources of food and manpower in times of crisis.[16] Exchange may, therefore, be seen not as the incentive for colonization of the islands of the Aegean, but as an indispensable enabling mechanism that promoted the survival of groups once established, particularly on smaller, more remote, and impoverished landfalls such as the so-called Amorgian islets of Epano and Kato Koufonisi, Donousa, Schinousa, or Keros.

Our understanding of trade in metals has been dramatically improved in recent years. Much current literature has been summarized in the volume *Bronze Age Trade in the Mediterranean*.[17] In general a clear pattern appears to have emerged from recent analyses. In the EBA Cyclades, Siphnos and Kythnos served as major sources for lead, silver, and copper. Both of these sources were replaced in the Middle Bronze Age by Laurion, which came to dominate the Aegean as the principal supplier of metals.[18] It is clear too that exchange in marble vessels and figurines played a role in EBA exchange, but slight progress has been made in this arena. There is little agreement among scholars as to the validity of attributing marble figurines to individual sculptural hands or workshops, and there is little basis for assigning such personalities or production centers to particular locations within the Cyclades, because the vast majority of marbles lack verifiable archaeological contexts.[19] For these reasons and because of their rarity, marble figurines are not likely ever to provide us with more than the crudest measurements of intra-Aegean exchange. Fewer than 2,000 figurines are known, and these were produced over some 600–700 years!

The study of ceramic fabrics promises in the long run to be of greater value in reconstructing patterns of exchange. Given the diversity of geology among the islands of the Aegean, it is in many cases possible to recognize imported products on the basis of both visual inspection and petrological analysis. The results of a long-term project conducted under the auspices of the Fitch Laboratory of the British School at Athens should soon be available. This study has focused spe-

---

[16] See J.F. Cherry, "Island Origins: The Early Prehistoric Cyclades," in B.W. Cunliffe ed., *Origins, the Roots of European Civilisation* (London 1987) 25–26; "Perspectives" 26–30.

[17] N.H. Gale ed., *Bronze Age Trade in the Mediterranean* (*SIMA* 90, Jonsered 1991). Of particular importance is the paper by Z.A. Stos-Gale and C.F. Macdonald, "Sources of Metals." Fig. 1, p. 254, provides a map of ore deposits sampled for lead-isotopic composition through 1990. On the subject of direct evidence for Bronze Age Cycladic metallurgy, see also Z.A. Stos-Gale, "Cycladic Copper Metallurgy," in A. Hauptman, E. Pernicka, and G.A. Wagner eds., *Old World Archaeometallurgy* (Der Anschnitt, Beiheft 7, Bochum 1989) 279–92. These papers should be read in conjunction with N.H. Gale and Z.A. Stos-Gale, "Cycladic Lead and Silver Metallurgy," *BSA* 76 (1981) 169–224. See also E. Pernicka, "Erlagerstätten in der Ägäis und ihre Ausbeutung im Altertum: Geochemische Untersuchungen zur Herkunftsbestimmung archäologischer Metallobjekte," *JRGZM* 34 (1987) 607–714. For the role of specific islands in prehistoric metalworking and trade, see discussion of Karpathos, Keos, Thera, Chios, and Melos in the following section of this review.

[18] Possible explanations for the replacement of Siphnos by Laurion as dominant supplier to Keos have been discussed by N.H. Gale, Z.A. Stos-Gale, and J.L. Davis, "The Provenance of Lead Used at Ayia Irini, Keos," *Hesperia* 53 (1984) 389–406. Evidence from the analysis of the small number of actual silver artifacts (as opposed to litharge samples) that have yet been examined is more equivocal: Laurion and Siphnos do not emerge so obviously as dominant sources.

[19] On the definition of sculptural hands, see P. Getz-Preziosi, *Sculptors of the Cyclades: Individual and Tradition in the Third Millennium B.C.* (Ann Arbor 1987); see ch. 7 for patterns of distribution, such as they are, given the lack of a proper excavated context for the vast majority of figures. For doubts about the use of a canon in the production of Cycladic marble figures and about the correctness of procedures employed to assign sculptures to hands, see C. Renfrew, *The Cycladic Spirit: Masterpieces from the Nicholas P. Goulandris Collection* (New York 1991) ch. 9 and pp. 137–41. Soon see also C. Chippindale and D. Gill, "Material and Intellectual Consequences of Esteem for Cycladic Figures" (in prep.) for discussion of the magnitude of the problem faced by archaeologists because such a substantial part of the corpus of marble figurines has been acquired through illegal excavations; Chippindale and Gill also adduce substantial art historical grounds for doubting that individual hands of prehistoric sculptors can be defined. J.F. Cherry, "The Individual in Prehistory: Reflections on Attribution Studies in the Bronze Age Aegean," in J.C. Crowley and R. Laffineur eds., *EIKON. Aegean Bronze Age Iconography: Shaping a Methodology* (Aegeum 10, in press).

cifically on the EBA and has included material from the sites of Keos *Ayia Irini*; Naxos *Cave of Zas, Grotta,* and *Palati*; Thera *Akrotiri*; Melos *Phylakopi*; Ios *Skarkos*; Amorgos *Markiani*; and Keros *Kavos*. It is anticipated that the final product will be presented in the form of a handbook that can be used in the field for fabric indentification.[20]

A second central issue in prehistory that benefits from a pan-Aegean perspective is the relationship between Crete and the islands of the Aegean in the MBA and earlier phases of the LBA, the time of the so-called Minoan Thalassocracy. Recent research on many of the Aegean islands leaves no doubt that contacts between Crete and the Cyclades became especially intense after the construction of the Old Palaces.[21] Exchange appears to have played a major role in motivating Cretan involvement in the affairs of the islands to its north. On many of these islands, local industries were deeply affected by the contact. Local styles of decoration, particularly for pottery, and local manufacturing techniques were abandoned in favor of Minoan-inspired prototypes. A number of these changes may well have resulted from elite emulation of the status goods produced by the Minoan civilization. Others, for instance the widespread adoption in the islands of Minoan forms of loomweights, may reflect subtler variation in the structure of Cycladic social and economic organization.[22]

Two items have been clarified by extensive recent debate. First, it is not possible to measure the extent of political control by the Cretans as a direct reflection of the extent of changes observable in the material culture of the islands. Political dominance by Crete may well have encouraged the adoption of Minoan ways in its overseas colonies. But conquest is, in and of itself, no real explanation for change in material culture: one can too easily point to a plethora of historical examples in which imperial control resulted in relatively few changes in the everyday life of the majority of the conquered.

Second, there is an enormous diversity in the settlement history of those island centers that were pulled within the Minoan orbit. The entirety of the southern Aegean was strongly affected by contact with Crete; the northern Aegean appears to have lain largely outside the sphere of Cretan cultural influence. In the west, no evidence for a heavily Minoanized settlement has been recognized north of Keos; in the east, Kos is the dividing line. In the central Cyclades, Naxos marks the limit. None of this is to say, of course, that evidence for *contact* with Crete cannot be recognized farther to the north. Minoan ceramic imports have long been acknowledged at Pefkakia in Thessaly, and on Samos, while Minoan artifacts appear to have made their way even to Troy, albeit in small quantities.[23]

The recent discovery of a Minoan sealing and roundel at the site of Mikro Vouni on Samothrace must be viewed within this general context.[24] The situation of these discoveries, however remarkable, should be distinguished from that of Cretan finds in the heavily Minoanized zone of the southern Aegean. Minoan finds north of an east–west line drawn between Attica

---

[20] This project is under the direction of S.J. Vaughan, to whom I am extremely grateful for the information summarized here. Her work will soon be published in S.J. Vaughan, *Early Bronze Age Cycladic Pottery Fabrics: Studies in Materials and Technology (Fitch Laboratory Occasional Paper 5,* in prep.). Vaughan emphasizes that the evidence supports her hypothesis that "already in the EBA there were well-established trade and exchange routes throughout the Cyclades and beyond" and that there was "very specialized ceramic production and trade reflecting skilled exploitation of the best raw materials available on each island, with connections perhaps for exchange with other items such as ores." Various special studies in press or in preparation examine the so-called EBA talc ware (S. Vaughan and D. Wilson, "Interregional Contacts in the EB II Aegean: The Talc Ware Connection," in C.W. Zerner and E.B. French eds., *Wace and Blegen: Pottery as Evidence for Trade in the Aegean Bronze Age 1939–1989,* in press), and ceramic fabrics from Amorgos *Markiani,* Melos *Phylakopi,* and Keros *Kavos.* Recent petrological studies of ceramics from Akrotiri on Thera and from Mikri Vigla on Naxos are described in the following section of this review. In addition to these, see also S.J. Vaughan, "Bronze Age Cycladic White Wares: A Question of Materials and Manufacturing Techniques," *AJA* 96 (1992) 342 (abstract). I thank D.E. Wilson for a preprint of his and Vaughan's paper on talc ware.

[21] Evidence for interaction between Crete and the islands, as understood in 1983, is summarized by papers in *Minoan Thalassocracy.* The current state of affairs is outlined in two papers by M.H. Wiener, "The Nature and Control of Minoan Foreign Trade," in Gale (supra n. 17) 325–50; and "The Isles of Crete? The Minoan Thalassocracy Revisited," in *TAW* III.1, 128–60.

[22] See, e.g., the arguments made in J.L. Davis, "Cultural Innovation and the Minoan Thalassocracy," in *Minoan Thalassocracy* 159–66.

[23] For Minoan finds in the eastern Aegean, see W.D. Niemeier, "The End of the Minoan Thalassocracy," in *Minoan Thalassocracy* 205–14 and discussion on p. 215; for the western coast of the Aegean, see J.B. Rutter and C.W. Zerner, "Early Hellado-Minoan Contacts," in *Minoan Thalassocracy* 75–82. For an as yet unverified report of MM I pottery at Troy, see D.F. Easton, "The Chronology of West Anatolia in the Early Bronze Age," *BICS* 35 (1988) 180–81; for stone vases of Minoan type at Troy, see P.M. Warren, *Minoan Stone Vases* (Cambridge 1969) 17; "Minoan Stone Vases as Evidence for Minoan Foreign Connexions," *PPS* 33 (1967) 37–56.

[24] See the following section of this review and infra n. 100. For earlier Linear A finds in the islands, see T.G. Palaima, "Linear A in the Cyclades: The Trade and Travel of a Script," *TUAS* 7 (1982) 15–22.

and Samos remain sporadic, and the material cultural assemblages in which they have been discovered are predominantly non-Minoan in character. The archaeological picture does not, however, entirely conform to predictions that "the strength of Minoan contacts is proportional to proximity to Crete."[25] Rather, there appears to have been a dramatic falloff in Minoan influence between the north and south Aegean, and even within the southern Aegean there are marked differences in the nature of Cretan influence.

More than a decade ago I argued that "there existed a zone in the Western Cyclades (encompassing at least the islands of Thera, Melos, and Keos) in which there was regular exchange between Cycladic settlements and Crete."[26] My argument in 1979 was that these islands had been preferentially supplied with Minoan products and that Minoan trading activities in the southern Aegean were to some extent directional (and thus purposeful). The principal settlements on Thera, Melos, and Keos were interpreted as three important ports along a "Western String" exchange route between Crete and the mainland. The subsequent definition of a similar "enriched" zone in the Dodecanese lends, I think, support to my proposition that one of the most important motives for such exchange was the acquisition of metals by Crete. The extent to which eastern Attica supplied the Minoan world with lead and silver has become much more clear in the past decade; copper now too can be added to the list of mineral products that reached Crete from Laurion. The sharp drop-off in evidence for Minoan contact to the north of Samos may suggest that Cretans in the eastern Aegean were also interested in the acquisition of a particular product, either one locally produced or that could be acquired through the medium of secondary distribution centers.[27]

This much is clear. The desire to colonize (i.e., to establish new Minoan settlements abroad) cannot have supplied the only motivation for Cretan activity in the Aegean, although it may explain archaeological evidence produced by recent excavations and surveys in the Dodecanese. There a remarkable increase both in the size and number of settlements occurred during the Minoan New Palace period, particularly on Rhodes, Kos, and Karpathos. These settlements were

apparently established *de novo* on virgin soil, and there is very little evidence for preexisting non-Minoan populations. The settlements of Trianda on Rhodes and Seraglio on Kos appear to have been of substantial size from the time of their foundation. Such a pattern, and the fact that the material culture of these sites was almost entirely Minoan in character, may well reflect purposeful large-scale colonization. But such an interpretation will not explain the Minoan presence in the Cyclades.

For example, it is now obvious that the settlement of Akrotiri on Thera was ancient when a Minoan presence was first felt; its history began already in the Neolithic period. Even at the time of most intense Cretan presence in the earlier stages of the Late Bronze Age, elements of the preexisting, non-Minoan, Cycladic material culture survived at Akrotiri and at contemporary centers like Phylakopi on Melos and Ayia Irini on Keos. There can be no doubt that local non-Minoan populations continued to occupy these sites, even if we allow for the possibility that one or all may have been administered by a Cretan overlord or that Minoan elements were present in the local population. The case for actual Cretan settlement seems strongest for Thera, partly because of the remarkable divergence of its settlement pattern from what was apparently the Cycladic norm. On both Keos and Melos, recent systematic surface surveys have reinforced a picture of islands dominated by a single "primate" center; the pattern of settlement on Thera appears to have been radically different and perhaps approximated that of New Palace Crete, with its dense array of towns, villages, and villas.

Such evidence does not suggest that the motivation for Minoan involvement as far north as Melos and Keos was primarily oriented toward conquest and colonization. Neither Ayia Irini nor Phylakopi seems to have expanded remarkably in size during the New Palace period and the countryside of both islands remained relatively vacant. Nor does evidence from the central and northern Cyclades attest to an expansion of Minoan population, although here the quality of our evidence is less adequate than in the western Cyclades.[28] At present, Delos (at approximately the same latitude as Keos and Samos) is the island farthest

[25] P.M. Warren, "The Thalassocracy of Minos," *Proceedings of the Classical Association, London* 67 (1970) 64.

[26] J.L. Davis, "Minos and Dexithea: Crete and the Cyclades in the Later Bronze Age," in J.L. Davis and J.F. Cherry eds., *Papers in Cycladic Prehistory* (*UCLAMon* 14, Los Angeles 1979) 143–57.

[27] See Niemeier (supra n. 23) 206 n. 18, where it is also

suggested that the acquisition of metals may have been a motivation in eastern Aegean–Cretan exchange.

[28] E. Schofield, "The Western Cyclades and Crete: A 'Special Relationship'?" *OJA* 1 (1982) 9–25, for the earlier evidence; for pertinent recent data, see the discussions of Naxos and Paros in the following section of this review.

north on which Minoan imports have been recognized.[29] Andros, Tinos, Syros, and Mykonos remain virtual blanks; nowhere in the Aegean is a systematic program of surface exploration and excavation more necessary.

The past decade has, however, produced new evidence from the central Cyclades. Finds from surface investigations at Mikri Vigla in western Naxos, although difficult to date with precision, document contact with Crete in the MBA and early LBA, and reinforce the picture offered by older discoveries at Aïla in the southeast. Discoveries both at Grotta (the capital, or Chora, of Naxos) and, more surprisingly, on the islet of Kato Koufonisi have shown that at a time contemporary with LM I on Crete, a range of Minoan and mainland ceramics similar to those found in the so-called "Western String" was also reaching the central islands. What is missing at present is any quantified information. Thus, although we now may have a somewhat better idea of the "content" and spatial distribution of the trade network that served the central Cyclades, we still lack any measure of its magnitude. Nor is there much evidence that contact with Crete had there the same profound effect on the material culture of native non-Minoan peoples as at Akrotiri, Phylakopi, and Ayia Irini.

Other arguments posed recently in support of Minoan political control of the Aegean purport to find their justification in historical Egyptian documents: namely, the description of Crete and the "Islands in the Middle of the Great Green" as a single entity is seen as providing evidence for Minoan hegemony.[30] Ultimately, however, the conflict that has resulted in the division of many Aegean prehistorians into two camps—one of Cycladic "nationalists," the other of Minoan "imperialists"—may be unresolvable. Indeed one might well debate the wisdom of using prehistoric archaeological data for the reconstruction of political events. Nonetheless, the islands of the Aegean present an extraordinary opportunity for prehistorians interested in the processes of cultural contact and change to investigate a wide range of case studies in a variety of settings. The laboratory-like benefits of archaeology on islands, in particular the well-boundedness of

social units and the diversity of environments, should in the future permit us to explain in much greater detail the material consequences of the Thalassocracy of Minos.

The Late Cycladic III period in the Aegean offers a similar opportunity for a synthetic comparative study of the processes by which Mycenaean material culture was adopted in the islands of the Aegean, a question largely forgotten in the recent rush to document the Minoan presence overseas. Mycenaean material culture was perhaps even more all-pervasive in the islands than was Minoan.[31] But is this to be taken as evidence for the settlement of mainlanders in the islands? Many of the same issues need to be faced that are being confronted in discussion of the Minoan Thalassocracy.[32] The only good stratigraphical sequence that bridges the earlier and later parts of the LBA, that reconstructed at Ayia Irini on Keos, does not suggest any obvious gap in the settlement sequence at the time when Mycenaean material culture came to dominate Minoan. Indeed, at that site, as in other Cycladic settlements of the early LBA, there had always existed considerable evidence for contact with the Greek mainland. The principal change that had occurred by the time of LH III was not the replacement of Minoan and Minoanized by mainland traditions, but rather the subtraction of Crete as a significant influence on local life-styles.

As in the case of the Minoan Thalassocracy, in the Mycenaean empire a great amount of diversity can be recognized in the nature of the responses of individual islands to contact with Mycenaean mainlanders. In the far north on Thasos, Mycenaean ceramic traditions were adapted and incorporated into local ceramic repertories, but standard Mycenaean wares appear to have reached the island only infrequently. Within the Aegean there are differences too in burial customs. Most obvious are the large cists used for burial in LB III Chios and Psara, a sharp contrast to the chamber tombs of the Dodecanese. In Euboia and the northern Sporades, the chamber tomb appears to have been standard. The chamber tomb was also present on Naxos, while on Paros and Tinos, a variety of tholos tomb was introduced. On Karpathos the larnax

---

[29] See discussion in J.L. Davis, "Ἐπεὶ οὔτοι πῖαρ ὑπ'οὖδας: Thoughts on Prehistoric and Archaic Delos," *TUAS* 7 (1982) 23–33.

[30] See W.-D. Niemeier, "Mycenaean Elements in the Miniature Fresco from Thera?" in *TAW* III.1, 267–82; "Creta, Egeo e Mediterraneo agli inizi di bronzo tardo," in M. Marazzi, S. Tusa, and L. Vagnetti eds., *Traffici micenei nel Mediterraneo: problemi storici e documentazione archeologica* (Taranto 1986) 245–70; and esp. Y. and E. Sakellarakis, "The

Keftiu and the Minoan Thalassocracy," in *Minoan Thalassocracy* 197–203.

[31] M. Marthari, "The Mycenaean Expansion in the Cyclades," in K. Demakopoulou ed., *The Mycenaean World: Five Centuries of Early Greek Culture 1600–1100 BC* (Athens 1988) 56–57.

[32] Perhaps the most insightful discussion of the problem is that by J.C. Wright, "Umpiring the Mycenaean Empire," *TUAS* 9 (1984) 58–70.

was employed and burial customs appear to have been related to those of Crete. The forms of burial practiced elsewhere, including the well-investigated island of Keos, remain a mystery. More generally, the absence of evidence that large numbers of intact Mycenaean vases have been looted over the years by perspicacious *archaiokapiloi* may in itself suggest that burial in chamber tombs never acquired the prominence in many islands that it had in the Dodecanese.

A REVIEW OF RECENT WORK

My specific goal in this section is to summarize recent scholarship that pertains to the islands of the Aegean. Much of it will be pertinent to issues already discussed above. Readers will notice that my definition of "recent" varies from one part of the Aegean to another. Even in an extensive format, there remain certain absolute limitations on space, and it makes little sense to consider in detail literature that has already passed into more general syntheses and is readily accessible. I, therefore, assume that the reader will have ready access to the *Gazetteer*. For the Bronze Age Cyclades, I have not generally taken into account those publications encompassed by Barber's comprehensive synthesis of Cycladic prehistory, *The Cyclades in the Bronze Age*. For other islands, I have attempted to provide an overview of significant research published since 1980.[33] I have paid most attention to new fieldwork, relatively little to art historical matters. In the case of Early Cycladic art or the Thera frescoes, the literature is so vast that it warrants separate reviews.[34] My references to secondary literature attempt only to epitomize a portion of recent scholarship, but I hope that I have provided readers with sufficient clues to allow them to find their way into more specialized publications, should they desire to do so. I

have summarized most extensively those studies that will be least accessible to readers in North America.

Presentation in this section follows the current organization of administrative districts within the Greek Archaeological Service, beginning with Keos in the first Ephoreia and concluding with the 22nd Ephoreia of the Dodecanese and Amorgos.

Keos

Work on Keos in the past decade has concentrated on publishing results of earlier excavations at the site of Ayia Irini. Seven volumes of the final excavation report have appeared, all since 1983, giving Ayia Irini the longest well-documented prehistoric sequence in the Cyclades. In addition, no less than three separate surface survey projects are providing the details of the overall prehistoric settlement system of the island.

Habitation at Ayia Irini appears to have begun somewhat later than at the FN site of Kephala nearby. EBA levels at Ayia Irini were extensive but remain largely unpublished.[35] Pottery from period I deposits, the earliest at Ayia Irini, is distinctly different from that from Kephala and lacks several distinctive features characteristic of that site, including pattern-burnishing and scoops, although there are general similarities in shapes, and the wares are still within a Neolithic tradition. After period I there appears to be a break in the sequence, inasmuch as period II represents a fully developed EB II phase of occupation, distinguished by close relations with eastern Attica.[36] Period III is characterized by the introduction of Anatolianizing ceramic shapes (constituting about 10% of the pottery in assemblages), at least some of which were locally produced; their introduction was not marked by discontinuities in the life of the settlement, and continuity with previous traditions was the rule.[37] In neither period is there evidence for any

---

[33] Since many publications in Greece, particularly journals, have often been published many years later than their cover date, in composing this report I decided to consider reports of fieldwork for inclusion if they were summarized in *AR* 27 (1981) or "Chronique" 1981 or later, even in cases where the original report abstracted had been composed many years prior.

[34] Fortunately, excellent recent syntheses are readily available. See esp. n. 19, supra, as well as P. Getz-Preziosi, *Early Cycladic Art in North American Collections* (Richmond 1987); Getz-Preziosi, *Early Cycladic Sculpture: An Introduction* (Malibu 1985); J.L. Fitton, *Cycladic Art* (Cambridge, Mass. 1990); J.E. Coleman, "'Frying Pans' of the Early Bronze Age Aegean," *AJA* 89 (1985) 191–219; C. Renfrew, "The Goulandris Museum of Cycladic and Ancient Art," *AR* 32 (1986) 134–41; and L. Goodison, *Death, Women, and the Sun* (*BICS* Suppl. 53, London 1989) ch. 1. These publications are rich with references to earlier studies of Cycladic art. For the Thera frescoes and other contemporary wall paintings from the islands of the Aegean, see discussions of Keos, Thera, Melos, and Rhodes, below.

[35] All finds earlier than the MBA will be published by D.E. Wilson and M.E. Eliot in *Ayia Irini: Periods I–III* (*Keos* IX, in prep.). I am grateful to David Wilson for the opportunity to read and to summarize briefly parts of his working manuscript for the volume.

[36] D.E. Wilson, "Kea and East Attica in Early Bronze II: Beyond Pottery Typology," in J.M. Fossey ed., Συνεισφορά *McGill: Papers in Greek Archaeology and History in Memory of Colin D. Gordon* (Leiden 1987) 35–49.

[37] Wilson argues for contemporaneity between Ayia Irini II and the "green" period at Poliochni; and between Ayia Irini III, the "red" and "yellow" phases of Poliochni, and, in part, Emborio I. Wilson convincingly demonstrates that the closest parallels for the Anatolian-style pottery from Ayia Irini III are to be found in southwestern Asia Minor. The most complete published summary of evidence relevant to later EBA Keos is now: D.E. Wilson and M. Eliot, "Ayia Irini, Period III: The Last Phase of Occupation at the E.B.A. Settlement," in *Prehistoric Cyclades* 78–87; see also Vaughan and Wilson (supra n. 20).

Fig. 2. Ayia Irini, Keos. Stone and gold beads strung as a necklace from MBA grave 24. (Courtesy John C. Overbeck)

direct contact with the Peloponnese; imported wares are recognized from period I, including probable Melian products, and quantities of imported ceramics reached as high as 30% in period II. It is indeed increasingly clear that exchange played a significant role in the life of the settlement from the time of its foundation.

The Middle Bronze Age at Ayia Irini has been divided into two principal periods, IV and V, the former subdivided into three subphases. The evidence for both periods IV and V has now been fully presented.[38] There was a break in occupation at Ayia Irini after period III. The earliest period IV deposits at the site are appreciably later than the beginning of the MH period on the Greek mainland and it is clear that a gap exists in the Ayia Irini sequence roughly contemporary with EH III and the earlier stages of the Middle Bronze Age. The cemeteries of period IV are among the very few cemeteries known in the MBA Cyclades (fig. 2). From the beginning of period IV the settlement was fortified, its principal gateway guarded by a horseshoe-shaped tower. This earliest defensive system was destroyed and eventually replaced by a system set farther north on the neck of the peninsula to encompass a somewhat larger area within the town. The construction of this new system

(of large roughly squared limestone blocks with rectangular towers) marks the beginning of period V, which must be on the basis of Minoan imports roughly contemporary with MM IIB/MM IIIA. As in the EBA, MBA Keos was closely linked through exchange to other areas of the Aegean. Ties to Crete are evident already from the beginning of period IV, although local ceramic traditions are dominant (fig. 3). In period V, there is evidence for the local use of the Cretan linear script and for Cretan-style administrative practice, as represented by a roundel of Minoan type and an inscribed tablet fragment. Aspects of material culture became increasingly Minoanized in the course of the MBA (and in the earlier stages of the LBA) as local potters copied Cretan shapes and many elements of Cretan technology were introduced to the island, including a Minoan system of metrology. Crete influenced local religious practices, and Minoan-style wall paintings were executed locally (figs. 4–5).[39]

Fig. 3. Ayia Irini, Keos. Fragment of an MBA barrel-jar with red and black matt-painted decoration. (Courtesy John C. Overbeck)

[38] J.C. Overbeck, *Ayia Irini: Period IV: The Stratigraphy and the Find Deposits* (*Keos* VII.1, Mainz 1989); J.L. Davis, *Ayia Irini: Period V* (*Keos* V, Mainz 1986). Further discussion and documentation of the material of period IV will be included in the second part of *Keos* VII, now in preparation by J.C. Overbeck.
[39] The context of the tablet with Linear A signs found in a stratum of period V has been discussed by Davis (supra n. 38) 99 (also *GORILA* I, KE 1); for the roundel, *GORILA* II, KE Wc 2. Signs adopted from the Cretan script replaced the older system of marks that had been used since the beginning of period IV when marking pottery had first become wide-

spread; see A.H. Bikaki, *Ayia Irini: The Potters' Marks* (*Keos* IV, Mainz 1984). For the full corpus of lead weights (from which it has been deduced that a Minoan metrological system was used locally), see K.M. Petruso, *Ayia Irini: The Balance Weights. An Analysis of Weight Measurement in Prehistoric Crete and the Cycladic Islands* (*Keos* VIII, Mainz 1992). Technological innovations of Minoan type include the so-called "fireboxes," which arguably were employed for the production of aromatics, and potter's wheel disks. These and other standardized ceramic shapes have been discussed by H.S. Georgiou, *Ayia Irini: Specialized Domestic and Industrial Pottery* (*Keos* VI, Mainz 1986). Other evidence of metals and

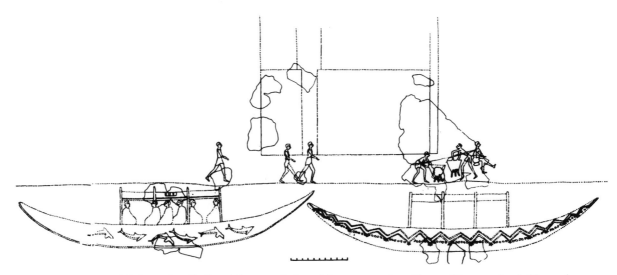

Fig. 4. Ayia Irini, Keos. Detail of a miniature painting: ships, men, and cauldrons. (Courtesy Lyvia Morgan)

As yet no overview of the settlement in any period of the LBA has appeared in the series of final excavation reports. Deposits from house A, published in 1983, continue to provide the most detailed picture of the nature of the material culture at the site in periods VI and VII.[40] The stratigraphy of these periods is now, however, understood in considerable detail as is the architectural development of the site. Two principal subgroups of material have been recognized within period VI: an earlier group that contains LM IA types but in which the LH I style is not represented, and a later one in which the LH I style, the LM IA style, and mainland matt-painted types contemporary with LH I are represented.[41] These

divisions of period VI are followed by the three subdivisions distinguishable in period VII. An early phase (VIIa), which bridges the gap between periods VI and VII, is marked by the first importation of LM IB/LH II ceramics to the site, and is earlier in date than the main destruction deposits of house A. These are in turn assigned to a middle phase of period VII (VIIb) and are characterized by the appearance of the Cretan Marine Style and the so-called Alternating Style. A late phase follows the destruction of house A but is still contemporary with the latest part of LH II (VIIc). In the early LBA, the area of houses C, F, and EJ seems to have consisted of a few independent establishments with large open spaces between them,

metalworking at both Ayia Irini and Kephala has been summarized recently by Z.A. Stos-Gale, "Lead Isotope Evidence for Trade in Copper from Cyprus during the Late Bronze Age," in *Greek Prehistory* 265–82, esp. 276, 282, and fig. 13; and by Z.A. Stos-Gale and N.H. Gale, "The Role of Thera in the Bronze Age Trade in Metals," in *TAW* III.1, 77, and figs. 6–7 on 78, 84. For a general overview of the contexts of industrial activities at Ayia Irini, see E. Schofield, "Evidence for Household Industries on Thera and Kea," in *TAW* III.1, 201–11. The more than 30 near-life-size terracotta figures of Minoan style found in the temple at Ayia Irini have now received their definitive publication in M.E. Caskey, *The Temple at Ayia Irini: The Statues* (*Keos* II.1, Princeton 1986). On the wall paintings from Ayia Irini, see E.N. Davis, "The Cycladic Style of the Thera Frescoes," in *TAW* III.1, 214–27, and L. Morgan, "Island Iconography: Thera, Kea, Milos," in *TAW* III.1, 252–65. Of particular interest is Morgan's reconstruction of fragments from the northeast bastion in the fortifications of Ayia Irini as parts of a miniature fresco, thematically related to the miniatures of the West House at Akrotiri on Thera.

[40] W.W. Cummer and E. Schofield, *Ayia Irini: House A* (*Keos* III, Mainz 1983).

[41] J.L. Davis and J.F. Cherry, "Spatial and Temporal Uniformitarianism in Late Cycladic I: Perspectives from Kea and Milos on the Prehistory of Akrotiri," in *TAW* III.1, 185–200. The latest of the two period VI subphases, best represented in deposit A of room 18 in house A, *cannot*, as recently has been argued by Warren (infra n. 152), be the result of a destruction that occurred contemporarily with the Seismic Destruction Level (SDL) at Akrotiri (on these deposits, see the discussion of Thera infra). The relevant deposits at Akrotiri produced no trace of the Late *Helladic* I style and were presumably deposited *before* its inception on the Greek mainland, while the LH I style is clearly represented in the deposit in house A. The house A deposit must, therefore, be later in date than the SDL at Akrotiri; its overall character is, in fact, more similar to that of the Volcanic Destruction Level (VDL) at Akrotiri (particularly in terms of the suite of mainland imports represented) than it is to the SDL. There can be little question that pottery of the LH I style and of contemporary matt-painted styles reached the southern Cyclades since mainland imports are well represented in LC I levels at Phylakopi on Melos, and are found already in the SDL at Akrotiri (infra n. 153). Once again, the danger of drawing supposititious correlations needs to be emphasized.

Fig. 5. Ayia Irini, Keos. Detail of a miniature painting: town by a river. (Courtesy Lyvia Morgan)

in contrast to the impression given by published plans of Ayia Irini, which show walls of all phases of the LBA, whether contemporary or not.[42]

Systematic investigation of the LH III settlement has emphasized that reoccupation following the main period VII destruction was substantial.[43] There seems to have been no gap in occupation at the site after period VII and a sequence of deposits following the general destruction of the town in period VIIb and contemporary with LH IIB and LH IIIA:1 on the Greek mainland can be distinguished stratigraphically. LH IIIA:1 material from most parts of the site appears to have been laid down as the result of another widespread destruction. Deposits from several different parts of the site indicate continuation of settlement in LH IIIA:2 as do remains of structures built outside the fortifications near the former (period VII) main gateway to the town. Continued use of burnished and matt-painted wares in LH IIIA:1, and of conical cups and tripod cooking pots, attests to the survival of these types into LH III alongside Mycenaean types proper; there is strong continuity in local ceramic traditions.

One objective of a recent systematic surface survey (1983–1984) in northwest Keos was to determine the character of settlement and land use in the immediate hinterland of Ayia Irini.[44] Results suggest that Keos may have followed a rather different pattern of de-

[42] For preliminary observations on the character of period VII subphases, see E. Schofield, "Ayia Irini, Keos, in Late Cycladic II," *BICS* 32 (1985) 155; and E. Schofield, "Destruction Deposits of the Earlier Late Bronze Age from Ayia Irini, Keos," in *Prehistoric Cyclades* 179–83.

[43] Remains of period VIII (i.e., the LH III settlement) are numerous. No general discussion has yet appeared in print, although the sequence of LH IIIC phases from the temple has been described and some representative pottery illustrated; see M.E. Caskey, "The Temple at Ayia Irini, Kea: Evidence for the Late Helladic IIIC Phases," in *Prehistoric*

Cyclades 241–54. My summary here is drawn from the text of an unpublished paper entitled "Ayia Irini, Keos: Late Helladic III," by C. Morris and C. Hershenson. I am grateful to both of them for a copy of it and for allowing me to summarize their conclusions.

[44] J.F. Cherry, J.L. Davis, and E. Mantzourani, *Landscape Archaeology as Long-Term History: Northern Keos in the Cycladic Islands* (*Monumenta Archaeologica* 16, Los Angeles 1991). Chs. 6–9 discuss results of the survey pertinent to the prehistory of the island and review evidence resulting from all earlier work on the island.

velopment in the EBA than did many other Cycladic islands. The population of the island (at least of its northwest part) appears to have been concentrated at the site of Ayia Irini alone and there is no Keian parallel to the scatter of small EC settlements and cemeteries recognized on so many other islands. Evidence available from two other surveys that have ranged more extensively supports our hypothesis that the settlement at Ayia Irini dominated the settlement system of Keos as a whole.[45] Other sites are both tiny in size and lack evidence for the imported ceramic wares that bear such vivid testimony to the interaction between Ayia Irini and the outside world. No pottery earlier than that at Kephala and Paoura has been recognized, nor has survey located material that might be employed to close gaps in the Ayia Irini sequence between periods I and II, and between periods III and IV. Finds of the late Middle and early Late Cycladic periods are most plentiful, but these are almost exclusively the remains of large storage jars and other coarse wares that were perhaps employed in rural settings by a population largely resident at Ayia Irini itself. LB III finds have been especially scarce.

Survey results have cast most light on Neolithic Keos. Detailed collection of surface materials at Paoura and Kephala has allowed the size of those sites to be estimated with greater precision. Analysis of lithics from both suggests that Paoura's closest ties are with Saliagos; the assemblage of Kephala is distinct from that of Paoura and its lithics have strong affinities with those of mainland sites. Paoura may well have supported a population of 75–130 individuals,

while Kephala was certainly a village of considerably smaller scale. Two new small aceramic sites in the northwest part of the island near Kephala have been assigned to the later Neolithic period on the basis of lithic attributes.[46]

Mineralogical field study has succeeded in relocating sources of lead ore, long known to exist on the island and mined for a short time in the later 19th and early 20th centuries. The deposits are distinguishable from those of Laurion on the basis of their lead-isotope ratios and are low in silver content. There is as yet no firm evidence that they were exploited in prehistoric times.[47]

The Northern Sporades

The principal development in the prehistory of the northern Sporades has been the publication of results of excavations at the site of Ayios Petros.[48] The site lies inside a large bay on the southwest side of the islet of Kyra Panayia. In the Neolithic Ayios Petros was attached to the adjacent mainland of Kyra Panayia, but even during the Palaeolithic there appears to have existed a sea lane between it and the island of Alonnisos to the southwest.[49] Most of the site is now submerged but even originally it seems to have been less than two-tenths of a hectare in area. Stratification was shallow (only a little more than a meter in depth) and much eroded but nonetheless excavation produced conclusive evidence that the principal period of occupation was contemporary with the latter part of the EN period and the beginning of the MN period in Thessaly; ^{14}C dates of 6740 ± 120 B.P. and 5860 ± 400 B.P. have been published.[50] Some LN, EBA (of

---

[45] Thus far the results of extensive survey by H.S. Georgiou and N. Faraklas in the northern part of the island have been published; see H.S. Georgiou and N. Faraklas, "Ancient Habitation Patterns of Keos: Locations and Nature of Sites on the Northwest Part of the Island," *Ariadni* 3 (1985) 207–66. Survey teams from the University of Athens have operated principally in the territories of the Classical city-states of Poieessa and Karthaia. For specifically prehistoric finds, see G. Galani, L. Mendoni, and H. Papayeoryiadou, "Επιφανειακή έρευνα στήν Κέα," *Arhaiognosia* 3 (1982–1984) 237–44.

[46] L.E. Talalay, "Body Imagery of the Ancient Aegean," *Archaeology* 44:4 (1991) 46–49, has also discussed the character of settlement at Kephala, the control of local resources, and the relationship between cemeteries and territorial definition. For the most authoritative recent discussion of Kephala and nearby sites, see R. Torrence, "The Chipped Stone," 173–98, and T.M. Whitelaw, "Investigations at the Neolithic Sites of Kephala and Paoura," 199–216, in Cherry et al. (supra n. 44).

[47] "Sources of Metals" 257–59; Stos-Gale and Gale (supra n. 39) 86; and Pernicka (supra n. 17). These assessments contrast with views expressed in M.E. Caskey et al., "Metals in Keos: A First Approach," in P.G. Marinos and G.C. Koukis

eds., *The Engineering Geology of Ancient Works, Monuments and Historical Sites: Preservation and Protection* (Rotterdam 1988) 1739–45.

[48] Most recently Neolithic remains have also been reported in the Kyklopi Cave on Yioura (the most remote of the northern Sporades); see "Travel Guide," *Archaeology* 45:2 (1992) 7.

[49] N. Efstratiou, *Ayios Petros: A Neolithic Site in the Northern Sporades* (*BAR-IS* 241, Oxford 1985). Survey of Kyra Panayia by Efstratiou revealed no additional prehistoric finds; see also "First Colonization" 167, for further discussion of sea level fluctuations and of the possibility that the northern Sporades were tied to each other and the adjacent mainland during the Palaeolithic.

[50] Efstratiou (supra n. 49) 167, appendix V; S.G.E. Bowman, J.C. Ambers, and M.N. Leese, "Re-evaluation of British Museum Radiocarbon Dates Issued between 1980 and 1984," *Radiocarbon* 32 (1990) 59–79. Efstratiou argues that there are parallels at Ayios Petros with ceramics of the second phase of Thessalian EN (Achilleion phase). These elements could not, however, be defined at Ayios Petros as a distinct stage in the life of the settlement, but were found together with ceramic elements of the sort that characterize the classic MN Sesklo phase in Thessaly.

Troy I character), and MBA (Gray Minyan) pottery in surface levels and in a pit reflect later use.[51] Palaeolithic artifacts have been reported at Ayios Petros and at several locations on Alonnisos.

Stone foundations for structures with both rectangular and curving walls appear to have supported mudbrick superstructures. Two child burials were excavated amidst the habitation levels while other human bones were found scattered. Artifactual evidence does not suggest that those who used the site of Ayios Petros were particularly isolated from adjacent mainlands. Nearly all of the pottery appears to have been produced locally, but stylistic affinities indicate continuing contact with the Thessalian mainland. Most distinctive are carinated bowls with red-patterned decoration on a creamy ground. Imported materials include Melian obsidian and flint that appears to have been Thessalian in origin. The stone used for axes, on the other hand, was probably of local derivation, quarried on the island of Psathoura, to the north of Kyra Panayia. The extensive collection of terracotta figurines (50 in number) from the site is noteworthy given the fact that most are from secure contexts; they include male as well as female and animal types. Features are for the most part rendered with deep incisions, some with white filling. Animal bones include a full range of domesticates. It is convincingly argued that the site was most likely a per-

manent, rather than a seasonal, occupation; if this interpretation is correct, Ayios Petros would be the earliest published permanent settlement yet known in the Aegean islands.

Euboia and Skyros

Euboia. Our picture of earliest settlement on Euboia has been greatly illuminated by the publication of the results of recent surveys and excavations designed to supplement older investigations by Theoharis and by members of the British and American Schools at Athens.[52] More than 60 Neolithic and EB I sites are now known, for the most part small settlements of limited duration. Analysis particularly of finds from the sites of Psahna *Varka*, Psahna *Glyfa*, Psahna *Votsika*, Eretria *Seïmen Mnima*, Politika *Spilaio Marmara*, Karystos *Plakari*, and Chalkis *Manika* have allowed the earlier prehistory of the island to be divided into six tentative phases: an Older (Αρχαιότερη) Neolithic I and II (roughly coincident with EN on the mainland); a Newer (Νεώτερη) Neolithic I, approximately equivalent with the earlier phases of the mainland LN; two stages of Final Neolithic (the latest equivalent to the Attic-Kephala culture); and EH I.[53] No Euboian phase corresponding in character to mainland MN has yet been noted. Each of these stages is defined with reference to characteristic ceramic and lithic artifacts, and to patterns in settlement.[54] Surface survey has

[51] Efstratiou (supra n. 49) 166, appendix IV, reports provisional results of spectroscopic analyses of samples of Gray Minyan pottery that suggest that, in their composition, they resemble most closely the Mycenaean pottery of Volos in Thessaly. Y. Liritzis, L. Orphanidis-Georgiadis, and N. Efstratiou, "Neolithic Thessaly and the Sporades: Remarks on Cultural Contacts between Sesklo, Dimini, and Aghios Petros Based on Trace Element Analysis and Archaeological Evidence," *OJA* 10 (1991) 307–13 found, however, no evidence that Neolithic pottery from Ayios Petros had been imported from Thessaly.

[52] A. Sampson, *Neolithic and Protohelladic*; see also Sampson, "Ωρεοί: Ταξιάρχης," *ArchDelt* 37 B' (1982) 174 (prehistoric remains reported at the site of Panayitsa, near Oreoi); P. Kalligas, "Ερέτρια (ευρέτερη περιοχή): Μαλακώντας," *ArchDelt* 36 B' (1981) 201 (a prehistoric settlement at Plakakia in the vicinity of Eretria); A. Sampson, "Καστέλλι Πισώνα," *ArchDelt* 38 B' (1983) 153 (Neolithic finds from excavations at Kastelli *Pisonas*, on a summit overlooking the Lelantine Plain); "Ζουγκλέικα Αγιάννας," *ArchDelt* 38 B' (1983) 154 (Neolithic axes and terraces at Ayianna *Zougkleika*); "Καμάρι," *ArchDelt* 38 B' (1983) 154 (Neolithic pottery from caves).

[53] Sampson, *Neolithic and Protohelladic*, draws parallels between the material from these phases and specific groups of finds from the Greek mainland or elsewhere in the Aegean: Older Neolithic II is compared with material from Nea Makri; Newer Neolithic I, with the Arapi and Tsangli phases of Thessaly, with the LN I of Corinth, and with Saliagos on Antiparos; and Final Neolithic (FN), with Ke-

phala on Keos, and Neolithic finds from the Athenian Agora. Most of these Euboian sites appear to have been settlements, although human bones from Politika *Spilaio Marmara* are of the Older Neolithic II phase and presumably derive from a burial. Older Neolithic I sites are poorly known and the character of the ceramics suggests isolation from mainland traditions.

Pre-Neolithic finds have also been reported on Euboia; see *Neolithic and Protohelladic* 23; "First Colonization" 165–67. For other recent reports of pre-Neolithic finds from the island, see A. Sampson, "Παραλία Αγιάννας," *ArchDelt* 38 B' (1983) 154 (Middle Palaeolithic at Aiyianna *Sarakeniko*); "Κερασία," *ArchDelt* 38 B' (1983) 155 (pre-Neolithic stone tools at Kerasia *Panayia* and Kerasia *Nero*); E. Sarantea, "Εργαστήρια κατασκευής Παλαιολιθικών εργαλείων στην περιοχή σπηλαίου Εφτακονάκων Μακρυκάπας στην Εύβοια," *AAA* 18 (1985) 81–85; and E. Sarantea, *Προϊστορικά ευρήματα Νέας Αρτάκης Εύβοιας* (Athens 1986).

[54] Representative species of shell in each phase are described (*Neolithic and Protohelladic* 47–49): two pierced *pecten jacobeus* from Politika *Spilaio Marmara* were used as jewelry. Murex shells were found at Vasiliko *Linovrohi*. Flint tools are abundant, but obsidian relatively rare before FN. Other artifacts of special interest include Newer Neolithic I fragments of schematic human figurines and animal figurines from Psahna *Varka* (*Neolithic and Protohelladic* 84–85) and FN bases with matt and cloth impressions from Tharrounia *Skoteini Cave* (*Neolithic and Protohelladic* 144).

been most extensive in central Euboia and it is not surprising that the area around Eretria and Chalkis is best represented by newly discovered sites. The greatest numbers of sites appear to belong to the Final Neolithic and EH I periods; these seem to have been times of settlement expansion. All parts of the island were inhabited, including inland and coastal locations in the north and south.[55] For the EBA as a whole more than a hundred sites are now known from excavation or surface investigations.[56] As for the Neolithic, these are concentrated in the central parts of the island.

The most intensively surveyed part of Euboia is the area around the bay of Karystos in the south.[57] The entirety of the Paximadi peninsula southwest of Karystos has now been investigated, and 19 concentrations of prehistoric material have been recognized. All belong to the Final Neolithic and early part of the Early Bronze Age. The focus of settlements appears to have been in the north of the peninsula, where flat land and water are more accessible. The earliest remains yet located in southern Euboia belong to the Late Neolithic and come from the cave of Ayia Triada, north of Karystos; they include obsidian and black-burnished pottery.[58] Fragments of human bone suggest that the cave may have been used as a place of burial, while just below it LN and FN habitation remains have been discovered in several rock-shelters. West of Karystos, FN finds have been recorded at two locations: a small site on the summit of the Kazara ridge and a larger settlement on the ridge of Plakari, both in defensible positions a short distance from the sea. Limited salvage excavations at Plakari have uncovered architectural remains with pattern-burnished pottery similar in character to that from Kephala on Keos.[59] In contrast, several EBA sites were located on the shore of the Paximadi peninsula: Ayia Pelayia on the northeast side,[60] Ayia Paraskevi at the south end, and Akri Rozos on the northwest. On the east side of the bay of Karystos another EBA site was found at Ayia Irini.

Finds of the MBA and LBA in contrast are relatively scarce here in the extreme south of Euboia. A large site was established in the MBA to the northeast of Karystos at Ayios Nikolaos; finds include plentiful evidence for metalworking, Gray Minyan and matt-painted pottery, bronze artifacts, and a lead pottery clamp. The settlement was apparently not inhabited in the LBA and as yet there have been no indisputable LBA finds reported in southern Euboia.[61]

In addition to the preceding general surveys and trials, more extensive excavations have been pursued at several locations. The most important of these have been at the apparently massive EBA site of Chalkis

---

[55] The distribution of sites by date (as summarized in *Neolithic and Protohelladic*) is as follows: Older Neolithic I, 9; Older Neolithic II, 8; Newer Neolithic I, 15; FN I, 4; FN II, 18; EH I, 23. These figures are now supplemented by more recent data, particularly that from survey in southern Euboia (infra ns. 57, 61).

[56] *Manika* I, 334–76 summarizes much of the evidence and includes commentary on a catalogue of EBA sites; many new sites have been identified since earlier investigations by Theoharis and by members of the British and American Schools. See also a report of EH II remains at Drosia *Gaidaros*: A. Sampson, "Δροσιά," *ArchDelt* 38 B′ (1983) 154. Kalligas has provided a detailed review of prehistoric research on the island before the 1980s: P.G. Kalligas, "Euboea and the Cyclades," in *Cycladica* 88–98, and publishes a number of older finds including a marble figurine from Makrohorifo, just south of Chalkis; he also discusses various Neolithic and EBA artifacts thought to come from the vicinity of Makrikapa, in east-central Euboia (including gold and silver vessels); most are now in the collections of the Chalkis Museum, the Metropolitan Museum of Art, and the Benaki Museum (see E. Davis, *The Vapheio Cups and Aegean Gold and Silver Ware* [New York 1977] 63–65). For general trends in the history of MBA and LBA settlement on Euboia, see *Manika* I, 336, 342.

[57] See D.R. Keller, *Archaeological Survey in Southern Euboea, Greece: A Reconstruction of Human Activity from Neolithic Times through the Byzantine Period* (Diss. Indiana Univ.

1985). I am grateful to Donald Keller for a copy of his dissertation.

[58] See also *Neolithic and Protohelladic* 92, 145.

[59] Pottery from the excavations at Plakari has been published by D.R. Keller, "Final Neolithic Pottery from Plakari, Karystos," in P. Spitaels ed., *Studies in South Attica* 1 (*Miscellanea Graeca* 5, Ghent 1982) 47–67. The presence of copper ore from the site is noted by Keller and Cullen (infra n. 61). All obsidian probably originated on Melos and the raw material does not seem to have been used in an economical fashion. Unworked nodules of obsidian appear to have been imported directly from Melos and are most plentiful on Cape Mnima, at the southern tip of the peninsula.

[60] Highly diagnostic EB II types, including sauceboats, found at Ayia Pelayia, represent the latest stage of Bronze Age occupation yet recognized on the Paximadi peninsula (Keller and Cullen, infra n. 61).

[61] Since 1984, the Canadian Karystia Expedition has completed survey of the Paximadi peninsula and parts of the southeastern coast of the island. Prehistoric finds have been reported but not yet described in detail. See D.R. Keller and M. Wallace, "The Canadian Karystia Project, 1986," *EchCl* 31 (1987) 227; Keller (supra n. 57) 237 n. 5.6; and Keller and T. Cullen, "Prehistoric Occupation of the Paximadhi Peninsula, Southern Euboea," *AJA* 96 (1992) 341 (abstract). I am grateful to Keller and Cullen for a copy of the full text of their paper.

Fig. 6. Skoteini Cave, Tharrounia, Euboia. Fragments of figurines. (Courtesy Adamantios Sampson)

Manika, at Tharrounia *Skoteini Cave,* the largest known cave on the island, and at Classical Eretria. The existence of prehistoric remains in the Skoteini Cave has long been known. Excavations since 1986 have, however, uncovered stratified deposits, which, when published, promise to clarify considerably the Late and Final Neolithic sequence of Euboia.[62] The earliest traces of human presence can be dated to Newer Neolithic I in the Euboian sequence (equivalent to early LN on the mainland); higher strata are of Final Neolithic, Early Helladic, and LH III date. Finds of exceptional interest include an EH clay sealing and a pithos handle that had been stamped repeatedly with a seal; various EH metal tools and items of jewelry; copper tools and needles from the FN levels; Neolithic stone and clay figurines, including steatopygous females and animal figurines (fig. 6); an image of an ithyphallic man accompanied by a naked woman, both rendered in relief on a Neolithic pithos; and well-stratified deposits of Neolithic pottery (fig. 7). Human bones were mixed within the Neolithic levels; the discovery of a skull separated from the rest

Fig. 7. Skoteini Cave, Tharrounia, Euboia. Neolithic vase with incised decoration. (Courtesy Adamantios Sampson)

[62] Few details concerning the excavations have as yet been published; see *AR* 33 (1987) 15; "Chronique" 1986, 562; 1987, 672. My description is summarized from a longer report, kindly provided by the excavator, Adamantios Sampson.

Fig. 8. Manika, Euboia. Foundations of EBA buildings in Zousi plot. (Courtesy Efi Sakellaraki)

of the skeleton seems to point to the practice of secondary burial. Some 400 m from the cave the remains of a badly eroded Neolithic cemetery has been excavated, including eight slab-built graves (four intact); multiple burial of skulls suggests the practice of secondary burial in two of these. Remains of an open-air FN settlement have also been excavated on a plateau above the cave.

The site of Manika, north of the Euripos near Chalkis, has been the target of especially intensive investigation. Although long known, only in the course of the past decade has the true extent and importance of Manika begun to be clarified.[63] Recent

investigations have focused on the EBA community although it is clear that the settlement continued to be inhabited in the MBA and LBA (fig. 8). The earliest strata are dated to a stage late in EH I. Most architectural remains are contemporary with EH II on the Greek mainland. The final major stage of EBA occupation, less widespread than the preceding EH II phase, belongs to the so-called Lefkandi I phase and is characterized by Anatolian elements in ceramics and metallurgy; after this the settlement appears to have been further reduced in size. The cause of this diminution is unclear: no obvious evidence for destruction either by human or natural forces has yet

[63] For earlier research see Kalligas (supra n. 56). The main recent bibliography includes *Manika* I–II, principally the results of research in 1982–1986; fieldwork in 1983–1984 has also been briefly described by A. Sampson and E. Sakellaraki, "Μάνικα," *ArchDelt* 38 B′ (1983) 139–40, and by Sakellaraki, "Μάνικα," *ArchDelt* 39 B′ (1984) 120–23. For more detailed presentations of results, see: E. Sakellaraki, "Νέοι τάφοι στη Μάνικα Χαλκίδας (οικόπεδο Παπασταματίου)," *Αρχείον Ευβοϊκών Μελετών* 27 (1986–1987) 5–21 (the excavation of tombs in 1986–1987); E. Sakellaraki, "Μάνικα Χαλκίδας. Στρωματογραφική έρευνα στον οικισμό: οικόπεδο Ζούση," *ArchDelt* 41 B′ (1986) 101–270 (a report on several structures and a discussion of the settlement *in toto*); "Από τη Εύβοια και τη Σκύρο," *AAA* 19 (1986) 30–35 (excavation of graves and soundings within the settlement in 1984–1985); and "New Evidence from the Early Bronze Age Cemetery at Manika, Chalkis," *BSA* 82 (1987) 233–64 (a full publication of eight tombs excavated

in 1984). *Manika* II contains an overview of recent work at the site and detailed plans showing the locations of the many test excavations. There is also an extensive discussion of the ground stone industry in *Manika* II, 80–104.

The extremely detailed presentation of excavations in the Zousis plot describes complexes of rectangular and apsidal rooms, some of which appear to have had two stories (122–24, 131–32). The pottery has been extensively described. Extraordinary finds included a bronze ring with incised decoration on its bezel (109, 224–26, no. 425), a terracotta "teddy-bear" (140, no. 9), stone vessels (217–18, nos. 388–92), stone pestles (218–19, nos. 393–94), a stone pebble figurine (141, no. 9), a terracotta quadruped figurine (140, no. 10), two bronze chisels (224, nos. 423–24), a stamp seal (266, no. 427), and a leg from a terracotta anthropomorphic figurine (266, no. 428). Few terracotta whorls and no loomweights were found. Ground stone and obsidian chipped stone tools were common (220–24, 226–34).

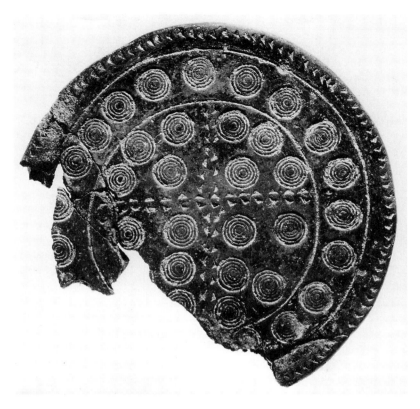

Fig. 9. Manika, Euboia. Fragment of frying pan with impressed decoration. (Courtesy Efi Sakellaraki)

been identified. There had previously been a continuity in architecture, ceramics, and burial customs at Manika; the settlement of the Lefkandi I phase did not represent a major break with previous traditions. Indeed, Anatolian types are most often found in funerary contexts (and even there are not common); they, like Cycladic imports in earlier stages of the EBA, appear to have been selectively chosen as grave gifts because of their prestige value as *exotica*. More common imported goods include Melian obsidian, and andesite, which was used for the manufacture of a substantial portion of all ground stone tools.

The biggest surprise of recent years has been the suggestion of the enormity of the size of Manika. In 1985, its maximum extent was estimated at 45–50 ha, but this estimate has recently been revised upward to about 80 ha.[64] From the results of augering and remote sensing, it has been suggested that areas situated between the various soundings that define the maximum extent of the settlement were compactly settled. Even if we may assume, as seems likely, that settlement was not contemporary in all parts of the site, Manika must have been one of the largest settlements in the Aegean in the EBA; it is certainly the only pre-palatial island settlement with a claim to rival contemporary Anatolian and Near Eastern centers in its scale.[65] It has also been argued that the settlement from its initial stages was, in some sense of the word, "organized":

---

[64] See H. Marukian, E. Kambouroglou, and A. Sampson, "Coastal Evolution and Archaeology North and South of Chalkis in the Last 5000 Years," in A. Raban ed., *Archaeology of Coastal Changes* (BAR-IS 404, Oxford 1988) 71–79. See also Sakellaraki, *ArchDelt* 41 (supra n. 63) 103, regarding the extent of the settlement.

[65] Estimates for sizes of many principal EBA sites on Crete are an order of magnitude smaller (T.M. Whitelaw, "The Settlement at Fournou Korifi, Myrtos and Aspects of Early Minoan Social Organization," in O. Krzyszkowska and L. Nixon eds., *Minoan Society* [Bristol 1983] 339). The largest

mainland sites are generally smaller than 4 ha (see D. Konsola, *Η πρώιμη αστικοποίηση στους πρωτοελλαδικούς οικισμούς* [Athens 1984] 94–102). In the Cyclades, settlements were still smaller (C. Broodbank, "The Longboat and Society in the Cyclades in the Keros-Syros Culture," *AJA* 93 [1989] 319–37). Nor were there habitations in the northern Aegean that approached Manika in size (C. Renfrew, *The Emergence of Civilisation* [London 1972] 236–44). For estimates of sizes for Near Eastern and Anatolian sites, see also Renfrew.

that all architectural remains thus far explored are
oriented to the cardinal points and take their cue from
similarly aligned streets.[66] The town may also have
been fortified.[67]

The cemetery of Manika lay to the south, adjacent
to the settlement; its maximum extent has not yet
been determined with certainty, but it appears to have
covered at least 6 ha.[68] Within this area, the density
of tombs varies; many appear to be grouped in clusters. Approximately 200 tombs with inhumation burials have thus far been investigated: burial chambers
of varying sizes cut into the bedrock were entered via
shaft-like antechambers, some with steps leading
down from ground level; slabs or built walls blocked
passage into the main chamber. The state of preservation of most of the human remains is poor but
adequate for certain generalizations about the nature
of burial customs. Bodies were placed into the tombs
in contracted positions. It is possible that some tombs
never held more than a single burial, but most contained multiple burials. The earlier burials were swept
aside when necessary to make room for additions;
sand or pebbles were sometimes used to separate
layers of older bone from newer. Other graves appear
to have been employed as ossuaries. Traces of burning
inside some tombs reflect burial ritual. Cycladic and
Anatolian types of pottery are both found with some
frequency: frying pans are especially common (fig. 9),
recovered in over 20 graves.[69] Types such as sauceboats, especially common in settlement levels, are
rarely found in the cemetery.

These newly excavated graves and buildings provide clearer contexts for a number of EBA artifact
types that had not been well documented in excavated
contexts. Scientific analyses have shown that bone
tubes of Cycladic type with incised decoration once
contained azurite, presumably used as a paint.[70] More
than 10 anthropomorphic figurines of marble and of
bone or shell have thus far been reported (figs. 10–

Fig. 10. Manika, Euboia. Marble figurine. (Courtesy Efi Sakellaraki)

11); terracotta figurines, and both terracotta and
stone zoomorphic vessels are also represented. The
marble anthropomorphic figures include schematic
types, examples reminiscent of Plastiras and Louros
features, canonical folded-arm figurines, and two
seated figures. This corpus is an important addition
to the still relatively small body of EBA marble figures
that have been found in the Aegean in secure undis-

---

[66] Cf. Sakellaraki, *ArchDelt* 41 (supra n. 63) 104, 122, but
see also Sakellaraki, *BSA* (supra n. 63) 236 where there is
said to be no evidence for town planning at the site.

[67] On fortifications, see Sakellaraki, *ArchDelt* 41 (supra n.
63) 101, 134, and 266. Characteristics of EBA architecture
at Manika and elsewhere in Euboia have been reviewed in
A. Sampson, "The Type of the Early Helladic House in
Euboea," in *Manika* II, 120–23; and Sampson, "Architecture
and Urbanization in Manika, Chalkis," in R. Hägg and D.
Konsola eds., *Early Helladic Architecture and Urbanization*
(*SIMA* 76, Göteborg 1986) 47–50.

[68] On tomb form and burial ritual especially see *Manika*
II; Sakellaraki, *BSA* (supra n. 63) 256–64; A. Sampson, "The

Early Helladic Graves of Manika: Contribution to the Socioeconomic Conditions of the Early Bronze Age," in R. Laffineur ed., *Thanatos: Les coutumes funéraires en Égée à l'Âge
du Bronze* (*Aegeum* 1, Liège 1987) 19–28; M. Fountoulakis,
"Some Unusual Burial Practices in the Early Helladic Necropolis of Manika," in *Thanatos* 29–33.

[69] Important new evidence suggests that these vessels were
at least sometimes brought to the grave containing food,
since animal bones have been found in them. See Sakellaraki,
BSA (supra n. 63) 240, 264, and Coleman (supra n. 34) 202–
204.

[70] Cf. Sakellaraki, *BSA* (supra n. 63) 251, 264 on the use
of these and other vessels as containers for paint.

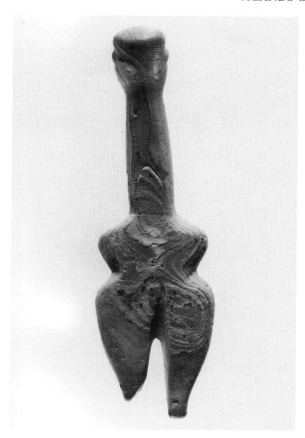

Fig. 11. Manika, Euboia. Bone figurine. (Courtesy Efi Sakellaraki)

turbed archaeological contexts.[71] Metal artifacts are especially common. The 50-odd artifacts consist of both silver and bronze, and include a curved knife, chisels, pins with pyramidal, conical, spherical, double-spiral, and roll-tops, tweezers, a cosmetic scraper, razors, rings, necklaces, and bangles. A number of these types find closest typological parallels in the eastern Aegean and in Anatolia.[72] Of three stone seals,

one has a spiral, another, a leaf-shape imprint, and the third, a geometric design.[73]

Rescue excavations at Classical Eretria in the Vouratsas plot, near the northeast corner of the later agora, have recovered deep prehistoric deposits extending well beneath the level of the water table. Finds reportedly date to the later phases of EH and to the beginning of the MBA, and there is a thin overlying stratum containing Minyan, Minoan, LH IIIB, and LH IIIC types. The greater part of the pottery may be dated to EH II, EH III, and early MH; proto-Minyan handmade bowls are well represented. The earlier finds were associated with architectural remains, including a storeroom that still contained a 15-cm thick stratum of carbonized grains and pulses on its floor. A well-preserved potter's kiln has been now moved to the Eretria Museum.[74] The exact date of the kiln is not entirely certain, since excavation beneath the water table made it impossible to record detailed stratigraphy, but it is clear that it is earlier than the Geometric period and much of the associated pottery was of EH types.

The prehistoric settlement explored by tests in the Vouratsas plot probably lay on a low headland by the sea. Excavations on the acropolis of Eretria have also yielded prehistoric finds. Most of the prehistoric pottery recovered there may, however, have been incorporated within mudbricks, subsequently decayed, and reused after the Bronze Age for fill, particularly for the core of the northeast tower of the fortifications. Finds from the acropolis belong mainly to the later stages of the Middle Helladic period and the Late Bronze Age (only LH IIIA–C is definitely attested). Elsewhere, in an area close to the western circuit of the historical city wall, Neolithic stone axes have been reported.[75]

Several other sites on Euboia have been explored through more limited excavation; results have not yet been published in detail. In the mountains of central

---

[71] The various figures found in excavations at Manika are reviewed and discussed by E. Sakellaraki, "Nouvelles figurines cycladiques et petite glyptique du bronze ancien d'Eubée," AntK 34 (1991) 3–12. See also Manika II, 70–71.

[72] For the typology of metal finds, see V. McGeehan Liritzis, "The Early Bronze Age Metals from Manika, Euboea," in Manika II, 105–19; also E. Sakellaraki, BSA (supra n. 63) 250–51.

[73] Manika II, 72; also Manika I, 459–60, and Sakellaraki, ArchDelt 41 (supra n. 63) 266.

[74] See A. Tuor, "Die prähistorische Grabung in G 10," AntK 24 (1981) 83–84; "Zur bronzezeitlichen Siedlung in G 10," AntK 25 (1982) 158–60. On the overall distribution of prehistoric material at Eretria, see also C. Krause, "Zur städtbaulichen Entwicklung Eretrias," AntK 25 (1982) 137–

44, esp. 138–39. On study of the material from the recent excavations, see P. Ducrey, "Les activités de l'École suisse d'archéologie en Grèce," AntK 28 (1985) 143. For the most detailed description of prehistoric Eretria, see P. Ducrey, "Érétrie, une cité de la Grèce antique," DossPar 94 (1985) 8–10, and S. Müller, "Des Néolithiques aux Mycéniens," DossPar 94 (1985) 12–16. I.R. Metzer, "Die Keramik von Eretria," Ἀρχεῖον Εὐβοϊκῶν Μελετῶν 26 (1984–1985) 221–52 also reviews the evidence for prehistoric occupation and for Dark Age settlement.

[75] AR 35 (1989) 23. The character of Neolithic occupation remains unclear. Müller (supra n. 74) 15 has suggested that Cretan LN imports (!) are present among finds from Tuor's excavations in the area of the later Agora.

Fig. 12. Excavations at Kaloyerovrysi, Euboia. (Courtesy Adamantios Sampson)

Euboia east of Chalkis, most of a small EH–MH site at Fylla *Kaloyerovrysi* has been explored (fig. 12). Both rectangular and apsidal buildings were associated with EH levels; obsidian was notably rare as was fine Ur-firnis pottery, surprising given the proximity of the site to Chalkis *Manika*. MH buildings of two different phases lay above the EH levels; the highest phase is reported to date to the transitional period between the Middle and Late Bronze Age. MH cist graves and the remains of a plundered shaft grave of early LH date were excavated among the MH buildings.[76]

In the northwest part of the island a second MH settlement was investigated at Aidipsou *Koumbi*. Foundations of two separate late MH buildings were found stratified over an earlier MH structure; on the floor of the latter was a thick burnt layer. Beneath it was a cist grave, also of MH date.[77] Within the limits of the inland mountain village of Avlonari *Ayios Yior-yios* in the east-central part of the island, south of ancient Kyme, excavations have uncovered an EH II ossuary, consisting of a rectangular built tomb that

had been covered with slabs and contained parts of two to three dozen disarticulated incomplete human skeletons; among the grave goods was a marble bowl of Cycladic type. Remains of a pillaged Mycenaean chamber tomb were also investigated nearby.[78] At Mourteri on the south side of the gulf of Kyme, two buildings have been excavated, one rectangular, the other apsidal; the pottery was exclusively of EH II, and obsidian was noticeably scarce among the non-ceramic finds.[79] At Amarynthos on the coast in the west central part of the island, excavation has produced Neolithic, EBA, MBA, and LBA finds; parts of buildings and a section of a possible fortification wall of the Early Helladic period have been explored.[80] Most recently, abundant EB, MB, and LB finds were recovered in renewed tests.[81] At Linovrochi, a coastal site east of Lefkandi, the construction of irrigation facilities uncovered structures of EH I and II; subsequent archaeological investigations revealed part of a probable apsidal building.[82] Elsewhere on the island, a figurine and vase were found in a grave at Eretria

[76] See A. Sampson, "Καλογερόβρυση Φύλλων," *ArchDelt* 38 Β′ (1983) 154; *Manika* II, 122, fig. 115. My description of this site is summarized from a text kindly provided by the excavator, Adamantios Sampson.

[77] A. Sampson, "Αιδηψός: Κουμπί," *ArchDelt* 37 Β′ (1983) 175–76; "Κουμπί Αιδηψού," *ArchDelt* 38 Β′ (1983) 141. See *Gazetteer* G87.

[78] *Manika* I, 332, 366, figs. 124–26; "Άγιος Γεώργιος Αυλωναρίου," *ArchDelt* 38 Β′ (1983) 141, 154–55.

[79] A. Sampson, *Ευβοϊκή Κύμη* (Athens 1981) 56–58; 31–32 for FN finds from surface collections and from excavations at the site of Potamia *Kastri* near the northern end of the bay; and 47–52 for general discussion of patterns of

prehistoric settlement in the area of Kyme, including brief descriptions of several new Neolithic, EBA, MBA, and LBA findspots.

[80] L. Parlama, "Μικρή ανασκαφική έρευνα στον προϊστορικό λόφο της Αμαρύνθου," *AAA* 12 (1979) 3–14.

[81] "Chronique" 1988, 668.

[82] Sakellaraki, *AAA* 19 (supra n. 63) 36–37; *Manika* II, 123, pl. 161; *Manika* I, 361–63, fig. 76. E. Sakellaraki, "Ιδιωτικές συλλογές," *ArchDelt* 38 Β′ (1983) 152 has described various prehistoric finds of EH and LH IIIC date that are in the care of the community of Vasiliko; these include a Phi-figurine from Lefkandi *Xeropolis* and a Mycenaean stirrup jar from Linovrochi.

Magoula;[83] prehistoric remains have been investigated at Petries; a Mycenaean tholos tomb previously excavated at Aliveri *Katakalos* has been studied and restored;[84] and a previously looted Mycenaean chamber tomb has been excavated at Limni *Fasouli* in the northwest.[85]

Skyros. The prehistoric antiquities of the island of Skyros have been extensively investigated in recent years. All archaeological bibliography relevant to the island has been synthesized, and artifacts from unpublished excavations have been described and illustrated as have various prehistoric chance finds in the collection of the local museum.[86] Skyros seems to have been most extensively settled in the EBA; 10 sites with characteristic EBA pottery have been identified. All are in the more fertile northwest part of the island, three along a coastal strip near the modern capital, the only part of Skyros where there is evidence for continuity in habitation between the Neolithic and Bronze Age.[87] Parlama postulates two separate foci of residence at the Chora in the EBA, one on the acropolis above the modern town, the other north along the coast; complete vases turned over to museum authorities suggest that there were EBA cemeteries in at least four nearby locations. Several vases find close parallels in the Cyclades, as does a pair of bone tubes with incised triangles and herringbone pattern. A fragment of a schematic marble figurine of "violin" type comes from the tiny island of Atsitsa, just off the northwest coast.[88]

In addition to this program of surface reconnaissance and recapitulation, excavations have been started at the most promising of the EBA sites, a low peninsula called Palamari, which lies on the northeast coast of the island and faces toward the islands of Ayios Efstratios and Limnos. Reports have summarized results of field campaigns in 1981, 1985, and 1986.[89] Remains of architecture observable on the surface suggest that the site was quite large, on the order of 10 ha; of this, an area of ca. 260 m^2 has thus far been excavated. Some traces of possible defenses on the neck of the peninsula are of uncertain date. Within the town, the buildings appear to have been built entirely of stone with roofs of schist slabs.

A series of important stratified habitation deposits appear to range in date from EB II through the beginning of the MBA, and EH I pottery has been observed in excavated surface levels and in surface collections.[90] The earliest architectural remains yet investigated are associated with pottery that contains a mixture of Helladic and Cycladic elements, as at Ayia Irini on Keos farther south. There are glazed sauceboats and saucers, but also sherds with *Kerbschnitt* and other impressed patterns. In the following phase of occupation, the sauceboats continue but Anatolian types are present, as in phase I of Lefkandi and in period III at Ayia Irini. In one instance the Anatolianizing deposits are overlain by house Alpha, which itself contained gray-burnished wares and part of a possible duck-vase with incised decoration that

---

[83] *Manika* II, 123, pl. 162; *Manika* I, 364; Sakellaraki (supra n. 71) 3, 5, fig. 2, 11, no. 2, pl. 2.2 and pl. 1.3 for a schematic figurine and a vase found with it.

[84] For Petries, see *Manika* II, 120, pl. 160. For Katakalos, see A. Sampson, "Αλιβέρι," *ArchDelt* 39 B' (1984) 125, and *Gazetteer* F91.

[85] E. Touloupa, "Λίμνη," *ArchDelt* 33 B' (1978) 130; see *Gazetteer* G98.

[86] L. Parlama, *Η Σκύρος στην εποχή του χαλκού* (Diss. Univ. of Ioannina 1984). See also A. Sampson, "Αρτεμίσι," *ArchDelt* 38 B' (1983) 155, where abundant Neolithic pottery and obsidian are reported at Artemisi in the southern part of the island.

[87] Parlama dates another 13 sites to the EBA on the basis of finds of obsidian alone; while such an assignment is possible, it is not demonstrable given the frequency with which obsidian was used in all phases of the Aegean Neolithic and Bronze Age.

[88] Parlama (supra n. 86) publishes a fragmentary EC pyxis lid (107–108, pl. 53, bottom right) and a small EBA bottle from Chalandriani on Syros (105, pl. 53, bottom left); the former has a close parallel in a more complete lid from Skyros (pls. 49–50), and the latter has parallels not only on Skyros (pl. 48.10–11), but also on Euboia at Kyme *Kastri Potamias* (supra n. 79), and among finds from the EBA cemetery on Epano Koufonisi. For the material from Koufonisi, see F. Zafeiropoulou, "The Chronology of the Kam-

pos Group," in *Prehistoric Cyclades* 33, fig. 1g. The pyxis lid from Skyros together with the two incised bone tubes have more recently been republished, with reference to parallels at Manika on Euboia, by E. Sapouna-Sakellaraki, "Κυκλαδικά της Σκύρου," in *Φίλια Επη* I (*Βιβλιοθήκη της εν Αθήναις Αρχαιολογικής Εταιρείας* 103, Athens 1986) 293–99.

[89] M.D. Theochari and L. Parlama, "Palamari, an Early Bronze Age Settlement at Skyros," in Hägg and Konsola (supra n. 67) 51–55; L. Parlama, "Νεώτερα στοιχεία από την ανασκαφή του προϊστορικού οικισμού στο Παλαμάρι της Σκύρου," in *Ιδρυμα Ν.Π. Γουλανδρή, Μουσείο Κυκλαδικής Τέχνης, Διαλέξεις 1986–1989* (Athens 1990) 125–34; ns. 11–12 briefly summarize the results of the 1987 season. In addition, see A. Sampson, "Παλαμάρι Σκύρου," *ArchDelt* 38 B' (1983) 141, and E. Sapouna-Sakellaraki, "Σκύρος," *ArchDelt* 38 B' (1983) 150 for results of emergency excavations in 1983; EH III pottery is there reported.

[90] See Parlama (supra n. 86) 91–94 for the most complete published description of the 1981 excavation season, including the fullest description of the character of the EB II and Lefkandi I ceramics from the site, with several photographs and drawings. Among other pottery that characterizes these phases are sizable quantities of the talc ware found at Ayia Irini and other Cycladic sites (see Vaughan and Wilson, supra n. 20).

finds its closest parallels in Phylakopi I.2. Red-burnished bowls, which can be paralleled both in Troy V and in the Middle Cycladic period, were recovered from a pit dug into Anatolianizing deposits before the construction of house Alpha.[91] Immediately to the west, in house Gamma, Anatolianizing types were excavated on a floor beneath the main deposit of the house, which contained a jug of Phylakopi I type, with pottery, including a relief-decorated "face-pot" that is said to find its closest parallels in Troy IV–V and the "brown" phase of Poliochni.

House Gamma is also of interest for its architecture and non-ceramic contents. Its one fully explored room has stone-built interior fixtures that include a raised platform, a bin, and a hearth; various storage jars, querns, and handstones, all in a good state of preservation, suggest that the building was abandoned in haste. Metal artifacts include a piece of lead sheeting and a roll-top pin of bronze; metals also appear to have been worked at the site.

There are few traces of Middle Bronze Age activity later in date than the abandonment of the settlement at Palamari: only a handful of badly worn sherds from Atsitsa have possible parallels among the Minoan and Minoanizing shapes of Ayia Irini period V, and can be added to the Minyan and matt-painted sherds noted years ago at Papa tou Houma. Documentation is similarly in short supply for the earlier phases of the LBA. Of 100 Mycenaean vases now in the museum of Skyros (all but one with some recorded findspot), none is earlier in date than LH IIIA:2. Virtually all of these vases were found in the vicinity of the modern Chora and probably derive from tombs in cemeteries that existed north, south, and east of its acropolis. No unplundered tomb has yet been excavated but like the looted tombs investigated by Theoharis at Krokos, most are likely to have been chamber tombs of standard Mycenaean type.[92] Evidence of a Mycenaean presence elsewhere on Skyros is meager.

Thasos

A review of the prehistory of the island with a gazetteer of prehistoric sites has recently been published.[93] The Neolithic of the island remains poorly known and unrepresented in excavations. Late Neolithic ceramic types of the sort characteristic in Macedonia have been recognized as have white-painted dark-ground types evocative of the southern Aegean. Links with Macedonia continued in the EBA, but the MBA is a blank. The most significant Bronze Age center on Thasos is at Theologos *Kastri,* a naturally fortified plateau in the southwestern part of the island. Some 300 m² of the settlement have been excavated; contemporary stone-built tombs in cemeteries nearby at Tsiganadika, Vrysoudes, and Kentria contained local imitation Mycenaean pottery and weapons, knives, and tools that also find antecedents in the south. The burials for the most part contained multiple inhumations although cremations are also represented. The analysis of finds from these graves suggests local mining and metalworking already by the end of the LBA.[94]

Since 1986 the small site of Skala Sotiros *Profitis Elias,* located on a small hill in the northwest part of the island, within the village of Skala Sotiros, has been explored. There, immediately beneath building levels of the sixth to fourth century B.C., are remains of a small (ca. 1400 m² in extent) habitation of the EBA, surrounded by a fortification wall, the earliest phase of which was built in part with masonry of herringbone style.[95] Excavations inside the fortifications have yielded the remains of several buildings. Floors associated with a structure destroyed in a conflagration contained numerous complete pots, some filled with the remains of carbonized seeds (mostly legumes),

---

[91] For the fullest discussion of the stratigraphy of houses A and B, see Parlama (supra n. 89) 124–26. The exact chronology of these post-Lefkandi I groups remains to be sorted out. It is important to note that thus far no EH III painted wares have been published from the site.

[92] Parlama (supra n. 86) 136, also reports unverified local testimony that suggests the existence on Skyros of large cist graves of the variety found on Psara in the Mycenaean period.

[93] C. Koukouli-Chrysanthaki, "Die frühe Eisenzeit auf Thasos," *Südosteuropa zwischen 1600 und 1000 v. Chr.* (Berlin 1982) 119–43; H. Matthäus, "Thasos im Altertum," in G.A. Wagner and G. Weisgerber eds., *Antike Edel- und Buntmetallgewinnung auf Thasos* (Bochum 1988) 13–39; Koukouli-Chrysanthaki, "Θεολόγος," *ArchDelt* 35 B' (1980) 422.

[94] E. Pernicka and G.A. Wagner, "Thasos als Rohstoffquelle für Bunt- und Edelmetalle im Altertum," in Wagner and Weisgerber (supra n. 93) 224–31, suggest the

possibility that local iron and copper were also being worked at the end of the Bronze Age on Thasos. Matsas (infra n. 100) mentions gold objects, probably of local metal, from latest LBA graves at Kastri as well as evidence for the working of local copper in the Chalcolithic phases of the settlement at Kastri. Analysis of lead artifacts from graves at Kastri points to compositions compatible with those of Thasian ores: see E. Pernicka, G.A. Wagner, and W. Todt, "Chemische und isotopische Zusammensetzung früheisenzeitlicher Bleiartefakte aus Thasos," in C. Koukouli-Chrysanthaki, *Προϊστορική Θάσος* (in press).

[95] C. Koukouli-Chrysanthaki, "Οικισμός της Πρωιμής Εποχής του Χαλκού στη Σκάλα Σωτήρος Θάσου," *AEMT* 1 (1987) 389–406; "Οικισμός της Πρωιμής Εποχής Χαλκού στη Σκάλα Σωτήρος Θάσου (II)," *AEMT* 2 (1988) 421–31. For reports in the Greek press on later seasons, see *AR* 35 (1989) 97.

part of a hearth, and various small finds, among them chipped and ground stone, bone pins, needles, and spindle whorls.

These deposits appear to mark the end of the EBA settlement; by that time the circuit was no longer serving a defensive function. From an older phase of habitation, two fragments of a stele in local schist and decorated in relief with the figure of a warrior have been retrieved, both reused as building material in the earliest phase of the western peribolos of the settlement. The head of the warrior was engraved with shallow incision; he wears a necklace, holds his right hand raised to his breast, and grasps a dagger in his left; set obliquely to his chest is a spear and a double-bladed axe is stuck through his broad belt. The closest parallels for this stele are in Troy I. Several fragmentary anthropomorphic schematic marble figurines, and parts of two others that were reused as building material within the circuit wall of the settlement, also find their closest parallels at Troy. These finds clearly predate construction of the peribolos but thus far soundings have failed to recognize earlier habitation levels. Parallels for ceramics from the earlier levels of Skala Sotiros are with Troy I, Sitagroi Va, and Emborio IV–V, from the later levels with Troy II–IV and later phases of the Macedonian EBA. Finds other than pottery from the excavations include obsidian, several metal objects, and a gold button-shaped ornament.

Elsewhere, in the southwest part of the island, at the site of Limenaria *Tsines*, two hematite mines (of some 15–20 in the vicinity) are thought to be prehistoric in date: handmade pottery, some of it Neolithic, has been found at the mouth of one mine and appears to postdate the mining. Bone and stone tools have been found in both mines and appear to have been employed for the extraction of minerals; the presence of horn from the Saiga antelope, extinct before the

Neolithic, and the absence of bones from domestic species suggest that the mines were principally worked in the Palaeolithic, and dates of 15,000–12,000 B.C. have been advanced.[96] If correct, these would be the oldest underground mines yet documented in Europe; Thasos would still have been attached to the adjacent mainland at this time.

Samothrace

Investigation of prehistoric Samothrace began in 1974 following rescue excavations on the coast southwest of modern Chora, at the site of Mikro Vouni; a wider program of regional survey, geological investigation, and ethnography has followed.[97] Systematic survey elsewhere on Samothrace suggests that the settlement pattern in the Bronze Age was characterized by a high degree of nucleation. Mikro Vouni itself appears to have been a narrow-necked peninsula in prehistoric times. Excavations have thus far investigated levels of the FN, the earlier phases of the EBA, and of LH III; one sounding is nearly 8 m deep.[98] Nine phases of construction have been recognized, and surface collection suggests that the settlement was approximately 1 ha in extent. The earliest material from Mikro Vouni is compared with that of Kum Tepe Ia and Ib, Poliochni "black," and Emborio VII–VI; the latest, to the middle phases of Troy VI.[99]

The very recent announcement of Minoan documents, found amid destruction debris (including fragments of white plaster with red decoration) in the penultimate architectural phase of the site, is particularly exciting.[100] These include a roundel and a nodule of types well known in Crete and generally found in administrative contexts. The Samothracian roundel may be of local clay, and was stamped repeatedly around its edges with a Minoan "cushion" sealstone engraved with Cretan hieroglyphic signs; it perhaps had Linear A signs written in ink on one side. The

[96] C. Koukouli-Chrysanthaki and G. Weisgerber, "Θέση Τσίνες: Προϊστορικό ορυχείο," *ArchDelt* 37 B′ (1982) 322–24; "Λιμενάρια Θάσου," *ArchDelt* 38 B′ (1983) 319; "Ορυχείο ώχρας στη θέση Τζίνες," *ArchDelt* 39 B′ (1984) 268. See also C. Koukouli-Chrysanthaki et al., "Prähistorischer und junger Bergbau auf Eisenpigmente auf Thasos," in Wagner and Weisgerber (supra n. 93) 241–44, where ^{14}C dates of ca. 6400 B.C. on artifacts of deer antler used for mining tools have been reported. The dates are based on the calcium in the antler, not collagen, and thus offer only a terminus ante quem for its age.

[97] D. Matsas, "Μικρό Βουνί Σαμοθράκης: Μία προϊστορική κοινότητα σ' ένα νησιώτικο σύστημα του ΒΑ Αιγαίου," *Anthropologika* 6 (1984) 73–94; "Σαμοθράκη," *Arhaiologia* 13 (Sept.–Nov. 1984) 35–43, esp. 36. A selection of pottery from surface collections at the site is catalogued and illustrated.

[98] D. Matsas, "Σαμοθράκη 1987: Αρχαιολογικές και εθνοαρχαιολογικές εργασίες," *AEMT* 1 (1987) 499–502. Views of architectural remains are included; an LBA "spit rest" and an FN anthropomorphic vessel are illustrated. Elsewhere, prehistoric remains have been reported at the site of Mantrouda in the southern foothills of the central massif of the island (E. Skarlatidou, "Παναγία η Μαντάλω," *ArchDelt* 35 B′ [1980] 434) and on the acropolis of Vrihou, west of Chora, where early Iron Age remains have been recently investigated. I thank D. Matsas for information about this site.

[99] "Chronique" 1989 reports that in 1988 lower levels of occupation were reached, with remains substantially earlier in date (ca. 5500–5000 B.C.) than previously reported.

[100] D. Matsas, "Samothrace and the Northeastern Aegean: The Minoan Connection," *Studia Troica* 1 (1991) 159–79.

nodule had been pressed against a peg wound round with string and had clearly been used to seal a wooden container; afterward it had been stamped, leaving a leaf-shaped imprint. The discovery of a mudbrick marked with a linear sign amid the destruction debris suggests that writing was practiced locally. The associated pottery has been described in some detail and is compared to that from early subphases of Troy VI and with the Poliochni "brown" phase. Carbon-14 dates for two samples of associated bone have thus far been reported (with a combined calibrated date of 2030–1785 at a probability of two standard deviations).

Lesbos, Chios, Psara, and Limnos [101]

Lesbos and Limnos. A sounding beneath the Hellenistic cemetery of ancient Mithymna on Lesbos reached prehistoric levels for the first time.[102] Also of interest is the publication of a single Neolithic sherd, perhaps from the site of Halakies in the south of the island.[103] On Limnos, continuing excavations, begun at the site of Myrina *Riha Nera* in 1986, have uncovered in several soundings parts of a complex of EBA buildings with at least three phases of habitation; associated finds are said to be contemporary with the "yellow" and "green" phases of Poliochni.[104] At Poliochni itself restoration work has clarified some details of the architectural history of the prehistoric settlement.[105]

Of more interest than the results of new excavations are those offered by recent metallurgical analyses of EBA finds from older excavations at Poliochni on Limnos and at Thermi on Lesbos.[106] Of 33 objects available for analysis from Thermi (phases III–V), only three included tin as a constituent. In the longer-lived settlement of Poliochni, among 74 samples analyzed (from the "blue" to "yellow" phases), the quantity of tin bronzes was found to increase throughout the life of the settlement, reaching more than 50% by the "yellow" phase. Arsenic was used alternatively with tin as an alloy to produce bronze; tin in one example from Thermi appears to have been alloyed

with iron (the well-known "tin bangle" from period IV, the earliest Aegean artifact in which tin is the principal constituent). In several instances at Thermi, brasses were also identified.

For the most part, the isotopic signatures of the lead contained in the copper from which unalloyed copper artifacts and arsenic bronzes were fashioned are the same as those from contemporary artifacts found in the Troad and at Yortan. Deposits in northwest Anatolia may be the most probable candidates for the source of the copper. Lead-isotope ratios appear to rule out Laurion as the source for even a single artifact of those from the "yellow" phase at Poliochni. The majority of copper-based artifacts that have an isotopic signature compatible with those of Aegean ores have incompatible chemical compositions. Chemical and lead isotopic analyses of artifacts from both Thermi and Poliochni suggest, however, that tin bronze was not invented or produced in the north Aegean. Tin bronze appears to have been exported to the northeast Aegean from a source as yet unknown. Imported tin does not appear to have been added to copper from sources that had previously been used locally either unalloyed or alloyed with arsenic. The fact that these "local" sources continued to be exploited after tin bronze had become widespread suggests that the EB II period was a time when copper became available from a broader geographical range of deposits.

Of the five silver objects from Poliochni that have been examined (including a double spiral-headed pin from the "blue" period, probably the earliest well-stratified silver artifact from the Aegean), all are of pure metal; they are not from the same ore and appear to have been extracted by cupellation.[107] Levels of silver were found to be so high in lead objects that it is clear that the lead had not been desilvered. The isotope ratio of the silver pin suggests that the silver from which it was made came from outside the Aegean area; of the other objects, some are compatible with Laurion and Siphnian isotopic fingerprints.

[101] I am grateful to M. Özdoğan for the information that there has been no relevant recent archaeological work conducted under Turkish auspices on the islands of Tenedos or Imbros.

[102] A. Arhontidou-Argyri, "Χρονικά Κ′ Εφορείας Αρχαιοτήτων Ετους 1986," *Lesviaka* 12 (1986) 72.

[103] *Kastro Tigani* 105, n. 413.

[104] Arhontidou-Argyri (supra n. 102) 56, 68–69. A paper entitled "Mycenaean Events from Lemnos," was delivered by Arhontidou-Argyri at the International Congress of Mycenology in Rome–Naples, October 1991.

[105] M. Ricciardi and S. Tinè, "Poliochni 1986–1987: Interventi di restauro conservativo e valorizzazione," *ASAtene* 64–65 (1986–1987) 389–401; see also P. Belli, "L'abitato di Poliochni," in P. Darcque and R. Treuil eds., *L'habitat égéen*

préhistorique (Paris 1990) 321–30, for an overview of work at the site and for references to other prehistoric sites on the island. See also *AR* 35 (1989) 91–92; 36 (1990) 62.

[106] F. Begemann, D. Schmitt-Strecker, and E. Pernicka, "The Metal Finds from Thermi III–IV: A Chemical and Lead-Isotope Study," *Studia Troica* 2 (in press); E. Pernicka et al., "On the Composition and Provenance of Metal Artefacts from Poliochni on Lemnos," *OJA* 9 (1990) 263–97. Three new ^{14}C dates for EBA levels at Thermi and one from Poliochni have been published: see Begemann et al. (supra); and M. Korfmann ed., *Demircihüyük* II: *Naturwissenschaftliche Untersuchungen* (Mainz 1987) xviii, fig. 4.

[107] For the pin, see K. Branigan, *Aegean Metalwork of the Early and Middle Bronze Age* (Oxford 1974) no. 2064.

A particularly exciting development is the discovery that in the northeast Aegean isotopic and chemical compositions of copper-based metals vary so uniformly through time that their composition can itself be used as a means to assign poorly stratified finds to a place in the Trojan stratigraphical sequence. Thus the types of metal used for bronze artifacts of Anatolian types at the site of Kastri on Syros can be tentatively dated to Troy IIg, providing support for the contemporaneity of the Kastri I phase in the Cyclades with EB II at Troy.

Chios. The final publication of the results of excavations at the prehistoric site of Emborio in southeastern Chios (1952–1955), the best anchorage between the Chora of the island and Kato Fana, and at Ayio Gala in the northwest (1938) has provided for the eastern Aegean a well-documented sequence of levels spanning the Later Neolithic and EBA.[108] Ten periods, numbered from top to bottom, were defined on the basis of excavated deposits: period I, the latest of the EBA periods, is contemporary with Troy II; period VII ceramics have close parallels in FN material at Kephala on Keos;[109] and period X corresponds to an early phase of the mainland Greek Late Neolithic. Still earlier material lay beneath the water table and was not investigated. Wheelmade pottery was first introduced in period I, along with an Anatolian tankard shape that is closely paralleled in the Cyclades among ceramics of the Kastri Group. MBA and LBA finds were not assigned to periods.

The deepest and earliest stratified sequence of deposits at Emborio was excavated in area A, on flat ground northwest of the acropolis between it and the historical Greek sanctuary. EBA, as well as LBA, deposits were also explored at the northern edge of the acropolis, and on its western ascent. In the EBA the minimum extent of the settlement has been estimated at approximately 3 ha. Before the EBA the settlement may not have included the acropolis itself. Slopes southwest of the acropolis served as a cemetery: a rock-cut EBA tomb and two Mycenaean cist graves were found in trials.[110]

Architectural remains were for the most part scrappy, although there were substantial stone walls even in the lowest stratum (period X) reached in area A; human skulls were found buried beneath one floor of period X. An adolescent had also been buried beneath a wall of a room that dated to period VIII. A spring in area A was later converted into a well, and was finally abandoned only in period II. At the end of period IV, the settlement appears to have been destroyed by fire at a time approximately contemporary with the earlier stages of the Aegean EBA; this is the only evidence of violent destruction recognized at Emborio. After the destruction, the ruins of the destroyed houses were deliberately filled with stones to build a level platform, which ultimately supported the foundations of period II houses.

For the most part, finds later than the EBA were found only in mixed levels. Burnished gray wares and matt-painted types were both represented. Most of the gray ware and matt-painted ware belongs to the LBA, but there are also types that find parallels in Troy III–V. The matt-painted (most often in bichrome red and black) pottery, though apparently of local production, looks ultimately to Crete for inspiration, and the limited range of motifs represented (e.g., spirals, foliate bands, wavy bands) is similar to the local Minoanizing pottery of the Dodecanese. The absence of light-on-dark imitations distinguishes it from the local Minoanizing wares of Rhodes and Kos. There is also no evidence that a full range of Minoan specialty implements (e.g., fireboxes) or tools (e.g., discoid loomweights) was introduced at Emborio; the lack of obvious Cretan imports also appears to distinguish Chios from its neighbors to the south.[111]

The most substantial Mycenaean remains come from the north edge of the acropolis in area F. Building levels of the LBA for the most part were dated to LH IIIC, although two floors in area F contained non-Mycenaean style pottery that may belong to earlier phases of the LBA.[112] The pottery in LH IIIC levels has its closest stylistic ties to Attica and Euboia; and the bulk of it appears to be Mycenaean rather than

---

[108] In addition to the British investigations, rescue excavations in the Baha plot (on the south shore of the harbor at Emborio) have explored what appears to be an undisturbed Neolithic stratum: see L. Ahilara, "Αρχαιολογικά Χρονικά της Χίου," *Hiaka Hronika* 17 (1985) 77–80. The relative chronology of Emborio has recently been reevaluated in *Kastro Tigani* 72–83. See also the analysis of a copper ingot from Emborio, in Stos-Gale and Gale (supra n. 39) 81, fig. 10, and 82.

[109] Hood's view that period X of Emborio was contemporary with the beginning of EN on the Greek mainland has not been widely accepted; it is unfortunate that only a single ^{14}C date (from period IV) is available for the site as a whole.

[110] See S. Hood, "Mycenaeans in Chios," in J. Boardman and C.E. Vaphopoulou-Richardson eds., *Chios: A Conference at the Homereion in Chios* (Oxford 1986) 169, for discussion of the use of cists for Mycenaean burials and a comparison between graves on Chios and those in the cemetery at Arhontiki on Psara. Similar cist graves may have been used on Skyros (supra n. 92).

[111] Note, however, the presence of a strainer-vase (*Emporio* 575), fig. 256.2675), and a single discoid loomweight of Minoan type (*Emporio* 633).

[112] Several sherds may date stylistically to LH IIIB, as do the four vases found in a cist grave (*Emporio* 582–83).

Anatolian in character, although several local shapes of Anatolian derivation are represented.[113] The LH IIIC town on the acropolis was destroyed by burning; on the west slope, a contemporary destruction level was recognized, with a later poorly preserved phase of LH IIIC stratified above it.

A variety of small finds from Emborio has been published: most belong to the Neolithic and EBA. They include terracotta spoons, one (and possibly two) terracotta stamp seal(s), a lump of clay used for sealing, possible crucibles, stone molds (one, of LBA date, for a butterfly pendant), loomweights, spindle whorls, terracotta figurines (mostly of Mycenaean types), an ox protome with incised decoration of EBA date, fragments of several stone vases, including a lamp of a type characteristic of the Cretan New Palace period, and an assortment of ground stone tools, chipped stone, and bone tools.[114] Among the most distinctive of the various copper or bronze finds are pins of familiar Aegean EBA varieties, a flat axe, a complete Mycenaean knife, and a fragment of a copper ingot of LBA type. Metal finds that are clearly Neolithic in date are few; they include the tip of a knife or dagger blade and a ring pendant with an attached suspension loop. A phallic pendant of spondylus shell has close parallels in the Cyclades. One faience bead comes from an EBA context, another,

cylindrical in shape, from a Mycenaean level. Three fragments of amber, also of Mycenaean date, are Baltic in origin.[115] The animal bones from both Neolithic and Bronze Age levels included characteristic Neolithic domesticates.[116]

The dating of finds from the two caves excavated at Ayio Gala before World War II has been controversial. No stratification was recognized in the lower cave; excavated material appears to have washed into it through a hole in its roof. In the nearby upper cave, two distinct strata were recorded, the lower of which contained ceramics of a character similar to the bulk of the finds from the lower cave. The character of the finds from the lower cave is not closely paralleled either at Emborio or at Tigani on Samos. Most scholars view the finds from Ayio Gala as largely earlier than those of Emborio period X and partly contemporary with the Middle Neolithic of the Greek mainland.[117] Small finds from Ayio Gala include terracotta human heads from figurines or attachments to vessels, bowls of steatite, part of a stone schematic figurine, bone tools, stone and shell pendants, celts, and stone bracelets.

Finds from elsewhere on the island echo the sequence of Emborio. At least 14 sites with traces of definite or possible prehistoric activity can be added to those listed in the *Gazetteer*.[118] They are dominantly of EBA and LH III date.[119]

---

[113] For a fuller discussion of the Mycenaean finds from Emborio and elsewhere in Chios, see Hood (supra n. 110) 169–80.

[114] For the chipped stone, see S. Hood and P.G. Bialor, "The Chipped Stone and Obsidian Industries of Emporio and Ayio Gala," in *Emporio* 699–713. Obsidian is notably scarce in all levels at Emborio and in both caves at Ayio Gala; local flint and even limestone was used in its place. Certain other features of the assemblage (e.g., the small and totally expended cores) suggested to Bialor that obsidian was in short supply. Somewhat counterintuitively, a higher percentage of obsidian was found in earlier levels than in the later levels at Emborio; there are only two tanged arrowheads, both from post-Neolithic strata.

[115] For the analysis of the amber, see C.W. Beck and C.A. Shustak, "Amber from Emborio," in *Emporio* 727–30.

[116] J. Clutton-Brock, "The Animal Bones," in *Emporio* 678–97.

[117] Felsch, *Kastro Tigani* 96–98, argues that the stratigraphy in the upper cave was inverted, with characteristic forms of the EBA in the lower deposits and Neolithic types in the upper. Parallels with ceramics characteristic of the Larisa, Arapi, and Otzaki A phases of the Greek mainland suggested to him that the upper cave was already occupied at an early phase of the mainland Greek Late Neolithic. Complete vases from the lower cave are compared to types of Hacılar VI

and are dated still earlier. Since the earliest types found in the upper cave are not represented either in the sequence of Emborio or Tigani, Felsch suggests that both the Emborio and Tigani sequences began later than the Arapi phase of the Greek mainland Late Neolithic. See also J.B. Rutter, who, in a review of the Emborio publication (*AJA* 88 [1984] 410–11), dated the earliest levels at Emborio to the Final Neolithic of the western Aegean, considerably later than material from the Ayio Gala caves. Hood preferred to view the material from both caves as representing cultural traditions contemporary with, but different from, those of Emborio. In his reconstruction, habitation at Ayio Gala began later than Emborio period X and overlapped in date with periods VIII/IX–VI/V; the earliest phases of occupation at both sites were viewed as contemporary with the later stages of the mainland Greek Early Neolithic.

[118] See *Emporio* 2–9; also, E. Yalouris, "Notes on the Topography of Chios," in Boardman and Vaphopoulou-Richardson (supra n. 110) 141–68, where detail is added to the discussion of some sites—particularly, a map of the (probably) fortified EBA site of Petranos in the southwest part of the island (147, 148, fig. 2).

[119] Among finds from them, a marble dagger pommel comes from Kato Fana (*Gazetteer* 370), two marble handles from Dotia, and a stone axe from the town of Chios (*Emporio* 6, fig. 3).

Psara. Excavations in the LH III cemetery at Arhontiki were resumed in 1983 after a hiatus of more than 20 years.[120] In addition, the northwest and southwest coasts of the island have been systematically explored. The cemetery is located on the west coast of the island within the bay of Ayios Nikolaos, 3 km north of the modern town of Psara. Most of the graves, cists with built entrances, appear to have been used for multiple burials or as ossuaries; in one large grave excavated in 1984, the first articulated inhumation was discovered amid the remains of earlier interments. Among the grave goods were beads of clay, glass paste, faience, gold, and semiprecious stones such as carnelian, a cylinder seal, pins, bronze tools and weapons, and spindle whorls of both clay and stone. West of the cemetery are remains of walls that belong to a settlement. Excavation in upper levels produced ceramics of Mycenaean date, contemporary with those from the cemetery; surface finds, however, suggest also Neolithic and EBA occupation.

On the tiny island of Daskaleio, just off the coast of Arhontiki in the bay of Ayios Nikolaos and perhaps once joined to the adjacent mainland, are remains of similar character and date; 300 m east of Arhontiki, EBA occupation levels have been found buried beneath 5 m of alluvium.

The Northern Cyclades

Little new information has become available in recent years from the northern islands of the Cyclades.[121]

Syros. Of particular importance is an ongoing project that seeks to prepare a complete final publication for the results of 19th-century excavations on Syros, at the site of Halandriani; the vast majority of graves and grave goods from investigations in 1861, in the 1870s, and in 1898 remain unpublished. One preliminary report has appeared thus far in which a score of ceramic and marble vessels are described and illustrated, most for the first time.[122] Other recent research has focused on the analysis of metal artifacts from the nearby site of Kastri; much of the copper appears to have come from outside the Aegean and is similar in composition to that in use at Troy.[123]

Delos. Recent excavations in the sanctuary of Apollo on Delos have explored Mycenaean strata just outside the fifth-century B.C. prytaneion and beneath the *prodomos* of the prytaneion. Mycenaean material had been employed to fill cavities in the bedrock, a leveling operation apparently conducted in conjunction with the establishment, beneath the prytaneion itself, of a round cutting in the bedrock (arguably a fountain), 5 m in diameter.[124] These remains are in a sector of the sanctuary where Mycenaean activities had not previously been recorded. Investigations in 1990 launched a systematic attempt to document more thoroughly all pre-Archaic architecture.

---

[120] Full reports have thus far appeared only in the local journal of the island: A. Tsaravopoulos et al., "Αρχαιολογική έρευνα στα Ψαρά," *Ta Psara* 49–51 (1984) 5–11; N. Zafeiriou et al., "Αρχαιολογική έρευνα Ψαρών," *Ta Psara* 49–51 (1984) 2–4; L. Ahilara, "Ανασκαφική δραστηριότητα στα Ψαρά κατά το 1985," *Ta Psara* 67–69 (1986) 10–11; A. Papadopoulou et al., "Ανασκαφική έρευνα στα Ψαρά 1986," *Ta Psara* 73–75 (1986) 2–7 (the most complete description of settlement remains). See also Ahilara (supra n. 108) 73–75. A paper by L. Ahilara, entitled "Mycenaean Events from Psara," was delivered at the International Congress of Mycenology in Rome–Naples, October 1991. See also *Gazetteer* 371.

[121] In addition to the new investigations on Syros and Delos described here, a find from one of the EC graves excavated at Diakoftis on Mykonos (*Gazetteer* 308) has been published (Hekman [infra n. 122] 24); see also E.-M. Bossert, "Zu einigen Figurgefäßen von den Kykladen und aus Westkleinasien," in *Beiträge zur Altertumskunde Kleinasiens. Festschrift für Kurt Bittel* (Mainz 1983) 121–38, esp. 127 fig. 2.3 where an EC vase from Mykonos, stamped with a seal, is illustrated.

[122] J.J. Hekman, "Chalandriani on Syros. An Early Bronze Age Cemetery in the Cyclades: Report of the Research Undertaken in 1990," *Netherlands Institute at Athens Newsletter* 3 (1990) 19–30. A detailed review of earlier research

on the island is included. I thank Mr. Hekman for providing me with information about his project. Cyprian Broodbank will also include statistics summarizing the total number of ceramic and marble objects from the Halandriani cemetery in his forthcoming publication of the pottery from the recent British investigations at Kavos on Keros. Various finds from the island of Syros have also been recently illustrated by F. Zafeiropoulou, *Το μουσείο της Σύρου* (Athens 1988).

[123] Most recently, see "Sources of Metals" 267. The interpretation of these data is another matter: see "Perspectives." It is not a foregone conclusion that bronzes from Troy were manufactured from northwest Anatolian copper; see the discussion of metallurgical analyses on Lesbos and Limnos summarized in this review. For variant opinions, see recently C. Doumas, "The EBA in the Cyclades: Continuity or Discontinuity," in *Greek Prehistory* 21–29; and J.A. MacGillivray, "Cycladic Society at the End of the Early Bronze Age," to be published in the proceedings of the 6th International Colloquium on Aegean Prehistory, Athens 1987.

[124] R. Étienne and A. Farnoux, "Délos. 1. Le prytanée. A. Sondages," *BCH* 112 (1988) 746–52; A. Farnoux, "Délos. 2. Nettoyage des murs de l'habitat pré-archaïque," *BCH* 114 (1990) 897–900. For a summary of recent work, see *AR* 36 (1990) 66.

The Western Cyclades[125]

Kythnos. Archaeological investigations of Bronze Age Kythnos in 1984–1985 included surface survey and the excavation of a previously unknown site at Skouries, east of the modern Chora in the northeast part of the island.[126] Amid fragments of baked clay from furnaces, pottery of the EC II period was found with obsidian tools and slag. Some 20 round buildings of schist slabs had apparently been erected to shelter smaller furnaces built inside them. Two have been excavated. Just to the southeast of Skouries at Yeronimos possible LBA pottery was excavated in association with a rectangular structure on a hilltop; there was reason to suspect that an EBA settlement associated with the mining operation at Skouries would have been located on the nearby bay of Ayios Ioannis. At Tsoulis, 2 km to the south, traces of an ancient surface mine suggest prehistoric copper mining; a fragment of an EC II jar came from surface deposits as did stone and obsidian tools.

Isotopic compositions of copper samples from the mines, furnaces, and various copper deposits on the island match those previously determined for the so-called "Kythnos Hoard," which is typologically of EC II date. The chemical composition of copper from slags and ores suggests that arsenical copper of the sort from which objects in the "Kythnos Hoard" were

manufactured was being produced on Kythnos. All but two objects in this hoard now appear, however, to have been found on Naxos, perhaps in the Cave of Zas, along with several similar tools now in Copenhagen.[127] Kythnos, nonetheless, appears to have been a major source for the copper used to manufacture copper-based artifacts in the southern Aegean in the EBA.[128]

Siphnos. Full publication of the results of interdisciplinary research on Siphnos has greatly transformed our impression of the importance of this island as a supplier of metals in prehistoric times.[129] Wide-ranging investigations of traces of ancient mining on the island have demonstrated that already in the earlier third millennium Siphnos served as a significant source of silver and lead in the Aegean.[130] A considerable amount of EBA pottery, and at least a small amount of FN, has been found on the surface in the vicinity of the mines at Ayios Sostis, in the northeast part of the island; most of the ceramics were mixed with debris from the mining, but a number of datable pieces come from within a deposit of mining debris (*Versatz*) inside one mine (no. 2) itself. Artifacts from Ayios Sostis have now been published in detail; they include objects directly connected with metallurgy, such as crucibles and tuyeres, as well as domestic vessels.[131] Several other lead and silver mines in other

---

[125] Of all the islands of the western Cyclades, the archaeological resources of Seriphos remain the most poorly known. Lately an EC sherd on a copper slag heap at Alivassos has been mentioned; see G. Weisgerber, "Bemerkungen zur prähistorischen und antiken Bergbautechnik," in *Silber, Blei und Gold* 112, n. 28.

[126] Z. Stos-Gale, N. Gale, and A. Papastamataki, "An Early Bronze Age Copper Smelting Site on the Aegean Island of Kythnos," in J. Ellis Jones ed., *Aspects of Ancient Mining and Metallurgy* (Bangor 1988) 23–30, and O. Hadjianastasiou and S. MacGillivray, "An Early Bronze Age Copper Smelting Site on the Aegean Island of Kythnos. Part II: The Archaeological Evidence," in *Aspects of Ancient Mining and Metallurgy* 31–34. Two ^{14}C dates are associated with charcoal inclusions in copper slags; see R.E.M. Hedges et al., "Radiocarbon Dates from Oxford AMS System: Archaeometry Datelist 11," *Archaeometry* 32 (1990) 226.

Also of interest is the recent reconsideration (and rejection) of claims of pre-Neolithic occupation at Maroula on Kythnos: see Perlès 1990 (supra n. 7) 125–26; finds may point instead to Neolithic or EBA activity. Earlier analysis by J.F. Cherry, "Four Problems in Cycladic Prehistory," in Davis and Cherry (supra n. 26) 25–32 reached the same conclusion.

[127] On the "Kythnos Hoard," see J.L. Fitton, "*Esse Quam Videri*: A Reconsideration of the Kythnos Hoard of Early Cycladic Tools," *AJA* 93 (1989) 31–39. The discovery of a significant number of metal tools in recent excavations at the Cave of Zas would tend to support Fitton's and Renfrew's suggestion that the Cave of Zas was the original findspot of this hoard (but also see infra n. 177 for bronzes from the Koronas Cave on Naxos).

[128] "Sources of Metals" 266–67. Present evidence suggests that Kythnos was a principal source not only for the Cyclades but also for Crete in the EBA, although data for Crete is still exiguous.

[129] H. Matthäus, "Sifnos im Altertum," in *Silber, Blei und Gold* 17–58, has summarized comprehensively the evidence for prehistoric archaeological discoveries on the island before the mid-1980s. Various finds from older excavations are reillustrated; a selection of obsidian tools and debitage recovered at the sites of Vorini and Platy Yialos in the course of the recent investigations by the Max Planck Institute is illustrated in fig. 9, p. 29. On artifacts from Platy Yialo, see also E. Pernicka et al., "Alte Blei-Silber-Verhüttung auf Sifnos," in *Silber, Blei und Gold* 197; for Vorini, see also G.A. Wagner and G. Weisgerber, "Andere Blei-Silbergruben auf Sifnos," in *Silber, Blei und Gold* 168–69. For EBA pottery from Ayios Andreas, see Vaughan and Wilson (supra n. 20). Matthäus reports finds that are possibly of FN date at several sites, including Ayios Sostis (p. 30); Gropengiesser 1987 (infra n. 131) 13, 35, n. 291, also mentions material that may be typologically of the later Neolithic from the site of Akrotiraki (*Gazetteer* 312) in the southeast part of the island. With it were terracotta implements probably associated with metallurgy.

[130] The extent to which its gold deposits were exploited, if at all, in prehistoric times remains unclear.

[131] H. Gropengiesser, "Siphnos, Kap Agios Sostis: Keramische prähistorische Zeugnisse aus dem Gruben- und Hüttenrevier," *AM* 101 (1986) 1–39; *AM* 102 (1987) 1–54. These papers fully describe material found at Ayios Sostis both on the surface and inside mine no. 2; for commentary on prehistoric artifactual material presented in *Silber, Blei*

parts of the island may also have been in use in prehistoric times.[132]

The scarcity of slags has raised the possibility that ore from the mines of Siphnos was smelted elsewhere, in areas where fuel supplies were more abundant. Whatever the case, lead-isotope analyses of lead and silver finds from the Cyclades suggest that a substantial amount of the Siphnian metals was being used in the EBA, even at Ayia Irini, which was located near a competing source at Laurion.[133] Continued use of the mines of Siphnos in the LBA has been postulated on the basis of thermoluminescence dates of slag samples at Ayios Sostis, but no lead-isotope analyses of LBA artifacts have yet indicated a Siphnian provenance.

Melos. The new British School excavations at Phylakopi and an intensive survey of parts of the island (1974–1977) resulted in a burst of publication in the early and mid-1980s.[134]

A report on the results of excavations in the Mycenaean sanctuary at Phylakopi represents the most recent contribution to the final publication of that campaign. The sanctuary consists of two parts, an east and a west shrine: the latter constructed first, during a time contemporary with LH IIIA on the Greek mainland; the former added in LH IIIB just inside an extension to the main fortification wall of the settlement. The entire complex was severely damaged at a time when LH IIIC styles were current (in phase 2b), approximately contemporary with the destruction of the citadel at Koukounaries on Paros; parts of the complex were reused, only to be abandoned finally in a later stage of LH IIIC.

A street and a courtyard (the latter with a possible sacred stone or baetyl in its corner) offered access to both shrines.[135] Within the sanctuary, benches and platforms served for the display of objects. A number of drain-tile fragments may derive from terracotta channels that were used to conduct water from the roof of the east shrine; interior walls of the sanctuary were extensively coated with white plaster, perhaps in part painted red; and coarser plain plaster is likely to have been employed to seal its roof. A few fragments of plaster with painted designs almost certainly derive ultimately from levels earlier in date than the building of the sanctuary. The buildings as a whole were well constructed, but there is no good reason to believe that the cult center was directly controlled by those who resided in the contemporary Mycenaean megaron at Phylakopi.

Pottery ranged in date from LH I/LM I to LH IIIC, although pre-LH III material is present only in small quantities as stray finds in later contexts.[136] The assortment of terracotta figures and figurines from the sanctuary, probably both votives and cult images, is unparalleled elsewhere in prehistoric Greece: not only female, animal, and chariot-group figurines of well-known Mycenaean varieties were recovered, but also female figures with bell-skirts of Cretan types, wheel-made bovine figurines, a possible fish rhyton, bird-askoi, a crudely fashioned large female figure with explicitly represented genitalia, and a large (45 cm), exquisitely modeled and decorated figure, the so-called "Lady of Phylakopi." Most unusual are several capped male figures with elongated bodies and ex-

---

und Gold, see Gropengiesser 1987, 53–54. Among the pottery are numerous examples of bases with matt, or leaf, impressions and a possible fragment of a Cycladic frying pan. A pattern-burnished sherd and a fragment of a "cheese-pot" are the clearest examples of FN. For an obsidian "Saliagos point" from Ayios Sostis, see G.A. Wagner et al., "Early Bronze Age Lead-Silver Mining and Metallurgy in the Aegean: The Ancient Workings on Siphnos," in P.T. Craddock ed., *Scientific Studies in Early Mining and Extractive Metallurgy* (BMOP 20, London 1980) 81, pl. 1. See also H. Gropengiesser, "Prähistorische Keramik von Siphnos," in *Kolloquium zur ägäischen Vorgeschichte (Schriften des deutschen Archäologen-Verbandes* 9, Mannheim 1987) 63, where further reference is made to surface finds from the site of Akrotiraki; the oldest material there is compared to the FN of Kephala on Keos. Impressed wares from Ayios Ioannis, also in the southeast, are compared to Thessalian EN types, and it is claimed that they represent the earliest Neolithic ceramics yet recognized in the Cyclades, a claim that remains to be substantiated.

[132] Near a mining shaft at Ayios Ioannis, the outline of a ship pecked on the bedrock finds a parallel on Naxos among the probable EC rock-carvings from Korphi t'Aroniou; see Weisgerber (supra n. 125) 107, 109, fig. 102.

[133] See E. Pernicka and G.A. Wagner, "Die metallurgische Bedeutung von Sifnos im Altertum," in *Silber, Blei und Gold*

200–11; and Gale, Stos-Gale, and Davis (supra n. 18) 389–406. The process by which Laurion after the EBA replaced Siphnos as the dominant source of lead and silver in the Aegean is discussed at length in the latter paper.

[134] See C. Renfrew and M. Wagstaff eds., *An Island Polity: The Archaeology of Exploitation in Melos* (Cambridge 1982); C. Renfrew, *The Archaeology of Cult: The Sanctuary at Phylakopi* (London 1985); see also specialized studies in *Prehistoric Cyclades,* and, for analyses of lead and litharge, Stos-Gale and Gale (supra n. 39) 87, fig. 20. A third volume, reporting results of excavations in the town elsewhere than in the sanctuary, is in preparation. Meanwhile, for a summary of pertinent results, see C. Renfrew, "Phylakopi and the Late Bronze I Period in the Cyclades," in *TAW* I, 403–21.

Claims of Palaeolithic and Neolithic tools of obsidian have been reported by the popular press but remain unsubstantiated ("Chronique" 1985, 841).

[135] See P. Warren, "Of Baetyls," *OpAth* 18 (1990) 203–204.

[136] Several objects from earlier excavations at Phylakopi are published for the first time or republished. Most notable are an ivory ring (*CMS* I, 410; see Renfrew 1985 [supra n. 134] 295–96) and various figurine fragments (276). On the small finds in general, see C. Renfrew and J.F. Cherry, "The Other Finds," in Renfrew 1985 (supra n. 134) 299–359.

plicitly rendered genitalia. There is some parallelism between types found in the two shrines. Nearly identical pairs are represented in several instances, and within the west shrine, the distribution of figures and figurines on platforms in its corners may indicate a male-female dichotomy in cult practices.

Probable votive gifts comprise sealstones, a scarab of a Syro-Palestinian type, a small human head worked in sheet gold by repoussé, two bronze figurines of a "smiting god" or "Reshef," their best parallels in Syria and Palestine, and a terracotta mold for the manufacture of flat chisels. Other metal objects included projectile points, knives, an attachment in the form of a small bird, rings, awls, pins, and lead clamps. Beads, mostly of glass paste, were common in the sanctuary but rare elsewhere; two were of faience. One fragment of ivory probably belonged to a handle, another to a sword or dagger pommel. Numerous fragments of ostrich shell may all derive from a rhyton, fabricated from a single egg. Pieces of tortoise shells preserve drill holes and served as sound-boxes for a lyre. Two triton shells may have provided musical accompaniment for ritual activities. Various spinning and weaving equipment was probably not associated with worship.

Among stone finds are fragments of vessels of Cretan New Palatial types, pedestaled lamps or censers in local tuff with chevron decoration, and a pendant in semiprecious stone of a reclining lion or dog, possibly of Egyptian manufacture. Ground stone tools were manufactured primarily from local volcanics; marble slabs were imported. A comparison of chipped stone assemblages from inside and outside the sanctuary delineated certain patterns: in the course of LB III, as the frequency of domestic use and discard of obsidian declined within the settlement as a whole, more obsidian was brought to the shrines and its use was increasingly incorporated into ritual activities. Analysis of faunal remains, however, did not detect patterns in consumption that would point to special sacrificial practices.

Additional fieldwork sponsored by the British School in 1989 intensively surveyed a number of sites (most of them already known from earlier survey), including several of the Early Cycladic period.[137] New fragments of frescoes retrieved in the recent excavations have been described, and new reconstructions have been proposed for wall paintings previously discovered at Phylakopi (fig. 13). Finally, a considerable quantity of unpublished pottery of Cycladic and Minoan MBA types from older excavations on Melos has also been catalogued and illustrated.[138]

The Southern Cyclades[139]

Ios. Explorations on the island of Ios since 1983 have made the first substantial contributions to our understanding of the prehistory of the island since early in this century; new sites have been located and new information gathered about those previously charted.[140] Of greatest significance has been the discovery in 1984 of the site of Skarkos, north of ancient Ios near a large natural harbor on the west coast of the island (fig. 14).[141] Excavations were started in 1986 following systematic surface collection and have con-

---

[137] On these surface collections, see *AR* 36 (1990) 67, and *Annual Report of the Managing Committee, the British School at Athens* 1989–1990, 26. The results will be published by R. Catling and G. Sanders. In association with this project, a republication by R. Arnott of the finds from the 1897 excavations at Pelos is in preparation. I am grateful to Mr. Arnott for this information; a summary of his paper, "The Early Cycladic I Cemetery of Pelos, Melos: Approaching a Republication of the Excavation," will be published in *BICS* as part of the minutes of the Mycenaean Seminar for 1992. Another member of this team recently described the distribution of Keros-Syros sites on the island and the characteristics of lithics from various Melian sites, within the context of a reconsideration of the causes that lay behind the emergence of a prismatic obsidian blade technology in the Aegean EBA. See T. Carter, "Blood and Tears: A Cycladic Case Study in Microwear Analysis. The Use of Obsidian Blades from Graves as Razors," to appear in the proceedings of the Sixth International Flint Symposium, October 1991, Madrid.

[138] For Phylakopi MBA pottery, see *Minoan Influence* 358–75. For frescoes, see Morgan (supra n. 39) 252–66. Morgan suggests that a fresco composition involving presentation of cloth to a goddess with associated monkeys, thematically related to the frescoes of Xesti 3 at Akrotiri, may have adorned the walls of the Pillar Crypt at Phylakopi and nearby rooms.

[139] Elsewhere in the southern Cyclades, the publication of an EBA bracelet from Folegandros is of interest; the archaeological resources of the island itself remain largely unexplored. See R. Arnott, "An Early Cycladic Bracelet from Pholegandros in the Fitzwilliam Museum," *BICS* 36 (1989) 117–26.

[140] See also *AR* 33 (1987) 49 for a report of a prehistoric settlement and EBA cemetery located at Halara Manganariou in the south of the island. R. Arnott, "Early Cycladic Objects from Ios Formerly in the Finlay Collection," *BSA* 85 (1990) 3–14, has recently published several marble figurines, marble vases, obsidian blades, and a lead figurine (of dubious authenticity), formerly in the collection of George Finlay and now in the collection of the British School at Athens.

[141] M. Marthari, "Σκάρκος: Ένας πρωτοκυκλαδικός οικισμός στην Ιο," in *Ιδρυμα* (supra n. 89) 97–100. My account is based on this publication, supplemented by information concerning the results of the 1990 and 1991 excavation seasons, kindly provided by Mariza Marthari.

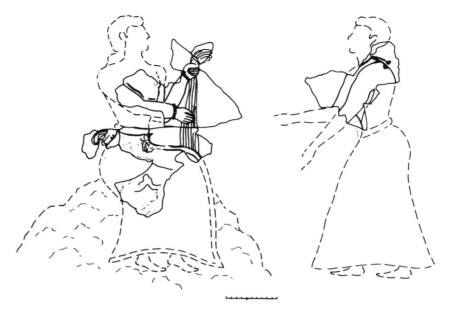

Fig. 13. Phylakopi, Melos. Presentation scene. Wall painting from the Pillar Crypt. (Courtesy Lyvia Morgan)

tinued through 1991. Squares, a road, and parts of contemporary building complexes have thus far been exposed. Beneath surface levels was a deep destruction layer, which rested on the floors of the buildings and dates both their destruction and final period of use to the EBA (fig. 15). Finds include EC II sauceboats (fig. 16) and saucers, loomweights, a large number of spindle whorls, many implements of ground

and chipped stone, bronze and lead objects, and two marble figurines similar to the Apeiranthos type. The walls of the structures are preserved to an extraordinary height, in places nearly 3 m; most of the buildings had a second story. All architectural remains excavated thus far appear to belong to the Keros-Syros phase of EC II; no pottery diagnostic of the Kampos group or of the succeeding Kastri group has

Fig. 14. Skarkos, Ios. General view. (Courtesy Mariza Marthari)

Fig. 15. Skarkos, Ios. Walls of EBA buildings. (Courtesy Mariza Marthari)

Fig. 16. Skarkos, Ios. Fragments of EC II sauceboats. (Courtesy Mariza Marthari)

been recognized. After the abandonment of the settlement, several cist and pithos graves of transitional MC/LC I date were dug into the EC debris.

Thera and Therasia. In recent years much progress has been made toward setting the site of Akrotiri within the context of the overall settlement history of the island of Thera.[142] Additional prehistoric settlements have been located both on Thera and Therasia.[143] It is now clear that these islands were densely settled in the centuries before the final eruption of the Santorini volcano and that their settlement patterns at the time of the eruption were more similar to those of Crete in the New Palace period than to those of other Cycladic islands, such as Melos and Keos.[144]

Limited excavation has continued at Akrotiri. Room 7 of the West House has been investigated and there have been stratigraphical tests north, south, and east of the West House. The western facade of Xesti (Ashlar) 5 has been cleared as has a terraced platform to its west. Excavation has also progressed in Xesti 3 (fig.

---

[142] Results of the first 20 years of work at Akrotiri will be summarized in C. Doumas ed., *Ακρωτήρι Θήρας: Είκοσι χρόνια έρευνας. Συμπεράσματα–Προβλήματα–Προοπτικές* (in press).

[143] Results of research prior to 1980 are conveniently summarized with relevant bibliography in C.G. Doumas, *Thera: Pompeii of the Ancient Aegean* (London 1983). For a later summary including the most important bibliography of the early 1980s, see R. Barber, *The Cyclades in the Bronze Age* (Iowa City 1987) ch. 8. More recent work is discussed in

many of the papers included in *TAW* III, where a current overview of the stratigraphy of the site as a whole is offered by C. Doumas, "Archaeological Observations at Akrotiri Relating to the Volcanic Destruction," in *TAW* III.3, 48–50.

[144] Evidence for the overall pattern of settlement on Thera and Therasia has been discussed by Davis and Cherry (supra n. 41), with a gazetteer of sites described in print up to 1989 on pp. 190–91. This gazetteer should be supplemented by the addition of newly located sites described by M.A. Aston and P.G. Hardy, "The Pre-Minoan Landscape of Thera: A

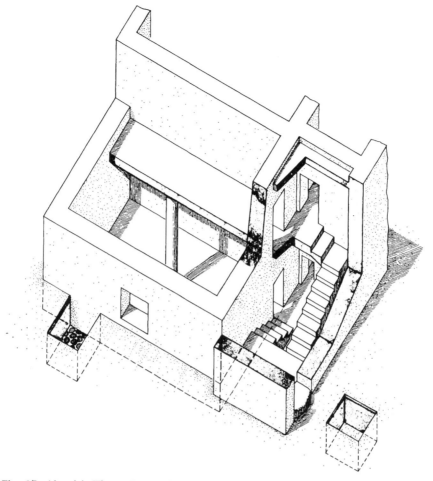

Fig. 17. Akrotiri, Thera. Isometric drawing of the eastern part of Xeste 3. (After C. Palyvou, in *TAW* III, 52 fig. 6)

17), within rooms 3B and 14.[145] Other subsidiary explorations have demonstrated that the level of the roads within the settlement was raised prior to the final volcanic destruction of the site; the removal of volcanic debris west of room Delta 15 (fig. 18) revealed hollows left by wooden furniture embedded in the ash.[146] Excavation has been most extensive in the

House of the Ladies, where investigation was resumed in 1987 after a hiatus of some 15 years. Many constructional details of the building are now clarified; the original interpretation of room 9 as a lightwell (a unique architectural feature at Akrotiri) is supported. Of special interest among recent finds is part of a horns of consecration, cut from volcanic stone.[147] Re-

Preliminary Statement," in *TAW* III.2, 348–60. Places in which the pre-eruption surface of the island is visible have begun to be mapped and the morphology of the pre-eruption island reconstructed; in several places, pre-eruption artifacts have been reported for the first time on the surface of the pre-eruption soils, notably in a quarry at Megalohori and on the caldera slopes at Megalo Vouno, but the material has not yet been adequately examined or closely dated. Finds of later MC and LC date from the Mavromatis quarry near Akrotiri have now been described in more detail and appear to extend over an area of at least 5 ha. On Mavromatis, see C. Televantou, "Ορυχεία Μαυρομμάτη," *ArchDelt* 37 B′ (1982) 358–59; and *Minoan Influence* 358.

[145] For tests outside the West House, see C. Doumas, "Ανασκαφή Θήρας (Ακρωτήρι)," *Prakt* 1985, 169–70; "Ανασκαφή Θήρας (Ακρωτηρίου)," *Prakt* 1987, 241–44; *Ergon*

1990, 108–109. Beneath the plateia west of Xesti 5, several bedrock-hewn chambers, perhaps originally chamber tombs, appear to have been reused by Middle Cycladic potters for cleaning and storing clay. Stone vases and other EC artifacts were recovered in the course of their excavation, some of them perhaps intentionally removed from the chambers by the potters: see *Prakt* 1985, 171–75. For Xesti 3, see *Prakt* 1987, 244–45; *Ergon* 1990, 113.

[146] For roads, see *Prakt* 1985 (supra n. 145) 175; for excavation west of room Delta 15, see *Ergon* 1988, 129.

[147] *Prakt* 1987 (supra n. 145) 245–54; *Ergon* 1990, 109–11. Fragments of earlier relief and other painted fresco have been found embedded in the floors of the upper story, and seem to have been recycled from older ruined structures. See also T. Sali-Axioti, "The Lightwell of the House of the Ladies and Its Structural Behaviour," in *TAW* III.1, 437–40.

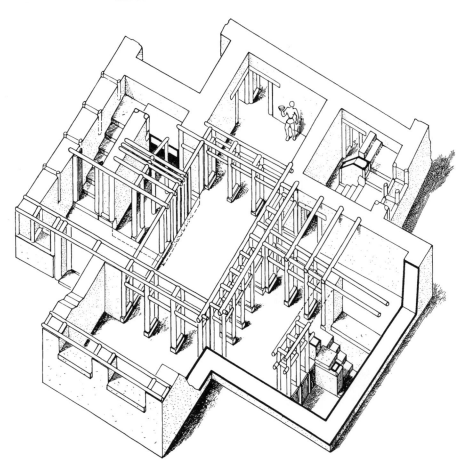

Fig. 18. Akrotiri, Thera. Isometric drawing of the southern entrance of sector Delta, rooms
15 and 16. (After C. Palyvou, in *Prehistoric Cyclades*, 141 fig. 6)

cently published frescoes include depictions of three youths and an adult from Xesti 3, room 3B, which may represent a male initiation ritual.[148]

Akrotiri was settled already in the Neolithic and was inhabited throughout the EBA.[149] The EBA settlement appears to have been of substantial size. Evidence for Neolithic occupation remains slim; 16 sherds have shapes and decoration paralleled in finds from Saliagos. Sherds of the EBA are plentiful. Almost all of the material is highly fragmentary and its dating, for the most part, depends on stylistic criteria.

More than 75% of the total EBA pottery comes, in fact, from the final destruction levels of the settlement, presumably the result of recycling of various kinds (e.g., through incorporation in mudbricks or roofing). All major phases of the EC period appear to be present, and there are types characteristic of the Kampos and Kastri assemblages. The overall distribution pattern of the Neolithic and EC sherds suggests that the focus of the earliest occupation at Akrotiri was in the southwestern part of the excavated area, in the vicinity of Xesti 3.

---

[148] For illustrations, see C. Doumas, "Ἀνασκαφή Θήρας (Ἀκρωτηρίου)," *Prakt* 1986, 208–11; *Ergon* 1988, 130, fig. 103; *Ergon* 1989, 116, figs. 109–11. Final study of the frescoes from the West House has now been completed; a volume will be published shortly by the Greek Archaeological Society: C.A. Televantou, *Ἀκρωτήρι Θήρας: Οι τοιχογραφίες της Δυτικής Οικίας*.

[149] P. Sotirakopoulou, "Early Cycladic Pottery from Akrotiri," *BSA* 81 (1986) 297–312. The extent of the EBA occupation had been described before this but the evidence had not been set forth in detail. See also Sotirakopoulou, "The Earliest History of Akrotiri: The Late Neolithic and Early Bronze Age Phases," in *TAW* III.3, 41–50. These two papers are complementary and should be read together.

Akrotiri was destroyed twice in the initial stages of the LBA.[150] A crisp description of the stratigraphy of the West House and of soundings beneath its floors has provided valuable details concerning the later history of Akrotiri.[151] On the floors of the West House lay deposits of the Volcanic Destruction Level (commonly now abbreviated VDL); beneath them were homogeneous deposits that had been used as fill. These deposits appear to derive from debris accumulated in a destruction that wracked the site at a very early stage of the LBA. The fact that so many buildings were damaged and subsequently required extensive reconstruction suggests that the destruction was caused by an earthquake. The deposits from the West House and others of similar character elsewhere are commonly said to belong to the Seismic Destruction Level (SDL) of Akrotiri.[152]

Still further below the rooms of the West House intact vases and sherds of late MC types have been found in pits of uncertain function that were cut into the bedrock.[153] Earlier stages of the MC period, including types characteristic of Phylakopi I, are represented, but not in well-stratified deposits.[154] This phase in the island's history has, however, been more systematically explored in excavations in two other locations, Ftellos and the Karayeoryis quarries.[155]

Both sites were discovered (and badly disturbed) during modern quarrying.

There should no longer be any debate over the dating of the final destruction of Akrotiri or concerning its relative position in the Minoan chronological sequence.[156] Akrotiri was abandoned in LM IA at a time before the LM IB style on Crete had developed. The explosion of the Santorini volcano appears to have occurred as a single event; there was no appreciable delay between the depositions of the various strata of volcanic ejaculates from its eruption. It is highly unlikely that the LM IB style developed in the interval between the abandonment of the settlement and the final eruption of the volcano.

Evidence from elsewhere in the Aegean leads to these same conclusions. It has been established for some years that the eruption of the Theran volcano, as represented by volcanic ash deposited in soil at Phylakopi on Melos, occurred at a time when LM IA and LC I styles were current, and not even at the very end of the LC I period.[157] Recent excavations both in East Crete and in the Dodecanese have revealed layers of Theran ash stratified over deposits of LM IA and beneath LM IB floors, with pieces of pumice from the eruption in LM IA contexts. The cumulative evidence in all cases suggests that the fall of ash occurred before

---

[150] M. Marthari, "The Destruction of the Town at Akrotiri, Thera, at the Beginning of LC I: Definition and Chronology," in *Prehistoric Cyclades* 119–33; and C. Palyvou, "The Destruction of the Town at Akrotiri, Thera at the Beginning of LC I: Rebuilding Activities," in *Prehistoric Cyclades* 134–47.

[151] M. Marthari, "The Chronology of the Last Phases of Occupation at Akrotiri in the Light of the Evidence from the West House Pottery Groups," in *TAW* III.3, 57–70.

[152] It was only in the course of the rebuilding of the settlement in the wake of this SDL that the walls of the houses were decorated with pictorial frescoes. The SDL and the general rebuilding of the town that followed it must not be confused with the earthquake damage and more ad hoc reconstruction that occurred soon before the final volcanic destruction of the settlement. On this point, see E.N. Davis (supra n. 39) 226, and comments by C. Renfrew, in *TAW* III.1, 70. Most recently, P.M. Warren, "A New Minoan Deposit from Knossos, c. 1600 B.C., and Its Wider Relations," *BSA* 86 (1991) 339, has drawn attention to stylistic similarities between material from the SDL and pottery in a deposit from Knossos that he dates to a newly defined transitional MM III/LM IA phase. His suggestion that the same earthquake was responsible for the destruction of Knossos, Akrotiri, and other southern Aegean sites, such as Ayia Irini on Keos, cannot be entirely correct (supra n. 41).

[153] Some pottery of MC character from Akrotiri is analyzed by A.G. Papagiannopoulou, in *Minoan Influence* 26–69; for additional observations on the technology of production, see

also A. Papagiannopoulou, "Some Changes in the BA Pottery Production at Akrotiri," in *TAW* III.1, 57–66. Most of the material comes from deposits of the SDL in trench A between Xesti 2 and room Delta 20, as described by Marthari (supra n. 150), but included are finds of Phylakopi I style from the so-called Sacrificial Fire Deposit (S. Marinatos, *Thera* III, 19–24) and from soundings beneath the West House. Papagiannopoulou also catalogues the small amount of mainland Gray Minyan pottery that has thus far been recognized in pre-VDL deposits at Akrotiri, describes a selection of Minoan imports of MM II and later date, and discusses in some detail the process of Minoanization of the local ceramic industry.

[154] A selection of material has been recently discussed by Sotirakopoulou (supra n. 149).

[155] For a preliminary presentation of finds from the Karayeoryis quarry, see *Minoan Influence* 321–23; a full publication of this material by M. Marthari will appear in *BSA*. A report on the 1981 season of excavation at Ftellos has now appeared: M. Marthari, "Θήρα: Φτέλλος," *ArchDelt* 36 B′ (1981) 373.

[156] See C. Renfrew, "Summary of the Progress in Chronology," in *TAW* III.3, 242.

[157] See A.C. Renfrew, "Phylakopi and the Late Bronze I Period in the Cyclades," in *TAW* I, 412–16; J.L. Davis and J.F. Cherry, "Phylakopi in Late Cycladic I: A Pottery Seriation Study," in *Prehistoric Cyclades* 148–61; and Davis and Cherry (supra n. 41) 198.

the introduction of the LM IB style. Mainland Greek imports to Thera support this chronology. The stylistic character of the LH I pottery from Akrotiri places the abandonment of the settlement some time before the beginning of LH II, which in turn appears to have begun earlier than LM IB.[158] The eruption of the Theran volcano can consequently not be held directly responsible for the well-known and widespread horizon of LM IB destructions on Crete.[159]

The *absolute* date of the Theran eruption continues to be far more controversial, and is bound up with arguments over the acceptability of a proposed "high" chronology for the Aegean as a whole. For a number of years it has been obvious that many ^{14}C dates from Akrotiri were too early to fit traditional chronologies that placed the volcanic destruction of the site ca. 1500 B.C. Recently arguments have been proffered for moving its destruction into the later 17th century B.C. Supporting data can be divided into three categories: ice cores, tree-rings, and ^{14}C dates. Fluctuations in acidity levels within ice cores from Greenland in many cases are demonstrably correlated with major

volcanic events. Volcanic fallout may also affect the growth rings of trees. The study of cores and of tree-rings (both in the United States and Ireland) suggests that a major volcanic event occurred in the later 17th century, and neither the ice cores nor tree-rings indicate a major eruption ca. 1500. Recently reported ^{14}C dates of samples from short-lived plant matter retrieved from the VDL at Akrotiri in the main seem to *support* a date in the 17th century for the eruption. There are very few artifactual synchronisms between Greece and Egypt during the early LBA. The dates and contexts of relevant imports and exports are in almost all cases disputable, and the evidence on which the traditional Aegean chronology has been based seems capable of accommodating a higher chronology.[160]

Many specialized studies of artifacts from Akrotiri have recently appeared. Metallurgical analyses have shed light on the nature of local industries and their sources for raw material.[161] Chipped stone tools were manufactured almost totally of imported Melian obsidian. Yiali sources are hardly represented, but char-

[158] See Y.G. Lolos, "On the Late Helladic I of Akrotiri, Thera," in *TAW* III.3, 51–56. See P. Warren and V. Hankey, *Aegean Bronze Age Chronology* (Bristol 1989) 97–98, and esp. 214 on the date of the Theran destruction relative to LH II and the relationship of LH II to LM IB.

[159] See J.S. Soles and C. Davaras, "Theran Ash in Minoan Crete: New Excavations on Mochlos," in *TAW* III.3, 82–95; P.P. Betancourt et al., "Excavations at Pseira: The Evidence for the Theran Eruption," in *TAW* III.3, 96–99. From a Cycladic perspective, it never did appear plausible that the final desertion of Akrotiri had actually occurred at a time contemporary with LM IB in Crete. It has been difficult to imagine that the absence of LM IB styles at Akrotiri could be explained by a stylistic time lag between the inception of LM IB on Crete and its introduction to Thera, despite the undeniably close relationship between LM IB vase painting and the Thera frescoes noted, among others, by L. Morgan, "Morphology, Syntax, and the Issue of Chronology," in *Prehistoric Cyclades* 165–78. The masses of LM IB pottery found both at Phylakopi on Melos and at Ayia Irini on Keos, even farther north than Thera, suggest that commerce with Crete was frequent and that certain settlements in the Cyclades were *au courant* with the latest Minoan fashions both before and after the Theran eruption.

[160] The bibliography on this subject is far too extensive to be summarized here. For a review of the state of the controversy before *TAW* III, see S.W. Manning, "The Bronze Age Eruption of Thera: Absolute Dating, Aegean Chronology, and Mediterranean Cultural Interactions," *JMA* 1 (1988) 17–82. For a balanced picture of the results of *TAW* III as they pertain to this issue, see S.W. Manning, "The Thera Eruption: The Third Congress and the Problem of the Date," *Archaeometry* 32 (1990) 91–100; "The Santorini Eruption: An Up-date," *JMA* 2 (1989) 303–13; S. Hood, "The Third International Congress on Santorini (Thera)," *Kadmos* 29 (1990) 84–86; and S. Sherratt, "Fallout from the Aegean Big Bang," *Antiquity* 65 (1991) 998–1001. All basic bibliog-

raphy through 1989 can be found in the two reviews by Manning.

Most recently, evidence pertaining to the date of the eruption of the Thera volcano has been critically examined within the context of a general overview of the evidence for the relative and absolute chronologies of the Aegean, Anatolia, the Levant, and Egypt during the Bronze Age in S.W. Manning, *The Absolute Chronology of the Aegean Early Bronze Age: Archaeology, Radiocarbon, and History* (Sheffield 1992). Manning here proposes and discusses a revised absolute chronology for the entire Cretan Bronze Age and, in addition to radiocarbon dates from Akrotiri, reconsiders those available for Ayia Irini on Keos. Warren and Hankey have continued to defend a lower chronology, based largely on artifactual synchronisms, and would place the eruption of the Santorini volcano in the later 16th century (supra n. 158, 215); see also P.M. Warren, "The Minoan Civilisation of Crete and the Volcano of Thera," *Journal of the Ancient Chronology Forum* 4 (1990–1991) 29–39. Muhly has recently claimed that the artifactual synchronisms between Greece and the Near East support a low chronology; his arguments have been countered by Manning: J.D. Muhly, "Egypt, the Aegean, and the Late Bronze Age Chronology in the Eastern Mediterranean: A Review Article," *JMA* 4 (1991) 235–47; S.W. Manning, "Response to J.D. Muhly on Problems of Chronology in the Aegean Late Bronze Age," *JMA* 4 (1991) 249–62. See also Manning, "Thera, Sulphur, and Climatic Anomalies," *OJA* 11 (in press).

[161] Stos-Gale (supra n. 39) 276, 281, fig. 12 (copper); Stos-Gale and Gale (supra n. 39) 85–88 (lead and litharge). See also Y. Bassiakos et al., "Provenance Studies of Theran Lead," in *TAW* III.2, 337–45, who report lead ore (cerousite) from the excavations at Akrotiri. From the description of the samples and their composition it seems more likely that they are of litharge; see Stos-Gale and Gale (supra n. 39) 85–88.

acteristically MBA/early LBA rhyolite denticulated bifaces are present.[162] Ostrich eggs were fashioned into rhyta.[163] There have been attempts to reconstruct the metrological system in use at Akrotiri on the basis of ceramic container capacity.[164] Artifacts associated with cloth production imply that weaving at Akrotiri had, as at other Cycladic sites, become Minoanized through the introduction of the warp-weighted loom; a peculiar lack of spindle whorls ties Akrotiri more closely to Crete than to her island neighbors.[165] The number of lead weights from the site has nearly doubled in recent years. It has been argued that the fractional units within the system of measure on which these weights are scaled find parallels both in Linear A and Linear B. It has also been suggested that at Akrotiri, such weights, as well as rarer weights of stone, were used for the measurement of heavy goods, wool in particular.[166]

Imported ceramics attest to considerable interaction between Akrotiri and other areas of the Aegean. Chemical and petrological analyses have had some success in defining the local products of Akrotiri.[167] The local character of the LC I ceramic industry at Akrotiri emerges distinct from that of Crete and other islands, despite the fact that many aspects of Minoan technology were blended with earlier Cycladic production techniques.[168] Even in the EBA, ceramic assemblages at Akrotiri were complex mixtures of imports from several locations with geologically distinct clays outside Thera.[169]

A tentative reconstruction of some aspects of the agricultural economy of prehistoric Thera is now also possible. Pre-eruption soils in the vicinity of Akrotiri were more mature in their development than previously thought.[170] Analysis of palaeobotanical remains has begun, in particular of Spanish vetchling (*Lathyrus clymenum*), a crop well represented in the West House. Examination of these pulses and the contaminants and weed seeds found with them suggests that the various deposits of vetchling in the West House came from different fields, probably of quite small size. Informed speculation about the economic and social

---

[162] T.D. Devetzi, "The Stone Industry at Akrotiri: A Theoretical Approach," in *TAW* III.1, 19–23; A. Moundrea-Agrafioti, "Akrotiri: The Chipped Stone Industry," in *TAW* III.1, 390–406. Rhyolite bifaces are of a type previously recognized on Keos and Melos (see R. Torrence, "Other Silaceous Materials," in Davis [supra n. 38] 95–96. Thus far analyses of chipped stone appear to support Torrence's position that obsidian trade at this time was *not* highly regulated by central authority or in the hands of specialist craftsmen (R. Torrence, *Production and Exchange of Stone Tools: Prehistoric Obsidian in the Aegean*, Cambridge 1986); contra Barber (supra n. 143) 117–19, who has been dismissive of Torrence's arguments.

[163] J.A. Sakellarakis, "The Fashioning of Ostrich-Egg Rhyta in the Creto-Mycenaean Aegean," in *TAW* III.1, 285–308, where eggs from Akrotiri and from Phylakopi on Melos are considered.

[164] L. Katsa-Tomara, "The Pottery-Producing System at Akrotiri: An Index of Exchange and Social Activity," in *TAW* III.1, 31–40; C. Doumas and A.G. Constantinides, "Pithoi, Size, and Symbols: Some Preliminary Considerations on the Akrotiri Evidence," in *TAW* III.1, 41–43.

[165] I. Tzachili, "All Important Yet Elusive: Looking for Evidence of Cloth-Making at Akrotiri," in *TAW* III.1, 380–89.

[166] A. Michailidou, "Μετρικό σύστημα και σχέσεις παραγωγής στο Αιγαίο, στην Υστέρη Εποχή του Χαλκού," *Meletimata tou K.E.R.A.* 10 (1990) 65–96; and "The Lead Weights from Akrotiri: The Archaeological Record," in *TAW* III.1, 407–19. Michailidou also notes her forthcoming publication of a potsherd from Akrotiri that has been incised with a record of commodities in Linear A; this is the first such document from the site. On the weights from Akrotiri, see also Petruso (supra n. 39).

[167] V. Kilikoglou et al., "A Study of Middle and Late Cycladic Pottery from Akrotiri," in *TAW* III.1, 441–48; and E. Aloupi and Y. Maniatis, "Investigation of the Technology of Manufacture of the Local LBA Theran Pottery: The Body and Pigment Analysis," in *TAW* III.1, 459–69, offer technological observations on locally produced ceramics, including analyses of clay bodies, pigments, and firing temperatures. On deposits of talc and other minerals locally available to the residents of Thera before the eruption, see W.L. Friedrich and C.G. Doumas, "Was There Local Access to Certain Ores/Minerals for the Thera People before the Minoan Eruption? An Addendum," in *TAW* III.1, 502–503.

[168] M. Marthari, "Investigation of the Technology of Manufacture of the Local LBA Theran Pottery: Archaeological Consideration," in *TAW* III.1, 449–58; "The Local Pottery Wares with Painted Decoration from the Volcanic Destruction Level of Akrotiri, Thera: A Preliminary Report," *AA* 1987, 359–79. Several specific shapes from the VDL have also been the subject of special investigations. See C. Gillis, "Statistical Analyses and Conical Cups: A Preliminary Report from Akrotiri, Thera," *OpAth* 18 (1990) 63–93, and R.B. Koehl, "The Rhyta from Akrotiri and Some Preliminary Observations on Their Functions in Selected Contexts," in *TAW* III.1, 350–60.

[169] S.J. Vaughan, "Petrographic Analysis of the Early Cycladic Wares from Akrotiri, Thera," in *TAW* III.1, 470–87. See also other studies by Vaughan (supra n. 20).

[170] S. Limbrey, "Soil Studies at Akrotiri," in *TAW* III.2, 377–82; but see also O. Rackham's skepticism concerning the potential of agricultural production on the island to explain its prosperity in the Bronze Age and in particular its density of settlement: "Observations on the Historical Ecology of Santorini," in *TAW* III.2, 384–91. On in-progress analyses of additional faunal remains from Akrotiri and preliminary data from the West House, see C. Trantalidou, "Animals and Human Diet in the Prehistoric Aegean," in *TAW* III.2, 392–405; on shell, including triton shells and murex, see L. Karali-Yannacopoulou, "Sea Shells, Land Snails, and Other Marine Remains from Akrotiri," in *TAW* III.2, 410–15; E. Aloupi et al., "Analysis of a Purple Material Found at Akrotiri," in *TAW* III.1, 488–90.

organization of landholding in prehistoric Thera may be possible in the near future.[171]

Only about 1 ha of the site of Akrotiri has been excavated. Local topography and test excavations suggest that the site originally covered some 20 ha, and that its harbor probably lay in what is now the valley of Ayios Nikolaos, some 200–300 m west of the current excavations.[172] Means of access, lighting and ventilation, and drainage all appear to have influenced the plan of the town and the overall density of its habitations, as did a lack of open courts within the houses. One principal purpose of narrow alleys was to provision the interiors of buildings with light and ventilation. The design of individual structures can

be analyzed in terms of general architectural models.[173] In this way a basic architectural vocabulary for the site can be compiled, one that serves not only to permit generalization about the architectural idiom of Akrotiri but also encourages attempts to explain any variation from the expected.[174]

The art of Thera continues to attract considerable attention from art historians, and justifiably so. But even the recent literature is already so voluminous that only a separate review could do it justice.[175] Several papers delivered at the most recent Thera and the Aegean World Congress are of particular importance.[176] Paintings from the West House have been newly reconstructed in light of architectural analyses.

[171] See A. Sarpaki, "'Small Fields or Big Fields?' That Is the Question," in *TAW* III.2, 422–31; also A. Sarpaki and G. Jones, "Ancient and Modern Cultivation of Lathyrus Clymenum L. in the Greek Islands," *BSA* 85 (1990) 363–68. Recent entomological studies of material from the West House are also of interest and have revealed species not now native to Greece but common in the Near East. See *Ergon* 1989, 117.

[172] C. Palyvou, "Notes on the Town Plan of Late Cycladic Akrotiri, Thera," *BSA* 81 (1986) 179–94. Palyvou is cautious in estimating the size of the town, noting only that it was large "by the standards of the time." This becomes clearer when the likely area of the site is compared with that of contemporary Aegean centers: see discussion by Wiener in *TAW* III.1 (supra n. 21) 129–31.

[173] C. Palyvou, "Architectural Design at Late Cycladic Akrotiri," in *TAW* III.1, 45–56; Ακρωτήρι Θήρα: Οικοδομική τέχνη και μορφολογικά στοιχεία στήν Υστεροκυκλαδική αρχιτεκτονική (Diss. Athens Polytechnic Univ. 1988).

[174] In this regard, Palyvou has emphasized the special characteristics of Xesti 4, including its ashlar facades with courses diminishing regularly in height from bottom to top; most masons' marks found at Akrotiri come from this building alone (see discussion in *TAW* III.1, 56). For other recent discussions of specific features of Theran architecture, see C. Palyvou, "Observations sur 85 fenêtres du cycladique récent à Théra," 123–39, and A. Michailidou, "The Settlement of Akrotiri (Thera): A Theoretical Approach to the Function of the Upper Storey," 293–306 in Darcque and Treuil (supra n. 105).

[175] For a catalogue of the various frescoes and a review of major studies of them through 1988, see S.A. Immerwahr, *Aegean Painting in the Bronze Age* (University Park, Pa. 1990) 185–88, and Immerwahr's own discussion in ch. 4. An atlas illustrating the Theran frescoes accompanied by brief informative texts by C. Doumas has been promised by the Thera Foundation. I thank D.A. Hardy for this information.

[176] Several papers in *TAW* III considered the local character of the Theran style of wall painting in comparison with Cretan frescoes, those from other Cycladic islands, and from Rhodes: among them, see E.N. Davis (supra n. 39); R. Laffineur, "Composition and Perspective in Theran Wall-Paintings," in *TAW* III.1, 246–50. S.A. Immerwahr, "Swallows and Dolphins at Akrotiri: Some Thoughts on the Relationship of Vase-Painting to Wall-Painting," in *TAW* III.1, 237–

44 examines the relationship between Cycladic pottery decoration and fresco painting.

C. Televantou, "New Light on the West House Wall-Paintings," in *TAW* III.1, 309–24, offers new reconstructions for the paintings of the West House. The interpretation of the iconography of the West House paintings remains a popular topic. See especially L. Morgan, *The Miniature Wall Paintings of Thera: A Study in Aegean Culture and Iconography* (Cambridge 1988). S. Hiller has seen the miniature West House frescoes as a reflection of a vanished Minoan epic poetry: "The Miniature Frieze in the West House—Evidence for Minoan Poetry," in *TAW* III.1, 229–34. The localities represented in these same frescoes was reconsidered by J.W. Shaw, "Bronze Age Harboursides," in *TAW* III.1, 420–36, by J.A. MacGillivray, "The Therans and Dikta," in *TAW* III.1, 363–69, and by G. Heiken, F. McCoy, and M. Sheridan, "Palaeotopographic and Palaeogeologic Reconstruction of Minoan Thera," in *TAW* III.2, 370–76. W.-D. Niemeier, "Mycenaean Elements in the Miniature Fresco from Thera," in *TAW* III.1, 267–82 argues strongly against the presence of Mycenaean iconography in the miniature frescoes of the West House, and suggests instead that they illustrate the Minoan Thalassocracy. On the interpretation of the Xesti 3 frescoes, see especially Morgan (supra n. 39), and N. Marinatos, "Minoan-Cycladic Syncretism," in *TAW* III.1, 370–76. J. Vanschoonwinkel, "Animal Representations in Theran and Other Aegean Arts," in *TAW* III.1, 327–47 has surveyed animal representations at Akrotiri.

Other recent studies of the iconography of the Thera frescoes include: N. Marinatos, "Role and Sex Division in Ritual Scenes of Aegean Art," *Journal of Prehistoric Religion* 1 (1987) 23–34 (West House and Xesti 3); "A Puberty Rite at Thera: Evidence from New Frescoes," *Journal of Prehistoric Religion* 3–4 (1989–1990) 49–51 (Xesti 3); C. Doumas, "Conventions artistiques à Thera et dans la Méditerranée orientale à l'époque préhistorique," in P. Darcque and J.-C. Poursat eds., *L'iconographie minoenne* (*BCH* Suppl. 11, Athens 1985) 29–34; N. Marinatos, "An Offering of Saffron to the Minoan Goddess of Nature: The Role of the Monkey and the Importance of Saffron," in T. Linders and G. Nordquist eds., *Gifts to the Gods: Proceedings of the Uppsala Symposium 1985* (*Boreas* 15, Uppsala 1987) 123–32; and S. Morris, "A Tale of Two Cities: The Miniature Frescoes of Thera and the Origins of Greek Poetry," *AJA* 93 (1989) 511–35. C. Televantou, "Τα κοσμήματα από την προϊστορική

The walls of this house had been decorated at least twice with wall paintings: of the earlier series only a few aniconic elements have been recognized. Three new cities have been added to the miniature fresco in room 5, for a total of five in all. Fragments of a previously unrecognized town belong to the west wall; on the north wall the well-known fragments that depict a "meeting on the hill" and a "shipwreck" are associated with previously unpublished ships and a town on a hill; the "Nilotic landscape" of the east frieze appears to have provided landscape context for a third town; and the more completely preserved frieze of the south wall has been altered slightly through additions and repositionings.

The Central Cyclades

Naxos. Recent fieldwork on Naxos has included systematic site survey, continuing excavations at the important prehistoric center of Grotta-Palati (the Chora of the island), and concerted efforts to explore Neolithic remains.[177] Only a decade ago the very existence of permanent Neolithic settlement could be doubted.[178] Today, there are well-stratified finds from two locations: the western edge of the shore at Grotta and the Cave of Zas, high on the central massif of the island. The sequence at Grotta appears to begin earlier than that in the Cave of Zas, and is in part contemporary with material from Saliagos.[179]

Finds from Grotta come from a rescue excavation near a place where more than half a century ago "sub-Neolithic" material was reported and from a sounding at nearby Kokkinovrachos.[180] These discoveries coupled with the presence of "sub-Neolithic" material on Palati suggest that the Neolithic site was extensive.

Pottery from the lowest levels inside the main chamber of the Cave of Zas shares features with that from the Saliagos culture, notably white-painted patterns, but crusted and pattern-burnished wares suggest that

Θήρα," *ArchEph* 1984, 14–54, discusses jewelry from Akrotiri in detail, with illustrations both of actual finds (mostly bronze and bone pins and stone beads) and of their depictions in the wall paintings, and, in "The Theran Wall-painting: Artistic Tendencies and Painters," in Crowley and Laffineur (supra n. 19), has defined hands of individual painters.

[177] For the results of general survey, see R. Treuil, "Prospection archéologique à Naxos en 1981," in *Les Cyclades* 59–65; for work (1982–1984) in the region of Kinidaros *Akrotiri* and the *Phaneromeni Monastery,* see *AR* 30 (1984) 53; "Chronique" 1985, 839; and R. Treuil, "Naxos," *ArchDelt* 38 B′ (1983) 350. I thank R. Treuil for kindly providing information about the project. A Bronze Age site has been reported at Kalamadikou, and prehistoric sites at a number of other locations have been noted; one is probably a cemetery. A source of flint and associated debitage at Stelida to the southwest of the Chora of Naxos has been studied, but its exploitation in prehistoric times has not yet been conclusively demonstrated (see M. Séfériadès, "Un centre industriel préhistorique dans les Cyclades: Les ateliers de débitage du silex de Stelida," in *Les Cyclades* 67–80). The results of palynological investigations at Grotta and two other locations on the island are described in J. Josette Renault-Miskovsky, "Les connaissances actuelles sur les végétations et les climats quaternaires en Gréce, d'après les données de l'analyse pollinique," in *Les Cyclades* 99–109.

The current state of Neolithic and EBA research on the island has recently been summarized in *Cycladic Culture.* For maps showing the locations of excavations conducted at the capital of Naxos under the auspices of the Greek Archaeological Society, see V.K. Lambrinoudakis, "Ἀνασκαφή Νάξου," *Prakt* 1985, suppl. pls. 6.1 and 6.2, facing p. 160. The results of investigations prior to the 1980s have been summarized with extensive bibliography and a gazetteer of prehistoric sites by V. Fotou, "Les sites de l'époque néolithique et de l'âge du bronze à Naxos," in *Les Cyclades* 15–57. For the history of research on Naxos, see also V. Lambrinoudakis, "Archaeological Research on the Early Cycladic Period in Naxos," in *Cycladic Culture* 25–26.

In 1989–1990, a large EC cemetery was explored at Kato Sangri in the western part of Naxos: Lambrinoudakis in *Cycladic Culture* 26. The excavation of a grave at Panormos *Korfari ton Amygdalion* has also been described: O. Hadjianastasiou, "Πάνορμο," *ArchDelt* 36 B′ (1981) 378. In the east of the island a new prehistoric site, fortified with rounded towers, has been reported at Zas *Kastelli;* see "Chronique" 1989, 818; also C. Doumas, "Cycladic Culture," in *Cycladic Culture* 20; "Weapons and Fortifications," in *Cycladic Culture* 92.

Aside from systematic fieldwork a number of individual prehistoric artifacts from the island have been published for the first time. These include EC stone and terracotta objects from graves in the region of Panormos (Bossert, supra n. 121), among them a terracotta vessel of the "teddy-bear" type. Many previously unillustrated EC finds from Naxos have been illustrated in *Cycladic Culture,* several of which are also illustrated in F. Zafeiropoulou, *Naxos: Monuments and Museum* (Athens 1988). These include: marble palettes, stone vessels, querns, pestles, hammers, chipped stone, a sealstone, stone beads, figurines, sling stones, terracotta vases (including a bell-shaped cup and a spouted jar of the Kastri group), jugs and a tankard from Panormos, a bone spindle whorl, bronzes (some from the Koronas Cave in the northern part of the island), lead rivets, and a silver-plated bronze dagger.

[178] See *Les Cyclades* 64–65.

[179] The evidence from both sites has been summarized by K. Zachos, "The Neolithic Period in Naxos," in *Cycladic Culture* 29–32. A selection of metal, ceramic, and stone artifacts from recent excavations at the Cave of Zas is presented.

[180] See O. Hadjianastasiou, "A Late Neolithic Settlement at Grotta, Naxos," in *Greek Prehistory* 11–20, with more general comments on the distribution of Neolithic pottery in the Cyclades. Also Hadjianastasiou 1989 (infra n. 185) 209, n. 17, and "Οικόπεδο Δημητροκάλλη," *Prakt* 1985, 153–57, where the excavation in the Dimitrokalli plot and the context of this early material is described in more detail.

the cave was first inhabited somewhat later than the abandonment of the settlement at Saliagos itself.[181] Higher levels share features with FN Kephala on Keos. The sequence appears to continue unbroken into the EBA, providing an important bridge between the later Neolithic and transitional EBA sequences of the Greek mainland and the eastern Aegean.

The later EBA stratum is characterized by Kastri Group types, and contained a substantial number of bronze tools and ornaments. Around a hearth were scattered pieces of unbaked clay with 15 seal impressions, made by an estimated five different seals bearing linear motifs. The highest levels contained finds of the historical periods mixed with Middle and Late Cycladic wares, including LH IIIC, and much Minyan and MC matt-painted. A strip of gold from a Neolithic stratum is the earliest gold object from the Cyclades; copper axes, awls, pins, and spatulas are also represented in Neolithic contexts. Domesticated crops were similar to those exploited on the Greek mainland; barley played a prominent role in the diet. Two large leaf-shaped, bifacially retouched, obsidian spearheads are exceptional components in the lithic assemblage; as on the Greek mainland, there appears to have been a shift from percussion to pressure-flaking at the end of the Neolithic. Other small finds of particular interest include a marble bowl and two bird-heads carved from bone.

Surface investigations in 1985 at the site of Mikri Vigla and the publication of Middle and early Late Cycladic finds from Grotta have shed light on the later prehistory of Naxos. Mikri Vigla is a promontory on the west coast, some 8 km south of the Chora.[182] Artifacts and traces of architecture are abundant on the surface, and have been mapped by the Greek Archaeological Service and the British School at Athens. Fragments of monochrome painted wall plaster were associated with the most impressive building (structure 7): to the east of it a rescue excavation yielded fragments of an MC storage jar. Local and imported pottery from surface collections ranges in date from EC through LC III; polychrome and mono-

chrome matt-painted varieties of probable Melian origin, Middle Minoan imports, and Gray Minyan are represented—types very scarce in Naxian contexts.[183] Later pots and terracotta lamps imitate shapes of Minoan origin.

Approximately 140 fragments of figurines were collected, for the most part small (some minute), standing, and anthropomorphic. They are diverse in style and as a group quite unique in the Cyclades; general parallels with Cycladic marble sculpture and Cretan coroplastic suggest that their production began in the EBA. Other small finds include discoid loomweights of Minoan type, fragments of emery, and marble objects (including a bowl and probably a folded-arm figurine). Petrographical analyses and stylistic observations indicate that substantial quantities of pottery were being imported, both from Melos and Crete.[184]

Elsewhere on the island, evidence for settlement in the later Bronze Age has been recognized in the Kalandos area (in the extreme south of Naxos), at Sangri, at Rizokastellia, and at Grotta itself.[185] Rescue excavations in a building plot (the Dimitrokalli plot) at the west end of Grotta, immediately south of the causeway that leads to Palati, have produced well-stratified deposits of the early LBA, the first published from the site. Excavations included the reexamination of a 10-m stretch of paved road cleared before World War II and subsequently backfilled. On the floor of a building to the south of the road were local and imported pots of LC II and LM IB types, covered by destruction debris of rubble and mudbrick; these included a jug, probably imported from the Dodecanese, Marine Style sherds, and fragments of a vase by the so-called Reed Painter. This was a site well situated within the Minoan orbit and in close contact with centers of the southern and western Cyclades.

Large-scale excavations at the Chora of Naxos were completed in 1985. Work had been resumed in 1978, the principal goal being to complete excavation of various parts of the LH IIIA to LH IIIC settlement explored in earlier campaigns (1949–1974), but not

---

[181] In addition to Zachos (supra n. 179), finds from the Cave of Zas are discussed in Zachos, "Ἀνασκαφή Σπηλαίου Ζάς Νάξος: Κατάσταση 1987," *ArchDelt* 42 B' (in press), a report on excavation seasons in 1985 and 1986; and in Zachos, "Late Neolithic Origins of Cycladic Metallurgy," and A. Douzougli, "The 'Attic-Kephala' Culture: A New Approach to an Aegean Culture," both to be published in the proceedings of the 6th International Colloquium on Aegean Prehistory, Athens 1987. I am extremely grateful to Douzougli and Zachos for allowing me to read and make reference to these papers in advance of their publication.

[182] R.L.N. Barber and O. Hadjianastasiou, "Mikre Vigla:

A Bronze Age Settlement on Naxos," *BSA* 84 (1989) 63–162.

[183] Middle Minoan dark-ground styles appear best represented, but one sherd of the LM IB marine style was present.

[184] S. Vaughan, "Appendix 2: Petrographic Analysis of Mikre Vigla Wares," in Barber and Hadjianastasiou (supra n. 182) 150–59.

[185] O. Hadjianastasiou, "Naxian External Connections in the Late Bronze Age," *BSA* 84 (1989) 205–15. The excavations themselves are more fully described with a plan in Hadjianastasiou, *Prakt* 1985 (supra n. 180) 153–57, and suppl. pl. 5, facing p. 152.

fully published. In 1982–1985, however, new excavations in the Plateia Mitropoleos explored a segment of the LH IIIC fortification wall of the town, nearly 18 m long, and buildings just inside it. Foundations for the wall are of unworked stones; on these lay a superstructure of mudbricks. Buildings of LH IIIB date outside the fortification show that the town had been larger before its construction.[186] Two lumps of raw caolinite and montmorillonite clay were found in an LH IIIC context, and appear to have been imported to Naxos, perhaps from Melos.

Paros.[187] Important new discoveries continue to be made at Koukounaries, on the southwest side of the bay of Naoussa in northern Paros. Excavations at Koukounaries began in 1976. Yearly campaigns have uncovered the remains of a long-lived settlement that had begun already in the Saliagos phase of the Cycladic Neolithic. Early Cycladic artifacts attest to occupation, but the settlement appears to have been deserted between the EBA and LH IIIC, when habitation was established anew.[188] In LH IIIC the site was well fortified with Cyclopean walls and the plateau on top was occupied by a "mansion"; in its ruins were large numbers of ceramic, stone, bronze, lead, and ivory artifacts. The complex was destroyed in a massive conflagration, promoted, no doubt, by a hostile attack: the body of an adult, killed by a wound to the head, had been hastily buried before the wound healed; the bodies of other humans and livestock were left amid the debris.

More recent investigations have defined the extent of Mycenaean settlement more accurately. Defenses on the southern approaches to the acropolis have been explored, and to the east the Mycenaean fortifications have also been located.[189] On the Lower Plateau, east of the upper acropolis, extensive and deep EBA strata (containing EC I material) have been explored beneath the LH IIIC levels; a tanged point of Saliagos type, a marble pendant in female steatopygous form, and ceramics suggest that Koukounaries was inhabited already in the Neolithic period.[190]

Excavations beneath the temenos of the Athena temple on the Middle Plateau have revealed, at the lowest levels, remains of building materials and artifacts of LH IIIC (including a pierced triton shell), contemporary with destruction levels of the megaron on the Upper Plateau; on the bedrock itself are EBA layers. Ash mixed with animal bones and shell suggest that from Geometric times this area was the focus for rituals. The cemetery of the Mycenaean settlement was located in a valley northwest of Koukounaries. Three excavated tombs resemble mainland tholos tombs and have chambers (rectangular with rounded corners) with stone walls and corbeled roofs built in Cyclopean style; all were robbed.[191]

All finds from excavations ca. 1900 on the citadel of Paroikia (the modern Chora of the island) have been recently reexamined.[192] The principal architectural remains should be dated to the final phase of Phylakopi I and are contemporary with the earlier part of period IV at Ayia Irini. A small amount of pottery is both earlier and later in date than main deposits. One of the earliest finds is a large fragment from a burnished rolled-rim FN bowl. Several sherds from burnished tankards are contemporary with Ayia Irini period III; a fragment of a hat-vase belongs to

---

[186] See Lambrinoudakis, *Prakt* 1985 (supra n. 177) 144–61; Lambrinoudakis and F. Zafeiropoulou, "Ἀνασκαφή Μητροπόλεως Νάξου," *Prakt* 1985, 162–67, with earlier references. Subsequent to completion of the excavations in the Plateia Mitropoleos, the most significant structures were roofed in situ to form a subterranean museum. Subsidiary investigations in conjunction with the building of the roof provided additional details concerning the prehistoric settlement. See *Ergon* 1989, 122–25. The study of Mycenaean pottery from Archaeological Society excavations at Grotta is currently being undertaken by M.B. Cosmopoulos, who delivered a paper entitled "Mycenaean Naxos: An Overview of the Evidence," at the International Congress of Mycenology in Rome–Naples, October 1991.

[187] Aside from excavated finds, EBA stone (including a schematic figurine) and ceramic artifacts, perhaps from southwestern Paros, have been published; one vessel has parallels in the Kastri Group. See O. Hadjianastasiou, "Πρωτοκυκλαδικά ευρήματα από την Πάρο," *ArchEph* 1983, appendix 1-4.

[188] The results of campaigns in the 1970s and early 1980s have been summarized in recent papers by D.U. Schilardi, "The LH IIIC Period at the Koukounaries Acropolis, Paros," in *Prehistoric Cyclades* 184–206, and "The Decline of the Geometric Settlement of Koukounaries at Paros," in R. Hägg ed., *The Greek Renaissance of the Eighth Century B.C.: Tradition and Innovation* (Stockholm 1983) 173–83. Surface reconnaissance in the Naoussa area has resulted in the discovery of new EBA sites: see Schilardi, in *Prehistoric Cyclades* 184, with references. There is limited evidence for rehabitation in later LH IIIC after the destruction of the citadel; a substantial Protogeometric settlement followed.

[189] D. Schilardi, "Ἀνασκαφή στην Πάρο," *Prakt* 1985, 111–12; *Ergon* 1990, 105–107.

[190] *Ergon* 1988, 134; *Ergon* 1989, 121.

[191] For the Mycenaean cemetery, see D. Schilardi, "Ἀνασκαφή Πάρου," *Prakt* 1986, 169, 203–204; "Ἀνασκαφή Πάρου," *Prakt* 1987, 236–40. For soundings on the Middle Plateau within and around the Athena temple precinct, see *Prakt* 1985 (supra n. 189) 130–31, 142; *Prakt* 1986, 191–97, 203; *Prakt* 1987, 235–36; *Ergon* 1988, 134; *Ergon* 1989, 118–19.

[192] J.C. Overbeck, *The Bronze Age Pottery from the Kastro at Paros* (*SIMA-PB* 78, Jonsered 1989); several additional finds from Rubensohn's excavations are illustrated by Papagiannopoulou, *Minoan Influence* 336–37.

Fig. 19. Paroikia, Paros. MBA barrel-jar with light-on-dark decoration. (Courtesy John C. Overbeck)

Fig. 20. Paroikia, Paros. Beaked jug with matt-painted decoration. (Courtesy John C. Overbeck)

an EC type best known in funerary contexts. Later material includes familiar Melian types such as the paneled cup, a single bell-cup of LM IB date, and deep bowls of LH IIIC. In general there appears to have been less Minoan influence on the development of MBA pottery at Paroikia and less contact with the Greek mainland than at Ayia Irini or Phylakopi. The main deposits are characterized by Gray Minyan of developed mainland varieties, MC burnished wares, and matt-painted barrel-jars and jugs (figs. 19–20); duck-vases and the extensive use of potters' marks are features in common with the earlier MBA at Phylakopi and Ayia Irini.

Elsewhere on Paros at Tripiti, Mycenaean pithos sherds have been reported, and on Antiparos at Ayia Kyriaki, part of a much damaged cist grave containing an EC figurine was excavated in 1983.[193]

The Amorgian Islands. Extensive illicit excavation on Keros since the late 1950s has resulted in the illegal

export from Greece of a great many EC marble figurines and vases. Some 500 objects have been attributed to the so-called "Keros Hoard," which was reputedly recovered at Kavos in the southwest part of the island. The presence of so many marble objects on so small an island is astonishing, and the nature of prehistoric activity on Keros was the center of much discussion in 1983 at the British Museum conference on EC art; several participants suggested that Kavos had served as a prehistoric ritual center in the EBA Aegean.[194] Investigations at the site were resumed in 1987, and included a systematic collection of surface artifacts.[195] Preliminary analysis of finds suggests that Kavos and, in the later stages of EC II, a settlement on the adjacent islet of Daskaleio were parts of a single large settlement.[196] Adjacent to this settlement was a deposit of special character in which marble artifacts and certain ceramic types were discarded in greater quantities than elsewhere on the site.

The earliest pottery is of Keros-Syros EC II types, but Kastri varieties are also represented.[197] Occasional sherds reminiscent of Phylakopi I are found but are extremely rare; their date is uncertain. Visual and petrological analysis suggests that an exceptionally high percentage (50–60%) of pottery from the site was imported from elsewhere in the Cyclades. Ce-

---

[193] O. Hadjianastasiou, "Πάρος" and "Αντίπαρος," *Arch-Delt* 38 B′ (1983) 350.

[194] See discussion in *Cycladica* 16, 27–29, 33–35.

[195] *Annual Report of the Managing Committee, the British School at Athens* 1986–1987, 32–34.

[196] *Gazetteer* 337–38.

[197] I am grateful to Cyprian Broodbank for sharing with me a draft copy of his report on the ceramics found in the recent explorations of Kavos, and for allowing me to summarize several of his conclusions here. Broodbank also notes a pyxis of Kampos Group type in the Naxos Museum, assigned to Keros, but not definitely to the site of Kavos.

ramic analysis demonstrates that the forms prominent in the special deposit are all compatible with funerary material, and may also suggest that imported goods were brought to the island by its own inhabitants. While a full interpretation of the site's function has not yet been offered, these observations do not actively support the hypothesis that Kavos was an international sanctuary.[198]

Elsewhere in this group of tiny and sparsely populated islets, excavations on Kato Koufonisi have explored part of a settlement of LC II date.[199]

Samos

Neolithic finds were recovered in several stratified soundings and in various isolated pits in the bedrock that were explored in the late 1960s while examining the Hellenistic settlement at Tigani. The publication of these finds has forced a revision of the older relative chronology established for Tigani. The various pits have been assigned to four chronological phases (I–IV) based on stratification in the soundings; several phases have been subdivided on the basis of stylistic criteria. The latest deposits appear to correspond to Emborio phases VII–VI in date (i.e., they antedate the beginning of the EBA); the possibility has been raised that phase I of Tigani began prior to the beginning of the Late Neolithic on the Greek mainland. No indisputable stylistic similarities with Troy I or the EBA sequence from Thermi on Lesbos have been noted; it has been suggested, however, that the earliest ("black") phase of settlement at Poliochni on Lemnos may be only slightly later than Tigani period IV. Several artifacts from Tigani do, however, find parallels in EBA levels elsewhere in the Aegean area and habitation probably continued at the site, despite the absence of an undisturbed EBA stratum.

Recently published finds from the excavations in the Heraion on Samos may close the gap between its sequence of EBA settlements and the Tigani sequence.[200] There, at some remove from EBA levels previously uncovered, four stages of construction were identified within prehistoric levels more than 2 m deep. Part of a fortification wall appears to have sported a rounded tower, and was apparently a predecessor of a previously investigated EBA enceinte. The fortifications rest on earlier habitation levels that lay beneath the water table and could not be investigated. The fourth and latest phase of occupation seems to have been contemporary with the EBA settlement already known at the Heraion. By then the fortifications investigated in this sounding were out of use and a rectangular building, part of a larger complex, extended the area of habitation beyond that previously enclosed within the settlement. The new evidence from the Heraion also points to the existence of a substantially larger prehistoric settlement than previously suspected. At Tigani, the overall distribution of finds also suggests that estimates for the size of the settlement in the later stages of the Neolithic require revision.

Newly published and republished small finds from Tigani include 11 stone vases, and several figurines, both terracotta and marble.[201] In the lithic industry, blades of obsidian are dominant, with a few obsidian arrowheads in Tigani III, a situation that contrasts remarkably with that at Emborio and Ayio Gala on Chios, where obsidian played a palpably subordinate role.[202] Despite close stylistic relationships recognizable in the ceramic styles of the two islands, it is not clear that there was much direct exchange in pottery. It has, in fact, been suggested that in the Neolithic a cultural dividing line should be drawn between them, with Samos looking away from Chios toward the Cyclades and the southeast Aegean.[203]

The Dodecanese

The past decade has witnessed a veritable explosion of new information relevant to the prehistory of the southeast Aegean, although as yet excavation has been limited and survey non-intensive. In the early 1980s, the absence of clear evidence for pre-LBA settlement on most of these islands was particularly odd, as was the paucity of documentation for contact between the Dodecanese and Crete, the Cyclades, or the Greek

---

[198] Contrast the opinion expressed in Renfrew (supra n. 19) 99–100.

[199] Hadjianastasiou 1989 (supra n. 185) 206, 215, n. 59. Parts of two vessels from the settlement are illustrated on pl. 40d–e. The sherd on pl. 40e may well derive from a burnished krater of "Aiginetan" type and, if so, would point to mainland, as well as Minoan, imports at the site. Several previously unillustrated terracotta vases from Apano Koufonisi have now been published in *Cycladic Culture* 172–73, nos. 178–80; additional EC terracotta vessels and stone figurines from both Apano and Kato Koufonisi are illustrated in Zafeiropoulou (supra n. 177) 30, 32–33, 37, 40.

[200] See H. Kyrieleis, H.J. Kienast, and H.-J. Weißhaar, "Ausgrabungen im Heraion von Samos 1980/81," *AA* 1985, 409–18; Felsch (*Kastro Tigani* 39, n. 92) sees no evidence for overlap between stratified deposits from Tigani and from the Heraion.

[201] Cf. the head of a small marble figurine from the Heraion (Kyrieleis et al. [supra n. 200] fig. 42.1).

[202] *Emporio* 699–712.

[203] Cf. A. Sampson, "The Neolithic of the Dodecanese and Aegean Neolithic Culture," *BSA* 79 (1984) 246, fig. 6. Local sources of flint do seem to have been available on Chios; see Hood and Bialor (supra n. 114).

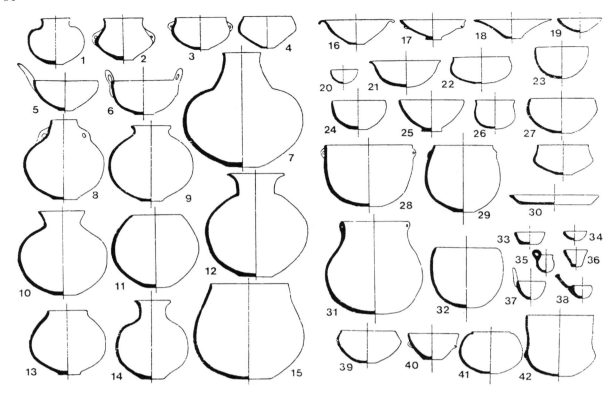

Fig. 21. Characteristic Neolithic pottery types in the Dodecanese. (Courtesy Adamantios Sampson)

mainland in pre-Mycenaean times—despite attested exchange between Crete and the Anatolian coast, notably with Knidos and Iasos.[204]

Neolithic. The picture now emerging for later phases of the Neolithic is one of a relatively dense distribution of sites, with similarities in material culture to Late Chalcolithic centers of Western Anatolia.

The general characteristics of Neolithic settlement can be outlined.[205] Earliest settlement is represented best by the lower phase of occupation in the Kalythies Cave on Rhodes, and is contemporary with the beginning of the Late Neolithic period on the Greek mainland. The Late Neolithic of the Dodecanese has been divided into four phases (Late Aegean Neolithic 1–

4), broadly contemporary with the Late Chalcolithic of Anatolia; each phase has been defined on the basis of stratified deposits from recent excavations and from extensive surface finds (fig. 21).[206] All Neolithic sites thus far investigated in the Dodecanese are small in comparison to those on either the Anatolian or Greek mainlands. Caves were frequently chosen for occupation.

Final reports on the results of recent excavations at five Neolithic sites in the Dodecanese have already appeared: the cave at Kalythies *Ayios Yioryios* on Rhodes; the cave at Arhangelos *Koumelo* on Rhodes; and open-air sites at Partheni on Leros and at Kastro on Alimnia.[207] These and sites on Yiali (below) were

[204] Evidence prior to 1982 is summarized in J.L. Davis, "The Earliest Minoans in the Southeast Aegean," *AnatSt* 32 (1982) 33–41.

[205] For discussion, see Sampson (supra n. 203) 239–49; *Neolithic Dodecanese*; "Νεολιθικά ευρήματα από τη Ρόδο," *AAA* 12 (1979) 24–39; "Το Ν.Α. Αιγαίο στα Νεολιθικά χρόνια," *ArchEph* 1983, appendix 5-13; "Topographical Survey of Prehistoric Sites in the Dodecanese," in D.R. Keller and D.W. Rupp eds., *Archaeological Survey in the Mediterranean Area* (BAR-IS 155, Oxford 1983) 283–85; and "Periodic and Seasonal Usage of Two Neolithic Caves in Rhodes," in *Dodecanese* 11–16.

[206] See *Kastro Tigani* 136–37 for an initial evaluation of the chronological system developed by Sampson and its interconnections with the Neolithic sequence proposed for

Samos. An earlier find from Kalymnos, published by A. Furness ("Some Early Pottery of Samos, Kalimnos and Chios," *PPS* 22 [1956] pl. 19), is there republished and identified correctly as a "scoop" of FN type (pp. 112–13, n. 487).

[207] *Neolithic Dodecanese.* The existence of the site of Partheni on Leros was previously known from investigations by Hope Simpson and Lazenby (*Gazetteer* 367). Material from Kalythies and Partheni is also illustrated in Sampson (supra n. 203) 241, figs. 2–3, and 243, fig. 4; material from the Koumelo Cave in Sampson 1979 (supra n. 205). For Partheni, see also S. Marketou, "Παρθένι, θέση Κονταρίδα," *ArchDelt* 35 B' (1980) 557; for preliminary reports on the Koumelo Cave, the Ayios Yeoryios Cave, the Kastro of Alymnia, Partheni on Leros, and for prehistoric material of less

Fig. 22. Kalythies Cave, Rhodes. Neolithic pottery. (Courtesy Adamantios Sampson)

initially identified or examined as part of a general survey of prehistoric archaeological resources in all islands of the Dodecanese (with the exception of Astypalaia) during 1977–1980. The purpose of that project was to supplement and clarify earlier reports summarized in the *Gazetteer*: 60 new prehistoric sites were recorded, 35 of them on Rhodes. Several of these have, however, yielded only finds of chipped stone and are not conclusively of pre-Mycenaean or even prehistoric date.[208] Thus far little evidence for occupation anywhere in the southeast Aegean prior to the Late Neolithic has been recognized.[209]

Three phases of the Late Neolithic have been recognized in the Kalythies Cave excavations (fig. 22). The most recent corresponds to the second phase of occupation at Tigani on Samos. Here as elsewhere in the Neolithic Dodecanese, Melian obsidian is common (80% of the chipped stone), but obsidian from Yiali and Anatolia is also represented. Plant remains were

recovered by sieving and impressions of plants were found on pottery. Plentiful human and faunal remains include a full range of basic Neolithic domesticates (cow, pig, sheep, goat, and dog), all but dog apparently raised for meat rather than for secondary products, as well as various species of birds, fish (including a tunny-sized specimen), and crustaceans. Only selected joints of deer appear to have been brought to the site. Fox, hare, and marten may have been deliberate live imports to the island, and the earliest domesticated chicken and black rat in Europe may also be attested.[210] Human bones belong to at least four infants and eight older individuals; juveniles and adults are mainly represented only by hand and foot bones and front teeth. The cave may, therefore, have served as a site of permanent burial only for infants, while the bones of juveniles and adults were transferred to another location for secondary burial.

closely determinable date at Pylonas *Cave of Halil* and at Arhangelos *Limani Papakonstanti*, both on Rhodes, see Sampson, "Ἀρχάγγελος" and "Ἅγιος Γεώργιος Καλυθιῶν," *ArchDelt* 34 B' (1979) 448–49; "Ἀνασκαφικές ἐργασίες: Ρόδος," *ArchDelt* 35 B' (1980) 558–59.

[208] *Neolithic Dodecanese* 96–115 contains a gazetteer that includes Neolithic, EBA, and some later findspots on Rhodes, Kos, Karpathos, Symi, Alymnia, Leros, Patmos, Halki, and Tilos. For a more complete list of pre-Mycenaean sites on Kos, see *Neolithic Dodecanese* 229–32. Four of the five sites catalogued for Karpathos are discussed in more detail in *Karpathos, Saros and Kasos* (see under A4–A6, E39, E40, and J56). For finds of Cycladic Keros-Syros type pottery at the site of Vathy *Elliniko* on Astypalaia (*Gazetteer* 365),

see C. Doumas, "Περιόδειαι," *ArchDelt* 29 B' (1973–1974) 981. For the site of Harkadio on Tilos, see C. Doumas, "Τῆλος," *ArchDelt* 30 B' (1975) 369–72.

[209] See "First Colonization" 170–71 with reference to excavations in the Harkadio Cave on Tilos. See also the results of investigations in a cave at Erimokastro on Rhodes where dwarf elephant bones and possible traces of human occupation have been noted, but in unstratified contexts; and A. Sampson, *Η Νεολιθική κατοίκηση στο Γυαλί της Νίσυρου* (Athens 1988) 210 where the possibility of Middle Palaeolithic material from Yiali is raised.

[210] P. Halstead and G. Jones, "Bioarchaeological Remains from Kalythies Cave, Rhodes," in *Neolithic Dodecanese* 135–45.

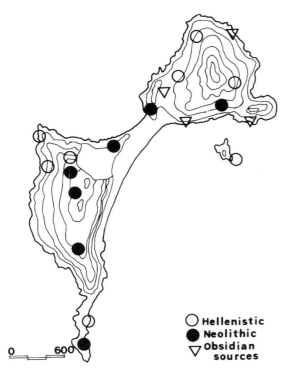

Fig. 23. Yiali. Obsidian sources and archaeological sites. (Courtesy Adamantios Sampson)

Excavations at the Koumelo Cave on Rhodes uncovered two superimposed surfaces: the lower of these was contemporary with the uppermost level of the Kalythies Cave, the top with the Final Neolithic of the Cyclades. Above Neolithic levels the cave was filled with a deep deposit of ash, apparently ejected by the Minoan eruption of the Santorini volcano.[211] On the tiny currently uninhabited island of Alimnia between Rhodes and Halki, excavations also uncovered parts of a settlement, including walls from both

apsidal and rectangular structures. Habitation was contemporary with the latest phase of occupation at the Koumelo Cave, as were badly eroded buildings at Partheni on Leros.

Neolithic settlements have also been investigated on the tiny island of Yiali (fig. 23).[212] Prehistoric remains are rare in the northeast where deposits of obsidian are located. On the neck that joins the northeast to the southwest part of the island, pottery and ground stone finds of FN and EBA date have been excavated (fig. 24); only here has EBA pottery been recognized.[213] FN finds are widespread in the south, and include terrace walls and the foundations for a three-room house with curving walls (fig. 25). Many vessels were associated with its destruction deposits as were two crucibles for melting copper. Remnants of over 70 rectangular cist graves have been excavated. No bones or grave goods were found in any, despite sieving, but from the Neolithic pottery around them there can be little doubt about their date. Ground stone tools were widespread. All appear to have been manufactured from local materials, with handstones of sandstone, limestone, and andesite, and querns mostly of andesite. Axes were not common.

Recent fieldwork in the Dodecanese does not suggest that Yiali ever served as a major supplier of obsidian to the Aegean; organized quarries have not been recognized. Although irregular flakes found both on Yiali and Alimnia were employed as tools for expedient purposes, regular types of chipped stone tools even on Yiali itself were manufactured of Melian (and perhaps Anatolian) obsidian and of flint.[214]

Early Bronze Age. Sites appear to have decreased in number between the Neolithic and the EBA. Contact with the adjacent Anatolian mainland seems to have been frequent. The earlier parts of the EBA are the

---

[211] Problems in assigning volcanic ash found outside Thera to the Minoan eruption of Santorini are discussed by R.B. Galloway et al., "Radio-isotope Analyses of Aegean Tephras: Contribution to the Dating of Santorini Volcano," in *TAW* III.3, 135–44. There the likelihood of a post-Neolithic eruption of the Yiali volcano, virtually contemporaneous with that of Santorini, is asserted—a suggestion that found little support from others in attendance at the *TAW* conference; see the discussion of this paper on pp. 144–45. More generally on the identification of volcanic ash likely to be Theran in origin, see D.G. Sullivan, "Minoan Tephra in Lake Sediments in Western Turkey: Dating the Eruption and Assessing the Atmospheric Dispersal of the Ash," in *TAW* III.3, 114–18, and the following discussion on p. 119.

[212] For the distribution in the Aegean of obsidian from Yiali, see Sampson (supra n. 209) 216–18, supplemented by references in J.L. Davis et al., "Keos and the Eastern Aegean: The Cretan Connection," *Hesperia* 52 (1983) 365–66. This obsidian does not appear to have been extensively used because of its poor fracturing properties. It was thus appar-

ently not the availability of obsidian that attracted early inhabitants to the island. See also H.G. Buchholz and E. Althaus, *Nisyros, Giali, Kos: Ein Vorbericht über archäologisch-mineralogische Forschungen auf griechischen Inseln* (Mainz 1982); and R. Torrence and J.F. Cherry, *Archaeological Survey of the Obsidian Source on Giali in the Dodecanese* (unpubl. ms. in British School of Archaeology at Athens).

[213] Sampson (supra n. 209) 23 has suggested that some lithics may be earlier in date than the Neolithic. Matt-impressions are present on the bases of so-called "cheese-pots" (p. 101). Neolithic pottery and obsidian from both Melos and Yiali have also been found on the islet of Pergousa, just to the west of Nisyros (*Neolithic Dodecanese* 252).

[214] Although Melian obsidian is not at all rare in the Dodecanese, the quantities in which it is found and a general scarcity of evidence for other kinds of Cycladic imports may be indicative of much more limited interaction between the Cyclades and Dodecanese than among the Cyclades themselves, or between the Cyclades and the Greek mainland (see also Melas 1988 [infra n. 237] 290).

Fig. 24. Yiali. Excavations in sector A. (Courtesy Adamantios Sampson)

least well documented.[215] It has been suggested that finds from the Aspri Petra Cave on Kos should be dated to EB II because one-handled cups and spouted jugs are present; other sherds from surface collections at Troulli on Kos and on Astypalaia may also belong to EB II. In recent excavations material of similar character has been found at Ayios Fokas on Kos and on the island of Yiali. Finds from Askloupi and Messaria on Kos, from Muskebi on the Anatolian mainland, from Lindos on Rhodes, and from Nisyros have sometimes been dated to EB III, but it has most recently been argued that the material from Askloupi and Messaria is of EB II date. EB II parallels from Tsilimbiri on Kos and from new excavations of graves at Tavla near Antimaheia on Kos have been adduced.[216]

Rescue excavations at Seraglio on Kos and Asomatos on Rhodes should clarify the EBA sequence considerably.[217] At Seraglio, a fortified settlement of EB III has been revealed in deep soundings beneath the later Bronze Age town; it was itself built on top of earlier levels of EB III, including the remains of a potter's kiln. Part of a single long house, possibly with one "ellipsoidal" wall, has been cleared. Ceramics

Fig. 25. Yiali. Foundations of a Neolithic house. (Courtesy Adamantios Sampson)

---

[215] For general discussion of the distribution and character of EBA material in the southeast Aegean, see *Neolithic Dodecanese* 118–19; Sampson 1983 (supra n. 205) 12. For an update, see T. Marketou, "Asomatos and Seraglio: EBA Production and Interconnections," *Hydra: Working Papers in Middle Bronze Age Studies* 7 (1990) 40.

[216] For Tavla, see H. Kantzia, "Αντιμάχεια: Κτήμα Ελ. Ζαβού," *ArchDelt* 39 B' (1984) 335.

[217] Marketou (supra n. 215).

(wheelmade red-burnished bowls, duck-vases, and tankards) find close parallels both in Anatolia and in the western Aegean. At Asomatos near Kremasti, west of Trianda on the north coast of Rhodes, two long "megaron-like" buildings have been uncovered, and were associated with similar pottery. They belong to the latest phase of the site and overlay parts of houses on a different orientation. Fortifications are surmised because of the density of architectural remains.[218]

Middle Bronze Age. The Middle Bronze Age in the Dodecanese remains a mystery on which recent explorations have shed little light.[219] The settlement at Asomatos came to an abrupt end in EB III. On the basis of finds (mainly carinated bowls[220]) from compressed levels found stratified in several soundings between EB III and LB I layers,[221] it has been argued that occupation at Seraglio was continuous from the end of the EBA to the LBA, but it is far from clear that all phases of the MBA are represented. A kiln for firing the bowls has also been investigated.[222] Minoanizing pottery with light-on-dark decoration, widespread in the Dodecanese and often assigned to the MBA, is more likely to belong to the earlier phases of the LBA, both in the southeast Aegean and in the Cyclades where it was imported.[223] As yet, there is little evidence for earlier versions of this style.[224]

Later phases of the MBA are best represented by finds from Mt. Filerimos on Rhodes, high above the northern coastal plain, southeast of Trianda.[225] At Profitis Elias on the most eastern spur of this massif, survey and excavation have yielded unstratified finds and traces of architecture. Jugs more Anatolian than Cretan in appearance were found with carinated and conical cups; some pottery belongs to LM IA. The existence of MBA material on Mt. Filerimos itself has now been clearly demonstrated. The only well-strati-

fied group of finds (excavated in 1925) comes from a floor, not clearly associated with other architectural features, southwest of the later Athena temple; finds of similar character were probably excavated in a fill beneath the temple itself and in other parts of the acropolis. Only undecorated pots were found on the floor; most have their closest parallels in MBA Crete. Small finds are both of MBA and LBA varieties and include a stone lid of MM type, a spindle whorl, a terracotta scuttle, a discoid loomweight, stone vases, marble pommels, and a bronze mirror.

Late Bronze I and II. LB I patterns of settlement contrast radically with their predecessors. In northern Rhodes, the focus of activity shifted from Mt. Filerimos to Trianda on the coastal plain below, where there is, for the first time, evidence for widespread habitation. Recent excavations have filled out the picture of occupation sketched by extensive Italian excavations before World War II.[226] The LB I settlement at Trianda was large by island standards, and has been estimated at over 12 ha. Moreover, the thoroughly Cretan character of the settlement has been reinforced by new discoveries. Buildings had plastered floors and walls; characteristically Minoan architectural features such as the *polythyron* and ashlar masonry were employed; and new fresco fragments, including one with a painted lily and another with a double-axe and sacral knot are in the Minoan idiom. Horns of consecration in stone suggest Cretan religious practices, as do new bronze figurines of Minoan types.

Results from recent excavations at Trianda in the Theoharis plot have been fully published. Excavations there in 1975, 1978, and 1980 uncovered structures within an area of approximately 360 m².[227] Three main constructional phases were recognized, Trianda

---

[218] On Asomatos, see Marketou (supra n. 215) 40–47.

[219] *Neolithic Dodecanese* 119–20.

[220] See Marketou (supra n. 215) fig. 5b.

[221] Marketou (infra n. 230) 101–104. See also the report of MBA pottery, including fragments of polychrome bird-jugs (infra n. 236).

[222] Marthari et al. (infra n. 223) 175.

[223] Marketou (infra n. 230) 103; M. Marthari, T. Marketou, and R.E. Jones, "LB I Ceramic Connections between Thera and Kos," in *TAW* III.1, 171–84; Davis et al. (supra n. 212) 361–66.

[224] Recently published results of excavations in the Theoharis plot at Trianda on Rhodes (infra n. 227) provide the only well-documented evidence in support of an early date for Dodecanesian light-on-dark wares. Only a single sherd from a pre-LM IA context has been published and the bulk of the ware clearly belongs to the LBA.

[225] T. Marketou, "New Evidence on the Topography and Site History of Prehistoric Ialysos," in *Dodecanese* 27–28; M.

Benzi, "Evidence for a Middle Minoan Settlement on the Acropolis of Ialysos (Mt. Philerimos)," in *Minoan Thalassocracy* 93–104 (including p. 102, for the possibility of MM material from the region of Ayios Isidoros in the central western part of Rhodes).

[226] For older bibliography, see *Gazetteer* 348. The recent bibliography is already extensive. In addition to references already cited (supra n. 225), see Doumas (infra n. 230) and Marketou (infra n. 230). Papagiannopoulou, *Minoan Influence* 218–22, remarks on the character of pottery from both older and recent excavations at Trianda and at Seraglio on Kos.

[227] L. Papazoglou-Manioudaki, "Ανασκαφή του Μινωικού οικισμού στα Τριάντα της Ρόδου," *ArchDelt* 37 Α' (1982) 139–87. Initial results of this excavation had previously been described in a preliminary report by C. Doumas and Papazoglou, "Santorini Ash from Rhodes," *Nature* 287 (1980) 322–24.

I, II, and III, and two architectural subphases distinguished within the third phase.[228] Both Trianda I and II were explored mainly in soundings beneath the courtyard of a large building of Trianda III. No trace of the LM IA style was recognized in the pottery of Trianda I. It is necessary, therefore, to redate the earliest occupation at Trianda to the later MBA, approximately contemporary with finds from Mt. Filerimos. Trianda I appears to be the earliest stratum at the site; in places, excavation reached bedrock and Trianda should still be viewed as a new foundation in the New Palace period of Crete.

The character of the shapes and decoration of pottery in Trianda I is overwhelmingly Minoan, and Cretan features such as discoid and cylindrical loomweights, a bull figurine, a stone vase, potters' disks, fragments of faience, and frescoes decorated with bands or curvilinear motifs are all represented.[229] Other small finds include fragments of small gold bands, a bronze sickle, bronze needles, and a lead rod. The cause for the destruction of Trianda I is not readily apparent. Phase II, on the other hand, showed obvious traces of destruction by fire, perhaps precipitated by an earthquake. The damaged remains of the settlement were soon partly covered by a layer of volcanic ash from the Santorini eruption; the latest pottery sealed beneath the ash belongs to the LM IA style. The Minoan LM IB style is only represented in strata above the ash layer. Elsewhere on Rhodes, layers of ash from the Santorini eruption have been investigated: near the airport at Paradeisi and on the east coast at Kolymbia the layer exceeded a half meter in thickness.[230]

In Trianda IIIA, a large house with rooms around a central court was built in the Theoharis plot. Many walls are quite substantial and ashlar masonry was sparsely employed; in the western part of the house, a second story was reached by wooden stairs within stairwells. After a destruction (perhaps caused by an earthquake), lighter less consequential walls, which infringed on the area of the courtyard, were added to the complex in Trianda IIIB. Individual stratigraphical levels could not be assigned to phase IIIA; the final abandonment levels of phase IIIB are dominated by LM IB/LH II ceramic types.[231]

Other recent soundings at Trianda have provided important details concerning the extent and duration of the prehistoric settlement. Excavations since 1982 in the Markos plot (300 m west of the Theoharis plot) have exposed the most western part of the Minoan/Mycenaean settlement, including parts of an LM IA building with a *polythyron*.[232] In the Kattavenos plot (300 m south of the center of the Italian excavations at Trianda), LM IB remains lay above volcanic ash, with LM IA remains beneath.[233] These and other recent soundings suggest that the southern part of the LM IA settlement had been abandoned after the eruption of the Thera volcano; in LM IB, new structures, including a possible defensive system, were built above the ash layer in northern parts of the site, and the settlement decreased in size. Imports from Crete continued in LM IB and Cypriot wares were also present.

Evidence of expansion of settlement in LB I is also evident in areas east and west of Trianda: contemporary remains have been explored in five other locations. These are spread over an area of more than 14 km along the coast, and from the village of Trianda to the foot of Mt. Filerimos. In addition, on the east coast of Rhodes LB I artifacts have been excavated in

---

[228] Phases defined by the new excavations can be approximately equated with those defined by A. Furumark ("The Settlement at Ialysos and Aegean History c. 1550–1400 B.C.," *OpArch* 6 [1950] 150–271) as follows: Trianda II=Furumark Trianda I; Trianda IIIA and B=Trianda IIA and B, respectively. Trianda I, on the other hand, represents an initial stage in the settlement not defined by earlier investigators.

[229] There are several striking differences between this Minoanized assemblage from Trianda and contemporary deposits in the Cyclades. Obsidian from Melos was present but scarce; mainland matt-painted and Minyan wares do not appear to be represented at all; and there is little evidence for the importation of Cycladic pottery. Not surprisingly, imports from Western Anatolia are indicative of exchange between Rhodes and the adjacent mainland; see Papazoglou-Manioudaki (supra n. 227) 171–72.

[230] On Theran ash, see T. Marketou, "Santorini Tephra from Rhodes and Kos: Some Chronological Remarks Based on the Stratigraphy," in *TAW* III.3, 100–12; C. Doumas, "The Prehistoric Eruption of Thera and Its Effects," in *Dodecanese* 34–38.

[231] Later Mycenaean finds include a bronze arrowhead, and a phi-figurine was recovered nearby at the so-called Pyrgos of Paraskevas; see Papazoglou-Manioudaki (supra n. 227) 181.

[232] See S. Marketou, "Οδός Ιερού Λόχου (οικόπεδο Κωνστ. Μάρκου, Κτ. Μερ. 551," *ArchDelt* 39 B´ (1984) 325–26, where long parallel walls perhaps belonging to a drainage work of LM IB date are reported as well as frescoes, Cypriot vases, and limestone horns of consecration. This is the plot described as plot 3 and marked on T. Marketou's map in *Dodecanese* (supra n. 225) 29, fig. 4; there a possible defensive function is suggested for the long walls.

[233] S. Marketou, "Πάροδος 9ης Μαΐου (βόθρος οικοπέδου Κατταβενού)," *ArchDelt* 39 B´ (1989) 327.

the cave of Koumelo[234] and are represented among surface finds from Kolimbia-Theotokos.[235]

Results from recent excavations at Seraglio on Kos echo those from Trianda.[236] The LM IA town at Seraglio also increased markedly in size, and two architectural phases have been recognized. After the first was destroyed by earthquake, there was a major reorganization of the town and a main street was established that led from the harbor up the hill to the main focus of the settlement. The second phase of the settlement was destroyed before the end of LM IA (probably also by earthquake); remains of human victims were found in its rubble. As at Trianda, a layer of volcanic ash covered this debris in part, but the ash appears to have fallen measurably later than the earthquake destruction.

Recent research on Karpathos, Kasos, and Saria paints a picture similar to that being established for Rhodes and Kos.[237] Here too there is considerable question about the date and extent of earlier (i.e., pre-Mycenaean) settlement. Surface investigations have documented considerable activity in the later Neolithic period and during transitional Neolithic/EBA phases, but finds are extremely worn and difficult to

parallel either in the Cyclades or on Crete. EBA and earlier MBA assemblages have not yet been well defined.

By the later MBA, it seems clear that Karpathos, Kasos, and Saria had been drawn into the Minoan orbit. The finest Minoan Kamares types characteristically found at Phylakopi or Ayia Irini already in the earlier MBA, however, have not yet been reported and there is only slight evidence for the importation of Cycladic wares.[238] Definite or possible finds have been published from more than 40 separate locations. Accumulating data suggest the existence of an extensive Minoanized center at Pigadia, capital of modern Karpathos. This settlement lay in the southeast part of the island on the south side of a large bay that faced the southern tip of Rhodes.[239] The focus of prehistoric occupation appears to have been the coastal plain, bordered on the west by the hill of Skopi and on the east by the acropolis of Sissimos; chamber tombs, some as early as MM III/LM IA, were dug into the slopes of both.

The existence of prehistoric settlement at the Xenona site has long been recognized, but it is now obvious that occupation in the Pigadia area was much

---

[234] See Sampson, in *Dodecanese* (supra n. 205) 13–14; in the Koumelo Cave, early LBA pottery (said to be of LM/LC and Cypriot types, including a base-ring jug) was found to be stratified both above and below the ash layer (*Neolithic Dodecanese* 214). See also *Neolithic Dodecanese* 74. Layers of ash associated with archaeological finds have also been recognized on Tilos, Karpathos, and Halki. For further remarks see Melas 1983 (infra n. 237) 58.

[235] Melas 1988 (infra n. 237) 300–302.

[236] See T. Marketou, "Marine Style Pottery from the Seraglio in Kos," *BSA* 82 (1987) 165–69, and brief reports on recent rescue excavations in the Seraglio, including I.H. Papahristodoulou, "Οδός Βεροιοπούλου 40 (οικόπεδο Ελ. Χατζηστέργου)," *ArchDelt* 34 Β' (1979) 452–54 (pure Mycenaean finds, including a phi-figurine, from soundings near the temple of Demeter); "Οδός Ελ. Βενιζέλου 30 (οικόπεδο Ν. Τουφεξή)," *ArchDelt* 34 Β' (1979) 456–57 (two prehistoric building levels, equivalent to Morricone's first and second city, in a sounding near the northeast corner of Morricone's zone I; from the foundation levels for the walls of the older phase came sherds with representations of birds, apparently in the Cycladic Black and Red style; in higher levels LM I and LH II–IIIB types were represented, along with jugs of the familiar Dodecanesian light-on-dark style; "Οδός Τσαλδάρη και 25ης Μαρτίου (οικόπεδο Ειρ. Σοφού)," *ArchDelt* 35 Β' (1980) 552–53 (in the Pizzoli zone of earlier Italian excavations; four major stratified levels were recognized, dating from later MM to LH IIIB/C); "Οδός Μ. Αλεξάνδρου και Ελ. Βενιζέλου (οικόπεδο αφών Χατζησάββα)," *ArchDelt* 35 Β' (1980) 553 (LH architectural remains farther west than the previously postulated limits of the settlement); "Οδός Ελευθερίου Βενιζέλου και Αγ. Παρασκευής (οικόπεδο αδελφών Βασιλείου)," *ArchDelt* 36 Β' (1981) 409 (opposite zone I of the Italian excavations; five architectural phases recognized, dating from MM to LH

IIIC; two potter's kilns of MM/LM IA date; EBA sherds); "Οδός Απέλλου και Κολοκοτρώνη (οικόπεδο Δ. Μυλωνά)," *ArchDelt* 38 Β' (1983) 396 (reached the top of Mycenaean levels); "Οδός Ελ. Βενιζέλου και Κολοκοτρώνη (οικόπεδο Σ. Διακαναστάση)," *ArchDelt* 38 Β' (1983) 396 (excavation of part of the Mycenaean settlement); H. Kantzia, "Οδός Κολοκοτρώνη 25 (οικόπεδο Αντ. Θαλασσινού)," *ArchDelt* 39 Β' (1984) 329–30 (LH III above MM/LM IA; stratified EBA including part of a wall and a partly intact potter's kiln); "Γωνία των οδών Ιω. Θεολόγου και Απέλλου (οικόπεδο Γεωρ. Πιζάνια)," *ArchDelt* 39 Β' (1984) 330 (LH III, MM/LM IA, with EBA just above virgin soil); "Οδός Ηφαίστου (οικόπεδο Δεσπ. Καλογήρου)," *ArchDelt* 39 Β' (1984) 331 (reached top of LH IIIC stratum).

[237] For recent work on these islands, see M. Melas, "Minoan and Mycenaean Settlement in Kasos and Karpathos," *BICS* 30 (1983) 53–61; "Survey of Karpathos, Kasos and Saria, Dodecanese," in Keller and Rupp (supra n. 205) 287–89; *Karpathos, Saros and Kasos*; "Exploration in the Dodecanese: New Prehistoric and Mycenaean Finds," *BSA* 83 (1988) 283–311. See also "Σπήλαιο Ελληνοκαμάρας," *ArchDelt* 37 Β' (1982) 417 for explorations by the Ephoreia of Caves in the cave of Ellinokamaras on Kasos (for earlier bibliography see *Gazetteer* 359). For copper in Karpathos in the LBA, see Stos-Gale (supra n. 39) 276.

[238] *Karpathos, Saros and Kasos* no. 558, from the site of Palio Mitato (D23), appears to be a sherd from a Melian jug.

[239] A large limestone figure found there was presented by J.T. Bent to the British Museum in 1886. Melas (*Karpathos, Saros and Kasos* 147–48) has suggested that it may have served as a cult statue; cf. Renfrew's remarks concerning similarly "colossal" figures from the southeastern Cyclades ("Speculations on the Use of Early Cycladic Sculpture," in *Cycladica* 24–30).

more extensive; some 150 m to the east of Xenona, a principal focus of LB I settlement has been identified at Vroulidia. Here recent construction work afforded opportunities to examine stratigraphy. Finds are of types characteristically found at Minoan and Minoanizing centers elsewhere in the southern Aegean and include plentiful conical cups, red wall-plaster, pottery of MM III/LM I varieties, and extensive deposits of murex shells.

Elsewhere on Karpathos, on Saros, and on Kasos, similar ceramics are widespread, if not so closely datable. Sites are generally small with undistinguished finds (occasional loomweights of Minoan type are notable); most are located on, or near, coasts. Pottery actually imported from Crete appears to be exceptional outside Pigadia. Trapeza (L60) on Kasos is an exception; Minoan finds were plentiful there and ashlar masonry was possibly employed. On Kasos the primary focus of occupation seems to have shifted from the southwest area, that part of the island closest to Crete, to the north coast at some time between LB I and LB III.

Minoan finds have also been recognized on many of the smaller islands of the southeast Aegean, e.g., at Garipa on Telos,[240] and at Pontamos *Ayioi Anargyroi* on Halki.[241]

Late Bronze III. Study of the Mycenaean period in the southeast Aegean continues to be hampered by a lack of properly excavated and completely published settlement sites; fullest information comes from excavations conducted in the 1920s and '30s when these islands were under Italian occupation.[242] Recent syntheses of previous archaeological investigations on Rhodes provide convenient points of departure for any discussion of the complex history of settlement in the Dodecanese during the Mycenaean period.[243] Findspots are concentrated in the more fertile areas of the north, particularly around Trianda, but chamber-tomb cemeteries have been recognized in most other parts of the Rhodian periphery and at several sites in the interior.[244]

Since thousands of tombs have been looted and their contents transferred to museum collections outside Greece, a great many artifacts both on Rhodes and abroad have little or no context. A pleasant exception are tombs in the Lindos area excavated in 1925 in a salvage operation designed partly to compensate for damage done by tomb-robbers. The results of these excavations have recently been published, and many tomb-groups now divided between Turkish and Danish museums have been reassembled on paper.[245] It has also been possible, in most cases, to relocate the sites of the original excavations.

The restudy of Mycenaean finds from Italian excavations at Trianda (Ialysos) has clarified the later history of northern Rhodes. There the identity of those who used the numerous chamber tombs (of LH IIB–IIIC date) at Makra Vounari and Moschou Vounari has long been at issue. Very little pottery later than LH IIIA:1 was published in the report of Italian excavations at Trianda, nor have excavations on Mt. Filerimos yielded substantial numbers of LBA finds.[246] Furumark, in his reanalysis of the excavations of Trianda, all but ignored the scanty Mycenaean evidence and assumed that the settlement was abandoned in LH IIIA:1.

It is now clear, however, that substantial numbers of LH IIIA:2 sherds were found in the older excavations; these were distributed over so large an area that it is unlikely that they were transported from elsewhere, despite a lack of associated architectural remains.[247] Current excavations at Trianda may resolve the matter soon. Thus far they have produced some evidence for occupation later than LH IIIA:1, including a few sherds of LH IIIB; LH IIIC is possibly also represented.

The first chamber tombs at Ialysos were built in LH IIB/IIIA:1; weapons were prominent in these earliest burials.[248] Minoan influence and imports had almost totally disappeared. Elsewhere on Rhodes, contemporary finds are thinly distributed. In LH IIIA:2, however, an island-wide pattern in the geographical

[240] A. Sampson, "Μινωικά από την Τήλο," *AAA* 13 (1980) 68–73; "Γαρίπα," *ArchDelt* 34 B' (1979) 461.

[241] Melas 1988 (supra n. 237) 307.

[242] See M. Benzi, "Mycenaean Rhodes: A Summary," in *Dodecanese* 59–72.

[243] C. Mee, *Rhodes in the Bronze Age: An Archaeological Survey* (Warminster 1982), subsumes bibliography and discussion included in the *Gazetteer,* and reevaluates much unpublished material from earlier excavations; see also Benzi (supra n. 242).

[244] More recently Sampson, in *Neolithic Dodecanese* 101, has reported the presence of Mycenaean pottery in a cave at Kakoskali near Arhangelos on Rhodes.

[245] S. Dietz, *Excavations and Surveys in Southern Rhodes: The Mycenaean Period* (*Lindos* IV.1, Copenhagen 1984).

[246] For a current summary of the evidence, see M. Benzi (supra n. 225) 100–102; and M. Martelli, "La stipe votiva dell'Athenaion di Jalysos: Un primo bilancio," in *Dodecanese* 104–20, esp. 115, n. 1.

[247] M. Benzi, "Mycenaean Pottery Later than LH IIIA:1 from the Italian Excavations at Trianda on Rhodes," in *Dodecanese* 39–55.

[248] Benzi (supra n. 242); see also "Tombe micenee di Rodi riutilizzate nel TE IIIC," *SMEA* 23 (1982) 323–44 (where contexts are clarified for chamber tombs at Ialysos, Kalavarda, and Mandriko); and "Rhodes in the LH IIIC Period," in *Greek Prehistory* 253–62. My summary is based largely on Benzi's account in *Dodecanese,* the most comprehensive and authoritative recent conspectus of the evidence.

distribution of tombs was established that persisted until LH IIIC. LH IIIB finds are, however, strangely uncommon, and it has been argued that this situation reflects an actual decrease in settlement.[249] In LH IIIB, there was a substantial decrease in the number of tombs built or in use at Ialysos and perhaps more generally in northwest Rhodes. In other parts of the island, the number of tombs in use also appears to have decreased substantially, except in the southeast where there are slightly more IIIB finds than in previous periods.

LH IIIC, on the other hand, witnessed a sudden increase in the number of burials at Ialysos; many older tombs were reused and more Mycenaean figurines were deposited in burials. Most interments appear to date early in LH IIIC. A "continuous but thin thread" seems to have been maintained between the Argolid and Rhodes throughout the IIIC period, but at most sites there is no pottery of the later stages of LH IIIC. It has been suggested that there may have been internal migration in early IIIC from other parts of the island into the Ialysos area.[250]

Recent research on Kos, Karpathos, Kasos, and Saria has also clarified the pattern of Mycenaean settlement. In Karpathos, Kasos, and Saria there remains an unexplained gap in the local sequence of habitation during LM IB and LM II, a peculiar absence given the presence of substantial amounts of LM IB at

Trianda on Rhodes. In LH III, there appear to have been far fewer sites than in MM III/LM IA and none has yet been located on Saria; most settlements and cemeteries were in naturally fortifiable locations where no evidence of earlier LB I occupation has been recognized. LM/LH IIIA and earlier LH IIIB types of ceramics are well represented; the later phases of LM/LH IIIB and IIIC are curiously absent. Imports from the mainland have been recognized but Cretan types remained dominant, in contrast to the situation on Rhodes and Kos.[251] Cemeteries with chamber tombs of Mycenaean type became the rule on Kos, Kalymnos, and Astypalaia.[252]

Excavations at Kardamaina (ancient Halasarna) on the south coast of Kos may help sort out details of Dodecanesian relative chronology in LB III; a stratigraphical sequence of deposits is said to run unbroken from LH IIIA:1 through Greek and Roman times.[253] Mycenaean finds have now also been recognized even on smaller islands of the southeast Aegean such as Leros.[254]

Amorgos

Many new prehistoric sites have been reported on Amorgos and the locations of older finds identified with greater certainty through recent surface explorations. Some 18 sites can now be dated to the Early Cycladic period.[255] A fortified EC stronghold at Mar-

[249] C. Mee, "The LH IIIB Period in the Dodecanese," in *Dodecanese* 56–58.

[250] On the issue of internal migration and more generally concerning regional variation in material culture during LH IIIC, see C. Macdonald, "Problems of the Twelfth Century B.C. in the Dodecanese," *BSA* 81 (1986) 125–51; on LH IIIC pottery in the eastern Aegean, see S. Sheratt, "The Development of Late Helladic IIIC," *BICS* 32 (1985) 161. See also J.H. Crouwel, "Fragments of Another Octopus Stirrup Jar from Kalymnos in Amsterdam," *BABesch* 59 (1984) 63–68 (two fragments of an unpublished LH/LM IIIC vessel said to have been found on Kalymnos).

[251] See *Karpathos, Saros and Kasos* 180; but also R. Jones and C. Mee, "Provenance Studies of Aegean Late Bronze Age Pottery," in R.E. Jones, *Greek and Cypriot Pottery: A Review of Scientific Studies* (The British School at Athens, Fitch Laboratory Occasional Paper 1, Athens 1986) 510. For Arkasa *Vonies* on Karpathos, see O. Zahariadou, "Θαλαμοειδής τάφος στην Αρκάσα Καρπάθου," *ArchDelt* 33 A′ (1978) 249–95; and A. Sampson, "Αρκάσα Καρπάθου," *ArchDelt* 34 B′ (1979) 459–60. The principal burial (of LB III date) in this case had been deposited in a terracotta larnax; various bronzes were included with it. Evidence for LBA settlement in the area, particularly at Arkeseia, is also discussed by Zahariadou.

[252] For the publication of a recently explored LH III chamber tomb on Kos at Kastello (or Kastelles), southeast of the modern Chora, see L. Papazoglou, "Μυκηναϊκός θαλαμωτός τάφος στο Κάστελλο Κώ," *AAA* 14 (1981) 62–75, and I.H. Papahristodoulou, "Καστέλλες," *ArchDelt* 34 B′ (1979) 458–59; for a chamber tomb at Messaria on Kos, see Papah-

ristodoulou, "Μεσαριά," *ArchDelt* 34 B′ (1979) 457–58; also Papazoglou 65–66, n. 9. For LH/LM chamber tombs on Kalymnos, see *AR* 30 (1984) 70. For the investigation of two chamber tombs on Astypalaia at Synkairos, located on the north shore of the island between Steno and Trito Marmari, see C. Doumas, "Αστυπάλαια," *ArchDelt* 30 B′ (1975) 372 (finds included a bronze spearhead, a fishhook, lead weights, chisels, and spatulas; bones in one tomb were fully disarticulated and in both tombs they showed strong signs of burning); for Mycenaean Astypalaia in general, see Macdonald (supra n. 250) 148.

[253] G. Aleura et al., "Ανασκαφή στην Καρδαμαίνα (Αρχαία Αλασάρνα) της Κώ," *ArchEph* 1985, Chronika 1–18 (for description of the prehistoric material, see p. 18).

[254] Marketou (supra n. 207); A. Sampson, "Ανασκαφικές εργασίες: Ρόδος," *ArchDelt* 35 B′ (1980) 559.

[255] L. Marangou, "Evidence for the Early Cycladic Period on Amorgos," in *Cycladica* 99–115. Marangou also publishes 1) fragments of EC pottery from various surface collections; and 2) previously unpublished vessels of terracotta and marble and six marble figurines that are now in the collection of the museum of Chora on Amorgos; L. Marangou, "Ανασκαφή Μινώας Αμοργού," *Prakt* 1985, 199–200, describes EC finds subsequently acquired by the museum. Marangou, "Découvertes récentes à Amorgos," in *Les Cyclades* 121, mentions fragments of frescoes from the site of Xylokeratidi, on the east side of the bay of Katapola, and Marangou, "Evidence for the Early Cycladic Period on Amorgos," in *Cycladica* 99, no. 3, makes reference to numerous Mycenaean sherds there. See also Marangou, "Ανασκαφή Μινώας Αμοργού," *Prakt* 1984, 388, where remains of a fortification,

kiani has been surveyed and excavated.[256] Two seasons of excavations documented stratified finds mainly of Grotta-Pelos, Kampos, and Kastri types. Burnished rolled-rim bowls with "tubular tunnel lugs" dominate in the earliest levels and are associated with a circuit of fortifications, the oldest recorded in the Cyclades.

Elsewhere on Amorgos, excavations both on the acropolis and in the lower town of Minoa have yielded finds of the Neolithic and EBA, principally in post-Bronze Age contexts (such as the filling of a tower in the Geometric fortifications), but also unmixed in bedrock pockets.[257] A fragmentary EC folded-arm figurine, found in the filling of a Roman cistern, is the first EBA marble figurine found on Amorgos in proper excavation since the 19th century.[258]

BEYOND PHYLAKOPI: TOWARD A PAN-AEGEAN PREHISTORY

The study of the prehistory of the Aegean islands has long been hampered by the absence of a flexible relative chronology based on a series of published deposits from settlement contexts. In the absence of competition, the stratigraphy of a single well-documented and long-lived site, Phylakopi on Melos, monopolized center-stage for much of this century. The dominance of this type-site has often encouraged the proliferation of uniformitarian assumptions about Aegean island prehistory and it has consequently been very difficult either to define or explain variation in material culture between one part of the Aegean and another.

It could still be said in 1979 that our comprehension of the cultural history of the Cycladic EBA had not improved greatly since the results of the first excavations of Phylakopi were published in 1904. Already then three main groups of material dating to the EBA were recognized and there was considerable consensus about the order in which they were to be arranged:

finds from the Pelos cemetery on Melos were early, material from the fortified acropolis of Kastri on Syros fell in the middle, and the first city at Phylakopi at the end.[259] No single site in the Cyclades had a stratified sequence that could be argued to span the totality of the EBA. At Phylakopi itself, it could be doubted that the site had been occupied at a time contemporary with EH II on the Greek mainland.[260]

Although Phylakopi was admirably published by the standards of its day, because of the method of its publication, any reevaluation of its conclusions in light of subsequent developments in Aegean prehistory is a formidable task. The contexts of finds from the excavations were generally described only with reference to successive broad phases or "cities" into which the history of the settlement was divided. Groups of finds were not published as units; in most cases, it is not possible to determine which specific finds were found associated in a single excavation level.[261] Furthermore, since the publication of Phylakopi, various additional "groups" have been defined, consisting of artifactual types that have consistently been found in association with each other in Cycladic graves. There has been considerable controversy over the relative chronology of some of these groups; it has even been suggested that the so-called Kampos group, often assigned to a stage intermediary between the Grotta-Pelos and Keros-Syros assemblages, may not represent a chronologically significant development at all but rather a series of wealthy burials for "socially conspicuous individuals."[262]

Many of these chronological conundrums may soon be resolved. Our understanding of the Neolithic in the islands is improving at a rapid pace. In another decade deposits of the Cycladic EBA will have been published from Ayia Irini on Keos (periods II and III), from the equally important site of Skarkos on Ios, and from Markiani on Amorgos. The stratigraphy of these three sites will provide a broad geograph-

---

other architectural features, and EBA pottery are reported to have been found at Mandres tou Nikita Roussou and are to be associated with tombs excavated nearby by Tsountas at Kat' Akrotiri (*Gazetteer* 340).

[256] See *Annual Report of the Managing Committee, the British School at Athens* (1986–1987) 32; (1987–1988) 28; (1988–1989) 23; and (1989–1990) 19; *AR* 36 (1989–1990) 69; and Renfrew (supra n. 19) 44, 45, 96.

[257] See Marangou 1985 (supra n. 255) 184–86, 191, 196–98. The Neolithic pottery from Minoa includes white-painted types: see Hadjianastasiou in *Greek Prehistory* (supra n. 180) 18. See also Marangou 1984 (supra n. 255) 357, 377, and 380 for possible EC from both the Acropolis and lower town, and p. 388 for a report of EC surface finds on the east slope of the Acropolis.

[258] *Ergon* 1990, 113, 114, fig. 157.

[259] See esp. the discussion in J.E. Coleman, "Chronological and Cultural Divisions of the Early Cycladic Period: A Crit-

ical Approach," in Davis and Cherry (supra n. 26) 48–50; C. Renfrew, "Terminology and Beyond," in Davis and Cherry (supra n. 26) 51–63; and J.E. Coleman, "Remarks on 'Terminology and Beyond'," in Davis and Cherry (supra n. 26) 64–65.

[260] J.L. Caskey, "Greece, Crete, and the Aegean Islands in the Early Bronze Age," in *CAH*³ I, ch. 36a, 794–95.

[261] It has sometimes been possible to reconstruct more specific contexts by recourse to the original excavation records: namely, D. Mackenzie, *Daybook of the Excavations at Phylakopi in Melos, 1896, 1897, 1898 and 1899* (unpublished transcript by Colin Renfrew), or by a close reading of the text of the excavation report itself (e.g., E.T. Blackburn, *The Cyclades in the Middle Bronze Age* (M.A. thesis, Univ. of Cincinnati 1964).

[262] See C. Renfrew, "From Pelos to Syros: Kapros Grave D and the Kampos Group," in *Prehistoric Cyclades* 41–54.

ical scope and should allow, for the first time, the construction of a relative chronology for the EBA Cyclades that is based almost entirely on settlement stratigraphy. Of special importance will be the publication of material of the initial phases of the EBA at Markiani: these finds in tandem with recently excavated "pre-city" deposits at Phylakopi and transitional Neolithic–EBA strata from the Cave of Zas on Naxos should permit firm definition of the beginning of the Cycladic EBA.

The position of the Keros-Syros phase of the Cycladic EBA is solidly established as contemporary with EH II on the Greek mainland. Ayia Irini period II, the principal deposits at Skarkos, and pre-city phase A2 from Phylakopi will allow this stage to be more tightly defined both in the western and southern Cyclades. The final stages of the EBA present greater problems. The Kastri Group and its Euboian equivalent, Lefkandi phase I, remain poorly understood. Although its type features have been recognized at many sites in both the northern and southern Cyclades, only at Ayia Irini is there abundant contextual information from an excavated settlement. There it is clear that the Anatolian features in the ceramics are displayed in only a small minority (about 10%) of the pottery in use. There is an obvious continuity in material culture from the preceding Keros-Syros phase. The hypothesis that the Cyclades were invaded and settled by new immigrants at the time of the Kastri Group is weak. It has often been argued that the sites of Kastri on Syros and Panormos on Naxos were settled by Anatolian newcomers, but neither has been fully published and it is not possible, as at Ayia Irini, to assess the extent of Anatolian influence on their ceramics. Kastri types from Mt. Kynthos on Delos are totally devoid of stratigraphical context.

Ceramic characterization studies of Kastri Group ceramics are badly needed. The possibility that Anatolian types were brought to some Cycladic islands through exchange with the eastern Aegean cannot be excluded. The suggestion that sites such as Kastri were established as forts by Anatolian invaders is even less convincing now that the site of Markiani on Amor-

gos appears to have been fortified already at the very beginning of the EBA. It seems less likely that the Kastri phase was the only, or even a special, time of troubles in the EBA Cyclades. The existence of weapons manufactured from bronze of a composition similar to that employed for bronzes in use at Troy also need not point to invaders from that part of the Aegean. More recent analyses of metal artifacts from Troy and the islands of the northeast Aegean suggest that a northwest Anatolian provenance for the Trojan bronzes themselves is in doubt, and it now is generally agreed that the Anatolian ceramic types that characterize the Kastri Group are of southwestern Anatolian, rather than Troadic, derivation.[263] The Kastri phase may be more plausibly seen as a phase of increased interaction between the Cyclades and the southeast Aegean.

After Ayia Irini period III and the abandonment of Kastri, the ground is very shaky until the inception of Ayia Irini period IV. There is certainly a gap in the stratigraphy of Ayia Irini between periods III and IV. Period III must be more or less contemporary with the later stages of EH II on the mainland, while period IV does not begin until the earliest phases of the mainland and Cretan MBA have passed. Periods equivalent to mainland EH III and earlier MH are completely unrepresented. More serious is the fact that almost no evidence has yet been recognized *anywhere* in the Cyclades for occupation contemporary with EH III on the Greek mainland, nor is there a stratigraphical sequence in the Cyclades that bridges fully the centuries of transition between the Cycladic EBA and MBA. This fact has led to the provocative suggestion that there is a general "gap" in the Cycladic sequence: whether this is an accident of excavation or reflects a time of generally thin settlement remains to be determined.[264]

With the start of period IV at Ayia Irini, we again have a firm footing. Indeed, periods IV and V at Ayia Irini appear to cover most of the later MBA.[265] Details of chronology become controversial again at the very end of the MBA. In Cretan terms, the latest imports in period V at Ayia Irini appear to date to the begin-

[263] On the relevant analyses from Kastri, see Z.A. Stos-Gale, N.H. Gale, and G.R. Gilmore, "Early Bronze Age Trojan Metal Sources and Anatolians in the Cyclades," *OJA* 3 (1984) 23–43. On the southwestern Anatolian origin of Kastri Group types, see M.J. Mellink, "The Early Bronze Age in West Anatolia: Aegean and Asiatic Correlations," in G. Cadogan ed., *The End of the Early Bronze Age in the Aegean* (Leiden 1986) 139–52, and Wilson and Eliot (supra n. 35).

[264] For arguments pro and con, see "Perspectives"; references in n. 123 (supra); Warren and Hankey (supra n. 158)

25–29; and J.B. Rutter, "The 'Early Cycladic III Gap': What It Is and How to Go about Filling It without Making It Go Away," in *Prehistoric Cyclades* 95–107. Arguments are summarized and discussed at length in Manning 1992 (supra n. 160).

[265] Recent excavations at Phylakopi have not produced detailed stratigraphy for the MBA. For this and other information concerning the second city of Phylakopi, I am grateful to Robin Barber, who has allowed me to study his unpublished report on newly excavated Middle Cycladic pottery.

ning of MM III. The earlier stage of period VI has been considered more or less contemporary with the Seismic Destruction Level at Akrotiri on Thera, and both have been dated in Cretan terms to the very beginning of LM IA. This is also the time when the Second City of Phylakopi was destroyed. There would, therefore, appear to be a gap in the Ayia Irini sequence. On Crete, the transitional MM/LM phases have never been closely defined; refinements there should allow the nature and duration of this gap to be described in greater detail.

The beginning of the LBA in the Cyclades is clearly represented by deposits of early period VI at Ayia Irini and from the Seismic Destruction Level at Akrotiri. The publication of these deposits will provide definitions for early LC I that are practicable within the Cyclades. It would be unwise to redefine the beginning of LC I in reaction to revisions in Cretan terminology. Subtle definitions of MM III and LM I, of the sort currently being proposed by Minoan specialists, could only be distinguished in the islands of the Aegean were substantial quantities of Cretan imports present. This is rarely the case, even in the Cyclades, where Minoan pottery never amounts to more than a fraction of the total in an assemblage.

For the remainder of the LBA, recent publications have clarified many details of relative chronology. The eruption of the Santorini volcano represents a pivotal stage and it is now obvious that the material in the Volcanic Destruction Deposits at Akrotiri is contemporary with a later, but not the latest, stage of LM IA on Crete. Stratigraphy at Phylakopi on Melos suggests that only some time after the eruption of the Santorini volcano did the first LM IB imports reach that site.[266] Times contemporary with LM IB on Crete and LH II on the Greek mainland are well represented by Ayia Irini period VII, which can itself now be subdivided. Plentiful finds of the LB III period have been illustrated, including destruction deposits at Koukounaries on Paros (dated to an early stage of LH IIIC), a long sequence of ceramic assemblages in the sanctuary at Phylakopi (LH IIIA–C), and groups in the temple at Ayia Irini (LH IIIC). Publication of LH IIIA–B deposits from Ayia Irini will also be invaluable.

We thus seem well on our way to establishing a relative chronology for the Cyclades that reflects the full range of variation within these islands as a whole. If this goal is to be accomplished we must resist the temptation to impose rigid chronological frameworks on a pan-Cycladic or pan-Aegean scale. Rather the stratigraphical sequences of each and every site and island need first to be considered individually and only then related to those of other islands: it is particularly important that stratified groups of material from Cycladic settlements continue to be published, rather than selections of finds arranged by phases established at some other site such as Phylakopi or Ayia Irini. Such a procedure is complicated, but the complexity is only reflective of the truly intricate nature of the archaeological record itself. Our purpose after all is not to establish a chronological system of mnemonic simplicity for students.

Enormous progress is also being made in sorting out the relative chronology of other islands and island groups of the Aegean. More detailed publication of finds from excavations in the prehistoric settlements at Manika should clarify the material cultural sequence of Euboia for Bronze Age periods earlier than the first phase of Lefkandi. Our understanding of later EBA and MH phases will profit from the complete publication of the results of excavations in the Vouratsas plot at Eretria, and from Palamari on Skyros. In the northern Aegean, stratigraphy from Skala Sotiros and Kastri on Thasos will be of great importance in linking the cultural sequences of the northern Aegean to those of the south, both in the EBA and LBA. Emborio on Chios and Tigani and the Heraion on Samos also emerge as pivotal sites that tie the later Neolithic and EBA Cyclades to the eastern Aegean and Anatolia.

Recent developments in the Dodecanese have already made important contributions to our understanding of the cultural history of the latest MBA and earlier LBA. The systematic inventory of archaeological remains and the identification of new sites have radically changed our picture of the density and distribution of settlements, particularly in the Middle and Late Bronze Ages. The earlier MBA is, however, still poorly understood, as is the EBA. The investigation of EB III levels at Asomatos on Kos is thus of great importance. We are still a long way from understanding the significance of substantial gaps in habitation sequences present on many of the islands of the Dodecanese.

It should also be evident from this review that relative chronology has not been the only, or perhaps even the principal, emphasis of recent fieldwork in the Aegean islands. Excavations such as those of house A on Keos or the sanctuary on Melos have been published with an opulence of detail that makes it now possible to begin to reconstruct the social and

---

[266] See Davis and Cherry (supra n. 41).

economic organization of prehistoric island centers for the first time. The full documentation of sequences at Akrotiri, Melos, and Keos permits us to hypothesize about the processes responsible for changes in material culture there. Intensive surveys on Keos and Melos, and systematic efforts also to inventory prehistoric resources in parts of Naxos, Ios, Siphnos, Keros, Amorgos, Euboia, Skyros, Chios, in the Sporades, and in the Dodecanese are giving us the first reliable pictures of patterns in settlement within entire prehistoric island landscapes.

It seems fair to say that the Aegean islands should no longer be viewed as a backwater but as one of the best-documented areas of prehistoric Greece, or even of prehistoric southern Europe.[267] Great progress has been made. The relative chronology of settlement is much better known than it was only a decade ago, and, perhaps of greater importance, excavations of settlement sites have established local stratigraphical sequences in all major parts of the Aegean. The publication of current excavations and advances in the study of absolute chronology promise to resolve long-standing problems in relative chronology and should make it possible for archaeologists to shift at last the focus of their efforts from matters of chronology to the reconstruction of the societies and economies of the islands of the prehistoric Aegean.[268] Indeed, the next decade promises to be exciting.

DEPARTMENT OF CLASSICS (M/C 129)
UNIVERSITY OF ILLINOIS AT CHICAGO
BOX 4348
CHICAGO, ILLINOIS 60680

---

[267] Indeed, the prehistoric archaeology of Melos has been employed as one principal case in a textbook now widely used in archaeology classes in North America: see C. Renfrew and P. Bahn, *Archaeology: Theories, Methods, and Practice* (London 1991) 438–45.

[268] Two important syntheses of available evidence for absolute and relative chronology in the Aegean are in press and deserve special notice: see Coleman (supra n. 8) and especially the detailed treatment of the islands provided by Manning 1992 (supra n. 160).

Addendum: 1992–1999

JACK L. DAVIS, IOULIA TZONOU-HERBST, AND AARON D. WOLPERT

INTRODUCTION

In the nearly eight years since the publication of "Review of Aegean Prehistory I: The Islands of the Aegean" (RAP I), there has been an unprecedented explosion in the intensity of archaeological exploration of the Aegean islands.[269] Now familiar is the archaeology of entire clusters of islands (e.g., the northern Sporades, the Turkish islands of Imbroz [Imbros] and Bozcaada [Tenedos], and the north-

ern Cyclades), once virtual *terrae incognitae*, while many a long-standing crux in scholarship has been addressed by focused investigations (e.g., the "mystery" of supposed Mesolithic artifacts at Maroula on Kythnos; the location of the settlement associated with the cemetery at Chalandriani on Syros). Our knowledge of earliest prehistory has grown substantially: "Investigation of the insular Neolithic is one of the youngest, yet fastest growing, areas of Aegean archaeology."[270] Above all, it is especially encouraging

---

[269] Davis has been primarily responsible for sections of this review that are concerned with Keos, the northern Sporades, the northern Cyclades, and the Turkish islands of the Aegean; Tzonou-Herbst with Lesbos, Chios, Limnos, the southern Cyclades, and the central Cyclades; and Wolpert with Euboia, Skyros, Thasos, Samothrace, the western Cyclades, and the Dodecanese. We all acknowledge indispensable assistance from Jean Wellington and Michael Braunlin of the Burnam Classics Library of the University of Cincinnati, and from Nancy Winter of the Blegen Library of the American School of Classical Studies at Athens. We also thank all those who have sent us information or have otherwise helped us to assemble bibliography: Claire Palyvou (whose important contributions to RAP I were inadequately recognized), Phoebe Acheson, Christos Agouridis, Lillian Ahilara, Cyprian Broodbank, Tristan Carter, Christos Doumas, Efi Karantzali, Anthi Koutsoukou, Toula Marketou, Mariza Marthari, Eleni Panagopoulou, Vasif Sahoglu, Efi Sakellaraki, Adamantios Sampson, Eleni Skafida, Sharon Stocker, Ioanna Venieri, and Andreas Vlachopoulos.

In addition to the abbreviations used in RAP I, the following abbreviations are used in this appendix:

AEMel	*Αρχείον Ευβοϊκών Μελετών.*
Das Neolithikum	E. Alram-Stern, *Das Neolithikum in Griechenland, mit Ausnahme von Kreta und Zypern* (Die Ägäische Frühzeit, 2. Serie; Forschungsbericht 1975–1993 1, Vienna 1996).
Kaloyerovrysi	A. Sampson, *Καλογερόβρυση: Ενας οικισμός της Πρώιμης και Μέσης Χαλκοκρατίας στα Φύλλα της Εύβοιας* (Athens 1993).
Kea-Kythnos	L.G. Mendoni and A. Mazarakis-Ainian eds., *Kea-Kythnos: History and Archaeology. Proceedings of an International Symposium Kea-Kythnos, 22–25 June 1994* (Μελετήματα 27, Paris 1998).
"Late Neolithic Remains"	A. Sampson, "Late Neolithic Remains at Tharrounia, Euboea: A Model for the Seasonal Use of Settlements and Caves," *BSA* 87 (1992) 61–101.
Limnos	*Λήμνος Φιλτάτη: Πρακτικά του 1ου Συνεδρίου Δημάρχων του Αιγαίου, Μύρινα Λήμνου, 21–24 Αυγούστου 1992* (Athens 1994).
Poliochni	C.G. Doumas and V. La Rosa eds., *Η Πολιόχνη και η Πρώιμη Εποχή του*
Poliochni on Limnos	*Χαλκού στο βόρειο Αιγαίο. Διεθνές Συνέδριο, Αθήνα, 22–25 Απριλίου 1996* (Athens 1997). L.G. Mendoni ed., *Πολιόχνη, Λήμνωι εν Αμιχθαλόεσσηι: Ενα κέντρο της Πρώιμης Εποχής του Χαλκού στο βόρειο Αιγαίο* (Athens 1997).
Protohistoric Thasos	C. Koukouli-Chrysanthaki, *Πρωτοϊστορική Θάσος: Τα νεκροταφεία του οικισμού Καστρί* (Δημοσιεύματα του Αρχαιολογικού Δελτίου 45, Athens 1992).
Skoteini	A. Sampson, *Σκοτεινή Θαρρουνίων: Το σπήλαιο, ο οικισμός και το νεκροταφείο* (Athens 1993).
Urla	*International Symposium: The Aegean in the Neolithic, Chalcolithic, and Early Bronze Age. Municipality of Urla, 13–19 October 1997. Abstracts.*
Wace and Blegen	C. Zerner ed., *Wace and Blegen: Pottery as Evidence for Trade in the Aegean Bronze Age, 1939–1989. Proceedings of the International Conference Held at the American School of Classical Studies at Athens, December 2–3, 1989* (Amsterdam 1993).

[270] C. Broodbank, "Colonization and Configuration in the Insular Neolithic of the Aegean," in P. Halstead ed., *Neolithic Society in Greece* (Sheffield Studies in Aegean Archaeology 2, Sheffield 1999) 15. See also G.A. Papathanassopoulos, *Neolithic Culture in Greece* (Athens 1996); and Broodbank, *An Island Archaeology of the Early Cyclades* (Cambridge 2000). Also of particular relevance for Neolithic and EBA settlement in the Cycladic islands are papers delivered at a one-day colloquium entitled "The Early Bronze Age in the Cyclades in the Light of Recent Research at Settlement Sites," held 1 November 1998 on the island of Syros. Participants discussed, among other topics, recent discoveries and research on Amorgos, Andros, Astypalaia, Keros (Dhaskalio-Kavos), Ios (Skarkos), Keos (surface survey in the southern part of the island), Melos (Adamas), Mykonos, Naxos (Cave of Zas and Iria), Paros (Marapas), and Thera (Akrotiri). Two papers from the symposium at Urla have comparable themes: N. Efstratiou, "The Neolithic of the Aegean Islands: A New Picture Emerging," in *Urla* 13; and V. Sahoglu, "New Evidence for the Relations between the Izmir Region, the Cyclades and the Greek Mainland during the Third Millennium B.C.," in *Urla* 43.

that archaeological histories are being written for individual islands of the Aegean, although few have yet been the targets of systematic intensive survey; in many instances artifacts have been reported but remain to be documented in a scientific manner. Important interpretive studies have also appeared recently and deserve mention here.[271]

Brief summaries of recent bibliography follow, with islands grouped in the same manner as in RAP I.

A REVIEW OF RECENT WORK

Keos

In 1994, a conference dedicated to the archaeology of Keos and Kythnos provided a welcome venue for the exposition and evaluation of both old and new research; papers were published promptly.[272] Communications concerned with prehistoric settlement may be divided into three groups: those elaborating results of excavations at Ayia Irini; those setting settlement on Keos in its larger Aegean context; and those documenting the natural resources of the island.

Studies of Ayia Irini included discussions of the overall organization of the Late Bronze I–II town and its antecedents; the Mycenaean settlement (Ayia Irini period VIII); the stratigraphy of the Temple; wall paintings from the Northeast Bastion of the LBA fortifications; modifications to the plan of the fortifications; palaeogeographic reconstruction of the coastline of the Ayia Irini peninsula; conical cups of the early LBA; and discussions of lead and copper ores on Keos and the likelihood that they were worked at Ayia Irini. Authors of other papers considered interaction between Keos and adjacent areas of the Aegean and compared settlement patterns on Keos with prehistoric distributions on other islands and with patterns documented through ethnographic research.[273]

[271] Significant bibliographical resources include *Das Neolithikum*, esp. ch. 5, "Inseln der Ägäis," 449–80; W. Ekschmitt, *Die Kykladen: Bronzezeit, geometrische und archaische* (Kulturgeschichte der antiken Welt, Mainz 1993); E. Karantzali, *Le Bronze ancien dans les Cyclades et en Crète: Les relations entre les deux regions. Influence de la Grèce continentale* (*BAR-IS* 631, Oxford 1996); E. Lanzillotta and D. Schilardi eds., *Le Cicladi ed il mondo egeo: Seminario internazionale di studi: Roma, 19–21 novembre 1992* (Rome 1996); L.G. Mendoni, D. Dimitropoulos, I. Exarhoulea, H. Tzavali, F. Myrilou, and G.A. Zahos, Ιστορία του τοπίου και τοπικές ιστορίες από το φυσικό περιβάλλον στο ιστορικό τοπίο: Πιλοτική εφαρμογή στις Κυκλάδες. Επιλεκτική βιβλιογραφία (Athens 1997); and A.-L. Schallin, *Islands under Influence: The Cyclades in the Late Bronze Age and the Nature of Mycenaean Presence* (*SIMA* 111, Jonsered 1993).

Other recently published works have considered stone tools (e.g., T. Carter, "Blood and Tears: A Cycladic Case Study in Microwear Analysis: The Use of Obsidian Blades as Razors?" in M.A. Bustillo and A. Ramos-Milán eds., *Siliceous Rocks and Culture: Consejo Superior de Investigaciones Científicas* [Madrid 1997] 537–51; Carter, "Knowledge Is Power: Craft Specialization and Social Inequality in the Southern Aegean Early Bronze Age," *AJA* 102 [1998] 414–15 [abstract]); sculpture (e.g., J. Sakellarakis, C. Doumas, E. Sapouna-Sakellaraki, and S. Iakovides, *The Dawn of Greek Art* [Athens 1994] 14–15, 37–39; J.-L. Zimmermann, *Armonie di marmo: Sculture cicladiche del Museo Barbier-Mueller di Ginevra: Dal 14.12.1993 al 12.2.1994* [Lugano 1993]; C. Marangou, "Anthropomorphic and Zoomorphic Figurines of the Early Bronze Age in the North Aegean," in *Poliochni* 649–65); stone vessels (e.g., P. Getz-Gentle, *Stone Vessels of the Cyclades in the Early Bronze Age* [University Park, Pa. 1996]); relations among mainland Greece, the Aegean islands, and Crete (e.g., T. Carter, "Reverberations of the 'International Spirit': Thoughts upon 'Cycladica' in the Mesara," 59–77, and P.M. Day, D.E. Wilson, and E. Kiriatzi, "Pots, Labels, and People: Burying Ethnicity in the Cemetery at Aghia Photia, Siteias," 133–49, in K. Branigan ed., *Cemetery and Society in the Aegean Bronze Age* [Sheffield Studies in Aegean Archaeology 1, Sheffield 1998]; and R.L.N. Barber, "Hostile Mycenaeans in the Cyclades?" in

R. Laffineur ed., *Polemos: Le contexte guerrier en Égée à l'Âge du Bronze* [*Aegaeum* 19, Liège 1999] 133–39); and Cycladic exchange networks in terms of seafaring and local industry (e.g., C. Agouridis, "Sea Routes and Navigation in the Third Millennium Aegean," *OJA* 16 [1997] 1–24; A.G. Papagiannopoulou, "The Change in LC Pottery Production and Its Trade Implications," in C. Gillis, C. Risberg, and B. Sjöberg eds., *Trade and Production in Premonetary Greece: Aspects of Trade. Proceedings of the Third International Workshop, Athens 1993* [*SIMA-PB* 134, Jonsered 1995] 55–60; Papagiannopoulou, *The Influence of Middle Minoan Pottery on the Cyclades* [*SIMA-PB* 96, Göteborg 1991]). For maps of the islands of the Aegean with archaeological sites indicated, see B. Lambrinoudakis, L. Mendoni, C. Doumas, and E. Simantoni-Bournia, Αρχαιολογικός Ατλας του Αιγαίου: Από την προϊστορία έως την ύστερη αρχαιότητα (Athens 1998); and for Cycladic biogeography see A. Troumbis, "Η βιολογική ποικιλότητα στις Κυκλάδες: Φυσική και ανθρώπινη ιστορία," in L.G. Mendoni and N. Margaris eds., Κυκλάδες: Ιστορία του τοπίου και τοπικές ιστορίες: Από το φυσικό περιβάλλον στο ιστορικό τοπίο (Athens 1998) 141–44.

[272] *Kea-Kythnos.*

[273] The ninth volume in the *Keos* series describes pottery and other finds of the Neolithic and Early Bronze Age: D.E. Wilson, *Ayia Irini: Periods I–III. The Neolithic and Early Bronze Age Settlements 1: The Pottery and Small Finds* (*Keos* IX.1, Mainz 1999). For the EBA through LB I–II town, refer to E. Schofield, "Town Planning at Ayia Irini, Kea," in *Kea-Kythnos* 117–22; W.W. Cummer, Schofield, and Davis will examine the stratigraphy, architecture, and finds from the Western Sector of the site, including Houses C, EJ, F, and J, in a forthcoming volume. The Mycenaean settlement is discussed in C.R. Hershenson, "Late Helladic IIB at Ayia Irini, Keos," in *Kea-Kythnos* 161–68 (deposits between the major destruction of House A in period VIIb and the arrival of earliest LH IIIA imports); and C. Morris and R. Jones, "The Late Bronze Age III Town of Ayia Irini and Its Aegean Relations," in *Kea-Kythnos* 189–99 (transition from "Minoan" to "Mycenaean" settlement and a discussion of contacts between the Mycenaean world and Ayia Irini in LH III).

Recent information on the stratigraphy associated with the Temple is found in M.E. Caskey, "Ayia Irini: Temple

The Northern Sporades

Skiathos. An important EBA settlement has been investigated at Kefala, in the northern part of Skiathos; a few Mycenaean sherds have been reported.[274]

Alonnisos. Systematic research since 1994 on Alonnesos has located 14 open-air sites with Middle Palaeolithic or Mesolithic finds. The island does not appear to have been connected to the mainland for most of the last glaciation or in the early Holocene.[275] Test excavations on the islet Mikro Kokkinokastro in 1994–1995 produced evidence for seasonal occupation during the Early and Middle Bronze Age; Palaeolithic and Neolithic stone tools were found mixed in surface levels.[276]

Yioura and vicinity. Excavations at the Cave of Cyclope on Yioura have been completed (1992–1996); Mesolithic, Early Neolithic, Middle Neolithic, and Late Neolithic strata have been investigated. Twenty-six radiocarbon samples have calibrated ages ranging from 8400 to 3500 B.C. It has been argued that the Cave of Cyclope is "the oldest human settlement ever found on an island in the Aegean sea." Dozens of fishhooks from Mesolithic deposits are said to demonstrate an "astonishing boom in fishing." Pigs, caprines, fish, and birds are well represented in these same levels. Contact with other parts of the Aegean already in the Mesolithic is demonstrated by small amounts of obsidian, and honey-colored chert occurs in EN strata.[277]

Surveys of adjacent islands and islets have brought previously isolated and relatively unknown parts of the northern Sporades to the archaeological map of the Aegean. There are pre-Neolithic remains on Kyra Panayia, Pappous, and Psathoura. Specifically Middle Palaeolithic remains have been reported on Ayios Petros; Middle and Late Palaeolithic on the islet of Gramiza; and Middle Palaeolithic on the islet of Psathoura. Mesolithic finds have been recorded on the islet of Sphika off Kyra Panayia. Evidence for the Neolithic has also been found on Kyra Panayia itself (Pigadi); at Ayios Petros, not far from the previously known site; on the islets of Psathoura and Pappous; on the island of Peristera (Phanari); and on Piperi and Skantzoura. The Bronze Age is represented by artifacts from Psathoura.[278]

Studies," in *Kea-Kythnos* 123–38. For the Northeast Bastion wall paintings, see L. Morgan, "The Wall Paintings of the North-East Bastion at Ayia Irini, Kea," in *Kea-Kythnos* 201–10 (the drawings of plant panels and the miniature fresco published in RAP I [supra 30–31, figs. 4 and 5] are revised; the miniature fresco includes the earliest representations in Aegean wall painting of chariots and horses, as well as dogs and deer). Fortifications are reevaluated in M.E. Caskey and N. Tountas, "Ayia Irini: Some New Architectural Details," in *Kea-Kythnos* 695–97; and for related palaeogeography, see N. Mourtzas and E. Kolaïti, "Αλληλεπίδραση γεωλογικών και αρχαιολογικών παραγόντων: Εξέλιξη των προϊστορικών και ιστορικών οικισμών και κατασκευών σε σχέση με τις μεταβολές του επιπέδου της θάλασσας στις ακτές της νήσου Κέας," in *Kea-Kythnos* 679–93. For statistical analysis of conical cups, refer to C. Gillis, "Pottery and Statistics: A Pilot Study," in *Kea-Kythnos* 155–60; and for metallurgy, N.H. Gale, "The Role of Kea in Metal Production and Trade in the Late Bronze Age," in *Kea-Kythnos* 737–58 (Gale confirms sources of silver and copper ores on Kea but is skeptical about their use in the Bronze Age); A. Papastamatakis, "Μεταλλουργικές δραστηριότητες στην Κέα κατά την αρχαιότητα: Νεώτερα στοιχεία," in *Kea-Kythnos* 759–65; E. Davi, "Εμφάνιση γαληνίτου στο κρυσταλλοσχιστώδες της νήσου Κέας," in *Kea-Kythnos* 713–16; and L.G. Mendoni, *Αρχαιολογία και ιστορία της νήσου Κέας* (Vourkariani, Kea 1991) 107–108.

Aegean interactions are considered in *Kea-Kythnos* by M. Marthari, "The Griffin Jar from Ayia Irini, Keos, and Its Relationship to the Pottery and Frescoes from Thera," 139–54; A.-L. Schallin, "The Nature of Mycenaean Presence and Peer Polity Interaction in the Late Bronze Age Cyclades," 175–87; L. Hitchcock, "Blending the Local with the Foreign: Minoan Features at Ayia Irini, House A," 169–74; and H. Georgiou, "The Role of Maritime Contacts in the Urban Development of the Prehistoric Cyclades," 211–16.

For surface survey results and interpretation, see L.G. Mendoni, "Αρχαία Κέα: Ιστοριογραφία και αρχαιολογικές έρευνες," in *Kea-Kythnos* 17–48; J.F. Cherry and J.L. Davis, "Northern Keos in Context," in *Kea-Kythnos* 217–26; and H. Georgiou and N. Faraklas, "Αρχαία κατοίκηση στην Κέα: Το βόρειο τμήμα της ανατολικής πλευράς του νησιού," *Ariadne* 6 (1993) 7–57. T. Whitelaw, "An Ethnoarchaeological Study of Rural Land Use in North-West Keos: Insights and Implications for the Study of Past Aegean Landscapes," in Doukellis and Mendoni (infra n. 315) 163–86 introduces an ethnographic perspective.

[274] A. Sampson, *Η Σκίαθος από τους προϊστορικούς χρόνους μέχρι των αρχών του 20ου αιώνος* (Athens 1977) 9.

[275] E. Panagopoulou, E. Kotjabopoulou, and P. Karkanas, "Γεωαρχαιολογική έρευνα στην Αλόννησο: Νέα στοιχεία για την Παλαιολιθική και την Μεσολιθική στον Αιγαιακό χώρο," in A. Sampson ed., *Αρχαιολογική έρευνα στις βόρειες Σποράδες* (Thessaloniki, in press).

[276] P. Arahoviti, A. Intzesiloglou, Z. Malakasioti, B. Rontiri, and E. Skafida, "Ανασκαφική έρευνα στη νησίδα Μ. Κοκκινόκαστρο, Αλοννήσου," *ArchDelt* 50 B' (in press).

[277] A. Sampson, "The Neolithic and Mesolithic Occupation of the Cave of Cyclope, Youra, Alonnessos, Greece," *BSA* 93 (1998) 1–22; Sampson, "Excavation at the Cave of Cyclope on Youra, Alonnessos," in *Das Neolithikum* 507–20. See also Sampson, "La grotte du Cyclope: Un abri de pêcheurs préhistoriques?" *Archéologia* 328 (1996) 54–59; and Sampson, "Νέα στοιχεία για τη Μεσολιθική περίοδο στον ελληνικό χώρο," *Αρχαιολογία και τέχνες* 61 (1996) 46–51. A large and well-preserved fishbone assemblage is being studied by J. Powell.

[278] Sampson, *Das Neolithikum* (supra n. 277) 511–12. See also A. Sampson, "Παλαιολιθικές θέσεις στην Εύβοια και στις βόρειες Σποράδες," *Αρχαιολογία και τέχνες* 60 (1996) 51–56, where Palaeolithic sites on Alonnisos, Kyra Panayia, Gramiza, Yioura, and Psathoura are mentioned.

Euboia and Skyros

Euboia. The final publication of results of excavations at the Late Neolithic site of Tharrounia *Skoteini Cave*[279] describes the stratigraphy of the cave and the primary context of artifacts, and also includes reports on human osteology, faunal and botanical remains, and technical and chemical analyses of Neolithic industries.[280] Trenches immediately inside the main chamber of the cave uncovered deep LN levels. Successive floors preserving pottery and food remains in situ are indicative of regular occupation in LN II. In upper levels (Tharrounia 3–4), pottery of both LN IIA and LN IIB was recorded.[281] Under the LN II deposit was a "transitional" LN I/II stratum with a striking absence of clearly defined floors, in sharp contrast to the preceding LN IB occupation. This thick stratum of Tharrounia 2, like Tharrounia 3–4, contained "successive floors of ashes, burning, and terra rossa, with fine-grained soil and stones between them as a result of erosion."[282]

LN IIB was characterized by the type of "cheese-pot" common in the Dodecanese and by scoops, rolled-rim bowls, and lug handles of a sort well known at Kolonna (Aigina), the Agora (Athens), and Volos *Pevkakia.* Pattern-burnished pottery is common in Tharrounia 3 levels, but much less frequently found in Tharrounia 4; pithoid jars are decorated with plastic or incised motifs. A pithos fragment with schematic human figures with conspicuous genitalia is unique but finds broad parallels in Thessaly, Chios *Ayio Gala,* and Paradimi in Thrace, and even farther afield in the Bulgarian Neolithic.[283] A remarkable volume of pottery was recovered from Tharrounia 2, including gray- and black-burnished pottery, matt-painted wares, pithoi with plastic rope decoration, and white-on-dark pottery previously found only on Euboia at Karystos *Ayia Triada.* Matt-painted pottery was also common in Tharrounia 1, along with black-burnished pottery, gray ware, incised wares, and a little Urfirnis. In addition to pottery, some 180 bone tools were found; obsidian blades are represented, but they do not appear to have been produced in any significant quantity at the site: cores and crested blades are nearly absent. Clay, stone, and marble figurines are mostly of LN I date and include a wide range of types: phalloi; anthropomorphic and zoomorphic figures; and ax-shaped pieces related to Rachmani acroliths.

To the LN IIB phase belongs a small settlement excavated some 150 m northwest of the cave, on an adjacent plateau.[284] Architecture exposed there in several trial trenches was for the most part inconsequential; surface finds included millstones, grinders, obsidian blades, as well as "opal" blades and scrapers said to be indicative of pre-Neolithic occupation.[285] Cist graves excavated in a disturbed cem-

[279] *Skoteini*; see also "Late Neolithic Remains," where the stratigraphy and finds from the cave as well as from the nearby settlement and necropolis are summarized.

[280] E. Stravopodi, "An Anthropological Assessment of the Human Findings from the Cave and the Cemetery," in *Skoteini* 378–91; E. Kotjabopoulou and K. Trantalidou, "Faunal Analysis of the Skoteini Cave," in *Skoteini* 392–434 (the large majority of animal bones are assigned to Neolithic domesticates); L. Karali, "Θαλάσσια όστρεα και χερσαία μαλάκια από το σπήλαιο Σκοτεινή," in *Skoteini* 370–77 (only one fish skeleton was recovered; marine *and* land mollusks were also scarce); M. Mangafa, "Αρχαιοβοτανική μελέτη του σπηλαίου Σκοτεινής στα Θαρρούνια Εύβοιας," in *Skoteini* 360–69; V. Kilikoglou and Y. Maniatis, "Technological Study of Neolithic Ceramics from Tharrounia and Psachna, Euboea," in *Skoteini* 438–41; M. Beloyianni, "Αποτυπώματα πλέγματος στις βάσεις αγγείων από το σπήλαιο Σκοτεινή Θαρρουνίων," in *Skoteini* 346–59; C. Perlès, "Les industries lithiques taillées de Tharrounia," in *Skoteini* 448–95; C. Sugaya, "The Stone Axes of Tharrounia," in *Skoteini* 442–47; G. Stratouli, "Οστέϊνα εργαλεία από το περιεχόμενο της εργαλειοθήκης του παραγωγού της Νεώτερης Νεολιθικής," in *Skoteini* 496–526 (a unique cylindrical stamp seal is illustrated in pls. 221, 224–26); E. Andreopoulou-Mangou, "Χημική εξέταση χάλκινων αντικειμένων από το σπήλαιο Σκοτεινή Θαρρουνίων Εύβοιας," in *Skoteini* 435–37 (copper-arsenic artifacts from LN II and EH strata all exhibit approximately the same

chemical signature).

[281] For stratigraphy see "Late Neolithic Remains" 62–68 and *Skoteini* 21–33. The relative chronology of Skoteini Cave as understood by the excavator is described in table 1 in "Late Neolithic Remains" 93. Tharrounia 4 corresponds roughly with Gymno LN IIB in Euboia, Rachmani I in Thessaly, and Sitagroi IV; Tharrounia 3 with Botsika LN IIA, Eutresis II/III, Otzaki B/C, and Sitagroi III; Tharrounia 2 with Varka 2, Eutresis I, Otzaki A, and Sitagroi II; Tharrounia 1 with Varka 1, Korykeio, Arapi-Tsangli, and Sitagroi I. Organic samples submitted for radiocarbon dating are described in *Skoteini* 33–41; dates are presented in "Late Neolithic Remains," and compared to those from contemporary sites.

[282] "Late Neolithic Remains" 67.

[283] For the clearest illustration, see *Skoteini* 206, fig. 202; L. Orfanidi and A. Sampson, "Ειδώλια και ειδωλοπλαστική," in *Skoteini* 202–18 discuss the ritual content of this representation; see also a summary of their argument in "Late Neolithic Remains" 80.

[284] For local geography and geomorphology, see *Skoteini* 15–21.

[285] Pre-Neolithic remains found on Euboia are reviewed in E. Sarantea-Micha, "Παλαιολιθικά λατομεία: Εργαστήρια κατασκευής εργαλείων," *Αρχαιολογία και τέχνες* 60 (1996) 42–47; E. Sapouna-Sakellaraki, "Παλαιολιθικά στην Εύβοια: Μια νέα προσέγγιση," *Αρχαιολογία και τέχνες* 60 (1996) 48–50; and Sampson 1996 (supra n. 278).

etery ca. 400 m west of the cave also date to LN II, though in general even the undisturbed graves lacked offerings. Graves were circular, petaloid, or trapezoidal, and were constructed of vertical slabs. Some had been reused, and there was evidence of secondary mortuary ritual.

Pre-Neolithic and Bronze Age remains in the cave were scarce. No certain Mesolithic material was recovered, but the presence of large rocks made it impossible to reach bedrock; a heavily calcified bear metapodial found in LN IIA levels may point to use of the cave prior to the Neolithic. A few LH sherds (mostly LH IIIA:2/IIIB) and a Mycenaean *Psi* figurine are insufficient to confirm any presumed cultic use for the cave. More abundant EH remains (mostly EH II, equivalent to Manika phase 2), associated with ash, suggest occasional occupation and use of the cave for storage (seeds were scattered throughout EH strata).[286] The excavator suggests that even during the Late Neolithic the cave was only seasonally occupied (spring to autumn), serving as a pen for flocks and a sheltered location for semipermanent storage (fragments of some 700 pithoi were recovered). He suggests that animals were herded into smaller southward-facing shelters in winter (as they are still today) by herdsmen resident in various lowland sites

that have been recently discovered between Tharrounia and Aliveri.

At Fylla *Kaloyerovrysi* in mountainous central Euboia,[287] a few EH I sherds were discovered, but the first architectural remains were associated with intensified occupation in EH II (phase II), during which period a type of coarse pottery found widely in Euboia is predominant. The site is thought to have been seasonally occupied in this phase, and after a gap in habitation, pottery of advanced Minyan style is found in phase III. In a MH–LH transitional phase (IV), LH I Polychrome Matt-painted "Mainland" pottery and contemporary lustrous decorated wares completely supplant Minyan traditions, while MH matt-painted traditions continue. At the periphery of the excavated area are six cist graves: one is reminiscent of shaft graves at Eleusis and in the Argolid and had been reused. An EH II cist grave was found ca. 100 m away. Other sites located in the vicinity of Kaloyerovrysi include several of EN, LN, and EH I–II date.[288]

Excavations have continued at several other prehistoric sites in Euboia, among them Aidipsos *Koumbi*, Chalkis *Manika*, Amarynthos *Palaiochora*, Karystos *Ayios Yioryios Kampos*, Kerinthos, and Classical Eretria.[289] Excavations at Eretria *Magoula*, located 5 km

---

[286] For post-Neolithic prehistoric remains see A. Kapetanios, "Πρωτοελλαδική περίοδος στη Σκοτεινή," in *Skoteini* 304–13; and S. Katsarou, "Υστεροελλαδικά ευρήματα από το σπήλαιο Σκοτεινή," in *Skoteini* 314–22.

[287] *Kaloyerovrysi*. Along with rough site plans and photographs are brief physical scientific studies: E. Stravopodi, "Μελέτη του ανθρωπολογικού υλικού των τάφων της περιοχής Καλογερόβρυσης," in *Kaloyerovrysi* 161–62; K. Trantalidou, "Παρατηρήσεις σε μικρά ανασκαφικά σύνολα: Το οστεολογικό υλικό της Καλογερόβρυσης," in *Kaloyerovrysi* 163–68; L. Karali, "Το μαλακολογικό υλικό από την Καλογερόβρυση," in *Kaloyerovrysi* 169–73.

[288] A survey of the fortifications at Fylla *Vrakos* also turned up EH material; see *Annual Report of the Managing Committee, the British School at Athens*, 1993–1994, 21–22.

[289] Metallurgical remains associated with MH–LH transitional pottery at Aidipsos *Koumbi* are discussed in *ArchDelt* 42 B′ (1987) 200–201 and in A. Sampson, "Ένας μεσοελλαδικός οικισμός στην Αιδιψό," *AAA* 20 (1987) 172–83. In LH I, building phases did not correspond to subdivisions based on the conventional ceramic chronology. In the Papastamatiou plot at Exo Panayitsa near Chalkis *Manika*, 18 plundered EH chamber tombs of the standard Manika type were excavated: seashell jewelry, marble figurines, and a fragmentary marble pyxis were recovered. One other chamber tomb was intact, the entrance to its narrow dromos blocked by a vertical slab. The corpse inside the chamber was covered with shells and outfitted with a one-handled cup, a headless marble Cycladic figurine, and a greenstone statuette of a seated figure with parallels at Herakleion *Teke* and Archanes *Fourni* on Crete

(*ArchDelt* 42 B′ [1987] 207). Some 40 additional tombs were found unplundered nearby in the Beliyiannis plot, near the site of the projected Chalkis–Artaki bus station; some were in a poor state of preservation. Grave offerings included Cycladic frying pans, a riveted dagger, marble vessels of several kinds, and imported Cycladic marble figurines (*ArchDelt* 43 B′ [1988] 193; *ArchDelt* 44 B′ [1989] 157). Six other EH tombs were excavated on the Kyrana property (*ArchDelt* 43 B′ [1988] 193), while excavations east of the Zousi property uncovered substantial EH II–III architectural remains (*ArchDelt* 45 B′ [1990] 156–57), including a boundary wall thought to mark the edge of the settlement. Domestic architecture was reported also on the Ellenikos property: five rooms dating to EH II–III flanked a courtyard (*ArchDelt* 48 B′ [1993] 194). On the Papadiotis property, part of a large apsidal building with two EH phases of occupation was discovered (*ArchDelt* 43 B′ [1988] 193; *ArchDelt* 44 B′ [1989] 157–59). Along Chrysanthemon Street other EH II–III structures were divided into distinct complexes by pebble-paved roads (*ArchDelt* 42 B′ [1987] 204–207). For a cautious perspective on Anatolian connections at Manika within a Helladic context, see A. Sampson, "Manika and Mainland Greece in Early Helladic III: Ceramic Evidence for Relations with the Aegean and Anatolia," in *Wace and Blegen* 159–64.

At Amarynthos *Palaiochora*, five small soundings on this previously explored hill revealed a history of occupation extending from EH I through Roman and Byzantine times (*ArchDelt* 43 B′ [1988] 196–202); stratigraphy, architecture, and pottery have been discussed by E. Sapouna-Sakellaraki, "Έρευνα στην προϊστορική Αμάρυνθο και στη

east of Eretria on the road to Amarynthos, have uncovered a domestic complex of rectilinear buildings flanking a paved courtyard equipped with storage cists; to the north are fragmentary remains of what may have been an apsidal structure. The buildings are of EH II date and were leveled by later MH building activity.[290] New investigations have also been initiated at Kastri *Lichadas* on the northern coast of Euboia, where an imposing hill rises 60 m above sea level; extensive survey in the 1960s had reported prehistoric remains there.[291] Excavations in 1992 and 1994 uncovered only a few remains of architecture but did produce an impressive ceramic sequence including EH, LH IIIC, Submycenaean, Geometric, Classical–Hellenistic, and Roman pottery. Neolithic occupation is *not* attested. EH pottery is most similar to that from Poliochni phases "blue" and "green." MH sherds occur less frequently but types are similar to those found in Boiotia, and there is no Yellow Minyan. Transitional MH–LH and Mycenaean pottery is even more poorly represented. Among finds other than pottery were lithics, spindle whorls, buttons, and spools.[292]

Finally, construction work at Lefkandi *Xeropolis* un-covered an enigmatic MH cist grave complex at the northwest end of the site.[293] Chamber 1 consisted of a nearly trapezoidal compartment (L. 2.80–3.00 m; W. 1.40 m; Depth 0.70–1.00 m) cut partly into bedrock: large rocks supported upper courses of fieldstones on three sides; a huge vertical slab closed its short side; and three large cover slabs sealed it. Chamber 2 was smaller (L. 1.15–1.40 m; W. 0.60–0.70 m; Depth 1.10 m). A narrow opening linking the two chambers (W. 0.60 m) was blocked by fill, and it is consequently unclear if chamber 2 served as a dromos for chamber 1 or was itself a burial chamber.[294] Only fragmentary bones and a few MH sherds were found on the sandy floors of both chambers; the tomb may have been looted already in the LBA. Under the chambers was a layer of reddish clay that contained the remains of several MH graves. Lefkandi I pottery was found in the lowest stratum.

Skyros. A new phase of excavation began in 1990 at the site of Palamari, reinforcing the impression of continuous habitation through four successive phases, Palamari I–IV.[295] Work has concentrated on House Gamma, House Delta, and Street 1 (L. 13 m), which

---

Μαγούλα Ερέτριας," *AEMel* 28 (1988–1989) 91–104. It is clear that Amarynthos, like Chalkis *Manika* and Eretria *Magoula*, was inhabited in an EH phase that predates Lefkandi I and that a destruction layer separated its Lefkandi I phase from phases of later MH date that are characterized by Gray and Yellow Minyan pottery. There is a kind of incised polychrome pottery with parallels in Lefkandi III. Most Mycenaean pottery is of LH IIIC date. Near Amarynthos at Aliveri *Karavos* three built cist tombs contained MH II incised and Gray Minyan pottery; scattered EH and Mycenaean sherds were recorded, as well as a gold-covered copper handle and a couple of Mycenaean figurines. On ΔΕΗ property near Karystos *Ayios Yioryios Kampos*, an abundance of EH sherds, including sauceboats and various impressed and corded urfirnis wares, was excavated (*ArchDelt* 47 B′ [1992] 177–78). LBA material reportedly gathered from the "acropolis" of Kerinthos by local collectors has been published (E. Sapouna-Sakellaraki, "Mycenaean Kerinthos," in D. Evely, I.S. Lemos, and S. Sherratt eds., *Minotaur and Centaur: Studies in the Archaeology of Crete and Euboea Presented to Mervyn Popham* [*BAR-IS* 638, Oxford 1996] 106–10), including an amygdaloid seal dating to LM IB/LH II and kylix sherds and a fragmentary Mycenaean *Psi* figurine from the later Mycenaean period. Stratified prehistoric remains at Classical Eretria (*AR* 41 [1994–1995] 29–31; *AR* 43 [1996–1997] 53–54) now complement previously discovered deposits preserved in pockets in the bedrock (*AR* 40 [1993–1994] 36–37). Two distinct strata belong to the late MH and early LH periods; Minyan pottery and bichrome matt-painted kraters are reported. In a room next to a Cyclopean fortification or retaining wall, two MH infant burials and secondary deposits of LN and EH sherds were found beneath a MH floor.

[290] *ArchDelt* 42 B′ (1987) 210–13; for stratigraphy, architectural remains, and pottery, refer to Sapouna-Sakellaraki 1988–1989 (supra n. 289), esp. fig. 39.

[291] L. Sackett, V. Hankey, R.J. Howell, T.W. Jacobsen, and M.R. Popham, "Prehistoric Euboea: Contributions towards a Survey," *BSA* 61 (1966) 37.

[292] E. Sapouna-Sakellaraki, "Ανασκαφή στο Καστρί Λιχάδας Ευβοίας το 1994," *AEMel* 31 (1994–1995) 101–37, with numerous photographs and drawings.

[293] *ArchDelt* 48 B′ (1993) 195–96; E. Sapouna-Sakellaraki, "A Middle Helladic Tomb Complex at Xeropolis (Lefkandi)," *BSA* 90 (1995) 41–54.

[294] These chambers share formal similarity with contemporary L-shaped structures at Eleusis.

[295] Palamari I corresponds to EB II, Palamari II to Lefkandi I–Kastri, Palamari III to Phylakopi I, and Palamari IV to the earliest MBA. See L. Parlama, M. Theochari, and E. Hatzipouliou, "Η κεραμεική της ΠΧ3 περιόδου από το Παλαμάρι της Σκύρου," in *Wace and Blegen* 187–93 (topographical map of the site, a plan of excavations, and illustrations of some finds of the late EBA); Parlama, "Το τέλος της Πρώιμης Χαλκοκρατίας στο Παλαμάρι της Σκύρου: Σχέσεις και προβλήματα χρονολογήσεως," *ArchDelt* 42 A′ (1987) 1–7; and *ArchDelt* 45 B′ (1990) 162–64 (excavations in House Gamma and House Delta). See also S. Vaughan and D. Wilson, "Interregional Contacts in the Aegean in Early Bronze II: The Talc Ware Connection," in *Wace and Blegen* 187–93 for a preliminary investigation proposing Skyros as a potential site of manufacture for so-called Talc ware (previously suggested in Parlama, *Σκύρος στην Εποχή του Χαλκού* [Diss. Univ. of Ioannina 1984]). Dolomitic marble and schist characteristic of Talc ware inclusions occur near Palamari.

passes between the houses. Room 2 of House Gamma dates to EB IIIB. Room 4 shows two phases of occupation, the later one dating to EB IIIB and the earlier with abundant pieces of lithic debitage, bone, and slag.[296] Room 1 of House Delta has three phases of occupation: transitional EB II/III, late EB III, and early MBA (with an abundance of proto-Minyan pottery). Work in 1995–1996 uncovered fortifications protecting the northwestern edge of the settlement from inland access. Projecting bastions were fronted by a double bulwark and ditch that ran parallel to the wall; the design of the fortifications recalls that from Kastri on Syros in late EB II.[297] Metallurgy and ceramic production reflect crafting traditions shared with Poliochni and the northeastern Aegean in general.[298]

Elsewhere on the island, at Basales, an intact Mycenaean chamber tomb has been excavated, containing more than 70 LH IIIB/IIIC vases (on one of which fish are painted); beads of gold, glass paste, and sardonyx; and earrings of bronze, iron, and gold.[299] Results of an extensive survey of the island (1979–1982) have been summarized: 23 EBA sites and three MBA sites are reported; Mycenaean artifacts are concentrated in several places near modern Chora.[300]

Thasos

Continuing excavations at the important EBA site of Skala Sotiros *Profitis Elias* have confirmed the stratigraphy and chronology previously proposed. Additional fragmentary stone stelae now complement the single one previously known; these reliefs remain unparalleled in the Aegean outside of Troy I. They can be dated only with reference to the fortification wall into which they were incorporated in the second half of the third millennium B.C.[301] Excavation in the hematite mines at Limenaria *Tsines* continued through 1992. A recent report summarizes mining techniques and tools used in mines T1 and T2. A calibrated date of 20,300 B.P. (bone collagen samples analyzed at the Institut für Teilchenphysik, Polytechnische Schule, Zurich) confirms previous suggestions, based on the presence of antler from Saiga antelope, that the mines had been exploited in the Upper Palaeolithic.[302]

Significant prehistoric remains have also been discovered in the Sideropoulos plot in Limenaria, where part of a Neolithic settlement has been explored. Artifacts corresponding to types from Sitagroi I, Paradimi I, and Karanovo III suggest that the site was settled late in the MN period; there is a typical assemblage of bone tools and lithics, biconical spindle whorls, loomweights, shell jewelry, and stone beads. An animal-headed stone bead is exceptional. Figurines are poorly preserved and of clay. Architectural remains are substantial: long retaining walls support a more or less level building surface on which were built (unfired) mudbrick houses, equipped with hearths, benches, and flat-bottomed waterproofed storage pits. The contracted skeleton of a child was found in one of these pits. There were other more irregularly shaped pits outside domestic structures; for the most part these contained household refuse (fish bones, shells, ovicaprid bones, cereal grains, pulses, and fruits).[303]

The four-volume final publication of cemeteries surrounding Theologos *Kastri* and another cemetery at Theologos *Larnaki* presents mortuary remains of the transition from the Late Bronze Age to the Early Iron Age and sets them in a broader regional con-

[296] *BCH* 120 (1996) 1292; *ArchDelt* 45 B′ (1990) 162–64.

[297] M. Theochari and L. Parlama, "Παλαμάρι Σκύρου: Η οχυρωμένη πόλη της Πρώιμης Χαλκοκρατίας," in *Poliochni* 344–56.

[298] E. Hatzipouliou, "Εξειδικευμένες δραστηριότητες στο Παλαμάρι της Σκύρου στο τέλος της τρίτης χιλιετίας," in *Poliochni* 357–61.

[299] *BCH* 118 (1994) 784; *ArchDelt* 48 B′ (1993) 197–98.

[300] L. Parlama, "Οι προϊστορικές εγκαταστάσεις της Σκύρου," *Διεθνές Συνέδριο για την Αρχαία Θεσσαλία στη Μνήμη Δημήτρη Ρ. Θεοχάρη: Πρακτικά* (Athens 1992) 257–66 (with distribution maps and a summary of bibliography relevant to the prehistory of the island); "Προϊστορική Σκύρος," *Αρχαιολογία και τέχνες* 42 (1992) 20–23.

[301] C. Koukouli-Chrysanthaki, "Ανασκαφή Σκάλας Σωτήρος," *AEMT* 3 (1989) 507–20 for remarks on the dramatic changes in the ceramic assemblage from two primary habitation phases, and 511–13 for further comments on the re-

liefs, including a report of a chance find of an engraved anthropomorphic stele in the area of Potos, which is not far from the primarily LBA–EIA site at Kastri. See also "Ανασκαφή Σκάλας Σωτήρος 1990," *AEMT* 4 (1990) 531–45, in particular 536–37 for a discussion of the reliefs. Hunter-warrior figurines found in contemporary Cycladic contexts and at Dikili Tash are cited as comparanda. A series of ^{14}C dates are discussed and compared to dates from Sitagroi Va and Pentapolis II: for contexts and material, see table 1 in *AEMT* 4 (1990) 535.

[302] C. Koukouli-Chrysanthaki and G. Weisgerber, "Προϊστορικά ορυχεία ώχρας στη Θάσο," *AEMT* 7 (1993) 541–58.

[303] D. Malamidou and S. Papadopoulos, "Ανασκαφική έρευνα στον προϊστορικό οικισμό Λιμεναρίων Θάσου," *AEMT* 7 (1993) 559–72, summarized in *AR* 43 (1996–1997) 85–86. A few EBA artifacts were found on the surface of the site.

text.[304] Continuity in cultural connections with central and eastern Macedonia throughout the LH IIIB–IIIC periods is noted, along with the replacement of imported Mycenaean pottery by Macedonian imitations in phase IB.[305] Scientific analyses do not support the assumption that metallurgical resources attracted Mycenaean interest in the island, as few of the artifacts sampled bore chemical signatures consistent with local deposits.

Samothrace

Minoan documents from Mikro Vouni (two roundels, an inscribed dome nodule, an uninscribed dome nodule with three sealings, and one direct sealing) are now published and have been interpreted in the wider context of Minoan and northeastern Aegean relations.[306] The sealing system observed on SA Wc2 is notable for the impression of multiple seals on one nodule, a practice known only in a series of documents from Knossos and Mallia. Radiocarbon dates from recently excavated bone samples bring the absolute date for the stratum more in line with the late-18th century B.C. absolute date for MM II/III that the excavator prefers.[307] The excavator argues that the inscription on the nodule SA Wa1 is in Linear A and not in Cretan Hieroglyphic, despite the fact that the roundel impressions and SA Wc2 in particular are most closely paralleled in the Knossos Hieroglyphic deposit. A lead weight also found in these ex-

cavations is apparently consistent with the Minoan metrological system. The artifacts of Minoan character in this deposit are primarily implements of trade; it has been suggested that Minoan elites were interested in metal that passed through Mikro Vouni. In other ways Samothrace was removed from developments in the southern Aegean: it occupied a "marginal" zone largely outside the distribution area of Melian obsidian.[308]

Lesbos, Limnos, and Chios

Lesbos. Archaeologists working on Lesbos have begun to escape from the shadow of the type-site Thermi to ask questions about initial colonization of the island, its settlement pattern, and the affinities of its material culture both to that of the adjacent Anatolian mainland and other islands of the Aegean. (Lesbos is located only 18 km from Turkey and discussion of its relations with the Anatolian mainland has remained a politically sensitive issue.)[309] It has been suggested that the first colonists originated in Chios or even in the Cyclades because the earliest sites on Lesbos are found in the Gulf of Kalloni (Halakies, Kourtir, Ayios Phokas, Makara), and because investigations on the mainland opposite Thermi at Altinova have yielded no pre-Bronze Age remains.[310] In the EBA, the nucleus of settlement around the Gulf of Kalloni may have been primarily influenced by contacts with the south Aegean, while the settlement

---

[304] The cemeteries near Theologos *Kastri* (Tsiganadika, Vrysoudes, and Kentria) are mentioned above in RAP I, 42 and n. 94. In addition to the meticulous description of the tombs, several specialist studies in *Protohistoric Thasos* should be noted: B. Herrmann, "Gräberfelder der Siedlung Kastri, Thassos: Identifikation der Skeletreste," 739–51; L. Karali, "Μελέτη του μαλακολογικού υλικού από τα νεκροταφεία Καστρί και Λαρνάκι," 756–59; L.C. Courtois, "Observations techniques sur les céramiques de Kastri (Bronze récent à Âge du Fer ancien)," 760–72; Z.A. Stos-Gale and N. Gale, "Sources of Copper Used on Thasos in Late Bronze and Early Iron Age," 782–93; E. Photos, "Late Bronze Age–Early Iron Age Copper and Iron Slags from Kastri and Paliokastro on Thasos," 795–801; and J. Henderson, "The Scientific Analysis of Vitreous Materials from Kentria and Theologos-Tsiganadika Tombs," 804–806. Several shorter papers consider other aspects of metallurgy, human osteology, faunal remains, and prehistoric ceramic fabrics.

[305] Macedonian or Thracian parallels for the mortuary architecture are not obvious.

[306] D. Matsas, "Minoan Long-Distance Trade: A View from the Northern Aegean," in R. Laffineur and W.-D. Niemeier eds., *Politeia: Society and State in the Aegean Bronze Age* (*Aegaeum* 12, Liège 1995) 235–47; E. Hallager, *The Minoan Roundel and Other Sealed Documents in the Neopalatial Linear A Administration* II: *Catalogue, Lists, Concordances* (*Ae-*

gaeum 14, Liège 1996) 198–201.

[307] The average calibrated dates are 1866–1742 B.C. at one standard deviation and 1876–1692 B.C. at two standard deviations; Matsas (supra n. 306) 236.

[308] V. Kilikoglou, A. Kyritsi, D. Matsas, and H.E. Moundrea-Agrafioti, "Study and Characterization of Obsidian Artefacts from Mikro Vouni, Samothrace, Greece," in *Urla* 22–23.

[309] N. Spencer, "Early Lesbos between East and West: A 'Grey Area' of Aegean Archaeology," *BSA* 90 (1995) 269–306.

[310] K. Lambrianides, *The Early Bronze Age Communities of Lesbos and Altinova: Exploring the Origin and Nature of Settlement, Culture and Exchange on the Aegean Coast of Anatolia, c. 5000–2400 B.C.* (Diss. Univ. of London 1995); Lambrianides, "Present-Day Chora on Amorgos and Prehistoric Thermi on Lesbos," in N. Spencer ed., *Time, Tradition and Society in Greek Archaeology: Bridging the "Great Divide"* (London 1995) 64–88; Lambrianides and Spencer, "Unpublished Material from the Deutsches Archäologisches Institut and the British School at Athens and Its Contribution to a Better Understanding of the Early Bronze Age Settlement Pattern on Lesbos," *BSA* 92 (1997) 73–107; and Lambrianides and Spencer, "The Development of Early Bronze Age Settlement on the Island of Lesbos and the Madra Çay Delta between Ayvalik and Dikili," in *Urla* 27–28.

at Thermi looked east. In addition to coastal sites such as Thermi, Plati, Halakies, Kourtir, Makara, Ayios Phokas, and Methymna, inland, often hilltop, sites such as Profitis Elias and Sarakinas were also settled.[311] Early MH pottery was excavated at the building site of the new archaeological museum in Mytilene.[312] At Makara, at the west entrance to the Gulf of Kalloni, Mycenaean tombs are reported, one quite large.[313]

Limnos. Poliochni is now being eclipsed by excavations at other equally important sites, but most recent publications still are concerned mainly with excavations there and the relations between Poliochni, the remainder of Limnos, the northeast Aegean, and the Aegean as a whole.[314] Results of new excavations at Poliochni (1986–present) have been summarized, together with specialized studies of material recovered from the site, its geology, and the social organization of the settlement.[315] The "black," "blue," and "green" phases of the site have been reinvestigated,

as has the so-called Granary. Magnetometer survey may have located the cemetery of Poliochni at the site of Ambeli tou Athanasiou.[316]

Research elsewhere on the island has been extensive. Sixteen prehistoric sites are now known in total.[317] Two "early urban sites, almost on a par with Poliochni," have been systematically excavated, one at Myrina[318] on the west coast, the other on the islet of Koukonisi in Moudros Bay. Myrina was apparently founded before Poliochni.[319] Finds at Koukonisi document contacts with the Troad, mainland Greece, the Cyclades, and Crete. The hiatus between the "yellow" and "brown" phases observed at Poliochni does not exist at Koukonisi, and unlike Poliochni and Myrina, the site flourished in the MBA. Pottery and figurines found on the surface point to a Mycenaean installation on the southern edge of the islet.[320] Two other prehistoric sites have been discovered, Playisou Molos in the southwest part of the island and

[311] K. Lambrianides and N. Spencer, "Some Reflections upon the Origins and Development of Early Bronze Age Settlement in Lesbos and Some New Evidence from Western Anatolia," in *Poliochni* 618–33.

[312] *ArchDelt* 43 B′ (1988) 454. The lithic assemblage from the Hatsakis property suggests a location primarily used in the initial stages of the knapping process; obsidian was not present, according to P. Avyerinou, "A Flaked-Stone Industry in Mytilene: Preliminary Report," in *Urla* 3–4.

[313] *Ελευθεροτυπία* (19 May 1994); *BCH* 119 (1995) 986.

[314] See, for example, the papers in *Poliochni on Limnos*: A. Di Vita, "Lo scavo di Poliochni: Una pagina significativa nella storia della Scuola archeologica italiana di Atene," 41–42; A. Archontidou-Argyri, "Η Πολιόχνη και τα νησιά του βορειοανατολικού Αιγαίου κατά την Εποχή του Χαλκού: Μερικές παρατηρήσεις," 20–22; A. Dova, "Η Λήμνος κατά τους προϊστορικούς χρόνους," 23–26; L. Parlama, "Το βόρειο Αιγαίο και η Πολιόχνη στην Πρώιμη Εποχή του Χαλκού," 27–28; M. Marthari, "Ο κυκλαδικός κόσμος στην Πρώιμη Εποχή του Χαλκού," 29–34; and C. Doumas, "Τα νησιά του βορειοανατολικού Αιγαίου και η συμβολή τους στον πολιτισμό," 35–38.

[315] For results of the new excavations, see the following in *Poliochni*: S. Tiné, "Poliochni: Risultati e prospettive del nuovo progetto di ricerca (1986–1996)," 13–23, and 14, fig.1, for a map showing new excavation trenches (1988–1995); A.G. Benvenuti, "Il saggio 'U' nel Vano 28 (il c. d. Granaio)," 24–33; V. Tiné, "Nuovi dati su Poliochni Nero," 34–57; A. Traverso, "Nuovi dati su Poliochni Azzurro," 58–77; M. Cultraro, "Nuovi dati sul Periodo Verde di Poliochni," 98–121; and V. La Rosa, "Qualche considerazione sulla Poliochni del Periodo Rosso," 122–33. See also Cultraro, *Poliochni del Periodo Giallo e le fasi finali del Bronzo antico nell'Egeo settentrionale* (Diss. Univ. of Pisa 1997). Annual reports are published in *ArchDelt* 43 B′ (1988) 465, 470; *ArchDelt* 44 B′ (1989) 411–12; and *ArchDelt* 47 B′ (1992) 540. Specialized studies include C. Marangou, "Μικρογραφικά αγγεία της Πολιόχνης (Πρώιμη Χαλκοκρατία)," in *Limnos*

47–64; E. Ciliberto, S. Scuto, and G. Spoto, "Osservazioni preliminari sulla forma e sulla composizione chimica e strutturale di pentole tripodate nella Poliochni Rossa," in *Poliochni* 134–144; C. Sorrentino, "Poliochni: Il materiale faunistico," in *Poliochni* 157–67; L. Karali, "Η σημασία των οστρέων της προϊστορικής Πολιόχνης," in *Poliochni* 195–200; and A. Moundrea-Agrafioti, "Η λιθοτεχνία της Πολιόχνης και η θέση της ως προς τις εργαλειοτεχνίες του αποκρουσμένου λίθου της Πρώιμης Εποχής του Χαλκού," in *Poliochni* 168–94. For site geology, refer to E. Bozzo and F. Merlanti, "Evidenze archeogeofisiche nel territorio di Poliochni (Lemnos)," in *Poliochni* 145–56; and Benvenuti, "Πολιόχνη 1991: Ερευνες υπεδάφους," in P.N. Doukellis and L.G. Mendoni eds., *Structures rurales et sociétés antiques: Actes du Colloque de Corfu (14–16 mai 1992)* (Annales littéraires de l'Université de Besançon 508; Centre de Recherches d'histoire ancienne 126, Paris 1994) 35–42. Social organization is discussed in S. Tiné, "Poliochni: Problemi di urbanistica e demografia," 201–10; and C.G. Doumas, "Πολιόχνη: Κοινωνικο-οικονομικές δομές," in *Poliochni* 211–22.

[316] *ArchDelt* 46 B′ (1991) 373–74.

[317] A. Archontidou-Argyri, "Λήμνος, Πρώιμη Εποχή Χαλκού: Ερευνα και προβληματισμός," in *Poliochni* 223–29. See maps in *Poliochni* 225 and in *Poliochni on Limnos* 24; and A. Dova, "Prehistoric Topography of Lemnos," in *Urla* 12–13.

[318] P. Avyerinou, "Ο οικισμός της Μύρινας: Πρώτες εκτιμήσεις," in *Poliochni* 273–81; A. Ahilara, "Μύρινα: Οι μνημειακές εγκαταστάσεις του Οικοπέδου Ευτ. Καζώλη," in *Poliochni* 298–310; and "Prehistoric Myrina in Lemnos Island," in *Urla* 2. See also reports in *ArchDelt* 43 B′ (1988) 465; *ArchDelt* 44 B′ (1989) 409; and *ArchDelt* 46 B′ (1991) 369.

[319] A. Dova, "Μύρινα Λήμνου: Οι αρχαιότερες φάσεις του προϊστορικού οικισμού," in *Poliochni* 282–97.

[320] C. Boulotis, "Κουκονήσι Λήμνου: Τέσσερα χρόνια ανασκαφικής έρευνας: Θέσεις και υποθέσεις," in *Poliochni* 230–72.

Ayios Ermolaos in the north; surface collections include pottery belonging to early Poliochni phases.[321] Theories that envisioned the population of the island moving to the southern Aegean after phase "yellow" should thus be reconsidered.

The role of the northeast Aegean in the development of metallurgy has continued to interest scholars;[322] recent studies have, however, also focused on relations with the Cyclades[323] and the Dodecanese. The Kastri group in the Cyclades now may provide evidence for the intensification of exchange between the Aegean and Asia Minor.[324] It seems clear that the Aegean was in some regards unified in the EBA, but that in other respects, there existed a divide between the northeast and southeast Aegean: this is particularly apparent if one examines the distribution of pattern-painted pottery and megaroid buildings.[325] The social and economic organization of settlements in the northeast Aegean and the Cyclades in the EBA was, however, very similar.[326]

Chios. Intensive surface survey centered on the sanctuary of Apollo Phanaios at Kato Fana in southwestern Chios is designed to situate it in a regional landscape that includes the ancient harbor and its affiliated settlement, and to relate finds from the region to the chronological sequence known at Emborio. In the first year of fieldwork prehistoric remains (flint, obsidian, sherds, architectural traces) were recovered from the Nepagos hill southwest of the sanc-

tuary and from the slopes northeast of the sanctuary at an EBA site. Future seasons will cover the area of Managros, at the head of the valley, where possibly prehistoric fortifications on the Kastri hill have been identified.[327]

The Turkish Islands of the Aegean
Imbros. An extensive diachronic survey of Imbros in 1995 by R. Osterhout and W. Held has been followed by systematic excavations at the site of Yenibademli Höyük, in the northeast part of the island, 1.7 km southwest of the village of Kaleköy (Kastro) in the valley of the Büyükdere (Megalos Potamos). Excavation was precipitated by an expansion of a military airbase. Initial habitation of the site is dated to the third millennium B.C. Troy I ceramic types have been recognized, but pottery and small finds also parallel those at Poliochni on Limnos and in Turkish Thrace. Local wares and imported Mycenaean pottery were also found.[328]

Survey sponsored by the Yenibademli excavations has located three other prehistoric sites in the southeastern part of the island. Two additional prehistoric sites were previously described, one at Alyke *Pyrgos*, west of Alyke, and another east of Alyke, on a low rise next to the sea. At the latter, parts of a fortification wall and foundations of buildings are preserved; surface sherds range in date from the EBA to the LBA.[329]

Tenedos. Recent rescue excavations have further

[321] P. Agallopoulou, "Δύο νέες προϊστορικές θέσεις και ένα αρχαίο λιμάνι στη Λήμνο," *ArchEph* 1994, 301–11.

[322] E.g., C. Doumas, "Η Λήμνος και η πρώιμη μεταλλουργία του Αιγαίου," in *Limnos* 11–17; and G. Nakou, "The Role of Poliochni and the North Aegean in the Development of Aegean Metallurgy," in *Poliochni* 634–48.

[323] C. Boulotis, "Καπελλόσχημα σκεύη από το Κουκονήσι της Λήμνου και τα πρωτοκυκλαδικά τους παράλληλα," in *Β' Κυκλαδολογικό Συνέδριο, Θήρα*, 31 *Αυγούστου–3 Σεπτεμβρίου 1995* (in press).

[324] P.I. Sotirakopoulou, "Κυκλάδες και βόρειο Αιγαίο: Οι σχέσεις τους κατά το δεύτερο ήμισυ της 3ης χιλιετίας π.Χ.," in *Poliochni* 522–42.

[325] M. Benzi, "The Late Early Bronze Age Finds from Vathy Cave (Kalymnos) and Their Links with the N.E. Aegean," in *Poliochni* 383–94; and T. Marketou, "Ασώματος Ρόδου: Τα μεγαρόσχημα κτήρια και οι σχέσεις τους με το βορειοανατολικό Αιγαίο," in *Poliochni* 395–413.

[326] M. Marthari, "Από τον Σκάρκο στην Πολιόχνη: Παρατηρήσεις για την κοινωνικο-οικονομική ανάπτυξη των οικισμών της Πρώιμης Εποχής του Χαλκού στις Κυκλάδες και τα νησιά του βορειοανατολικού Αιγαίου," in *Poliochni* 362–82.

[327] *Annual Report of the Managing Committee, the British School at Athens*, 1996–1997, 26–27, and 1997–1998, 27; L.A. Beaumont, "The Kato Phana Project, Southwest Chios," *AJA* 102 (1998) 368 (abstract); and *AR* 44 (1997–1998) 100–101; L.A. Beaumont and A. Archontidou, "New Work at Kato

Phana Chios: The Kato Phana Archaeological Project. Preliminary Report for 1997 and 1998," *BSA* 94 (1999) 255–77.

[328] R. Osterhout and W. Held, "Antik ve Bizans Çagi Anıtları Hakkında 1995 Yılında Imbros/Gökçeada'da: Yapılan Yüzey Araştırması," in *XIV. Araştırma Sonuçları Toplantısı* 2 (Ankara 1996) 61–69. This is the site of Ayios Floros, previously reported by I. Andreou and Y. Andreou, "Η Ιμβρος στην αρχαιότητα," *Αρχαιολογία και τέχνες* 41 (1991) 92–100, where foundations of an enclosure, walls of buildings, fragments of pithoi, and other sherds are reported; ceramics range in date from the EBA through the Mycenaean period. For prehistoric Imbros see also N. Fıratlı, *İmroz ve Bozcaada* (Istanbul 1964) 6. For the current excavations at Yenibademli Höyük, see the following papers by H. Hüryılmaz: "1996 Rettungsgrabungen in Yenibademli Höyük," in *Urla* 18; "Gökçeada-Yenibademli Höyük 1996: Yılı Kurtarma Kazısı," in *XIX. Kazı Sonuçları Toplantısı* 1 (Ankara 1998) 357–77; "Eine Gruppe frühbronzezeitlicher Menschenfiguren aus Yenibademli Höyük (Haghios Floros Tepe) auf Gökçeada (Imbros)," *Studia Troica* 9 (in press); and "Bronze Age Idols from Imbros (Gökçeada)," paper delivered at the "Symposium for James H. Ottaway, Jr., 11.–13. April 1999, Tübingen."

[329] Andreou and Andreou (supra n. 328). See also C. Friedrich, "Imbros," *AM* 33 (1908) 81–112, esp. 101–102, where three stone axes with earlier prehistoric parallels are described and illustrated.

investigated a previously known cemetery, with graves that date primarily between the eighth and second centuries B.C. In 1992–1993 graves of prehistoric date (third millennium B.C.) were found for the first time; both stone cists and pit burials are represented.[330]

The Northern Cyclades

Andros. From 1987 to 1990 the northwest part of Andros (that part closest to Attica) was surveyed. Sites range in date from the Late and Final Neolithic to the Late Cycladic period. There are exiguous MC and LC remains at Mazareko tou Fellou, suggested to be the remains of a peak sanctuary. A settlement site at Pori yielded sherds of later MC, LC, and LM I types; a chance find of an intact LH IIIB stirrup jar probably points to the existence of a nearby cemetery. At Plaka on the western coast, prehistoric sherds are reported.[331]

Mykonos. A Neolithic settlement has been excavated at Ftelia near the northern bay of Mykonos. Finds contemporary with the later Saliagos phase and the Kephala culture cover a low hill and adjacent flats by the shore, about a kilometer southeast of Mavrospelia.[332] At least three building phases are represented, the earliest founded on bedrock. Thick walls suggest that some structures may have had a second story; one figurine (tall, long-necked, and female) is reminiscent of EC types; there are a few copper objects. Survey and test excavations on islets near Mykonos (Strapodi and Rheneia) have yielded other prehistoric finds: there are massive quantities of worked obsidian on Rheneia, remains of prehistoric buildings, and traces of MC activity.[333]

A newly investigated Mycenaean tholos tomb (L. dromos 14 m; D. chamber 5.80 m; pres. H. chamber 2.70 m) is situated in a visually prominent location on the hill of Angelika, to the south of Chora.[334] Inside are low benches for extended burials and ossuaries, but skeletal material was fragmentary. Finds of LH IIIA:2/IIIB:1 date included a piriform jar, repaired anciently with lead; three rock-crystal seals; elements from at least two gold necklaces and faience beads from a third; and steatite buttons. Mycenaean and other prehistoric sherds have also been found near Chora inside a cave called the School of Mavros.[335]

Syros. Results from a new project to study the early excavations at Chalandriani by Stephanos and Tsountas have been published at length; the spatial characteristics of the cemetery and architectural features of the few surviving tombs are described.[336] It has been suggested that the large cemetery at Chalandriani can be understood only as a reflection of

[330] N. Sevinç, "Bozcaada (Tenedos) Nekropolü 1992: Yılı Kurtarma Kazısı," in *IV. Müze Kurtarma Kazıları Semineri (26–29 April 1993, Marmaris)* (Ankara 1994) 311–20; and Sevinç, "Tenedos Kurtarma Kazısı," in *V. Müze Kurtarma Kazıları Semineri (25–28 April 1994, Didim)* (Ankara 1995) 113–27.

[331] A. Koutsoukou, *An Archaeological Survey in N.W. Andros, Cyclades* (Diss. Univ. of Edinburgh 1992). Published preliminary reports include Koutsoukou, "Αρχαιολογική επιφανειακή έρευνα στην βορειοδυτική Άνδρο," *Πρακτικά Α΄ Κυκλαδολογικού Συνεδρίου: Τα περί Άνδρου* (Andriaka Chronika 21, Andros 1993) 99–110. The final report of the project will be published by the Kairios Library of Andros. Other Neolithic finds from the island have been discussed in C.A. Televantou, "Από τους οικισμούς της Νεολιθικής στους οικισμούς της Πρώιμης Εποχής του Χαλκού στην Άνδρο," at the conference "The Early Bronze Age in the Cyclades in the Light of Recent Research at Settlement Sites" (supra n. 270).

[332] A. Sampson, *Μύκονος: Ο Νεολιθικός οικισμός της Φτελιάς και η προϊστορική κατοίκηση στο νησί* (Athens 1997). See also *AR* 42 (1995–1996) 37. The site was previously reported by Tsakos, who illustrated a number of surface finds: K. Tsakos, "Μία νέα προϊστορική θέση στη Μύκονο: Ο τύμβος της Φτελιάς: Τάφος του Αίαντος," *Αρχαιογνωσία* 6 (1989–1990) 121–32; a small collection of animal bones is described by K. Trantalidou. Tsakos (125, n. 21) refers to an increasing number of EBA sites that have become known in recent years (see now P. Hadzidakis, "Μύκονος: Θέσεις της 3ης χιλιετίας π.Χ. στη Μύκονο," at the conference "The Early Bronze Age in the Cyclades in the Light of Recent Research at Settlement Sites" [supra n. 270]). Sampson mentions many other prehistoric sites: Palaiokastro in Ano Mera

(Neolithic and Middle Cycladic); Divouni (Neolithic and Early Cycladic); Glyskidia (Neolithic and probably EC); Karapeti (Neolithic); Anavolousa (MC); the islet of Baou (MC); Panayia Eleemonetria (MC); Kalo Livadi (MC); and the islet of Strapodi (MC). Middle Cycladic pottery is of mainland character. Two "menhirs," at Palaiokastro and Panayia Eleemonetria, may be of prehistoric date.

[333] See *AR* 43 (1996–1997) 96 for reference to a "porphyry workshop" on Strapodi.

[334] P.J. Hadzidakis, "Une tombe mycénienne dans l'île de Mykonos," *Archéologia* 333 (1997) 40–47. Mycenaean tholoi in the Cyclades remain rare: see W. Cavanagh and C. Mee, *A Private Place: Death in Prehistoric Greece* (*SIMA* 125, Jonsered 1998) 63, 78, 83; Cavanagh and Mee refer to *AM* 1898, where a tholos tomb on Mykonos is said to have been empty of contents. See G. Despines, "Ανασκαφή Τήνου," *Prakt* 1979, 228–35 for a full publication of the smaller Ayia Thekla tholos tomb on Tenos.

[335] See also *BCH* 119 (1995) 997: two rock-cut tombs of Mycenaean date are reported as well as a few Mycenaean sherds inside the Cave of Mavros. *AR* 43 (1996–1997) 96 mentions a Mycenaean tomb at Vryses.

[336] J.J. Hekman, "Chalandriani on Syros: An Early Bronze Age Cemetery in the Cyclades," *ArchEph* 1994, 47–74. Additional artifacts from Chalandriani are illustrated in earlier preliminary reports: J.J. Hekman, "Chalandriani on Syros: An Early Bronze Age Cemetery in the Cyclades: Report on the Research Undertaken in 1990," *Netherlands Institute at Athens Newsletter* 3 (1991) 19–30; and "The Early Cycladic Cemetery at Chalandriani on Syros: Report of the 1991 Topographical Survey," *Netherlands Institute at Athens Newsletter* 4 (1992) 17–43.

the dense pattern of EBA settlement that characterizes the island as a whole, but this conclusion is based on the assumption that there was no settlement directly associated with it.[337] On the contrary, however, recent trials have demonstrated that a substantial EBA habitation, greater than 1 ha in extent, *did* occupy the site of the modern village of Chalandriani.[338]

The Western Cyclades

Kythnos. Mesolithic finds in the Cave of Cyclope on Yioura sparked interest in Mesolithic remains elsewhere in the Aegean, and in 1996 the controversial site of Maroula on Kythnos was at last systematically explored. Although ^{14}C dates are not yet available, the typology of lithics and faunal remains suggests Mesolithic occupation; five burials and a kind of paved structure "indicating habitation on a permanent or seasonal basis" have been excavated. The finds from Maroula have been compared to lithics from Franchthi Cave, Theopetra Cave, and the Cave of Cyclope.[339]

The nature of Kythnian metallurgy has been reexamined as well. Other EC assemblages now complement remains previously associated only with slag heaps at Skouries and Tsoulis.[340] EC II sherds, obsidian blades, and slag have been recorded at Zoyaki and Lefkes on the southeastern coast and at Kakovolo *Kastella* in the northwest (where there are also architectural remains). These small sites cannot as yet be related to any larger mining or smelting center,

and no evidence for prehistoric artifacts was documented in the recent survey of the ancient polis center of Kythnos.[341]

Seriphos. Seriphos remains almost a blank as far as its prehistory is concerned. Slag at Kefala has continued to attract attention: "the appearance of the site and the slag and its chemical composition suggest also an EBA date for the site."[342]

Siphnos. Excavations have been renewed at the so-called Mycenaean citadel of Ayios Andreas. Possible monumental architecture has been observed at the eastern end of the rocky plateau that forms the top of the acropolis.[343]

Melos. Two graves have been investigated at Ribari, one an undisturbed circular rock-cut tomb. Fifty-five vessels were recovered from it, including a triple kernos, an incised pyxis, and a black-glazed askos.[344]

The Southern Cyclades

Pholegandros. A small prehistoric settlement with scattered EC II pottery has been located on the south side of Kastellos, on the northeast coast of Pholegandros.[345]

Therasia. A juglet found on Therasia in 1866 has recently been published. The suggested date is LC I early.[346]

Thera. Results of past excavations at Akrotiri have been summarized, and future goals for the site made explicit.[347] Final reports are beginning to appear in the series *Ακρωτήρι Θήρας* and elsewhere, and con-

---

[337] Hekman suggests that in the EBA a number of small settlements dispersed in the north of the island may have used the cemetery at Chalandriani communally. He also provides a general overview of prehistoric settlement on the island "based on unconfirmed reports and references," in F. Aron, *Πτυχές της αρχαίας Σύρου: Απανοσύρια* (Athens 1979). Aron reports four LN Saliagos-period sites on or near the southern coast; eight sites of EC I dispersed throughout the island; substantially more EC II sites; EC IIIA sites limited to the north; and two EC IIIB sites, also in the north. The 27 undocumented MBA sites are widely distributed. In the LBA there are 21 sites, 15 of them Mycenaean.

[338] M. Marthari, *Σύρος: Χαλανδριανή, Καστρί. Από την έρευνα και την προστασία στην ανάδειξη του αρχαιολογικού χώρου* (Athens 1998) 18, 22 describes rescue excavations carried out by the 21st Ephorate of Antiquities and cites the opinions of Tsountas, Caskey, and Renfrew in support of this position. The same publication describes a program of conservation that has restored the sites of Kastri and Chalandriani and has made them accessible to visitors.

[339] A. Sampson, "From the Mesolithic to the Neolithic: New Data on Aegean Prehistory," in *Urla* 12; and Sampson 1998 (supra n. 277) 21.

[340] O. Hadjianastasiou, "Σημειώσεις από Κύθνο," in *Kea-Kythnos* 259–73. A recent review of finds from Skouries appears in the same volume. Organic samples associated with

EC II sherds from the slag heaps are dated to the early third millennium B.C.: Z.A. Stos-Gale, "The Role of Kythnos and Other Cycladic Islands in the Origins of Early Minoan Metallurgy," in *Kea-Kythnos* 717–35, in particular 719–20 for ^{14}C results and the statement that "this site can be described as the earliest proven industrial metallurgical site in the Aegean."

[341] Georgiou (supra n. 273) and discussion following A. Mazarakis Ainian, "The Kythnos Survey Project: A Preliminary Report," in *Kea-Kythnos* 363–79.

[342] Stos-Gale in *Kea-Kythnos* 720.

[343] Y. Stavrakis, "Mycenaean Citadel Investigated," *Archaeology* 52:1 (1999) 29.

[344] *AR* 43 (1996–1997) 56.

[345] O. Hadjianastasiou, "Κάστελλος: Μία προϊστορική θέση στη Φολέγανδρο," *Καθημερινή: Επτά Ημέρες* (28 July 1996) 4; and *ArchDelt* 43 B' (1988) 504.

[346] V. Economidou, "A Late Cycladic I Juglet from Therasia in the British Museum (BM 1926.4-10.9)," *BSA* 90 (1995) 155–56.

[347] C. Doumas ed., *Ακρωτήρι Θήρας: Είκοσι χρόνια έρευνας (1967–1987). Συμπεράσματα, προβλήματα, προοπτικές* (Βιβλιοθήκη της εν Αθήναις Αρχαιολογικής Εταιρείας 116, Athens 1992). A second volume, *Ακρωτήρι Θήρας: Τριάντα χρόνια έρευνας (1967–1997)*, is in preparation.

tinuing excavations have brought to light fragments of at least two clay tablets and a pithos with a Linear A inscription.[348] Also recently recovered are sealings with representations of chariots, bull-leaping scenes, and heraldic griffins. The distribution of EC figurines may reflect their cultic reuse in the LC I period.[349] Excitement surrounding the Thera frescoes continues, as does interest in the nature and date of the prehistoric eruption of Santorini itself.[350] The replacement of the existing roof by a new bioenvironmental envelope will protect the site, visitors, and the excavation personnel.[351]

Recently published specialized reports include studies of the environment of Akrotiri, metal technology, and pottery.[352] An abundance of LH/LM IA cups on Thera is indicative of a trade route between the Argolid and Crete that passed through Thera. A scarcity of ritual vases and the presence of many pouring vessels in Xesti 3 suggest that the building had a special function that involved the use of liquids.[353]

Close affinities between pottery of the Cyclades and that of the Dodecanese and Euboia demonstrate that there were contacts among these areas already at the beginning of the LN period.[354] Study

[348] A. Michailidou, Ἀκρωτήρι Θήρας: Η μελέτη των ορόφων στα σπίτια του οικισμού (Diss. Univ. of Thessaloniki 1991); P.I. Sotirakopoulou, Ἀκρωτήρι Θήρας: Η Νεολιθική και η Πρώιμη Εποχή του Χαλκού επί τη βάσει της κεραμεικής (Βιβλιοθήκη της εν Αθήναις Αρχαιολογικής Εταιρείας 191, Athens 1999); C.A. Televantou, Ἀκρωτήρι Θήρας: Οι τοιχογραφίες της Δυτικής Οικίας (Βιβλιοθήκη της εν Αθήναις Αρχαιολογικής Εταιρείας 143, Athens 1994); A. Sarpaki, Η παλαιοεθνοβοτανική της Δυτικής Οικίας Ακρωτηρίου Θήρας: Η μελέτη μίας περίπτωσης (Βιβλιοθήκη της εν Αθήναις Αρχαιολογικής Εταιρείας, Athens, in press); and Televantou, Δυτική Οικία: Επίχριστες ζωγραφιστές τράπεζες προσφορών (Βιβλιοθήκη της εν Αθήναις Αρχαιολογικής Εταιρείας, Athens, in press). Continuing excavations are summarized in Prakt 1992, 176–88; Ergon 1992, 75–81; Prakt 1993, 164–87; Ergon 1993, 83–91; Prakt 1994, 155–66; Ergon 1994, 56–62; Prakt 1995, 127–36; Ergon 1995, 52–57; and Ergon 1996, 75–77. For a plan of the excavation with the most recent names of buildings and areas, see Prakt 1994, 156, and 155–59 for explanations of nomenclature.

[349] P.I. Sotirakopoulou, "The Early Bronze Age Stone Figurines from Akrotiri on Thera and Their Significance for the Early Cycladic Settlement," BSA 93 (1998) 107–65.

[350] The "First International Symposium on the Wall Paintings of Akrotiri" was held on Thera, 30 August–4 September 1997. The proceedings are being edited in Oxford by S. Sherratt. Subjects discussed include the technique of the Theran wall paintings and a comparison with examples from Egypt and the Levant; modes of representation; and the architectural/functional, environmental, social, and religious/symbolic dimensions of the wall paintings. Televantou's final publication (supra n. 348) of the frescoes from the West House has challenged previous assumptions and contributed essential new information: earlier figureless fresco decoration (dating at the latest to a transitional MC–LC I phase) was succeeded by the later pictorial program, which dates to LC I. Reconstruction of this pictorial program has forced revisions to the architectural plan of the West House, especially the interior arrangement of rooms 4 and 5. The "Priestess" does not belong to room 4; at least five towns are represented in the Miniature Frieze. Televantou suggests that the frieze depicts the timeless relationship of Therans to the sea. See also C.D. Cain, The Question of Narrative in Aegean Bronze Age Art (Diss. Univ. of Toronto 1997); and I. Kaïnadas, "Η φύση και το περιβάλλον των Κυκλάδων στις τοιχογραφίες της Σαντορίνης," in Mendoni and Margaris (supra n. 271) 86–92; A. Vlachopoulos, "The Reedbed Wall-Painting

from Akrotiri: Towards an Interpretation of the Iconographic Programme of Room 3b of Xeste 3," BICS 42 (1997–1998) 235–46; and D. Evely ed., Fresco: A Passport into the Past. Minoan Crete through the Eyes of Mark Cameron (Athens 1999).

For the eruption, J. Driessen and C.F. Macdonald, The Troubled Island: Minoan Crete before and after the Santorini Eruption (Aegaeum 17, Liège 1997) 85–104 summarize current opinions regarding the Santorini eruption and its effects on Crete. Fouqué's geological study (1879) has recently been translated and annotated by A.R. McBirney: F.A. Fouqué, Santorini and Its Eruptions (Baltimore 1998). See also M. Wiener, The Date of the Theran Eruption and Its Implications for Aegean Prehistory and Egypto-Aegean Relations (in prep.).

[351] Synthesis and Research International, "'ASPIRE'—Innovative Protection of a Bronze Age City at Akrotiri, Santorini," in E. Fitzgerald and J.O. Lewis eds., European Solar Architecture: Proceedings of a Solar House Contractors' Meeting, Barcelona 1995 (Dublin 1995) 165–69; and N. Fintikakis, C. Doumas, N. Kaiser, and S. Sgouropoulos, "The Innovative Protection of the Bronze Age City at Akrotiri, Santorini," in Solar Energy in Architecture and Urban Planning, Fourth European Conference: Proceedings of an International Conference, Berlin, Germany, 26–29 March 1996 (Bedford 1996) 97–100. See also articles in Καθημερινή (20 December 1998) 49, 58–59, and Καθημερινή (22 December 1998) 3.

[352] A. Sarpaki, "A Palaeoethnobotanical Study of the West House, Akrotiri, Thera," BSA 87 (1992) 219–30; E. Panagiotakopulu, P.C. Buckland, P.M. Day, C. Doumas, A. Sarpaki, and P. Skidmore, "A Lepidopterous Cocoon from Thera and Evidence for Silk in the Aegean Bronze Age," Antiquity 71 (1997) 420–29; A. Michailidou, "Investigating Metal Technology in a Settlement: The Case of Akrotiri at Thera," Αρχαιογνωσία 8 (1993–1994) 165–80.

[353] M. Marthari, "The Ceramic Evidence for Contacts between Thera and the Greek Mainland," in Wace and Blegen 249–56; and A. Papagiannopoulou, "Xeste 3, Akrotiri, Thera: The Pottery," in C. Morris ed., Klados: Essays in Honour of J.N. Coldstream (BICS Suppl. 63, London 1995) 209–15.

[354] Sotirakopoulou (supra n. 348); see also P.I. Sotirakopoulou, "Οι πρωϊμότατες φάσεις του Ακρωτηρίου: Νεολιθική και Πρώιμη Εποχή του Χαλκού," in Doumas 1992 (supra n. 347) 185–99; and Sotoirakopoulou, "Late Neolithic Pottery from Akrotiri on Thera: Its Relations and the Consequent Implications," in Das Neolithikum 581–607.

of EC pottery at Akrotiri has contributed to the solution of a major chronological problem. Kastri-phase ceramic forms coexist with types dating to Phylakopi I-ii in sealed EC contexts. It has been argued that this discovery invalidates Rutter's theory that there was a gap in occupation in the Cyclades in EC III. Phylakopi I-ii is thought to be equivalent to early EC III, and Phylakopi I-iii to late EC III/early MBA.[355]

The Central Cyclades

Naxos. More of the extensive Neolithic settlement at Grotta has come to light, and part of a LN house has been excavated at Kokkinovrahos. Further discussion of work at the Cave of Zas has been published.[356] Motifs on sealings from Zas differ significantly from those found at Lerna and other mainland Greek sites, but have parallels in the east Aegean, Anatolia, and on Crete;[357] similarities with seals from Skarkos point to the existence of a local Cycladic tradition.[358] Robbed EC cemeteries have been located at Oskelos, Spedos and Skales, Marathos, Pateoura, and Hliaris. There is an EC IIIB settlement at Glei-

soures.[359] Contributing also to the reconstruction of the EC landscape on Naxos are further published results from the systematic survey begun in 1981.[360] Surface sherds suggest that there was a MC–LC settlement 800 m northeast of the hill of Mikri Vigla.[361] A Mycenaean chamber tomb (with pottery from the middle phase of LH IIIC) has been discovered 400 m distant from tombs A and B at Aplomata.[362] Complete Mycenaean vases were found in the area of the Metropolis Square in Chora in the course of its conversion into an open-air museum.[363] Excavations in the interior of the Archaic temple at Gyroulas, Sangri, confirm that this area was in use already in Mycenaean times.[364]

Studies of pottery from Naxos have demonstrated that the island lay on a trade route between mainland Greece and Crete; contacts with Crete begin in the MM period.[365] Mycenaean influences on the LH IIIA:1–2 pottery from Grotta are strong; in contrast, in the early LBA and in LH IIIB, styles on Naxos were more independent of regional trends.[366] Dynamic local pottery production on Naxos in LH IIIC should be seen as an indication

[355] Sotirakopoulou 1992 (supra n. 354); and P.I. Sotirakopoulou, "The Dating of the Late Phylakopi I as Evidenced at Akrotiri on Thera," *BSA* 91 (1996) 113–36.

[356] For previously known Neolithic remains in the Grotta area, see above, RAP I, 59. A report on Kokkinovrahos was published in *ArchDelt* 43 B′ (1988) 496. See K. Zachos, "Ἀρχαιολογικές ἔρευνες στο Σπήλαιο του Ζα Νάξου," in I.K. Probonas and S.E. Psarras eds., *Πρακτικά του Α′ Πανελληνίου Συνεδρίου: Η Νάξος δια μέσου των αιώνων, Φιλώτι, 3–6 Σεπτεμβρίου 1992* (Athens 1994) 99–113 for a report on the Cave of Zas; also K. Flint-Hamilton, *Palaeoethnobotany of the Zas Cave on Naxos* (Diss. Duke Univ. 1994). For an analysis of the Zas cave in terms of local characteristics that differentiate functions for well-known caves in the Neolithic Aegean, see K.L. Zachos, "Zas Cave on Naxos and the Role of Caves in the Aegean Late Neolithic," in Halstead (supra n. 270) 153–63.

[357] A. Dousougli-Zachos, "Sas-Höhle," *CMS* V, Suppl. 1B (Berlin 1993) 103–109.

[358] Marthari (supra n. 326).

[359] *ArchDelt* 43 B′ (1988) 498–500.

[360] See above, RAP I, 59, n. 177; see now R. Dalongeville and J. Renault-Mikovsky, "Paysages passés et actuels de l'île de Naxos," 9–57, on regional geomorphology and palynology, and I. Erard-Cerceau, V. Fotou, O. Psychoyos, and R. Treuil, "Prospection archéologique à Naxos (région nord-ouest)," 59–96, in R. Dalongeville and G. Rougemont eds., *Recherches dans les Cyclades: Résultats des travaux de la RCP 583* (Collection de la Maison de l'Orient Méditerranée 23, Lyons 1993) for survey results (sparse Neolithic, MBA, and LBA remains bracketing a rich EBA record).

[361] *ArchDelt* 43 B′ (1988) 497. For Mikri Vigla, see above, RAP I, 60.

[362] *ArchDelt* 43 B′ (1988) 494–96; and A. Vlachopoulos,

Η Υστεροελλαδική ΙΙΙΓ περίοδος στη Νάξο: Τα ταφικά σύνολα και οι συσχετισμοί τους με το Αιγαίο (Diss. Univ. of Athens 1995). Five chamber tombs in the cemetery of Kamini are published in this dissertation, as are previously unpublished finds from tombs Alpha, Beta, and Gamma at Aplomata. The still-unpublished tomb Delta is described. A. Mastrapas, "Σφραγιδόλιθος μυκηναϊκού τάφου των Απλωμάτων Νάξου," in Probonas and Psarras (supra n. 356) 135–46 redates the seal from tomb Beta at Aplomata to the end of the 15th century B.C.

[363] *Ergon* 1994, 63–64; for a plan of the excavations at Metropolis Square, see 63, fig. 50. V. Lambrinoudakis, "Προσπάθεια συστηματικής διαχείρισης αρχαιολογικών χώρων της Νάξου," *Επετηρίς Εταιρείας Κυκλαδικών Μελετών* 12 (1995) 458–80 discusses the transformation of this area into an open-air museum. The archaeological sites of coastal Grotta are mapped on 466, fig. 1, and the area proposed as part of an archaeological park is shown on 467, fig. 2.

[364] *Ergon* 1991, 91.

[365] O. Hadjianastsiou, "Naxian Pottery and External Relations in Late Cycladic I–II," in *Wace and Blegen* 257–62.

[366] M.B. Cosmopoulos, "Ceramic Regionalism and Artistic Interaction: The LH IIIA1–IIIA2 Evidence from Grotta," in R. Laffineur and P.P. Betancourt eds., *TEXNH: Craftsmen, Craftswomen and Craftsmanship in the Aegean Bronze Age* (*Aegaeum* 16, Liége 1997) 369–76; and Cosmopoulos, "Reconstructing Cycladic Prehistory: Naxos in the Early and Middle Late Bronze Age," *OJA* 17 (1998) 127–48. For a general plan of the area of Grotta, see 130, fig. 2a; there is a plan of LH IIIA:1–IIIB:1 Grotta on p. 131. See also now M.B. Cosmopoulos, *Μυκηναϊκή Νάξος: Η πρώτη πόλη της Γρόττας* (Βιβλιοθήκη της εν Αθήναις Αρχαιολογικής Εταιρείας, Athens, in press).

of the revival of economic activity rather than a disruption.[367]

Paros. In 1991, major excavations at Koukounaries were completed, and in 1993 preparation for publication began.[368] An EC "monumental" building (est. L. 10 m) lies beneath the LH IIIC building at the northeast edge of the Upper Plateau. Both its size and style of masonry are exceptional for EC II.[369] The citadel flourished in the "Developed" phase of LH IIIC and was destroyed early in the "Advanced" phase of LH IIIC. The site had a Mycenaean palatial character: megaronlike plans have been restored for the Mansion's upper floor. Skeletons of horses and a bronze horse-bit were recovered in the vicinity.[370] Relations between Koukounaries and the rest of the Cyclades in LH IIIC have been reconsidered.[371]

The Amorgian Islands. Prehistoric sherds were noted on the hill of Profitis Elias on Schoinousa.[372] A bedrock depression containing a deposit of early EC II sherds and complete vessels was excavated on Koufonisi. On Keros, preliminary results from fieldwork in 1987 at Daskaleio-Kavos indicate that pottery found in the so-called special deposit area probably derives from a disturbed cemetery. Vases deposited in graves appear to have been preferentially chosen from a broader repertory of ceramics in use in the community. It it clear that residents of the community themselves actively maintained regular connections with other islands.[373]

The Dodecanese[374]
Kalymnos. In a series of articles reconsidering remains from Vathy Cave,[375] pottery from the later EBA and Minoan and Mycenaean pottery of the LBA have been discussed. Included in the prehistoric pottery that the initial excavator identified as Neolithic was actually a substantial quantity of LN pottery, some scattered EB II sherds, much EB III pottery, and a few sherds datable to the MBA. A hiatus in occupation is evidently marked between EB II and EB III, and it is the latter phase that has received recent attention. Three primary classes of pottery have been identified: Red-Slipped and Burnished ware (bowls with incurved rims, two-handled tankards), Dark-Faced Incised ware (duck vases), and Dark-on-Light Patterned ware (various hand-built forms). A two-handled, narrow-necked jar with plastic decoration recalls pots from Lerna IV, Troy III, and Poliochni "yellow." The assemblage for the most part corresponds to an eastern Aegean later EBA *koine* encompassing Troy IV–V, Heraion IV–V, and contemporary deposits from Seraglio and Asomatos on Rhodes. The

[367] A.G. Vlachopoulos, "Νάξος: Η φυσιογνωμία και ο χαρακτήρας ενός ακμαίου Μυκηναϊκού νησιωτικού κέντρου του 12 αι. π.Χ.," in *A΄ Διεθνές Διεπιστημονικό Συμπόσιο: "Η περιφέρεια του Μυκηναϊκού κόσμου," Λαμία, 25–29 Σεπτεμβρίου 1994. Πρακτικά* (Lamia 1999) 303–14; Vlachopoulos, "Naxos and the Cyclades during the LH IIIC Period," *BICS* 42 (1997–1998) 237–38; and Vlachopoulos, "Ο κρατήρας της Γρόττας: Συμβολή στη μελέτη της ΥΕ ΙΙΙΓ εικονιστικής κεραμεικής της Νάξου," in N.C. Stampolidis ed., *Φως κυκλαδικόν: Τιμητικός τόμος για τον Νικόλαο Ζαφειρόπουλο* (Athens 1999) 74–95.

[368] For a plan of the bay of Naousa with its archaeological sites, see D.U. Schilardi, "Παρατηρήσεις για την ακρόπολη των Κουκουναριών και την Μυκηναϊκή Πάρο κατά τον 12 αι. π.Χ.," *Επετηρίς Εταιρείας Κυκλαδικών Μελετών* 12 (1995) 502, fig. 2. For the acropolis of Koukounaries, see 503, fig. 3. See also *Ergon* 1993, 111.

[369] This structure is described in *Ergon* 1991, 83; and *Prakt* 1991, 220–55, with a plan of the building on p. 228.

[370] Schilardi (infra n. 371) 631 discusses LH IIIC chronology, with the bronze bit noted on 633 and 638; the equid remains are published in Schilardi (supra n. 368) 481–506.

[371] D.U. Schilardi, "Paros and the Cyclades after the Fall of the Mycenaean Palaces," in J.-P. Olivier ed., *Mykenaïka* (*BCH* Suppl. 25, Paris 1992) 621–39.

[372] *ArchDelt* 46 B΄ (1991) 381–82.

[373] *ArchDelt* 43 B΄ (1988) 500–501; C. Broodbank, "Perspectives on an Early Bronze Age Island Centre: An Analysis of Pottery from Daskaleio-Kavos (Keros) in the Cycla-

des," *OJA* 19 (forthcoming).

[374] Toula Marketou kindly provided us with an unpublished annotated report that discusses all the areas of the Dodecanese mentioned in this review in significantly more detail. Several scholars have considered trade routes and interaction spheres of the north- and southeastern Aegean in recent years, among them M. Benzi, "Problems of the Mycenaean Expansion in the South-Eastern Aegean," in E. De Miro, L. Godart, and A. Sacconi eds., *Atti e memorie del secondo Congresso internazionale di micenologia, Roma–Napoli, 14–20 ottobre 1991*, 3: *Archeologia* (Incunabula Graeca 98, Rome 1996) 947–78; and P.P. Betancourt, "The Trade Route for Ghyali Obsidian," in Laffineur and Betancourt (supra n. 366) 171–75. The Neolithic–EBA transition and Anatolian–Aegean interaction have received particular attention; see the following abstracts in *Urla*: O. Kouka, "Zur Organisation der insularen Gesellschaften der Nord- und Ostägäis während der Frühbronzezeit," 24–25; M. Marthari, "Skarkos on Ios, the Cyclades, and the Eastern Aegean: The EBA 'International Spirit' in the Light of New Evidence," 33; M. Özdoğan, "From the Neolithic to the Early Bronze Age: Diffusion, Colonization and Marginality in the Northern Aegean," 38; and P.I. Sotirakopoulou, "The Cyclades, the East Aegean Islands and Western Asia Minor: Their Relations in the Aegean Late Neolithic and Early Bronze Age," 45–46; see also Marketou (infra n. 393).

[375] Excavated in 1922 and published in preliminary form in 1928 by A. Maiuri, "Jalisos: Scavi della Missione archaeologica italiana a Rodi," *ASAtene* 6–7 (1923–1924) 83–341.

presence of pattern-painted ware, however, distinguishes Kalymnos, Kos, and Rhodes from Samos and links the southeastern Aegean to the Phylakopi I ceramic assemblage. This fact raises the possibility that the EBA pottery at Vathy Cave is at least partly contemporary with the assemblage from Asomatos and is therefore later than Heraion phases IV–V.[376]

Minoan pottery previously subsumed under the generic label of "Kamares" is now reclassified as imported Minoan, Light-on-Dark and Dark-on-Light local wares, and plain local pottery. The term "local" is used to refer to pottery of the southeastern Aegean that has a distinctive non-Cretan fabric and construction. The presence of a possible "Cycladic White" beaked jug, decorated in the Curvilinear style, and of local imitations of MM vessels, suggests limited use of the site in the MBA. LM IA–IB imports are rare. Decorated local wares were probably imported from Kos, although a dark red micaceous fabric is characteristic of pottery still made on Kalymnos today.[377]

It continued to be the case in LM IB–IIIA:1 that most pottery from Vathy Cave was locally produced. In LH IIIA:2–IIIB a wide range of imports appears (although local Mycenaean imitations are also attested). Standard Mycenaean shapes and motifs prevail among the imported pots, while local pottery has "a southeast Aegean fabric of domestic character, found in settlement deposits rather than in tombs."[378] Fewer than 10 LH IIIC sherds have been reported, but pictorial-style sherds include one from an octopus stirrup jar that belongs to the Pitane-Kalymnos-Kos group "Late Eastern Style." The motif of *agrimi* flanking an abstract tree on a sherd from a collar-necked jar (FS 63) differs markedly from another sherd with a similar theme from this site that is on display in the British Museum and is closer in style to unconventional depictions from Seraglio and Lefkandi. The latest prehistoric material from the cave is of middle LH IIIC date, although later LH IIIC pottery has been found in nearby tombs at Perakastro.

It is suggested that Vathy Cave had a cultic function in the early LBA, despite the absence of contemporary settlements in the area. For the later LBA, it is argued that the cave served as a temporary refuge; a lack of domestic pottery at that time is explained as either an accident of preservation or the result of biased discard by the excavator.

Karpathos.[379] Trenches excavated at Afiarte *Kontokefalo* in the south of the island uncovered part of a structure equipped with a pithos, a lentoid Minoan seal in carnelian, and a group of conical cups. The deposit can be dated by the presence of a LM IA kyathos.[380]

Kos. At the southern edge of the Koutsouradi property in Seraglio, a LM IA Minoan polythyron has been found under unimpressive Mycenaean remains. The polythyron measures 5.25 m in length and dates to the period between the seismic destruction of the site and the fall of Theran tephra, approximately contemporary with similar Minoanizing building programs at Akrotiri and Trianda.[381]

Prehistoric remains (including MBA–LM IA finds, Mycenaean sherds, and gold jewelry) have also been reported from the eastern side of the same hill, at Seraglio *Halbazia*;[382] in addition, MBA, LM IA, and Mycenaean material was found on the Saroukou property.[383] Conical cups are ubiquitous at Seraglio in LM IA–B. Authentic Minoan imports are relatively rare. Light-on-Dark decorated ware is common and is similar to that found at Iasos and Miletos.

Rhodes. The pace of archaeological investigation on Rhodes has not slowed. Prehistoric settlements and cemeteries in the area of Ialysos have received particular attention.[384] It remains unclear whether the evidence supports Minoan colonization of the island or changes in settlement strategies and lifeways enacted by a local population in LM IA and following the eruption of Santorini. Nor is the process that led to the replacement of Minoan by Mycenaean material culture well understood.[385]

More MBA remains are now known than in 1992.

[376] Benzi (supra n. 325).
[377] M. Benzi, "The Late Bronze Age Pottery from Vathy Cave, Kalymnos," in *Wace and Blegen* 275–88.
[378] Benzi (supra n. 377) 282.
[379] See Καθημερινή (6 September 1992) for a map of archaeological remains on the island.
[380] *ArchDelt* 47 B′ (1992) 646; *ArchDelt* 48 B′ (1993) 553–55.
[381] *ArchDelt* 45 B′ (1990) 493–96.
[382] *ArchDelt* 46 B′ (1991) 486–92.
[383] *ArchDelt* 45 B′ (1990) 496.
[384] At the northern edge of the settlement (property of the Kostas brothers), 31 pit burials (three with pithos inhumations) were excavated; none had associated grave offerings, but one grave contained a horse: *ArchDelt* 43 B′

(1988) 616–17 and Marketou 1998 (infra n. 385) 60–61. Ca. 160 m southeast of this location an extension of the cemetery was excavated on the Ioannides property. Thirteen pit graves, four pithos burials, and two built cists have been reported, all dug into a LM IA stratum. Most also lacked associated offerings, but one of the burial pithoi contained several LM IA semiglobular cups. LH IIIA:2 remains were found nearby, but the graves themselves were scattered amid three LM IA walls.
[385] A striking change at the LM IA–IB transition appears characteristic of sites in many parts of the island. See *ArchDelt* 42 B′ (1987) 614–15 for evidence at Ayia Triada. Information on the Paraskeva property at Trianda will be published in a future *ArchDelt* B′ volume. An up-to-date review of evidence for the Minoan transformation of mate-

In addition to those from Mt. Filerimos, stratified MBA levels have been found in several locations in Trianda and elsewhere on the island.[386] The picture of MBA settlement that is emerging for Trianda is one of small pockets of occupation, dispersed within the limits of the later LBA town and throughout the Ialysia. Local wheelmade unpainted, red monochrome, and matt-painted pottery is dominant. There are a few Minoan and Koan imports.[387] The settlement pottery changes dramatically early in LM IA: ceramics from this phase are "mostly local, made from a soft clay of a rather poor quality compared to that in use in the Middle Bronze Age," and are decorated with simple matt-painted designs.[388] Following a seismic destruction in LM IA, there was substantial rebuilding in a clearly Minoanizing style similar to that seen at Akrotiri and Seraglio. This settlement covered more than 17 ha at the time of the Theran eruption.[389] Pottery was largely Minoan in inspiration but was locally produced. Imports include pieces from eastern Crete, Light-on-Dark styles from Kos, and a single Egyptian sherd.

Reoccupation of the site in LM IB–II after the fall of Santorini tephra was restricted to the northern part of the earlier town.[390] Large parallel walls were built across a polythyron complex and were extended further south in LH IIIA. It is suggested that profound geomorphological changes caused by earthquakes as-

sociated with the Theran eruption made construction of such walls as flood-control devices necessary; the ultimate failure of this strategy led to the abandonment of the town in LH IIIA:2.[391]

The megaroid buildings at Asomatos have been described in more detail and compared to contemporary architecture in the northeastern Aegean. Structures were built next to each other at the western edge of the previously excavated EBA necropolis, and were oriented east–southeast by west–northwest. The main chamber of the northwesternmost building is 6.30 m in length and is equipped with a central hearth; maximum dimensions of the entire structure are 11.70 × 7.65 m.[392] Ceramics resemble those of the later EBA from Seraglio. A distributional analysis of pottery preserved in situ in one structure revealed that storage jars, "table-ware open shapes," and fine pottery were segregated by room.[393]

A joint Danish-Greek survey at Kattavia in the vicinity of Lindos has found Epipalaeolithic remains and abundant Neolithic stone tools. Several newly discovered Mycenaean settlements have been located in the area where Mycenaean chamber tombs were excavated in the early 20th century.[394]

Nine new Mycenaean chamber tombs (LH IIIA:2–IIIC) were excavated (1993–1996) on the hill of Asprospilia, north of Pylona. The tombs are unexceptional in construction and form, but calcified textile

---

rial culture can be found in T. Marketou, "Excavations at Trianda (Ialysos) on Rhodes: New Evidence for the Late Bronze Age I Period," *RendLinc* 9 (1998) 39–82. Marketou defines four primary objectives: 1) investigation of the plan and extent of successive settlements; 2) systematic documentation of stratigraphy; 3) analysis of the diachronic development of the town; and 4) examination of native–Minoan interaction and external connections between the settlement and the rest of the Mediterranean. See also T. Marketou, "Excavations at Trianda (Ialysos) on Rhodes: New Evidence for the Late Bronze Age I Period," *BICS* 41 (1996) 133–34.

[386] For the site on Profitis Elias (Koronellos property), see now *ArchDelt* 42 B′ (1987) 615–16. Some 250 m south of the edge of the LM IA settlement at Trianda (as defined in 1988), on the Tsakiris-Marouklas property, excavations have explored a MBA stratum with architectural remains; the structure appears to be a house with a narrow corridor and pebble-paved court, similar to the Asomatos megaron (*ArchDelt* 43 B′ [1988] 611–14; *ArchDelt* 44 B′ [1989] 502), but on a smaller scale. Architectural remains are now known also from the Metaxotos property (east of the Tsakiris-Marouklas plot), where conical cups, plaster, a bronze nail, and animal bones were found with MBA sherds (*ArchDelt* 45 B′ [1990] 487–88). See also *ArchDelt* 47 B′ (1992) 640–41 for MBA remains on the Kavallieros property and a MBA pithos burial immediately to the east (*ArchDelt* 45 B′ [1990] 487). Among notable sites elsewhere is the Kostaridis property near Hellenistic Rhodes, which has yielded significant MBA remains. See Marketou 1998 (su-

pra n. 385) 42.

[387] Marketou 1998 (supra n. 385) 63–64 argues that "settlement in Ialysos had a long local history before the organisation of the Late Bronze Age IA town. In that sense Trianda cannot be considered as a Minoan settlement colony. The strong Minoan features of the settlement [rather] indicate the prosperity of the town. . . . Minoanising styles could be seen as part of a new prestige concept of an emergent Rhodian élite."

[388] Marketou 1998 (supra n. 385) 46.

[389] A second polythyron is currently being excavated in the southwestern sector of the settlement. Fresco fragments from various monumental buildings are reported, and two have been fully published (Marketou 1998 [supra n. 385] 59–60 and 81, pl. IX). The spatial estimate includes the LBA remains from the Siatras property, which represents the southernmost limit of the prehistoric settlement yet documented (*ArchDelt* 47 B′ [1992] 641–43).

[390] For LM IB–LH IIIA remains, see *ArchDelt* 43 B′ (1988) 614–15 (Tsavaris property) and *ArchDelt* 44 B′ (1989) 500–501 (Liamis property).

[391] The thick alluvial deposits on the floodplain and the thin soil of Mt. Filerimos are cited in support of this hypothesis.

[392] *ArchDelt* 44 B′ (1989) 503; *ArchDelt* 45 B′ (1990) 480; and Marketou (supra n. 325).

[393] T. Marketou, "Early Bronze Age Pottery from Rhodes," in *Urla* 32–33.

[394] *AR* 41 (1994–1995) 60.

remains have been preserved in tomb 1 on piriform jars and on a beaked jug (LH IIIA:2 late). Several layers of what appears to be linen are preserved on the rim and neck of each jar, and on the rim, neck, and handle of the jug. In at least one instance, clay seems to have been used to fasten the fabric to the pot and to hold it in place, suggesting that the cloth had been wrapped tightly over the vessels in order to preserve their contents.[395] These tombs also contained two coarse clay torch-holders or wall brackets (comparable to finds from the Menelaion, Tiryns, and Enkomi), a unique chariot-group figurine, and a conical rhyton decorated with a painted "Master of Animals" and a bucranium modeled in relief.[396]

Fourni. A map of archaeological sites on Fourni has been published.[397]

Amorgos

Neolithic and EBA levels at Minoa on Amorgos are much better known now than in 1992.[398] Late or Final Neolithic pottery, obsidian tools, and a clay figurine are stratified in the lowest deposits reached in soundings beneath the remains of the historical sanctuary on the acropolis. Surface finds nearby suggest that the Neolithic settlement was limited to the eastern edge of the hill. EC pottery has been noted on lower terraces at the south side of the acropolis, in the opposite direction from the tombs excavated by Tsountas.[399] The Cycladic figurine previously found in a Roman cistern has been the subject of much discussion.[400]

Elsewhere on the island, obsidian blades and EC II sherds with incised and painted decoration were found at Ayiali *Asomatos* on the Theologiti property, and a chance discovery was made of a Cycladic marble figurine in the modern capital of Chora.[401] Soil micromorphological studies at Markiani have identified erosional events that may have resulted from nucleation in population in the early EBA.[402] The MBA of Amorgos is represented only by sherds found in the rescue excavation of two plundered Mycenaean chamber tombs at Xylokeratidi on the north side of the bay of Katapola. New LBA finds from Xylokeratidi have also been reported, and a Mycenaean alabastron appears to have been found at Karlas near Xenotafia.

DEPARTMENT OF CLASSICS
UNIVERSITY OF CINCINNATI
CINCINNATI, OHIO 45221-0226
JACK.DAVIS@UC.EDU
TZONHERB@UCLINK4.BERKELEY.EDU
WOLPERAD@EMAIL.UC.EDU

[395] *ArchDelt* 48 B′ (1993) 542–44; E. Karantzali, "New Mycenaean Finds from Rhodes," in P.P. Betancourt et al. eds., *Meletemata: Studies in Aegean Archaeology Presented to Malcolm H. Wiener as He Enters His 65th Year* (Aegaeum 20, Liège 1999) 403–408.

[396] The wall brackets come from tombs 1 and 5A (LH IIIA:2 late), the chariot-group figurine from tomb 3 (LH IIIA:2 late/IIIB:1), and the rhyton (FS 199) from tomb 2 (LH IIIA:2 late). See also E. Karantzali, "A New Mycenaean Pictorial Rhyton from Rhodes," in V. Karageorghis and N. Stampolidis eds., *Eastern Mediterranean: Cyprus–Dodecanese–Crete, 16th–6th Cent. B.C. Proceedings of the International Symposium Held at Rethymnon, Crete, in May 1997* (Athens 1998) 87–104.

[397] *ArchDelt* 43 B′ (1988) 507, fig. 17.

[398] For annual reports and site plans see *Prakt* 1988, 160–77; *Prakt* 1989, 267–86; *Prakt* 1990, 236–70; *Prakt* 1991, 281–305; *Prakt* 1992, 189–99; *Prakt* 1993, 188–208; *Prakt* 1994, 237–38; *Prakt* 1995, 69; *Prakt* 1996, 84–88; and *Prakt* 1997, 63–67.

[399] L. Marangou, "Νέες μαρτυρίες για την ιστορία της αρχαίας Αμοργού," *Επετηρίς Εταιρείας Κυκλαδικών Μελετών* 15 (1994) 307–32.

[400] L. Marangou, "Κυκλαδικό ειδώλιο από τη Μινώα Αμοργού," *ArchEph* 1990, 159–76.

[401] *ArchDelt* 47 B′ (1992) 648–49. For other recently recorded EBA sites, refer to the map in Marangou (supra n. 399) 309, fig. 1.

[402] C.A.I. French and T.M. Whitelaw, "Soil Erosion, Agricultural Terracing and Site Formation Processes at Markiani, Amorgos, Greece: The Micromorphological Perspective," *Geoarchaeology* 14 (1999) 151–89. Underneath *modern* terracing was found evidence for a discontinuous sequence of erosional events, the first of which was correlated with initial habitation and site clearance. Following the abandonment of the site in the later third millennium B.C., the slopes stabilized and withstood further erosion until the next primary phase of occupation in the Hellenistic period. There is no evidence for EBA or Hellenistic terracing. See also L. Marangou, C. Renfrew, and C. Doumas, *Markiani: An Early Fortified Site on Amorgos* (Athens, in prep.).

Review of Aegean Prehistory II: The Prepalatial Bronze Age of the Southern and Central Greek Mainland

JEREMY B. RUTTER

Dedicated to the memory of Klaus Kilian

INTRODUCTION

This review of a modest slice of mainland Greek prehistory is designed for twin audiences and has twin goals. On the one hand, it is targeted at archaeologists, ancient historians, Classicists, and others who, though they take an interest in Aegean prehistory and may even have some familiarity with it, hardly consider themselves specialists in this subdiscipline of Old World archaeology. For this audience, the purpose of what follows is to provide an outline, with helpful but by no means exhaustive references, to the principal discoveries made, questions addressed, and novel research strategies employed in the archaeology of roughly the first three-quarters of the Bronze Age on the southern and central Greek mainland. At the same time, this review is addressed to specialist Aegean prehistorians, not with the aim of making them aware of discoveries or intellectual currents about which they may be ignorant, but rather with the intent of encouraging them, through a consideration of the current state of our field, to take whatever future action they may feel is appropriate to improve upon the present state of our knowledge.[1]

[1] The publication of this review has been made possible in part by a generous subvention from the Institute for Aegean Prehistory. I am very grateful to Tracey Cullen and Fred Kleiner for the invitation extended to me to write it, and to Julia Pfaff for executing the drawings that accompany it.

This summary, reflecting the priorities and choices of just one individual, is a highly personal one, with all the potential for sins of both commission and omission that single authorship of such a review entails. I apologize to all colleagues in advance for any and all unintentional offenses or slights that such errors on my part may occasion.

Without the helpful response from numerous friends and colleagues to my appeals for information, offprints, and preliminary reports on their most recent research, the content of this review would have been much poorer. I would like to thank Susan Alcock, Sebastiaan Bommeljé, Shelby Brown, Hector Catling, William Cavanagh, Georgia Chatze-Speliopoulou, John Cherry, Elmar Christmann, John Coleman, Michael Cosmopoulos, Joost Crouwel, Katie Demakopoulou, Oliver Dickinson, Søren Dietz, Angelika Dousougli-Zachos, Jeannette and Björn Forsén, John Fossey, Mihalis Fotiadis, Elizabeth French, Noel Gale, Giampaolo Graziadio, Robin Hägg, Paul Halstead, Stefan Hiller, the late Klaus Kilian, to whose memory this review is dedicated, Imma Kilian-Dirlmeier, Georgios Korres, Cynthia Kosso, Sturt Manning, Josef Maran, Hartmut Matthäus, Christopher Mee, Penelope Mountjoy, Sylvie Müller, William Murray, Gullög Nordquist, Thanasis Papadopoulos, Daniel Pullen, Jörg Rambach, James Roy, Curtis Runnels, Efi Sakellaraki, Zophia Stos-Gale, Gilles Touchais, Lucia Vagnetti, Karen Vitelli, Joanita Vroom, Gisela Walberg, Peter Warren, Hans-Joachim Weisshaar, Berit Wells, Martha Wiencke, David Wil-

son, James Wright, Eberhard Zangger, and Carol Zerner. John Bennet, John Cherry, and Daniel Pullen were kind enough to read portions of the manuscript in draft form and suggested many improvements. I owe a special debt of gratitude to Jack Davis for helpful references on a wide range of topics, for encouragement and sympathy, for a helpfully critical reading, and above all for leading the way.

The following abbreviations are used in this paper:

ATMA	S. Dietz, *The Argolid at the Transition to the Mycenaean Age: Studies in the Chronology and Cultural Development in the Shaft Grave Period* (Copenhagen 1991).
BA Trade	N.H. Gale ed., *Bronze Age Trade in the Mediterranean* (*SIMA* 90, Jonsered 1991).
Celebrations	R. Hägg and N. Marinatos eds., *Celebrations of Death and Divinity in the Bronze Age Argolid* (Stockholm 1990).
"Chronique"	"Chronique des fouilles," *BCH*.
Chronology	P.M. Warren and V. Hankey, *Aegean Bronze Age Chronology* (Bristol 1989).
Contributions	N.C. Wilkie and W.D.E. Coulson eds., *Contributions to Aegean Archaeology: Studies in Honor of William A. McDonald* (Minneapolis 1985).
EHAU	R. Hägg and D. Konsola eds., *Early Helladic Architecture and Urbanization* (*SIMA* 76, Göteborg 1986).
Gazetteer	R. Hope Simpson and O.T.P.K. Dickinson, *A Gazetteer of Aegean Civilisation in the Bronze Age 1: The Mainland and Islands* (*SIMA* 52, Göteborg 1979).

Originally published in *AJA* 97 (1993) 745–97.

The spatial coverage undertaken for this review includes those portions of the Greek mainland south of a roughly east–west line connecting the mouth of the Spercheios River with the southeast corner of the Gulf of Arta (see below, fig. 3). Epirus, Thessaly, Macedonia, and Thrace are thus omitted from consideration, but Akarnania, Aetolia, the southern half of Eurytania, and the Ionian islands from Lefkas south are included. Also included, aside from the entire Peloponnese and the central Greek nomes of Attica, Boiotia, Phocis, Locris, and the southern half of Phthiotis, are the islands of the Saronic Gulf (most notably Aegina and Salamis), islands located just off the southeastern coast of the Argolid (such as Hydra and Spetses), and islands off the southwest coast of the Cape Malea peninsula (Elaphonisos and Kythera),

but the large island of Euboea, since it was covered thoroughly in last year's review,[2] is not considered here.

The period of time surveyed encompasses the entire Early and Middle Bronze Ages (EBA and MBA, respectively), known throughout the area in question as the Early Helladic (EH) and Middle Helladic (MH) periods, as well as the earlier part of the Late Bronze Age (LBA), variously termed the Late Helladic (LH) or Mycenaean period. The terminal date for my chronological coverage is provided by the construction, at some point during the LH IIB or LH IIIA1 periods in the 15th century B.C., of the first Mycenaean architectural complexes generally recognized by the term "palaces" as the administrative seats of centralized kingdoms.[3]

Iconography	R. Laffineur and J.L. Crowley eds., *EIKΩN: Aegean Bronze Age Iconography: Shaping a Methodology* (*Aegaeum* 8, Liège 1992).
L'habitat	P. Darcque and R. Treuil eds., *L'habitat égéen préhistorique* (*BCH* Suppl. 19, Paris 1990).
Nichoria	W.A. McDonald and N.C. Wilkie eds., *Excavations at Nichoria in Southwest Greece* II: *The Bronze Age Occupation* (Minneapolis 1992).
Problems	E.B. French and K.A. Wardle eds., *Problems in Greek Prehistory* (Bristol 1988).
"RAP I"	J.L. Davis, "Review of Aegean Prehistory I: The Islands of the Aegean," *AJA* 96 (1992) 699–756.
Thalassocracy	R. Hägg and N. Marinatos eds., *The Minoan Thalassocracy: Myth and Reality* (Stockholm 1984).
Thanatos	R. Laffineur ed., *Thanatos: Les coutûmes funéraires en Égée à l'Age du Bronze* (*Aegaeum* 1, Liège 1987).
"Tierkopfge-fässe"	H.-J. Weisshaar, "Frühhelladische Tierkopfgefässe," in *Gedenkschrift für Gero von Merhart zum 100. Geburtstag* (*Marburger Studien zur Vor- und Frühgeschichte* 7, Marburg 1986) 327–35.
Transition	R. Laffineur ed., *Transition: Le monde égéen du Bronze moyen au Bronze récent* (*Aegaeum* 3, Liège 1989).
Twilight	J. Forsén, *The Twilight of the Early Helladics: A Study of the Disturbances in East-Central and Southern Greece towards the End of the Early Bronze Age* (*SIMA-PB* 116, Jonsered 1992).
Wace and Blegen	C.W. and P.C. Zerner eds., *Wace and Blegen: Pottery as Evidence for Trade in the Aegean Bronze Age, 1939–1989* (Amsterdam, forthcoming).

Periodicals whose actual date of publication is considerably later than the date printed on the volume's spine have been cited with both dates in order to stress when a given excavation report first became available. The UMI numbers for all doctoral dissertations completed at universities in the United States have been provided to facilitate the acquisition of these unadvertised and ordinarily little-known works, in either microfilm or photocopied form, directly from the publisher: University Microfilms International, 300 North Zeeb Road, Ann Arbor, Michigan 48106, U.S.A.

[2] "RAP I" 713–21.

[3] The only exception to the rule that the entire area under consideration here falls within the Helladic cultural orbit is the island of Kythera. Once an EH population had either moved off the island on its own initiative or been driven away from it by Minoan fishermen or colonists, Kythera appears to have become culturally Minoan through the end of the period surveyed: J.N. Coldstream and G.L. Huxley eds., *Kythera. Excavations and Studies Conducted by the University of Pennsylvania Museum and the British School at Athens* (London 1972) 272–303; Coldstream, "Kythera: The Change from Early Helladic to Early Minoan," in R.A. Crossland and A. Birchall eds., *Bronze Age Migrations in the Aegean* (London 1973) 33–36; *Gazetteer* 121–22, sites C50–C55; J.B. Rutter and C.W. Zerner, "Early Hellado-Minoan Contacts," in *Thalassocracy* 75–83, esp. 75–76 and ns. 4–8; G.L. Huxley, "Kythera and the Minoan Maritime Economy," in E. Acquaro et al. eds., *Momenti precoloniali nel Mediterraneo antico* (Rome 1988) 65–71.

For the date of the earliest Mycenaean palaces in ceramic terms, see H.W. Catling, "Excavations at the Menelaion, Sparta, 1973–76," *AR* 23 (1977) 24–42, esp. 27–31; K. Kilian, "L'architecture des résidences mycéniennes: Origine et extension d'une structure de pouvoir politique pendant l'Age du Bronze récent," in E. Lévy ed., *Le système palatial en Orient, en Grèce et à Rome* (Leiden 1987) 203–17; Kilian, "Zur Funktion der mykenischen Residenzen auf dem griechischen Festland," in R. Hägg and N. Marinatos eds., *The Function of the Minoan Palaces* (Stockholm 1987) 21–38; Kilian, "Μυκηναϊκά ανάκτορα της Αργολίδας," *Πρακτικά*

For the most up-to-date reports on work accomplished in Greece in the field as well as in museums and laboratories, the reader is referred to the annual reviews published in *Archaeological Reports (AR)* and in the "Chronique des fouilles" section of the *Bulletin de correspondance hellénique (BCH)*.[4] Of the scores of distinct field, museum, and laboratory projects cited over the past 15 years in the pages of these two bulletins, only those of particular relevance to the themes selected for consideration here are mentioned in what follows. The last synthetic, comprehensive examination of the Greek mainland during the various periods surveyed here, Hope Simpson's and Dickinson's *Gazetteer of Aegean Civilisation in the Bronze Age 1: The Mainland and Islands* (Göteborg 1979), provides a useful terminus post quem for the period of scholarly activity covered in the present review.[5]

GENERAL DEVELOPMENTS

Despite the rich dividends paid over the past 15 years by investment in both continuing and freshly initiated excavation projects, another brand of fieldwork has come to the fore that promises to have an equivalently potent impact on the course of archaeological research in this area—surface survey, particularly of the systematic and intensive variety.[6] Table 1 lists the principal programs of intensive survey so far undertaken on the Greek mainland, along with a selection of extensive survey projects for comparison;[7] figure 1 indicates the locations of the various survey areas and provides a convenient visual display of their relative sizes and distribution throughout the Peloponnese and central Greece. Of the 16 projects identified in table 1, only the University of Minnesota Messenia Expedition (UMME) had been undertaken

---

του Β´ Τοπικού Συνεδρίου Αργολικών Σπουδών (Athens 1989) 33–40; Catling, *Some Problems in Aegean Prehistory c. 1450–1380 B.C.* (Oxford 1989) 7–10; M.K. Dabney and J.C. Wright, "Mortuary Customs, Palatial Society and State Formation in the Aegean Area: A Comparative Study," *Celebrations* 45–53, esp. 48 and n. 31; R.L.N. Barber, "The Origins of the Mycenaean Palace," in J.M. Sanders ed., *ΦΙΛΟΛΑΚΩΝ: Lakonian Studies in Honour of Hector Catling* (London 1992) 11–23. For the dating in calendar years, my preference is for the higher chronology championed since 1987 chiefly by Betancourt and Manning (see table 2; P.P. Betancourt, "Dating the Late Bronze Age with Radiocarbon," *Archaeometry* 29 [1987] 45–49, esp. table 1; S.W. Manning, "The Bronze Age Eruption of Thera: Absolute Dating, Aegean Chronology and Mediterranean Cultural Interrelations," *JMA* 1 [1988] 17–82; Manning, "The Thera Eruption: The Third Congress and the Problem of the Date," *Archaeometry* 32 [1990] 91–100) rather than for the dates roughly a century later upheld by Warren and Hankey in *Chronology* 145–48, 169 table 3.1 and more recently by P.M. Warren, "The Minoan Civilization of Crete and the Volcano of Thera," *Journal of the Ancient Chronology Forum* 4 (1990–1991) 29–39. For a critical assessment of *Chronology*, which focuses on the periods of concern in the present review and with which I am largely in agreement, see the review by J. Maran in *Acta Praehistorica et Archaeologica* 22 (1990) 179–86. For the most recent overviews on absolute dating at either end of the Mycenaean era, see S.W. Manning, "Thera, Sulphur, and Climatic Anomalies," *OJA* 11 (1992) 245–53; S.W. Manning and B. Weninger, "A Light in the Dark: Archaeological Wiggle Matching and the Absolute Chronology of the Close of the Aegean Late Bronze Age," *Antiquity* 66 (1992) 636–63; Manning, "Santorini, Ice-cores and Tree-rings: Resolution of the 1645 or 1628 Debate?" *Nestor* 19 (1992) 2511–12.

[4] For the authorship of these two annual bulletins, both of which have far wider spatial and chronological scopes than those encompassed in the present review and are there-

fore precluded from being synthetic or analytical in their approach, see "RAP I" 700 n. 2.

[5] As it did for J.L. Davis in his assessment of recent developments in the Aegean islands ("RAP I" 700). General surveys of Aegean prehistory contemporary with or more recent than the *Gazetteer* lack its mainland Greek focus and necessarily devote considerable attention to developments on Crete: S. Hood, *The Arts in Prehistoric Greece* (Harmondsworth 1978); R. Treuil et al., *Les civilisations égéennes du Néolithique et de l'Age du Bronze* (Paris 1989); O.T.P.K. Dickinson, *The Aegean Bronze Age* (Cambridge, forthcoming). For a recent survey of developments in Mycenaean archaeology specifically, see the magisterial overview by the late K. Kilian, "Mycenaeans Up to Date: Trends and Changes in Recent Research," in *Problems* 115–52. The more recently published survey included in W.A. McDonald and C.G. Thomas, *Progress into the Past: The Rediscovery of Mycenaean Civilization*[2] (Bloomington 1990) 353–472 is in several important respects not as up to date. Now over a decade old, Dickinson's essay on the Bronze Age in the Peloponnese (infra n. 24), though it has somewhat different chronological and geographical foci, anticipates a number of themes in the present survey and is still very much worth reading.

[6] For a brief but eloquent statement on the rise to prominence of surface survey as an alternative to excavation among the fieldwork options open to archaeologists working in Greece, see A. Snodgrass and J. Cherry, "On *Not* Digging Up the Past," *The Cambridge Review* 109 (1988) 9–13.

[7] The inspiration for, and a good deal of the data in, table 1 were contributed by Cynthia Kosso, to whom I am exceptionally grateful for sharing with me the chapters dealing with archaeological survey from her recently completed *Public Policy and Agricultural Practice: An Archaeological and Literary Study of Late Roman Greece* (Diss. Univ. of Illinois at Chicago 1993). Note also the important role played by the analysis of recent survey data in S.E. Alcock, *Graecia Capta: The Landscapes of Roman Greece* (Cambridge 1993) 33–72.

Table 1. Sizes and Site Densities of All Intensive and Selected Extensive Survey Projects Conducted on the Southern and Central Greek Mainland since 1965[8]

Survey Project	Area Surveyed (km²)	Total Sites	Sites per km²	EH Sites	MH Sites	LH Sites	"Prehistoric" Sites
Intensive							
Berbati-Limnes Survey[9]	25	122	4.9	13 [1]	0 [1]	19 [1]	—
Cambridge/Bradford Boeotian Expedition (1979–1982 seasons only)[10]	21	81	3.9	5–10 [3]	9 [4]	8–17 [4]	—
Laconia Survey[11]	70	ca. 461	6.6	ca. 45 [1]	ca. 15 [1]	ca. 20 [1]	—
Megalopolis Survey[12]	77	306	4.0	? [0]	? [0]	? [0]	—
Methana Survey[13]	10	103	10.3	21+ [3]	3–4 [0]	5–8 [2]	—
Nemea Valley Archaeological Project (NVAP)[14]	50	89	1.8	21 [2]	2 [1]	8 [2]	—
Oropos Survey[15]	15	53+	3.5+	9 [1]	2 [1]	3 [1]	8 (all Bronze Age)
Pylos Regional Archaeological Project (PRAP) (1992 season only)[16]	12	18	1.5	1? [0]	2–4 [2–3]	6 [3]	—
Southern Argolid Exploration Project (AEP)[17]	44	328	7.5	28–34 [2–3]	5 [2]	27–37 [4–5]	—
Stanford Skourta Plain Project (SSPP)[18]	32	120	3.8	15–26 [0]	3–6 [0]	14–18 [0]	—
Extensive[19]							
Aetolia Survey	5500	800+	0.15	3 [1?]	8–9 [2–3]	8–10 [9]	ca. 90 (Stone Age–early Iron Age)
Eastern Phocis Survey	216	19	0.09	5 [4]	5 [3–4]	8 [7]	—
Opountian Locris Survey	—	22	—	4 [3]	5 [4]	9 [7]	—
Perachora Peninsula Survey	—	31	—	11–13 [3]	3–5 [1?]	8 [5]	—
Phocis-Doris Expedition	—	44	—	7 [0]	7 [2]	14 [4]	—
University of Minnesota Messenia Expedition (UMME)	3800	455	0.12	22–35	58–107	168–195	—

[8] References in the following notes 9–19 to brief summaries of progress made in individual field seasons (either in the form of reports to *AR* or of paper abstracts published in *AJA*) are provided only for seasons not covered, insofar as finds of Bronze Age date are concerned, in more substantial preliminary reports. Preliminary reports are only cited if they contain some mention of Bronze Age settlement patterns or if they are the only preliminary reports of any real consequence to have appeared involving a particular survey project. The figures cited under "Area Surveyed," in the cases of intensive surveys, refer not to the entire survey area but rather to the area covered by intensive fieldwalking. The percentage of the total survey area intensively explored varies considerably from project to project (e.g., ca. 20% for the Berbati-Limnes Survey and the Methana Survey vs. ca. 63% for the Nemea Valley Archaeological Project). The figure given for the total area of the Eastern Phocis Survey is no more than a rough approximation based upon the maps published in Fossey 1986 (infra n. 19); no comparable attempt has been made to measure his survey areas in Opountian Locris and the Perachora peninsula. The area surveyed by the Phocis-Doris Expedition has likewise not

been estimated since its boundaries are not specified with any particular precision. Under the headings for the three major chronological subdivisions of the mainland Greek Bronze Age or Helladic era, ranges reflect the extent to which sites were *certainly* occupied (lower number) as opposed to either *possibly* or *probably* occupied (upper number). Since the figures in these three columns refer to sites occupied during broad but nevertheless discrete intervals of time, the same site may be counted under two or even all three headings. The bracketed figures represent the numbers of sites for each period included in the *Gazetteer*. The figures under "LH Sites" include sites of all phases of the Mycenaean period, not merely LH I–II. Sites reported as "prehistoric" could not be more closely dated. The data from the University of Minnesota Messenia Expedition (UMME), all of which were included in the *Gazetteer*, have been presented here for comparative purposes; neither the area covered by that project nor those of the more recently published regional overviews of settlement patterns cited in n. 20 infra are indicated on fig. 1.

[9] B. Wells, C.N. Runnels, and E. Zangger, "The Berbati-Limnes Archaeological Survey: The 1988 Season," *OpAth* 18

(1990) 207–38; Wells, Runnels, and Zangger, "In the Shadow of Mycenae," *Archaeology* 46:1 (1993) 54–58, 63; *AR* 36 (1990) 14; 37 (1991) 22. The overall site total listed in table 1 does not include 15 standing monuments (only one of which is prehistoric, of LH date); neither this figure nor the period subtotals include the so-called Mastos, the principal prehistoric site in the Berbati valley and the only one mentioned in the *Gazetteer*: 39 site A5.

[10] J. Bintliff and A.M. Snodgrass, "The Cambridge/Bradford Boeotian Expedition: The First Four Years," *JFA* 12 (1985) 123–61; J. Bintliff, "The Boeotia Survey," in S. Macready and F.H. Thompson eds., *Archaeological Field Survey in Britain and Abroad* (London 1985) 196–216; Bintliff, "The Development of Settlement in South-west Boeotia," in P. Roesch and G. Argoud eds., *La Béotie antique* (Paris 1985) 49–70; Bintliff and Snodgrass, "Off-site Pottery Distributions: A Regional and Interregional Perspective," *CurrAnthr* 29 (1988) 506–13; *AR* 32 (1986) 40–41; 33 (1987) 23–24; 35 (1989) 44–46; 36 (1990) 33–34; 37 (1991) 33–34; 38 (1992) 29.

[11] W.G. Cavanagh and J. Crouwel, "Laconia Survey 1983–1986," Λακωνικαί Σπουδαί 9 (1988) 77–88; W.G. Cavanagh, S. Hirst, and C.D. Litton, "Soil Phosphate, Site Boundaries and Change Point Analysis," *JFA* 15 (1988) 67–83; *AR* 34 (1988) 26; 35 (1989) 37; 36 (1990) 21–22; Cavanagh and Crouwel, "Melathria: A Small Mycenaean Rural Settlement in Laconia," in Sanders (supra n. 3) 77–86.

[12] J.A. Lloyd, E.J. Owens, and J. Roy, "The Megalopolis Survey in Arcadia: Problems of Strategy and Tactics," in Macready and Thompson (supra n. 10) 217–24; Lloyd, "Farming the Highlands: Samnium and Arcadia in the Hellenistic and Early Roman Imperial Periods," in G. Barker and J. Lloyd eds., *Roman Landscapes: Archaeological Survey in the Mediterranean Region* (London 1991) 180–93; *AR* 28 (1982) 24; 29 (1983) 28–29; 30 (1984) 26–27; Roy, Lloyd, and Owens, "Two Sites in the Megalopolis Basin," in Sanders (supra n. 3) 185–94.

[13] C. Mee, D. Gill, H. Forbes, and L. Foxhall, "Rural Settlement Change in the Methana Peninsula, Greece," in Barker and Lloyd (supra n. 12) 223–32; *AR* 31 (1985) 21–22; 32 (1986) 28; 33 (1987) 19–20; 34 (1988) 22–23.

[14] J.F. Cherry, J.L. Davis, A. Demitrack, E. Mantzourani, T. Strasser, and L. Talalay, "Archaeological Survey in an Artifact-Rich Landscape: A Middle Neolithic Example from Nemea, Greece," *AJA* 92 (1988) 159–76; L. Roberts, "Early Bronze Age Settlement in Southern Greece: New Data from the Nemea Valley," *AJA* 92 (1988) 252 (abstract); J.L. Davis, "If There's a 'Room at the Top', What's at the Bottom? Settlement and Hierarchy in Early Mycenaean Greece," *BICS* 35 (1988) 164–65; J.C. Wright, J. Cherry, J.L. Davis, E. Mantzourani, S.B. Sutton, and R.F. Sutton, "The Nemea Valley Archaeological Project: A Preliminary Report," *Hesperia* 59 (1990) 579–659, esp. 603–17, 646–59; Wright, Cherry, Davis, and Mantzourani, "Early Mycenaean Settlement in the Nemea Region," in G. Korres ed., *The Prehistoric Aegean and Its Relations to Adjacent Areas (Proceedings of the 6th International Colloquium on Aegean Prehistory*, Athens, forthcoming).

[15] M.B. Cosmopoulos, "Αρχαιολογική έρευνα στην περιοχή του Ωρωπού," *ArchEph* 1989 (1991) 163–75; *AJA* 94 (1990) 328, and 95 (1991) 332 (abstracts). I am greatly indebted to Michael Cosmopoulos for a brief summary of the results of the third (1991) season of the Oropos Survey, thus far unpublished. The total number of new sites located by this survey (53) should be adjusted upward slightly to take cognizance of sites previously known within the survey area such as the Amphiaraion and the prehistoric site at

Skala Oropou (*Gazetteer* 221 site A57).

[16] I am very grateful to the director of the Pylos Regional Archaeological Project (PRAP), J.L. Davis, for supplying me with a copy of his preliminary report on the progress made during the first of what is projected to be three seasons of fieldwork (1992–1994) devoted to extensive survey in an area of some 250 km² (the block indicated in fig. 1) in southwestern Messenia and intensive survey of ca. 50 km², including the entirety of the Englianos ridge, in the immediate vicinity of the Mycenaean palace at Pylos.

[17] The beginning of intensive surface survey in the southern Argolid actually dates back to a single season of work in 1972: M.H. Jameson, "The Southern Argolid: The Setting for Historical and Cultural Studies," in M. Dimen and E. Friedl eds., *Regional Variations in Modern Greece and Cyprus: Toward a Perspective on the Ethnography of Greece (New York Academy of Sciences Annals* 268, New York 1976) 74–91. A continuous program of systematic intensive survey in this area, however, began only in 1979: T.H. van Andel, C.N. Runnels, and K. Pope, "Five Thousand Years of Land Use and Abuse in the Southern Argolid, Greece," *Hesperia* 55 (1986) 103–28; Runnels and van Andel, "The Evolution of Settlement in the Southern Argolid, Greece: An Economic Explanation," *Hesperia* 56 (1987) 303–34; van Andel and Runnels, *Beyond the Acropolis: A Rural Greek Past* (Stanford 1987); C.N. Runnels, D.J. Pullen, and S.H. Langdon, *Artifact and Assemblage: Finds from a Regional Survey of the Southern Argolid* 1: *The Prehistoric and Early Iron Age Pottery and Lithic Artifacts* (Stanford, forthcoming); M.H. Jameson, C.N. Runnels, and T.H. van Andel, *A Greek Countryside: The Southern Argolid from Prehistory to Present Day* (Stanford, forthcoming).

[18] M.H. Munn and M.L.Z. Munn, "Studies on the Attic-Boeotian Frontier: The Stanford Skourta Plain Project, 1985," in J. Fossey ed., *Boeotia Antiqua* 1 (Amsterdam 1989) 73–127; M.H. Munn, "New Light on Panakton and the Attic-Boeotian Frontier," in H. Beister and J. Buckler eds., *Boiotika* (Munich 1989) 231–44; M.H. Munn and M.L.Z. Munn, "On the Frontiers of Attica and Boeotia: The Results of the Stanford Skourta Plain Project," in A. Schachter ed., *Essays in the Topography, History, and Culture of Boeotia (Teiresias* Suppl. 3, Montreal 1990) 33–40; *AJA* 95 (1991) 332 (abstract).

[19] S. Bommeljé et al., *Aetolia and the Aetolians: Towards the Interdisciplinary Study of a Greek Region* (Utrecht 1987); Bommeljé et al., *An Inland Polity* (Utrecht 1993); J.M. Fossey, *The Ancient Topography of Eastern Phokis* (Amsterdam 1986); Fossey, *The Ancient Topography of Opountian Lokris* (Amsterdam 1990); Fossey, "The Perakhora Peninsula Survey," *EchCl* 34:9 (1990) 201–11; E.W. Kase, G.J. Szemler, N.C. Wilkie, and P.W. Wallace eds., *The Great Isthmus Corridor Route: Explorations of the Phokis-Doris Expedition* 1 (Dubuque 1991); W.A. McDonald and G.R. Rapp, Jr., eds., *The Minnesota Messenia Expedition: Reconstructing a Bronze Age Environment* (Minneapolis 1972). As a complement to the work of Fossey in eastern Phocis, Kase and his coworkers further west in the region north of Amphissa, and Bommeljé and his coworkers still further west in Aetolia, see also S. Müller, "Delphes et sa région à l'époque mycénienne," *BCH* (forthcoming). The UMME survey in Messenia was amplified somewhat by a supplementary survey conducted in the "Five Rivers Area" near the site of Nichoria (F.E. Lukermann and J. Moody, "Nichoria and Vicinity: Settlements and Circulation," in G. Rapp, Jr., and S.E. Aschenbrenner eds., *Excavations at Nichoria in Southwest Greece* I: *Site, Environs, and Techniques* [Minneapolis 1978] 78–112), the results of which have not been included in table 1.

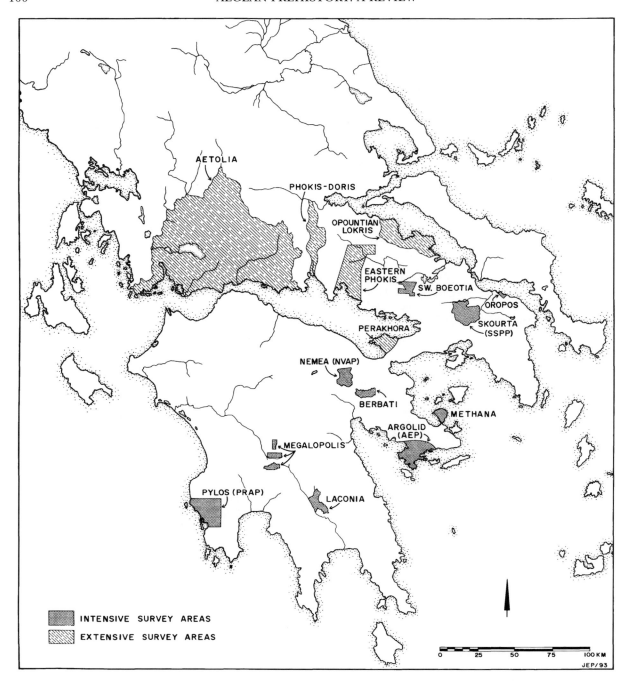

Fig. 1. Locations of intensive and selected extensive survey projects listed in table 1 (except for UMME in Messenia)

and published before the appearance of the *Gazetteer*, with the result that the site totals for Messenia were grossly inflated in that volume relative to those of other regions within southern Greece. Fieldwork on the first intensive surveys conducted on the southern Greek mainland began in 1979, the year of the *Gazetteer*'s publication (Cambridge/Bradford Boeotian Expedition, Southern Argolid Exploration Project). Of all the intensive surveys listed in table 1, only the

Pylos Regional Archaeological Project (PRAP), freshly launched in 1992, and the Oropos Survey are still ongoing projects in the field. Thus, as a phenomenon affecting our understanding of mainland Greek pre-history, the practice of systematic intensive survey made a sudden appearance at the end of the 1970s and flourished throughout the 1980s, but may turn out to be a less prominent strategy of field research in this particular region of Greece during the 1990s.[20]

Discussion of the implications of this new form of fieldwork for period- or region-specific problems, like the impact of recent discoveries generated by excavation, may be postponed for the sections of this essay devoted to particular periods and cultures. But some of what is new and exciting, as well as problematic, about the information derived from surveys applies to all times and regions and is therefore best summarized separately and in advance. To date, intensive survey on the southern Greek mainland[21] may be viewed as having gone through two distinct stages of development and recently to have entered a third. The first stage, encompassing roughly the period between 1978 and 1984, witnessed the beginning of about half of the projects listed in table 1. The principal concern of the practitioners of intensive survey in the field was to devise methodologies appropriate for their specific research goals and geographical region, but in their publications they were above all concerned with demonstrating the superiority of their approach to survey over the extensive, typically non-systematic strategies that had flourished in Greece since the 19th century.[22]

The second stage, lasting from 1984 through 1992, revealed through the clear dominance of intensive over extensive surveys that the debate over the relative merits of the two strategies had been decisively settled, insofar as fieldwork on the Greek mainland was concerned, in favor of intensive survey.[23] The repeated demonstration that intensive surveys were successful

---

[20] At the time of writing, more intensive survey projects are in progress on both Crete and Cyprus than on the southern and central Greek mainland, but this is unlikely to remain the case for very long. It is more difficult to generalize in an equivalent way about extensive survey projects. The bulk of Fossey's fieldwork in eastern Phocis, Opountian Locris, and Boeotia took place in the later 1960s, contemporaneously with the later stages of the surveying undertaken by McDonald and his colleagues on the UMME project in Messenia. Kase and his coworkers on the Phocis-Doris Project conducted their field research in the later 1970s. Fossey's work on the Perachora peninsula was concentrated in the late 1970s and early 1980s. Finally, S. Bommeljé, P.K. Doorn, and J.A.C. Vroom, who began their work in Aetolia in the 1980s, have continued to pursue active fieldwork through to the present. For a convenient summary of extensive survey work affecting the EH II–III and MH periods, see *Twilight* 177–82. Overviews of settlement patterns within some of the principal regions of the southern and central Greek mainland that have been published since the *Gazetteer* but are not included in table 1 are T.J. Papadopoulos, *Mycenaean Achaea*: Pts. 1–2 (*SIMA* 55.1–2, Göteborg 1978, 1979); M. Koumouzelis, *The Early and Middle Helladic Periods in Elis* (Diss. Brandeis Univ. 1980; UMI 80-24537) 237–56; K. Kilian, "Ἡ διοικητική οργανώση της Πύλου και η αρχαιολογική ιεραρχία των οικισμών της Αργολίδας στη μυκηναϊκή εποχή," *Πρακτικά του Β' Τοπικού Συνεδρίου Μεσσηνιακών Σπουδών* (Athens 1984) 55–68; A. Foley, *The Argolid, 800–600 B.C.: An Archaeological Survey* (*SIMA* 80, Göteborg 1988) 171–99; J.M. Fossey, *Topography and Population of Ancient Boeotia* 1–2 (Chicago 1988); P.B. Phaklares, *Αρχαία Κυνουρία: Ανθρωπίνη δραστηριότητα και περιβάλλον* (Athens 1990); O.T.P.K. Dickinson, "Reflections on Bronze Age Laconia," in Sanders (supra n. 3) 109–14.

[21] There is a certain degree of "cultural lag" detectable between the progress of intensive survey in the Aegean islands and that on the neighboring Greek mainland. The Melos survey, for example, was both initiated and published well in advance of the first mainland equivalent (J.F. Cherry, "A Preliminary Study of Site Distribution" and "Appendix A: A Register of Archaeological Sites on Melos," in C. Renfrew and M. Wagstaff eds., *An Island Polity: The Archaeology of Exploitation in Melos* [Cambridge 1982] 10–23 and 291–

309, respectively). The significant advances in survey theory and methodology achieved during the 1980s are reflected in the final publication of the Northern Keos survey, which has appeared before the first complete publication of any mainland survey (J.F. Cherry, J.L. Davis, and E. Mantzourani, *Landscape Archaeology as Long-Term History: Northern Keos in the Cycladic Islands* [*Monumenta archaeologica* 16, Los Angeles 1991]). Note also from an island the work of D.R. Keller, *Archaeological Survey in Southern Euboea, Greece: A Reconstruction of Human Activity from Neolithic Times through the Byzantine Period* (Diss. Indiana Univ. 1985; UMI 85-27015).

[22] For the concern with appropriate intensive survey methodologies in an embryonic form, see many of the papers dealing with projects in Greece included in D.R. Keller and D.W. Rupp eds., *Archaeological Survey in the Mediterranean Area* (*BAR-IS* 155, Oxford 1983) 207–302. For the debate over intensive vs. extensive approaches to surface survey, see R. Hope Simpson, "The Limitations of Surface Surveys," and J.F. Cherry, "Frogs around the Pond: Perspectives on Current Archaeological Survey Projects in the Mediterranean Region," in Keller and Rupp (supra) 45–47 and 375–416, esp. 390–94, respectively; R. Hope Simpson, "The Analysis of Data from Surface Surveys," and J.F. Cherry, "Common Sense in Mediterranean Survey?" *JFA* 11 (1984) 115–17 and 117–20, respectively.

[23] Of the projects listed in table 1, the Aetolia Survey is unique in having employed from its inception in the mid-1980s an extensive strategy. The rationale for doing so in this particular case is simple and compelling: the area being surveyed is enormous and, in relation to areas of the mainland to both south and east, very poorly documented archaeologically. In addition, the terrain and ground cover across most of Aetolia make intensive strategies virtually counterproductive, except in a few zones that together constitute only a small percentage of the survey area's overall extent. Steep relief, dense ground cover, or simple inaccessibility caused by the reluctance of landowners to permit survey on their property have made intensive survey impossible in some sections of virtually every project's study area, but in most regions of the Peloponnese and east-central Greece such obstacles to an intensive survey's success involve a far smaller component of the total landscape than in Aetolia.

in identifying a vastly larger total number of sites within a given area persuaded those interested in the study of diachronic change in settlement patterns that data generated by extensive strategies were simply not close enough to any ancient reality for interregional analyses of such data to inspire any confidence.[24] This stage witnessed the first lengthy publications on individual mainland Greek intensive surveys, in the form of preliminary reports in which methodological issues were at least initially of primary concern.[25] In more recent preliminary reports, there has been a somewhat greater emphasis on the presentation of artifactual data, although there continues to be a substantial interest in questions of method.[26] During this same period the first synthetic analyses of the data generated by one of the earliest of these mainland Greek intensive surveys, the Southern Argolid Exploration Project, appeared,[27] as did some reminders that extensive programs of survey still have an impressive amount of new information to contribute when conducted in areas and for periods of time that are still quite poorly known archaeologically, such as the Greek northwest in prehistory (fig. 2a–b).[28]

The third stage has begun only within the past year and is characterized by two highly significant developments: first, the appearance of the final publications of several of the intensive survey projects conducted during the 1980s,[29] and second, the initial interregional comparisons of the available data from such projects, whether in preliminary or in final form.[30] On the eve of the flood of interregional comparative studies that is bound to result from the publication of vast quantities of information of a fundamentally different character than has hitherto been available, it is worth taking the time to comment briefly on some of the problems raised in the preliminary reports on mainland Greek intensive surveys concerning their interpretation. Masses of new information from the intensive surveys listed in table 1 have been collected, whether by superior or inferior sampling strategies and field recording techniques. What should we keep in mind as we brace ourselves for the onslaught of these staggering quantities of fresh data and prepare to choose between a wide variety of interpretative approaches?

The collection of these data has been conditioned by our desire to investigate patterns of settlement, that is, mankind's adaptations on a regional scale to particular natural environments. Our ultimate goal is to document and explain variety in such settlement patterns across space and through time. To this end we need to be particularly sensitive, in seeking to digest the new data and to assess the interpretations derived from those data, to three broad areas of concern: the nature of the environment in which ancient populations found themselves, the ways by

---

[24] Studies of mainland Greek settlement patterns employing the data from extensive surveys include C. Renfrew, *The Emergence of Civilisation: The Cyclades and the Aegean in the Third Millennium B.C.* (London 1972) 225–64; Renfrew, "Patterns of Population Growth in the Prehistoric Aegean," in P.J. Ucko, R. Tringham, and G.W. Dimbleby eds., *Man, Settlement and Urbanism* (London 1972) 383–99; O.T.P.K. Dickinson, "Parallels and Contrasts in the Bronze Age of the Peloponnese," *OJA* 1 (1982) 125–38; Foley (supra n. 20) 22–33 and tables 1–2; J.M. Fossey, "Settlement Development in Greek Prehistory," in J.M. Fossey ed., *ΣΥΝΕΙΣΦΟΡΑ McGill* 1: *Papers in Greek Archaeology and History in Memory of Colin D. Gordon* (Amsterdam 1987) 17–33; Cosmopoulos (infra n. 46) 1–12. For the demonstration that an intensive strategy can result in the recognition of 50–100 times the number of sites per unit area identified with an extensive strategy, see Cherry in Keller and Rupp (supra n. 22) 391–93, fig.1; Bintliff in Macready and Thompson (supra n. 10) 208; Bintliff and Snodgrass (supra n. 10) 127–37, table 4.

[25] Bintliff in Macready and Thompson (supra n. 10); Bintliff and Snodgrass 1985 (supra n. 10); Lloyd et al. (supra n. 12); Bintliff and Snodgrass 1988 (supra n. 10).

[26] Cherry et al. (supra n. 14); Cosmopoulos 1989 (supra n. 15); Wright et al. (supra n. 14); Wells et al. 1990 (supra n. 9).

[27] van Andel and Runnels (supra n. 17); Runnels and van Andel (supra n. 17).

[28] Bommeljé et al. 1987 (supra n. 19); Kase et al. (supra n. 19). The Bronze Age in the Spercheios River valley at the extreme northeast of the area covered in this review has likewise not received the attention it deserves until quite recently, under the aegis of F. Dakoronia, Ephor of Antiquities in Lamia: *Μάρμαρα: Τα υπομυκηναϊκά νεκροταφεία των τύμβων* (Athens 1987); "Late Helladic III, Submycenaean and Protogeometric Finds," in Kase et al. (supra n. 19) 70–74, fig. 7-1. For a review of recent fieldwork on Bronze Age sites in the region southeast of Lamia, see F. Dakoronia, "Homeric Towns in East Lokris: Problems of Identification," *Hesperia* 62 (1993) 115–27. See also J. Vroom, "The Kastro of Veloukhovo (Kallion): A Note on the Surface Finds," *Pharos* 1 (1993) 103–28.

[29] Runnels et al. (supra n. 17); Jameson et al. (supra n. 17); B. Wells and C.N. Runnels eds., *The Berbati-Limnes Archaeological Survey 1988–1990* (Stockholm, forthcoming). In this context, it is also appropriate to draw attention to the appearance of the second volume on the Aetolia Survey (Bommeljé et al. 1993, supra n. 19), which documents a comparable increase in the numbers of known sites in that region of west-central Greece.

[30] *Twilight* 176–96; Kosso (supra n. 7); Alcock (supra n. 7). The first study is restricted to the EH II through MH periods, the second to the late Hellenistic, Roman Imperial, and early Byzantine eras, and the last for the most part to Hellenistic and Roman times.

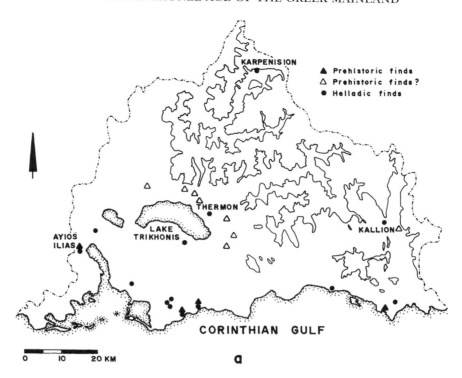

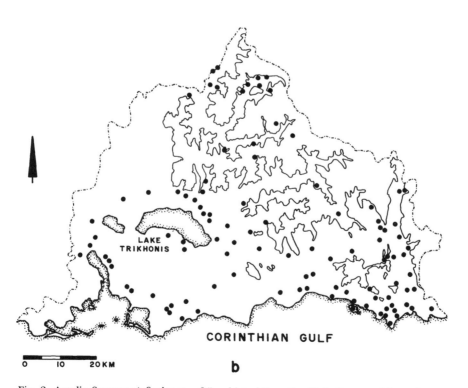

Fig. 2. Aetolia Survey: a) findspots of "prehistoric" and/or Helladic material as of 1986 (after S. Bommeljé et al., *Aetolia and the Aetolians* [Utrecht 1987] fig. 2.2); b) findspots of all prehistoric material, from the Stone Age through the early Iron Age, as of 1992 (S. Bommeljé and J. Vroom). Contour interval at 1000 m in both maps.

which we are measuring time, and the definition and characterization in terms of size and function of the locales of past human activity that we refer to as "sites."

The nature of the ancient Greek landscape was no more constant through either time or space than was

the pattern of human settlement within it. Thus, establishing how and when this landscape underwent significant change must be considered an ingredient critical to the appropriate interpretation of intensive survey data.[31] As important as the shape of the landscape are the resources, whether faunal,[32] botanical,[33]

---

[31] See, e.g., J.C. Kraft, G. Rapp, Jr., and S.E. Aschenbrenner, "Late Holocene Paleogeographic Reconstructions in the Area of the Bay of Navarino: Sandy Pylos," *JAS* 7 (1980) 187–210; van Andel et al. (supra n. 17); C. Baeteman, "Late Holocene Geology of the Marathon Plain (Greece)," *Journal of Coastal Research* 1 (1985) 173–85; J.C. Kraft et al., "The Pass at Thermopylae, Greece," *JFA* 14 (1987) 181–98; O. Psychoyos, *Déplacements de la ligne de rivage et sites archéologiques dans les régions côtières de la mer Égée au Néolithique et à l'Age du Bronze* (*SIMA-PB 62*, Jonsered 1988); E.A.W. Finke [now E. Zangger], *Landscape Evolution of the Argive Plain, Greece: Paleoecology, Holocene Depositional History, and Coastline Changes* (Diss. Stanford Univ. 1988; UMI 88-26140); T.H. van Andel and E. Zangger, "Landscape Stability and Destabilization in the Prehistory of Greece," in S. Bottema, G. Entjes-Nieborg, and W. van Zeist eds., *Man's Role in the Shaping of the Eastern Mediterranean Landscape* (Rotterdam 1990) 139–57; T.M. Niemi, "Paleoenvironmental History of Submerged Ruins on the Northern Euboean Gulf Coastal Plain, Central Greece," *Geoarchaeology* 5 (1990) 323–47; T.H. van Andel, E. Zangger, and A. Demitrack, "Land Use and Soil Erosion in Prehistoric and Historical Greece," *JFA* 17 (1990) 379–96; Zangger, "Tiryns Unterstadt," in E. Pernicka and G. Wagner eds., *Archaeometry '90* (Basel 1991) 831–40; Zangger, "Prehistoric Coastal Environments in Greece: The Vanished Landscapes of Dimini Bay and Lake Lerna," *JFA* 18 (1991) 1–15; J.C. Kraft, "Geology of the Great Isthmus Corridor," in Kase et al. (supra n. 19) 1–16; Zangger, "Prehistoric and Historic Soils in Greece: Assessing the Natural Resources for Agriculture," in B. Wells ed., *Agriculture in Ancient Greece* (Stockholm 1992) 13–19; Zangger, "Neolithic to Present Soil Erosion in Greece," in J. Boardman and M. Bell eds., *Past and Present Soil Erosion* (Oxford 1992) 133–47; Zangger, *Geoarchaeology of the Argolid* (Berlin, forthcoming); Zangger, "The Island of Asine: A Palaeogeographic Reconstruction," *OpAth* (forthcoming).

[32] For recent summaries of the exploitation of animals during the Aegean Bronze Age, see S. Payne, "Zoo-Archaeology in Greece: A Reader's Guide," in *Contributions* 211–44; P. Halstead, "Man and Other Animals in Later Greek Prehistory," *BSA* 82 (1987) 71–83; C. Trantalidou, "Animals and Human Diet in the Prehistoric Aegean," in D. Hardy ed., *Thera and the Aegean World* III.2: *Earth Sciences* (London 1990) 392–405. For a critical evaluation of the prehistoric evidence in Greece for pastoralism in general, and for transhumant pastoralism in particular, see J.F. Cherry, "Pastoralism and the Role of Animals in the Pre- and Protohistoric Economies of the Aegean," in C.R. Whittaker ed., *Pastoral Economies in Classical Antiquity* (*Cambridge Philological Society* Suppl. 14, Cambridge 1988) 6–34; P. Halstead, "Present to Past in the Pindhos: Diversification and Specialization in Mountain Economies," *RStLig* 56 (1990) 61–80.

For the earliest secure evidence for draft animals in the Aegean as well as for the introduction of the plow into Aegean agriculture, see D.J. Pullen, "Ox and Plow in the Early Bronze Age Aegean," *AJA* 96 (1992) 45–54. For the publication of the first faunal collection from a Bronze Age site on the southern Greek mainland to rival and in some ways (e.g., in sheer quantity) surpass that published by N.-G. Gejvall, *Lerna I: The Fauna* (Princeton 1969), see A. von den Driesch and J. Boessneck, "Die Tierreste von der mykenischen Burg Tiryns bei Nauplion/Peloponnes," *Tiryns* XI (Mainz 1990) 87–164, helpfully summarized in a review of the whole volume by O.T.P.K. Dickinson in *CR* 42 (1992) 397–98. For recent contributions on invertebrate fauna in particular, see also L. Karali-Yannacopoulou, "Sea Shells, Land Snails and Other Marine Remains from Akrotiri," in Hardy (supra) 410–15; D.S. Reese, "Recent and Fossil Invertebrates (with a Note on the Nature of the MH I Fauna)," in *Nichoria* 770–78. (The animal bones from Nichoria were published by R.E. Sloan and M.A. Duncan, "Zooarchaeology at Nichoria," in Rapp and Aschenbrenner [supra n. 19] 60–77; part of this report has been amplified by E.A. Mancz, *An Examination of Changing Patterns of Animal-Husbandry of the Late Bronze and Dark Ages of Nichoria in the Southwestern Peloponnese* [Diss. Univ. of Minnesota 1989; UMI 89-18286].)

For the introduction of the horse into the Aegean and the history of draft animals in the later Bronze Age, see J. Crouwel, *Chariots and Other Means of Land Transport in Bronze Age Greece* (Amsterdam 1981) esp. 32–41; and R. Drews, *The Coming of the Greeks: Indo-European Conquests in the Aegean and the Near East* (Princeton 1988) esp. 74–84; both of these require updating in view of the new evidence for EH III horses from Tiryns published by von den Driesch and Boessneck (supra) 92, and from Thebes cited by Fossey (supra n. 20) 419 n. 49. The new material from Tiryns also provides unambiguous evidence for the presence of the lion in the Argolid throughout the Mycenaean era, albeit, as J. Cherry has cautioned me, not necessarily as a wild endemic species (von den Driesch and Boessneck [supra] 110–11); see also Dickinson (supra) 398. For recent studies on the use of the lion in Aegean Bronze Age art, see I. Pini, "Das Motiv des Löwenüberfalls in der spätminoischen und mykenischen Glyptik," in P. Darcque and J.-C. Poursat eds., *L'iconographie minoenne* (*BCH* Suppl. 11, 1985) 153–66; N. Marinatos, "Celebrations of Death and the Symbolism of the Lion Hunt," in *Celebrations* 143–47; E.F. Bloedow, "On Lions in Mycenaean and Minoan Culture," in *Iconography* 295–305, esp. 300–301; Laffineur in *Iconography* 109 n. 33; Bloedow, "Löwenjagd im spätbronzezeitlichen Griechenland," *Altertum* 38 (1993) 241–50.

[33] For the natural vegetation of the southern Greek mainland, see O. Rackham, "Land-Use and the Native Vegetation

or mineral,[34] that were available to the human populations that settled within it.

Archaeological time can be measured in both absolute and relative terms. In the context of the mainland Greek Bronze Age, relative dating is most effectively achieved through seriating ceramics from stratified excavation contexts, although objects of stone, metal, and bone or ivory from the same contexts may also be useful for this purpose. In light of the range of artifactual materials as a rule recovered during intensive surface surveys, the overwhelming majority of Bronze Age occupational components identified at survey sites are recognized and dated with the aid of stone tools and pottery, for the most part highly fragmentary and heavily worn. Although a fair amount of progress has been made over the past decade on the chronology of Helladic stone and bone tools as well as stone vessels,[35] potsherds still represent the "artifactual category of choice" for dating episodes of Bronze Age activity wherever evidence of this is found. Yet there are numerous problems with the use of pottery for this purpose. In the first

---

of Greece," in M. Bell and S. Limbrey eds., *Archaeological Aspects of Woodland Ecology* (*BAR-IS* 146, Oxford 1982) 177–98; O. Rackham, "Observations on the Historical Ecology of Boeotia," *BSA* 78 (1983) 291–352; H. Allen, "A Postglacial Record from the Kopais Basin, Greece," in Bottema et al. (supra n. 31) 173–82; S. Jahns, "Preliminary Notes on Human Influence and the History of Vegetation in S. Dalmatia and S. Greece," in Bottema et al. (supra n. 31) 333–40. For cultivated plants in the same region, see J.M. Hansen, "Paleoethnobotany in Greece: Past, Present and Future," in *Contributions* 171–81; C. Runnels and J. Hansen, "The Olive in the Prehistoric Aegean: The Evidence for Domestication in the Early Bronze Age," *OJA* 5 (1986) 299–308; G. Jones, "Agricultural Practice in Greek Prehistory," *BSA* 82 (1987) 115–23; Hansen, "Agriculture in the Prehistoric Aegean: Data versus Speculation," *AJA* 92 (1988) 39–52; L. Foxhall, *Olive Cultivation within Greek and Roman Agriculture: The Ancient Economy Revisited* (Diss. Univ. of Liverpool 1990).

[34] The mineral wealth of Greek landscapes has traditionally been described in terms of sources of metallic ores, e.g., Z.A. Stos-Gale and N.H. Gale, "The Sources of Mycenaean Silver and Lead," *JFA* 9 (1982) 467–85; V. McGeehan-Liritzis, "The Relationship between Metalwork, Copper Sources and the Evidence for Settlement in the Greek Late Neolithic and Early Bronze Age," *OJA* 2 (1983) 147–80; E. Pernicka, "Erzlagerstätten in der Ägäis und ihre Ausbeutung im Altertum: Geochemische Untersuchungen zur Herkunftsbestimmung archäologischer Metallobjeckte," *JRGZM* 35 (1989) 607–714; Z.A. Stos-Gale and C.F. Macdonald, "Sources of Metals and Trade in the Bronze Age Aegean," in *BA Trade* 249–87; Gale and Stos-Gale, "Lead Isotope Studies in the Aegean (The British Academy Project)," in A.M. Pollard ed., *New Developments in Archaeological Science* (*ProcBritAc* 77, Oxford 1992) 63–108, although this focus has recently been corrected by studies of important raw materials employed for both chipped stone (e.g., obsidian: Torrence, infra n. 35) and ground stone (e.g., andesite: C. Runnels, *A Diachronic Study and Economic Analysis of Millstones from the Argolid, Greece* [Diss. Indiana Univ. 1981; UMI 81-19022]; C. Runnels and R. Cohen, "The Source of the Kitsos Millstones," in N. Lambert ed., *La grotte préhistorique de Kitsos (Attique)* [Paris 1981] 233–39). With respect to the sources of metalliferous ores, the most important discovery over the past 15 years involving the southern Greek mainland in the Bronze Age has been the revelation that the Laurion area of eastern Attica was a major source not merely of lead and

silver ores (e.g., Stos-Gale and Gale, supra; Gale and Stos-Gale, "Thorikos, Perati, and Bronze Age Silver Production in Laurion, Attica," *Miscellanea Graeca* 5 [1982] 97–103; N.H. Gale, Z.A. Stos-Gale, and J.L. Davis, "The Provenance of Lead Used at Ayia Irini, Keos," *Hesperia* 53 [1984] 389–406; P. Spitaels, "The Early Helladic Period in Mine No. 3 (Theatre Sector)," in *Thorikos* VIII [Gent 1984] 151–74; M. Waelkens, "Tool Marks and Mining Techniques in Mine Nr. 3," in *Thorikos* IX [Gent 1990] 114–43), as in late Archaic and Classical times, but also of copper ores (Gale and Stos-Gale, "Bronze Age Copper Sources in the Mediterranean: A New Approach," *Science* 216:4541 [1982] 11–19; Z.A. Stos-Gale, N.H. Gale, and U. Zwicker, "The Copper Trade in the South East Mediterranean Region: Preliminary Scientific Evidence," *RDAC* 1986, 122–44; Stos-Gale and Macdonald, supra). For bronze artifacts dating from the periods surveyed here, see D.N. Tripathi, *Bronzework of Mainland Greece from c. 2600 B.C. to c. 1450 B.C.* (*SIMA-PB* 69, Göteborg 1988), helpfully reviewed by R. Laffineur in *Annales d'archéologie égéenne de l'Université de Liège* 6 (*Aegaeum* 6, Liège 1990) 186–87, and by H. Matthäus, in *Gnomon* 63 (1991) 657–58.

[35] For chipped stone tools in particular, see Runnels (infra n. 72); R. Torrence, *Production and Exchange of Stone Tools: Prehistoric Obsidian in the Aegean* (Cambridge 1986); H. Blitzer, "Middle to Late Helladic Chipped Stone Implements of the Southwest Peloponnese, Greece. Part I: The Evidence from Malthi," *Hydra* 9 (1991) 1–73; P.N. Kardulias, "The Ecology of Bronze Age Flaked Stone Tool Production in Southern Greece: Evidence from Agios Stephanos and the Southern Argolid," *AJA* 96 (1992) 421–42. For ground stone implements, see C.N. Runnels, "Trade and the Demand for Millstones in Southern Greece in the Neolithic and the Early Bronze Age," in A.B. Knapp and T. Stech eds., *Prehistoric Production and Exchange: The Aegean and Eastern Mediterranean* (Los Angeles 1985) 30–43; Runnels, "Early Bronze Age Stone Mortars from the Southern Argolid," *Hesperia* 57 (1988) 257–72; P. Warren, "Lapis Lacedaemonius," in Sanders (supra n. 3) 285–96. For publications stressing the importance of lithic artifacts in general, see C. Runnels, "Lithic Artifacts from Surface Sites in the Mediterranean Area," in Keller and Rupp (supra n. 22) 143–48; H. Blitzer, "The Chipped Stone, Ground Stone, and Worked Bone Industries," in *Nichoria* 712–56. For bone implements, see O.H. Krzyszkowska, *The Bone and Ivory Industries of the Aegean Bronze Age: A Technological Study* (Diss. Univ. of Bristol 1981) and Blitzer (supra).

Table 2. Suggested Absolute Chronology for the Prepalatial Phases of the Helladic Bronze Age

Relative Chronological Phase	Suggested Calendar Years B.C.
Early Helladic I	3100/3000–2650
Early Helladic II: Early	2650–2450/2350
(Lerna IIIA–B and Thebes group A)	
Early Helladic II: Late	2450/2350–2200/2150
(Lerna IIIC–D, Lefkandi I, and Thebes group B)	
Early Helladic III	2200/2150–2050/2000
Middle Helladic I	2050/2000–1950/1900
Middle Helladic II	1950/1900–1750/1720
Middle Helladic III	1750/1720–1680
Late Helladic I	1680–1600/1580
Late Helladic IIA	1600/1580–1520/1480
Late Helladic IIB	1520/1480–1445/1415

After S.W. Manning, *The Absolute Chronology of the Aegean Early Bronze Age: Archaeology, Radiocarbon, and History* (Sheffield 1993).

instance, ceramic specialists are constantly revising their opinions as to which types of pot belong when.[36] Some periods are poorly defined ceramically, particularly in areas where relatively few excavations have been undertaken.[37] Some periods, even if relatively well defined ceramically by several excavated sequences, may nevertheless be difficult to recognize from the kinds of ceramic fragments that a surface survey is likely to recover.[38] Finally, there is the fundamental question of how many sherds datable to a given period are considered necessary to prove that a particular site was in fact occupied during that period. Recognition of these problems involving the primary evidence for dating sites, along with explicit statements concerning what percentages of the finds actually recovered are presented in the final report and how these items were selected, should be considered extremely important in a surface survey's final publication.

Relative dating is critical for the sequencing of distinct patterns of settlement through time. Absolute dating, on the other hand, is significant for determining the pace of change in such patterns (table 2). There is currently considerable disagreement among Aegean prehistorians concerning absolute dating, both with respect to the date of the volcanic explosion of Santorini at some point in the second quarter of the second millennium B.C. and with regard to the beginning of the Early Bronze Age sometime in the second half of the fourth.[39] One result of this dis-

---

[36] E.g., the fine gray-burnished class of pottery generally known as Gray Minyan is ordinarily considered to be a hallmark of the MH period, but it was in fact first produced across a large portion of the central and southern Greek mainland in the EH III period (J.B. Rutter, "Fine Gray-burnished Pottery of the Early Helladic III Period: The Ancestry of Gray Minyan," *Hesperia* 52 [1983] 327–55; G.C. Nordquist, "A Note on EH III Fine Gray-burnished Pottery from Asine," *OpAth* 18 [1990] 241–43) and survives in considerable quantities in some areas into the LH I period (J.L. Davis, "Late Helladic I Pottery from Korakou," *Hesperia* 48 [1979] 234–63; *ATMA* 199–204). As a class, it therefore cannot be used as a simple means of identifying MH occupation, although it has often enough been so employed in the past.

[37] E.g., the lack of a well-established Neolithic through Early Iron Age ceramic sequence in west-central Greece accounts for the large numbers of sites located recently by the Aetolia Survey at which occupation can be no more closely dated than "prehistoric" (table 1, fig. 2a–b).

[38] J.B. Rutter, "Some Thoughts on the Analysis of Ceramic Data Generated by Site Surveys," in Keller and Rupp (supra n. 22) 137–42; Cherry, Davis, and Mantzourani (supra n. 21) 224; *Twilight* 194–95. Coarse wares may prove to be more helpful indicators of date than fine wares for a substantial percentage of the total sites located by intensive survey, even when detailed typologies of the vessels produced in such wares have yet to be established: D.C. Haggis and M.S. Mook, "The Kavousi Coarse Wares: A Bronze Age Chronology for Survey in the Mirabello Area, East Crete," *AJA* 97 (1993) 265–93.

[39] Supra n. 3. See also now S.W. Manning, *The Absolute Chronology of the Aegean Early Bronze Age: Archaeology, Radiocarbon, and History* (Monographs in Mediterranean Archaeology 1, Sheffield 1993) who, in contrast to the positions adopted by Warren and Hankey in *Chronology*, advocates a high dating for the Theran eruption and a low date for the beginning of the EBA. I am very grateful to Sturt Manning for assisting me with the selection of absolute date ranges to include in table 2. For another recently published survey of Aegean chronology that advocates a significantly higher date for the beginning of the EBA, see J.E. Coleman, "Greece and the Aegean from the Mesolithic to the End of the Early Bronze Age," in R.W. Ehrich ed., *Chronologies in Old World Archaeology*[3] (Chicago 1992) 1:247–79, 2:203–21. For additional titles documenting the current state of ferment in the absolute dating of the Aegean Bronze Age, see "RAP I" 736 and n. 160.

agreement over the length of various intervals of the Helladic relative chronological system will be that estimates of the number of sites occupied per unit time in a given area may vary appreciably. It is nevertheless true that displaying site densities diachronically in terms of the numbers of sites occupied per century is a far more satisfactory way to represent changes in such densities than the conventional bar graph that simply plots site numbers against archaeological periods, regardless of the highly variable duration of such periods.[40] The discriminating reader of the forthcoming final publications of intensive surveys executed during the 1980s will therefore have to pay as much attention to how issues of absolute chronology between 3500 and 1500 B.C. are treated as to how details of relative chronology are handled.

Defining a "site"—that is, distinguishing a concentration of artifactual debris from the blanket of similar man-made litter often referred to as "background noise," which covers virtually the entire Greek landscape—and establishing a site's limits, and hence size, have been central concerns of those practicing intensive survey on the Greek mainland from the beginning.[41] Those most familiar with the problems of site definition—that is, intensive surveyors themselves—candidly admit that site definition is as much an act of interpretation as of pure observation.[42] Since the methodology of site recognition is likely to be as project-specific as the reconstruction of the environment through time and the criteria employed to measure that time in both relative and absolute terms, we should once again expect final publications of intensive surveys to be explicit on the questions of how sites are distinguished and their extents measured. We have a further right to expect that equally explicit

criteria will be provided for the attribution of functions to sites and for the identification of site hierarchies. Of critical importance for such interpretations are assessments not merely of the size and environmental setting of each site but also of the significance of the artifacts recovered at each. For every chronologically discrete component recognized at a site, what are the numbers and functional ranges of these items, what are the relative frequencies of imported as opposed to local products, and are the imports likely to have come to the site as raw materials or as finished goods? The task of identifying imports should not be restricted to one or another artifactual class, although until recently such work has focused largely on fragmentary ceramic containers and chipped stone tools of obsidian.[43]

However legitimate it may be to expect the final reports on the intensive survey projects of the 1980s to be explicit about their methodologies and criteria on all these fronts, it is already clear from the preliminary reports in print that the survey strategies adopted in the field have varied considerably. It is virtually certain that the approaches adopted toward environmental reconstruction, chronology, and site definition and interpretation will mirror to some degree those differences in field techniques and that they will therefore themselves be quite variable. To what extent this variability will hamper the attempts of synthesists to undertake interregional comparisons of settlement patterns can hardly be predicted as yet. Aside from stressing the basic inadequacy of extensive survey data for such efforts, I have sought in the preceding pages merely to draw attention to some of the problems posed by the richer data from systematic and intensive surveys. I suspect that a valid compari-

---

[40] For the sensible suggestion that settlement density should be expressed in terms of sites occupied per unit time rather than per archaeological period, see *Twilight* 186. Even graphs such as van Andel et al. (supra n. 17) 125 fig. 15 or Runnels and van Andel (supra n. 17) 324 fig. 15, though they provide some estimate of each period's absolute duration, overemphasize changes in settlement pattern from period to period by representing the site numbers for each period in the form of a single bar.

[41] E.g., Cherry in Keller and Rupp (supra n. 22) 394–97; Bintliff and Snodgrass 1985 (supra n. 10) 127–37; Bintliff and Snodgrass 1988 (supra n. 10); Cherry et al. (supra n. 14) esp. 159–63; Wright et al. (supra n. 14) 603–17.

[42] Snodgrass and Cherry (supra n. 6) 12; M. Fotiadis, "Units of Data as Deployment of Disciplinary Codes," in J.-C. Gardin and C.S. Peebles eds., *Representations in Archaeology* (Bloomington 1992) 132–48.

[43] For provenience studies involving pottery, see the comprehensive review by R.E. Jones, *Greek and Cypriot Pottery:*

A Review of Scientific Studies (Athens 1986), to be supplemented by a few more recent studies: C.W. Zerner, "Middle and Late Helladic I Pottery from Lerna," *Hydra* 2 (1986) 58–74; M. Attas, J.M. Fossey, and L. Yaffe, "An Archaeometric Study of Early Bronze Age Pottery Production and Exchange in Argolis and Korinthia (Corinthia), Greece," *JFA* 14 (1987) 77–90; A.B. Knapp and J.F. Cherry, *Provenance Studies and Bronze Age Cyprus: Production, Exchange, and Politico-Economic Change* (Madison, Wis., forthcoming). For obsidian, see Torrence (supra n. 35). For andesite, see Runnels (supra n. 34) and Runnels and Cohen (supra n. 34). For metals, see Pernicka (supra n. 34) and Stos-Gale and Macdonald (supra n. 34). The materials used for most ground stone implements as well as the cherts used for much of the Bronze Age chipped stone toolkit on the Greek mainland remain underinvestigated insofar as provenience is concerned: see Runnels (infra n. 72) on distinct varieties of chert and their potential significance.

son of one intensive survey's data set with that from another will rarely be a simple or straightforward process.

A second area of intellectual inquiry in mainland Greek prehistory within which greatly increased activity may be expected in the near future is that of gender studies generally and the definition of women's special role in the transmission of material culture through time and across space in particular. The reasons for an increased emphasis on what may be considered by many to be simply contemporary feminism in archaeological garb are first, a significant rise in archaeological publications of all kinds devoted to exploring women's experiences in both the past and the present, and second, a growing interest within

Aegean prehistory specifically in industries that are likely to have been in the hands of women throughout much of the mainland Greek Bronze Age, notably weaving and pottery production.[44] To these may be added an enhanced emphasis of late on the roles played by women in prehistoric Aegean religion.[45]

THE EARLY BRONZE AGE (EARLY HELLADIC I– III, CA. 3100/3000–2050/2000 B.C.)

Enough comprehensive syntheses have been published over the past decade to provide the general reader with several detailed overviews of what is currently known about EH material culture, especially that of its most distinctive and best documented subdivision, the EH II phase.[46] In what follows, my goals

[44] With regard to the subjects of women's roles in Classical and prehistoric Greek antiquity, as well as in contemporary archaeology, I have benefited enormously from conversations with Shelby Brown and from reading her "Feminist Research in Archaeology: What Does It Mean? Why Is It Taking So Long?" in N.S. Rabinowitz and A. Richlin eds., *Feminist Theory and the Classics* (New York, forthcoming). From her extensive bibliography, I have selected the following titles as representative of the growing volume of literature on gender studies in archaeology generally: M.W. Conkey and J.D. Spector, "Archaeology and the Study of Gender," *Advances in Archaeological Method and Theory* 7 (1984) 1–38; L. Gibbs, "Identifying Gender Representation in the Archaeological Record: A Contextual Study," in I. Hodder ed., *The Archaeology of Contextual Meanings* (Cambridge 1987) 79–101; M. Ehrenberg, *Women in Prehistory* (London 1989); J.M. Gero and M.W. Conkey eds., *Engendering Archaeology: Women in Prehistory* (Cambridge, Mass. 1991); M.W. Conkey and S.W. Williams, "Original Narratives: The Political Economy of Gender in Archaeology," in M. di Leonardo ed., *Gender at the Crossroads of Knowledge: Feminist Anthropology in the Postmodern Era* (Berkeley 1991) 102–39; R. Gilchrist, "Women's Archaeology? Political Feminism, Gender Theory and Historical Revision," *Antiquity* 65 (1991) 495–501; E. Engelstad, "Images of Power and Contradiction: Feminist Theory and Post-processual Archaeology," *Antiquity* 65 (1991) 502–14; A. Wylie, "The Interplay of Evidential Constraints and Political Interests: Recent Archaeological Research on Gender," *AmerAnt* 57 (1992) 15–35.

For weaving in prehistoric Greece, see J. Carington Smith, *Spinning, Weaving and Textile Manufacture in Prehistoric Greece* (Diss. Univ. of Tasmania 1975); E.J.W. Barber, *Prehistoric Textiles: The Development of Cloth in the Neolithic and Bronze Ages* (Princeton 1991); J. Carington Smith, "Spinning and Weaving Equipment," in *Nichoria* 674–711; M. Beloyianni, "Αποτυπώματα πλέγματος στις βάσεις και στα πλευρά κεραμεικών αγγείων απο Τσούγκιζα (Νεμέας)," *AAA* (forthcoming), part of a Ph.D. dissertation entitled *Basketry and Matting in Prehistoric Greece*, in progress at the University of Athens. For women's roles in prehistoric pottery production on the Greek mainland, see H.B. Lewis, *The Manufacture of Early Mycenaean Pottery* (Diss. Univ. of Min-

nesota 1983; UMI 83-18093); T. Cullen, "Social Implications of Ceramic Style in the Neolithic Peloponnese," in W.D. Kingery ed., *Ancient Technology to Modern Science* 1 (Columbus 1985) 77–100; K.D. Vitelli, "Potters, Cooks, and Social Change," *AJA* 97 (1993) 343 (abstract); Vitelli, *Franchthi Neolithic Pottery* 1: *Classification and Ceramic Phases 1 and 2* (Bloomington 1993) xx, 217; Vitelli, *Shaping Clay, Shaping Culture: Early Potters and the Development of the Craft* (London, forthcoming).

[45] The greater quantity of representational art found on Crete and in the central Aegean islands than on the Greek mainland during the periods surveyed here explains why most of the recent literature on women's roles in Aegean prehistoric religion concerns Minoan and Cycladic rather than Helladic cult: R. Hägg, "Die göttliche Epiphanie im minoischen Ritual," *AM* 101 (1986) 41–62; W.-D. Niemeier, "Zur Deutung des Thronraumes im Palast von Knossos," *AM* 101 (1986) 63–95; N. Marinatos, "Role and Sex Division in Ritual Scenes in the Aegean," *Journal of Prehistoric Religion* 1 (1987) 23–34; L. Goodison, *Death, Women and the Sun: Symbolism of Regeneration in Aegean Religion* (*BICS* Suppl. 53, London 1989), reviewed by C. Renfrew in *Antiquity* 64 (1990) 969–70, and by T. Cullen in *JFA* 18 (1991) 498–501.

[46] R. Treuil, *Le Néolithique récent et le Bronze ancien égéens: Les problèmes stratigraphiques et chronologiques, les techniques, les hommes* (Paris 1983); D.J. Pullen, *Social Organization in Early Bronze Age Greece: A Multi-dimensional Approach* (Diss. Indiana Univ. 1985; UMI 85-16653); M. Wiencke, "Change in Early Helladic II," *AJA* 93 (1989) 495–509; M.B. Cosmopoulos, *The Early Bronze 2 in the Aegean* (*SIMA* 98, Jonsered 1991); *Twilight*. See the forthcoming reviews of Forsén's *Twilight* by myself and of Cosmopoulos's book by Forsén in *OpAth* (forthcoming). The chronological and spatial coverages of each of these five synthetic studies, though somewhat different, in combination provide very full coverage of the EH II and III periods; for recent developments affecting our understanding of the EH I period, see below pp. 759–61.

See also J. Maran, *Die deutschen Ausgrabungen auf der Pevkakia-Magula in Thessalien* III: *Die mittlere Bronzezeit* (Bonn 1992) I: 301–28, 335–59, 370 fig. 25; Manning (supra n. 39). Maran is working on a Habilitationschrift at the

are to identify the major achievements of EH scholarship over the past 15 years, to survey briefly those topics that have attracted the most attention in the recent literature, and to highlight certain areas of research that in my opinion deserve further attention.

One of the more significant advances in recent years has been a greatly improved understanding of the EH period in the southern and western Peloponnese, that is, throughout a good part of the region covered by this review that lies outside the so-called "heartland" of mainland Greek Bronze Age cultures,[47] the modern nomes of the Argolid, Corinthia, Attica, Boeotia, and Euboea. This improved knowledge, resulting from the publication of excavations at the sites of Kouphovouno and Ayios Stephanos in Laconia,[48] Voïdhokoilia in Messenia,[49] and Ayios Dhimitrios, Strephi, Olympia, and Elis in Elis,[50] will soon be further enhanced by the final publication of the Laconia Survey and by preliminary reports on the Pylos Project.[51] By contrast, the nomes of Arcadia in the center

of the Peloponnese and Achaea in the north continue to be poorly documented, despite recent reports of important discoveries at the sites of Sphakovouni and Steno in Arcadia and Aigion in Achaea.[52] North of the Isthmus of Corinth and outside of the "heartland," recent fieldwork involving the EH period has focused more on the location of new sites than on their excavation. Among the more promising of these are Mitrou in Locris, Amphissa in Phocis, and the underwater site at Platygiali near Astakos in Aetolia.[53]

The principal discoveries affecting our understanding of EH material culture, however, have as before been made in the northeastern Peloponnese and east-central Greece. Deep soundings as well as the exposure of substantial horizontal expanses of EH settlements at the major sites of Tiryns in the Argolid, Kolonna on Aegina, and Thebes in Boeotia have provided us with a series of settlement sequences that can be profitably compared with the heretofore paradigmatic stratification for the later EH and MH periods

---

University of Heidelberg with a working title of *Kulturwandel auf dem griechischen Festland und den Kykladen im späten dritten Jahrtausend v. Chr.*, scheduled to be published as a monograph upon its completion. I have not seen J. Renard, *Habitat et mode de vie dans le Peloponnèse au bronze ancien* (Diss. Université de Paris I 1991), cited in *Nestor* 19 (1992) item 920146.

[47] For the definition of a "heartland" of the cultures of the mainland Greek Bronze Age, a region to which his own study was limited, see Pullen (supra n. 46) 47–52.

[48] J. Renard, *Le site Néolithique et Helladique ancien de Kouphovouno (Laconie): Fouilles de O.-W. von Vacano (1941)* (*Aegaeum* 4, Liège 1989); R. Janko ed., *Excavations at Agios Stephanos in Lakonia* (London, forthcoming). For summaries of the EH occupations at both sites, see *Twilight* 105–106.

[49] The excavations conducted by Georgios S. Korres at this extremely important site have recently been summarized in English, with full references to the extensive preliminary reports in Greek: G.S. Korres, "Excavations in the Region of Pylos," in J.-P. Descoeudres ed., *ΕΥΜΟΥΣΙΑ. Ceramic and Iconographic Studies in Honour of Alexander Cambitoglou* (Sydney 1990) 1–11, esp. 2–5 for the EH period. See also the summary in *Twilight* 101–103.

[50] For Ayios Dhimitrios, see C. Zachos, *Ayios Dhimitrios, a Prehistoric Settlement in the Southwestern Peloponnesos: The Neolithic and Early Helladic Periods* (Diss. Boston Univ. 1987; UMI 87-04824). For Strephi, see Koumouzelis (supra n. 20) 27–55. For the two sites at Olympia, see Koumouzelis (supra n. 20) 125–91; J.B. Rutter, "A Group of Distinctive Pattern-decorated Early Helladic III Pottery from Lerna and Its Implications," *Hesperia* 51 (1982) 459–88, esp. 480–88; H. Kyrieleis, "Neue Ausgrabungen in Olympia," *AntW* 21 (1990) 177–88; *AR* 34 (1988) 27; 36 (1990) 30; and 37 (1991) 31. For the ancestry of the incised and impressed pottery that is particularly characteristic of EH III strata at these two Olympian sites, see further J. Maran, "Überlegungen

zur Abkunft der FH III-zeitlichen ritz- und einstichverzierten Keramik," *Hydra* 2 (1986) 1–28; Maran, "Ein Nachtrag zur FH III-zeitlichen ritz- und einstichverzierten Keramik," *Hydra* 3 (1987) 3–4. For Elis, see Koumouzelis (supra n. 20) 55–63; and M. Koumouzelis, "La tombe préhistorique d'Elis: Ses relations avec le Sud-Est Européen et les Cyclades," *AAA* 14 (1981) 265–72. See also the summaries of the EH occupation at all five sites in *Twilight* 84–95.

[51] Supra ns. 11 and 16. For an up-to-date assessment of Laconia in the Bronze Age, see Dickinson (supra n. 20).

[52] For the relative dearth of excavated sequences in Achaea and Arcadia, see *Twilight* 82–84 and 95–98, respectively. For preliminary notices on the excavations by T. Spyropoulos of a major settlement sequence at Sphakovouni and what are claimed to be six EH metallurgical furnaces at Steno, see *ArchDelt* 37B′ (1982) [1989] 116 and 120–21, respectively; see also "Chronique" 1987, 532 and 1990, 740 for the former, "Chronique" 1981, 792 and 1990, 740 as well as *AR* 37 (1991) 26 for the latter. Most of the rich assortment of artifactual material from Sphakovouni on display in the new Archaeological Museum in Tripolis appears to be of Neolithic rather than EH date. For Aigion, see the preliminary report by L. Papazoglou-Manioudake in *ArchDelt* 39B′ (1984) [1989] 94–95, 98, summarized in *AR* 38 (1992) 21.

[53] For Mitrou, see Fossey, *Opountian Lokris* (supra n. 19) 50. For Amphissa, see "Chronique" 1989, 628–29, based upon the preliminary report by G. Rethemiotakes in *ArchDelt* 35B′ (1980) [1988] 265–67. For Platygiali, see *AR* 33 (1987) 28; 35 (1989) 56; A. Delaporta, I. Spondyles, and Y. Baxevanakes, "Πρωτοελλαδικός οικισμός στο Πλατυγιαλί Αστάκου (πρώτες παρατηρήσεις)," *Ανθρωπολογικά Ανάλεκτα* 49 (1988) 7–19; "Platyiali-Astakos: A Submerged Early Helladic Site in Akarnania," *Enalia Annual* 1 (1990) 44–46.

excavated by Caskey at Lerna in the 1950s.[54] The final site report on the settlement at Lithares in Boeotia has furnished an unusually complete plan for an EH II village as well as copious artifactual evidence for the earlier stages of that particular chronological phase.[55] Reports on excavations at smaller-scale EH settlements at Rouph in Attica, Aetopetra and Tsoungiza in the Corinthia, and Kephalari Magoula in the Argolid have helpfully supplemented findings at the larger sites, especially in the cases of the last two sites with respect to the EH I phase.[56] The sites of Nea Makri in Attica and Vouliagmeni in the Corinthia have furnished useful new evidence on EH funerary behavior; Thorikos in southeastern Attica has provided the earliest definitive evidence for EH mining; and a bay on the north coast of the island of Dhokos,

just off the southeastern coast of the Argolid, may be the site of the earliest shipwreck yet located in the Aegean.[57] Finally, five subterranean chambers at Koropi in Attica filled with all sorts of EH II artifactual debris constitute a genuine riddle of a site insofar as function is concerned.[58]

Caskey's excavations at the Argive coastal site of Lerna, in concert with his supplementary excavations at Eutresis in Boeotia, continue to provide the chronological backbone for the Early Bronze Age throughout southern and central Greece.[59] But since the beginning of the EH period and the transition to it from the preceding Neolithic era were not represented at Lerna, the definition of the beginning of the Bronze Age has not been particularly clear in the Peloponnese. One result of this has been that practitioners

---

[54] For Kolonna, see H. Walter and F. Felten, *Alt-Ägina III.1: Die vorgeschichtliche Stadt: Befestigungen, Häuser, Funde* (Mainz 1981); *Twilight* 114–17; Maran (supra n. 46) 323–28.

For the recent excavations at Tiryns, see the series of excavation reports for the 1976–1981 excavation seasons published by K. Kilian in *AA* 1978, 449–70; 1979, 379–411; 1981, 149–94; 1982, 393–430; and 1983, 277–328, supplemented by the reports on the EH pottery recovered during four of these seasons by H.-J. Weisshaar in *AA* 1981, 220–56; 1982, 440–66; and 1983, 329–58. For the 1984 and 1985 seasons, see "Chronique" 1985, 776–78 and 1986, 689–91. The results of both the recent as well as previous excavations at the site, insofar as the EH period and the transition to MH are concerned, are helpfully summarized in *Twilight* 38–49. The classification of EH pottery employed at Tiryns has been critiqued by J.M. Fossey and M.K. Mogelonsky in "The Typology of Early Helladic Pottery: A Comparison of the Vouliagmeni (Perakhora)-Asine System with the Proposed Tiryns System," *PZ* 58 (1983) 106–13.

For Thebes, see K. Demakopoulou and D. Konsola, "Λείψανα πρωτοελλαδικού, μεσοελλαδικού και υστεροελλαδικού οικισμού στη Θήβα," *ArchDelt* 30A (1975) [1978] 44–89; Konsola, *Προμυκηναϊκή Θήβα: Χωροταξική και οικιστική διαρθρώση* (Athens 1981); T. Spyropoulos, *Αμφείον: Ερευνα και μελέτη του μνημείου του Αμφείου Θηβών* (Sparta 1981); S. Symeonoglou, *The Topography of Thebes from the Bronze Age to Modern Times* (Princeton 1985) esp. 15–19; Aravantinos (infra n. 62); J. Maran, "Die Schaftlochaxt aus dem Depotfund von Theben (Mittelgriechenland) und ihre Stellung im Rahmen der bronzezeitlichen Äxte Südosteuropas," *ArchKorrBl* 19 (1989) 129–36. The most important excavations for the EH period at Thebes since the publication of Konsola's 1981 synthesis and the termination of Symeonoglou's coverage in 1980 are those by V. Aravantinos at 26 Pelopidou and at the corner of Dirke and Eurydike streets (*ArchDelt* 37B' [1982] (1989) 165–68), by Aravantinos at 27 Pelopidou and in the Christodoulou plot on Oidipodos (*ArchDelt* 38B' [1983] (1989) 129–31), and by C. Piteros in the Liangas property at Oidipodos 1 (*ArchDelt* 38B' [1983] (1989) 131–34), all five of which are summarized in "Chronique" 1990, 763–66 and *AR* 37 (1991) 34–35. Also important for its stratification is the excavation of the Koropoule plot on the northwest flank of the Kadmeia reported by K. Demakopoulou (*ArchDelt* 33B' [1978] (1985)

108–12). For a convenient summary of what is presently known about the EH settlement history of Thebes, see *Twilight* 130–35; Maran (supra n. 46) 310–11.

[55] H. Tzavella-Evjen, Λιθαρές (Athens 1984); *Lithares, an Early Bronze Age Settlement in Boiotia* (Los Angeles 1985); "Lithares Revisited," in Fossey (supra n. 18) 5–12; *Twilight* 128–30.

[56] For Rouph, see M. Petritake, "Λείψανα πρωτοελλαδικού οικισμού στο Ρουφ," *ArchDelt* 35A (1980) [1986] 147–85. For Aetopetra, see E. Chatzipouliou-Kallire, "Λείψανα πρωτοελλαδικού και μεσοελλαδικού οικισμού στο λόφο Αετόπετρα: Πρώτα αποτελέσματα δοκιμαστικής ανασκαφικής έρευνας," *ArchDelt* 33A (1978) [1985] 325–36. For Tsoungiza, see D.J. Pullen, "The Early Bronze Age Settlement on Tsoungiza Hill, Ancient Nemea," in *L'habitat* 331–46; Wright et al. (supra n. 14) 625–29. For Kephalari Magoula, see Dousougli (infra n. 60) 173–75, 199–204. For convenient summaries of the discoveries at these four sites, see *Twilight* 110, 72, 70–71, and 49–50, respectively.

[57] For chamber tombs at Nea Makri and Vouliagmeni, see E. Theocharake's report in *ArchDelt* 35B' (1980) [1988] 82–84 and E. Chatzipouliou-Kallire, "An Early Helladic II Tomb by Lake Vouliagmeni, Perachora," *BSA* 78 (1983) 369–75, respectively. For the EH mine at Thorikos, see Spitaels (supra n. 34). For the possible shipwreck off the north coast of Dhokos, see G.A. Papathanasopoulos, "Το πρωτοελλαδικό ναυάγιο της Δοκού," *AAA* 9 (1976) 17–23; N. Tsouchlos et al., "Dokos Project," *Enalia Annual* 1 (1990) 10–43; G. Papathanasopoulos et al., "Dokos 1990," *Enalia Annual* 2 (1990) [1992] 4–38; *AR* 38 (1992) 10.

[58] O. Kakavoyanni, "Subterranean Chambers of Early Helladic Date at Koropi, Attica," in *EHAU* 37–39; "Πρωτοελλαδικός οικισμός στο Κορωπί," in *Wace and Blegen*.

[59] The classic expressions of the evidence from these sites (J.L. Caskey, "The Early Helladic Period in the Argolid," *Hesperia* 29 [1960] 285–303; J.L. and E.G. Caskey, "The Earliest Settlements at Eutresis: Supplementary Excavations, 1958," *Hesperia* 29 [1960] 126–67) were the bases for the summaries of the period's chronology as presented in E. Vermeule, *Greece in the Bronze Age* (Chicago 1964) 27–44 and by Caskey himself in *CAH* I, pt. 2³ (1971) 777–93. For the continuing importance of these two sites into the 1990s, see, e.g., Maran (supra n. 46) 302–309, 335–41.

of intensive survey have often not been able to date site occupations any more closely than "Final Neolithic to EH I," and consequently the definition of the transition from the Neolithic to the Early Bronze Age in terms of changes in settlement patterns has been blurred. The recent success of Dousougli, Weisshaar, and Pullen in isolating a distinctive ceramic inventory characteristic of the later EH I phase in the Argolid and the Corinthia marks an important step toward bringing this transition into sharper focus. Defined through excavations at Kephalari Magoula and Tsoungiza and by large collections of surface materials at Makrovouni and Talioti, this "Talioti" ceramic assemblage is important not only in chronological but also in spatial terms. Since it differs appreciably from the contemporary assemblage recovered at Eutresis, which has for so long defined the EH I phase for the entire Helladic mainland, it makes possible the recognition of regional ceramic types for the first time in this earliest phase of the Bronze Age.[60]

By far the best-known subdivision of the mainland Greek Early Bronze Age is that termed EH II. The broad outlines of cultural change during this interval of some three to four centuries have recently been sketched by Wiencke, who discerns within it two principal stages of development.[61] Peculiar to the latter is a building form, variously termed the "corridor house" or the House of Tiles type, which has been recognized over the past decade at some half-dozen or more sites from Thebes in Boeotia to Akovitika in Messenia (fig. 3).[62] Such structures exhibit a characteristic ground plan and elevation: rectangular, freestanding, and composed of a linear series of square to rectangular halls, they are flanked on the long sides by corridors, which often serve as stairwells leading up to a second story. They also share a number of other features, such as relatively high and broad socles of fieldstones, rectangular rooftiles of terracotta and occasionally of schist, and aligned off-center doorways. Unlike the later Minoan and Mycenaean traditions of monumental architecture or that of contemporary Troy, this newly recognized EH II tradition makes no use of cut stone masonry nor of half-timbered construction. Aside from rectangular corridor houses, it features fortifications (as at Lerna and Thebes, and possibly at Kolonna as well), a very large cylindrical building, the so-called Rundbau at Tiryns, which may have functioned as a communal granary, and a few large, circular tumuli whose function is at present uncertain.[63] In contradistinction to the earliest forms of monumental architecture in Minoan Crete, this early tradition of large-scale buildings on the Greek mainland seems to consist exclusively of structures for the living: monumental tombs are unattested until the EH III phase, at which point the first of the burial tumuli appear; they go on to become quite common in the subsequent MH period.[64] Ordinary EH II domestic architecture has enough in

---

[60] A. Dousougli, "Makrovouni–Kefalari Magoula–Talioti: Bemerkungen zu den Stufen EH I und II in der Argolis," *PZ* 62 (1987) 164–220; H.-J. Weisshaar, "Die Keramik von Talioti," *Tiryns* XI (Mainz 1990) 1–34; D.J. Pullen, "The Earlier Phases of the Early Bronze Age at Tsoungiza Hill, Ancient Nemea, Greece," *AJA* 92 (1988) 252 (abstract). For a significantly different EH I ceramic assemblage typical of the southern Argolid, which may represent an earlier stage of EH I in the northeastern Peloponnese, see D.J. Pullen, "The Early Bronze Age in the Southern Argolid: Argo-Corinthian and Saronic Gulf Cultural Spheres," *AJA* 88 (1984) 257 (abstract).

[61] Wiencke (supra n. 46). For the absolute duration of EH II, see Manning (supra n. 39).

[62] P.G. Themelis, "Early Helladic Monumental Architecture," *AM* 99 (1984) 335–51; Pullen (supra n. 46) 263–67; M.H. Wiencke, "Building BG at Lerna," in *EHAU* 41–45; V.L. Aravantinos, "The EH II Fortified Building at Thebes: Some Notes on Its Architecture," in *EHAU* 57–63; D.J. Pullen, "A 'House of Tiles' at Zygouries? The Function of Monumental Early Helladic Architecture," in *EHAU* 79–84; S. Hiller, "Early and Late Helladic 'Megara': Questions of Architectural Continuity in Bronze Age Greece," in *EHAU* 85–89; J.W. Shaw, "The Early Helladic II Corridor House: Development and Form," *AJA* 91 (1987) 59–79; Wiencke (supra n. 46) 496, 503–505; J.W. Shaw, "The Early Helladic II Corridor House: Problems and Possibilities," in *L'habitat* 183–94.

[63] For the Rundbau, see P. Haider, "Zum frühhellad-

ischen Rundbau in Tiryns," in *Forschungen und Funde: Festschrift B. Neutsch* (Innsbruck 1980) 157–72; K. Kilian, "The Circular Building at Tiryns," in *EHAU* 65–71. For EH II tumuli, see n. 64.

[64] The well-known R-graves on Lefkas constitute the single undeniable exception to this generalization (K. Branigan, "The Round Graves of Levkas Reconsidered," *BSA* 70 [1975] 37–49; S. Müller, "Les tumuli helladiques: où? quand? comment?" *BCH* 113 [1989] 1–42, esp. 5–15; *Twilight* 235–37). Their typological anomalousness is likely to be a reflection of their location at the northwestern limits of the area surveyed here, as far away from any known corridor house as is possible within this region.

There is no evidence that the newly discovered EH II tumulus within the Altis at Olympia served a funerary purpose (J. Rambach, pers. comm., August 1992; see also Kyrieleis, supra n. 50).

Both the date and the function of the so-called Ampheion at Thebes, a plundered cist within a very large tumulus, continue to be disputed (Spyropoulos [supra n. 54]; I. and E. Loucas, "La tombe des jumeaux divins Amphion et Zethos et la fertilité de la terre béotienne," in *Thanatos* 95–106; *Twilight* 133–34, with extensive references to assessments of this monument in publications dating between 1976 and 1991). Thus this structure, however impressive, hardly constitutes convincing evidence for the existence of monumental funerary architecture in the EH II "heartland."

For the most recent synthetic treatment of mainland Greek tumuli throughout the Bronze Age, see Müller (supra). For

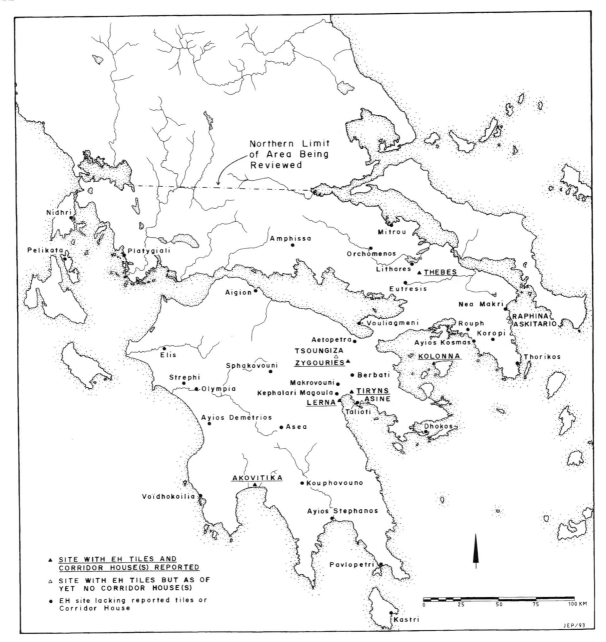

Fig. 3. Locations of important sites of the Early Helladic period. (Incorporating data from *EHAU* figs. 2–3)

common with the corridor house in terms of materials and specific design features to have persuaded most specialists that the corridor house is an indigenous

development. On the other hand, there is as yet no real consensus concerning the function or range of functions that it may have had.[65] During the EH II

---

the suggestion that the earliest and largest EH tumuli known—those of EH II date in the Altis at Olympia and covering the House of the Tiles at Lerna, and perhaps the Ampheion at Thebes—served a ritual rather than funerary function, see *Twilight* 232–37.

[65] See my review of *EHAU* in *BibO* 45 (1988) 661–68 for a more extended treatment of several of the issues associated with EH II monumental architecture and EH urbanization.

For a significant addition to our understanding of EH architecture since the publication of *EHAU*, see Pullen (supra n. 56). For a recent reexamination of how the sealings from room XI of the House of the Tiles may have been used, see S.T. Stewart, "Bureaucracy and Packaging at Lerna: Evidence from the Clay Sealings in the House of the Tiles at Lerna," *AJA* 92 (1988) 253 (abstract).

phase, individual buildings exposed in excavations, as well as whole sites whose boundaries have been established by surface survey, vary sufficiently in size to show clearly that a hierarchy of such units existed.[66] Konsola, employing a multivariate approach to investigate the degrees of urbanization manifested in excavated EH settlements, has detected a differently defined hierarchy among EH II sites, which she considers to be absent in both the preceding EH I and succeeding EH III phases.[67]

The nature of the transition between the EH II and EH III phases has been the focus of considerable discussion and debate over the past 15 years. At the time of the *Gazetteer's* publication, analysis of this transition was typically focused on what were perceived as profound differences distinguishing EH III material culture from that of the preceding phase. The type site for this transition in the northeastern Peloponnese was Lerna, where, in addition to dramatic changes in much of the artifactual assemblage, a burnt destruction horizon separated these two phases. J.L. Caskey, the excavator of Lerna, had invoked an invasion of the Peloponnese by warlike newcomers to explain this sudden change in material culture.[68] The discovery of a seemingly unrelated EBA assemblage in the mid-1960s in the basal levels of a deep sounding at Lefkandi on the south-central coast of Euboea initially had little impact on interpretations of the EH II–III transition. Even though he correctly identified the relative chronological position of this new assemblage (which he christened "Lefkandi I") and recognized its western Anatolian affinities, Renfrew in his extremely influential survey and interpretation of the Aegean Early Bronze Age saw

no significant formal connection between it and the assemblages that he considered to precede (EH II = "Korakou culture") and follow (EH III = "Tiryns culture") it.[69] In spite of his predisposition to avoid using invasionist hypotheses to explain cultural change, Renfrew frankly admitted that the shift in material culture was so pronounced and abrupt in the case of the EH II–III transition that it stood out as "more marked than any other subsequently seen in Greek prehistory, or any previously documented since the development of farming life."[70] Thus, although by the later 1970s the practice of invoking invasions was generally frowned upon as an old-fashioned and oversimplified interpretative strategy, in this particular instance that explanation still attracted a wide following.[71]

But scholarly opinion on this issue began to shift in the very year of the *Gazetteer's* publication. First, attention was directed toward some of the continuities in material culture between the EH II and III phases at Lerna, initially in terms of the pottery of the two periods and subsequently in terms of the chipped stone tools and terracotta anchor-shaped objects of uncertain use.[72] Second, and far more importantly, stratified settlement sequences spanning the EH II–III transition were published from the major sites of Kolonna on Aegina, Thebes in Boeotia, and Tiryns in the Argolid, which revealed that the abrupt and pervasive changes in material culture combined with a violent destruction that characterized this transition at Lerna were anything but typical.[73] At Tiryns, within sight of Lerna across the Gulf of Argos, the German excavations of the late 1970s and early 1980s demonstrated that even a site within the immediate vicinity

[66] For the existence of a hierarchy of settlements during the EH II period, see Pullen (supra n. 46) 344–64; Runnels and van Andel (supra n. 17), esp. 311–14; Kilian (supra n. 20) 63; *Twilight* 189–90, 192. The number of steps in this hierarchy is disputed, two (Pullen) or three (Runnels and van Andel) being identified in the southern Argolid and as many as four in the main Argive plain (Kilian). For the notion that the presence of a corridor house at a site is in and by itself an indicator of a site's loftier position within a regional settlement hierarchy, see Pullen (supra n. 46) 359.

[67] D. Konsola, *Η πρώιμη αστικοποίηση στους πρωτοελλαδικούς οικισμούς* (Athens 1984), summarized by Pullen (supra n. 46) 359–63, and applied diachronically to the three phases of the EH period in D. Konsola, "Stages of Urban Transformation in the Early Helladic Period," in *EHAU* 9–19. The hierarchy identified by Konsola, consisting of just two tiers, is limited to excavated sites of the EH II period. Pullen (supra n. 46) 355, on the other hand, argues on the basis of site size alone for the existence of a two-tiered hierarchy among sites explored by surface survey in the southern Argolid as early as EH I. Mee (pers. comm.) has

suggested that a similar two-tiered settlement hierarchy existed on Methana in the EH period, again on the basis of site size.

[68] Caskey (supra n. 59) 299–302, reiterated with flourishes by Vermeule (supra n. 59) 29–31.

[69] Renfrew, *Emergence* (supra n. 24) 103–105, for an assessment of the "Lefkandi I" assemblage based on the work of David French, who drew attention to its potential significance as early as 1968 (*Twilight* 204).

[70] Renfrew, *Emergence* (supra n. 24) 116.

[71] *Gazetteer* 373–74; S. Hood's paper, "Evidence for Invasions in the Aegean Area at the End of the Early Bronze Age," in G. Cadogan ed., *The End of the Early Bronze Age in the Aegean* (Leiden 1986) 31–68, though published in the mid-1980s, was actually delivered at Cincinnati in 1979.

[72] J.B. Rutter, *Ceramic Change in the Aegean Early Bronze Age* (Los Angeles 1979); C.N. Runnels, "The Bronze Age Flaked-Stone Industries from Lerna: A Preliminary Report," *Hesperia* 54 (1985) 357–91; H.-J. Weisshaar, "Ägäische Tonanker," *AM* 95 (1980) 33–49.

[73] See supra n. 54.

could produce contemporary, yet significantly different assemblages of pottery from those in use at Lerna, and this within a stratified sequence that also featured at least two destruction levels, one *at* and one shortly *after* the end of the EH II phase. At Kolonna, the Austrian excavators claimed that the EH II to III transition at their site was gradual rather than abrupt and featured a major destruction horizon not at or near the end of the EH II phase but rather toward the end of EH III (Kolonna V). Finally, at Thebes, excavations by the Greek Archaeological Service have revealed a culturally distinct horizon between levels characterized by typical EH II and EH III artifactual types. This intermediate horizon, in which EH II ceramic forms occur together with forms typical of the "Lefkandi I" assemblage, has been termed "group B" by Konsola to distinguish it from the canonical EH II pottery typical of "group A" deposits at Thebes.[74] Although burnt destruction levels occur in both "group B" and subsequent EH III strata at Thebes, it has thus far been impossible to establish whether these destructions were site-wide or, instead, more localized events.[75]

Shortly after I was given the responsibility of publishing the EH III pottery from Lerna and just before the results of these important new excavations at Tiryns, Kolonna, and Thebes began to be reported, I suggested that many of the new features that distinguish the EH III pottery of Lerna IV from that of the preceding EH II settlement, or Lerna III, owed their existence to a process of fusion between the standard EH II ceramic repertoire and that of the "Lefkandi I" assemblage.[76] One of the weaknesses of Caskey's invasion theory had been that much of the material culture of those whom he identified as invaders, namely the EH III inhabitants of Lerna IV, had no obvious antecedents either locally within the northeastern Peloponnese or anywhere outside that area.[77] In proposing that the EH III ceramic assemblage at Lerna was a hybrid product of originally distinct EH II and "Lefkandi I" ceramic traditions, I was in effect suggesting that Caskey's invaders could be traced back to central Greece.[78] For there, not only at Thebes but at coastal sites in eastern Attica (Raphina) and on both Aegina (Kolonna) and Euboea (Lefkandi, Manika), as well as at other inland sites in Boeotia (Eutresis, Orchomenos), the EH II and "Lefkandi I" ceramic traditions have repeatedly been shown to have coexisted for some time before the appearance of an EH III ceramic assemblage identifiable as the merged product of these two. By contrast, nowhere in the Peloponnese has the "Lefkandi I" ceramic assemblage been attested. Thus, if the "Lefkandi I" assemblage is admitted to be ancestral to the EH III ceramic types of both the Peloponnese (Argolid, Corinthia, Achaea, Arcadia, and Elis) and central Greece (Boeotia, Attica, Phocis, and Euboea), the fusion process must have taken place somewhere in central Greece. How long this process lasted, and what the resulting hybrid ceramic inventory of the EH III phase signifies in human terms, are questions for which answers must await the discovery and publication of a good deal

---

[74] Konsola (supra n. 54) 119–23, 143–46.

[75] Relatively few of the finds associated with these various destruction deposits have as yet been published. In addition, the locations at which these discoveries have been made are fairly small building lots scattered throughout the heart of modern Thebes, in the southern part of the ancient city's acropolis known as the Kadmeia (*Twilight* 131–33).

[76] Rutter (supra ns. 36 and 72), summarized in *Twilight* 204–10. This view is presented in considerably greater detail in J.B. Rutter, *Lerna* III: *The Pottery of Lerna IV* (Princeton, forthcoming).

[77] Renfrew, *Emergence* (supra n. 24) 116; Dickinson (infra n. 122) 32.

[78] For an invasionist interpretation of the artifactual novelties appearing in central Greece at the end of the EH II period, see S. Hiller, "Zum archäologischen Evidenz der Indoeuropäisierung Griechenlands," in *Symposia Thracica* A' (1982) 183–210; "Die Ethnogenese der Griechen aus der Sicht der Vor- und Frühgeschichte," in W. Bernhard and A. Kandler-Palsson eds., *Ethnogenese europäischer Völker* (Stuttgart 1986) 21–37. For the view that "Lefkandi I" ceramic types are indicative of population movements into the Cyclades, Euboea, and east-central Greece from western Anatolia in general, or specifically from southwestern Anatolia,

or from one or more of the large islands in the northeastern Aegean (e.g., Lemnos), see, respectively, R.L.N. Barber, *The Cyclades in the Bronze Age* (London 1987) 28–29, 137–39; M. Mellink, "The Early Bronze Age in West Anatolia: Aegean and Asiatic Correlations," in Cadogan (supra n. 71) 139–52; and C. Doumas, "Early Bronze Age in the Cyclades: Continuity or Discontinuity," in *Problems* 21–29. For an interpretation of these types as trade goods, see J.L. Davis, "Perspectives on the Prehistoric Cyclades," in P. Getz-Preziosi, *Early Cycladic Art in North American Collections* (Richmond 1987) 4–45, esp. 32. For a noncommittal description of the new ceramic features that accompany "Lefkandi I" pottery types in the stratified EBA sequence at Ayia Irini on Keos, see D.E. Wilson and M. Eliot, "Ayia Irini, Period III: The Last Phase of Occupation at the E.B.A. Settlement," in J.A. Macgillivray and R.L.N. Barber eds., *The Prehistoric Cyclades* (Edinburgh 1984) 78–87; for the hybrid Cycladic-Helladic nature of the EBA pottery from this site, as well as for the suggestion that its inhabitants played the role of middlemen in a trade in metals between the Laurion area of southeastern Attica and the Cyclades to the east and south of Keos, see D.E. Wilson, "Kea and East Attike in Early Bronze II: Beyond Pottery Typology," in Fossey (supra n. 24) 35–49.

more evidence. For the time being, it seems clear from the multiple building levels represented by the "Lefkandi I" strata at Lefkandi itself, as well as from the number of EBA levels in which "Lefkandi I" ceramic types occur at Pefkakia on the Thessalian coast just south of Volos, that the "Lefkandi I" and later EH II ceramic assemblages were in concurrent use for as much as a century or even longer.[79]

Whether or not the appearance of EH III pottery should be interpreted as the result of an invasion depends, among other things, upon the extent to which the new features of this ceramic assemblage can be shown to be associated with other artifactual novelties, signs of violence, indications from collections of human bone for the introduction of a new population element, or evidence for a change in language.[80] Forsén has recently conducted a thoroughgoing review of Caskey's hypothesis that the Peloponnese was invaded at the end of the EH II phase by warlike newcomers and subsequently infiltrated at the transition to the MH period by smaller and less bellicose human groups.[81] From a detailed examination of the evidence from 89 excavated sites in the Peloponnese and east-central Greece, she concludes that destruction levels that may be closely dated and interpreted with some confidence as site-wide do not cluster either spatially or temporally. Rather, such destructions seem to occur haphazardly more or less throughout the EH II and EH III phases. Thus, Caskey's contention that the burning of the House of the Tiles at Lerna was just one of many in a widespread horizon of more or less contemporary destructions does not stand up to close scrutiny. Much the same is true of the set of artifactual novelties that Caskey attributed to his warlike invaders, items such as apsidal buildings, terracotta "anchors," stone shaft-hole hammer-axes, and large non-funerary tumuli such as that raised over the House of the Tiles. Not only did these distinctive artifactual types appear at different times in different regions within the larger study area but they appear to have entered the area from several different directions. It is consequently difficult to associate them as a group with any single population movement.

In showing that Caskey's criteria for an invasion of the northeastern Peloponnese, based on his discoveries at Lerna, do not apply at other sites even within the Argolid, much less further afield, Forsén's study should mark the starting point of a new generation of investigations into the significance of the EH II–III transition. Full publication of the relevant strata at Lerna, Tiryns, Thebes, and Lefkandi is clearly a prerequisite to further progress. The suggestion has been made, on the basis of the stratification observed at Tiryns, that Lerna may have been abandoned for a short but critical interval during this transition.[82] The argument in favor of a brief hiatus in Lerna's occupation would have been far stronger had the Tirynthian evidence been supported by that from Asine and Berbati, as was originally claimed but as has since been disproved.[83] In point of fact, there is probably no hiatus in settlement at either Lerna or Tiryns at any point during this transition. Instead, the significant differences in material culture between the two at various stages during the transition probably reflect the differing circumstances in which the change in question occurred. And if these circumstances could differ appreciably between two sites less than five hours' walk apart, they could presumably differ even more noticeably at sites further removed from each other. It is therefore a mistake to identify *any* particular site during this period of transition as

---

[79] E. Christmann, "Die Magula von Pevkakia (Volos) und die Frühbronzezeit in Thessalien: Chronologie und externe Kontakte," in *La Thessalie: Quinze années de recherche 1975–1990* (Lyons, forthcoming), abstracted from his 1990 dissertation for the University of Heidelberg entitled *Die Keramik der frühen Bronzezeit von der Pevkakia-Magula bei Volos, Thessalien;* also Manning (supra n. 39).

[80] For an investigation of the kinds of evidence that might warrant invoking the invasion hypothesis in a prehistoric setting, see I. Rouse, *Migrations in Prehistory: Inferring Population Movement from Cultural Remains* (New Haven 1986). For an evaluation of the evidence for changes in language toward the end of the Aegean EBA, see A. Morpurgo Davies, "The Linguistic Evidence: Is There Any?" in Cadogan (supra n. 71) 93–123. For recent book-length surveys on the question of when either Indo-Europeans or Greek-speakers or both first appeared in Greece, see M. Sakellariou, *Les Proto-*

Grecs (Athens 1981); C. Renfrew, *Archaeology and Language: The Puzzle of Indo-European Origins* (London 1987); Drews (supra n. 32); J.P. Mallory, *In Search of the Indo-Europeans: Language, Archaeology and Myth* (London 1989). See also the group of articles in *Antiquity* 62 (1988) responding to Renfrew's book: C. Ehret, "Language Change and the Material Correlates of Language and Ethnic Shift," M. and K.V. Zvelebil, "Agricultural Transition and Indo-European Dispersals," and A. and S. Sherratt, "The Archaeology of Indo-European: An Alternative View," pp. 564–74, 574–83, and 584–95, respectively. I have not seen A. Martinet, "The Indo-Europeans and Greece," *Diogenes* 145 (1989) 1–16.

[81] *Twilight.*

[82] Weisshaar 1982 (supra n. 54) 462–63.

[83] D.J. Pullen, "Asine, Berbati, and the Chronology of Early Bronze Age Greece," *AJA* 91 (1987) 533–44.

the type-site in terms of the stratification at which all other sites can be relatively dated.[84] In the short term, correlating occupational strata during this period of transition at any two sites may pose some serious difficulties. Yet in the long term, the very differences between the transitional processes at a growing number of sites should prove to be far more informative concerning the nature and pace of, and ultimately the reasons for, that transition than a greater degree of homogeneity in material culture would ever have been.

We should therefore welcome the variety in the stratigraphic sequences spanning the EH II–III transition that we have been finding rather than insist that they be uniform. At the same time, we should be doing our best to recover more in the way of non-artifactual data, which has all too often been ignored. For example, human skeletal remains of this period, with the exception of the bones from two or three cemeteries, have not been systematically collected.[85] Yet they may provide us with the best evidence available, particularly as early as the third millennium B.C., for the detection of intrusive population elements. Greater attention paid to the recovery of faunal and botanical remains might also pay rich dividends. We already have reason to believe that the domesticated horse first appeared in southern Greece

in the EH III period. It is not unreasonable to expect that the introduction of this domesticate might have entailed changes in the ranges of plants and animals being exploited by the inhabitants of this area. Alternatively, perhaps the appearance of the horse is more significant for the changes it accompanied than for the changes it may have caused.[86] On another front, the dramatic differences between the EH II and EH III repertoires of cooking pottery suggest that a shift in the manner of food preparation, possibly signaling a change in diet as well, may have been a facet of this cultural transition.[87] Finally, a good deal of evidence from the Argolid for a major episode of alluviation in the later Early Bronze Age indicates that important changes in the environment may have occurred, whether natural and the result of a climatological shift or anthropogenic and the consequences of a failure to make adequate provision against topsoil runoff through the construction and maintenance of terrace walls.[88]

EH tombs and burial customs, though occasionally the subject of synthetic analyses, have not attracted very much attention for the simple reason that EH tombs are not very numerous and rarely contain very much in the way of grave goods.[89] The vast majority of known EH tombs date from the EH II phase; EH III tombs are rare, especially those of adults, and EH

---

[84] The most useful variety of chronological chart should thus be of the sort published recently by Maran (supra n. 46) 370 fig. 25, in which the stratigraphic sequences at eight different sites are correlated without any single site being accorded greater significance. For a similar emphasis on the need to get away from dependence on a single site and instead to rely upon numerous localized sequences based on settlement stratigraphy, see "RAP I" 753–56.

[85] For studies of EH human remains published during the past 15 years, see N.I. Xirotiris, "The Indo-Europeans in Greece: An Anthropological Approach," *JIES* 8 (1980) 201–10; J.H. Musgrave and S.P. Evans, "By Strangers Honor'd: A Statistical Study of Ancient Crania from Crete, Mainland Greece, Cyprus, Israel and Egypt," *Journal of Mediterranean Anthropology and Archaeology* 1 (1981) 50–107; M. Fountoulakis, "Το ανθρωπολογικό υλικό της Μάνικας Χαλκίδας," in A. Sampson, *Μάνικα: Μία πρωτοελλαδική πόλη στην Χαλκίδα* (Chalkis 1985) 393–458; Fountoulakis, "Some Unusual Burial Practices in the Early Helladic Necropolis of Manika," in *Thanatos* 29–33. For later Bronze Age human remains, see S.C. Bisel and J.L. Angel, "Health and Nutrition in Mycenaean Greece: A Study in Human Skeletal Remains," in *Contributions* 197–210; S.C. Bisel, "The Human Skeletal Remains," in *Nichoria* 345–58.

[86] For the arrival of the horse in the Bronze Age Aegean, see supra n. 32.

[87] Among those vessels identifiable from their coarse red-

dish-brown fabric and fire-blackened surfaces as cooking pottery, common EH II shapes are hole-mouthed jars, deep ring-based bowls with vertical or incurving upper profiles, shallow baking dishes, and stands. In the EH III ceramic repertoire, baking dishes, stands, and ring bases have all disappeared; the common types are wide-mouthed jars with everted rims, either without handles or with a single vertical strap to the shoulder; also quite frequent are pedestal-footed cups with multiply perforated bodies, rim-handled wide-mouthed jars decorated with coarse incisions, and shoulder-handled cups which are essentially miniature versions of the shoulder-handled jars (Rutter [supra n. 76 and infra n. 110]). No frequently found shape is common to both the EH II and EH III inventories of cooking pottery.

[88] van Andel, Zangger, and Demitrack (supra n. 31) 382–85; van Andel and Zangger (supra n. 31) 145–48.

[89] For EH tombs in general, see Pullen (supra n. 46) 88–156, summarized in D.J. Pullen, "Mortuary Practices in Early Bronze Age Greece: Identifying Patterns of Prehistoric Behavior," *AJA* 90 (1986) 178 (abstract); D.J. Pullen, "Early Helladic Burials at Asine and Early Bronze Age Mortuary Practices," in *Celebrations* 9–12. For the large numbers of tombs excavated over the past decade at Manika on Euboea, some quite richly furnished, see "RAP I" 716–19 and ns. 63, 68. For tumulus and intramural burials at the end of the EH period, see *Twilight* 232–40.

I tombs are virtually nonexistent. When one considers how much of our appreciation of both Early Minoan (EM) and Early Cycladic (EC) material culture stems from discoveries made in the tombs and cemeteries of Crete and the central Aegean islands, one is compelled to wonder whether the Helladic mainland may not have been equally rich in terms of representational art or artifacts produced from metal or exotic stones.

The nature of EH II representational art has rarely been explored, probably because of a commonly held perception that not very much of it exists.[90] But the corpus of EH II representational art has been sufficiently augmented over the past 15 years by finds of terracotta objects from settlement contexts that its general character and the ways in which it differs from contemporary art on Crete and in the Cyclades have become clearer. Perhaps the most numerous items within this enlarged corpus are figurines of quadrupeds, sheep and cattle.[91] A cache of bull figurines found at Lithares, taken as evidence for a shrine in preliminary reports, is no longer so interpreted in the site's final publication. This change of opinion, reflecting an altogether appropriate degree of caution on the part of the excavator, draws attention to how little is known about EH II religion, a topic conspic-

Fig. 4. Terracotta figurine fragment of a yoked pair (?) of oxen, from Tsoungiza. (After D.J. Pullen, *AJA* 96 [1992] 50, fig. 1)

uously absent from general surveys of the period.[92] A recently discovered fragment of a bovid figurine from Tsoungiza (fig. 4) has been reasonably interpreted as part of what was once a yoked pair of oxen.[93] Whatever its original function, this humble fragment provides us with the earliest evidence from anywhere in the Aegean for the use of oxen as draft animals, almost certainly to pull a plow.

[90] See M.H. Wiencke, "Art and the World of the Early Bronze Age," in Cadogan (supra n. 71) 69–92, and M.B. Cosmopoulos, "The Development of Iconography in the Early Bronze 2 Aegean," in *Iconography* 87–96 for such analyses, which, however, are not restricted to representational art. For figurines and models as well as miniature containers, see now C. Marangou, *EIΔΩΛIA: Figurines et miniatures du Néolithique récent et du Bronze ancien en Grèce* (*BAR-IS* 576, Oxford 1992). Whether or not EH II representational art flourished in media and forms (e.g., stone and metal vessels, jewelry, seals, and weapons) likely to be found only in tombs is a question that cannot yet be answered with any confidence in view of the relatively small number of EH II tombs that have been excavated and published, particularly in areas of the mainland exhibiting little contact with, and hence influence from, the Cyclades. Pullen's 1985 review of the evidence (supra n. 89) makes abundantly clear that the only site in the Peloponnese at which substantial numbers of EH tombs have been found is Pavlopetri in southeastern Laconia. These tombs have not been excavated, however, so their dating to the EH period rests entirely on their form and we are ignorant of their contents. By contrast, a number of fairly large EH II cemeteries in Attica (Aghios Kosmas, Tsepi), Boeotia (Lithares, Likeri, Paralimni), and Euboea (Manika) have been excavated. The finds from these central Greek tombs, when published, typically resemble those from contemporary Cycladic cist graves and occasionally contain anthropomorphic stone or bone figurines (e.g.,

"RAP I" figs. 10–11).
[91] W.W. Phelps, "Prehistoric Figurines from Corinth," *Hesperia* 56 (1987) 233–53 and Cosmopoulos (supra n. 90) 90, in addition to the titles cited in ns. 92 and 94 below. Phelps considers several of these figurines to be images of slaughtered and gutted animals because of the slits in their bellies, but Pullen (supra n. 32) 50 n. 55 has drawn attention to the problems connected with such an interpretation and prefers to interpret the slashes in purely technological terms, as provisions made for the thorough firing of the artifacts in question. For numerous examples of EH II zoomorphic figurines, see Pullen (supra n. 32) 52–53, ns. 57–65, and Marangou (supra n. 90) 286–87 nos. BA 755–797. For an anthropomorphic foot in terracotta that may be of EH II date, see J. and B. Forsén, "A Prehistoric Foot from Argolis," *Journal of Prehistoric Religion* 6 (1992) 24–30.
[92] Tzavella-Evjen 1984 (supra n. 55) 21–22, 169–70, 206, 213–14. See also the small EH II structure excavated at Perachora-Vouliagmeni by J.M. Fossey, sometimes considered to be a shrine on the basis of the "plastic vase in the form of a ram" found on its floor (*ArchDelt* 28B' [1973] (1977) 150), which may resemble a zoomorphic rhyton without context illustrated by Weisshaar ("Tierkopfgefässe," 329–30 and n. 29, pl. 16.2). Weisshaar considers most of the sauceboats and rhyta with zoomorphic protomes to have been cult vessels.
[93] Pullen (supra n. 32).

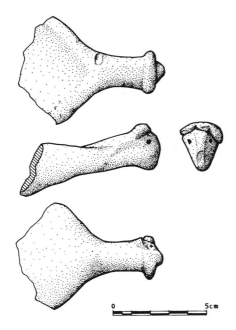

Fig. 5. Sauceboat spout fragment terminating in bull's (?) head, from Tiryns. (After "Tierkopfgefässe," fig. 1.1)

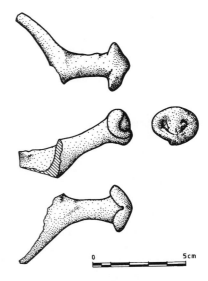

Fig. 6. Sauceboat spout fragment terminating in ram's head, from Tiryns. (After "Tierkopfgefässe," fig. 1.2)

Protomes of the same two domesticates occasionally decorate the ends of sauceboat spouts (figs. 5–6) or, less frequently, the ends of tubular spouts on closed vessels, which may be considered the EH II antecedents of later Aegean zoomorphic rhyta.[94] Similar protomes are also found attached at the base of the handle on such closed shapes as askoi (fig. 7) and jugs (fig. 8). In the case of a small stone vase found at Tiryns, such a protome even serves as a handle.[95] Given the location of these protomes at the bases of handles on closed vases and their occasional function as handles when placed near the rim of either open or closed shapes,[96] we may be justified in identifying as handles the spouts of sauceboats decorated with such protomes. That is, when ornamented with a protome in such a way as to block the end of its spout, a sauceboat may have functioned as a dipper, the "spout" playing the role of a handle.

Two-dimensional renditions of representational motifs in or on fired clay, like the three-dimensional versions just surveyed, take several different forms. For example, a row of scorpions added in a light-firing slip over a dark-slipped ground decorates the handle of an askos from Tiryns (fig. 9).[97] A terracotta hearth rim from the same site is decorated in relief with a frieze of quadrupeds, one of which appears to be suckling its young (fig. 10).[98] Four of the 70 seal devices that can be restored from sealings found in the House of the Tiles at Lerna bear representational motifs. Three feature single, centrally placed spiders, and the last a set of four narrow-necked jugs, which from their shape would be more at home in a "Lefkandi I" than an ordinary EH II ceramic assemblage (fig. 11).[99] A comprehensive listing and detailed analysis of EH II representational art lie outside the scope of this essay. My purpose here is merely to draw attention to the peculiar range and character of EH II pictorialism in the Peloponnese. For example, the human figure is altogether absent, despite the pres-

[94] "Tierkopfgefässe," esp. 329–30; Cosmopoulos (supra n. 90) 89.

[95] "Tierkopfgefässe," 331, pl. 16.1.

[96] Aside from the protome on the stone vase cited in n. 95, a long-necked protome from near the rim of a small closed shape also found at Tiryns may likewise have functioned as a handle ("Tierkopfgefässe," 329, fig. 1.3, pl. 14.2).

[97] H.-J. Weisshaar, "Ein tirynther Gefäss mit frühbronzezeitlicher Tierdarstellung," AM 96 (1981) 1–5. The patterned ornament on this vase's shoulder is almost certainly abstract rather than representational.

[98] H.-J. Weisshaar, "Reliefpithoi und Herdplatten aus Tiryns," in W. Müller ed., Fragen und Probleme der bronzezeitlichen ägäischen Glyptik (CMS Beiheft 3, Berlin 1989) 315–

22, esp. fig. 11a–b. See also J.C. Lavezzi, "Early Helladic Hearth Rims at Corinth," Hesperia 48 (1979) 342–47; A. Dousougli-Zachos, "Ein frühhelladischer Stempelroller aus Ton," in Müller (supra) 19–25; and M. Caskey, "Thoughts on Early Bronze Age Hearths," in Celebrations 13–21.

[99] M.C. Heath, "Early Helladic Clay Sealings from the House of the Tiles at Lerna," Hesperia 27 (1958) 81–121, esp. 104 types S4–S5, 111 type S55, 112 type S61, 114, pls. 20, 22, 25, 28, 29; M.H. Wiencke, "Lerna," in CMS V.1 (Berlin 1975) 28–114, esp. 52 nos. 57–58, 86 no. 109, 90 no. 115. For another spider on a sealing from Asine, see O. Frödin and A.W. Persson, Asine: Results of the Swedish Excavations, 1922–1930 (Stockholm 1938) 236–37, fig. 172.5; Cosmopoulos (supra n. 90) 91.

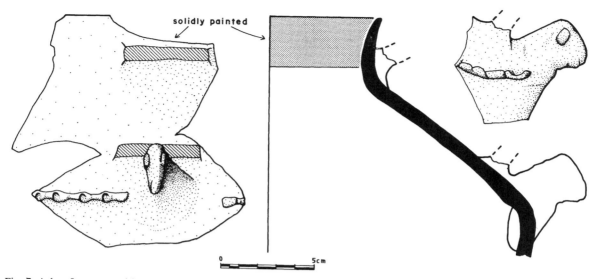

Fig. 7. Askos fragment with zoomorphic protome at base of handle, from Makrovouni. (After "Tierkopfgefässe," fig. 2)

ence of human products such as vases (fig. 11d) and the yoke linking a pair of oxen (fig. 4). Equally distinctive are the range of artifactual types that serve as vehicles for such art and the selection of particular locations on these vessels for the display of representational motifs. For example, animal protomes on terracotta vessels, although relatively rare, are more often intelligible as an adjunct or appendage to a handle than as an ornamental elaboration of a spout or mouth. In other words, such protomes function less often like the heads of zoomorphic rhyta, which are such a common feature of Aegean art of the Middle and Late Bronze Ages, than might have been expected. Peloponnesian pictorialism in this period is thus quite different, for example, from that which flourishes in the contemporary Cyclades with its emphasis on three-dimensional human and zoomorphic forms in stone and incised two-dimensional representations of ships and fish on dark-burnished frying pans.

The topic of trade in the Early Bronze Age has been the focus of as much recent scholarly discussion and debate as any other aspect of human activity in the Aegean during the third millennium B.C.[100] Some of the goods being passed around, particularly volcanic stones such as obsidian from Melos and andesite from several potential sources in the Saronic Gulf (Aegina, Methana, Poros), had been playing a role in mainland Greek exchange networks for centuries be-

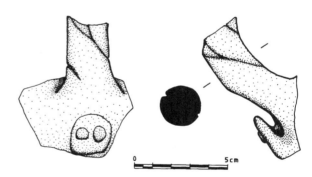

Fig. 8. Jug fragment with zoomorphic protome at base of handle, from Makrovouni. (After "Tierkopfgefässe," fig. 1.6)

[100] The word "trade" is used here as an umbrella term to describe a wide range of modes of exchange including commerce for profit, reciprocity, and redistribution. In practice, it has ordinarily not been possible to differentiate among these modes with the data available. On this point, see T.H. van Andel and C.N. Runnels, "An Essay on the 'Emergence of Civilization' in the Aegean World," *Antiquity* 62 (1988) 234–47, esp. 237. For other treatments of trade in the Early Bronze Age involving the Greek mainland, see Rutter and Zerner (supra n. 3) 75, 81; Pullen (supra n. 46) 332; Wiencke (supra n. 46) 500–501, 508; A. Sampson, "Early Helladic Contacts with the Cyclades during the EBA 2," in R. Laffineur ed., *Annales d'archéologie égéenne de l'Université de Liège 2* (*Aegaeum* 2, Liège 1988) 5–10; M.B. Cosmopoulos, "Ex-

change Networks in Prehistory: The Aegean and the Mediterranean in the Third Millennium B.C.," in R. Laffineur and L. Basch eds., *Thalassa: L'Égée préhistorique et la mer* (*Aegaeum* 7, Liège 1991) 155–68. For an intriguing investigation of trade in the EBA Cyclades, which, inter alia, suggests specific connections between trading activity and Early Cycladic iconography, see C. Broodbank, "Ulysses without Sails: Trade, Distance, Knowledge and Power in the Early Cyclades," *WorldArch* 24 (1993) 315–31. For a recent overview of trade during the Neolithic era in the Aegean, see C. Perlès, "Systems of Exchange and Organization of Production in Neolithic Greece," *JMA* 5 (1992) 115–64; the theoretical issues raised in this extremely stimulating paper are as applicable to the EBA as to the Neolithic.

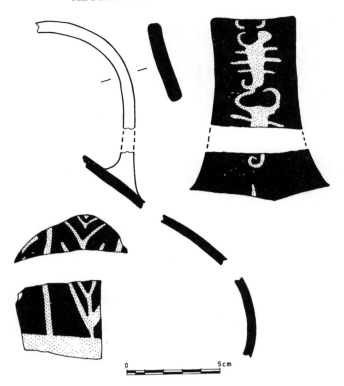

Fig. 9. Light-on-dark painted askos fragments decorated with scorpions on back of handle, from Tiryns. (After H.-J. Weisshaar, *AM* 96 [1981] fig. 1)

fore the beginning of the EH period.[101] Other items, however, whether as raw materials (e.g., metal ores) or as finished goods (e.g., andesite mortars), began to circulate for the first time in the Early Bronze Age.[102] A complete list of the commodities exchanged would no doubt include perishable foodstuffs, textiles, and items made out of wood and hides in addition to the more durable items that have survived and thus can be positively documented.[103]

Although many of these durable items can be identified as imported in the EH contexts in which they are found, reconstructions of the mechanisms whereby they arrived at their places of discovery can usually be little more than educated guesses. As raw materials, obsidian, chert, andesite, and metallic ores were probably accessible to anyone who was willing and able to travel to the appropriate quarries or mines

to help himself.[104] Blades of obsidian and chert, on the other hand, like querns or mortars of andesite, are more likely to have been distributed from centers of production located somewhere other than at the

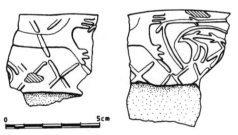

Fig. 10. Terracotta hearth rim decorated in relief with quadrupeds, from Tiryns. (After H.-J. Weisshaar, in *Fragen und Probleme der bronzezeitlichen ägäischen Glyptik* [Berlin 1989] fig. 11a–b)

---

[101] For obsidian, see Torrence (supra n. 35); for andesite, see Runnels in Knapp and Stech (supra n. 35) and Runnels and Cohen (supra n. 34).

[102] For metal ores, see Gale, Stos-Gale, and Davis (supra n. 34), McGeehan-Liritzis (supra n. 34), Spitaels (supra n. 34), Pullen (supra n. 46) 336–38, and Wilson (supra n. 78); for andesite mortars, see Runnels 1988 (supra n. 35).

[103] For an impressive list of goods that might have been

traded within the EBA Aegean, see van Andel and Runnels (supra n. 100) 243. Note that there is as yet no evidence for the exchange during the Early Bronze Age of liquid produce in specially produced transport containers, the equivalents of the later Cycladic duck askoi, Minoan and Mycenaean stirrup jars, Canaanite jars, and Iron Age amphoras.

[104] Pullen (supra n. 46) 333–38. See also supra ns. 101–102.

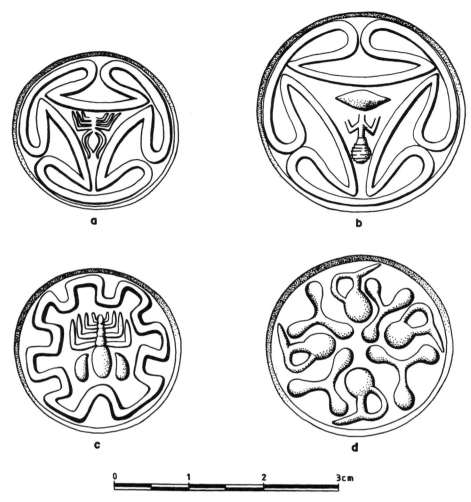

Fig. 11. Seal types reconstructed from sealings found in the House of the Tiles at Lerna. (After *CMS* V.1 [Berlin 1975] nos. 57, 58, 115, and 109, respectively)

source of each raw material.[105] Blades could be produced from Melian obsidian nodules by a knapper working at Lerna, and metallic ores from the Laurion area could be smelted by smiths working at Raphina or Kolonna: that is, at none of the sources of the four materials in question did an EBA settlement arise whose inhabitants were prepared to exploit the nearby mineral wealth by controlling access to it and becoming specialized producers of tools or other implements.[106]

Truths about EH exchange networks are occasionally revealed in strange ways. For example, in studying the chipped stone from EH and MH levels at Lerna, Runnels found relatively few formal differences between the toolkits of Lerna III (EH II) and Lerna IV (EH III). The principal differences between the chipped stone assemblages of these two horizons are the results of economic rather than technological change: a higher frequency in Lerna III of locally produced obsidian pressure blades, in tandem with a substantial number of imported chert pressure blades, serves as evidence not only for specialized craftsmen but also for extensive exchanges of their products, evidently involving the stockpiling of these at local

---

[105] For obsidian and chert blades, see Runnels (supra n. 72) 360; for andesite mortars, see Runnels 1988 (supra n. 35). See also the discussion in Perlès (supra n. 100).

[106] For evidence of metallurgy at sites located at some distance from the sources of the ore, see Walter and Felten (supra n. 54) 23–26, figs. 17–20; Pullen (supra n. 46) 222–23 (Kolonna IV), 239–40 (Raphina, with full references to Theochares' preliminary reports). For an examination of settlement locations with respect to ore sources during this period, see McGeehan-Liritzis (supra n. 34).

centers and their redistribution to lower-level sites in the regional site hierarchy. In other words, the principal difference between the chipped stone industries of these two periods lay in the exchange of tool blanks: such exchange existed during the later EH II horizon represented by Building BG and the House of the Tiles, but not during the subsequent EH III phase.[107]

Attas's employment of neutron activation analysis (NAA) to study the traffic in pottery within the northeastern Peloponnese succeeded, among other things, in establishing that ordinary vessel types were exchanged between EH II communities, despite the fact that each produced the same shape decorated in the same fashion.[108] These vessels were in some instances small open shapes, sauceboats and bowls, which could not have served as transport containers but rather must have been exchanged for their own sake. Pullen has noted that there is no spatial patterning in Attas's NAA data.[109] The lack of directionality in these EH II pottery exchanges suggests that pottery may have been exchanged less for economic than for social reasons during EH II, that is, chiefly to promote stylistic uniformity and hence a sense of societal cohesion.[110]

Hypotheses concerning the mechanics of specific exchange networks such as the two briefly outlined above require testing against other bodies of EH II lithic and ceramic data. At this point it seems to be impossible to generalize about the nature of EH II exchange mechanisms, but it does look as though trade during the EH III phase worked in a significantly different way, with respect to both ceramics and chipped stone.

Systematic intensive surveys have had an enormous impact on our understanding of the shifting patterns of human settlement on the Greek mainland during the third millennium B.C. To begin with, most survey directors have reported locating approximately 10 times as many EH sites as had previously been documented in their survey areas (table 1).[111] But to present the figures for total sites occupied at one time or another over roughly a thousand years is, of course, to tell only a small part of the story. For example, several surveys (Berbati, Methana, Nemea, Southern Argolid) have reported a sharp decline in the number of sites from EH II to EH III,[112] while at least two (Laconia, Skourta Plain) report finding no evidence whatsoever for EH III occupation.[113]

The two last surveys call for additional comment. In the area of the Skourta plain, the absence of EH III pottery, which can be very difficult to recognize when heavily worn and highly fragmentary, is preceded by an even more striking absence of EH II sherd material, which is notoriously easy to identify even when small and worn. Although a sizable number of sites dating from the very beginning of the Bronze Age have been located in this upland plain (table 1), they all appear to have been abandoned by the onset of the EH II phase. The fact that it was uninhabited for much of the EH period may explain why the Skourta plain exhibits no evidence for a major episode of erosion during the EH II phase, which has been documented in both the southern Argolid and the Argive plain and which has been attributed to overly aggressive clearing by farmers of the natural vegetation on hillslopes.[114]

---

[107] Runnels (supra n. 72), esp. 388. The EH II situation with respect to the production by specialized craftsmen of obsidian and chert blades is paralleled in the earlier Neolithic (Perlès [supra n. 100] 125–37, 148–50).

[108] M. Attas, *Regional Ceramic Trade in Early Bronze Age Greece: Evidence from Neutron Activation Analysis of Early Helladic Pottery from Argolis and Korinthia* (Diss. McGill Univ. 1982); Attas et al. (supra n. 43).

[109] Pullen (supra n. 46) 338–41, tables 6.3, 6.4, fig. 91.

[110] J.B. Rutter, "Early Helladic Pottery: Inferences about Exchange and Production from Style and Clay Composition," in *Wace and Blegen*. For the export of pottery from Attica to the Cycladic island of Keos, see Wilson (supra n. 78).

[111] Only the Boeotia survey, among intensive surveys for which more than a single season's results are available, reports a significantly smaller increase in the number of EH sites identified. Bintliff's theory of a "cumulative disappearance of sites" (also called "cumulative site-loss" or "progressive disappearance") to explain the relatively small numbers of prehistoric sites located in the Boeotia survey perhaps no longer needs to be invoked in the face of the more plentiful

comparative data now available from other intensive surveys (table 1). If site density is expressed as the number of sites per unit area surveyed, the Bronze Age figures from Boeotia are not wildly out of line with those from other areas. What *is* different about the figures for the Boeotia survey is the larger number of prehistoric sites known in the area before survey began. Table 1 also shows that the increase in the number of EH sites is routinely far greater than that noted for MH sites (again, with the exceptions of the Boeotia and Pylos surveys) and is often comparable to (Berbati, Boeotia, Skourta Plain, Southern Argolid) or even in excess of (Laconia, Methana, Nemea, Oropos) that recorded for LH sites.

[112] Wright et al. (supra n. 14) 640–41 (Nemea); van Andel et al. (supra n. 17) 113; Runnels and van Andel (supra n. 17) 311–15, 326 (Southern Argolid); J. Forsén, pers. comm. (Berbati); C. Mee, pers. comm. (Methana).

[113] *AR* 36 (1990) 21 (Laconia); Munn and Munn 1990 (supra n. 18) 34 (Skourta Plain).

[114] For the lack of evidence for EH II–III occupation in the Skourta plain, see Munn and Munn 1990 (supra n. 18) 34; for man's role in triggering a major episode of soil erosion during the EH II phase in the northeastern Pelo-

The dearth of EH III cultural remains in Laconia, on the other hand, is part of a far more widespread phenomenon characteristic of Messenia as well.[115] The recent publication of the Bronze Age remains from Nichoria shows that the earliest datable post-Neolithic material from this Messenian site consists of pottery that finds its closest parallels in late Lerna IV rather than in Lerna V, and which may therefore be better described as very late EH III than MH I.[116] Whatever the precise chronological label for it may be, in view of how similar this pottery is to that of the early MH period, and if this is indeed the first pottery to be produced in the southern Peloponnese after material dated to the EH II phase on typological grounds, there appears to have been a substantial lacuna in Laconian and Messenian prehistory equivalent to most of the duration of Lerna IV. But perhaps such a lacuna is illusory. Could it be that the relatively high numbers of EH sites identified in the Laconia Survey (table 1) reflect a longer-lived EH II culture in the southern than in the northern Peloponnese?[117]

What can one say about those intensively surveyed areas that have yielded evidence for EH III occupation? While it is true that the decline in site numbers from the EH II to the EH III phase is not as drastic when expressed as sites occupied per unit time instead of simple totals for each period,[118] the drop in site density is nevertheless pronounced. Since there is no evidence for an increase in average site size in EH III—if anything, most EH III sites appear to have been smaller than their EH II predecessors—there ought to have been a significant drop in population at or toward the end of the EH II phase. But there is no obvious indication of higher mortality at this time in the form of a rise in the number of burials[119] nor of emigration in the sudden appearance of Helladic cultural traits elsewhere. The problem may be simply that we have exaggerated the suddenness of the changes in settlement pattern between the EH II and EH III phases by neglecting to date periods of occupation at EH II sites as precisely as possible. That is, the decline in site numbers may have been a phenomenon that began well before the end of EH II and culminated in EH III rather than beginning at that time.[120]

There is evidence for the development of increasing social complexity at the level of the individual site during the course of the long EH II phase, which may prove to be connected with the emergence of a hierarchy of settlement at the regional level.[121] At the moment, however, not enough data have been published for an informed judgment to be made on such

ponnese, see Zangger in Boardman and Bell (supra n. 31) 136, with support from pollen data published by Jahns (supra n. 33) and evidence for contemporary usage of the plow published by Pullen (supra n. 32); for the Skourta plain as a region exhibiting no evidence of a major erosional episode in the EBA or subsequently, see Zangger (supra) 136–38. In reviewing the evidence for such erosional episodes in Greece, Zangger draws attention to how their dates vary (LN in Thessaly, EH II in the Argolid, and never in the case of the Skourta plain): "Thus there is no general pattern for environmental reconstruction. Each area must be examined individually" (p. 138). The same emphasis on the variability of individual spatial units might equally well be applied to reconstructions of the transition from EH II to EH III culture or to reconstructions of the mechanics whereby raw materials or particular categories of finished goods were exchanged.

[115] Rutter (supra n. 72) 15; Dickinson (supra n. 20) 110.

[116] R.J. Howell, "The Middle Helladic Settlement: Pottery," in *Nichoria* 43–204, esp. 43–46, 83–86, figs. 3-1a through 3-4, pls. 3-1 through 3-3 (MH I group A). Howell is aware of the parallels between this earliest "MH" deposit from Nichoria and EH III pottery from the Argolid, as is Dickinson (supra n. 20) 110.

[117] For this suggestion, which Dickinson (supra n. 24) 133 has described as a "counsel of despair," see Rutter (supra n. 72) 15 and n. 38.

[118] For such an approach to the comparison of site densities between periods, see supra n. 40.

[119] Perhaps the mass grave represented by the fill of the

Cheliotomylos well is representative of an unsettled subphase within EH II when there was unusually high mortality due to either warfare or disease: T.L. Shear, "Excavations in the North Cemetery at Corinth in 1930," *AJA* 34 (1930) 403–31, esp. 405–406; F.O. Waage, "An Early Helladic Well near Old Corinth," *Hesperia* Suppl. 8 (1949) 415–22; Pullen (supra n. 46) 113–15; *Twilight* 72–73. But this continues to be a unique discovery insofar as the large number of individuals comprising both sexes and several different age groups is concerned. For an estimate of a population decline in the southern Argolid from ca. 1900 during the EH II phase to 500 or less in EH III and the ensuing MH period, see Runnels and van Andel (supra n. 17) 325 n. 6.

[120] For an interesting discussion of these and other issues (e.g., the problem of the relative "visibility" of EH II vs. EH III pottery), see *Twilight* 176–96. Note especially Forsén's comparison (195) of our understanding of EH patterns of settlement before and after the advent of systematic intensive survey. By focusing here on the EH II–III transition, I do not mean to give it any special significance. Many of the same kinds of issues and problems would arise in a consideration of the transition from FN to EH I or from EH III to the MH period. Unfortunately, the evidence available for the earlier of these two transitions is still too sparse for much to be said about it. The later transition from EH III to MH is surveyed by Forsén (supra) 176–96.

[121] For the increasing complexity of EH II society with time, see Wiencke (supra n. 46); for settlement hierarchies during this phase, supra ns. 66–67 and Wiencke (supra) 499.

critical questions as when and where a distinct settlement hierarchy can first be discerned, of how many
levels or tiers such hierarchies consisted (and was this
number a constant from region to region and subphase to subphase), and what connections existed
between the appearance of a hierarchy of settlement
and the rise of monumental architecture in the form
of corridor houses and fortification systems. The
kinds of information recovered through intensive surface survey have opened up a number of new ways
of investigating particular cultures or periods of time.
Yet much of intensive survey's potential is dependent
on the accurate identification and closest possible dating of the heavily weathered artifacts recovered. The
ability to assign increasingly more precise dates to
these worn and fragmentary artifacts and to comment
upon their function when they were whole can only
come about through more finely tuned chronologies
and significant contextual associations. These, in turn,
are the products of excavation rather than survey.

THE MIDDLE BRONZE AGE (MIDDLE HELLADIC
I–III, CA. 2050/2000–1680 B.C.) AND THE
EARLY MYCENAEAN PERIOD (LATE HELLADIC
I–IIB, CA. 1680–1445/1415 B.C.)

Shortly before the *Gazetteer*'s appearance, one of its
authors published a thorough survey of the MH period and the first century or two of the subsequent
Mycenaean era, which today remains the most comprehensive synthesis of the half-millennium represented by this segment of mainland Greek pre-

history.[122] Yet enough new material has been found
or published during the past 15 years to make Dickinson's classic survey now more a point of departure
than the last word on the subject.

The terminology ordinarily employed to describe
the mainland Greek Middle Bronze Age continues to
be a bit awkward. At its beginning, the labels "EH III"
and "MH" put far too much emphasis on changes
that seem relatively minor: first, the switch by potters
from iron-based to manganese-based slips as materials
with which to decorate vases; and second, a significant
increase in the exchange of certain categories of finished goods between mainland coastal sites and the
islands of the Cyclades and Crete.[123] The reason behind the first change has yet to be investigated in any
detail; the second is usually considered to reflect Minoan and Cycladic enterprise, the mainlanders playing the passive role of disadvantaged natives being
irradiated by their more progressive and outward-
looking neighbors across the water to the east and
south. At its other chronological terminus, MH culture is distinguished from the earliest stage of Mycenaean culture by a more impressive array of changes:
first, the appearance of enormous wealth, in the form
of locally produced as well as imported goods, at a
handful of sites in the southwestern and northeastern
Peloponnese and perhaps one or two more in central
Greece; and second, the aping of Minoan fashions in
ceramics, certain categories of metalwork (chiefly
weaponry, jewelry, and containers), and possibly also
funerary architecture.[124] This later set of changes,

[122] O.T.P.K. Dickinson, *The Origins of Mycenaean Civilisation* (*SIMA* 49, Göteborg 1977).

[123] For the problems associated with Helladic terminology,
see R.A. McNeal, "Helladic Prehistory through the Looking-
glass," *Historia* 24 (1975) 385–401. For Caskey's recognition
that most of the cultural differences traditionally associated
with the EH–MH transition in fact applied to the earlier EH
II–III transition, see supra n. 59 and J.L. Caskey, "Aegean
Terminologies," *Historia* 27 (1978) 488–91. For Howell's
championing of a new terminology for the cultural continuum from EH III through MH, see R.J. Howell, "The
Origins of the Middle Helladic Culture," in R.A. Crossland
and A. Birchall eds., *Bronze Age Migrations in the Aegean*
(London 1973) 73–106. Dickinson (supra n. 122) 17–31, esp.
19–20, was willing to endorse Howell's suggestion but Caskey
was not ("Discussion" in Crossland and Birchall, 99–100).
For more recent considerations of the EH III–MH transition, see J.B. Rutter, "Some Comments on the Nature and
Significance of the Ceramic Transition from Early Helladic
III to Middle Helladic," *Hydra* 2 (1986) 29–57, esp. 29–33;
Runnels (supra n. 72); *Twilight*, esp. 21–22, 248–60; Maran
(supra n. 46) 369–72. For the rise in mainland Greek contacts
with other Aegean cultural spheres at the beginning of the
MH period, see Rutter and Zerner (supra n. 3); Nordquist

1987 (infra n. 142) 62–68; C.W. Zerner, "New Perspectives
on Trade in the Middle and Early Late Helladic Periods on
the Mainland," in *Wace and Blegen*.

[124] For some general summaries of these changes during
the past dozen years, see J. Muhly, "On the Shaft Graves at
Mycenae," in M.A. Powell, Jr., and R.H. Sack eds., *Studies
in Honor of Tom B. Jones* (Neuenkirchen-Vluyn 1979) 311–
23; H. Matthäus, "Minoan Influence on the Greek Mainland
during the Sixteenth Century B.C. and the Origins of Mycenaean Civilization," *TUAS* 5 (1980) 37–44; O.T.P.K. Dickinson, "Cretan Contacts with the Mainland during the Period
of the Shaft Graves," and R. Hägg, "Degrees and Character
of the Minoan Influence on the Mainland," in *Thalassocracy*
115–18 and 119–22, respectively; S. Dietz, "Some Notes on
the Pattern of Foreign Influences in the B-Circle of Mycenae
(The Ceramic Evidence)," *Schriften des deutschen Archäologen-Verbandes* 9 (1987) 113–19; Dietz, "On the Origin of the
Mycenaean Civilization: Some Recent Results," in *Studies in
Ancient History and Numismatics Presented to Rudi Thomsen*
(Aarhus 1988) 22–28; G. Touchais, "Le passage du Bronze
moyen au Bronze récent en Grèce continentale: État de la
question," S. Dietz, "The Concept of the Middle Helladic III
Period in a Historical Perspective," and O. Dickinson, "'The
Origins of Mycenaean Civilisation' Revisited," in *Transition*

though clearly important, evidently took place gradually rather than suddenly, over a period of time commonly referred to as the Shaft Grave era ("Schachtgräberzeit"). This term, encompassing several shorter-lived ceramic phases (MH III, LH I, early LH IIA), has until recently served to mask the precise sequence in which several critical changes occurred. Aside from refining a ceramic relative chronology in order to sequence these changes as a preliminary to explaining them, archaeologists need to address the question of why the pace of cultural change during the three to four centuries prior to the Shaft Grave era should have been so slow, particularly in comparison to contemporary developments on Crete and even in the Cyclades. In what follows, I will first survey advances affecting all phases of the MH period before moving on to topics that are peculiar to the period of cultural ferment that is the Shaft Grave era.

Of special significance for the MH period as a whole, I would single out four recent contributions to the body of scholarly knowledge, which I list here in roughly their sequence of publication. First, Zerner has presented the evidence from Lerna for the EH III–MH transition and for the first stage of the full MH period.[125] In this groundbreaking study, she identified and carefully began the process of defining two groups of ceramic fabrics that were imported to Lerna in large quantities throughout the MH period and into the earliest Mycenaean phase, LH I. The first of these she termed "Gold Mica Fabric," after the biotite inclusions that make this fabric relatively easy

to recognize.[126] Earlier scholars had suggested that these were Aeginetan products on the grounds that several categories of painted vases containing the distinctive biotite inclusions were particularly common on Aegina and that these same categories were widely distributed all around the Saronic Gulf, at the geographical center of which the island of Aegina is located.[127] Zerner's contribution has been to extend this identification to three or four unpainted classes, including cooking pottery, and to arrange for the petrographic characterization of samples taken from all these decoratively distinct but petrographically linked classes.[128] With these petrographic characterizations she has made an even stronger case for Aegina as the source of this pottery, while significantly expanding the functional and chronological ranges as well as the sheer quantity of pottery produced within this distinctive ceramic tradition. The actual centers of production, though presumably located in the vicinity of the island's principal prehistoric site at Kolonna on the northwest coast, have yet to be located.

The second fabric category of imported pottery richly represented in the MH village of Lerna V has been termed "Lustrous Decorated" by Zerner. Like the Aeginetan material just described, "Lustrous Decorated" pottery includes fired fabrics of several different grades of fineness, which are linked, in this case, not so much by distinctive inclusions as by the use of a lustrous iron-based paint that often serves as the ground for abstract motifs overpainted in matt white and purple.[129] In their ranges of shapes and

113–21, 123–29, and 131–36, respectively. For recent surveys of mainland Greek funerary architecture at the transition from the MH period to the Mycenaean era, see O. Pelon, "L'architecture funéraire de Grèce continentale à la transition du Bronze moyen et du Bronze récent," in *Thanatos* 107–16; S. Hiller, "On the Origins of the Shaft Graves," and Y.G. Lolos, "The Tholos Tomb at Koryphasion: Evidence for the Transition from Middle to Late Helladic in Messenia," in *Transition* 137–44 and 171–75, respectively. For studies of the transition focused on Messenia rather than the Argolid, see R. Hägg, "On the Nature of the Minoan Influence in Early Mycenaean Messenia," *OpAth* 14 (1982) 27–37; G.S. Korres, "The Relations between Crete and Messenia in the Late Middle Helladic and Early Late Helladic Period," in *Thalassocracy* 141–52; Y.G. Lolos, *The Late Helladic I Pottery of the Southwestern Peloponnesos and Its Local Characteristics* (SIMA-PB 50, Göteborg 1987).

[125] C.W. Zerner, *The Beginning of the Middle Helladic Period at Lerna* (Diss. Univ. of Cincinnati 1978; UMI 79-04772).

[126] Zerner (supra n. 125) 148–50, 156–58; C.W. Zerner, "Middle Helladic and Late Helladic I Pottery from Lerna," *Hydra* 2 (1986) 58–74, esp. 64–66, fig. 1; Zerner, "Middle Helladic and Late Helladic I Pottery from Lerna: Part II, Shapes," *Hydra* 4 (1988) 1–10, esp. 1–5, figs. 1–23; J. Maran,

Kiapha Thiti: Ergebnisse der Ausgrabungen II.2: 2. Jt. v. Chr.: Keramik und Kleinfunde (*Marburger Winckelmann-Programm 1990*, Marburg 1992) 179–99 ("Goldglimmerkeramik"); Zerner (supra n. 123).

[127] Maran (supra n. 126) 179–80 identifies D. Fimmen, J.P. Harland, D. French, S. Hiller, and R. Wünsche as scholars who have played significant roles in the identification of painted Aeginetan ceramics during the MH and early Mycenaean periods. To these may now be added H. Siedentopf (infra n. 138).

[128] Zerner's unpainted Aeginetan classes, or wares, are Plain, Dark-Burnished, and Coarse (or Kitchen Ware): see the list in S. Dietz, C. Zerner, and G. Nordquist, "Concerning the Classification of Late Middle Helladic Wares in the Argolid," *Hydra* 5 (1988) 15–16. For the chronological differentiation of Aeginetan shapes and decoration, see Zerner 1988 (supra n. 126). Maran (supra n. 126) 195–98 has since added a class of solidly painted Aeginetan pottery in which the paint's color varies from red to dark gray or black on a single vase and thus appears to signal an iron-based rather than manganese-based paint or slip.

[129] Zerner 1986 (supra n. 126) 66–68, fig. 1; Zerner 1988 (supra n. 126), esp. 6–10, figs. 24–41.

patterns, the vases produced in this "Lustrous Decorated" category are Minoanizing but not purely Minoan. Their place of production is as yet unknown, but was in all probability a single site located on the coast of the southeastern Peloponnese or on the island of Kythera.[130] Both "Gold Mica" and "Lustrous Decorated" vessels often bear simple incised or impressed marks made before firing (so-called potters' marks), but the marking systems associated with the two fabric groups differ systematically insofar as the locations of the marks and their actual forms are concerned.[131] With her dissertation and subsequent publications charting the developments through time of the "Gold Mica" and "Lustrous Decorated" repertoires in terms of the stratification observed at MH–LH I Lerna, Zerner has provided an exceedingly useful relative chronology,[132] and at the same time has sketched the outlines of two remarkably widespread ceramic distribution networks. From published sources alone,[133] a distribution map showing where vessels of the "Gold Mica" fabric group have so far been noted can be drawn (fig. 12). A similar map drawn for the "Lustrous Decorated" group would not have as many sites indicated and would show a more southerly distribution.[134]

Evidence for the economic and probably political preeminence of the inhabitants of Aegina during the MH period is by no means restricted to their exports of ceramic containers, which were probably accompanied by andesite grinding stones (as ballast?) in the ships carrying this pottery to mainland coastal sites. During these centuries the site of Kolonna boasted the most impressive fortifications in the Aegean world after those of Troy. The careful disentanglement by Walter and Felten of several stages of EH III and MH defensive systems at the site, together with their presentation of some of the ceramic evidence for dating them, has made abundantly clear how atypical Kolonna is for either a mainland Greek or a Cycladic site of the later third and early second millennia B.C.[135] In addition to far-flung trade networks, monumental public architecture, and a system of marking ceramic vessels prior to firing that must be in some way connected with their surplus production of tablewares, storage vessels, and cooking pots for export, the Aeginetans at Kolonna can lay claim to the earliest known Aegean shaft grave, which furthermore may have held the earliest royal burial attested within the Helladic cultural sphere.[136] The more we learn about Kolonna during the Middle Bronze Age, the more

[130] Zerner 1986 (supra n. 126) 67; Dickinson (supra n. 20) 110–11; Zerner (supra n. 123).

[131] Zerner 1986 (supra n. 126) 65, 67; Zerner 1988 (supra n. 126) figs. 2–3, 7–8, 12, 16–23 (Aeginetan "Gold Mica"), 31–32, 34, 36 ("Lustrous Decorated"). Examples of comparable marks on other imported "Gold Mica" vases are common at numerous sites throughout the southern Aegean, especially at Ayia Irini on Keos (A.H. Bikaki, *Keos* IV: *Ayia Irini: The Potters' Marks* [Mainz 1984] passim), Tiryns (H. Döhl, "Bronzezeitliche Graffiti aus Tiryns I: Vor dem Brand eingeritzte Zeichen," *Kadmos* 17 [1978] 115–49), Kiapha Thiti (Maran [supra n. 126] 184, 187–88, 195 and n. 374), Korakou (Davis [supra n. 36] 246 nos. 106–13, 252 nos. 250–52, 254, figs. 7, 8, 11), and, of course, Kolonna on Aegina (Walter and Felten [supra n. 54] 125–26, pls. 124–25).

[132] The relative chronological subdivisions MH I, MH II, MH III, and LH I applied to the illustrations in Zerner 1988 (supra n. 126) make possible the cross-dating of strata containing such types elsewhere (e.g., Maran [supra n. 126] 180–99 passim, 206 n. 430). For a recent discussion of the various subdivisions of the MH period proposed since Blegen published his excavations at Korakou in 1921, see Lambropoulou (infra n. 147) 8–28, appendices B–C.

[133] The approximately 30 publications consulted for the preparation of this map are too numerous to list here. Dietz cites many of them in presenting a map of findspots of the Aeginetan Polychrome painted class, produced for the most part in the form of two large open shapes, kraters and basins (*ATMA* 303–305, fig. 91). These are datable primarily to LH I, though a very few may be earlier and a fair number remained in use, or were perhaps even produced, as late as LH IIA (Maran [supra n. 126] 198–99).

[134] Rutter and Zerner (supra n. 3) 77–80; Dickinson (supra

n. 20) 110–11; Zerner (supra n. 123).

[135] Walter and Felten (supra n. 54). Kolonna was, to be sure, recognized as atypical for a MH site well before this publication appeared (e.g., Dickinson [supra n. 122] 33), but the extent of its differences from any contemporary site in the western Aegean during the period ca. 2200–1700 B.C. has only become clear over the past 15 years. The EH III phases of the fortified town are numbered IV–VI, the MH phases VII–X. For the chronological placement of these relative to the sequences excavated at Lerna, Eutresis, and Lefkandi on the mainland, Ayia Irini and Phylakopi in the Cyclades, and Argissa and Pefkakia in Thessaly, in addition to the EM III–MM III ceramic sequence on Crete, see Maran (supra n. 46) 323–28, 370 fig. 25. The only other fortified town of the MBA in the western Aegean at all comparable is Ayia Irini on Keos, which is not resettled and fortified for the first time until halfway through the period: J.L. Davis, *Keos* V: *Ayia Irini: Period V* (Mainz 1986) 104–105; "RAP I" 709 n. 38. For the impact of Aeginetan commerce at an ordinary northeastern Peloponnesian coastal site, see Nordquist 1987 (infra n. 142) 62–64.

[136] For the shaft grave at Kolonna, which contained a bronze sword, gold diadem, and fine decorated pottery of both Minoan and Cycladic (Melian and possibly Kean) manufacture, see H. Walter, "Ανασκαφή στο λόφο Κολόννα, Αίγινα, 1981–1982," *AAA* 14 (1981) 179–84; R. Higgins, "A Gold Diadem from Aegina," *JHS* 107 (1987) 182; Hiller (supra n. 124) 139, who reasonably suggests that this tomb may be better described as a "remarkable example of a stone-built tomb" rather than a shaft grave, for the simple reason that no shaft above the tomb survives. For MM ceramic imports at Kolonna, see S. Hiller, "Minoan and Minoanizing Pottery on Aegina," in *Wace and Blegen*. For yet another

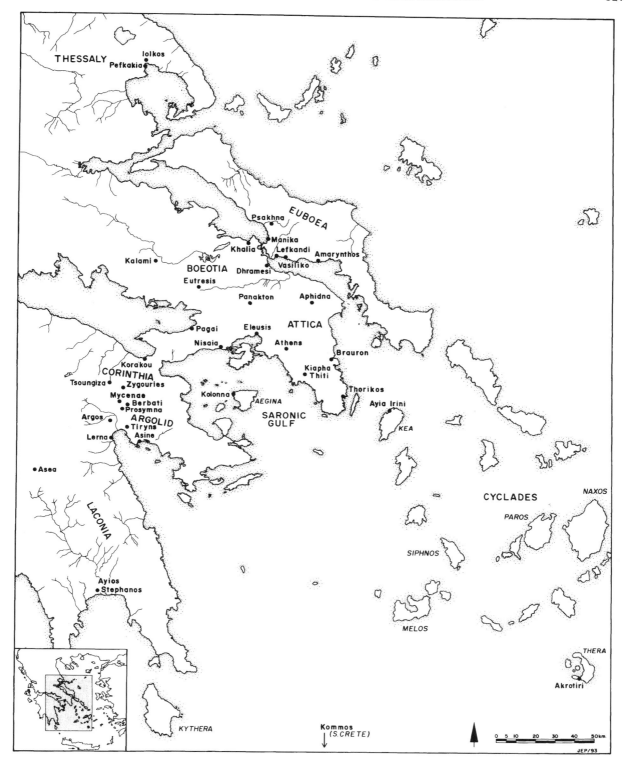

Fig. 12. Distribution of pottery of Middle Helladic and early Mycenaean (LH I–II) date considered to have been manufactured on Aegina

---

unusual find at Kolonna, see C. Reinhold, "Ein minoischer Steinhammer in Ägina," *ArchKorrBl* 22 (1992) 57–62. The only mainland Greek tombs that can possibly be identified as "royal," yet which also predate the shaft grave at Kolonna, are some of the larger R-graves on Lefkas (supra n. 64).

Fig. 13. Aeginetan barrel jar decorated with a frieze of manned ships, from
Welter's excavations at Kolonna. (After H. Siedentopf, *Alt-Ägina* IV.2: *Mattbemalte Keramik der Mittleren Bronzezeit* [Mainz 1991] pl. 35.158)

tempting it is to view certain novel and striking forms
of behavior characteristic of the Shaft Grave period,
such as the placement in tombs of large quantities of
movable wealth in the form of imported ceramics,
weaponry, and gold jewelry, as imitations by the mainlanders of customs learned not from the Minoans but
rather from closer neighbors on Aegina with whom
they were in far more frequent contact.[137] One final

expression of Aeginetan cultural supremacy during
the MH period in the west-central Aegean takes the
form of a small number of matt-painted barrel jars,
or pithoi, found at Kolonna during Welter's excavations of over 50 years ago. Long known and often
illustrated but only recently published in full, two of
these are decorated with longboats and one with a
human figure who seems to be standing on top of and

---

[137] In citing the shaft grave at Kolonna as a model imitated
by the earliest Mycenaean elite of the Argolid, Hiller (supra
n. 124) suggests that this form of grave may have imitated
still earlier prototypes in the Cyclades to the east. For inter-

action between the Cyclades and mainland Greece during
the MBA, see J.C. Overbeck, "The Hub of Commerce: Keos
and Middle Helladic Greece," *TUAS* 7 (1982) 38–49.

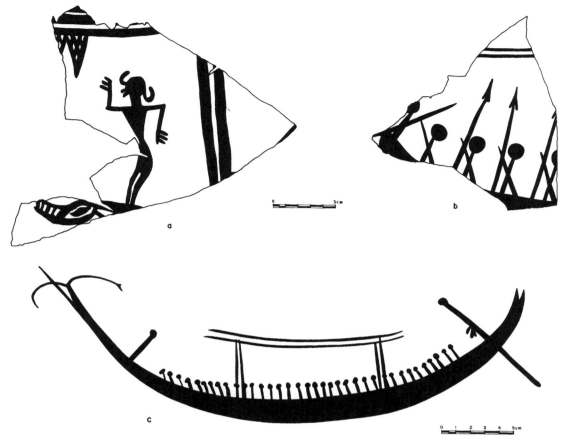

Fig. 14. Aeginetan barrel jar fragments (a–b) and reconstructed ship (c) from reconstructed jar illustrated in figure 13, all drawn to approximately the same scale. (After H. Siedentopf, *Alt-Ägina* IV.2: *Mattbemalte Keramik der Mittleren Bronzezeit* [Mainz 1991] pls. 14.75, 38.162, and fig. 4, respectively)

riding a large fish (figs. 13–14).[138] The latter has no close parallel in Aegean prehistoric art of which I am aware, but the longboats seem typologically as well as chronologically intermediate between the incised EC II ships that decorate a number of so-called "frying pans" found in graves at Chalandriani on Syros and the polychrome LC I ships of the well-known Fleet Fresco from the West House at Akrotiri on Thera.[139] The functions of the earlier "frying pans" and of the later frescoes are much disputed and so the social

---

[138] H. Siedentopf, *Alt-Ägina* IV.2: *Mattbemalte Keramik der Mittleren Bronzezeit* (Mainz 1991) 18–19, 24–25, 55 no. 75, 62 nos. 158, 162, fig. 4, pls. 14, 35–38. The two pieces illustrating ships are also discussed by S. Hiller, "Pax Minoica versus Minoan Thalassocracy: Military Aspects of Minoan Culture," in *Thalassocracy* 27–31. The same body of material included in Siedentopf's study formed the basis of R. Wünsche's "Die Entwicklung der mittelhelladischen matt-bemalten Keramik," *MüJb* 28 (1977) 7–27, esp. 15 and ns. 38–42 for the figured scenes. The fish-rider, perhaps the earliest version known of the "boy-on-a-dolphin," has been identified as a prehistoric representation of Apollo Delphinios by S. Hiller, "Fisch oder Schiff: Zu einem bemalten mittelbronzezeitlichen Gefässfragment aus Ägina," *Pantheon* 30 (1972) 439–46.

[139] For longboats on the EC II "frying pans," see J.E.

Coleman, "'Frying Pans' of the Early Bronze Age Aegean," *AJA* 89 (1985) 191–219, esp. 202–204, 207–209 nos. 13–19, 25–27, 211 no. 54, ill. 5, pls. 34–35, 37; "RAP I" 718 n. 69, fig. 9; C. Broodbank, "The Longboat and Society in the Cyclades during the Keros-Syros Culture," *AJA* 93 (1989) 319–37, as well as his more recent article on EC II trade (supra n. 100). For the Fleet Fresco, see L. Morgan, *The Miniature Wall Paintings of Thera: A Study in Aegean Culture and Iconography* (Cambridge 1988) and the study in press by C.A. Televantou, Ακροτήρι Θήρας: Οι τοιχογραφίες της Δυτικής Οικίας (Athens, forthcoming). For thematically related miniature frescoes illustrating ships from Ayia Irini on Keos, see "RAP I" 709–10, n. 39, fig. 4. See also the formidable amount of recent bibliography on Theran wall painting assembled by Davis in "RAP I" 738–39 n. 176.

contexts in which such ship representations were displayed at least in part as symbols of status are uncertain.[140] The ships from Kolonna, on the other hand, decorate large containers designed to hold surplus agricultural produce, presumably a dimension in terms of which status was measured on MH Aegina. In view of the rarity of representational art during this period, even on Aegina, its limited spatial distribution may not appear significant. Yet can it really be coincidental that all three examples of such art occurring on the large and constantly growing corpus of painted Aeginetan ceramics were found at Kolonna itself?[141] The spears indicated on the fragment illustrated here as figure 14b suggest that these ships were at least in some cases conceived of as warships. Thus, these Aeginetan symbols alluded to raiding or warfare in addition to—perhaps even instead of—trade or the simple fetching of mineral raw materials (e.g., obsidian, metalliferous ores, etc.) from sources that were open to all.

In terms of its iconography, then, as well as in its fortification and at least one exceptionally wealthy burial, Kolonna has emerged as a Middle Helladic site without peer on the Greek mainland. For a typical coastal site on the mainland during this same period with which to contrast Kolonna, we are no longer dependent on the well-stratified and continuously occupied but only partially published site of Lerna. With Dietz's publication of a major extramural cemetery and Nordquist's marvelously thorough synthesis of

the evidence for all aspects of MH life at the nearby site of Asine just across the Gulf of Argos, we now know considerably more about Asine than we do about any other MH site published.[142] Despite extensive excavation over the past 60 years, the site has produced no public architecture, no particularly wealthy tombs or households, and no compelling evidence for craft specialization or anything that might be properly called a local industry.[143] There are some possible indications of social ranking in residential structures of varying sizes and room numbers, as well as in burials accompanied by different classes and quantities of grave goods, which have been placed in tombs exhibiting different degrees of architectural complexity. The variability in burial practices, however, may be as much due to differences in gender or age as to any other social variables.[144] Though by no means an impoverished site, at least to judge from a substantial number of securely identified imports and the range of external contacts for which these are evidence, MH Asine was probably not as well-to-do a community as nearby Lerna. Neither site, however, has anything to compare with the varied evidence for both economic and military power that contemporary Kolonna exhibits. At a still humbler level is a site like the late MH hamlet of Tsoungiza whose tiny population, recent resettlement, and inland location make it appear very poor and isolated in comparison with larger coastal sites to both the north and south.[145] By the end of the MH period, then, there may be evi-

---

[140] For the symbolic meaning of longboats, see Broodbank (supra n. 139) 335–37. For approaches to determining the function of Theran frescoes, see N. Marinatos, *Art and Religion in Thera: Reconstructing a Bronze Age Society* (Athens 1984), esp. 31–33; Morgan (supra n. 139) 155–65; and W.-D. Niemeier, "Iconography and Context: The Thera Frescoes," in *Iconography* 97–104.

[141] For other representations of ships in MH through LH I or in Middle Cycladic art, see M. Wedde, "Aegean Bronze Age Ship Imagery: Regionalisms, a Minoan Bias, and a 'Thalassocracy'," in *Thalassa* (supra n. 100) 73–94, esp. 93 n. 77; S.A. Immerwahr, "Some Pictorial Fragments from Iolkos in the Volos Museum," *ArchEph* 1985 (1987) 85–94; E. Protonotariou-Deïlaki, "La céramique prémycénienne des tumuli d'Argos," *Études argiennes* (*BCH* Suppl. 6, 1980) 41–52, esp. fig. 26; T.D. Atkinson et al., *Excavations at Phylakopi in Melos* (London 1904) 91, 104, pls. V.8c, XII.23. The seven small ships painted directly below a large running spiral pattern on the matt-painted neck-handled jug from Argos, dating from MH III or perhaps LH I, recall the association on EC II "frying pans" of ships with densely packed, incised and impressed spirals presumably intended to represent the sea. The emphasis placed on steering oars in these MH and MC representations of ships is, however, altogether absent from the EC II renderings.

[142] S. Dietz, *Asine* II: *Results of the Excavations East of the*

Acropolis 1970–1974 1: *General Stratigraphical Analysis and Architectural Remains* (Stockholm 1982); 2: *The Middle Helladic Cemetery, the Middle Helladic and Early Mycenaean Deposits* (Stockholm 1980); S. Dietz, "Kontinuität und Kulturwende in der Argolis von 2000–700 v. Chr. Ergebnisse der neuen schwedisch-dänischen Ausgrabungen in Asine," *Kleine Schriften aus dem vorgeschichtlichen Seminar Marburg* 17 (1984) 23–52; G.C. Nordquist, *A Middle Helladic Village: Asine in the Argolid* (Uppsala 1987); Nordquist, "New Middle Helladic Finds from Asine," *Hydra* 8 (1991) 31–34; R. Hägg and G.C. Nordquist, "Excavations in the Levendis Sector at Asine, 1989," *OpAth* 19 (1992) 59–68; for a summary of the preceding as well as earlier publications on MH Asine, see Lambropoulou (infra n. 147) 221–37. For a stratified MH II to LH I ceramic sequence from the site placed in the broader context of developments throughout the Argolid during this period, see *ATMA* 37–105. For the geomorphological setting of the site in the Bronze Age, see Zangger, forthcoming (supra n. 31).

[143] Nordquist 1987 (supra n. 142) 107–11.

[144] Nordquist 1987 (supra n. 142) 69–106.

[145] For MH Tsoungiza, see Wright et al. 1990 (supra n. 14) 629; J.B. Rutter, "Pottery Groups from Tsoungiza at the End of the Middle Bronze Age," *Hesperia* 59 (1990) 375–458.

dence for a three-stage hierarchy among MH settlements. But for most of the period's duration, the vast majority of sites were probably comparable to Asine and Lerna, with no site on the mainland rivaling Kolonna on Aegina and few hamlets on the scale of Tsoungiza being founded.

The resettlement of Tsoungiza late in the MH period, as recent intensive survey in addition to both old and new excavations have shown, is but one instance of a far more widespread episode of colonization of the interior. Such resettlements may have occurred not only in other valleys of the northeastern Peloponnese (e.g., Zygouries in the Kleonai valley to the east of Ancient Nemea, Ayia Irini in the Phlius valley to the west) but perhaps also in valley systems as far away as Attica (e.g., Kiapha Thiti just inland of Vari, Panakton in the Skourta plain), Phocis (e.g., Koumoula, just northeast of and above Delphi), and the southeastern Argolid at much the same time.[146] In virtually all of the Peloponnesian cases, abandonments near or at the end of the EH III period are followed by resettlement several centuries later in the MH III phase. Whether this pattern of desertion and resettlement is the result of common factors, and to what extent the growth in the number of late MH sites in Attica and Phocis is part of this same resettlement phenomenon, must remain open questions pending the publication of more data from both surveys and excavations. Preliminary analysis of the data so far available from the Corinthia and the Argolid suggests that significant differences exist between the pattern of MH settlement in the northern, coastal Corinthia and that on the interior to the south, as well as between the latter and that in the southeastern Argolid.[147] As Lambropoulou is careful to point out, the abandonment of sites in this region during or at the end of the EH III phase and their MH III resettlement are two separate events, which therefore merit individual explanations: although the MH III resettlement of sites in the interior of Attica may parallel events on the interior of the Corinthia, the preceding abandonments of the Skourta plain and Kiapha Thiti in Attica and of the Nemea valley in the Corinthia all took place at different times. The point worth stressing in all of this is that our understanding of MH relative chronology has become sufficiently refined, thanks to excavated and published sequences at sites such as Asine, Kolonna, and Lerna, that we are now able to detect discontinuities in occupation at individual sites through excavation as well as within whole valley systems through intensive surface survey. The intermittent periods of occupation and abandonment within the MH period should not come as such a surprise in view of what we have known for some time about fluctuations in settlement densities within both the EH and LH periods. The fact that they do

---

[146] For the depopulation of the Nemea and neighboring valley systems during roughly the first three-quarters of the MH period, followed by the colonization of the interior of both the Argolid and the Corinthia, see Wright et al. 1990 (supra n. 14) 609, 640–42; Rutter (supra n. 145) 452–55. For a similar phenomenon in Attica, see H. Lauter, "Die protomykenische Burg auf Kiapha Thiti in Attika," in *Transition* 145–49 and Maran (supra n. 126) 200–204 (Kiapha Thiti); Munn and Munn 1990 (supra n. 18) 34–35 (survey of Skourta plain), *AR* 38 (1992) 29–31, and pers. comm. (excavations of 1991–1992 at Panakton). For another possible parallel in Phocis, see G. Touchais, "Le matériel de l'habitat préhistorique de Koumoula," in *L'antre corycien* (*BCH* Suppl. 7, 1981) 183–93, 252–57. Müller (supra n. 19) ns. 23–24, on the other hand, views this site as one seasonally occupied by transhumant pastoralists over a longer period of time; for critiques of the projection backward into prehistory of models of transhumant pastoralism, see Cherry (supra n. 32) and Halstead (supra n. 32). Note also J. Knauss, "Deukalion, die grosse Flut am Parnass und der Vulkanausbruch von Thera," *AntW* 18:3 (1987) 23–40, esp. 34–40 (for the view that a natural catastrophe caused the abandonment of Koumoula in LH I). The evidence from the southeastern Argolid is more tenuous in that it consists entirely of material collected during intensive surface survey: G. Nordquist, "The Middle Helladic Pottery from the Southern Argolid," *Hydra* 5 (1988) 17–31, esp. 21–23.

[147] A. Lambropoulou, *The Middle Helladic Period in the*

Corinthia and the Argolid: An Archaeological Survey (Diss. Bryn Mawr 1991; UMI 91-28582) 144–47, 284–95. To the sites in the Corinthian interior showing evidence of resettlement in the late MH period may probably be added, to judge from the finds on display in the Nemea Museum, the site of Ayia Irini in the Phliasian plain west of Tsoungiza (*Gazetteer* 67–68 site A71). Further south, Prosymna on the northern fringe of the Argive plain not far east of Mycenae shows a pattern of desertion after EH III and reoccupation in MH III identical to that at Tsoungiza (Lambropoulou 257–67). On the other hand, Berbati, just to the north in its own valley, was occupied throughout the MH period (Lambropoulou 253–56), during which time, as in the EH III phase, it was the only site in that valley to be occupied (supra n. 9). As was true of the coastal plain in the Corinthia, most of the MH sites located in the Argive plain appear to have been continuously occupied throughout the period (Lambropoulou 291), but the brief report by Dietz (*ATMA* 287) on the site of Profitis Elias near Ayios Adrianos excavated in 1981 by Kilian and Deïlaki suggests that this site may have been initially settled only late in the MH period. For the connection of the resettlement of the Nemea valley with the rise to power of an elite at nearby Mycenae, see Davis (supra n. 14); Wright et al., forthcoming (supra n. 14); J.C. Wright, "An Early Mycenaean Hamlet on Tsoungiza at Ancient Nemea," in *L'habitat* 347–57; Rutter (supra n. 145) 452–55; Lambropoulou (supra) 284–95, 349–53.

come as a surprise is eloquent testimony to how little interest, relatively speaking, the MH period has until recently attracted.

A brief recapitulation of the four areas in which the most progress has been made toward a fuller understanding of Helladic culture during the Middle Bronze Age makes clear how fundamentally we should revise our previous conception of that period. Through a fuller understanding of the production capacities and distribution zones of the Aeginetan and "Lustrous Decorated" ceramic traditions, an enhanced appreciation of the extraordinary site of Kolonna, a balanced and unusually detailed examination of a typical MH coastal site in the form of Asine, and finally a growing awareness of the changing nature of the pattern of settlement within the period, MH society is emerging as considerably more varied and complex than conventionally portrayed. A number of other developments have played a role in this transformation. For example, in the aftermath of a Workshop on Middle Bronze Age Pottery held at the Swedish Institute in Athens in June, 1985, a new periodical by the name of *Hydra* was created "to serve as the vehicle for the exchange of information of

scholars working on the Middle Bronze Age in the Aegean."[148] The publication of a stratified MH and early Mycenaean settlement sequence from the site of Nichoria in Messenia for the first time makes available ceramic, lithic, and faunal assemblages from a continuously occupied site in the southern Peloponnese.[149] These will soon be able to be compared with similar assemblages recovered from the sites of Ayios Stephanos and the Menelaion in Laconia[150] where, however, the sequences of MH and early Mycenaean occupation, especially the former, are not as fully documented as at Nichoria. Within the "heartland" of Helladic culture, two sites have emerged as particularly large MH centers, which continue to be prominent in the early Mycenaean era. Unfortunately, the Bronze Age remains of Argos and Thebes lie buried under flourishing modern towns, with the result that they are accessible to archaeologists almost exclusively in the form of rescue excavations conducted in scattered and usually fairly small building plots. Several summary syntheses of the large number of such salvage operations provide a helpful overview of the extent and prosperity of these two settlements during the first half of the second millennium B.C.[151] Other

[148] *Hydra* 1 (1985) 1. Coedited by G. Nordquist (Department of Classical Archaeology, University of Uppsala, Sweden) and C. Zerner (Archivist, American School of Classical Studies at Athens, Greece), 10 issues of *Hydra* have now appeared, the most recent during 1992.

[149] R.J. Howell, "Middle Helladic Settlement: Stratigraphy and Architecture," in *Nichoria* 15–42 and Howell (supra n. 116); Blitzer, in *Nichoria* (supra n. 35) 712–56; Mancz (supra n. 32); O.T.P.K. Dickinson, "Part I: The Late Helladic I and II Pottery," in *Nichoria* 469–88.

[150] For Ayios Stephanos (*Gazetteer* 112–13 site C17), see supra n. 48; R. Janko, "A Stone Object Inscribed in Linear A from Ayios Stephanos, Laconia," *Kadmos* 21 (1982) 97–100, now classified as HS ZgI in *GORILA* V (1985) 16; J.B. Rutter, "Stone Vases and Minyan Ware: A Facet of Minoan Influence on Middle Helladic Laconia," *AJA* 83 (1979) 464–69. For the Menelaion (*Gazetteer* 107–108 site C1) in MH and early Mycenaean times, see H.W. Catling, "Excavation and Study at the Menelaion, Sparta 1978–1981," *Λακωνικαί Σπουδαί* 6 (1982) 28–43; Catling, "Study at the Menelaion, 1982–1983," *Λακωνικαί Σπουδαί* 7 (1983) 23–31; Catling 1989 (supra n. 3), esp. 7–10; *AR* 23 (1977) 24–35; 27 (1981) 16–19; 32 (1986) 29–30; and 35 (1989) 36. Koumouzelis's pulling together of the scattered MH material known from Elis deserves mention here as another example of relatively recent and helpful efforts to establish a regional MH sequence in an area outside of the "heartland" of the northeastern Peloponnese and east-central Greece: Koumouzelis (supra n. 20) 192–211.

[151] For summaries of MH finds at Argos, see *ATMA* 281–85; Maran (supra n. 46) 355–58. For a full listing of all known MH findspots at Argos and a general discussion of

the implications of their temporal and spatial distributions for the nature of the MH site there, see G. Touchais, "Argos à l'époque mésohelladique: Un habitat ou des habitats?" in A. Pariente and G. Touchais eds., *Argos et l'Argolide: Archéologie et l'urbanisme* (Paris, forthcoming). For the MH tombs at Argos, especially the tumuli along the southeast flank of the Aspis, see E. Protonotariou-Deïlaki, *Οι τύμβοι του Αργους* (Athens 1980); Protonotariou-Deïlaki (supra n. 141); E. Morou's report on a cemetery located on Herakles Street in *ArchDelt* 36B′ [1981] (1989) 107–109; E. Protonotariou-Deïlaki, "Burial Customs and Funerary Rites in the Prehistoric Argolid," in *Celebrations* 69–83; *ATMA* 132–40. Note the discovery in early 1989 by F. Pachiyianni at Argos of a boar's tusk helmet in a MH tomb: C.D. Fortenberry, *Elements of Mycenaean Warfare* (Diss. Univ. of Cincinnati 1990; UMI 90-32620) 108 and n. 18, 116.

For summaries of MH finds at Thebes, see Konsola (supra n. 54), esp. 58–61, 111–16, 126–34, 152–55, 166–70; Symeonoglou (supra n. 54), esp. 19–25; Maran (supra n. 46) 310–11. For recent publications of the MH finds themselves, see Demakopoulou and Konsola (supra n. 54); D.N. Konsola, "Preliminary Remarks on the Middle Helladic Pottery from Thebes," *Hydra* 1 (1985) 11–18. For a warrior burial of the Shaft Grave era, see M. Kasimi-Soutou, "Μεσοελλαδικός τάφος πολεμιστή απο τη Θήβα," *ArchDelt* 35A (1980) [1986] 88–101. Important discoveries of MH and early Mycenaean material since the publication of Konsola's 1981 synthesis and the termination of Symeonoglou's coverage in 1980 include: four of the five locales listed supra n. 54 (i.e., all except 27 Pelopidou); excavations by Aravantinos at 23 Dirkes (*ArchDelt* 36B′ [1981] (1988) 188–89; 37B′ [1982] (1989) 167) and 30 Oidipidos (*ArchDelt* 37B′ [1982] (1989)

recently excavated sites within the "heartland" that have produced significant quantities of MH settlement material include Eleusis, Plasi, and Kiapha Thiti in Attica,[152] Chaironeia, Distomo, Drosia, and Vlicha in Boeotia,[153] Aetopetra and Tsoungiza in the Corinthia,[154] and Kephalari, Kephalari Magoula, and Midea in the Argolid (fig. 15).[155] Outside of the "heartland" to the west and north, only Antikyra, Kirrha, and Koumoula in Phocis and Mitrou and Smixi in Locris have produced anything more than a few MH sherds.[156] In the southern and western Peloponnese, only at Koukounara *Gouvalari* has any excavation been conducted recently at a MH settlement.[157] The task of publishing the MBA levels from the important Thessalian coastal site of Pefkakia, not far beyond the northern boundary of the area considered here, has led Maran to undertake a thoroughgoing review of the MH stratification at major sites in

central Greece (including Aetolia and the Ionian islands) and the Peloponnese, as well as in the Cyclades, Thessaly, and Macedonia.[158] Here is a comparative stratigraphic essay that will prove as useful to those working on topics within the Aegean Middle Bronze Age as was Eva Hanschmann's magnificent stratigraphic analysis of EBA sites covering much the same area but written 16 years earlier.[159]

Whereas large numbers of MH tombs have been excavated at Argos and Thebes over the past 15 years, relatively few have been investigated elsewhere (fig. 16).[160] At Voïdhokoilia in western Messenia, an early MH tumulus, inside of which an early Mycenaean tholos was later sited, itself covers the core of a small EH II settlement in a stratified sequence that has no close parallel at any other site yet known on the Greek mainland.[161] At Kokkolata on Kephallenia, however, something vaguely comparable has been detected by

169), respectively summarized in "Chronique" 1989, 632 and 1990, 764, as well as in *AR* 36 (1990) 38 and 37 (1991) 34; excavations by Sampson on the M. Loukou property on Pelopidou (*ArchDelt* 35B' [1980] [1988] 217–20, summarized in *AR* 35 [1989] 45–46); and excavations by K. Demakopoulou at 58 Epameinonda, 25 and 5 Pelopidou, and 3 Zengine (*ArchDelt* 30B' [1975] [1983] 128–33; 34B' [1979] [1987] 165; 35B' [1980] [1988] 215–17, respectively summarized in "Chronique" 1984, 784; 1988, 642; and 1989, 632, as well as in *AR* 30 [1984] 33; 34 [1988] 32; and 35 [1989] 46).

[152] For Eleusis, see the report by K. Preka on MH and early Mycenaean remains in *ArchDelt* 38B' [1983] [1989] 27–29, summarized in "Chronique" 1990, 717. See also M.B. Cosmopoulos, "The Early and Middle Helladic Pottery from Eleusis," *AJA* 97 (1993) 344–45 (abstract) for a report on the progress of a project to publish all the EH and MH pottery retained from early excavations at the site. For Plasi, see *AR* 31 (1985) 11 and "Chronique" 1988, 621. For the late MH occupation at Kiapha Thiti, also in Attica, see Maran (supra n. 126) and Lauter (supra n. 146).

[153] For the Toumba Balomenou at Chaironeia, see *Ergon* 1989 (1990) 49–52, summarized in "Chronique" 1990, 763 and *AR* 36 (1990) 40. For Distomo, see A. Kyriazopoulou's report in *ArchDelt* 37B' (1982) [1989] 217–20, summarized in "Chronique" 1990, 762. For Drosia, see E. Touloupa's report in *ArchDelt* 33B' (1978) [1985] 117–19, summarized in "Chronique" 1986, 709 and *AR* 32 (1986) 40. For Vlicha, see E. Sapouna-Sakellaraki, "Γλύφα η Βλύχα Βοιωτίας: Η μυκηναϊκή Αυλίδα?" *AAA* 20 (1987) 191–210. Note the title of a dissertation in progress as of March 1992 at the University of Heidelberg's Institut für Ur- und Frühgeschichte: K. Sarri, *Die Keramik der Mittelbronzezeit von Orchomenos.*

[154] For Aetopetra, see Chatzipouliou-Kallire (supra n. 56). For the late MH resettlement of Tsoungiza, also in the Corinthia, after a long abandonment, see supra n. 145.

[155] For Kephalari and Kephalari Magoula, two sites about a kilometer apart, see the report by C.B. Kritzas in *ArchDelt* 29B² (1974) [1979] 242–43 and 246–47, summarized in "Chronique" 1980, 599 and *AR* 26 (1980) 28. For Midea,

see P. Åström, K. Demakopoulou, and G. Walberg, "Excavations in Midea 1985," *OpAth* 17 (1988) 7–11, esp. 9–11; P. Åström et al., "Excavations in Midea 1987," *OpAth* 18 (1990) 9–22, esp. 16–22; P. Åström et al., "Excavations in Midea, 1989–1990," *OpAth* 19 (1992) 11–22, esp. 15–22; G. Walberg, "Excavations on the Lower Terraces at Midea," *OpAth* 19 (1992) 23–39, esp. 25.

[156] For Antikyra, see the report by E. Baziotopoulou-Valavane in *ArchDelt* 37B' (1982) [1989] 206, summarized in "Chronique" 1990, 762. For Kirrha, see the reports by M. Tsipopoulou in *ArchDelt* 35B' (1980) [1988] 255–60 and by D. Skorda in *ArchDelt* 36B' (1981) [1988] 235; 37B' (1982) [1989] 220; and 38B' (1983) [1989] 188–89, summarized in "Chronique" 1989, 629 and 1990, 761 as well as in *AR* 35 (1989) 47 and 37 (1991) 37. For the resettlement of Koumoula, also in Phocis, not long before the end of the MH period, see Touchais (supra n. 146). For Mitrou, see Fossey (supra n. 53). For Smixi, see the report by F. Dakoronia in *ArchDelt* 34B' (1979) [1987] 186, summarized in *AR* 34 (1988) 34. Note the title of a dissertation in progress as of March 1992 at the University of Heidelberg's Institut für Ur- und Frühgeschichte: E. Welli, *Die mittelhelladische Keramik von Kirrha bei Delphi.*

[157] The fieldwork undertaken by G. Korres on previously known MH buildings at Gouvalari consisted of a cleaning operation to establish the stratigraphy: *Ergon* 1987 (1988) 104, summarized in *AR* 35 (1989) 37.

[158] Maran (supra n. 46) 301–84 (regions outside Thessaly), 205–300 (Thessaly).

[159] E. Hanschmann and V. Milojčić, *Die deutschen Ausgrabungen auf der Argissa Magula in Thessalien* III: *Die frühe und beginnende mittlere Bronzezeit* (Bonn 1976) 107–229.

[160] For MH burial customs in general, see Nordquist 1987 (supra n. 142) 91–106; C. Zerner, "Ceramics and Ceremony: Pottery and Burials from Lerna in the Middle and Late Bronze Ages," in *Celebrations* 23–34; G.C. Nordquist, "Middle Helladic Burial Rites: Some Speculations," in *Celebrations* 35–41; Protonotariou-Deïlaki 1990 (supra n. 151).

[161] Korres (supra n. 49), esp. 5–8.

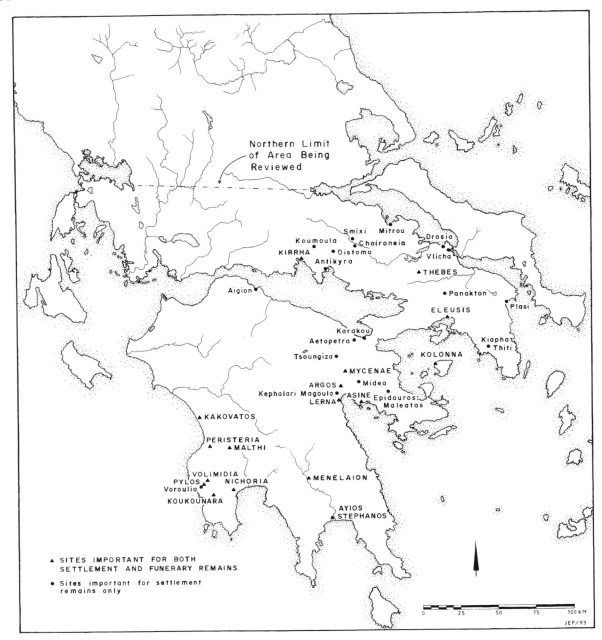

Fig. 15. Locations of important settlement sites of the Middle Helladic and early Mycenaean periods

Kalligas in the placement of a pair of small tholos tombs of LH IIIB date within a MH tumulus.[162] Müller's recent survey of all Helladic tumuli makes clear what a heterogeneous assortment of constructions they are in terms of date, location, and size as well as in the details of their use as places of burial.[163] More common and more widely distributed during the MH period than in any other, these tumuli nevertheless clearly cluster in Messenia, Elis, and the Argolid, at least within the Peloponnese. A pair of cist graves

[162] P.G. Kalligas, "Κεφαλληνιακά III," *AAA* 10 (1977) 116–25.

[163] Müller (supra n. 64). Note the more recent review of this category of architecture by Forsén in *Twilight* 232–37, 255–56, plus the addition to Müller's catalogue of a newly

recognized late MH tumulus at Corinth (Rutter [supra n. 145) 455–58) and several more of both MH and Mycenaean date at Kanalos near Gargalianoi in Messenia (E. Papakonstantinou in *ArchDelt* 37B′ [1982] (1989) 135, summarized in *AR* 37 [1991] 32). For the identification of Grave Circles

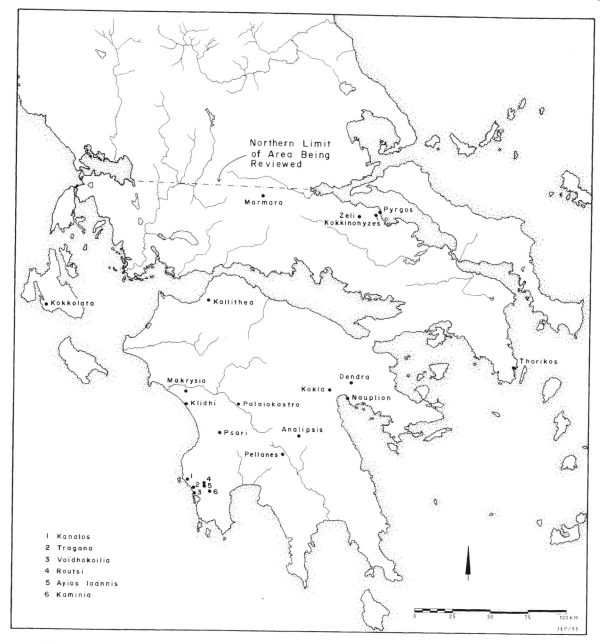

Fig. 16. Locations of Middle Helladic and early Mycenaean sites important for their funerary remains only

from Pyrgos, near Livanates in Locris, are unusual not so much for their form or contents as for their place of discovery, an area as yet rather poorly documented throughout the Bronze Age.[164]

The Shaft Grave era—that period during which burials were made in Grave Circles A and B at Mycenae—corresponds in ceramic terms to three phases, MH III, LH I, and the beginning of LH IIA, repre-

---

A and B at Mycenae as tumuli, as well as for the discovery of three MH or early Mycenaean tumuli at the west end of the chamber tomb cemetery of Dendra, see E. Protonotariou-Deïlaki, "The Tumuli of Mycenae and Dendra," in *Celebrations* 85–106. For the MH tumulus at Ayios Ioannis *Papoulia* and the early Mycenaean tumulus at Kaminia, see

G.S. Korres's reports in *Ergon* 1978 (1979) 46 and 1980 (1981) 34–35, summarized in "Chronique" 1979, 363–65 and 1981, 797–800, in *AR* 26 (1980) 33 and 28 (1982) 25, and in Korres (supra n. 49) 9–10.

[164] F. Dakoronia, "Mittelhelladische Gräber in Ost-Lokris," *AM* 102 (1987) 55–64; Dakoronia 1993 (supra n. 28).

senting some 100–150 years.[165] This era has been the subject of an enormous amount of scholarly literature over the past 15 years. Rather than seeking to summarize this scholarship, I will instead indicate what appear to me to be some common foci of interest within it.

A good deal of effort has been devoted to subdividing the Shaft Grave period into shorter phases, each lasting on the order of a generation, or roughly 30 years. Studies of this kind differ appreciably one from the next depending on whether they are based on funerary assemblages or settlement deposits or both, whether they focus on discoveries at a single site or at several sites within a larger region, and whether the chronology proposed is a stepping stone to some other kind of analysis or an end in itself. For example, several intriguing studies have concentrated on establishing the relative chronology of the burials in the two Shaft Grave circles at Mycenae with the aim of describing the nature of early Mycenaean social rank-

ing and the process of its emergence.[166] Those publishing deposits of settlement pottery from such sites as Korakou, Tsoungiza, Asine, Nichoria, and Kiapha Thiti, on the other hand, have typically aimed at little more than definitions of local ceramic sequences, although there has also been a fair amount of interest in identifying the relative proportions of locally made and imported pottery in such deposits, as well as the sources of the imported pottery.[167] Between these extremes are studies that are not restricted to either tomb finds or settlement assemblages but encompass both, either at the site or at the regional level, and again principally with the aim of defining chronological intervals in terms of ceramic types.[168] Local ceramic sequences based on settlement rather than funerary types are, of course, highly desirable from the point of view of archaeologists conducting intensive surface survey.[169] These increasingly refined pottery sequences should enable correlations of stages in the emergence of social stratification (as determined

---

[165] For a relatively short Shaft Grave era lasting roughly a century, see Dickinson (supra n. 122) 18 fig. 1, 29–31, 50–51; for a significantly longer Shaft Grave era, see *ATMA* 316–21, fig. 93.

[166] I. Kilian-Dirlmeier, "Beobachtungen zu den Schachtgräbern von Mykenai und zu dem Schmuckbeigaben mykenischer Männergräber," *JRGZM* 33 (1986) 159–98; A. Xenaki-Sakellariou, "Problèmes chronologiques des tombes du Cercle A de Mycènes," in *Transition* 177–82; R. Laffineur, "Mobilier funéraire et hierarchie sociale aux cercles des tombes de Mycènes," in *Transition* 227–38; G. Graziadio, "The Chronology of the Graves of Circle B at Mycenae: A New Hypothesis," *AJA* 92 (1988) 344–72, a preliminary to Graziadio, "The Process of Social Stratification at Mycenae in the Shaft Grave Period: A Comparative Examination of the Evidence," *AJA* 95 (1991) 403–40. The references cited in Graziadio's two articles constitute by themselves a full bibliography through 1990 of the scholarly literature on the Shaft Graves and the period of time that they span. For the appearance of Circle A at Mycenae in the Shaft Grave era and the nature and interpretation of its monumentalization in later Mycenaean times, see C. Gates, "Rethinking the Building History of Grave Circle A at Mycenae," *AJA* 89 (1985) 263–74; R. Laffineur, "Le cercle des tombes de Schliemann: cent dix ans après," in *Thanatos* 117–26; R. Laffineur, "Grave Circle A at Mycenae: Further Reflections on Its History," in *Celebrations* 201–206. For what makes Mycenae an unusual Mycenaean site from the Shaft Grave era until near the close of the LBA, see E. French, "'Dynamis' in the Archaeological Record at Mycenae," in M.M. Mackenzie and C. Roueché eds., *Images of Authority: Papers Presented to Joyce Reynolds on the Occasion of Her 70th Birthday* (Cambridge 1989) 122–30.

[167] For Korakou, see O.T.P.K. Dickinson, "Late Helladic IIA and IIB: Some Evidence from Korakou," *BSA* 67 (1972) 103–12; and Davis (supra n. 36). For Tsoungiza, see J.B.

Rutter, "A Ceramic Definition of Late Helladic I from Tsoungiza," *Hydra* 6 (1989) 1–19; Rutter (supra n. 145); Rutter, "A Group of Late Helladic IIA Pottery from Tsoungiza," *Hesperia* 62 (1993) 53–93. For Asine, see *ATMA* 37–105. For Nichoria, see Howell (supra n. 149) and Dickinson (supra n. 149). For Kiapha Thiti, see Maran (supra n. 126). The reports of this kind that were composed, though not necessarily published, in the 1970s focused on the definition of temporal intervals. One result of the growing number of published sequences of settlement pottery has been an increasing emphasis on regional variation. With respect to the sources and quantities of imported pottery, which by itself constitutes a useful index of regional variation, various Aeginetan wares (e.g., matt-painted, solidly coated, and cooking pottery) have received the most attention. Other categories of imported pottery, whose centers of production have yet to be established with any precision, are largely of LH I date: Mainland Polychrome matt-painted (*ATMA* 217–23, 301–303), Gray Minyan (*ATMA* 199–204), Light on Dark-slipped-and-Burnished (*ATMA* 212–13), and Fine Orange (*ATMA* 214–15).

[168] At the site level, see Zerner (supra ns. 126 and 160) for Lerna, Dietz (supra n. 142; *ATMA* 37–105) and Nordquist 1987 (supra n. 142) for Asine. At the regional level, see *ATMA* for the Argolid and Lolos (supra n. 124) for Messenia. I have not seen the Greek dissertation by A. Sabur entitled *Η εξελίξη της μυκηναϊκής κεραμεικής στην Βοιωτιά* (1987), cited in *AR* 34 (1988) 32.

[169] The fact that several recent surveys have been closely linked to specific excavation programs is hardly coincidental (e.g., the Laconia Survey and the excavations at the Menelaion, the Nemea Valley Survey and the excavations at Tsoungiza, and the Skourta Plain Survey and the excavations at Panakton). Other survey projects have been able to rely upon local prehistoric sequences established by earlier excavations at nearby sites (e.g., Berbati, Pylos).

from the analysis of funerary data) with changes in settlement patterns (as documented by surface survey), both in the immediate vicinity of later palatial sites (e.g., Mycenae and Pylos, through the Nemea Valley, Berbati-Limnes, and Pylos Regional Surveys) and in areas far removed from such centers (e.g., the Skourta plain, the Oropos area, the Methana peninsula, and the southern Argolid).[170]

One unfortunate development stemming from the intense recent interest in refining chronological precision within the Shaft Grave era has been the rise of several different terminologies for the various subphases defined. Thus, for example, Kilian-Dirlmeier's phases 1–4 cover the same time span as Dietz's MH IIIA–B, LH IA–B, and LH IIA, while Graziadio employs the terms Early Phase and Late Phases I and II to describe stages within the use of Grave Circle B alone. In some cases, the above authorities have commented in detail on how and why their own relative chronology differs from those employed by others, but due presumably to time constraints they have not always managed to provide as full a critique as desirable of competing relative chronologies.[171] For the time being, we must accept the fact that no universally accepted terminology exists, so that tables illustrating one's own point of view in comparison with those of other specialists are virtually mandatory.[172] In the

midst of so much evidence for disagreement, it is important to underscore one important point on which all authorities do agree: namely, that during the earliest phase of the Mycenaean era known as LH I, the amount of decorated Mycenaean pottery is very small in comparison to the quantities of matt-painted and fine unpainted (i.e., Minyan, whether Yellow, Black, or Red) pottery in use. It is for this reason that Dietz's typology of MH III and LH I shapes is so welcome, despite its strictly northeastern Peloponnesian focus, for Furumark's original typology of Mycenaean pottery and Mountjoy's helpfully illustrated updating of it do not cover the vast majority of ceramic types in use during most of the Shaft Grave era.[173]

How the rise to dominance of the fine, lustrous-painted class of pottery that we call "Mycenaean" should be interpreted is still very much an open question, as is where the production center (or centers) of the earliest Mycenaean decorated pottery was (or were) located.[174] Progress on answering these and other questions concerning the early stages of Mycenaean culture will be made as more is learned about regional variation during the Shaft Grave era.[175] Pottery is certainly one sphere of material culture in which regional differences are already well documented. Settlement architecture, on the other hand,

---

[170] For the beginnings of investigations of this type, see Wright et al., forthcoming (supra n. 14), Davis (supra n. 14), and Wright (supra n. 147).

[171] Laffineur (supra n. 166) provides a critique of Kilian-Dirlmeier (supra n. 166), as do Graziadio 1991 (supra n. 166) 414–15, 430–34, and Dietz (ATMA 264). Graziadio 407 n. 38 also supplies a brief comment on Laffineur. Dietz's critical assessment (ATMA 25–26) of Graziadio's 1988 schema does not permit a convenient yet comprehensive comparison of the rival chronologies espoused by these two scholars.

[172] For such tables, see Graziadio 1988 (supra n. 166) 345 table 1 and Graziadio 1991 (supra n. 166) 433 table 4; Laffineur (supra n. 166) 234; ATMA 26 fig. 1.

[173] A. Furumark, Mycenaean Pottery: Analysis and Classification (Stockholm 1941) esp. 472–77; P.A. Mountjoy, Mycenaean Decorated Pottery: A Guide to Identification (SIMA 73, Göteborg 1986) esp. 9–16. The northeastern Peloponnesian focus of Dietz's typology may severely limit its use in other regional contexts. His classification scheme is also restricted to finds from tombs, with the result that, for example, Aeginetan matt-painted basins and kraters, very common in Argive, Corinthian, and Attic settlement contexts of the Shaft Grave era, are not included as types (ATMA 224–27), although Dietz describes their distribution in some detail in a separate section (303–305, fig. 91). For Messenia, two recent publications provide a welcome complement to Dietz's

treatment of the Argive material: first, Lolos (supra n. 124) has provided an extremely valuable regional perspective with his publication of both settlement deposits (e.g., Malthi, Volimidia, Koukounara Katarrachaki, Peristeria, Voroulia, Pylos, and Nichoria) and tomb material (Malthi, Nichoria, Kaminia, Koukounara, Voïdhokoilia, Tragana, Pylos, Volimidia, Routsi, Peristeria, Kakovatos, Klidhi, and Makrysia) from virtually all of this region's excavated early Mycenaean sites as far north as the Alpheios valley in Elis; second, Howell and Dickinson (supra n. 149) have recently published what appears to be a continuous MH III through LH II settlement sequence from Nichoria.

[174] For the stylistic ingredients of Mycenaean decorated pottery of the LH I period, see O.T.P.K. Dickinson, "The Definition of Late Helladic I," BSA 69 (1974) 109–20; Mountjoy (supra n. 173) 9. For what appears to be a typical northeastern Peloponnesian ceramic assemblage of the LH I period, containing very little decorated Mycenaean pottery, see Davis (supra n. 167).

[175] For an introduction to regionalism in Mycenaean ceramics of all phases, see P.A. Mountjoy, "Regional Mycenaean Pottery," BSA 85 (1990) 245–70. For technical aspects of early Mycenaean pottery production, which are as likely to have varied regionally as are combinations of shape and decoration, see Lewis (supra n. 44). For other items of material culture subject to regional variation, see Dickinson (supra n. 122) 87–99 and supra n. 24.

is not, for the simple reason that so little of it datable to this period has been recovered.[176] Far more commonly located and excavated are early Mycenaean tombs—cist graves, shaft graves, tumuli, tholoi, and chamber tombs—with the result that the funerary architecture and burial customs of this period were already quite well known before the *Gazetteer* appeared.[177] They have since become even better documented thanks to a number of important recent discoveries (fig. 16). In the Peloponnese, the excavations of tholoi at Klidhi in Elis, Psari and Routsi in Messenia, Kallithea in Achaea, Pellanes in Arcadia, and Kokla in the Argolid merit special mention; the

last was found unrobbed in 1981 and thus furnished valuable evidence for funerary ritual in addition to a rich array of grave goods.[178] Large cemeteries of chamber tombs at Nauplion in the Argolid and Palaiokastro in Arcadia, the earliest of which date from the early Mycenaean era, have received preliminary publication, while many of the chamber tombs at Mycenae dug in the last century have at last received the full publication they deserve.[179] A richly furnished cist grave of LH IIB date from Argos has also been fully published.[180] North of the isthmus, preliminary reports of early Mycenaean chamber tombs at Kokkinonyzes and Zeli in eastern Locris are welcome

---

[176] A pair of LH I "megara" at Tsoungiza (Wright et al. [supra n. 14] 631–32, fig. 19) and the fortifications at Kiapha Thiti (Lauter [supra n. 146]) are the only major additions to the corpus of early Mycenaean settlement architecture predating the LH II "mansions" at the Menelaion (supra n. 150) to have been discovered over the past 15 years (fig. 15). For excavations of early Mycenaean settlement deposits not already mentioned, see the reports of E. Papazoglou on a LH II "megaron" found in Aigion (*ArchDelt* 37B' [1982] (1989) 149–50, summarized in "Chronique" 1990, 753–54 and *AR* 37 [1991] 28, respectively) and the report of F. Pachiyianni-Kaloudi and K. Lazaridi on a stratified final MH through LH sequence at Eleusis (*ArchDelt* 34B' [1979] (1987) 37–40, summarized in *AR* 34 [1988] 12). For Thebes, see supra n. 151. For the fortified Mycenaean site at Vlicha where earlier remains dating to the LH IIB–IIIA1, LH IIA, and LH I phases have been excavated, see Sapouna-Sakellaraki (supra n. 153), esp. 197–203.

[177] Dickinson (supra n. 122) 59–65. For more recent overviews, see esp. R. Hägg and F. Sieurin, "On the Origin of the Wooden Coffin in Late Bronze Age Greece," *BSA* 77 (1982) 177–86; O.T.P.K. Dickinson, "Cist Graves and Chamber Tombs," *BSA* 78 (1983) 55–67; Pelon (supra n. 124).

[178] For the LH I tholos tomb surrounded by a LH II–IIIC cemetery of chamber tombs at Kallithea, see T. Papadopoulos's reports in *Ergon* 1987 (1988) 89–91, and 1988 (1989) 24–26; and *Prakt* 1987 (1991) 69–72 and 1988 (1991) 32–35, summarized in "Chronique" 1988, 632–34; 1989, 622; and 1990, 752. For the five tumuli at Klidhi cleared in the early 1980s, one with a tholos at its center, see E. Papakonstantinou's reports in *ArchDelt* 36B' (1981) [1988] 148–49; 37B' (1982) [1989] 133–34; and 38B' (1983) [1989] 109–10, summarized in "Chronique" 1989, 615 and 1990, 744–46; in *AR* 36 (1990) 32 and 37 (1991) 32; and in Korres (supra n. 49) 10–11. For the tholos at Kokla, see the preliminary reports by K. Demakopoulou in *ArchDelt* 36B' (1981) [1988] 94–97; 37B' (1982) [1989] 83–85; and 38B' (1983) [1989] 76; see also K. Demakopoulou, "The Burial Ritual in the Tholos Tomb at Kokla, Argolis," in *Celebrations* 113–23, a companion piece to which is O. Pelon, "Les tombes à tholoi d'Argolide: Architecture et rituel funéraire," in *Celebrations* 107–12, and A. Demakopoulou, "Argive Mycenaean Pottery: The Evidence from the Necropolis at Kokla," in *Wace and Blegen*. For the rock-cut LH II tholos at Pellanes, the site of two other such tombs excavated in 1926 (*Gazetteer* 123 site C56), see T. Spyropoulos's report in *ArchDelt* 37B' (1982)

[1989] 112–13, and the summaries in "Chronique" 1983, 761–62 and 1990, 733, as well as in *AR* 28 (1982) 24; 29 (1983) 29; and 37 (1991) 27. For the large tholos at Psari, see G. Chatze's reports in *ArchDelt* 37B' (1982) [1989] 137–38 and 38B' (1983) [1989] 111–13 and the summaries in "Chronique" 1983, 764 and 1990, 744, in *AR* 29 (1983) 30; 32 (1986) 31; 36 (1990) 33; 37 (1991) 33; and 38 (1992) 27; and in Korres (supra n. 49) 10.

[179] For the Evangelistria cemetery at Nauplion, see E. Deïlaki's report in *ArchDelt* 29B² (1974) [1979] 202–203, summarized in "Chronique" 1980, 603 and *AR* 26 (1980) 30. For Palaiokastro, see the summary in *AR* 35 (1989) 34. For Mycenae, see A. Xenaki-Sakellariou, Οι θαλαμώτοι τάφοι των Μυκηνών: Ανασκαφές Χ. Τσούντα (1887–1898) (Paris 1985). I have not seen E. Krigas, Η προϊστορική Αναλίψις Αρκαδίας (Diss. Univ. of Athens 1983), cited in *AR* 30 (1984) 26, which may contain an equally full publication of the finds from the tholos and other built tombs at this important site in Arcadia (*Gazetteer* 123–24 site C58).

The excavation, beginning in 1979, of a cemetery of previously plundered chamber tombs at Aidonia, in the southwestern Corinthia not far west of modern Nemea, has not yet been the subject of a formal preliminary report, although three gold rings of LH II date from one of these tombs have been published (K. Krystalle-Votse, "Τα δακτυλίδια απο τα Αηδόνια Κορινθίας," in Φιλία Έπη εις Γεώργιον Ε. Μυλώναν δια τα 60 έτη του ανασκαφικού του έργου Γ [Athens 1989] 34–43). These and other finds of the same date in precious materials, in addition to the LH II–IIIB pottery and bronzes from the tombs, have been on exhibit in the museum in Ancient Nemea since the mid-1980s. The goldwork from these tombs has allowed a group of stylistically very similar Mycenaean jewelry, on exhibition in the Michael Ward Gallery in New York from April to June 1993 (R. Reif, "Rare Gold Baubles: Small, Ancient and Radiant," *N.Y. Times* [4 April 1993] H:39), to be identified as probably having come from the same tomb or tombs and hence to have been exported illegally from Greece (W.H. Honan, "Greece Sues Gallery for Return of Mycenaean Jewelry," *N.Y. Times* [26 May 1993] C:14). I am particularly grateful to James Wright for bringing these developments to my attention.

[180] D. Kaza-Papageorgiou, "An Early Mycenaean Cist Grave from Argos," *AM* 100 (1985) 1–21; for an equally well furnished LH I child's cist grave from Tiryns, see "Chronique" 1981, 789–92 and *AR* 27 (1981) 14–16, fig. 21.

additions to the corpus of Bronze Age tombs known from this underexplored region.[181] Even more valuable is the publication, from an inland location in Phthiotis not far south of the Spercheios River, of a tumulus cemetery at Marmara that may date in part from the very end of the Bronze Age but the earliest tombs in which appear to have been dug during the Shaft Grave era.[182]

The gradually growing body of evidence for close links between tumuli and tholoi as funerary forms, not only from sites in Messenia and Triphylia such as Voïdhokoilia, Kaminia, and Klidhi but also from the other side of the Mycenaean mainland at Thorikos in southeastern Attica, has by now all but proven that tholoi developed directly out of tumuli. In all likelihood, the Mycenaean tholos represents the merging of a mainland tradition of burial below ground surface in pits, cists, and small chambers set into a low tumulus, on the one hand, and on the other, a Minoan tradition of burial above ground in large circular tomb chambers with corbeled side walls, as long ago maintained by Hood and more recently supported by Pelon.[183] As in the case of the Shaft Grave circles at Mycenae, some of the most recent and most stimulating work on tholos tombs has taken the form of studies evaluating their social and political significance.[184] How Mycenaean tholoi were built has been the subject

of a fairly heated debate, sometimes with important implications for how this form of burial architecture is likely to have been disseminated around the Aegean.[185] Chamber tombs, too, have been analyzed from a number of different perspectives. For example, how does their architecture vary from region to region? How can they be used to provide statistics for rises and falls in the populations of the settlements adjacent to them? And how might the design and siting of such tombs reflect Mycenaean funerary ritual, aesthetics, or social structure?[186]

The wealth of the grave goods deposited in the shaft graves at Mycenae, in the contemporary tholoi of Messenia, and in tombs of both kinds in central Greece at sites such as Thebes and Thorikos is as astonishing today as ever, especially in view of how poorly MH graves were furnished over the preceding three centuries. This material wealth is accompanied by an abundance of pictorial art in numerous media that is no less striking, particularly because of the aniconic nature of virtually all MH art. The individual motifs, as well as the scenes and objects in and on which these appear, are in most cases derived from Minoan art. Whether they were transmitted to the mainland directly from Crete or indirectly through the islands, by Minoan artisans working for Helladic patrons or by Cycladic and Helladic artisans schooled

---

[181] For Kokkinonyzes, see the report by F. Dakoronia in *ArchDelt* 35B′ (1980) [1988] 244–45, summarized in "Chronique" 1989, 630 and *AR* 35 (1989) 48. For Zeli, see the reports by F. Dakoronia in *ArchDelt* 32B′ (1977) [1984] 104; 33B′ (1978) [1985] 139; and 35B′ (1980) [1988] 240–42, summarized in "Chronique" 1986, 706 and 1989, 629 and in *AR* 32 (1986) 42; 34 (1988) 35; and 35 (1989) 49.

[182] Dakoronia 1987 (supra n. 28); J. Maran, "Zur Zeitstellung der Grabhügel von Marmara," *ArchKorrBl* 18 (1988) 341–55.

[183] S. Hood, "Tholos Tombs of the Aegean," *Antiquity* 34 (1960) 166–76; O. Pelon, *Tholoi, tumuli, et cercles funéraires* (Paris 1976); Dickinson (supra n. 177) 57–58, 63–64. For Thorikos, see J. and B. Servais-Soyez, "La tholos 'oblongue' (Tombe IV) et le tumulus (Tombe V) sur le Vélatouri," *Thorikos* VIII (Gent 1984) 14–67; O. Pelon, "Jean Servais et l'architecture funéraire de Thorikos," *Bulletin de liaison de la Société des Amis de la Bibliothèque Salomon Reinach* 4 (1986) 9–17.

[184] J.C. Wright, "Death and Power at Mycenae: Changing Symbols in Mortuary Practice," and P. Darcque, "Les tholoi et l'organization socio-politique du monde mycénien," in *Thanatos* 171–84 and 185–205, respectively; C.B. Mee and W.G. Cavanagh, "Mycenaean Tombs as Evidence for Social and Political Organization," *OJA* 3 (1984) 45–64; I. Kilian-Dirlmeier, "Das Kuppelgrab von Vapheio (Lakonien): Die Beigabenausstattung in der Steinkiste. Untersuchungen zur Sozialstruktur in späthelladischer Zeit," *JRGZM* 34 (1987) 197–212.

[185] W.G. Cavanagh and R.R. Laxton, "The Structural Mechanics of the Mycenaean Tholos Tomb," *BSA* 76 (1981) 109–40; B.S. Frizell, "The Tholos Tomb at Berbati," and B.S. Frizell and R. Santillo, "The Construction and Structural Behavior of the Mycenaean Tholos Tomb," *OpAth* 15 (1984) 25–44 and 45–52, respectively; W.G. Cavanagh and R.R. Laxton, "Problem Solving and the Architecture of Tholos Tombs," and B.S. Frizell and R. Santillo, "The Mycenaean Tholos—A False Cupola?" in *Problems* 385–95 and 443–46, respectively.

[186] For regional variation in chamber tomb design, see L. Kontorli-Papadopoulou, "Some Aspects concerning Local Peculiarities of the Mycenaean Chamber Tombs," in *Thanatos* 145–60. For a study of Mycenaean demography based principally on the excavations of chamber tomb cemeteries, see M.J. Alden, *Bronze Age Population Fluctuations in the Argolid from the Evidence of Mycenaean Tombs* (SIMA-PB 15, Göteborg 1981), critically reviewed by J.F. Cherry in *BibO* 41 (1984) 196–99 and by myself in *ArchNews* 13 (1984) 71–72. For the interplay between chamber tomb design and these tombs' placements and functions, see W.G. Cavanagh, "Cluster Analysis of Mycenaean Chamber Tombs," in *Thanatos* 161–69; R. Laffineur, "Weitere Beiträge zur Symbolik im mykenischen Bestattungsritual," *Schriften des deutschen Archäologen-Verbandes* 9 (1987) 125–32; W.G. Cavanagh and C. Mee, "The Location of Mycenaean Chamber Tombs in the Argolid," in *Celebrations* 55–64; C.B. Mee and W.G. Cavanagh, "The Spatial Distribution of Mycenaean Tombs," *BSA* 85 (1990) 225–43.

in Minoan workshops, are questions to which answers have long been, and continue to be, elusive. The mechanisms of this transmission process are virtually certain to have been multiple rather than single, to have differed from region to region within the Peloponnese and central Greece, and to have varied according to the material and function of the objects in question. The sheer range of these decorated objects in both material and functional terms is astounding, as are in some cases the quantities of a single class of object (e.g., bronze swords, amber beads) deposited with a single interment. It is probably correct to see in all of these variables—function of object, material, quantity, and nature of decoration—denominations in terms of which status came to be measured toward the end of the MH period within mainland Greek societies.[187]

The principal functional categories that can be distinguished among the grave goods of the Shaft Grave era in the Argolid are drinking and pouring vessels, jewelry, weaponry, and containers of various shapes and sizes (boxes, small and large jars, etc.).[188] The first of these categories is traditional though by no means universal in MH graves. The remaining three, however, are all additions to the mainland Greek funerary assemblage from the MH III period onward. All are prefigured in the MH II shaft grave at Kolonna (see above p. 776) but not, to my knowledge, in any contemporary or somewhat earlier Minoan or Cycladic burial. Thus, perhaps not merely a tomb form but also the functional patterning of a new

funerary assemblage was adopted by an emerging elite in the MH III Argolid after an Aeginetan model. Elements of this new package of grave goods—but, perhaps significantly, not the form of tomb nor the stele that marked its position[189]—were adopted somewhat later in regions such as Messenia and Attica by emerging local elites for essentially the same purpose, that is, to mark differences in status. Although the various regional ranking systems appear to have made use of many of the same artifact types as indices of status, the tomb forms employed to express differences in rank appear to have varied significantly from one region to the next (e.g., shaft grave in the Argolid, tholos tomb in Messenia), to have changed with time within the same region (e.g., the shift from shaft grave to tholos in the Argolid during the LH IIA phase), and probably to have expressed differing levels of status even though the same in form (e.g., burial in Argive tholoi restricted to smaller groups of higher status than burial in Messenian tholoi).[190]

Important elements in the recognition of male rank during the Shaft Grave era, which are not attested earlier, are items of both offensive and defensive weaponry such as swords, daggers, and boar's tusk helmets. All three of these classes of object not only signified a certain degree of status if owned but could be elaborated to indicate higher rank, the first two by means of decoration with representational art and the last by increasing the number of tusks with which such helmets were embellished.[191] That is, not only may such objects have functioned more as indicators of

---

[187] For analyses of ranking in the Shaft Grave burials at Mycenae in such terms, see above all (supra n. 166): Kilian-Dirlmeier, Laffineur 1989, and Graziadio 1991.

[188] For encyclopedic publications of the metal vessels from the Shaft Graves at Mycenae and from contemporary tombs elsewhere on the Greek mainland, see H. Matthäus, *Die Bronzegefässe der kretisch-mykenischen Kultur* (*Prähistorische Bronzefunde* 2.1, Munich 1980); E.N. Davis, *The Vapheio Cups and Aegean Gold and Silver Ware* (New York 1977); R. Laffineur, *Les vases en métal précieux à l'époque mycénienne* (Göteborg 1977). For an equally thorough assessment of bronze spearheads and arrowheads, see R.A.J. Avila, *Bronzene Lanzen- und Pfeilspitzen der griechischen Spätbronzezeit* (*Prähistorische Bronzefunde* 5.1, Munich 1983). See also O. Höckmann, "Lanze und Speer im spätminoischen und mykenischen Griechenland," *JRGZM* 27 (1980) 13–158. For objects of faience, see K.P. Foster, *Aegean Faience of the Bronze Age* (New Haven 1979); Foster, "Faïence from the Shaft Graves," *TUAS* 6 (1981) 9–16. For gold diadems, see B. Kling, "Evidence for Local Style on the Shaft Grave Diadems," *TUAS* 6 (1981) 29–38. For jewelry, see R. Laffineur, "Mycenaean Artistic Koine: The Example of Jewelry," *TUAS* 9 (1984) 1–13.

For Mycenaean drinking behavior and its material correlates, see J.C. Wright, "Empty Cups and Empty Jugs: The

Social Role of Wine in Minoan and Mycenaean Society," in P. McGovern and S. Fleming eds., *The Origins and Ancient History of Wine* (forthcoming).

[189] For the grave stelai at Mycenae, see G. Kopcke, "Treasure and Aesthetic Sensibility—The Question of the Shaft Grave Stelai," *TUAS* 6 (1981) 39–45; Graziadio 1991 (supra n. 166) 411. For simpler but roughly contemporary stelai at Argos, see Protonotariou-Deïlaki 1980 (supra n. 151) 164–68, figs. ΣT3–ΣT6 and (supra n. 160) 81–82, figs. 26–28.

[190] For such regional and chronological distinctions in tomb form and usage, see Dickinson (supra n. 24) 133–35; Dickinson (supra n. 177) 60–66; Pelon (supra n. 124).

[191] For swords and daggers of the Shaft Grave era, see S. Hood, "Shaft Grave Swords: Mycenaean or Minoan?" *Πεπραγμένα του Δ' διεθνούς Κρητολογικού Συνεδρίου Α'* (Athens 1980) 233–42; Fortenberry (supra n. 151) 143–49, 164–67, 174–75, 307. For the iconography of the decoration of early Mycenaean swords and daggers, see R. Laffineur, "Iconographie mycénienne et symbolique guerrier," *Art & Fact: Revue des historiens, archéologues et orientalistes de l'Université de Liège* 2 (1983) 38–49; Laffineur, "Mycenaeans at Thera: Further Evidence?" in *Thalassocracy* 133–38. Such decoration could be either incised or executed by means of inlays in precious metals. For the use of the latter technique as an indicator of status in the form either of recurring

rank than as serviceable weaponry but they provide, through their decorative elaboration, vehicles for the articulation of a practically endless series of status gradations. The manipulation of representational art in this fashion to express the rank of its owner is by no means limited to weaponry in this period. Laffineur has recently drawn attention to how the iconography of seals may have been similarly exploited.[192] One might add the chariot as an example of both an image and a physical object that appears to have been employed more for the rank it implied than for either its speed or its military effectiveness.[193]

There may be close to universal agreement that one of the chief functions of representational art during the Shaft Grave era was to enhance individual status, but there exists far less in the way of a consensus on

the distinction between Mycenaean and Minoan art, especially by the beginning of the LH IIA phase.[194] One category of pictorial art that probably did not function to promote its owner's status and that is unambiguously Helladic rather than Minoan is that which appears on painted pottery, particularly on the class of LH I vessels decorated in the Mainland Polychrome matt-painted style.[195] A recently found fragment of a large narrow-necked jar from Tsoungiza of LH I date, handmade in a coarse fabric and decorated in a single color of dark brown matt paint (fig. 17), is to my knowledge unique in vase painting of the Shaft Grave period in its depiction of a human being. The vase to which it belonged has close parallels in terms of both shape and decorative syntax among large matt-painted jars found in graves A, I, and N

---

pictorial motifs or of complex scenes on daggers, see A. Xenaki-Sakellariou and C. Chatziliou, *"Peinture en metal" à l'époque mycénienne* (Athens 1989). For the decoration of dagger and sword hilts and pommels, sometimes with representational forms, see A. Xenaki-Sakellariou, "Poignées ouvragées d'épées et poignards," in *Aux origines de l'hellénisme: La Crète et la Grèce: Hommage à Henri van Effenterre* (Paris 1984) 129–37. See also T.J. Papadopoulos, "A Mycenaean Inlaid Dagger from Messenia (?) in Japan," in *Φιλία Έπη εις Γεώργιον Ε. Μυλώναν δια τα 60 έτη του ανασκαφικού του έργου* A (Athens 1986) 127–35 and I. Kilian-Dirlmeier, "Remarks on the Non-Military Functions of Swords in the Mycenaean Argolid," in *Celebrations* 157–61.

For boar's tusk helmets, see Fortenberry (supra) 103–26 and esp. 121–23, 306 for their function as markers of status; A.P. Varvarigos, *Το οδοντόφρακτον μυκηναϊκόν κράνος: Ως προς την τεχνικήν της κατασκευής του* (Athens 1981); Morgan (supra n. 139) 109–15. For the hunting of boar, see C.E. Morris, "In Pursuit of the White Tusked Boar: Aspects of Hunting in Mycenaean Society," in *Celebrations* 45–53.

[192] R. Laffineur, "The Iconography of Mycenaean Seals and the Status of Their Owners," in *Aegaeum* 6 (supra n. 34) 117–60; Laffineur, "Iconography as Evidence of Social and Political Status in Mycenaean Greece," in *Iconography* 105–12. For Mycenaean glyptic in general, see J.G. Younger, *The Iconography of Late Minoan and Mycenaean Sealstones and Finger Rings* (Bristol 1988); Younger, *A Bibliography for Aegean Glyptic in the Bronze Age* (*CMS* Beiheft 4, Berlin 1991).

For the identification of early Mycenaean artists and workshops, see Younger, "The Mycenae-Vaphio Lion Group," *AJA* 82 (1978) 285–99; J.H. Betts, "The 'Jasper Lion Master': Some Principles of Establishing LM/LH Workshops and Artists," *CMS* Beiheft 1 (1981) 1–15; Betts and Younger, "Aegean Seals of the Late Bronze Age: Masters and Workshops: Introduction," *Kadmos* 21 (1982) 104–21; Younger, "Origins of the Mycenae-Vaphio Lion Master," *BICS* 26 (1979) 119–20; Younger, "Aegean Seals of the Late Bronze Age: Masters and Workshops III: The First Generation Mycenaean Masters," *Kadmos* 23 (1984) 38–64; J.F. Cherry, "Beazley in the Bronze Age? Reflections on Attribution Studies in Aegean Prehistory," in *Iconography* 123–44, esp. 135.

[193] For Mycenaean chariots, which make their first appearance on the Greek mainland in the Shaft Grave era, see Crouwel (supra n. 32); P.A.L. Greenhalgh, "The Dendra Charioteer," *Antiquity* 54 (1980) 201–205; K. Kilian, "Mycenaean Charioteers Again," *Antiquity* 56 (1982) 205–206; M.A. Littauer and J.H. Crouwel, "Chariots in Late Bronze Age Greece," *Antiquity* 57 (1983) 187–92; Drews (supra n. 32) 158–96; Fortenberry (supra n. 151) 233–54.

[194] For a classic statement of the problem, see J. Hurwit, "The Dendra Octopus Cup and the Problem of Style in the Fifteenth Century Aegean," *AJA* 83 (1979) 413–26. For distinctions between Minoan and Mycenaean iconography during this period, see J.H. Betts, "The Seal from Shaft Grave Gamma: A 'Mycenaean Chieftain'?" *TUAS* 6 (1981) 2–8; R. Laffineur, "Early Mycenaean Art: Some Evidence from the West House in Thera," *BICS* 30 (1983) 111–22; W.-D. Niemeier, "Zum Problem von Import und Imitation minoischer Keramik in frühmykenischer Zeit," in *Origines* (supra n. 191) 111–19; Laffineur, "Iconographie minoenne et iconographie mycénienne," and A. Xenaki-Sakellariou, "Identité minoenne et identité mycénienne à travers les compositions figuratives," in Darcque and Poursat (supra n. 32) 245–66 and 293–309, respectively; Laffineur 1983, 1984 (supra n. 191); Laffineur 1990, 1992 (supra n. 192); W.-D. Niemeier, "Mycenaean Elements in the Miniature Fresco from Thera," in D. Hardy ed., *Thera and the Aegean World* III.1: *Archaeology* (London 1990) 267–82 and subsequent discussion between R. Laffineur and W.-D. Niemeier.

[195] Davis (supra n. 167) 241–43, 256–58; Graziadio 1988 (supra n. 166) 351–52, n. 35; Graziadio 1991 (supra n. 166) 416, fig.1; *ATMA* 217–23, 301–303. For a discussion of this particular class in the context of other pictorial pottery of the Shaft Grave era, see J. Crouwel, "Pictorial Pottery from Mycenae at the Time of the Shaft Graves," in *Transition* 155–65, esp. 158–60, 165. To judge from its wide distribution and its discovery in rich tombs, the Mainland Polychrome matt-painted class was a highly valued category of ceramic that conferred status on its owners. There is, however, no particularly good reason to see in the occasional pictorial images that decorate some specimens of this class additional indicators of prestige.

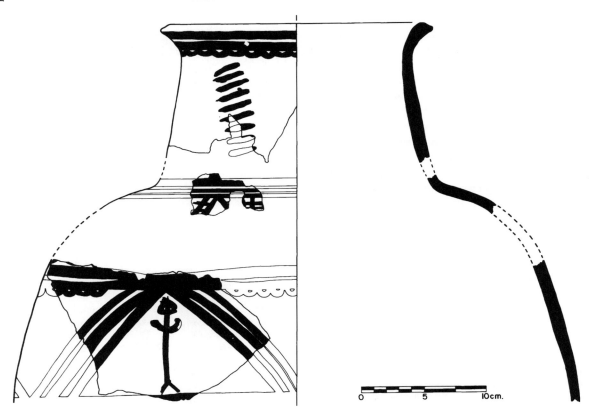

Fig. 17. Fragmentary LH I matt-painted jar decorated with human figure in belly zone, from Tsoungiza

in Circle B at Mycenae.[196] Like the birds and griffins that decorate Mainland Polychrome matt-painted jugs and jars, the antecedents of the stick figure on the Tsoungizan jar are probably Cycladic rather than Minoan.[197] Such evidence for Cycladic influence of some kind on Helladic pictorial art is a salutary reminder that the mainlanders were not dependent

entirely on Crete for the stimuli that transformed MH into Mycenaean material culture.

Other sources of external stimuli, as early as LH I and possibly from the very beginning of the Shaft Grave era, are a group of small islands located just north of eastern Sicily and another small island at the northwest end of the Bay of Naples.[198] Two features

[196] G.E. Mylonas, *Ο τάφικος κύκλος β των Μυκηνών* (Athens 1973) pls. 14a–b (A-4), 95a, c (I-97), 140a–b (N-159), and 221–22.

[197] For various aspects of a peculiarly Cycladic impact on the shapes, decorative syntaxes, and decorative motifs of mainland Greek pottery during the LH I phase, see J.L. Davis, "The Mainland Panelled Cup and Panelled Style," *AJA* 82 (1978) 216–22; G. Graziadio, "Le influenze minoiche e cicladiche sulla cultura tardo medio-elladica del Peloponneso," *SMEA* 19 (1978) 165–203; Crouwel (supra n. 195); P. Betancourt and G. Myer, "Cycladic and Other Highly Micaceous Imports into Lerna V: Evidence from Ceramic Petrography," and M. Marthari, "The Ceramic Evidence for Contacts between Thera and the Greek Mainland," in *Wace and Blegen.*

[198] A partial bibliography of the rapidly growing body of recent literature on early Mycenaean contacts with the West includes, in order of appearance: M. Marazzi and S. Tusa, "Die mykenische Penetration im westlichen Mittelmeerraum: Probleme und Voraussetzungen bei der Gestaltung einer Forschung über die italienischen und sizilianischen

Handelszentren," *Klio* 61 (1979) 309–51; W.D. Taylour, "Aegean Sherds Found at Lipari," in L. Bernabò Brea and M. Cavalier, *Meligunis-Lipara* IV: *L'acropoli di Lipari nella preistoria* (Palermo 1980) 793–817; M. Benzi and G. Graziadio, "Note sulla provenienza delle ceramiche micenee rinvenute in Italia meridionale," in *Aparchai: Nuove ricerche e studi sulla Magna Grecia e la Sicilia antica in onore di Paolo Enrico Arias* (Pisa 1982) 19–33; L. Vagnetti, "Quindici anni di studio e ricerche sulle relazioni tril mondo egeo e l'Italia protostorica," and "Lipari (Messina)," in L. Vagnetti ed., *Magna Grecia e mondo miceneo: Nuovi documenti* (Taranto 1982) 9–40 and 132–35, respectively; M. Marazzi, "Contributi allo studio della 'Societa Micenea' III: documentazione e valore dei primi traffici d'Oltremare," *Quaderni urbinati di cultura classica* 15 (1983) 147–70; M. Cavalier and L. Vagnetti, "Frammenti di ceramica 'matt-painted' policroma di Filicudi (Isole Eolie)," *MEFRA* 95 (1983) 335–44; Cavalier and Vagnetti, "Materiali micenei vecchi e nuovi dale Acropoli di Lipari," *SMEA* 25 (1984) 143–54; E. French, "Problems in Mycenaean Contact with the Western Mediterranean," *TUAS* 9 (1984) 31–32; A.F. Harding, *The Mycenaeans and*

of these early Mycenaean contacts with the West are particularly striking: first, the early date and frequency of the Mycenaean pottery from Filicudi and Lipari in the Aeolian islands and from Vivara cannot be matched by Mycenaean (as opposed to Minoan) exports to areas east or south of the Aegean, although comparable early Mycenaean ceramic exports have now been found to the north at Torone in the Chalkidike;[199] and second, although there are a few pieces of what are probably correctly identified as LM I and LC I imports among the quantities of Aegean pottery found on these island sites in the southern Tyrrhenian Sea, their number is very small in relation to that of the Mycenaean imports.[200]

More is conventionally considered to be known about early Mycenaean than about MH religious practices due to the far greater role played by representational art in the LH I–II phases.[201] At the same time, the problem of distinguishing Helladic from Minoan elements in the iconography of this period limits our ability to distinguish securely between Mycenaean and Minoan behavior or practice. Moreover, we ordinarily have no way of determining the reason an object identified as a Minoan product entered a Mycenaean depositional context. Was it an element of booty or tribute, a simple trade item, or just a gift? If such an object is decorated with a scene or motifs agreed to be religious when in a Minoan context, are

---

Europe (London 1984), esp. 244–61; M. Cavalier and L. Vagnetti, "Arcipelago eoliano," M. Marazzi, "Importazioni egeo-micenee dall'isola di Vivara (Procida)," L. Re, "Importazioni di ceramica d'uso corrente sull'isola di Vivara," and O.T.P.K. Dickinson, "Early Mycenaean Greece and the Mediterranean," in M. Marazzi, S. Tusa, and L. Vagnetti eds., *Traffici micenei nel Mediterraneo: Problemi storici e documentazione archeologica* (Taranto 1986) 141–45, 155–61, 162–65, and 271–76, respectively; T.R. Smith, *Mycenaean Trade and Interaction in the West Central Mediterranean 1600–1000 B.C.* (*BAR-IS* 371, Oxford 1987), critically assessed by L. Vagnetti in *AntJ* 69 (1989) 348–49; E. Lattanzi et al., "Nota preliminare sul sito protostorico di Capo Piccolo presso Crotone," *Klearchos* 113–16 (1987) 25–44; M. Marazzi, "La più antica marineria micenea in occidente," and A.M. Bietti Sestieri, "The 'Mycenaean Connection' and Its Impact on the Central Mediterranean Societies," *DialArch* 6 (1988) 5–22 and 23–51, respectively; F.-W. von Hase, "Ägäische Importe im zentralen Mittelmeergebiet in späthelladischer Zeit (LHI–IIIC)," in T. Bader et al., *Orientalisch-ägäische Einflüsse in der europäischen Bronzezeit* (Bonn 1990) 80–108; R.E. Jones and L. Vagnetti, "Traders and Craftsmen in the Central Mediterranean: Archaeological Evidence and Archaeometric Research," and A. and S. Sherratt, "From Luxuries to Commodities: The Nature of Mediterranean Bronze Age Trading Systems," in *BA Trade* 127–47 and 351–86, respectively; L. Vagnetti, "Appendice III. Le ceramiche egeo-micenee," in L. Bernabò Brea, *Meligunìs-Lipára* VI: *Insediamenti dell'Età del Bronzo* (Palermo 1992) 263–305, esp. 293–96; L. Vagnetti, "Mycenaean Pottery in Italy: Fifty Years of Study," L. Re, "Mycenaean Plain and Coarse Ware from Italy," M. Marazzi, "Early Aegean Presence in the Gulf of Naples: Old and New Discoveries," and S. Tusa, "The Bronze Age Settlements at Vivara (Naples): The Local Context," in *Wace and Blegen*; G. Graziadio, "La Grecia continentale all'inizio del Tardo Bronzo e le rotte protomicenee verso occidente," in M. Marazzi and S. Tusa eds., *Dinamiche ed incontri di culture marinare nel Basso Tirreno nei sec. XVI e XV a.C. Le presenze micenee nel golfo di Napoli* (forthcoming); Graziadio, "Aegean Trade Circuits and Trade-Routes in the Shaft Grave Period" (unpublished manuscript, 1992).

[199] The material from Torone dates to LH I, LH IIA, and LH IIB: A. Cambitoglou and J.K. Papadopoulos, "Excavations at Torone, 1989," *MeditArch* 4 (1991) 147–71, esp. 161–62, figs. 22–23, pl. 25.2–4; J.K. Papadopoulos, "Macedonia in the Second Millennium B.C.," *AJA* 96 (1992) 362 (abstract); A. Cambitoglou and J. Papadopoulos, "The Earliest

Mycenaeans in Macedonia," in *Wace and Blegen*; A. Cambitoglou and J.K. Papadopoulos, "Excavations at Torone, 1990," *MeditArch* 5–6 (forthcoming). For early Mycenaean contacts with the northern Aegean and beyond, see Harding (supra n. 198) 235–44; S. Hiller, "Mycenaean Relations with Their Northern Neighbors," *TUAS* 9 (1984) 14–30; J. Bouzek, *The Aegean, Anatolia and Europe: Cultural Interrelations in the Second Millennium B.C.* (Prague 1985) 30–91; K. Kilian, "Il confine settentrionale della civiltà micenea nella tarda età del bronzo," in Marazzi et al. (supra n. 198) 283–93. I have not seen C. Sueref, "Presenza micenea in Albania e in Epiro: Problemi ed osservazioni," *Iliria* 19.2 (1989) 65–78, cited by Vagnetti 1992 (supra n. 198) 293 n. 119.

For early Mycenaean contacts with the eastern Mediterranean, see O. Negbi, "Were There Connections between the Aegean and the Levant at the Period of the Shaft Graves?" *TUAS* 6 (1981) 46–47; J. Maran, "Die Silbergefässe von El-Tod und die Schachtgräberzeit auf dem griechischen Festland," *PZ* 62 (1987) 221–27. See also Dickinson 1986 (supra n. 198).

[200] Graziadio 1992 (supra n. 198). I am very grateful to G. Graziadio for allowing me to cite information from this manuscript in advance of its publication.

[201] R. Hägg, "Official and Popular Cults in Mycenaean Greece," and R.B. Koehl, "The Functions of Aegean Bronze Age Rhyta," in R. Hägg and N. Marinatos eds., *Sanctuaries and Cults in the Aegean Bronze Age* (Stockholm 1981) 35–39 and 179–87, respectively; J. Chadwick, "What Do We Know about Mycenaean Religion?" and R. Hägg, "Mycenaean Religion: The Helladic and the Minoan Components," in A. Morpurgo Davies and Y. Duhoux eds., *Linear B: A 1984 Survey* (Louvain 1985) 191–202 and 203–25, respectively; J. van Leuven, "The Religion of the Shaft Grave Folk," in *Transition* 191–201; W.-D. Niemeier, "Zur Ikonographie von Gottheiten und Adoranten in den Kultszenen auf minoischen und mykenischen Siegeln," in Müller (supra n. 98) 163–84; Niemeier, "Cult Scenes on Gold Rings from the Argolid," and R. Hägg, "The Role of Libations in Mycenaean Ceremony and Cult," in *Celebrations* 165–70 and 177–84, respectively; K. Kilian, "Mykenische Heiligtümer der Peloponnes," in H. Froning, T. Hölscher, and H. Mielsch eds., *Kotinos: Festschrift für Erika Simon* (Mainz 1992) 10–25, esp. 11–13; J.C. Wright, "The Spatial Configuration of Belief: The Archaeology of Mycenaean Religion," in S. Alcock and R. Osborne eds., *Placing the Gods: The Landscape of Greek Sanctuaries* (Oxford, forthcoming).

we justified in inferring anything about Mycenaean religious behavior from the motifs or scene in question? The religious iconography on luxury objects such as gold rings or even on items made from less valuable materials such as stone seals can therefore rarely be convincingly argued to reflect Mycenaean religious ideology or ritual practice.

Actual locations where cult was practiced in MH and early Mycenaean times—sanctuaries or shrines—appear to have been extremely rare. In fact, no MH cult locales whatsoever have been identified, to my knowledge.[202] Only in the later sanctuary of Apollo Maleatas near Epidauros has the nature of the finds, in non-funerary contexts adjacent to an early Mycenaean settlement, suggested the existence of a contemporary cult place.[203] This site has been compared with Minoan peak sanctuaries on the basis of the Minoan character of some of the finds (seals, steatite rhyton fragment with figured decoration in relief, bronze double-axes), the locale of their discovery (just north and downslope from a hilltop settlement on Mt. Kynortion exhibiting three phases of Mycenaean occupation on top of two EH phases), and their association with quantities of animal bones from strata containing much evidence for burning. The presence of numerous bronze weapons other than double-axes (e.g., swords and daggers with the pommels for both, spearheads) sets the Maleatas finds apart from those recovered at typical Minoan peak sanctuaries, but weapons are found in other Minoan cult places (e.g., the Arkalochori Cave[204]) and thus there is no need to see in the presence of this weaponry an aspect of Helladic rather than Minoan religious behavior.

CONCLUSION

One way to measure progress since the *Gazetteer*'s publication in our understanding of the societies occupying the southern and central Greek mainland during roughly the first three-quarters of the Bronze Age is to single out several major issues and assess how answers to them have recently changed.[205]

How and why, for example, has thinking about the transition from the Neolithic to the Bronze Age developed? In this case, aside from some progress in describing settlement assemblages near the beginning of the EH period and developing a better sense of the changes in settlement patterns between the Final Neolithic (or Late Neolithic II) period and the EH I phase (see above pp. 760–61), not much else appears to have happened. The reason why this is so has to do with the lack of excavated FN and EH I settlements and the virtual non-existence of funerary remains on either side of what, in view of the terminology in use, should be a transition of major significance. At a number of locales in both the Peloponnese and central Greece, as in other areas of the Aegean, whether to the north in Thessaly (at Pefkakia and Sesklo) and Macedonia (at Sitagroi), to the south in Crete (at Knossos), or in the approximate center in the Cyclades (at Kephala on Keos and the Cave of Zas on Naxos), the production, or at least presence, of metal artifacts in Neolithic levels has been documented. There is therefore no real basis for the distinction between the end of the Neolithic and the beginning of the Early Bronze Age on the grounds that metallurgy made its initial appearance in the EH period.[206]

[202] For the nonexistence of recognized MH cult locales, see Nordquist 1987 (supra n. 142) 111.

[203] V. Lambrinoudakis, "Remains of the Mycenaean Period in the Sanctuary of Apollon Maleatas," in Hägg and Marinatos (supra n. 201) 59–65, with extensive references to earlier preliminary reports. The architecture associated with these finds consists of a terrace wall and a patch of the original floor of the terrace. Associated with these were copious animal bones and extensive evidence of burning, interpreted as the remains from repeated burnt offerings of sacrificial animals on an open-air altar located on the terrace. West of this "altar terrace" were found walls defining three rooms, one of them paved. All three are dated to the early Mycenaean period and assigned to a sacral building on the grounds that the LH I–II pottery associated with the rooms consists of the same types as that found in the area of the "altar terrace." The earliest pottery from this part of the Apollo Maleatas sanctuary is firmly assigned to the LH I period by Dietz (*ATMA* 287).

[204] For the Arkalochori Cave, see H. Hazzidakis, "An Early Minoan Sacred Cave at Arkalochori in Crete," *BSA* 19 (1912) 35–47. For Minoan peak sanctuaries, see A.A.D. Peatfield, "The Topography of Minoan Peak Sanctuaries," *BSA* 78 (1983) 273–80; Peatfield, "Palace and Peak: The Political

and Religious Relationship between Palaces and Peak Sanctuaries," in Hägg and Marinatos (supra n. 3) 89–93; B. Rutkowski, "Minoan Sanctuaries: The Topography and Architecture," in Laffineur (supra n. 100) 71–99; Peatfield, *The Peak Sanctuaries of Minoan Crete* (Diss. Univ. of London 1989); Peatfield, "Minoan Peak Sanctuaries: History and Society," *OpAth* 17 (1990) 117–31; Peatfield, "Rural Ritual in Bronze Age Crete: The Peak Sanctuary at Atsipadhes," *Cambridge Archaeological Journal* 2 (1992) 59–87.

[205] Every Aegean prehistorian would no doubt come up with a somewhat different list if asked to identify the four most important questions at issue during this millennium and a half of the mainland Greek Bronze Age. My aim here has been to focus on episodes of major cultural change, which by chance are fairly evenly distributed throughout the time period being surveyed.

[206] For a thorough review of the evidence, see McGeehan-Liritzis (supra n. 34); V. McGeehan-Liritzis and J. Taylor, "Yugoslavian Tin Deposits and the EBA Industries of the Aegean," *OJA* 7 (1987) 211–25; V. McGeehan-Liritzis and N.H. Gale, "Chemical and Lead Isotope Analysis of Greek Late Neolithic and Early Bronze Age Metals," *Archaeometry* 30 (1988) 199–225. For the Cave of Zas on Naxos, see "RAP I" 740 n. 181.

What has happened to change our thinking about the eventful transition from the EH II phase (as typified in Renfrew's Korakou culture) to EH III (the floruit of his Tiryns culture)? On this front, there have been numerous developments (see above pp. 763–66). But the result has not been to provide a more definitive response to the questions of what happened and why. Rather, an old explanatory model (Caskey's theory of a double invasion at the transitions from EH II to III and from EH III to MH, based on his excavations at Lerna) has had to be scrapped with the realization that the transitions in question are manifested in quite different ways in the different regions that make up our study area. In this case, the question of what happened at the EH II–III transition has not really been altered but the response to it has been "pluralized" as we have come to appreciate that the process of cultural change in question was a long-lived rather than short-term one, which began earlier in the north of the study area than in the south. The stages in this cultural metamorphosis vary considerably from region to region, both in number and in nature.[207]

What caused a dramatic rise in material wealth toward the end of the MH period, initiating the Shaft Grave era (MH III–LH IIA ceramic phases)? In this period of three to four generations a social hierarchy was gradually articulated, at least in terms of the material correlates that make it visible to archaeologists, by means of the goods deposited with individual burials. There is no evidence for a hierarchy marked in this way during the preceding three centuries (EH III–MH II ceramic phases). That is, the emergence of a distinct social group, or elite, which chose to employ this new wealth as a means of self-identifica-tion, appears to have been as new as the wealth itself. What, then, happened that could have led to the emergence of this elite first in the Argolid and Messenia, and caused it to distinguish itself with a particular range of artifactual types? The answers that have been in vogue over the past 15 years identify, in the emerging elites, small Peloponnesian groups who somehow managed to gain control over the flow into the Aegean of a valuable raw material, either tin or gold. With control over this resource, the mainlanders were able to negotiate a "special relationship" with one or more Minoan palaces, giving them access to both artisans and other valuable raw materials, and resulting in the lavish and unusually diverse grave goods found in the Shaft Graves.[208] As in the case of the EH II–III transition, we are now not so much in a position to answer the question as to approach it with more varied and potentially valuable information at our disposal. The emergence of Kolonna on Aegina as a potent center of production and probably as the principal agent responsible for the distribution of both its finished goods (pottery) and its raw materials (andesite)[209] has introduced into the Middle Bronze Age a hitherto neglected candidate for the title of "the Aegean's first state."[210] Whether or not the site of Kolonna was the home of an administrative structure to rival those of Protopalatial Crete, one must now consider the possibility that the emerging stratified societies on the Greek mainland, especially those in the Argolid, may have been aping Aeginetan rather than Minoan customs in their choices of how to bury their most prominent families. The recent recognition that major areas of the interior in some regions (e.g., the Corinthia and perhaps also Attica) appear to have been colonized at the time the Shaft Grave era began

---

[207] Cf., e.g., the variability in ceramic assemblages attested during the EH III phase in Boeotia, Elis, and the Argolid: J.B. Rutter, "Early Helladic III Vasepainting, Ceramic Regionalism, and the Influence of Basketry," in *Problems* 73–89.

[208] For tin as the valuable raw material in question, see Dickinson (supra n. 122) 51–57. For gold, see E. Davis, "The Gold of the Shaft Graves: The Transylvanian Connection," *TUAS* 8 (1983) 32–38. If control over metal resources was of such importance, it is perhaps surprising that a site like Thorikos, in a district that had been a major source of lead, silver, and copper ores for centuries, did not become a greater center of power than it did. For Dickinson's critique of his own theory that the wealth of the Shaft Grave princes stemmed from their control of a metal that was in high demand, see Dickinson (supra n. 198) 274 and Dickinson 1989 (supra n. 124) 136, both with references to the critique of the same theory by Harding (supra n. 198) 280–81.

[209] The andesite may well have been marketed in the form of millstones or other finished goods, such as the EH tripod mortars to which Runnels has drawn attention (1988 [supra n. 35]).

[210] For a selection of recent literature on the emergence of the state in the Aegean, see P. Halstead, "From Determinism to Uncertainty: Social Storage and the Rise of the Minoan Palace," in A. Sheridan and G. Bailey eds., *Economic Archaeology* (Oxford 1981) 187–213; J.F. Cherry, "Evolution, Revolution, and the Origins of Complex Society in Minoan Crete," and J. Lewthwaite, "Why Did Civilization Not Emerge More Often? A Comparative Approach to the Development of Minoan Crete," in O. Krzyszkowska and L. Nixon eds., *Minoan Society* (Bristol 1983) 33–45 and 171–83, respectively; J.F. Cherry, "The Emergence of the State in the Prehistoric Aegean," *PCPS* 30 (1984) 18–48; Cherry, "Polities and Palaces: Some Problems in Minoan State Formation," in C. Renfrew and J.F. Cherry eds., *Peer Polity Interaction and Socio-Political Change* (Cambridge 1986) 19–45; L.V. Watrous, "The Role of the Near East in the Rise of the Cretan Palaces," in Hägg and Marinatos (supra n. 3) 65–70; K. Branigan, "Some Observations on State Formation in Crete," and P. Halstead, "On Redistribution and the Origin of Minoan-Mycenaean Palatial Economies," in *Problems* 63–71 and 519–30, respectively; van Andel and Runnels (supra n. 100) 234–47.

may also play a role in new suggestions about how the princes of Mycenae (and Messenia?) acquired their wealth. The discovery that exchanges with the central Mediterranean were fairly common and had begun by the dawn of the Mycenaean era has already had an impact on explanations of the Shaft Grave phenomenon.[211]

Finally, where, when, and why did the combination of administrative headquarters, manufacturing center, and royal residence that we call a Mycenaean palace first appear? At present, the leading contender is the earliest of several superimposed "mansions" at the Menelaion in Laconia, although Kilian has suggested that a partially excavated structure at Kakovatos might be even earlier.[212] In either case, the building in question cannot be dated before the beginning of the LH II period; indeed, it is quite possible that Mycenaean palaces were not built until as late as the LH IIB phase. Thus, it continues to be the case that the palace form did not make its initial appearance on the mainland until long after the Shaft Grave era had begun and possibly not until it was actually over.[213] In view of the probable date of its appearance, the Mycenaean palace is likely to have come into being as a result of the chain of LM IB disasters that overwhelmed all the Neopalatial centers of Crete except Knossos. Further progress on identifying and explaining the appearance of the earliest Mycenaean palaces must await the full publication of the LH II–IIIA1 "mansions" at the Menelaion, as well as of the LH IIIA1 palace built over impressive late MH and early Mycenaean structures on the summit of the citadel at Tiryns. Additional information concerning the date at which Mycenaean palatial administrative and ceremonial complexes were instituted

may also be forthcoming from the Pylos survey in the form of evidence for a significant shift in the settlement pattern in the environs of the palace. In the meantime, the refinement of regional ceramic chronologies during the potentially crucial LH IIB and LH IIIA1 phases will have done much to make the eventual dating of the event much more precise than would have been possible 15 years ago.[214]

Not one of the preceding four questions about the causes of major changes in the cultural history of the mainland Greek Bronze Age has yet been satisfactorily answered. Does this signify that little or no recent progress has been made in the archaeology of this area and time period? Not at all. Impressive advances have been made in identifying regional variation[215] and refining relative chronologies in all phases of the Bronze Age. One consequence of this has been that we are now willing to view the EH II–III transition less as an event and more as a process that took place over a far longer period of time than previously thought and in significantly different ways, with different material correlates, depending on where the process is being tracked. Much the same could be said, and for the same reasons, about the MH–LH transition. Thanks to the rise in intensive surface survey as a mode of fieldwork, such cultural transitions are now examined as much in terms of changes in settlement pattern as any other set of variables. This is good news indeed, for it is in terms of changing settlement patterns that the transitions from the Neolithic to the Bronze Age and from the prepalatial to the palatial stages of Mycenaean culture may prove to be most clearly identifiable. Once again, these last two transitions are likely to occur over time intervals and in sets of differential stages that vary considerably from re-

---

[211] Dickinson 1989 (supra n. 124); Vagnetti 1992 (supra n. 198) 293–96. Long-distance trade with sites in the Tyrrhenian Sea to the west and by way of Troy with sites in the Black Sea to the northeast are considered by A. and S. Sherratt (supra n. 198) 370 to account for the wealth of, respectively, the early Messenian tholoi and the Shaft Graves at Mycenae.

[212] For the Menelaion, see Catling, supra ns. 3 and 150. For Kilian's candidate at Kakovatos, see Kilian in Lévy (supra n. 3) 212, fig. 8; Kilian in Hägg and Marinatos (supra n. 3) 33, fig. 9.

[213] For the gap between the rich early Mycenaean burials in the tholoi of Messenia and the Shaft Graves of Mycenae, and the emergence of complex bureaucracies housed in the mainland's first true palaces, see Dickinson 1989 (supra n. 124) 131. Like Dickinson (see also ns. 2–3), I am not persuaded by Kilian's reconstruction of an early Mycenaean

palace at Pylos resembling a Minoan palace in its form.

[214] For the relative chronology of the LH IIB and IIIA1 phases, see Dickinson (supra n. 167); Catling (supra n. 3); B. Santillo Frizell, *An Early Mycenaean Settlement at Asine: The Late Helladic IIB–IIIA1 Pottery* (Göteborg 1980); P.A. Mountjoy, *Four Early Mycenaean Wells from the South Slope of the Acropolis at Athens* (*Miscellanea Graeca* 4, Gent 1981); Lewis (supra n. 44); P.A. Mountjoy, "The Ephyraean Goblet Reviewed," *BSA* 78 (1983) 265–71; Mountjoy (supra n. 173) 37–66; *Chronology* 96–99, 145–46; J.B. Rutter, "Late Helladic IIB Pottery Deposits from Tsoungiza," *Hesperia* (forthcoming).

[215] Certain regions, however, especially in the west (Aetolia, Akarnania, and the Ionian islands), remain seriously underexplored, as should be apparent from the fact that they have scarcely been mentioned in this review.

gion to region. From what we already know of such major transitions (e.g., the EH II–III and MH–LH examples just discussed), they begin in different regions and take place at different rates. One kind of interesting investigation that still lies some years in the future will be the comparative analysis of these episodes of relatively rapid cultural change. But such analyses will only be possible when our understanding of spatial and temporal variation within each of these episodes has improved considerably. For the time being, there is plenty of basic fieldwork and primary analysis of artifactual data still crying out to be done.

DEPARTMENT OF CLASSICS
DARTMOUTH COLLEGE
HANOVER, NEW HAMPSHIRE 03755
INTERNET JEREMY.RUTTER@DARTMOUTH.EDU

Addendum: 1993–1999

JEREMY B. RUTTER

INTRODUCTION

Since my earlier review of the prepalatial Bronze Age of the Greek mainland (RAP II), exciting discoveries of Early Helladic material have been made at Petri in the southern Corinthia and Geraki in Laconia, while the rich finds from excavations between 1992 and 1994 at the Minoan peak sanctuary of Ayios Georgios on Kythera have now been extensively and widely illustrated in conference papers and preliminary publications.[216] Yet more progress has undeniably been made over the past half-dozen years in the slice of prehistoric Aegean space and time surveyed here through publication than through new fieldwork, whether excavation or survey. By drawing attention to this recent asymmetry in the balance between

initial discovery and final publication, I have no wish to ignore or even downplay the significance of current or very recently completed programs of field research. I mean only to applaud the reversal of a trend that has for altogether too long been dominant in this branch of the larger discipline, and to express the hope that final publications of important fieldwork will continue to appear as rapidly as they have of late.

Perhaps the most striking example of this upswing in publications involves intensive surface survey. The prehistoric findings of no fewer than four major field projects conducted mainly during the 1980s have been comprehensively reported, supplemented by substantial preliminary reports on three new survey programs of the 1990s.[217] The stage is now set for an assessment of the impact of these projects on the

---

[216] I am grateful to the following friends and colleagues for providing news and information that contributed to the content of this addendum: Eva Alram-Stern, Cyprian Broodbank, John Cherry, Jack Davis, Angelika Douzougli-Zachou, Florenz Felten, Walter Gauss, Stefan Hiller, Konstantinos Kalogeropoulos, Michael Lindblom, Joseph Maran, Sylvie Müller, Claus Reinholdt, Christina Shriner, Sharon Stocker, Judith Weingarten, Gert van Wijngaarden, Aaron Wolpert, and James Wright.

For initial reports on the discoveries at Petri, see M. Kostoula, "Πετρί Νεμέας: Τά ανασκαφικά δεδομένα," in Α΄ Αρχαιολογική Σύνοδος Νότιας και Δυτικής Ελλάδος, Πάτρα, 9–12 Ιουνίου 1996 (forthcoming), a prolegomenon to her dissertation in progress at the University of Heidelberg with the working title of Die frühhelladische Siedlung von Petri bei Nemea. For the most recent reports on Geraki, with references to the two earlier preliminary reports that focus on mapping, remote sensing, and survey activities at the site, see J.H. Crouwel, M. Prent, J. Fiselier, and J.A.K.E. de Waele, "Geraki, an Acropolis Site in Lakonia: Preliminary Report on the Third Season (1997)," Pharos 5 (1997) 49–83, esp. 58–62, 67–72, fig. 5, pls. VII–VIII; J.H. Crouwel, M. Prent, R. Cappers, and T. Carter, "Geraki, an Acropolis Site in Lakonia: Preliminary Report on the Fourth Season (1998)," Pharos 6 (forthcoming); and J. Weingarten, J.H. Crouwel, M. Prent, and G. Vogelsang-Eastwood, "Early Helladic Sealings from Geraki in Lakonia, Greece," OJA 18 (1999) 357–76. For Ayios Georgios, see J.A. Sakellarakis, "Το μινωικό ιερό των Κυθήρων," in Λοιβή: Εις μνήμη Α.Γ. Καλοκαιρινού (Heraklion 1994) 195–203; J.A. Sakellarakis and J.-P. Olivier, "Un vase en pierre avec inscription en Linéaire A du sanctuaire de sommet minoen de Cythère," BCH 118 (1994) 343–51; E. Sapouna-Sakellarakis, Die bronzenen Menschenfiguren auf Kreta und in der Ägäis (Prähistorische Bronzefunde 1.5, Stuttgart 1995) 121–34; Y. Sakellarakis, "Minoan Religious Influence in the Aegean:

The Case of Kythera," BSA 91 (1996) 81–99; Y. Sakellarakis, "Μινωικό χάλκινο ειδώλιο σκορπιού από τα Κύθηρα," in B.C. Petrakos ed., Έπαινος Ιωάννου Κ. Παπαδημητρίου (Βιβλιοθήκη της εν Αθήναις Αρχαιολογικής Εταιρείας 168, Athens 1997) 423–72; and several papers delivered at the 8th Cretological Congress (Heraklion, September 1996), the proceedings of which are scheduled for publication in the fall of 2000.

The following abbreviations, in addition to those used in RAP II, are found below:

AATU	A. Pariente and G. Touchais eds., Argos et l'Argolide: Topographie et urbanisme. Actes de la Table Ronde internationale, Athènes–Argos, 28 avril–1er mai 1990 (Athens 1998).
Beyond the Site	P.N. Kardulias ed., Beyond the Site: Regional Studies in the Aegean Area (Lanham 1994).
Polemos	R. Laffineur ed., Polemos: Le contexte guerrier en Égée à l'Âge du Bronze (Aegaeum 19, Liège 1999).
Politeia	R. Laffineur and W.-D. Niemeier eds., Politeia: Society and State in the Aegean Bronze Age (Aegaeum 12, Liège 1995).
Techne	R. Laffineur and P.P. Betancourt eds., TEXNH: Craftsmen, Craftswomen and Craftsmanship in the Aegean Bronze Age (Aegaeum 16, Liège 1997).

[217] In the chronological order of their printing, the final publications are M.H. Jameson, C.N. Runnels, and T.H. van Andel, A Greek Countryside: The Southern Argolid from Prehistory to Present Day (Stanford 1994); C. Runnels, D.J. Pullen, and S. Langdon eds., Artifact and Assemblage: The Finds from a Regional Survey of the Southern Argolid, Greece 1: The Prehistoric and Early Iron Age Pottery and the Lithic Artifacts (Stanford 1995); W. Cavanagh, J. Crouwel, R.W.V.

study of mainland Greek prehistory and for a comparison with the impact of other regional studies elsewhere in the Aegean and wider Mediterranean world.[218] An important component of such surface survey continues to be the study of environmental change by geomorphologists, geologists, geographers, and palaeoclimatologists.[219]

Recently published final reports on excavations conducted over the past 40 years include a pair of volumes devoted to J.L. Caskey's EH findings of the 1950s at Lerna, one to H. Walter's excavation in 1982 at Kolonna on Aegina of the earliest known shaft grave, one to A. Sampson's discoveries of Neolithic through Late Helladic III date in excavations of the early 1990s at Spelaio Limnon near Kastria in Arcadia, and one to V. Milojčić's Early Bronze Age findings during the decade 1967–1977 at Pefkakia in coastal

Thessaly.[220] These comprehensive final reports, in tandem with two major topical syntheses on prehistoric funerary behavior and the earliest stages of metallurgy in the Aegean,[221] have had a substantial impact on several of the topics singled out for special comment in my original review,[222] as has a constant flow of significant periodical literature.

EARLY BRONZE AGE

The transition from the terminal stage of the Neolithic (variously termed Final Neolithic, Late Neolithic, or Chalcolithic) to the earliest phase of the Bronze Age, EH I, continues to be rather unclear, but is certainly better understood with the publication of substantial bodies of the latest Neolithic pottery from stratified sites such as Aria and Franchthi Cave in the Argolid, Aigeira in Achaia, and Kolonna on Aegina.[223]

Catling, and G. Shipley, *Continuity and Change in a Greek Rural Landscape: The Laconia Survey* 2: *Archaeological Data* (*BSA* Suppl. 27, London 1996); B. Wells and C. Runnels eds., *The Berbati-Limnes Archaeological Survey 1988–1990* (Stockholm 1996); and C. Mee and H. Forbes eds., *A Rough and Rocky Place: The Landscape and Settlement History of the Methana Peninsula, Greece* (Liverpool 1997). The preliminary reports are J.L. Davis, S.E. Alcock, J. Bennet, Y. Lolos, and C.W. Shelmerdine, "The Pylos Regional Archaeological Project, Part I: Overview and the Archaeological Survey," *Hesperia* 66 (1997) 391–494; J. Forsén, B. Forsén, and M. Lavento, "The Asea Valley Survey: A Preliminary Report of the 1994 Season," *OpAth* 21 (1996) [1997] 73–97; M.B. Cosmopoulos, "Archäologische Forschungen im Gebiet von Oropos: Die vorgeschichtliche Besiedlung," *PZ* 73 (1998) 52–68. An initial report on a fourth new survey project, now underway on the island of Kythera, has appeared: C. Broodbank, "Kythera Survey: Preliminary Report on the 1998 Season," *BSA* 94 (1999) 191–214.

[218] Such an assessment has, in fact, been commissioned from J.F. Cherry, to appear as part of the ongoing series of "Reviews of Aegean Prehistory" in *AJA*, tentatively entitled "The Impact of Archaeological Surveys and Regional Analysis on Aegean Prehistory, 1970–2000."

[219] Again in the chronological sequence of their appearance, relevant recent publications include E. Zangger, *The Geoarchaeology of the Argolid* (Berlin 1993); Zangger, "The Island of Asine: A Palaeogeographic Reconstruction," *OpAth* 20 (1994) 220–39; Zangger, "Landscape Changes around Tiryns during the Bronze Age," *AJA* 98 (1994) 189–212; P.A. James, C.B. Mee, and G.J. Taylor, "Soil Erosion and the Archaeological Landscape of Methana, Greece," *JFA* 21 (1994) 395–416; G. Rapp, Jr., and J.C. Kraft, "Holocene Coastal Change in Greece and Aegean Turkey," in *Beyond the Site* 69–90; B. Wells, "A Prehistoric Environmental Catastrophe: The Case of Berbati and Limnes," in K.A. Sheedy ed., *Archaeology in the Peloponnese: New Excavations and Research* (Oxford 1994) 65–76; C.N. Runnels, "Environmental Degradation in Ancient Greece," *Scientific American*, 272:3 (March 1995) 72–75; S.C. Stiros, "Palaeogeographic Reconstruction of the Heraion-Vouliagmeni Lake Coast since Early Helladic Times," *BSA* 90 (1995) 17–22; K. Lambeck, "Sea-Level Change and Shoreline Evolution

in Aegean Greece since Upper Palaeolithic Times," *Antiquity* 70 (1996) 588–611; S. Stiros and R.E. Jones eds., *Archaeoseismology* (Fitch Laboratory Occasional Paper 7, Exeter 1996); E. Zangger, M.E. Timpson, S.B. Yazvenko, F. Kuhnke, and J. Knauss, "The Pylos Regional Archaeology Project, Part II: Landscape Evolution and Site Preservation," *Hesperia* 66 (1997) 549–641.

[220] M.H. Wiencke, *Lerna, a Preclassical Site in the Argolid* IV: *The Architecture, Stratification, and Pottery of Lerna III* (Princeton 2000); J.B. Rutter, *Lerna, a Preclassical Site in the Argolid* III: *The Pottery of Lerna IV* (Princeton 1995); I. Kilian-Dirlmeier, *Alt-Ägina* IV.3: *Das mittelbronzezeitliche Schachtgrab von Ägina* (Mainz 1997); A. Sampson, *Το Σπήλαιο των Λίμνων στα Καστριά Καλαβρύτων: Μια προϊστορική θέση στην ορεινή Πελοπόννησο* (Athens 1997); E. Christmann, *Die deutschen Ausgrabungen auf der Pevkakia-Magula in Thessalien* II: *Die frühe Bronzezeit* (Bonn 1996).

[221] W. Cavanagh and C. Mee, *A Private Place: Death in Prehistoric Greece* (*SIMA* 125, Jonsered 1998); V. McGeehan-Liritzis, *The Role and Development of Metallurgy in the Late Neolithic and Early Bronze Age of Greece* (*SIMA-PB* 122, Jonsered 1996).

[222] See RAP II above, 144–47.

[223] A. Douzougli, *Αρια Αργολίδος: Χειροποίητη κεραμεική της Νεότερης Νεολιθικής και της Χαλκολιθικής περιόδου* (Athens 1998); K.D. Vitelli, *Franchthi Neolithic Pottery* 2: *The Later Neolithic Ceramic Phases 3 to 5* (Franchthi 10, Bloomington 1999); E. Alram-Stern, "Aigeira/Achaia and the Settlement Pattern in the Peloponnese in the Final Neolithic and EH I," in *Η προϊστορική έρευνα στην Ελλάδα και οι προοπτικές της: Θεωρητικοί και μεθοδολογικοί προβληματισμοί. Αρχαιολογικό Συμβούλιο στη μνήμη του Δ.Ρ. Θεοχάρη, Θεσσαλονίκη–Καστοριά, 26–28 Νοεμβρίου 1998* (Thessaloniki 1999) 1–9; H.-J. Weisshaar, "Keramik des Südwest-Ägäischen Chalkolithikums von Ägina," in C. Dobiat ed., *Festschrift für Otto-Herman Frey zum 65. Geburtstag* (Marburger Studien zur Vor- und Frühgeschichte 16, Marburg 1994) 675–89. On this topic, see also A. Douzougli-Zachou, "Η Αργολική Πεδιάδα στην Υστερη Νεολιθική και Πρωτοχαλκή Εποχή: Σύνοψη της προβληματικής από μία διεπιστημονική προσέγγιση," in *AATU* 23–39; and D.J. Pullen, "The Pottery of the Neolithic, Early Helladic I, and Early Helladic II Periods," in Runnels, Pullen, and Langdon (supra n. 217) 6–42.

A helpful synthesis of the Early Bronze Age in the Peloponnese by Renard went to press just before the final survey and excavation reports cited above appeared, with the unfortunate result that it is in some respects already badly out of date, and the same probably applies to Harrison's slightly earlier overview of settlement patterns throughout Greece.[224] Excavations conducted at newly reported EH sites have without exception produced only EH II material,[225] but ongoing excavations at Kolonna, a reevaluation of the material recovered in the 1930s at Asea, and the recent final publications from Lerna and Pefkakia have presented EH III as well as EH II cultural remains.[226] A survey of ongoing research on prehistoric activity on and around the Athenian Acropolis that went to press in 1998 includes some EH II material, but nothing positively identifiable as EH III.[227] The restudied site of Deriziotis Aloni in Messenia, excavated in the 1950s by the team then working under Blegen at the nearby Mycenaean palace at Pylos, joins Nichoria, also in Messenia, as the only other site in the southern Peloponnese to have produced EH III remains; in both cases, the pottery in question dates to the very end of the EH III period and is not preceded by any traces of EH I–II settlement.[228] Wiencke's detailed study of the House of the Tiles, of its equally grand but less fully cleared predecessor, Building BG, and of the full sequence of EH II fortifications at Lerna puts the study of EH monumental settlement architecture on a new footing, for Lerna now provides the only known example of a corridor house or of an EH II fortification system for which both the buildings and their contents have been published in full.[229] Welcome complements to this long-awaited volume are recent assessments of ordinary EH II settlement architecture and of population levels and "urbanism" in the Argolid during this era.[230] Burial customs of the EH II period have also received a good deal of attention, whether in the form of freshly published tombs or more synthetic treatments of the subject.[231] Considerations of EH metallurgy, on the other hand, have been relatively sparse of late and have usually been embedded in broader studies devoted to metallurgy throughout the Aegean world in the Early Bronze Age.[232] Textiles, lithics, and figurines of the EH period have also received only occasional attention recently.[233] Major contributions to the study of EH pottery, by contrast,

[224] J. Renard, *Le Péloponnèse au Bronze ancien* (*Aegaeum* 13, Liège 1995); S.G. Harrison, *Settlement Patterns in Early Bronze Age Greece: An Approach to the Study of a Prehistoric Society* (Diss. Univ. of Nottingham 1992), which I have not seen.

[225] F.K. Haniotes and N. Voutiropoulos, "New Evidence from Platygiali, an Early Bronze Age Settlement in Western Greece," *BSA* 91 (1996) 59–80; Kostoula (supra n. 216); Crouwel et al. 1997 and forthcoming (supra n. 216); Sampson (supra n. 220); K. Demakopoulou, "Ευρήματα της Πρωτοελλαδικής Εποχής στο Αργος: Ανασκαφή οικοπέδου Γ. Λεμπετζή," in *AATU* 57–70. The absence of EH III is also reported by some regional surface surveys in Laconia (Cavanagh et al., supra n. 217), the Oropos area of eastern Attica (Cosmopoulos, supra n. 217), and the Berbati and Limnes valleys of the Argolid (Wells and Runnels, supra n. 217).

[226] F. Felten and S. Hiller, "Ausgrabungen in der vorgeschichtlichen Innenstadt von Ägina-Kolonna (Alt-Ägina)," *ÖJh* 65 (1996) 29–111; J. Forsén, "Prehistoric Asea Revisited," *OpAth* 21 (1996) [1997] 41–72; Wiencke (supra n. 220) and Rutter (supra n. 220); Christmann (supra n. 220).

[227] W. Gauss, "Neue Forschungen zur prähistorischen Akropolis von Athen," in F. Blakolmer ed., *Österreichische Forschungen zur Ägäischen Bronzezeit* (Wiener Forschungen zur Archäologie 3, forthcoming).

[228] S.R. Stocker, *Deriziotis Aloni: A Small Bronze Age Site in Messenia* (M.A. thesis, Univ. of Cincinnati 1995); for the late reoccupation of Nichoria after a long gap, see RAP II above, 123 and n. 116.

[229] Wiencke (supra n. 220).

[230] S. Harrison, "Domestic Architecture in Early Helladic II: Some Observations on the Form of Non-Monumental Houses," *BSA* 90 (1995) 23–40; Renard (supra n. 224) 141–224; M.B. Cosmopoulos, "Le Bronze ancien en Argolide: Habitat, urbanisme, population," in *AATU* 141–56.

See also M.B. Cosmopoulos, "Social and Political Organization in the Early Bronze 2 Aegean," in *Politeia* 23–32.

[231] D.J. Pullen, "Modelling Mortuary Behavior on a Regional Scale: A Case Study from Mainland Greece in the Early Bronze Age," in *Beyond the Site* 113–36; M. Koumouzeli, "Πρωτοελλαδικό οστεοφυλάκειο στο Σπήλαιο Λίμνης Βουλιαγμένης Περαχώρας," *ArchDelt* 44–46A (1989–1991) [1996] 223–38; and Cavanagh and Mee (supra n. 221) 15–22, a survey that includes discussion of EH III funerary behavior and draws attention to the absence thus far of positively identifiable EH I burials.

[232] C. Reinholdt, "Der Thyreatis-Hortfund in Berlin: Untersuchungen zum vormykenischen Edelmetallschmuck in Griechenland," *JdI* 108 (1993) 1–41; G. Nakou, "The Cutting Edge: A New Look at Early Aegean Metallurgy," *JMA* 8:2 (1995) 1–32; McGeehan-Liritzis (supra n. 221); G. Nakou, "The Role of Poliochni and the North Aegean in the Development of Aegean Metallurgy," in C.G. Doumas and V. La Rosa eds., *Η Πολιόχνη και η Πρώιμη Εποχή του Χαλκού στο βόρειο Αιγαίο. Διεθνές Συνέδριο, Αθήνα, 22–25 Απριλίου 1996* (Athens 1997) 634–48. Only Renard (supra n. 224) 275–79 restricts her survey to EH metal types, and then only to finds from the Peloponnese. See also Z. Stos-Gale, A. Sampson, and E. Mangou, "Analysis of Metal Artifacts from the Early Helladic Cemetery of Manika on Euboea," *Aegean Archaeology* 3 (1996) 49–62.

[233] M.P. Beloyanni, "Αποτυπώματα πλέγματος σε προϊστορική κεραμεική της Τσούγκιζας," *AAA* 22 (1989) [1995] 171–82; Renard (supra n. 224) 280–81 (textiles), 236–46 (stone tools and ornaments), and 271–74 (figurines); A. Karabatsoli, *La production de l'industrie lithique taillée en Grèce centrale pendant le Bronze ancien (Lithares, Manika, Nemée, Pefkakia)* (Diss. Univ. de Paris X 1997); E. Andrikou, "An Early Helladic Figurine from Thebes, Boeotia," *BSA* 93 (1998) 103–106.

have been numerous, especially for the EH II and EH III phases.[234] Thanks to the detailed publication of a lead seal found at Tsoungiza in the 1980s, a renewal of interest in the Lerna sealings, and the recent discoveries of quantities of EH II sealings at Petri and Geraki, studies of EH glyptic art and sealing practices have become extraordinarily prominent in the past few years and will no doubt provoke an extensive literature reevaluating EH II social and economic organization in the near future.[235]

With the publication of complete ceramic sequences spanning the momentous transition between the EH II and III phases from two of the most important settlements thus far excavated on the Greek mainland, namely Lerna and Pefkakia, it is now possible to see even more clearly than just a few years ago how differently this transition manifests itself in disparate regions.[236] Continuing excavations at the fortified island sites of Kolonna and Palamari (Skyros) promise to provide further information of considerable sig-nificance for how this transition began in the later EB 2 period and how it proceeded in insular rather than mainland environments.[237] On the heels of Manning's recent exploration of the transition in the context of climatic changes that may have precipitated the collapse of EBA cultures further to the east, Maran has now placed it at the heart of an exhaustive and wide-ranging investigation of intercultural contacts having a more northern and western focus.[238] Considerations of space preclude further comment here on such broadly based overviews of the profound cultural changes in question, but these works, like the rash of recent publications on EH II sealing practices, will undoubtedly spawn a good deal of scholarly debate in the next few years.[239]

MIDDLE BRONZE AGE AND EARLY MYCENAEAN PERIOD

Among recent publications dealing with Middle Helladic and early Mycenaean (LH I–II) topics, site

---

[234] EH II pottery: Pullen (supra n. 223); N. Boroffka and T. Stapelfeldt, "Bemerkungen zu einer balkanischen Gefässform: Die Saucière," *Arheologia Moldovei* 18 (1995) 277–88; Y. Vichos, "Ship (?) Engraving on a Jug Handle from the Cargo of the Dokos EH II Wreck," *Enalia Annual* 3 (1995) 46–47; Wiencke (supra n. 220). EH III pottery: G. Nordquist, "The Pottery of the Early Helladic III and Middle Helladic Periods," in Runnels, Pullen, and Langdon (supra n. 217) 43–51; Rutter (supra n. 220). Ceramic assemblages of all three phases of the EH period, as well as other terracotta implements, are reviewed by Renard (supra n. 224) 247–70, 274. Interesting for its application of a novel combination of analytical techniques (electron microprobe analysis, X-ray diffraction, and petrological analysis) to distinguish local from imported fabrics at Lerna is C.M. Shriner, *Ceramic Technology at Lerna, Greece, in the Third Millennium B.C.: Economic and Social Implications* (Diss. Indiana Univ. 1999), of which a portion has now been published as C. Shriner and M.J. Dorais, "A Comparative Electron Microprobe Study of Lerna III and IV Ceramics and Local Clay-rich Sediments," *Archaeometry* 41 (1999) 25–49.

[235] D.J. Pullen, "A Lead Seal from Tsoungiza, Ancient Nemea, and Early Bronze Age Aegean Sealing Systems," *AJA* 98 (1994) 35–52; J. Aruz, "Seal Imagery and Sealing Practices in the Aegean World," in P. Ferioli, E. Fiandra, G.G. Fissore, and M. Frangipane eds., *Archives before Writing* (Rome 1994) 211–35; Renard (supra n. 224) 288–95; Kostoula (supra n. 216); J. Weingarten, "Another Look at Lerna: An EH IIB Trading Post?" *OJA* 16 (1997) 147–66; Crouwel et al. 1997 and forthcoming (supra n. 216); Weingarten et al. (supra n. 216).

[236] See RAP II above, 145. For Lerna, Wiencke (supra n. 220) and Rutter (supra n. 220)—reviewed in *AJA* 101 (1997) 409–11; *Acta praehistorica et archaeologica* 29 (1997) 160–62; and *AntCl* 66 (1997) 648–49. For Pefkakia, Christmann (supra n. 220)—reviewed in *Starinar* 47 (1996) 318–20; and *AnzAW* 50 (1997) 193–200—and J. Maran, *Die deutschen Ausgrabungen auf der Pevkakia-Magula in Thes-salien III: Die mittlere Bronzezeit* (Bonn 1992)—reviewed in *CR* 44 (1994) 374–75; *JHS* 114 (1994) 218–19; *SMEA* 36 (1995) 157–58; *AJA* 99 (1995) 542–44; and *Germania* 76 (1998) 901–904.

[237] For Kolonna, Felten and Hiller (supra n. 226). For Palamari, L. Parlama, "Το τέλος της Πρώιμης Χαλκοκρατίας στο Παλαμάρι της Σκύρου: Σχέσεις και προβλήματα χρονολογήσεως," *ArchDelt* 42A (1987) [1994] 1–7; M.D. Theochari and L. Parlama, "Παλαμάρι Σκύρου: Η οχυρωμένη πόλη της Πρώιμης Χαλκοκρατίας," 344–56, and E. Hatzipouliou, "Εξειδικευμένες δραστηριότητες στο Παλαμάρι της Σκύρου στο τέλος της τρίτης χιλιετίας," 357–61, in Doumas and La Rosa (supra n. 232). Publication of the EBA remains from Ayia Irini, Keos, also furnishes important new data on this transition, notwithstanding the abandonment of that site before the beginning of EB 3 and throughout the ensuing MB 1 phase (D.E. Wilson, *Ayia Irini: Periods I–III. The Neolithic and Early Bronze Age Settlements* 1: *The Pottery and Small Finds* [*Keos* IX.1, Mainz 1999]; see J.L. Davis, RAP I above, 28, ns. 35–37, and 78–79, n. 273, for relevant bibliography).

[238] S. Manning, "Cultural Change in the Aegean c. 2200 B.C.," in H. Nüzhet Dalfes, G. Kukla, and H. Weiss eds., *Third Millennium B.C. Climate Change and Old World Collapse* (Berlin 1997) 149–71; J. Maran, *Kulturwandel auf dem griechischen Festland und den Kykladen im späten 3. Jt. v. Chr.: Studien zu den kulturellen Verhältnissen in Südosteuropa und dem zentralen sowie östlichen Mittelmeerraum in der späten Kupfer- und frühen Bronzezeit* (Bonn 1998), which incorporates the points made in J. Maran, "Neue Ansätze für die Beurteilung der Balkanisch-Ägäischen Beziehungen im 3. Jahrtausend v. Chr.," in P. Roman ed., *The Thracian World at the Crossroads of Civilizations* 1 (Bucharest 1997) 171–92.

[239] Maran's book (supra n. 238), although in print for less than a year at the time of this writing, has already inspired a lengthy response from R. Peroni, "'Kulturwandel' e formazioni economico-sociali: Osservazioni a proposito della monografia di Joseph Maran," *SMEA* 40 (1998) 155–65.

reports and ceramic studies have once again played a dominant role. The former include two articles devoted to the major MH center of Argos, six articles and a book on various aspects of the fortified town of Kolonna, a final report on the strata of late MH and early Mycenaean date directly overlying EH II levels at the northern Arcadian cave site of Spelaio Limnon, the final publication of the Mycenaean cemetery at Medeon in Phocis excavated by the French School in the early 1960s, a preliminary report on early Mycenaean tumuli explored much more recently at Glypha in Phthiotis, and the final publication of the early Mycenaean cemetery at the southeastern Arcadian site of Analipsis, investigated by Rhomaios in the mid-1950s and comprising one large and about 10 smaller tholos tombs.[240] Publications with an emphasis on ceramics include, aside from portions of the final survey publications cited above,[241] two articles on the organization of ceramic production, a preliminary report on the pottery of traditional MH types from Tiryns, a reevaluation of the MH pottery published by Holmberg from Asea, a dissertation devoted chiefly to the MH pottery from Boeotian Orchomenos, the initial work on a dissertation devoted to the Aeginetan system of potmarks, a report on chemical analyses of early Mycenaean sherds from the Argive site of Prophitis Ilias near Katsingri, a study of Minoan and Minoanizing pottery of early Mycenaean date from the Menelaion, and an analysis of the earliest stages of Mycenaean pictorial vase painting.[242]

---

[240] Argos: N. Divari-Valakou, "Ευρήματα από το Μεσοελλαδικό οικισμό του Αργους: Ανασκαφή οικοπέδου Β. Τζάφα," in *AATU* 85–101; G. Touchais, "Argos à l'époque mésohelladique: Un habitat ou des habitats?" in *AATU* 71–84. Kolonna: C. Reinholdt, "Entwicklung und Typologie mittelbronzezeitlicher Lanzenspitzen mit Schäftungsschuh in Griechenland," *Mitteilungen der Berliner Gesellschaft für Anthropologie, Ethnologie und Urgeschichte* 14 (1993) 43–52; H. Walter and H.-J. Weisshaar, "Alt-Ägina: Die prähistorische Innenstadt westlich des Apollontempels," *AA* 1993, 293–97; W.-D. Niemeier, "Aegina: First Aegean 'State' outside of Crete," in *Politeia* 73–80; I. Kilian-Dirlmeier, "Reiche Gräber der mittelhelladischen Zeit," in *Politeia* 49–53, a forerunner of her final publication of the Aegina shaft grave (supra n. 220), which itself features an extensive appendix devoted to Middle Minoan and Middle Cycladic ceramic imports at the site, as well as locally produced Minoanizing pottery; G. Graziadio, "Egina, Rodi e Cipro: Rapporti interinsulari agli inizi del Trado Bronzo," *SMEA* 36 (1995) 7–27; Felten and Hiller (supra n. 226). Spelaio Limnon: Sampson (supra n. 220). Medeon: S. Müller, *Les tombes mycéniennes de Médéon de Phocide: Architecture et mobilier* (Diss. Univ. Lumière [Lyon II] 1995). Glypha: M.-P. Papakonstantinou, "Early Mycenaean Tumuli at Glypha in Phthiotis (Ancient Antron)," *BICS* 41 (1996) 137–38. Analipsis: K. Kalogeropoulos, *Die frühmykenischen Grabfunde von Analipsis (Südöstliches Arkadien) mit einem Beitrag zu den Palatialen Amphoren des griechischen Festlandes* (Βιβλιοθήκη της εν Αθήναις Αρχαιολογικής Εταιρείας 175, Athens 1998). Note also the preliminary reports on recent prehistoric excavations at Eleusis by M. Cosmopoulos: "The University of Manitoba Excavation at Eleusis: An Interim Report," *EchCl* 39 (1995) 75–94; and "Recherches sur la stratigraphie préhistorique d'Eleusis: Travaux 1995," *EchCl* 40 (1996) 1–26.

[241] Supra n. 217. See also Gauss (supra n. 227) for the Athenian Acropolis; and B. Wells, G. Ekroth, and K. Holmgren, "The Berbati Valley Project: The 1994 Season," *OpAth* 21 (1996) [1997] 189–209, esp. 193–94, for a small body of MH pottery found during soundings around the Mycenaean tholos tomb at Berbati, at some distance from the main prehistoric settlement in the valley (at the Mastos) and thus far the only site in the entire valley aside from the Mastos to have produced material of this date.

[242] G. Nordquist, "Who Made the Pots? Production in the Middle Helladic Society," in *Politeia* 201–207; Nordquist, "What about Production? Production in the Middle Helladic Frame," in C. Gillis, C. Risberg, and B. Sjöberg eds., *Trade and Production in Premonetary Greece: Production and the Craftsman* (*SIMA-PB* 143, Jonsered 1997) 15–27; C. Belardelli, "Materiali di tradizione mesoelladica dagli strati micenei di Tirinto," in E. De Miro, L. Godart, and A. Sacconi eds., *Atti e memorie del secondo Congresso internazionale di micenologia, Roma–Napoli, 14–20 ottobre 1991, 3: Archeologia* (Incunabula Graeca 98, Rome 1996) 1137–44, a prolegomenon to her forthcoming publication in the *Tiryns* series tentatively entitled *The Middle Helladic Painted Pottery from Tiryns*; Forsén (supra n. 226); K. Sarri, *Orchomenos in der mittleren Bronzezeit* (Diss. Univ. of Heidelberg 1998); M. Lindblom, "Aeginetan Potters' Marks at Asine: A Pilot Study," *OpAth* (forthcoming) and Lindblom, "Manufacture and Markings: Aeginetan Pots and Prefiring Marks," in E. Konsolaki ed., *First International Conference on the History and Archaeology of the Argo-Saronic Gulf* (forthcoming), both of which are preliminaries to a dissertation in progress at the University of Uppsala with the working title of *Aeginetan Potters' Marks: A Diachronic Study of Distribution, Appearance, and Function*; H. Mommsen, T. Beier, D. Heimermann, A. Hein, D. Ittameier, and C. Podzuweit, "Neutron Activation Analysis of Selected Sherds from Prophitis Ilias (Argolid, Greece): A Closed Late Helladic II Settlement Context," *JAS* 21 (1994) 163–71; H.W. Catling, "Minoan and 'Minoan' Pottery at the Menelaion, Sparta," in D. Evely, I.S. Lemos, and S. Sherratt eds., *Minotaur and Centaur: Studies in the Archaeology of Crete and Euboea Presented to Mervyn Popham* (*BAR-IS* 638, Oxford 1996) 70–78; J.H. Crouwel and C. Morris, "The Beginnings of Mycenaean Pictorial Vase Painting," *AA* 1996, 197–219. Note also the spate of more recent publications: C.R. Hershenson, "Late Helladic IIB at Ayia Irini, Keos," in L.G. Mendoni and A. Mazarakis-Ainian eds., *Kea-Kythnos: History and Archaeology* (Paris 1998) 161–68; G.-J. van Wijngaarden, "Production, Circulation and Consumption of Mycenaean Pottery (Sixteenth to Twelfth Centuries B.C.)," 21–47, and L. Vagnetti, "Mycenaean Pottery in the Central Mediterranean," 137–61, in J.P. Crielaard, V. Stissi, and G.-J. van Wijngaarden eds., *The Complex Past of Pottery: Production, Circulation and Consumption of Mycenaean and Greek Pottery (Sixteenth to Early Fifth Centuries B.C.)* (Amsterdam 1999); P.A. Mountjoy, *Regional Mycenaean Decorated Pottery* (Berlin 1999); G.-J. van Wijngaarden, *Use and Appreciation of Mycenaean Pottery outside Greece: Contexts of LH I–LH IIIB Finds in the Levant, Cyprus and Italy* (Diss. Univ. of Amsterdam 1999).

The early Mycenaean settlement of Prophitis Ilias and the early Mycenaean pottery from Tiryns are the subjects of two dissertations nearing completion at German universities.[243]

Other aspects of MH and early Mycenaean life that have received a fair amount of attention over the past six years are burial customs and religion.[244] In a class by themselves under the latter heading are the spectacular discoveries made by J.A. Sakellarakis and his team at the Minoan peak sanctuary of Ayios Georgios on Kythera, many of which are now on dis-

play in the newly refurbished Piraeus Museum.[245] Settlement architecture, aside from that published in site reports mentioned above, has figured prominently only in a general survey of the megaron form during the Bronze Age on both sides of the Aegean.[246] The topic of early Mycenaean political organization has attracted a good deal of recent attention, not only due to conferences and symposia organized around the themes of the ruler, the state, and warfare, but also as a direct result of the dramatic increase in data generated by surface survey.[247] Finally, the arrival of

---

[243] D. Ittameier at Heidelberg, with the working title of *Der Prophitis Ilias von Katsingri: Eine mykenische Siedlung in der Argolis*; H. Stülpnagel at Freiburg, with the working title of *Frühmykenische Keramik von Tiryns*. In this connection, note the reevaluation of the Mycenaean pottery excavated by Blegen in the Prosymna cemetery, K.S. Shelton, *The Late Helladic Pottery from Prosymna* (*SIMA-PB* 138, Jonsered 1996), the outgrowth of a 1993 Ph.D. dissertation at the University of Pennsylvania; and a study of 16th–14th century B.C. pottery found at Midea, A.M. Liakopoulou, *Early Mycenaean and LH IIIA:2 Pottery from the Mycenaean Citadel of Midea* (M.A. thesis, Univ. of Cincinnati 1995).

[244] Burial customs: S. Voutsaki, *Society and Culture in the Mycenaean World: An Analysis of Mortuary Practices in the Argolid, Thessaly and the Dodecanese* (Diss. Univ. of Cambridge 1993); Cavanagh and Mee (supra n. 221) 23–39 (MH), 41–60 (early Mycenaean); E. Sapouna-Sakellaraki, "A Middle Helladic Tomb Complex at Xeropolis (Lefkandi)," *BSA* 90 (1995) 41–54; L. Kontorli-Papadopoulou, "Mycenaean Tholos Tombs: Some Thoughts on Burial Customs and Rites," in C. Morris ed., *Klados: Essays in Honour of J.N. Coldstream* (*BICS* Suppl. 63, London 1995) 111–22; S. Voutsaki, "Social and Political Processes in the Mycenaean Argolid: The Evidence from Mortuary Practices," in *Politeia* 55–66; Müller (supra n. 240); Papakonstantinou (supra n. 240); J.C. Wright, "Thugs or Heroes? The Early Mycenaeans and Their Graves of Gold," in R.H. Howland ed., *Mycenaean Treasures of the Aegean Bronze Age Repatriated* (Washington, D.C. 1997) 5–17; A. Kanta, "Late Bronze Age Tholos Tombs, Origin and Evolution: The Missing Links," in J. Driessen and A. Farnoux eds., *La Crète mycénienne* (*BCH* Suppl. 30, Paris 1997) 229–47; Y.G. Lolos, "Mycenaean Burial at Pylos," in J.L. Davis ed., *Sandy Pylos: An Archaeological History from Nestor to Navarino* (Austin 1998) 75–78; Kilian-Dirlmeier (supra ns. 220 and 240); Kalogeropoulos (supra n. 240); O. Pelon, "Les tombes circulaires dans l'Égée de l'Âge du Bronze: État des recherches sur les tombes à tholos," *Topoi* 8 (1998) 95–158; S. Voutsaki, "Mortuary Evidence, Symbolic Meanings and Social Change: A Comparison between Messenia and the Argolid in the Mycenaean Period," 41–58, and W. Cavanagh, "Innovation, Conservatism and Variation in Mycenaean Funerary Ritual," 103–14, in K. Branigan ed., *Cemetery and Society in the Aegean Bronze Age* (Sheffield 1998).

Religion: J.C. Wright, "The Spatial Configuration of Belief: The Archaeology of Mycenaean Religion," in S. Alcock and R. Osborne eds., *Placing the Gods: Sanctuaries and Sacred Space in Ancient Greece* (Oxford 1994) 37–78; D.S. Reese, "Equid Sacrifices/Burials in Greece and Cyprus: An

Addendum," *Journal of Prehistoric Religion* 9 (1995) 35–42; J.C. Wright, "The Archaeological Correlates of Religion: Case Studies in the Aegean," in *Politeia* 341–48; H.-G. Buchholz, "Zur religiösen Bedeutung mykenischer Igel," *Journal of Prehistoric Religion* 9 (1995) 9–14; R. Hägg, "The Religion of the Mycenaeans Twenty-four Years after the 1967 Mycenological Congress in Rome," in E. De Miro, L. Godart, and A. Sacconi eds., *Atti e memorie del secondo Congresso internazionale di micenologia* 2: *Storia* (Rome 1996) 599–612; R. Jung, "Menschenopferdarstellungen? Zur Analyse minoischer und mykenischer Siegelbilder," *PZ* 72 (1997) 133–94; R. Hägg, "Did the Middle Helladic People Have Any Religion?" *Kernos* 10 (1997) 13–18; R. Hägg, "Ritual in Mycenaean Greece," in F. Graf ed., *Ansichten griechischer Rituale: Geburtstag-Symposium für Walter Burkert* (Stuttgart 1998) 99–113.

[245] For various preliminary assessments of this remarkable material, which includes an unusually large number of bronze figurines (both anthropomorphic and zoomorphic, among them a unique scorpion) and stone vases (one with a Linear A inscription), see supra n. 216. The recently launched Kythera Survey has, after just one season in the field, already produced some surprising results: evidence for several small Minoan(izing?) settlements of Neopalatial date on the interior of the island, as well as prepalatial Minoanizing sherds from two of the EBA sites so far discovered, also in inland locations. I am very grateful to Cyprian Broodbank for sharing this information with me prior to its formal publication and for allowing me to mention it here.

[246] K. Werner, *The Megaron during the Aegean and Anatolian Bronze Age* (*SIMA* 108, Jonsered 1993). See also J. Maran, "Structural Changes in the Pattern of Settlement during the Shaft Grave Period on the Greek Mainland," in *Politeia* 67–72.

[247] In chronological order of publication: J.C. Wright, "From Chief to King in Mycenaean Greece," 63–80, and R. Laffineur, "Aspects of Rulership at Mycenae in the Shaft Grave Period," 81–94, in P. Rehak ed., *The Role of the Ruler in the Prehistoric Aegean* (*Aegaeum* 11, Liège 1995); Voutsaki, in *Politeia* (supra n. 244); W.G. Cavanagh, "Development of the Mycenaean State in Laconia: Evidence from the Laconia Survey," *Politeia* 81–88; S. Deger-Jalkotzy, "Mykenische Herrschaftsformen ohne Paläste und die griechische Polis," in *Politeia* 367–77; E.F. Bloedow, "Human and Environmental Interaction in the Emergence and Decline of Mycenaean State and Society," in *Politeia* 639–48; Wright, in *Politeia* (supra n. 244); S. Voutsaki, "The Creation of Value and Prestige in the Aegean Late Bronze Age," *Journal*

the Greeks continues to be a much debated subject, still without any general consensus on when or whence this group of Indo-European speakers made their initial appearance in the southern and central Aegean world.[248]

Space considerations permit only a few summary comments on the significance of the latest literature concerning the MH through LH II (ca. 2050–1430 B.C.) phases. The unusual importance of Kolonna throughout the period in question has been even more amply demonstrated in the past few years by studies of its surprisingly early and rich shaft grave, its large-scale production for export of ceramics (and

probably also andesite millstones), and the extensive ceramic and now also architectural evidence for its close ties with both the Protopalatial and Neopalatial polities of Minoan Crete.[249] The flood of literature on various aspects of the Shaft Graves at Mycenae that was characteristic of the 1970s and 1980s shows no signs of letting up, although most of this has taken the form of relatively short contributions, many of them conference papers.[250] Extended studies of other sites with rich early Mycenaean or MH remains, both in the Peloponnese and central Greece, show signs of assuming greater importance in the years to come. Chief among those studies that

of European Archaeology 5:2 (1997) 34–52; Lolos (supra n. 244); J.L. Davis, "The Palace and Its Dependencies," 53–68, and J. Bennet, "The Linear B Archives and the Kingdom of Nestor," 111–33, esp. 125–29, in Davis (supra n. 244); P.E. Acheson, "The Role of Force in the Development of Early Mycenaean Polities," in *Polemos* 97–104; J. Bennet and J.L. Davis, "Making Mycenaeans: Warfare, Territorial Expansion, and Representations of the Other in the Pylian Kingdom," in *Polemos* 105–20; J. Bennet, "Pylos: The Expansion of a Mycenaean Center," in M.L. Galaty and W.A. Parkinson eds., *Rethinking Mycenaean Palaces: New Interpretations of an Old Idea* (Los Angeles 1999) 9–18; A. Wolpert, *A "Social Rupture" Contextualized: Competitive Destruction and Ceramic Traditions at the Transition from Chiefdom to State on the Southeastern Greek Mainland, MH III–LH I* (M.A. thesis, Univ. of Cincinnati 1999); J.C. Wright, "Die Entwicklung von Sekundärstaaten: Die mykenische Kultur als Fallstudie," in H. Nissen, C. Strahm, and M. Heinz eds., *Theorie des sozialen Wandels. Tagung: Genese und Struktur der primären Hochkulturen* (Bielefeld, forthcoming).

[248] D.W. Anthony, "Horse, Wagon and Chariot: Indo-European Languages and Archaeology," *Antiquity* 69 (1995) 554–65; O. Carruba, "L'arrivo dei Greci, le migrazioni indoeuropee e il 'Ritorno' degli Eraclidi," *Athenaeum* 83 (1995) 5–44; C.G. Doumas, "Early Helladic III and the Coming of the Greeks," *Cretan Studies* 5 (1996) 51–61; M. Finkelberg, "Anatolian Languages and Indo-European Migrations to Greece," *CW* 91 (1997) 3–20; R. Drews, "PIE Speakers and PA Speakers," *JIES* 25 (1997) 153–77.

[249] See RAP II above, 125–30; Kilian-Dirlmeier (supra ns. 220 and 240); Lindblom (supra n. 242); Niemeier (supra n. 240). The shaft graves of Mycenae, Lerna, Thebes, and other mainland Greek sites now seem more than ever patterned after the model of the grave of the warrior-hero buried next to, and just outside, a major gate leading into the fortified lower town of Kolonna from the east in the MH II period; for more extended comments, see my review of Kilian-Dirlmeier (supra n. 220) in *AJA* 103 (1999) 357–58.

[250] For publications through 1993, see RAP II above, 135–42. Shaft Grave artifacts and personnel: P. Taracha, "Weapons in the Shaft Graves of Mycenae: Aspects of the Relative Chronology of Circle A and B Burials," *Archeologia War* 44 (1993) 7–34; H. Hughes-Brock, "Amber in the Aegean in the Late Bronze Age: Some Problems and Perspectives," in C.W. Beck, J. Bouzek, and D. Dreslerova eds.,

Amber in Archaeology (Prague 1993) 219–29; R.B. Koehl, "The Silver Stag 'BIBRU' from Mycenae," in J.B. Carter and S.P. Morris eds., *The Ages of Homer: A Tribute to Emily Townsend Vermeule* (Austin 1995) 61–66; J.H. Musgrave, R.A.H. Neave, and A.J.N.W. Prag, "Seven Faces from Grave Circle B at Mycenae," *BSA* 90 (1995) 107–36; K. Demakopoulou, E. Mangou, R.E. Jones, and E. Photos-Jones, "Mycenaean Black Inlay Metalware in the National Archaeological Museum, Athens: A Technical Examination," *BSA* 90 (1995) 137–54; R. Laffineur, "A propos des 'Gamaschenhalter' des tombes à fosse de Mycènes," in De Miro et al. (supra n. 242) 1229–38; Laffineur, "*Polychrysos Mykene*: Toward a Definition of Mycenaean Goldwork," in A. Calinescu ed., *Ancient Jewelry and Archaeology* (Bloomington 1996) 89–116; P. Muhly, "Furniture from the Shaft Graves: The Occurrence of Wood in Aegean Burials in the Bronze Age," *BSA* 91 (1996) 197–211; O. Dickinson, "Arts and Artefacts in the Shaft Graves: Some Observations," in *Techne* 45–49; J.C. Younger, "The Stelai of Mycenae Grave Circles A and B," in *Techne* 229–39; J.-C. Poursat, "Les armes en Égée au Bronze moyen: Quelques remarques," in *Polemos* 427–31; C.R. Floyd, "Observations on a Minoan Dagger from Chrysokamino," in *Polemos* 433–42, esp. 439–40.

Shaft Grave iconography: L. Morgan, "Of Animals and Men: The Symbolic Parallel," in Morris (supra n. 244) 171–84; N.R. Thomas, "The War Animal: Three Days in the Life of the Mycenaean Lion," in *Polemos* 297–311; S. Hiller, "Scenes of Warfare and Combat in the Arts of the Aegean Late Bronze Age: Reflections on Typology and Development," in *Polemos* 319–30. Sociopolitical dimensions of the Shaft Graves: I. Tournavitou, "The Shaft Grave Phenomenon: A Dead End?" in C. Gillis, C. Risberg, and B. Sjöberg eds., *Trade and Production in Premonetary Greece: Aspects of Trade* (*SIMA-PB* 134, Jonsered 1995) 111–23; Maran (supra n. 246); Kilian-Dirlmeier (supra n. 220); S. Deger-Jalkotzy, "Military Prowess and Social Status in Mycenaean Greece," in *Polemos* 121–31. Mainland Greek external contacts in the Shaft Grave era: S. Hiller, "Die Schachtgräber von Mykene in ägyptischem Kontext," *Minos* 29–30 (1994–1995) 7–31; G. Graziadio, "Trade Circuits and Trade-Routes in the Shaft Grave Period," *SMEA* 40 (1998) 29–76; S. Dietz, "The Cyclades and the Mainland in the Shaft Grave Period: A Summary," *Proceedings of the Danish Institute at Athens* 2 (1998) 9–36; R. Barber, "Hostile Mycenaeans in the Cyclades?" in *Polemos* 133–39.

have already appeared is Kalogeropoulos's publication of the cemetery of early Mycenaean tholoi at Analipsis on the border between Arcadia and Laconia, a work distinguished not only by a wealth of first-rate illustrations but also by a painstaking analysis of the 208 Palace Style jars known or suspected to be mainland Greek rather than Minoan products. Based on a dissertation recently completed at Heidelberg, this volume also features an equally useful, though necessarily briefer and less detailed, survey of LBA gray wheelmade wares found throughout the southern and western Aegean as well as in southern Italy,

the Dodecanese, and northwestern Anatolia.[251] One can only hope that more publications of this quality by a new generation of Aegean prehistorians, predominantly Greek and western European, will soon appear, for they are bringing to our attention major bodies of material long known but, until recently, undeservedly ignored.[252]

DEPARTMENT OF CLASSICS
DARTMOUTH COLLEGE
HANOVER, NEW HAMPSHIRE 03755-3506
JEREMY.RUTTER@DARTMOUTH.EDU

---

[251] Kalogeropoulos (supra n. 240) 42–60 (wheelmade gray wares of the LBA). The portion of this study devoted to Helladic Palace Style jars (85–179) is a fitting complement to the study of the analogous class of Minoan vase painting published by W.-D. Niemeier, Kalogeropoulos's supervisor at Heidelberg, as *Die Palaststilkeramik von Knossos: Stil, Chronologie und historischer Kontext* (Berlin 1985).

[252] See also the publication of the Mycenaean cemetery at Medeon by Müller (supra n. 240) with its comprehensive discussion of built LBA chamber tombs throughout the Aegean and as far east as Cyprus and Ugarit (esp. 74–

138); the investigation of the traffic in Mycenaean pottery to both the east and central Mediterranean by van Wijngaarden (supra n. 242); the study of MH Orchomenos by Sarri (supra n. 242); the reassessment of the Mycenaean pottery from Prosymna by Shelton (supra n. 243); and the dissertations by Ittameier and Stülpnagel and thesis by Liakopoulou on more recently discovered material from Prophitis Ilias, Tiryns, and Midea (supra n. 243). S.R. Stocker is undertaking a long-term study of the MH material from Blegen's excavations at Pylos.

Review of Aegean Prehistory III:
Crete from Earliest Prehistory through the Protopalatial Period

L. VANCE WATROUS

Dedicated to Sinclair Hood

INTRODUCTION

This article has three aims: 1) to present the basic framework of Minoan archaeology from earliest prehistory through the Middle Minoan II period, 2) to highlight recent work done on these periods, and 3) to discuss some of the broader issues raised by this material.[1] One of the main obstacles in understanding pre- and protopalatial Crete is that a high proportion of the published material is from unstratified and poorly dated tomb groups excavated early in this century. For this reason I have given first priority to setting out the primary evidence in correct chronological sequence. In this respect, this

[1] Publication of this review and of the previous two reviews in this series was made possible by a generous grant to *AJA* by the Institute for Aegean Prehistory. The editors and I are grateful for this support.

I would also like to acknowledge the help of the following scholars who have personally taken me around their site and explained it to me and have generously given me permission to reproduce illustrations of their work: P. Betancourt (Pseira), K. Branigan (Agia Kyriaki), G. Cadogan (Pyrgos), P. Croft (Lemba), C. Davaras (Pseira), D. Haggis (Kavousi survey), B. Hayden (Istron survey), S. Hood (Knossos), A. Kanta and A. Tsigkanaki (Monasteraki), A. Karetsou (Mt. Jouktas), J. and E. Lagarce (Ras Ibn Hani), V. La Rosa (Agia Triada and Phaistos), T. Marketou (Trianda), O. Pelon (Mallia), J.-C. Poursat (Mallia), I. and E. Sakellarakis (Archanes/Phourni), J. and M. Shaw (Kommos), J. Soles (Mochlos), M. Tsipopoulou (Agia Photia and Petras), A. Vasilakis (Trypeti), and A. Zois (Vasiliki). The following scholars have aided me by discussing their research with me or by providing me with unpublished manuscripts or information: D. and D. Arnold, H. Blitzer, G. Cadogan, P. Day, R. Hägg, E. and B. Hallager, I. Hamilakis, S. Hiller, R. Hope Simpson, A. Karetsou, K. Kopaka, E. Lax, A. MacGillivray, N. Momigliano, J. Moody, J. and P. Muhly, K. Nowicki, N. Özgüç, S. Paley, A. Peatfield, J. Rutter, I. Sakellarakis, A. Sarpaki, J. Shaw, D. Slane, T. Strasser, S. Swiny, L. Vagnetti, D. Vallianou, M. Vlasakis, J. Weingarten, T. Whitelaw, M. Wiener, D. Wilson, J. Younger, C. Zerner, and A. Zois. W. and E. Myers sent me copies of their photographs.

This article, written during the fall and winter of the 1993/1994 academic year during my tenure as a Whitehead Visiting Professor at the American School of Classical Studies at Athens, would definitely have not been possible without the library and staff of the School. Because this article is a summary account, I have been unable to include all of the research done by colleagues working on Crete; to those whose work I have omitted, I offer my apologies. H. Blitzer edited the manuscript and, additionally, endured me while I was writing it.

The following abbreviations are used in this article:

Andreou	S. Andreou, *Pottery Groups of the Old Palace Period in Crete* (Diss. Univ. of Cincinnati 1978).
Branigan	K. Branigan, *Aegean Metalwork of the Early and Middle Bronze Age* (Oxford 1974).
Chronology	P. Warren and V. Hankey, *Aegean Bronze Age Chronology* (Bristol 1989).
Ehrich	R. Ehrich ed., *Chronologies in Old World Archaeology*[3] I–II (Chicago 1992).
Festòs	D. Levi, *Festòs e la civiltà minoica* I–II (*Incunabula Graeca* 60, 77, Rome 1976, 1988).
Function	R. Hägg and N. Marinatos eds., *The Function of the Minoan Palaces* (SkrAth 4, 35, Stockholm 1987).
Levant	P. Gerstenblith, *The Levant at the Beginning of the Middle Bronze Age* (ASOR Dissertation Series 5, Philadelphia 1983).
Mochlos	R. Seager, *Explorations in the Island of Mochlos* (Boston 1912).
MSV	P. Warren, *Minoan Stone Vases* (Cambridge 1969).
Myrtos	P. Warren, *Myrtos: An Early Bronze Age Settlement in Crete* (London 1972).
Pepragmena 1981	Πεπραγμένα του Δ′ Διεθνούς Κρητολογικού Συνεδρίου (Athens 1981).
Pepragmena 1990	Πεπραγμένα του ΣΤ′ Διεθνούς Κρητολογικού Συνεδρίου (Chania 1990).
Society	O. Krzyszkowska and L. Nixon eds., *Minoan Society* (Bristol 1983).
Soles	J. Soles, *The Prepalatial Cemeteries at Mochlos and Gournia and the House Tombs of Bronze Age Crete* (*Hesperia* Suppl. 24, Princeton 1992).
Thalassocracy	R. Hägg and N. Marinatos eds., *The Minoan Thalassocracy: Myth and Reality* (SkrAth 4, 32, Stockholm 1984).

Originally published in *AJA* 98 (1994) 695–753.

157

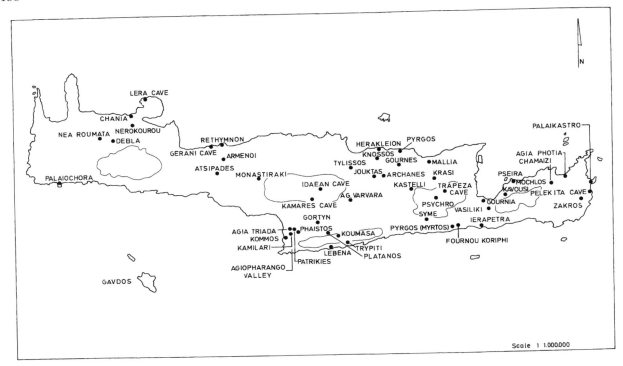

Fig. 1. Map of Crete with principal sites mentioned in the text

study differs from the first two articles in this series,[2] which focused primarily on recently recovered evidence. As will be seen below, the format adopted here follows from the current state of archaeological research on Crete. The article begins with a review of the history of Minoan archaeology because it is this history more than anything else that has determined the nature of the discipline today. Due to limitations of time and space, some of the broader interpretative problems arising from the archaeological material cannot be treated here.

This article is not intended to be a complete report on all of the archaeological work being carried out on Crete. That service is provided by *Archaeological Reports* (*AR*), *Bulletin de correspondance hellénique* (*BCH*), *Κρητικά Χρονικά* (*CretChron*), *Αμάλθεια* (Historical-Ethnographic Society of

Lasithi), and *Κρητική Εστία* (Historical, Ethnographic and Archaeological Society of Crete, Chania). The official Greek publications of all Greek excavations, which greatly outnumber foreign projects, are *Αρχαιολογικόν Δελτίον* (*ArchDelt*), *Το Έργον*, and *Πρακτικά της εν Αθήναις Αρχαιολογικής Εταιρείας* (*Prakt*). Since the *Deltion*, whose reports include the many Service rescue excavations, is at present six years behind schedule, I have contacted a number of Greek archaeologists directly in an effort to present as up-to-date a discussion as possible.

HISTORY OF RESEARCH

Since the beginning of this century the British, Italian, French, and American archaeological schools have undertaken a continuing and systematic series of excavations on Crete (fig. 1).[3] As a con-

---

van Effenterre   H. van Effenterre, *Le palais de Mallia et la cité minoenne: Étude de synthèse* I–II (*Incunabula Graeca* 76, Rome 1980).

VTM   S. Xanthoudides, *The Vaulted Tombs of Mesara* (London 1924).

Yule   P. Yule, *Early Cretan Seals: A Study of Chronology* (*Marburger Studien zur Vor- und Frühgeschichte* 4, Mainz 1981).

[2] J. Davis, "Review of Aegean Prehistory I: The Islands of the Aegean," *AJA* 96 (1992) 699–756 and J. Rutter, "Re-

view of Aegean Prehistory II: The Prepalatial Bronze Age of the Southern and Central Greek Mainland," *AJA* 97 (1993) 745–97.

[3] The Italian and French Schools have published valuable retrospectives of their work on Crete. See A. Di Vita, V. La Rosa, and M. Rizzo eds., *Creta antica* (Rome 1984), which gives an overview of Italian archaeological investigations from 1894 to 1984. For French excavations on Crete, see C. Tiré and H. van Effenterre, *Guide des fouilles françaises en Crète* (Paris 1978) and O. Pelon, *Guide de Malia* (Paris 1992).

sequence, our knowledge of certain sites, notably Mallia, Phaistos, and Knossos, has become quite detailed. For Mallia alone the French excavators have published 20 volumes. Crete also has a long and singular tradition of Ephors who were both active excavators as well as distinguished scholars of prehistory, such as Xanthoudides, Marinatos, Platon, Alexiou, Davaras, and Sakellarakis.

Systematic excavation on Crete began at the turn of this century. This early (1900–1940) period saw excavation at a large number of important settlements, e.g., Agia Triada, Amnissos, Chamaizi, Gournia, Kavousi, Knossos, Mallia, Mochlos, Palaikastro, Phaistos, Pseira, Tylissos, Vathypetro, Vasiliki, and Vrokastro, as well as at sanctuaries (Arkalochori, Mt. Jouktas, Kamares Cave, Petsophas, Psychro Cave) and numerous tombs on the north coast and in the Mesara. These excavations were often massive in scale, exposing whole palaces and their dependencies, urban blocks of houses, and large deposits from caves and tombs. After World War II the pace of Greek and foreign excavation began to increase rapidly. At present there are more prehistoric excavations on Crete than in any other region of Greece, in part because of the richness and complexity of the Minoan archaeological record. Since 1950 there have been major Bronze Age excavations on Crete at Agia Photia, Agia Triada, Archanes, Armenoi, Atsipades, Chania, Gerani Cave, Herakleion, Idaean Cave, Jouktas, Kamilari, Karphi, Kato Syme, Kavousi, Knossos, Kommos, Lebena, Lera Cave, Makriyialos, Mallia, Mochlos, Monasteraki, Myrtos, Palaikastro, Patrikies, Petras, Pseira, Trypeti, Vasiliki, and Zakros (fig. 1). The number of smaller excavations in that period was enormous. Archaeological survey on the island also had an early beginning, due largely to the work of John Pendlebury.[4] Following Pendlebury's example, surveys in the Amari Valley, around Rethymnon, Palaiochora, Viannos, and in the eparchy of Agios Vasilios were undertaken by Sinclair Hood and other British archaeologists.[5]

During the pre-World War II years, general works such as Arthur Evans's *Palace of Minos* and Pendlebury's *Archaeology of Crete* dominated the field of Minoan archaeology.[6] All of this changed after the 1950s with an explosion of specialized studies on many aspects of Minoan civilization, a trend that has continued (and accelerated) to the present day. Some idea of the vastness of this bibliography can be grasped by reading Hiller's bibliography on Minoan studies, which lists 443 articles and books for the 12 years between 1965 and 1977. It is impossible even to summarize these studies here, but mention should be made of the variety of subjects covered: administration, architecture, chronology, cult, economy, fresco painting, funerary customs, iconography, international connections, ivories, metalwork, palaeobotany and palaeozoology, physical anthropology, politics, sculpture, seals, society, stone vases, tools, toponymy, trade, vase painting, and writing. These studies have given us a much clearer and more objective picture of Minoan civilization than was possible even 25 years ago.

One basic study must be discussed. The recent publication of Warren and Hankey, *Aegean Bronze Age Chronology* (Bristol 1989), has provided prehistorians with a useful reference that brings together in painstaking detail the evidence for relative and absolute Aegean chronology. The frequency with which it is cited below is a testimony to its value. With the new ^{14}C dates for the Early Minoan period, we can now see that the traditional sequence for Early Bronze Age Crete was too short. Instead of beginning at ca. 2900 B.C. and carrying through to 2500 B.C., EM I is now estimated to span 3500–2900 B.C. Similarly, the previous dates for EM II of 2500–2200 B.C. have been stretched to 2900–2300/2150 B.C. As a result, it is evident that the EM II civilization took much longer to develop than previously envisioned, a fact that has consequences for earlier interpretations of prepalatial Crete (see below). The date for the end of the protopalatial period, however, remains more controversial, be-

---

[4] J. Pendlebury walked from one end of the island to the other recording sites. See his remarks in *The Archaeology of Crete: An Introduction* (London 1939) 8–9 on his experience, as well as the still valuable lists of sites compiled in his book.

[5] T. Dunbabin, "Antiquities of Amari," *BSA* 42 (1947) 184–93; S. Hood, P. Warren, and G. Cadogan, "Travels in Crete, 1962," *BSA* 59 (1964) 50–99; Hood, "Minoan Sites in the Far West of Crete," *BSA* 60 (1965) 99–113; S. Hood and P. Warren, "Ancient Sites in the Province of Ayios Vasilios," *BSA* 61 (1966) 163–91; Hood and Warren, "Some

Ancient Sites in South-West Crete," *BSA* 62 (1967) 47–56.

[6] In the early 1960s two general books on Minoan Crete, R. Hutchinson, *Prehistoric Crete* (London 1962) and F. Schachermeyr, *Die minoische Kultur des alten Kreta* (Stuttgart 1964), appeared. Both systematized the work done up until the 1950s, especially that of Evans. S. Hiller's *Das minoische Kreta nach den Ausgrabungen des letzten Jahrzehntes* (Vienna 1977) summarizes archaeological work on Minoan Crete from 1965 to 1977; see 17–39 for bibliography.

cause it is affected by the current disagreement over the "high" ¹⁴C dates from Thera.[7] Warren and Hankey, who reject the new Thera dates, date the protopalatial period to 1900–1700/1650 B.C. This is unlikely. Kemp and Merrillees have shown that MM II pottery (e.g., the Qubbet el-Hawa vase) appears in Egypt by "the first part of the Twelfth Dynasty," i.e., between 1990 and 1890 B.C., which would give us an end date for MM II of no later than ca. 1800 B.C.[8] This fits exactly with the higher dates of MM III and LM IA required by the new Theran ¹⁴C dates.

Anthropological thinking, especially in the areas of cultural evolution, systems theory, and ecology, over the last 20 years has affected Minoan archaeology in subtle but important ways.[9] The means by which archaeologists conceptualize ancient culture have matured, especially in the areas of social organization, cultural change, and the environment. This intellectual self-appraisal has had certain practical effects on recent fieldwork in Crete. A number of new excavations have been smaller, more precise in the recording of their finds, and have focused on specific problems. Excavators have adopted a broader approach to the past, with a new emphasis on interdisciplinary methods, borrowing from geology, soil studies, physical anthropology, ethnography, palaeozoology, and palaeobotany, and employing scientific methods of dating and determining the provenance of pottery and metals. One of the greatest benefits of this approach is that it has encouraged some (but not all) excavators working on Crete to be more rigorous in the interpretations of their finds.

Since 1970 archaeologists have begun to ask new questions about Minoan population, land use, and the political organization of regions on the island, questions that have led to an even greater emphasis on survey. Intensive regional surveys have covered or are under way in the Lasithi Plain, Akrotiri peninsula of Chania, Western Mesara Plain, Istron/Mesaleri area (East Crete), Sphakia, the island of Pseira, and the areas of Kavousi, Mallia, Atsipades, Gournia, and Praesos.[10] Less systematic surveys have been carried out in the areas of the Agiopharango Valley/South Coast, Gavdos Island, Knossos, Kommos, Mochlos, Palaikastro, Siteia, and Zakros/Ziro.[11] As a consequence, we now have a good deal of detailed evidence for the patterns of settlement on Crete.

[7] See the recent non-partisan summary by S. Manning, "The Thera Eruption: The Third Congress and the Problem of the Date," *Archaeometry* 32 (1990) 91–100.

[8] B. Kemp and R. Merrillees, *Minoan Pottery in Second Millennium Egypt* (Mainz 1980) 255–56. See G. Cadogan, "Early Minoan and Middle Minoan Chronology," *AJA* 87 (1983) 516 for the MM II date of the Qubbet el-Hawa vase.

[9] A good survey of the intellectual history of archaeology over the last two decades appears in B. Trigger, *A History of Archaeological Thought* (Cambridge 1989) 289–411.

[10] Lasithi: V. Watrous, *Lasithi* (*Hesperia* Suppl. 18, Princeton 1982). Chania area: J. Moody, *The Environmental and Cultural Prehistory of the Khania Region of West Crete: Neolithic–Late Minoan III* (Diss. Univ. of Minnesota 1987). Western Mesara: V. Watrous et al., "A Survey of the Western Mesara Plain in Crete: Preliminary Report of the 1984, 1986, and 1987 Field Seasons," *Hesperia* 62 (1993) 191–248. Istron area: B. Hayden, J. Moody, and O. Rackham, "The Vrokastro Survey Project, 1986–1989: Research Design and Preliminary Results," *Hesperia* 61 (1992) 293–353. Pseira: R. Hope Simpson and P. Betancourt, "Intensive Survey of Pseira Island, Crete," *AJA* 94 (1990) 322–23 (abstract). Kavousi: D. Haggis, *The Kavousi-Thriphti Survey: An Analysis of the Settlement Patterns in an Area of Eastern Crete in the Bronze Age and the Early Iron Age* (Diss. Univ. of Minnesota 1992). Mallia: S. Müller, "Routes minoennes en relation avec le site de Malia," *BCH* 115 (1991) 545–60; Müller, "Prospection de la plaine de Malia," *BCH* 116 (1992) 742–53, with earlier references. Praesos: *AR* 39 (1992–1993) 77–79. Gournia: L.V. Watrous, "Gournia Again Focus of Exploration," *Newsletter of the American School of Classical Studies at Athens* 32 (1993) 1, 3. The survey in the valley around Atsipades is continuing under the direction of A. Peatfield.

[11] Ayiopharango Valley/South Coast: D. Blackman and K. Branigan, "An Archaeological Survey of the South Coast of Crete, between the Ayiopharango and Christostomos," *BSA* 70 (1975) 17–36; Blackman and Branigan, "An Archaeological Survey of the Lower Catchment of the Ayiopharango Valley," *BSA* 72 (1977) 13–84; and Vasilakis 1989 (infra n. 22). Knossos: S. Hood and D. Smyth, *Archaeological Survey of the Knossos Area*² (Oxford 1981). Kommos: R. Hope Simpson, V. Watrous, and J. Shaw, "The Archaeological Survey," in *Kommos* I (Princeton, in press). Mochlos: J. Soles and C. Davaras, "Excavations at Mochlos, 1989," *Hesperia* 61 (1992) 413–16 and fig. 1. Palaikastro: J. Driessen and A. MacGillivray, "The Neopalatial Period in East Crete," in R. Laffineur ed., *Transition: Le monde égéen du Bronze moyen au Bronze récent* (*Aegaeum* 3, Liège 1989) 99–112. Sphakia: L. Nixon et al., "Archaeological Survey in Sphakia, Crete," *EchCl* 7 (1988) 159–73; 8 (1989) 201–15; 9 (1990) 213–20. Siteia: M. Tsipopoulou, *Archaeological Survey at Aghia Photia, Siteia* (Partille 1989). Zakros: N. Schlager, "Untersuchungen zur prähistorischen Topographie im aussersten sudösten Kretas: Zakros bis Xerokampos," in W. Schiering ed., *Ägais-Kolloquium* IX (Mannheim 1987) 64–82. See also I. Tzedakis et al., "Les routes minoennes: rapport préliminaire, défense de la circulation ou circulation de la défense?" *BCH* 113 (1989) 43–75. The island of Gavdos is being surveyed by K. Kopaka (University of Crete). New surveys in 1994 are planned for the areas of Sisi near Mallia and Ziros in East Crete.

The result of the research outlined above is that today the Minoan archaeologist faces an archaeological record of breadth and depth that is unique in the prehistoric Aegean. This level of published detail calls for a synthesis as well as a consideration of how perceptions of these data have changed during the last generation.

Finally, one should mention that the archaeological museums on Crete have been transformed in the last decade. New museums have opened in Rethymnon and Archanes within the last three years and a new museum at Kastelli Kissamou is under construction at present. The new collection at Rethymnon is now stunningly displayed in a modern setting housed inside the Venetian Fortezza of the city. In addition, the collections at Chania, Siteia, and Ierapetra have been reorganized and greatly augmented in handsome new quarters.

EARLIEST PREHISTORY—NEOLITHIC

When does the human prehistory of Crete begin? For many years the conventional answer was the beginning of the seventh millennium B.C., when the site at Knossos (stratum X) was founded.[12] But recently there has been a spate of publications suggesting that the extinction of Pleistocene animals on Crete was caused by human visitors to the island prior to the Neolithic period.[13] Because Pleistocene animals are absent from early settlement contexts, it is believed that many, such as pygmy hippopotamus, pygmy elephant, and deer (*Candiacervus cretensis*), apparently do not survive to the time of the earliest known settlement of the island. The only dated find of these Pleistocene animals is a hippopotamus bone from the upland plain of Katharo, dated by radiocarbon to 12,135 ± 485 B.P.[14] Lax and Strasser have argued that it was the Neolithic inhabitants of Crete who caused the extinction of many Pleistocene animals through their destruction of these animals' environments (by means of their farming, pastoralism, and the introduction of new animal species). This is probably true for certain early animals, such as the endemic mouse and shrew, since they occur in Neolithic contexts and then disappear from the later archaeological record. But some Pleistocene species do not appear in Neolithic habitation levels, which may mean that the earliest settlers predate the Neolithic period. What has changed our perception of this question is the recent discovery and excavation of the site of Aetokremnos on Cyprus.[15] This small kill-site produced deposits of shells, and pygmy hippopotamus and elephant bones, with a range of dates extending from the 10th through the 12th millennium B.C. Aetokremnos shows that hunter-gatherer groups from the Asian mainland had begun to visit the island during the 12th millennium B.C. One suspects that similar events took place on Crete and it is only a matter of time before such a site is found.[16]

The earliest known permanent settlement of an Aegean island took place on Crete, at Knossos. Strasser and Broodbank's recent discussion of the Knossos colonization stresses that this was neither an accidental discovery nor one example of many such colonization attempts on the Aegean islands.[17] Rather, the colonization of Crete was a unique, long-range, deliberately planned effort by a group of agriculturalists, probably motivated by Crete's advantageous environment. The first settlers arrived on the island with a well-developed continental economy based on their former environment (probably the Anatolian coast, since Knossian bread wheats are known in Anatolia but not in the earliest mainland Greek Neolithic sites). The material culture of the first settlers shows some changes in the Early Neolithic II–Middle Neolithic period,[18] but

[12] See Moody (supra n. 10). For the date of the Knossos basal level, see Coleman (infra n. 36) I, 263 and II, 211, table 1.

[13] J. Cherry, "The First Colonization of the Mediterranean Islands: A Review of Recent Research," *JMA* 3 (1990) 145–221. Most recently discussed by E. Lax and T. Strasser, "Early Holocene Extinctions on Crete: The Search for the Cause," *JMA* 5 (1992) 203–24. For the domesticated livestock of the Neolithic settlers, see C. Groves, "Feral Mammals of the Mediterranean Islands: Documents of Early Domestication," in J. Clutton-Brock ed., *The Walking Larder* (London 1990) 46–58.

[14] F. Bachmayer and H. Zapfe, "Ein absolutes Altersdatum für den fossilen Zwergflusspferde der Insel Kreta," *AnzWien, Mathematisch-Naturwissenschaftliche Klasse* 8 (1985) 165–66.

[15] A. Simmons, "Preliminary Report on the Excavations at Akrotiri-Aetokremnos (Site E): 1987, 1988, 1990," *RDAC* 1989, 7–14.

[16] The process described for sixth-millennium B.C. settlement on Cyprus (N. Stanley-Price, "Khirokitia and the Initial Settlement of Cyprus," *Levant* 9 [1977] 66–89, esp. 78–86) was probably similar to that on pre-Neolithic Crete.

[17] C. Broodbank and T. Strasser, "Migrant Farmers and the Neolithic Colonization of Crete," *Antiquity* 65 (1991) 233–45.

[18] See C. Broodbank, "The Neolithic Labyrinth: Social Change at Knossos before the Bronze Age," *JMA* 5 (1992) 39–75. Because of his assumptions, Broodbank fails to provide a convincing explanation for the changes he demonstrates. See also T. Whitelaw, "Lost in the Labyrinth? Comments on Broodbank's 'Social Change at Knossos before the Bronze Age'," *JMA* 5 (1992) 225–38.

the subsistence base seems not to have been modified in response to the local environment or indigenous domestication. Apparently because of their small population and isolation, the early settlers did not adapt to the Cretan environment in ways that would have encouraged population growth and expansion.

Early Neolithic sites have rarely been recognized on Crete and only three—Knossos, Gerani Cave, and Lera Cave—are known in any detail.[19] Intensive surveys on Crete have shown that Neolithic settlement on all parts of the island continued to be sparse until the Final Neolithic period. Only then did settlements begin to spread over the many different ecological zones of Crete. On the Akrotiri peninsula of Chania, for example, Moody's survey records an increase in the number and types of sites in the FN period.[20] In Sphakia in West Crete, upland areas are first settled in this period.[21] In the Western Mesara, one possible MN site, at Kannia, is succeeded by nine new FN settlements. These sites include open settlements and caves on the Mesara coasts, in the central plain, in the Asterousia Mountains, and on Mt. Ida.[22] In the coastal plain of Kavousi, the earliest sites date to the FN period.[23] Further west, in the Istron area, three FN settlements are established on the coast and the island of Pseira was first inhabited at this time.[24] Caves and open sites in the plain of Lasithi, high in the Dictaean mountain range, are first occupied in the FN–EM I period.[25] All of these new sites may be partly interpreted as seasonal and complementary dwellings of a relatively small overall population, but their large numbers and the expansion of the settlement at Knossos from 3 ha in EN to perhaps 5 ha by the FN period indicate a real increase in the Final Neolithic population.[26]

Vagnetti's publication has provided us with a better understanding of FN Phaistos.[27] The Italian excavators report finding FN pottery and walls in their trenches across the Phaistos ridgetop, indicating that the FN settlement was perhaps 5.6 ha in size. Rectangular house walls with beaten mud floors and hearths are similar to those at FN Knossos, but a circular house, 2.5 m in diameter, has its closest parallels in Neolithic II Cyprus.[28] Our knowledge of religion on Crete in this period is dependent on the few known figurines, usually found in secondary domestic contexts. A female figurine from Phaistos may have served a religious function, as it was found with a piece of meteoritic iron, and a red-painted Triton shell.[29] Larger (up to 14 cm) three-dimensional clay female figurines may have been a feature of domestic cult, as in Cyprus and Anatolia, while the smaller schematic stone examples were probably worn as amulets.[30] Final Neo-

---

[19] For Knossos, see J. Evans, "Neolithic Knossos: The Growth of a Settlement," *PPS* 37 (1971) 95–117, with earlier bibliography. The Lera Cave, overlooking the Bay of Stavros on the northwestern tip of the Akrotiri peninsula of Chania, was a settlement from EN to EM I. The excavators noted numerous parallels between the EN pottery of Lera and Knossos. For Gerani Cave, see brief reports only by I. Tzedakis in *ArchDelt* 25 (1970) Chronika 474–76; 26 (1971) 508. For Lera Cave, see A. Guest-Papamanoli and A. Lambraki, "Les grottes de Lera et de l'Arkoudia en Crète occidentale aux époques préhistoriques," *ArchDelt* 31A (1976) 178–293.

For various aspects of Neolithic Crete see A. Zois, Κρήτη—Εποχή του λίθου (Athens 1973); I. Sakellarakis, "Neolithic Crete," in D. Theocharis, *Neolithic Greece* (Athens 1973) 131–46; and T. Strasser, *Neolithic Settlement and Land-Use on Crete* (Diss. Indiana Univ. 1992).

[20] Moody (supra n. 10) 292–94.

[21] Nixon et al. (supra n. 11) 171.

[22] For Kannia, see L. Vagnetti, "Tracce di due insediamenti neolitici nel territorio dell'antica Gortina," *AntCr* 1 (1973) 1–9. For the Mesara, see Watrous et al. (supra n. 10) 223. Asterousias: A. Taramelli, "Cretan Expedition VIII: The Prehistoric Grotto at Miamu," *AJA* 1 (1897) 287–312; Blackman and Branigan 1977 (supra n. 11) 67 and fig. 34; A. Vasilakis, "Προϊστορικές θέσεις στη Μονή Οδηγήτριας," Κρητική Εστία 3 (1989) 70. Two of these sites have now been excavated. Traces of FN pottery are reported under the tholos tomb at Agia Kyriaki, D. Blackman and K. Branigan, "The Excavation of an Early Minoan Tholos

Tomb at Ayia Kyriaki, Ayiopharango, Southern Crete," *BSA* 77 (1982) 44. A. Vasilakis excavated and published an FN house near Kaloi Limenes, "Ανασκαφή νεολιθικού σπιτιού στους Καλούς Λιμένες της Νότιας Κρήτης," in Ειλαπίνη (Herakleion 1987) 45–53.

[23] Haggis (supra n. 10) 270.

[24] Hayden et al. (supra n. 10) 320 and 322, fig. 15. For Pseira, Κρητική Εστία 3 (1989/1990) 296.

[25] Watrous (supra n. 10) 9–10 and map 4.

[26] See Evans (supra n. 19).

[27] L. Vagnetti, "L'insediamento neolitico di Festòs," *ASAtene* 34/35 (1972/1973) 7–138.

[28] Circular house, Vagnetti (supra n. 27) 27–29, figs. 17–18. V. Karageorghis, *Cyprus* (London 1982) 26–30 for an introduction to the sites of Vrysi, Sotira, and Philia-Drakos A.

[29] Vagnetti (supra n. 27) 90, fig. 78.24. Pernier's excavations produced a similar context: a female figurine, miniature pots, and seashells. See L. Pernier, *Il palazzo minoico di Festòs* I (Rome 1935) 105, fig 48.

[30] For the Phaistos figurines: Vagnetti (supra n. 27) 90, fig. 78.24–25. This interpretation is suggested by Cypriot and Minoan figurines. Cypriot cult figurines: E. Peltenburg, "Chalcolithic Figurine from Lemba, Cyprus," *Antiquity* 51 (1977) 140–43 argues that Cypriot figurines were probably pendants based on the existence of larger cult statuettes, such as the example from Lemba. In his excavations in Anatolia, at Çatal Hüyük and Hacılar, J. Mellaart likewise distinguished two types of figurines, larger clay statuettes found in shrines and in deposits of stored

lithic burials have rarely been identified, as they were probably simple inhumations within settlements, rock shelters, or caves.[31]

The material record of Final Neolithic Crete exhibits increased signs of widespread Aegean contacts. The FN pottery at Phaistos (and Knossos) has extensive parallels overseas, especially with the eastern Aegean.[32] The FN pottery from Nerokourou near Chania has now been published and shows affinities with the eastern Aegean, the Peloponnese, and the "Attic-Kephala" culture.[33] Copper and obsidian at FN Phaistos also point to international contacts.[34] Davaras's recent excavation in the Pelekita Cave on the east coast of the island likewise produced FN pottery and a phallic-shaped idol with Cypriot parallels.[35] These new signs of Cretan overseas contacts are part of a wider pattern of internationalism that occurs throughout the Aegean and the Near East at this time.[36]

EARLY MINOAN I

Early Minoan I is the period par excellence of settlement expansion on Bronze Age Crete. Intensive surveys have documented the distribution and density of new settlement on the island. In the Western Mesara, the number of sites doubles in the EM I period.[37] To the south in the Agiopharango Valley, the increase is even more dramatic, from two FN sites to at least 11 EM I sites.[38] In other areas of the island, it is clear that many new settlements are established along the coast and in the interior.[39] By this time most (but not all) caves occupied in FN are no longer inhabited. Settlement hierarchy changes in EM I. In the Mesara virtually all of the FN settlements are small sites (farmsteads or camps?) except for Phaistos, but in EM I hamlet-sized settlements make their appearance. Located in the mountains south of Chania, Debla (phase 1), the only published EM I settlement on the island, fits this category, for it was probably a seasonal farmstead.[40] Interdisciplinary survey work in the Mesara has shown that this spread of new settlements brought in its wake a period of widespread erosion probably caused by the settlers' stripping of the vegetation cover from the land.[41]

We rely chiefly on burials for what we know about EM I Crete.[42] Inhumation in caves or rock shelters continues to occur.[43] For this period the most important recent discovery is the EM I–II cemetery excavated by Davaras at Agia Photia on the north coast near Siteia.[44] This necropolis consists of 252 tombs (an estimated 50 more tombs having been de-

food or granaries and a smaller schematic "ex-voto" (based on the former type) found in houses: "Excavations at Çatal Hüyük, 1962," *AnatSt* 13 (1963) 82, and "Excavations at Çatal Hüyük, 1963," *AnatSt* 14 (1964) 40–81, esp. 95 and ns. 42–44. Cypriot figurine as a pendant amulet: V. Karageorghis, *The Civilization of Prehistoric Cyprus* (Athens 1976) pl. 25. Cretan figurine as a pendant amulet: B. Rutkowski, *Petsophas* (Warsaw 1991) pl. X.4.

[31] See L. Vagnetti and P. Belli, "Characteristics and Problems of the Final Neolithic in Crete," *SMEA* 19 (1978) 150 and 142, table 1. The excavation at the Ayia Kyriaki tholos showed that, although FN pottery occurred at the site, the tomb was constructed in EM I: Blackman and Branigan 1982 (supra n. 22) 44–46.

[32] Vagnetti (supra. n. 27) 126–28, who includes Knossos parallels.

[33] L. Vagnetti et al., *Scavi greco-italiani a Nerokourou (Kydonias* 1, Rome 1989) 11–97.

[34] Vagnetti (supra n. 27) fig. 133.4. A. Evans's excavation at FN Knossos produced a copper ax, *PM* II, 14, fig. 3f. Only two other metal examples are known from FN Crete: a silver/lead bead from Agios Nikolaos (N. Tod, "Excavations at Palaikastro, II," *BSA* 9 [1902/1903] 336–43) and from Mochlos (*Mochlos* 93, fig. 48). For obsidian from Phaistos, see Vagnetti (supra n. 27) 115, fig. 127.

[35] C. Davaras, *ArchDelt* 34 (1979) Chronika 402–404, and pl. 215c. Cf. P. Dikaios, *Khirokitia* (Oxford 1953) pl. 95.194.

[36] J. Coleman, "Greece, the Aegean and Cyprus," in Ehrich I, 255–64; J. Mellaart, *The Chalcolithic and Early Bronze Age in the Near East and Anatolia* (Beirut 1966) 114–17.

[37] Watrous et al. (supra n. 10) 223 n. 60. Because of extensive alluviation in the Mesara, the number of EM I and II sites discovered by the survey is much smaller than must have existed, pp. 197–204.

[38] Blackman and Branigan 1977 (supra n. 11) 67–68; Vasilakis 1989 (supra n. 22) 71–74.

[39] Because of the difficulty of distinguishing LN from EM I pottery, several surveys have treated the two ceramic phases as one period, e.g., Watrous (supra n. 10) 9, 67–68; Hayden et al. (supra n. 10) 320–21.

[40] P. Warren and I. Tzedakis, "Debla: An Early Minoan Settlement in Western Crete," *BSA* 69 (1974) 299–342.

[41] See K. Pope's important report on the geology and soils of the Western Mesara in Watrous et al. (supra n. 10) 197–204.

[42] There is relatively little detailed knowledge about the EM I phase at Minoan settlements because, in many cases, it is the basal stratum sealed or destroyed by later Minoan remains. *Chronology* 13–14 lists 10 useful EM I deposits, of which three (either small or unpublished) come from settlements.

[43] Burials: Kyparissi, S. Alexiou, "Πρωτομινωικαί ταφαί παρά το Κανλί Καστέλλι Ηρακλείου," *CretChron* 5 (1951) 275–94. Pyrgos: S. Xanthoudides, *ArchDelt* 4 (1918) 136–70. The upper level at Pyrgos contained larnakes and so probably dates to MM I. Partira: C. Mortzos, "Πάρτιρα: Μία πρώιμος μινωική κεραμεική ομάς," *Επετηρίς Επιστημονικών Ερευνών* 3 (1972) 386–421.

[44] C. Davaras, "Πρωτομινωικόν νεκροταφείον Αγίας Φωτιάς Σητείας," *AAA* 4 (1971) 392–97; Davaras, *ArchDelt* 27, Chronika (1972) 648–50. See *Chronology* 14.

Fig. 2. Tomb 195, cemetery of Agia Photia. (After C. Davaras, *AAA* 4 [1971] 394, fig. 7)

Fig. 4. Incised pan from cemetery of Agia Photia. (After C. Davaras, *Guide to Cretan Antiquities* [Athens 1976] 131, fig. 77)

stroyed), most of which are simple oval chambers dug into the shallow bedrock with a small doorway (facing north and out to sea) plugged with an upright slab (fig. 2). Often a single vase, usually a Pyrgos ware chalice, stood on the small paved floor of the antechamber in front of the door. The inhumation lay in the interior chamber, on a floor strewn with sea pebbles. Finds included vases (fig. 3), bronze daggers, a sword, knives, a socketed spearhead, fishhooks, chisels, masses of obsidian blades, stone axes, two animal-shaped amulets of lead, and a few stone vases.

Davaras drew attention to the similarity of form between the Agia Photia tombs and those in the Cyc-

lades, especially on the island of Ano Kouphonisi. The pottery at Agia Photia—pans (fig. 4), pyxides, incised bottles (fig. 5), fruitstands, and jugs (some of which may be imports)—is similar to the Kampos Group in the Cyclades. A large proportion of the ca. 2,000 unpublished vases are said to be of Cycladic type. Crucibles from the cemetery are of a type known from Syros and Thermi.[45] Recent analyses of

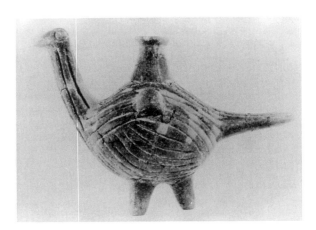

Fig. 3. Bird vase from cemetery of Agia Photia. (After C. Davaras, *Guide to Cretan Antiquities* [Athens 1976] 130, fig. 76)

Fig. 5. Incised bottle from cemetery of Agia Photia. (After C. Davaras, *Haghios Nikolaos Museum* [Athens, n.d.] fig. 6)

---

[45] K. Branigan, *Pre-Palatial. The Foundations of Palatial Crete: A Survey of Crete in the Early Bronze Age*[2] (Amsterdam 1988) 239.

the bronze objects from Agia Photia indicate a Cycladic source for the metal.[46] Another EM I cemetery has been reported at Nea Roumata southwest of Chania where a small, circular built tomb with a slab floor has been compared to similar tombs from Syros.[47] Most Early Minoan burials in North Crete were made in caves (often in caves inhabited in the Neolithic period) or rock shelters and are accompanied by stone idols, a few vases, obsidian blades, and perhaps an occasional copper tool or dagger.[48] At least five types of idols, all schematic variations of the Cycladic Pebble form (*Brettidolen*), are known from EM I burials.[49] The tholos tomb at Krasi, built in EM I, remains a unique type at this time in the north. Its basal level, usually dated to EM I but perhaps actually EM I–IIA, is said to have produced a lead amulet(?), gold foil, bronze knives, needles, silver jewelry, a foot amulet, and a clay spindle whorl.[50] The earliest Cretan seals, e.g., that from Krasi, may date to EM I, but more probably are EM IIA.[51]

In southern Crete, EM I is the great era of settlement foundation and tholos tomb construction. Branigan's newly revised book on the Mesara tombs lists 25 tholos tombs built in this period.[52] It is only in this period that burials receive special preparations: individuals are now buried in built tombs, with a few personal belongings, and are given offerings. Unfortunately, almost all of the tholoi discovered in the last quarter century have been robbed, and are known only from short reports of rescue excavations published by the Archaeological Service.[53] The single exception is the publication of the British excavation at the (robbed) tomb of Agia Kyriaki in the Ayiopharango Valley on the south

coast.[54] A typical burial offering at Ayia Kyriaki consisted of a jug, three cups, and a bowl or jar. A bowl and fruitstand were used in a ceremony held in front of the tomb.

In his fundamental survey of Aegean metalwork, Branigan describes EM I Crete as one of the leading metallurgical centers in the Aegean.[55] Recent research requires a modification of this view. The EM I tomb deposits in Crete (at Pyrgos, Kyparissi, and perhaps Krasi) containing metal objects (bronze daggers, awls, chisels cast in open molds, and gold foil jewelry) are now recognized to span the EM I–IIA period: thus, the early date for the beginnings of Cretan metallurgy is less certain. The earliest Cretan crucibles, from Agia Photia, are of a Cycladic type; the EM round-heeled dagger is also probably a foreign type, as it is known earlier in the Near East.[56] Gale's lead isotope analyses of metal objects from the Mesara tholoi show that the composition of the Cretan artifacts there is consistent with an ore source on the island of Kythnos.[57] Early Minoan metalworkers seem to have been dependent on Cycladic sources for their copper (as well as silver and probably gold), rather than having significant indigenous sources as Branigan believed. Certainly the amounts of imported obsidian and pottery evident in EM I contexts point to regular Cycladic-Cretan connections. The above evidence suggests that the Cycladic contribution to Early Minoan metallurgy has probably been underrated.

The dramatic rise in the number of FN–EM I settlements has generally been explained either through immigration or population growth.[58] The most likely candidate for a foreign settlement on

[46] N. Gale, "The Provenance of Metals for Early Bronze Age Crete—Local or Cycladic?" *Pepragmena* 1990 I, 299–316.

[47] I. Tzedakis, "Le passage en Minoen ancien en Crète occidentale," in C. Nicolet ed., *Aux l'origines de l'hellénisme* (Paris 1984) 3–7; H. Catling, "Archaeology in Greece, 1984–1985," *AR* 31 (1984/1985) 67.

[48] See supra n. 43.

[49] K. Branigan, "Cycladic Figurines and Their Derivatives in Crete," *BSA* 66 (1971) 57–78 and fig. 1, nos. 1–4 and 8.

[50] S. Marinatos, *ArchDelt* 12 (1929) 102–41. In his report Marinatos clearly distinguishes a lower level with EM I pottery and the finds noted in the text. This level may have continued into EM IIA, for the low pedestaled goblet (pl. 4.2) resembles EM IIA examples at Knossos; cf. D. Wilson, "The Pottery and Architecture of the Early Minoan IIA West Court House at Knossos," *BSA* 80 (1985) 300–302, figs. 10–11, P 29–34, 43–46. I am indebted to D. Wilson for these parallels.

[51] One seal comes from the lower level (EM I/II?) at Krasi, Marinatos (supra n. 50) 122, fig. 15, no. 56, 123, fig. 16; and *CMS* II.1, nos. 195–203 from the middle level at Lebena Tomb II, which produced EM I pottery but may

be mixed since seal *CMS* II.1, no. 201 is later.

[52] K. Branigan, *Dancing with Death* (Amsterdam 1993) 143–48, plus eight additional possible tombs.

[53] Much of the material from the robbed tholoi can be seen in private collections. See, e.g., L. Marangou ed., *Minoan and Greek Civilization from the Mitsotakis Collection* (Athens 1992).

[54] The robbed Agia Kyriaki tholos was excavated and published by Blackman and Branigan 1982 (supra n. 22) 1–57. It is a measure of our ignorance that Blackman and Branigan's report presents the fullest published collection of painted EM I–II pottery from the Mesara. When published, Alexiou's excavation of the unrobbed tholoi at Lebena will be an extremely important contribution to our knowledge of EM Crete.

[55] Branigan 101–105.

[56] For the dagger at fourth-millennium B.C. Byblos: M. Dunand, *Fouilles de Byblos* I (Paris 1937) pl. 189, nos. 6773 and 6776, cited by Branigan 101.

[57] Gale (supra n. 46) 301 and fig. 1.

[58] See the discussion in P. Warren, "Crete 300–1400 B.C.: Immigration and the Archaeological Evidence," in R. Crossland and A. Birchall eds., *Bronze Age Migrations in the Aegean* (London 1973) 41–50.

Crete is the habitation site (probably now covered by the nearby village) associated with the cemetery at Agia Photia. Certainly the high proportion of foreign features there relative to other cemeteries, such as that at Pyrgos (also on the north coast), must be significant in this regard.[59] The evidence from Agia Photia, however, is unique. Does this mean that foreign settlement was rare in Crete at this time? Final Neolithic settlements established in defensive locations, especially in marginal environments, can also be suspected as intrusive. Examples of such settlements include Katalimata (Ierapetra), Trapeza (near Kamilari village), Gortyn acropolis, and Pseira.[60] In the Western Mesara, there are some possible signs of newcomers.[61] On the other hand, new EM I sites founded in areas adjacent to older settlements probably do represent a growth in local population. Such patterns are relatively common in Crete and have been noted in Lasithi, the Mesara, and the Agiopharango Valley.[62] The implication seems to be that the EM I population expansion throughout Crete was to a great extent the result of local population growth. During the FN–EM I period this mixing of indigenous settlers with newcomers in Crete creates the regional character of the succeeding Minoan population.

A new explanation for FN–EM I population growth focuses on changes in local subsistence.[63] With the introduction of certain new technologies— the ability to plow heavier soils and to make cheese out of milk—and of new crops, mainly olives and grapes, the settlers were for the first time able to take advantage of vast tracts of virgin land. On Crete it may be possible to recognize two phases in this transition: 1) a greatly increased focus on pastoralism with some agricultural changes, and 2) a balance reached between fully developed agriculture and herding. The first phase (FN–EM I) is represented by the widespread occupation of caves and open sites. The location of and finds from these new sites in the interior of the island, many of them caves (such as Miamou and Psychro), indicate that the inhabitants were small groups relying heavily on pastoralism supplemented by seasonal agriculture.[64] The appearance of EM I seasonal sites such as Debla where the inhabitants grew and processed emmer wheat, barley, and oats and kept herds of sheep/goat mainly for their secondary products (viz., milk/cheese, wool, and hides) is an archaeological manifestation of this new subsistence strategy. During the second phase (EM I–IIA) new crops may have been introduced and large open settlements established, primarily near arable land. The small faunal assemblage from the EM II occupation in the Sedoni Cave (630 masl) near Zoniana (Rethymnon) offers some evidence for diversified animal husbandry since sheep, goat, cow, and pig as well as deer are present.[65]

---

[59] Moreover, the results of Tsipopoulou's survey (supra n. 11) make it difficult to believe that the cemetery of ca. 300 tombs at Agia Photia served a population entirely descended from the inhabitants of the only nearby Neolithic site, the Kouphota Cave.

[60] For FN at Katalimata, see W. Coulson and M. Tsipopoulou, "Preliminary Investigations at Chalasmeno, Crete, 1992–1993," *Aegean Archaeology* 1 (in press). I am indebted to K. Nowicki for this reference.

[61] The circular house at Phaistos and certain pottery motifs in the Mesara resemble features of the Erimi culture on Cyprus. Cf. S. Alexiou, "New Light on Minoan Dating: Early Minoan Tombs at Lebena," *ILN* 1960, 227, figs. 14, 15, and 20 and Blackman and Branigan (supra n. 22) figs. 7, 10, and 11 with P. Dikaios and J. Stewart, *The Stone Age and the Early Bronze Age in Cyprus* (SwCyprusExp IV:1A, Lund 1962) figs. 37 and 42; I. Todd, "Vasilikos Valley Project, 1977–1978," *RDAC* 1979, 13–68, pls. 4–5.

[62] Lasithi: Watrous (supra n. 10) 9–10. Mesara: Watrous et al. (supra n. 10) 223–24. This is based on the identification of these sites as permanent settlements, an assumption that rests on the fact that the sites are substantial, equal in size, and similar in their catchment areas. Agiopharango: Blackman and Branigan 1975 (supra n. 11) 67 and fig. 34.

[63] The "secondary products revolution" discussed in A. Sherratt, "Plough and Pastoralism: Aspects of the Secondary Products Revolution," in I. Hodder, G. Isaac, and N. Hammond eds., *Pattern of the Past: Studies in Honour of David Clarke* (Cambridge 1981) 261–306.

[64] See, e.g., the evidence from Magasa, R. Dawkins, "Excavations at Palaikastro IV," *BSA* 11 (1904/1905) 260–68. The olive apparently first appears in Middle to Late Neolithic levels in pollen cores from West Crete, Moody (supra n. 10) 285–86. Ovicaprids show a marked increase in FN levels at Knossos; see the discussion in P. Halstead, "Counting Sheep in Neolithic and Bronze Age Greece," in Hodder et al. (supra n. 63) esp. 324–31.

[65] Direct evidence for subsistence during EM I–IIA is scant. The tripod cooking pot, known in Chalcolithic levels from western Anatolia and the Near East, first appears in Crete in EM I. The Cretan adoption of this shape may have been accompanied by dietary introductions as well. The faunal remains from the Sedoni Cave, excavated by E. Gavrilaki for the Greek Archaeological Service, will be published by I. Hamilakis, "Στοιχεία γιά την Πρωτομινωική κτηνοτροφία: Ζωοαρχαιολογικές μαρτυρίες από το Σπήλαιο Σεντόνι Ζονιανών," *Άνθρωπος και Σπηλαιοπεριβάλλον* (Athens, in press). Hamilakis cautions that more large, properly collected assemblages are needed to prove his hypothesis concerning diversification.

Fig. 6. View of Trypeti, from the northeast. (After A. Vasilakis, *Αρχαιολογία* 30 [1989] 53, fig. 2)

EARLY MINOAN II

Intensive surveys have documented that settlement expansion continues in Early Minoan II but at a demonstrably slower pace. In the Lasithi Plain, five relatively large EM II settlements at the edge of the plain replace the more numerous FN–EM I campsites high on the mountain slopes.[66] In the area around Phaistos, the number of settlements drops slightly (perhaps a sign of urban nucleation), in contrast to the continuing growth in the Agiopharango Valley to the south.[67] In the Chania area, settlements grow in number and size.[68] In the Isthmus of Ierapetra settlement dispersion apparently does not take place until EM II, since the Gournia hill, Vasiliki, Fournou Koriphi, and Myrtos/Pyrgos are all founded at this time. While new sites are established in all parts of Crete, settlement hierarchy does not change, but continues as in EM I. In the Western Mesara, the EM II settlement hierarchy, that is, one village-sized settlement (Phaistos), a few hamlet-sized (50–100+ m in length) communities, and many smaller sites, probably single farmsteads, is the same as in EM I. While growth occurs at the lower levels of the hierarchy, large settlements, such as Knossos and Phaistos, do not reveal any increase in size during EM I–II.[69]

Despite recent work at several EM II settlements, our knowledge of EM II Crete is still dangerously dependent on cemeteries. The one splendid exception is Peter Warren's excavation and publication of the site of Myrtos (Fournou Koriphi), which has provided new and vivid documentation of an EM II hamlet.[70] Established in EM IIA on a steep, arid hill overlooking the sea, Fournou Koriphi was a small community in EM IIB, consisting of five or six households (perhaps 25–30 persons in total).[71] Irregular, one-story houses of stone and mudbrick with flat roofs had plastered walls (at times painted red) and packed earth floors. The settlement was protected by an outer wall and a tower at its southern, seaward entrance. Houses were entered

---

[66] Watrous (supra n. 10) 11 and map 5.

[67] Blackman and Branigan 1977 (supra n. 11) 68.

[68] Moody (supra n. 10) 298–99.

[69] Knossos: Whitelaw (supra n. 18) 227–28. Phaistos: T. Whitelaw, "The Settlement at Fournou Korifi, Myrtos and Aspects of Early Minoan Social Organization," in *Society* 338–39 to which EM deposits under the Italian storerooms should be added.

[70] *Myrtos.*

[71] As reinterpreted by Whitelaw, in *Society* (supra n. 69) 323–46. The cultural assumptions and formalistic method of C. Tenwolde, in "Myrtos Revisited: The Role of Relative Function Ceramic Typologies in Bronze Age Settlement Analysis," *OJA* 11 (1992) 1–24 make his study unconvincing.

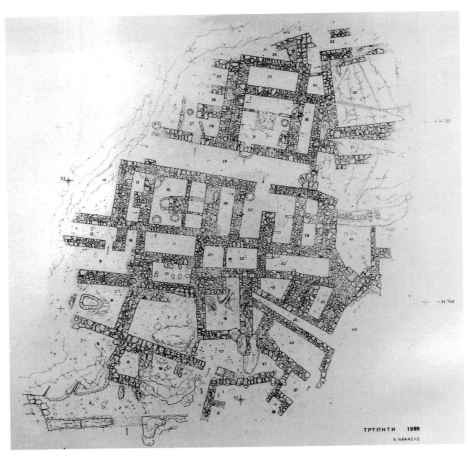

Fig. 7. Plan of the site of Trypeti. (Courtesy A. Vasilakis)

through doorways with wooden doors set on stone pivots; some rooms were entered from the roof. Rooms were fitted with benches, working platforms, cupboards, and hearths or cooking holes. Each house had a cooking area, storage places for food and vases, and work areas. One completely preserved house plan (rooms 72–74, 79–82, 88) is similar to those at Trypeti and Agia Triada. This house was entered through a corridor, into a line of outer workrooms where weaving, milking, and grinding of grain may have taken place. The central room had a roof support, cupboard, and storage vases lined along the south wall. A narrow room to the east held vases and perhaps a ladder to the roof. A narrow room to the west had a hearth and cooking ware and thus can be identified as the kitchen.

The Myrtos community practiced mixed farming, of barley, wheat, grapes, and olives, and animal husbandry involving cattle, pig, and especially sheep and goat. Domestic industries included textile and

perhaps pottery manufacture. Perforated stone weights may have been used on fishing nets; two clay balls may have been sling bullets. Stone stamp seals were used and one stamped clay sealing probably sealed a container. Two stone "kernoi," perhaps gameboards, were found in situ set at the edge of the open central court of the settlement. The original publication suggested that evidence for external relations at the site was limited to obsidian, a copper chisel, and possibly some Vasiliki vases (but see below).

Recent excavations have revealed an EM II settlement at Trypeti on the south coast.[72] Trypeti was founded in EM I on a small, steep hilltop on a cove (fig. 6). Preliminary reports indicate a community of perhaps eight houses built on either side of a wide central street (fig. 7). Two architectural phases have been observed in the houses. Pottery of the EM I– MM I periods is reported. The one-story houses often have a large central rectangular room with

[72] A. Vasilakis, "Ο Πρωτομινωικός οικισμός Τρυπητής," Αρχαιολογία 30 (1989) 52–56; "Τρυπητή," Κρητική Εστία 2 (1988) 331–32; 3 (1989/1990) 287; and "Πρωτοανακτο-

ρικός οικισμός Τρυπητής στη Νότια Κρήτη," Πεπραγμένα του Θ΄ Διεθνούς Κρητολογικού Συνεδρίου, in press.

Fig. 8. Aerial view of Vasiliki. (W. and E. Myers and G. Cadogan, *The Aerial Atlas of Ancient Crete* [Berkeley 1992] fig. 41.2, courtesy W. and E. Myers)

narrower side rooms used as storerooms entered from above. The central room could possess a bench, cupboard, and a shallow hearth in the floor. Carbonized wheat, barley, peas, vetch, figs, bones of cattle, sheep/goat, pig, hare, and bird, seashells (Triton, snails, murex, limpets, clams), and fishbones were present in many of the rooms. Stone tools, including querns, handstones, axes, hammers, pestles, and weights, occurred most commonly in the lowest stratum but also in later levels. Bone tools as well as obsidian and chert blades, cores, points, and knapping debris were found. A clay sealing, stamped twice, and a "kernos" set in a house floor are reported. Imports to the hamlet included obsidian, a copper pin, and (in the nearby tholos tomb) two silver beads.

Two prepalatial houses at Agia Triada have recently been uncovered ca. 100 m southeast of Tholos A.[73] The EM II settlement at Agia Triada may thus have consisted of two adjacent communi-

ties, east and west of the tholos tombs A and B. The West House had a large storeroom, with a pi-shaped central roof support (as at Myrtos) and contained Agios Onouphrios and dark-ground vases, five pithoi, a stool, tripod cooking (?) tray, and many obsidian blades. The narrow north room is similar to examples at Myrtos and Trypeti. Built over part of the West House, the East House had a large room, with central support, which consisted of a storage area, with pithoi, a stone pestle, and obsidian, and a work area, with a quern, stone pounder, and small vases. A wall added on the east enclosed an apsidal space. Both houses were provided with benches along their exteriors. The houses were abandoned in EM IIB.

The patient excavations (1970–present) of A. Zois at Vasiliki have greatly improved our understanding of this complicated and important site (figs. 8–9).[74] Founded in EM IIA, the settlement consisted of at least four houses, Θ and Ξ on the north edge

[73] C. Laviosa, "Saggi di scavo ad Hagia Triada," *ASAtene* 31/32 (1969/1970) 407–15; "L'abitato prepalaziale di Haghia Triada," *ASAtene* 50/51 (1972/1973) 350–53.

[74] A. Zois, annual reports in *Prakt* 1972 through 1982. A short but useful summary appears in W. and E. Myers

and G. Cadogan, *The Aerial Atlas of Ancient Crete* (Berkeley 1992) 276–81. A. Zois and C. Mortzos will republish the vases saved from Seager's excavation in the volume Βασιλική II.

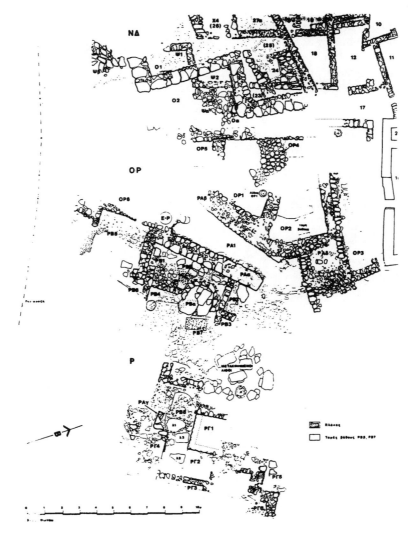

Fig. 9. Plan of the site of Vasiliki, sector OP. (Courtesy A. Zois)

of the hilltop and two on the south. The remains of Θ and Ξ consist of regular cells, filled in with packing, to create a foundation for the houses.[75] House Θ was entered from the north from a paved area. The floor packing of the houses contained Koumasa ware, obsidian blades and knapping debris, ground stone tools, a ceramic jug, bronze tweezers, and caprid bones. Structure Π may have been a separate house or a work area for Θ; it produced obsidian. Structures Θ, Π, and Ξ were destroyed in EM IIA.

Zois's investigations have shown that the great "House on the Hilltop" reconstructed by Seager was

a conflation of houses of different dates.[76] The actual architectural sequence was more complicated. In the first phase of EM IIB the hilltop was reorganized. A large structure (Zois's Red House) was built on the southern half of the hilltop. A large paved court was laid out west and to the north of the Red House. The structure almost certainly had two stories, with red-painted walls and floors, a mudbrick and pisé superstructure, and a flat roof made with beams, reeds, and plaster. There were entrances from the north court, on the south (room 16), and from room 13. There are two groups of small rooms (15, 16, 28, 33, and 36–38) used as basement maga-

[75] For Minoan architectural foundations, see A. Zois, "Pour un schema evolutif de l'architecture minoenne. Les fondations: Techniques et morphologie," in P. Darcque and R. Treuil eds., *L'habitat égéen préhistorique* (*BCH* Suppl. 19, Paris 1990) 75–93.

[76] A. Zois, *Βασιλική* I (Athens 1976) 34–35.

zines on the south slope at a lower level. Seager found many jugs and cups in room 42, which may have served as a pantry. Room 39 was supplied with an 8-m-deep well. Many pithoi were found south of room 43. Certain details make it probable that the Red House structure is in fact two houses: first, the doorway in room 13/34 that opens out onto a space (3.50 m in width) between rooms 13 and 39, and second, the presence of two separate paved courts and two complexes of rooms, with large ones on the north (1–3, 6, 13, and 39–42) and smaller rooms (storage annexes?) on the south.[77] Two broken bronze axes and a knife, much obsidian, and many whole vases were found in the Red House.[78] Zois's new finds include a steatite seal and a large vase, stamped with a seal motif typical of EM II.[79] A Koumasa-type marble figurine with folded arms (FAF) was found in the packing of the east wall of the structure. Probably out of context, the find is nevertheless important because it indicates that Cretan folded-arm figurines were made for use by the living, not just for burials.[80] Amphoras and loomweights were found between the two houses that comprise the Red House.

During EM IIB, two new houses (Zois's West House and the Southwest House) were built on top of the paved court next to the Red House. The West House consists of a large central room (5) around which were added storage annexes and other rooms. The new excavations found over 70 loomweights placed in room 27a of the Southwest House. The Red and West Houses met their end by fiery destruction in EM IIB. The Southwest House produced no floor deposits (except for some pithoi)

and contained no signs of fallen roofing, so it may have been abandoned rather than destroyed.

The EM IIA–B settlement at Vasiliki apparently consisted of two to four houses.[81] Zois's excavations on the southeast slope (area P) revealed fragments of scrappy walls that may belong to a continuation of the EM IIB settlement, or to the EM III–MM I period. Excavations in 1991 under the paved floor of structure PBb produced a carbonized olive stone of EM IIB date.[82] EM II Vasiliki was thus a hamlet, ca. 80 × 40 m in extent,[83] whose inhabitants farmed, kept livestock, wove textiles, and made bronze tools in molds.[84] They had access to foreign materials, copper and obsidian, perhaps via two large EM II settlements on the north coast of the Isthmus.[85] Close to two excellent clay sources (north and south of the present-day village of Vasiliki), the inhabitants of EM II Vasiliki may have produced pottery for export.

Our limited knowledge of major Early Minoan II settlements comes from small soundings.[86] Trial trenches dug at Mallia in the last 15 years have revealed traces of irregular EM II house walls under the palace and its immediate surroundings, indicating that the site reached village size in EM II.[87] Recent trenches at Knossos revealed the basement of a single house (West Court House).[88] Imported pottery in this house included Agios Onouphrios vases from the Mesara, pithoi, and EC II sauceboats. EM IIA levels found in the palace area and along the Royal Road indicate that building and extensive terracing took place at Knossos in EM IIA, including the construction of an EM IIA or IIB stone-paved ramp leading to the top of the tell where the north-

[77] That the "Red House" is actually two houses is also suggested by the fact that the west wing is surrounded by a double wall, a construction usually found on external walls.

[78] The most complete account of Seager's excavations appears in Zois (supra n. 76).

[79] A stray find, the seal is published in *CMS* V.1, no. 27. The vase is mentioned in *Prakt* 1979, 326.

[80] As R. Barber and J. Davis have suggested for Cycladic figurines, cf. L. Fitton ed., *Cycladica* (London 1984) 10–23.

[81] According to Seager, his trials on the lower slopes of the hill produced no signs of EM settlement, R. Seager, "Excavations at Vasiliki, Crete, in 1906," *Transactions of the Free Museum of Science and Art* 2 (1907) 113. The same is true for Zois's investigations.

[82] I am grateful to the excavator for showing me his unpublished reports of the 1990–1993 excavations from which this summary is drawn.

[83] New excavations to the north and south may well reveal more EM II structures. The local topography sug-

gests that most of the settlement is already revealed.

[84] The EM II bronze bivalve mold for a double ax from Vasiliki indicates that metallurgical activity was carried out in the settlement. See K. Mavriyannaki, "Μινωική μεταλλική μήτρα από την Βασιλική της Ιεράπετρας," Κρητολογία 9 (1984) 140–76.

[85] These sites were discovered in 1992 and 1993 by the Gournia Survey under the direction of myself and C. Davaras.

[86] Fragmentary house remains have been uncovered at Phaistos, Knossos, and Mallia. See *Chronology* 15 for bibliography.

[87] See van Effenterre I, 82–92. Reports on the more recent sondages have appeared in the *BCH* Chronique sections: 110 (1986) 814 and 817; 113 (1989) 770–85; 114 (1990) 908–10 and 921; 115 (1991) 735.

[88] Wilson (supra n. 50) 281–364. Wilson has recently reconstructed an adjacent mudbrick upper story using the basement roof as a veranda overlooking a terraced area to the west (where the later West Court was). There is no evidence for this reconstruction.

Fig. 10. Aerial view of the tholos tombs at Moni Odigitria. (W. and E. Myers and G. Cadogan, *The Aerial Atlas of Ancient Crete* [Berkeley 1992] fig. 30.4, courtesy W. and E. Myers)

west corner of the later palace was located.[89] Walls of two houses are known at Phaistos.[90] All of these buildings at the later Minoan centers are no more advanced than the architecture at Vasiliki. The only possible exception is at Palaikastro where fragments of large walls were recorded, although nothing else is known about them.[91]

The burials of EM II Crete are of two main types, the tholos tombs of the Mesara and the house tombs of the north coast. Despite Branigan's excellent study of the tholoi,[92] our ability to understand these tombs fully is hindered by the fact that the only excavations of unrobbed tombs are either unpub-

lished or were carried out early in this century (and are therefore incomplete by present-day standards). Meanwhile the list of plundered tholoi grows longer each year.[93] It is a sad fact that Blackman and Branigan's publication of their (re)excavation of the robbed Agia Kyriaki tholos provides our most complete picture of the range of vases offered at an EM II tholos.[94] Many of the tholoi had additional structures built next to or around them. The best-preserved outer complex of a tholos comes from the recently excavated tombs at Moni Odigitria where a paved and enclosed court, with an entrance and auxiliary rooms, can be seen (fig. 10).[95]

[89] D. Wilson, "Early Minoan Knossos: An Overview," in N. Momigliano and D. Evely eds., *Knossos: A Labyrinth of History. Papers Presented in Honour of Sinclair Hood* (Oxford, in press).

[90] Pernier (supra n. 29) 117, 119; and D. Levi, "L'archivo di cretule a Festòs," *ASAtene* 19/20 (1957/1958) 168–69, figs. 348–49.

[91] Dawkins (supra n. 64) pl. X.

[92] Branigan (supra n. 52), a fully revised version of his earlier *Tombs of Mesara*, London 1970.

[93] See the finds, including pottery, stone vases, Koumasa-type figurine, gold and stone jewelry, bone seals, bronze weapons, and stone tools in Marangou (supra n. 53).

[94] Blackman and Branigan 1982 (supra n. 22).

[95] The Greek Archaeological Service excavation (undertaken by A. Vasilakis) of the *looted* tombs yielded 275 vases, 20 stone vases, 11 necklaces, 3 gold diadems, a gold bracelet, 5 bronze objects, and stone tools, including obsidian blades; the excavation remains unpublished.

Only two Mesara tombs, Platanos A and Lebena IIa, have stratified EM II levels. The EM II level at Platanos Tholos A was poor in finds; Xanthoudides mentions 14 triangular daggers, a few gold beads, a diadem attachment, and an electrum pendant.[96] Tholos A at Agia Triada produced pottery, 13 seals,[97] at least one stone vase,[98] and probably most (but not necessarily all) of the 35 short bronze daggers from the tomb, and a few pieces of gold jewelry.[99] The unrobbed tombs at Lebena are unfortunately still unpublished, but preliminary reports indicate that EM II burial levels contained clay vases, including a rhyton, two stone spouted bowls, a bronze dagger, stone figurines, seals, amulets, a gold diadem, necklaces of clay and steatite beads, and obsidian blades.[100] Outside the Mesara to the north, at Archanes, Tholos E had an EM II basal level that produced bone and steatite seals, a few clay and stone vases, a Koumasa-type figurine, jewelry (many steatite and bone pendants and beads, a gold bead, a bronze ring, and bits of gold), obsidian blades, and animal bones.[101] Branigan's new study of the Mesara tholos tombs describes the local EM II burial customs.[102] The deceased were buried with their daily possessions, which included clay vases (jug, cups, bowls), jewelry (necklace, pendants, gold diadems), a sealstone, a bronze toilet article, tool, or weapon, and perhaps a stone figurine. Reviewing the evidence from newer excavations, Branigan comes to the conclusion, surely correct, that the tholoi were fully vaulted in stone.[103]

New excavations and Soles's study of house tombs have helped clarify the dates and architectural details of the prepalatial tombs on the north coast.[104] Much of Soles's work has focused on Mochlos. There, the cemetery consists of three large wealthy tombs on the upper West Terrace and smaller tombs

on the South Slope. The only tomb at Mochlos with a secure, pure EM II deposit is Tomb I, which produced clay vases, stone bowls, jugs, a triangular bronze dagger and cutter, a necklace of electrum, gold, amethyst, and crystal beads, and a Syrian cylinder seal.[105] The deposits in the other tombs spanned longer periods (e.g., EM II–MM I). The range of EM II grave goods at Mochlos seems to include clay vases, stone vases (bowls, ladles, pyxides, jars, and teapots), steatite and bone seals, and jewelry (clay, bone, stone and gold pendants, gold diadems, floral sprays, bands, appliqués, rings, necklaces of clay, steatite, and crystal and gold beads). Occasionally a tomb might contain a bronze dagger, a knife and toilet articles, obsidian blades, and rarely, a stone figurine. A cache of EM IIB gold jewelry placed in a silver vase was found next to Tomb VI in 1971.[106]

Evidence of extensive Cretan trade with the Cyclades and the mainland in EB II has continued to build. A Minoan settlement was established on the island of Kythera in EM II. The site has close ceramic ties with West Crete but since no associated architecture was found, it has been suggested that it may have been seasonally occupied.[107] Various explanations for the colonization of Kythera—trade with the mainland, fishing opportunities, population pressure—have been suggested. Imports into Crete in EM II include masses of obsidian, invariably found on every EM II site (especially along the north coast), metals, clay and stone vases, marble figurines, and jewelry.[108] Signs of Cycladic influence have been observed in EM II ceramic shapes and bronze weapon and tool types, jewelry, figurines, and grave (cist) forms.[109] In contrast, the list of EM II exports (a few clay vases and perhaps a dagger) in the Aegean is relatively short.[110] Undoubtedly the

---

[96] In *VTM* 89, Xanthoudides explained the poverty of the EM II level relative to the upper stratum by suggesting that it had been robbed. But if so, why were the 14 daggers of valuable bronze not taken?

[97] The Agia Triada seals: *CMS* I.2, 11–14, 32, 35, 46, 49, 61, 75, 76, 87, 91.

[98] Stone vase: L. Banti, "La grande tomba a tholos di Haghia Triada," *ASAtene* 13/14 (1930/1931) no. 78.

[99] E.g., the gold pendant, Banti (supra n. 98) 194, fig. 63, no. 164.

[100] Lebena tombs: Myers et al. (supra n. 74) 164–67 with bibliography. The finds—pottery, stone vases, bronze objects, jewelry, seals—made by the Greek Archaeological Service rescue excavations, mentioned in *ArchDelt*, remain otherwise unpublished.

[101] I. Sakellarakis, *Prakt* 1975, 292–307.

[102] Branigan (supra n. 52) 67–80, 119–41.

[103] Branigan (supra n. 52) 41–56.

[104] Soles.

[105] *Mochlos* 18–22; Soles 50.

[106] C. Davaras, "Early Minoan Jewellery from Mochlos," *BSA* 70 (1975) 101–14; Soles 58–62; Higgins (infra n. 137) 54–55.

[107] Excavation: J. Coldstream and G. Huxley, *Kythera* (London 1972) 83–91 and 272–74; Coldstream and Huxley, "The Minoans of Kythera," *Thalassocracy* 108. J. Rutter and C. Zerner, "Early Hellado-Minoan Contacts," in *Thalassocracy* 75–76 and n. 5 suggest the EM II settlement may have been seasonal.

[108] For Cretan imports, see Branigan (supra n. 45) 185–86; 245–47. I. Sakellarakis, "The Cyclades and Crete," in J. Thimme ed., *Art and Culture of the Cyclades* (Karlsruhe 1977) 145–53.

[109] Branigan (supra n. 49) 60; Branigan, "A Transitional Phase in Minoan Metallurgy," *AJA* 72 (1968) 219–22; S. Stucynski, "Cycladic Imports in Crete: A Brief Survey," *TUAS* 7 (1982) 50–59.

[110] Branigan (supra n. 49) 76–78; Rutter and Zerner (supra n. 107) 81; *Chronology* 17.

most significant contribution to the question of EM II external relations has been made by the Oxford program of lead isotope analysis of metal objects from Agia Photia and seven Mesara tholos tombs.[111] The analyses have shown the Agia Photia metal to be from the Cyclades and the Mesara copper to be primarily from Kythnos, but also Lavrion, and perhaps Cyprus (with two examples from a local Cretan source). Early Minoan lead objects analyzed from Archanes and Mochlos have compositions consistent with origins at Lavrion and Siphnos.[112] Cretan contact with areas outside the Aegean seems to have been slight. A silver cylinder seal from Mochlos, now identified as being of mid-third-millennium Syrian manufacture, and a hippopotamus bone at Knossos are the only Near Eastern imports known.[113] Possible Egyptian finds in Crete are limited to two stone bowl fragments from Knossos.[114]

Recent research indicates that the intensive trade of EM II Crete was not confined to coastal sites such as Mochlos, but was carried out among regions within the island.[115] This study of the Early Minoan wares at Knossos, using stylistic analysis, thin-section petrography, and scanning electron microscopy, has shown that several sizable ware groups (fine painted bowls, fine gray ware goblets and pyxides) were imported from the Mesara to Knossos in EM IB and EM IIA. These imports at Knossos mark the earliest known range of specialized pottery types that were distributed between regions in Crete. Analyses of Knossian fabrics indicate that standardization of clays in ceramic production also increases, especially after EM IIA, in EM IIB and

EM III.[116] Mesara imports at Knossos seem to cease in EM IIB and other contacts develop with East Crete. As at Knossos, pottery from the Mesara was also imported to Fournou Korifi in EM IIA. Petrographic and stylistic study of the larger EM IIB assemblage at Myrtos indicates that over half of the pottery was imported to the site. Possible changes in the scale of ceramic distribution and transport are indicated by many amphoras and other large vessels as well as Vasiliki ware, the famous "Goddess of Myrtos," and cooking pots imported from the Isthmus of Ierapetra.[117] A few small vases at Fournou Korifi may still be Mesara imports as in EM IIA. Other finds point to the same pattern: the well-known type of stone pyxis lid surmounted by a dog, surely the product of a single workshop, is known at Mochlos, Agia Triada, and Zakros.[118] The contents of the Mesara tombs—obsidian, copper, marble vases, and gold and silver jewelry—all indicate intensive trade relations between the Mesara and the North Coast.[119] The excavators of the tholos tomb at Agia Kyriaki on the south coast were able to distinguish 35 pieces of Vasiliki ware imported from East Crete.[120]

During the last 20 years discussion concerning EM II Crete has been dominated by the question of its social organization and complexity. Some have argued that EM II Crete had reached a level of sociopolitical ranking implying wealthy elites.[121] These elite families would have had some form of authority and power within their communities, which could then be seen as antecedent to later palatial organization. Other scholars have been more skeptical.[122]

---

[111] Gale (supra n. 46).

[112] Z. Stos-Gale and C. MacDonald, "Sources of Metals and Trade in the Bronze Age Aegean," in N. Gale ed., *Bronze Age Trade in the Mediterranean* (*SIMA* 90, Jonsered 1991) 249–88.

[113] J. Aruz, "The Silver Cylinder Seal from Mochlos," *Kadmos* 23 (1984) 186–87. O. Krzyszkowska, "Wealth and Prosperity in Pre-palatial Crete: The Case of Ivory," *Society* 166 and n. 7 where the date is given as "likely" EM II.

[114] *Chronology* 125. Such finds are possible (since Egyptian stone vases were traded as far north as Ebla in EB II) but their uniqueness, as well as Warren's methodology for dating Egyptian imports to Crete (see below), raises suspicions. In addition, one of the vases comes from a mixed context.

[115] D. Wilson and P. Day, "Ceramic Regionalism in Prepalatial Crete: The Mesara Imports from EM I to EM IIA Knossos," *BSA* 89 (in press), with a contribution by V. Kilikoglou.

[116] P. Day, V. Kilikoglou, and D. Wilson, "Technological and Cultural Change in Early Bronze Age Knossos: A Multi-disciplinary Approach to the Ceramic Record," pre-

sented at the Second European Meeting on Ancient Ceramics, Barcelona, November 1993.

[117] P. Day et al., "Pottery Importation in Early Minoan IIB Myrtos Fournou Korifi, Crete: A Reassessment," Proceedings of the 29th International Symposium on Archaeometry, Ankara, forthcoming.

[118] P. Warren, "The First Minoan Stone Vases and Early Minoan Chronology," *CretChron* 19 (1965) 13.

[119] *VTM*, passim; Branigan 1970 (supra n. 92) 56–85.

[120] Blackman and Branigan 1982 (supra n. 22) 39–41.

[121] K. Branigan, "Early Minoan Society: The Evidence of the Mesara Tholoi Reviewed," in Nicolet (supra n. 47) 29–37; J. Evans, "The Early Minoan Occupation of Knossos: A Note on Some New Evidence," *AnatSt* 22 (1972) 115–28; J. Soles, "Social Ranking in Prepalatial Cemeteries," in E. French and K. Wardle, *Problems in Greek Prehistory* (Bristol 1988) 49–62; Whitelaw, in *Society* (supra n. 69); P. Warren, "The Genesis of the Minoan Palace," in *Function* 47–56.

[122] J. Cherry, "Evolution, Revolution, and the Origins of Complex Society in Minoan Crete," in *Society* 33–46; V. Watrous, "The Role of the Near East in the Rise of the

The main claims for an EM II ranked society are as follows:

1) There are architectural forerunners of the palaces in EM II Crete that signal social ranking and the existence of local chiefs.[123] The principal evidence for this argument used to be the large "House on the Hill" at Vasiliki. Zois's investigations at the site have shown that there is no large, single house, however, but several small ones.[124] Nor was there a paved central court since there is no evidence for EM II structures on the west side of the hilltop. In addition, storage facilities at Vasiliki are not centralized, but probably occur as annexes to each individual house. Sporadic excavations of EM II levels at regional centers, e.g., Knossos, Phaistos, and Chania, where one would expect such architecture, have only produced fragments of small houses. Nothing approaching the size or planned complexity of the Greek mainland EH II corridor house is known on Crete. There does not seem to exist any sign of the kind of social stratification visible in the MM II architecture at Quartier Mu at Mallia or the complex administration of the sealings from MM II Monasteraki.

2) The prepalatial cemeteries at Mochlos, Gournia, and Mallia show signs of social and economic ranking.[125] More recent work at Mochlos has shown that the differences between Soles's larger "elite" tombs on the West Terrace and those on the South Slope are minimal. Soles's careful investigations at Mochlos have indicated that in EM II the West Terrace tombs are smaller than previously thought (I/II and IV/VI, rooms III and V being later additions).[126] Moreover, excavation on the South Slope has uncovered a tomb (L) as large as the West Terrace examples.[127] In addition, the architectural elaborateness of the tombs does not necessarily cor-

respond to the wealth of their contents.[128] "Ivory" objects and gold and silver jewelry are hard to accept as signs of social ranking because examples of such objects occur in both parts of the Mochlos cemetery.[129] Not surprisingly the tomb contents do show some variation in wealth, but any evidence for deliberate or ascribed social or political hierarchy is missing.

The danger in inferring social rank from differing burial data is illustrated by the situation at Gournia. The argument that the Gournia house tombs and the separate Sphoungaras rock shelter burials were indicative of a local social ranking has been thrown into doubt by the discovery in 1992 of a separate and sizable EM II settlement on the hill above Sphoungaras.[130] This find implies that the two cemeteries belong to two different settlements, rather than to different classes of the same community. The same situation exists in the Mesara where the cemetery of Phaistos at Ieroditis consists of individual inhumations, while those at Agia Triada are buried in tholos tombs.[131]

3) Early Minoan technology shows a steady and incremental growth leading up to (and thus explaining) the material achievements of the protopalatial period. This argument is an outgrowth of the basic studies made of Minoan metal objects, seals, and stone vases. In order to evaluate this claim we must consider these studies in some detail. The question of the ceramic sequence is discussed separately below (see below, Early Minoan III).

In his first general study of Minoan metalwork,[132] Branigan grouped the metal objects, mostly from the Mesara tombs, by typology and then dated them to the Early Minoan period. Subsequent studies have shown that the Mesara tomb deposits continue

Cretan Palaces," in *Function* 65–70; J. Cherry, "The Emergence of the State in the Prehistoric Aegean," *PCPS* 1984, 18–48.

[123] *Myrtos* 260–61; Branigan (supra n. 45) 48–49, 118–23.

[124] A. Zois's review of this issue in prepalatial architecture, "Gibt es Vorläufer der minoischen Paläste auf Kreta? Ergebnisse neuer Untersuchungen," in D. Papenfuss and V. Strocka eds., *Paläste und Hütte* (Mainz 1982) 207–15, found no evidence of any kind for ranking. If future excavation at Vasiliki shows that the walls in area P belonged to small, poorly built EM II houses, that might constitute evidence for social ranking.

[125] Soles (supra n. 121).

[126] Soles 43–60.

[127] J. Soles and C. Davaras, "Excavations at Mochlos, 1989," *Hesperia* 61 (1992) 420–24 and fig. 4.

[128] Soles 71 notes, for instance, that Tomb XIX is mod-

est in construction, but one of the richest in contents. Nor can the "orthostate" construction of the West Terrace tombs be cited as an elite feature, since it does not use real orthostates nor occur outside the tombs (where it would have been visible).

[129] South Slope tombs with "elite" material: gold jewelry in Tombs IX, XIX–XXIII (Soles 84 for Tomb IX); silver in Tomb XX; "ivory" in Tomb XVIII. Moreover, any comparison of the West Terrace and South Slope tombs must also take into account the much higher proportion of robbed tombs on the South Slope.

[130] These sites were found in 1993 by the Gournia Survey, under the direction of C. Davaras and myself.

[131] Watrous et al. (supra n. 10) 224. The tombs at Mallia mentioned by Soles are almost entirely protopalatial.

[132] K. Branigan, *Copper and Bronzeworking in Early Bronze Age Crete* (Lund 1968).

well into the protopalatial period.[133] Many studies of the Mesara tholoi, however, have continued to treat them as Early Minoan monuments.[134] While it is true that most of the circular tombs were originally built in EM I (or EM II), the final form of these complexes consisted of the original tholos and many later annexes whose total contents were mostly MM I in date. For example, Tholos A at Agia Triada for which we have a relatively full (if select) publication spans the EM I–MM II period.[135] The pottery, which is the most numerous and precisely dated class of artifact in Tholos A, may give us a rough idea of which finds date to each chronological period. Banti published 159 vases from the complex. Of these, 28 can be dated to EM I–II; 37 to EM III–MM IA, and 94 to MM IB–II. The implications of this chronological sequence have not been thoroughly appreciated. Most of the metal objects, for instance, almost certainly date not to the Early Minoan period, but to MM IA–II (see below).

In a subsequent study of metalworking of the Early and Middle Bronze Age Aegean,[136] Branigan defined new artifact types and metallurgical techniques for EM II Crete and laid out the chronological contexts for Minoan metal artifacts, again largely from the Mesara. Very few of these objects are from pure EM II levels; most are from EM II–MM I/II contexts. The Early Minoan dates he assigns to many of the objects, especially the weapons and tools from unstratified contexts, are too early, since one cannot assume, as he does, that these objects are contemporary with EBA parallels in the northern

Aegean.[137] He also overestimates the advanced state of Early Minoan metallurgy.[138] Finally, by considering all of the artifacts of the EM III, MM IA, MM IB, and MM II periods together in one section, he infers that the history of Minoan metallurgy from EM II to MM II was one of uninterrupted continuity.[139] This argument is circular.

The seals of the EM II–MM II period have recently been admirably organized into stylistic groups and dated by Yule.[140] Yule identified two main prepalatial groups of seals, the Parading Lions/Spiral and Border/Leaf complexes, which he dates to EM III–MM IA and EM II–MM IA(–?), respectively.[141] His dating of these groups is unlikely, however, since it would mean that the manufacture of seals in the Mesara virtually ceased in the MM IB–II period. Subsequent reviews of Yule's study by Hood and Younger have pointed out that these dates are too early.[142] As Younger has shown, the Border/Leaf group is a chronological extension of the Parading Lions/Spiral group. Since the Border/Leaf group uses both ivory/bone and stone and overlaps with the MM II Phaistos sealings, it is dated by Younger to the MM IA–II period. Younger thus dates the Parading Lions/Spiral group predominantly within the MM IA period.[143]

Yule compares the EM II and EM III–MM IA groups of seals. While EM II seals come in diverse shapes (conoids, discs, L-shaped, foot-seals, rings, hammerhead signets, and plate signets), they are most commonly decorated with random or cross-hatched lines. EM III–MM IA seals assume a more

---

[133] K. Branigan, "The Mesara Tholoi and Middle Minoan Chronology," *SMEA* 5 (1968) 7–23; G. Walberg, *Provincial Middle Minoan Pottery* (Mainz 1983) 90–137.

[134] Branigan's book (supra n. 52), for example, features the subtitle "Life and Death in Southern Crete, c. 3000–2000 B.C." The correct dates are ca. 3500–1800 B.C.

[135] Banti (supra n. 98). Any bias in Banti's list of pottery is likely to favor the earlier periods, as she specifically mentions, on p. 178, "numerossime" MM I vases from the annex of which she only publishes representative examples.

[136] Branigan.

[137] See R. Higgins, *Greek and Roman Jewellery* (Berkeley 1980) 53, for the same conclusions. Branigan's conclusion that the Mesara was a leading center of metalworking in the Aegean during the EM I–MM II period is based on assumptions not generally accepted, i.e., that the number of bronzes in the tombs relative to other parts of the Aegean is not accidental, that Mesara bronzeworking was based mainly on local ore sources, and that the use of deliberate arsenical and tin alloys in the Mesara was in advance of practices elsewhere.

[138] Branigan 106–108. Contra Branigan: the only spear from a certain EM context is that from Agia Photia, and it may be Cycladic in origin. The Mochlos arrowhead, the

only possible example known from Crete before MM IB, comes from Tomb XIX. Seager (*Mochlos* 71) dates the arrowhead to MM I, later than the main "EM II–III" contents of the tomb. The tomb should probably be dated EM II and MM I and the arrowhead to MM I (see below). There are no type I saws from an EM II context; the only type I from a secure context dates to MM IB (Branigan 168). There are no known EM II tin bronzes. Gale (supra n. 46) 301 suggests that the earliest tin bronzes in Crete date to MM I. The only "short sword" from an EM context is that from Agia Photia, so again it may be an Early Cycladic product; the only other example (Branigan 164) from a good context is MM I–II.

[139] Branigan 114; and K. Branigan, *The Foundations of Palatial Crete* (London 1970) 78–83.

[140] Yule. See also I. Pini, "Ein Beitrag zur chronologischen Ordnung der frühkretischen Siegel," *Pepragmena* 1981 I, 421–35; and "Eine frühkretische Siegelwerkstatt?" *Pepragmena* 1990 I, 115–27.

[141] Yule 208–10.

[142] S. Hood, *Antiquity* 58 (1984) 70–71; and J. Younger, in *GGA* 240 (1988) 188–224.

[143] Younger (supra n. 142) and personal communication.

regular repertoire of shapes, i.e., gables, half-ovoids, zoomorphs, and three-sided prisms. The most frequently occurring motifs include leaves, loops, hatched triangles, and crosshatching. Using the list of securely dated prepalatial seals in Pini's 1981 study, we can form a more precise idea of EM II–MM IA seal development.[144] For the EM II period there are 20 securely dated seals and one sealing.[145] The shapes represented are cones (4), plate signets (2), rings (2), feet (2), pyramoids (2), zoomorphs (2), a disc, hemisphere, pyramid, hammerhead signet, stump signet, and a rod. The motifs on the 19 seals and the one sealing are crosshatched lines (12), random lines (4), chip carving/lines, crossed lines, and a cross.

For the EM III–MM IA period the seal shapes represented are stamp cylinders (9), cones (6), discoids (5), three-sided prisms (2), step pyramids (2), plate, half-cylinder, triangle, button, zoomorph, wand, scarab, and fly. Decorations consist of spirals (7), rosettes (6), leaves or petals (4), crosshatched lines (4), vases (3), double axes (3), ?deer (3), loops (2), men (2), goats, meander, zigzags, lions, random lines, drill holes, leg, hand, fish, and chip cuts. Two important conclusions emerge from this comparison: EM II seal carving is relatively simple compared with that in EM III–MM IA and there is minimal overlap in seal shape and motif between the two periods.

In his study *Minoan Stone Vases (MSV)*, Warren concluded that many vessels (vase types 1, 3, 4, 7, 8, 10, 17, 20, 22, 28, 29, 31, 36, 37, and 41) were manufactured uninterruptedly from EM IIB through MM II and onward.[146] These "transitional" vases are dated from their contexts (mainly mixed) and on the basis that they show the same technique (incision) and material (steatite) as EM II examples. From this he inferred that the bulk manufacture of Minoan stone vases began in ca. 2300 B.C., i.e., in EM III or late EM II.

Let us consider the evidence for the dating of this transitional group. Warren's alabastron type 1A is dated EM III–MM I. It is a Mesara form with a precise 12th-Dynasty parallel, noted by Warren, which suggests a date of late MM IA (table 1); all three secure contexts are MM I.[147] The "bird's nest" bowl (type 3) occurs primarily in MM I–II contexts in the Mesara.[148] None are found in EM II contexts. This vase shape occurs only in harder stone material and thus should date to MM IB and later. Block vases (type 4) are also not found in any secure Early Minoan context. The earliest example is from Lebena Tomb IIa dated to MM IA.[149] Of the 37 block vases with find contexts, all examples of type 4 vases are in MM IA, MM IA–II, or LM I contexts; most are in MM IA–II contexts.[150] Bowl type 7 is dated to EM III–MM I. The earliest (numerous) certain contexts are MM I–II.[151] The earliest secure contexts for Warren's bowl type 8 are MM I; other find contexts are EM II–MM I, LM I, and LM III.[152] Not one of the 50 examples of Warren's cup type 17A occurs in a secure EM II context. As Warren notes, the large numbers found in the Mesara tombs indicate their popularity in MM I.[153] The tumbler (type 20) is typical.[154] It occurs at Mochlos in Tomb VII, where the only clay vases published by Seager are EM II, and in the Mesara tombs. Warren thus dates the type to EM III–MM I. The vase, however, must be MM IA–II as the earliest safe contexts are MM IB–II and as the Eastern parallels (see below) show. The same situation obtains with jug type 22D. In *MSV* it is noted that vase type 22D is found primarily in secure MM IB–II contexts, except for Mochlos Tombs I and VI, for which Seager only published "EM II" vases. Thus in *MSV* the shape is dated to EM II–MM I.[155] Both of the Mochlos tombs have later MM material in them, however, and so this vase type is clearly protopalatial. Miniature amphoras (type 28) dated EM III–MM I/II come only from secure MM I and MM II contexts.[156] Miniature goblets (type 29A) come exclusively from mixed EM II–MM I tomb contexts. Two examples (P 372 and 377 in *MSV*) imitate MM IA eggcups.[157] Bowl type 31 comes from mixed EM II–MM I tomb contents and secure MM I–II settlement contexts at Knossos, Phaistos, and Chamaizi.[158]

---

[144] Pini 422–23.

[145] Omitted are the five considered transitional EM II/III from Maronia and Mochlos and *CMS* II.1 196, whose date Yule 191 doubts.

[146] *MSV* 182–84. Warren's early dating for his transitional vases is also dependent on the dates given to the Mochlos tombs by Seager. These dates are discussed below.

[147] *MSV* 4–5.

[148] *MSV* 7–11.

[149] *MSV* 11–14. The Lebena vase is on p. 12.

[150] See P. Muhly, *Minoan Libation Tables* (Diss. Univ. of Minnesota 1981) 242–52.

[151] *MSV* 20–21.

[152] *MSV* 21–24.

[153] *MSV* 38–39.

[154] *MSV* 44–45.

[155] Jug type 22D is discussed in *MSV* 47. MM objects in the Mochlos tombs: Tomb I, "MM III sherds" as well as the carnelian seal (I s); Tomb VI, cup (VI 6), the breccia jug (VI 4), seal (VI 26).

[156] *MSV* 71–72.

[157] *MSV* 72–73.

[158] *MSV* 76–78.

Table 1. Chronology for Sites and Areas in Crete and the East

	Knossos	Phaistos	Mallia	Gournia	Vasiliki	Mochlos	Pyrgos (Myrtos)	Egypt	Anatolia	Levant
2200 B.C. EM III	Upper East Well		E.C. XVIII, 51-56		Period IV (Pits I, II)		Gap	F.I.P.	EB III B	EB IV
2100 B.C. MM IA	West Court Houses		Premier Charnier	North	Seager's Well	Material from Tombs II–VII, IX–XI, XIII, XV–XX, XXII		XI Dynasty	Tarsus EB IIIB Kultepe Level 11	Ras Shamra III A3 (Ugarit Moyen I) Byblos JI–II
2000 B.C. MM IA	R.Road S Base, Lower	Patrikies	South Houses	Trench	House B	House D	Pyrgos II a–b	1963 B.C.	Karum Kanish II	MB I Byblos "Dépôts des offrandes"
1900 B.C. MM IB–II	Early West Magazines	Festos Ia	Town Group	Early Gournia:	House A	Hesperia 61 (1992) 428.	Pyrgos II c–d	XII Dynasty		Ugarit Moyen II
1800 B.C.	Trial KV: Village	Festos Ib–II	Quartier Mu	Houses Aq,Ek					Karum Kanish Ib	Byblos Royal Tombs I–III

This leaves the following EM II vase types: 10A, 29B, 37B, and 41. How often do these vases continue to be made after EM IIB? Bowl type 10A is a North Coast type found in EM II and EM II–MM I contexts; of the 49 examples cited in *MSV*, one (from Kamilari) is from a secure MM I context.[159] EM II miniature goblets (29B) differ completely from the MM I forms (29A).[160] Spouted bowl 37B is an EM II type; three examples have been found in MM I–II contexts.[161] The teapot, type 41, is important because it closely imitates the ceramic form, which in turn can be closely dated.[162] Type 41A mimics the EM II clay shape; type 41D imitates the MM IA carinated teapot. Type 41B copies the MM IA/B Patrikies form and type 41C the MM IB–II shape.

From the analyses above we can conclude that 1) there are relatively few EM II stone vase types; 2) very few stone vase types actually continue from EM II into MM I; 3) there is an explosion in the number and range of new vase types, especially small ones, in MM I (as discussed below, a good many of these new shapes have Egyptian parallels); and 4) many stone vases come from EM II–MM I (e.g., Mochlos) or EM II–MM II (Mesara tombs) contexts. These vases should be dated to MM IA–II (see below).

Does Early Minoan technology show a continuous development from EM II to MM I as claimed above? While it is difficult to trace the technical development of Early Minoan metal objects because they often cannot be precisely dated, it does seem that some of the Early Minoan dates assigned by Branigan to metal objects are too early. On the other hand, EM II and EM III–MM IA seals and stone vases do not show a continuous development but rather tend to cluster into two separate groups.[163] Prepalatial artifacts therefore do not illustrate a clear tradition of continuous development from EM II to MM I and cannot be used to infer such a development for prepalatial Crete.

4) Given the probable size of the EM II settlements at Knossos, Phaistos, and Mallia, cross-cultural parallels would suggest that they had reached some form of social hierarchy.[164] As Soles has pointed out, this is not necessarily true, for there exist many examples in anthropological literature of large, relatively egalitarian communities.[165] One cannot prove or disprove the above assertion; one can only state that the evidence on Crete does not at present support such an inference.

Thus, there is at present no archaeological evidence for a ranked society in EM II Crete that can be seen as an antecedent to palatial organization.

EARLY MINOAN III

The end of the EM IIB period was marked by the abandonment and destruction of many sites on Crete. Traces of destruction by fire have been found at Vasiliki, Fournou Koriphi, Pyrgos/Myrtos, and Mallia.[166] It is becoming clear from recent excavations that for the period immediately following EM IIB, that is, EM III, evidence for occupation on large sites is extremely limited, and many smaller sites were abandoned during this period. The excavators at Pyrgos/Myrtos have recognized a gap in occupation, between period I (EM II) and period II (MM IA). The earliest post-EM II architecture at the site is defined by deposits containing polychrome pottery (i.e., MM IA).[167] At Phaistos there is little published evidence for EM III. A deposit over the EM II house under cortile LXX produced pottery stylistically assignable to MM IA, but some could be earlier.[168] Excavations at Kommos have found very little evidence of occupation at the site during the EM III–early MM IA period.[169] Palaikastro may have been abandoned at this time, perhaps for the nearby peak of Kastri.[170] Knossos is one of the few sites at which EM III stratigraphic levels have been identified. A terrace wall running under the west

---

[159] *MSV* 76–77. Bowl types 10B and 10C come from MM I–LM I contexts and are a different shape from type 10A. Cf. *MSV* P 150–60 and P 161–73.

[160] Cf. *MSV* P 388–91 and P 369–87.

[161] *MSV* 94–95.

[162] *MSV* 98–99.

[163] See Yule 226–29 on the "discontinuous development" of early Cretan seals.

[164] Whitelaw, in *Society* (supra n. 69) 337–40.

[165] Soles 50 and n. 1 with bibliography.

[166] For Mallia, see the report of a burnt level with whole EM IIB vases in Amouretti (infra n. 174).

[167] See Cadogan (infra n. 229) 71.

[168] D. Levi, "Gli scavi a Festòs nel 1956 e 1957," *ASAtene* 35/36 (1957/1958) 169–78.

[169] P. Betancourt, *Kommos* II (Princeton 1990) 62–64.

[170] Relevant stratigraphy at Palaikastro is given for one area, d32: an upper MM IB level is characterized by the

types of cups shown in R. Dawkins, "Excavations at Palaikastro," *BSA* 9 (1902/1903) 302, fig. 2, nos. 1–2. For no. 1, cf. *ArchEph* 1972, Chronika, pl. Ca; for no. 1a, cf. Walberg (supra n. 133) 133; nos. 2 and 2a are carinated cups. The next lower level (0.50 m) consists of a few sherds shown on p. 199, fig. 2, whose decoration closely resembles that of Gournia North Trench examples, for which an MM IA date has been argued. At 1.00 m below, a thickly packed stratum of EM II vases (Dawkins, *BSA* 10 [1903/1904] 201, fig. 3b) was encountered, *separated by 0.50 m of deposition from the earlier, MM IA level*, suggesting a passage of time between the two levels. The settlement at the nearby citadel of Kastri has produced MM IA vases: L. Sackett et al., *BSA* 60 (1965) pl. 72b–c. In addition to the above information, the earliest published evidence of the post-EM II reoccupation of Palaikastro is the MM IA and MM IB vases in Sackett et al. (supra) pl. 72d–e.

facade of the first palace and at the northwest angle of the palace has been dated variously to EM III and MM IA.[171] If EM III, this wall may have formed a platform for prepalatial structures; if MM IA, it may have been associated with the construction of the first palace. Four other deposits said to be EM III have been uncovered in various parts of the site.[172] More recently the British excavators at Knossos have redated the three houses (A, B, and C) and a well found beneath the West Court to EM III.[173] At Mallia a small deposit stratified over an EM II destruction level is probably EM III (table 1).[174]

Recent surveys also indicate that the countryside was largely deserted during the EM III period. The 1992–1993 survey of Gournia and the northern Isthmus of Ierapetra has shown that following the EM II period, the rural landscape is first resettled in the MM IA period. Similarly, the Western Mesara Survey found minimal evidence of settlement outside of Phaistos during the EM III–MM IA period.[175] Virtually no EM III–MM IA material was found in the Agiopharango Valley in southern Crete.[176]

Many tombs show the same discontinuity of use. A minimal list of tombs with a gap between EM II and MM IA includes Agia Eirene; Agios Onouphrios; Agia Triada B; Archanes Tholos A and Building 6; Lebena Tombs I, IB, II, IIa, and III; Mallia, Western Ossuary; Mochlos Tomb XXII; Palaikastro Tomb II; and Platanos Tholoi A and Γ.[177] As will be argued below, this list can be lengthened considerably.

Signs of Cretan foreign contact with the Cyclades, the Greek mainland, or the Near East during this period are absent.[178]

Our understanding of developments during this period is clouded by problems of chronological and stylistic definition at the beginning and end of EM III. Early Minoan III has been defined as a ceramic *style*, but not stratigraphically.[179] Seager created an impression of cultural continuity between EM II and EM III, still accepted today, by describing many of the vases and "deposits" at Mochlos as "EM II/III" or "EM III."[180] In 1971, excavation next to Tomb VI at Mochlos uncovered a deposit of pottery that was described as EM II/III.[181] The pottery from the deposit consisted of Vasiliki ware (68%), "white-on-black" EM III styles (15%), dark-burnished fabrics (7%), and polished buff and Koumasa style (3%). Given the apparent homogeneity of the deposit, there seems little reason not to call it EM IIB. The excavators' decision to use the term "EM II/III" was based on caution, dictated by our relative ignorance of EM IIB and EM III pottery and the lack of deposits of EM III stratified over EM IIB. The only meaningful stratified EM II and EM III deposits are known at Knossos.[182] There EM IIB is described as being mainly dark-on-light and red- or black-slipped wares, with lesser amounts of dark-on-light and Vasiliki wares. Thus, from a stylistic perspective, much of the pottery traditionally identified as EM II/III or EM III could be either chronologically EM IIB or MM IA.

---

[171] Wilson (supra n. 89).

[172] Wilson (supra n. 89).

[173] G. Cadogan et al., "Early Minoan and Middle Minoan Pottery Groups at Knossos," *BSA* 88 (1993) 21–28 have placed several deposits from Knossos in a relative ceramic sequence and labeled them with conventional terms, e.g., EM III, MM IA. While the sequence may well be correct, there is no evidence that permits these groups to be assigned conventional chronological labels (viz., EM III, which is dated ca. 2300–2200 B.C.). Specifically, the deposits labeled "EM III" may be earlier than the Royal Road South Fill (called "MM IA"), but both groups may in fact date to the chronological span conventionally assigned to MM IA (ca. 2100–1900 B.C.). The time to assign these unpublished deposits conventional chronological terms is when they are fully published, with their Cretan and Aegean correlations. There is no basis for the assumption that a continuous ceramic sequence can be translated into a chronologically uniform development.

[174] M.-C. Amouretti, *Fouilles exécutées à Mallia: Le centre politique* II (*EtCret* 18, Paris 1970) 51–54 and fig. 5.

[175] Watrous et al. (supra n. 10) 68.

[176] Blackman and Branigan 1977 (supra n. 11) 68.

[177] See the lists in *MSV* 193–97 and Soles 201.

[178] Cyclades, A. MacGillivray, "The Relative Chronology of Early Cycladic III," in A. MacGillivray and R. Barber eds., *The Prehistoric Cyclades* (Edinburgh 1984) 73–74. Mainland: Rutter and Zerner (supra n. 107) 76–77.

[179] A. Zois, "Υπάρχει ΠΜ III Εποχή;" Πεπραγμένα του Β′ Διεθνούς Κρητολογικού Συνεδρίου (Athens 1968) 141–56. Walberg's (supra n. 133) identifications of EM III and MM IA pottery (Walberg phase 1) are of limited value because they are not based on stratified settlement deposits, but are rearrangements of published pottery according to her own stylistic criteria. One cannot assume, as Walberg does, that vases from different regions of Crete with shared morphological features are contemporary (circular argument) nor that individual vases identified stylistically as part of groups ("EM III" or phase 1) can actually be dated to conventional chronological periods. The amount of chronological variation found within her vase "shapes" indicates this.

[180] *Mochlos*, Tombs I–XII, XIII, XV, XVI–XVIII, XIX–XXII, XXIII.

[181] Davaras (supra n. 106); Soles 58–59.

[182] See Cadogan et al. (supra n. 173) and esp. Wilson (supra n. 89).

The end of the EM III period is also poorly defined. The clearest sign of this is the controversy surrounding the EM III–MM IA ceramic sequence in East Crete. All agree that EM III–MM IA is a long period, usually assigned 300 years, but with no chronological fixed points.[183] Thus, the phases of this period have been dated stylistically, i.e., by the appearance of certain shapes and decoration and the use of polychromy, but such a ceramic sequence can only be relative. We have no idea when polychromy[184] actually appears within the chronological period conventionally assigned to EM III–MM IA. Moreover, the decision to use the appearance of polychromy to mark the beginning of MM IA and to date this to ca. 2100 B.C., as is usually done, is arbitrary and without supporting evidence.[185] As conventionally dated, East Cretan "EM III" style is the most advanced regional style on the island. A priori, there seems little reason for East Cretan ceramics to be stylistically ahead of those of Central Crete. What is known about monumental architecture and overseas contacts (discussed below) all indicates that Central Crete was the most advanced region of the island in MM IA.

Zois, who studied this problem extensively, observed that the only Minoan site in East Crete with evidence for EM III stratified over EM II and under MM IA was Vasiliki.[186] The EM IIB houses on the site were destroyed, apparently by fire. The following phase of occupation (Seager's period IV) was extremely meager, and only in MM IA is the site extensively reoccupied. Seager, in his 1904 excavation report, noted that the period IV inhabitants of the settlement "built their hovels only over the southeast corner, as there are no signs of their ware on any other part of the hill."[187] In his 1907 excavation report Seager writes, "The area in which the sherds of period IV were found was small, measuring about eight by ten metres. . . . The settlement is even less extensive than that of the preceding pe-

riod (Period III or EM II) and seems to have consisted of poorly built hovels huddled against the massive outer walls of the big house of Period III, already in ruins."[188]

At the time that Vasiliki was being dug, Edith Hall excavated the classic source for East Cretan EM III ware, the Gournia North Trench.[189] Harriet Boyd, the director of the excavation, described the North Trench deposit as containing "thousands upon thousands of sherds" with "a very large proportion" of the decorated sherds being "Light on Dark pieces" and "many" similarly decorated fragments of "Dark on Light," as well as "a considerable number" of "local proto-naturalistic style of Class IV" (Boyd's designation for Kamares style), with only "a few pieces" of Vasiliki and Koumasa styles.[190] Hall, who excavated and published the North Trench group, also specifically notes the absence of Vasiliki and red-on-buff (Koumasa style) wares in the deposit.[191] She does not identify the deposit as immediately succeeding EM II (that is, EM III), but carefully distinguishes it as later than the stratified sequence of period IV at Vasiliki (pits I and II) where three strata were observed. These strata contained the following wares (starting from the top and proceeding to the bottom): 1) white-on-dark and Vasiliki ware; 2) Vasiliki ware and red-on-buff geometric style (Koumasa style); and, finally, 3) only Vasiliki ware.[192] The two lower strata must date to EM IIB. The top level is either late EM IIB or EM III. In the end, Hall viewed the Gournia North Trench deposit as contemporary with Knossian MM IA, which is almost certainly correct (table 1). In the EM IIB deposits at Fournou Koriphi, Vasiliki ware is extremely common,[193] but in the North Trench deposit it is virtually absent. In addition, the main shapes of the North Trench—cups, jugs, and bridge-spouted jugs—and their decoration are new and unrelated to EM IIB antecedents.[194] There must therefore be a considerable chronological gap

[183] See *Chronology* 169; Cadogan (supra n. 8) 517.

[184] *Pace* P. Betancourt, *The History of Minoan Pottery* (Princeton 1985) 53–63.

[185] N. Momigliano, "MM IA Pottery from Evans' Excavations at Knossos: A Reassessment," *BSA* 86 (1991) 219 has pointed out that in MM IA polychromy is much less common than usually believed.

[186] See Zois's comments in Myers et al. (supra n. 74) 276.

[187] R. Seager, "Excavations at Vasiliki, 1904," *Transactions of the Department of Archaeology, University of Pennsylvania* I (Philadelphia 1905) 218.

[188] Seager (supra n. 81) 118.

[189] E. Hall, "Early Painted Pottery from Gournia," in *Transactions of the Department of Archaeology, University of*

Pennsylvania I.3 (Philadelphia 1904) 191–206.

[190] H. Boyd, "Gournia," in *Transactions* (supra n. 189) 186.

[191] Hall (supra n. 189) 193.

[192] Seager (supra n. 81) 118. Hall (supra n. 189) 193.

[193] *Myrtos* 93–94.

[194] For cups, cf. *Myrtos* figs. 64–65 with Hall (supra n. 189) pl. XXVI and Andreou fig. 6. For jugs, cf. *Myrtos* figs. 68–73 with Hall (supra n. 189) pl. XXXI and Andreou fig. 6. For bridge-spouted jars, cf. *Myrtos* figs. 85–88 with Hall (supra n. 189) pls. XXIX–XXX and Andreou fig. 7. This scheme makes the spiraliform style of the North Trench overlap the second phase (defined by the presence of spirals) of MM IA at Knossos, as S. Hood in *CretChron* 15/16 (1961/1962) 94.

between EM IIB deposits at Fournou Koriphi and the Gournia North Trench deposit.

This reconstruction agrees with Seager's description of the "EM III" well deposit from Vasiliki, which he dates later than the strata in the EM II–III pits.[195] As Seager noted, the well contents were not a gradual accumulation, but were dumped in all at once. Seager distinguished two levels in the major construction (Houses A and B) at Vasiliki in his period V. These can now be securely dated to MM IA/B and MM IB/II.[196] By the process of elimination, the evidence above suggests that Seager's well group is MM IA (in Knossian terms) material dumped into the well, probably at the start of reconstruction at Vasiliki. More recent study by Andreou has shown that some of Seager's "EM III" deposits at Mochlos are also later. The deposit under House D, dated EM III/MM I, is contemporary with Vasiliki House B, Pyrgos/Myrtos II, and Knossian MM IA (table 1).[197] The excavators at Mochlos acknowledge a gap in prepalatial occupation of the site,[198] which they date to MM IA. This is unlikely, given the fact that 14 of the Mochlos tombs contain MM IA pottery.[199] Since MM IA is a well-documented period[200] of occupation for the Mochlos settlement, this gap then probably occurs in the EM III chronological (not stylistic) period.

A Middle Bronze date for the "EM III" East Cretan style can also be derived independently, by means of ceramic parallels from outside of Crete. The kantharos from House D at Mochlos, for example, is an Anatolian shape characteristic of MB I,[201] decorated in typical MB I Syro-Cilician style.[202] From the same deposit at Vasiliki comes a Cycladicizing jug with parallels from Phylakopi Iii.[203] The decoration of early Barbotine ware follows

Anatolian fashion.[204] Amiran has pointed out that the deep rounded cups characteristic of "EM III" deposits in Crete also have close parallels, including the same vestigial handles, in the MB I Levant.[205] The MB I phase in the Levant is dated ca. 2000–1900 B.C. and thus corresponds to MM IA.[206]

The scheme proposed here has the advantage of offering a solution for some of the problems of the old chronology, namely, that 1) the tombs at Mochlos and Archanes were full of costly materials imported from the Cyclades at a time when the Cyclades were experiencing depopulation and turbulence; 2) excavations at Mochlos, Gournia, and Vasiliki, showed that "EM III" was a period of prosperity for the first two sites and one of extreme poverty for nearby Vasiliki; and 3) East Cretan "EM III" pottery is supposed to represent a chronological period but it has not been isolated stratigraphically (and it is found in the same deposits as Central Cretan MM IA at Mallia, Mochlos, Pyrgos, and Palaikastro).

One hesitates to step into the whirlpool of Early Cycladic chronology, but it may be significant that the "gap" noticed on many Cretan sites in EM III corresponds closely in time to late EC III when at least some Cycladic sites (e.g., Agia Eirene on Kea) are deserted, and that the spread of new settlements on Crete early in MM IA also seems to correspond to the time when Phylakopi Iii is established.

MIDDLE MINOAN IA

Excavation of MM IA levels at major settlements on Crete is extremely limited. In addition, recognition of MM IA deposits has been hampered by problems of ceramic definition.[207] Several houses (A, B, and C) from the Knossos West Court, however, have

---

[195] Seager (supra n. 81) 119: "Moreover, scattered sherds of the mottled (Vasiliki) ware were found in almost every metre, but in much smaller numbers than was the case in the pits where the cruder light on dark ware, identical with the sherds from the Gournia dump, was found side by side with the mottled ware which at first retained its old popularity. Thus we must suppose that the contents of the well are of a slightly later date and represent Period IV at its highest stage of development."

[196] Andreou 73–75, 102–103, and 172.

[197] Andreou 71–73.

[198] Soles and Davaras (supra n. 11) 417.

[199] See the list of MM IA tombs in Soles 201.

[200] See R. Seager, "Excavations on the Island of Mochlos, Crete, in 1908," *AJA* 13 (1909) figs. 6–8 and 13.1, 3–5, and 7.

[201] Cf. the Mochlos kantharos (Seager [supra n. 200] 292, fig. 13, upper right) to Anatolian examples (S. Lloyd and J. Mellaart, *Beycesultan* II [London 1965] passim).

[202] *Levant* 68–70, fig. 23, nos. 1–4, 21–23.

[203] Cf. the Mochlos jug (Seager [supra n. 200] 292, fig.

13, lower left) with examples from Phylakopi (T. Atkinson, *Phylakopi* [London 1904] pl. 9).

[204] V. Watrous, "The Anatolian Origin of Minoan Barbotine Decoration," *Proceedings of the Tenth Congress of the Turkish Historical Society* (Ankara 1990) 133–37.

[205] E.g., *Mochlos* fig. 49, nos. 58–60; R. Amiran, "The Middle Bronze I and the Early Minoan III," *CretChron* 23 (1971) 52–57, esp. 55–56, and cf. fig. 1, nos. 1–5 and pl. IA'.

[206] *Levant* 101–108 and table 9 for the chronology of MB I in the Near East.

[207] Three recent ceramic studies, based on stratigraphic deposits, have redefined MM IA and MM IB–II pottery. In all cases, the authors have shown that pottery assigned by Evans to MM IA should be dated MM IB or MM II: Andreou; Momigliano (supra n. 185) 149–272; and A. MacGillivray, *Pottery of the Old Palace Period at Knossos and Its Implications* (Diss. Univ. of Edinburgh 1986). Thus Hood's "EM III" deposit at Knossos has been dated later because the Helladic import in the deposit has been dated to MH I. See Coleman (supra n. 36) 270.

been identified as dating to MM IA.[208] The deposits from these houses have produced loomweights, vases for food processing, several large pithoi, and numerous Cycladic-looking vases.[209] The early hypogaeum underneath the South Porch of the palace cannot be dated precisely, but Momigliano's recent restudy of the associated pottery shows it is mostly MM IA.[210] A clay jar stopper, stamped with two different seals (one from the MM I Parading Lions group), was found on the floor of an "EM III/MM IA" house near the south front of the palace.[211] Nevertheless, Knossos seems to have grown considerably in this period, since MM IA pottery has been found widely beyond the edge of the earlier Early Minoan settlement. According to Hood's survey of the Knossos area, MM IA was a period of rapid expansion for Knossos, and the site may have been fortified in that period.[212] Evidence for the size of MM IA Phaistos is more fragmentary but it does appear that the settlement grew, perhaps substantially, during this period.[213]

MM IA Mallia is a large settlement, as scattered finds from south, west, and north of the later palace area indicate.[214] At this time a wall of immense limestone boulders, probably for purposes of fortification, was constructed north of area A and between the north edge of the town of Mallia and the coast.[215] At Palaikastro numerous deposits, including some with MM IA eggcups, indicate that the settlement was also sizable in this period.[216] On the hilltop of Vasiliki, Seager's Houses A and B as well as Zois's

Houses Γ, Φ, and X were built.[217] On the south slope of the hill, Zois's 1990–1993 excavations have revealed two massive walls (PA 1 and PAb), separated by a corridor, that probably date to this period. Wall PAb ends at the northeast in a rectangular mass, which resembles a tower. If so, these walls may be part of an early fortification. Remains of well-built structures have also been found on the central hilltop (E-50), and on the south slope (PB 1).[218]

At Mochlos substantial deposits of MM IA vases were found in blocks A and C and under House D.[219] Excavations there in 1993 revealed an MM IA building.[220] Gournia produced a very large deposit of MM IA pottery (North Trench Deposit) that had been dumped over the north edge of a massive wall.[221] Thus, Gournia may have been fortified in MM IA.

Smaller excavated sites of this period are few in number: Chamaizi, Agia Photia, Pyrgos/Myrtos, and Patrikies (fig. 1). In the mountains southwest of Siteia, the oval-shaped structure built (over an EM settlement) on a hilltop near the village of Chamaizi has been called an MM IA peak sanctuary, because of the offering table and figurines discovered there.[222] Davaras's reinvestigation of this building has revealed new details that suggest its domestic character.[223] Ten rooms, with household pottery, pithoi (one inscribed with the Linear A sign for wine), loomweights, and stone tools, face out onto a small paved court with a cistern.[224] Axes, an adz, a chisel, and a sickle (as well as a spearhead) recov-

[208] Momigliano (supra n. 185) 206–36 and 185–95.

[209] Momigliano's reexamination of these deposits suggests that they are mixed, containing prepalatial and MM II vases (supra n. 185) 167–77, 206–35. For the Cycladic-looking examples: pyxides (*PM* I, 166–68, fig. 118b); askos (*PM* IV, 79–80); and other vases (H. and J. Pendlebury, "Two Protopalatial Houses at Knossos," *BSA* 30 (1928/1930) 60, fig. 5.8, and pl. 12a.10. As the parallels for the Cycladic imports are with Phylakopi Iii (cf. the Knossos askos and Phylakopi, pl. IX.11, and other examples in MacGillivray [supra n. 178] 73), which is in turn connected with MH I contexts at Lerna and other mainland sites (see Coleman [supra n. 36] 268 for references), these Cycladicizing vases, and the prepalatial groups they are a part of, are better referred to as Middle Bronze I (MM IA) than earlier, *pace* Wilson (supra n. 89). MacGillivray [supra n. 178] 74 states that the evidence for Cycladic contacts is far more plentiful in Crete in MM IA than during the EB II period.

[210] Momigliano (supra n. 185) 195–98.

[211] S. Hood and V. Kenna, "An Early Minoan Sealing from Knossos," *AntCr* 1 (1973) 103–106. As Weingarten (infra n. 329) 3–4 notes, if this sealing was stamped by two seal owners, it could be a sign of supra-household administration.

[212] Hood and Smyth (supra n. 11) 8. Possible fortification wall at Knossos: S. Hood, "Archaeology in Greece,

1960–61," *AR* 1960–1961, 27.

[213] The Western Mesara Survey (see Watrous et al., supra n. 10) found MM IA pottery to the west of the hill of Ephendi Christou. The Italian excavations have revealed MM IA deposits in the area of the palace and in Chalara (*ASAtene* 19/20 [1957/1958] 170–77; 45/46 [1967/1968] 66; *Festòs* I, 288–94).

[214] van Effenterre 30–41 and map on 52. Müller 1992 (supra n. 10).

[215] van Effenterre 266–67. Only two stretches of this wall are known.

[216] *Chronology* 18 lists the deposits.

[217] Seager (supra n. 81) 123–29; and A. Zois, *Prakt* 1980, 331–36.

[218] A. Zois has kindly supplied me with this information from his unpublished 1992 report to the *Εργον*.

[219] Seager (supra n. 200) 273–303.

[220] J. Soles and C. Davaras, "1993 Excavations at Mochlos," *AJA* 97 (1993) 45–46 (abstract).

[221] Hall (supra n. 189).

[222] N. Platon, "Το ιερόν Μαζά και τα Μινωϊκά ιερά κορυφής," *CretChron* 5 (1951) 122–24.

[223] C. Davaras, "The Oval House at Chamaizi Reconsidered," *AAA* 5 (1972) 283–88.

[224] Some of these objects come from the original excavation. See S. Xanthoudides, "Εκ Κρήτης," *ArchEph* 1906, 116–55.

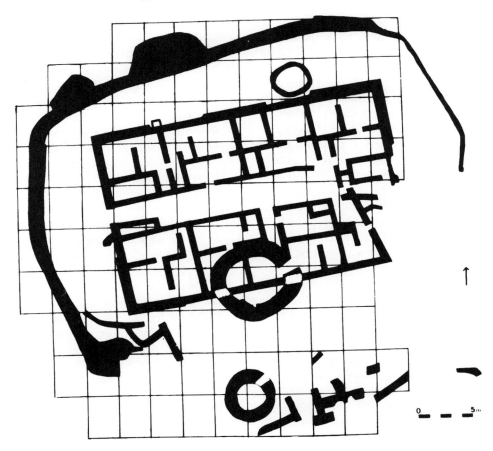

Fig. 11. Plan of building at Agia Photia. (After M. Tsipopoulou, in E. French and K. Wardle eds., *Problems in Greek Prehistory* [Bristol 1988] 32, fig. 1)

ered outside the house also may have been for domestic use. The large number of stone vessels, some of them duplicates, may indicate the presence of a workshop.[225] The Chamaizi house may well have been built late in MM IA, since some of the pottery has parallels with Patrikies, but it must have continued into MM IB, since a number of the vases are protopalatial, including the "Chamaizi pots" whose MM IB–II workshop has been found at Mallia.[226]

Excavations in 1985–1986 at the headland of Agia Photia east of Siteia have revealed a large rectangular, one-story building that consists of groups of rooms (22 in total) opening onto an inner court, originally with a single entrance on the west (figs. 11–12).[227] Located next to the building is a silo-like structure (*kouloura*) identified as a place for storage. A fortification wall with four apsidal towers is preserved around three sides of the building. Finds from the building, domestic pottery, numerous ground stone tools, many obsidian blades (as well as cores and debris), hearths, a bronze ax, and a loomweight, indicate that it was used for living and working quarters. The published pottery from the building appears to span MM IA and MM IB. After the abandonment of the building, two additional koulouras were built on the site in MM II. The complex is distinctive for several reasons: its fortification walls, unparalleled architectural plan, and large

---

[225] Xanthoudides (supra n. 224) pl. 11, nos. 2–3, 15–16. In addition, the stone object, pl. 9.10, looks like a mold for metal.

[226] MM IA-style vases include Xanthoudides (supra n. 224) pl. 9.6–10. Cf. pl. 9.6 and the teapots in N. Bonacasa, "Patrikies—Una stazione medio-minoica fra Haghia Triada e Festòs," *ASAtene* 45/46 (1967/1968) 7–54. MM IB–II

vases are shown in pl. 8.4 and pl. 9.1–3 ("Chamaizi vases") and 11. The "Chamaizi vase" workshop at Mallia is published in H. and M. van Effenterre, *Fouilles exécutées à Mallia: Maisons* IV (*EtCret* 22, Paris 1976) 66–84.

[227] M. Tsipopoulou, "Αγία Φωτία Σητείας: Το νέο εύρημα," in French and Wardle (supra n. 121) 31–48; Myers et al. (supra n. 74) 66–69.

Fig. 12. Aerial view of Agia Photia. (W. and E. Myers and G. Cadogan, *The Aerial Atlas of Ancient Crete* [Berkeley 1992] fig. 6.2, courtesy W. and E. Myers)

number of ground stone tools. Its exposed position on the coast and the evidence for food processing and imports point to its involvement in maritime trade.

The site of Patrikies sits on the ridge that runs between Phaistos and Agia Triada. During excavations, six rooms of a larger complex (hamlet?) and a paved road were revealed.[228] Large amounts of pottery were recovered, especially teapots. Because of the specialized nature of the pottery, Patrikies has been identified as the site of a ceramic workshop. At Pyrgos/Myrtos a settlement was established on the hilltop in MM IA.[229] Small MM IA settlements share certain characteristics: they are new foundations, fortified or built on defensible locations, and they

show signs of specialized production and foreign contacts.[230]

Survey results also show that the countryside is tentatively resettled at this time. In the northern Isthmus of Ierapetra, survey in 1992–1993 revealed that, after the abandonment of many EM II sites, the region is first resettled, in small numbers, in MM IA. In the Western Mesara, the number of settlements drops sharply after EM II; moreover, half of the MM IA sites are new foundations.

Burials thus continue to provide the bulk of the artifactual information for MM IA Crete. The most impressive early second-millennium B.C. cemetery known on Crete is at Archanes, on the southern hilltop of Phourni. The cemetery appears to be

[228] Bonacasa (supra n. 226); *Festòs* I, pl. 16 illustrates additional vases from the site.

[229] G. Cadogan,"Pyrgos, Crete, 1970–7," *AR* 24 (1976–1977) 71–74.

[230] S. Alexiou pointed to the defensive location of a

number of MM I sites—Chamaizi, Kastri (Palaikastro), Kastello (Tzermiado), Boubouli (Viannos), Volakas (Koumasa), and Vigla (Apesokari)—in "Τείχη και ακροπόλεις στη μινωική Κρήτη," *Κρητολογία* 8 (1979) 41–56.

Fig. 13. Plan of the Phourni cemetery at Archanes, south sector. (After I. and E. Sakellarakis, *Archanes* [Athens 1991] 67, fig. 40)

grouped into four architectural complexes: Tholos E, Building 16 and perhaps 19; Tholos Γ, Buildings 5, 8, 9, 13, and 24–26; Tholos B and Building 7; and Building 6 (fig. 13).

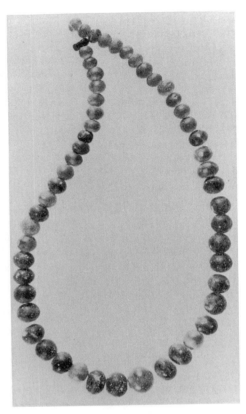

Fig. 14. Necklace of amethyst and sard from Tholos E, Phourni cemetery (Archanes). (After I. and E. Sakellarakis, *Prakt* 1975, pl. 240d)

Tholos E, the earliest structure at Phourni, was built in EM II (see above). In the upper level of the tholos were 56 MM IA burials, found in 29 larnakes, two pithoi, and in the earth between the containers. Burials consisted of skeletal remains, personal possessions, burnt animal offerings (caprid, cattle, bird, fish, and perhaps pig and hare), seashells, and pebbles. Possessions included bone/ivory and steatite seals, necklaces (fig. 14), pendants and a ring of bone/ivory, silver, faience, amethyst, sard, steatite, and bronze, obsidian blades, pottery, and a few stone mortars and vases.[231] The upper layer is dated to MM IA by the excavators, but several finds, e.g., a bronze ring of the signet type and a juglet, indicate that some of the burials there continued into the MM IB–II period.[232] Building 16 contained burials similar to those in the upper level of E, and may have served as an annex to the tholos.[233] The small apsidal vaulted Building 19 also served to hold later

---

[231] I. and E. Sakellarakis, *Prakt* 1975, 268–92.
[232] For the signet ring, see Higgins (supra n. 137) 68–69 for its late date. For the juglet, D. Levi, "La tomba a tholos di Kamilari presso a Festòs," *ASAtene* 23/24 (1961/1962)

85, fig. 113c; *Festòs* II, pl. 38f.
[233] I. and E. Sakellarakis (supra n. 231) 307–12; *Prakt* 1976, 392–98.

burials of the MM IB–III period.[234] Larnax burials at Archanes apparently begin in MM IA; the occurrence of these burials alongside simple inhumations within Tholos E might be taken as a sign of increased wealth and social stratification. The finds recorded inside the larnakes, however, do not differ much from those accompanying inhumations.

A second tholos (Γ) was constructed north of E in MM IA.[235] Tholos Γ, 3.60 m in diameter, was vaulted and buttressed by adjoining buildings. In the upper burial layer were 11 larnakes and a pithos. Except for animal bones in the pithos, there were no other finds in this level. Why those larnakes were found empty remains a mystery. Underneath the larnakes, a leveling course of stones had been laid on the bedrock over which earth had been spread. All of the rich finds (e.g., fig. 15) from Tholos Γ were found in the earth floor and among the stones and probably should be dated to the MM IA period.[236] The 269 objects included 13 stone and two ivory figurines; 15 pendants of ivory, two of faience, and one of gold; an ivory, silver, and bronze pin; 38 beads of gold, two of rock crystal, and one of ivory; eight ivory seals; three bronze daggers (fig. 16); a few clay and stone vases; obsidian blades; animal bones; and seashells. Evidence of Cycladic contact,

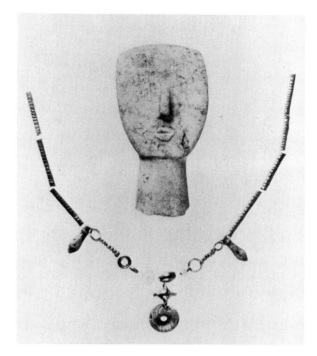

Fig. 15. Finds from Tholos Γ, Phourni cemetery (Archanes). (After I. Sakellarakis in J. Thimme and P. Getz-Preziosi eds., *Art and Culture of the Cyclades* [Karlsruhe 1977] 153, fig. 148)

---

[234] I. and E. Sakellarakis 1976 (supra n. 232) 351–85; *Prakt* 1977, 481. All the vases illustrated in I. Sakellarakis and E. Sapouna-Sakellaraki, *Archanes* (Athens 1991) 124, pl. 102 are MM IB or later. The cup, from the lower level of the tomb, in *Prakt* 1976, 377, fig. 13 is MM IB/II. The small larnax in *Prakt* 1976, 355, fig. 5 is MM III; cf. Betancourt (supra n. 169) figs. 31 and 40. See also C. Maggidis, "Tomb 19, Phourni (Archanes): Originality and Variety in the MM I Burial Architecture," in Πεπραγμένα (supra n. 72).

[235] I. and E. Sakellarakis, *Prakt* 1972, 327–51; 1973, 179–81.

[236] The excavators group the two strata together and date them to EM III, *Prakt* 1972, 349 n. 2. Such an early dating may have been influenced by the Spedhos-type figurines in the deposit, which they regard as EC II (*Prakt* 1977, 148). All discussions of the Cycladic folded-arm figurines agree that the duration of their manufacture is uncertain. Renfrew concluded that they probably continued into the MBA: C. Renfrew, "The Development and Chronology of the Early Cycladic Figurines," *AJA* 73 (1969) 26. More specifically, a Spedhos-type figurine (Atkinson [supra n. 203] pl. 30.2) comes from a First City context on Phylakopi, which is almost certainly MC I (Renfrew [supra] 25, Phyl. 2). The ceramic "EM III" parallels cited differ considerably in their shape, necks, and decorations from the Archanes examples. Closer parallels follow. The small jug (*Prakt* 1972, pl. 290b, middle) has single knobs on its belly, an early form of Barbotine typical of MM IA; cf. *BSA* 86 (1991) 27, no. 27 and pl. 31, no. 27. The globular body and short neck of the jug (*Prakt* 1972,

pl. 290b, right) have MM IA parallels; cf. A. Zois, Προβλήματα χρονολογίας της Μινωικής κεραμεικής (Athens 1969) pl. 8, bottom, 10, no. 7022; 18, no. 7003, left. The miniature juglet (*Prakt* 1972, pl. 290b, left) has a good MM IB parallel at Kamilari: Levi (supra n. 232) 79, fig. 102, bottom left. Just outside the entrance of the tomb another burial produced two vases. The conical cup (*Prakt* 1973, pl. 177b) is an MM IA type (E. Fiandra, in Πεπραγμένα του Γ′ Διεθνούς Κρητολογικού Συνεδρίου [Athens 1973] pl. 19a) that continues into early MM IB (Festòs I, pl. 16, l and p). The slender double jug (*Prakt* 1973, pl. 179a) is a common MM IB type (*ASAtene* 23/24 [1961/1962] 79, fig. 102a).

The evidence of strong Cycladic contacts in the deposits also makes an EM III date difficult to accept. The chronological sequence of Cycladic imports at Knossos is clear: imports occur in large numbers in EM IIA and begin again in MM IA. There are virtually no signs of Cycladic contact at Knossos in EM IIB and EM III: Wilson (supra n. 89) where Wilson and MacGillivray's ongoing study of Cycladic imports at EM II–MM II Knossos is cited. The excavators at Archanes note that the distinctive stone-packed lower level in Tholos Γ is also found in the bottom level of the adjacent Building 13, which like Γ, is built on bedrock. This level of Building 13, which contains gold, obsidian, and ivory objects similar to those in Γ, is probably contemporary with the lower level in Γ. It is dated to MM IA in *Prakt* 1973, 186–87. All of the arguments above point strongly to an MM IA date for the lower level in Tholos Γ.

Fig. 16. Three bronze daggers from Tholos Γ, Phourni cemetery (Archanes). (After I. Sakellarakis in J. Thimme and P. Getz-Preziosi eds., *Art and Culture of the Cyclades* [Karlsruhe 1977] 147, fig. 135)

in the Spedhos-type figurines, metals, and obsidian, is pronounced.[237]

Built next to Tholos Γ, Building 13 may be contemporary with the lower level in Γ; it produced child burials, jewelry, a human figurine, an animal horn, a gold bird-shaped pendant, and seashells.[238] North of Tholos Γ, Building 7 was constructed in MM IA to hold burials. Despite being partly destroyed by Tholos B, which was erected over it, the building produced a rich series of burials, on the floor or in larnakes. Finds included personal possessions, clay vases (cup, juglet, bowl, conical cups, jug, jars), a bronze knife and tweezers, ivory and steatite seals, an Egyptian faience scarab (fig. 17, upper), jewelry (ivory and gold pendants, a gold band, and necklaces of crystal, sard, amethyst, steatite, and faience beads), and the remains of offerings, a

stamped sealing, a clay "sheepbell," a steatite figurine of a male with his hands on his chest, a stone kernos and bird's nest bowl, animal bones including a boar's tusk, obsidian, and seashells.[239]

During the MM IA period, Tholos B was built over Building 7.[240] During the protopalatial period five annexes were added around three sides of the tholos forming a large rectangular, two-story structure. Funerary finds indicate that these rooms were used continuously for burials until the LM IIIA period. Building 6, originally a single room, was constructed in MM IA at the highest part of the cemetery. The two eastern rooms contained 196 burials accompanied by jewelry (necklaces, pendants, and rings), 16 seals, and an Egyptian scarab (fig. 17, lower), as well as offerings such as stone and clay vases, "sheepbells," and many seashells. Four of the seals bear hieroglyphic inscriptions, the earliest examples of literacy found on Crete (fig. 18). One extraordinary seal has 14 faces (fig. 19). Along the east

Fig. 17. Egyptian faience scarabs from Phourni cemetery (Archanes): upper, from Building 7; lower, from Building 6. (After I. and E. Sakellarakis, *Archanes* [Athens 1991] 97, fig. 69)

---

[237] I. and E. Sakellarakis (supra n. 235) 349–51; I. Sakellarakis, "The Cyclades and Crete," in J. Thimme and P. Getz-Preziosi eds., *Art and Culture of the Cyclades in the Third Millennium B.C.* (Karlsruhe 1977) 147–53.

[238] I. and E. Sakellarakis, *Prakt* 1973, 186–87.

[239] Building 7: I. and E. Sakellarakis, *Prakt* 1967, 153–57; 1971, 277–81. This level in Building 7 was not sealed from above and may have contained finds of a protopala-

tial or later date, since an LM III kylix was found in one larnax.

[240] I. and E. Sakellarakis 1967 (supra n. 239) 153–57; 1971 (supra n. 239) 277–82. Tholos B was originally dated to the Old Palace period, *Prakt* 1966, 176. Only finds from its final LM IIIA use remained in the tholos chamber, but MM IA pottery (Lahanas, infra n. 241) resting against the south face of its retaining wall dates its construction.

Fig. 18. Hieroglyphic seal from Building 6 at Phourni cemetery (Archanes). (After I. and E. Sakellarakis, *Archanes* [Athens 1991] 102, fig. 75)

side of Building 6 a 3-m-high terrace raised it above the level of surrounding buildings and provided a paved area in front of its entrance. Many conical cups as well as other cups and a human figurine with its hand on its chest were found on the paved platform. Excavation below and to the east of the terrace revealed some 300 vases thrown down from the paved area above: the finds—kernoi, figurines, and many cups—seem to have come from some form of ceremony carried out in front of Building 6. The excavators date the building to MM IA, but the associated pottery is MM IA–II.[241]

---

[241] Finds from the paved area: *Prakt* 1973, 174. Seals: *CMS* II.1, 391–94. None of the more than 70 vases from inside Building 6 have been published. The associated deposit below and to the east of Building 6 appears in I. and E. Sakellarakis, "Αποθέτης κεραμεικής της τελευταίας φάσεως των προανακτορικών χρόνων εις Αρχάνες," *ArchEph* 1972, Chronika, 1–11. The deposit was dated to EM III–MM IA in *ArchDelt* 21 (1966) Chronika 411–12.

The pottery illustrated from this deposit spans MM IA–MM II. Parallels follow. Carinated cup (*ArchEph* 1972, pls. Eb), cf. *Festòs* I, 738, no. 3313; *Festòs* II, pls. 130–34. Teapot (*ArchEph* 1972, pl. IAb), cf. *Festòs* II, pl. 30h. Tumbler (*ArchEph* 1972, pl. Ba, middle), cf. *Festòs* II, pl. 119d. Large cylindrical cup (*ArchEph* 1972, pl. Ea), cf. *Festòs* II, pls. 126a–d; 127f. Straight-sided cup (*ArchEph* 1972, pl. Da), cf. *BSA* 86 (1991) 170 no. 9. Eggcups (*ArchEph* 1972, pl. Ba, right, G) are not the MM IA type (*Pepragmena* 1990 I, 482, fig. 3) and also show developed, post-MM IA decoration. The spherical cup (*ArchEph* 1972, pl. Za, left) is a type that continues into MM II (*BSA* 86 [1990] 250–51, type 2). For the carinated cup (*ArchEph* 1972, pl. Γa) see the example from an MM IB context at Mallia, H. Chevalier et al., *Fouilles exécutées à Mallia: Sondages au Sud-Ouest du Palais* (*EtCret* 20, Paris 1975) no. 6. The crinkled rim of the goblet in pl. 2, upper left, is an Anatolian metalli-

Fig. 19. Hieroglyphic seal from Building 6, Phourni cemetery (Archanes). (After I. and E. Sakellarakis, *ArchDelt* 21 [1966] pl. 441a)

---

cizing feature that is known there only after 1900, see E. Davis, "The Silver Kantharos from Gournia," *TUAS* 4 (1979) 34–45. For the unique metallicizing kernos (*ArchEph* 1972, pl. IG) see T. and N. Özgüç, *Kültepe Kazısı Raporu 1949* (Ankara 1953) pl. 55, no. 528. Other examples from Kültepe II–Ib are on display in the Konya Museum.

After writing this article, I was shown the unpublished Ph.D. thesis of Alexandros Lahanas, *Ein Keramik Depot aus Archanes und seine Bedeutung für die Entwicklung der mittelminoischen Keramik* (Freiburg 1994) by I. Sakellarakis. Lahanas correctly dates, on stylistic grounds, the pottery from this deposit to the MM IA, MM IB, and MM II periods.

The Phourni cemetery provides us with important new information on chronology, burial customs, the appearance of literacy,[242] overseas contacts, and social organization. The Phourni deposits illustrate a chronological sequence of assemblages useful for defining certain aspects of cultural development in EM II–MM II Crete. The EM II deposit (Tholos E, lower stratum) consists of many objects of bone, obsidian, and steatite as well as lesser amounts of clay, gold, bronze, and local stone. Imports are probably limited to materials from the Aegean islands. Possessions and offerings (two stone vases and animal sacrifices) are relatively few and simple. In the upper, MM IA level of Tholos E there is a greater incidence of seals; likewise, there is a greater range of clay vases. Bronze and shell objects appear and jewelry comes in varied materials (sard, amethyst, alabaster, rock crystal, faience, and silver make their first appearance in the MM IA level). The use of bone, obsidian, flint, and steatite is less frequent than in EM II.

The basal level of Tholos Γ (MM IA) is similar in most respects to the upper stratum of E but is richer. The deposit contained many objects of ivory/bone, obsidian, marble, gold, and bronze. Imported materials (including lead) are more common and there is a greater variety in the materials and forms of jewelry (fig. 15). Building 7, also of MM IA date, produced a variety of new seal shapes and the first Egyptian object, a faience scarab (fig. 17, upper). From Building 13 came a human figurine and a gold bird-shaped pendant. Clay and stone vases remain a minor component of both EM II and MM IA deposits. The first bifacial seals, a clay figurine, "sheepbells," and miniature pots appear in MM IA. Burials made in larnakes, pithoi, or jars are often accompanied by animal bones, seashells, and pebbles. Generally the MM IA deposits at Phourni are larger than the EM II deposit and are much more numerous, suggesting a sharp rise in population at Archanes. Signs of greater wealth are unmistakable in the number of personal seals, foreign imports (from the Cyclades and perhaps lead from Lavrion), and particularly the more varied imported materials used in jewelry.

In 1972 I. and E. Sakellarakis suggested, on the basis of the finds from Tholos Γ at Archanes, that island peoples had settled there.[243] There is now more evidence to suggest that not only Archanes but many north coast settlements received island and eastern immigrants at the beginning of the MM I period. Cist graves, a Cycladic form of burial, appear for the first time on Crete in MM IA, at many sites along the north coast, at Archanes ("enclosures"), Mallia, Pseira, Sphoungaras, and Zakros.[244] Pithos burials, a type characteristic of western Anatolia (and rare in the Aegean), appear at this time along the whole north coast of Crete from Chania to Zakros.[245] At MM IA Knossos Cycladic-style vases were produced in local clay.[246] The suggestion that Cretan settlements grew in MM IA partly as a result of immigration fits the evidence from the Aegean islands and western Anatolia, which at this time show signs of unrest and population movement.[247]

MM IA burials at Mallia are numerous and of many types: burials in rock crevices, pithos or larnax burials, cist tombs, and house tombs. House tombs also varied in size. A well-preserved medium-sized example, the "House of the Dead" was a rectangular building with a stuccoed and painted atrium and seven inner rooms that contained inhumation, cist, and pithos burials continuing into the protopalatial period. Offerings included stone vases, an offering table, a teapot, lamps and juglets, and a clay imitation of an Egyptian stone vase.[248]

The first phase of the tomb at Chrysolakkos dates to MM IA.[249] According to Soles's new reconstruction, the paved terrace along the west facade of

---

[242] J.-P. Olivier, "The Relationship between Inscriptions on Hieroglyphic Seals and Inscriptions," in T. Palaima ed., *Aegean Seals, Sealings and Administration* (*Aegaeum* 5, Liège 1990) 11–19 and the important article by J. Younger, "New Observations on Hieroglyphic Seals," *SMEA* 28 (1990) 85–92 on the use of the hieroglyphic script on seals.

[243] I. and E. Sakellarakis (supra n. 235) 350–51 and I. Sakellarakis, "Τά κυκλαδικά στοιχεία των Αρχανών," *AAA* 10 (1977) 93–115. This view was criticized by C. Doumas, "Προϊστορικοί κυκλαδίτες στη Κρήτη," *AAA* 9 (1976) 69–80.

[244] I. Pini, *Beiträge zür minoischen Gräberfunde* (Wiesbaden 1968) 9.

[245] Pini (supra n. 244) 11–13; T. Wheeler, "Early Bronze Age Burial Customs in Western Anatolia," *AJA* 78 (1974)

415–25.

[246] A. MacGillivray et al., "Dark-faced and Incised Pyxides and Lids from Knossos: Problems of Date and Origin," in French and Wardle (supra n. 121) 91–93.

[247] For the Aegean islands, see Coleman (supra n. 36) 266–69. Western Anatolia, M. Mellink, "The Early Bronze Age in West Anatolia," in G. Cadogan ed., *The End of the Early Bronze Age* (Leiden 1986) 139–52.

[248] Soles 173–76 with references. The Vapheio cups in H. and M. van Effenterre, *Fouilles exécutées à Mallia: Étude du site et exploration des nécropoles* (*EtCret* 13, Paris 1963) pl. 38 indicate use continued into the MM IB–II period.

[249] The pottery from Chrysolakkos has been republished: V. Stürmer, "La céramique de Chrysolakkos," *BCH* 117 (1993) 123–87.

Chrysolakkos was bounded by a rubble and mud-brick wall topped by a series of rounded capping stones that are unparalleled outside of Egypt.[250] A long corridor, with alternating stone orthostates and niches, ran along the east facade and joined several other rooms that formed a shrine. These rooms were fitted with benches, a plaster bin, and a clay hearth. In front of the facade is a raised altar and a kernos set into the floor at its base. The corridor resembles the "corridor chapel" placed in front of the facade of Old Kingdom mastabas with its alternating niches set along the facade to receive wooden panels.[251] The interior of the great structure, mostly covered by the second building phase, contained rooms for burials. The pointed-bottomed cups offered there have no Minoan parallels, but are quite a common shape in Egypt.[252] It is at this time, in the late prepalatial period, when Chrysolakkos was built, that undeniable evidence for social ranking can be found in the Mallia cemeteries.

Ceramic studies enable us to identify much of the material in the "EM II Mochlos tombs" as actually dating to MM IA or MM IB. Iconography and style, now often neglected in archaeological studies, also allow us to appreciate more fully the extent of Cretan overseas connections in this period. For example, Mochlos Tomb II, the richest in the cemetery, contains many MM IA objects. Two jugs date to this period.[253] A clay bowl in Tomb II is unique.[254] One of the two seals in the tomb is engraved with a design of antithetical cynocephalus apes, an Egyptian motif.[255] Many of the stone vases from the Mochlos tombs have been dated too high. In *MSV*, Warren lists parallels for the vases in the Mochlos tombs and dates the parallels to EM II or EM III on the basis of the Mochlos examples. Warren's careful lists establish two things: 1) most of the parallels are from the unstratified Mesara tombs where the contexts are EM II–MM IB/II, and 2) in at least a dozen cases, vases called "Early Minoan" by Seager and Warren have secure and exclusive MM I–II contexts.[256] At least five stone vases are imitations of Egyptian vase shapes and are not likely to be earlier than the 12th Dynasty (see below).[257] Other finds from the tombs can be dated on the basis of associated artifacts to MM IA. They include one or perhaps two long daggers, a socketed arrowhead, two knives, and rhyta of a woman and a bull.[258]

In earlier studies, the gold jewelry from the Mochlos and Mesara tombs was taken as a sign of

---

[250] Soles 163–66. Cf. P. Demargne, *Fouilles exécutées à Mallia: Exploration des nécropoles* I (*EtCret* 7, Paris 1945) pl. 53.3 and D. Arnold, *Building in Egypt* (Oxford 1991) 148 and n. 151.

[251] Cf. Demargne (supra n. 250) pl. 38.2 and W. Smith, *The Art and Architecture of Ancient Egypt* (Baltimore 1958) 35–38 and fig. 8.

[252] Cf. cups, Demargne (supra n. 250) pl. 39.3 and Stürmer (supra n. 249) 139–40, figs. 54–57. Cf. A. Kelley, *The Pottery of Ancient Egypt* 1 (Toronto 1976) pl. 21.1 and vol. II, pls. 36.1:27 and 37.5:173–93 and Dunand (supra n. 56) pl. 151, no. 4035.

[253] Cf. *Mochlos*, fig. 3, IIb and Momigliano (supra n. 185) 254, fig. 33, types 5 and 6 (MM IA); *Mochlos*, fig. 3, IIr and *Festòs* I, pl. 94 (MM IB).

[254] *Mochlos*, fig. 3, IIL. H. Frankfort took it as Near Eastern: *Studies in the Early Pottery of the Near East* 2 (London 1927) 122. He cites Eastern parallels for the decoration: *Iraq* 15 (1953) 63, fig. 1; 66, fig. 4. The bowl shape is Minoan, but the metope and butterfly decoration is derived from the East where it is a hallmark of Syro-Cilician painted wares at the beginning of the MBA, at Mersin, Tarsus, Ugarit, and Alalakh. See *Levant* 68–70 and figs. 20.1; 23.1–14, 21–23. The vase dates to MB I in the Near East (ca. 2000–1900 B.C.) and thus is MM IA. See *Levant* 101–108 and table 9 for absolute dates of the MB I period in the Near East.

[255] *PM* I, 83; Pendlebury (supra n. 4) 72; V. Kenna, *Cretan Seals* (Oxford 1960) 18. As Yule 33–35 observes, the shape of this early seal (type 3a–b) can be dated primarily to MM IA–II. Since this type of motif is entirely absent in EM II Crete, the seal should date no earlier than the beginning of the Middle Kingdom when strong contacts between Crete and Egypt begin (see below).

[256] All references are to Mochlos vases in *MSV*. Two bowls (types 8C and E) dated by Warren to EM II–MM I/II, from Mochlos Tombs II and XIX; secure contexts: MM IB–II at Mallia and MM II at Phaistos. A bowl (type 10) dated EM II–MM I by Warren, from Mochlos Tomb XVII; secure context: MM IB onward at Kamilari. Two jars (type 20) dated EM III–MM I by Warren, from Mochlos Tombs VII and XIX; secure contexts: MM IB onward at Kamilari (an imitation of the MM I clay tumbler!). Four jugs (type 22) dated EM II–MM I by Warren, from Mochlos Tombs I and VI; secure contexts: MM I–II at Chamaizi, Mallia, and Kamilari. Three miniature amphoras (type 28) dated EM II–MM I/II by Warren, from Mochlos Tombs II and V; secure contexts: MM I at Palaikastro and MM II at Mallia. Since specific stone vase shapes change as rapidly as their ceramic counterparts (e.g., *MSV* 98–100), the Mochlos vases must be Middle Minoan (MM I–II) in date, not earlier.

[257] *MSV* 71–72; 92 recognizes *Mochlos* fig. 7, nos. IIj, k, and o as Egyptianizing. Three others are also probably Egyptianizing: cf. *Mochlos* IId and A. Spencer, *Catalogue of the Egyptian Antiquities in the British Museum* 5 (London 1980) pl. 20, nos. 216 and 218; *Mochlos* fig. 7, IIe to be compared to pl. 12.109 and pl. 14.135 and *Mochlos* fig. 18, IV.3 and F. Petrie, *Funeral Furniture and Stone and Metal Vases* (London 1937) pl. 27, no. 533, without a base.

[258] Dagger, *Mochlos* fig. 44 XIX 27; second dagger, fig. 44 XXI 22; arrowhead, fig. 45 XIX 34; knives, fig. 45 XIII m and n; rhyta, figs. 28 II 14 and 32 XIIg.

the wealth and commercial status of EM II Crete. Branigan cites the diadems, for example, as an EM II development and compares the blossoming of Cretan goldworking to the jewelry from Troy IIg.[259] This is problematic because there is only one EC II gold diadem from the Cyclades. There are no certain EM II examples from Crete, but there are 18 post-EM II examples as well as 51 "EM II–III/MM I" examples.[260] Much of this Minoan jewelry should be compared to hoards of similar objects found in MB I contexts at Kültepe, Byblos, and Egypt.[261] Similarly, gold bracelets from Cretan tombs find precise parallels at MB I Kültepe and Byblos.[262] Distinctive gold discs, with two perforations, are known from tombs at Platanos and Kültepe Ib.[263] Gold bosses from Mochlos also have parallels at Kültepe.[264] Similar earrings are found at Mochlos and MB I Byblos.[265] Additional gold diadems, beads, and pendants from the tombs at Platanos, Kalathiana, Koumasa, and Mochlos have now been dated to the MM IB–II period.[266] Seager compared the necklace of gold tubular beads from Tomb III to the common Egyptian "mummy" beads.[267] Precise Egyptian parallels exist.[268] The gold leaf pendants from Mochlos Tombs II, IV, and XIX have an MM IB–II parallel from Mallia.[269] It is evident that much of the gold jewelry from the Mochlos and Mesara

tombs is better dated to the beginning of the Middle Minoan period.

The rich finds from the Mesara tholoi are unstratified, but a few can be identified as MM IA in date on the basis of parallels stratified elsewhere. It has not been recognized that much of the Mesara material spans the MM IA–II period. Platanos produced an enormous number of stone vases; three imitate MM IA ceramic shapes.[270] Many groups of vases, bird's nest bowls, bridge-spouted jars, calyx bowls, two-handled and spouted bowls, goblets, cups, and block vases probably begin to be produced in this period and certainly continue well into the protopalatial period.[271] Platanos produced many Egyptianizing stone vases: 11 tubular vases, eight pear-shaped alabastra, three cylindrical vases, 11 miniature alabastra, and 15 block vases that are MM IA–II in date.[272] A large number of the bronze daggers from Platanos also probably date to this period.[273] Over half of the 78 published seals from Platanos belong to the late prepalatial period.[274] Many are part of Yule's Parading Lions/Spiral group, and nearly all were imported from abroad.[275] One figurine is of a type common at Phylakopi Iii.[276] Gold beads, diadems, bosses, and rings similar to examples from Mochlos are found at Platanos but cannot be dated precisely. Gold pendants in the shape of a

---

[259] Branigan 106 and 108. An inspection of Branigan's list of these diadems and their attachments on pp. 183–84 shows that there are no examples from a secure EM II context, but only from mixed or post-EM II deposits. The Cretan gold jewelry bears little resemblance to the Trojan IIg collection.

[260] Branigan 183–84.

[261] Cf. the diadems (*Mochlos* II.1 in figs. 8 and 9 and *VTM* pl. 39b, no. 236) with T. Özgüç, *Kültepe-Kanesh* II (Ankara 1986) pls. 63.1–4, 64.1. Cf. the diadem (*Mochlos* II.7 in fig. 9) with the similarly decorated example in Özgüç (supra) 119 and fig. 23 dated to ca. 2000 B.C. See also the diadems from the MB I Tomb II at Byblos in P. Montet, *Byblos et l'Égypte* (Paris 1928) pl. 98, nos. 645–46. The peaked diadems from Crete are paralleled at MB I Kültepe. Cf. *Mochlos* II.4 and 6 in fig. 8 as well as the example from Lebena Tomb I in *ILN* 1960, 225, fig. 6 with Özgüç (supra) pl. 63.4 from level 1.

[262] Cf. *VTM* pl. 57, nos. 491, 493 and Özgüç (supra n. 261) pl. 63, nos. 6, 7, 10, 11, 13–16. *Mochlos* II.18f and h and Montet (supra n. 261) pl. 104, nos. 690–91.

[263] Cf. *VTM* pl. 57, middle, and Özgüç (supra n. 261) pl. 65.8–15. The Kültepe discs are thought to have been used to cover the eyes of the deceased.

[264] Cf. *Mochlos* II.12 in fig. 9 and Özgüç (supra n. 261) pl. 72.6–7.

[265] Cf. *Mochlos* fig. 9, II.15 and Dunand (infra n. 305) pl. 189, no. 17,755.

[266] Higgins (supra n. 137) 58–59.

[267] *Mochlos* 78 and fig. 20, III.19.

[268] Spencer (supra n. 257) pl. 20, no. 235 and also the MB I example from Byblos, Montet (supra n. 261) pl. 94, nos. 627–28.

[269] *Mochlos* fig. 10, II.35; fig. 20, IV.14; fig. 43, XIX.23. Cf. van Effenterre 496, fig. 677.

[270] *VTM* pl. 54, nos. 1673, 1886, and 1990.

[271] For these vases, see *VTM* 98–104.

[272] Pear-shaped alabastra: *VTM* 100, nos. 1690, 1691, 1682–84, 1689, 1966; cf. Petrie (supra n. 257) pl. 29, no. 605. Cylindrical jars: *VTM* 101, nos. 1637, 1640, 1904; cf. Petrie (supra n. 257) pl. 12, nos. 109–27 and comments in *MSV* 75–76. Miniature amphoras: *VTM* 100–101, nos. 1665, 1668, 1669, 1671, 1672, 1675, 1697, 1991, 2497; cf. *MSV* 71–72 and P 355–57. Block vases: *VTM* 99, nos. 1619, 1620, 1622–25, 1627–29, 1633, 1636; cf. F. Petrie, *Prehistoric Egypt* (London 1920) pl. 42, figs. 213–14 as well as Muhly (supra n. 150) 242–52. Tubular vases: *VTM* 101, nos. 1638–41, 1697, 1916, 1990, 2497, 2515, 2516; cf. Petrie (supra n. 257) pl. 27, nos. 551 and 595.

[273] Branigan 8–10, types II–IV are MM IA, while types V and VI probably span MM IA–II.

[274] See *VTM* 112–23 and Yule 208–10, with Younger's important review (supra n. 142).

[275] O. Krzyszkowska, "Ivory in the Aegean Bronze Age," *BSA* 83 (1988) 229 identifies these seals as made from Egyptian hippopotamus tusk.

[276] *VTM* pl. 58, no. 225; Branigan (supra n. 49) 64.

bee and a claw that imitate Egyptian types are MM IA–II.[277] Tholos A at Agia Triada also produced MM IA finds: pottery, stone vases, 21 seals, some of the bronze weapons, figurines, and jewelry.[278] The unpublished Lebena tombs have artifacts identified as coming from MM IA levels. These include seals and stone and clay vases.[279] The two Egyptian scarabs are important finds because of their secure context: they establish the overlap of MM IA and the 12th Dynasty of the Middle Kingdom. The stone vases include an Egyptianizing miniature goblet and an Egyptianizing block vase ("kernos").[280] At Pyrgos/Myrtos a paved road was constructed south of the settlement leading to a small courtyard in front of a large house tomb with two ossuaries. Offerings there included a rhyton in the shape of a dove and cups.[281]

There has much recent work on Minoan peak sanctuaries.[282] A. Karetsou's excavations on Mt. Jouktas have produced masses of new evidence that modify Evans's earlier views on the sanctuary.[283] Present evidence indicates that the sanctuary at Jouktas began in MM IA.[284] Excavation of the MM IA–II burnt level on bedrock has shown that the protopalatial sanctuary already covered an area of at least ca. 200 × 100 m. The neopalatial architectural features, the open court, terracing, and rooms presently visible on the site cover the fragmentary remains of protopalatial walls, which suggests that the MM I–II shrine was an open area, perhaps terraced, but simpler in plan than in MM III–LM I.[285] The stepped structure, built next to a deep (over 10 m) chasm in the bedrock, probably served as an altar in the MM IB–II period. Pottery from within the chasm dates to MM I–III, most of it being protopalatial.[286] Next to the altar was found a large stone kernos (with ca. 100 cupules) and, in a depression in the bedrock, a cache of bronze double axes.[287] The massive peribolos wall (over 700 m in length) encircling the mountaintop, dated by Evans to MM IA, has now been shown to be Late Minoan, probably LM IIIC, in date.[288] MM I–II levels in the sanctuary have produced ash, animal bones, and shells and include large numbers of pots (conical cups, eggcups, tumblers, goblets, bridge-spouted jars, jugs, shallow bowls, miniature vases, cooking pots, pithoi); male figurines (which greatly outnumber the female figurines); clay representations of human heads, hands, and torsos; animal figurines (sheep/goat, pig, birds, snakes, and bucrania); clay balls; schematic representations of floral branches, women crouching in childbirth, and phalloi; clay "offering tables"; miniature stone vases; fragments of gold foil; a gold pendant depicting a scorpion, insect, and snake; seals; and bronze votive double axes.[289]

---

[277] Fly, *VTM* pl. 57, no. 487; cf. C. Aldred, *Jewels of the Pharaohs* (New York 1971) 189 and pl. 29. Claw, *VTM* pl. 57, no. 489; cf. J. Bourriau, *Pharaohs and Mortals: Egyptian Art in the Middle Kingdom* (Cambridge 1988) 149.

[278] The 10 MM IA–II Egyptianizing shapes are listed below (infra n. 309). MM IA seals, *CMS* I.2, 20, 22, 25–28, 37–39, 52, 54, 55, 57, 59, 60, 62–65, 82, 89. Bronze weapon, i.e., Banti (supra n. 98) 207.

[279] Seals, *CMS* II.1, 193, 205–209, and scarabs, nos. 180, 201, and 204. According to James Weinstein (personal communication), these three scarabs date to the 12th Dynasty. Stone vases, *MSV* 12, 27, 73, and 77. Pottery, Alexiou (supra n. 61) 227, fig. 19.

[280] Block vase, *MSV* 12. Egyptianizing goblet, Alexiou (supra n. 61) 226, fig. 11, left.

[281] Cadogan (supra n. 229) 70–84.

[282] Aside from the excavations summarized here, mention should be made of B. Rutkowski's (supra n. 30) republication of the finds from the peak sanctuary of Petsofas above Palaikastro. For the protopalatial period Rutkowski (p. 18, fig. 1) reconstructs the shrine as an open sacrificial area with terraces on one side. The volume provides a catalogue of the clay finds (except pottery): male and female figurines, votive torsos, arms and legs, animal figurines (cattle, sheep, goats, pigs, birds, agrimia, beetles, turtles, weasels), balls, models of fruit and grain, and miniature vases.

[283] Karetsou's excavations at Jouktas were carried out mainly between 1974 and 1985. Reports of her work appear in *Prakt* 1974, 228–39; 1975, 330–42; 1976, 408–18; 1977, 419–20; 1978, 232–58; 1979, 280–81; 1980, 337–53; 1981, 405–408; 1984, 600–14; 1985, 286–96. A summary of her research from 1974 to 1979 appeared in "The Peak Sanctuary of Mt. Jouktas," in R. Hägg and N. Marinatos eds., *Sanctuaries and Cults in the Aegean Bronze Age* (Stockholm 1981) 137–53.

[284] In January 1994 the excavator discussed her work and unpublished study at Jouktas with me and clarified several points. According to Karetsou, the shrine was probably established in MM IA and the few EM II sherds found on bedrock are unrelated to the later sanctuary. Her reasons are that 1) while there are a few EM II sherds on bedrock there is an enormous amount of MM IA in the lowest burnt levels, and 2) unlike the EM II sherds, the MM IA finds—conical cups, sheep bells, figurines, pithoi—have a ritual character. She also believes the small amount of white-on-dark wares in these levels is probably MM IA in date.

[285] See the plan in *Prakt* 1985, opp. p. 289.

[286] I am indebted to A. Karetsou for this information, which comes from E. Banou's unpublished study in 1993 of the pottery from inside the chasm.

[287] *Prakt* 1974, 233 and pl. 173a.

[288] *Prakt* 1979, 280–81.

[289] The list above is preliminary and, with future study, will undoubtedly grow. For MM I–II levels, *Prakt* 1974, 247–49; bronze axes, *Prakt* 1974, 232 and pl. 173a.

Fig. 20. View of the Agios Vasilios Valley and the peak sanctuary of Atsipades (center, background). (Courtesy A. Peatfield)

In 1989 Peatfield excavated a complete peak sanctuary at Atsipades in the inland valley of Agios Vasilios south of Rethymnon (fig. 20).[290] This peak sanctuary was chosen for excavation because it was a small rural shrine, unlike the great urban sanctuaries at Jouktas and Petsofas. Finds at Atsipades were distributed over a limited area (less than 200 m²) on two terraces. No traces of architecture were found. Votive activity on the upper terrace was confined to a natural hollow in the bedrock at the east end. There waterworn pebbles brought from the river in the valley below were laid out to form a floor around an artificial earth platform, lined with schist-like stones, which apparently supported an (unknown) object that was the central feature of the shrine. Vase fragments (as well as two clay offering tables) were plentiful around the platform; especially numerous were vase forms connected with libations—rhyta and painted bridge-spouted jars. While cups, dishes, jars, lamps, and cooking pots were common at the site, signs of burning and animal bones were absent. On the lower terrace the votives as well as cups and dishes were concentrated in the rock clefts.[291] The pottery on the site is predominately protopalatial and the shrine appears not to have been used after MM II. It is claimed that EM I (but no EM II) pottery has also been identified at the site, but the relationship of that pottery with the later shrine is unclear. Animal (mostly bovine)

Fig. 21. Animal figurines from the Atsipades peak sanctuary. (Courtesy A. Peatfield)

[290] The preliminary report of the excavation is A. Peatfield, "Rural Ritual in Bronze Age Crete: The Peak Sanctuary at Atsipadhes," *Cambridge Archaeological Journal* 2 (1992) 59–87. The excavator estimates that some 80% of the site was dug.

[291] Peatfield (supra n. 290) 67, fig. 7.

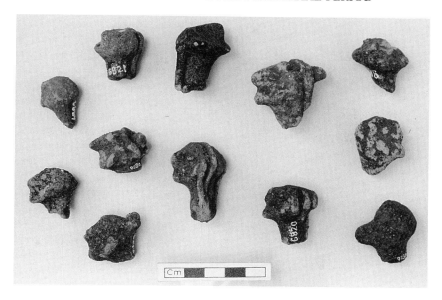

Fig. 22. Heads of male figurines, Atsipades peak sanctuary. (Courtesy A. Peatfield)

figurines (fig. 21), male and female human figurines (figs. 22–23), and clay phalloi (fig. 24) were numerous. Aside from its lack of neopalatial finds, the shrine differs from those at Jouktas and Petsofas in that the votives at Atsipades are limited to a few basic types.

The most recent excavation of a Minoan peak sanctuary has taken place at the peak of Agios Georgios on the island of Kythera.[292] Excavations at the shrine have produced an unprecedented number of bronze figurines (over 50), a votive hand and legs, model swords in bronze, an oxhide ingot fragment, melting debris, stone vases and offering tables (including unworked chunks of Peloponnesian antico rosso), seashells, sea pebbles, and MM I/II–LM IB pottery. Pottery and some fragments of relief ware with a plastic seashell, fish, and horns of consecration are said to be protopalatial. The large amounts of MM III–LM I bronze at the sanctuary indicate the settlers at Kastri had ready access to copper, which may explain why the Minoans chose to settle on Kythera.

Peatfield's researches have clarified many details about the nature of peak sanctuaries.[293] Surveys have modified some of Peatfield's conclusions. There seems to have been a hierarchy of peak shrines: regional sanctuaries, e.g., Jouktas, Kophi-

nas, and Vysinas, as well as local examples belonging to one or several small communities, such as Agia Pelagia (Gournia), Ephendi Christos (Phaistos), Ieroditis (Agia Triada), Vigla (Pobia), Arolithia (Matala), and Aphratias (Kalamaki). The smaller peak sanctuaries do not necessarily exhibit the same range of finds recovered at regional peak shrines. This probably means that there exist many more peak sanctuaries than are currently acknowl-

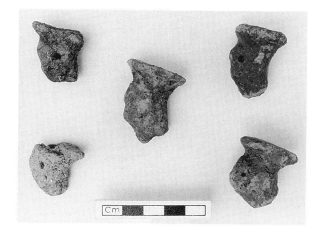

Fig. 23. Heads of female figurines, Atsipades peak sanctuary. (Courtesy A. Peatfield)

[292] Accounts of the excavations have appeared in the Greek newspapers, e.g., Ελευθεροτυπία (12 October 1992), Τα Νέα (11 September 1993), and in an article, A. Elder, "Embarkation for Kythera," The Athenian 18 (1993) 20–24. The excavator graciously showed me his finds and discussed them with me prior to publication.

[293] A. Peatfield, "The Topography of Minoan Peak Sanctuaries," BSA 78 (1983) 273–79, and Peatfield, "Minoan Peak Sanctuaries: History and Society," OpAth 18 (1990) 117–31.

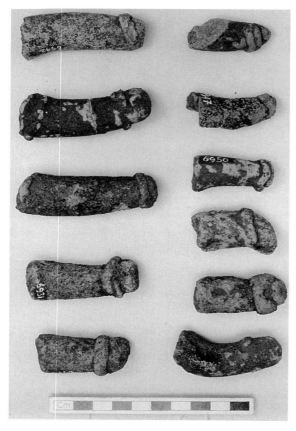

Fig. 24. Clay phalloi from the Atsipades peak sanctuary.
(Courtesy A. Peatfield)

edged.[294] Peatfield's study has shown that peak sanctuaries are thickly distributed across the center and east of the island.[295] It is still uncertain whether the absence of such shrines in western Crete is merely the result of a lack of investigation or is an accurate

reflection of the situation. Despite substantial variations in the offerings at the different peak sanctuaries, the impression gained is that a similar cult was practiced at all of these shrines.[296]

The most recent study of Aegean cult places dates the beginning of worship in caves to MM IA.[297] While it is clear that the earliest artifacts date to MM IA in a number of caves, such as Kamares, Trapeza, the Idaean Cave, at Psychro, and at Agios Charalambos (Lasithi), in most cases burials have also been recognized in these caves and there is nothing to distinguish the cave assemblages from those found in tombs.[298]

Relatively little attention has been paid to MM I foreign connections or how they relate to contemporary events in the Near East. The EB III–MB I sequence in the Near East is important for Minoan (and Aegean) archaeology because it provides a context for understanding foreign imports and signs of influence in Crete. Several cities of Anatolia and Syro-Cilicia, e.g., Kültepe, Tarsus, Ebla, Ugarit, and Byblos, were destroyed by fire at the end of the Early Bronze period.[299] Tarsus was destroyed at the end of EB III, ca. 2200 B.C.[300] Ebla was destroyed twice, at ca. 2250/2200 and again ca. 2000 B.C. During this interim (level IIB2) the palace (G) was not rebuilt and the city is said to have entered a period of economic recession.[301] There are few signs of trade during this period (EB IV, ca. 2250–2000 B.C.) until after 2000 B.C. Imported goods or foreign ceramic influences at Kültepe after level 12 until Karum Kanish II are apparently few.[302] Trade began to revive at the end of this period and by ca. 1950 B.C. with the establishment of Assyrian merchants in Anatolia it had become extremely active. Texts relate that ca. 2000/1950 B.C. the MB I cities

[294] E.g., Peatfield (supra n. 290) 59, fig. 1. See L.V. Watrous, "Some Observations on Minoan Peak Sanctuaries," in W.-D. Niemeier and R. Laffineur eds., *Politeia* (*Aegaeum* 9, in press).

[295] Peatfield (supra n. 290).

[296] At Atsipades hundreds of phalloi were dedicated; they are rare at Jouktas and Petsofas. Small animal figurines are numerous at Jouktas and Petsofas, but are said to be rare at Atsipades. Ash deposits and votive limbs are common at Petsofas and Kophinas but are few at Atsipades.

[297] B. Rutkowski, *Cult Places of the Aegean* (New Haven 1986) 47–71.

[298] The primary data are gathered in L. Tyree, *Cretan Sacred Caves: Archaeological Evidence* (Diss. Univ. of Missouri 1974). For the Idaean cave, see A. Vasilikis, "Μινωική κεραμεική από το Ιδαίον Άντρον," *Pepragmena* 1990 I, 125–30. Votives different from normal funerary offerings, i.e., belonging to a sanctuary, only begin in neopalatial

times. Protopalatial cave offerings are discussed by Tyree (supra) 64–70. According to the excavator of the Idaean Cave, the first archaeological signs that the cave had become a shrine begin in MM III (personal communication).

[299] Kültepe was burnt three times during the EB III period. T. Özgüç, "New Observations on the Relationship of Kültepe with Southeast Anatolia and North Syria during the Third Millennium," in J. Canby et al. eds., *Ancient Anatolia* (Madison 1986) 31–47.

[300] Mellink (infra n. 302).

[301] P. Matthiae, *Ebla* (Turin 1977) 107–13.

[302] Özgüç (supra n. 261) and K. Emre, "The Pottery of the Assyrian Colony Period according to the Building Levels of the Kaniş Karum," *Anatolia* 7 (1963) 87–99. M. Mellink, "Anatolian Chronology," in Ehrich 218. At Ugarit, for example, the "Plain Simple ware" of the nearby Amuq Plain and Ebla IIB2 is unknown. For a recent summary of Syria at this period, see G. Schwartz and H. Weiss, "Syria, ca. 10,000–2000 B.C.," in Ehrich I, 238–40.

at Kültepe and in Syro-Cilicia began a period of intense commerce in metals (silver, gold, and tin) and textiles. The MB I levels at these sites produce increased amounts of metal objects, imported pottery, and seals.

Relations between Egypt and Syria-Palestine follow the same pattern. With the fall of the Old Kingdom in Egypt, Egyptian trade with Syria-Palestine ceased until the Middle Kingdom. Egyptian objects are not found there in any number until the beginning of the 12th Dynasty when the expansion of trade began in Egypt and overseas. With the resumption of royal control over Egypt (and the royal monopoly on foreign trade) beginning in the 12th Dynasty (ca. 1963 B.C.), Egyptian objects begin to appear regularly at the coastal emporia of the Levant, at sites such as Byblos.[303] Additionally, Egyptian material in the Levant formerly dated to the First Intermediate period is now generally regarded as beginning in the late 11th Dynasty and only becomes abundant in the 12th Dynasty.[304] The mass of Egyptian and Egyptianizing objects at MB I–II Byblos includes miniature vases modeled on Egyptian funerary types (unguent jars). Many of these vases are similar to the Cretan examples.[305] This situation in Egypt and Syria-Palestine has important implications for Cretan foreign relations and particularly for the date of Egyptian and Egyp-

tianizing objects found on Crete. The date and distribution of Egyptian objects in the Near East make it likely that the many Egyptian and/or Egyptianizing objects from "EM–MM" contexts on Crete were part of the same trade pattern and date no earlier than the beginning of the 12th Dynasty, ca. 1963 B.C., that is, late MM IA.

Signs of Minoan trade increase dramatically in MM IA. Within Crete interregional imports and similarities in regional ceramic styles indicate intensive internal trade.[306] Within the Aegean MM IA pottery from Central and East Crete is exported in some quantity to Aegina and the Greek mainland.[307] One MM IA dagger and two other MM I–II examples from Platanos have been shown to be made from Kythnian ore.[308] The Mesara tholoi contain much evidence for foreign contact during this period. Tholos A at Agia Triada has one genuine Egyptian Old Kingdom stone vase and over a dozen Egyptianizing vases: carinated bowls, cylindrical jars, miniature amphoras, and alabastra.[309] Two of the Platanos gold beads are decorated with granulation, a Near Eastern technique that first appears at Byblos ca. 2000 B.C. and is introduced into Crete shortly thereafter.[310] Pini has identified a large group (87 examples) of MM IA seals probably made by one workshop located in the Lebena-Kaloi Limenes area of South Crete.[311] These seals are marked

[303] See Montet (supra n. 261). For the date of the 12th Dynasty see K. Kitchen, "Supplementary Notes on the Basics of Egyptian Chronology," in P. Åström ed., *High, Middle or Low?* Pt. 3 (*SIMA-PB* 80, Göteborg 1989) 152–62.

[304] J. Weinstein, "Egyptian Relations with Palestine in the Middle Kingdom," *BASOR* 217 (1975) 1–16. Warren dates Egyptian and Egyptianizing vases in Crete as early as their wide range of parallels in Egypt allows. He then assumes that they arrived in Crete immediately after this early date. This practice is unconvincing in the extreme. Thus he takes the Old Kingdom vase in EM II–MM II Tholos A at Agia Triada as a sign of EB II trade (*Chronology* 125–26). W. Ward, *Egypt and the East Mediterranean World 2200–1900 B.C.* (Beirut 1971) 91–104, has criticized Warren's use of Egyptian parallels. In addition, the many Old and Middle Kingdom objects in later Cretan contexts indicate that Warren's assumption that Egyptian objects must have been traded soon after manufacture is invalid. See, for example, L. Pomerance, "The Possible Role of Tomb Robbers and Viziers of the 18th Dynasty in Confusing Minoan Chronology," in *Pepragmena* 1981, 447–53. Ward's dating of Egyptian material in the Levant is generally regarded as too high (see J. Weinstein, "The Chronology of Palestine in the Early Second Millennium B.C.E.," *BASOR* 288 [1992] 36–37). Ward has revised his dates somewhat in "Scarab Typology and Archaeological Context," *AJA* 91 (1987) 509–12. He now dates the Montet jar, with its potpourri of Egyptian and Egyptianizing finds, to ca. 1950–1900 B.C. (= late MM IA).

[305] See M. Dunand, *Fouilles de Byblos* II (Paris 1950) pl. 203 and *VTM* pls. 53–54.

[306] *Chronology* 17–20 for examples. Note the Cycladicizing pyxis (Knossian?) from Koumasa, *VTM* pl. 18, upper. Stylistic links are collected in Zois (supra n. 179) and Walberg (supra n. 133).

[307] Rutter and Zerner (supra n. 107) 75–83. The first Minoan exports appear in Cyprus (H. Catling and V. Karageorghis, "Minoika in Cyprus," *BSA* 55 [1960] 109–10).

[308] Gale (supra n. 46) 314, fig. 6, nos. 9382, 9384, and 9392.

[309] Numbers are those in Banti (supra n. 98) 155–251. Carinated bowls (nos. 80, 87, 88, 90, 92): cf. Petrie (supra n. 257) pl. 23.386. Cylindrical jars (nos. 96, 98, 99, 103): cf. Petrie (supra n. 257) pl. 27.545 and Ward 1971 (supra n. 304) 105, fig. 19. Miniature amphoras (nos. 105, 106): cf. Ward 1971 (supra n. 304) 104–105. Alabastra (no. 108 and HM 373 in *MSV* 5): cf. Ward 1971 (supra n. 304) 104–105, fig. 19, no. 22 (12th Dynasty) and Petrie (supra n. 257) pl. 29.628 (12th Dynasty) and pl. 29.606–607 (12th Dynasty). The Old Kingdom parallels for the Cretan jars only indicate that material from the widely robbed Old Kingdom tombs was on the international market. The 12th Dynasty parallels provide a date for the Egyptian trade to Crete.

[310] Higgins (supra n. 137) 22–23; H. Maxwell-Hyslop, *Western Asiatic Jewellery* (London 1971) 36–37.

[311] Pini 1990 (supra n. 140) 115–27.

by their material ("glazed steatite") and their high proportion of Egyptian details.

Near Eastern features begin to appear in Cretan metalwork in this period. Several daggers from Cretan tombs are either Eastern imports or Minoan imitations of Eastern forms.[312] The Mochlos dagger, found in Tomb XI with MM IA pottery, has been called a Near Eastern type.[313] A second imported dagger, from the Trapeza Cave, may be as early.[314] Branigan pointed out that some of the Mesara daggers exhibit Syro-Cilician influence in their new shape and hafting details. A dagger from Koumasa, for example, has distinctive features found at Middle Bronze I Ugarit.[315] In MM IB–II Eastern imports and technological influence on Minoan metalworking become more substantial.[316]

The first ceramic exchanges between Crete and the Near East also begin in the MM IA period.[317] Minoan vases with close Eastern parallels appear at this time.[318] Miniature stone and clay vases imitating Egyptian funerary vessels flood the cemeteries. One of the hallmarks of MM IA deposits in the Mesara is the handmade squared-off conical cup with two rim bands. This shape is probably an imitation of the common Early Dynastic cylindrical jar.[319] MM IA cemeteries also produce larnakes, a container new to the Aegean. The tub and chest forms of larnakes are known in Old Kingdom Egypt.[320]

In the early second millennium B.C. Crete enters the vastly expanded network of international trade in the Near East.

MIDDLE MINOAN IB–II

Throughout Crete, MM IB ushers in a period of tremendous population expansion. The Minoan town at Knossos reached its greatest size by MM IB: houses are known to extend onto Gypsades Hill south of the palace, to the foot of the Acropolis to the west, and for over a quarter of a mile north of the palace.[321] The extent of MM IB Knossos has been estimated at ca. 75–112 ha.[322] In the Western Mesara, Bronze Age settlement reached its greatest density in MM IB. Settlement hierarchy is clearly defined. Phaistos was a state center measuring at least 0.90 × 1.0 km in size. Fragmentary protopalatial houses are known from Agia Photini, Chalara, the palace west court, from near the tourist pavilion, and the Church of Agios Georgios by the current parking lot.[323] Surrounding Phaistos were many village-sized settlements, around which were hamlets and farmsteads. Sites with specialized functions, e.g., ports (Kommos) and sanctuaries (Kophinas), appear. In the upland Plain of Lasithi, the number and size of settlements increase sharply.[324] The Chania survey recorded an increase from 31 to 94 settlements within its area.[325] A hierarchy of settlements develops, with many small sites growing up around larger centers. Rural farmsteads, sometimes called "villas" or "forts," agricultural terrace walls, and dams appear in MM II.[326] One can appreciate the proportions of this growth by comparing the size of Cretan settlements to other Aegean centers:

[312] See K. Branigan, "Byblite Daggers in Cyprus and Crete," *AJA* 70 (1966) 123–26. This should be read, however, with S. Dietz in "Aegean and Near-Eastern Metal Daggers in Early and Middle Bronze Age Greece," *ActaArch* 42 (1971) 1–22.

[313] Dietz (supra n. 312) 17 considers Mochlos XI.22 in fig. 45 an Eastern type and compares it with examples from Byblos.

[314] Dietz (supra n. 312) 20, who cites an EB IIIB parallel from Tarsus.

[315] K. Branigan, "Further Light on Prehistoric Relations between Crete and Byblos," *AJA* 71 (1967) 117–21.

[316] K. Branigan, "A Transitional Phase in Minoan Metallurgy," *BSA* 63 (1968) 185–203.

[317] E.g., an MM IA jar from Lapithos, Catling and Karageorghis, "Minoika in Cyprus," *BSA* 55 (1960) 109–10, fig. 2, and an EC III/MC I amphora imported to Knossos, H. Catling and J. MacGillivray, "An EC III Vase from the Palace at Knossos," *BSA* 78 (1983) 1–8.

[318] The number of generic similarities between Minoan and Eastern vases in this period is large. A selected list of close parallels follows: 1) the Mochlos teapot (*Mochlos* fig. 32, XIIIc) is a Near Eastern type, cf. H. Goldman, *Excavations at Gözlü Kule, Tarsus* II (Princeton 1956) fig. 273, no. 571; R. Amiran, *Pottery of the Ancient Holy Land* (Jerusalem

1969) pl. 22.7; 2) the carinated teapot (*Mochlos* figs. 49, no. 75, and 50, nos. 90 and 92) is an Anatolian type, cf. Lloyd and Mellaart (supra n. 201) 226, fig. P59, no. 29; 3) the carinated pedestaled bowl (*Mochlos* fig. 32, XX 1 and *PM* I fig. 122, no. 12) is a Syro-Cilician type, cf. Goldman (supra) fig. 287; 4) the East Cretan rounded cup is an Eastern shape: see Amiran (supra n. 205).

[319] MM IA conical cup, Fiandra (supra n. 236) pl. 21d and g; pl. 22d. Cf. Ward 1971 (supra n. 304) 99, fig. 16.2 and 4 and Petrie (supra n. 257) pl. 7.18 and 29.

[320] Pini (supra n. 244) 11, who believes the Cretan larnakes were derived from Egypt; see also B. Rutkowski, "The Origin of the Minoan Coffin," *BSA* 63 (1968) 219–28.

[321] Hood and Smyth (supra n. 11) 8.

[322] Hood and Smyth (supra n. 11) 10.

[323] Watrous et al. (supra n. 10) 225.

[324] Watrous (supra n. 10) 12.

[325] Moody (supra n. 10) 302–304.

[326] S. Marinatos excavated a lone house in the Mesara, whose earliest deposit was protopalatial, *ArchDelt* 9 (1924/1925) 57. A fort or farm complex in East Crete, containing domestic pottery and loomweights, and a nearby dam have been partly investigated and published, I. Tzedakis et al., "Les routes minoennes: Le poste de

Knossos, ca. 100 ha, Phaistos, ca. 90 ha, Phylakopi, 2 ha, and Agia Eirene, 1 ha.[327]

Recent studies have reevaluated Evans's reconstruction of the Old Palace at Knossos. There is scant architectural evidence, and thus the form of the Old Palace remains vague.[328] Aside from the koulouras, much of the evidence is indirect, that is, protopalatial deposits under the west and east wings of the palace. By MM II there is evidence for a sophisticated literate bureaucracy within the palace.[329] MacGillivray has also argued that the Old Palace at Knossos was originally constructed as a single unit including the west and east wings and central court[330] rather than as separate blocks, or "insulae," around the central court as envisioned by Evans.[331] While MM II deposits in the west and east wings of the palace area indicate the presence of structures there, the architectural plan is in fact unknown. The existence of the west facade of Evans's MM IB–II palace has been called into question.[332] The massively walled Keep dated by Evans to EM III was apparently constructed in MM IB possibly to store produce and/or to support a tower alongside the north entrance passage.[333] The Royal Road, traced for almost a kilometer to the west of the palace, was cut through the MM IA town. Almost certainly this creation of a centralized street system came at the same time as the construction of the first palace. Thus, a consensus of opinion presently exists that the Old Palace was built in late MM IA when the Royal Road was constructed and the tell at Knossos was leveled to form its foundation.[334] What little evidence there is suggests that it was the first palace to be built in Crete. The absence of protopalatial ash-

lar orthostates at Knossos, the masonry technique used at the first palaces at Phaistos and Mallia, may also be due to its early date of construction. The territory of the Knossos palace has recently been estimated to include the area between Gournes and Agia Pelagia on the north and the Pediada villages of Kastelli and Agia Varvara on the south (fig. 1).[335]

Poursat's excavation and ongoing publication of Quartier Mu have given us a clear example of wealthy business establishments of the MM II period.[336] Quartier Mu consists presently of two large houses, built in early MM II. Next door are five small workshop establishments: that of a seal engraver, a potter, and perhaps two or maybe three metalworkers. These establishments had a second-floor workshop and living quarters downstairs, each entered separately. The seal engraver's workshop yielded 150 seals, worked material of steatite and rock crystal, broken and unfinished seals, and tools.[337] A total of about 550 seals have been identified as belonging to this workshop, most of which are three-sided prisms of steatite.[338] A second workshop produced pottery, ceramic reliefs, different types of shells (including Tritons) as well as Agrimi horns used for funerary and perhaps other kinds of cult.[339] Molds for bronze tools come from other workshops.

Houses A and B are large (each with 30+ rooms on the ground floor) and have an elegant stuccoed section with vestibules, polythera, a light well, suites, a lustral basin, staircases leading to the second floor, and a magazine section. Nine tablets, 13 medallions, two inscribed cones, 16 noduli, and various types of sealings were found in Quartier Mu. Hieroglyphic

---

Χοιρόμανδρες et le contrôle des communications," *BCH* 114 (1990) 43–65. See also A. MacGillivray, "The Cretan Countryside in the Old Palace Period," in R. Hägg and N. Marinatos eds., *The Minoan Villa* (Stockholm, in press). MacGillivray's claim for a deserted MM I countryside is contradicted by recent survey data.

[327] M. Wiener, "The Isles of Crete? The Minoan Thalassocracy Revisited," in D. Hardy et al. eds., *Thera and the Aegean World* III.1: *Archaeology* (London 1990) 131; Hood and Smyth (supra n. 11) 8.

[328] G. Cadogan, "What Happened at the Old Palace of Knossos?" in *Function* 71 and J. MacGillivray, "The Early History of the Palace at Knossos," in Momigliano and Evely (supra n. 89).

[329] I. Pini, "The Hieroglyphic Deposit and the Temple Repositories at Knossos," in Palaima (supra n. 242) 33–60 and J. Weingarten, "Sealings and Sealed Documents at Bronze Age Knossos," in Momigliano and Evely (supra n. 89).

[330] MacGillivray (supra n. 328).

[331] *PM* I, 203–204.

[332] N. Momigliano, "The 'Proto-palatial Façade' at Knossos," *BSA* 87 (1992) 165–75.

[333] K. Branigan, "The Early Keep, Knossos: A Reappraisal," *BSA* 87 (1992) 153–63. The construction of much of the present palace cannot be dated any earlier than MM II. Pendlebury (supra n. 4) 129 dated the Keep, the present form of the West Magazines, the Koulouras and West Court (which he excavated), and the single East Wing to MM II.

[334] MacGillivray (supra n. 328) 70–72.

[335] G. Cadogan, "An Old Palace Period Knossos State?" in Momigliano and Evely (supra n. 89).

[336] See B. Detournay, J.-C. Poursat, and F. Vandenabeele, *Fouilles exécutées à Mallia: Le Quartier Mu* II (*EtCret* 26, Paris 1980) and Poursat's summary, "Ateliers et sanctuaires à Malia," in *Society* 273–76.

[337] *BCH* 102 (1978) Chronique 831–34; van Effenterre 551–61.

[338] Yule 212–13.

[339] *BCH* 105 (1981) Chronique 964–65.

inscriptions occur on tablets, pottery, medallions and cones, and on impressions stamped on noduli and sealings from the upper floor.[340] An archives complex, with a variety of document types (e.g., noduli related to the delivery of goods and cones for chests or doors), has been identified near the east entrance of House A. Tablets were used in storage areas to keep track of produce. Both the long two-sided rectangular tablets and the medallions were probably first drafts used in the storage rooms and workshops. Crescents may have been connected with goods brought into the storerooms. In addition, Houses A and B produced hundreds (350) of stone vases, bronze cauldrons, and a bowl, seals, moldmade ceramic reliefs (including a sphinx), several swords including one with a gold-covered handle, and five spearheads. A number of the finds, human and animal figurines as well as miniature and Chamaizi vases and offering tables, point to the existence of domestic shrines. The area above room IV 4 in House B was a storeroom for costly objects. In addition to domestic dwellings, the large houses had an administrative role, which involved production, storage, record-keeping, and redistribution. Glimpses of the wealth of these households appear in the finds and in the records: one tablet records the number 7,000 (sheep?). It appears that each family had a group of clients who worked for them (and were fed in return). International connections are apparent in the sealings (Anatolia), reliefs (Egypt and Anatolia), stone and faience beads (of Egyptian shape), a sword (Syria), and two stone anchors. The international mercantile character of Quartier Mu is reminiscent of the contemporary houses from the karum at Kültepe-Kanish.

The French excavators have uncovered much new evidence for the urban development of Mallia in the MM IB–II period.[341] Areas of the protopalatial town outside of the palace include the open court called the "Agora" and the large specialized building at its southwest corner ("Crypte Hypostyle"); Houses A and B (south of the palace), which together flanked a narrow entrance into the town protected by a tower; the Southwest Building; and houses in quarters Alpha, Beta, Gamma, Mu, and Thêta.[342] Because of its cache of stone funerary vases, the protopalatial Villa Alpha near the cemetery has been identified as a priest's house.[343] The paved road west of the palace was constructed in MM IA.[344] Beginning in the early 1980s a series of trial trenches sunk around and inside the Late Minoan palace at Mallia have uncovered walls and floors from lower levels, which because of their size and orientation have been interpreted as belonging to the first palace.[345] Sondages under the central court have found surfaces of packed whitish earth identified as belonging to the protopalatial central court. Along the south border of the central court a water channel of protopalatial date was found, perhaps defining the edge of the protopalatial court.[346] These trials have also established the MM II stratigraphy of the two great swords found in the palace at Mallia.[347] Pelon, the excavator, also claims to have discovered a foundation deposit in a cist containing an MM IA jug connected with the construction of the early palace.[348] The case for the existence of an early palace at Mallia seems convincing, but evidence for its plan and date of construction remains minimal. The discovery of a clay bar inscribed in hieroglyphic, in a protopalatial context in the town some distance west of the palace, should indicate that literacy at Mallia was not strictly limited to the palace and its appendages.[349]

[340] See J.-C. Poursat, L. Godart, and J.-P. Olivier, *Fouilles exécutées à Mallia: Le Quartier Mu* I: *Écriture hiéroglyphique crétoise* (*EtCret* 23, Paris 1978) and J.-C. Poursat, "Hieroglyphic Documents and Sealings from Mallia, Quartier Mu: A Functional Analysis," in Palaima (supra n. 242) 24–33. The economic holdings described on the tablets from Quartier Mu are separate from the administration of the first palace and do not necessarily tell us anything about the latter, pace T. Palaima, "Administration in Minoan and Mycenaean Society," in Palaima (supra n. 242) 93.

[341] J.-C. Poursat, "La ville minoenne de Malia: Recherches et publications récentes," RA 1988, 72–74, 77–80.

[342] Agora: H. and M. van Effenterre, *Fouilles exécutées à Mallia: Le centre politique* I: *L'agora (1960–1966)* (*EtCret* 17, Paris 1966). "Crypte Hypostyle": Amouretti (supra n. 174). Quartier Thêta: H. and M. van Effenterre, *Fouilles exécutées à Mallia: Maisons* IV: *Le Quartier Thêta* (*EtCret* 22, Paris 1976). Synthesis in van Effenterre 155–200 and for the First Palace, 201–28; discussion in J. MacEnroe, *Mino-*

an House and Town Arrangement (Diss. Univ. of Toronto 1979) 17–20, 182–89. For the tower at Mallia, see Y. Spence, "Was There a Guarded Southern Entrance Way to the First Palace at Mallia?" *BSA* 85 (1990) 369–74.

[343] van Effenterre 181–84.

[344] *BCH* 113 (1989) Chronique 770.

[345] Reports have appeared in the Chronique section of *BCH*: *BCH* 108 (1984) 881–87; 110 (1986) 814; 113 (1989) 711–77; 115 (1991) 726–35; 116 (1992) 1–36.

[346] O. Pelon, "Particularités et développement des palais minoens," in E. Levy ed., *Le système palatial en Orient, en Grèce et à Rome* (Leiden 1987) 187–201.

[347] O. Pelon, "L'épée à l'acrobate et la chronologie maliote II," *BCH* 107 (1983) 679–703.

[348] O. Pelon, "Un dépôt de fondation au palais de Malia," *BCH* 110 (1986) 9–16.

[349] S. Müller and J.-P. Olivier, "Prospection à Malia: Deux documents hiéroglyphiques," *BCH* 115 (1991) 65–70.

An ongoing survey of the urban extent of Mallia will eventually inform us about the size and development of the site.[350] Several studies on the size of the territory controlled by the first palace at Mallia have suggested that this area extends from Gournes in the west to Chamaizi in the east, and includes the upland Plain of Lasithi and the Mirabello/Isthmus of Ierapetra as far as Pyrgos in the south; it has also been defined by a common ceramic style called the "Mallia Town Group."[351] Poursat has posited a similar area of influence on the basis of Chamaizi juglets (whose workshop has been found at Mallia) and hoards of bronze tools.[352] These suggestions are convincing as areas of palatial commercial contact, but whether that can be translated into political terms is harder to determine. One notices too a lack of Cycladic imports at Mallia, unlike Knossos.[353] What is distinctive about protopalatial Mallia is its evidence for Eastern connections, particularly with Egypt. One wonders whether the two north coast palace states had not already developed separate economic spheres.

Levi's monumental publication of his excavations at Phaistos has provided the best documentation for the development of an Old Palace on Crete.[354] The architectural phasing of the Old Palace has been controversial, but the weight of opinion now favors three phases, roughly equivalent to Knossian MM IB, MM IIA, and MM IIB.[355] Levi reports that in its earliest phase the First Palace consisted only of three groups of rooms (LIX, LX, LXIV, LXI, LXIII, LXIV; LXIIIa–e; and LIII, LI, LIV, LV, LXII) with an ashlar orthostate facade and central entrance facing onto the (lower) paved west court (fig. 25). The southern block (partly covered today by the Second Palace) extended up to the area of the central court, but the nature of these rooms is unclear. Aside from its monumentality, the most distinctive palatial feature of the structure is its west facade built of massive ashlar orthostates, a masonry technique orig-

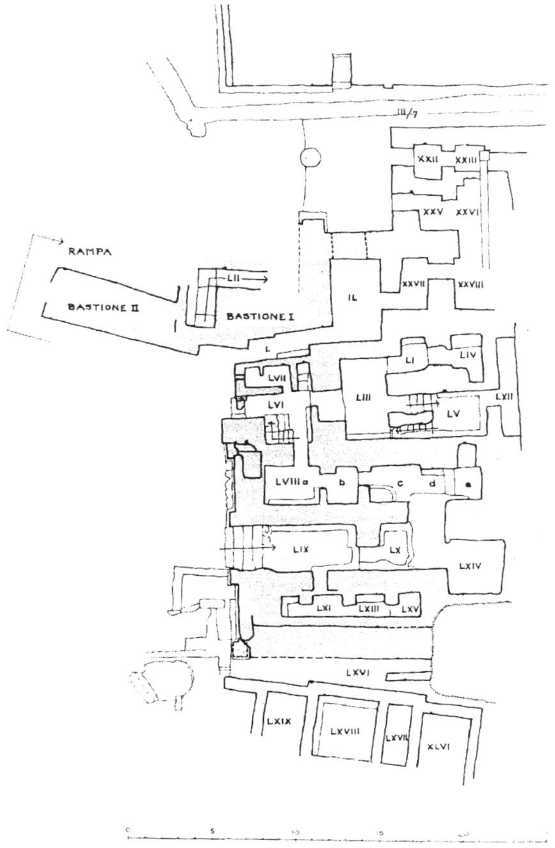

Fig. 25. Plan of Levi's excavation of the First Palace at Phaistos. (After D. Levi, *The Recent Excavations at Phaistos* [Lund 1961] fig. 2, courtesy Italian School of Archaeology at Athens)

inating in Syria.[356] During MM IB a paved ramp ran from the level of the lower west court to a second paved court to the north. According to Levi, at the beginning of MM II the palace was enlarged to include the northern block of magazines dug by Pernier and the corridor (III) leading eastward to

---

[350] See Müller 1992 (supra n. 10).

[351] G. Cadogan, "Lasithi in the Old Palace Period," *BICS* 37 (1990) 72–74. For the Mallia Town Group, see Andreou 134–63.

[352] J.-C. Poursat, "Town and Palace at Malia in the Protopalatial Period," in *Function* 75.

[353] van Effenterre 536–37 makes this point. He mentions, 436 n. 136, one possible MC I import. A second possible import is a "Cycladic idol" referred to in *BCH* 113 (1989) Chronique 771.

[354] *Festòs*. My account of Phaistos is based on Levi's first volume, which must be supplemented by E. Fiandra, "I periodi struttivi del primo palazzo di Festòs," *CretChron* 15/16 (1961/1962) 112–26 and *Festòs* II, esp. 299–307. On many essential points these primary sources do not agree.

I am grateful to V. La Rosa for discussing Levi's excavations at Phaistos with me. S. Damiani Indelicato, *Piazza pubblica e palazzo nella Creta minoica* (Rome 1982) 85–120 must be used with care.

[355] See the summary in *Chronology* 47–52.

[356] Watrous (supra n. 122) 69. The Syrian constructions, with orthostates, set on a protruding plinth, and with their upper surfaces drilled with dowel holes (for a wooden framework), are identical to examples at Mallia (and Chrysolakkos). The early and wide geographic distribution of this technique in the Near East leaves little doubt as to its eastern origin. See G. Hult, *Bronze Age Ashlar Masonry in the Eastern Mediterranean* (Göteborg 1983) 44–49, 66–67.

the area of the later central court. The tripartite west facade of the north block repeats that of the lower southern section. Later in MM II rooms were added to the northwest "shrine" and koulouras to the middle court. While the paved corridor between the north and south blocks of the First Palace might well be taken to imply the existence of a "central" court, the earliest architectural elements (i.e., colonnade and pavement) of the central court are dated, according to Levi, to MM III.[357] The fact that the central court shows no signs of construction between EM I and the time that the MM pavement was laid down could argue for its use as an open area already in MM IB.[358] Levi's reconstruction of the architectural development of the palace is not entirely convincing. The presence of two paved courts in MM IB and the deliberate symmetry of the west facades of the north and south blocks, which are laid along a single line at the east edge of these two courts, argue for their contemporaneity. In addition, there does not seem to be any appreciable chronological difference between the earliest pottery in the levels below the north and south blocks.[359]

The earliest artifacts from the First Palace, found in the MM II destruction level, help us to understand the palace's function. The north block contained storage magazines and complexes where food was prepared and served (rooms V–IX, XIX, XX), each opening directly onto the west court by a door. An alcove (with shelves?) of an archive room in the southeast portion of the storage wing yielded over 6,500 sealings. Protopalatial Linear A inscribed objects were found in room 25 (18 tablets, one sealing, and five roundels), room 51 (three sealings and five roundels), and between rooms LIII and LV (one tablet). A small MM II complex of six rooms, with benches, tables, two clay hearths, cult objects (Triton shell, stone offering tables), and areas for food preparation and storage, opened onto the west court, which contained an open-air hearth; the complex is generally called a shrine.[360] It is more accurate, however, to say simply that within this complex people were served food (accompanied by

rite or ceremony) at the palace's expense.[361] The southern block of the palace is organized into two areas: 1) the rooms (LIX, LX, LXIV) leading from the entrance (with annexes LXI, LXIII, and LXV for the storage of pottery and a potter's wheel) to the magazines (LVIIIa–e); and 2) the complex of residential rooms and workrooms (LI, LIII, LIV, LV, LXII). The benches and hearth in the first area as well as the many pitchers and cups and the nine pithoi (one with the remains of grapes) indicate that wine and perhaps food was dispensed here. The second area included signs of residence: a possible bedroom dais in LIV, a cosmetic palette, loomweights, a hearth with animal bones, and possible signs of manufacturing and domestic activities, viz., a mortar, grindstone, whetstones, stone vases, inlays, lamps, stone and bronze tools, and a potter's wheel. This second area is connected by a staircase (and the presence of sealings) to the upper floor. Thus it is likely that the workshops were actually upstairs, as in Quartier Mu at Mallia.[362] The upper floors (Levi's phase II) gave evidence of a wider variety of activities, viz., food preparation, weaving of textiles (many loomweights), bronzeworking (lost-wax mold of a human hand),[363] a small shrine(?) (LI), and sealings from an administrative system. Sealings from the upper floor have been found in rooms LI, LXIV, LV, and in rooms 10 and 11 to the northeast. The main group of sealings along with inscribed tablets, bars, and roundels was found in room 25 in the north storage block. The inscriptions are written in an early form of Linear A and mention men, vases, wine, grain, and figs.[364] The preserved inscriptions all record relatively small amounts of agricultural goods.

There has been much progress in understanding protopalatial administration at Phaistos and elsewhere. Fiandra's early studies made two main contributions: they showed how the sealings were used and how the administrative system worked. She documented that the clay sealings at Phaistos were used mainly to seal the wooden pommels or knobs of boxes and doors as well as jars and basketry. The

---

[357] See *Festòs* I, 262–81 and note the spacing of the column bases of the colonnade vis-à-vis corridor III. Pernier (supra n. 29) 353–75 dated a group of rooms (XL–XLIII) northeast of the palace to the protopalatial period because they rested on a "probable MM I" level. The pottery illustrated is MM III, however.

[358] See Vagnetti (supra n. 27) 12–13, and fig. 2a.

[359] *Pace* Fiandra (supra n. 354) 116–17 with pls. ΚΣΤ′ nos. 1–3 and ΙΘ′, Κ′ nos. 1–2. On present evidence the pottery below the north and south blocks appears to be a mixture of MM IA and MM IB.

[360] G. Gesell, *Town, Palace, and House Cult in Minoan Crete*

(Göteborg 1985) 11, 120–24.

[361] Muhly (supra n. 150) 270 minimizes (rightly, in my opinion) the religious character of the complex.

[362] Identified by K. Branigan, "Craft Specialization in Minoan Crete," in *Society* 26.

[363] C. Laviosa, "Una forma minoica per fusione a cera perduta," *ASAtene* 29/30 (1967/1968) 499–510. Laviosa lists some of the Near Eastern and Egyptian antecedents for this type of statue mold.

[364] *GORILA* 1 (Paris 1976) 286–319; 2 (Paris 1979) 89–96.

sealed objects were constantly being opened and resealed; broken sealings were stored in room 25 as records of transactions.[365] By comparing the Phaistos sealing system to identical examples throughout the Near East (where written documents explain the bureaucratic system that the sealings were a part of), Fiandra hypothesized that the Phaistos sealings were made by officials who oversaw the redistribution of palace stores to guard against theft. The sealings were kept so that if necessary they could be checked against written orders for the redistributions. This sealing system is relatively simple in comparison with that of the neopalatial system. It is generally accepted that this sealing system derived from the East.[366] Weingarten's recent review of Minoan sealing administration emphasizes the lack of earlier precedents for this MM II sealing practice and sees it as an importation to the island at the time of the first palaces.[367] Within the protopalatial period the Minoans introduce two new practices to their system: crescent-shaped sealings meant to hang by a cord and flat-based nodules pressed directly on leather strips that may have been written documents. The MM II administration at Phaistos used Linear A, while those at Knossos and Mallia used cursive hieroglyphic script, as well as hieroglyphic engraved seals and sealings stamped with two or more different seals.[368] Hieroglyphic seals are interpreted as belonging to high officials as opposed to the lower status of "non-literate" seal owners.[369] It is the complete absence of this distinction between types of seals and any complex sealing practice in

EM II–III Crete that makes it difficult to believe in any developed social ranking in Crete before late MM IA. The transactions recorded in the Hieroglyphic Deposit from the Palace at Knossos differ from those at Phaistos because the seals used on the sealings rarely repeat: thus, they do not directly reflect palatial storeroom accounting (where certain seals, presumably those of palace officials, predominate). Weingarten has noted antecedents for the multiple stamping system (as well as for the motifs of the Phaistos seals) at MB II (ca. 1750 B.C.) Karahöyük in Anatolia.[370]

New archaeological evidence from Phaistos and Mallia and the flurry of studies on aspects of the Old Palaces bear directly on one of the most discussed questions in Aegean archaeology, namely, the process whereby palatial or state society was first developed on Crete in MM I.[371] The architectural development of the Minoan centers is clearly a central aspect of this process. At present three reconstructions have been suggested.[372] The first sees an early stage of urban construction over which the first palaces were superimposed. Van Effenterre hypothesized that at Mallia the "Agora" and its street system as well as the "Crypte Hypostyle" comprised the political center of the settlement before the first palace. They thus represent a "democratic" stage of political development at Mallia before the superimposition of palatial control.[373] The pottery associated with the hypothetical first palace and the "Agora" and "Crypte Hypostyle," however, does not allow any chronological distinction. Moreover, there is no

[365] E. Fiandra, "A che cosa servivano le cretule di Festòs," in Πεπραγμένα (supra n. 179) 383–97 and Fiandra, "Ancora a proposito delle cretule di Festòs," BdA 60 (1975) 1–25.

[366] The similarity of the MM II system to Egyptian practice even extends to the flaring pommels and their containers—see Fiandra, in Πεπραγμένα (supra n. 365) 386–94 and pls. ΡΛΖ′–ΡΝΔ′ and Fiandra 1975 (supra n. 365) 10–17. J. Weingarten, "The Sealing Structures of Minoan Crete: MM II Phaistos to the Destruction of the Palace of Knossos," OJA 5 (1986) 280 gives additional Eastern parallels for the Phaistos pommels and suggests that the wooden containers may have been imported from the East to Crete.

[367] J. Weingarten, "Three Upheavals in Minoan Sealing Administration: Evidence for Radical Change," in Palaima (supra n. 242) 105. See also the remarks following Pini's suggestion (supra n. 329) that prepalatial seals were used as part of an administrative system, 55–60.

[368] Detournay et al. (supra n. 336) 157–229. Weingarten (supra n. 329) 7–11 notes two possible exceptions to this difference in scribal tradition between North and South Crete in MM II.

[369] Poursat interprets hieroglyphic seals used with a "non-literate" seal on sealings as the countermark of the

supervising official. J.-C. Poursat, "Fonction et usage des sceaux en Crète à l'époque des premiers palais," in W. Müller ed., Fragen und Probleme der bronzezeitlichen ägäischen Glyptik (Berlin 1989) 222.

[370] J. Weingarten, "The Multiple Sealing System of Minoan Crete and Its Possible Antecedents in Anatolia," OJA 11 (1992) 25–37, esp. 33 and n. 11; Weingarten, "The Sealing Structure of Karahöyük and Some Administrative Links with Phaistos on Crete," OA 29 (1991) 1–33; and J. Aruz, "Crete and Anatolia in the Middle Bronze Age: Sealings from Phaistos and Karahöyük," in M. Mellink, E. Porada, and T. Özgüç eds., Aspects of Art and Iconography: Anatolia and Its Neighbors (Ankara 1993) 36–51.

[371] For reasons of time and space, this complex question cannot be fully addressed here, but will be considered in detail in V. Watrous and D. Hadzi-Vallianou, The Plain of Phaistos, in preparation.

[372] For the earlier idea that the palaces can be explained exclusively as an outgrowth of Early Minoan society, see supra.

[373] van Effenterre 33–41, 155–74 for his "archaeopalatial" period at Mallia, and H. and M. van Effenterre (supra n. 342) 142–44 for the prepalatial role of the "Agora" and the "Crypte Hypostyle." Damiani Indelicato (supra n. 354) esp. 123–39.

Fig. 26. View of the MM I–II settlement of Monasteraki, south sector. (Courtesy A. Kanta)

evidence for the political functions adduced by van Effenterre for the "Agora" and the first palace.[374]

The second view stresses the evolutionary form of the first palaces worked out during MM IB–II.[375] This seems true for certain aspects of the palaces. The MM IB storage facilities at Knossos and Phaistos are augmented in MM II by the addition of koulouras in the West Court and a magazine for pithoi in the east wing at Knossos. Similarly, the administrative system of the palaces undergoes development.[376] If it could be proved that the palaces controlled the fine Kamares ware workshops whose products are exported overseas beginning in MM II, then that could be seen as an evolved feature of the later first palaces.

The third view does not necessarily exclude the second. It simply emphasizes that all of the basic characteristics of the palaces are apparent from the very beginning of their construction. Thus, at Phaistos it seems probable that the First Palace built in MM IB consisted of the southern block (residences and workshops), the north block (storage magazines), two west courts, perhaps one kouloura, and a central court.[377] Both architectural and later administrative evidence indicates that this complex at Phaistos should be regarded as a "palace," that is, as the residence of a powerful authority, assisted by a literate bureaucracy, which controls a system of redistribution. Architecturally the Phaistos building differs in distinctive ways from earlier Minoan techniques: in its monumentality, ashlar orthostates and

timber-braced superstructure, cut limestone blocks, frescoed floors and walls, and its facade. These features, which cannot be derived from earlier Minoan practice, are employed to differentiate the building from the more traditional residential structures of the Phaistos community. While no sealings or tablets have been found in MM IB contexts at Phaistos, the developed nature of the MM II administrative system and the continuity of function apparent within the rooms of the MM II palace leave little doubt that the MM IB building served a similar purpose.[378] What seems to distinguish the MM IB palace at Phaistos is its architectural pretension, its storage block, and its inclusion of the west courts as part of its plan (and function).

Ongoing excavations at Monasteraki promise to document a provincial town of protopalatial date. The settlement of Monasteraki sits on the top and slopes of Charakas, a steep, flat-topped hill overlooking the widest part of the Amari Valley. Part of Monasteraki's importance must have derived from its location on a natural route between the Mesara and the coastal plain of Rethymnon. The ceramic finds at Monasteraki resemble the pottery at Phaistos. The settlement was founded in MM I and passed through two or possibly three architectural phases. It was apparently abandoned—no skeletal material and virtually no metal has been found on the site—before being destroyed by fire in MM II. The site was not reinhabited until Hellenistic times, which greatly increases the potential value of the

[374] See J. MacEnroe's review of Damiani Indelicato (supra n. 354) in *AJA* 88 (1984) 75.

[375] K. Branigan, "A Dynamic View of the Early Palaces," in *Pepragmena* 1990, 147–59.

[376] MacGillivray (supra n. 328).

[377] S. Damiani Indelicato, "A New Kouloura at Phaistos," *AJA* 88 (1984) 229–30.

[378] For the already evolved nature of the MM II sealing system, see Weingarten (supra n. 366) 281.

Fig. 27. Building west of open area at Monasteraki. (Courtesy A. Kanta)

information to be gained from excavation. During the protopalatial period the settlement was extremely large, measuring perhaps 20 ha in area. In MM I–II it must have been the main settlement in the Amari Valley. The recent excavations, directed by A. Kanta, have focused on three areas on the hilltop. The first area (fig. 26), on the south slope of the hilltop, has revealed a number of small rooms (probably part of a house or, at any rate, a larger structure), one of which produced ca. 150 clay sealings, the context of which is still unclear. Immediately south of these rooms was a possible ramp and a retaining wall along the south side of which was a fill with many MM IB–II conical cups. In this area was found a protopalatial clay two-storied house model.[379] While this model is different in plan from the MM III Archanes house model, it clearly is an earlier example in the same tradition. The context of the sealings is as yet unclear.

The second area is immediately to the north on the flat saddle at the summit of the hill. Excavations there have shown that the limestone bedrock was trimmed and a level of earth packing was laid down to form a flat open area, which may have been a court. The north edge of the "court" was supported by a cyclopean retaining wall (fig. 26) and on the

terrace below (north) there was a line of storage magazines containing pithoi that had been partly dug by German excavators during World War II.[380] The south side of the "court" is formed by a massive cyclopean terrace wall. At the west end of the "court" sits a (domestic?) building built of immense limestone blocks. Its interior rooms are fitted with large threshold blocks, a round cut-limestone column base, and a doorway with L-shaped doorjambs of (non-local) sandstone (fig. 27). The house faces onto a flagstone court to the west.

The third area under investigation is on the southeast corner of the summit, which is separated from the north by a rock outcropping. Current excavation there is revealing part of a large building, apparently a single structure, of more than 60 rooms (fig. 28). This two-story structure was built of rubble and wooden beams with a second story of mudbrick. Most of the rooms are quite small (a few are long and rectangular); all seem to have been basement storerooms. No certain exterior entrance has yet been found. The 1993 excavations revealed rooms on the north, with pithoi and masses of carbonized material and a few vases at an upper level that were from the second floor. Some 700 clay sealings, most of them fallen from the upper floor, have

[379] The house model is illustrated in L. Godart and I. Tzedakis, *Témoignages archéologiques et épigraphiques en Crète occidentale du Néolithique au Minoen récent IIIB* (Rome 1992) pl. 87, I.

[380] E. Kirsten and K. Grundmann, "Die Grabung der Charakeshohe bei Monasteraki, I, II," in F. Matz ed., *Forschungen auf Kreta* (Berlin 1951) 27–71.

Fig. 28. Building in southeast sector at Monasteraki. (Courtesy A. Kanta)

been found in the building. For the most part, finds from the upper floor have been relatively scarce and it is uncertain how much of the structure had an upper story. Two deposits found within the building, the skeleton of an animal with conical cups set next to it and a cache of miniature vases, may represent cult activity. The character of this southern structure remains uncertain (domestic or official?), although its sprawling, diffuse plan vaguely resembles the plan of MM I house structures at Mallia.[381]

Ultimately the chief importance of Monasteraki may be the more than 900 clay sealings from the site, which promise to shed much light on the nature of MM II administration. These clay bullae preserve clear imprints on their undersides of the containers, apparently of wood and basketry, that they sealed (fig. 29).[382] The face of each sealing is stamped several times with different seals. The administrative system for storage at Monasteraki seems to closely resemble that at Phaistos (including the presence of door and knob sealings). Likewise, many of the Monasteraki seal motifs are also found

at Phaistos. Although no inscribed tablets or roundels have yet been recovered, one loomweight inscribed with a Linear A sign indicates the existence of literacy at Monasteraki. At present Monasteraki gives the impression that it was controlled by a central administration, housed perhaps in the building north of the "court." The Monasteraki "court" resembles that at Gournia in shape and topographical siting.

Cemeteries of the MM IA period continue to be used into the protopalatial period. Publication of MM I–II pottery deposits and ceramic studies have helped to make this clear.[383] Many "MM IA" deposits actually consist of MM IA and MM IB and even MM II style vases. The composition of these widespread deposits tells us that the late MM IA–MM IB/II period should be considered a single cultural continuum. At Mallia the tomb at Chrysolakkos was thoroughly reconstructed in MM IB.[384] The tomb was given a monumental limestone facade in ashlar orthostates with a paved terrace around it. A room with an elaborate stuccoed platform may have

---

[381] See van Effenterre 157, fig. 223 (houses south of the palace) and 183, fig. 254 (Villa A).

[382] Only a few of the sealings have been published: from the old excavations, Kirsten and Grundmann (supra n. 380) pl. 38.1 and 3; from the new excavations, *BCH* 111 (1987) 578, figs. 99–102 and Godart and Tzedakis (supra n. 379) pls. 77–86. A. Tsigkanaki is undertaking the publication of these seals.

[383] A list of deposits appears in *Chronology* 51, to which Archanes Tholos C, Buildings 6 and 13, Knossos West Court Houses and Vat Room Deposit, and the "House of the Dead" at Mallia should be added. Middle Minoan ceramic studies, G. Walberg, *Kamares: A Study of the Character of Palatial Middle Minoan Pottery* (Uppsala 1976) and Walberg (supra n. 133) with bibliography.

[384] Soles 166–71.

Fig. 29. Sealing from Monasteraki. (After A. Kanta, *BCH* 111 [1987] 578, figs. 99–100)

served as a shrine. Even though it was robbed, the tomb of Chrysolakkos produced figurines, stone vases, seals, bone/ivory inlays, a bronze vase and weapons, gold diadems, appliqués and pendants (including the famous bee pendant), an indication of its rich contents.[385] This tomb certainly contrasts sharply with contemporary burials around it, in the Second Charnier and the Pierres Meulières, which contained only a few pots, stone vases, lamps, and personal possessions. At Gournia four house tombs had MM IB–II burials. In Tomb I were two clay kantharos imitations, the famous silver kantharos, clay vessels, seven stone vases, tweezers, two seals, a necklace of silver beads, a gold-plated bead, and ivory inlays (from a box?). Tomb II contained MM IA–IB/II ware, conical cups, seven stone vases, three bronze tweezers, and a zoomorphic amulet. Outside the tomb a conical cup was found next to a kernos. Poorly published Tombs VII and VIII held cookpots, three bronze knives, and a fragment of gold.[386] Along the shore (at Sphoungaras), MM IA–II burials consisted of larnakes and pithoi next to which were found jugs, cups, and bowls.[387] At Knossos the earliest of the chamber tombs at Mavrospelio date

to MM II.[388] In Tomb XVII pithos burials were redeposited in a pit with MM II pottery, beads of amethyst (of 12th Dynasty type), steatite, faience and crystal, seals, a stone jug, and a lump of meteoritic iron.

The Mesara tholoi continue to be used well into the protopalatial period. The Kamilari tholos tomb is particularly useful for protopalatial burial customs since it was only constructed at the beginning of the protopalatial period. During the MM IB–II period, offerings at Kamilari included bridge-spouted jars, miniature juglets and pithoi, cups, jugs, teapots, stone vases, seals, conical cups, and a few pieces of jewelry.[389] Most of the (published) material from the tholos tombs at Agia Triada dates to the protopalatial period. This includes masses of pottery, especially from the annexes, stone vases, including the Old Kingdom imported pyxis,[390] bronze weapons,[391] jewelry (beads of rock crystal, carnelian, faience; pendants of gold and ivory/bone), and 21 of the seals.[392] Tholoi A and B at Platanos continue at least into MM II. These tombs contained MM IB–II pottery,[393] many stone vases,[394] over 30 bronze daggers,[395] a short sword and two

[385] Demargne (supra n. 250) pls. 61–68. For a discussion of the date of the pendant, see G. de Pierpont, "Réflexions sur la destination des édifices de Chrysolakkos," in R. Laffineur ed., *Thanatos: Les coutumes funéraires en Égée à l'âge du bronze* (Aegaeum 1, Liège 1987) 84–85.

[386] Soles 3–28, 39–40.

[387] E. Hall, *Excavations in Eastern Crete: Sphoungaras* (Philadelphia 1912) 55–60. Soles 51 is right to point to the difference in wealth between these two groups of protopalatial tombs. The distinction between the tombs does not hold completely, for House Tombs VII and VIII held simple larnax burials like those at Sphoungaras.

[388] E. Forsdyke, "The Mavrospelio Cemetery at Knossos," *BSA* 28 (1926/1927) 243–96.

[389] Levi (supra n. 232) 7–148; *Festòs* I, 703–43.

[390] Pace *Chronology* 125. Stone vases, Banti (supra n. 98) nos. 79, 87, 92, 96, 98–108.

[391] Branigan 160–61: 279, 314, 316, and a short sword, *BSA* 63 (1968) 203 no. 25.

[392] MM IB–II seals from Tholos A at Agia Triada: *CMS*

I.2, 9, 29, 44, 58, 70, 72, 78, 80, 81, 83, 85, 86, 90, 94, 96–101, and 103.

[393] Some 25 examples are published in *VTM*, e.g., pl. 9.

[394] Banti (supra n. 98), e.g., bridge-spouted jars, bowls, bird's nest bowls, cups. There are over a dozen Egyptianizing shapes: alabastra, nos. 108 (cf. Ward 1971 [supra n. 304] 104–105, fig. 19, no. 22) and HM 373 (cf. *MSV* 5 [HM 373] and Petrie [supra n. 257] pl. 29.606–607); bowls, nos. 87, 88, 90, 92 (cf. Petrie [supra n. 257] pl. 23.385–86); cylindrical jars, nos. 96, 98–100, 102, 104 (cf. Ward 1971 [supra n. 304] 97–104 and Petrie [supra n. 257] pls. 2.22, 5.161–62, 173); miniature amphoras, nos. 105–106 (see *MSV* 71–72).

[395] Branigan 10–12, types V, VI, and IX, which span MM IA–II and types X and XIV, which are MM IB–II: 159–61, nos. 230–53, 274–76, 280–82, 287–90, 309, 313, and the tin bronze HM 1934 in K. Branigan, "The Mesara Tholoi and Middle Minoan Chronology," *SMEA* 5 (1968) 20–23. See also Branigan (supra n. 312).

Fig. 30. Clay sistrum from Building 9, Phourni cemetery (Archanes). (After I. and E. Sakellarakis, *Archanes* [Athens 1991] 121, fig. 99)

double axes,[396] 30 seals,[397] an Old Babylonian cylinder seal,[398] three Egyptian scarabs,[399] and several amulets.[400] Gold jewelry of late MM IA–II date includes three gold diadems,[401] 22 gold beads,[402] and gold discs, rings, and pendants.[403] The Koumasa tombs had MM IB–II clay and stone vases, animal and human figurines, seals, at least seven bronze

long daggers,[404] stone palettes, a gold diadem, and jewelry including a gold bead in the form of a lion, its mane rendered in granulation.[405]

The cemetery at Phourni in Archanes continued in use in MM IB–II. Three rooms (Building 9) built over Building 13 produced larnax and pithos burials, in addition to a clay sistrum (fig. 30), bull figurines and a rhyton, along with MM IB vases.[406] North of Tholos Γ two rooms (8), built over an earlier structure (Building 29), contained more protopalatial burials.[407] South of Tholos Γ, Building 18, constructed over traces of an earlier structure (Building 24), held burials of the MM IB–II period.[408] North of Tholos Γ the large Building 5 was constructed over an older structure (Building 25).[409] Buildings 5, 6, 8, 9, 13, 16, 18, and 19 contained substantial protopalatial deposits (fig. 31). Materials characteristic of MM IA burials, including seals of ivory/bone and steatite, obsidian blades, gold bands, pendants and bosses, necklaces with beads of bone, crystal, steatite, faience, seashells, silver rings, and stone vases, continued to be found in these protopalatial levels. Distinctive of the protopalatial deposits are the large number and types of clay vases offered as well as the presence of clay figurines (human and animal) and bull rhyta similar to those found on contemporary peak sanctuaries. Individual burials were often marked by a single cup or jug, and perhaps animal bones (including bird and fish), an obsidian blade, pebbles, and seashells. A single burial of a child in a jar with a silver ring, a cup, and three sacrificed animals might be interpreted as a case of inherited wealth.[410] Unique finds include a clay sistrum and a lapis lazuli cylinder seal.[411] Relative to the large number of deceased in these upper levels, the burials appear markedly poorer in possessions than in MM IA, a change most easily seen

[396] Branigan 164, nos. 481, 521, and 522.

[397] MM IB–II seals from Platanos: *CMS* I.2, 241, 242, 247, 255, 260, 261, 269, 270, 275, 277, 279, 281, 282, 284, 285, 289, 293, 298, 301–303, 306, 307, 324, 328, 330, 332, 337, 349.

[398] V. Kenna, "Ancient Crete and the Use of the Cylinder Seal," *AJA* 72 (1968) 322–24.

[399] W. Ward, "The Scarabs from Tholos B at Platanos," *AJA* 85 (1981) 70–73 and Ward 1987 (supra n. 304) 507–32.

[400] *VTM* pl. 15, nos. 1026, 1145–47, and 1252.

[401] *VTM* pl. 57, nos. 481–83. See Higgins (supra n. 137) 58.

[402] *VTM* pl. 57, upper two rows.

[403] *VTM* pl. 57; nos. 487 (fly) and 489 (claw) are imitations of 12th-Dynasty Egyptian types of jewelry, cf. Bourriau (supra n. 277) 141 and 149.

[404] Branigan 160–61, types 10–11, 13–14.

[405] *VTM* pls. 3–5, 19–24, 26, 29–32.

[406] *Prakt* 1971, 281; 1972, 351–52; 1973, 181–86. Sistrum, Sakellarakis and Sapouna-Sakellaraki (supra n. 234) 121, fig. 99; bull figurine and rhyton, *Prakt* 1972, pl. 277.

[407] Room 8, *Prakt* 1971, 281–82; 1973, 177–81; 1982, 495–99.

[408] *Prakt* 1976, 344–51. The juglet (*Prakt* 1976, 350, fig. 3) from the lower level of Building 18 dates to the MM IB–II period, cf. Zois (supra n. 236) pl. 17, MM IB; *Festòs* I, pl. 196a–c, e and g, MM II.

[409] *Prakt* 1967, 159–61; 1971, 281; 1972, 319–27.

[410] *Prakt* 1976, 359–60.

[411] Cylinder seal, *Prakt* 1967, pl. 152. Building 5 is dated to the MM IA period by the excavators, but its pottery indicates it continued into a later date. The low conical cup (*Prakt* 1972, pl. 270a) is MM II–III (Fiandra [supra n. 236] pl. 31a–g). The small amphora is of the same date (Levi [supra n. 232] 55, fig. 59a). The basket-shaped kalathos (pl. 275a) is a protopalatial shape (*Festòs* I, pl. 117d).

Fig. 31. Pottery from Building 6, Phourni cemetery (Archanes). (After I. and E. Sakellarakis, *Archanes* [Athens 1991] 101, fig. 24)

in the jewelry. Signs of overseas contacts reach a peak in this period: obsidian, probably sard, gold, silver, lead, and bronze from the Aegean; ivory and lapis from the Near East; and possibly ivory, gold, and faience from Egypt.

Recent studies have shown that the widespread and intense trade connections usually associated with LM I Crete had already begun in the protopalatial period. Relatively little is known about Middle Bronze I–II levels in the Aegean islands, but Minoan pottery and other objects have been found at a number of sites. While MM IA is presently unknown at Phylakopi, MM IB–II vases (and local imitations) are found in the City Iii level.[412] Papaiannopoulou's recent study[413] of the saved Minoan pottery from Phylakopi records two Barbotine vases, over three dozen MM II–IIIA cups, and a few jugs or amphoras and hole-mouthed jars as well as a figurine. Palatial-quality vases, with parallels at Knossos and Phaistos, predominate (as a result of

sorting?). Three possible East Cretan cups are mentioned. Minoan imports appear on Kea (period IV) in small quantities at the beginning of the Middle Bronze Age and they increase rapidly until the end of the period when their numbers are said to be "immense." Kamares ware from palatial workshops occurs.[414] The few soundings made under LM I levels at Akrotiri on Thera have also produced MM II pottery, mostly fine Kamares cups as well as one or two East Cretan examples.[415] On Samos an MM IA type goblet and MM II–III pottery have been found.[416] At Knidos painted Minoan pottery and cooking pots are said to begin in MM I.[417] On Rhodes MM II pottery, stone vases, a spindle whorl, and a loomweight have been found on the acropolis at Ialysos. The high proportion of Minoan-type artifacts (12 out of 13) in the floor deposit at Ialysos led Benzi to call the finds evidence for a Minoan settlement.[418] The Minoan town site of Trianda on Rhodes is said to be founded in MM III, but the

[412] R. Barber, "The Status of Phylakopi in Creto-Cycladic Relations," in *Thalassocracy* 179–81.

[413] A. Papaiannopoulou, *The Influence of Middle Minoan Pottery on the Cyclades* (Göteborg 1991) 84–116.

[414] J. Caskey, "Investigations in Keos," *Hesperia* 41 (1972) 376, fig. 8, nos. D8–10, 382 and pl. 83. The pottery of period IV is now published in J. Overbeck, *Keos VII: Ayia Irini, Period IV* (Mainz 1989); see 11 for a summary.

[415] S. Marinatos, *Thera* VI (Athens 1974) 31 and pl. 67b. See the more recent catalogue in Papaiannopoulou (supra n. 413) 51–53.

[416] The MM I eggcup reported in J. Davis, "The Earliest Minoans in the South East Aegean: A Reconsideration of the Evidence," *AnatSt* 32 (1982) 32, fig. 2 has a mono-

chrome interior and is Momigliano's type 3 (supra n. 185) 246, fig. 30. It is from north-central Crete and, on present evidence, should date to MM IA. For other Minoan finds, see W.-D. Niemeier, "The End of the Minoan Thalassocracy," *Thalassocracy* 206–207.

[417] Reported in M. Mellink, "Archaeology in Asia Minor," *AJA* 82 (1978) 321.

[418] M. Benzi, "Evidence for a Middle Minoan Settlement on the Akropolis at Ialysos (Mt. Philerimos)," *Thalassocracy* 93–105. For the Profitis Elias site, see T. Marketou, "New Evidence on the Topography and Site History of Prehistoric Ialysos," in S. Dietz ed., *Archaeology in the Dodecanese* (Copenhagen 1988) 27–28. Marketou identifies the pottery as local.

published pottery, a Patrikies-type teapot and carinated cups, looks like material from MM IA–II.[419]
Minoan pottery of the Old Palace period is known
from Mikre Vigla on Naxos.[420] Protopalatial pottery
has been found on Kasos and Karpathos.[421] A Minoan settlement, with Minoan artifacts, burials, and
a peak sanctuary, was established at Kastri on
Kythera by MM IA and continued until LM IB.[422]
The Italian excavations at Iasos report Kamares
ware, pithoi, conical cups, lamps, and loomweights
in a large building.[423] MM II pottery has also been
reported at Miletos.[424]

Beginning in MB I, Minoan pottery was for the
first time traded to the Greek mainland.[425] Sites receiving Minoan pottery include Kolonna on Aegina,
Asine, Athens, Argos, Agios Stephanos in Laconia,
Eutresis, Lerna, Mycenae, and Iolkos and Pefkakia
in Thessaly. On Aegina, Hiller reports that the earliest Minoan imports are MM IA eggcups, followed
by some 30 MM II vases, most of which are Kamares
ware cups.[426] At Lerna the amount of imported Minoan pottery as well as Minoanizing imitations is
said to be in excess of 200 vases.[427] Minoan imports
at Lerna consist of Barbotine fine ware and larger
storage containers. The Minoan route using the
"Western String" of islands ending in Lavrion seems
to have been motivated by the Minoan desire to
acquire copper, silver, and lead.[428] Thus it appears

that the route defined by Davis for LB I already
existed in MM II. Papaiannopoulou's study indicates that MM I–II pottery in the Cyclades was
mainly fine ware exported for its own sake; by MM
III, Minoan ceramic exports were commonly larger
vases traded as containers.[429] She also stresses how
beneficial the trade in Minoan ceramics and metals
must have been to the Cycladic middlemen.[430]

A wide range of foreign imports first appears in
Crete in the protopalatial period. Cypriot pottery in
MM IB contexts has been found at Kommos.[431] Copper objects analyzed from the Mesara tombs are
consistent with a Cypriot source.[432] Substantial
amounts of tin first appear in Minoan objects of
protopalatial date,[433] signaling commercial ties with
the East (Syria?). On the other hand, Middle Helladic pottery on Crete is conspicuously rare.[434] The
famous silver kantharos from Gournia is a sign of
Cretan trade, probably for metals with Anatolian
Cappadocia.[435] Egyptian scarabs appear in tombs at
Archanes, Gournes, and Lebena.[436] Wiener has emphasized the importance of the Near East in the
metals trade with MM IB–II Crete.[437]

Within the Aegean three Minoan "routes" leading
to different areas are discernible: 1) Kythera, Agios
Stephanos, and the Argolid (Lerna); 2) the "Western
String" of islands (Thera, Melos, Kea) to Lavrion;
and 3) Kasos, Karpathos, and Rhodes to the Ana-

[419] Marketou (supra n. 418) 28–29 and fig. 5L. Papazoglou-Manioudaki, *ArchDelt* 37 (1982) 142–51. Patrikies-
type teapot, 149, no. 7 (with incorrect reference in n. 30)
and pl. 62.7; this necked spout with an outturned rim
should be compared to Patrikies-phase examples, Bonacasa (supra n. 226) 47, fig. 36 and *Festòs* I, pls. 98 and 102.
The Trianda example dates to MM IA–B. The carinated
cups, pls. 62.1, 4, and 9, 63.11–12, and p. 150, fig. 5, TP
163, represent a common protopalatial type. Papaiannopoulou (supra n. 413) 309 mentions MM IA pottery
from Trianda.

[420] R. Barber and O. Hadjianastasiou, "Mikre Vigla: A
Bronze Age Settlement on Naxos," *BSA* 84 (1989) 107–
108 and 140.

[421] E. Melas, *The Islands of Karpathos, Saros and Kasos in
the Neolithic and Bronze Age* (Göteborg 1985) 173.

[422] Coldstream and Huxley, in *Thalassocracy* (supra n.
107) 107–12.

[423] C. Laviosa, "The Minoan Thalassocracy, Iasos and
the Carian Coast," *Thalassocracy* 183–85.

[424] Discussion in *Thalassocracy* 189; A. Papaiannopoulou, "Were the S.E. Aegean Islands Deserted in the MBA?"
AnatSt 35 (1985) 86–87.

[425] Rutter and Zerner (supra n. 107) 75–83.

[426] S. Hiller, "Minoan and Minoanizing Pottery on
Aegina," in C. and P. Zerner and J. Winder eds., *Wace and
Blegen: Pottery as Evidence for Trade in the Aegean Bronze Age,
1939–1989* (Amsterdam 1993) 197–99. Hiller lists other
Minoan imports or Minoan-type artifacts from MH con-
texts: stone vases, loomweights, a stone kernos, and a pot-

ter's wheel.

[427] Rutter and Zerner (supra n. 107) 79 n. 14.

[428] For the Late Cycladic I period, see J. Davis, "Minos
and Dexithea: Crete and the Cyclades in the Later Bronze
Age," in J. Davis and J. Cherry eds., *Papers in Cycladic
Prehistory* (Los Angeles 1979) 143–57.

[429] Papaiannopoulou (supra n. 413) 267–73.

[430] Papaiannopoulou (supra n. 413) 273–79.

[431] V. Watrous, "Late Bronze Age Kommos: Imported
Pottery as Evidence for Foreign Contacts," *Scripta Mediterranea* 6 (1985) 12.

[432] Stos-Gale and Macdonald (supra n. 112) 267.

[433] Branigan 150–51, nos. 554, 780, 4, 375, 73, 93,
3351, 1467, 537, 122, 702A, and 956A. The MM IB–II
dates are indicated typologically (375, 537, 1467) or by
find context (554, 754, 702A, and 956A). No. 93 is said to
have come from the lower (EM II and later?) level at Platanos A. EM–MM I: 73, 3351, 122. See Gale's remarks
(supra n. 46) on the probable MM I date of the tin bronze
9402.

[434] Rutter and Zerner (supra n. 107) 81–82.

[435] Davis (supra n. 241).

[436] Listed in *Chronology* 129. The authors' citation of
literature on the chronology of scarabs is selective; they do
not acknowledge Ward's 1987 article (supra n. 304) lowering the dates of exported scarabs. C. Lambros-Phillipson,
Hellenorientalia (Göteborg 1990) 51–54 collects the evidence.

[437] M. Wiener, "The Nature and Control of Minoan
Foreign Trade," in Gale (supra n. 112) 327–34.

tolian mainland (Iasos, Knidos, and Miletos) and to Cyprus and the Near East. These routes may to some extent be regionally organized, that is, route 1 seems to be connected with Chania and western Crete, route 2 with Knossos and north-central Crete, and route 3 with eastern Crete (including Mallia). Along route 3 Yiali obsidian was imported to Mallia.[438] Poursat believes that Minoans must have traveled to Egypt in MM II because local clay vases with relief scenes based on Egyptian wall paintings are known.[439] Two silver Egyptian objects of the 12th Dynasty are claimed to be made from Lavrion silver.[440] Fresco fragments of kyanos blue found in an MM II context at Knossos can be linked to Egypt.[441] Obsidian from southern Anatolia (the Çiftlik area) appears in MM I contexts at Knossos and in Tholos B at Platanos.[442] The eastern trade route, via Cyprus to the ports of Syro-Cilicia, points to Minoan acquisition of metals (silver, tin, and copper). Many seals of the Old Palace period were carved from Near Eastern raw materials (agate, onyx, carnelian, sard, lapis lazuli).[443] The Egyptian diorite statuette of User from the palace at Knossos may, like the similar royal statuettes found at Byblos, be a sign of links with Middle Kingdom Egypt.[444] Signs of Near Eastern technology appear in MM IB–II metalwork, in the form of copies of eastern artifact types and new techniques of alloying, casting, and granulation.[445]

Evidence for Minoan trade outside the Aegean first appears in MM IA. The earliest object is the famous MM IA jar found in Tomb 806A at Lapithos in northern Cyprus.[446] MM IB–II pottery, mostly cups, has been found at Karmi on Cyprus, and in Syria–Palestine at Ugarit, Qatna, Beirut, and Byblos. Kemp and Merrillees have studied Minoan im-

ports in Egypt.[447] MM IB–II sherds are known from Lisht, Harageh, Kahun, Abydos, and Qubbet el-Hawa near Aswan. The contexts of these vases in Egypt range from the 12th to the 13th Dynasties. Knossian and Phaistian potters also made for export clay vases in imitation of foreign metal vases.[448] Warren and Hankey have argued that the silver vases in the Tôd treasure, which probably date to the 12th Dynasty, are Minoan (or can be taken as evidence of similar Minoan work).[449] Since the one gold and 153 silver Tôd cups are a single group, technically and stylistically, the standard shapes in the deposit may indicate their place of manufacture. The four main shapes (accounting for over 90% of the vases) are the hemispherical and shallow cups, kantharoi, and conical cups.[450] These shapes are elements of the Anatolian MB I ceramic repertoire.[451] None are Aegean. Only two unique shapes in the Tôd treasure are standard Minoan vase forms, the globular cup and cylindrical cup.[452] Thus, an Anatolian source for the Tôd vases seems likely. Objects mentioned in Near Eastern written documents supplement the list of Minoan exports. A Mari tablet mentions clothing and a pair of leather shoes from Crete.[453] A tablet of ca. 1800 B.C. records tin sent to Mari from the Caspian area for Cretans and others at Ugarit. Two Mari tablets refer to a Cretan weapon and Cretan products being sent from Mari to Babylon.

While Minoan trade is now better documented, the structure of that trade remains less clear. Was protopalatial trade mainly controlled by the palace or were other sectors of society also involved? Wiener stresses the importance of the palace in protopalatial overseas metals trade.[454] Metal products convincingly associated with the palace at Mallia in-

[438] F. Chapoutier and P. Demargne, *Fouilles exécutées à Mallia: Palais* III (*EtCret* 6, Paris 1942) 54 and pl. 52.26.

[439] J.-C. Poursat, "Une thalassocracie au Minoen moyen II?" in *Thalassocracy* 87.

[440] N. Gale in discussion, *Thalassocracy* 87.

[441] S. Immerwahr, *Aegean Painting in the Bronze Age* (University Park, Pa. 1990) 16.

[442] C. Renfrew, J. Cann, and J. Dixon, "Obsidian in the Aegean," *BSA* 60 (1965) 239. As Wiener notes (supra n. 437), the Anatolian obsidian comes from an area near metal sources in the Taurus Mountains and is a sign of Cretan-Anatolian metals trade (see A. Yener and P. Vandiver, "Tin Processing at Göltepe, an Early Bronze Age Site in Anatolia," *AJA* 97 [1993] 207–38), just as Melian obsidian is a sign of Cretan-Cycladic metals trade in the EBA.

[443] Yule 192–97.

[444] *PM* I, 286–90.

[445] Branigan 114–29, esp. 122–23 and fig. 10.

[446] See Cadogan (supra n. 8) 514–17.

[447] Kemp and Merrillees (supra n. 8).

[448] *Chronology* pls. 6–11.

[449] *Chronology* 131–34. The examples adduced in *Chronology* 132–33 show only that Minoan potters imitated a few of the types of metal vessels found in the Tôd cache. For the eastern origin of the Tôd vases, see E. Davis, *The Vapheio Cups and Aegean Gold and Silver Ware* (Diss. New York Univ. 1973) 69–79.

[450] See F. Bisson de la Roque et al., *Le trésor de Tôd* (Cairo 1953): hemispherical cups, pls. 12–13, 22–27; shallow cups, pl. 14; kantharoi, pl. 17; conical cups, pls. 19–21.

[451] See Lloyd and Mellaart (supra n. 201): hemispherical cups, 90, fig. P4, nos. 9 and 11; shallow cups, 92, fig. P5, nos. 10–12; kantharoi, 92, fig. P5, nos. 23–27; and conical cups, 90, fig. P4, nos. 15, 16, 18, and 92, fig. P5, nos. 13–16.

[452] Bisson de la Roque (supra n. 450) pl. 15, nos. 70583 and 70580.

[453] Wiener (supra n. 437) 329.

[454] Wiener (supra n. 437) 330–34.

clude the two MM II swords and the molds for axes and blades (from the area adjacent to the Mallia palace).[455] At Knossos a crystal core, gold, alabaster, Giali (?) obsidian, and faience and shell inlays as well as clay sealings, ca. 400 loomweights, and miniature faience vases are probably indirect evidence for palace workshop activity.[456] MacGillivray's study of Kamares ware production centers at Knossos postulates workshops serving Knossos, Phaistos, Mallia, Vasiliki, and Palaikastro.[457] The excavation of Quartier Mu (producing, e.g., the mold for a "Kamares" lobed bowl and the stone anchors) serves as a warning that "palatial" workshops of artisans fed through redistribution and maritime trade were not limited to the palace but were also controlled by families living outside the palace. We do not know the exact relationship between these families and the residents of the palace. It is very likely that they were closely related, as at LBA Ugarit, but their commercial and political interconnections remain unknown. Links between Kamares ware workshops and the palaces are equally tenuous. As MacGillivray points out, the kilns for the Knossian area seem to have been located some 3 km south of Knossos.[458] Certainly quantities of Kamares ware were destined for the palaces but, equally, quantities have been found in other sectors of palatial towns. Similarly there is no evidence that the palaces had any predominant role in the distribution of Kamares ware either in Crete or overseas. "Palatial" goods such as Kamares ware, precious metals, and artwork should probably be regarded as coming from groups of wealthy families or royalty located at the principal Minoan towns.[459] The construction of a large architectural complex at the port of Kommos, however, may have been initiated by the palace at Phaistos.[460] There is now an impressive body of literature based on Near Eastern texts that illustrates the wide range of possibilities for the structure of protopalatial trade. The royal monopoly of Egypt seems exceptional. Far more normal in the Near East is the situation in which private commerce and royal trade (a mixture of commerce, gift exchange, and internal taxation) exist side by side.[461]

Finally, one of the most distinctive features of Minoan civilization is its early adoption of representational art under strong Syrian and Egyptian influence.[462] Prepalatial representations on seals, pottery, and even sculpture are for the most part abstract.[463] In the late prepalatial period (MM IA), figural representations on Minoan seals, made of ivory imported from Syria and Egypt, become common. On the earliest (MM IA–IB) group featuring pictorial motifs, the range of subjects is relatively limited: lions, spiders, scorpions, and goats.[464] The successive MM IA–II group, distinctive for its highly pronounced Egyptian influence in its shapes and motifs, features a wider repertoire: man, deer, boar, goat, lion, ape, calf, fly, lily, ship, and jug as well as hieroglyphic characters (e.g., sistrum, leg, and double ax).[465] Many of these early motifs are derived from Syrian or Egyptian workshops.[466] The Mallia Workshop group (MM II) depicts men, goats, pottery, fish, waterbirds, bucrania, ships, spiders, scorpion, octopus, dog, double ax, and a fly.[467] The MM II Phaistos sealings add to the Mallia repertoire with scenes of galloping animals in a landscape, an owl, and a Triton shell. Egyptian motifs include the bull and battlement, ape, griffin, bee, and Tu-art.[468] A few pictorial motifs are depicted on pottery[469] and the sphinx also makes its appearance on seals and ceramic relief.[470]

[455] O. Pelon, "Minoan Palaces and Workshops: New Data from Malia," in *Function* 269–72.

[456] *PM* I, 165–75, 248–70. For a discussion of the MM IA–II Vat Room deposit, see Momigliano (supra n. 185) 167–71; K. Branigan, "The Economic Role of the First Palaces," in *Function* 247–49 and ns. 4 and 6.

[457] J. MacGillivray, "Pottery Workshops and the Old Palaces in Crete," in *Function* 273–79.

[458] MacGillivray (supra n. 457) 276.

[459] See the careful discussion in M. Wiener, "Trade and Rule in Palatial Crete," in *Function* 264–65.

[460] See J. Shaw, "Excavations at Kommos (Crete) during 1986–1992," *Hesperia* 62 (1993) 184–85 and 164, fig. 10b.

[461] See the comments by W. Helck and B. Foster on Egyptian and Old Babylonian trade in *Function* 267. For the Near East, see P. Garelli ed., *Le palais et la royauté* (Paris 1974); M. Heltzer, *Goods, Prices and the Organization of Trade in Ugarit* (Wiesbaden 1978); Heltzer, *The Internal Organization of the Kingdom of Ugarit* (Wiesbaden 1982); C. Zaccagnini, "Aspects of Ceremonial Exchange in the Near East during the Late Second Millennium B.C.," in M.

Rowlands, M. Larsen, and K. Kristiansen eds., *Centre and Periphery in the Ancient World* (Cambridge 1987) 57–65; E. Gaal, "The Social Structure of Alalah," in M. Heltzer and E. Lipinski eds., *Society and Economy in the Eastern Mediterranean* (Louvain 1988) 94–110.

[462] See the excellent summary in Immerwahr (supra n. 441) 26–37.

[463] Cretan figurines in stone and clay are, for religious reasons, an obvious exception.

[464] Yule 208–209: the Parading Lions/Spiral group.

[465] Yule 210–11: Border/Leaf Complex.

[466] Yule 210–11; Pini 1981 (supra n. 140) 421–35; and Pini 1990 (supra n. 140) 115–27. P. Yule, "Early and Middle Minoan Foreign Relations: The Evidence from Seals," *SMEA* 25 (1987) 161–75.

[467] Yule 212–13.

[468] *CMS* II.5, nos. 253–326.

[469] G. Walberg, *Tradition and Innovation: Essays in Minoan Art* (Mainz 1986) 6–38.

[470] J.-C. Poursat, "Le sphinx minoen: un nouveau document," *AntCr* 1 (1973) 111–14.

The Old Palace period is brought to a close by a series of destructions in MM II, observed at Phaistos, Knossos, Mallia, Monasteraki, Pyrgos/Myrtos, and Palaikastro as well as at other sites.

CONCLUSIONS

During the last 20 years it has become increasingly apparent that excavation must go hand in hand with other techniques if it is to answer some of our current questions about Minoan Crete. Surveys, for example, have not only documented changing patterns of settlement, but they provide us with a general context that is invaluable in interpreting excavation finds. Surveys also present a unique diachronic perspective. We now know that defensively located settlements, for example, are not confined to the EM II period but are also characteristic of the FN, EM I, and MM I periods. The systematic use of watersieving to recover organic remains has the potential to answer basic questions about the evolving Minoan exploitation of the environment, about economic organization, population, and diet. Many problems involving chronology, trade, and religion in Minoan archaeology are in fact Aegean, or even Mediterranean, problems and are most profitably approached from a wider perspective. Much would be learned, for instance, about the structure of Minoan overseas trade by the thorough excavation and publication of an EBA Cycladic settlement connected with a mined ore source.

Studies of Early and Middle Minoan pottery deposits have helped to define these ceramic phases. Thanks to recent research we now know that the EM IIA and EM IIB periods are very different in some ways. Research on Middle Minoan pottery has made clearer the strongly regional character of Minoan Crete. For the EM I–MM II periods, however, we still lack a continuous stratigraphy (or even part of one) based on a single site. At Phaistos, for example, we have published deposits of FN, but nothing from EM I through MM IA. For Knossos there are informative publications of EM IIA and MM IA, but no EM I, EM IIB, EM III, MM IB, or MM II. Both sites possess excavated material from these missing periods but it has not been published. Consequently we depend on deposits from widely separated areas of Crete and from tombs for our ceramic sequence. In the past this has resulted in controversies concerning dating and has hindered our understanding of important historical questions, such as the development of Minoan social complexity, Aegean interrelations, and the evolution of Linear B. What is needed is the publication of as full as possible a sequence of deposits from a single site. Knossos is the obvious place for this to happen.

Scholars of Early Minoan Crete have reconstructed a society at the threshold of palatial achievement made up of elite families whose centralized authority included control of specialized workshops. These families are thought to have reached a peak of prosperity and technical proficiency during the "international era" of the Aegean EB II period. A generation of research has confirmed some of these claims and cast doubt on others. Current multidisciplinary ceramic analyses are beginning to demonstrate the highly specialized nature of EM II ceramic production and the volume of long-distance trade in pottery within Crete. Similarly the startling amount and range of Cretan access to Aegean metals have also been documented by scientific and archaeological work.

On the other hand, recent excavation and research have yet to yield any evidence for a complex sociopolitical organization in Early Minoan Crete. Some aspects of EM II material culture are indeed sophisticated and rich, but if the culture of EM II Crete is compared with that of other areas in the contemporary Aegean or with later MM IA achievements, it is relatively modest. Future research may well modify this view. We need an excavation of a large EM II settlement, at one of the later palatial sites, or at Koumasa, Platanos, or Agia Triada, only the cemeteries of which have been investigated. Such an excavation would correct the present bias in our EM II evidence toward tomb material. Because so many Early Minoan tomb groups are unstratified, the publication of the tombs at Lebena and Agia Photia would be particularly valuable. Data for most aspects of the all-important economic component of EM II society continue to be extremely rare—the excavations at coastal Myrtos, for example, produced no fish bones and only one olive stone—largely due to the lack of watersieving for organic remains. It is disturbing that while such economic questions are being actively discussed in the literature, many current well-financed foreign excavations in Crete are failing to watersieve. A large program of analyses of Cretan metal artifacts is another desideratum, as it would undoubtedly yield valuable information on Minoan society, technology, and trade.

The EM III period has generally been regarded as one of smooth transition and continuity between EM II and MM I. This prevailing view is based on past scholarship dealing with pottery, stone vases, and seals. Faced with a lack of stratigraphy for the EM III period, these studies created a uniformitarian sequence from EM IIB to MM IB based exclusively on style. The production of seals and stone vases during the EM II–MM I period is not, however, an uninterrupted tradition. Recent excavation and survey work have also shown that there was a widespread, but by no means total, discontinuity of settlement on Crete at the end of the Early Minoan period, and that there is no basis for assuming that this period proceeded without interruption. All of this indicates rather strongly that previous continuous stylistic sequences, while perhaps internally correct, have little historical validity. EM III as it is understood in the current literature is simply a stylistic creation. Much that has been called "EM III" could easily be EM IIB or MM IA. The hard truth is that we know next to nothing about Crete during the EM III period.

This EM III controversy closely resembles the old problem, debated in the 1970s, of Late Minoan II— whether it was a style or a chronological period— and I believe it has the same solution. Before the mid-1970s it was thought that LM II was a Knossian style contemporary with LM IB in the rest of the island. Subsequent excavation and stylistic analysis showed that LM II is a chronological period, with its own ceramic style,[471] which had been missed by earlier excavators because it was rare and ill defined. This suggests that once EM III levels at Knossos are fully published, EM III material will eventually be recognized by excavators in the rest of the island. It may well turn out that no discrete decorative "style" exists for EM III and that we will recognize the pottery of the period in terms of certain shapes and their relative incidence within an assemblage. Excavation might help: a stratified EM II–MM I sequence certainly exists at the major centers and possibly at some smaller sites, such as Chamaizi, Gournia, Koumasa, and Mochlos.

In the past, our image of the MM IA period has been vague, largely because of chronological problems. Consequently, studies of the early Middle Minoan period have been relatively rare, particularly in comparison with the amount of research on the Early Minoan period. This has certainly tended to obscure the importance of MM IA and its development. Over the last 20 years, however, studies of chronology, pottery, seals, and metalwork have helped us to comprehend better what was actually achieved during the period. It is now clear, for instance, that exported Minoan pottery, our best evidence for the development of Cretan trade with the rest of the Aegean, is rare in EM II and increases dramatically in quantity and distribution in MM IA–

II. This should cause us to reevaluate the older view that most of the rich finds from the EM II–MM I/II Cretan tombs should be dated to EM II. Most would now agree that MM IA is a long period and one of dynamic development. Little is known about the early, first phase of MM IA but the evidence seems to indicate that there is initial recovery and great population growth, visible at major centers, and probably the beginning of an influx of new settlers at this time.

During the later, second phase of MM IA, the first true Aegean urbanization takes place on Crete.[472] The major population centers are reorganized: street systems, open squares, fortifications, and the first palaces are constructed. Literacy is introduced. Wealthy burials signal continued recovery and at the same time settlements spread across the countryside. Foreign imports from tombs at Archanes, Mochlos, and from the Mesara are a sign of the renewed international relations that are made possible by the stabilization of the Near East and the opening up of maritime contacts in the eastern Mediterranean with the rise of the 12th Dynasty in Egypt. Foreign influence is apparent in the number of imports and in new burial customs, architecture, ceramics, and seals. The Egyptian scarabs from Lebena and Archanes indicate that this later phase of MM IA corresponds roughly to the 20th century B.C. Peak sanctuaries are established in MM IA, and at the end of the period the first palaces are constructed at Knossos and Mallia. With the consolidation of these city-states, direct international relations are established with other polities outside the Aegean. Like their counterparts in the Near East, these Minoan states enter an era of widespread prosperity.

The outlines of the protopalatial period were securely established by excavators early in this century. For this reason, the period has been relatively neglected until recently. Several excavations—at Phaistos, Phourni cemetery (Archanes), Quartier Mu at Mallia, and Monasteraki—have helped to fill certain gaps in our knowledge. Levi's excavations at Phaistos have revealed a large portion of the Old Palace, but now need to be supplemented with tests to resolve important problems of relative dating for certain sectors of the palace. The revelation of Quartier Mu at Mallia makes one wish for excavation of another MM IB–II sector of the city (further

---

[471] This view was put forth by M. Popham, in "Late Minoan II Crete: A Note," *AJA* 79 (1975) 372–74.

[472] The archaeological correlates of urban states are

usefully listed in C. Redman, *The Rise of Civilization* (San Francisco 1978) 218.

out from the palace?) to understand better the range of urban dwellings and daily life at Mallia. The important excavations at Monasteraki, when fully published, will help fill out our picture of an MM IB–II provincial town. Sites such as Chamaizi and Agia Photia throw into relief the problem of rural "villas" or farms and their functions. Claims for lines of Minoan "forts" linked by paved roads in East Crete need further substantiation: the complete publication of one of these complexes would be helpful. The identification by survey and subsequent excavation of rural constructions, such as check dams and built terraces, is particularly exciting. More such work needs doing to document Minoan land use and engineering capabilities. Two areas of prime importance begging for intensive survey work are the Knossos-Archanes region and the plain of Rethymnon.

Some 20 years ago two scholars, C. Renfrew in *The Emergence of Civilisation* (London 1972) and K. Branigan in *The Foundations of Palatial Crete* (London 1970), presented an influential outline for the cultural development of pre- and protopalatial Crete.

This sequence was one of rapid cultural development during the EM I–II periods followed by a continuous and uneventful transition into the protopalatial period. Twenty years of excavation and research on Crete have documented a different pattern. Cultural development in EM I–II Crete appears to have been gradual and relatively modest; there is at present no evidence for social ranking in EM II Crete. Society in EM II Crete was sharply interrupted at the end of the period by widespread turbulence and the abandonment of many settlements. Only in the subsequent MM IA period is order gradually restored to the island. In MM IA, Minoan Crete first achieves urbanization, sociopolitical complexity, literacy, and wealth based on international trade, all cultural features we traditionally associate with civilization.

DEPARTMENT OF ART HISTORY
605 CLEMENS HALL
STATE UNIVERSITY OF NEW YORK AT BUFFALO
BUFFALO, NEW YORK 14260

Addendum: 1994–1999

L. VANCE WATROUS

The account below is summary and selective, covering the years since the publication of my previous review of Crete from its earliest prehistory through the protopalatial period (RAP III).[473]

RECENT FIELDWORK

Surveys for this period in Crete have been carried out recently in and around Mallia and Gournia, around Ziros, in the Agios Vasilios Valley, and on Gavdos.[474] The continuing "Minoan Roads" project in East Crete is yielding interesting information on farmsteads, ceramic workshops, terraces, roads, quarries, peak sanctuaries, and "guardhouses."[475]

Excavations at Poros, the port of Knossos, show that the site already had international connections by the EM I period.[476] Early Minoan levels yielded areas associated with the working of metal (including molds, crucibles, and slag) and obsidian, and much Early Cycladic pottery. At Chrysokamino in East Crete an Early Minoan copper smelting site was excavated.[477] The final, Early Minoan floor level yielded a hearth, clay pot bellows, clay furnaces, and much slag. Some of the copper ore has been linked to the island of Kythnos. The fired clay pot bellows were found with a ledge of baked clay adhering in a ring around their exterior, which indicates that they were set into the floor (or, in the heat, became fused with the floor), thus explaining the so-called postholes reconstructed at the site. Excavations at Kalo Chorio have resulted in the first publication of an EM I settlement in East Crete.[478] Rescue excavations in the Asterousias Mountains near Moni Odigitria at Skaniari to Lakko have revealed a new tholos tomb with an annex and a separate building for burials, offerings, and storage.[479] At Knossos, excavations uncovered an EM III house and a unique Cycladic jar from that period.[480] A large terrace wall under the west and north facades of the Knossos palace may have supported a building or buildings in EM III or MM IA. Sondages at Mochlos yielded remains of EM II and

---

[473] My thanks to Harriet Blitzer, who edited the manuscript for this addendum. To those whose work I have inadvertently neglected, my apologies.

Please note the following corrections to my earlier review above: p. 179, right column: delete the words "end of the" in the sentence "The end of the EM IIB period . . ."; p. 180, right column, last sentence: read "Thus, from a stylistic perspective, much of the pottery traditionally identified as EM II/III or EM III could be EM IIB"; p. 181, right column, lines 30–31: read "The top level is EM IIB"; p. 182, left column, line 28: for "A Middle Bronze date," read "A later date"; p. 192, right column, line 23: for "all were imported from abroad," read "all were of ivory imported from abroad"; p. 193, n. 279, line 4: for "12th Dynasty," read "11th or 12th Dynasty"; p. 196, right column, lines 7–13: read "While it is clear that the earliest cult artifacts date to MM IA at some caves, such as Kamares, the Idaean Cave, and Psychro, other caves (Trapeza and Agios Charalambos) were simply burial places"; p. 199, left column, last sentence: for "The absence of protopalatial ashlar orthostates . . . construction," read "Ashlar orthostates were used at all three of the first palaces."

The following abbreviations are used below:

Pepragmena 1995   Πεπραγμένα του Ζ΄ Διεθνούς Κρητολογικού Συνεδρίου I–II (Athens 1995).

Techne   R. Laffineur and P.P. Betancourt eds., *TEXNH: Craftsmen, Craftswomen and Craftsmanship in the Aegean Bronze Age* (Aegaeum 16, Liège 1997).

[474] Mallia: *BCH* 120 (1996) 921–28; *ArchDelt* 44 (1989) Chronika 464–66; 46 (1991) Chronika 437–38. Gournia: *AJA* 99 (1995) 313 (abstract). Ziros: K. Branigan, "Prehistoric and Early Historic Settlement in the Ziros Region, Eastern Crete," *BSA* 93 (1998) 23–90. Agios Vasilios: Κρητική Εστία 4 (1991–1993) 279–85; *AR* 41 (1994–1995) 64. Gavdos: Κρητική Εστία 5 (1994–1996) 242–44.

[475] Αρχαιολογία 43 (1993) 70–78; Κρητική Εστία 4 (1991–1993) 306–19; 5 (1994–1996) 359–66; 6 (1997–1998) 195–236; 7 (1999) 317–26.

[476] *ArchDelt* 48 (1993) 450–58; N. Dimopoulou, "Workshops and Craftsmen at Poros-Katsambas," in *Techne* 433–38.

[477] *AR* 43 (1996–1997) 113–14; *AJA* 101 (1997) 374 (abstract); 103 (1999) 273 (abstract); P.P. Betancourt et al., "Research and Excavation at Chrysokamino, Crete, 1995–1998," *Hesperia* 68 (1999) 343–70.

[478] *AJA* 99 (1995) 313 (abstract); D. Haggis, "The Typology of the EM I Chalice and the Cultural Implications of Form and Style in Early Bronze Age Ceramics," in *Techne* 291–300.

[479] Κρητική Εστία 5 (1994–1996) 336–37; *AR* 44 (1997–1998) 114.

[480] N. Momigliano and D. Wilson, "Knossos 1993: Excavations outside the South Front of the Palace," *BSA* 91 (1996) 1–55; D. Wilson, "Knossos before the Palaces: An Overview of the Early Bronze Age (EM I–III)," in D. Evely, H. Hughes-Brock, and N. Momigliano eds., *Knossos: A Labyrinth of History* (Oxford 1994) 23–44. Wilson has made the important observation that the settlement at Knossos was physically reorganized in EM IIA.

EM III–MM IA houses.[481] Excavators at the prepalatial settlement at Trypeti on the south coast of Crete have now identified a total of 46 rooms, including a storeroom with murex shells, a cistern, two steatite seals, and a copper pin.[482]

Protopalatial houses at Poros (Herakleion) produced evidence of foreign trade: signs of bronzeworking and seal carving as well as an Egyptian scarab in a MM IB context.[483] Excavations below the west wing of the neopalatial palace at Galatas in central Crete have revealed eight rooms—kitchens, workshops, and storage areas—belonging to a large protopalatial building decorated with red and blue painted plaster.[484] The large scale of food preparation, industrial activities, and storage in these rooms suggests that the building belonged to a centralized authority. At Kommos, a monumental MM IIB structure (Building AA) was uncovered below the Late Minoan harbor complex.[485] The building produced some 40 fragments of imported pottery from Cyprus and elsewhere. Work near the tholoi at Agia Triada indicates that the ossuary next to Tholos B was independent of the tomb and was walled shut in MM II.[486] The small rooms south of Tholos A contained MM IA–B burials.

Digging at the EM III–MM II settlement at Chamalevri in West Crete produced evidence for the production of pottery, textiles, and stone tools.[487] A Syrian cylinder seal of a type dated to 1850–1600 B.C. was found at Mochlos in Tomb L.[488] At Petras, excavation revealed a "palatial" MM II building, complete with a MM IIB hieroglyphic archive containing clay bars, medallions, crescents, noduli, chest sealings, and nodules beneath the neopalatial administrative center.[489] Plans and brief reports on two MM II sites in the Amari Valley, Monasteraki and Apodoulou, have now appeared.[490] In the summer of 1999 the exhibition "Minoan and Mycenaean Flavours," held at the National Archaeological Museum in Athens, displayed cooking pots and a pithos from these two sites that, according to analyses, had contained olive oil, vegetables, fruit, meat, and resinated wine (for the catalogue to the exhibition, see Y. Tzedakis and H. Martlew eds., *Minoans and Mycenaeans: Flavours of Their Time*, Athens 1999).

Excavation at Kato Syme has thrown light on the sanctuary's beginnings.[491] Founded in MM IB, the sanctuary went through three architectural phases within the protopalatial period. The earliest structure on the site, Building V, was large (at least 21 m long) and possessed a stone-paved floor and column bases. Building U, the MM II successor of V, had at least 22 rooms, with plaster floors. The north wing of the building was used for the storage and preparation of food as well as for the collection of cult paraphernalia. Spacious benched rooms in the south wing served for gatherings. A wide doorway in Building U led to an open area consisting of three terraces facing onto a "plateia" that was used by the worshippers. Apparently a paved road connected Building U to the natural focus of the sanctuary, the large spring on the site. In MM IIB, Building U was destroyed by

[481] J.S. Soles and C. Davaras, "Excavations at Mochlos, 1992–1993," *Hesperia* 65 (1996) 175–230.

[482] Κρητική Εστία 4 (1991–1993) 292–96; A. Vasilakis, "Τρυπητή 1986–1991: Ζητήματα του προανακτορικού μινωϊκού πολιτισμού στη νότια κεντρική Κρήτη και η ανασκαφή του οικισμού Τρυπητής," in *Pepragmena* 1995, I, 69–80.

[483] Supra n. 476.

[484] Κρητική Εστία 7 (1999) 224–39.

[485] J. Shaw, "Kommos in Southern Crete: An Aegean Barometer for East–West Interconnections," in V. Karageorghis and N. Stampolidis eds., *Eastern Mediterranean: Cyprus–Dodecanese–Crete, 16th–6th Cent. B.C. Proceedings of the International Symposium Held at Rethymnon, Crete, in May 1997* (Athens 1998) 13–24, esp. addendum on p. 23. I am also indebted to Aleydis Van de Moortel for the specific details about these finds.

[486] *ArchDelt* 45 (1990) 431; 46 (1991) 407; Κρητική Εστία 4 (1991–1993) 296–301; 5 (1994–1996) 326–32; 7 (1999) 273–84.

[487] Κρητική Εστία 4 (1991–1993) 241–44; 5 (1994–1996) 251–64. M. Vlasaki, "Craftsmanship at Khamalevri in Rethymnon," in *Techne* 37–44.

[488] C. Davaras and J. Soles, "A New Oriental Cylinder Seal from Mochlos," *ArchEph* 1995, 29–66. See also J. Aruz, "Syrian Seals and the Evidence for Cultural Interaction between the Levant and Crete," in I. Pini and J.-C. Poursat eds., *Sceaux minoens et mycéniens* (*CMS* Beiheft 5, Berlin 1995) 1–21.

[489] *ArchDelt* 48 (1993) 493–95; *AJA* 102 (1998) 391 (abstract); Κρητική Εστία 5 (1994–1996) 344–58; 7 (1999) 298–310.

[490] Monasteraki: Κρητική Εστία 4 (1991–1993) 274; 5 (1994–1996) 312–14. Apodoulou: Κρητική Εστία 3 (1989–1990) 276–78; 4 (1991–1993) 275–79; 5 (1994–1996) 308–12; G. Godart and Y. Tzedakis, "Les recherches à Apodoulou," in *Pepragmena* 1995, I, 353–58; A. Tzigkounaki, "Παλαιοανακτορική εγκατάσταση Αποδούλου: Η χρονολόγηση και η σχέση της με γειτονικά κέντρα," in *Pepragmena* 1995, II, 895–914.

[491] Reports on the Syme excavations appear in *Praktika* from 1972 to the present. See also A. Lebessi and P. Muhly, "The Sanctuary of Hermes and Aphrodite at Syme, Crete," *NatGeogRes* 3 (1987) 102–13; A. Lebessi, P. Muhly, and J.-P. Olivier, "An Inscription in the Hieroglyphic Script from the Syme Sanctuary, Crete," *Kadmos* 34 (1995) 63–77. Most recently, *Prakt* 1993, 209–30; 1994, 239–44; 1995, 245–60. See *BCH* 118 (1994) 816 for MM IB pottery at the site.

an earthquake and immediately afterward a small open-air sacrificial area (Ub) surrounded by a peribolos wall was built on its ruins. Protopalatial finds from Syme include clay chalices, a kantharos, stone vases, seals, and clay figurines. One vase bears a sealing of the Lion/Spiral Group known from the Mesara. Area Ub, which continues into MM III, produced many clay and stone vases inscribed with Linear A. A tablet inscribed in hieroglyphic script from Building U implies that some sort of authority was involved with the administration of the sanctuary in protopalatial times. The excavators rightly point out that this casts doubt on the commonly believed theory that rural Minoan sanctuaries were initially only local gathering places for popular cult, and were then brought under palatial control in the neopalatial period.

RECENT STUDIES

Environment and Subsistence

Though not strictly speaking a study of Minoan Crete, O. Rackham and J. Moody's book *The Making of the Cretan Landscape* (Manchester 1996) must be mentioned. The authors lovingly describe the landscape of Crete and the geological, faunal, and human forces that over millennia have shaped the island's topography. For those interested in the earliest prehistory of Crete, Reese's collection of 26 articles on Pleistocene and Holocene fauna of Crete is a treasury: studies of Pleistocene pygmy elephants and hippopotamuses as well as deer, birds, otters, badgers, turtles, mice, and fish.[492] Holocene animals and their relation to man are discussed; no certain evidence for human occupation on pre-Neolithic Crete has yet appeared. Hamilakis has assembled an admirable collection of the evidence for Minoan cultivation of olives and vines, though he overemphasizes the un-

reliability of the data for the prepalatial period, and thus concludes that oil and wine only became important in the protopalatial period as items connected with social ceremonies such as feasts and gift-exchange.[493] This seems doubtful—there is strong evidence for ceremonial drinking and libation as early as EM II or even earlier. Signs of surplus production for trade in the protopalatial period should not be confused with the beginnings of olive and grape cultivation.[494] For example, Blitzer, in her evaluation of artifactual and ethnographic evidence (as well as palynological data from the eastern Mediterranean), concludes that olive cultivation was already a basic element of the Early Minoan economy.[495] In fact, pollen cores taken near Chania have produced large quantities of olive pollen in Late Neolithic levels, suggesting the appearance of olive cultivation by that period.[496] These cores also indicate that the climate became drier during the Early Minoan period (some pollen from trees presently typical of central Europe disappears during the course of the Early Bronze Age). Strasser's examination of the *koulouras* at the palaces has shown that they were not granaries, and that the role of grain storage in the emergence of the first palaces has been exaggerated.[497]

Artifacts

Vasilakis has published a new and complete study of 960 gold and silver objects from Early Minoan Crete.[498] He identifies the northern Aegean as the source of EM gold and metalworking technology. Zois's exhaustive catalogue of Early Minoan sites in Crete, *Η Πρώιμη Εποχή του Χαλκού* I–VII (Athens 1997), has appeared. Zielinski, in a recent dissertation on the sociopolitical aspects of Cyclopean architecture, delineates seven political territories and their

---

492 D. Reese ed., *Pleistocene and Holocene Fauna of Crete and Its First Settlers* (Monographs in World Archaeology 28, Madison 1996).

493 Y. Hamilakis, "Wine, Oil, and the Dialectics of Power in Bronze Age Crete: A Review of the Evidence," *OJA* 15 (1996) 1–32. On the same question, A. Sarpaki also stresses the importance of systematically collecting botanical data: "Η αρχαιολογική ορατότητα της αμπέλου στην Κρήτη και στον ελλαδικό χώρο την προϊστορική εποχή," in *Pepragmena* 1995, II, 841–62. See now D. Wilson and P. Day, "EM IIB Ware Groups at Knossos: The 1907–1908 South Front Tests," *BSA* 94 (1999) 1–62. Wilson and Day conclude that many of the EM IIB shapes were used for the ceremonial drinking of wine.

494 As do Hamilakis (supra n. 493) and C. Runnels and J. Hansen, "The Olive in the Prehistoric Aegean: The Evidence for Domestication in the Early Bronze Age," *OJA* 5

(1986) 299–308.

495 H. Blitzer, "Olive Cultivation and Olive Production in Minoan Crete," in M.-C. Amouretti and J.-P. Brun eds., *Oil and Wine Production in the Mediterranean Area* (*BCH* Suppl. 26, Paris 1993) 163–76.

496 J. Moody, O. Rackham, and G. Rapp, "Environmental Archaeology of Prehistoric N.W. Crete," *JFA* 23 (1996) 273–97.

497 T. Strasser, "Storage and States on Prehistoric Crete: The Function of the Koulouras in the First Minoan Palaces," *JMA* 10 (1997) 73–100.

498 A. Vasilakis, *Ο χρυσός και ο άργυρος στην Κρήτη κατά την Πρώιμη Περίοδο του Χαλκού* (Herakleion 1996). Also *CretChron* 1990, 35–50. M. Effinger, *Minoischer Schmuck* (*BAR-IS* 646, Oxford 1996) is a typological study of all Minoan jewelry.

social hierarchies.[499] Poursat has promptly published the five important "house/workshops" in Quartier Mu at Mallia.[500]

In a recent study, Vagnetti has documented the numerous ceramic parallels between Final Neolithic Crete and the Aegean.[501] An important study of EM I–IIA pottery imported from the Mesara to Knossos, combining the identification of ceramic wares and petrography, supplies a detailed description of specialized Early Minoan ceramic production.[502] The *Techne* conference in 1996 produced a series of excellent papers on ceramic themes. Three distinct ceramic traditions (South Coast, Mirabello, and Vasiliki wares) present at EM IIB Myrtos/Fournou Koriphi have been identified.[503] A definitive study establishes that true ceramic specialization existed in Early Minoan Crete and that "if a complex ceramic system was already present in EM Crete, then the term [ceramic specialization] cannot aid us in discriminating between Pre- and Protopalatial systems, i.e., it may not, in itself, indicate change in the overall sociopolitical system."[504]

Having discerned major differences in the labor investment and economic organization of ceramic production at Mallia and at Myrtos/Pyrgos, Knappett correctly questions whether Myrtos/Pyrgos was part of a centralized state focused on Mallia in the protopalatial period.[505] Carinci has made a convincing case for the location of ceramic workshops at Phaistos and Agia Triada in the protopalatial period.[506] Pottery from Tholos E (EM II–MM II) at Archanes has been partly published, and MacGillivray has carried out an excellent study of the protopalatial pottery from Knossos.[507]

A reexamination of EM seals shows that they are made of bone, not of imported ivory as was once believed.[508] Sbonias in a study of prepalatial seals makes many interesting points about the sociopolitical development of EM II–MM I Crete.[509] Seals before EM III are homogeneous in motif and are not made of exotic materials, and thus were probably for local use only. EM seals are simpler than their EH counterparts. By MM IA, seals are large, varied in shape, made of ivory, and have complicated imagery. By MM IB, seals become smaller, are made of local materials (bone, paste, soft stones), and a few exceptional examples (e.g., *CMS* II, Suppl. 1, no. 391) stand out as elite items. During MM IA, the wide distribution of certain stylistic groups of seals in Crete is a sign of extensive trade, competition, and innovation. In contrast, by MM IB every large settlement has its own glyptic group, and each seal group displays regionalism and close contact with its palatial center.

Foreign Contacts and Trade

Betancourt has reviewed the evidence for Minoan–Near Eastern connections in the early Middle Bronze Age.[510] A comparison of the types of goods exchanged between Egypt and Byblos and between Egypt and Crete suggests that in the area of funerary customs, the Minoans were open to Egyptian ideas, since MM I–II tombs contained large numbers of Egyptianizing burial goods.[511] Minoan seals and amulets drew extensively, but not randomly, on Egyptian prototypes. In their borrowing of Egyptian amuletic motifs and shapes, the Minoans focused on a single type, called "amulets of assimilation," because

[499] J.P. Zielinski, *Cyclopean Architecture in Minoan Bronze Age Crete: A Study in the Social Organization of a Complex Society* (Diss. Univ. at Buffalo 1998). Zielinski, "Sociopolitical Complexity in the Minoan Prepalatial Period: A Reassessment," *AJA* 100 (1996) 354 (abstract).

[500] J.-C. Poursat, *Artisans minoens: Les maisons-ateliers du Quartier Mu* (*EtCret* 32, Paris 1996). See also *Guide de Malia au temps des premiers palais: Le Quartier Mu* (Paris 1992).

[501] L. Vagnetti, "The Final Neolithic: Crete Enters the Wider World," *Cretan Studies* 5 (1996) 29–39.

[502] D. Wilson and P. Day, "Ceramic Regionalism in Prepalatial Central Crete: The Mesara Imports at EM I to EM IIA Knossos," *BSA* 89 (1994) 1–87.

[503] T. Whitelaw, P. Day, E. Kiriatzi, V. Kilikoglou, and D. Wilson, "Ceramic Traditions at EM IIB Myrtos, Fournou Korifi," in *Techne* 265–74.

[504] P. Day, D. Wilson, and E. Kiriatzi, "Reassessing Specialization in Prepalatial Cretan Ceramic Production," in *Techne* 279–80.

[505] C. Knappett, "Ceramic Production in the Protopalatial Mallia 'State': Evidence from Quartier Mu and Myrtos Pyrgos," in *Techne* 305–12; Knappett, "Assessing a Polity in

Protopalatial Crete: The Malia-Lasithi State," *AJA* 103 (1999) 615–39.

[506] F. Carinci, "Pottery Workshops at Phaistos and Haghia Triada in the Protopalatial Period," in *Techne* 317–22.

[507] D. Panagiotopoulos, "Η κεραμεική του θολωτού τάφου Ε στο Φουρνί Αρχανών," in *Pepragmena* 1995, II, 729–40. J.A. MacGillivray, *Knossos: Pottery Groups of the Old Palace Period* (*BSA* Studies 5, London 1998).

[508] O. Krzyszkowska, "Early Cretan Seals: New Evidence for the Use of Bone, Ivory and Boar's Tusk," in I. Pini ed., *Fragen und Probleme der bronzezeitlichen ägäischen Glyptik* (*CMS* Beiheft 3, Berlin 1989) 111–26.

[509] K. Sbonias, *Frühkretische Siegel* (*BAR-IS* 620, Oxford 1995).

[510] P.P. Betancourt, "Middle Minoan Objects in the Near East," in E. Cline and D. Harris-Cline eds., *The Aegean and the Orient in the Second Millennium* (*Aegaeum* 18, Liège 1998) 5–12.

[511] V. Watrous, "Egypt and Crete in the Early Middle Bronze Age: A Case of Trade and Cultural Diffusion," in Cline and Harris-Cline (supra n. 510) 19–28.

they provided strength or protection by assimilating the powers that certain animals possessed naturally or by association with a kindred deity. Many of these amulets in Egypt were associated with maternal protection, particularly during childbirth.

Karantzali compares and contrasts the ceramic and sculptural traditions shared by the Cyclades and Crete in the Early Bronze Age.[512] Aruz has concluded that while there is no evidence for actual exchange of seals between MBA Crete and central Anatolia (Karahöyük), some of the motifs shared by the two areas point to interaction.[513] In addition, she suggests that the griffin, sphinx, and blocky lion motifs on the MM II Phaistos sealings derive from the area of Syria and central Anatolia.

There have been several studies of early administrative practices on Crete. Olivier and Godart have published a new corpus of hieroglyphic inscriptions.[514] Weingarten has concluded that the MM IIB deposit of sealings from the Phaistos palace represents an accumulation over many years (not an administrative "year" as usually claimed) and that the iconographic clusters of motifs within the sealings may correspond to social groups.[515] Poursat has suggested that MM II discs, perforated sherds, and miniature vases may have served as tokens in a counting system.[516] Tzigkanaki has completed her doctoral thesis on the MM II sealings at Monasteraki. When published, this study will be an extremely valuable contribution to our knowledge of protopalatial administration. Vlasaki and Hallager have presented all known prepalatial sealings from West Crete and have concluded that seals were used in the administration of production, trade, and perhaps storage during the prepalatial period.[517] While focused primarily on the neopalatial period, Hallager's exhaustive study of Minoan sealed documents, roundels, and nodules traces their development from the MM II period onward.[518]

Religion

Nowicki has identified new features (e.g., an area of pebbles) associated with peak sanctuaries and has suggested that all peak sanctuaries evolved from the one on Mt. Jouktas.[519] A recent study offers a critical review of writings on Minoan extraurban sanctuaries and argues that when royal dynasties arose in MM IB Crete, they consolidated their power by establishing an official cult center within their territory that transcended earlier ancestral cults located at local tombs.[520] This is much like the process in Early Iron Age Greece where incipient poleis founded rural shrines in key locations in order to mark out their territories. Iconographic analysis of votives at extraurban shrines does not corroborate the idea that the Minoans practiced a unified cult on peaks distinct from that in caves or at springs. Cave and peak sanctuaries share a wide range of basic concerns (female maturation/childbirth, crop fertility, and male initiation) that imply multiple deities. They also differ in some specific ways (e.g., only peak sanctuaries have votives related to health and human sexuality). Nevertheless, even among themselves, peak sanctuaries sometimes have votive assemblages that differ markedly from one another, such as the assemblages from Atsipades and Petsophas.

In other words, the labels "peak sanctuary" and "cave sanctuary" are probably misleading terms. It seems more likely that each territory had a main rural sanctuary on a high place, whether on a peak, in a cave, or next to a spring, and that the rites celebrated (and their social functions) at these shrines overlapped significantly. Each shrine had distinctive regional features, due probably to the number and nature of local deities and the ways in which they were worshipped. Jones's study of finds from peak and cave sanctuaries also concludes that these shrines show local variations on island-wide practices.[521] His

[512] E. Karantzali, "Απόψεις πάνω στις πολιτιστικές σχέσεις Κρήτης και Κυκλάδων την Πρώιμη Εποχή του Χαλκού: Η μαρτυρία των αγγείων και των ειδωλίων," in *Pepragmena* 1995, I, 445–82.

[513] J. Aruz, "Crete and Anatolia in the Middle Bronze Age: Sealings from Phaistos and Karahöyük," in M. Mellink, E. Porada, and T. Özgüç eds., *Aspects of Art and Iconography: Anatolia and Its Neighbors. Studies in Honor of Nimet Özgüç* (Ankara 1993) 35–54.

[514] J.-P. Olivier and L. Godart, *Corpus hieroglyphicarum inscriptionum Cretae* (*EtCret* 31, Paris 1996).

[515] J. Weingarten, "Two Sealing Studies in the Middle Bronze Age, I: Karahöyük, II: Phaistos," in P. Ferioli et al. eds., *Archives before Writing* (Rome 1994) 261–98. In the discussion (298–305) following Weingarten's paper, the points she raised were contested by E. Fiandra.

[516] J.-C. Poursat, "Les systèmes primitifs de comptabilité

en Crète minoenne," in Ferioli et al. (supra n. 515) 247–53. In this context, one wonders about the EM II "counters" from Myrtos/Fournou Koriphi (P. Warren, *Myrtos* [Oxford 1972] pl. 79e).

[517] M. Vlasaki and E. Hallager, "Evidence for Seal Use in Pre-palatial West Crete," in Pini and Poursat (supra n. 488) 251–70.

[518] E. Hallager, *The Minoan Roundel* (*Aegaeum* 14, Liège 1996).

[519] K. Nowicki, "Some Remarks on the Pre- and Protopalatial Peak Sanctuaries in Crete," *Aegean Archaeology* 2 (1994) 31–48.

[520] V. Watrous, *The Cave Sanctuary of Zeus at Psychro* (*Aegaeum* 15, Liège 1996).

[521] D. Jones, *Peak Sanctuaries and Sacred Caves in Minoan Crete* (*SIMA-PB* 156, Jonsered 1999).

quantitative analysis reveals further patterns, such as the lack of coiffured female figurines from caves and the absence of evidence for any uniform dining ritual at peak or cave shrines.

The volume *Cemetery and Society in the Aegean Bronze Age* features articles on the Mesara tholoi, Cycladic imports in these tholoi, mortuary feasting, and the ethnicity of the community using the EM I–II Agia Photia cemetery.[522] Rethemiotakis's thorough study of clay human figurines in Minoan Crete links the sharp increase in the production of such figurines to the rise of peak sanctuaries in late MM IA.[523] He demonstrates that protopalatial figurines evolve toward realism from an earlier abstract style. Maggidis's study of Building 19 at the Archanes cemetery also considers the extensive evidence within the burial data for MM IA social stratification.[524] He points out that the appearance of fixed altars at tombs, often in association with paved areas, benches, and antechambers, is a sign of new funerary ceremony and social ranking in MM I Crete.[525] Goodwin's investigation of the orientation of the entrances of approximately 30 Early Minoan tombs in the Mesara has identified two distinct groups, one with a solar alignment and one with a lunar alignment. She concludes that, at minimum, by EM I the Minoans understood right-angle geometry and had a system of "degrees" similar to our own for breaking down a circle, perhaps based on the number 6 as the basic unit.[526]

Chronology and Cultural Implications

The absolute and relative chronological framework for the Early Minoan period presented in table 2 is adapted from S. Manning's monograph, *The Absolute Chronology of the Aegean Early Bronze Age: Archaeology, Radiocarbon, and History* (Sheffield 1995). I have supplied the site phases and their relative correlations, including quotations from the excavators' site reports. This new chronology introduces two significant changes for Crete: 1) The EM II period (ca. 2700–

2200 B.C.) is lengthened and its end occurs later, and 2) a short EM III (ca. 2200–2100 B.C.) period corresponds to the Egyptian First Intermediate period and EB IV in the Levant. The advantage of lengthening the EM II period is that the rich tombs at Mochlos, which in ceramic terms have been called EM II/III or EM III, can be dated to EM IIB and thus are correlated in time with the international era of Troy IIg, EB III Levant, and Sixth Dynasty Egypt.

A second advantage of this Early Minoan chronology is that it allows the destructions reported at EM II sites, such as Myrtos, Mallia, and Vasiliki, to have variously occurred over a 250-year period, rather than belonging to a single horizon. The EM IIB scenario on Crete then resembles events in the EH II mainland, as recently reconstructed by J. Forsén in *The Twilight of the Early Helladics* (Jonsered 1992).

EM IIB thus becomes a relatively long period (ca. 2450–2200 B.C.). Wilson has described the sharp break between EM IIA and EM IIB ceramics at Knossos.[527] This is also true for other aspects of Cretan culture during these two periods. In contrast with the preceding chronological period, EM IIB witnesses the rise of local leaders ("chieftains"), increased interregional hostility, extended international trade with the Near East, and a progressive abandonment of the rural countryside.

In 1994, I wrote that "there is at present no archaeological evidence for a ranked society in EM II Crete" (RAP III, 179). Despite the fact that the evidence for EM II social complexity is still scarce and indirect, I have changed my mind on this issue, partly as a result of our findings of the 1992–1994 surface survey carried out around Gournia. During EM IIB, the site of Vasiliki appears to be the dominant settlement in the northern Isthmus of Ierapetra. At Vasiliki itself an important development occurred in EM IIB: an annex (Zois's West House) was added to the large, two-storied Red House (see above, RAP III,

[522] See the following articles in K. Branigan ed., *Cemetery and Society in the Aegean Bronze Age* (Sheffield Studies in Aegean Archaeology 1, Sheffield 1998): K. Branigan, "The Nearness of You: Proximity and Distance in Early Minoan Funerary Behaviour," 13–26; J.M. Murphy, "Ideologies, Rites and Rituals: A View of Prepalatial Minoan Tholoi," 27–40; T. Carter, "Reverberations of the 'International Spirit': Thoughts upon 'Cycladica' in the Mesara," 59–77; Y. Hamilakis, "Eating the Dead: Mortuary Feasting and the Politics of Memory in the Aegean Bronze Age Societies," 115–32; P.M. Day, D.E. Wilson, and E. Kiriatzi, "Pots, Labels and People: Burying Ethnicity in the Cemetery at Aghia Photia, Siteias," 133–49.

[523] G. Rethemiotakis, Ανθρωπομορφική πηλοπλαστική

στην Κρήτη (Βιβλιοθήκη της εν Αθήναις Αρχαιολογικής Εταιρείας 174, Athens 1998). See also A. Pilali-Papasteriou, Μινωϊκά πήλινα ανθρωπόμορφα ειδώλια της συλλογής Μεταξά (Thessaloniki 1992).

[524] C. Maggidis, "Burial Building 19, Phourni (Archanes): Variety and Originality in MM I Burial Architecture," in *Pepragmena* 1995, II, 561–76.

[525] C. Maggidis, "Minoan Tomb Altars and Shrines," *AJA* 103 (1999) 286 (abstract).

[526] M. Goodwin, *The Archaeology of Early Minoan Crete* (M.A. thesis, Bryn Mawr College 1998). I am indebted to the author for the information presented here.

[527] Wilson (supra n. 480).

Table 2. Comparative Chronology of the Aegean and Near East, ca. 2500–1800 B.C.*

Period / Date	Knossos	Mallia	Vasiliki	Mochlos	Cyclades	Troy	Tarsus	Kültepe	Ebla	Egypt
2500 B.C. / EM IIA				Wealthy Tombs 1-8, 9,10, 13, 19, 20, 21, 23, possess: bronze, gold, Syrian seal.	EC IIA	II	EB II	Mound 17-14		Dynasty V
2400 B.C. / EM IIB	South Front Early Houses Deposit		Seager III		EC IIB		Final EB II Destruction		Mardikh IIB1	Dynasty VI ca. 2340-2180 B.C.
2300 B.C.	RRN, floor V		Red House West Houses	→	Lefkandi I / Kastri Phases	International contacts / Trade with the Cyclades	EB IIIA		Sargonic Period	International trade
EM IIB	Imported Egyptian stone vases		Access to obsidian, copper.		Anatolian Contacts	IIg Fortifications City looted	Contacts with Syria and West Anatolia	Mound 13-12	Destruction ca. 2250 B.C.	
2200 B.C.		Destruction by fire	Destruction by fire / Seager IV	"time of retrenchment"	EC III	III		Three destructions in EB II-III	IIB2	
EM III / 2100 B.C.	Upper East Well / "period of isolation"		"poorly built hovels"	"decline in population"	Kea, Kastri deserted	Decline	EB IIIB	Mound 11 / Little sign of trade	"Economic Recession"	F.I.P. ca. 2180-2134 B.C. Peak period of drought and famine
MM IA / 2000 B.C.	West Court Houses	Premier Charnier	Seager V	Blocks A, C, D, MMIA Building and Tombs 1-3, 7, 11, 13, 16-17, 22	MC I	IV	MB I	Karum Kanesh IV-III	EB IV Destruction	Dynasty XI
1900 B.C.	RR Basement, lower level	South Houses	Houses A, Β, Γ, Φ, Χ		Phylakopi Iii	V		Karum Kanesh II	IIIA	— 1963 B.C. Dynasty XII
MM IB-II / 1800 B.C.	Early West Magazines / Trial KV: Village	Town Group / Quartier Mu		House D	Exports to Crete, Mainland / Increase in overseas interconnections	Renewed international contacts		Old Assyrian Trade / Karum Kanesh Ib	Foreign contacts	Expansion of foreign trade

* This table supersedes table 1 in RAP III, page 178, above. Revised May 2000.

170–71). This structure was of inferior construction (no second floor) and produced only pithoi and loomweights. Seager referred to the West House as "sheds" and "servants' quarters or storerooms."[528] The West House resembles a work and storage structure ancillary to the Red House, with its own living quarters. Thus, it seems reasonable to interpret the West House as an EM IIB predecessor of the menial resident-workshops ("ateliers") attached to Houses A and B in MM II Quartier Mu at Mallia. If this interpretation is correct, the Red House-West House unit is direct evidence of complex social ranking in EM IIB Crete. The Red House could have been the residence of an EM IIB "chieftain" who probably had some form of control over the local production and export of Vasiliki ware.[529]

In contrast to EM II, the EM III period on Crete emerges as an era of isolation and retraction, as it is elsewhere in the contemporary Aegean and Near East. In EM III, areas of the island are abandoned, some sites are deserted or shrink in size, signs of interregional and international trade virtually disappear, and ceramic styles become severely regionalized. It would seem better, therefore, to date the "time of retrenchment" and "population decline" noted at Mochlos to the EM III period rather than to MM IA.[530]

What caused these trends in EM III is harder to define. A number of factors seem apparent, but their relative importance and interaction are obscure. The destruction of EM IIB Vasiliki by fire, for instance, suggests armed hostility. But the parallelism of events in EM III Crete and the contemporary Cyclades and mainland implies a wider cause. The scale and intensity of Anatolian material cultural features across mainland Greece and the Aegean islands in EH/EC IIB–III

surely imply the movement of Anatolian peoples into these areas of the Aegean.

In the Near East at this time, similar types of events were taking place, and in that context we know that one of the basic causes was climatic change. In a recent collection of environmental studies, Nüzhet Dalfes, Kukla, and Weiss have gathered evidence for a period of severe desiccation, famine, and population loss/migration across the eastern Mediterranean toward the end of the third millennium B.C. While Crete seems to have been spared most of the immigration apparent on the mainland, it does suffer the same types of environmental changes and demographic losses recorded in Egypt, Anatolia, Syria, and Palestine.[531]

Our understanding of the MM IA period has not changed greatly since 1994. MM IA is a period of recovery, population growth, and renewed contacts with the Aegean and the Near East. At the end of the period, the introduction of literacy, the establishment of extraurban sanctuaries, and the reorganization of urban centers signal the appearance of the first states on Minoan Crete.

The implications of the above outline for research on Cretan state formation are important. In Crete, the later prepalatial period is not an unchanging cultural continuum. Rather, this period consists of three chronological phases, each with its own diverse events and cultural trends. Any convincing explanation for the rise of the Minoan palaces must take each of these distinct phases into account.

DEPARTMENT OF ART HISTORY
605 CLEMENS HALL
STATE UNIVERSITY OF NEW YORK AT BUFFALO
BUFFALO, NEW YORK 14260-4640
WATROUS@ACSU.BUFFALO.EDU

---

[528] Seager (supra n. 187) 210; see also H.B. Hawes et al., *Gournia, Vasiliki and Other Prehistoric Sites on the Isthmus of Hierapetra, Crete* (Philadelphia 1908) 49.

[529] For the location of the production source of Vasiliki ware, see Whitelaw et al. (supra n. 503) 268.

[530] Soles and Davaras (supra n. 481) 180 and n. 8.

[531] H. Nüzhet Dalfes, G. Kukla, and H. Weiss eds., *Third*

Millennium B.C. Climate Change and Old World Collapse (Berlin 1997). The climatic data for the Aegean are collected and discussed in J. Moody and V. Watrous, "Climate Change and the Aegean Bronze Age," paper given at the "International Congress: Archaeology of the Ancient Near East," Copenhagen, 22 May 2000.

Review of Aegean Prehistory IV:
The Stone Age of Greece from the Palaeolithic to the Advent of the Neolithic

CURTIS RUNNELS

INTRODUCTION*

The Stone Age of Greece was overlooked in the heroic age of prehistoric archaeology when the Palaeolithic of Europe was brought to light with its rich record of human fossils, stone tools, and painted caves. Serious research on the early prehistory of Greece began only in the 1960s, and even so it has been pursued in fits and starts, perennially short of money and people, and with a surprising lack of interest and support from institutions.

The reasons for this neglect are difficult to evaluate properly because of the lack of historical study of the problem, but some possible factors can be suggested. One must be the long and successful career of classical archaeology that focused the attention of archaeologists firmly on the great monuments of the historical past. When this fact is put beside the tendency for prehistoric archaeology and classical archaeology to be taught in entirely different academic departments in Europe and North America, it is likely that students with different interests were urged by helpful advisors to seek "appropriate" areas for fieldwork. As their advisors were no doubt under the impression that Greece "was for the Classicists," students who wished to study the Palaeolithic were encouraged to seek fieldwork opportunities in Europe, the Near East, or Africa.[1]

Those who consider prehistoric research in Greece face a daunting problem. Because of its position at the boundary between the African and European plates, Greece is active geologically with much uplift, folding, and tectonism, and older deposits have been destroyed or masked through erosion and deposition. Recent studies have shown that the effects of humans on the landscape in the last 8,000 years have been greater than previously thought, and erosion triggered by extensive clearance of vegetation from hillslopes for agricultural purposes has contributed significantly to the destruction or burial of early archaeological sites. The transgression of the Mediterranean in the Holocene has further complicated the picture by submerging large areas of coastal shelf. Offshore sites are submerged beneath 40–120 m of water and may lie under thick mantles of sediments eroded from the mainland interior.[2] As a consequence of these geologic and anthropogenic changes, early sites are preserved only in places where they have escaped the ravages of a landscape constantly on the move. It is understandable that prehistorians often prefer to carry out their research in areas with a better record of preservation.

There are theoretical reasons for investigating prehistory in regions outside of Greece. The origins of humans and the early stages of human evolution are

---

* Publication of this review and of the previous reviews in this series was made possible by a generous grant to *AJA* by the Institute for Aegean Prehistory. The editors and I are grateful for this support.

The following people helped to improve this paper with their valuable suggestions and advice. Tjeerd van Andel read the text in an early version, and Tracey Cullen, Jack Davis, Julie Hansen, Priscilla Murray, and Catherine Perlès read the final draft in the face of a looming deadline. Mark Rose supplied me, at short notice, with valuable references to tunny fishing. Their generous cooperation is very much appreciated. I would also like to thank the participants of the First International Conference on the Palaeolithic of Greece and Adjacent Areas in Ioannina in September 1994, for sharing their views and discussing with me some of the issues presented in this paper. Eliza McClennen prepared the maps and Michael Hamilton helped with the preparation of photographs. Geoff Bailey contributed

the photograph of Klithi Cave (fig. 8). The writing of this paper was completed while I was a Visiting Fellow of the McDonald Institute for Archaeological Research at the University of Cambridge. Unless otherwise specified, all dates are given in uncalibrated radiometric years.

[1] For the different approaches to archaeology, see C. Renfrew, "The Great Tradition versus the Great Divide," *AJA* 84 (1980) 287–98; and A.M. Snodgrass, *An Archaeology of Greece: The Present State and Future Scope of a Discipline* (Berkeley 1987) 1–18.

[2] The effects of erosion on the burial of sites are discussed in M.H. Jameson, C.N. Runnels, and T.H. van Andel, *A Greek Countryside: The Southern Argolid from Prehistory to the Present Day* (Stanford 1994) 228–46. See also E. Zangger, *The Geoarchaeology of the Argolid* (Berlin 1993). Changes in sea level are illustrated in T.H. van Andel and J.C. Shackleton, "Late Paleolithic and Mesolithic Coastlines of Greece and the Aegean," *JFA* 9 (1982) 445–54.

Originally published in *AJA* 99 (1995) 699–728.

being traced in Africa, which is widely regarded as the homeland of the human race. The later developments that brought humans from Africa into Eurasia have been of comparatively lesser interest, although there has been much new enthusiasm for the subject in recent years. Research on the later periods of prehistory has also been directed to areas outside of Greece. The origins of the Neolithic have been sought in southwest Asia since the time of Raphael Pumpelly and Vavilov, and Greece is usually regarded as on the margins of the region of primary cultural development.[3]

Despite the combined effects of these factors, a complete reversal of our view of Stone Age Greece has occurred in the last decade, and Greece has moved from its position on the margins of European prehistory to a position near the center. This change is the result chiefly of the growing theoretical interest in the emergence of modern humans between 100,000 and 40,000 B.P., and the continuing interest in the origins of agriculture and its spread to Europe in the early Holocene. For the former problem, new fossils and dating techniques have shown that the area encompassing the Balkans, Turkey, and southwest Asia was the center of activity in a key period of human evolution. The importance is based on geography, for these lands lay athwart the passage from Africa into Europe and Asia that was traversed, perhaps repeatedly, by hominids migrating from the heartland of humanity. The second area of interest is of longer standing, but new evidence, chiefly from regional surface surveys, indicates that Greece was the center of the earliest Neolithic cultures on European soil. The new importance of Palaeolithic archaeology can perhaps be gauged by the support for the first conference on the Palaeolithic of Greece and adjacent areas that was convened in Epirus in September 1994. This conference brought together scientists from many countries who are working in Greece and the Balkans, and the generous support for the conference provided by the Greek Ministry of Culture and the large number of participants are indications of the emergence of a new and vigorous discipline.

HISTORY OF RESEARCH

Early Studies

The first indication that a Stone Age sequence existed in Greece comparable with that known from Europe came with the publication of a short paper by George Finlay in 1869.[4] In this little-known pamphlet Finlay drew attention to the similarities between artifacts collected in Greece, chiefly stone axes and obsidian tools, and those found in the newly explored Swiss Neolithic lake villages. He concluded that early prehistoric remains existed in Greece, but sporadic reports of Stone Age finds in the following decades were not followed up with systematic research.[5] The lack of research is understandable when we recall that most of the early finds were made by travelers and classical scholars who had no interest in pursuing the subject once they had made their reports. It was not until the beginning of this century that the pioneering excavations of Christos Tsountas demonstrated for the first time that there was a rich field for prehistoric research in Greece. Tsountas explored the Thessalian plain between Volos and Larisa mapping such prehistoric mounds that could be reached by train. For the purposes of excavation, he focused his efforts beginning in 1901 on two sites, Sesklo and Dimini, which were easily reached from the city of Volos.[6] These sites were perhaps not the best choices for establishing a cultural sequence as they were disturbed by much post-Neolithic cultural activity, making the stratification difficult to decipher. Tsountas was nevertheless able to separate the materials from his excavations into two periods (Neolithic A and B) of considerable length and antiquity, which he thought were more or less comparable with the better-known Neolithic sequences of Europe. Although Tsountas did not have a means of dating his finds, his excavations

---

[3] There is a large literature on these subjects. For summaries of the current views on early human migrations, see P.A. Mellars, M.J. Aitken, and C.B. Stringer, "Outlining the Problem," *Philosophical Transactions of the Royal Society of London* 337 (1992) 127–30; W. Roebroeks and T. van Kolfschoten, "The Earliest Occupation of Europe: A Short Chronology," *Antiquity* 68 (1994) 489–503; and W. Roebroeks, "Updating the Earliest Occupation of Europe," *CurrAnthr* 35 (1994) 301–305. For Neolithic Greece, see J.-P. Demoule and C. Perlès, "The Greek Neolithic: A New Review," *Journal of World Prehistory* 7 (1993) 355–416; and J.M. Hansen, "Agriculture in the Prehistoric Aegean: Data versus Speculation," *AJA* 92 (1988) 39–52.

[4] G. Finlay, Παρατηρήσεις ἐπὶ τῆς ἐν Ἑλβετίᾳ καὶ Ἑλλάδι προϊστορικῆς ἀρχαιολογίας (Athens 1869).

[5] An example of what was perhaps a handaxe was shown to Lenormant by an Argos physician, who claimed it was found associated with extinct animal bones at Megalopolis in Arcadia: F. Lenormant, "L'âge de la pierre en Grèce," *RA* 1867, 16–19.

[6] C. Tsountas, Αἱ προϊστορικαί ἀκροπόλεις Διμηνίου καὶ Σέσκλου (Athens 1908). For a historical overview of this period of research, see K. Gallis, "A Short Chronicle of Greek Archaeological Investigations in Thessaly from 1881 until the Present Day," in B. Helly ed., *La Thessalie: Actes de la table-ronde 21–24 juillet 1975* (Lyons 1979) 1–30.

established the existence of a prehistoric culture on Greek soil evidently much older than the Bronze Age civilization discovered by Schliemann, and inaugurated a period of systematic archaeological research.

Despite the success of Tsountas in Thessaly, the discovery of earlier Stone Age cultures came only after further decades of neglect and disinterest. The first systematic excavations of pre-Neolithic sites in Greece were conducted at the Zaïmis and Ulbrich caves in the Megarid and Argolid, respectively, by the geologist and speleologist Adalbert Markovits beginning in the late 1920s. The results of these excavations were either ignored or deprecated by the few scholars who came to know of them, but there is no question that Markovits was the first to identify the Palaeolithic and Mesolithic in Greece. The important start made by Markovits was not followed up, and the very existence of this work was long forgotten: today the finds and even the caves themselves have been lost.[7] His position as a pioneer in Greek prehistory, however, is well established.

After Markovits, serious fieldwork was held up by the tragic disruptions created by economic depression, invasion, and war. The only notable exception was the excavation of Palaeolithic layers in the Seidi Cave in Boeotia in 1941 by R. Stampfuss. At the end of the war the finds, which had been removed from Greece, were misplaced, and the publication of the excavations in a not very fashionable journal was ignored for a long time.[8] The excavations of Markovits and Stampfuss were indications to the few who studied their publications that early prehistoric cultures existed in Greece.

Neolithic research in these same decades fared much better, with important excavations carried out by scholars from many countries. One reason for the greater interest in the Neolithic, apart from the fact that Tsountas was well known to the international intellectual community and had published his findings in a widely available monograph, was the theoretical interest focused on the Greek Neolithic in the 1920s by V. Gordon Childe. He saw the Neolithic of the Balkan peninsula as the result of the diffusion of the Neolithic way of life from its point of origin in the Near East, and he drew attention to the similarity of the Neolithic remains in Greece to finds being made in the Near East. Childe stimulated further interest in the subject by placing the Greek Neolithic in a wider Near Eastern context.[9] As new information was made available by topographic surveys and excavations, Thessaly was recognized as a center of a highly developed Neolithic civilization, perhaps the oldest manifestation of the village farming way of life in Europe. From the 1920s to the 1960s, Neolithic sites were discovered in the Cycladic islands, Crete, the Peloponnese, and the Ionian islands, and the new technique of radiocarbon dating showed these sites to be roughly contemporary with Neolithic sites elsewhere in the Balkans, but somewhat younger than the earliest sites in the Near East.[10] This steady growth of the field, despite the interruptions of economy and war, is in sharp contrast with the failure of prehistorians to follow the lead of Markovits and Stampfuss. Discerning minds realized, however, that there was potential for further research.

Recent Research

Investigation of the Palaeolithic and Mesolithic since the Second World War can be divided into two phases, the first representing the work of a few pioneers who carried out the initial scientific study of the subject beginning in 1958, and the second phase encompassing the work of projects since 1979 and continuing to the present day.

Sustained systematic research on the Palaeolithic and Mesolithic of Greece began in 1958–1959, coincidently the centennial of the publication of Darwin's *On the Origin of Species*. Palaeolithic discoveries were made in several parts of Greece, more or less by accident. In 1958, Michael Jameson discovered a Middle Palaeolithic stone tool on the slopes of Mt. Profitis Elias near Didyma in the southern Argolid, and this chance find was followed by exploration and excavation supported by the American School of a number of nearby caves, unfortunately without significant positive result.[11] In the same

---

[7] The most useful discussion of Markovits's excavations is found in C. Perlès, *Les industries lithiques taillées de Franchthi (Argolide, Grèce) 2: Les industries du mésolithique et du néolithique initial (Franchthi* 5, Bloomington 1990) 120–22; see also S.S. Weinberg, "The Stone Age in the Aegean," *CAH* I, 1 (Cambridge 1970) 557–672.

[8] See summary in Weinberg (supra n. 7); and R. Stampfuss, "Die ersten altsteinzeitlichen Höhlenfunde in Griechenland," *Mannus* 34 (1942) 132–47; E. Schmid, "Die Seïdi-Höhle: eine jungpaläolithische Station in Griechenland," *IVème Colloque international de spéléologie, Athènes 1963* (Ath-

ens 1965) 163–74.

[9] For discussion of Neolithic Greece in a broad setting, see Demoule and Perlès (supra n. 3) and D. Theocharis, *Neolithic Greece* (Athens 1973) 17–57.

[10] Demoule and Perlès (supra n. 3). See also T.H. van Andel and C. Runnels, "The Earliest Farmers in Europe," *Antiquity* 69 (1995) 481–500.

[11] P. Bialor and M.H. Jameson, "Palaeolithic in the Argolid," *AJA* 66 (1962) 181–82; Jameson et al. (supra n. 2) 326–35.

year a German team directed by Vladimir Milojčić discovered two flint flakes of characteristic Palaeolithic type while excavating a deep well at the Classical and Neolithic site of Argissa on the Peneios River in Thessaly. This accidental discovery was followed by a campaign of research involving many specialists directed toward the recovery of fossil animal bones and lithic artifacts from the banks of the river. A large number of Palaeolithic artifacts were discovered associated with fossil animal bones, and the results of this research were published in 1965.[12] In 1960 men from the village of Petralona in the Chalkidiki discovered a complete fossilized cranium in a deep cavern. Initially identified as a classic Neanderthal, the fossil created great excitement and proved in a dramatic way the existence of prehistoric humans in Greece. Lastly, Jean Servais discovered Palaeolithic artifacts in Elis in 1960 and this discovery was followed by a systematic campaign of research and publication supported by the French School.[13] Chance finds of stone tools, some of which may be Palaeolithic, were made in the Ionian islands and the Sporades in the years that followed.[14]

This evidence of undoubted Palaeolithic artifacts provided by these first discoveries attracted the attention for the first time of prehistorians who specialized in the study of the Palaeolithic. Two men have the distinction of being the first Palaeolithic archaeologists to work in Greece on a significant scale. The better known of these was Eric Higgs of the University of Cambridge who undertook an ambitious survey of Thrace, Macedonia, and Epirus in 1962 with the specific purpose of discovery of Palaeo-

lithic materials. The effects of this project are hard to calculate, but it certainly drew international attention for the first time to the Palaeolithic potential of Greece. His discovery of numerous sites in Epirus, some of which were extraordinarily rich in Palaeolithic artifacts, encouraged Higgs to concentrate his efforts there. Between 1963 and 1967 he excavated one open site at Kokkinopilos and rock shelters at Asprochaliko and Kastritsa, publishing the results of the survey and excavations in a series of detailed and influential papers in the *Proceedings of the Prehistoric Society*.[15] Only shortly after the first efforts of Higgs, Augustus Sordinas began exploration of the Ionian islands for his Harvard dissertation. The research was carried out chiefly between 1964 and 1968. Although his dissertation work focused on the evidence for the Neolithic and the Bronze Age, he also began an intensive survey of Corfu for Palaeolithic and Mesolithic sites. His survey was followed by trial excavations at two sites, the Upper Palaeolithic rock shelter at Grava in southwestern Corfu and the Mesolithic and Neolithic open site of Sidari on the north coast.[16]

The projects described above were exploratory, recalling to mind more the efforts of the early antiquarian topographers in Greece, pioneers who sketched the broad outlines of the picture, rather than the contemporary classical archaeologists who were conducting research and excavation on a large scale, reflecting the interests of a mature discipline with a long history of research. The early projects succeeded in identifying the most likely areas where sites of the Palaeolithic and Mesolithic periods were

---

[12] V. Milojčić, J. Boessneck, O. Jung, and H. Schneider, *Paläolithikum um Larissa in Thessalien* (Bonn 1965).

[13] The Petralona find was first described by P. Kokkoros and A. Kanellis, "Découverte d'un crâne d'homme paléolithique dans la péninsule chalcidique," *L'Anthropologie* 64 (1960) 438–46. The French discoveries in Elis were published in a series of papers: J. Servais, "Outils paléolithiques d'Élide," *BCH* 85 (1961) 1–9; A. Leroi-Gourhan, "Découvertes paléolithiques en Élide," *BCH* 88 (1964) 1–8; J. Chavaillon, N. Chavaillon, and F. Hours, "Une industrie paléolithique du Péloponnèse: Le Moustérien de Vasilaki," *BCH* 88 (1964) 616–22; Chavaillon et al., "Industries paléolithiques de l'Élide I: Région d'Amalias," *BCH* 91 (1967) 151–201; and Chavaillon et al., "Industries paléolithiques de l'Élide II: Région du Kastron," *BCH* 93 (1969) 97–151. For summaries of the French work, see C. Perlès, *Les industries lithiques taillées de Franchthi (Argolide, Grèce)* 1: *Présentation générale et industries paléolithiques* (Franchthi 3, Bloomington 1987) 205; and C. Runnels, "A Prehistoric Survey of Thessaly: New Light on the Greek Paleolithic," *JFA* 15 (1988) 277–90.

[14] For typical examples: G.A. Cubuk, "Altpaläolithische

Funde von der Mittelmeerterrassen bei Nea Skala auf Kephallinia (Griechenland)," *ArchKorrBl* 6 (1976) 175–81; A.N. Poulianos, "Petralona: A Middle Pleistocene Cave in Greece," *Archaeology* 24 (1971) 6–11; Theocharis (supra n. 9) gives other examples.

[15] S. Dakaris, E.S. Higgs, and R.W. Hay, "The Climate, Environment and Industries of Stone Age Greece: Part I," *PPS* 30 (1964) 199–244; E.S. Higgs and C. Vita-Finzi, "The Climate, Environment and Industries of Stone Age Greece: Part II," *PPS* 32 (1966) 1–29; and E.S. Higgs et al., "The Climate, Environment and Industries of Stone Age Greece: Part III," *PPS* 33 (1967) 1–29. See also G.N. Bailey et al., "Asprochaliko and Kastritsa: Further Investigations of Palaeolithic Settlement and Economy in Epirus (Northwest Greece)," *PPS* 49 (1983) 15–42.

[16] A. Sordinas, *The Prehistory of the Ionian Islands. The Flints and Pottery* (Diss. Harvard Univ. 1968); "Investigations of the Prehistory of Corfu during 1964–1966," *BalkSt* 10 (1969) 393–424; *Stone Implements from Northwestern Corfu, Greece* (Memphis 1970).

preserved, and used trial excavations to test the stratigraphy and to obtain samples for classification and dating.

The next logical step was the careful excavation of key sites other than Kastritsa and Asprochaliko in order to obtain a stratigraphic profile and large samples of artifacts and biological materials to permit typological analyses to place the archaeological cultures in established European and Near Eastern sequences and to reconstruct the palaeoenvironments of the Greek cultures. Unfortunately, few excavations were undertaken, and these were mostly of an exploratory nature. In Thessaly, new research was carried out by Demetrios Theocharis who continued to add to the existing collections, but did not conduct any excavations. Freund and Schmid restudied the materials from Stampfuss's excavations at Seidi and the Thessalian finds of Milojčić, and Schmid carried out supplementary excavations in Seidi to confirm the stratigraphy of the site.[17] In the Peloponnese the Kephalari Cave near Argos was the object of rescue excavations by the German Archaeological Institute in the 1970s.[18] In Elis, the French conducted no follow-up excavations. The Greek Archaeological Service carried out small-scale excavations near the town of Nafplion, but the results of these excavations are not published.[19] The only sustained and systematic excavation project directed toward the study of the Palaeolithic and Mesolithic periods took place in the southern Argolid at Franchthi Cave. Excavations were begun there under the direction of Thomas Jacobsen of Indiana University in 1967 and were continued until 1979 with the support of the University of Pennsylvania, Indiana University, and the American School of Classical Studies at Athens.[20]

Despite the spotty record of excavation, the early Stone Age of Greece moved in the short interval from 1958 to 1976 from the status of *terra incognita* into the mainstream of European prehistoric archaeology. Franchthi Cave, for instance, was recognized as one of the key type sites for European prehistory because the stratigraphic succession could be traced from the beginning of the Upper Palaeolithic to the end of the Neolithic, a period of as much as 25,000 years. The success of the excavations at Franchthi also drew scholarly attention to the strategic location of Greece athwart the prehistoric land and sea routes from the Near East to Europe. The study of Stone Age Greece was no longer regarded as something of an oddity or a sideshow to the important research taking place in Europe and the Near East, but was seen as well placed for playing an important part in the study of European prehistory. The pace of prehistoric research in Greece, however, was not sustained. By the mid-1970s research in the two richest areas, Epirus and Thessaly, was at an end, and the pioneers in the field, namely Higgs, Milojčić, and Theocharis, were dead. In the southern Argolid, the excavations at Franchthi were over by 1979, and the many specialists involved in this large interdisciplinary project turned to the study of the excavated materials. Thus ends the first phase of modern Stone Age research in Greece.

The second phase begins in 1979 with the Stanford University Environmental and Archaeological Survey of the Southern Argolid under the direction of Michael Jameson and Tjeerd van Andel.[21] This project had as one of its major goals the continuation of the Palaeolithic research begun by Jameson and Jacobsen, and in the first season an archaeological and geological survey of the region was carried out around Franchthi Cave that recovered data for the reconstruction of the palaeoenvironment in the Pleistocene and early Holocene. In this same period, a University of Cambridge team returned to Epirus under the direction of Geoffrey Bailey to pick up the threads of Higgs's research program and to undertake an entirely new excavation in the small rock shelter of Klithi near the town of Konitsa.[22] For some years these two projects constituted virtually the only Palaeolithic research being conducted in Greece, but the pace has accelerated noticeably since the mid-1980s, with surface reconnaissance in Thessaly, the Argolid, and Epirus directed specifically toward the identification of Palaeolithic and Meso-

[17] D. Theocharis, Ἡ αὐγή τῆς Θεσσαλικῆς προϊστορίας (Volos 1967); Theocharis (supra n. 9); Schmid (supra n. 8); G. Freund, "Zum Paläolithikum Thessaliens," *PZ* 46 (1971) 181–94.

[18] L. Reisch, *Pleistozän und Urgeschichte der Peloponnes* (Diss. Friedrich-Alexander Univ. 1980); Reisch, "The Transition to Middle Palaeolithic in Greece and the Southern Balkan," in A. Ronen ed., *The Transition from Lower to Middle Palaeolithic and the Origins of Modern Man* (Oxford 1982) 223–31.

[19] Perlès (supra n. 13) 204; G. Kourtessi-Philippakis, *Le paléolithique de la Grèce continentale* (Paris 1986) 138–39.

[20] Since 1987 nine fascicles have been published in the series *Excavations at Franchthi Cave, Greece* (Bloomington) under the general editorship of Thomas W. Jacobsen.

[21] Jameson et al. (supra n. 2) 326–35.

[22] See G. Bailey, "The Palaeolithic of Klithi in Its Wider Context," *BSA* 87 (1992) 1–28, for a summary of the project and a list of references to earlier publications.

lithic sites, and surveys and excavations in the island of Kefallinia, in the Boila Cave (Epirus), and Theopetra Cave (Thessaly) among other places.[23]

At the time of writing there are active Palaeolithic research projects being conducted by a large number of scholars with an international background in nearly every part of Greece. The intensity of recent research can be gauged by an examination of the collective results of the first phase of research that were summarized in 1970 by Saul Weinberg in the *Cambridge Ancient History*.[24] In that landmark publication, Weinberg's section on the Palaeolithic and Mesolithic took up a mere seven pages of the printed text, reporting on the work of half a dozen scholars and excavations. Some may recall that when Weinberg wrote his paper the number of archaeologists doing Palaeolithic fieldwork in Greece could be counted, literally, on one hand. The improvement can be measured by the scale and composition of the First International Conference on the Palaeolithic of Greece and Adjacent Areas held in Ioannina, just 30 years after Weinberg's article. This conference was convened in Epirus in the heart of the region first explored by the late Eric Higgs, with the generous support of the Greek Ministry of Culture. There were nearly 100 participants at the conference from at least 10 nations, with reports on most parts of Greece, from Thrace to the southern reaches of the Peloponnese, and from Thessaly to the western Ionian islands.[25] The topics of these papers and the discussions that followed them revealed not only the new interest in and enthusiasm for Stone Age research in Greece, but also a useful convergence of thinking about the principal problems to be addressed by future research in this area. I can confidently predict that the pace of research will increase exponentially in the coming decade.

SIGNIFICANT ISSUES IN EARLY PREHISTORY

In the early days of European prehistoric archaeology, an understandable emphasis was placed on the study of stone tool typology, stratification, and regional chronology. The first step in archaeology is to build reliable regional cultural histories that permit the placement of new finds within relative chronological sequences, allowing comparisons of finds within smaller areas and between larger regions. Once cultural histories are available attention can be turned to questions about human behavior. How do humans go about colonizing previously uninhabited areas? How have humans adapted to the changing climatic demands of the glacial and interglacial periods? How can the study of stone tools and biological remains from archaeological sites be used to understand the dynamics of human evolution? The transition from cultural history to the analysis of problems that are sometimes termed "behavioral" or "social" is the mark of a mature science, and the move to a problem-oriented European prehistory began more than 50 years ago.[26] It is evident that Greek prehistory is moving rapidly in this direction, and several key issues have emerged in recent years that are likely to be the primary focus of future research.

A central question in Greek Palaeolithic studies is the timing of the first entry of human beings into the peninsula. The history of the movement of humans from the African homeland through the Near East into Europe and Asia is obscure. One long-standing hypothesis attributes the first dispersion to *Homo erectus*.[27] According to this hypothesis the distribution of Acheulean lithic industries rich in handaxes in Europe marks the settlement of the continent by *Homo erectus*. It is true that the earliest fossils outside of Africa are indeed *Homo erectus*, but such fossils are absent from Europe, and even the dating of the Acheulean in Europe is fraught with controversy.[28] Interest has shifted in recent years to the hypothesis that Europe was settled after 500,000 B.P. by archaic *Homo sapiens*, the ancestors of both the classic Neanderthals and anatomically modern *Homo sapiens*. The picture is complicated by the ex-

---

[23] A large number of reports on recent Palaeolithic surveys and excavations are being published in G. Bailey et al. eds., *Proceedings of the First International Conference on the Palaeolithic of Greece and Adjacent Areas* (British School of Archaeology at Athens, in press). For a summary account of this conference, see G. Bailey, "The Balkans in Prehistory: The Palaeolithic Archaeology of Greece and Adjacent Areas," *Antiquity* 69 (1995) 19–24. For Kefallinia, see G. Kavvadias, Παλαιολιθική Κεφαλωνιά (Athens 1984). Lithic artifacts that may be Palaeolithic or Mesolithic have been noted and collected in the course of numerous regional surveys directed toward the recovery of information about all periods. Particularly worth noting are the patinated stone tools of generally Middle Palaeolithic type discovered in the Nemea Valley Archaeological Project and the Pylos Regional Archaeological Project, but not yet published (J.L.

Davis, personal communication, 1995). These finds are an indication that the discovery of Palaeolithic and Mesolithic sites is likely to become a regular feature of regional surveys.

[24] Weinberg (supra n. 7).

[25] Bailey et al. (supra n. 23). The summary of the Palaeolithic offered in 1986 by Kourtessi-Philippakis (supra n. 19), although longer than Weinberg's summary of 1970 (supra n. 7), included few sites or publications not known to Weinberg.

[26] C. Gamble, *The Palaeolithic Settlement of Europe* (Cambridge 1986) is an example of this new direction in Palaeolithic studies.

[27] Gamble (supra n. 26) 177–79; Roebroeks and van Kolfschoten (supra n. 3).

[28] See Roebroeks, and Roebroeks and van Kolfschoten (supra n. 3).

istence of two early Palaeolithic technocomplexes in Europe, the Acheulean and the chopper/flake tool industry called Clactonian, which some scholars consider to be an indication of the long-term presence of humans on the continent, or perhaps the existence of more than one hominid group. It must be acknowledged that our understanding of the events after one million years ago, when hominids established themselves outside of Africa, is very uncertain. It is for this reason that it is a matter of importance to know when Greece was first inhabited. It is likely that this peninsula would have been inhabited by the first hominids to pass from the Near East into Europe, and some early sites must survive that throw light on this period.

Another problem is connected with the origins of modern humans. Here two hypotheses are competing for attention.[29] In one view, Eurasia (including Greece) was initially populated by a migration of *Homo erectus* from the African homeland that occurred between one and two million years ago. According to this hypothesis, often called the "Multiregional" theory, anatomically modern *Homo sapiens* evolved from this widely spread *Homo erectus* population, perhaps passing through the stage of archaic *Homo sapiens* (represented in Greece by the Petralona cranium). This multiregional theory predicts the evolution of local populations into *Homo sapiens* in widely separated geographical locations, although allowing for the possibility of gene flow. In another view, usually called the "Replacement" theory, anatomically modern humans evolved from *Homo erectus* in only one restricted geographical area, which is located in Africa on the basis of anatomically modern human fossils that date to as much as 120,000 B.P., and migrated from Africa about 100,000 B.P. to replace archaic humans throughout their range in Europe, the Near East, and Asia. This theory has gained support in recent years as new dates from Israel show modern humans there already by 100,000 B.P., and genetic studies place the emergence of modern *Homo sapiens* in Africa.[30]

It is not necessary to go into a detailed discussion of the evidence for and against these different hypotheses. The important point is that the debate on the origins of modern humans has brought renewed attention to Greece, which is the logical point of first entry for human migrants to Europe. The emergence of modern humans is closely bound up with the well-documented archaeological transition from the Middle to the Upper Palaeolithic. This transition is marked by the disappearance of the Mousterian, a lithic technocomplex rich in side scrapers and points made on short broad flint flakes, and its replacement by the Upper Palaeolithic technocomplexes dominated by tools made on long thin blades, typically points with retouched "backs" and end scrapers. This transition was for a long time dated to approximately 35,000 B.P. and considered to represent a clear-cut boundary between the passing of the Neanderthals as the makers of the Mousterian, and the coming of modern humans with their new blade-tool technology. It is now evident that the transition occurred before 40,000 B.P. in the Near East and slightly later as one moves westward into the Balkans and Europe.[31] The associations of fossil human groups with the different industries have also been challenged. The discovery of modern humans in Israel in association with the Mousterian as early as 100,000 B.P., and Neanderthals in France in association with an Upper Palaeolithic industry as late as 32,000 B.P., is an unexpected reversal of the usual assumptions, and, if sustained by future research, indicates that the picture is very complicated.[32] Industries in the Balkans and Greece appear to have characteristics of both the Mousterian and an Upper Palaeolithic industry (the Aurignacian), and some have proposed that these industries are evidence of "acculturation" that occurred as the result of contact between classic Neanderthalers and the advancing wave of modern humans.[33] A detailed study of the transition from the Middle to the Upper Palaeolithic in Greece is likely to have useful implications for the broader study of modern human origins.

A full study of the Palaeolithic in Greece requires more than stone tools. To add the dimension of human behavior, more attention must be given to the search for human fossils. Fossil-bearing deposits of

[29] Mellars et al. (supra n. 3) offer a summary of the problem. See also P. Mellars, "Archaeology and the Population-dispersal Hypothesis of Modern Human Origins in Europe," *Philosophical Transactions of the Royal Society of London* 337 (1992) 225–34.

[30] N. Mercier and H. Valladas, "Thermoluminescence Dates for the Palaeolithic Levant," and H.P. Schwarcz, "Chronology of Modern Humans in the Levant," in O. Bar-Yosef and R.S. Kra eds., *Late Quaternary Chronology and Paleoclimates of the Eastern Mediterranean* (Tucson 1994) 13–20 and 21–31, respectively.

[31] For the dating of the Middle/Upper Palaeolithic tran-

sition, see C. Stringer and C. Gamble, *In Search of the Neanderthals* (London 1993) 39–60; and Schwarcz (supra n. 30).

[32] Stringer and Gamble (supra n. 31) 123–42; Mercier and Valladas (supra n. 30).

[33] On acculturation, see P. Allsworth-Jones, *The Szeletian and the Transition from Middle to Upper Palaeolithic in Central Europe* (Oxford 1986); F.B. Harrold, "Mousterian, Chatelperronian and Early Aurignacian in Western Europe: Continuity or Discontinuity?" in R.L. Ciochon and J.G. Fleagle eds., *The Human Evolution Source Book* (Englewood Cliffs, N.J. 1993) 585–603; Runnels (supra n. 13).

the Pleistocene are very rare in Greece, and human fossils are likely to be discovered only after extensive searching. The well-preserved Petralona cranium in the Chalkidiki suggests that the search will be successful in the long run, although the skull remains an isolated and enigmatic find. It was found cemented in a stalagmite unassociated with other fossils or artifacts. The cranium is no longer considered a classic Neanderthal, as it was called in early publications, but its exact classification and age remain a subject of considerable controversy. Current opinion holds that it should be classified as an archaic form of *Homo sapiens*, perhaps ancestral to classic Neanderthals and anatomically modern humans, and the designation of *Homo heidelbergensis* is one suggested name for the species.[34] The most reliable estimate of its age is based on the radiometric dating of the stalagmitic stone layer that covered the fossil, which dates to ca. 160–240,000 B.P. The skull must be older, and most authorities assign it an age between 200 and 400,000 B.P.[35] No Neanderthals have been discovered in Greece, and the excavations of Upper Palaeolithic sites such as Franchthi have turned up only very fragmentary human remains, mainly teeth and bone fragments. A heavily mineralized occipital from a human skull, now in the archaeological museum of Volos, was found on the banks of the Peneios River in the 1970s. It may date between 50 and 30,000 B.P., but it has not been studied and published.[36] The fact remains that we have very little fossil evidence for the Palaeolithic period.

Other interesting questions are connected with the Upper Palaeolithic. After 30 years of research it is clear that some puzzling gaps remain in the archaeological record, even if we allow for the small number of systematic excavations, and the absence of early Upper Palaeolithic remains is striking. The sequences tested in cave excavations are all younger than 28,000 B.P., yet the earliest Upper Palaeolithic (Aurignacian) was established in the Balkans by 38,000 B.P.[37] There is evidently a hiatus of as much

as 10,000 years between the beginning of the Upper Palaeolithic in the Balkans and the Upper Palaeolithic in some parts of Greece. A related problem is the apparent discontinuity in the distribution of Upper Palaeolithic sites in Greece during the last glacial. Cave sites are known in Epirus, Boeotia, and the Argolid, but are curiously rare in the western Peloponnese, Thessaly, Macedonia, and Thrace. This patchiness of settlement is typical of Palaeolithic Europe as a whole, and is not adequately explained.[38] The rarity of Upper Palaeolithic open-air sites, as opposed to caves and rock shelters, is puzzling, especially as the number of intensive surface surveys has increased in the past decade. We may add to this list of questions the apparent abandonment of almost all the known Upper Palaeolithic sites before the end of the Pleistocene, producing a significant hiatus in occupation between about 13,000 and 10,000 B.P.

Yet another major area of research concerns the origins and significance of the Mesolithic period in Greece. The rarity of Mesolithic sites is remarkable: at present there are 12 sites considered to be Mesolithic in the entire country. At Franchthi Cave, the only site where the transition from the Palaeolithic to the Mesolithic has been tested by excavation, it is probable that there was an interruption in the cave sequence between the two periods.[39] The significance of the Mesolithic and its connection, if any, with the Palaeolithic are very difficult to evaluate when great tracts in the country appear to have been uninhabited during this period. The paucity of the Mesolithic record has a bearing on another important problem in early Greek prehistory, namely the origins of agriculture. The Neolithic emerged first in the Near East, in its broadest geographical sense, and was established only later in Europe according to our present understanding, and the details of this important revolution in economic and social organization are today a focus of debate.[40] One hypothesis regards the spread of the Neolithic as the result

---

[34] C.B. Stringer et al., "The Significance of the Fossil Hominid Skull from Petralona, Greece," *JAS* 6 (1979) 295–98; C. Stringer, "The Dating of European Middle Pleistocene Hominids and the Existence of *Homo erectus* in Europe," *Anthropologie* 19 (1981) 2–14; M.H. Day, *Guide to Fossil Man*,⁴ (Chicago 1986) 91–98; C.B. Stringer, personal communication, 1994.

[35] G. Hennig et al., "ESR-dating of the Fossil Hominid Cranium from Petralona Cave, Greece," *Nature* 292 (1981) 533–36; A.G. Wintle and J.A. Jacobs, "A Critical Review of the Dating Evidence for Petralona Cave," *JAS* 9 (1982) 39–47; A. Poulianos et al., "Petralona Cave Dating Controversy," *Nature* 299 (1982) 280–82; A.G. Latham and H.P. Schwarcz, "The Petralona Hominid Site: Uranium-series Re-analysis of 'Layer 10' Calcite and Associated Palaeomagnetic Anal-

yses," *Archaeometry* 34 (1992) 135–40.

[36] For Franchthi human bone, see T. Cullen, "Mesolithic Mortuary Ritual at Franchthi Cave, Greece," *Antiquity* 69 (1995) 270–89. For the Thessalian skull fragment, see Theocharis 1967 (supra n. 17) 32–33, pl. V, where the heavily mineralized calvaria is pictured: L. Angel is quoted as saying that the fossil "should not be classified as Neanderthal in the classic sense of the term."

[37] Mellars (supra n. 29).

[38] Gamble (supra n. 26) 367–78; and Runnels (supra n. 13).

[39] C. Perlès, "Long-Term Trends at Franchthi: A Synthetic and Comparative Approach," in Bailey et al. (supra n. 23).

[40] See van Andel and Runnels (supra n. 10).

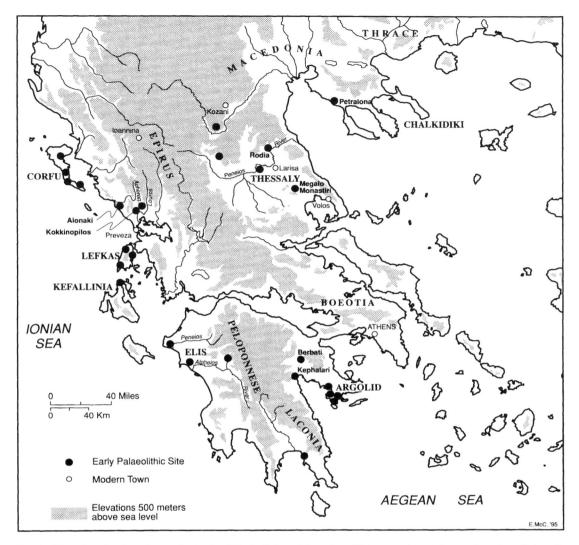

Fig. 1. Map showing locations of principal Early Palaeolithic sites. This map shows sites assigned traditionally to the Lower and Middle Palaeolithic (300,000–30,000 B.P.). Thessaly, Epirus, and Elis have numerous small scatters of lithic artifacts, chiefly of Middle Palaeolithic type (100,000–30,000 B.P.), which are not indicated individually on this map.

of demic diffusion from the Near East outward to Europe, Central Asia, and North Africa, while another holds that the Neolithic emerged as the result of local processes whereby indigenous Mesolithic communities more or less independently changed their economies from foraging to farming.[41] A growing number of archaeologists see the spread of the Neolithic as a complex process involving in some cases the physical movement of Near Eastern farmers into new lands, and in other cases a mixed and dynamic process involving the interaction of migrants

with indigenous populations of Mesolithic foragers.[42] Greece is the portion of Europe that lies closest to the Near East and it is logical to assume that evidence from this first frontier will be of primary significance for the understanding of the transition from the Mesolithic to the Neolithic.

AN OVERVIEW OF EARLY GREEK PREHISTORY

The Early Palaeolithic

The Palaeolithic in Greece is divided roughly into two periods. The division between the two periods

---

[41] A.J. Ammerman, "On the Neolithic Transition in Europe: A Comment on Zvelebil & Zvelebil (1988)," *Antiquity* 63 (1989) 162–65. R. Dennell, *European Economic Prehistory* (London 1983) 152–68 offers one view of the "indigenist" hypothesis.

[42] For a discussion of demic diffusion, see A. Ammerman and L.L. Cavalli-Sforza, *The Neolithic Transition and the Genetics of Populations in Europe* (Princeton 1984); and C. Renfrew, *Archaeology and Language* (New York 1987) 145–59.

Fig. 2. View of the Thessalian plain. The Peneios River is visible in the plain. Early Palaeolithic findspot 30 (Rodia) is located in the center of the picture, along the horizontal white line.

is based chiefly on chronology and the dominant stone tool industries. The Early Palaeolithic is a long period (300,000–30,000 B.P.) that includes the traditional periods of the Lower and Middle Palaeolithic, terms often applied arbitrarily to cultural phenomena that may overlap in time and space. The archaeological cultures of the Early Palaeolithic were once associated with fossil human forms, either *Homo erectus* or archaic *Homo sapiens* (e.g., Neanderthals). The Upper Palaeolithic (30,000–10,000 B.P.) period is usually correlated with early forms of anatomically modern *Homo sapiens*. Even this two-part division is open to question, because specific forms of early humans can no longer be identified as the makers of particular stone tool industries, and it is used here only as a rough indication of chronological position in the cultural sequence.

The earliest Palaeolithic finds are found in northern Greece (fig. 1). The Petralona cranium when it was first discovered was classified as a Neanderthal, and Mousterian artifacts in Thessaly, the Argolid, and Epirus were once thought to provide the archaeological background for the fossil. After a careful reexamination of the fossil in the 1970s, its classification was changed and its date was pushed back to 200,000 B.P. or earlier, evidence that an earlier Palaeolithic horizon was to be expected in Greece.[43]

Until recently, however, the only archaeological find belonging to the time of the Petralona cranium was a handaxe found by Eric Higgs near Kozani in 1962 and classified as belonging to the Acheulean, a stone tool industry of the Lower Palaeolithic.[44] Since Higgs's time claims have been made for early stone tools in the Petralona cavern, and amateurs have reported Early Palaeolithic implements in many parts of Greece. On the basis of the reports, the majority of these objects are without secure stratigraphic or geologic contexts and in some cases are not certainly of human manufacture.[45] Until these artifacts have been published in the professional literature it is not possible to evaluate them further. Even the Kozani handaxe remains an isolated chance find with no context or date.

The first published Early Palaeolithic materials from a datable context were found in the southern Peloponnese, where Ludwig Reisch found a non-Mousterian flake assemblage in Laconia associated with a raised beach level that may belong to the last interglacial (ca. 125,000 B.P.) or earlier, and in eastern Thessaly, where my colleagues and I identified six sites with a chopper/flake tool industry near Larisa and the village of Megalo Monastiri.[46] The Thessalian site near the village of Rodia (fig. 2), north of Larisa, can be dated by its geologic context to approxi-

[43] Stringer et al. (supra n. 34).

[44] E.S. Higgs, "A Hand Axe from Greece," *Antiquity* 38 (1964) 54–55.

[45] E.g., E. Sarantea, *Προϊστορικά ευρήματα Νέας Αρτάκης Ευβοίας* (Athens 1986); A. Andreikos, *Οι κατώτερες*

παλαιολιθικές λιθοτεχνίες της Δυτικής Ηπείρου και του Ιονίου (Athens 1993); Poulianos (supra n. 14).

[46] Reisch 1980 and 1982 (supra n. 18); C. Runnels and T.H. van Andel, "The Lower and Middle Paleolithic of Thessaly, Greece," *JFA* 20 (1993) 299–317.

Fig. 3. Early Palaeolithic artifacts from findspot 30 (Rodia) in Thessaly. Typical notched pieces are visible on the left and right. The raw material is massive quartz or fine-grained quartzite.

mately 300–400,000 B.P. The distinctive chopper/flake tools belong to a pebble tool tradition where quartz pebbles were flaked to produce large, simple bifacial cores (classified as choppers or chopping tools) and flakes. The cores are flaked along one side to form a long cutting edge. The technique of prepared flake removals from flat cores, which is called the Levallois technique, is absent. This technique, common in Middle Palaeolithic industries, is rare in chopper/flake tool traditions. The Thessalian cores were worked instead by direct hard hammer percussion. The resulting flakes were typically retouched on the edges, and often more than one edge has been modified to create scrapers, piercing tools, and knives (fig. 3). The characteristic feature of the industry is the frequent occurrence of large notches manufactured by the removal of a single flake by direct percussion (the so-called Clactonian technique). These notches may occur singly or be grouped on a flake to create a denticulate. No complete handaxes have yet been found with this industry, but some fragmentary bifacial pieces could be from handaxes. The Thessalian pebble tool complex has similarities with the Clactonian industry, which belongs, like the Acheulean, to the Lower Palaeolithic in Europe.

In Epirus a number of Lower Palaeolithic sites have been identified in the course of a joint American-Greek survey of the Nome of Preveza. A handaxe and other artifacts were discovered in a secure geologic context at the site of Kokkinopilos near Preveza.[47] The handaxe is a pointed type occurring throughout Europe in the late Acheulean and not unknown in the early Middle Palaeolithic (fig. 4). It, and associated artifacts, are made from flint cobbles rather than quartz pebbles. Other sites in the Preveza survey produced chopper/flake tools using techniques similar to the Clactonian, and it is probable that both Acheulean and chopper/flake industries are present in western Greece.

Many reports of possible Lower Palaeolithic artifacts from other parts of Greece were made at the First Palaeolithic Conference in Ioannina, and it is certain that new finds will follow.[48] The increased rate of discovery of Lower Palaeolithic sites has been made possible by our growing understanding of Pleistocene deposits and their associated geologic fea-

---

[47] Runnels et al., "Human Settlement and Landscape in the Preveza Region, Epirus, in the Pleistocene and Early Holocene," in Bailey et al. (supra n. 23); C. Runnels and T.H. van Andel, "A Handaxe from Kokkinopilos, Epirus, and Its Implications for the Paleolithic of Greece," *JFA* 20 (1993) 191–203.

[48] There are many reports of poorly dated chance finds in Bailey et al. (supra n. 23), but they are an indication that the rate of discovery and reporting is increasing. Kourtessi-Philippakis reports a possible stone tool from a geologic context in Corfu that could be as much as 750,000

B.P. in age. The implement is an isolated find, and even if it is not intrusive, or a naturally fractured stone, the dating of the context, which is based on palaeomagnetism, remains open to question. In light of the Early Palaeolithic artifacts discovered on the mainland opposite Corfu, however, further research on Corfu should be encouraged: see G. Kourtessi-Philippakis, "Les plus anciennes occupations humaines dans le territoire épirote et aux confins de l'Illyrie méridionale," in P. Cabanes ed., *L'Illyrie méridionale et l'Épire dans l'antiquité* II (Paris 1993) 11–16.

Fig. 4. Early Palaeolithic handaxe (biface) from Kokkinopilos, Epirus. (Photo J.R. Wiseman)

tures, permitting us to pinpoint the places where archaeological materials of a particular age are likely to be best preserved, and by the growing number of regional surveys that include specialists trained in the recognition of Palaeolithic artifacts.

The limited array of Early Palaeolithic finds can only be interpreted with caution because they are widely scattered in space and time and any conclusions are certain to require major modifications as new finds appear. Nevertheless it is possible to draw a few simple inferences. There is as yet no evidence for humans in Greece before 400,000 B.P., and this fact supports those who postulate a late entry of humans into Europe. It is always difficult to base an argument on negative evidence, and we cannot rule out an earlier human presence that may have been small, tentative, and short-lived, leaving few traces. If humans entered Greece and the rest of Europe relatively late in the Pleistocene, it is likely that these early humans were not *Homo erectus* but were an archaic form of *Homo sapiens*. Once humans were established in Greece, they appear to have left more than one lithic industry. In Thessaly we see a chopper/flake tool industry, made chiefly from quartz pebbles, and evidently without handaxes. In Epirus there are materials belonging to a chopper/flake tool tradition, but there are also handaxes and other arti-

facts that may belong to the Acheulean. There is nothing unusual about finding chopper and handaxe industries in close proximity, and both traditions are widely attested throughout Europe. A recent summary has evaluated the different hypotheses that account for these two traditions and found that there can be no definite conclusion made at this time, but some evidence suggests that two industries, the Acheulean and Clactonian, are at least partly contemporary.[49]

Early human sites show a marked preference for the availability of water. In Epirus, sites are closely connected with karstic features such as poljes, which are depressions created by tectonic faulting that become plugged with erosional sediments and fill with water on a seasonal basis to form swamps or shallow lakes.[50] The Thessalian landscape is not karstic, and sites are situated instead on the interfluves between the channels of a braided river system.[51] This distribution of sites suggests a pattern of foraging that had a seasonal basis. Larger base camps or aggregation sites may exist on the now submerged coastal plains, and early humans probably moved to the interior only in the spring and summer when melting snow filled the lakes and rivers with water. The presence of water and new vegetation attracted animals to the lakes and rivers, providing the hunters

[49] N. Ashton et al., "Contemporaneity of Clactonian and Acheulian Flint Industries at Barnham, Suffolk," *Antiquity* 68 (1994) 585–89.

[50] Runnels and van Andel (supra n. 47).
[51] Runnels and van Andel (supra n. 46).

with concentrated and predictable resources. Camps on the banks of the river channels or the margins of lakes were ephemeral working sites where raw materials were worked to produce weapons and tools for processing animal and plant food. This is the reason for the many cores and retouched tools still to be found in these places. The small number of sites makes further interpretation very risky. The destruction of sites and the dispersal of artifacts have certainly removed large portions of the record. One last observation is possible. Even if we allow for post-depositional disturbance and destruction of sites, the quantity of artifacts found on the surviving sites is very small when compared with the concentrations of thousands of handaxes and other artifacts on sites in Africa or the Near East. The poverty of the Greek sites may be in part a function of the relative brevity of the Greek Palaeolithic, a period of 0.3 million years versus 1.6 million years in Africa, and the possibility that we have mainly the seasonal hunting stands of highly mobile foragers.

The later Early Palaeolithic (100,000–30,000 B.P.), also known as the Middle Palaeolithic in traditional terms, produced much evidence of human activity. The Middle Palaeolithic is marked by the flake tool industry called the Mousterian (after a French type site), and the Mousterian is found from western Europe in a continuous band through the Balkans to the Near East and beyond.[52] The Greek Mousterian is sometimes found with a few small handaxes, and usually contains large numbers of scrapers, points, and other tools. The use of cores prepared in the Levallois fashion in order to remove large flat flakes for blanks that will be retouched to create different tool types is the most conspicuous feature of the industry. Another feature of the Greek Mousterian is the presence of distinctive bifacially flaked foliates ("leafpoints") made by direct percussion on large flakes (fig. 5).[53] The chronology of the Middle Palaeolithic in Greece is uncertain. The beginning of the period is marked by the transition from the Acheulean to the Mousterian, which is poorly understood and nowhere well dated. Some authorities believe that the "transition" is more a

Fig. 5. Early Palaeolithic bifacial foliate ("leafpoint") from Galatas, Epirus. (Photo M. Hamilton)

product of archaeological classification than a real boundary. It is clear in any case that flake tool industries of broadly Mousterian character are already present in the Near East as early as 200,000 B.P., and somewhat later in some parts of western Europe.[54] The earliest Mousterian in Greece is considerably later than that from neighboring regions. A thermoluminescence determination of ca. 100,000 B.P. for the Mousterian industry in the lowest levels of the stratified sequence from the Asprochaliko Cave in Epirus suggests that the Mousterian was established in Greece only after the last interglacial.[55] Other dates for the Greek Mousterian are younger. An in situ Mousterian site in the southern Argolid was

[52] Stringer and Gamble (supra n. 31) 143–77.

[53] See Runnels (supra n. 13) for a listing of bifacial foliates in Greece.

[54] See Stringer and Gamble (supra n. 31) 143–77; R. Grün, P. Mellars, and H. Laville, "ESR Chronology of a 100,000-Year Archaeological Sequence at Pech de l'Azé II, France," *Antiquity* 65 (1991) 544–51, have the late Acheulean at ca. 190,000 B.P.; J.L. Bischoff et al., "Uranium-series Isochron Dating of El Castillo Cave (Cantabria, Spain): The 'Acheulean'/'Mousterian' Question," *JAS* 19 (1992) 49–62

place the boundary between 100,000 and 200,000 B.P. See also Mercier and Valladas (supra n. 30) and Schwarcz (supra n. 30).

[55] J. Huxtable et al., "Thermoluminescence Dates and New Analysis of the Early Mousterian from Asprochaliko," *CurrAnthr* 33 (1992) 109–14; G. Bailey, V. Papaconstantinou, and D. Sturdy, "Asprochaliko and Kokkinopilos: TL Dating and Reinterpretation of Middle Palaeolithic Sites in Epirus, North-west Greece," *Cambridge Archaeological Journal* 2 (1992) 136–44.

dated to ca. 52,000 B.P. by a uranium/thorium (U/Th) assay of pedogenic calcium carbonate crusts that covered the artifacts.[56] Mousterian sites in Thessaly are stratified in deposits being exposed by the down-cutting of the Peneios river and are bracketed by radiocarbon and U/Th dates that range from ca. 45,000 to 30,000 B.P.[57] The Mousterian vanishes from the Greek record before 30,000 B.P., as it does throughout Europe.

Who was responsible for the Mousterian in Europe and Greece? For decades it was thought that the Mousterian people were Neanderthals, but this comfortable assumption has been destroyed by recent evidence from Israel and France showing that remains of modern *Homo sapiens* are found with Mousterian tools and Neanderthals with tools of Upper Palaeolithic type.[58] It is difficult to determine the identity of the stone tool makers as few fossil hominids have been found in direct association with tools. In the absence of such associations in Greece, the identity of the Mousterian people must be a matter of speculation. There are sufficient finds, however, of Neanderthals with Mousterian sites in Europe and Israel to make the association between the two the most probable hypothesis, and in this paper I will assume that the Greek Mousterian was produced by Neanderthals.[59] The location and dating of the origins of the Neanderthals is also a mystery, but the present consensus is that Neanderthals are derived from European populations of archaic *Homo sapiens* (or perhaps *Homo heidelbergensis*) represented by fossils such as Petralona, Steinheim, Swanscombe, and Arago.[60] Some authorities accept a controversial date for a Neanderthal in Israel of 220,000 B.P., but others place the first appearance of Neanderthals much later, between 160,000 and 125,000 B.P.[61] When did Neanderthals enter Greece? The evidence from Asprochaliko shows that the Mousterian was already present early in the last glacial, and the coincidence of the appearance of the Mousterian in Greece and the Near East has suggested to some scholars that Neanderthals may have taken refuge in the Mediterranean region to escape severe glacial conditions in Europe.[62] If this hypothesis is cor-

rect, parts of central and northern Europe were intermittently abandoned by Neanderthals who moved south after ca. 60,000 B.P., pushing into Spain, Italy, Greece, Turkey, and perhaps to the Near East.[63]

An early glacial migration of Neanderthals into Greece explains the otherwise puzzling abundance of Middle Palaeolithic sites in Greece, which mark a horizon of intense activity between 100,000 and 30,000 B.P. European Neanderthals were attracted no doubt by the vast coastal plains on the continental shelf exposed by lower sea levels. The broad plains available around Greece were not simple extensions of existing environments, but were habitats that have entirely vanished from the present-day Mediterranean. They were areas of low-lying land with a relatively mild climate during glacial winters. Free from snow, and with abundant water, they provided refuges for trees and other plants and supported herds of grazing animals.[64] The Neanderthals would have frequented these plains in glacial winters and would penetrate the interior during the spring and summer when melting snow supplied lakes and rivers with water and the new vegetation attracted large herbivores. The rivers and lakes would have been especially attractive in the high summer and early fall as surface water dwindled, and remaining water sources served to concentrate plant and animal resources, which the Neanderthals no doubt found to be predictable and dependable as they made their way down to winter encampments on the coastal plain.

The distribution of Mousterian sites in Greece reveals the importance of water to the Neanderthals. The greatest concentrations of sites are located along the Peneios River in Thessaly, the rivers and numerous lakes of southern Epirus, and the Alpheios and Peneios rivers in Elis. Sites are rare in the arid lands of central Greece and the eastern Peloponnese, at least in those areas that have been searched in a reasonably systematic manner. In the dry interior valley of Berbati, a Swedish-American survey identified only one certain Middle Palaeolithic site and no more than a dozen stone tools in an area of 60 km².[65] In the arid southern Argolid an intensive

[56] Jameson et al. (supra n. 2) 326–35.

[57] Runnels (supra n. 13); Runnels and van Andel (supra n. 46).

[58] Stringer and Gamble (supra n. 31) 195–217.

[59] For a summary of evidence for Neanderthal associations with the Mousterian, see Harrold (supra n. 33).

[60] Stringer and Gamble (supra n. 31) 64–69.

[61] See Mercier and Valladas (supra n. 30) for an early dating of Neanderthals.

[62] Huxtable et al. (supra n. 55).

[63] Stringer and Gamble (supra n. 31) 143–77.

[64] J.C. Shackleton et al., "Coastal Paleogeography of the Central and Western Mediterranean during the Last 125,000 Years and Its Archaeological Implications," *JFA* 11 (1984) 307–14; T.H. van Andel, "Late Quaternary Sea-level Changes and Archaeology," *Antiquity* 63 (1989) 733–45.

[65] B. Wells et al., "The Berbati-Limnes Archaeological Survey: The 1988 Season," *OpAth* 18 (1990) 207–38.

American survey produced no more than five sites and a few dozen artifacts in an area of 250 km².[66] By way of contrast, more than 30 sites with hundreds of stone tools were discovered along one small segment (8 km) of the Peneios River in Thessaly.[67] Epirus offers a very clear illustration of the connection between Middle Palaeolithic sites and water. Sites are very numerous in the region west of a line from Ioannina to Preveza down to the Ionian Sea. This area has perennial streams and rivers and is dotted with lakes, many of which are filled karstic poljes. Mousterian sites are found here in abundance. The site of Kokkinopilos alone yielded 5,000 artifacts to Higgs's collecting teams, and thousands more have eroded from the site in the intervening years. My survey of the district of Preveza added as many as 20 findspots to those discovered by Higgs and his colleagues farther north. Some of these findspots are as rich as Kokkinopilos. Alonaki, near the mouth of the Acheron River, is littered with artifacts over an area of more than a square kilometer. More than 150,000 stone tools were counted on the surface at Alonaki, chiefly belonging to the Early Palaeolithic or the early Upper Palaeolithic. This figure serves as a useful contrast with the paucity of lithics from the Argolid.[68]

The association of Mousterian sites with water suggests that the Neanderthals used more planning and scheduling than is sometimes thought. Stringer and Gamble have assembled the evidence for the unplanned and unstructured foraging activities of Neanderthals, but Jameson and his colleagues contend that late Mousterian sites in the southern Argolid show some evidence of logistical or strategic planning.[69] They point to the pattern of small sites distributed around Franchthi Cave, which they postulate was a base camp, or at least a home base that supported the smaller satellite foraging and supply sites discovered by their survey, some of which were located near supplies of flint and water, while others were located at strategic points in the landscape suitable for hunting stands. The excavations in Franchthi did not penetrate below the Upper Palaeolithic layers, and the evidence for the Mousterian consists of a dozen artifacts that appear to

have been "kicked-up" from lower levels, and as a consequence the hypothesis that this was a base camp remains unconfirmed.[70] The still unpublished Kephalari Cave near Argos has a long sequence of layers rich in Mousterian and is a better candidate for a home base, perhaps serving the entire Argolid.[71] A distinct pattern in the distribution of Palaeolithic finds was identified in the Argolid and Berbati surveys. Assuming that Franchthi and Kephalari served as base camps, specialized flintworking camps and hunting stands are located at less than a day's walk from each cave. Isolated finds of spearpoints and similar artifacts that probably represent hunting losses are found at distances requiring more than a day's walk from the base camp, often at elevations of 700 or 1,000 m.[72] This three-level distribution pattern is suggestive of logistical foraging activity centered upon a base camp.

The concentration of Mousterian artifacts near seasonal lakes in southern Epirus also offers evidence of logistical planning in the Middle Palaeolithic. The large numbers of artifacts at sites where water, flint, and other resources were concentrated suggest repeated visits by small numbers of Neanderthals over large periods of time. The repetitive seasonal use of the same sites along the line of movement from the interior hills to the coastal plains is a form of logistical foraging normally thought to have been introduced in the Upper Palaeolithic by modern *Homo sapiens*. Here too, however, the hypothetical base camps are missing. The excavations by Higgs in Asprochaliko demonstrated that this shelter was too small, and the deposits too shallow, to qualify as a base camp, and we must look again to the vanished coastal plains as the most likely place to find the home bases.[73]

If the timing of the Neanderthal origins and their entry into Greece is open to question, the ultimate fate of the Neanderthals is even more puzzling. The only excavated sites where the transition from the Middle to the Upper Palaeolithic can be traced remain unpublished, but the preliminary reports suggest that there is an apparent hiatus between the latest Middle Palaeolithic and the earliest Upper Palaeolithic. Kephalari Cave may preserve evidence

---

[66] Jameson et al. (supra n. 2) 326-35.

[67] Runnels and van Andel (supra n. 46).

[68] Runnels et al. (supra n. 47). See also Higgs and Vita-Finzi (supra n. 15) to gain an idea of the richness of the Epirote sites.

[69] Stringer and Gamble (supra n. 31) 143-77; Jameson et al. (supra n. 2) 326-35.

[70] Perlès (supra n. 13) 49-51.

[71] Reisch 1980 (supra n. 18).

[72] Isolated finds of Mousterian tools at high interior elevations are documented in Wells et al. (supra n. 65) and Jameson et al. (supra n. 2) 329.

[73] See discussion in Bailey (supra n. 22).

of the transition, but the layers in question are thin and have very few artifacts, a difficulty complicated by a lack of dates for the sequence and full publication. In Thessaly the latest Middle Palaeolithic sites are associated with a dated stratigraphic sequence. The recent investigations of these sites demonstrate that they overlap in time the earliest Upper Palaeolithic Aurignacian industry in the Balkans, and show evidence of what is called acculturation.[74] The specific Aurignacian elements are blades, often retouched along one edge, burins, and a variety of end scrapers made on small flakes. These tool types are found with Mousterian sidescrapers and Levallois flakes on the same site, and are made of the same raw materials. The presence of typical Mousterian artifacts and tool types usually associated with the Aurignacian on the same sites in Thessaly is interpreted as evidence for cultural borrowings by late Neanderthals who had some kind of contact with modern humans. The most significant feature of the Thessalian sites is that they disappear from the record before 30,000 B.P., and after this time there are no more Mousterian sites anywhere in Greece or the rest of Europe.[75] In Greece the Mousterian is not immediately replaced by Upper Palaeolithic, and large areas of Thessaly, the Peloponnese, and Epirus appear to have been uninhabited or infrequently visited for several millennia. I believe that this is evidence for the disappearance of the Neanderthals, whose home ranges were not immediately taken over by modern humans. There is at present no consensus on the fate of the Neanderthals, but it is widely accepted that they were replaced by modern humans who migrated from the Near East through the Balkans into western Europe between 40,000 and 30,000 B.P.

One curious and unexplained phenomenon is why Middle Palaeolithic sites appear to be concentrated in the west, chiefly in Epirus, while Thessaly and the Peloponnese were only occupied by Mousterian people for a short interval at the end of the period (ca. 45,000–30,000 B.P.). One explanation may be that Neanderthals were displaced from Epirus as Aurignacian peoples spread down from the central Balkans

into northwestern Greece. Another, perhaps related, possibility is that the movement of Mousterian people south into the interior was encouraged by the reduction in size of the northwestern coastal plains in the period 45,000–30,000 B.P. when the climate was often warmer.[76]

The Upper Palaeolithic

Greece was sparsely occupied in the millennia following the disappearance of the Neanderthals. The earliest Upper Palaeolithic culture in Europe, the Aurignacian (ca. 40,000–25,000 B.P.), is extremely rare in Greece. The Aurignacian industry is based on blades (*sensu stricto*) with many carinated end scrapers and burins, and, where preservation is good, distinctive bone points with split bases. It is an industry that can be distinguished from the Mousterian, although in Greece it appears to be everywhere mixed with Mousterian elements, such as sidescrapers and Levallois flakes.[77] The Aurignacian may be present in the lowest Upper Palaeolithic layers at Franchthi Cave and Kephalari Cave, but it is in such small quantities that its very identification is open to question. There are two surface sites in Achaia that may be Aurignacian, as is the recently discovered open-air site of Spilaion in Epirus (fig. 6).[78]

The scarcity of stratified and dated sites requires an explanation. It is possible that the expansion of the Aurignacian coincided with a relatively warm interstadial phase when Greece's coastal plains contracted, or the Aurignacian people were few in number and could concentrate on areas with rich and dependable resources with no pressure to occupy districts of marginal productivity.

Evidence of wider occupation in Greece comes only after the Aurignacian, sometime after 25,000 B.P. The coincidence of the expansion of Upper Palaeolithic occupation with the beginning of the last major cold phase of the glacial period draws attention once more to the coastal plains, which reached their greatest extent ca. 20,000 to 18,000 B.P. The new archaeological cultures are known as Gravettian or Epigravettian and are characterized by an abundance of small blades, many of which are

[74] See discussion in Runnels (supra n. 13).

[75] For the end of the Middle Palaeolithic in Greece, see Runnels (supra n. 13).

[76] Priscilla Murray is credited with the suggestion that the late dispersal of Middle Palaeolithic sites in Greece could be the result of the displacement of Neanderthals by the makers of the Aurignacian. See Mellars (supra n. 29) for possible movements of Aurignacian peoples in the Balkans.

[77] Runnels (supra n. 13).

[78] See Mellars (supra n. 29) for the Aurignacian. Aurignacian sites in Achaia are described by A. Darlas, "Η Ωριγνάκια λιθοτεχνία του Ελαιοχωρίου Αχαΐας," *ArchEph* 128 (1989) 137–59; see Runnels (supra n. 13) for a summary of the Greek Aurignacian. A new Aurignacian site was discovered in 1992 at Spilaion, near Preveza, Epirus, as part of the Nikopolis Survey (Runnels et al. [supra n. 47]), but it has not yet been studied in detail.

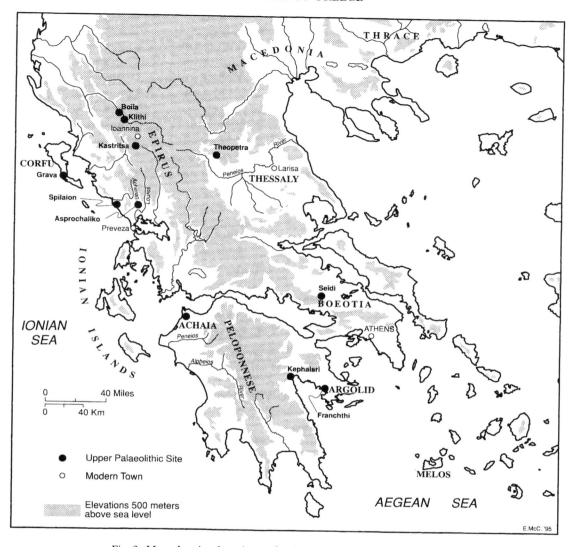

Fig. 6. Map showing locations of principal Upper Palaeolithic sites

no more than 1 or 2 cm in length. These "bladelets" have been steeply retouched along one or both edges to form small points, and these "backed" bladelets were mounted in the grooves of wooden, bone, or antler points to create spears and arrows.[79] The other tool types in these industries reflect the emphasis on small-scale hunting implements, and include geometric microliths (also used to arm projectiles) and a wide variety of steep end scrapers on blades and flakes used to work wood and hides. The Epigravettian is known almost entirely from cave sites, and appears to be very rarely found on open-air sites.[80] Several caves have been excavated, provid-

ing us for the first time with more than one well-stratified and well-dated sample.

The most important site is Franchthi Cave, where there is a sequence of Palaeolithic deposits ranging from 25,000 to 11,000 B.P. The Palaeolithic occupation of the cave was not continuous. Several distinct gaps, or hiatuses, have been detected in the stratification of the cave representing periods when there was no deposition of sediments or when sediments were eroded away. A large hiatus in the occupation of the cave occurred at the end of the last glacial maximum between 18,000 and 13,000 B.P. The cave deposits are nevertheless rich in artifacts. The lithic in-

---

[79] G. Bailey reports that the microscopic study of backed bladelets from Klithi shows that they were used as projectile points and hide working awls: G. Bailey et al., "Active

Tectonics and Land-use Strategies: A Palaeolithic Example from Northwest Greece," *Antiquity* 67 (1993) 292–312.

[80] Bailey et al. (supra n. 15).

dustries have been published by Catherine Perlès and she recognizes six distinct lithic phases at Franchthi, which are characterized by fluctuations over time in the frequency of certain common tool types and by changes in the knapping techniques employed to manufacture them.[81] The chief tool types are backed bladelets and microliths, the latter typically small geometric tools in the form of triangles and trapezes that served as inserts in wooden or bone hafts to make knives and points. They were made by snapping blades into small segments, usually retouching the margins to give them their final forms.

The thick stratification at Franchthi is not the result of continuous habitation, but represents episodes of use by small bands that visited the site on a periodic, seasonal basis. Because the rate of sedimentation was very slow in the cold, dry conditions of the last glacial, the length of these intervals or of the interruptions between them is difficult to compute. Nevertheless, the Palaeolithic occupation of Franchthi is remarkable because of the few signs of change from top to bottom in the sequence. After a short phase at the base of the sequence with some possible Aurignacian, the successive lithic phases recognized by Perlès are all dominated by the same types, e.g., backed bladelets, end scrapers, and microliths, which vary in percentage and type from one phase to another.[82]

The cave is at present directly on the coastline, but it was up to 7 km inland during the last glacial maximum.[83] The rich grazing provided by the vast coastal plain attracted a diverse fauna, both ungulates and the predators that preyed upon them. Faunal remains from the excavations include a number of large herd ungulates such as bison and ass that are characteristic species of the plains, and the excellent hunting was presumably the chief attraction of the cave. Very few plant remains have survived from the Palaeolithic levels, but these suggest that plant collecting played a relatively small role in the economy of the site. Fish and shellfish remains are conspicuous by their rarity, and the sea was undoubtedly too distant to be of much use.[84]

The picture we have is one of a very conservative, even simple, pattern of exploitation. The picture of a simple hunting camp is reinforced by the lack of art, ornament, or permanent burial. A recent study of the human remains from the cave reported seven human bones and teeth from Palaeolithic levels at the site. These were found scattered in the deposits, probably dispersed by carnivores, rodents, and later human activities at the site. It is interesting to note the presence of two shed milk teeth in this small sample, a clear indication that children accompanied adults at the Franchthi encampment.[85] A complete group, including adults and children, is evidence that the cave served as a base camp at times. Considering that this way of life endured for as much as 25,000 years, we can also say that it was a successful adaptation.

We have more excavated sites for this period than for any other. Other sites, both published and unpublished, include Theopetra Cave in Thessaly, Seidi Cave in Boeotia, Kephalari Cave in the Argolid, Grava Cave in Corfu, and Asprochaliko, Kastritsa, Klithi, and Boila in Epirus.[86] With the possible exception of the large cavern at Kephalari, these sites are small, perhaps better classified as rock shelters or overhangs than caves (fig. 7). The majority of these sites do not show any evidence of Upper Palaeolithic occupation until after 20,000 B.P. Only Kephalari and Asprochaliko have Middle Palaeolithic components. Both sites are unpublished, but preliminary reports suggest that there is a hiatus at each between the Middle and Upper Palaeolithic.

Bailey has recently noted that it is clear from the

---

[81] The Franchthi Cave stratigraphic sequence is marked by a number of gaps, or unconformities, that range in length from 200 to more than 8,500 years. These gaps occur when deposits are not being laid down or later erosion has removed them. For the Franchthi discontinuities, see W.R. Farrand, "Discontinuity in the Stratigraphic Record: Snapshots from Franchthi Cave," in P. Goldberg, D.T. Nash, and M.D. Petraglia eds., *Formation Processes in Archaeological Context* (Madison 1993) 85–96. The lithic phases are discussed in Perlès (supra n. 13).

[82] Perlès (supra n. 13).

[83] T.H. van Andel and S.B. Sutton, *Landscape and People of the Franchthi Region* (Franchthi 2, Bloomington 1987); Jameson et al. (supra n. 2) 195–210.

[84] For Franchthi plant remains, see J.M. Hansen, *The Palaeoethnobotany of Franchthi Cave* (Franchthi 7, Bloomington 1991). For shellfish, see J.C. Shackleton, *Marine Molluscan Remains from Franchthi Cave* (Franchthi 4, Bloomington 1988).

For fauna, see S. Payne, "Faunal Evidence for Environmental/ Climatic Change at Franchthi Cave (Southern Argolid, Greece) 25,000 B.P.–5000 B.P.: Preliminary Results," in J.L. Bintliff and W. van Zeist eds., *Palaeoclimates, Palaeoenvironments, and Human Communities in the Eastern Mediterranean Region in Later Prehistory* (BAR-IS 133, Oxford 1982) 133–37.

[85] Cullen (supra n. 36) 274.

[86] The results of these excavations are summarized in Kourtessi-Philappakis (supra n. 19); Bailey (supra n. 22); Reisch 1980 (supra n. 18); and Bailey et al. (supra n. 23). Many small test excavations have taken place in caves and rock shelters that have been reported in the popular press, but have not been published (e.g., T. Spyropoulos, "Εἰσαγωγή εἰς τὴν μελέτην τοῦ Κοπαϊδικοῦ χώρου," AAA 6 [1973] 201–14). The descriptions suggest that backed bladelet industries are the usual finds, and that some late Palaeolithic sites are yet to be intensively investigated in regions such as Boeotia.

Fig. 7. Grava Cave (Corfu), an example of a typical small rock shelter utilized in the later Upper Palaeolithic

scattered state of the evidence and the small size and thin deposits at these sites that we are dealing with a small part of the extended range of the human groups that occupied them.[87] Ranging over hundreds of square kilometers, from the coastal plains to the high elevations of the interior mountain valleys, small bands of humans utilized extensive tracts of land in a highly specialized version of a logistical foraging pattern. Klithi Cave in northern Epirus gives the best picture of one of these specialized hunting camps (fig. 8).[88] The cave was excavated between 1983 and 1988, reaching a depth of 2.9 m below surface. Ten major stratigraphic units were recognized and have been dated to between 16,000 and 13,000 B.P. The cave was occupied briefly after the last glacial maximum when the interior mountain valleys were free of glaciers. Located in the steepsided valley of the Voïdomatis River just above the

Konitsa plain, this area was probably inaccessible in the winter because of the snow pack and nearby glaciers. Visited only in the warmest months, it was used for the specialized hunting of chamois and ibex. This is demonstrated by the bones and horns of these animals in the site, which are very numerous. The horizontal excavation of the deposits revealed a very small area that was occupied in the cave. The occupation debris is nevertheless abundant. There are hundreds of thousands of tools, many of them backed bladelets and shouldered points used for projectiles and end scrapers useful for making and repairing weapons and processing of meat and hides from animals. Analysis of the abundant stone tools and bone fragments, which show little sign of weathering or abrasion, suggests that the site was occupied only infrequently, and probably by very small groups of people, perhaps no more than 5–10 persons. Klithi

[87] Bailey (supra n. 22).
[88] Bailey (supra n. 22) summarizes the excavations and

gives a complete list of publications.

Fig. 8. View of Klithi Cave, Epirus. The shallow rock shelter is visible in the center of the photograph, in the side of the gorge cut by the Voïdomatis River. (Photo G. Bailey)

was occupied during a relatively brief period and was abandoned as soon as there was a significant re-turn to colder, dryer conditions.[89]

The foregoing model of seasonal movement over a large territory was originally proposed by Eric Higgs in the 1960s, and was in turn based on the concept of Site Catchment Analysis developed by Higgs and Claudio Vita-Finzi. In a series of influential papers Higgs and his colleagues argued for a pattern of sea-sonal movement in the Upper Palaeolithic that in some ways resembled the transhumant pattern of the modern Sarakatsani and other pastoralists who move their flocks of sheep and goats from summer fields in the mountains to winter pasture near the present coast.[90] Higgs considered the different posi-tions of Kastritsa and Asprochaliko, including their

suitability for summer or winter habitation (based on mean daytime temperatures in different seasons as measured by buried thermometers), as indications that these caves were stopping places along a path of seasonal movement followed by red deer during the glacial period. In this model humans closely fol-lowed the herds of deer much as the Sarakatsani followed their flocks of sheep. Higgs pointed to the existence of modern transhumant routes that passed the caves, more as examples of a similar pattern than as a claim for the continuity of this behavior.

In the 1980s, Geoffrey Bailey and his colleagues challenged this simple but compelling model, and proposed a subtle but significantly different model to replace it.[91] They noted that the two caves used by Higgs to construct his model, Kastritsa and

[89] Bailey (supra n. 22) 27.

[90] Higgs and Vita-Finzi (supra n. 15); Higgs et al. (supra n. 15).

[91] Bailey (supra n. 22); Bailey et al. (supra n. 79) 302; Bailey et al. (supra n. 15); Bailey et al., "Epirus Revisited:

Seasonality and Inter-site Variation in the Upper Palaeo-lithic of North-West Greece," in G. Bailey ed., *Hunter-Gatherer Economy in Prehistory: A European Perspective* (Cambridge 1983) 64–78.

Asprochaliko, were very different from each other. Kastritsa was used in a much more intensive manner (as measured by the density of artifacts and bones in the sediments) than Asprochaliko, despite its much smaller size. There are also significant differences in the species of animals available to the inhabitants of the two caves. They draw attention also to the rather careful selection of the small shelters such as Kastritsa, Asprochaliko, and Klithi, which are on the margins of areas where the bedrock tends to control the type of vegetation available for browsing herbivores. The pockets of suitable grazing pasture for the animals are often small and rather circumscribed by rugged ridges that create topographic barriers. From their hidden shelters, just out of sight of the circumscribed areas supporting herds of grazing animals, small parties of human hunters were able to cull their quarry from their preferred habitats and to ambush them as they passed through narrow defiles between one area of grazing and another. This very carefully thought out pattern of foraging was successful as long as the colder drier climate of the last glacial encouraged growth of shrubby vegetation ideal for the support of large herbivores.

In this model, seasonal mobility of animals such as red deer, horse, cattle, ibex, and chamois is still assumed and hunters certainly shifted their settlements to take advantage of these movements. A different perspective is offered, however, by the revised model. The hunters do not follow the herds, like modern transhumants, but shift their camps on a seasonal basis within a very large territory to take maximum advantage of the circumscribed animal habitats. The known sites (Klithi, Kastritsa, and Asprochaliko) are not the base camps, but seasonal encampments that are part of a complex and hierarchical settlement pattern that included major base camps, perhaps open-air sites, on the coastal plains.

This well-balanced existence apparently did not include the intense ritualistic and artistic activities that are well known from the densely inhabited regions of southwestern France and northeastern Spain. Cave art and mobiliary art are unknown from the Greek Palaeolithic, except for small quantities of pierced animal teeth and marine shells that evidently served as ornaments.[92] Burials are unknown, and the only stratified human remains known are the scattered finds of teeth and bone fragments in the Franchthi sediments.[93] Perhaps if the putative base camps and aggregation sites on the coastal plains are located and explored, we shall learn something of the intellectual life of the Palaeolithic people.

The last glacial began to break up by 16,000 B.P., and by 10,000 B.P. the global climatic conditions that characterize the Holocene were established. Sometime during this period of transition from the Pleistocene to the Holocene, most of the Palaeolithic sites in Greece were abandoned.

The Mesolithic

In 1865 Sir John Lubbock divided prehistory into two great periods: the Palaeolithic and the Neolithic. This simple classification was based chiefly on the predominant type of edged stone tools in common use: flaked tools in the Palaeolithic and polished implements in the Neolithic.[94] Other criteria have been added over the years, but the basic classification has survived. After its introduction an unconformity between the two periods was noticed. When climatic and economic factors were added to the other criteria for the definition of the terms, the "Palaeolithic" turns out to correspond to hunters and foragers who lived in the Pleistocene epoch and the "Neolithic" to village farming peoples in the Holocene. Excavations in Europe, however, revealed the existence of foragers who continued to hunt and gather in the early Holocene until they were replaced by Neolithic farmers. Some scholars considered that the logic of climatic and economic factors of definition required a separate designation for Holocene foragers, and the term "Mesolithic" was proposed.[95]

The concept of the "Mesolithic" has been debated since its introduction. The term has been retained by some archaeologists working in Europe, but it has lost ground in other regions. Archaeologists in closely neighboring areas such as the Balkans or the Near East sometimes use the term "Epipalaeolithic" instead of Mesolithic. The term "Epipalaeolithic" suggests that this phase is regarded as a continuation of the Palaeolithic into the Holocene, with a hint that it is a kind of Palaeolithic twilight where foragers attempted to adjust to the new climatic conditions of the present age, and in this sense it is often justified.[96] Whether "degenerate" or merely "transi-

---

[92] For Palaeolithic shell ornaments from Franchthi, see Shackleton (supra n. 84) 49–53; for ornaments made from animal teeth, see Higgs et al. (supra n. 15) 24.

[93] Cullen (supra n. 36) 274 n. 6.

[94] Sir J. Lubbock, *Pre-Historic Times* (London 1865).

[95] The first use of "Mesolithic" was by the Irish archae-

ologist H. Westropp in 1866: see B. Gräslund, *The Birth of Prehistoric Chronology* (Cambridge 1987) 38; and G. Clark, *Mesolithic Prelude: The Palaeolithic–Neolithic Transition in Old World Prehistory* (Edinburgh 1980) 1–7.

[96] Clark (supra n. 95) 4.

tional," the Mesolithic is often thought of as the tail end of the Palaeolithic, a slightly uncomfortable term to cover an awkward segment of prehistory that does not fit well in the sequence. There have been attempts in recent years, most notably by Grahame Clark, to reevaluate the Mesolithic and to depict it as a formative era standing apart from the other prehistoric periods, but this effort has not been altogether successful.[97] Despite these reservations, the evidence from Greece suggests that the Mesolithic is a period stratigraphically, chronologically, and economically distinct from the Palaeolithic and Neolithic.

The Mesolithic period belongs to the early Holocene, an era of rapid changes in global climate as the result of the change from cold, dry glacial conditions to the warmer, wetter regime of the modern climate. The exact effects of this climatic change on Greece are difficult to measure, because the proxy data used to reconstruct past climates, such as pollen from cores, tree rings, and biological remains from excavations, are few and far between in Greece for the late Pleistocene and early Holocene. The general consensus, however, is that the rise in temperature and precipitation encouraged the expansion of arboreal species, chiefly pine and deciduous oak. The change in vegetation was accompanied by changes in the fauna, with the disappearance of many large herbivores and an increase of woodland species such as red deer and pig. These changes were more dramatic in coastal areas where marine transgression submerged the coastal plains.[98]

Until the 1960s the existence of a Mesolithic period in Greece was uncertain. Although Perlès has demonstrated that the caves explored by Markovits in the 1920s and 1930s were probably Mesolithic, Markovits's findings were ignored for a long time.[99] The first definitive evidence for the Mesolithic came in 1964 with the excavations at Sidari in Corfu and in 1967 at Franchthi Cave in the Argolid (fig. 9). These two sites are the only Mesolithic sites yet tested by modern excavation methods. In the last five years the picture of the Mesolithic has changed rapidly as the result of substantial new finds from surface surveys.

It is necessary to review the results of the two excavations before turning to the new finds.

The Franchthi Cave excavations were carried out in four areas within the cave, which were tested with a series of deep trenches. The long sequence of Mesolithic layers, up to 4 m thick in some areas, has been divided by the excavators into two phases dated by conventional uncalibrated radiocarbon determinations: the Lower Mesolithic (ca. 9500–9000 B.P.) and the Upper Mesolithic (ca. 9000–8000 B.P.). Perlès uses the lithics to distinguish a third phase, the Final Mesolithic, but she stresses the essential continuity that connects the phases. In this paper, I will consider the Upper Mesolithic as including Perlès's Final Mesolithic. The latest Palaeolithic levels are separated from the Lower Mesolithic by a hiatus of approximately 300–600 years.[100] In addition to the stratigraphic break that separates the Mesolithic from the Palaeolithic, the Mesolithic at Franchthi has many novel features. The lithic assemblage of the Lower Mesolithic lacks the geometric microliths and backed bladelets of the Final Palaeolithic and is made up instead of simple flakes, often with multiple retouched edges formed by a small nibbling retouch. Notches and denticulates are the most common tool types, and the entire assemblage is remarkable more for the many types that it does not have than for any definite character. Melian obsidian, present in the Upper Palaeolithic, is definitely part of the Mesolithic assemblage, although very rare (ca. 1%). It is evidence nevertheless of maritime contact with the obsidian sources of Melos. The faunal remains, although they have not been published in detail, also reflect a break with the Palaeolithic pattern. Most of the great herbivores disappear and are replaced by red deer with smaller numbers of pig. There is more evidence of plant collecting in this phase, and carbonized remains of wild barley, oats, and nuts such as almonds and pistachios are common. An increase in fish bones and changes in the species of marine shell reinforce our view that the cave inhabitants had a familiarity with the sea, albeit with fish found chiefly in coastal lagoons and estuar-

[97] Clark (supra n. 95) 101–103.

[98] The evidence for the manifold changes in early Holocene climate and environment is summarized in Jameson et al. (supra n. 2) 165–68, 194–213, 335–38.

[99] Perlès (supra n. 7) 120–22.

[100]The exact length of the Mesolithic period at Franchthi is unknown, but may be as much as 1,500 radiocarbon years. Deposition of Mesolithic deposits may have begun as early as 10,500 B.P. in some parts of the cave, but the

generally accepted beginning of the Mesolithic is placed later, ca. 9500 B.P. For a discussion of the Franchthi chronology, see Hansen (supra n. 84) 119–20, 129, 135. Perlès (supra n. 7) 107–15 discusses the differences in lithics from phase VI (latest Palaeolithic) to phase VII (Lower Mesolithic). The stratigraphic break between the Palaeolithic and Mesolithic is documented in Farrand (supra n. 81) 92–94.

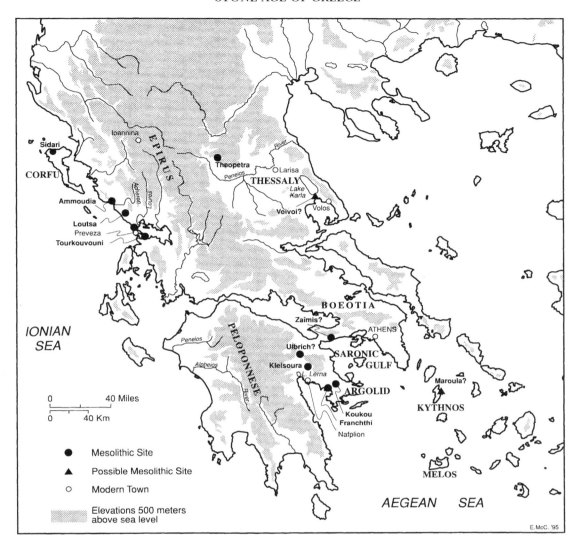

Fig. 9. Map showing locations of principal Mesolithic sites. Voivoi and Maroula are generally not considered to be Mesolithic, but are shown for reference. The precise locations of Zaïmis and Ulbrich are unknown.

ies.[101] Fragments of andesite querns imported from the Saronic Gulf were probably used to crush plant materials as well as to shape shell and stone ornaments and perform other tasks.[102]

The most spectacular recent discovery from the Lower Mesolithic is a cemetery near the mouth of the cave. One intact burial had been excavated earlier, the flexed inhumation of a young man at the mouth of the cave, at that time the earliest human burial recorded in Greece. Reanalysis of the human bone remains by Tracey Cullen and Della Cook has shown that this well-known burial lay above a small community cemetery, with five inhumations, two cremations, and the scattered remains from another two to five individuals.[103] At least one other burial (Upper Mesolithic) can be reconstructed from another area and six to 25 individuals are represented by the *disiecta membra* collected from Mesolithic levels

---

[101] For the changes in plants, fauna, and shellfish, see Hansen, Payne, and Shackleton (supra n. 84). For Melian obsidian, see Perlès (supra n. 7) 30. The important and interesting remains of pelagic fish are discussed by M. Rose, *With Line and Glittering Bronze Hook: Fishing in the Aegean Bronze Age* (Diss. Indiana Univ. 1994) 429–45; and Rose, "Fish-

ing at Franchthi Cave, Greece: Changing Environments and Patterns of Exploitation," *OWAN* 18:3 (1995) 21–26.

[102] C.N. Runnels, *A Diachronic Study and Economic Analysis of Millstones from the Argolid, Greece* (Diss. Indiana Univ. 1981) 100–101.

[103] Cullen (supra n. 36).

throughout the cave. The human remains reveal that adults, adolescents, infants, and neonates were present in the group that occupied the cave. The interpretation of the Franchthi community is significantly altered by discovery of adult men and women of different ages and of children among the dead. The conclusion is inescapable that we are dealing with a permanent settlement with the full spectrum of the social group. The sophistication and complexity of thought revealed by the different treatment of the dead, some of whom were inhumed while others were cremated, is mirrored by the richness of the material culture evident from the profusion of artifacts, particularly in the Upper Mesolithic phase, from the rest of the cave during the 1,500 (radiocarbon) years of the settlement's history.

The Upper Mesolithic is evidently a continuation of the culture established in the Lower Mesolithic. The lithic assemblage is marked by a return of microlithic geometrics and backed bladelets, with an increase in the percentage of Melian obsidian to ca. 3%, evidence of an increased contact with the Cycladic islands. Other finds, which are present throughout the Mesolithic sequence, suggest a permanent settlement with a complex economy. Andesite continued to be imported from the Saronic Gulf, and the presence of carbonized remains is an indication that wild cereals were being collected. Stone and shell ornaments are present, and bone was used to fashion fishing tackle and possibly parts of clothing (buckles or toggles). An increased interest in the sea is supported by the occurrence for the first time of pelagic fish, including remains of large tunny, which were taken in the open sea. The presence of pelagic fish at Franchthi coincides with the increase in the quantity of imported Melian obsidian.[104]

The excavators are still in the process of publishing their finds, but several inferences are possible for the Mesolithic at Franchthi as a whole. The presence of tunny, when put beside the imported obsidian and andesite, underscores an emphasis on marine resources and long distance trade and communication. The thickness of the deposits, the density of the finds, and wide range of new kinds of tools and artifacts (such as the querns), together with the human burials, suggest a more sustained human exploitation of the cave and its environs.

Is the precocious settlement at Franchthi Cave,

with its resemblance to the Natufian of the Near East, indicative of developments elsewhere in Greece during the Mesolithic period? There is no way to know. Our data are too few. The site of Sidari is the only other Mesolithic site to be excavated in recent times, and it is a small, shallow tell on the north coast of the island of Corfu later in date and considerably less rich in finds (fig. 10). It was excavated in 1964 by Augustus Sordinas and has three major units: Mesolithic, Neolithic, and Early Bronze Age.[105] The Mesolithic deposits are on virgin soil. The lowest deposit consists chiefly of charcoal, marine shells, flints, and bones of animals and fish in an anthropogenic soil rich in carbon and ash. Finds of some interest not reported by Sordinas, but present in the collections housed in the Corfu Archaeological Museum, are large pieces of burned daub that may be from simple structures or shelters. The deposit is dated to ca. 5870 ± 340 B.C. (i.e., 7820 ± 340 B.P. in uncalibrated radiocarbon years). On the basis of the lithics the Mesolithic component at Sidari (level D) belongs to the Upper Mesolithic, if we compare it with the Franchthi Cave sequence, but the date indicates that the site is at least partly contemporary with Early Neolithic sites in eastern Greece and Crete. The lithics from Sidari closely resemble those from Franchthi, particularly in the small scale of the artifacts and presence of geometric microliths, which are made by simple retouch on fragments of flakes or blades and not by the microburin technique. Obsidian is completely absent. Sordinas noted the apparent importation of the distinctive flint used to make the tools, and from this and the coastal location of the site, he concluded that the Mesolithic people are unrelated to the former Palaeolithic inhabitants of the island and had an economy focused on the exploitation of marine resources.

The only other Mesolithic sites tested by excavation are the Ulbrich Cave in the Argolid and Zaïmis Cave in the Megarid investigated by Markovits between 1928 and 1933. The finds from these excavations are lost and the locations of the caves themselves are no longer certain. The Ulbrich Cave is said to be midway between Nemea and Nafplion, and Zaïmis was evidently along the line of the modern highway between Megara and Corinth, and may have been destroyed in its construction. Markovits's reports have been closely examined by Perlès who be-

[104] T.W. Jacobsen, "17,000 Years of Greek Prehistory," *Scientific American* 234:6 (1976) 76–87 illustrates Mesolithic artifacts and fish remains. The appearance of pelagic fish in the Upper Mesolithic is documented by Rose 1995 (supra n. 101). The increase in obsidian is discussed in T.W.

Jacobsen and D.M. Van Horn, "The Franchthi Cave Flint Survey: Some Preliminary Results (1974)," *JFA* 1 (1974) 305–308.

[105] Sordinas 1970 (supra n. 16).

Fig. 10. View of the Mesolithic site of Sidari, Corfu. The low mound is in the center of the photograph, and the stratification is visible in the sea scarp.

lieves that Markovits was correct in attributing the pre-ceramic layers to the early Holocene, and hence to the Mesolithic. As Perlès notes, it is interesting that Markovits considered the evidence to show that the inhabitants of Zaïmis and Ulbrich were primarily fishers.[106] He compared the lithics to the Tardenoisian of France. In the absence of further evidence, nothing more can be said about these sites.

Other sites mentioned in the literature as possible candidates for the Mesolithic include Theopetra Cave and Voivoi in Thessaly and Maroula in Kythnos. Theopetra Cave in western Thessaly near Kalambaka is currently being excavated and is not yet published, but reportedly has a Mesolithic component. The site of Voivoi in Thessaly on the shore of the former Lake Karla was once considered as a possible Mesolithic site by Theocharis, but he changed his mind when

it was possible to compare the finds with the material from Franchthi Cave, and Voivoi is now regarded as Neolithic.[107] The site of Maroula on the island of Kythnos is something of a puzzle. It was initially described as a Mesolithic site in a brief report, but a later analysis suggested a Neolithic or Bronze Age attribution for the site.[108] Until the site is excavated our questions may not be answered, but the discovery of a probable early Holocene site at Aetokremnos in Cyprus is a stimulus to reexamine any island site that may belong to the late Pleistocene or early Holocene.[109]

A number of new Mesolithic sites have been identified recently. A small cave (F35, Koukou Cave) in the Fournoi Valley, about 5 km from Franchthi Cave, was discovered by an American team in the 1970s. The simple flint implements from the surface of the

[106] Perlès (supra n. 7) 120–22.

[107] Perlès (supra n. 7) 120 for a summary of Voivoi. Theopetra Cave is being excavated by N. Kyparissi-Apostolika for the Ephoreia of Palaeoanthropology and Speleology: see report in Bailey et al. (supra n. 23).

[108] The curious site of Maroula is discussed in detail by Perlès (supra n. 7) 125–26; and J.F. Cherry, "Four Problems in Cycladic Prehistory," in J.L. Davis and J.F. Cherry

eds., *Papers in Cycladic Prehistory* (Los Angeles 1979) 26–32.

[109] A.H. Simmons, "Humans, Island Colonization and Pleistocene Extinctions in the Mediterranean: The View from Akrotiri *Aetokremnos*, Cyprus," *Antiquity* 65 (1991) 857–69; and A.H. Simmons and P.E. Wigand, "Assessing the Radiocarbon Determinations from Akrotiri *Aetokremnos*, Cyprus," in Bar-Yosef and Kra (supra n. 30) 247–64.

site, chiefly simple flakes with notches and multiple retouched edges, and the lack of ceramics suggest comparison with the Lower Mesolithic at Franchthi, but the sample is too small to be conclusive. Several lithic scatters in the same region may be Mesolithic, but are too small and too disturbed to support definitive identification.[110]

A reconnaissance of the Berbati and Limnes valleys on the northern edge of the Argive plain by a Swedish-American team identified two open-air sites in the Kleisoura Gorge, which together produced a collection of nearly 1,000 flint artifacts.[111] The two sites (findspots 200 and 201) are only a few hundred meters apart, and there is no apparent difference between the collections made at the sites, which may be contemporary (fig. 11). A close analysis of the lithics shows them to be very similar to the Lower Mesolithic industry at Franchthi, and a radiocarbon date of 10,000 B.P. from one of them shows that they belong to the beginning of the Holocene.[112] A pollen core from nearby Lake Lerna shows that the region supported a deciduous oak forest and must have been well watered.[113] A reconstruction of the Argive Plain as the result of a detailed geological study can be used to show that the Kleisoura Mesolithic sites were about 18 km from the coast in the early Holocene.[114] It is probable that there are other Mesolithic sites in the region, and one of the Kleisoura sites could possibly be Markovits's Ulbrich Cave (one of the findspots is close to a mostly collapsed rock shelter that could loosely be described as a cave), but there is no way to confirm this hypothesis.

A survey in southern Epirus (the Nomos Prevezas) has produced evidence of six possible Mesolithic sites on the Ionian Sea littoral.[115] Three sites are found in paleosols in a dune field west of the town of Preveza. The dune field lies directly on the present shoreline and consists of fossil dunes with stratified deposits of paleosols capping them (fig. 12). Both fossil dunes and paleosols are overlain today by active dunes. The sites consist of dense concentrations of flint implements embedded in the paleosols. Their distribution is governed by modern building activity and they are also uncovered by shifting dunes, exposing the relatively hard and stable surfaces of the paleosols. Geological study shows that the coastal

Fig. 11. View of Mesolithic site at findspot 201 (Kleisoura) in Berbati, Argolid. The shallow shelter is visible in the right center of the photograph, on the line of the cultivated field. The stratified deposits are found in front of the projecting rocks.

environment between Preveza and the Acheron River was a complex and rapidly changing network of lagoons, swamps, estuaries, and braided streams separated by dunes and small rises, which were sometimes stable for periods long enough for shallow soils to form. The sites are thought to be campsites situated among the dunes in protected swales or on dunes stabilized by vegetation that overlooked estuaries and streams. The lithics are rich in trapezoidal microliths (used as arrowheads) and other projectile points. The industry is made up otherwise of very small flake tools with multiple retouched edges fashioned with tiny nibbling retouch. Blades are rare, and there are many notches and denticulates. No ceramics have been found and only one piece of ob-

[110] Jameson et al. (supra n. 2) 335–40.

[111] B. Wells, C.N. Runnels, and E. Zangger, "In the Shadow of Mycenae," *Archaeology* 46:1 (1993) 54–63; C. Runnels, "The Palaeolithic and Mesolithic Remains from the Berbati-Limnes Survey," in B. Wells and C. Runnels eds., *The Berbati-Limnes Archaeological Survey 1988–1990* (Stockholm, in press).

[112] J. Kozlowski, personal communication, 1994.

[113] S. Jahns, "On the Holocene Vegetation History of the Argive Plain (Peloponnese, Southern Greece)," *Vegetation History and Archaeobotany* 2 (1993) 187–203.

[114] Zangger (supra n. 2).

[115] Runnels et al. (supra n. 47).

Fig. 12. View of one of the possible Mesolithic sites on the Ionian coast west of Preveza, Epirus. Microlithic artifacts are found in the paleosol in the foreground, exposed by the removal of sand from a dune for construction purposes.

sidian, evidently not of Melian origin. A fourth site similar to these three is located near the mouth of the Acheron River, near the village of Ammoudia. Two other sites are located on limestone spurs with commanding views of the sea at Loutsa near the Acheron valley and on the headland of Tourkovouni at the end of the Ayios Thomas peninsula east of Preveza. Burned daub was noted at the Loutsa site suggesting the presence of a structure or structures at some sites.

Until these sites are fully published it is possible to draw only very preliminary conclusions, but it is notable that the sites are located with a clear orientation to the present coastline and in positions where they would have had access to marine and estuarine resources. The small scale of the flint industries is another feature of the traditional picture of Mesolithic exploitation patterns, which were focused on a mixed economy of hunting and fishing.

The presence of Mesolithic sites chiefly in Epirus and the Argolid suggests that the Mesolithic has a rather discontinuous distribution in Greece. It is clear that large areas were uninhabited during the Mesolithic, particularly areas such as eastern Thessaly that have substantial numbers of Neolithic sites beginning about 9,000 years ago. From this we can conclude that any hypothesis of experimentation with domestication in the Mesolithic leading to the

indigenous and independent development of the Neolithic village farming economy must be abandoned.[116] There is a considerable body of evidence to demonstrate that the earliest Neolithic cultures reached Greece in the seventh millennium B.C. as the result of demic diffusion from the Near East, and the distribution of Mesolithic sites suggests that there may have been an earlier wave of migration that paved the way for Neolithic settlers to follow.

In my view, the Greek Mesolithic may be unconnected with the Palaeolithic, but is separated from it by a hiatus of unknown length. As a working hypothesis, I consider the presently available evidence to point to the introduction of the Mesolithic by seafaring people who are unrelated to the Pleistocene inhabitants of Greece. The Mesolithic represents the first stage or wave of demic diffusion that culminated in the establishment of the Neolithic farming village way of life in Greece.

An early Holocene site in Cyprus, and perhaps another in Kythnos, point to a passage by sea, with travelers perhaps attracted by the isolated large islands with indigenous fauna unprepared for human predation. When these stocks were exhausted, the seafarers worked their way through the islands to the mainland where they established themselves either permanently, or on a seasonal basis, to carry out a mixed economy based on hunting, fishing, and

---

[116] See van Andel and Runnels (supra n. 10).

collecting. The distribution of sites is significant because the earliest Mesolithic sites (Franchthi, Koukou, Kleisoura sites) are found in southern Greece and later Mesolithic sites (Sidari, Preveza sites, Acheron sites) are in northwestern Greece—all with a coastal location suggesting an east to west settlement by seafarers.

One factor indicating an intrusive Mesolithic is the similarity of the cultural materials at all of the Greek sites, particularly of the lithic assemblages. It should also be noted that the Mesolithic features are completely different from those of the preceding Palaeolithic, but resemble those found at contemporary sites in the eastern Mediterranean. The presence of formal burials, with evidence of ritual activity, is perhaps one of the chief features that connects Franchthi with contemporary sites in the Near East.[117] Other shared features include increased use of marine and riverine resources, a special emphasis on the hunting of red deer or some other cervid, the use of wild cereals and querns to grind them, and the use of exotic raw materials such as obsidian to manufacture stone tools.

EARLY GREEK PREHISTORY IN BROAD PERSPECTIVE

It is possible only to sketch the relationships between the existing evidence and the questions proposed earlier in this paper to guide research. The archaeological record does not show a steady occupation of the region after an initial settlement, but reveals a complicated picture of renewed human settlement separated by sometimes long periods with little evidence of human activity. The entry of early humans into Greece occurred as the result of two separate movements of people. The first, ca. 300,000 B.P., brought archaic *Homo sapiens* into Greece, perhaps filling a void left by an earlier pioneering movement of *Homo erectus* from Africa into Europe that failed to take hold. If supported by future research, this finding will require modification of the multiregional hypothesis for the origins of modern humans, adding weight to the hypothesis that *Homo erectus* may not have reached Europe at all, and that the colonization of Europe was carried out by a later hominid of generalized *Homo sapiens* type. The evidence also indicates that a separate and later movement ca. 100,000 B.P. brought Neanderthals or other archaic *Homo sapiens* into Greece from central and southeastern Europe. It is an open question whether Greece was inhabited continuously during this period.

Another influx of immigrants into the Balkans took place between 40,000 and 30,000 B.P., bringing anatomically modern *Homo sapiens* into contact with resident Neanderthal populations, and which, for unknown reasons, was followed by the disappearance of the Neanderthals. Yet another hiatus appears to interrupt the record at this point, and it is not until after 28,000 B.P. that moderns appear to have established themselves more or less permanently in Greece, although on a limited and patchy basis. If this reconstruction is correct, the evidence supports the replacement theory for the origins of modern humans, although suggesting that it must be seen as a complex process of discontinuous regional movements. The central tenet of the replacement theory is that modern humans evolved in Africa between 200,000 and 100,000 B.P., and migrated into the Near East by 100,000 B.P. where they overlapped with archaic humans for nearly 60,000 years. The archaic humans in their turn may have encountered modern humans moving northward from Africa as they themselves moved southward into the Balkans and southwest Asia. In the Near East, where the overlap between the two human groups is seen most clearly, it is not yet clear whether the archaic and modern humans were in the same region at the same time, or if they alternated in their movements in and out of the area.[118] Modern humans appear to have been confined to the Near East until 40,000 B.P. or even later. Only after the transition from the Middle Palaeolithic to the Upper Palaeolithic is registered in the Near East does the earliest Upper Palaeolithic, the Aurignacian, appear in the Balkans before 40,000, reaching western Europe later still. From this we can conclude that modern humans began a new expansion into Europe after a long period in the Near East that ultimately resulted in the extinction of the Neanderthals and other archaic humans for unknown reasons.

The Upper Palaeolithic in Greece is separated from what comes before and after by breaks in the stratigraphic record. There is no evidence that the Upper Palaeolithic settlement of Greece involved all parts of the country. The islands were not inhabited, although the presence of obsidian at Franchthi

---

[117] A comprehensive study of the structural features of the Mediterranean Mesolithic is found in Clark (supra n. 95) 59–100.

[118] O. Bar-Yosef and R.S. Kra, "Dating Eastern Mediterranean Sequences: Introductory Remarks," in Bar-Yosef and Kra (supra n. 30) 1–12.

in the final Upper Palaeolithic indicates a knowledge of and access to the resources of some islands.[119] There are many unsettled questions about this period, but I think that the most likely hypothesis is that modern humans entered Greece in the Upper Palaeolithic as the result of numerous small movements of people, probably entering the region at separate times and from different directions. The Epirote Palaeolithic may be the result of movements of small bands across the Adriatic plain from Italy or the northwestern Balkans, while separate groups may have found their way into the Peloponnese by following the coastal plains southward along the east coast.

The nature of Upper Palaeolithic inhabitation of Greece and the rest of Europe is discontinuous in both space and time. This fact has been discussed before, but there is no good explanation for it, and we are unlikely to make progress without more evidence. I suspect that there are at least two factors that must be considered. There were undoubtedly very small numbers of humans in this period and in the absence of population pressure many areas would simply have been passed over for better habitats. We are hampered in discussing the merits of different regions by the lack of detailed proxy evidence for reconstructing palaeoenvironments for small areas and within reasonably narrow chronological limits. If we could do this, we would possibly find that some regions were too dry, were glaciated, or were otherwise unsuitable for habitation in the late Pleistocene. Another factor in Greece is the effect of marine transgression and other geologic processes on the preservation of the archaeological record. The Upper Palaeolithic settlement took place during the last glacial when sea levels were depressed by as much as 120 m, exposing large coastal plains, which were lost again with the rapid rise of the sea in the late Pleistocene. In Greece this had a major impact on the preservation of sites. In a country with a long coastline and a mountainous interior the loss of the plains meant the loss of 40–70% of the land most likely to have been occupied.[120] This factor had a greater impact in the Upper Palaeolithic than in the Middle Palaeolithic or the Mesolithic when sea levels were lower by only 40 m, making the propor-

tional losses of coastal plains much less. It is also a remarkable fact that most of the Upper Palaeolithic sites in Greece are found in caves or rock shelters, and that open sites are rare. The open Upper Palaeolithic sites that have been found by surveys often are no more than small scatters of stone tools on bare rock or on thin relict soils, and it is possible that many such sites were removed altogether by post-Pleistocene erosion.

When we turn to the Mesolithic, it is clear that the most recent evidence contributes to a revised understanding of the period. The Mesolithic of Greece can be attributed to the movements of people by sea that ultimately brought people from the Near East to Greece in the Neolithic period when the pattern of the Greek economic and social structure for all subsequent periods was established. A review of the Neolithic as a whole is not necessary here, and it is sufficient to note that the evidence from Greece confirms Childe's hypothesis that the earliest Neolithic of southeastern Europe was the result of diffusion of agriculturalists from the Near East, even if the process of diffusion is more complicated than he originally thought.

CONCLUSION

When we regard the great sweep of Greek prehistory before the Bronze Age, it is clear that much progress has been made in our understanding of the earliest periods. A few decades ago almost nothing was known of early Greek prehistory, and someone writing of it in 1960 may have said something very like what Dr. Johnson said of British prehistory more than two centuries ago: "All that is really *known* of the ancient state of Britain is contained in a few pages. We *can* know no more than what old writers have told us; yet what large books have we upon it, the whole of which, excepting such parts as are taken from those old writers, is all dream. . . ."[121] The prospects of writing a reasonably coherent prehistory of Greece have tolerably improved. It must be admitted, however, that the gaps in our knowledge are equally apparent. We do not know whether Greece was settled during the first migration of early humans from Africa, and we still have no good idea of the identity of the hominids who first penetrated

---

[119] Evidence for habitation of the Mediterranean islands is summarized by J.F. Cherry, "The First Colonization of the Mediterranean Islands: A Review of Recent Research," *JMA* 3 (1990) 145–221. For Mesolithic obsidian, see C. Renfrew and A. Aspinall, "Aegean Obsidian and Franchthi Cave," in Perlès (supra n. 7) 257–70.

[120] See van Andel, in Jameson et al. (supra n. 2) 203, table 3.8, and fig. 3.27, for a graphic illustration of the impact of marine transgression on the Franchthi coastal plains.

[121] J. Boswell, *The Life of Samuel Johnson, LL. D.*,[3] (London 1799) 356. Emphasis is Dr. Johnson's.

the fastnesses of the Greek mountains or wandered its now lost and forgotten shores.

The rarity of human fossils in the Palaeolithic is a major impediment to further progress, and for all periods and areas complete inventories of existing sites are lacking. The small number of excavations is simply unacceptable. It is humbling to acknowledge that large regions, such as Macedonia, Thrace, and much of central Greece and the Peloponnese, remain to be explored. The finds from existing excavations and surveys are inadequately published, and in the case of Asprochaliko, Kastritsa, Kephalari, and some other sites, it seems that the results of the excavations are unlikely ever to be published. When the loss of information from Markovits's and Stampfuss's excavations is added to the list of unfinished work, I sometimes feel as if we are doomed to repeat, like Sisyphus, the labors of basic research.

Finally, there are some areas about which little can be said. The existence of obsidian in Mesolithic and Upper Palaeolithic layers at Franchthi Cave is an indication that we will eventually find evidence for activity during these periods on the Cycladic islands. An early Holocene site in Cyprus is a harbinger of what is to be found on some of the larger Mediterranean islands, and Crete is likely to have played an important role in the transmission of Mesolithic and Neolithic culture to the mainland. No reliable report of pre-Neolithic antiquity exists for Crete, but the Mesolithic seafarers could not have overlooked this island with its strategic position in the Aegean and its abundance of untapped natural resources.[122] After due adjustments are made for geologic and geomorphic changes that serve to mask early sites and control their discovery, Crete will no doubt yield many secrets to persistent investigators.

The most important conclusion is that Greece is no longer on the fringe, but is a central part of the prehistoric world that stretched without boundary from western Europe to the Near East. In early prehistoric times people moved in both directions on this great east–west axis as on a highway, now seeking new lands, now retreating in the face of global climatic changes, and sometimes, in moments that we can only dimly imagine, meeting others who were like themselves and yet different. The prehistory of Greece is not the story of continuous development beginning from an initial settlement, or enduring inhabitation by a stable population, but is a patchwork of migrations and new settlements followed by long periods of adaptation, interruption, and abandonment: a cultural pattern that endured for three thousand centuries and set its stamp upon the cultural history of this country.

DEPARTMENT OF ARCHAEOLOGY
BOSTON UNIVERSITY
BOSTON, MASSACHUSETTS 02215
RUNNELS@BU.EDU

---

[122] The lack of existing or published evidence for pre-Neolithic habitation of Crete is summarized in Cherry (supra n. 119) 158–65. An interesting argument for the visitation of Crete in the early Holocene is the evidence for faunal extinctions discussed in E. Lax and T.F. Strasser, "Early Holocene Extinctions on Crete: The Search for the Cause," *JMA* 5 (1992) 203–24.

Addendum: 1995–1999

CURTIS RUNNELS

INTRODUCTION

Our knowledge of the Palaeolithic and Mesolithic Aegean has grown since 1995, albeit at a modest rate, with significant new information coming from excavations in Epirus, the Argolid, and Thessaly, supplemented with data from systematic regional surveys. Recent publications have made available the results of projects not yet complete at the time of the original publication of this review (RAP IV, above). In this addendum new evidence is briefly reviewed for the light it throws on the major problems that remain. In this fast growing field it is not feasible to include all the new information that is flowing from surveys, excavations, and chance finds, making it necessary to choose carefully the material that is to be included. Accordingly, my focus here is on those accounts available in published or in-press accounts, while brief reports of the Greek Archaeological Service in government publications, articles in the popular press, and publications not receiving peer review (e.g., Internet Web sites) have been excluded. What remains is sufficiently interesting to serve as an indication of the progress made in the last four years.

RECENT RESEARCH AND PUBLICATION

Significant developments since 1995 have included the publication of the proceedings of the 1994 conference in Ioannina on the Palaeolithic archaeology of Greece and adjacent areas (hereafter ICOPAG) and the appearance of the final report on the decade-long British research project centered on Klithi in northern Epirus.[123] Some of the papers published in the ICOPAG conference volume touch upon significant excavations and surveys in Greece's neighboring regions (e.g., Yarımburgaz Cave in northwestern Turkey and Konispol Cave in Albania) that are outside the scope of this review, and a large section of the ICOPAG report is devoted to Klithi, which is superseded by the final publication that has appeared since the conference. The most important contributions in the ICOPAG volume for our subject are the reports of new discoveries of Palaeolithic materials (e.g., from open-air sites in Thrace, Lefkas, Zakynthos, the Mani, and Achaia) where they had not been reported before. The widespread distribution of Palaeolithic materials shown by these new finds is evidence of the richness of the Palaeolithic record in Greece, which is even now largely unexplored. It is worth remarking that these new discoveries confirm the general conclusion that the Middle Palaeolithic is the best-represented period in Greece, while the Lower Palaeolithic, Late Upper Palaeolithic, and Mesolithic periods remain conspicuous by their rarity. A large number of reports in the ICOPAG volume are concerned with Theopetra Cave (Thessaly), which has been under excavation since 1987 by a team directed by N. Kyparissi-Apostolika (Ephorate of Caves and Palaeoanthropology). In addition to the five papers in this volume, Theopetra has been the subject of an international conference held at Trikala in 1998.[124] This important site reportedly has evidence of occupation beginning in the Middle Palaeolithic ca. 44,000 B.P. and continuing through the Upper Palaeolithic, Mesolithic, and into the Neolithic, although it is probable that there are significant hiatuses in the stratigraphic record and that occupation in this cave, as at Franchthi Cave, was not continuous. Among the more significant finds reported from the excavations are burials in the Palaeolithic and Mesolithic levels and a hominid footprint from the Middle Palaeolithic levels. As one of the few Palaeolithic sites to be systematically excavated in recent years, the final publication of the results are eagerly awaited.

The results of the major excavation project centered on Klithi Cave in northwestern Epirus have now been published in two large volumes. This excavation was part of a major restudy of the Palaeolithic record and palaeoenvironment of Epirus begun by E.S. Higgs. The regional research project combined new excavations and survey with an examination of old exca-

---

[123] G.N. Bailey, E. Adam, E. Panagopoulou, C. Perlès, and K. Zachos eds., *The Palaeolithic Archaeology of Greece and Adjacent Areas: Proceedings of the ICOPAG Conference, Ioannina, September 1994* (*BSA* Studies 3, London 1999); G.N. Bailey ed., *Klithi: Palaeolithic Settlement and Quaternary Landscape in Northwest Greece* (Cambridge 1997).

[124] N. Kyparissi-Apostolika, personal communication, 1998; "Theopetra Cave—Twelve Years of Excavation and Research," an international conference sponsored by the Greek Ministry of Culture and the Prefecture of Trikala, November 1998.

vation and survey data from the work of Higgs and his team. A thorough review of this important publication is outside the scope of this addendum, and it is sufficient to say that the results emphasize or support previously published conclusions.[125] Klithi was a specialized hunting camp occupied mainly between 16,000 and 13,000 B.P. by hunters pursuing ibex and chamois and was only one part of an extensive logistical network of specialized sites. Bailey's early hypothesis that this cave was a major base camp has been abandoned. The attention paid by the excavators to the investigation of horizontal exposures of deposits at Klithi succeeded in showing that spatial patterning was not preserved in the way that was hoped, and Bailey and his colleagues emphasize that the disturbing activities of human and natural forces in caves and rockshelters make it difficult to interpret the stratification and spatial distribution of artifacts and features. It is becoming increasingly clear from publications such as the Klithi volumes that the contexts and stratigraphy of open-air sites and caves are difficult to decipher, a finding that is reinforced by the ICOPAG reports on Theopetra Cave and Farrand's study of the Franchthi Cave stratigraphy discussed below.

The Argolid, like Epirus, continues to be a focus of attention because of the high concentration of Palaeolithic and Mesolithic sites. New research projects have built upon the foundations laid by earlier ones; two open-air prehistoric sites in the Kleisoura Gorge (Berbati) on the northern edge of the Argive plain, explored originally by a Swedish-American team, have been the subject recently of trial excavations by a team directed by M. Koumouzelis (Ephorate of Caves and Palaeoanthropology) and J.K. Kozlowski (Jagiellonian University, Krakow).[126] The excavation in Cave 1 is particularly important for the stratigraphic sequence that includes an Early Aurignacian level dated to ca. 34,000–26,000 B.P., a later Upper Palaeolithic level dated to ca. 19,000–16,000 B.P., and a Mesolithic level dated to ca. 10,000 B.P. and perhaps later.

Another valuable addition to the literature is a newly completed volume on the stratigraphy of the Franchthi Cave by William Farrand (University of Michigan).[127] Franchthi Cave is of critical importance as a stratified, systematically excavated, and well-published sequence of deposits from the beginning of the Upper Palaeolithic to the end of the Neolithic period. Farrand's study of the Franchthi stratification reinforces the observations already made concerning Theopetra (and noted by Bailey's team in Epirus) that the sequence of deposits is not continuous in any of the caves or rockshelters that have been excavated in Greece. At Franchthi the interruptions in the stratigraphy are sometimes short (e.g., 600–800 years between the Palaeolithic and Mesolithic deposits), but at important points in the cultural record they are sometimes quite large, particularly the gap in the Pleistocene record between ca. 18,000 and 13,000 B.P. This gap in the Franchthi Palaeolithic sequence corresponds to the main periods of occupation of the Kleisoura shelters and Klithi. The combination of discontinuities in the stratigraphic record and lack of overlap in occupational sequences at key sites such as Franchthi, Theopetra, and Kleisoura make regional comparisons difficult at best.

Other notable research concerns surface survey finds of Early Palaeolithic artifacts in the Langadas Survey (eastern Macedonia) directed by K. Kotsakis and S. Andreou (University of Thessaloniki). These artifacts are retouched flakes, mainly of quartz, that closely resemble Palaeolithic artifacts found in Thessaly that belong to two different periods, a Lower Palaeolithic dated to ca. 300,000 B.P. and a Middle Palaeolithic dated to 45,000–30,000 B.P.[128] A long sequence of Palaeolithic and Mesolithic sites in the Preveza region of Epirus were investigated as part of the Nikopolis Survey directed by J.R. Wiseman (Boston University) and K. Zachos (Museum of Archaeology, Ioannina).[129] The Preveza finds include a series of Early Palaeolithic sites associated with karstic features of the landscape that suggest a structured, logistical pattern of land use focused on perennial

---

[125] Bailey (supra n. 123); for earlier publications on the Epirus project, see Bailey (supra n. 22).

[126] J.K. Kozlowski, personal communication, 1998; M. Koumouzelis, J.K. Kozlowski, M. Nowak, K. Sobczyk, M. Kaczanowska, M. Pawlikowski, and A. Pazdur, "Prehistoric Settlement in the Klisoura Gorge, Argolid, Greece (Excavations 1993, 1994)," *Préhistoire européenne* 8 (1996) 143–73; B. Wells and C. Runnels eds., *The Berbati-Limnes Archaeological Survey, 1988–1990* (*SkrAth* 4°, 44, Stockholm 1996) 23–35. It should be noted that Koumouzelis et al. have changed the numbering of the sites so that their Cave 1 and Cave 4 correspond to FS 201 and FS 200 in Wells

and Runnels.

[127] W.R. Farrand, *Depositional History of Franchthi Cave: Stratigraphy, Sedimentology, and Chronology* (*Franchthi* 12, Bloomington 2000).

[128] K. Kotsakis and S. Andreou, personal communication, 1998. For the Thessalian industries, see Runnels and van Andel (supra n. 46).

[129] C. Runnels and T.H. van Andel, "The Early Stone Age Prehistory of the Nome of Preveza (Greece): A Palaeoenvironmental and Archaeological Study of Landscape and Settlement," in J.R. Wiseman and K. Zachos eds., *Landscape Archaeology in Southern Epirus, Greece* 1 (Princeton, in press).

water sources by Neanderthals or other archaic *Homo sapiens*. A large open-air site at Spilaion at the mouth of the Acheron River is remarkable for preserving evidence of spatial patterning detected by mapping, detailed sampling, and application of Geographic Information Systems.[130] Some 150,000 artifacts belonging to the early Upper Palaeolithic (Aurignacian) were found on the surface in discrete clusters that appear to be the remains of flintknapping episodes and not the result of chance factors such as erosion. Spilaion is exceptional because of the preservation of such patterning, which resulted from the removal by erosion of fine-grained sediments on a surface with a low gradient and irregular surface that trapped the artifacts. These conditions are unusual for such early sites, most of which remain to be excavated or studied in detail. Palaeolithic and Mesolithic sites near the Acheron River were placed in a rough chronological framework based on a program of thermoluminescence and uranium/thorium dates; they range from before ca. 200,000 B.P. for the earliest Palaeolithic to the Middle Palaeolithic, which dates from before the last interglacial (ca. 130,000 B.P.) until ca. 52,000 B.P. and after. The latest Middle Palaeolithic sites and the early Upper Palaeolithic site of Spilaion could not be closely dated. The Mesolithic sites were dated to between 10,000 and 7000 B.P.[131]

Finally, it is worth bearing in mind that significant new finds are in the offing. New regional surveys are reporting Palaeolithic finds as a matter of course.[132] Among the more notable discoveries is a Mesolithic site excavated on the island of Yioura in the northern Sporades, a Middle Palaeolithic open-air site at Maara in Macedonia, and hominid fossils comparable to the Petralona cranium from the Mani.[133] Yioura is a pre-ceramic cave site with up to 3 m of stratified deposit dating from approximately 10,500 to 8500 B.P. It is notable for its large concentration of fish remains, land snails, and bone fishing tackle. The lithic industry consists of small numbers (less than 50) of obsidian and flint flakes, end scrapers,

denticulates, and geometric microliths largely comparable to those found at Franchthi Cave and Kleisoura on the mainland. The site of Maara is a cave near a significant spring where tools of quartz and flint of Middle Palaeolithic type were excavated in association with the fossilized remains of Pleistocene animals including cave bear, mammoth, horse, and various cervids. The deposit has been dated to 50,000 B.P. by an unspecified method of dating. The fossilized human remains from the site of Apidima in the Mani, which have yet to be published in detail, are nevertheless of interest for the possible comparison of these fossils with the isolated Petralona cranium from the Chalkidike. Unfortunately, the dating and taxonomic position of the Apidima fossils, which are essentially unstratified finds, are very uncertain. New approaches to palaeoenvironmental reconstructions are also adding to our understanding of the early prehistory of Greece, especially the critical Oxygen Isotope Stage (OIS) 3 from 60,000 to 30,000 B.P., which saw the greatest period of human activity in the Greek world. The OIS 3 turns out to be a highly unstable period of climate requiring precise dating, as yet unavailable, to properly correlate human settlement and climate. Such correlations will remain elusive until a larger sample of well-dated sites is available. In a similar fashion, the detailed modeling of shorelines that is now possible for the period of rapid climatic change that marked the transition from the Pleistocene to the Holocene, and which undoubtedly had an impact on settlement patterns and economy, also affects the recovery of archaeological sites from the late Pleistocene and early Holocene that are probably submerged by marine transgression.[134]

CONCLUSIONS

In the last four years the steadily accumulating new information on the Greek Palaeolithic and Mesolithic has not changed the picture significantly and tends to support previously published conclusions. Lower Palaeolithic remains are still rare and appear

---

[130] C. Runnels, E. Karimali, and B. Cullen, "The Early Upper Palaeolithic Site of Spilaion and the Study of Artifact-Rich Surface Sites," in Wiseman and Zachos (supra n. 129).

[131] Runnels and van Andel (supra n. 129).

[132] J.L. Davis, S.E. Alcock, J. Bennet, Y.G. Lolos, and C.W. Shelmerdine, "The Pylos Regional Archaeological Project, Part 1: Overview and the Archaeological Survey," *Hesperia* 66 (1997) 414–17.

[133] A. Sampson, "The Neolithic and Mesolithic Occupation of the Cave of Cyclope on Youra, Alonnessos, Greece," *BSA* 93 (1998) 1–22; Sampson, "Παλαιολιθικές θέσεις στην

Εύβοια και στις βόρειες Σποράδες," Αρχαιολογία και τέχνες 60 (1996) 51–56; K. Trandalidou, "Πηγές του Αγγίτη: Θέση διέλευσης παλαιολιθικών κυνηγών-συλλεκτών στη γη της σημερινής Ανατολικής Μακεδονίας," Αρχαιολογία και τέχνες 60 (1996) 19–23; T.K. Pitsios, "Ο Ταινάριος Ανθρωπος,"Αρχαιολογία και τέχνες 60 (1996) 68–72.

[134] T.H. van Andel, "Middle and Upper Palaeolithic Environments and the Calibration of ^{14}C Dates beyond 10,000 B.P.," *Antiquity* 72 (1998) 26–33; K. Lambeck, "Sea-Level Change and Shore-line Evolution in Aegean Greece since Upper Palaeolithic Times," *Antiquity* 70 (1996) 588–611.

in Greece only about 300,000 B.P. and after. In this period the human population remained very small and dispersed and only became noticeably more abundant in the later Middle Palaeolithic period, chiefly in OIS 3, where precise dating remains the greatest challenge.

The early Upper Palaeolithic, as indicated by the presence of Aurignacian materials at Elaiochori in Achaia,[135] Spilaion (Epirus), and Kleisoura in the Argolid, testifies to the existence of anatomically modern *Homo sapiens* in Greece. Sites with Upper Palaeolithic remains are sharply reduced in number and are mainly confined to caves and rockshelters. The conclusion that the human population was significantly larger in the Middle Palaeolithic than in the earlier and later periods is inescapable. The evidence for interruptions, hiatuses, and abandonments that emerges from a study of the survey results and the excavations at Klithi and Franchthi supports the conclusion that in some periods, e.g., the Upper Palaeolithic period (ca. 26,000–13,000 B.P.), humans were few and far between on the landscape. The slowly developing picture gathered especially from regional surveys demonstrates the patchy distribution of humans. The discovery of Upper Palaeolithic and even early Holocene habitation in Theopetra Cave notwithstanding, large parts of Thessaly, Macedonia, Thrace, and the Peloponnese (e.g., Messenia) were devoid of significant populations well into the Holocene, indeed often well after the beginning of the Neolithic.

The existence of population peaks in the Middle Palaeolithic, and again in the early Holocene, appears to be a pan-Mediterranean phenomenon linked to glacial climatic conditions and changes in the size of human populations.[136] Finally, in discussions with a number of colleagues in the years following my earlier review of this material, it has become clear that the major remaining question is the degree to which the picture of discontinuous human habitation in this region is the result of incomplete research or is a reflection of reality. The tendency of the newly reported results and the growing body of research to largely corroborate existing evidence is an indication that the picture has not and probably will not change radically in the near future from what we have before us now.

DEPARTMENT OF ARCHAEOLOGY
BOSTON UNIVERSITY
675 COMMONWEALTH AVENUE
BOSTON, MASSACHUSETTS 02215-1406
RUNNELS@BU.EDU

---

[135] For Elaiochori in Achaia, see Darlas (supra n. 78).

[136] M.C. Stiner, N.D. Munro, T.A. Surovell, E. Tchernov, and O. Bar-Yosef, "Paleolithic Population Growth Pulses Evidenced by Small Animal Exploitation," *Science* 283 (1999) 190–94.

Review of Aegean Prehistory V:
The Neolithic and Bronze Age of Northern Greece

STELIOS ANDREOU, MICHAEL FOTIADIS, AND KOSTAS KOTSAKIS

INTRODUCTION

In this article we summarize the state of research on the Neolithic and Bronze Age in the Greek provinces of Thessaly, Macedonia, Thrace, and Epirus.*

Emphasizing field projects undertaken in the last two decades, we review the main conclusions of those projects, and outline many new questions that arise as a result of the recent research.

---

* This review would have been impossible without the help of many colleagues and friends, who gave us site tours, supplied us with offprints and manuscripts of their project reports, and generously responded to our queries: V. Adrimi-Sismani, A. Batziou-Efstathiou, M. Besios, A. Cambitoglou, E. Christmann, P. Chrysostomou, J.L. Davis, A. Douzougli, N. Efstratiou, D.V. Grammenos, B. Hänsel, A. Hondroyanni, G. Karametrou, S. Kotsos, H. Koukouli-Chrysanthaki, Z. Malakasioti, D. Malamidou, S. Morris, J. Papadopoulos, S. Papadopoulos, A. Papanthimou, A. Papasteriou, M. Pappa, E. Poulaki, V. Rondiri, C.N. Runnels, M. Savina, T.F. Tartaron, G. Toufexis, R. Treuil, K. and D. Wardle, N. Wilkie, C.L. Zachos, and H. Ziota. T. Cullen, D.V. Grammenos, P. Halstead, G.H. Hourmouziadis, A. Kalogirou, and K.D. Vitelli provided incisive comments on large sections of the manuscript. A. Vargas and M. Magafa helped design the maps and, together with P. Skoufis, ensured communication between continents.

We repeatedly and extensively discussed among ourselves most of the issues we treat. The closest collaboration has been between Andreou and Kotsakis, who wrote the sections on Thessaly, central and eastern Macedonia, and Thrace, with Kotsakis writing primarily about the Neolithic, and Andreou about the Bronze Age. The note on the history of research in Macedonia, the sections on western Macedonia and Epirus, and the short concluding note on the earliest Neolithic were written by Fotiadis.

The following abbreviations are used in this review:

Achilleion	M. Gimbutas, S. Winn, and D. Shimabuku, *Achilleion: A Neolithic Settlement in Thessaly, Greece, 6400–5600 B.C.* (Los Angeles 1989).
AEMT	*Το Αρχαιολογικό Εργο στη Μακεδονία και Θράκη* (Thessaloniki).
Ancient Thessaly	*Διεθνές Συνέδριο για την Αρχαία Θεσσαλία στη Μνήμη του Δ.Ρ. Θεοχάρη* (Athens 1992).
ArchMak	*Αρχαία Μακεδονία* (International Symposia, Thessaloniki).
Argissa III	E. Hanschmann and V. Milojčić, *Die deutschen Ausgrabungen auf der Argissa-Magula in Thessalien III: Die frühe und beginnende mittlere Bronzezeit* (BAM 13, Bonn 1976).
Atlas	C.J. Gallis, *Ατλας των προϊστορικών θέσεων της ανατολικής Θεσσαλίας* (Larisa 1992).
BAM	*Beiträge zur ur- und frühgeschichtlichen Archäologie des Mittelmeer-Kulturraumes.*
Coleman	J.E. Coleman, "Greece, the Aegean and Cyprus," in R.W. Ehrich ed., *Chronologies in Old World Archaeology*[3] (Chicago 1992) 247–79.
Dimini	G.H. Hourmouziadis, *Το νεολιθικό Διμήνι* (Volos 1979).
Egnatia	*Εγνατία. Επιστημονική Επετηρίδα της Φιλοσοφικής Σχολής. Τεύχος Τμήματος Ιστορίας και Αρχαιολογίας* (Thessaloniki).
Feuer	B. Feuer, *The Northern Mycenaean Border in Thessaly* (BAR-IS 176, Oxford 1983).
Gazetteer	R. Hope Simpson and O.T.P.K. Dickinson, *A Gazetteer of Aegean Civilisation in the Bronze Age 1: The Mainland and Islands* (SIMA 52, Göteborg 1979).
Grammenos	D.V. Grammenos, *Νεολιθικές έρευνες στην κεντρική και ανατολική Μακεδονία* (Library of the Athens Archaeological Society 117, Athens 1991).
Halstead 1984	P. Halstead, *Strategies for Survival: An Ecological Approach to Social and Economic Change in the Early Farming Communities of Thessaly, N. Greece* (Diss. Univ. of Cambridge 1984).
Halstead 1989	P. Halstead, "The Economy Has a Normal Surplus: Economic Stability and Social Change among Early Farming Communities of Thessaly, Greece," in P. Halstead and J. O'Shea eds., *Bad Year Economics: Cultural Responses to Risk and Uncertainty* (Cambridge 1989) 68–80.
Halstead 1994	P. Halstead, "The North–South Divide: Regional Paths to Complexity in Prehistoric Greece," in C. Mathers and S. Stoddart eds., *Development and Decline in the Mediterranean Bronze Age* (Sheffield Archaeological Monographs 8, Sheffield 1994) 195–219.
Iolkos	I. Kolliou ed., *Νεότερα δεδομένα των ερευνών για την αρχαία Ιωλκό. Πρακτικά Επιστημονικής Συνάντησης 12 Μαΐου 1993* (Volos 1994).
Kastanas	B. Hänsel, *Kastanas: Ausgrabungen in ein-*

Originally published in *AJA* 100 (1996) 537–97.

Table 1. Archaeological Phases and Chronology for Northern Greece: Neolithic and Bronze Age

Archaeological Phases			Years B.C. Calendrical
Early Neolithic			6700/6500–5800/5600
Middle Neolithic			5800/5600–5400/5300
Late Neolithic			5400/5300–4700/4500
Final Neolithic			4700/4500–3300/3100
Early Bronze Age			3300/3100–2300/2200
(Middle Bronze Age)	} Later Bronze Age {		2300/2200–1700/1500
Late Bronze Age			1700/1500–1100

Modern geopolitical divisions—states, administrative districts, and the boundaries between them—provide a framework for organizing our knowledge and narrative. However alien they may be to the Neolithic and Bronze Age, such divisions continue to play powerful and multiple roles in the production of archaeological knowledge; they are devices as much as they are obstacles.[1] Our way of coping with their ill effects is indirect. In the body of the review we treat each modern province (Περιφέρεια) in turn, beginning with Thessaly, continuing with western, central, and eastern Macedonia and Thrace, and ending with Epirus. We resist, however, the temptation to develop grand syntheses of the prehistory of each province, or of northern Greece as a whole. The effort to write such syntheses would entrap us in a labyrinth of assumptions and theoretical presuppositions that we are not prepared to accept, and it would entail leaps of faith and, ultimately, violence to the archaeological evidence. We prefer instead to be as synthetic in our scope and conclusions as circumstances in each province allow. We cannot overstress the fact that our conclusions, drawn upon the work of hundreds of researchers, are provisional. We expect—in fact, we hope—that they will be challenged in the very near future. That is all the more likely for northern Greece today, since many field projects are currently in progress, and they have thus far been reported only in preliminary fashion.

We focus here on questions of regional significance, and on interregional comparisons and comparisons between archaeological phases. The state of archaeological knowledge is uneven across the regions with which we are concerned, with the result that we cannot be wholly consistent from one region to the next in the questions we address, nor can we attempt interregional comparisons in all crucial respects. Our strategy is therefore opportunistic: we exploit the particular strengths of archaeological knowledge in each region, and we point out the weaknesses.

We have adopted the broadest chronological framework and terminology, and we use calendrical rather than radiocarbon dates (table 1).[2] Even this

---

em Siedlungshügel der Bronze- und Eisenzeit Makedoniens, 1975–1979: Die Grabung und der Baubefund (Prähistorische Archäologie in Südosteuropa 7, Berlin 1989).

Kotsakis   K. Kotsakis, Κεραμεική τεχνολογία και κεραμεική διαφοροποίηση: Προβλήματα της γραπτής κεραμεικής της Μέσης Νεολιθικής εποχής του Σέσκλου (Diss. Univ. of Thessaloniki 1983).

La Thessalie   Θεσσαλία. Δεκαπέντε χρόνια αρχαιολογικής έρευνας, 1975–1990. Αποτελέσματα και προοπτικές. Πρακτικά Διεθνούς Συνεδρίου, Λυών, 17–22 Απριλίου 1990. La Thessalie. Quinze années de recherches archéologiques, 1975–1990. Bilans et perspectives. Actes du colloque international, Lyon, 17–22 avril 1990, vols. A–B (Athens 1994).

Pefkakia I   H.-J. Weisshaar, Die deutschen Ausgrabungen auf der Pevkakia-Magula in Thessalien I: Das späte Neolithikum und das Chalkolithikum (BAM 28, Bonn 1989).

Pefkakia III   J. Maran, Die deutschen Ausgrabungen auf der Pevkakia-Magula in Thessalien III: Die mittlere Bronzezeit (BAM 30, Bonn 1992).

Sitagroi   C. Renfrew, M. Gimbutas, and E.S. Elster eds., Excavations at Sitagroi: A Prehistoric Village in Northeast Greece 1 (Los Angeles 1986).

[1] It is small consolation that political boundaries often follow geographical ones (e.g., coasts, massive mountains, steep climatic gradients). Geographical boundaries, and the regions they define, are negotiable, and have limited authority outside particular political fields. See M. Fotiadis, "Regions of the Imagination: Archaeologists, Local People, and the Archaeological Record in Fieldwork, Greece," Journal of European Archaeology 1:2 (1993) 154–56 and 161–62.

[2] "B.C." in this review always indicates calendrical dates, whether obtained by calibration of radiocarbon measurements or by other means, including estimation. We do not use "b.c." or "B.P.," except when quoting uncalibrated radiocarbon measurements as published.

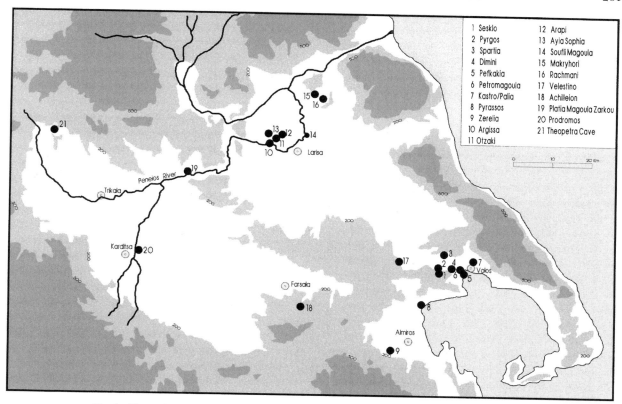

1 Sesklo	12 Arapi
2 Pyrgos	13 Ayia Sophia
3 Spartia	14 Soufli Magoula
4 Dimini	15 Makryhori
5 Pefkakia	16 Rachmani
6 Petromagoula	17 Velestino
7 Kastro/Palia	18 Achilleion
8 Pyrassos	19 Platia Magoula Zarkou
9 Zerelia	20 Prodromos
10 Argissa	21 Theopetra Cave
11 Otzaki	

Fig. 1. Thessaly. Principal sites mentioned in the text. Contours at 200 and 500 masl.

broad framework cannot be followed in all its details in every province. Particularly troublesome is the phase we designate as "Middle Bronze Age," which can be identified only in Thessaly and parts of Macedonia. Where the phase remains elusive, we resort to the broader term "later Bronze Age," covering the time period from ca. 2300/2200 to ca. 1100 B.C. Subdivisions within the phases shown in table 1 are possible for many sites and regions. These are discussed along with the other data from the respective sites and regions.[3]

THESSALY

The pioneering work of Tsountas and Wace and Thompson during the early 20th century has made Thessaly the focal point of Neolithic research in Greece (fig. 1).[4] Long before any systematic framework was established in other parts of Greece, research in Thessaly possessed an elaborate chronotypological system suitable for describing the culture history of the area. To some extent this privileged

position is still held today, and some of the central issues of Greek prehistory, such as the beginning of a farming economy or the emergence of social complexity, revolve around research in Thessaly, although questions of culture history and chronology are still discussed.

The refinement of the chronological framework was the main objective of the German and Greek excavations carried out from 1953 to 1977 at a number of Thessalian sites. This approach was the natural outcome of a long-established concern with the importance of the Aegean for European chronology. In the last decade or so, research in Thessaly has moved into a phase of synthesis, with less emphasis on excavation and more on the analysis of excavated data. At the same time, new issues have been put forward and new methods and approaches adopted.

Gulf of Volos

The most intensively excavated area of Thessaly is its coastal region. Research, which started here

---

[3] For the perplexities surrounding the date of the earliest Neolithic, see E.F. Bloedow, "The Date of the Earliest Phase at Argissa Magoula in Thessaly and Other Neolithic Sites in Greece," *MeditArch* 5–6 (1992–1993) 49–57.

[4] For an account of the Greek archaeological research in Thessaly carried out from 1881 to 1975, see C.J. Gallis,

"A Short Chronicle of Greek Archaeological Investigations in Thessaly from 1881 until the Present Day," in *La Thessalie, Actes de la Table-Ronde 21–24 juillet 1975, Lyon* (Collection de la Maison de l'Orient méditerranéen 6, Lyons 1979) 1–30.

at the turn of the century and continues to date, has produced a fairly complete excavation record covering extensive parts of settlements and cemeteries from the Early Neolithic to the Late Bronze Age.

Sesklo (fig. 1:1). A new period of research was initiated at Sesklo in 1956 by D.R. Theocharis. With shorter or longer intervals, this period lasted until 1981, and is partly summarized in *Νεολιθική Ελλάς* and partly in a number of preliminary reports.[5] The initial objective was the reexamination of the stratigraphy of the mound, but the focus of investigation gradually shifted to the extended Middle Neolithic settlement outside and around the tell of Sesklo. Theocharis named this part of the settlement the *polis* (Sesklo B), in contrast to the original *acropolis* of Tsountas (Sesklo A), and he put forward a model of urban development and population concentration that had no antecedents in the Greek Neolithic.[6]

The total excavated area approaches 4,500 m² and the estimated area of the settlement amounts to 12 ha, unequally divided between the acropolis and the polis. The acropolis, where Tsountas's original excavation had been conducted, is in the form of a tell, 8.5 m high and ca. 0.3 ha in area. The polis stretches out on the flat slope to the northwest, on the edge

of a dissected terrace of Tertiary lacustrine marls. Both parts are flanked on the north and south by deeply cut streams that, by Tsountas's time, had already eroded a large part of the tell.

The stratigraphy of the site, clarification of which was one of the principal aims of Theocharis, was checked in a number of trenches. On the tell itself, the stratigraphic sequence was uniform.[7] The lowest part was characterized by the absence of pottery and was considered "preceramic."[8] The rest of the stratigraphy was divided into Early Neolithic and Middle Neolithic, each further subdivided into three phases. The Early and the Middle Neolithic end stratigraphically with an extensive destruction.[9] The Late Neolithic, already investigated by Tsountas, was not studied stratigraphically to any extent by Theocharis.[10]

No significant architectural finds support the division of the Early Neolithic period into three parts. The division rests mostly on observations of ceramic change. The architectural evidence, though tenuous, points to small rectangular houses built with pisé walls and posts or with stone socles and mudbrick.[11] By contrast, the MN phases (I, II, IIIA, IIIB) correspond to architectural episodes of rebuilding houses and floors.[12] The MN IIIB phase ends with a wide-

[5] D.R. Theocharis, *Νεολιθική Ελλάς* (Athens 1973) 36, 40, 60–77, 102. Theocharis, "Ανασκαφαί εν Σέσκλω," *Prakt* 1962, 24–35; *Prakt* 1963, 40–44; *Prakt* 1965, 5–9; *Prakt* 1966, 5–7; *Prakt* 1968, 24–30; *Prakt* 1971, 15–19; *Prakt* 1972, 8–11; and *Prakt* 1977, 159–61; Theocharis, *Το Εργον της Αρχαιολογικής Εταιρείας* 1976, 88–99. K. Kotsakis, "Τρία οικήματα του οικισμού του Σέσκλου. Ανασκαφική έρευνα," *Anthropologika* 2 (1981) 87–108; Kotsakis 37–41. Results of research on different groups of finds, after Theocharis's death, are included in A. Christopoulou, *Microwear Analysis of the Chipped and Ground Stone Tools from Sesklo A* (Diss. Univ. of London 1979); H.-A. Moundrea-Agrafioti, *La Thessalie du sud-est au Néolithique: Outillage lithique et osseux* (Diss. Univ. of Paris X–Nanterre 1981); M. Wijnen, "Building Remains of the Early Neolithic Period at Sesklo," in *Ancient Thessaly* 55–63; A. Christopoulou, "Ιχνη χρήσης στα λειασμένα λίθινα εργαλεία του Σέσκλου Α," in *Ancient Thessaly* 64–69; A. Papaefthimiou-Papanthimou, "Εργαλεία υφαντικής από το Σέσκλο," in *Ancient Thessaly* 78–82; A. Pilali-Papasteriou, "Οι σφραγίδες από το Σέσκλο και τα προβλήματα της θεσσαλικής νεολιθικής σφραγιδογλυφίας," in *Ancient Thessaly* 83–90; A. Papaefthimiou-Papanthimou, *Οι ανασκαφές του Δ.Ρ. Θεοχάρη στο νεολιθικό οικισμό του Σέσκλου: Πήλινα μικροαντικείμενα* (Athens, in press).

[6] Theocharis 1973 (supra n. 5) 65.

[7] M. Wijnen, *The Early Neolithic I Settlement at Sesklo: An Early Farming Community in Thessaly, Greece* (Leiden 1982) 10–15, 99.

[8] The existence of a true "preceramic" phase in Thessaly has often been questioned, e.g., by C. Perlès, "New Ways with an Old Problem: Chipped Stone Assemblages as an Index of Cultural Discontinuity in Early Greek Prehistory," in E.B. French and K.A. Wardle eds., *Problems in Greek Prehistory* (Bristol 1988) 484–86; *Achilleion* 26–27; Perlès, "La

néolithisation de la Grèce," in O. Aurenche and J. Cauvin eds., *Néolithisations* (*BAR-IS* 516, Oxford 1989) 115–16; E.F. Bloedow, "The 'Aceramic' Neolithic Phase in Greece Reconsidered," *MeditArch* 4 (1991) 2–35. For the opposite view, see M. Tellenbach, "Materialien zum präkeramischen Neolithikum in Süd-Ost-Europa. Typologisch-stratigraphische Untersuchungen zu lithischen Gerätschaften," *BerRGK* 64 (1983) 92–94, 123–24. See also infra p. 597.

[9] Wijnen (supra n. 7) 11. Contrary to the MN, the EN destruction was not observed in other parts of the settlement. Therefore it would not be wise to treat it as a general feature of the Sesklo stratigraphy.

[10] Theocharis reports levels belonging to the FN "Rachmani" phase from the acropolis and ascribes them to three subphases. See *Prakt* 1966, 6. No further information is available from this stratigraphic section. Weisshaar's (*Pefkakia* I, 85) reconstruction is insubstantial.

[11] Wijnen (supra n. 5) 56–63.

[12] *Prakt* 1968, 25; *Prakt* 1971, 15; Kotsakis 46–51. Also, K. Kotsakis, *Σέσκλο. Οι ανασκαφές του Δ.Ρ. Θεοχάρη 1956–1977: Η στρωματογραφία και η αρχιτεκτονική της Μέσης Νεολιθικής περιόδου* (in preparation), where the architecture and stratigraphy of Sesklo are discussed in detail. B. Otto, *Die verzierte Keramik der Sesklo- und Diminikultur Thessaliens* (Mainz 1985) 66 attempts to subdivide the MN sequence of Sesklo into six subperiods (MN IA, IB, IIA, IIB, IIIA, IIIB) on the basis of stylistic observations on the pottery published by Tsountas. The stratigraphic support for this subdivision is insufficient and contradicts some of Theocharis's observations. See Theocharis 1973 (supra n. 5) 79, 119 and *Prakt* 1968, 27–30. I. Aslanis, *Η προϊστορία της Μακεδονίας* I: *Η Νεολιθική εποχή* (Athens 1992) 88–93, repeats Otto's scheme.

spread destruction, observed both at the tell and at the extended settlement.[13] The majority of the architecture at Sesklo, such as the famous "potter's workshop," belongs to this final phase.[14]

The stratigraphy of the polis (Sesklo B) was in many respects different from that of the acropolis (Sesklo A).[15] As a rule, deposits at Sesklo B are much shallower than those of Sesklo A, and their stratigraphic order appears discontinuous, varying from trench to trench. Moreover, large areas of Sesklo B are devoid of cultural deposits. The evidence in the extended settlement points toward a pattern of habitation of considerable spatial and temporal discontinuity, with parts of the site remaining either temporarily or totally uninhabited.[16] There is no such evidence at Sesklo A, where spatial discontinuity is limited. Dispersed traces of EN habitation are also present at Sesklo B, occasionally near the surface, but LN material is absent.

Significant differences between the two areas of the settlement are observed in architecture as well. All the buildings explored at Sesklo A are freestanding, sometimes with considerable space around them, or built around yards. By contrast, buildings at Sesklo B form tight clusters, sharing walls and facilities. At least some of these clusters preserve facilities for food-processing and storage, normally distributed in separate rooms.[17] A typical example of a Sesklo A dwelling is given by house 39: it is spacious (8.5 × 5.5 m), with one entrance on its narrow west side, and no internal divisions. Three areas are distinguished inside: a stone-built platform associated

with storage vessels, a hearth situated next to it, and a work area with grinders, querns, and an oven on the far east end. The arrangement integrates essential needs of the household in one defined unit.[18]

The differences between the two areas in the Middle Neolithic are emphasized by the stone "fortification walls" that encircle part of the tell. The walls were observed initially by Tsountas and since then their defensive function has been debated.[19] Their size and construction make it more probable that they served as retaining walls, supporting terraces on which houses were founded.[20] Whatever the practical purpose of these features, they represent the concern of the inhabitants for maximizing the available space on the tell itself, a concern absent from Sesklo B. At the same time, the effort to separate the two parts of the settlement stresses further their differences during the Middle Neolithic.

Closely related to the dual habitational pattern at Sesklo is the spatial distribution of pottery, which was preserved thanks to the extended final MN destruction. The frequency of painted pottery is consistently higher at Sesklo A than Sesklo B. Together with differences in ceramic technology, this discrepancy between the two areas seems but another aspect of the dual settlement pattern at Sesklo.[21] In this respect, the original acropolis-polis model might still be relevant, as it implies a deeper difference between the two areas. The size of the population, however, given the more or less dispersed habitation at Sesklo B, was probably a 10th or less of the high figure (3,000–4,000) estimated by Theocharis. Moreover, the

---

[13] *Prakt* 1972, 8–9; Kotsakis 46–51. This widespread destruction level permits a clear and positive chronological correlation of the final deposits as well as of the houses, floors, and constructions associated with them in different parts of the settlement.

[14] Excavations uncovered 22 MN houses, and a considerable number of partly preserved other structures. They were all built with stone socles and mudbrick. For an earlier discussion of the architecture of Sesklo, based on preliminary reports, see R. Elia, *A Study of the Neolithic Architecture of Thessaly, Greece* (Diss. Boston Univ. 1982) 128–33, 169–74, 216–33. For the "potter's house," see *Prakt* 1968, 27–30. This house is reconstructed by Theocharis 1973 (supra n. 5) fig. 16 as a two-storied building, a reconstruction that has been widely accepted, e.g., in A. Sherratt ed., *The Cambridge Encyclopedia of Archaeology* (Cambridge 1980) fig. 15.6. Examination of the stratigraphic evidence, however, does not clearly support the existence of the second floor.

[15] K. Kotsakis, "The Use of Habitational Space in Neolithic Sesklo," in *La Thessalie* A, 125–30; *contra* Wijnen (supra n. 7) 14–15.

[16] Kotsakis (supra n. 15) 127–28 notes that this pattern resembles that of the extended LN sites of central Macedonia and contrasts with the pattern of persistent occu-

pation of tell sites (see infra p. 585). It is extremely interesting, however, that at Sesklo both patterns are present simultaneously, especially if a socially recognized significance was attached to the tell part of the settlement, which physically represented the long lineage of the households of the community.

[17] E.g., houses A, Γ, and Z2, Kotsakis (supra n. 5) fig. 3.4.

[18] This arrangement is seen in the well-known house model from Platia Magoula Zarkou; see K.I. Gallis, "A Late Neolithic Foundation Offering from Thessaly," *Antiquity* 59 (1985) 20–24.

[19] Theocharis 1973 (supra n. 5) 65; *Dimini* 85.

[20] Kotsakis (supra n. 12): at least one house was founded on top of one of these walls. Most of the MN houses were founded on varying levels, and the whole settlement on the tell must have had a steplike, terraced appearance.

[21] Kotsakis 55–56, 95–102. For the technological differences between the two areas of Sesklo, see Y. Maniatis, V. Perdikatsis, and K. Kotsakis, "Assessment of In-site Variability of Pottery from Sesklo, Thessaly," *Archaeometry* 30 (1988) 264–74. The archaeometric analysis on a small stratified sample from both areas has found a marked preference for calcareous clays in Sesklo A, non-calcareous in Sesklo B. Macroscopic examination of the pottery from both areas seems to support this conclusion.

instability of the extended part of the settlement contrasts with the permanent "urban" characteristics of a polis, and the supposed fortification walls of the acropolis can be more reasonably interpreted as retaining constructions. Finally, although the differences between the polis and the acropolis are clear, they need not imply a formally stratified society with a well-defined elite controlling social production. It is rather a difference in scale, which, at least as far as pottery is concerned, results in a certain inequality of access to raw materials and produce.[22]

An interesting methodological lesson can be learned from the example of Sesklo. The complex intrasite variability of the archaeological features shows clearly that comparisons among sites are potentially misleading. Given the generally limited extent of excavations in Greece, it is unwise to describe excavation sequences as "typical" and to base comparative conclusions on them. Most of the syntheses of the Neolithic in Thessaly have not considered this important factor of latent variability within sites.[23]

Little is known about Sesklo after the Neolithic, mainly because the higher levels had already been removed by Tsountas. In the area of Sesklo B, there are no traces of Bronze Age habitation, except for MBA cist graves, common at Sesklo A as well.[24] Traces of massive retaining walls on the mound must also belong to this period, although their exact date is obscure.[25] Houses of the Middle Bronze Age are reported from the western side of the tell, but evidently this part of the Bronze Age settlement did not spread as far as the Sesklo B area. Particularly interesting is the observation of traces of EBA habitation in area E, ca. 130 m southeast of Sesklo A, across the Seskouliotis ravine.[26]

Pyrgos (fig. 1:2). On a low hill that overlooks the Gulf of Volos, ca. 250 m north of Sesklo, lies the small site of Pyrgos (25 m in diameter), already identified

by Tsountas and excavated by the ΙΓ′ Ephoreia in 1979.[27] The excavators explored a deposit containing mainly LN "classical Dimini" pottery and a level with FN "Rachmani" pottery, including incised sherds with white or pink filling, and crusted ware. A thick layer of burnt debris separates the two deposits. The inventory of finds and the few architectural remains point to a more or less permanent settlement. If this small site is directly associated with LN Sesklo, it would match the MN pattern of dispersed habitation around the acropolis. In this case the site could represent a small cluster of households placed a few hundred meters away from Sesklo, overlooking the extended plateau, where the prime farmland lies.

Further to the north, two previously known sites, Spartia (fig. 1:3) and Palaiokastron, have recently been reinvestigated.[28] Together with Pyrgos and Sesklo, they seem to have flanked, during the Late Neolithic, the Tertiary plateau of lacustrine marls of excellent arable qualities (100–200 masl). Unlike Pyrgos, they are long-lived sites, occupied until Hellenistic times or later. Spartia and Palaiokastron are situated on the main pass linking the eastern plain of Thessaly with the small coastal plain of Volos. Sesklo is connected to the coastal area via a route that passes from the Seskouliotis stream to Dimini, Petromagoula, and Pefkakia (fig. 1:4–6). To the southwest the route continues to the Aerino plateau, where four more prehistoric sites were located, of which Persoufli Magoula is also a site of considerable longevity. Another pass, at 300 masl, leads over low mountains to the area of Pyrassos (fig. 1:8) on the present coast of the Pagasitikos Gulf.

Dimini (fig. 1:4). The well-known site of Dimini was reinvestigated by Hourmouziadis in 1974–1976. The main objective was to reexamine the architecture and to consider the relationship of the site to neighboring settlements in an attempt to integrate

[22] Kotsakis 264–300; K. Kotsakis, "Aspects of Technology and Distribution of MN Pottery at Sesklo," in *Science in Archaeology. Proceedings of a Meeting Held at the British School at Athens, January 1985* (Athens 1986) 1–2.

[23] E.g., Y. Mottier, *Die deutschen Ausgrabungen auf der Otzaki-Magula in Thessalien* II (*BAM* 22, Bonn 1981) 39–54, regards the Otzaki sequence as typical and bases on it the relative chronology of the excavated MN Thessalian sites. On these grounds she views the Sesklo sequence (p. 43) as contemporary with the deeper levels of MN Otzaki, and argues for an early abandonment of Sesklo. The available ^{14}C dates from the last MN phase at Sesklo, however, argue clearly against such a conjecture, as does the A3β-γ pottery of the "degenerate" (pl. E, I/3-2-1, no. 72) style, which is very common in MN IIIB Sesklo and appears also in final MN levels at Otzaki.

[24] MBA cist graves have been found as far as the mod-

ern village of Sesklo, more than 1 km away: Theocharis 1976 (supra n. 5) 99. For a detailed dating of the Sesklo graves, see *Pefkakia* III, 222–26.

[25] C. Tsountas, Αι προϊστορικαί ακροπόλεις Διμηνίου και Σέσκλου (Athens 1908) 110.

[26] Theocharis 1976 (supra n. 5) 88; Το Εργον της Αρχαιολογικής Εταιρείας 1977, 88–93. A few EBA or MBA copper objects have been analyzed by McGeehan-Liritzis and Gale (infra n. 46) 205–206, 211–15, 221–23. There is one occurrence of a tin-bronze alloy, but no identification of the source of the copper was possible.

[27] A. Batziou, "Πύργος: Ενας δορυφορικός προϊστορικός οικισμός," *Anthropologika* 2 (1981) 108–20.

[28] Tsountas (supra n. 25) 4, nos. 3–5; M. Di Salvatore, "Ricerche sul territorio di Pherai: Insediamenti, difese, vie e confini," in *La Thessalie* B, 93–124.

archaeological information in a systemic framework, characteristic of the 1970s.[29] Research was directed toward the excavation of particular features and the restoration of the entire settlement. Spatial information became available on a large scale,[30] although the intensity of the investigation was not uniform throughout the settlement.

The tell of Dimini lies on the higher western edge of the coastal plain of Volos. It sits on an outcrop of schist, at 18 masl and 3 km from the present coast. A major episode of alluviation, dated by ^{14}C to the fourth millennium B.C., has formed the plain, pushing the coast away from Neolithic Dimini.[31] The other sites on the Gulf of Volos, Pefkakia and Petromagoula (fig. 1:5–6), have retained their coastal location.

Clarification of the function of the six concentric perimeter walls at Dimini, uncovered by Stais and Tsountas, was the initial objective of the reexamination. Hourmouziadis carefully evaluated the architectural evidence, and concluded that the purpose of the perimeter walls was to enclose four main domestic areas or "courtyard groups." The four wards were situated at a lower level around a central court. Each ward contained a larger building and a number of storage or food preparation facilities as well as work areas.[32] Communication was ensured through

the radiating entrances. According to Hourmouziadis, the pattern of the six concentric perimeter walls was the outcome of the gradual growth of the settlement and reflected the insistence of the inhabitants on dividing their settlement into well-demarcated areas using internal boundaries. The walls also satisfied the need to support and maximize the available space on the small rocky spur of Dimini.

The previous interpretation of the walls as defensive constructions was seriously questioned by Hourmouziadis. He argued that their size and location do not conform with their presumed purpose of preventing hostile intrusions. He could find no evidence, for instance, that the height of the walls exceeded the measure of a simple boundary wall.[33] His main argument, however, derived from his view of social organization: he argued that a Neolithic fortified acropolis, defending the central part of the settlement, would imply a stratified social structure, incompatible with the presumed "Neolithic mode of production."[34] It must be remembered, however, that a territorial demarcation, in any form, primarily controls access, physically or symbolically, to the settlement or to a part of it.[35] Such barriers to access, mainly perimetric ditches, are not uncommon in Neolithic settlements.[36] In any case, the interpretation of the walls at Dimini is a reminder that ar-

---

[29] Hourmouziadis, *Dimini* 25–27, describes this system as a threefold structure comprising the subsystems of the organization of space, economy, and non-productive activities.

[30] Several scholars have taken advantage of the recent spatial data: P. Halstead, "Dimini and the 'DMP': Faunal Remains and Animal Exploitation in Late Neolithic Thessaly," *BSA* 87 (1992) 44–55; A. Tsuneki, "The Manufacture of *Spondylus* Shell Objects at Neolithic Dimini, Greece," *Orient* 25 (1989) 1–21; L. Skafida, "Νεολιθικά ανθρωπόμορφα ειδώλια του Διμηνίου," in *Ancient Thessaly* 166–79; and Z. Malakasioti, "Μικρά ευρήματα με εγχάρακτη διακόσμηση," *AAA* 15 (1982) 173–81.

[31] E. Zangger, "Prehistoric Coastal Environments in Greece: The Vanished Landscapes of Dimini Bay and Lake Lerna," *JFA* 18 (1991) 1–7 and esp. fig. 1. Contrary to Zangger, E.M. Kambouroglou, "Η γεωμορφολογική εξέλιξη του κόλπου του Βόλου από τη Νεολιθική εποχή μέχρι σήμερα," in *La Thessalie* A, 41–52, maintains that the rise of sea level was the main geomorphological activity in the area, gradually flooding the Volos plain toward Dimini. Only in late antiquity did alluviation prevail, extending the plain toward the sea. Nevertheless, anthropogenic FN and BA alluviation remains a plausible suggestion, and conforms with observations made in the Larisa plain. See A. Demitrack, *The Late Quaternary Geologic History of the Larissa Plain, Thessaly, Greece. Tectonic, Climatic and Human Impact on the Landscape* (Diss. Stanford Univ. 1986); T.H. van Andel, Zangger, and Demitrack, "Land Use and Soil Erosion in Prehistoric and Historical Greece," *JFA* 17 (1990) 379–96; Demitrack, "A Dated Stratigraphy for the Late Quaternary in Eastern Thessaly and What It Implies about Landscape Changes,"

in *La Thessalie* A, 38. Also van Andel, K. Gallis, and G. Toufexis, "Early Neolithic Farming in a Thessalian River Landscape, Greece," in J. Lewin, M.G. Macklin, and J.C. Woodward eds., *Mediterranean Quaternary River Environments* (Rotterdam 1995) 131–43.

[32] *Dimini* 110–40.

[33] *Dimini* 59.

[34] *Dimini* 83–98. In two subsequent articles, Hourmouziadis explains more clearly what he believes to be the basic elements of a "Neolithic mode of production," which he considers incompatible with an antagonistic social reality involving aggression and defense: G.H. Hourmouziadis, "Εισαγωγή στο νεολιθικό τρόπο παραγωγής," *Anthropologika* 1 (1980) 118–29 and *Anthropologika* 2 (1981) 39–54. Nevertheless, in the case of Dimini, equal access to household production, as suggested by Hourmouziadis, would seem inconsistent with the seclusion of the productive units behind stone walls.

[35] According to Hourmouziadis, *Dimini* 51, Neolithic Dimini extended outside the acropolis, covering an area of 3 ha, though in a less organized fashion. The extent of the settlement was confirmed by subsequent research in the area of modern Dimini: V. Adrimi-Sismani, *ArchDelt* 32 B′ (1977) 131–34. We have already seen a similar arrangement at Sesklo.

[36] Ditches have been reported from a number of LN sites in Thessaly. For Arapi Magoula and Argissa Magoula, see H. Hauptmann and V. Milojčić, *Die Funde der frühen Dimini-Zeit aus der Arapi-Magula, Thessalien* (BAM 9, Bonn 1969) 3, and Milojčić, "Bericht über die Ausgrabungen auf der Gremnos-Magula bei Larissa 1956," *AA* 71 (1956) 160–63.

chitectural features need to be examined in their particular social and economic context.[37]

Another point of divergence from older literature on Dimini concerns the "central megaron." According to Hourmouziadis's observations, the typical "megaron" form at Dimini resulted from a later, EBA modification of the central court area. The modification was related to the demographic decline of the mound and the deterioration of the communal character of the central court, which was then taken over by a single household, apparently an eminent one.[38]

The reconstruction of the gradual formation of the "megaron" at Dimini is convincing and warns against the strict typological approach to architecture. The dating, however, of the Dimini "megaron" to the Early Bronze Age is not supported by decisive stratigraphic evidence, since all the deposits there had already been dug by Stais and Tsountas.[39] Moreover, similar LN architectural finds from Sesklo, Ayia Sophia, and possibly Visviki seem to point to an earlier dating.[40]

Within the limitations of the uneven scale of excavation, Dimini offers an opportunity to observe the spatial arrangement of various finds, including food preparation and storage facilities. They are fairly evenly distributed across the discrete domestic areas and tend to be located indoors rather than in the open areas. A good example is house N, which contained four food preparation and two storage facilities, though not all of them were in use at the same time.[41] Of the other facilities scattered throughout the site, one was identified as a specialized pottery workshop.[42] The composition of the faunal assemblage related to food preparation and consumption was found by Halstead to vary insignificantly within the different domestic areas, which may indicate generally equal access to produce; the possibility remains, however, that some domestic units consumed more meat than others.[43] The majority of faunal remains were classified as sheep/goat, while the percentages of pigs and cattle fluctuated. Eight intramural infant cremation burials were uncovered, all placed near hearths and in pots, some made especially for this purpose.[44] Figurines are present almost everywhere but their distribution shows a strong concentration in the three peripheral domestic areas rather than the central court.[45] Objects made of *Spondylus* have a similar distribution. A concentration of finished rings was identified in house N, while an even greater concentration of buttons and cylinder beads was found in the area of the pottery workshop (area C). Regardless of the possible interpretation of this pattern, which can partly be due to uneven intensity of excavation, the quantity and type of objects prove that LN Dimini was a significant node in the extended exchange network of *Spondylus*.[46]

[37] I. Aslanis, "Οι οχυρώσεις στους οικισμούς του βορειοελλαδικού χώρου κατά τη Χαλκολιθική περίοδο και η περίπτωση του Διμηνίου," in M.B. Sakellariou ed., *Ποικιλία* (Μελετήματα 10, Athens 1990) 19–53, wishes to restore the "defensive" interpretation of the Dimini perimeter walls on the basis of perceived similarities with the Chalcolithic settlements of Bulgaria and Rumania. Also, Aslanis, "Die Siedlung von Dimini: Ein neues Rekonstruktionsbild," in *Settlement Patterns between the Alps and the Black Sea—5th to 2nd Millennium B.C.* (Museo civico di storia naturale, Sezione scienze uomo 4, Verona 1995) 35–43.

[38] *Dimini* 106, 110 and fig. 6.

[39] The EBA dating of the Dimini "megaron" has been questioned by P. Halstead, review of *Dimini* in *JHS* 101 (1981) 206–207.

[40] Theocharis 1973 (supra n. 5) figs. 18 and 23; V. Milojčić, "Die Grabung auf der Agia Sofia-Magula," in Milojčić et al., *Die deutschen Ausgrabungen auf Magulen um Larisa in Thessalien* (BAM 15, Bonn 1976) 5–6. Particularly useful is the dating of the Ayia Sophia "megaron," although this has been only partially uncovered and is not altogether comparable to the megara at Dimini and Sesklo. To these examples one may add the recently found LN "megara" at Makriyalos in Pieria; see infra p. 573.

[41] *Dimini* 133–59. See also Halstead 1984, ch. 5.2.3. As Halstead (supra n. 30) 31–32 has pointed out, the interior location of food-producing facilities is in contrast to earlier Neolithic practice. For house N, see *Dimini* 149–50.

[42] G.H. Hourmouziadis, "Ένα ειδικευμένο εργαστήριο κεραμεικής στο νεολιθικό Διμήνι," *AAA* 10 (1978) 207–26. Also Hourmouziadis, "Die Spezialisierung im Neolithikum," in D. Papenfuss and V.M. Strocka eds., *Palast und Hütte* (Mainz 1982) 125–35.

[43] Hourmouziadis has repeatedly stressed the uniform distribution of food refuse, tools, and pottery in all parts of the settlement. See *Dimini* 67. The inability to estimate the quantity of animal bone deposited was attributed to retrieval factors: Halstead (supra n. 30) 56. For the archaeobotanical remains from the recent excavations, see H. Kroll, "Kulturpflanzen aus Dimini," in U. Körber-Grohne ed., *Festschrift Maria Hopf* (Archaeo-Physika 8, Cologne 1979) 173–89.

[44] G.H. Hourmouziadis, "Εισαγωγή στις ιδεολογίες της ελληνικής προϊστορίας," *Politis* 17 (1979) 33. Also Hourmouziadis, *Αρχαία Μαγνησία: Από τις παλαιολιθικές σπηλιές στο ανάκτορο της Δημητριάδας* (Athens 1982) 81, fig. 52. Halstead (supra n. 30) 33, reports additional infant bones found together with the faunal remains.

[45] Skafida (supra n. 30) 166–79, table 1, fig. 1. With two exceptions, the figurines are schematic—cruciform or acrolithic. See also C. Marangou, *Ειδώλια: Figurines et miniatures du Néolithique Récent et du Bronze Ancien en Grèce* (BAR-IS 576, Oxford 1992) 38–40 for the figurines found by Tsountas.

[46] Tsuneki (supra n. 30) table 1. Also P. Halstead, "*Spondylus* Shell Ornaments from Late Neolithic Dimini, Greece: Specialised Manufacture or Unequal Accumulation?" *Antiquity* 67 (1993) 603–609, table 1. According to Tsuneki

The poor preservation of the post-LN architectural remains has led to conflicting reconstructions of the later occupational history of the mound. The circuit walls were possibly replaced by a ditch, and occupation became more sparse and horizontally discontinuous.[47] Halstead argues for the transformation of the hill into a segregated elite area in the Final Neolithic and Early Bronze Age. He considers the segregation of the hill as part of a process, begun in the Late Neolithic, toward an institutionalized hierarchical organization.[48] Whether the end of the Neolithic at Dimini is marked by crisis and disintegration or by continuity and consolidation of a central authority remains an open issue.

A conspicuous change is manifest near the end of the Middle Bronze Age, when the hill was again demarcated by a mudbrick perimeter wall. From that period onward the evidence of occupation is limited to a few burials.[49] The transformation of former habitation mounds to burial grounds was a practice not uncommon at Thessalian sites during the later

part of the Middle Bronze Age, and may represent a type of bounded burial, existing in the region prior to the appearance of the first tholoi and built tombs.[50] According to Halstead, the move may be related to the action of elites wishing to isolate their burial grounds.

The most important development for the understanding of the later history of the site has been the excavation of an extensive LBA settlement on the alluvial plain at the foot of the mound. Since 1978 the Archaeological Service has excavated several blocks of houses flanking a wide street. Surface finds and trial trenches indicate that the town was ca. 10 ha in size.[51] The latest architectural remains were found a little below the surface, and the excavation provides a picture of the layout of the settlement in its last phase, which was characterized by pottery of the late LH IIIB or early IIIC style. Earlier deposits, reached in small trenches beneath the floors, show successive habitation from the Middle Bronze Age onward.[52]

(supra n. 30) 13, the *Spondylus* rings were exclusively manufactured in house N, and beads and buttons in area C. Halstead (pp. 607–608), however, points out that waste products from the manufacture of rings, buttons, and beads were found in almost every part of the settlement, which suggests a more dispersed production of these objects. He proposes, therefore, that these objects were unequally accumulated by individual domestic groups as exchange tokens for "social surplus." This exchange may also have included copper artifacts. A copper flat ax and an earring have been analyzed and discussed by V. McGeehan-Liritzis and N.H. Gale, "Chemical and Lead Isotope Analyses of Greek Late Neolithic and Early Bronze Age Metals," *Archaeometry* 30 (1988) 201–207, 211–15, 222–23. The Dimini artifacts were made of arsenical copper, the provenance of which cannot be identified. For a more general discussion of personal ornaments in the Thessalian Neolithic, see N. Kyparissi-Apostolika, "Κοσμήματα της νεολιθικής Θεσσαλίας," in *Ancient Thessaly* 185–90.

[47] Tsountas (supra n. 25) 30–31, 65–68, 363. *Gazetteer* 275. Dating these modifications with any accuracy is impossible.

[48] Halstead 1984, chs. 5.2.4 and 8.1.2–3. House remains dated to the EBA have recently been found in the lower ground, south of the mound, but no details have been published. See V. Adrimi-Sismani, "Η μυκηναϊκή πόλη στο Διμήνι: Νεότερα δεδομένα για την Ιωλκό," in *Iolkos* 22. The massive foundations of a large building between the first and second perimeter walls on the southwest, found during the early period of excavations, may, according to Halstead 1984, ch. 5.2.4, represent the remains of a FN central building. Hourmouziadis and Adrimi-Sismani argue for the identification of the same building with the elite residence or the "palace" of the LBA settlement: *Dimini* 107–10, 149, fig. 6 and pl. 1; Adrimi-Sismani, "Μυκηναϊκός οικισμός Διμηνίου," in *Ancient Thessaly* 275–76, pl. 59a. The documentation offered by Tsountas, however, is insufficient to decide the matter one way or another.

[49] For the MBA wall and contemporary habitation on the lower ground, see Adrimi-Sismani in *Iolkos* (supra n. 48) 23. For the date of the cist graves, see *Pefkakia* III, 217–18. For the cist graves and the two tholos tombs, see *Gazetteer* 147–52.

[50] For other instances of Thessalian habitation mounds transformed into burial grounds, see Halstead 1984, ch. 5.2.5; and J. Maran, "Zum mittelbronzezeitlichen Bebauungsschema auf der Pevkakia-Magula bei Volos," in *La Thessalie* A, 209 and ns. 12–13. For the same practice in southern and central Greece, see Maran, "Structural Changes in the Pattern of Settlement during the Shaft Grave Period on the Greek Mainland," in R. Laffineur and W.-D. Niemeier eds., *Politeia: Society and State in the Aegean Bronze Age (Aegaeum* 12, Liège 1995) 69–72. The mortuary reuse of habitation mounds may imply an attempt by an elite to appropriate symbolically the past qua conspicuous ruins. In most cases, however, it is uncertain that the burials belong to an elite group.

[51] V. Adrimi-Sismani, *ArchDelt* 32 B′ (1977) 132–34; *ArchDelt* 35 B′ (1980) 272; *ArchDelt* 43 B′ (1988) 238–39; Adrimi-Sismani, in *Ancient Thessaly* (supra n. 48) 272–78; and in *Iolkos* (supra n. 48) 17–44; and Adrimi-Sismani, "Ο μυκηναϊκός οικισμός Διμηνίου," in *La Thessalie* A, 225–32.

[52] The pottery of the latest floor deposits displays stylistic traits that have been related to LH IIIB1, IIIB2, or even early LH IIIC styles; see Adrimi-Sismani in *La Thessalie* A (supra n. 51) 226–29, figs. 12–18; also in *Ancient Thessaly* (supra n. 48) 273–75. This variability could be due to the idiosyncracy of LH IIIB and IIIC pottery in Thessaly; cf. E.S. Sherratt, "Regional Variation in the Pottery of Late Helladic IIIB," *BSA* 75 (1980) 175–202; Sherratt, "The Development of Late Helladic IIIC," *BICS* 32 (1985) 161–62. Deposits with LH IIB and LH IIIA pottery were also found. Handmade burnished pottery of distinctive shapes was found along with the Mycenaean in the earlier and later LBA levels: Adrimi-Sismani in *Iolkos* (supra n. 48) 27, figs.

The 45-m stretch of street was 5 m wide, paved with pebbles and flanked by walls with no openings. The houses, with a stone socle and mudbrick superstructure, were comprised of several rooms around courtyards, where wells were located. Walls and floors were occasionally plastered. One of the most regularly planned houses had a main room with a hearth and two smaller rooms at the back. A fenced corner in one of the rooms of another house contained a bull figurine and a possible altar, probably indicating a domestic shrine. Several rooms were used for storage and as specialized working areas, including a space with traces of metalworking. Finally, a potter's kiln was uncovered at the eastern limits of the settlement.[53]

The layout indicates a complex, well-organized community, with central planning and craft specialization. The two tholos tombs and a possible central building at the top of the tell point to the existence of a central authority. Dimini offers the most complete picture of a Thessalian LBA community, so far unique in the region.

Pefkakia (fig. 1:5). Pefkakia Magoula, another important coastal site on the Gulf of Volos, had been investigated in the late 1950s by Theocharis, but systematic research was undertaken in 1967 by Milojčić and lasted until 1977. The magoula was formed on the slopes of a rocky promontory.[54] It now extends over 2 ha, but it has suffered much erosion from rising sea level and repeated human interventions. The Neolithic settlement must have been small, limited primarily to the top of the promontory. By contrast, trenches dug at lower levels on the side of the tell revealed thick deposits from the Bronze Age and few traces of the Neolithic.[55]

The information on the Neolithic sequence comes from a single trench, 13 × 10 m, on the top of the mound. A small area produced deposits of the Late Neolithic ("classical Dimini"). The rest was taken up by a sloping outcrop of the natural rock that lay immediately under the levels of the succeeding phases.[56] Three FN architectural phases were defined with rectangular houses built on stone foundations and with clay floors. Plans cannot be reconstructed, but the state of preservation was best in the last phase, where parts of four houses were distinguished. They were arranged in parallel rows separated by narrow alleys. One of the houses contained several small pits and storage vessels, a large rectangular pit lined with mudbrick and filled with ash, and a rectangular clay hearth. Under the floor, near the lined pit, was a burial furnished with two obsidian cores.[57] A stone platform cutting into the house wall recalls the food-processing facilities of house N at Dimini. It is not clear, however, whether this construction was approached from the outside.[58]

In the previous, second, phase, preservation was poorer, but enough survived to indicate that the orientation of houses was the same and that storage facilities were abundant. The orientation of houses was different in the earliest phase. Parts of two houses were defined, while a wall 1.20 m thick was located on their west side. The excavator interpreted this wall as defensive, but its location makes the defensive function again ambiguous; it might well be an internal boundary as at Dimini.

Pefkakia is the only site that stratigraphically completes the sequence of Neolithic phases in Thessaly as reconstructed by Milojčić. For this reason it holds a central position in the chronological debate still continuing in northern Greek and Balkan archaeology.[59] The main argument revolves around ceramic wares and their stratigraphical position. In general terms, the pottery from Pefkakia displays elements characteristic of the Aegean FN phase, such as redslipped wares and crusted wares, "elephant lugs," and

---

7–9; Adrimi-Sismani 1977 (supra n. 51) 131–34. In the final LBA levels, wheelmade "pseudo-Minyan" gray ware was also found: Adrimi-Sismani, in *Ancient Thessaly* (supra n. 48) 273, pl. 56ε; K. Kilian, "Mycenaeans Up to Date," in French and Wardle (supra n. 8) 132–33, n. 4. For non-Mycenaean wares in LBA Thessaly, see *Pefkakia* III, 107–108, 174–76, 214–15, 222–27, 274–78, 286; *Argissa* III, 117, ns. 97–98. Also Feuer 85–86, 98, 103–104, 127, 131–38, 187; and Avila (infra n. 88) 37, 50–51, 56.

[53] Adrimi-Sismani in *Iolkos* (supra n. 48) 31–36, figs. 4, 17, 18. The bovine figure recalls those found in the LH IIIC shrine at Phylakopi, shown in C. Renfrew, *The Archaeology of Cult: The Sanctuary at Phylakopi* (Oxford 1985) 248, 276–80, 425, pl. 39. For the kiln, see V. Adrimi-Sismani, "Μυκηναϊκός κεραμικός κλίβανος στο Διμήνι," in *Η περιφέρεια του μυκηναϊκού κόσμου: Διεθνές διεπιστημονικό*

συμπόσιο, *Λαμία 25–29.9.1994* (forthcoming).

[54] The promontory may have been flanked during most of the site's life by two small bays: Kambouroglou (supra n. 31).

[55] *Pefkakia* I, fig. 1, trench G-H V; E. Christmann, "Die Magula von Pevkakia und die Frühbronzezeit in Thessalien: Chronologie und externe Kontakte," in *La Thessalie* A, 201.

[56] *Pefkakia* I, pl. 146.

[57] Halstead 1984, ch. 5.2.4, relates the lined pit with the burial underneath and points out the similarities with the Ayia Sophia Magoula burials; see Milojčić (supra n. 40) 6–7.

[58] *Dimini* pl. 5.

[59] H.-J. Weisshaar, "Varna und die ägäische Bronzezeit," *ArchKorrBl* 12 (1982) 321–29.

plastic decoration.[60] Ten uncalibrated ^{14}C dates from the site are tightly clustered between 3820 ± 70 b.c. and 3560 ± 65 b.c., and the difference between the six "Dimini" phase dates and the four "Rachmani" ones is very small.[61] Clearly then, the LN–FN sequence at Pefkakia was relatively short and must be placed around the accepted date for the LN–FN boundary near the end of the fifth millennium B.C. The short duration is also confirmed by the minimal changes in the layout of the houses from one architectural phase to the next. Furthermore, repeated episodes of leveling, an expected activity in building on a slope, must have obliterated and disturbed a good part of the original deposits. The particularly poor state of preservation of the architectural remains, especially in the lower phases, and the high frequency of pottery from earlier phases in almost all of the excavated deposits support such a claim.[62]

Despite the series of ^{14}C dates, the excavator proposed a much lower date for the "Dimini" and "Rachmani" levels at Pefkakia, making the last phase synchronous with EH I and part of EH II. That dating was based on the presence of a small number of EH II Urfirnis sherds in the upper Rachmani deposits.[63] A small amount of black-on-red LN pottery of eastern Macedonian origin found in the lower Rachmani levels was thus dated by analogy equally low. This dating has been regarded with much skepticism by archaeologists working in southern as well as in northern Greece.[64]

It is clear then that the Pefkakia sequence repre-

sents only a small fraction of the total assumed time span between the end of the Late Neolithic and the beginning of the Early Bronze Age. Consequently, an exact stratigraphic definition of the "Rachmani" phase is still wanting. This generally holds for all sites reported to have "Rachmani" deposits, where even the stratigraphic succession from the "Dimini" phase is assumed rather than shown.[65] On the other hand, it has to be pointed out that the long and convoluted discussion of the comparative chronology at Pefkakia has overshadowed the significance of the presence of imports, which reveal the long-distance connections of the site, already in the Late Neolithic.[66]

The Early Bronze Age at Pefkakia was represented by substantial deposits and architectural remains. The extent of the settlement appears to have been larger than during the Neolithic, since EBA deposits have also been found at the base of the mound. The remains were originally described by Milojčić, who reported a defensive wall with a bastion in an early phase, a large apsidal building with a hearth and several episodes of rebuilding, and the so-called "Trojan megaron" in the final phase. Recently, Christmann has subdivided the EBA levels into seven building phases. He assigned the circuit wall to phase 3, the reconstructions of the apsidal building to phases 5–7, and the "megaron" to the two subphases of phase 7.[67]

During the Early Bronze Age Pefkakia maintained its overseas connections, but their scope was now broader, and oriented toward the south and east rather than the north.[68] The presence of the solid

[60] *Pefkakia* I, 16–25, 44; E. Christmann, "Thessalien im dritten Jahrtausend," *Thraco-Dacica* 14 (1993) 42–43; Coleman 257.

[61] *Pefkakia* I, 139.

[62] Coleman 276–77; pottery of the "Sesklo," "Tsangli," "Arapi," "Otzaki," and "Dimini" phases is present in almost all levels of the trench. See *Pefkakia* I, pls. 137–38.

[63] *Pefkakia* I, 25, 142–43, pl. 145; H.-J. Weisshaar, "Ausgrabungen auf der Pevkakia Magula und der Beginn der frühen Bronzezeit in Griechenland," *ArchKorrBl* 9 (1979) 385–92; also Weisshaar (supra n. 59); Weisshaar, "Galepsos und Urfirnis: Bemerkungen zur relativen Chronologie der Rachmani-Kultur," in J. Lichardus ed., *Die Kupferzeit als historische Epoche. Symposium Saarbrücken und Otzenhausen 6.–13.11.1988* (Bonn 1991) 240–43.

[64] Coleman 257, 276–77; C. Renfrew, "Sitagroi in European Prehistory," in *Sitagroi* 478–79; Grammenos 86–91; R. Treuil, *Le Néolithique et le Bronze Ancien égéens: Les problèmes stratigraphiques et chronologiques, les techniques, les hommes* (*BEFAR* 248, Athens 1983) 73–74; Christmann (supra n. 55) 203 and (supra n. 60) 41–44 has demonstrated that Weisshaar's position is unacceptable, also arguing that a phase contemporary with EH I, which is absent from Pefkakia, is represented at Petromagoula.

[65] Renfrew (supra n. 64) 478 suggests that a hiatus must

be assumed in the Pefkakia sequence; Milojčić, *Otzaki* III (infra n. 98) 134–37; Treuil (supra n. 64) 77–78.

[66] Notable among the other finds are two copper adzes from the second phase of Rachmani levels: *Pefkakia* I, 48, pl. XIX.

[67] Christmann (supra n. 55) 201 with earlier references. Also E. Christmann, *Die deutschen Ausgrabungen auf der Pevkakia-Magula in Thessalien* II: *Die frühe Bronzezeit* (*BAM* 29, Bonn, in press). For EBA deposits at the base, see *Pefkakia* III, 59.

[68] EH II and EC II imports were present in all seven phases. Phases 4–6 run parallel with Argissa II. "Anatolianizing" features in the pottery first appeared in phase 6, but were mainly present, together with Anatolian imports, in phase 7, which displays affinities with Lefkandi I and Keos III and late EH II. Cf. J.L. Davis, "Review of Aegean Prehistory I: The Islands of the Aegean," *AJA* 96 (1992) 96–97, ns. 36–37; also J. Rutter, "Review of Aegean Prehistory II: The Prepalatial Bronze Age of the Southern and Central Greek Mainland," *AJA* 97 (1993) 764–65, ns. 78–79. "Anatolianizing" features, however, were also present in the transitional phase together with EH III patterned ware. See Christmann (supra n. 55) 201–203 and (supra n. 60) 43–46; see also infra n. 70.

perimeter wall and the expansion of the exchange network might indicate increased centralization of the social structure, but decisive evidence is lacking.

The MBA habitation at Pefkakia is considerably better understood.[69] The MBA sequence has been divided into seven phases, preceded by a transitional phase between the Early and Middle Bronze Age.[70] From phase 2 onward, the settlement was closely compacted, in a pattern that lasted until phase 6. The stone-built oblong houses stood on terraces along the slope of the mound. Internal arrangements varied but houses were consistently divided into a number of rooms. Storage facilities in various forms were abundant, and a few industrial installations were also found.[71]

Buildings were closely packed, leaving little free space. They give the impression of self-contained units, partitioned into separate spaces, often with a discrete function. The repeated occurrence of infant burials inside the houses, occasionally marked with stone slabs, may further stress the self-containment of the household. Similarly, the increasing importance of hunting during the Bronze Age may also have been part of a strategy to sustain the self-sufficiency of the household through individual or privately negotiated acts.[72] In phase 7 a significant change is observed in the southern part of the mound, where the former habitation area was occupied by cist graves of infants and some adults.[73]

Material culture began changing already in the earlier MBA levels, but the changes can be seen more clearly after phase 3. The most obvious was the gradual adoption of a new type of table ware, Gray Minyan, and the appearance of several types of matt-painted vessels. Gray Minyan became the dominant fine ware after phase 4. Matt-painted sherds were already present in the transitional phase, but fine and coarse matt-painted pots appeared mainly after phase 5.[74] Domestic plain wares relate Pefkakia to the inland sites of the region, such as Argissa. By contrast, special pottery products, such as Gray Minyan and matt-painted pottery, differentiate the site from the inland regions, particularly during the later Middle Bronze Age. In that period pottery was also coming from central Greece, the northeastern Peloponnese, Aegina, the Cyclades, and possibly other areas not easily identifiable.[75]

A less detailed picture is available for the LBA settlement. Previous research had already shown that the southern terrace of the mound was reinhabited in a period corresponding to the LH III pottery phase. A cemetery with rectangular built tombs was placed at the edge of the magoula, and a substantial building nearby was abandoned in the period corresponding to LH IIIA. Recent research has demonstrated that the settlement extended well beyond the mound, acquiring a size of ca. 8 ha.[76] Parts of a substantial building with plastered walls, benches, and extensive storage space were found at some distance to the southeast, and parts of a second to the southwest. The building had two phases, the second of which contained late LH IIIB–early LH IIIC pottery. After that period the settlement seems to have been abandoned.

---

[69] *Pefkakia* III. Habitation probably expanded in that period also: A. Batziou-Efstathiou, "Αποτελέσματα των πρόσφατων ανασκαφικών ερευνών στη Νέα Ιωνία και στην περιοχή Πευκακίων," in *Iolkos* 59–69.

[70] *Pefkakia* III, 4–5, plan I. The remains of this transitional phase are scanty, and the extent of changes in the architecture from the underlying EBA levels cannot be evaluated: *Pefkakia* III, 6–7, 61. Absolute dates are not available, and relative dating is established through comparative stratigraphy. The period from the transitional to the third phase has been related to EH III, and phases 3–6 may correspond to the MH period. Phase 7 displays affinities with Shaft Grave period contexts. The earlier five MBA phases at Pefkakia are broadly related to the early five MBA phases at Argissa. The limited and selected set of data, however, cautions against detailed comparisons.

[71] *Pefkakia* III, 7–33, 51–55, 61–64.

[72] The contribution of hunting to the diet increased in Bronze Age Thessaly. At Pefkakia it rose to 21%: A. von den Driesch, "Haus- und Jagdtiere im vorgeschichtlichen Thessalien," *PZ* 62 (1987) 7, esp. fig. 2. Halstead 1984, ch. 7.3, sees hunting as a way of buffering risk. See also P. Halstead, "Man and Other Animals in Later Greek Prehistory," *BSA* 82 (1987) 74–75, where the archaeozoological evidence of Pefkakia is discussed in the general context of Neolithic and Bronze Age subsistence. Animal remains from Pefkakia are presented in B. Jordan, *Tierknochenfunde aus der Magula Pevkakia in Thessalien* (Diss. Univ. of Munich 1975); G. Hinz, *Neue Tierknochenfunde aus der Magula Pevkakia in Thessalien 1: Die Nichtwiederkäuer* (Diss. Univ. of Munich 1979); K.-P. Amberger, *Neue Tierknochenfunde aus der Magula Pevkakia in Thessalien 2: Die Wiederkäuer* (Diss. Univ. of Munich 1979).

[73] Burials were occasionally furnished with pots and a few other objects: *Pefkakia* III, 31. For similar cases, see supra n. 50.

[74] "Matt-painted" here designates the possible use of manganese-based paint in decoration. The technique appeared at a time when EH III patterned ware was still present in the deposits: *Pefkakia* III, 31 n. 1,204. After phase 5, polychrome and wheelmade matt-painted pots appeared as well: *Pefkakia* III, 149–73. For LBA matt-painted pottery and plain wares, see *Pefkakia* III, 174–76 and 285–89.

[75] Maran is cautious in the macroscopic identification of imports and points out that in cases such as Gray Minyan it is difficult to distinguish imports from Thessalian products: *Pefkakia* III, 81.

[76] A. Batziou-Efstathiou, "Νεότερες ανασκαφικές έρευνες στην ευρύτερη περιοχή της μαγούλας 'Πευκάκια'," in *Ancient Thessaly* 279–85, figs. 1–2, pls. 60–63; Batziou-Efstathiou (supra n. 69).

Petromagoula (fig. 1:6). The excavations at Petromagoula might be crucial for understanding the FN–EBA sequence in coastal Thessaly. The site lies on the former coastline midway between Pefkakia and Dimini. The stratigraphic sequence presents two main architectural phases with a maximum depth of deposit of 2.80 m down to bedrock. No complete architectural plans were found, but houses with stone socles and a circuit wall are reported. Storage facilities were abundant both indoors and outdoors. The finds included a group of copper and lead objects.[77]

The pottery of Petromagoula displays affinities with the "Rachmani" levels at Pefkakia. It also includes incised pieces (absent from Pefkakia) related to groups dating to the beginning of EH I.[78] It is probable that the very beginning of the Bronze Age is present at Petromagoula, in contrast to Pefkakia. In that case, Petromagoula may date closer to the end of the Final Neolithic, thus narrowing the gap left by the high ^{14}C dates of Pefkakia.

Compared to the Middle Neolithic, intensity of occupation in the wider area of the Volos bay, including the hills around Sesklo, seems to have increased during the Late and Final Neolithic. Seen in this light, the foundation of Petromagoula would be part of a regional trend, which could also be responsible for the alluviation of the Dimini bay through the anthropogenic erosion of higher ground.[79]

Kastro/Palia (fig. 1:7). Modern buildings impede the investigation of the impressive tell of Kastro/Palia at the tip of the gulf, near the western edge of modern Volos.[80] Several crucial aspects relating to its stratigraphy and history during the Neolithic and Bronze Age remain obscure, and the interpretation of earlier and recent finds, especially in respect to the organizational aspects of the site and its importance in the regional LBA settlement network, is at best equivocal.

Over several years the ΙΓ′ Ephoreia has excavated over a dozen test pits spread over the site mainly as part of rescue operations.[81] The new excavations confirmed some of Theocharis's claims and challenged others. Up to 2 m thick, the EBA and MBA deposits contained remains of apsidal and rectangular houses with stone walls, clay and paved floors, and occasional infant burials.[82] During the Middle Bronze Age Kastro/Palia participated in the same exchange network as Pefkakia.[83]

Less substantial were the LBA deposits. Recent excavations were unable to locate further traces of the building designated a "palace" by Theocharis. Various architectural phases were represented in the deposits, dated by pottery of LH IIB–LH IIIB2 styles. Finally, despite several instances of burnt and ashy layers, no destruction horizon has been identified in any LBA phase or between the LBA and Protogeometric levels.[84]

It would be an exaggeration to say that the LBA

---

[77] L. Hadjiaggelakis, "Ο προϊστορικός οικισμός της Πετρομαγούλας," *Anthropologika* 5 (1984) 75–85. The lead and copper objects are discussed and analyzed in McGeehan-Liritzis and Gale (supra n. 46) 205, 209–15, 222–23. A possible source for the lead object is Lavrion.

[78] Hadjiaggelakis (supra n. 77) figs. 10–11; C.L. Zachos, *Ayios Dhimitrios: A Prehistoric Settlement in the Southwestern Peloponnesos: The Neolithic and Early Helladic Periods* (Diss. Boston Univ. 1987) 134; Christmann (supra n. 55) 201 and (supra n. 60) 44.

[79] Halstead 1984, table 6.4; and supra n. 31.

[80] *Gazetteer* 272–73. For the location of the site, see P. Marzolff and W. Boser, *Die deutschen archäologischen Forschungen in Thessalien: Demetrias* III (*BAM* 19, Bonn 1980) plans I–II. The two early excavators of Kastro, Tsountas and Theocharis, argued for its identification with Homeric Iolkos, a view that has been recently challenged (infra n. 91).

[81] Z. Malakasiotou, "Νεότερα δεδομένα για την αρχαία Ιωλκό στα Παλιά του Βόλου," in *Iolkos* 47–57; *ArchDelt* 36 B′ (1981) 352–53; *ArchDelt* 43 B′ (1988) 239–41. The total depth of deposits including those of the later periods (Protogeometric–Geometric and Early Christian–Ottoman) averaged ca. 9 m.

[82] The earliest occupation at Kastro/Palia may date to EB I: *Gazetteer* 272. The three successive EBA building phases distinguished by Theocharis have affinities with EBA Argissa II and III and some parallels with Lefkandi I and Ayia Irini III (*Argissa* III, 126–29, pls. 60–62).

[83] Similar MBA and early LBA wares, including polychrome-decorated and Minoan pots, occur at Kastro/Palia and Pefkakia: *Pefkakia* III, 219–22; see also J.B. Rutter and C.W. Zerner, "Early Hel025ado-Minoan Contacts," in R. Hägg and N. Marinatos eds., *The Minoan Thalassocracy: Myth and Reality* (Athens 1982) 82, no. III, 6S; S.A. Immerwahr, "Some Pictorial Fragments from Iolkos in the Volos Museum," *ArchEph* 1985, 85–94.

[84] Malakasiotou, in *Iolkos* (supra n. 81) 51–53. Finds include fragments of pictorial-style vases and figurines of Mycenaean types. Earlier Mycenaean-style pottery in very small numbers has been reported but not illustrated, and was found together with pottery designated as "Middle Helladic." The characteristics of early LBA assemblages in Thessaly have not yet been determined with precision. It is generally accepted that MH burnished ware continued and that pre-LH IIB pottery was rare in the area around Volos and absent further inland. Consequently, it is probable that some of the Thessalian deposits generally reported as MH could date to the LBA. On the other hand, the plan, extent, and specific date of occupation during the period of LH IIIC pottery and the transition from LH IIIC to Protogeometric remain undetermined; see Malakasiotou (supra n. 53. M. Sipsie-Eschbach, *Protogeometrische Keramik aus Iolkos in Thessalien* (Prähistorische Archäologie in Südosteuropa 8, Berlin 1991) 186–88, has recently published a few small stratified deposits from Theocharis's test pits.

history of the site has become any clearer after the recent investigations. The remains display strong horizontal and vertical discontinuities and, for that reason, assessments of the size and density of LBA occupation would be speculative. In view of the growing evidence from Dimini and Pefkakia, however, LBA Kastro/Palia emerges as a less prominent settlement than previously thought.

Rescue excavations over many years in the nearby district of Nea Ionia have unearthed an extensive cemetery, ca. 500 m to the north of the settlement, representing most periods of occupation at Kastro/Palia.[85] Twenty new cists and one pit, with LH IIB and LH IIIA style pottery, have recently been added, found underneath 3.50 m of alluvium.[86] The graves held single adult inhumations in a contracted position and were generally poor in grave goods. The most common finds were Mycenaean alabastra and piriform jars, but a bronze dagger, sealstone, bronze ring, a few beads, and decorated bone pins have also been found. One grave stands out: in addition to pots of fine quality, it contained a type CII sword with an alabaster pommel, and a razor.[87]

The proximity of the tholos tomb at Kapakli to the settlement has been a crucial component of the argument for the dominance of Kastro/Palia in the Volos area. Avila has restudied the finds and proposed a new date in LH IIIA for the main period of use.[88] The construction, size, and contents of the tholos exemplify the strong contrasts characterizing Thessalian society during this period. It may be suggested that an important medium for the expression of these contrasts was the varied use of the contemporary Mycenaean material culture by the different segments of the population. Avila contrasts the high craftsmanship of the gold objects with the much lower technological standards displayed by local Mycenaean (LH I–LH IIIA1) pottery.[89] These contrasts may indicate dissimilar modes and levels of adoption of cultural traits from southern Greece by the elite and the rest of the community. At the same time, they may display the different levels of incorporation of Thessalian society into the Mycenaean cultural system.[90]

Finally, in recent years the identification of the settlement at Kastro/Palia with Homeric Iolkos has been questioned on archaeological, literary, and topographical grounds. The incentive was undoubtedly the discovery of the extensive LBA settlement at Dimini. The presence of three closely spaced and equally large contemporaneous settlements along the coast of Volos poses difficulties for the recognition of a regional hierarchical structure on the basis of differences in settlement size. Similarly, the absence of clearly differentiating elements in terms of monumentality, craft specialization, administrative features, and burial practices among the three sites impedes unequivocal recognition of a political and administrative center for the area. Therefore, the identification in coastal Thessaly of a state, resem-

---

[85] Summary of research in Batziou-Efstathiou (supra n. 69) 59–60. D. and M. Theocharis, "Εκ του νεκροταφείου της Ιωλκού," AAA 3 (1970) 198–203, explored 20 cist graves buried underneath the alluvium and dated by LH IIB- and IIIA-style pottery. Two other distinct burial grounds can be related to the settlement. Sixteen LBA cist graves were excavated by Tsountas at the edge of the mound. More LBA cist graves have been found recently in the same area (unpublished). For the tholos tomb excavated by Kourouniotis at Kapakli ca. 500 m to the northwest, see below.

[86] A. Batziou-Efstathiou, "Μυκηναϊκά από τη Νέα Ιωνία Βόλου," ArchDelt 40 A′ (1985) 17–71. A total of 208 graves belonging to various periods from the EBA to Early Christian have been explored since 1981: Batziou-Efstathiou (supra n. 69) 59.

[87] Two jugs stand out for their decorative and technological superiority; see Batziou-Efstathiou (supra n. 86) 54–56 and 77–79. An almost identical jug, a cup, and sword were found in another grave excavated by D. and M. Theocharis (supra n. 85) fig. 2. Single burials in a contracted position, primarily in cist graves, seem to be the rule, at least since the third millennium B.C. in Thessaly. For a discussion of EBA and MBA burials in Thessaly, see Halstead 1984, ch. 5.2.4–5 and figs. 5.4–5. Presumably the practice continued through the LBA. For LBA single inhumations, see Halstead 1984, ch. 5.2.5, and Feuer 70, where

inland examples are discussed.

[88] A.J. Avila, "Das Kuppelgrab von Volos-Kapakli," PZ 58 (1983) 15–60. The stylistic affinities of some ornaments leave open the possibility of a longer use of the tomb (Avila 49–56). The 20 burials were arranged in groups, and grave goods were concentrated in four of the burials. The tomb (10 m in diameter) was rich in gold ornaments along with silver objects, glass paste, and ivory. It also contained Mycenaean, red-burnished, and Gray Minyan pottery (presumably all of LBA date; Avila 23, 55–56).

[89] The differences between local Thessalian Mycenaean and Peloponnesian Mycenaean pottery are seen in the treatment of the clay, modeling techniques, surface treatment, decoration, and firing. Avila (supra n. 88) 57 observes that, occasionally, local non-Mycenaean pottery displays a higher technological standard. The differences, therefore, do not stem from technological skills alone, but also from the particular role of pottery in the Thessalian "market," and from economic aspects such as the level of mechanization or the scale of production. One may assume two distinct modes of ceramic production between early LBA Thessaly, on the one hand, and the Argolid, on the other. There is great scope for further work on local non-Mycenaean and Mycenaean patterns of ceramic technology, production, circulation, and consumption.

[90] Avila (supra n. 88) 57.

bling in organizational features the Mycenaean states of central and southern Greece, is problematic.[91]

Almiros area. An intensive survey has been initiated in the area southeast of Almiros, around the Hellenistic city of Halos. Preliminary results confirm the known pattern of prehistoric occupation in the coastal area and further inland around Zerelia Magoula (fig. 1:9). A LBA rock-cut chamber tomb at Kato Mavrolofos makes a useful addition to the few other examples in Thessaly. Pottery of LH IIIA2 and LH IIIB was associated with at least six burials. Metal finds were missing but the plundered tomb was fairly rich in glass and carnelian beads, conical and biconical "buttons," and glass and steatite seals.[92]

Eastern Plain

No major excavation has been conducted in the eastern Larisa plain since the intensive activity of the mid-1960s. During the last 20 years, however, the results of these early excavations have gradually appeared in an impressive number of volumes presenting in detail the evidence on which the preliminary synthesis by Milojčić had been based.

Argissa (fig. 1:10). Among the first sites to be excavated by Milojčić in the Larisa area, Argissa Magoula is a large tell with an estimated area of 5 ha, the cumulative result of a long history of shifting occupation through the Neolithic and Bronze Age.[93]

The publication of the excavation was completed in 1981 with the presentation of the MBA levels and the few later finds. Architectural remains of the EBA habitation were very sparse. The only evidence for

the earlier part of the period are the three successive ditches that probably marked the western limit of the site, carrying on a Neolithic tradition. The remains of two rectangular post-framed houses with facilities for storing and processing food inside and outside, on top of the earlier ditches, indicate the expansion of habitation during the later part of the period.[94] The MBA stratigraphy was divided into seven building phases with a sterile level at the bottom of the sequence.[95] The two large post-houses of the last EBA phase were succeeded in the next phase by three smaller, elongated ones built with mudbricks. From the second phase onward habitation became dense. Narrow alleys separated the houses, which were usually packed with hearths, bins, and storage facilities. An emphasis on storage inside houses characterizes all MBA phases. The plan in the excavated part of the settlement was more or less stable, but the position of the houses shifted laterally from one phase to the next. In the sixth phase the plan became very irregular, and houses with different orientations covered the excavated area. The last MBA and the following LBA phase were much eroded.[96]

As at MBA Pefkakia, access to domestic space was restricted, in contrast to the pattern of the last EBA phase, when several domestic activities took place outside. On the other hand, functional partitioning within the house (persistent at Pefkakia) was not evident at Argissa. At the community level, the arrangement of spaces in the excavated part appears less complex than at Pefkakia: no indications of terracing or large-scale constructions involving commu-

---

[91] Hourmouziadis 1982 (supra n. 44) 33–35 suggests that Homeric Iolkos refers to the area rather than to a particular site. This is supported by the fact that Pefkakia and Dimini were abandoned at the end of the 13th or early 12th century B.C., while Kastro/Palia continued through the Protogeometric period. On the basis of the archaeological evidence from Dimini and the reinterpretation of literary sources, it has been proposed recently that Dimini should be identified with Homeric Iolkos: Adrimi-Sismani, in *Ancient Thessaly* (supra n. 48) 277–78; and in *Iolkos* (supra n. 48) 36–43; B.G. Intzesiloglou, "Ιστορική τοπογραφία της περιοχής του κόλπου του Βόλου," in *La Thessalie* B, 34–42; and Intzesiloglou, "Νέα αποτελέσματα για τη θέση της Ιωλκού," in *Iolkos* 71–82. For a discussion of the problems and possible forms of LBA state organization in Thessaly, see Feuer 41–45 and Halstead 1984, ch. 6.4.6.

[92] A. Efstathiou, Z. Malakasioti, and R. Reinders, "Halos Archaeological Field Survey Project," *Newsletter of the Netherlands Institute at Athens* 3 (1990) 31–45; B.J. Haagsma et al., "Between Karatsadagli and Baklali," *Pharos* 1 (1993) 147–64; Malakasioti et al., "A Neolithic Site in the Almiros Plain near Karatsadhagli (Thessaly, Greece)," *Pharos* (in press); Malakasioti, *ArchDelt* 39 B′ (1984) 140, fig. 2, pl. 43;

and Malakasioti, "Θαλαμοειδής μυκηναϊκός τάφος στον Κάτω Μαυρόλοφο Αλμυρού," in *Ancient Thessaly* 267–71. For a discussion of chamber tombs in Thessaly, see Feuer 76 and Halstead 1984, ch. 5.2.5 and figs. 5.4–5. The restricted distribution of chamber tombs in Thessaly and their rich finds support their characterization as elite burials.

[93] *Argissa* III, 12; *Atlas* no. 50. The largest part of the mound has been eroded by the Peneios River.

[94] *Argissa* III, 12–17.

[95] E. Hanschmann, *Die deutschen Ausgrabungen auf der Argissa-Magula in Thessalien* IV: *Die mittlere Bronzezeit* (BAM 23, Bonn 1981) 5–15. For the synchronization of the Argissa MBA phases with those of Pefkakia, see supra n. 70. Maran, *Pefkakia* III, 228–30, points out that the change in material culture between the EBA and MBA levels at Argissa is much less pronounced than suggested by Hanschmann. For the hiatus in the stratigraphy, see *Argissa* III, 115–17, and *Pefkakia* III, 239–41.

[96] For storage facilities, see Hanschmann (supra n. 95) pls. G–H. For LBA deposits, see Hanschmann (supra n. 95) 117–19; Feuer 124. A group of handmade pottery indicates the continuity of the local ceramic tradition into the LBA. The Mycenaean pottery at the site belongs to LH IIIA2 and LH IIIB.

nal labor were identified. Whether this variance simply reflects the difference between a site built on a flat surface and one built around a natural knoll, or differences in community organization between a coastal and an inland settlement, remains an open question. Similarly, the precise meaning of the often-mentioned inland/coastal distinction in Bronze Age Thessaly remains obscure. The near absence at Argissa of imports of pottery from southern Greece marks a difference from Pefkakia, and demonstrates the crosscutting, but not overlapping, exchange networks of the two communities.[97]

Otzaki (fig. 1:11). The publication of the old excavations at Otzaki Magoula by Milojčić was completed in 1983 with the presentation of the stratigraphy and the Neolithic architecture. The excavated area of less than 400 m² represents a very small fraction of the total area of the magoula, estimated at 9 ha.[98]

In the 4 m of MN deposits there were as many as 16 reconstructions of houses, some with further subphases. Throughout the Middle Neolithic the general layout of the settlement remained stable, despite successive rebuildings of individual houses. The main characteristic of this layout was its compactness and the limited open space, in contrast to sites such as Achilleion or Sesklo A. The rectangular houses, occasionally of the "Tsangli" type with internal buttresses, had a stable plan, with one, and rarely two, rooms. All houses were built of mudbrick, with the exception of the latest MN phase, where lines of postholes mark a change in the building technique. Posts

were also used in the earlier phases for the support of walls and roofs.

The information provided for the plans and phases of the buildings is rich, but the function of rooms and of the limited open space between them has not been determined. Storage and food-processing facilities are not mentioned, with the exception of the occasional hearth. Apart from pottery, which was abundant, the number of other finds is astonishingly limited.[99] The significance of that pattern is unclear.

The rich architectural remains of the MN period contrast strongly with the poor preservation of the LN and FN levels. The bulk of information for these periods came from ditches and pits that had been dug from and through LN levels, where no substantial architectural remains were found to support stratigraphic observations.[100] A number of deep and wide ditches, similar to those found in other sites from the Early Neolithic onward, were also identified and characterized as defensive. The same interpretation was given to a strong earthen construction with a wooden-post frame.[101] The defensive function, however, is incompatible with at least one of the ditches, which runs through the middle of the settlement, while the course of the others and the character of the earthen construction are indeterminable. The difficulty of approaching the function of these constructions in a more meaningful way is exacerbated by the absence of information on their contents, except for pottery.[102]

Ayia Sophia (fig. 1:13). About 3 km northwest of

---

[97] At Argissa, as at Pefkakia, matt-painted pottery appears in the earliest MBA levels: Hanschmann (supra n. 95) 114. Few Gray Minyan and even fewer matt-painted sherds were found at Argissa, which does not necessarily indicate a lack of long-distance contacts. Indeed, contacts may have existed with areas to the north and west. At the moment, however, it is not easy to distinguish these exchanges, not least because of our poor knowledge of MBA communities further north and west; see Hanschmann (supra n. 95) 109–16; *Pefkakia* III, 231–35, 285–89.

[98] V. Milojčić, *Die deutschen Ausgrabungen auf der Otzaki-Magula in Thessalien* II: *Das mittlere Neolithikum: Die mittelneolithische Siedlung* (*BAM* 20, Bonn 1983); Milojčić, *Die deutschen Ausgrabungen auf der Otzaki-Magula in Thessalien* III: *Das späte Neolithikum und das Chalkolithikum: Stratigraphie und Bauten* (*BAM* 20, Bonn 1983).

[99] For a detailed publication of the MN pottery and the few other finds, see Mottier (supra n. 23) 20–38, 72. The pottery is divided into monochrome, incised, painted red-on-white, and scraped wares, but the frequencies of wares, types, and motifs are not recorded. There are notable differ-

ences in the pottery repertoire from the coastal area, both in shapes and motifs.

[100] Military trenches dug during the Balkan wars of 1912 have significantly affected the shape of the mound: Milojčić, *Otzaki* III (supra n. 98) 7. Milojčić, on the basis of the stratigraphy of the pits, assigned the black-burnished "Larisa" ware to FN, but evidence from Platia Magoula Zarkou and other sources, discussed below, has since shown this assignment to be erroneous. Similarly, much of the ceramic material that defines the "Otzaki A–C" and "Rachmani" phases does not come from closed contexts but from pits and ditches: H. Hauptmann, *Die deutschen Ausgrabungen auf der Otzaki-Magula in Thessalien* III (*BAM* 21, Bonn 1981) 42, 66, 134. K.I. Gallis, "Results of Recent Excavations and Topographical Work in Neolithic Thessaly," in *La Thessalie* A, 58, strongly doubts the validity of the Otzaki scheme.

[101] Milojčić, *Otzaki* III (supra n. 98) 12–13, 22–23, 28–29, 33–35.

[102] The ceramic material has been exhaustively published by Hauptmann (supra n. 100).

Otzaki lies Ayia Sophia Magoula, the last site excavated by Milojčić in the Larisa region. It is a low and extended mound, rising only 3 m above the plain and covering 2 ha.[103] The brief excavation explored an area of 400 m² in the center, where many pits had been sunk. The stratigraphical observations on these pits allowed Milojčić to define the sequence succeeding the LN "Otzaki" phase. Deposits of earlier LN phases were also found but have not yet been published.

An important LN feature was uncovered. A platform constructed of mudbricks, with three consecutive phases, occupied a central part of the site. It was connected to the lower parts of the mound. On top of the platform the porch of a building, interpreted as a "megaron," was uncovered. Two mudbrick walls formed a sort of gateway to the east. The arrangement recalls the central court at Dimini, which also stood higher than the surrounding courtyards and was connected to them by gateways. The platform area at Ayia Sophia was separated during the final LN by a ditch, possibly surrounding the central part.

The significance of the terraced area is highlighted by its proximity to a unique feature with a possibly ritual significance. Immediately to the east, an earlier artificial mound, with a clay platform on its top, covered three successive small rectangular structures of mudbrick, associated with two burials. The structures were filled with fine compact earth, mixed with a few fragments of human and animal bone. The surface of the artificial mound was burnt hard, and a circular pit with a clay rim was constructed at the top. The pit was filled with ashes.[104]

The association of a probable megaron with a feature related to the ritual treatment of the dead is not a common characteristic of Neolithic Greece, and it is not, therefore, easy to decipher. Halstead argued that the mound represented a "revered minority burial" and that its association with the megaron reinforces the evidence available from other sites for the emergence of an institutionalized elite during the LN period.[105] Alternatively, the association of the megaron with a place of mortuary ritual could imply a form of symbolic control over the dead by a certain privileged group, materialized in this revered spot. The find only permits a glance into ritual in Neolithic communities, an area little understood, yet with a potentially significant role.

Soufli Magoula (fig. 1:14). A group of EN cremations was found at Soufli Magoula and published by K.I. Gallis of the IE′ Ephoreia.[106] The cemetery was found (accidentally) at the perimeter of the magoula, where in 1958 Biesantz had excavated a small group of LN cremations in urns. The new finds consisted of 15 concentrations of human bones, ceramic vessels and sherds, animal bones, and traces of fire. In almost all cases a miniature bowl was found with the cremation, and one cremation was accompanied by a stone ax. The burials had been made in shallow, irregular depressions, dug into the levels of the early settlement. Two deeper round pits approximately 1 m in diameter, constructed with care, were interpreted as incinerators. They contained ashes, human and animal bone, and some sherds but no complete vessels.

The reconstruction of the burial procedure in its details is not possible from the available information. Selection of particular parts of the skeleton for burial, mainly the skull and the limbs,[107] is evident. More meaningful perhaps is the presence of the burials in the habitation area of the settlement, the deposits of which covered the cemetery soon after.

Velestino (fig. 1:17). The area of Velestino (ancient Ferai) is one of the few naturally watered spots in the arid southern part of the eastern plain. The area was densely inhabited since the Early Neolithic, with the population living in dispersed settlements.[108] These settlements were abandoned by the Early Bronze Age, with the exception of a huge tell, known as Magoula Bakali, in the vicinity of the Hyperia spring. Excavations at the foot of the tell uncovered remains of an extended MBA settlement and ceme-

---

[103] Milojčić (supra n. 40) 1–14; *Atlas* no. 42. The site is reported to have EBA and MBA phases. Evidence for Bronze Age habitation has also been found ca. 100 m south of the magoula. See *Atlas* no. 52. A short study of the *Spondylus* objects from Ayia Sophia has been published by A. Tsuneki, "A Reconsideration of *Spondylus* Shell Rings from Agia Sofia Magoula, Greece," *Bulletin of the Ancient Orient Museum* 9 (1987) 1–15. Tsuneki sees evidence for craft specialization and mass production, but the size of the sample hardly justifies such conclusions.

[104] Milojčić (supra n. 40) 6–7, pl. 4.

[105] Halstead 1984, ch. 5.2.3; Halstead 1994, 203.

[106] K.I. Gallis, Καύσεις νεκρών από τη Νεολιθική εποχή στη Θεσσαλία (Athens 1982) 23–63.

[107] N.I. Xirotiris, "Αποτελέσματα της ανθρωπολογικής εξετάσεως των καμένων οστών από τη Σουφλί Μαγούλα και την Πλατιά Μαγούλα Ζάρκου," in Gallis (supra n. 106) 190–99.

[108] *Atlas* nos. 270–74, 280, 331. O. Apostolopoulou-Kakavoyianni, "Τοπογραφία της περιοχής των Φερών Θεσσαλίας κατά την προϊστορική περίοδο," *ArchDelt* 34 A′ (1979) 189–200.

tery. During the Late Bronze Age, habitation spread further east and north, over an area of almost 25 ha. The MBA cemetery of cist and pit graves was succeeded by a LBA cemetery of small cist graves with contracted burials accompanied by few grave goods. A potter's kiln, where LH IIIC pots were fired, was excavated at the periphery of the settlement.[109]

The settlement pattern in the area of Velestino is an example of the aggregation of smaller Neolithic communities into larger, long-lasting Bronze Age settlements. This pattern, common in inland Thessaly,[110] is very different from that observed in the coastal areas, where settlement was more stable, and communities may have continued their autonomous existence until the end of the 13th century.

The eastern Thessalian plain has also been the focus of significant palaeoenvironmental research. Demitrack has studied alluviation cycles on the plain and the possible impact of human settlement on the landscape. Her studies indicate the existence of a series of alluvial fans at the edges of the plain and a series of Peneios alluvia, dated to the Pleistocene and Holocene. The middle Holocene episode of alluviation (the Girtoni alluvium) has been dated to 7000–6000 B.P. and has been tentatively related to the activity of farmers in the Middle and Late Neolithic.[111]

An extensive survey program has been undertaken in the eastern plain during the last 20 years by the IE′ Ephoreia (Larisa).[112] One hundred and three new sites have been added to those previously known, raising the total of prehistoric sites in eastern Thessaly to 255. Most of the additions are low mounds or are located in hilly areas. The pattern that emerges shows an initial slight preference for habitation in the plains rather than the hilly areas, followed by an expansion to the open plains in the Late Neolithic, and recolonization of the hills and uplands in the Late Bronze Age. A marked increase was noted in the number of settlements in the LN period and a sharp decline during the Middle and Late Bronze Age. The FN period presents the sharpest drop in the number of sites, which, in view of the length of the period, is difficult to explain.[113] The general trends accord well with the data from the whole of Thessaly presented by Halstead, with the exception of the coastal area, where settlement was more stable.[114]

Site dimensions as reported by Gallis are systematically larger than those used by Halstead, and the discrepancy affects estimates of population size and the perception of social structure.[115] The incompatibility of the two data sets stems from the employment of different measuring techniques, none of which, however, complies with the requirements of modern survey work.[116] A more accurate estimate of size would require intensive, systematic sampling of Thessalian sites.

Western Plain

The western plain of Thessaly displays a lower concentration of settlement in the prehistoric period with the exception of the hilly area near Farsala. This sparseness of habitation is usually attributed to unwelcoming physiographical characteristics and also to the low intensity of archaeological work. Apart

---

[109] A. Doulgeri-Intzesiloglou, "Οι νεότερες αρχαιολογικές έρευνες στην περιοχή των αρχαίων Φερών," in *La Thessalie* B, 76–78; Apostolopoulou-Kakavoyianni (supra n. 108) 181–83; A. Batziou-Efstathiou, "Μυκηναϊκός κεραμεικός κλίβανος," in *La Thessalie* A, 215–24. Halstead 1984, ch. 5.2.5, suggests that Magoula Bakali was an artificially segregated habitation area, surrounded by ramparts and perhaps occupied by an elite.

[110] Halstead 1984, table 6.4.

[111] Demitrack, in *La Thessalie* A (supra n. 31) figs. 1–6, and Demitrack 1986 (supra n. 31); van Andel et al. 1990 (supra n. 31) 386–88.

[112] *Atlas* 85–195. The catalogue of prehistoric sites includes data on their topography, size, and date, an account of research prior to 1991, and a brief inventory of surface finds. See also Gallis (supra n. 100) 57–60. Work on figurines collected from sites of the east Thessaly survey has been published by G. Toufexis, "Νεολιθικά ειδώλια της περιοχής Τυρνάβου," *Πρακτικά Πρώτου Συνεδρίου Τυρναβίτικων Σπουδών, Τύρναβος 9–10 Σεπτεμβρίου 1990* (Tirnavos 1991)

21–29; Toufexis, "Neolithic Animal Figurines from Thessaly," in *La Thessalie* A, 163–68. Also K.I. Gallis and L. Orphanidis, "Twenty New Faces from the Neolithic Society of Thessaly," in *La Thessalie* A, 155–62.

[113] According to Gallis, the visibility of the Final Neolithic is negatively affected by the poor preservation of crusted wares, which he treats as the sole reliable indicator of the period: *Atlas* 229–30. Another period of low visibility is perhaps the early part of the LBA, prior to the appearance of LH III-style pottery. See Feuer 51, 54, figs. 7, 11.

[114] Halstead 1984, chs. 6.1.6, 6.3, 6.4, and table 6.1, as a rule used the data provided by D. French's extensive survey.

[115] In a recent article this difference is used to support a higher figure for the size of the population during the Neolithic: J.-P. Demoule and C. Perlès, "The Greek Neolithic: A New Review," *Journal of World Prehistory* 7 (1993) 368–70.

[116] French (Halstead, personal communication) employed the actual size of the mound, and Gallis, the extent of sherd scatter (*Atlas* 34, 225).

from work at Achilleion and Platia Magoula Zarkou, no major prehistoric project has taken place during the last 20 years.[117]

Achilleion (fig. 1:18). The initial objective of the excavation at Achilleion (1973–1974) was the exploration of the "preceramic" phase that Theocharis had reported from the site.[118] A "preceramic" horizon was absent from the excavated area, however, and the cultural sequence at the site was divided into four main phases, covering without interruption most of the Early and Middle Neolithic. A long series of ^{14}C dates placed that sequence in the period 6500–5500 B.C.[119]

Traces of plastered floors and large pits were described by the excavators as houses and/or storage areas in the first phase. Rectangular houses (some built with pisé on stone socles, others around a frame of posts) appeared in succeeding phases. The general impression is one of a loose spatial arrangement. The area around the houses was littered with hearths, and ovens or food-processing facilities, and it seems probable that the greater part of everyday work took place outdoors; few traces of activity were found inside the houses. The architectural evidence does not, however, permit firm conclusions. During phase IVa, dated to the advanced Middle Neolithic, a deep ditch probably segregated the central part of the settlement.[120]

The continuous sequence of pottery at Achilleion permits the understanding of regional ceramic variation, an aspect often underestimated and interpreted in chronological terms. Contrary to the pattern at other sites, early painted ware continues at Achilleion up to the Middle Neolithic. Also, the absence of MN scraped ware (A3ε, A3ζ) from the Achilleion deposits contrasts with the dominance of this ware in the Larisa area during the same period.[121] With the exception of obsidian, little evidence is available concerning the contacts between Achilleion and other regions. According to Elster, the obsidian tools were not manufactured at the site, in contrast to tools made of other stones.[122]

Platia Magoula Zarkou (fig. 1:19). Founded on Pleistocene alluvium near the Peneios River, the tell of Platia Magoula Zarkou is today only 6–7 m high. Another 5 m of deposits lie below the present surface of the plain, providing a measure of alluviation in the area since the foundation of the site. Recent geomorphological work has established the chronology and sequence of alluviation and has shown that the size of the tell did not exceed 2 ha.[123]

The excavation investigated 10.5 m of deposits in one trench of 8 × 5 m in the center of the mound. Deposition began in the EN III phase and continued through the Middle and the early Late Neolithic, forming a mound ca. 5 m high. The site was reoccupied in the Early and Middle Bronze Age. The transition from the Middle to the Late Neolithic is

---

[117] Study of the material from the excavation at Prodromos continued: P. Halstead and G. Jones, "Early Neolithic Economy in Thessaly—Some Evidence from Excavations at Prodromos," *Anthropologika* 1 (1980) 93–117. Some survey work has been done on previously known sites: E. Nikolaou, V. Rondiri, and E. Skafida, "Η προϊστορική έρευνα στην ευρύτερη περιοχή των Σοφάδων," in *Σοφάδες* (Larisa 1994) 7–21; A. Koungoulos, "Νεολιθικές θέσεις περιφέρειας Τρικάλων," paper read at "2ο Συμπόσιο Τρικαλινών," Trikala, 10 November 1990.

[118] Less than 0.2% of the 260 × 200 m tell was sampled. Only the central area of the tell appears to have preserved intact cultural deposits, which may mean that the Neolithic settlement was significantly smaller than the area occupied by the tell today. See *Achilleion* 7–8, 19–22.

[119] For reservations about some of the ^{14}C dates, and about the calibration, see J. Nandris's review of M. Gimbutas ed., *Neolithic Macedonia, as Reflected by Excavation at Anza, Southeast Yugoslavia* (Los Angeles 1976), in *BIALond* 16 (1979) 263–64, and C. Runnels's review of *Achilleion* in *JFA* 17 (1990) 341–45.

[120] Similar ditches are known from Soufli Magoula, Nea Nikomedeia, Servia, and other EN and MN sites: Theocharis 1973 (supra n. 5) 65–66 and supra n. 36 for LN examples.

[121] The early painted ware disappears from Sesklo at the start of EN III: Wijnen (supra n. 7) 35–37. For the MN scraped ware, see Mottier (supra n. 23) 33–34. Scraped ware was very common in Platia Magoula Zarkou but absent from Tsani Magoula: J.-P. Demoule et al., "Transition entre les cultures néolithiques de Sesklo et de Dimini: Les catégories céramiques," *BCH* 112 (1988) 12–16. For regional variability of incised "barbotine" and "cardium" wares, which seem to be rare in Achilleion and in MN contexts, see G.H. Hourmouziadis, "Η διακεκοσμημένη κεραμική της Αρχαιοτέρας Νεολιθικής περιόδου εις την Θεσσαλίαν," *ArchEph* 1971, 165–77. For a general assessment of the regional variability of Neolithic pottery in Thessaly, see Halstead 1984, ch. 4.

[122] E.S. Elster, "The Chipped Stone Industry," in *Achilleion* 300, table 10.4. Also Elster, "Prehistoric Tools in Thessaly: Achilleion, Makrychori 2 and Plateia Magoula Zarkou," in *La Thessalie* A, 169–76. The quantity of obsidian at the site is considerably smaller than at other Thessalian Neolithic sites: C. Perlès, "L'outillage de pierre taillée néolithique en Grèce: Approvisionnement et exploitation des matières premières," *BCH* 114 (1990) table 3. See also Moundrea-Agrafioti (supra n. 5) 59–60.

[123] van Andel et al. 1995 (supra n. 31).

defined by a house floor, under which the well-known house model of Platia Magoula Zarkou was found, near a hearth.[124]

The main contribution of the Platia Magoula excavations to the chronological and culture-typological discussion about Thessaly is the stratigraphic definition of the so-called "Larisa" ware. Black-burnished pottery constitutes a long-recognized horizon of the Late Neolithic of Thessaly, with connections to areas to the north and south, but a particular variety of fine pots with white paint or plastic decoration had been distinguished by Milojčić and Hauptmann and placed in the Final Neolithic, immediately after the phase of "classical Dimini," on grounds of indirect stratigraphic evidence. Such an attribution was met with reservations by many, who proposed an earlier LN date for this pottery. The excavations at Platia Magoula Zarkou offered the necessary stratigraphic confirmation for dating "Larisa" ware to the beginning of the Late Neolithic.[125]

Although the place of "Larisa" ware in the Thessalian cultural sequence may now be fixed near the beginning of the Late Neolithic, the chronological distribution of the broader class of LN black-burnished wares is still obscure in its details. Their assumed absence from later LN levels cannot be inferred from Platia Magoula or Makryhori 2, where only part of the LN sequence is represented.[126] On the other hand, the regional variability of Neolithic pottery is still very little understood in Thessaly, and it is arguable that many of the differences observed

are regional rather than chronological.[127] Laboratory analysis of wares characteristic of the transition from the Middle to Late Neolithic has indicated various patterns of ceramic production and distribution. The Gray-on-Gray ware was probably produced in a few places, while the black-burnished wares had a less centralized production pattern. Such differences introduce an obvious element of variability in the distribution of wares that normally form the basis of the definition of phases in the Thessalian Neolithic.[128]

Information about the community of Platia Magoula comes from its cemetery, a few hundred meters to the north.[129] More than 60 cremations in pots of common domestic types were found in shallow pits. A stone wall of the same period possibly delimited the area. Occasionally, the urns were covered with an inverted vessel and/or were accompanied by another. A number of flint tools, some with traces of use or of fire, were also found. Red-fired sherds, in groups or singly, were found near, over, or inside many of the undecorated urns, as well as scattered throughout the cemetery, but figurines were conspicuously rare. Some parts of the body, such as the skull and limbs, were consistently selected for inclusion in the urns, which occasionally contained bones of different individuals.[130]

The cemeteries at Platia Magoula and Soufli Magoula are the only known cases of organized burial grounds in Neolithic Thessaly. There are obvious similarities between the two, but the location of the

---

[124] K.I. Gallis, "Die stratigraphische Einordnung der Larisa-Kultur: Eine Richtigstellung," *PZ* 62 (1987) 147–63; Demoule et al. (supra n. 121) 5–7, fig. 3; Gallis, "Archäologische Entdeckungen aus der Jungsteinzeit Thessaliens (Griechenland)," *Altertum* 39 (1993) 83–89. See also Gallis, "Η σωστή στρωματογραφική θέση της νεολιθικής κεραμεικής της γνωστής ως πολιτισμού της Λάρισας," *Πρακτικά του Α΄ Ιστορικού-Αρχαιολογικού Συμποσίου* (Larisa 1985) 37–55; C. Becker, "Die Tierknochenfunde von der Platia Magoula Zarkou: Neue Untersuchungen zu Haustierhaltung, Jagd und Rohstoffverwendung im neolithisch–bronzezeitlichen Thessalien," *PZ* 66 (1991) 14–78; G. Jones and P. Halstead, "Charred Plant-Remains from Neolithic–Bronze Age Platia Magoula Zarkou, Thessaly," *BSA* 88 (1993) 1–3; also Elster in *La Thessalie* A (supra n. 122) 169–76. The earliest levels were only reached in a portion of the original trench. For the house model, see Gallis (supra n. 18) 20.

[125] Hauptmann (supra n. 100) 75–76, 99–110. Gallis 1987 (supra n. 124) 162 proposed renaming the first Tsangli phase of the Late Neolithic "Tsangli-Larisa." Demoule et al. (supra n. 121) 50, on the basis of further work on the pottery from Platia Magoula Zarkou, argue for a separate ceramic phase, intermediate between the Middle and Late Neolithic, which they call the "Zarko phase." Much of the discourse on prehistoric Thessaly consists of claims of this sort. See also

Gallis (supra n. 100) 58–59.

[126] Black-burnished carinated pottery is attested from the "Arapi" and "Otzaki" phases. See Hauptmann and Milojčić (supra n. 36) 50–51; Milojčić, *Otzaki* III (supra n. 98) 10; Demoule et al. (supra n. 121) 35. For a small excavation at Makryhori 2, see Gallis 1987 (supra n. 124) 154–56.

[127] Cf. P. Halstead, "Λάρ'σα, Λάρ'σα, σ' είδα και λαχτάρ'σα," in *Ancient Thessaly* 210–16.

[128] G. Schneider et al., "Transition entre les cultures néolithiques de Sesklo et de Dimini: Recherches minéralogiques, chimiques et technologiques sur les céramiques et les argiles," *BCH* 115 (1991) 1–64. Schneider et al., "Production and Distribution of Coarse and Fine Pottery in Neolithic Thessaly, Greece," in E. Pernicka and G.A. Wagner eds., *Archaeometry '90. Proceedings of the 27th Symposium on Archaeometry Held in Heidelberg, April 2–6, 1990* (Basel 1991) 513–22. Schneider et al., "Production and Circulation of Neolithic Thessalian Pottery: Chemical and Mineralogical Analyses," in *La Thessalie* A, 61–70. For an experimental reconstruction of production techniques of Gray-on-Gray pottery, see K.D. Vitelli, "Experimental Approaches to Thessalian Neolithic Ceramics: Gray Ware and Ceramic Colour," in *La Thessalie* A, 143–48.

[129] Gallis (supra n. 106) 64–134.

[130] Xirotiris (supra n. 107) 199–215.

cemeteries is very different. The Soufli cemetery is adjacent to the settlement, and the pits with the cremations were dug in habitation deposits, while the Platia Magoula cemetery is set some distance from the settlement, and perhaps defined by a wall. One could hypothesize that the practice of segregating a part of the living space of the settlement, observed in the Middle and Late Neolithic, is repeated here at the symbolic level. A further step would be to suggest that LN groups had a pronounced perception of social order, which could be a reflection of an emerging stratified social structure. There are hints for such a development from LN contexts but, to a great extent, the issue remains open.

Geomorphological work at the site of Platia Magoula indicates that the first settlement was established in the active floodplain of the Peneios River. During the Early and Middle Neolithic, flooding resulted in the formation of a deep alluvium (the Girtoni alluvium), which covered the surroundings of the site.[131] Alluviation had ceased before the foundation of the cemetery. According to van Andel et al., that sequence of events has interesting implications for the adaptation of early farmers to their environment. The foundation of sites in an active floodplain suggests a farming practice that takes advantage of periodic flooding and benefits from crops sown in the spring, and may also imply seasonal occupation of the site. This conclusion is in contrast to the prevailing opinion that early farming in Thessaly was geared toward farming on light arable soils fed by rain and based on winter-sown crops.[132] The observations about Platia Magoula and their implications have been projected to other Thessalian sites with a similar setting. [133]

This model of early farming rests on the assumption that flooding occurred with a predictable regularity and that agriculture was based on spring-sown

crops. At present the stratigraphic evidence from other Thessalian sites is not detailed enough to support the identification of periodic flooding. Moreover, archaeobotanical evidence from EN sites is very limited, particularly regarding the weed component, a sensitive indicator of environmental conditions.[134] Another question for future research is the applicability of this model to other Neolithic sites.

Theopetra Cave (fig. 1:21). At the western edge of the plain, Theopetra Cave has been excavated by the Greek Archaeological Service since 1987. The cave has a long history of occupation starting in the Middle Palaeolithic. The Neolithic deposits were to a great extent disturbed, but ceramic evidence suggests occupation in all periods of the Neolithic. A series of 25 ^{14}C dates has been published, covering the period from 40,000 b.c. to 4450–4249 B.C.[135]

The potential importance of Theopetra Cave for Neolithic research lies in its long habitation from the Palaeolithic to the Neolithic, challenging the prevailing opinion that Thessaly was uninhabited for a long period before the EN.[136] The dates from the cave form a broadly continuous sequence covering the crucial period from 9000 B.C. to 6500 B.C. There is a hiatus between 6500 B.C. and 5200 B.C., but, according to the preliminary reports, archaeological material fills that hiatus. On the other hand, the sedentary or transient character of the Theopetra settlement is debatable, and the relation of the site to the potentially more stable open settlements of the plains remains unclear. Until the evidence from Theopetra is published, no firm conclusions can be drawn.

Research Perspectives

A major focus of prehistoric research in Thessaly in the last 25 years has been the refinement of the chronological framework and the relationship of

[131] van Andel et al. 1995 (supra n. 31) 140–41.

[132] P. Halstead, "Counting Sheep in Neolithic and Bronze Age Greece," in I. Hodder, G. Isaac, and N. Hammond eds., *Pattern of the Past: Studies in Honour of David Clarke* (Cambridge 1981) 311, 317–20; Halstead 1984, ch. 6.4.4; Halstead, "Traditional and Ancient Rural Economy in Mediterranean Europe: Plus ça change?" *JHS* 107 (1987) 83–85.

[133] T.H. van Andel and C.N. Runnels, "The Earliest Farmers in Europe," *Antiquity* 69 (1995) 490–98.

[134] H. Kroll, "Thessalische Kulturpflanzen," *ZfA* 15 (1981) 97–103, esp. table 1.

[135] G. Fakorellis, G. Maniatis, and N. Kyparissi, "Χρονολόγηση με ραδιοάνθρακα δειγμάτων από το σπήλαιο Θεόπετρας, Καλαμπάκας," in I. Stratis et al. eds., *Archaeometrical and Archaeological Research in Macedonia and Thrace. Proceedings of the 2nd Symposium of the Hellenic Archaeometrical Society, Thessaloniki, 26–28 March 1993* (Thessaloniki

1996) 99–116; N. Kyparissi-Apostolika, "Σπήλαιο Θεόπετρας: Μια σπάνια περίπτωση σπηλαιοκατοίκησης στην παλαιολιθική Θεσσαλία," paper read at "Α' Πανελλήνιο Σπηλαιολογικό Συνέδριο 'Ανθρωπος και Περιβάλλον,' Αθήνα 26–29.11.1992"; Kyparissi-Apostolika, "Prehistoric Inhabitation in Theopetra Cave, Thessaly," in *La Thessalie* A, 103–108; Kyparissi-Apostolika, "The Palaeolithic Deposits of Theopetra Cave in Thessaly (Greece)," in *First International Conference "The Palaeolithic of Greece and Adjacent Areas," Ioannina 6–11/9/1994* (Athens, in press).

[136] C. Runnels, "A Prehistoric Survey of Thessaly: New Light on the Greek Middle Paleolithic," *JFA* 15 (1988) 284; Perlès 1988 (supra n. 8) 485–86; Perlès, "Les débuts du Néolithique en Grèce," *La Recherche* 25 (1994) 646; Runnels, "Review of Aegean Prehistory IV: The Stone Age of Greece from the Palaeolithic to the Advent of the Neolithic," *AJA* 99 (1995) 723.

Thessaly with southern Greece and the Balkans, in a true Montelian fashion.[137] Leaving aside the question of relationships, which are to a great extent still intractable, the use of the Thessalian chronological scheme has shown its major weaknesses. Although these weaknesses had been pointed out quite early,[138] it has been only gradually realized that the stratigraphic evidence that supports the definition of phases on the basis of pottery types may not always be secure. It has also been realized that the variability of pottery, both within sites and across regions, cannot be interpreted in exclusively chronological terms. As a rule, excavations have been limited in extent, and do not permit evaluation of the various aspects of variability of the Thessalian assemblages. Finally, the scarcity of ^{14}C dates supporting the scheme limits its applicability considerably. The difficulties are exacerbated in the case of the Final Neolithic and the transition to the Early Bronze Age, where the very long time span defined by ^{14}C dates from surrounding areas is not compatible with the sparse archaeological remains from Thessaly. Similar problems, to a lesser extent, apply to the chronological sequence of the Bronze Age. Here, the difficulties are clearly seen at the outset and the close of the Late Bronze Age. Although the number of excavated sites in Thessaly is considerable, there is need for new extensive excavations with secure architectural remains and closed deposits.

Another weakness of chronological resolution in the Thessalian sequences arises from the processes of site formation, especially in mounds. Milojčić had perceptively observed the variability in the intrasettlement pattern and the shifts of habitation at sites such as Otzaki and Argissa, or the complexities of the formation processes at Ayia Sophia.[139] The interpretation, however, of the archaeological levels in terms of the reconstructed chronological phases needs still to be evaluated against the possible distortion caused by formation processes. It is worth noting in this respect that in the Bronze Age sequences of Argissa and Pefkakia, where the definition was based on architectural phases, the problems were minimized.

Understanding the processes of site formation is necessary for reconstructing intrasettlement spatial organization and arriving at demographic estimates. The case of Sesklo shows that there are diverging patterns of intrasettlement organization that need not have a temporal meaning. Bounded sites in the form of mounds seem to be the rule during the Neolithic, and are possibly related to specific patterns of social behavior and economic practice. Nevertheless, unrestricted, extended sites in the form of Sesklo B may also exist in numbers. Surface material from Thessalian sites has been collected primarily for use in dating, but also to some extent for determining intersettlement regional and temporal patterns. In evaluating the changes in size of settlements, there is no doubt that surface collection data are constrained by serious weaknesses, related to collection strategies and geomorphological and other postdepositional distortions. Despite the restrictions, a pattern seems to emerge, indicating a gradual shift from dispersed settlements in the Neolithic to nucleated, larger ones during the Bronze Age, especially in the Middle Bronze Age and the Late Bronze Age. Evidence from excavations also suggests a trend toward nucleation in the Bronze Age. Some nucleated sites are very large and exhibit new characteristics in the spatial arrangement of habitation.[140]

The farming economy of prehistoric Thessaly has been described by Halstead.[141] During the initial stages of the Neolithic, the small-scale economy relied on reciprocity and networks of obligations and alliances to cope with environmental uncertainties and the limitations of Neolithic production. A diversified agriculture based on a wide variety of domesticates and on breeding a range of livestock was a primary constituent of Neolithic subsistence. Diversification seems to be further stressed during the later Neolithic and the Bronze Age, and the scale

---

[137] V. Milojčić, *Hauptergebnisse der deutschen Ausgrabungen in Thessalien, 1953–1958* (Bonn 1960) 1–3, where the research objectives of this program are stated.

[138] Hourmouziadis (supra n. 121) 165–77.

[139] Milojčić, *Otzaki* III (supra n. 98) 5–6; *Argissa* III, 3–11; Milojčić (supra n. 40) 4.

[140] Typical examples are Velestino, Pefkakia, Argissa, and Dimini: Halstead 1994, 203; *Atlas* 232–34; Feuer 44. Grammenos reports a recently found LBA site at Dilofos, near Farsala, with an estimated size of ca. 60 ha, associated with an acropolis: D.V. Grammenos, "Ζητήματα της επιφανειακής έρευνας στη βόρεια Ελλάδα (Νεολιθική-Εποχή Χαλκού)," in *Α' Συνέδριο Ανθρωπολογίας, Κομοτινή, Νοέμβριος 1993*

(Komotini, in press).

[141] Halstead 1981 (supra n. 132) 307–39; Halstead (supra n. 72) 71–83; Halstead, "Like Rising Damp? An Ecological Approach to the Spread of Farming in Southeast and Central Europe," in A. Miles, D. Williams, and N. Gardner eds., *The Beginnings of Agriculture* (*BAR-IS* 496, Oxford 1989) 25–53; Halstead (supra n. 30) 33–48, 53–56; Halstead and Jones (supra n. 117) 106–108; P. Halstead and J. O'Shea, "A Friend in Need is a Friend Indeed: Social Storage and the Origin of Social Ranking," in C. Renfrew and S. Shennan eds., *Ranking, Resource and Exchange* (Cambridge 1982) 93–96; Demoule and Perlès (supra n. 115) 360–63.

of the economy expanded. It retained, nevertheless, its unspecialized character. Colonization of more marginal lands and amplification of animal husbandry in the final stages of the Neolithic and particularly during the Bronze Age are now discernible. Palynological evidence from Thessaly and elsewhere shows a change in the upland vegetation that could be related to forest degradation through intensive grazing.[142]

The Neolithic economic regime, based on reciprocity and social obligations, would have placed a heavy emphasis on the social organization of production. Throughout the period the social character of consumption and storage must have been stressed in various ways. Although the evidence for ritual or symbolic behavior is minimal in Thessaly, some form of ideological coercion stressing sharing between members of the community must be assumed. The decorated, open ceramic shapes, suitable for display of food consumption, and the presence of facilities for cooking and storage in open, public areas, at least in the Early and Middle Neolithic, are probable indications of an idealized economic reality.[143] The unequal distribution of painted pottery among households at Sesklo or its greater frequency in pits at Achilleion may attest to its ideological function. During the Early and Middle Bronze Age the eclipse of painted pottery was accompanied by a turn to a more private and self-contained household, with storage areas being increasingly moved inside the house. Storage vessels were common among the few painted pots of the Middle Bronze Age, probably stressing further the importance of private surplus.

The obligation for social sharing and the need for storage and diverse productive activities can create a social context for conflict and dissent among members of a community. The house models and the often "personalized" human figurines may represent, among other things, an emphasis on the productive unit and its members.[144] The rise of social elites could be precisely an expression or even a res-

olution of a long-term conflict between communal appropriation through sharing and production on the household level. On the other hand, the archaeological traces of these social hierarchies are admittedly faint prior to the Late Bronze Age in Thessaly. In tracing social hierarchy in Thessaly, we should expect not a cumulative evolutionary continuum but rather a process, marked with breaks and even regressions. Breaks in the cultural sequence, such as the "Rachmani" FN phase or the early part of the Early Bronze Age (fourth millennium B.C.), provided they are not simply gaps in archaeological evidence, should caution against a simplifying evolutionary reconstruction. Nor is it easy to observe in LBA Thessaly a complex sociopolitical formation as the culmination of an evolutionary process.

The recent evidence from excavations in the coastal area has shown the difficulties in recognizing the formation of a state during the Late Bronze Age. Despite the fact that the material culture of the area shows close affinities with that of central and southern Greece, the hierarchy of sites, a typical characteristic of southern Greek state organization, is here expressed in a random distribution, which displays little patterning in terms of size and location of sites.[145] The impression is one of small-scale polities. The appropriation of Mycenaean cultural traits, such as those observed in Thessaly, does not by necessity imply the adoption of the Mycenaean political and economic organization prevalent in some southern areas. What must be investigated is the particular political and ideological use of these traits, within and in opposition to a tradition of local political structures.[146]

Another aspect of Neolithic and Bronze Age economy is craft production, generally assumed, at least during the Neolithic, to have been primarily a household activity. This perception of an idealized, simple Neolithic self-sufficiency is gradually changing, as a result of more extensive research and a deeper understanding of the complexities involved. Studies of stone tools, pottery, and "prestige" objects indi-

---

[142] K.J. Willis, "The Vegetational History of the Balkans," *Quaternary Science Reviews* 13 (1994) 786; Willis and K.D. Bennett, "The Neolithic Transition—Fact or Fiction? Palaeoecological Evidence from the Balkans," *The Holocene* 4 (1994) table 1; S. Bottema, "Palynological Investigations in Greece with Special Reference to Pollen as an Indicator of Human Activity," *Paleohistoria* 24 (1982) 261–62, 287.

[143] Halstead 1994, 206–207; P. Halstead, "From Sharing to Hoarding: The Neolithic Foundations of Aegean Bronze Age Society?" in Laffineur and Niemeier (supra n. 50) 16–19. But see reservations infra n. 259.

[144] Contrary to the often assumed "religious" meaning

of figurines, Hourmouziadis has stressed their role in the representation of everyday activities. See G.H. Hourmouziadis, *Η ανθρωπόμορφη ειδωλοπλαστική της νεολιθικής Θεσσαλίας* (Volos 1973) 196–206. The so far unique house model from Platia Magoula Zarkou (supra n. 18) connects the house models with the human figurines.

[145] Halstead 1984, chs. 6.4.5–6; Halstead 1994, 203; Feuer 38–47.

[146] See Feuer, esp. 1–21, 179–203, for discussion of Thessaly's role in a "Mycenaean world" with a Mycenaean type of political and social organization.

cate extensive networks of exchange as well as specialized production centers for various classes of finds. Perlès has shown that obsidian tools were manufactured by specialized knappers, probably itinerant; and chemical analysis has indicated the circulation of specific classes of pottery among sites and the production of ceramics in special centers, occasionally concentrated in small areas, as in the case of LN Gray-on-Gray ware.[147] We still have a very limited understanding, however, of broader aspects of Neolithic society, such as social boundaries and disruptions, mobility and sedentism, inequality and gender, and conflict within and between communities.[148]

Very little work has been done on the modes of production and exchange in Bronze Age Thessaly. Non-systematic, macroscopic observations leave no doubt that pottery was exchanged between Thessalian sites and distant regions during the Early and Middle Bronze Age. For the Late Bronze Age there are indications from several sources—chemical analysis, pottery kilns, and macroscopic ceramic analysis—of different conditions and centers of pottery production, and the exchange of pottery between sites and with regions outside Thessaly. The picture, however, is still tentative.[149]

NOTE ON THE HISTORY OF RESEARCH IN MACEDONIA

Already in the early 20th century, Macedonia came to occupy a peculiar place in the consciousness of prehistorians. It was discussed in terms of what it had *not* been as often as in terms of what it was, in terms of deficiency as much as in terms of importance. It was considered, for example, a key province for the study of European prehistory, but also (especially its western part) a backward area in itself, with "a native tendency to isolation."[150] It was claimed to be the ancestral Bronze Age homeland of the legendary Dorians,[151] yet, as everyone knew, only upon leaving that home did the Dorians shed their primitive habits and achieve distinction. Examples are too many indeed. Macedonia was construed as a passage, or a highway, between lands of obvious importance, Europe and Old Greece or Anatolia,[152] and archaeologists from Rey to Rodden would invoke that condition as a justification for excavating in Macedonia.[153] As early as 1902, Schmidt had concluded, from a collection of potsherds in Berlin, that the province's connections were with the "northern hinterland" (i.e., central Europe).[154] Heurtley wrote his monumental book in hopes of "removing that impression . . . the slogan 'Macedonia goes with the North,'" and compensating for "the tacit omission of Macedonia from books dealing with the prehistory of the Aegean";[155] the land west of the Struma (Strymon) belongs primarily with the Aegean, he argued, at a time when few could pay attention. Other researchers, including S. Casson, would make it clear that Macedonia was European—not Mediterranean—by nature; they sought and found the province's northern character, not in its latitude vis-à-vis "mainland

---

[147] For craft production and specialization, see C. Perlès, "Systems of Exchange and Organization of Production in Neolithic Greece," *JMA* 5 (1992) 115–64. C. Perlès and K.D. Vitelli, "Technologie et fonction des premières productions céramiques de Grèce," *Terre cuite et société: La céramique, document technique, économique, culturel* (Juan-les-Pins 1994) 226–30; Perlès (supra n. 122) 1–42. For chemical analysis and discussion of the circulation of pottery in Thessaly, see supra n. 128. Also Y. Liritzis and J. Dixon, "Πολιτιστική επικοινωνία μεταξύ των νεολιθικών οικισμών Σέσκλου και Διμηνίου (Θεσσαλία)," *Anthropologika* 5 (1984) 51–62, where a local exchange of pottery between Sesklo and Dimini is observed. For the distribution of Neolithic pottery in the Thessalian plain, see V. Rondiri, "Επιφανειακή κεραμεική νεολιθικών θέσεων της Θεσσαλίας: Κατανομή στο χώρο," *Anthropologika* 8 (1985) 53–74. For intrasite analysis of pottery, see Maniatis et al. (supra n. 21) 272–74; Kotsakis (supra n. 22) 1–2; and Kotsakis 208–20, 264–71.

[148] For the potential role of conflict, see infra ns. 277–78.

[149] For pottery exchange in the EBA and MBA, see *Argissa* III, 41, 49–50, 59, 78–79; Hanschmann (supra n. 95) 109–16; Christmann (supra n. 55) 201–204; *Pefkakia* III, 285–89. For chemical analysis of Bronze Age pottery from various sites in Thessaly, see S.R. White, *The Provenance of Bronze Age Pottery from Central and Eastern Greece* (Diss. Univ. of Bradford 1981); White, S.E. Warren, and R.E. Jones, "The Provenance of Bronze Age Pottery from Thessaly in Eastern Greece," in A. Aspinall and S.E. Warren eds., *Proceed-*

ings of the 22nd Archaeometry Symposium (Bradford 1982) 323–32; Jones, *Greek and Cypriot Pottery* (Athens 1986) 121–32, where all previous work is discussed. For macroscopic studies of LBA pottery, see Feuer 143–77; also Avila (supra n. 88) 48–49. For recent kiln finds, see Batziou-Efstathiou (supra n. 109) 215–24; also Adrimi-Sismani, in *Η περιφέρεια* (supra n. 53).

[150] E.g., V.G. Childe, review of S. Casson, *Macedonia, Thrace and Illyria* (Oxford 1926), in *Man* 26 (1926) no. 99; W.A. Heurtley, *Prehistoric Macedonia: An Archaeological Reconnaissance of Greek Macedonia (West of the Struma) in the Neolithic, Bronze, and Early Iron Ages* (Cambridge 1939) 129–32.

[151] W.A. Heurtley, "A Prehistoric Site in Western Macedonia and the Dorian Invasion," *BSA* 28 (1926–1927) 159–94.

[152] E.g., S. Casson, "The Bronze Age in Macedonia," *Archaeologia* 74 (1924) 73–88.

[153] L. Rey, "Observations sur les sites préhistoriques et protohistoriques de la Macédoine," *BCH* 40 (1916) 257; R.J. Rodden and J.M. Rodden, "A European Link with Chatal Huyuk: Uncovering a 7th Millennium Settlement in Macedonia. Part I—Site and Pottery," *ILN* 2179 (1964) 564.

[154] H. Schmidt, "Die Keramik der makedonischen Tumuli," *ZfE* 37 (1905) 110–13.

[155] Heurtley (supra n. 150) xvii. The slogan echoes A.J.B. Wace and M.S. Thompson, *Prehistoric Thessaly* (Cambridge 1912) 233, who, however, applied it to northern Greece—at their time, Thessaly.

Greece," but in its very environment and climate, e.g., in the discharge pattern of its rivers.[156] And just as rivers overflow and spill onto broad vales, so did the idea: Macedonia became different from the Aegean in general, in its natural environment as much as in the character of its prehistoric culture; it became the Other of the Aegean.

The vision of Macedonia's Otherness took form in the context of late 19th- and early 20th-century quests for identities, for nations, races, and their origins, and was directed by the geopolitical concerns of the time.[157] We still live with the consequences,[158] however, and that fact cannot be accounted for in the present review. The most recent textbook on the Bronze Age in the Aegean, for example, once more largely omits discussion of "the northernmost parts of modern Greece" (and other circum-Aegean areas), since, "although demonstrably in contact with the Aegean cultures, [those parts] have an essentially different history."[159] That may well be so; but unless the boundary between "the Aegean cultures" and the north becomes the object of intensive investigation, and its problematical nature is fully documented, to speak of *essentially different histories* for the Aegean and the north can only have one effect, however unintended: it continues to reify Identity—in this case cultural—as a stable, homogeneous, inalienable essence, always the same. Did not, for example, the "contact" have any material consequences for "the Aegean cultures"? In the era of world system approaches, with their emphasis on interaction among centers, peripheries, and margins (to mention but one set of notions that has become available recently to prehistorians),[160] a "given," stable cultural identity for "the Aegean" is a notion that needs considerable justification. In the end, Macedonia in prehistory can be considered a part of "the Aegean" or "Europe"

only as long as the last two constructs continue to evade our analyses.

Questions of cultural origins had been prevalent in Heurtley's book,[161] "and the sections on racial contacts form[ed] a brilliant climax to the whole."[162] Invasions as well as local developments were invoked as explanations of change in "wares" and figurine types. But the work offered much more than this, and it was justifiably called "a scientific record of lasting value."[163] A ceramic cultural sequence was established, even an absolute chronology; while the latter was short by ca. 2,000 years, the former was remarkably close to the one that we rely on today for dating unstratified materials. Time was measured in thickness of deposits (in half-meters). Moreover, as the excavations were dispersed over a very wide area, from the Florina basin to the coast of Chalkidiki, regional differences were emerging.[164]

The departure of Heurtley's team from Macedonia in 1931 was followed by a 30-year period during which a minimum of fieldwork was carried out at prehistoric sites. When the joint Cambridge-Harvard excavations at Nea Nikomedeia began in 1961, the prehistory of the province was once more a "lacuna to fill,"[165] since much fieldwork had in the meantime been conducted in every area with which Macedonia was thought to be connected, from Anatolia to Hungary to Thessaly. The new project was also conceived with a view to Macedonia's key location—this time, however, in the context of the "spread" of Neolithic farming. Diffusion and ethnogenesis were no longer the leading concerns of mainstream European prehistory.[166] The project, staffed with people from departments of anthropology, comparative zoology, forestry, and the like,[167] brought to Greece "in one piece" a radically different set of questions and ethos of practice, a "scientific humanism" that had devel-

---

[156] Casson (supra n. 150) 1–5.

[157] The issue is treated in detail in M. Fotiadis, "Imagining Macedonia in Prehistory, ca. 1900–1930" (in preparation). See also K. Kotsakis, "The Powerful Past: Theoretical Trends in Greek Archaeology," in I. Hodder ed., *Archaeological Theory in Europe: The Last Three Decades* (London 1991) 65–90.

[158] E.g., Macedonia's natural environment is described in terms of its difference from the Aegean in N.G.L. Hammond, *A History of Macedonia* 1: *Historical Geography and Prehistory* (Oxford 1972) 3–5; and in E.N. Borza, *In the Shadow of Olympus: The Emergence of Macedon* (Princeton 1990) 24–28.

[159] O. Dickinson, *The Aegean Bronze Age* (Cambridge 1994) xviii. By contrast, see C. Renfrew, *The Emergence of Civilisation* (London 1972).

[160] See, e.g., A. Sherratt, "What Would a Bronze-Age World System Look Like? Relations between Temperate Europe and the Mediterranean in Later Prehistory," *Journal of European Archaeology* 1:2 (1993) 1–58; M. Rowlands, M. Larsen, and K. Kristiansen eds., *Centre and Periphery in*

the Ancient World (Cambridge 1987).

[161] Heurtley (supra n. 150).

[162] W. Lamb, review of Heurtley (supra n. 150), in *Man* 40 (1940) 29.

[163] V.G. Childe, review of Heurtley (supra n. 150), in *AntJ* 24 (1944) 155. Cf. Lamb (supra n. 162), with similar praises.

[164] Before the project was interrupted, plans were underway for excavating in the Bitola basin as well: W.A. Heurtley, "Prehistoric Macedonia: What Has Been and What Remains to Be Done," *Man* 31 (1931) 217.

[165] The phrase is Rey's from 1916 (supra n. 153).

[166] They survived, however, in many quarters; see the keen remarks of R. Dennell, *Early Farming in South Bulgaria from the VI to the III Millennia B.C.* (BAR-IS 45, Oxford 1978) 12–13.

[167] Grahame Clark was among them. See R.J. Rodden et al., "Excavations at the Early Neolithic Site at Nea Nikomedeia, Greek Macedonia (1961 Season)," *PPS* 28 (1962) 267–88; and Rodden and Rodden (supra n. 153).

oped outside Aegean prehistory.[168] That was an exciting moment for archaeology, all the more so since the site yielded an early radiocarbon date (6220 ± 150 b.c.) associated with domesticates, and a "shrine."[169] Nea Nikomedeia was, then, "the site of the oldest dated Neolithic community yet found in Europe,"[170] making Macedonia an important link in the long chain of evolution of European society. But the excitement was short-lived for many reasons, including the realization that, in regard to the spread of Neolithic farming, the conventional geographical boundary between western Asia and eastern Europe (the Hellespont-Bosporus strait) was "irrelevant and even misleading."[171] Still, the project at Nea Nikomedeia marked the beginning of the modern phase of prehistoric research in Macedonia and beyond. It was followed by excavations at several sites, including the important one at Sitagroi, and, in the 1980s, by the projects described individually in this review.

The first chair of prehistory at the University of Thessaloniki was created in 1964, and was occupied by N. Platon, whose area of fieldwork was Minoan Crete.[172] Only under his successors, D.R. Theocharis and G.H. Hourmouziadis after the mid-1970s, were courses in the prehistory of northern Greece offered as regular parts of the curriculum, and prehistoric research undertaken by the University in that area. Dissertations by students on northern Greek topics are now proliferating. Equally important, a few zealous women and men, with a declared interest in prehistory, have in recent decades joined the ranks of the ephoreias in Macedonia. The present review owes much to their field efforts.

WESTERN MACEDONIA

Environmental Change

During the first half of the Holocene, temperatures continued to rise in western Macedonia (west of the Axios River; fig. 2), and in the fifth millennium B.C. summers in the uplands may have been warmer than today by up to 4° C.[173] Cooler, more humid conditions, approximating those of the present, became progressively prevalent in the last two millennia of prehistory, especially after 2500 B.C. The effects of the extensive Neolithic habitation are hardly conspicuous in the region's palynological record.[174] A decrease of forest, in particular, is not in evidence until "about 3100–3300 B.P." (uncalibrated).[175] Whatever the exact chronology and scale of that decrease,[176] it seems to have affected the conifers; oak and, at 1,200–1,500 masl, beech continued to regenerate through much of the historical period. Nonetheless, the episode may have initiated a cycle of slope erosion and deposition of coarse sediments along the peripheries of valleys: a change to more frequent torrential discharge in streams is suggested by the appearance of the plane tree in the pollen record.[177] As a further result, surface outlets in some basins may have been blocked, and marshes may thus have formed or expanded, for example, in Kitrini Limni.[178] At the same time, the walnut and, in the lowlands, the olive were introduced as cultivated trees.

---

[168] See M. Fotiadis, "Modernity and the Past-Still-Present: Politics of Time in the Birth of Regional Archaeological Projects in Greece," *AJA* 99 (1995) 59–78, with further references.

[169] For a summary see, e.g., R.J. Rodden, "An Early Neolithic Village in Greece," *Scientific American* 212:4 (1965) 83–92. For the ironic legacy of Nea Nikomedeia, see Fotiadis (supra n. 1) 157–59. An addendum to that legacy is the recent treatment of the site as one of "quelques sites marginaux" by J.-P. Demoule, "Néolithique et Chalcolithique de Macédoine: Un état des questions," *ArchMak* 5 (1993) 374.

[170] Rodden (supra n. 169) 83.

[171] G. Clark and S. Piggott, *Prehistoric Societies* (New York 1965) 224. For the questions surrounding all four ¹⁴C dates from the site, see S. Bottema, *Late Quaternary Vegetation History of Northwestern Greece* (Groningen 1974) 147. The first volume of the final publication, containing the stratigraphy and a study of the ceramics, is now published: G. Pyke and P. Yiouni, *Nea Nikomedeia, the Excavation of an Early Neolithic Village in Northern Greece, 1961–1964* I: *The Excavation and the Ceramic Assemblage* (*BSA* Suppl. 25, Athens 1996).

[172] It was Platon who introduced all three authors of this review to prehistory.

[173] Esp. B. Huntley and I.C. Prentice, "July Temperatures in Europe from Pollen Data 6000 Years before Present," *Science* 241 (1988) 689 and fig. 3.

[174] Bottema (supra n. 142), esp. 279–84.

[175] Bottema (supra n. 142), esp. 261–66. Bottema has always insisted on dates around 3200 B.P. (in ¹⁴C years) for the changes in Macedonia; at best, that is a rough approximation. Fresh, well-dated cores from the western Macedonian basins would be very helpful. Cf. S. Bottema, "Développement de la végétation et du climat dans le bassin méditerranéen oriental à la fin du Pléistocène et pendant l'Holocène," *L'Anthropologie* 95 (1991) 724; and Bottema and H. Woldring, "Anthropogenic Indicators in the Pollen Record of the Eastern Mediterranean," in Bottema, G. Entjes-Neiborg, and W. van Zeist eds., *Man's Role in the Shaping of the Eastern Mediterranean Landscape* (Rotterdam 1990) 231–64. In the last article, the Macedonian evidence is treated in its broad geohistorical context, the authors' "B.O. phase."

[176] For inferring scale of deforestation from pollen evidence, see the cautions of Bottema and Woldring (supra n. 175), esp. 240–42.

[177] Bottema (supra n. 142) 274–77.

[178] M. Fotiadis et al., *Prehistory of Kitrini Limni, Northern Greece* I: *Surveys and Excavation 1987–1992* (in preparation).

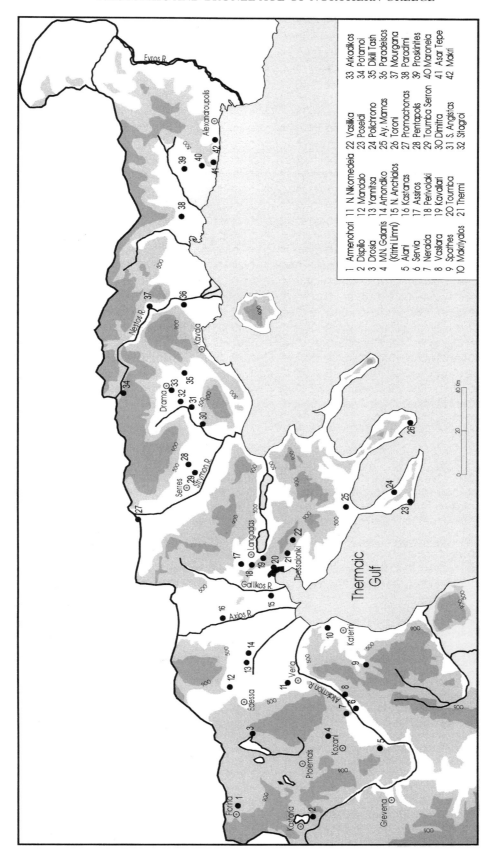

Fig. 2. Macedonia and Thrace. Principal sites mentioned in the text. Contours at 500 and 900 masl.

1 Armenohori
2 Dispilio
3 Drosia
4 MN Galanis (Kitrini Limni)
5 Alani
6 Servia
7 Neraida
8 Vasilara
9 Spathes
10 Makriyalos
11 N. Nikomedeia
12 Mamaio
13 Yannitsa
14 Armonidiko
15 N. Anchialos
16 Kastanas
17 Assiros
18 Perivolaki
19 Kavallari
20 Toumba
21 Thermi
22 Vasilika
23 Poseidi
24 Polichrono
25 Ay. Mamas
26 Toroni
27 Promachonas
28 Pentapolis
29 Toumba Serron
30 Dimitra
31 S. Angistas
32 Sitagroi
33 Arkadikos
34 Potamoi
35 Dikili Tash
36 Paradeisos
37 Mourgana
38 Paradimi
39 Proskinites
40 Maroneia
41 Asar Tepe
42 Makri

This is a puzzling pollen record. The vegetational and other changes it suggests are thought to be largely anthropogenic.[179] Assuming that the chronology is not in error by several hundred years, the changes occurred during the Late Bronze Age. Archaeologically, the period remains poorly known. Even so, an increase of population at a scale that would justify forest clearings can be precluded. It is more likely that clearings would result from new ways of exploiting the land's resources. Lumbering has been suggested,[180] and large flocks, requiring summer pastures and, hence, vertical transhumance, also are a possibility.[181] In either of these cases, the uplands (1,000–1,500 masl) should be affected most, and, in that respect, the pollen record may offer a clue: decline was noted among the conifers, which must have occupied the higher elevations, rather than in the oak forest. A further, tantalizing possibility suggests itself: in view of the region's archaeological record for the period 1500–1100 B.C., it is virtually impossible to explain either large, transhumant flocks or systematic lumbering; simply, there could not be enough consumers for the products *within* the region. Should we speculate, then, that the products (e.g., ship lumber, wool) were destined for an interregional trade network? Would that also mean that

western Macedonia was drawn, as "margin,"[182] into the world system of the eastern Mediterranean Late Bronze Age? These are questions, however, not conclusions, all the more so since the region's archaeological record would at this time suggest negative, rather than affirmative, answers.

Sea level change is a complicated matter, and studies that purport to reconstruct prehistoric shorelines on the basis of sea level curves derived from broad areas offer no reliable guides.[183] In zones of high seismicity, and of extensive deltaic progradation, such as the Gulf of Thessaloniki,[184] strictly local geological data are essential before the coastal environment can be reconstructed. For the time being, only one recent study fulfills that requirement, covering a small area, the "Gulf of Kastanas," for the last ca. 4,000 years.[185]

Material Sequence and Archaeological Phases

For the Neolithic, the material sequence of western Macedonia today rests firmly on stratified, correlatable deposits at several of the province's sites. In addition to Nea Nikomedeia, four sites have yielded ^{14}C dates—Servia and Servia V (Varytimides) in the Aliakmon valley,[186] Megalo Nisi Galanis in Kitrini Limni,[187] and Mandalo in the Yannitsa

[179] For a possible change in the pattern of rainfall, concurrent with the anthropogenic changes, see esp. S. Bottema, "The Prehistoric Environment of Greece: A Review of the Palynological Record," in P.N. Kardulias ed., *Beyond the Site: Regional Studies in the Aegean Area* (Lanham 1994) 59–61; see also Bottema and Woldring (supra n. 175) 261–62; N. Athanassiadis and A.M. Gerasimidis, "Μεταπαγετώδης εξέλιξη της βλάστησης στο Βόρα Αλμωπίας," *Scientific Annals of the Department of Forestry and Natural Environment, University of Thessaloniki* 29 (1986) 213–49; Athanassiadis and Gerasimidis, "Μεταπαγετώδης εξέλιξη της βλάστησης στο όρος Πάϊκον," *Scientific Annals of the Department of Forestry and Natural Environment, University of Thessaloniki* 30 (1987) 405–45; Athanassiadis, "Η ανάλυση γύρης και η σημασία της από ιστορικο-αρχαιολογική άποψη με βάση τα δεδομένα διαγράμματός της από το Βαρυκό Λιτοχώρου," *Scientific Annals of the Department of Forestry and Natural Environment, University of Thessaloniki* 31 (1988) 143–52.

[180] Bottema and Woldring (supra n. 175) 261, where the authors are speaking of western Turkey as well.

[181] The reader should be aware, however, of the arguments put forward against pastoral transhumance in Greek prehistory: M. Fotiadis, "Transhumance: Was It Indeed Practiced in the Prehistoric Mediterranean?" *AJA* 84 (1980) 207 (abstract); J.F. Cherry, "Pastoralism and the Role of Animals in the Pre- and Protohistoric Economies of the Aegean," in C.R. Whittaker ed., *Pastoral Economies in Classical Antiquity* (*PCPS* Suppl. 14, Cambridge 1988) 7–11; and P. Halstead, "Present to Past in the Pindhos: Diversification and Specialisation in Mountain Economies," in R. Maggi, R. Nisbet, and G. Barker eds., *Archeologia della pastorizia*

nell'Europa meridionale 1 (*RStLig* 56, Bordighera 1990) 61–80.

[182] In the strictly technical sense the term has in the context of world system analyses; see Sherratt (supra n. 160).

[183] G. Rapp, Jr., and J.C. Kraft, "Holocene Coastal Change in Greece and Aegean Turkey," in Kardulias (supra n. 179) 73; see also Kraft, I. Kayan, and O. Erol, "Geology and Paleogeographic Reconstructions of the Vicinity of Troy," in Rapp, Jr., and J.A. Gifford, *Troy: The Archaeological Geology* (Princeton 1982) 19 and n. 24, where the authors warn against the use of their curve for other regions. That warning has not been heeded in Aslanis (supra n. 12) 26, 67, 83.

[184] Progradation in the historical period is in the order of 40–50 km: e.g., J.C. Kraft and G.R. Rapp, Jr., "Geological Reconstruction of Ancient Coastal Landforms in Greece with Predictions of Future Coastal Changes," in P.G. Marinos and G.C. Koukis eds., *The Engineering Geology of Ancient Works, Monuments and Historical Sites* (Rotterdam 1988) 1,548.

[185] H.D. Schulz, "Die geologische Entwicklung der Bucht von Kastanas im Holozän," in *Kastanas* 375–93; for earlier work, see J. Bintliff, "The Plain of Western Macedonia and the Neolithic Site of Nea Nikomedeia," *PPS* 40 (1976) 241–62.

[186] C. Ridley and K.A. Wardle, "Rescue Excavations at Servia 1971–1973: A Preliminary Report," *BSA* 74 (1979) 226; R. Burleigh, J. Ambers, and K. Mathews, "British Museum Natural Radiocarbon Measurements XV," *Radiocarbon* 24 (1982) 277–78.

[187] M. Fotiadis and A. Hondroyanni-Metoki, "Κίτρινη Λίμνη: Διαχρονική σύνοψη, ραδιοχρονολογήσεις και η ανασκαφή του 1993," *AEMT* 7 (1993, in press); cf. below.

Tertiary zone.[188] Together, deposits from the five sites cover much of the Early Neolithic, the entire Middle and Late, and the first half of the Final Neolithic—that is, roughly, the late seventh, sixth, and fifth millennia B.C. Problematical periods are the Early and Final Neolithic—the first, because we lack secure ^{14}C dates (and deposits) from its beginning, the second, because none of the excavated deposits can be confidently assigned to the fourth millennium B.C. The sequence for the sixth and fifth millennia B.C. is more comparable to that of Thessaly than to that of eastern Macedonia,[189] which has prompted many researchers in recent publications to treat western Macedonia in the Neolithic as a province of Thessaly. This practice should be avoided. To call the Late Neolithic of the region "Late Dimini," for example, or to consider "Larisa wares" typical of LN sites in western Macedonia can only lead to confusion, especially since the applicability of such terms to Thessaly itself as a whole is far from self-evident.[190]

For the Bronze Age, one has still to rely on poorly correlated stratigraphies from sites across a very wide area, stretching from Thessaly to the Troad. That is so, despite ^{14}C dates from Servia, Mandalo, and, now, from Arhondiko near Yannitsa (fig. 2:6, 12, 14).[191] The two EBA phases at Servia are ceramically distinct, but their chronological ranges remain obscure.[192] Mandalo covers a large part of the third millennium; when the study of the contexts and their stratigraphic order progresses, certain questions of material sequence may find answers. Arhondiko may in the future help us to distinguish another phase

in the sequence, a "Middle" Bronze Age perhaps, around 2000 B.C. Mycenaean (LH IIIB and IIIC) fabrics appear at many sites, but their full contexts, where they exist, have yet to be studied and published. In short, knowledge of the Bronze Age material sequence in western Macedonia remains fragmentary, and one often resorts to annoyingly vague designations of time for particular archaeological contexts. The designation "later Bronze Age" is occasionally used in this review for contexts that, we think, should be dated in the range 2200–1100 B.C., but for which we may not be more specific.

Recent Projects

Middle Aliakmon valley: riverine zone. The landscape along the middle course of the Aliakmon changed dramatically in the mid-1970s with the damming of the river. A strip 30 km long and up to 3 km wide was flooded before the land was systematically surveyed. The site of Servia (fig. 2:6)—known since 1911, excavated in 1930 and again from 1971 to 1973—now lies under many meters of water, as does the nearby EN site Servia V, excavated in 1972–1973.[193] Of the sites that had been known in the area before the 1970s, some escaped inundation (e.g., Vasilara,[194] fig. 2:8), but the entire valley floor, including the terrace on which the Neolithic settlement of Servia was established,[195] is lost to archaeology. Recent surveys by the IZ' Ephoreia indicate the magnitude of the loss. Surveying along the shore of the newly formed lake, in parts of the terraces that are seasonally exposed, A. Hondroyanni-Metoki and G. Karametrou-Mentesidi have found 13 new settle-

[188] K. Kotsakis et al., "Carbon 14 Dates from Mandalo, W. Macedonia," in Y. Maniatis ed., *Archaeometry: Proceedings of the 25th International Symposium* (Amsterdam 1989) 679–85.

[189] For correlations with sequences in many parts of the Balkan peninsula one may consult, e.g., Demoule (supra n. 169) 389, table 2, or J.-P. Demoule, "Problèmes chrono-culturels du Néolithique de Grèce du Nord," in *La Thessalie* A, 83, table 1. Demoule's tables were prepared ca. 1990, however, and should be used with caution. Note a terminological difference between the two versions of the table (far left column).

[190] "Thessalocentrism" is not, however, the only trend; equally unproductive is the practice, popular among both Greek and other archaeologists, of invoking Vinca, Anza, and a host of other *Kulturkreis* labels originating in regions, nearby or distant, to the north of Macedonia.

[191] A. Papaefthimiou and A. Papasteriou, "Ανασκαφή Αρχοντικού, 1994. Προϊστορικός τομέας," *AEMT* 8 (1994, in press).

[192] Ridley and Wardle (supra n. 186) 217–26 discuss the material as well as the problems.

[193] Heurtley (supra n. 150) 43–56; Ridley and Wardle (supra n. 186) 185–230. Bibliographic guides to prehistoric

research in western Macedonia (begun in 1898) are supplied in H. Koukouli-Chrysanthaki, "Η δυτική Μακεδονία στην προϊστορία: Νεολιθική εποχή," in *Γ' Συνέδριο Ιστορίας, Λαογραφίας, Γλωσσολογίας, Παραδοσιακής Αρχιτεκτονικής Δυτικομακεδονικού Χώρου. Πρακτικά* (Thessaloniki 1982) 98–128; in H. Ziota, "Ο Νομός Κοζάνης στην προϊστορία: Ερευνα και προοπτικές," in *Δυτικομακεδονικά γράμματα* (Kozani 1990) 105–34; and in D. Kokkinidou and K. Trantalidou, "Neolithic and Bronze Age Settlement in Western Macedonia," *BSA* 86 (1991) 93–106.

[194] Located on a prominent butte over the Aliakmon course, Vasilara was excavated in 1994 by the IZ' Ephoreia; cf. Hondroyanni-Metoki (infra n. 196) 109–10. The site was first inhabited in the Late Neolithic, and continued to be occupied through the Bronze Age.

[195] Settlement at Servia was established on a surface of yellowish silt, probably of lacustrine origin, which was found topped with a (fossil) soil profile. That surface, at ca. 260 masl and 17 m above the braided river channel at the time of excavation, appears to have been safe from floods since the Early Neolithic: I.A. Morrison, "Servia Excavations: The Geomorphological Setting of the Site," *AAA* 6 (1973) 425–26.

ment sites since 1985, and the number is likely to rise.[196] Two of those sites (Goules-Varemenoi and Kranidia-Kryovrysi, both near Servia)[197] were founded in the Early Neolithic, and were occupied, continuously or not, to the Bronze Age and later. New foundations were laid in every archaeological phase, down to the later Bronze Age. The Bronze Age chronology of those sites is, for reasons outlined above, much less firm than their Neolithic chronology. Mycenaean sherds indicate activity at some sites toward the close of the Bronze Age,[198] but they do not, by themselves, guarantee extensive habitation, as the example of Servia demonstrates.[199]

When the chronological problem and the loss of the entire lower terrace are taken into account, little can still be said about the settlement pattern. Most clearly, the site of Servia no longer appears as a lonely outpost. The riverine zone of the middle Aliakmon has been extensively settled since the Early Neolithic—at least since an advanced phase of that period.[200] Site numbers increased in the course of the Neolithic. In the Late Neolithic, a small cave, within a few hundred meters of Servia, came into use.[201] Five of the recently found sites were inhabited during some part of the Final Neolithic,[202] two of them located less than 1.5 km from Servia. The well-documented LN abandonment at Servia does not represent a region-wide event. A literal interpretation of the chronological evidence from the two neighboring sites would in fact suggest that they were settled as Servia was abandoned, which may also be the case for Vasilara (5 km downstream).[203] Equally noteworthy, the two sites show no evidence of habitation in the Early Bronze Age, when Servia was reoccupied. At that time, the top of a towering hill

across the river from Servia (Neraida, 150 m above the valley floor, fig. 2:7) was also inhabited.[204] Settlements could be located at short distances from one another: around Servia, distances between archaeologically contemporary sites are in the order of 0.5–1 km.[205] Site abandonments are as much in evidence as site occupations—an observation that, without geomorphological and further archaeological data from the lost valley floor, will remain uninterpretable. Finally, the concentration of sites of all periods in the vicinity of the Servia bridge—nine confirmed sites within an area ca. 4 km²—perhaps indicates more than a preference for settlement in land of superior agricultural potential; it may also suggest that a trail between Thessaly and Macedonia, well traveled in the historical period,[206] was firm geographical knowledge in prehistory as well.

In 1993, a lowering of the lake exposed an orderly cemetery of pithos burials and cists. Forty-one graves in an area 0.3 ha in size were promptly excavated. Preliminary analysis of the goods deposited with the dead shows a date "in the advanced phases of the Early Bronze Age."[207]

Middle Aliakmon valley: terraces and Aiani. The area north of the Aliakmon is a terrace of Tertiary sediments with outcrops of limestone. It rises from 250 masl near the river to 650 masl near Kozani, and is flanked on the west, north, and east by mountains (1,300–1,850 masl). The largest part of that extensive surface (ca. 220 km²) has never been systematically surveyed, yet several sites are known. Some are located near springs (and old villages), as at Karyditsa and Amygdalia;[208] others occupy eccentric locations (e.g., hill slopes over deep ravines). As far as one can judge, none of the sites antedates the Late Neo-

---

[196] G. Karametrou-Mentesidi, *ArchDelt* 42 B' (1987) 418–19, 426, and 429–31; A. Hondroyanni-Metoki, "Από την έρευνα στην παραποτάμια-παραλίμνια περιοχή του Αλιάκμονα," *AEMT* 4 (1990) 105–19; Hondroyanni-Metoki and H. Ziota, "Προϊστορική έρευνα στην παραλίμνια περιοχή του Αλιάκμονα," *AEMT* 7 (1993, in press). The sites are severely disturbed by the lake waters; Hondroyanni-Metoki stresses that measurements of size (now between 0.2 and 4.5 ha) often are meaningless.

[197] Kranidia is currently being excavated: A. Hondroyanni-Metoki, "Αλιάκμων 1992: Προϊστορική ανασκαφή στα Κρανίδια," *AEMT* 6 (1992) 35–43; Hondroyanni-Metoki and Ziota (supra n. 196).

[198] Hondroyanni-Metoki (supra n. 196) 111–12.

[199] Ridley and Wardle (supra n. 186) 189.

[200] Comparison of the Servia V ceramics with those from EN Sesklo suggests a late date for the former site: M. Wijnen, in Ridley and Wardle (supra n. 186) 194. See also the single acceptable ¹⁴C date from Servia V (BM-

1157), 4955 ± 87 b.c.

[201] K. Rhomiopoulou and C. Ridley, "Prehistoric Settlement of Servia," *AAA* 6 (1973) 424.

[202] That is indicated by numerous analogies ("strainers," crusted sherds, and a variety of lugs and appendages on body sherds) with the FN material from Megalo Nisi Galanis (20 km to the north; see below).

[203] Ridley and Wardle (supra n. 186) 225–26.

[204] Test excavations by P. Pantos, *ArchDelt* 32 B' (1977) 229. The site (395 masl), today occupied by the relocated village of Neraida, commands the entire valley of the middle Aliakmon.

[205] The map in Hondroyanni-Metoki (supra n. 196) 108 is at a scale of 1:100,000.

[206] Hammond (supra n. 158) 109–10, 117–20.

[207] A detailed report on the burials will appear in Hondroyanni-Metoki and Ziota (supra n. 196).

[208] Hondroyanni-Metoki (supra n. 197); H. Ziota, *ArchDelt* 43 B' (1988) 402.

lithic. Intensive research will, however, be necessary before patterns emerge.[209] The important question is whether the settlement pattern here, in the relatively dry Tertiary zone, is different from that in the riverine zone, which has a distinctive—and privileged—pedology, hydrology, and even climate.

Aiani, a major center of the early historical period in Macedonia, is also located in the Tertiary zone (fig. 2:5). The main site, Megali Rahi, is a true acropolis, rising 40–80 m above its immediate surroundings, to 480 masl. Recent excavations of the IZ′ Ephoreia[210] indicate that the acropolis appears to have been occupied from the Bronze Age to the first century B.C. The earliest features, in a level area near the summit, are two small oval buildings with stone foundations, one of them with a rectangular hearth in the middle.[211] The buildings are associated with pots—including mugs with two handles—that the excavator compares with those of Armenohori (70 km to the north; fig. 2:1). The latter is "the only site which could date between the Early Bronze Age and the Early Iron Age [previously] excavated in western Macedonia."[212] However fragmentary, the evidence suggests habitation of the acropolis in the later Bronze and Early Iron Age as well. In the saddles and ridges below the acropolis, Karametrou found an abundance of LN (mainly black-burnished) ceramics, and a second extensive site of similar date was identified through exploration a few kilometers away.[213] At the northern foot of the acropolis, in a colluviated area, excavation revealed a series of later Bronze/Early Iron Age burials in pits and cists, along with a hearth-like structure and a pile of ca. 80 broken pots. The majority of the pots are "matt-painted," but the pile also included a complete Mycenaean pot and parts of others. At least one of the graves contained a Mycenaean alabastron next to a matt-painted bowl and a bronze pin.[214]

The finds of Aiani are important for several reasons.[215] First, the widespread distribution of LN material documented by the excavator raises the possibility of dispersed settlement on the Tertiary terraces around Megali Rahi. Second, the early buildings on the acropolis itself suggest occupation during a period (ca. 2000 B.C.?) for which, in western Macedonia, we know virtually nothing. Radiocarbon dates would, in this case, be extremely useful. Third, a pile of broken matt-painted pots and a hearth within a cemetery from the end of the Bronze Age raise intricate interpretative questions, as the excavator emphasizes. Fourth, the concurrence, in a few contexts, of local matt-painted and Mycenaean pots is notable, for it is without clear precedents in western Macedonia. The matt-painted pots of Macedonia, Epirus, and Albania have been the subject of much discussion and controversy in the past. Thanks to new excavations and to distribution studies carried out in the 1970s, it is now known that comparable techniques of matt-painting appear and disappear at different times in different regions, from Kosovo to southern Italy.[216] In western Macedonia they have been thought to occur both toward the end of the Bronze Age and in the Early Iron Age, yet the evidence for the date assigned to specific finds has often been superficial. The Aiani finds do not yet resolve such problems, but they may point to a date for the

[209] The head of a Mycenaean figurine and a Mycenaean amphora also come from the area, but they are without precise context: G. Karametrou-Mentesidi, ArchDelt 39 B′ (1984) 267; and Ancient Macedonia (Athens 1988) 135–36.

[210] Initiated by G. Karametrou-Mentesidi in 1983 and continuing to date.

[211] G. Karametrou-Mentesidi, "Από την ανασκαφική έρευνα στην Αιανή, 1989," AEMT 3 (1989) 46 and pl. 5.

[212] K.A. Wardle, "Cultural Groups of the Late Bronze and Early Iron Age in Northwest Greece," Godisnjak, Centar za balkanoloska ispitivanja, Sarajevo 15 (1977) 188. For more doubts about the chronology of Armenohori, see Treuil (supra n. 64) 86.

[213] Karametrou-Mentesidi (supra n. 196) 424, 429–30.

[214] Karametrou-Mentesidi (supra n. 211) 49 and figs. 7–9, and Karametrou-Mentesidi, "Ανασκαφή Αιανής 1990," AEMT 4 (1990) 76 and pls. 1–4; also Karametrou-Mentesidi, ArchDelt 43 B′ (1988) 399. The Mycenaean pots are not assigned to specific phases.

[215] For an older surface find with a mysterious inscription, see A. Panayotou, "An Inscribed Pithos Fragment from Aiane (W. Macedonia)," Kadmos 25 (1986) 97–101.

[216] See esp. A. Hochstetter, "Die mattbemalte Keramik in Nordgriechenland, ihre Herkunft und lokale Ausprägung," PZ 57 (1982) 201–19, for a discussion of previous views, and for differences between the western and central Macedonian varieties. For distribution maps in western Macedonia and Albania, see respectively K. Romiopoulou, "Some Pottery of the Early Iron Age from Western Macedonia," BSA 66 (1971) fig. 7, and K. Kilian, "Zur mattbemalten Keramik der ausgehenden Bronzezeit und der Früheisenzeit aus Albanien," ArchKorrBl 2 (1972) 116. For discussion of the Epirotic finds, assigned to the Iron Age, see Wardle (supra n. 212) 179; K.A. Wardle, "The Northern Frontier of Mycenaean Greece," BICS 22 (1975) 207; and I. Vokotopoulou, Βίτσα, τα νεκροταφεία μιας μολοσσικής κώμης (Athens 1986) 255–76. For finds from sites near Naousa, see Vokotopoulou, "La Macédoine de la protohistoire à l'époque archaïque," Magna Grecia, Epiro, e Macedonia. Atti del 24° Convegno di studi sulla Magna Grecia (Taranto 1985) 143–44.

first local production of matt-painted pots before the 11th century B.C.

Grevena and the upper Aliakmon catchment. The most striking discovery thus far reported by the interdisciplinary, comprehensive survey of the Nomos of Grevena undertaken by Carleton College[217] is that of "at least" 15 EN sites.[218] Most of those sites are less than 1 ha in area, and occupy terraces and relatively flat areas near major streams. Mudbrick features in many instances suggest a considerable degree of permanence. More fieldwork will be needed, however, before one can determine why, around 6000 B.C., people settled in a landscape dominated by deeply incised terraces, and why they left their hamlets soon after. Could the EN evidence produced by the Grevena project be indicative of a larger pattern, yet to be mapped in other parts of western Macedonia? The distribution of Bronze Age sites is no less interesting: some were found in higher elevations, near 1,000 masl, and those of the Middle Bronze Age— with occasional pieces of "Gray Minyan"— often "are on rather large, isolated hill tops."[219] In this last, important respect, Grevena in the Middle Bronze Age begins to sound a little like, for example, Messenia (see below, "New Questions").

Further north, along the eastern foothills of the Pindos range, several sites have been found in recent years.[220] At the same time, a LN site on the shore of Lake Kastoria, Dispilio (fig. 2:2), has come under excavation; intriguing finds include what may be the trace of a small flatboat, and a mysterious wooden tablet.[221]

Kitrini Limni area. Since the 1950s, strip mining and industry have brought havoc to the Ptolemais system of basins, creating new deep valleys and precipitous hills. Neolithic sites were first identified here in 1913, but systematic surveys did not begin until the mining had transformed an area ca. 50 km² in the central part of the system.[222] The southernmost and highest of the basins, Kitrini Limni (floor at 650 masl), has to date survived largely intact, and has been since 1987 the object of intensive surveys, excavations, and experimental methods.[223] Systematic survey has also been undertaken in the mountainous hinterland (Vermio), at elevations 850–1,480 masl. A summary of conclusions follows.

Neolithic settlement on the basin floor began no later than 5600 B.C., as the presence of various EN elements (e.g., bowls on low bases, with red-slipped surfaces and linear patterns in white paint) at one site confirms. Another site, 5 km away, as well as a remote cave on Mt. Vermio (940 masl), may have been used at that time. The location of the confirmed EN site, Megali Toumba Ayiou Dimitriou, is noteworthy: it is adjacent to the central and least dry part of the basin floor, yet a few meters above it, on a low ridge, commanding a view in all directions.[224] For a pioneer agricultural community settling in a newly opened landscape, there is hardly a more privileged location in all of Kitrini Limni. The site was occupied in the Middle, Late, and Final Neolithic as well, becoming eventually the most conspicuous mound on the basin floor, with more than 5 m of deposits. It was used again some time in the Bronze Age, perhaps as a burial ground.

At least three more sites on the basin floor were settled by the Middle Neolithic (as shown by the presence of distinctive pot profiles with red-slipped surfaces, occasionally with "flame" patterns, known, e.g., from MN Servia).[225] During the Late and Final Neolithic, on the other hand, 13 sites—some between 5 and 10 ha in area—were settled. While all those

---

[217] The project is directed by N.C. Wilkie. A substantial report will appear in *Hesperia*. See N.C. Wilkie, "The Grevena Project," *ArchMak* 5 (1993) 1,747–55; G. Toufexis, "Νεολιθικές έρευνες στο Ν. Γρεβενών," *AEMT* 7 (1993, in press); also M. Savina, "Some Aspects of the Geomorphology and Quaternary Geology of Grevena Nomos, Western Macedonia, Greece," in H. Reidl ed., *Beiträge zur Landeskunde von Griechenland* 4 (Salzburger geographische Arbeiten 22, Salzburg 1993) 57–75.

[218] Wilkie (supra n. 217) 1,751. One of the sites, Kremastos near the village of Knidi, is being excavated by G. Toufexis (IE' Ephoreia).

[219] Wilkie (supra n. 217) 1,752.

[220] H. Ziota, personal communication.

[221] G.H. Hourmouziadis, "Σήματα λυγρά," *AEMT* 7 (1993, in press); G. Anagnostou et al., "Ανασκαφές Δισπηλιού Καστοριάς: Το χρονολογικό πρόβλημα," *AEMT* 7 (1993, in press).

[222] G. Karametrou-Mentesidi, "Προϊστορικοί οικισμοί Κίτρινης Λίμνης (Σαριγκιόλ) Κοζάνης," in *Αμητός. Τιμητικός*

τόμος για τον καθηγητή Μ. Ανδρόνικο (Thessaloniki 1986) 391–416, with references to earlier work.

[223] A project of the IZ' Ephoreia, in collaboration with M. Fotiadis and others, currently overseen by H. Ziota. Preliminary reports: M. Fotiadis, "Κίτρινη Λίμνη, Νομού Κοζάνης, 1987: Προϊστορική έρευνα," *AEMT* 1 (1987) 51–61; Fotiadis, "Προϊστορική έρευνα στην Κίτρινη Λίμνη, Ν. Κοζάνης, 1988: Μία σύντομη έκθεση," *AEMT* 2 (1988) 41–54; H. Ziota et al., "Κίτρινη Λίμνη, τέσσερα χρόνια έρευνας," *AEMT* 4 (1990) 93–103; Fotiadis and Hondroyanni-Metoki (supra n. 187). See also A. Kalogirou, *Production and Consumption of Pottery in Kitrini Limni, West Macedonia, Greece, 4500 B.C.–3500 B.C.* (Diss. Indiana Univ. 1994); and Fotiadis (supra n. 178). Several other studies are in progress; those on the bone tools (R. Hristidou) and botanical remains (M. Mangafa) are nearly completed.

[224] The claim for EN components in another seven sites in the basin, in Aslanis (supra n. 12) 67–69, is spurious.

[225] Kalogirou (supra n. 223) 250–51; cf. Karametrou-Mentesidi (supra n. 222).

sites were clustered in 30 km² in the nearly flat basin bottom, a steep hill (Ag. Eleftherios, 853 masl), 2.5 km outside the basin, and overlooking a major trail (now, national road) to the Aliakmon valley, was also used in the Late or Final Neolithic.[226]

In the later part of the Final Neolithic, the basin floor appears to have lost much population. Typical EBA pieces are rare on the surface of the sites; small quantities were also found in "pockets" at the excavated site, Megalo Nisi Galanis (fig. 2:4). Here, potsherds from all the traditionally recognized EBA phases were identified, as well as a few later Bronze Age pieces.[227] Some FN deposits in the periphery of Megalo Nisi Galanis were found buried under a dark lacustrine clay, which indicates an expansion of marshes in the basin floor. That episode, however, has yet to be dated with precision, and need not, therefore, be the cause of site abandonments in the basin floor (cf. above, "Environmental Change"). Finally, while the Mt. Vermio survey was successful in identifying small sites (including several tumuli, situated over pastures at 1,050–1,150 masl), it located no definite Bronze Age sites.

The excavation at Megalo Nisi Galanis has identified two main phases, a "Late" and a "Final Neolithic." The LN deposits rest on a nearly level part of the basin floor, directly on a thin horizon of dark clay that covers the soft, clay marl substratum. Settlement began at a time when the red-slipped pots known from the Middle Neolithic were still being produced.[228] In the course of time, those were progressively replaced by dark-burnished pots with rounded profiles, and, later still, by "black-topped," distinctly carinated ones.[229] This last ceramic subphase has been dated at the site to the range 5200–4950 B.C.[230] The end of the Late Neolithic is, however, missing from the excavated trenches—the result of digging by the subsequent, FN occupants of the site; traces of that subphase (e.g., small sherds

with "classical Dimini," or comparable, patterns) are found in later deposits.

The Final Neolithic of Megalo Nisi Galanis is, in terms of ceramics and stone tools, comparable to the "Rachmani" phase in Thessaly (e.g., Pefkakia), and it shares many elements with the early part of the Final Neolithic in southern Greece (e.g., Kitsos Cave). Two dates from different contexts show habitation in the period 4700–4450 B.C.[231] Pottery now is much more abundant than before. Hemispherical and conical bowls in a wide range of capacities (0.12–9 liters) predominate, followed by jars with capacities up to 30–35 liters. What truly characterizes the ceramics of this phase, however, is a variety of clay bodies (calcareous and non-calcareous), surface treatments (including frequent application of white and pink "crusts"), pigments, and a broad range of new types of containers and other utensils (e.g., "strainers" and asymmetrical and angular vessels).[232] Taken together, the increase in the quantity of pottery and the proliferation of fabrics and shapes strongly suggest that the ceramic craft radically expanded, its products becoming useful in a large spectrum of diverse practices; one is tempted to speak of a "ceramic revolution," the full articulation of which with other crafts and activities needs to be systematically explored. The lithic material from the FN deposits comprises heavily used and reused blades (often as scrapers and drills) from a variety of high-quality cherts, obtained mostly as ready-made tools or blanks through long-distance trade. Obsidian of Melian texture is present in the uppermost deposits, which also contain objects from marine shell, and pieces of gold sheet and wire. In house construction, a calcareous concrete was used; it probably was a man-made material, prepared by mixing lime with a sandy sediment collected for the purpose from streambeds.[233] Some surfaces were covered with fine white plasters.

---

[226] F. Petsas, *Prakt* 1965, 27–28. EBA occupation is in evidence as well.

[227] Examples of both the earliest and the latest ceramic materials from Kitrini Limni are illustrated in Fotiadis and Hondroyanni-Metoki (supra n. 187); "tubular lugs," "corded" designs, and clay "anchors" should be added to the EBA material.

[228] Cf. "phase 6" at Servia, Ridley and Wardle (supra n. 186) 212–13.

[229] The groups of rounded dark-burnished pots and carinated "black-topped" vessels have some elements in common (e.g., "rippled" decoration), yet they appear to have been produced by two very different ceramic recipes, at least at Megalo Nisi Galanis (Fotiadis, personal observations, 1994; cf. Ridley and Wardle [supra n. 186] 216–17). The technology of the LN carinated pots is treated exten-

sively in Kalogirou (supra n. 223), esp. 72–106. For means by which the distinctive shine of the LN carinated pots could be achieved, see, e.g., Vitelli (supra n. 128) 143–44.

[230] Two dates: 6150 ± 90 B.P. (Beta-48508) and 6250 ± 170 B.P. (Beta-48507). Calibrations by the University of Washington Quaternary Isotope Lab Radiocarbon Calibration Program, rev. 3.0.3c. See also Fotiadis and Hondroyanni-Metoki (supra n. 187).

[231] Beta-48506: 5730 ± 80 B.P., and Beta-48509: 5710 ± 100 B.P.

[232] Kalogirou (supra n. 223) 107–80. The capacities cited for bowls are those that could be measured.

[233] Fotiadis 1988 (supra n. 223) 43–46. Samples are presently being analyzed by L. Joyner (Fitch Laboratory, British School at Athens).

By the end of the FN occupation, the settlement stood on a mound almost 9 ha in area and with its top 5 m above the basin floor. Most deposits thus far excavated at Megalo Nisi Galanis are secondary, and contexts—especially FN ones—are highly fragmentary. Nevertheless, that is the only site thus far excavated in western Macedonia with an almost complete LN sequence topped by a rich Final Neolithic.

Drosia (fig. 2:3).[234] Drosia is located in a small basin (ca. 8 km[2], 500 masl) in the upper catchment of the Agras River, east of Lake Vegoritis. The cultural horizon, up to 1.20 m thick, occupied a gentle rise, and extended over at least 1.4 ha. Excavation in 1992 by the IZ' Ephoreia in an area ca. 40 m[2] uncovered remains of house floors, made of clay set on an infrastructure of worked timbers. At least two such floors were identified ca. 10 m apart, and one of them preserved a small grinding facility, a slab supported by small stones. In the space between the two floors a pit was found, 3 m in diameter and 40 cm deep, containing a large amount of potsherds, stone tools, and animal bone. Outside that pit, the cultural deposits contained few artifacts.

The site must belong to the period 6000–5500 B.C., as is shown by hemispherical bowls with red-burnished surfaces and occasional bands of red paint, and by "barbotine" patterns on some of the larger vessels. The excavator calls attention to the relatively large number of ground stone tools (mainly axes or adzes from serpentinites) in comparison with the number of chipped stone blades and scrapers (made on both good- and poor-quality cherts). Three lower bodies of clay figurines, three "sling bullets," a "spool," and a chert "arrowhead" are also mentioned.

Drosia, then, is a single-period, EN/MN settlement with dispersed houses, the first site of its kind to be identified in this part of Greece.[235] It lies in a well-watered, fertile part of the landscape amid high mountains, but also along the main natural artery (Via Egnatia)[236] from the plains of central Macedonia to the upland basins of Pelagonia and Ptolemais. It may therefore have been not simply one more settlement of pioneer farmers in search of a cultivable patch, but also a station along the trails of prospectors and traders, a socially marked place in a sparsely populated landscape.[237] The finds ought to be examined with that possibility in mind. Eight thousand years after it was formed, the cultural horizon is extremely fragile, and hardly detectable from the surface, even though the house floors lie less than 50 cm below. The circumstances of discovery are instructive: the site was spotted as it was being bulldozed away, in the course of industrial development. One lesson is that such sites are difficult to detect, and, in certain areas, scores of them may lie hidden under recent alluvia.

Yannitsa area. In the low terraces flanking the plain of central Macedonia on the northern side, between the courses of the Loudias and the Axios, recent explorations by the IZ' Ephoreia have produced evidence for at least 15 new prehistoric sites. Information on most of them still is sketchy,[238] but one site, Yannitsa B (fig. 2:13), has been under excavation by P. Chrysostomou since 1989, and short reports appear regularly.[239] The site is located in a densely built area within the city limits of Yannitsa, and only small parts of it can be excavated. Late Neolithic deposits have been estimated to cover an area of 6–8 ha; in their southern quarter, in an area near springs, they appear to rest directly on deposits, up

[234] S. Kotsos, "Ανασκαφή νεολιθικού οικισμού στη βιομηχανική περιοχή Δροσιάς-Εδεσσας," *AEMT* 6 (1992) 195–202.

[235] Its only known parallels are Servia V in the Aliakmon valley, and the sites in the Grevena area.

[236] See N.G.L. Hammond, "The Via Egnatia in Western Macedonia," *ArchMak* 4 (1986) 247–55.

[237] The nearest contemporary sites known to date—Yannitsa to the east (see below), the sites of Kitrini Limni to the southwest, and those of the Bitola area to the northwest—lie already more than 50 km away. It must be remembered, however, that the sizable basins nearest to Drosia—Amyndaio and Florina—remain poorly explored; see K. Trantalidou, "Προϊστορικοί οικισμοί στις λεκάνες της Φλώρινας και του Αμυνταίου (δυτική Μακεδονία)," *ArchMak* 5 (1993) 1,593–622, where only one MN site, Monastiraki, is claimed for the area (p. 1,614). For the Bitola sites, see, e.g., D. Simoska and V. Sanev, *Prahistory* [sic] *in Central Pelagonia* (Bitola 1976), with catalogue and map.

[238] The most useful accounts are P. Chrysostomou, "Η topografία της βόρειας Βοττιαίας: Η αποικία της Πέλλας και οι χώρες τους," in *Μνήμη Δ. Λαζαρίδη: Πόλις και χώρα στην αρχαία Μακεδονία και Θράκη. Πρακτικά Αρχαιολογικού Συνεδρίου, Καβάλα, 1986* (Thessaloniki 1990), esp. 213–17; and Chrysostomou and P. Chrysostomou, "Νεολιθικές έρευνες στα Γιαννιτσά και στην περιοχή τους," *AEMT* 4 (1990) 169–77 (with remarks on the pattern of site distribution).

[239] P. Chrysostomou, "Ο νεολιθικός οικισμός των Γιαννιτσών Β," *AEMT* 3 (1989) 119–34; Chrysostomou, "Οι νεολιθικές έρευνες στην πόλη και την επαρχία Γιαννιτσών κατά το 1991," *AEMT* 5 (1991) 111–25; Chrysostomou, "Ο νεολιθικός οικισμός Γιαννιτσών Β: Νέα ανασκαφικά δεδομένα (1992–1993)," *AEMT* 7 (1993, in press); Chrysostomou and Chrysostomou (supra n. 238) 175–76. Archaeobotanical evidence is presented in S. Valamoti, "Γεωργικά προϊόντα από το νεολιθικό οικισμό Γιαννιτσά Β: Προκαταρκτική προσέγγιση μέσω των αρχαιοβοτανικών δεδομένων," *AEMT* 6 (1992) 177–84.

to 1 m thick, that clearly belong to the Early Neolithic. In one of the soundings into those EN deposits, Chrysostomou uncovered the remains of three superimposed structures, the lowest resting on the natural surface and being elliptical in plan, the others being rectangular. The small internal diameter of the elliptical structure appears to be ca. 4 m.[240] All three structures had walls built around frames of sturdy posts. The walls of the upper two structures rested in foundation trenches (50–60 cm wide, 40 cm deep), and the floor of one of them had been lined with a hard calcareous material.[241] From another sounding Chrysostomou reports a massive foundation, perhaps of a platform, constructed with fieldstones set in clay.[242]

The above are the earliest structural remains to be uncovered in northern Greece since the excavation of Nea Nikomedeia (fig. 2:11). An early date is suggested, first of all, by the associated pottery, which is characterized by an abundance of red-slipped, deep hemispherical bowls (often on ring bases, many with solid and linear patterns in white paint) and by small quantities of pots with impressed decoration.[243] Even more telling perhaps are a few "studs" ("earplugs"),[244] known to mark a very early ceramic Neolithic horizon from Iran to Thessaly.[245] A date around 6000 B.C. or earlier seems likely. A series of ^{14}C dates from the site is essential, and might also resolve remaining questions on the date of Nea Nikomedeia.[246]

The settlement stood near the coast of the Aegean,

ca. 25 km around the gulf from Nea Nikomedeia.[247] A third EN settlement appears to have been located between Yannitsa B and Nea Nikomedeia. Material of the Middle Neolithic is reported from yet another site, while later Neolithic components are claimed for more than 20 sites in the area.[248] It is worth remembering that one of the latter sites, Aravissos, is the source of a small hoard of gold objects (unfortunately, a "chance find") that have close parallels among the funerary furnishings from the cemetery of Varna (Bulgaria).[249]

Mandalo (fig. 2:12). A small mound (area under 0.5 ha, height 7–8 m), Mandalo is located on a narrow interfluve, ca. 40 masl, in the northwestern part of the Yannitsa terraces. A substantial portion of the mound (ca. 10%) was excavated from 1981 to 1988 by the University of Thessaloniki, and a group of 19 generally consistent radiocarbon dates now is available.[250] Two main periods of occupation have been distinguished, a "Late Neolithic" and an "Early Bronze Age," separated by an occupational hiatus of ca. 1,000 years. The "Late Neolithic" of the site spans the second half of the fifth millennium B.C. (12 useful dates, ca. 5700–5300 B.P.)—a time period that, according to the chronological framework we have adopted in this review (table 1), is part of the Final Neolithic. The ceramic and other parallels (e.g., implements for copper working, acrolithic figurines) also are with sites, in Greece and beyond, that belong to the Final Neolithic. If there is a discrepancy between the preliminary project reports and the pres-

[240] The correct scale of fig. 1 in Chrysostomou 1991 (supra n. 239) 112 is 1:50.

[241] Chrysostomou 1991 (supra n. 239) 111–13.

[242] Chrysostomou 1989 (supra n. 239) 122, and fig. 4 on p. 124 (correct scale is 1:30). Possible ditches are also reported in Chrysostomou 1993 (supra n. 239).

[243] Chrysostomou 1991 (supra n. 239) 113–15, figs. 6–12 and 14–15. The most noticeable difference from Nea Nikomedeia is the rarity, at Yannitsa, of red patterns on white background; cf. Rodden (supra n. 167) 284.

[244] One carved in marble and one in clay are reported in Chrysostomou 1989 (supra n. 239) 128 and fig. 7, lower left. They have rounded rather than (as from Nea Nikomedeia and the Near East) pointed tips, resembling therefore those from the first EN phases of Thessaly: D.R. Theocharis, *Η αυγή της θεσσαλικής προϊστορίας: Αρχή και πρώιμη εξέλιξη της Νεολιθικής* (Volos 1967) 82–84.

[245] E.g., R.J. Rodden, "Recent Discoveries from Prehistoric Macedonia: An Interim Report," *BalkSt* 5 (1964) 121; Theocharis (supra n. 244) found them most often in layers that he considered "preceramic" Neolithic.

[246] Demoule and Perlès (supra n. 115) 381. Cf. A. Whittle, *Neolithic Europe: A Survey* (Cambridge 1985) 41.

[247] Bintliff (supra n. 185) 256–57. Marine shell and fish vertebrae (unidentified) are common finds at Yannitsa B,

as at neighboring sites: Chrysostomou 1989 (supra n. 239) 121.

[248] Chrysostomou 1991 (supra n. 239) 117; Chrysostomou and Chrysostomou (supra n. 238) 173.

[249] Grammenos 109 and pl. 30.1–6; *Ancient Macedonia* (supra n. 209) 120–21; J. Makkay, "Comparisons of Some Chalcolithic and EBA Types from Anatolia, the Aegean and the SE Balkans," *ArchMak* 5 (1993) 821–23.

[250] For summary reports, see Kotsakis et al. (supra n. 188); A. Pilali-Papasteriou et al., "Νέος προϊστορικός οικισμός στο Μάνδαλο δυτικής Μακεδονίας," *ArchMak* 4 (1986) 451–65; A. Papanthimou and A. Papasteriou, "Ο προϊστορικός οικισμός στο Μάνδαλο: Νέα στοιχεία στην προϊστορία της Μακεδονίας," *ArchMak* 5 (1993) 1,207–16; A. Pilali-Papasteriou and A. Papaefthimiou-Papanthimou, "Νέες ανασκαφικές έρευνες στο Μάνδαλο δυτικής Μακεδονίας, 1985–1986," *Egnatia* 1 (1989) 15–28; Papaefthimiou-Papanthimou and Pilali-Papasteriou, "Η ανασκαφική έρευνα στο Μάνδαλο (1987–1990)," *Egnatia* 2 (1990) 411–21; and Papaefthimiou-Papanthimou and Pilali-Papasteriou, "Ο προϊστορικός οικισμός του Μανδάλου δυτικής Μακεδονίας μέσα στα πολιτιστικά πλαίσια της Υστερης Νεολιθικής," in *ΣΤ΄ Διεθνές Συμπόσιο Αιγαιακής Προϊστορίας* (Athens, in press).

ent account, then, it is strictly terminological, and need not be dwelt upon. No such discrepancy exists for the second period of occupation, the Early Bronze Age at the site, which covers the years 2900–2200 B.C. (five dates in stratigraphic order, ca. 4300–3850 B.P.).

In both periods, habitation structures were built with pisé, piled onto frames carried by large posts. White plasters and clays were commonly used for floors and hearths (cf. the FN phase at Megalo Nisi Galanis). House plans, however, have proven intractable, despite efforts[251] and the relatively broad exposures. Toward the end of the Neolithic occupation, a large wall made of fieldstones was erected. Almost 2.5 m wide and more than 1.4 m high, the wall may have ringed the settlement, or some part of it; alternatively, it may have formed a barrier on one side only. A second, outer wall is veiled in comparable uncertainties. Parts of those walls may still have been standing above ground 1,200 years later, during the EBA occupation.[252] A child burial in an urn also was part of the Neolithic settlement, and the remains of an adult were at some point reburied in a pit lined with mudbricks and a clay floor.[253]

To judge by the volume of debris (mainly building materials) accumulated in so small an area, habitation structures must have been tightly packed. Still, the community can never have numbered more than a few dozen people—that is, assuming that the community lived within the walled area, and not in houses dispersed in the plain below.[254] In the last instance, the walled site might even have been a chiefly estate. But the possibilities are many, and one must wait for the in-depth studies of the many classes of data.

One point is clear. Despite its small size, Mandalo cannot be thought of as a settlement marginal to the regional economic system, nor perhaps to the political one: inside the wall, a variety of productive activities took place, including the manufacture of textiles, perhaps at some scale;[255] and, toward the close of the fifth millennium, a coppersmith appears to have lived there.[256]

Makriyalos (fig. 2:10). The recently excavated Neolithic site of Makriyalos occupies a hill, ca. 1 km inland from the modern coast, in the rolling landscape of northern Pieria. Surface remains cover an area of ca. 50 ha. Of these, 6 ha were intensively excavated from November 1992 to June 1994, in one of the largest, best coordinated salvage efforts ever conducted in Greece.[257] The excavators have distinguished two components, with a minimum of spatial overlap. The earlier component is securely datable by the preponderance of characteristic black-burnished pots to the early part of the Late Neolithic. At that time the entire settlement was encircled by a system of ditches. Habitation structures within the circle were partly sunk into the ground; they survived as pits, often overlapping, in groups separated by extensive open spaces. One of those groups of pits was found littered with exceptionally large quantities of cultural residue, ranging from scraps of animal bone to complete figurines.

As the preliminary reports make clear, the concentric ditches—up to three—were maintained through substantial, continuous investments of labor. Dug and redug as a series of adjoining pits into the Tertiary substratum, the largest one reached in places a depth of 4 m, and widths exceeding 5 m. Subse-

---

251 See esp. K. Kotsakis, "Αποκατάσταση κατόψεων πασσαλόπηκτων οικημάτων με τη βοήθεια ηλεκτρονικού υπολογιστή στην ανασκαφή Μανδάλου, Δ. Μακεδονίας," in *Ειλαπίνη: Τόμος τιμητικός για τον καθηγητή Νικόλαο Πλάτωνα* (Iraklion 1987) 117–24.

252 The excavators found the upper parts of the walls amid EBA debris: Papanthimou and Papasteriou (supra n. 250) 1,208.

253 Pilali-Papasteriou et al. (supra n. 250) 455 and fig. 5.

254 A survey has identified the nearest contemporary ("LN") site ca. 3 km away: A. Papaefthimiou-Papanthimou and A. Pilali-Papasteriou, "Ανασκαφή στο Μάνδαλο (1988)," *AEMT* 2 (1988) 131.

255 Pilali-Papasteriou and Papaefthimiou-Papanthimou (supra n. 250) 24; A. Papaefthimiou-Papanthimou and A. Pilali-Papasteriou, "Ανασκαφές στο Μάνδαλο," *AEMT* 1 (1987) 177. Archaeobotanical evidence is presented in S. Valamoti, *The Plant Remains from the Late Neolithic/Early Bronze Age Site of Mandalo, Macedonia, Greece* (M.S. thesis, Univ. of Sheffield 1989).

256 For a well-dated clay crucible, see Papanthimou and Papasteriou (supra n. 250) 1,209 and fig. 2; also Pilali-

Papasteriou and Papaefthimiou-Papanthimou (supra n. 250) 24 for metal objects (needle, chisel, copper sheet, and ax) from both the fifth- and third-millennium deposits. Neutron activation analysis of obsidian has shown a Carpathian provenance; a Melian provenance was also indicated for one sample: V. Kilikoglou et al., "Carpathian Obsidian in Macedonia, Greece," *JAS* (in press). For chemical analyses of EBA pottery, see M. Kesisoglu, E. Mirtsou, and I. Stratis, "Μελέτη δειγμάτων κεραμεικής από το Μάνδαλο—Πρώιμη Εποχή Χαλκού," in Stratis et al. (supra n. 135) 161–68.

257 The project has been organized and overseen throughout by M. Pappa and M. Besios (ΙΣΤ' Ephoreia, Thessaloniki), and has involved a staff of ca. 150. See the informative reports of M. Pappa, "Νεολιθικός οικισμός Μακρυγιάλου," *AEMT* 7 (1993, in press), and of M. Besios and M. Pappa, "Νεολιθικός οικισμός Μακρυγιάλου," *AEMT* 8 (1994, in press). The excavated portion lay directly in the path of a new Thessaloniki–Athens railway. It has now been completely erased. Excavations were resumed in October 1995, for additional salvage work.

quently, a V-shaped ditch was dug through those irregular pits. Refuse from the settlement, including
human bone, frequently found its way into the ditch.
Not all of the accumulation, however, was due to accidents (e.g., collapsing ditch walls, or trapping of
loose debris from above): burials, both primary and
secondary, had intentionally been placed in the ditch.

Such evidence is intriguing. The ditches no doubt
served a variety of purposes, including defense
against raiders and against intrusions of the wild.
But the episodic nature of digging, the irregulari-
ties in proportions and sections, and, even more, the
episodes of partial infilling, at least with burials—
all of those also require explanation. One is re-
minded of remarks made by I. Hodder about ditches
at a British site: "the enclosure was less a thing than
a process. Ditches were continually being subdivided
and joined." For Hodder, the larger entity, the enclosure in this case, was the product of "segmented
labour activities" involving, among other things, competition between the social segments responsible for
the work.[258] In the enclosure of Makriyalos too, one
is tempted to see a process as much as a thing: the
ditches may well have constituted a field of conten-
tions not only between a human community and nature, but also among the social units—kin groups
or other—making up the community. Such a hypothesis deserves exploration.

The later component at Makriyalos yielded a very
high proportion—thus far unique outside Thessaly—
of "classical Dimini" ceramics, with painted as well
as incised patterns. The new settlement occupied
a smaller area, adjacent to that occupied before. The
density of structures in the inhabited space was
higher, but appears to have varied through time. Most
structures were, again, partly sunk into the soft
ground. They were found as roughly circular pits
of various depths and diameters, many preserving
evidence for superstructures supported on frames
of posts. One of the deepest pits was fitted with an
earthen staircase, and had served as storage space;

large jars had once stood on its floor. Gravel pavements outside the large pits had ovens built on them,
while small pits served as depositories—some for
seashell—or perhaps as cooking facilities.[259] In addition to the circular, partly subterranean structures,
a number of rectangular, "megaroid" buildings with
apsidal ends stood above ground. They appear to
form a coherent pattern, and possibly belong to a
distinct subphase. An infant cremation burial, bones
in a small urn, was also found within the settled area,
while several inhumations in pits were made at one
point beyond the edge of the inhabited area. Finally,
this settlement too, or some part of it, appears to
have been bounded or divided by ditches.

The salvage excavation of Makriyalos is a landmark, opening a new, vast potential for research into
Neolithic societies in Greece, thanks not only to the
size of the area exposed, but also to the fine grain
of observation. The contexts recovered—salvaged,
indeed—are immensely rich.[260] Neolithic settlements that spread over hill slopes, with houses separated by ample open spaces, have been known from
surface surveys in Macedonia since the 1970s.[261]
They have held the promise of large exposures, and
of contexts modified only by natural forces and agriculture, but not by repeated, long-term habitation.
Makriyalos, the first such settlement to be extensively
excavated, stands up to those promises. The presence, side by side, of two distinct components is also
interesting for at least two reasons: it provides a
unique basis for a comparative approach to the
phases of the local Neolithic; and it also hints at discontinuities in the habitation of prehistoric sites in
Greece—discontinuities one suspects, but cannot
easily document, while excavating mound sites.

Several other sites, contemporary with Makriyalos
and later, have been discovered in northern Pieria
in recent years, and some have been excavated.[262]

Mt. Olympos. Spathes (fig. 2:9), a 13th–12th century B.C. cemetery, with finds that might be equally at
home in Mycenaean Thessaly, was excavated in 1985–

[258] I. Hodder, "The Haddenham Causewayed Enclosure
—A Hermeneutic Circle," in Hodder, *Theory and Practice
in Archaeology* (London 1992) 232–33.

[259] Pits found filled with ashes may, but need not, be
places where fires were lit. They can also be places where
fires were put out—safe depositories for embers still burning, or storage for the resulting, highly useful ashes. The
issue becomes critical when one attempts to determine
whether hearths were indoors or outdoors, and whether,
therefore, food consumption involved hospitality and reciprocity or was a sign of emerging redistribution; e.g., Halstead 1989, 74–76; Halstead 1994, 206–207.

[260] The finds of Makriyalos display an incomparably

large variety in materials and types, including obsidian
and stones from distant sources, *Spondylus* shell as finished
ornaments and raw material, and several copper artifacts.

[261] See Kotsakis (supra n. 15) 127–28.

[262] E.g., K. Soueref, *ArchDelt* 41 B´ (1986) 141–42; Grammenos 140–42. M. Besios, "Ανασκαφές στη Β. Πιερία," *AEMT*
8 (1994, in press) where the rescue excavation of a LBA
cist grave cemetery near Korinos (15 single-burial graves)
is reported. Mycenaean pottery, gold jewelry, and a marble
Early Cycladic vessel were among the finds. Rubbish pits
were the only remains of the eroded and destroyed Bronze
Age settlement, and their contents included a stemmed
bowl in Gray Minyan fabric and Mycenaean pottery.

1987 by E. Poulaki-Pantermali (IΣΤ' Ephoreia).[263] Located on a steep, westward slope of Mt. Olympos, at 1,000–1,100 masl, the site overlooks a major high pass between Thessaly and Macedonia. No settlements are known in the area, but the valley floor below, 800–900 masl, has some potential for garden farming and tree orchards, and an intensive survey would be essential. In any case, the placing of the cemetery on a high slope with a broad horizon is noteworthy (though far from unique; see, e.g., above, the tumuli of Mt. Vermio).

The graves—34 excavated in an area of ca. 0.2 ha— were arranged in rows. The shafts, many of them exceeding 2 m in length, were carefully dressed and roofed with heavy slabs, and were sealed from above with red earth. They had been repeatedly opened for new burials, including children. The dead were often buried with a carved sealstone on their chests, and with personal and other items—jewelry, pots, bronze weapons, and some biconical and conical "buttons." An unspecified number of those items are of readily recognizable Mycenaean types (e.g., alabastra, both rounded and straight-sided, a juglet, two swords), and/or are objects usually found in graves in "Mycenaeanized" provinces (e.g., strings of glass paste and amber beads, the former with volute designs). The remains of another cemetery with comparable graves and furnishings have also been found at some distance along the same mountain pass.[264] As a consequence of those discoveries, the "border/ frontier boundary" of Mycenaean Thessaly in the area of Mt. Olympos may have to be drawn a little further west than Feuer drew it in 1983.[265] But, until a detailed publication of the grave contents appears, it is impossible to proceed with a more exacting interpretation. Did, for example, the graves belong to military personnel, dispatched by one of Thessaly's chiefs to guard a crossover into his territory? Or did they belong to a "wild bunch"—mountain bandits, living off booty from traffic through the pass? Lumbering may also have been carried out in the area, the cemetery being located at the altitude where oaks give way to a dense conifer forest (see "Environmental Change" above).

New Questions

The maps of Neolithic and Bronze Age site distributions in western Macedonia are rapidly being filled. Any attempt to analyze and interpret the emerging patterns, however, is compromised by the virtual absence of intensive surveys, especially of the kind that employ controlled (probability) sampling, and of geomorphological research. Only a few, tiny areas have undergone intensive surface survey (e.g., segments of the Aliakmon riverine zone; parts of the western watershed of Mt. Vermio). Geomorphic change, moreover, while evident to the trained eye in many areas, and also gleaned from the pollen record,[266] is nowhere adequately dated, nor are its magnitude and complexities documented by reference to quantified field data.

Take as an example the Kitrini Limni basin. In the center of the basin floor,[267] the surface on which some of the Neolithic settlements were established is today buried under a lacustrine clay at least 1 m thick. In theory, many small, especially EN, sites may lie under that deposit. The eastern quarter of the basin floor, on the other hand, is covered by large, coalescent alluvial fans, in part postdating the prehistoric occupation. What significance can one attach to the absence of prehistoric sites in that area? If none, and if no significance can be attached to the presence of only one confirmed EN site in the basin, how can one speak, for example, of the process of Neolithic colonization and the spread of agriculture in the basin?

In brief, the list of what one can infer from site distributions in western Macedonia today is considerably shorter than the list of what one should not attempt to infer. Let us focus on a few, specific, positive points, those that might pose challenges to established views, or reinforce them. It appears, for example, that for every site with an EN and/or MN (roughly 6500–5400 B.C.) component identified in recent years, two to three sites with later Neolithic (LN and/or FN) components have been identified.[268] Even when we consider the possibility that the later phases comprise a longer period of time than the earlier ones (table 1), that statistic still seems to lend

[263] E. Poulaki-Pantermali, "Ὄλυμπος 2," in Ἀμητός (supra n. 222) 706–708; Poulaki-Pantermali, "Ἀνασκαφή Ἀγ. Δημητρίου Ὀλύμπου," AEMT 1 (1987) 201–208; E. Pantermali, ArchDelt 40 B' (1985) 243; ArchDelt 41 B' (1986) 140–41; and ArchDelt 42 B' (1987) 363–64.

[264] Pantermali 1987 (supra n. 263); Poulaki-Pantermali, in AEMT (supra n. 263) 203–204. For references to other, old and new, Mycenaean finds from Mt. Olympos, see Poulaki-Pantermali, in Ἀμητός (supra n. 263) 705–706, 711–12; and Pantermali 1985 (supra n. 263) 240–41.

[265] Feuer 199.
[266] See also Savina (supra n. 217).
[267] Probability sampling was employed here, but it was limited to on-site survey, and to transects between some of the sites.
[268] In all, 30 late seventh/early sixth millennium (EN and/or MN) sites have to date been confirmed in western Macedonia, 15 of them in the Grevena area, five in the Aliakmon riverine zone, four in Kitrini Limni, four in the coastal plain, Monastiraki (supra n. 237), and Drosia.

support to the idea of a "Late Neolithic expansion,"[269] at the same time as it calls some critical elements of that idea into question. First of all, an increase of population in the later Neolithic phases (noted by many for several circum-Aegean areas) is beyond dispute; not only are there more LN and FN sites, but some of them (e.g., Megalo Nisi Galanis, and other sites in Kitrini Limni) are, by Aegean standards, massive. But that pattern does not seem to hold for every river valley and basin, as the evidence produced especially by the Grevena survey suggests. Furthermore, speculation that Greek Macedonia was virtually empty for the period 6500–5400 B.C. appears to have been rash.[270] The recent discoveries, accidental and systematic, of EN and MN sites in five different parts of western Macedonia strongly suggest that we have yet to learn a good deal about the late seventh and early sixth millennia B.C.

In almost all five areas (except, perhaps, Grevena), the confirmed early sites are located at, or very near, the lowest points of the landscape—that is, in proximity to groundwater or streams. A dispersal to a variety of locations, including locations in elevated, dry land (e.g., terraces north of the Aliakmon), is noticeable for the later sixth millennium B.C. The significance of that pattern—far from unique to western Macedonia[271]—has yet to be fully understood. The dispersal, for example, cannot be seen as strictly the result of population pressure. Nor is it obligatory to see locations in relatively dry land (e.g., on terraces) as "agriculturally marginal": the marginality in question depends as much on the goals of agricultural production as on pedology and rainfall.[272] Finally, the suggestion that farming in dry parts of the landscape was made possible by the development of the ard meets several difficulties, both evidential and theoretical.[273] In short, the Late Neo-

lithic expansion remains a fascinating issue, in need of field and analytical investigations.

Most remarkable is the occasional presence of later Neolithic material in sites that cannot have been selected for their farming potential.[274] The strategic location of Ag. Eleftherios (near Kitrini Limni) with regard to an important trail was noted earlier, but it is impossible to specify the function of the site in the regional network. The significance of such sites is that they hint at dimensions of Neolithic societies systematically marginalized in our analyses. In particular, the view of the Neolithic populations of mainland Greece as sedentary farmers, peaceful, hospitable, prudent, and devoted to nothing but production,[275] has detracted attention from the potential those "farmers" had for practicing mobility. When mobility is discussed, it is primarily in the context of orderly modes of exchange.[276] Yet practices of mobility also include common forms of aggression and tactics of warfare—raids, ambushes, cunning embassies, misleading footprints. We should be paying more attention to all the precautions taken against such dangerous traffic, from ditches and walls around settlements to means of territorial surveillance and of intelligence about distant places.[277] Rather than being skirted, the forms of aggression should be treated as central aspects of Neolithic political economies; they appear to us to contribute as much to the formation of value (especially "prestige" value) as "elite" pots and specialist craftsmen.

It is in the Bronze Age, however, that "high places," affording large views and, hence, possibilities for extended territorial surveillance, become occupied with some regularity (e.g., Megali Rahi, at Aiani, fig. 2:5; Neraida hill, fig. 2:7; and sites in the Grevena area). Whatever complex social transformation brings the new pattern about,[278] it is not peculiar to Mace-

---

[269] E.g., Demoule and Perlès (supra n. 115) 398; cf. Halstead 1994, 200 and passim.

[270] Demoule (supra n. 169); cf. Perlès (supra n. 136) 645–46.

[271] E.g., A. Sherratt, "Water, Soil and Seasonality in Early Cereal Cultivation," *WorldArch* 11 (1980) 313–30.

[272] As has been long recognized; for references and a relevant model, see M. Fotiadis, *Economy, Ecology and Settlement among Subsistence Farmers in the Serres Basin, Northeastern Greece, 5000–1000 B.C.* (Diss. Indiana Univ. 1985) 66–95. The interesting questions raised by A. Fleming, "Landscape Archaeology, Prehistory, and Rural Studies," *Rural History* 1 (1990) 11–13 are also pertinent.

[273] Fotiadis (supra n. 272), esp. 151–53.

[274] E.g., Rodohori Cave, F. Petsas, *ArchDelt* 19 B′ (1964) 356–59.

[275] In fact, dedicated to overproduction: e.g., Halstead

1989, 73–75; and Halstead 1994, 202, 206–207. Cf. Fotiadis (supra n. 1) 156; and Fotiadis (supra n. 168) esp. 68–76.

[276] Movement of households or villages at times of crop failure also is an attractive possibility: Halstead 1989, 73–75.

[277] For the frequency of aggression and warfare among supposedly peaceful Neolithic folk, see L.H. Keeley, *War before Civilization: The Myth of the Peaceful Savage* (New York 1996).

[278] For an interpretation that does not invoke an increase in warfare but considers changes in agricultural technology, see M. Fotiadis, "Settlement and Production in the Bronze Age of North Eastern Greece," *International Thracian Conference: The Bronze Age in the Thracian Lands and Beyond* (Milan 1986) 91–92. Cf. Dickinson (supra n. 159) 80–81.

donia, for the pattern is evident over much of Europe, from the Peloponnese to western Germany.[279] That is not to suggest that the processes that generated Mycenae of the Shaft Graves and the Bronze Age acropolises of western Macedonia differed merely in scale. The observation does, however, cast doubt on the common view that life in Bronze Age western Macedonia continued in isolation, becoming an impoverished version of Stone Age manners, with nothing socially important happening (except invasions).[280] There are important questions to be asked and investigated in the field: are the province's Bronze Age acropolis sites the marks of a new political economy and organization? Were they the central places (in the "Assiros" or any other model)[281] of a regional network of settlements yet to be systematically recorded? Were they also lookouts, signaling stations, or cult places? Speculation will not substitute for evidence, which in some cases (e.g., Neraida) has been destroyed.

CENTRAL MACEDONIA

Environmental Change

Pollen data from regions adjacent to central Macedonia (the area between the Axios and Strymon rivers, fig. 2) indicate a continuous expansion of deciduous forest during the early Holocene, both in the plains and the mountains, with a peak around 8000–7000 B.P. Forest expansion was succeeded by a decline, which at Philippoi is dated to 3500 B.P. and at Yannitsa to 4500 B.P., and may be partly attributable to human activity. Evidence for extensive clearing in the lowlands, possibly dating from the end of the second or beginning of the first millennium B.C., also comes from the mouth of the Strymon. The palynological evidence from the Yannitsa

plain indicates generally unstable conditions related to successive inundations and sedimentations of the area, between 8500 and 7000 B.P.[282] Geomorphological study in the Axios valley has shown that a marine transgression connected to the sea-level rise after 8000 B.C. culminated around 4000 B.C., creating a deep gulf and areas of brackish water. During the Bronze Age the settlement of Kastanas was on an island, but successive alluviations by the Axios and episodes of land rise resulted in the silting of the gulf by 200 B.C.[283] Environmental research has not confirmed any substantial changes in the climate during the last 8,000 years, although regional variation cannot be excluded.[284]

Material Sequence and Archaeological Phases

In contrast to eastern Macedonia, secure series of stratified ^{14}C dates are generally lacking from central Macedonia, with the exception of the Bronze Age sites of Kastanas and Assiros. The chronology of earlier periods is of necessity relative, and relies on comparisons of the local ceramic sequences with those of eastern Macedonia and the Balkans, and occasionally with Thessaly. To some extent, comparisons with other regions have resulted in a confusing terminology: the earliest levels are designated "Middle Neolithic" in Balkan terms but "Late Neolithic" according to Thessalian and southern Greek terminology. The same holds true for the "Chalcolithic" and "Final Neolithic."[285] In the discussion that follows we use the Aegean terminology.

The earliest deposits in the region, dating to the end of the Middle Neolithic or beginning of the Late Neolithic, come from a small excavation at Vasilika, where a specific class of painted pottery has been related to the Thessalian MN painted styles.[286] In

[279] For the complexities of the transformation in Central Europe, see S. Shennan, "Settlement and Social Change in Central Europe 3500–1500 B.C.," *Journal of World Prehistory* 7 (1993) 121–61.

[280] See, e.g., the evocative prose of Borza (supra n. 158) 72: "the dwellers in Macedonia continued to live in scattered unwalled villages, content—as far as we know—to exploit on a local level the rich natural resources of their hills and plains." Cf. Heurtley (supra n. 150) 132. Borza is contrasting Macedonia with the Mycenaean Bronze Age; that should serve as a good example of the construction of Macedonia's Otherness, noted earlier.

[281] For the Assiros model, see below.

[282] Yannitsa: Bottema (supra n. 171) 141–48, 159, 162–66; Strymon mouth: P. Morrison, *Holocene Landscape Evolution of the Langadas Basin, Macedonia: An Approach to the Evaluation of the Soil Resource for Prehistoric Settlement* (Diss. Univ. of Birmingham 1993) 83–85, fig. 3.3, where otherwise un-

published information is presented; Philippoi: J. Turner and J.R.A. Greig, "Vegetational History," in *Sitagroi* 45–54, with references to earlier work; Willis (supra n. 142) 784–85, table 8. The only pollen diagram from central Macedonia comes from Lake Volvi and is dated to the historical period. Bottema (supra n. 142) 265–66.

[283] Schulz (supra n. 185) 375–93.

[284] Turner and Greig (supra n. 282) 51; Morrison (supra n. 282) 75–76, 90.

[285] See Demoule (supra n. 189) table 1, which synchronizes cultures in "Aegean" (left) and "Balkan" (right) terms; Coleman 247–79.

[286] Grammenos 46–58, 91. For a surface find of MN "Thessalian" sherds found at Mesimeriani Toumba, see R.C.S. Felsch, "Bericht über neolithische Scherben aus Mesimeriani," in F. Schachermeyr, *Die ägäische Frühzeit* I: *Die vormykenischen Perioden* (Vienna 1976) 293–97.

terms of absolute chronology, however, two ^{14}C dates place MN Vasilika at around 5500 B.C.—rather early in comparison to the final Middle Neolithic of Thessaly.[287] Based on the evidence from Vasilika, the LN sequence of central Macedonia has affinities with "Sitagroi II" and "Sitagroi III," but this observation needs further corroboration. Deposits that could be securely assigned to the Final Neolithic are difficult to define.[288]

Kastanas remains the only site with a stratified sequence for the third millennium, yet the dearth of material in the earliest four building phases and the clustering of three ^{14}C dates in the later phases, between 2000 and 1800 B.C., preclude estimation of the time span represented by the site's stratigraphic sequence.[289] The chronology of the Early Bronze Age has to rely, therefore, on general ceramic affinities with adjacent areas, and firm definition of subphases is still wanting. Stratified deposits with ceramic affinities to the earlier MBA phases in Argissa Magoula have been found at Kastanas but the later part of the Middle Bronze Age and the early Late Bronze Age, equivalent to the prepalatial Late Bronze Age in central and southern Greece, are still poorly documented. Recently excavated material from Toroni, Ayios Mamas, and Toumba Thessalonikis promises to fill this gap.[290] The later LBA stratigraphy is more adequately recorded at Kastanas, Assiros, and Toumba Thessalonikis. Mycenaean pottery of LH IIIA, IIIB, and IIIC styles in LBA stratified deposits has been used to establish a chronological scheme. Four ^{14}C dates from the latest LBA phases at Assiros are fairly consistent and conform to the conventional chronology for the beginning of LH IIIC, around 1200. A long series from Kastanas offers dates around the 13th century B.C. for levels with LH IIIB pottery, but the late 13th-century date for levels with LH IIIC and Protogeometric pottery seems too high.[291]

Recent Projects

The majority of prehistoric sites in central Macedonia were first systematically described by D.H. French in the 1960s. Additional sites have been identified by the ΙΣΤ′ Ephoreia, and the number has risen to 220.[292] The temporal distribution of sites offers a rough account of the general trends of settlement. From the Late Neolithic to the Early Bronze Age a rise in density is observable. The increase in number of sites in the later Bronze Age is accompanied by a decrease in the size of those sites. On present evidence, therefore, a process of nucleation cannot be documented in central Macedonia, in contrast to Thessaly.[293] Most inventoried sites are tells, but a number of flat and inconspicuous Neolithic sites have recently been identified. Some of these are huge and reach dozens of hectares.[294]

[287] Bln-3185 (6630 ± 50 B.P., 5580–5480 B.C.) and Bln-3186 (6650 ± 50 B.P., 5585–5480 B.C.). See D.V. Grammenos, *Νεολιθικά θέματα από τη Μακεδονία και την ευρύτερη περιοχή* (Athens, in press).

[288] Grammenos 64–84. For a description of LN ceramics from central Macedonia, see Aslanis (supra n. 12) 179–89, 206–209. For the FN, see Treuil (supra n. 64) 90–93; J.-P. Demoule, "Les recherches récentes en Grèce septentrionale et les problèmes chronologiques et régionaux des cultures à céramique au graphite," in Lichardus (supra n. 63) 232; also Demoule, "La transition du Néolithique au Bronze Ancien dans le nord de l'Egée: Les données de Dikili Tash," in Maniatis (supra n. 188) 687–96.

[289] I. Aslanis, *Kastanas: Ausgrabungen in einem Siedlungshügel der Bronze- und Eisenzeit Makedoniens, 1975–1979: Die frühbronzezeitlichen Funde und Befunde* (Prähistorische Archäologie in Südosteuropa 4, Berlin 1985) 317–20. See also H. Willkomm, "Radiokohlenstoffdatierungen des Siedlungshügels Kastanas," in *Kastanas* 409–10.

[290] Aslanis (supra n. 289) 317–20; A. Cambitoglou and J.K. Papadopoulos, "Excavations at Torone, 1989," *MediterArch* 4 (1991) 162–67, where a stratigraphic sequence covering the EBA to early LBA, perhaps with regional characteristics, is summarily presented; ^{14}C dates are forthcoming. For Toumba Thessalonikis, see below. For Ayios Mamas, see B. Hänsel, "Erste Vorstellung eines neuen Projektes: Agios Mamas/Olynth," *AEMT* 7 (1993, in press).

[291] Assiros: *Radiocarbon* 24 (1982) 243–44; Kastanas: Willkomm (supra n. 289) 395–411. For discussion, see P. Warren and V. Hankey, *Aegean Bronze Age Chronology* (Bristol 1989) 159, n. 39; S.W. Manning and B. Weninger, "A Light in the Dark: Archaeological Wiggle Matching and the Absolute Chronology of the Close of the Aegean Late Bronze Age," *Antiquity* 66 (1992) 639–50. For PG-style pottery, see B. Hänsel, "Ergebnisse der Grabungen bei Kastanas in Zentralmakedonien 1975–1978," *JRGZM* 26 (1979) 189–90; and C. Podzuweit, "Spätmykenische Keramik von Kastanas," *JRGZM* 26 (1979) 204.

[292] D.H. French, *Index of Prehistoric Sites in Central Macedonia* (unpublished manuscript, Thessaloniki 1967); D.V. Grammenos and M. Bessios, "Από τους προϊστορικούς οικισμούς της κεντρικής Μακεδονίας, Θεσσαλονίκη 1992," in preparation. Also Grammenos (supra n. 287). For a list of Neolithic sites from central and eastern Macedonia, see Grammenos, "Διάγραμμα των χρονικών της νεολιθικής έρευνας στη νότια Βαλκανική από το 1984 κ.εξ.," *Μακεδονικά* 28 (1992) 263–65.

[293] S. Andreou and K. Kotsakis, "Διαστάσεις του χώρου στην κεντρική Μακεδονία: Αποτύπωση της ενδοκοινοτικής και διακοινοτικής χωροοργάνωσης," in *Αμητός* (supra n. 222) 57–86.

[294] Grammenos 30–31, 136–43; Andreou and Kotsakis (supra n. 293) 70–77, 82–84. For eastern Macedonia, see Fotiadis (supra n. 272) 407; Grammenos 104.

Langadas basin. Intensive survey since 1986 in the western Langadas basin has investigated the pattern of prehistoric human activity.[295] The tectonic basin is dominated by two lakes, remnants of a larger single lake that contracted during the Early and Middle Quaternary. Neolithic and Bronze Age sites are distributed unequally across the recent alluvium, the alluvial fans of the lower Pleistocene terrace, the heavier soils of the upper Pleistocene terrace, and further, on the surrounding mountains, where arable land was scarce, but not altogether unavailable. Two LN sites located in areas dominated by heavy, water-retentive soils are large and flat, reaching 30 ha. It has been suggested that their size is primarily due to a shifting, unrestricted occupation, interspersed with cultivated land.[296] Why this pattern was preferred to the more restricted habitation characteristic of tells is not immediately apparent. It may be suggested tentatively that proximity of habitation and fields facilitated the intensive cultivation of the land, compensating for the low workability of the heavy soil. In an area of relative aridity, such as that around Langadas, the productivity of this water-retentive soil in conditions of drought would be a vital advantage and would justify the extra labor required. Another possibility, to be explored in the future, is that the sites were seasonally occupied. The problem of aridity, however, was probably resolved in a different way in the case of Kavallari (fig. 2:19) and other Neolithic sites located near the lakes, in areas that were regularly inundated.[297]

Neither of the flat, extended sites continued to be occupied in the Bronze Age. The number of sites declines generally in the Early Bronze Age, but during the Late Bronze Age, habitation becomes increasingly more dense, limited to small, steep-sided tells and to sites on hill summits. Traces of perimeter walls are preserved in some cases, and can be assumed in others, but their function, whether protective or retaining or both, cannot be confirmed. New sites in high places with an unrestricted view of the surrounding landscape were established at the end of the period and continued to be occupied into the Early Iron Age. The shift to settlement near a greater variety of soils and landscapes denotes an emphasis on diversified production, which is also detectable in the impressive archaeobotanical evidence from Assiros.[298] The major settlements of Langadas developed on the alluvial fans of the lower terraces. One of these, Assiros, possibly evolved during the Late Bronze Age into a regional economic center.

Assiros (fig. 2:17). The 14-m-high tell of Assiros lies in the western part of the Langadas basin, and was extensively excavated in 1975–1979 and 1986–1989. Nine building phases were identified on the top, of which phases 9–5 cover the later Late Bronze Age. The phases are dated by the occurrence of LH III pottery, with LH IIIA2 in phase 9 and continuing with LH IIIC in phases 7–5. Earlier deposits were dug on a limited scale on the side of the mound, providing a tentative date for the beginning of occupation in the late Middle Bronze Age.[299]

A massive earthen bank and a casemate wall, repeatedly reconstructed at the edge, supported the buildings inside, and, according to the excavator, defended the site.[300] The layout of the settlement remained more or less stable through the successive rebuildings. Parallel narrow alleys separated elon-

[295] K. Kotsakis, "The Langadas Basin Intensive Survey. First Preliminary Report: The 1986 Season," *Egnatia* 1 (1989) 3–14; Kotsakis, "Το πρόγραμμα της εντατικής επιφανειακής έρευνας Λαγκαδά: Δεύτερη περίοδος 1987," *Egnatia* 2 (1990) 175–86; S. Andreou and Kotsakis, "Prehistoric Rural Communities in Perspective: The Langadas Survey Project," in P.N. Doukellis and L.G. Mendoni eds., *Structures rurales et sociétés antiques. Actes du colloque de Corfou, 14–16 mai 1992* (Centre de recherches d'histoire ancienne 126, Annales littéraires de l'Université de Besançon, Paris 1994) 17–25; Kotsakis and Andreou, "Επιφανειακή έρευνα Λαγκαδά: Περίοδος 1992," *AEMT* 6 (1992) 349–56.

[296] Andreou and Kotsakis (supra n. 293) 82–84; Andreou and Kotsakis (supra n. 295) 19–20. The pattern of extended habitation is similar to that of the well-known flat, extended sites from the Balkans. See R. Tringham and D. Krstić eds., *Selevac: A Neolithic Village in Yugoslavia* (Los Angeles 1990) 585–89; A. McPherron and D. Srejović, *Divostin* (Pittsburgh 1988) 35–142, 469–89; J.C. Chapman, "The Early Balkan Village," in S. Bökönyi ed., *Neolithic of Southeastern Europe and Its Near Eastern Connections* (Varia archaeologica hungarica 2, Budapest 1989) 38–40. For an inter-

pretation of the Macedonian sites as large "proto-urban" centers, see Grammenos 102; Grammenos (supra n. 140); Grammenos (supra n. 292) 255; Grammenos (supra n. 287). For the classification of soils, see Morrison (supra n. 282) 30–34.

[297] Morrison (supra n. 282) 244–46.

[298] G. Jones et al., "Crop Storage at Assiros," *Scientific American* 254:3 (1986) 87; Jones, "Agricultural Practice in Greek Prehistory," *BSA* 82 (1987) 121.

[299] For preliminary reports, see K.A. Wardle, "Excavations at Assiros 1975–9," *BSA* 75 (1980) 229–65; *BSA* 82 (1987) 313–29; *BSA* 83 (1988) 375–87; and *BSA* 84 (1989) 447–63. Also Wardle, "Assiros: A Macedonian Settlement of the Late Bronze and Early Iron Age," in *ArchMak* 3 (1983) 291–305. For the MBA phase of the site, see Wardle, "Mycenaean Trade and Influence in Northern Greece," in C.W. Zerner, P.C. Zerner, and J. Winder eds., *Wace and Blegen: Pottery as Evidence for Trade in the Aegean Bronze Age, 1939–1989* (Amsterdam 1993) 121. Phases 4–1 belong to the Early Iron Age.

[300] Wardle 1980 (supra n. 299) 236–39; Wardle 1988 (supra n. 299) 384.

gated blocks of rooms, which changed in their internal arrangement and function from one phase to the next. The buildings had mudbrick walls with a frame of posts. A destruction by fire at the end of phase 9 preserved an impressive quantity and variety of charred seeds, stored in six storerooms occupying half the excavated area. The storerooms were crowded with pithoi, large baskets, and smaller clay containers. The quantity and pattern of storage suggested a communal storeroom, in contrast to the next two phases (7 and 6) of the Late Bronze Age, which have been more extensively excavated, and date to the 12th century. Storage facilities in these phases were dispersed throughout the settlement, and storage appears to have been a more private affair than previously.[301] The settlement consisted of at least four large, elongated complexes with rectangular rooms separated by narrow streets. Open and roofed spaces were found in each complex, equipped with ovens, hearths, occasional pithoi, and other food-processing and storage facilities. The final LBA phase (5) shows few changes in the alignment and internal arrangement of the buildings. The smaller amount of pottery, particularly of Mycenaean type, precludes close dating.[302]

Handmade pottery with a limited variety of wares and shapes, mainly plain burnished ware, comprises the overwhelming majority of the finds at Assiros, as at all other Bronze Age sites in Macedonia. Matt-painted and incised vessels with white or pink fill or incrustation are a small portion of the ceramic repertoire and indicate a specialized production on a small scale. Mycenaean ceramics appear with increasing frequency, but remain, until the end of the Bronze Age, a very small fraction of the assemblages. Small shapes predominate, indicating that Mycenaean vases probably reached Assiros as "luxuries."[303]

Excavations at Assiros offer a wealth of information on an inland LBA settlement in central Macedonia, the result of the intensive strategy employed, with several aspects of prehistoric life and different types of evidence investigated. During the 13th and 14th centuries (phases 8 and 9), Assiros in all probability acquired a principal position in the regional economic structure, becoming the focus of agricultural storage, which exceeded the needs of this settlement. It has been suggested that a hierarchical political structure, analogous to that of the southern Greek palaces, had been established in central Macedonia by that time.[304] The bioarchaeological finds, however, along with the rest of the archaeological evidence, do not support a specialized and extensive agriculture, nor a centralized economy. Rather, they can be better understood in the context of a small-scale, diversified, intensive farming and animal husbandry regime.[305] Storage at Assiros, therefore, may not represent mobilization of surplus to serve an elite controlling production and exchange, but a reserve against the unpredictabilities of a subsistence economy. Assiros could have been the focal point of a regional settlement network with a hierarchical structure, but a small-scale and unstable network very different from the contemporary polities of Mycenaean Greece.[306] The regional evidence helps to clarify further the picture: in the western Langadas basin, the nearby tell of Perivolaki

---

[301] The storerooms of Assiros offered a wealth of information on storage techniques, crop-processing methods, and farming practices. The stored crops included einkorn, broomcorn, millet, bitter vetch, macaroni wheat, and hulled barley (pure crops), and emmer and spelt (a mixed crop). Flax, lentils, and unrecognizable seeds have also been found. See Jones (supra n. 298) 117–23; and Wardle 1989 (supra n. 299) 462.

[302] Wardle 1989 (supra n. 299) 455.

[303] For a discussion of pottery and other finds from the site, see Wardle 1980 (supra n. 299) 244–53. For an excellent summary of LBA Macedonian ceramics based on the sample from Assiros, see Wardle 1993 (supra n. 299) 121–24, 127–29, 130–33, with reference to previous work. According to macroscopic observations and some chemical analyses, Mycenaean-style pottery at Assiros falls into three broad groups, designated by Wardle as "local," "imports" from centers of the southern mainland, and "provincial," a non-homogeneous group. Coastal central Macedonia has been tentatively suggested as one of the sources for the last group. The earliest "local" Mycenaean sherd in Assiros was found in phase 9. By phases 7 and 6, "local" and "provincial" pottery predominated in the Mycenaean pottery

assemblages. Despite their long coexistence, the handmade and Mycenaean (wheelmade) wares apparently stem from two independent manufacturing traditions. Only occasionally did other Mycenaean objects find their way to Assiros, see, e.g., Wardle 1980 (supra n. 299) 253. For chemical analyses, see Jones (supra n. 149) 108–112, 494.

[304] Wardle 1989 (supra n. 299) 462; Wardle 1993 (supra n. 299) 127.

[305] G. Jones, "Weed Phytosociology and Crop Husbandry: Identifying a Contrast between Ancient and Modern Practice," *Review of Palaeobotany and Palynology* 73 (1992) 141–42; Halstead 1994, 202, 206, 209.

[306] Andreou and Kotsakis (supra n. 295) 21; S. Andreou and K. Kotsakis, "'Μυκηναϊκή παρουσία' και 'Μυκηναϊκή περιφέρεια': Η Τούμπα της Θεσσαλονίκης, μια θέση της Εποχής του Χαλκού στη Μακεδονία," forthcoming in *Η περιφέρεια* (supra n. 53). For a general discussion of settlement hierarchical networks in central Macedonia, see Kotsakis and Andreou, "Ιεραρχική οργάνωση στην κεντρική Μακεδονία στην Εποχή του Χαλκού," in *The Prehistoric Aegean and Its Relations to Adjacent Areas. Proceedings of the Sixth International Colloquium on Aegean Prehistory* (Athens, in press).

(fig. 2:18, Saratse) competes in size and construction with Assiros, indicating that the hierarchical system had more than one center in the basin, either contemporaneous or succeeding each other. This picture of small-scale networks is corroborated by the evidence from Toumba in Thessaloniki (see below).

Kastanas (fig. 2:16). Four seasons of excavation at Kastanas, a 14-m-high mound on the left bank of the Axios River, explored parts of another long-lasting Bronze Age and Iron Age settlement. The site, an island during the Bronze Age, was located near a coast occupied by several tells, the most imposing of which is the well-known mound of Axiochori (Vardaroftsa).[307]

The excavation revealed a deep stratigraphy with Bronze Age and Iron Age levels.[308] The Bronze Age was separated into 17 building phases: eight assigned to the Early Bronze Age and the beginning of the Middle Bronze Age, and the rest to the Late Bronze Age. A period of abandonment separated the two groups of building phases.[309] The architectural picture for the EBA phases is elusive. Sparse architectural traces indicate lines of posts with one possible apsidal building and a complex of post-framed rooms containing clay benches and food-processing facilities.[310] More information comes from the LBA phases. The characteristic features in phases 18–14 are parts of apsidal or rectangular freestanding buildings, laid out in a random way, without an apparent overall plan.[311] Hearths and food-processing facilities are concentrated mainly inside the buildings. A preference for larger, more widely spaced houses, and the adoption of mudbrick for construction of walls mark the beginning of the Late Bronze Age.

Such features have been exposed over a limited area, however, and their significance cannot be evaluated.

Transformations of the settlement layout are evident in the final part of the Late Bronze Age. The orientation of post-framed houses in phase 13, with ovens and hearths inside and outside, changed.[312] In phase 12, the independent buildings were replaced by complexes of rooms, built with mudbricks and supported by posts. The buildings were arranged in a more compact way, reminiscent of the layout at Assiros in phases 7–5. Food-processing facilities were appended in special, possibly roofed, areas outside the houses, while storage facilities were absent. It has been suggested that one of the complexes served a large number of occupants. The next change in settlement layout is dated to the 10th century B.C. or later.

Apart from stratigraphic and architectural evidence, the work at Kastanas has produced significant bioarchaeological data. According to Kroll,[313] a highly diversified subsistence system during the Early Bronze Age was succeeded in the Late Bronze Age by a more specialized and extensive system of agriculture and stock-raising. The end of the Bronze Age was marked by the adoption of a more balanced regime, namely, intensive small-scale cultivation of a wide variety of crops and a new interest in gathering and, especially, hunting.[314]

The changes in the layout of Kastanas and the organization of production during phases 18–14 of the Late Bronze Age have been regarded as evidence for a more centralized social organization, influenced by developments in southern, Mycenaean Greece.[315] Evidence from Assiros and the Langadas survey im-

---

[307] For the geomorphological study, see Schulz (supra n. 185) 375–93.

[308] *Kastanas* 25–62, esp. 52–54. The excavation has been promptly published in six informative volumes: H. Kroll, *Kastanas: Ausgrabungen in einem Siedlungshügel der Bronze- und Eisenzeit Makedoniens, 1975–1979: Die Pflanzenfunde* (Berlin 1983); A. Hochstetter, *Kastanas: Die handgemachte Keramik* (Berlin 1984); C. Becker, *Kastanas: Die Tierknochenfunde* (Berlin 1986); Hochstetter, *Kastanas: Die Kleinefunde* (Berlin 1987); *Kastanas*; and Aslanis (supra n. 289). See also Kroll, "Bronze Age and Iron Age Agriculture in Kastanas, Macedonia," in W. van Zeist and W.A. Casparie eds., *Plants and Ancient Man: Studies in Palaeoethnobotany* (Rotterdam 1984) 243–46. The only group of finds that remains unpublished is the wheelmade pottery.

[309] *Kastanas* 52–54. For the relative chronology of the earlier phases, see Aslanis (supra n. 289) 203–316, fig. 121. No Mycenaean pottery was found in the earliest LBA phase (19); LH IIIA2 pottery appears in phase 18, and LH IIIC pottery in phase 14. In phase 12, however, Middle Protogeometric pottery was found along with pottery preserving Mycenaean LH IIIC features. Quantities of wheelmade

pottery rose dramatically during this phase: Hänsel (supra n. 291) 189–91; Podzuweit (supra n. 291) 203–23. Phase 11 has been assigned to a period contemporary with Protogeometric. On the basis of similar Mycenaean pottery at Kastanas and Assiros, phases 18 and 17 of Kastanas may be correlated with phase 9 at Assiros, phases 16–14b at Kastanas with phase 8 at Assiros, and phases 14–13 with 7–5 at Assiros. The date of phase 12 at Kastanas remains an open problem, especially since ^{14}C determinations indicate a date in the 12th century B.C. or earlier. A similar assemblage is missing from Assiros but was recently found at the Toumba of Thessaloniki (see below).

[310] Aslanis (supra n. 289) 32–35, figs. 13–14; 45–53, figs. 23–24.

[311] *Kastanas* 70–146.

[312] *Kastanas* 337–38.

[313] Kroll 1983 (supra n. 308) 148–51.

[314] Becker (supra n. 308) 291.

[315] *Kastanas* 334–35. The evidence for influence from Mycenaean Greece comprises the adoption of mudbricks, the production of painted pottery, and the appearance of Mycenaean imported vases.

plies a centralized social organization in central Macedonia during the same period, yet there is little to suggest that the cause of social complexity was Mycenaean influence, or that its form and content were "Mycenaean."[316] Nor could one readily comply with the excavator's assertion that major changes in the settlement, such as those observed in phases 13 and 12, were the result of successive arrivals of northern populations and southern Aegean immigrants, respectively.[317] This constrained migrationist/diffusionist explanation overlooks important possible factors for short-term change in the life of past communities, such as times of dearth and famine, shifts in production, collapse of exchange networks, and intraregional antagonism and aggression.[318]

Despite the contrasting locations of Kastanas and Assiros, no significant differences can be observed in their material culture.[319] In architectural layout, however, the sites diverge. The communal storerooms at Assiros are conspicuously absent from the Axios site, as are the earthen banks and casemate walls at the edge. A possible explanation may lie in the rank of each site in its regional network: Kastanas in the Late Bronze Age may have been part of a polity of which it was not the center.[320]

Gallikos valley. Very little work has recently been done in the Gallikos valley. During excavations at

Toumba Nea Anchialos (fig. 2:15), a third-millennium pottery deposit and possibly the remains of an EBA pottery kiln were found in the area of the Archaic cemetery. Recent excavations at the tell have offered indications that the earliest phase of occupation there may be placed at the end of the Late Bronze Age.[321]

Area of Thessaloniki. Two Neolithic sites have been explored in the coastal plain of Thessaloniki by the ΙΣΤ′ Ephoreia. Stavroupolis is located on the hills to the west, and the other site in a flat area at the center of the city. Both sites are extended and flat. The latter, for which more information is available, has been dated to the final Middle Neolithic and early Late Neolithic, and the only remains of habitation were pits, similar to those at Makriyalos.[322]

Toumba Thessalonikis (fig. 2:20). Toumba Thessalonikis, or Toumba Kalamaria, is an imposing tell in the hills surrounding the small coastal plain of the inner Thermaic Gulf. The tell is 1.3 ha in area and stands 23 m above a plateau formed by the deposits of an Iron Age settlement spread around the base. Once a prominent feature of the landscape, it is now blocked by modern high-rise buildings. Excavations since 1984 by the University of Thessaloniki have uncovered deposits ranging from the late Early Bronze Age to the fourth century B.C.[323] Five

---

[316] Extensive agriculture and overproduction geared to a surplus for exchange and trade have been claimed for Kastanas. Questions have been raised, however, regarding the interpretation of the archaeobotanical evidence: Jones (supra n. 305) 141.

[317] *Kastanas* 335–37.

[318] Channeled ware, considered an indication of northern intruders, appears at Kastanas for the first time in phase 13, in extremely small quantities, and continues modestly into later phases: Hochstetter 1984 (supra n. 308) 188–94; for the "Mycenaean elements" in the architecture of phase 12, see Andreou and Kotsakis 1992 (infra n. 323) 265–66.

[319] A wider variety of Mycenaean pottery motifs was noted at Kastanas, although Mycenaean pottery appeared at the same time at both sites. Comparison of frequencies from the two sites, however, is inhibited by a lack of detailed quantitative data. The appearance of Protogeometric style is much more obvious at Kastanas than at Assiros, but the suggestion that Mycenaean pottery production continued on the former site during the Early Iron Age has been questioned by Wardle 1980 (supra n. 299) 252. Decorated and undecorated wares, including double cooking vessels with central European affinities, displayed a similar variety at both sites. Other finds relating to everyday activities were also identical. For the Mycenaean pottery of Kastanas in the wider Macedonian context, see Podzuweit (supra n. 291); C. Podzuweit, "Der spätmykenische Einfluss in Makedonien," in *ArchMak* 4 (1986) 467–84. For comparisons between the material culture of Assiros and

Kastanas, see Wardle 1993 (supra n. 299) 121–24, 127, 129, 133–35. For a detailed presentation and analysis of handmade LBA pottery from Kastanas and its relationship to material from other sites in the region and beyond, see Hochstetter 1984 (supra n. 308). For other finds, see Hochstetter 1987 (supra n. 308) 94–101.

[320] The nearby site of Axiochori, one of the largest mounds in Greek Macedonia, may be the equivalent of Assiros in the Axios area. Indeed, such a suggestion was made by Hänsel for the subsequent Early Iron Age: *Kastanas* 340–41.

[321] S. Andreou, "Αποθέτης κεραμεικής της Πρώιμης Εποχής του Χαλκού στη Σίνδο Θεσσαλονίκης," *ArchDelt* (in press). M. Tiverios, "Αρχαιολογικές έρευνες στη διπλή τράπεζα κοντά στη σημερινή Αγχίαλο και Σίνδο (1990–1992)—Ο αρχαίος οικισμός," *Egnatia* 3 (1991–1992) 211.

[322] M. Pappa and N. Kousoulakou, "Ανασκαφή στο χώρο της Διεθνούς Εκθέσεως Θεσσαλονίκης," *AEMT* 7 (1993, in press). The Stavroupolis site remains unpublished.

[323] K. Kotsakis and S. Andreou, in *AEMT* 1 (1987) 223–33; Kotsakis and Andreou, in *AEMT* 3 (1989) 201–13; Andreou, Kotsakis, and G. Hourmouziadis, "Ανασκαφή στην Τούμπα της Θεσσαλονίκης 1989," *Egnatia* 2 (1990) 381–403; Andreou and Kotsakis, in *AEMT* 5 (1991) 209–19; and *AEMT* 6 (1992) 259–72; Kotsakis and Andreou, in *AEMT* 7 (1993, in press); Andreou and Kotsakis, "Ανασκαφή Τούμπας Θεσσαλονίκης 1990–92," *Egnatia* 3 (1991–1992) 175–98; Andreou and Kotsakis (supra n. 306); I. Anagnostou et al., in *AEMT* 4 (1990) 277–87; A. Krahtopoulou and K. Tou-

building phases have been identified at the top of the mound. The earliest three (phases 5–3) belong to the later Late Bronze Age, and in their deposits little LH IIIC-style pottery was found. The penultimate phase (2) contained some pottery with compass-drawn concentric circles and new shapes more akin to Protogeometric shapes, along with Mycenaean-style features.[324]

Earlier Bronze Age phases have only been reached in trenches on the side of the mound. Habitation levels dating from the end of the third millennium have been found both at the bottom and near the top of the mound, indicating that the settlement had spread across the slope of the natural hill, in stepped terraces, reminiscent of the arrangement at Pefkakia during the Middle Bronze Age.[325] Architectural remains of the Middle Bronze Age were found in a small area at the bottom of the mound.[326] The layout changed in the Late Bronze Age, when massive casemate constructions (6 m wide × 3 m high) were erected midway down the slope, surrounding the tell. The houses were on the top of the mound, supported by a strong retaining wall.[327] The purpose of the massive constructions is not entirely clear. They had a retaining function, but at the same time they controlled access to the central part of the settlement on the top.

The LBA houses were tightly clustered. A system of narrow lanes separated large blocks of rooms in a layout that was maintained for the last three phases of the Late Bronze Age. The large buildings were constructed of mudbrick reinforced by wooden posts. They comprised living quarters and extensive storerooms with large pithoi. One 225-m² complex was uncovered, with storerooms occupying more than half the area.[328] The inventory of finds is similar to that from Assiros and Kastanas. Several bronze implements were collected, a hoard of which included a double ax and was found in one of the rooms of the large complex. The same complex also contained a bone horse bit of Central European type.[329] The earliest, unstratified, Mycenaean pottery dates to LH IIIA1. Later on, both imports and local products are found, although Mycenaean pottery never seems to have exceeded 5.5% of the total assemblage.[330]

The formation processes of the mound are very complex, and offer an idea of the difficulties involved in the interpretation of the stratigraphic sequence of some high Bronze Age tells. The successive construction of massive earthworks at different levels on the slope creates a stratigraphy that does not follow the regular principle of superposition of layers. It may even result in an "inverted" stratigraphy, where older layers are found above later ones. Of equal importance are the implications for the mobilization of a workforce to erect these ramparts. In this respect, tells like Toumba and Assiros stand apart from sites like Kastanas, where no traces of this intensive activity can be discerned. At Assiros the difference is amplified by the centralized storage of phases 9 and 8. At Toumba, information on storage is not as conclusive, but the scale of the collective effort inferred from the earthworks points again to a centralized social structure in the Late Bronze Age.

Thermi and Vasilika (fig. 2:21–22). The Neolithic sites of Thermi and Vasilika are located in the valley of Anthemous to the east of Thessaloniki. Limited salvage excavations were conducted here by the ΙΣΤ′ Ephoreia.[331] Vasilika and Thermi are flat, extended sites covering an area of 25 ha and 12 ha, respectively.

loumis, in *AEMT* 4 (1990) 289–97; Hourmouziadis, in *AEMT* 4 (1990) 269–75; Kotsakis et al., "Reconstructing a Bronze Age Site in CAD," in J. Hugget and N. Ryan eds., *Quantitative Methods in Archaeology 1994* (*BAR-IS* 600, Oxford 1995) 181–87.

[324] There are certain similarities between phase 2 at Toumba and phase 12 at Kastanas. The amount of wheelmade pottery at Toumba rises dramatically during phase 2. Also notable at Toumba is the absence of channeled ware from this and earlier phases.

[325] See supra p. 548.

[326] The latest of these levels contained incised pottery, a few sherds of dark-burnished, ribbed cups, and even occasional matt-painted sherds. These features comply to some extent with Heurtley's original definition of the MBA, see Heurtley (supra n. 150) 89–91. The levels must be later than those designated by Aslanis (supra n. 289) at Kastanas as early MBA.

[327] Kotsakis and Andreou 1989 (supra n. 323) figs. 6–9; Kotsakis and Andreou 1993 (supra n. 323) fig. 6.

[328] Andreou and Kotsakis 1992 (supra n. 323) fig. 4.

[329] Andreou et al. (supra n. 323) figs. 12, 14.

[330] For a discussion of Mycenaean pottery from Toumba, see Andreou and Kotsakis 1992 (supra n. 323) 266–68; Andreou and Kotsakis, forthcoming (supra n. 306). Petrographic analysis has identified locally produced and imported pottery: E. Kiriatzi, "Pottery Production in Late Bronze Age Central Macedonia, Greece: Toumba Thessalonikis" (unpublished manuscript, Sheffield 1995).

[331] Thermi: D.V. Grammenos et al., "Ανασκαφή νεολιθικού οικισμού Θέρμης, 1987," *Μακεδονικά* 27 (1990) 223–87. Also Grammenos et al., "Ανασκαφή νεολιθικού οικισμού Θέρμης Β και βυζαντινής εγκατάστασης παρά τον προϊστορικό οικισμό Θέρμη Α," *Μακεδονικά* 28 (1992) 381–501. Vasilika: Grammenos 30–31 and 36–37; Grammenos (supra n. 292) 234–39. For the lithics from Vasilika, see M. Kyriakidou, *Η λιθοτεχνία των φάσεων III και IV: Υστερες φάσεις της Νεώτερης Νεολιθικής του οικισμού των Βασιλικών, Ν. Θεσσαλονίκης* (M.A. thesis, Univ. of Thessaloniki 1991). Both excavations were complemented by studies of bioarchaeological remains, and other special groups of finds, included in the reports.

The small trench at Vasilika revealed a sequence that was divided into four phases mainly on the basis of pottery typology, spanning the period equivalent to Sitagroi I–III. The Thermi sequence was divided into three main building phases that were related to phase III at Vasilika. At Vasilika architectural remains are sparse, limited to the later deposits. They testify, however, to the use of mudbricks and stone socles.

The picture from Thermi is clearer, mainly because a larger area was excavated. The site's main feature is an open surface, ca. 60 m², paved with cobbles. In one of the trenches, deposits indicating a period of abandonment were found between two successive cobbled yards. Everyday activities took place in these yards, including food- and crop-processing and knapping a low-quality flint taken from a quarry some 12 km away. A hearth and several pits were related to food preparation activities. In the next phase (II), clay floors and traces of stone and post-built walls covered the cobbled yard. The general impression from the small excavation at Thermi is one of considerable discontinuity in the use of space, with activities shifting between open yards and habitation structures, and with temporary abandonments.[332]

Chalkidiki. Prehistoric research in Chalkidiki resumed the last few years, ending a long period of inactivity since Heurtley's work in the 1920s. While previous work in the area had focused on the flatter northern and western coasts, at mound sites such as Kritsana and Ayios Mamas (fig. 2:25), recent research has turned to the peninsula itself. Settlements here are often found on natural knolls by the sea and on rocky promontories, some of which, like the mounds in the plains, were occupied for long periods.

On the western side of the Kassandra peninsula, at Cape Poseidi, a sanctuary with successive buildings dating from the 10th century B.C. has been excavated since 1989 (fig. 2:23).[333] Beneath the earliest

apsidal temple, dated by Middle and Late Protogeometric pottery, a deep deposit of ashes and animal bone indicated an earlier altar. The deepest levels there, underneath deposits described as Protogeometric and Submycenaean, reportedly contained LH IIIC-style pottery along with handmade wares. It has been suggested that both the wheelmade and handmade pottery display closer affinities to Lefkandi wares than to local wares.[334] No LBA buildings have been found, but, if the earliest levels could be related to a sanctuary, then Poseidi would be the only specialized site known from Bronze Age northern Greece, with indications of ritual that are missing from the tells of central Macedonia. The location of the site on a prominent spot by the sea, however, and the Euboean connections implied by the pottery might indicate its close relationship to seafaring prospectors at the close of the Bronze Age.[335]

On the eastern side of the Kassandra peninsula, the EBA settlement of Polichrono (fig. 2:24) was located on the slope of a natural hill, ca. 100 m from the shore of the Gulf of Toroni.[336] Rescue excavations revealed successive terrace walls with scanty remains of habitation. A more interesting find was a small pit interpreted as a potter's kiln at the outer limit of the settlement, postdating the terrace walls.[337] Bowls with incurving rims and trumpet lugs, one-handled tankards, pointed cups, and pithoi with plastic decoration date the find to the later part of the third millennium.[338]

Toroni (fig. 2:26). Excavations over a number of years at the strategically located, steep promontory of Lekythos at Toroni have revealed extensive remains of occupation ranging from the Early Iron Age to the Ottoman period. A very significant development of recent years, however, has been the discovery of stratified remains belonging to a FN and Bronze Age settlement.

Prehistoric pottery of the third and early second

---

[332] There are only four pieces of obsidian of unspecified provenance reported from Thermi: Grammenos (supra n. 292) 234. For the lithics from Thermi, see A. Skourtopoulou, *Η λιθοτεχνία της Θέρμης Β* (M.A. thesis, Univ. of Thessaloniki 1993); A. Skourtopoulou and S. Dimitriadis, "Η θερμική επεξεργασία των πυριτικών λίθων στις λιθοτεχνίες του παρελθόντος: Το παράδειγμα του νεολιθικού οικισμού της Θέρμης Β," in Stratis et al. (supra n. 135) 331–50. A new project by the ΙΣΤ' Ephoreia was started in 1992 at Mesimeriani Toumba, a few kilometers south of Thessaloniki. The first report gives a preliminary account of the site morphology and describes successive floors and a part of a house belonging to the end of the LBA and the Early Iron Age from a 4 × 4 m trench. D. Grammenos and K. Skourtopoulou, "Μεσημεριανή Τούμπα Τριλόφου Νομού Θεσσαλονίκης: Ανασκαφική περίοδος 1992," *AEMT* 6 (1992) 339–47.

[333] I. Vokotopoulou, "Μένδη-Ποσείδι 1990," *AEMT* 4 (1990) 401–404.

[334] I. Vokotopoulou, "Ποσείδι 1992," *AEMT* 6 (1992) 445, figs. 5–6; Vokotopoulou and S. Moschonisiotou, "Ποσείδι 1994," *AEMT* 8 (1994, in press).

[335] J.D. Muhly, "The Crisis Years in the Mediterranean World: Transition or Cultural Disintegration?" in W.A. Ward and M.S. Joukowsky eds., *The Crisis Years: The 12th Century BC from beyond the Danube to the Tigris* (Dubuque 1992) 10–26.

[336] M. Pappa, "Εγκατάσταση της Εποχής του Χαλκού στο Πολύχρονο Χαλκιδικής," *AEMT* 4 (1990) 393–98.

[337] Heurtley (supra n. 150) 5–7; and Andreou (supra n. 321). Two other similar EBA firing pits are known from central Macedonia, at Ayios Mamas and Sindos.

[338] Pappa (supra n. 336) pls. 6–13.

millennium has been found in most places where excavation reached the rock beneath the later buildings.[339] The deposits have been disturbed by the intensive use of the site, and later architectural remains preclude an understanding of the settlement layout during the earliest periods. The traces of earliest occupation comprise a small number of burnished and white-painted FN sherds found on bedrock. EBA remains have been preserved more frequently: several closed deposits include architecture and floors belonging to different phases, occasionally accompanied by traces of destruction by fire. Among the EBA material, obsidian flakes, a "Trojan" anthropomorphic lid, not necessarily imported, several pieces of sauceboats, and a clay figurine have been found.[340]

Toroni is the only site in Greek Macedonia with a documented continuous stratigraphy from FN to the earliest part of the Late Bronze Age.[341] MBA levels with mudbrick walls contained dark-faced handmade pottery and also wheelmade Gray and Yellow Minyan wares, presumably imported. Moreover, imports from southern Greece continued to appear during the early Late Bronze Age. Toroni offers the earliest indication of imported Mycenaean pottery in the northern Aegean, with a handful of sherds of LH I, LH IIA, and LH IIB styles.[342] One rubble stone foundation was connected with a deposit of locally made two-handled bowls imitating Minyan shapes and associated with imported LH I and II sherds.[343] The later phases of the Late Bronze

Age, however, are poorly represented by a few sherds from handmade and Mycenaean wares.

The special relationship of Chalkidiki to the Aegean has been pointed out since the beginnings of prehistoric research in Macedonia on the basis of very limited evidence.[344] The comparison of the archaeological record from Toroni with that from Bronze Age tell sites in the rest of central Macedonia should allow a better evaluation of the impact Aegean connections may have had on local developments.[345]

Ayios Mamas (fig. 2:25). The recent resumption of investigations at the tell of Ayios Mamas promises to offer new evidence on the network of sites in Chalkidiki from the Neolithic to the Late Bronze Age.[346] Rescue excavations by the ΙΣΤ′ Ephoreia of an EBA cemetery immediately west of the tell have revealed an aspect of EBA communities so far unique in the archaeological record of central Macedonia.[347] The remains, comprising ca. 15 graves, were found amid burials of the Late Roman period. They displayed a variety of mortuary practices, such as contracted inhumations in pithoi sunk in shallow pits, or placed directly in pits strewn with pebbles, and one cremation of an infant. The graves were often delimited by rows of stones, and the pithoi selected for burials had plastic decoration and striated surfaces. Almost all burials were furnished with pots or copper/bronze ornaments. One of the best-preserved burials was furnished with a jug, cup, and a necked jar with vertically pierced lugs, which finds its best parallels in the Cyclades.[348] In the jar, 25 beads,

---

[339] A. Cambitoglou and J. Papadopoulos, "Excavations at Torone, 1986: A Preliminary Report," *MeditArch* 1 (1988) 188, 204–205, 207–208, 210–11, 215; "Excavations at Torone, 1988," *MeditArch* 3 (1990) 129; and Cambitoglou and Papadopoulos (supra n. 290) 152, 161–62, 164, 167, 169; also Cambitoglou and Papadopoulos, "The Earliest Mycenaeans in Macedonia, Greece," in Zerner et al. (supra n. 299) 289–302.

[340] Cambitoglou and Papadopoulos 1988 (supra n. 339) 205; Cambitoglou and Papadopoulos (supra n. 290) 161–62, figs. 24–25. A similar figurine was found at the western Macedonian site of Mandalo. Remains of houses with storage facilities possibly recalling those from MBA Argissa have also been reported: Cambitoglou and Papadopoulos (supra n. 290) 167, cf. *Argissa* III, pl. G.

[341] A series of 14C dates from various stratified deposits is forthcoming, see Cambitoglou and Papadopoulos (supra n. 290) 164. Although the pottery from Toroni displays many strictly local features, its publication is expected to clarify the ceramic sequence of the third and early second millennia over a broad area.

[342] Sixteen sherds of mostly open Early Mycenaean vessels have been found in stratified and mixed deposits. See Cambitoglou and Papadopoulos, in Zerner et al. (supra n. 339).

[343] The occurrence of LH I and II pottery with imported or imitation Minyan ware is a good indication that MBA wares continued in coastal Macedonia, as well as elsewhere, into the earlier LBA phases. Minyan pottery in the Chalkidiki sites of Ayios Mamas and Molyvopyrgos is better related to types common during the last phase of MH or the beginning of LH, see *Pefkakia* III, 382–83. The deposits at Toroni include both imported and local imitations of Minyan ware as well as handmade and wheelmade varieties: Cambitoglou and Papadopoulos 1988 (supra n. 339) 215.

[344] Heurtley (supra n. 150) 121–23.

[345] Metal sources in Chalkidiki were a possible attraction for the southern Aegean; see G.A. Wagner et al., "Archäometallurgische Untersuchungen auf Chalkidiki," *Der Anschnitt* 5–6 (1986) 183–85, fig. 19, where a possible northern origin is suggested for silver and lead used in some objects in the Shaft Graves of Mycenae; Z.A. Stos-Gale and C.F. Macdonald, "Sources of Metals and Trade in the Bronze Age Aegean," in N.H. Gale ed., *Bronze Age Trade in the Mediterranean* (SIMA 90, Jonsered 1991) 258–62, 267–68, 270–76.

[346] Hänsel (supra n. 290).

[347] M. Pappa, "Τούμπα Αγίου Μάμαντος Χαλκιδικής: Ανασκαφή νεκροταφείων," *AEMT* 6 (1992) 475–84.

[348] Pappa (supra n. 347) fig. 3.

shown by chemical analysis to be of faience, were deposited. The surviving evidence from the cemetery is very incomplete, as scattered fragments of EBA pithoi indicate; nevertheless an impression of considerable care is dominant.

New Questions

Recent research in the province has once more failed to identify traces of habitation prior to the late sixth millennium. A number of possible explanations can be put forth: obliteration of the remains of early human settlement by postdepositional factors, unsuitability of the area due to particular environmental conditions, or the occupation of the area by non-sedentary populations, invisible to research geared to stable farming sites. In the Langadas basin, for example, where survey was intensive, several episodes of erosion and alluviation after the Late Neolithic were identified.[349] The absence of sites, however, cannot be accounted for by geomorphological changes alone, unless early sites were ephemeral and were located exclusively on the alluviated or eroded areas—an interesting possibility, but one that clearly needs additional firmly dated regional geomorphic and archaeological support. In the meantime, it is difficult to decide whether Macedonia east of the Axios River was uninhabited from the Upper Palaeolithic to the Middle Neolithic, or has simply been insufficiently researched.

As a result of the uncertainties surrounding the time depth of settlement, major themes such as Neolithic colonization or Late Neolithic expansion can only be partly understood. Does the LN settlement pattern indicate the adoption of full-fledged farming by a population previously exploiting the aquatic resources of the region or does it depict the initial episodes of agricultural colonization of an empty area? Alternatively, does it represent the growth and expansion to less desirable locations of farming communities limited previously to specific niches? The extended sites that highlight the Neolithic settlement pattern imply a particular type of habitation and land use, but in view of the gaps in evidence, their relation to any of the alternatives remains obscure. What is perhaps more clear is the contrast between the extended sites and the tell sites that appear also during the same period. Tells represent

an option for continuity of settlement, which can be the result of economic choice but has also a definable ideological content.[350] They were prominent points in the landscape, the mark of a community's permanence and its inhabitants' lineage, an instrument for constructing the identities of prehistoric people.

The three recent large excavations on tells, focusing on the Late Bronze Age, and new data from surveys encourage discussion of political and economic aspects of the prehistoric communities of central Macedonia. The outstanding position of some settlements during the later Late Bronze Age in terms of capacity and centralization of agricultural storage, scale of public works, extent and size of occupation, and internal arrangement of houses suggests the operation of a hierarchical social organization, integrating neighboring sites. We have no details for the structure of this hierarchy, or for its ideological content, which is markedly invisible in the archaeological record. The range of the hierarchical networks, however, must have been relatively limited, judging from the scale of production, small number of sites involved, their proximity, and restricted size. The limited range is probably reflected in the absence of a strong symbolic expression of authority, which is also missing from the internal arrangement of houses at the settlements. This, however, remains an issue for future research, with the hope that information on mortuary practices will be forthcoming. Equally, the processes by which complexity rose and developed in the third and early second millennium B.C., or possibly earlier, are presently little understood.

A recurrent issue in research since Heurtley worked in the area has been the relationship of LBA Macedonia with the "Mycenaean world." This relationship has been perceived in different forms by various researchers, ranging from more or less regular trading contacts to the establishment of southern colonies along the coast of central Macedonia. The arguments put forth in support of these propositions, occasionally not without considerable excess, range from similarities observed in building techniques to assumed analogies in political organization, but the presence of Mycenaean-style pottery in the excavated deposits and on the surface of LBA

---

[349] The causes and exact dates of the alluviation-erosion episodes are not known, but there is at least one Neolithic site (Kavalari) in the Langadas basin that seems to have been partially buried under an alluvium of ca 1.25 m, either during, or right after, its use. For discussion of the absence

of earlier Neolithic phases in the Langadas basin and its relation to environmental or postdepositional factors, see Morrison (supra n. 282) 274–75.

[350] Chapman (supra n. 296) 38–40.

settlements remains the strongest evidence.[351] In recent years, considerable amounts of new data have been added, but researchers have only started to approach issues concerning the patterns of production, circulation, and consumption of this group of pottery, using quantitative and analytical data, vis-à-vis the overwhelmingly predominant handmade pottery. Although the relationship between Macedonia and the "Mycenaean world" never ceases to fascinate archaeologists, it is still too early to define meaningfully its intensity and nature.[352]

EASTERN MACEDONIA

Environmental Change

The environmental evidence from eastern Macedonia (the area between the Strymon and Nestos rivers) does not give a significantly different picture from that discussed above for central Macedonia, although it has been suggested that the Drama plain remained generally wooded, despite some small-scale fluctuations during the Bronze Age.[353] Erosion and alluviation from the Strymon and Angitis rivers have been noted in the two plains of Drama and Serres as major contributors to postdepositional distortion of the archaeological record.[354] The geomorphological evolution of the lakes and marshes at the bottom of the basins is not yet clearly understood, and human habitation in relation to this part of the plains is still unclear.

Material Sequence and Archaeological Phases

The Neolithic sequence in eastern Macedonia begins with Sitagroi I, dated by ^{14}C to 5500–5200 B.C. (late Middle Neolithic in Thessalian terms). The only

earlier case may be Toumba Serron (fig. 2:29), reported from surface finds as belonging to an earlier "Karanovo I" horizon.[355] The earlier phase of the LN sequence for the region is represented by Dikili Tash I and Sitagroi II, and is defined by the presence of "black-topped" and "rippled" pottery along with a variety of distinctive painted wares. It is dated by a series of ^{14}C dates from Sitagroi to ca. 5200–4800 B.C.[356] The later Late Neolithic, highlighted by "graphite" and "black-on-red" wares, is represented by the stratigraphic phases of Sitagroi III and Dikili Tash II. Absolute dates indicate that the sequences of the two sites are probably not coterminous, and Sitagroi III may continue into the Final Neolithic, i.e., after ca. 4500 B.C. The ^{14}C dates from Sitagroi III, however, are not decisive since they all derive from the early levels of the phase. In addition to the well-known sequences of Sitagroi and Dikili Tash, Pentapolis has supplied six dates for two EBA phases, which agree with the Sitagroi IV/Va ^{14}C sequence.[357] Combining the stratigraphic sequences of the three sites, a subdivision of the Early Bronze Age into two phases is possible. An earlier phase in which "channeled" ware is a well-known feature (Sitagroi IV–Va, Dikili Tash IIIA, Pentapolis I; ca. 3200–2500 B.C.) is roughly contemporaneous with EH I/II, and a later phase (Sitagroi Vb, Dikili Tash IIIB, Pentapolis II; ca. 2500–2200 B.C.) with late EH II/III.[358] It has not been possible, however, to identify a stratigraphically distinct MBA phase nor an early LBA phase, before 1400 B.C. Three ^{14}C dates covering the period 1200–1000 B.C. were obtained from the LBA settlement of Angista. The samples came from deposits that contained a few sherds of LH IIIC type.[359]

---

[351] For a recent summary, see Wardle 1993 (supra n. 299). Also Cambitoglou and Papadopoulos, in Zerner et al. (supra n. 339) 289–302; *Kastanas* 331–37; K. Kilian, "Mycenaean Colonization: Norm and Variety," in J.P. Descoeudres ed., *Greek Colonists and Native Populations* (Oxford 1990) 448–55; I. Vokotopoulou, "Macedonia—Geographical and Historical Outline," in I. Vokotopoulou ed., *Greek Civilization: Macedonia, Kingdom of Alexander the Great* (Athens 1993) 12; H. Koukouli-Chrysanthaki, "Macedonia in the Bronze Age," in Vokotopoulou (supra) 108–10, 116–23. For discussion of the arguments, see Andreou and Kotsakis (supra n. 306).

[352] For ceramic analysis along these lines, e.g., Wardle 1993 (supra n. 299) 131; Kiriatzi (supra n. 330). For other incentives for contact between Macedonia and southern Greece, see supra n. 345.

[353] Turner and Greig (supra n. 282) 51–53. Regional environmental work has been conducted in the Drama basin, in connection with the Sitagroi project: O. Rackham, "Charcoal," in *Sitagroi* 55–62; and D.A. Davidson, "Geomorphological Studies," in *Sitagroi* 25–40.

[354] Davidson (supra n. 353) 30; Fotiadis (supra n. 272)

99–143.

[355] Grammenos and Fotiadis (infra n. 360) 20–23, but for reservations, see Fotiadis (supra n. 272) 210–12.

[356] *Sitagroi* 169–74; R. Treuil ed., *Dikili Tash: Village préhistorique de Macédoine orientale* 1 (*BCH* Suppl. 24, Paris 1992) 33–37.

[357] D. Grammenos, "Ανασκαφή σε οικισμό της Εποχής του Χαλκού (Πρώιμης) στην Πεντάπολη του Νομού Σερρών," *ArchEph* 1981, 123. A hiatus in occupation between Sitagroi III and IV remains a plausible hypothesis: *Sitagroi* 482. Between Dikili Tash II–III, and III–IV (LBA), long hiatuses were suggested by the excavators: Treuil (supra n. 356) 33–36.

[358] S.W. Manning, *The Absolute Chronology of the Aegean Early Bronze Age* (Sheffield 1994) 161–64; *Sitagroi* 482–83.

[359] H. Koukouli-Chrysanthaki, "Οικισμός της Υστερης Εποχής του Χαλκού στον Σταθμό Αγγίστας Σερρών," *Anthropologika* 1 (1980) 78. Another date comes from Dikili Tash: Koukouli-Chrysanthaki, *Πρωτοϊστορική Θάσος: Τα νεκροταφεία του οικισμού Καστρί* (Athens 1992) 668–69; Treuil (supra n. 356) 36.

There are 76 reported prehistoric sites from eastern Macedonia, distributed mainly in the two major basins of Serres and Drama. Outside these areas, large parts of the region appear blank, but this reflects the intensity of research and lack of systematic reporting rather than the preferences of prehistoric communities.[360] The number of sites increases through the Neolithic, and, after a sharp decline and discontinuity during the Early Bronze Age, sites reach the highest number for all periods during the Late Bronze Age. A few LN and Bronze Age sites are caves.[361] These general trends are observed in both the Serres and Drama basins. In the Neolithic period, settlements tend to be located on the lower terraces, in areas providing light arable along with other types of land. In the Serres basin, more than half of the known sites are abandoned at the end of the Neolithic, and the number of sites in the Drama basin also declines. In the later Bronze Age, however, sites are established on higher ground with less light arable around and further away from the plain. At the same time, conspicuous locations on hilltops are selected.[362] The occupation of higher ground is a familiar LBA trait from the other regions discussed above, but whether it reflects an increase in antagonism and warfare or an economic decision is at pres-

ent difficult to determine.[363] The limited evidence is also not particularly helpful for defining regional hierarchical structures, such as those suggested for central Macedonia. Perhaps the rarity here of the large and distinctively high settlements seen in central Macedonia is a sign of diverging social trajectories between the two areas.[364]

Recent Projects

Dikili Tash (fig. 2:35). Excavations at Dikili Tash started in 1961 as a joint Greek-French project, and with long intermissions continue to date.[365] The mound is situated near a rich spring, at the edge of an extensive marshland, drained in recent times. The actual depth of the deposits and the extent of the settlement are among the problems investigated by recent work at the site. Geomorphological research at the present edge of the mound has shown that the archaeological deposits alternated with alluvial lake deposits, signifying the fluctuating levels of the marshland.[366]

The stratigraphy of the mound, already established by early excavations, is divided into four main phases that cover the Late Neolithic (Dikili Tash I–II), the Early Bronze Age (Dikili Tash III), and the Late Bronze Age (Dikili Tash IV), with hiatuses between

---

[360] The area of the Nestos delta was surveyed for prehistoric sites during excavations at Paradeisos. The absence of sites in the area is taken to indicate a large-scale infilling from alluviation: P. Hellström ed., *Paradeisos: A Late Neolithic Settlement in Aegean Thrace* (Medelhavsmuseet 7, Stockholm 1987) 13. For a catalogue and discussion of sites with references to previous work, see D. Grammenos and M. Fotiadis, "Από τους προϊστορικούς οικισμούς της ανατολικής Μακεδονίας," *Anthropologika* 1 (1980) 15–33; Grammenos, "Συμπεράσματα από τη μελέτη των προϊστορικών οικισμών της ανατολικής Μακεδονίας," in *Α΄ Τοπικό Συμπόσιο, 'Η Καβάλα και η Περιοχή της,' 18–20 Απριλίου 1977* (Thessaloniki 1980) 235–47; Grammenos, "Προϊστορικοί οικισμοί της ανατολικής Μακεδονίας," *Θρακικά Χρονικά* 36 (1980–1981) 95–100; Grammenos, "Bronzezeitliche Forschungen in Östmakedonien," in B. Hänsel ed., *Südosteuropa zwischen 1600 und 1000 v. Chr.* (Prähistorische Archäologie in Südosteuropa 1, Berlin 1982) 89–98; Grammenos (supra n. 287); and Grammenos 120–26. For a detailed description of sites and finds from the Serres basin, see Fotiadis (supra n. 272) 350–408. For the Drama basin, see E. Blouet, "Development of the Settlement Pattern," in *Sitagroi* 133–44. To the number of sites reported, a few have been added recently: K. Kasvikis, *Οικισμοί της Εποχής του Χαλκού στην ανατολική Μακεδονία* (M.A. thesis, Univ. of Thessaloniki 1995). No regional projects in eastern Macedonia have followed an intensive strategy.

[361] K. Trantalidou and A. Darlas, "Έρευνες στα σπήλαια του Νομού Δράμας, 1992," *AEMT* 6 (1992) 593–600.

[362] Fotiadis (supra n. 272) 281–83. These later Bronze Age sites are often one-period sites with shallow deposits,

and their absence from the lower areas can be attributed either to the effects of alluviation or to their low visibility: Blouet (supra n. 360) 139.

[363] Fotiadis (supra n. 278) 89–92 considers economic choice as a more plausible alternative.

[364] See, however, H. Koukouli-Chrysanthaki, *ArchDelt* 27 B΄ (1972) 527–29 for a large tell in the Strymon valley.

[365] For a detailed report of the first period of French excavations at Dikili Tash, see Treuil (supra n. 356); also M. Séfériadès, "Dikili Tash: Introduction à la préhistoire de la Macédoine orientale," *BCH* 107 (1983) 635–77. For a summary of results of the first period of Greek excavations, see H. Koukouli-Chrysanthaki and K. Romiopoulou, "Οι ανασκαφές στον ελληνικό τομέα του προϊστορικού οικισμού Ντικιλί Τας (1961–1967)," in *Ancient Thessaly* 226–47. For the more recent excavations, see Koukouli-Chrysanthaki, "Προϊστορικός οικισμός στο 'Ντικιλί Τας,'" *Prakt* 1986, 141–46; Koukouli-Chrysanthaki and Treuil, "Dikili Tash," *BCH* 111 (1987) 616–19; Koukouli-Chrysanthaki, *Prakt* 1987, 173–76; K. Peristeri and R. Treuil, *BCH* 112 (1988) 727–31; Koukouli-Chrysanthaki, *Prakt* 1989, 233–42; A Pariente, *BCH* 114 (1990) 799; P. Darcque, G. Touchais, and R. Treuil, *BCH* 116 (1992) 715–19; and Koukouli-Chrysanthaki, "Dikili Tash," *Το Έργον της Αρχαιολογικής Εταιρείας* 1993, 68–75.

[366] The archaeological deposits at the foot of the tell were dated to the EBA. Two stone features were uncovered in two separate locations (sectors II and IV). They probably date to the EBA and may represent circuit walls built to protect the site from the fluctuating marshes: Peristeri and Treuil (supra n. 365) 729; Darcque et al. (supra n. 365) 715.

Dikili Tash II (ending ca. 4500 B.C.) and III (starting ca. 3200 B.C.), and between the Early Bronze Age and the later Bronze Age.[367] Excavations at different locations of the mound display dissimilar stratigraphic sequences implying discontinuities and shifts in habitation from period to period.[368] Architectural remains were scanty in the Neolithic levels and mainly comprised traces of post-built walls and stone socles. Many hearths and ovens were found, but it is unclear whether they were located inside or outside houses. One feature deserves special notice: a potter's firing pit, found partly sunk in a floor, together with a large pit filled with ashes and another filled with clay, a silo filled with carbonized lentils, and two mysterious joined cavities. The assemblage belongs to Dikili Tash I. The firing pit had a single chamber containing deformed pots, charcoal, and ashes.[369] Apart from its contents, it resembles the common ovens found at the site, which implies that firing pottery was within the capacities of the regular household.

Recent excavations on the eastern plateau, below the top of the mound, have yielded complete plans of post-buildings arranged in regular rows, with occasional indications of an upper story. The houses are 10 m long × 5 m wide and are separated by narrow lanes.[370] This architecture was dated to the latest part of Dikili Tash II and provides the only information on the layout of a Neolithic settlement in eastern Macedonia. In another sector of the excavation, a thick destruction level of the early LN period was uncovered. The remains of pisé houses of undetermined plan, again with ovens and silos, were explored.[371]

Over a final destruction deposit on the eastern plateau, dating to the end of the Late Neolithic, sparse remains of EBA occupation were preserved, including post-built houses equipped with pits and horseshoe-shaped ovens. A long post-built house with internal partitions, at least 12 m long, was found there.[372] It was rebuilt at least three times, the last probably with a stone socle. Two hearths were located at the two ends and during the last phase the house was equipped with a stone platform. A street separated it from another house to the north. At the top of the mound, five occupation phases were identified through successive floors with hearths and ovens, but no house plans could be determined. EBA activity at the base of the mound is indicated by recent finds, but occupation on the mound itself during that period was possibly more limited than previously, as the absence of EBA deposits on the southern slope indicates.[373]

Another long apsidal building at the top of the mound is the sole structure dated to the Late Bronze Age. The building was constructed of mudbricks and was at least 10 × 4 m in size. Most remarkable were two elliptical plaques of clay, placed on an earlier floor, lying opposite one another, near the long walls of the building.[374] They had a square hollow in the middle filled with ashes, two round bowls on each side, and were decorated with parallel curvilinear grooves running around the edge of the plaques. Part of a clay figurine and several spindle whorls have also been reported from the building, which was destroyed twice by fire.[375]

Notable is the suggested use of flint from the Danube area for the flaked tool industry at the end of the Neolithic, while obsidian was represented by very few pieces. Copper objects were present in LN and EBA levels in very small numbers. Finally, a variety of objects made of bone, lead, shell, and clay were found mainly in the Neolithic deposits of the site.[376]

Sitagroi (fig. 2:32).   One of the main objectives of the Sitagroi project was the clarification of the chronological position of the Balkan LN and Chalcolithic

---

[367] Treuil (supra n. 356) 33–36.

[368] E.g., Peristeri and Treuil (supra n. 365) 729, 731. Also Koukouli-Chrysanthaki and Romiopoulou (supra n. 365) 235.

[369] Treuil (supra n. 356) 23, 43–44.

[370] Koukouli-Chrysanthaki 1993 (supra n. 365) 70–74.

[371] *AR* 1993–1994, 59; Darcque et al. (supra n. 365) 715–17.

[372] Koukouli-Chrysanthaki 1993 (supra n. 365) 69, 74; Koukouli-Chrysanthaki and Romiopoulou (supra n. 365) 235–47. The house was probably contemporary with the "Long House" of Sitagroi Vb.

[373] See Treuil (supra n. 356) 49–51; for building activities at the base of the mound, see supra n. 366.

[374] Treuil (supra n. 356) 52–57; M.S. Séfériadès, "Le bâtiment absidial en briques crues de Dikili Tash (Bronze Récent)," in J.-L. Huot, M. Yon, and Y. Calvet eds., *De l'Indus aux Balkans: Recueil à la mémoire de Jean Deshayes* (Paris 1985) 111–13.

[375] Séfériadès (supra n. 374) interprets the plaques as altars, and the building as a sanctuary. Treuil (supra n. 356) 56–57, however, takes a more skeptical view.

[376] Treuil (supra n. 356) 59–144. Archaeobotanical remains from the second period of research in the Greek sector are presented in M. Magafa, *The Plant Remains from the Late Neolithic/Early Bronze Age Site of Dikili Tash, Macedonia, Greece* (M.S. thesis, Univ. of Sheffield 1990); Magafa and K. Kotsakis, "A New Method for the Identification of Wild and Cultivated Charred Grape Seeds," *JAS* (in press). The archaeobotanical analysis of grape seeds shows that wine was produced on the site, but from wild grapes.

periods and their relation to the Aegean. The results in this respect were revolutionary for the whole of southeastern Europe and, since the completion of fieldwork in 1970, have been discussed repeatedly, despite the fact that the first volume of the final publication appeared only in 1986. We shall not, therefore, deal extensively with these results.[377] The excavation focused also on the placement of the prehistoric settlement in its broader palaeoeconomic context, thus carrying on a tradition seen earlier at Nea Nikomedeia.

In the deep trenches excavated at Sitagroi, only clay floors could be identified for the Neolithic phases. No substantial parts of buildings or features were unearthed, except for a number of hearths, pits, and the occasional wall of pisé or posts. The general pattern of habitation is suggested by the stratigraphy of the deep trench ZA, where house floors were found alternating with layers described as middens. In this — admittedly small — area, habitation was not continuous, and occasional, short-term abandonment may have taken place. This possibility finds support in the results of phosphate and particle-size analyses of the sediments.[378]

More information is available for the layout of the settlement during the Early Bronze Age. Houses were as a rule built of posts and elongated, possibly following a single orientation and regular layout.[379] During phase Va, houses at the top were probably closely packed together.[380] The apsidal "Burnt House" of that phase was 8 m long, with a concentration of food-processing and long-term storage facilities inside the apse. Various domestic activities were indicated by the presence of a hearth, and a number of vessels and tools in the main room.[381] The "Long House" (at least 15.5 m long) of phase Vb, in the same area, preserved less information, with the exception of a stone shaft-hole ax head and several intramural infant burials. During the same phase, evidence from trenches away from the top indicates

the existence of similarly long buildings and possibly a less packed arrangement of habitation. In the eroded uppermost level, traces of intensive storage and other domestic activities were not connected to house remains. Habitation continued after the late EBA phase, but no architectural remains have been found associated with the mixed deposits.[382]

It is not possible to correlate changes observed in the regional settlement pattern with changes in the pattern of habitation at Sitagroi. The vertical strategy of the excavation precludes obtaining information about changes in the general layout of the settlement, density of habitation, or architectural features. Consequently, the proposition that, during the Sitagroi III phase, a demographic growth at the settlement level should be correlated through nucleation to a decrease in the total number of sites in the Drama basin certainly needs further support.[383]

The Neolithic pottery of Sitagroi — especially that of phase III — is very rich in decoration and technically advanced.[384] Its distribution over an extensive area possibly signifies the existence of long-distance exchange networks, parallel to exchange networks of raw materials such as metal, flint, etc., but also perhaps foodstuffs. At the present level of research, it is impossible to place these potentially interconnected networks into a wider social and economic context, similar to that discussed in Thessaly, nor is it possible to define more closely their specific content and extent. Equally poorly understood are the consequences or causes of a shift in orientation toward the Aegean at the end of the Early Bronze Age, evident in the similarities in pottery from both areas, and, more importantly, in the occurrence of tin alloys.[385]

Toumba Dramas/Arkadikos (fig. 2:33).[386] A brief excavation at Arkadikos, near the town of Drama, was conducted in 1991. The site extends over 15 ha and provides a good example of a flat, extended site in eastern Macedonia. The excavations revealed a level

[377] *Sitagroi.* For recent discussions based on the Sitagroi sequence and its importance for northern Greek prehistory, see Grammenos (supra n. 292); Grammenos 85–95; Aslanis (supra n. 12) 129–40, 260–64; Coleman 261–62, 274; Demoule, in Lichardus (supra n. 288) 227–36; Manning (supra n. 358) 92–97, 161–64; Demoule, in Maniatis (supra n. 288) 690 defines, on grounds of pottery typology, three subphases of Sitagroi III (a–c) and inserts a hiatus between IIIa and IIIb.

[378] *Sitagroi* 175–82, 212–18. For the geoarchaeological analysis of formation processes, see *Sitagroi* 32–40.

[379] *Sitagroi* 207–208.

[380] *Sitagroi* 190.

[381] *Sitagroi* 191–203.

[382] For the "Long House," see *Sitagroi* 189–90; the rest of the Vb phase, *Sitagroi* 203–10; the "Bin Complex," *Sitagroi* 187–88; and for later Bronze Age phases, *Sitagroi* 470.

[383] *Sitagroi* 137.

[384] For the technological aspects of this pottery, see Jones (supra n. 149) 768–72, with earlier references.

[385] For ceramic form and decoration, changing subsistence practices, and orientation of contacts, see *Sitagroi* 446–49. For a discussion of technological aspects of metallurgy, see McGeehan-Liritzis and Gale (supra n. 46) 215–23.

[386] Grammenos 125.

of LN habitation with dense concentrations of post-holes, possibly representing repeated reconstructions of post-built houses.[387]

Dimitra (fig. 2:30). The site of Dimitra lies on a Neogene formation very close to the Angitis River alluvium, in the Serres basin. Two trenches were dug to investigate the stratigraphy. The Neolithic sequence was divided into three phases (Dimitra I–III), corresponding to phases I–III of Sitagroi, and habitation levels were also found dating to the Late Bronze Age (Dimitra IV). Very little was discovered in respect to architecture except for a LBA house/retaining wall associated with a destruction deposit. A wealth of material came from the Neolithic strata, including gold and copper beads from all phases, *Spondylus* rings and beads, and a good sample of bio-archaeological material, which was systematically collected.[388] Two ^{14}C dates from phase I appear extremely high in relation to the Sitagroi I dates.[389]

Pentapolis (fig. 2:28). A small-scale excavation was conducted at the low mound (2.5 m high) of Pentapolis in the central part of the Serres basin. The site is situated on the middle terraces surrounding the plain, in a landscape of high erosional activity and dominated by conglomerates and red clays. The brief excavation produced deposits showing two phases dated to the Early Bronze Age, and traces of later, LBA habitation, which have been eroded. A series of ^{14}C dates confirmed a chronological overlap with Sitagroi IV and V. The small trench preserved remains of mudbrick walls, floors, a hearth, and a clay bin.[390]

Stathmos Angistas (fig. 2:31). Stathmos Angistas

is a tell on the summit of a hill rising ca. 45 m above the surrounding alluvial valley of the Angitis River. Since the center of the Bronze Age settlement had been destroyed by a Macedonian tomb, LBA levels were explored only near the western edge of the site. The excavation revealed two main LBA strata.[391] Mudbrick terraces supported the edge, while floors with pithoi, clay bins, hearths, and an oven belonged to roughly rectangular houses with mudbrick walls. Handmade pottery, in plain coarse, coarse with plastic decoration, burnished, incised, and occasional painted and graphite-coated wares, comprised the majority of the ceramics. In addition a small amount of wheelmade Mycenaean pottery was found (0.08%). The two phases were dated by the presence of LH IIIA2/B and LH IIIC pottery, respectively. The presence of Mycenaean pottery along with the terraced formation of the mound gives Stathmos Angistas a "central Macedonian" appearance.[392]

Paradeisos (fig. 2:36). A small excavation was conducted for one month in 1976 at Paradeisos, situated strategically on the right bank of the Nestos River. Deposits were 1.7 m deep and belong mainly to the LN period, contemporary with Sitagroi III. Thin EBA deposits were also found, and LBA pottery on the surface testifies to the long life of the settlement.[393]

New Questions

As a result of sound fieldwork, analysis, and publication since the late 1960s, eastern Macedonia offers a chrono-typological framework for the Neolithic and Early Bronze Age that is more complete and secure

[387] K. Touloumis and K. Peristeri, "Ανασκαφή στον Αρκαδικό Δράμας, 1991," *AEMT* 5 (1991) 359–69; I. Anagnostou and A. Vargas-Escobar, "Ανασκαφή Αρκαδικού 1991," *AEMT* 5 (1991) 371–81; and Vargas et al., "Ανασκαφές στην προϊστορική τούμπα του Αρκαδικού Δράμας," *AEMT* 6 (1992) 577–85.

[388] Grammenos (supra n. 287) includes chapters on ceramic technology, petrographic analysis, metallurgical examination, and archaeobiological analysis; also Grammenos 48–63.

[389] 6060–5950 B.C. (Bln 3187) and 6370–6220 B.C. (Bln 3189). For a recent excavation of a contemporary site at Promachonas-Topolniča (fig. 2:27), see H. Koukouli-Chrysanthaki, "Προμαχώνας-Topolniča. Ενα πρόγραμμα ελληνοβουλγαρικής συνεργασίας," *AEMT* 6 (1992) 561–75; Koukouli-Chrysanthaki, I. Aslanis, and F. Konstantopoulou, "Προϊστορικός οικισμός Προμαχώνας-Topolniča," *AEMT* 7 (1993, in press); Koukouli-Chrysanthaki, Aslanis, and Konstantopoulou, "Προμαχώνας-Topolniča: Ελληνοβουλγαρικές έρευνες στον προϊστορικό οικισμό," *AEMT* 8 (1994, in press).

[390] Grammenos (supra n. 357) 91–153.

[391] Koukouli-Chrysanthaki 1980 (supra n. 359) 54–85. See also Koukouli-Chrysanthaki 1992 (supra n. 359) 475–76

for additional information about the stratigraphic sequence. EBA and Early Iron Age finds are also mentioned.

[392] For informative reviews of the existing evidence on LBA eastern Macedonia with emphasis on chronocultural issues and LBA ceramics, see H. Koukouli-Chrysanthaki, "Late Bronze Age in Eastern Macedonia," in *Thracia praehistorica* (Supplementum Pulpudeva 3, Sofia 1982) 231–58; also Koukouli-Chrysanthaki 1992 (supra n. 359) 442–63, 473–507, 559–61, 631–34, 668. The affinities of the material culture with that from central Macedonia are stressed. General affinities with the central and eastern Balkans and Aegean Thrace are also recognized. For a review with emphasis on economic and social issues, see Fotiadis (supra n. 278). Two isolated tumuli, dated to the end of the Bronze Age and the beginning of the Iron Age, were partially rescued in the highland passes near the villages of Potamoi (fig. 2:34) and Exohi, near the Greek-Bulgarian border. An undetermined number of cremations in urns were furnished with plain, graphite-coated, and incised pottery, and with a few Mycenaean pots. See D. Grammenos, "Τύμβοι της Υστερης Εποχής του Χαλκού και άλλες αρχαιότητες στην περιοχή του Νευροκοπίου Δράμας," *ArchEph* 1979, 26–71.

[393] Hellström (supra n. 360).

than most other areas in the Aegean can claim. In this respect, it offers a useful example for other regions with longer histories of research. Major issues that occupied the previous generation of archaeologists have been elucidated, and it would not be an exaggeration to say that the data from this area could be used with care as safe time pegs to assist the clarification of difficult chronological problems, even in areas as far removed as Thessaly. There is an urgent need, however, for the extension of the chronotypological framework to include the later Bronze Age, for which information is minimal. We now understand many aspects of the palaeoenvironment, but work done in the 1970s on the interaction between settlement and environment needs to be continued in a more intensive form. Finally, it is time to start translating the well-known cultural features of the region into human terms by investigating the changing relationships within and between eastern Macedonian communities, an aspect of prehistoric life that at present is very little understood.

THRACE

Greek Thrace is generally absent from reviews of Aegean prehistory. This is surprising since one would think that both the Rodopi plain to the south as well as the lower Evros valley to the east would attract researchers interested in prehistoric interaction among Anatolia, the Aegean, and the Balkans. Nevertheless, it was only a few years ago that a prehistoric excavation of some scale was undertaken by the Archaeological Service, which has also conducted smaller-scale excavations of early sites in the area.[394]

No secure stratified sequence has been sufficiently published for any period of western Thrace. In the absence of ^{14}C dates, comparisons with the material culture from sites in eastern Macedonia, southern Bulgaria, and the northeastern Aegean offer the only basis for dating archaeological assemblages. Recent excavations at the site of Makri promise to rectify the situation for the Neolithic period by providing a more secure stratigraphy for the fifth and early

fourth millennium B.C. than is presently provided by Paradimi, and may offer evidence for even earlier Neolithic occupation. Dating problems are more severe for the period 3500–1000 B.C. due to a general dearth of excavated sites and the absence of long, continuous stratigraphies.

Previously known sites with Neolithic and occasional EBA occupation are primarily mounds along the edges of the plain and near the coast, and caves with sparse traces of intermittent occupation from Late Neolithic to historical times.[395] Only recently have less conspicuous sites, some in elevated areas, been discovered, indicating at least for some periods more varied patterns of habitation than were suspected in the past.

The preliminary results of a recent joint project conducted by the Ephoreia of Komotini, the University of Thessaloniki, and A. Ammerman for the investigation of the plain of Rodopi and adjacent areas offer additional reasons for the general scarcity of prehistoric sites in the area. Eustatic sea-level rise, large-scale alluviation in deltaic areas and along floodplains, and the late formation of Lake Vistonis in the western part of the plain, though not accurately datable, possibly prohibit the recovery of prehistoric sites other than large mounds. Geomorphological changes may also have rendered large parts of the lowlands unattractive for occupation during certain periods of the prehistoric past. On the other hand, exploration of the Pleistocene terraces along the southeastern edge of the area identified a concentration of sites, some of small size, belonging to various prehistoric periods, including a few Middle Palaeolithic and several LN sites.[396] Whether the geomorphological changes were initiated by human activity and whether occupation of the Pleistocene terraces was related to economic and political processes are questions for future research.

Recent Projects

Paradimi (fig. 2:38). The early excavations at Paradimi in the 1920s by S. Kyriakides, an anthropologist, and E. Pelekides were published in 1981 by G.

[394] For a first synthesis of the data from the area with a catalogue of sites, see D. Theocharis, *Prehistory of Eastern Macedonia and Thrace* (Athens 1971). For a recent summary, see D. Triantafyllos, "Ancient Thrace," in V. Papoulia et al. eds., *Thrace* (Athens 1994) 37–41. For the only site excavated prior to the 1970s, and this on a very small scale, see G. Bakalakis and A. Sakellariou, *Paradimi* (Mainz 1981). Bakalakis was the initiator of research specifically conducted to collect surface data, followed by D. French and members of the Archaeological Service.

[395] Theocharis (supra n. 394) 11 and Appendix III. E.

Tsimbidis-Pentazos, "Ἀρχαιολογικαί ἔρευναι ἐν Θράκῃ," *Prakt* 1971, 87–88.

[396] N. Efstratiou, "Νεότερες ἐνδείξεις γιὰ τὴν προϊστορικὴ ἐγκατάσταση στὴν Θράκη," *AEMT* 5 (1991) 430–32. For more Neolithic and EBA sites in elevated areas, see D. Triantafyllos, *ArchDelt* 26 B' (1971) 430–31, 437; Triantafyllos, "Ἡ Θράκη τοῦ Αἰγαίου πρὶν τὸν ἑλληνικὸ ἀποικισμό," *Θρακικὴ ἐπετηρίδα* 7 (1987–1990) 299, 302, 304–305, 309, where LBA and Early Iron Age occupation on high ground is preceded by Neolithic settlement.

Bakalakis and A. Sakellariou. Bakalakis dug a small control trench (7 × 1 m) in 1965 to check the stratigraphy of the tell and correlate the abundant material produced by the earlier excavations with specific strata. The 4.5-m stratigraphy of Paradimi was divided into four main Neolithic phases, covering the span from the end of the Middle Neolithic to the Final Neolithic (roughly equivalent to phases Sitagroi I–III), and one phase belonging to the Early Bronze Age. The publication is heavily biased toward pottery, and gives little information on the settlement. The pottery comprises dark-faced vessels with carinated shapes, "black-topped" and "channeled" wares in the earlier phases, and graphite decoration as well as some "black on red" in the later Neolithic deposits.[397]

Paradimi is a well-known site, although the level of research hardly justifies its prominent position in the literature. The recent publication gives a somewhat clearer view of the evidence, but does not warrant the view that the Paradimi "culture" is unique, with features demonstrating its position at a crossroads between east and west, north and south.[398] Similar views have been expressed about Macedonia as a whole, and even Thessaly (see above); they are based, however, on perceptions of the geopolitical position of the sites and regions in question rather than on archaeological evidence.

Proskinites (fig. 2:39). A brief excavation at a site 5 km from the coast, near the village of Proskinites, south of Komotini, explored ca. 3.5-m-deep Neolithic deposits. The low mound is fairly large, ca. 8 ha, and is located at the boundary between the limestone hills and the Pleistocene terrace. The two 4 × 4 m trenches uncovered only elusive structural elements, probably from post-framed houses, more substantial remains of clay-lined pits, and rich furnishings in the form of pottery and other implements, including a rich repertoire of chipped stone, mainly from local chert and flint, and several large ground stone tools. Ceramic vessels, mainly monochrome or decorated with channeling, reportedly resemble the repertoires from Paradimi I–II, a few kilometers to the north, and the more distant site of Sitagroi I–II.[399]

Makri (fig. 2:42). The mound of Makri, 11 km west of Alexandroupolis, is typical of Neolithic sites in the area. It is located on a rocky outcrop rising ca. 50 masl on the face of which opens a cave with sparse remains of habitation from different periods. The mound is fairly small but trial trenches up to 50 m away from its base on the north side have uncovered habitation deposits underneath several meters of recent alluvium, indicating a settlement of ca. 1 ha. Some 200 m further north another trial trench revealed, beneath 2.50 m of alluvium, a deposit with flakes and tools yet no pottery, provisionally interpreted as a flint-knapping floor, not necessarily related to the main settlement.[400]

The site was also occupied in the historical period and the Bronze Age, but the prehistoric remains in the 250-m² excavated area belong exclusively to the Neolithic period. The 4-m-deep deposits of the settlement have been assigned to two periods, Makri I and II, separated by a destruction deposit and ending in a uniform destruction horizon. Monochrome pottery prevailed in both phases, with occasional incisions or impressions in Makri I, and rare painted "white-on-red" pottery was also found. In Makri II, monochrome pottery continued to be produced, with clays taken from six local sources; carinated shapes appeared along with channeled decoration.[401] Efstratiou assigns the later phase to the period covered by phases I–II at Sitagroi and Paradimi I–III, and attributes the rarity of painted pottery to regional variation. It is proposed that Makri I could date to a period earlier than Sitagroi I, possibly going back into the Early Neolithic, suggesting a closer connection with recently discovered assemblages in eastern Thrace and Anatolia.[402]

The possibly early date of the site is a new development for the prehistory of the northern Aegean. Furthermore, the extensive architectural remains of

---

[397] Bakalakis and Sakellariou (supra n. 394) 14–23.

[398] Bakalakis and Sakellariou (supra n. 394) 27–40, esp. 38.

[399] D. Triantafyllos, "Προσκυνητές-Ροδόπης," *Το Εργον της Αρχαιολογικής Εταιρείας* 1986, 50.

[400] Makri represents the first long-term excavation of a prehistoric site in the region; see D. Kallintzi and N. Efstratiou, "Ανασκαφή στη Μάκρη Εβρου," *AEMT* 2 (1988) 499–510; Efstratiou, in *AEMT* 3 (1989) 595–605; *AEMT* 4 (1990) 595–612; and *AEMT* 6 (1992) 643–54; N. Urem-Kotsos and N. Efstratiou, "Η συμβολή της κεραμεικής τυπολογίας

της Μάκρης στη μελέτη της προϊστορικής εξέλιξης στη Θράκη," *AEMT* 8 (1994, in press). Also Efstratiou and Kallintzi, *Ο αρχαιολογικός χώρος Μάκρης-Εβρου* (Komotini, in press).

[401] For a technological analysis of pottery from Makri, see P. Yiouni, "Η συμβολή των αρχαιομετρικών ερευνών στη μελέτη της νεολιθικής κεραμεικής," in Stratis et al. (supra n. 135) 135–48.

[402] Cf. infra n. 437. For a surface find of a clay figurine head possibly dating to the sixth millennium B.C., see Efstratiou (supra n. 396) 429–30.

Makri II offer an opportunity for the investigation of Neolithic social and economic organization that is unique in the area.

Buildings in Makri II were constructed with frames of posts with occasional use of mudbricks and stone. Traces of a possible stone enceinte wall need further clarification, but more important for the understanding of community organization is the concentration of storage facilities in the form of several clay bins and a large plastered pit in a central part of the settlement. The area, presumably roofed, was 60 m² in extent and was also furnished with a clay platform and three conical objects that have been alternatively interpreted as horns of consecration or as fire-stands. It is suggested that the complex may represent a communal storage area or centralized storage controlled by an elite. Information, however, on the general layout of the settlement is still insufficient, and no complete house plans have yet been documented. Nevertheless, numerous floors have been uncovered, often plastered and preserving a rich inventory of finds and features. Finally, there is evidence for the practice of intramural adult burial.[403]

Information on EBA patterns of occupation and material culture is sparse. It has been suggested that habitation continued in some of the earlier mounds and that affinities with the material culture from the northeastern Aegean and southern Bulgaria are displayed.[404] A major change has been recognized in the pattern of settlement during the Late Bronze Age. New sites were established during that period on eminent, naturally protected hilltops, away from the plain, in the upland areas near or away from the coast.[405] Two of the excavated sites, Ay. Georgios Maroneias and Asar Tepe (Kremasti Erganis) (fig. 2:40–41), both near the southeastern edge of the plain, also display large enceinte stone walls (ca. 1.40 m thick), with protected entrances and towers. More importantly, they contain areas segregated by additional walling at the very top, and rectangular or elliptical buildings inside. However, at Mourgana (fig. 2:37), another recently excavated small site, the post-framed houses were only protected by the precipitous natural formation of the hill.[406] The appearance of monumental constructions, the spatial segregation observed in some settlements, and the differences in construction and layout between settlements may imply changes in the sociopolitical organization of Thracian LBA communities. The low quality of current field data, however, prevents any detailed understanding of these new developments or of the processes that brought them about. Several issues remain open, such as the accurate dating of the enceinte walls or the economic implications of the shift in settlement to the upland areas.

EPIRUS

Epirus (fig. 3) is mountainous, difficult to explore and, because of ubiquitous steep grades, its landscape is subject to intense erosion and deposition. Fieldwork has been erratic. In view of those conditions, it is not surprising that few Neolithic sites are known in the province. It may in fact be more surprising that as many as 10–15 Neolithic sites are known.[407] A few are caves—that is, relatively stable, protected microenvironments. Others, masked by recently deposited sediments, were discovered "by chance," during construction of soccer fields or drainage ditches; they would have been undetectable by conventional surface surveys, however intensive. Such facts underline the rarity of stable areas in the Epirotic landscape, where Neolithic settlements might be easy to come upon. Remote sensing, in conjunction with GIS applications, should one day prove very useful in identifying surfaces, either buried or eroding, that

---

[403] A. Agelarakis and N. Efstratiou, "Skeletal Remains from the Neolithic Site of Makri, Thrace: A Preliminary Report," in Stratis et al. (supra n. 135) 11–21.

[404] Triantafyllos (supra n. 394) 40; Triantafyllos 1971 (supra n. 396) 430.

[405] Triantafyllos (supra n. 394) 42. Most sites were also occupied in the Iron Age and later periods, but had an earlier component dated to the LBA on the basis of wares decorated with incised and encrusted patterns or relief cordons, features also present in LBA eastern and central Macedonia; see Koukouli-Chrysanthaki 1992 (supra n. 359) 482–83, with a list of sites in Thrace. Koukouli-Chrysanthaki also discusses affinities with the central and northeastern Balkans. Notable is the absence of any trace of Mycenaean-type pottery from Thrace: Triantafyllos (supra n. 394) 42. Some caves were also reoccupied during the same period, Tsimbidis-Pentazos (supra n. 395) 87–88.

[406] For Asar Tepe and Ay. Georgios Maroneias, see Tsimbidis-Pentazos (supra n. 395) 90–93, 97–99; E. Tsimbidis-Pentazos, "Προϊστορικαί ακροπόλεις εν Θράκη," Prakt 1972, 86–91. For Mourgana, see D. Triantafyllos, "Αρχαιολογικές εργασίες στην Παρανέστια περιοχή," AEMT 4 (1990) 627–30.

[407] For summaries and bibliographic guides to older finds, see T. Papadopoulos, "Η Εποχή του Λίθου στην Ήπειρο," Dodoni 3 (1974) 125–34; T. Koungoulos, "Νεολιθικές εγκαταστάσεις Καστρίτσας Ιωαννίνων," Ηπειρωτική Εστία 1990, 3–24, where Neolithic material from the area of Kastritsa (fig. 3:2) also is discussed.

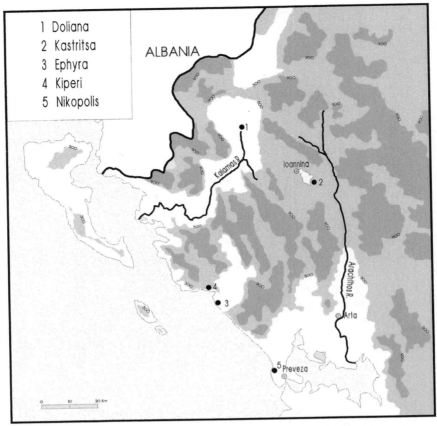

Fig. 3. Epirus. Principal sites mentioned in the text. Contours at 500 and 900 masl.

were settled in various phases during the Neolithic.[408]

Noteworthy, however, is the absence of Neolithic mound sites. That may suggest that settlements were relatively ephemeral, buildings were dispersed, limited use was made of earthen materials for construction, and/or that population density was never very high. By no means does it compel us to project the "Sarakatsani model" of pastoralism and transhumance onto the Neolithic;[409] the model is best reserved for the historical period or, at the earliest, for the Late Bronze Age.

The most interesting Neolithic find of recent years is a modest structure, dated to the range 3600–3100 B.C. (four ^{14}C dates), in the Doliana basin (ca. 300 masl; fig. 3:1). Here, in the vicinity of the headwaters of the Kalamas River,[410] excavations by the IB′ Ephoreia uncovered two superimposed "hut" floors (4.5 × 3.5 m) in association with hearths, an abundance of potsherds, and animal bone—a distinctive assemblage, without known parallels in the Neolithic and Early Bronze Age of Epirus.[411] The excavators named this assemblage "Doliana," cautiously also comparing the ceramics with those of Chalcolithic sites in Albania (Maliq phase IIb and Tren).[412] A pollen core from Gramousti, a former lake bottom 500 m west of the site, had previously been analyzed. The results are at odds with the archaeological record: forest reduction both preceded and, especially, followed the known Neolithic occupation, while in the

---

[408] These are the research strategies employed by the Nikopolis Project, a current joint venture of Boston University, the IB′ Ephoreia, and the 8th Ephoreia of Byzantine Antiquities: J. Wiseman, "Archaeology and Remote Sensing in the Region of Nikopolis, Greece," *Context* 9 (1992) 1–4; see also infra ns. 414 and 416.

[409] The objections to pastoral transhumance in the Neolithic have been voiced many times; see supra n. 181.

[410] The Doliana basin lies along a highly active fault: D. Sturdy, personal communication.

[411] A. Douzougli and K. Zachos, "Αρχαιολογικές έρευνες στην Ήπειρο και την Λευκάδα: 1989–1990," *Ηπειρωτικά Χρονικά* 31 (1994) 14–17 and pls. 3–5.

[412] For a ^{14}C date, calibrated to 4660–4092 B.C., from phase IIa at Maliq, see J. Guilaine and F. Prendi, "Dating the Copper Age in Albania," *Antiquity* 65 (1991) 574–78.

fourth millennium B.C. the oak forest regenerated.[413] Several episodes of intensified erosion and deposition during the Holocene also are attested by changing rates of sedimentation at Gramousti.

The Nikopolis Project has preliminarily reported ca. 20 secure Bronze Age sites in the lowlands of southwestern Epirus, many of them largely buried, and exposed only in road cuts and other scarps.[414] Two of those sites yielded ^{14}C dates within the second millennium B.C., but a ceramic chrono-typology remains an elusive objective. Bronze Age settlement appears to have been extensive in the vicinity of small coastal plains, such as the Acheron River mouth. A walled acropolis in "Cyclopaean" masonry, Xylokastra (or Ephyra), has been known in that area for some time (fig. 3:3);[415] the Nikopolis Project now adds possible terrace walls in the same masonry. Mycenaean ceramics are rare (ca. 50 out of 2,500 Bronze Age sherds) throughout the survey area. A reconstruction of the LBA site distribution with regard to land resources in southwestern Epirus ought to be within reach when the study of the survey data progresses.[416]

An important question concerns the nature of the acropolis at Xylokastra. Is it a Mycenaean "fort," or "trading post," comparable in its functions (at least initially) to, for example, the forts established by Europeans in North America in the 16th century and later? Or is it the material mark of an indigenous social transformation, indicating the emergence of a line of chiefs, who engaged in transactions with the polities of southern Greece, and managed to emulate some of their ways? The existence of burial tumuli within the acropolis, and of a tholos tomb at Kiperi (fig. 3:4), 10 km away,[417] is compatible with either of these scenarios. Authorities have as a rule favored the first scenario,[418] but the quality of evidence from the excavations at Xylokastra is less than satisfactory, and the interpretative efforts have been speculative. The site may, for example, have been a port of call along a probable "amber route"[419] (and it even yielded an amber bead),[420] but only well-designed fieldwork could substantiate such speculations.

As is well known, in the latter half of the second millennium B.C. quantities of bronze, especially in the form of weapons, were deposited in graves and buried as hoards throughout Epirus.[421] The pattern seems to set Epirus largely apart from the other provinces examined in this review, but its significance has yet to be fully realized. For some, those deposits constitute evidence for "pastoralist warriors or chieftains whose appreciation of fine craftsmanship and wide-ranging contacts enabled them to obtain suitable weapons."[422] Recent interpretations of somewhat analogous patterns in other periods and regions are geared to broader questions, and are informed by more sophisticated premises, such as the macroeconomic distinctions between "core" and "periphery," and between "gift" and "commodity." To A. and S. Sherratt, for example, the ritual deposition of metal might indicate a political economy that is out of step with the LBA Aegean "core," yet is already transformed by it through a "contagious process," the spread of the "desire for luxuries" among local elites.[423] S. Shennan adopts a comparable perspec-

---

[413] K.J. Willis, "The Late Quaternary Vegetational History of Northwest Greece III," *New Phytologist* 121 (1992), e.g., 146.

[414] T.F. Tartaron, "Prehistoric Settlement in Southern Epirus: Preliminary Results from Survey," *AJA* 98 (1994) 316 (abstract); Tartaron and K. Zachos, "The Mycenaeans and Epirus," forthcoming in *H περιφέρεια* (supra n. 53); see also supra n. 408.

[415] For a recent summary, see T. Papadopoulos, "Settlement Types in Prehistoric Epirus," in P. Darcque and R. Treuil eds., *L'habitat égéen préhistorique: Actes de la table ronde internationale, Athènes, 23–25 juin 1987* (*BCH* Suppl. 19, Paris 1990) 364.

[416] See now T. Tartaron, *Bronze Age Settlement and Subsistence in Southwestern Epirus, Greece* (Diss. Boston Univ. 1996).

[417] T. Papadopoulos, "Das mykenische Kuppelgrab von Kiperi bei Parga (Epirus)," *AM* 96 (1981) 7–24.

[418] Papadopoulos (supra n. 415); K.I. Soueref, *Μυκηναϊκές μαρτυρίες από την Ήπειρο* (Diss. Univ. of Thessaloniki 1986), e.g., 171; Feuer 88.

[419] See, e.g., A.F. Harding, "The Wessex Connection: Developments and Perspectives," in *Orientalisch-ägäische Einflüsse in der europäischen Bronzezeit: Ergebnisse eines Kollo-*

quiums (Römisch-Germanisches Zentralmuseum, Forschungsinstitut für Vor- und Frühgeschichte, Monograph 15, Bonn 1990) 139–43 and 153.

[420] In all, 12 amber beads are known from Epirus: Soueref (supra n. 418) 108.

[421] More than 80 weapons (daggers, swords, knives, axes, spearheads) are individually treated in Soueref (supra n. 418) 91–105. For a recently reported hoard, mainly of double axes, see E. Andreou, in *ArchDelt* 41 B' (1986) 114 and pls. 107–108. Contexts in general are poor, and that has encouraged the practice of connoisseurship with regard to the cultural identities and places of manufacture of the objects. Connoisseurship is effectively demonstrated in Soueref, who boldly juxtaposes the divergent opinions of various scholars. Local manufacture of some types of weapons has been argued by Wardle (supra n. 212) 190–98; the claim is not, however, repeated in Wardle 1993 (supra n. 299) 117–41.

[422] Feuer 88.

[423] A. and S. Sherratt, "Luxuries to Commodities: The Nature of Mediterranean Bronze Age Trading Systems," in Gale (supra n. 345), esp. 353–56 and 375.

tive: the Epirotic pattern should suggest to him an economy still in the "prestige mode," and, at once, "a tension between two different transactional orders," one of them taking the form of gift exchanges, the other arising from self-interested transactions.[424]

But these arguments are not only well informed by long-standing theoretical problems (and dilemmas that they attempt to resolve). They also — especially Shennan's — are aimed at interpreting thoroughly researched portions of the European archaeological record, and take into account a multitude of strands of local evidence.[425] For Epirus, the problem seems to be far more basic and discomforting: a scarcity of field data. The underdevelopment of prehistoric research — a chronic condition — has stunted progress. The archaeological imagination has always been resourceful in Epirus. It is time, however, for intensive fieldwork.

A NOTE ON THE EARLIEST NEOLITHIC

Good analytical work on the evidence for the earliest Neolithic in Greece has recently been published by Perlès.[426] The conclusion once more weighs heavily on the side of an allochthonous origin, and on colonization from the Near East. For Thessaly, in particular, "néolithisation" is regarded by Perlès as a fully exogenous process.[427] The Neolithic colonization of Greece, she further suggests, may not be an isolated event but an extension of a process already attested in the Near East, namely the "PPNB exodus."[428] Notwithstanding the reservations Perlès herself has about aspects of the relevant evidence, about her interpretation, and about similar interpretations

offered in recent decades, colonization at some scale appears to her to be beyond doubt, as does the (ultimately) Near Eastern origin of the colonists.

We take a more dim view of the evidence.[429] We think that questions about the earliest Neolithic in Greece will not be answered by "paper-and-pencil" operations but by fresh fieldwork. Exercises such as Perlès's have great analytical merit. The conclusions, however, can be only as good as the evidence upon which they rest, and here one meets with serious problems. For example, no northern Greek province (not even Thessaly)[430] has been researched thoroughly enough to justify the inference that it was uninhabited during the Pleistocene/Holocene transition and during the ensuing one or two millennia. The recent discoveries of probable Mesolithic sites in coastal Epirus,[431] and the tantalizing ^{14}C dates and finds from Theopetra Cave underline precisely this point. True, we cannot imagine that scores of Mesolithic sites will be discovered throughout northern Greece in the future; yet — it is worth remembering — the factors responsible for their scarcity in our records are not very well understood. Have we, for instance, been searching for Mesolithic sites in the wrong places? The pattern for the entire southern Balkan peninsula — if one can call ca. 15, widely dispersed, for the most part poorly dated occurrences a pattern — suggests a preference for locations near the (former) coast and other bodies of water. This observation will, no doubt, encourage some to invoke (once more) submergence and burial by alluviation as the reasons for the invisibility of the Mesolithic in northern Greece. Our aim is different, however —

---

[424] S. Shennan, "Commodities, Transactions, and Growth in the Central-European Bronze Age," *Journal of European Archaeology* 1:2 (1993) 59–72, esp. 66.

[425] It is in fact impossible to do justice to Shennan's argument (supra n. 424) without frequent reference to the rich data base for the Early Bronze Age in Central Europe.

[426] Perlès 1989 (supra n. 8) 109–27; Perlès (supra n. 136) 642–49; Perlès and Vitelli (supra n. 147) 226–33; Demoule and Perlès (supra n. 115), esp. 364–65. See also Bloedow (supra n. 8).

[427] van Andel and Runnels (supra n. 133) further amplify this view. See also Runnels 1995 (supra n. 136) 725. A different model, involving "borrowings" and interaction between colonizers and local Mesolithic groups, is envisaged for Franchthi and, perhaps, for Sidari: Perlès 1989 (supra n. 8) 117–20; Perlès (supra n. 136) 646.

[428] Perlès (supra n. 136) 648–49; J. Cauvin, "La néolithisation au Levant et sa première diffusion," in Aurenche and Cauvin (supra n. 8), esp. 14–24.

[429] Papers and comments on the earliest Neolithic in Europe — a veritable industry since the 1980s — as a rule cover very large areas (e.g., the whole of Greece, the Balkans, or the entire continent). Such broad perspectives are

dictated by the need for comparative treatment, but also by the scarcity of data pertinent to particular, relatively small regions. We cannot in this review delve into the larger picture and theoretical controversies for we must limit ourselves primarily to the evidence from northern Greece. For bibliography on the larger picture, see, e.g., Perlès (supra n. 136) passim; M. Zvelebil, "On the Transition to Farming in Europe, or What Was Spreading with the Neolithic: A Reply to Ammerman (1989)," *Antiquity* 63 (1989) 382–83; and C.N. Runnels and T.H. van Andel, "Trade and the Origins of Agriculture in the Eastern Mediterranean," *JMA* 1 (1988) 103–109.

[430] But see Runnels 1988 (supra n. 136) 284.

[431] Runnels 1995 (supra n. 136) 724–25. For Albania see K.M. Petruso, "Radiocarbon and Archaeomagnetic Dates from Konispol Cave, Albania," *Antiquity* 68 (1994) 335–39. Epipalaeolithic sites have in recent years also been claimed from the coast of Turkish Thrace: I. Gatsov and M. Özdoğan, "Some Epi-Paleolithic Sites from NW Turkey: Ağaçlı, Domalı and Gümüşdere," *Anatolica* 20 (1994) 97–120. Both the Epirotic and the Thracian finds are from surface surveys; their chronology is as yet problematic.

to direct future research to promising coastal spots and other areas rich in aquatic resources.

A second problematic area is the paucity of data from very early Neolithic sites in northern Greece—sites that, according to calibrated ^{14}C dates, were probably occupied ca. 6500 B.C. or earlier yet.[432] We concur with Perlès's assertion[433] that the chipped stone industry of "preceramic" Argissa (and Sesklo) has a distinctly Neolithic, rather than Mesolithic, character.[434] We find it methodologically unsound, however, to generalize from just two sites to the entire province of Thessaly. In short, the sample for Thessaly ca. 6500 B.C. is at this moment pitifully small to permit inferences of regional significance with regard to the nature and origin of the earliest Neolithic. Nothing militates against the possibility that some of the province's ca. 120 recorded EN sites conceal deposits roughly contemporary with those of "preceramic" Argissa and Sesklo, and that such deposits contain a chipped stone industry comparable to that of "aceramic" Franchthi.

There are further problems, including problems with chronology.[435] Demic diffusion from the Near East is considered the sole process by which Neolithic culture reached northern Greece, but was it? The evidence in favor of a positive answer is not as considerable as is currently thought.[436] But we wish to speculate no further, either about the earliest Neolithic of Thessaly, or about the "absence" of late seventh/early sixth millennium sites in Greek central and eastern Macedonia, and Thrace.[437] Rigorous, persistent fieldwork is in order. We only hope that the next wave of excavations into the Early Neolithic of northern Greece will be carried out by people who understand the difference between "strata" and deposits, people who, unlike our predecessors, will not subscribe to the "layer cake" view of the archaeological record (and of culture and history), and will be knowledgeable about, and attentive to, site formation processes. We also hope that they will document the data obtained from their researches in clear and incontrovertible ways.

DEPARTMENT OF ARCHAEOLOGY
UNIVERSITY OF THESSALONIKI
540 06 THESSALONIKI
GREECE
ANDREST@OLYMP.CCF.AUTH.GR

DEPARTMENT OF CLASSICS
UNIVERSITY OF CINCINNATI
CINCINNATI, OHIO 45221
FOTIADM@UCBEH.SAN.UC.EDU

DEPARTMENT OF ARCHAEOLOGY
UNIVERSITY OF THESSALONIKI
540 06 THESSALONIKI
GREECE
KOTSAKIS@OLYMP.CCF.AUTH.GR

---

[432] For this date see Bloedow (supra n. 8).

[433] Esp. Perlès 1989 (supra n. 8) 115–17.

[434] Some might regard this as too generous a concession, however: in the 1980s, Perlès examined the material collected by Milojčić in the 1950s. Milojčić's notion of "Steingeräte" may have been less inclusive than ours today, and his collection strategy may have systematically favored the discovery of pressure-flaked blades, at the expense of the products of a flake industry, such as those that later became known from, e.g., "aceramic" Franchthi. The same reservations may also hold for Theocharis's work.

[435] Of eight ^{14}C dates available from the earliest Thessalian Neolithic (the "preceramic"), three have appeared, without comment, in a table only: Coleman 209 (the dates are those from Argissa, with the prefix "H"); another two (UCLA-1657A and UCLA-1657D) are entangled in bizarre histories: Bloedow (supra n. 8) 50–53; no context for any of the eight dates has been adequately published. For disturbing problems with the dates from EN Achilleion as well, see Nandris (supra n. 119). Furthermore, we are doubtful that ^{14}C dates obtained early in the history of radiocarbon dating can be calibrated with confidence in the results.

[436] Cf. Runnels 1995 (supra n. 136) 725.

[437] Our colleagues in Turkish Thrace and Bulgarian Macedonia have, through systematic fieldwork, been able to resolve such dilemmas all the way to the borders of their countries with Greece: for Hoca Çeşme and Kovačevo, see respectively M. Özdoğan, Y. Miyake, and N. Özbaşaran Dede, "An Interim Report on Excavations at Yarımburgaz and Toptepe in Eastern Thrace," *Anatolica* 17 (1991) 81–82, and M. Lichardus-Itten, "Zum Beginn des Neolithikums im Tal der Struma (südwest-Bulgarien)," *Anatolica* 19 (1993), esp. 101–103.

Addendum: 1996–1999

STELIOS ANDREOU, MICHAEL FOTIADIS, AND KOSTAS KOTSAKIS

To the memory of Maria Mangafa (1964–1998), friend and collaborator

In this update to our earlier review of the Neolithic and Bronze Age of northern Greece (RAP V), we focus on recent developments in Thessaly, Macedonia, and Thrace.[438] Little new fieldwork has taken place in Epirus in the past few years and it is thus excluded from this brief discussion.

THESSALY

Large-scale public works in Thessaly during the last three years have prompted a campaign of extensive rescue excavations far surpassing in size and intensity any earlier archaeological project carried out in Thessaly. The Larisa area especially benefited from this opportunity, and archaeological work in that region is in progress. The immense quantity of material produced is only slowly entering the study phase and there are few concrete results to report as yet, although one can venture the prediction that the picture of Neolithic and Bronze Age Thessaly will change substantially when the new evidence becomes available in its totality. At present, preliminary reports permit a quick glance at this emerging picture.

Galini. Galini is a newly discovered site located east of Larisa near the homonymous village. It has been excavated to an extent of 0.17 ha.[439] The site was buried under 0.80 m of alluvial deposit and consists of numerous pits of varying size and shape dug into the natural subsoil. The distribution of the pits varies from closely packed in the southern part to widely dispersed in the northern. All of the pits were dated on the basis of pottery to the "Arapi" phase of the Late Neolithic and Galini is described as a single-period site. Of prime importance here is the adoption of an extended and unbounded pattern of hab-

itation, a practice that expands our perception of Neolithic settlement in Thessaly. It is now clear that the extended settlement seen at Sesklo B does not represent an isolated case in Thessaly.[440] As at Sesklo, this pattern is coeval with the tell sites that abound in the vicinity of Galini.

Rachmani (fig. 1:16). Rachmani is a well-known site dug by Wace and Thompson in the early 20th century, which gave its name to the elusive Final Neolithic of Thessaly. Rescue excavation here did not offer fresh evidence on the stratigraphic position of the FN "Rachmani" phase, mainly because it was confined to the western edge of the mound. It did, however, offer new information on the relationship of the settlement to its surroundings and particularly to the Gyrtoni alluvium, which reaches the edges of the mound. The new evidence indicates that Rachmani was situated on an active floodplain, perhaps similar to the setting of Platia Magoula Zarkou.[441]

Mandra. Mandra, with its concentric perimeter walls and ditches, is another previously known site that might have been excavated on a large scale.[442] The layout of the site recalls that of Dimini, with which Mandra is contemporary. Mandra's architecture indicates that the concentric pattern extends inland from the coastal area of eastern Thessaly and may represent a much more widespread practice of spatial organization among the Neolithic settlements of the region than had been previously realized.

Achilleion (fig. 1:18). A detailed study by Björk of the Early Neolithic pottery from Achilleion has been added to the information published from the site.[443] The author examines the technological and archaeological aspects of this pottery and discusses its possi-

---

[438] This addendum to RAP V was a collaborative effort: Andreou was responsible for the discussion of the Bronze Age in central Macedonia; Fotiadis wrote the section on western Macedonia; and Kotsakis compiled the information for Thessaly, eastern Macedonia, and Thrace. For information on Kastanas and Ayios Mamas, we wish to thank R. Jung, I. Aslanis, and B. Hänsel. We are also grateful to G. Toufexis for information on the new excavations in the Larisa region. Abbreviations used in RAP V above are also employed here.

[439] G. Toufexis, "Recent Neolithic Research in the Eastern Thessalian Plain, Greece," in *International Symposium: The Aegean in the Neolithic, Chalcolithic, and Early Bronze Age.*

Municipality of Urla, 13–19 October 1997 (forthcoming).

[440] Kotsakis (supra n. 15) 129; K. Kotsakis, "The Coastal Settlements of Thessaly," in G.A. Papathanassopoulos ed., *Neolithic Culture in Greece* (Athens 1996) 49–54; Kotsakis, "What Tells Can Tell: Social Space and Settlement in the Greek Neolithic," in P. Halstead ed., *Neolithic Society in Greece* (Sheffield Studies in Aegean Archaeology 2, Sheffield 1999) 66–76.

[441] Toufexis (supra n. 439).

[442] *Atlas* 145; Toufexis (supra n. 439).

[443] C. Björk, *Early Pottery in Greece: A Technological and Functional Analysis of the Evidence from Neolithic Achilleion, Thessaly* (SIMA 115, Jonsered 1995).

ble functional range. She suggests that the pottery was not used for storage and cooking and, following Vitelli's lead for the EN pottery from Franchthi Cave,[444] she favors a "symbolic" use. The distinction drawn between "domestic" and "symbolic" adopted in this study is debatable, however, and the contrast need not be as clear-cut as the author perceives.[445]

Theopetra Cave (fig. 1:21). Substantial work has been carried out in Theopetra Cave, which has clarified some aspects of the transition to the Neolithic. The preliminary results of this effort were presented in a conference held at Trikala in 1998. A series of ^{14}C dates bridges what had been thought to be a gap in occupation and it is now clear that the cave was used from the Middle Palaeolithic to the Final Neolithic. A closer look at lithics and other classes of archaeological evidence seems consistent with this scenario. There are still problems, however, with the stratigraphy of the cave, which, according to detailed lithostratigraphic analysis, shows substantial gaps and hiatuses. Nevertheless, the potential of the cave to increase our understanding of this crucial transitional phase remains considerable.[446]

WESTERN MACEDONIA

Middle Aliakmon valley: riverine zone. Excavations and surveys have continued at a fast pace. At the site of Aiani-Polemistra (on the left bank of the Aliakmon), a burnt building yielded a date (DEM-555) in the 19th–17th centuries B.C. associated with pottery comparable to that of the Thessalian Middle Bronze Age. The building was part of a sizable and long-lived settlement, founded in the Early Bronze Age. It was replaced by a new building, some walls of which were constructed of fieldstones set in the herringbone pattern familiar from sites along the Aegean coast but not previously attested in inland Macedonia.[447]

A number of burial grounds have also been excavated and preliminarily reported.[448] The earliest burial is an intramural cremation, with remains in an urn dated to the Late Neolithic. Most important, however, is the Bronze Age cemetery at Goules-Tourla (mentioned above, RAP V, 288). The dead, always single, were interred either in cists or, more often, in large pithoi, but two cremations were also identified. The bodies were placed in sharply contracted positions, those in pithoi being deposited through an opening in the belly of the vessel. One individual had been decapitated. Care was taken in closing all graves and, possibly, marking their location. Most of the dead were supplied with a used or "killed" cup (handles broken off), and a fifth of them were decorated with bronze jewelry. A triangular bronze dagger was also found. In short, the cemetery of Goules-Tourla is characterized by both orderliness (also reflected in the nearly uniform orientation of the graves) and variation. The date may well be in the very late third or early second millennium B.C. Some of the other cemeteries and isolated burials found in the area are dated to the very end of the Bronze Age, as indicated by the presence of matt-painted and Mycenaean IIIC pots. From one such grave, gold and bronze jewelry is reported, as well as an amber bead.[449]

Grevena area. A small excavation at Kremastos (670 masl) has demonstrated the permanent, agricultural nature of the EN sites first discovered in this area in the late 1980s. Substantial house remains (including evidence for ceilings or walls constructed with wooden planks), storage pits and jars, and charred seeds of emmer and pulses are among the finds from the site. Animal bone has not been preserved. Chipped stone tools were made of quartz. Pot profiles, fabrics, and decorative modes place the thin occupation horizon at a time near the end of the Early Neolithic. The site was briefly reoccupied in the Late Neolithic.[450]

Kremastos need not, of course, be representative of all 18 EN sites currently known in the upper Aliakmon catchment. Nor does the evidence answer the questions we raised earlier concerning the choice of settlement area and the reasons for abandonment

---

[444] K.D. Vitelli, *Franchthi Neolithic Pottery* 1: *Classification and Ceramic Phases 1 and 2* (*Franchthi* 8, Bloomington 1993) 213–18.

[445] Björk (supra n. 443) 113–35.

[446] N. Kyparissi-Apostolika, "The Significance of Theopetra Cave for Greek Prehistory," in M. Otte ed., *Préhistoire d'Anatolie: Genèse des deux mondes* I. *Actes du Colloque internationale, Liège, 28 avril–3 mai 1997* (Études et recherches archéologiques de l'Université de Liège 85, Liège 1998) 249–50; and Kyparissi-Apostolika, "The Neolithic Use of Theopetra Cave in Thessaly," in Halstead (supra n. 440) 142–52. A valuable compilation of research, literature, and finds gathered with meticulous care is presented in E. Alram-Stern, *Das Neolithikum in Griechenland, mit Ausnahme*

von Kreta und Zypern (Die Ägäische Frühzeit, 2. Serie; Forschungsbericht 1975–1993 I, Vienna 1996).

[447] A. Hondroyanni-Metoki, "Αλιάκμων 1994: Ερευνα οικισμού Εποχής Χαλκού," *AEMT* 8 (1994) 30–36.

[448] A. Hondroyanni-Metoki, "Από την έρευνα των νεκροταφείων στην κοιλάδα του μέσου ρου του Αλιάκμονα," in *Μνείας χάριν: Τόμος στη μνήμη Μαίρης Σιγανίδου* (Thessaloniki 1998) 287–97; H. Ziota and Hondroyanni-Metoki, "Αλιάκμων 1993: Προϊστορική έρευνα," *AEMT* 7 (1993) 36–41.

[449] Hondroyanni-Metoki (supra n. 448) 295.

[450] G. Toufexis, "Ανασκαφή στον Νεολιθικό οικισμό Κρεμαστός του Ν. Γρεβενών," *AEMT* 8 (1994) 17–26.

(RAP V, 290). An attempt to answer such questions has been made by Wilkie and Savina.[451] They invoke a possible climatic change and—disputing van Andel and Runnels[452]—point out that demic diffusion out of Thessaly may not have operated in favor exclusively of floodplains. We think that a satisfactory answer will have to be yet more complex, that it may be related to the exploratory practices of early farmers, and that it will entail revisions of our current conception of the objectives of those "farmers."

Kitrini Limni (fig. 2:4). Archaeologically contemporary with the Goules-Tourla cemetery in the Aliakmon valley, but larger and better preserved, is the cemetery of Xeropigado, 4 km to the east of Megalo Nisi Galanis.[453] Its extent is estimated at ca. 0.25 ha; three-fifths of the site has been excavated. Most of the 168 individual burials were placed directly into pits that were lined, covered, or simply dotted with fieldstones collected from nearby hills. The remains of a few cremations, on the other hand, were placed in jars or pithoi, as were sometimes the remains of children. Nine cist graves, all for children, were also identified. With a single (probable) exception, adult females were laid on their left, adult males on their right side. One or two used and/or "killed" cups accompanied most of the dead. Metallic goods were rarely deposited in the graves, but those found include two pieces of jewelry from precious metals or alloys; both pieces accompanied child burials.

Pebbles, snails, and fragments and components of tools were also placed with the dead in some cases. No group of burials stands out for its wealth, and no grave appears to have been conspicuously marked above ground. In brief, simple technology and a low degree of differentiation are the chief communal features of the cemetery, and they contrast sharply with the insistence on individual burials. Patterns of dental wear are indicative of relatively high rates

of meat consumption, higher than indicated for populations from later cemeteries in western Macedonia (e.g., the LBA cemetery of Spathes on Mt. Olympos).[454]

Mandalo (fig. 2:12). The small settlement of Mandalo on the northwestern flanks of the central Macedonian plain obtained its obsidian during the Final Neolithic from a Carpathian source. Melian obsidian is also present but may not have been brought in before the Early Bronze Age.[455] Such data need to be treated with caution, for the sample analyzed is small; one cannot yet speak, for example, of a realignment of exchange networks in the Bronze Age. Still, the presence at Mandalo of obsidian from Carpathia, ca. 800 km away, is remarkable, and not only because such obsidian is reported from the southern Balkans for the first time. We previously indicated that, notwithstanding its comparatively diminutive size (under 0.5 ha), Mandalo cannot be considered a settlement marginal to the economic and political systems of its time (RAP V, 294). The point is not that Mandalo is exceptional, but rather that the old idea of settlement hierarchy, based on site size, is an insufficient, possibly misleading, guide for approaching regional systems in the northern Greek Neolithic and Early Bronze Age; a rhizomatic, rather than a dendritic, model of those systems may be more realistic. The discovery of exotic obsidian at the site further underlines this point.[456]

Arhondiko (fig. 2:14). A large toumba (ca. 20 m high and more than 10 ha in area), Arhondiko was first occupied in the Neolithic, but excavations in the 1990s have concentrated on more recent periods. Two major architectural phases have been distinguished, the earlier of which is dated to the last 200–300 years of the third millennium, the second to the 21st–20th centuries B.C.[457] In the earlier phase buildings were constructed around frames of

[451] N.C. Wilkie and M.E. Savina, "The Earliest Farmers in Macedonia," *Antiquity* 71 (1997) 201–207.

[452] Supra n. 133.

[453] H. Ziota, "Προϊστορικό νεκροταφείο στην Κοιλάδα Κοζάνης: Μια πρώτη αναλυτική παρουσίαση της ανασκαφικής έρευνας (1995–1996)," in *Μνείας χάριν* (supra n. 448) 81–102.

[454] S. Triantaphyllou, "Prehistoric Cemetery Populations from Northern Greece: A Breath of Life for the Skeletal Remains," in K. Branigan ed., *Cemetery and Society in the Aegean Bronze Age* (Sheffield Studies in Aegean Archaeology 1, Sheffield 1998) 159–60.

[455] V. Kilikoglou et al., "Carpathian Obsidian in Macedonia, Greece," *JAS* 23 (1996) 343–49. All nine FN specimens analyzed were assigned to the "Carpathian 1" source; of the two EBA specimens, one was from the same source, the other from Demenagaki. None of the specimens is il-

lustrated or described; one wonders whether the "EBA" specimens could not be on recycled Neolithic material.

[456] Mandalo also boasts the earliest archaeological find of the saw-toothed grain beetle: S.M. Valamoti and P.C. Buckland, "An Early Find of *Oryzaephilus surinamensis* (L.) (Coleoptera: Silvanidae) from Final Neolithic Mandalo, Macedonia, Greece," *Journal of Stored Products Research* 31 (1995) 307–309. For the rhizomatic vs. the dendritic model, see especially G. Deleuze and F. Guattari, *A Thousand Plateaus: Capitalism and Schizophrenia* (Minneapolis 1987) 3–25.

[457] A. Papaefthimiou-Papanthimou and A. Pilali-Papasteriou, "Οι προϊστορικοί οικισμοί στο Μάνδαλο και στο Αρχοντικό Πέλλας," *AEMT* 10 (1996) 147–55. Note that there are confusing discrepancies between the tables of ^{14}C dates (pp. 149–50) and the ensuing commentary.

posts and their walls were built in the wattle-and-daub technique. Of special interest are concentrations of kitchen facilities, which include well-preserved domed ovens as well as storage bins. From one of the latter a substantial quantity of einkorn wheat was retrieved. The grain had been stored still dressed in its spikelets, presumably for protection from pests.[458] Buildings of the second phase, on the other hand, had substantial stone foundations. The ceramics of this later phase include a few pots and sherds decorated with bands of incisions, filled with a white substance. This decorative mode has been known from central Macedonia since the days of Stanley Casson, but its absolute chronology was until now in dispute.

Nea Nikomedeia (fig. 2:11). The recently published ^{14}C dates from Nea Nikomedeia might fully resolve the issue of the chronology of this site. If calibrated, most of those dates would fall in the last four centuries of the seventh millennium B.C., thus placing Nea Nikomedeia squarely within the Greek Early Neolithic, in an advanced phase of it. If we hesitate slightly on the matter, it is only because the new dates have been published without indications of provenience or further comments.[459] The duration of the settlement has been estimated to be 50–150 years, and three (rather than the original two) generations of buildings have been distinguished. Estimates of community size (500–700 individuals during the first two phases) may be toward the higher end, for they assume simultaneous occupation of all buildings.[460] The analysis of the ceramic material has demonstrated that several ceramic pastes were used at once, all of which probably derived from local sources, and none of them was reserved for any particular kind of vessel.[461] It has also been shown that the color of the so-called pink slipped ware from the site is in fact a pigment rather than a slip; it is made of crushed hematite mixed with clay.[462] Calculations of rates of ceramic production (pots per year) have been attempted, but should be treated with caution; they rest on an estimate offered by Rodden at the time of excavation and can no longer be verified, because only a fraction of the excavated pottery was kept.

Yannitsa area. The number of known EN sites in the central Macedonian plain has been growing.[463] The lack of ^{14}C dates, however, in combination with the near-invisibility of the MN period in the province, engenders discomforting questions: could it be that some of what is considered EN pottery is indeed later? On the other hand, a new excavation at Axos A (west of Yannitsa) may well have revealed an EN phase earlier than those represented at Nea Nikomedeia and Yannitsa B, but documentation of this phase of "monochrome pottery" remains inadequate.[464]

CENTRAL MACEDONIA

Stavroupolis. Rescue excavations at Stavroupolis revealed an extended occupation of over 4 ha. The deposits, with a maximum depth of 4 m, were divided into several architectural phases, all dated to the early Late Neolithic, on grounds of typological ceramic similarities. The earliest phase is distinguished by pit-dwellings, while subsequent phases display an architecture of rectangular houses with clay floors, hearths, and storage facilities.[465] The site was deserted before pottery types considered broadly contemporary with the "Dimini" phase made their appearance.

Kastanas (fig. 2:16). An investigation of the spatial distribution of activities in the settlement of Kastanas, taking into account all archaeological and bioarchaeological data, offers valuable insights regarding the communal relationships at the site during the penultimate phase of the Late Bronze Age (levels 16–14).[466] Activities related to small-scale storage, preparation, cooking (in portable hearths), and consumption of food occurred, along with spinning and sewing, mainly inside the small buildings of the earliest level (16). Long-term storage, on the other hand, was confined to a very small freestand-

[458] S. Valamoti, "Αρχαιοβοτανικά κατάλοιπα από τον οικισμό του Αρχοντικού: Ανασκαφική περίοδος Σεπτεμβρίου 1993," *AEMT* 7 (1993) 155–58, with a long list and discussion of the species identified; A. Papaefthimiou-Papanthimou and A. Pilali-Papasteriou, "Ανασκαφή Αρχοντικού 1993," *AEMT* 7 (1993) 149.

[459] Pyke and Yiouni (supra n. 171) 195.

[460] Pyke and Yiouni (supra n. 171) 47–48.

[461] Pyke and Yiouni (supra n. 171) 76–77, 186. These conclusions parallel nicely those of Vitelli for EN Franchthi; see, e.g., K.D. Vitelli, "Pots, Potters, and the Shaping of Greek Neolithic Society," in W.K. Barnett and J.W. Hoopes eds., *The Emergence of Pottery: Technology and Innovation in Ancient Societies* (Washington, D.C. 1995) 60.

[462] Pyke and Yiouni (supra n. 171) 65–69.

[463] P. Hrisostomou, "Η Νεολιθική κατοίκηση στη βόρεια παράκτια ζώνη του άλλοτε Θερμαϊκού κόλπου (επαρχία Γιαννιτσών)," *AEMT* 10 (1996) 167; N. Merousis and A. Stefani, "Προϊστορικοί οικισμοί του Νομού Ημαθίας," *Μακεδονικά* 29 (1993–1994) 354.

[464] Hrisostomou (supra n. 463) 62–64.

[465] D. Grammenos, S. Kotsos, and A. Hatzoudi, "Σωστικές ανασκαφές στο Νεολιθικό οικισμό της Σταυρούπολης," *AEMT* 11 (1997, in press).

[466] C. Becker, "Zur Rekonstruction von Aktivitätsmustern in spätbronzezeitlichen Haushalten, untersucht am Fundmaterial aus Kastanas (Nordgriechenland)," *PZ* 70 (1995) 96–114.

ing structure, at the entrance of which is evidence for increased meat consumption. In the next level (15), the space of the small storeroom and the residential unit next to it was taken over by an extensive oval house with a large permanent hearth and sizable storage facilities inside. A similar hearth was also placed in an outer court.

Finally, in level 14b, the total area was taken over by a large "megaron" with one permanent hearth placed inside. The scale of storage, preparation, and consumption of foodstuffs was greater than ever before, both within the structure and in the surrounding open space, and it is suggested that the house served a large crowd. Moreover, the artifact-rich deposits imply a more elaborate material culture and a greater variety of activities. One may conclude from the analysis presented by Becker that a series of transformations in communal relationships occurred during the period between ca. 1250 and 1150 B.C. The evidence from the early phase implies a social regime of small, spatially distinct yet interdependent residential units, sharing surpluses on occasions of group consumption and feasting. In the later levels, however, there is a shift to larger and stronger residential groups, which stress their presence through increased storage facilities and collective public consumption.[467]

The recently finished, thorough study of the Mycenaean-style pottery from Kastanas completes the series of publications of the prehistoric levels of the site, making it the only fully published prehistoric excavation in Macedonia.[468] As seems to be the rule

in the area, a limited amount of LH IIIA2- and IIIB-style pottery appears for the first time in level 16 of Kastanas. Numbers rise considerably with the first appearance of early and middle LH IIIC-style pottery in levels 14 and 13, respectively, to reach the highest point in the earliest Early Iron Age level 12, in which, however, late LH IIIC-style and Early Protogeometric pottery occur together.[469]

Toumba Thessalonikis (fig. 2:20). Continuing work at Toumba has refined the earlier stratigraphy of the site. Two early LBA architectural phases (6 and 7) have been defined. Decorated pottery in these early phases was limited to matt-painted and incised categories, which contrasts with the situation during the later phase 5, when LH IIIA2- and IIIB-style pottery was present. Three earlier architectural phases (8–10), separated from 6 and 7 by an extensive destruction horizon, seem compatible with MBA and late EBA dates. The construction of stone walls during the early phases was generally more meticulous than later on, employing occasionally the herringbone pattern familiar from other Aegean sites, but no complete house plans can be made out. Later LBA walls, however, do not suggest any major reorientation of the earlier settlement plan, apart from the fact that later habitation was confined to the very top of the mound, above the imposing LBA earthen ramparts.[470]

Mesimeriani Toumba. The site of Mesimeriani lies on the hilly area at the southern edge of the Thermaic Gulf, a few kilometers from the present coast. Following a Neolithic (Middle and Late?) phase extending to ca 4.5 ha, habitation contracted during

---

[467] Perhaps, after a short regression, the process of expansion of the residential unit took a more concrete and stable form in level 12, again related to food preparation and consumption on a larger scale. See *Kastanas* 52–53, 171–79.

[468] R. Jung, *Kastanas: Ausgrabungen in einem Siedlungshügel der Bronze- und Eisenzeit Makedoniens, 1975–1979: Die Drehscheibenkeramik der Schichten 19 bis 11* (Prähistorische Archäologie in Südosteuropa, Berlin, in press).

[469] Jung (supra n. 468). A new ^{14}C date of 965±49 B.C. has been provided for the immediately following level 11, with Middle Protogeometric pottery. This allows a date for level 12 in the late 11th or early 10th century B.C. More ^{14}C dates from short-lived samples are expected and may resolve the problematic dating of level 12; see supra n. 291. A similar assemblage has been found at Toumba Thessalonikis, but Aegean-style painted pottery is lacking from the Early Iron Age levels of Assiros. For Toumba, see supra n. 324 and S. Andreou and K. Kotsakis, "Η προϊστορική τούμπα της Θεσσαλονίκης: Παλιά και νέα ερωτήματα," *AEMT* 10 (1996) 369–87; for Assiros, see K. Wardle, "Change and Continuity: Assiros Toumba at the Transition from Bronze to Iron Age," *AEMT* 10 (1996) 427–42. For further discussion of the Mycenaean pottery

from Kastanas, see below.

[470] For a general review of excavation results, see Andreou and Kotsakis (supra n. 469). For technological aspects of the Toumba pottery, see V. Kiriatzi, "Η μελέτη της τεχνολογίας ως δείκτης ανθρώπινης συμπεριφοράς: Παρατηρήσεις στην κατασκευή κεραμεικής της ΥΕΧ από την Τούμπα Θεσσαλονίκης," *ArchMak* 6 (1999) 585–97. For quantified accounts of the Mycenaean ware from the site and a discussion of the possible meaning of Mycenaean pottery in Macedonian contexts, see S. Andreou, "Looking South through a Wine Glass: LH III Pottery from the Toumba of Thessaloniki" (in preparation); S. Andreou, "Μυκηναϊκή κεραμική και μακεδονικές κοινωνίες κατά την Εποχή του Χαλκού" in *Β′ Διεθνές Διεπιστημονικό Συμπόσιο: "Η περιφέρεια του Μυκηναϊκού κόσμου," Λαμία, 26–30 Σεπτεμβρίου 1999* (Lamia, forthcoming). For the evidence of wine making at Toumba, see M. Mangafa and K. Kotsakis, "A New Method for Identification of Wild and Cultivated Charred Grape Seeds," *JAS* 23 (1996) 409–18; and Mangafa et al., "Αμπελοκαλλιέργεια στην προϊστορική Μακεδονία: Τα δεδομένα της προϊστορικής τούμπας Θεσσαλονίκης," *Πρακτικά Ε′ Τριημέρου Εργασίας: Αμπελο-οινική ιστορία στο χώρο της Μακεδονίας και Θράκης* (Athens 1998) 158–69.

the Early Bronze Age to a large (1 ha), well-defined mound. By the Early Iron Age, the mound had attained a height of 16 m. The LBA deposits were very shallow and MBA levels were not easily definable. The EBA deposits, on the other hand, were particularly thick (12 m). They comprised a series of 17 reconstructions of post-framed, rectangular buildings, the most recent of which provided a ^{14}C date of 2194–1931 B.C. Although no complete house plans have been preserved, the remains of a heavily burnt room reveal the same concentration of food storage and preparation facilities seen also at contemporary sites in eastern and western Macedonia.[471] The importance of the room and of the activities taking place in it are underlined by the discovery of large relief fragments of clay with curvilinear motifs, possibly decorating a wall or structure.[472]

Ayios Mamas (fig. 2:25). Unlike Mesimeriani, Ayios Mamas, located on a peninsula during the Bronze Age, provides a long stratigraphy and a wealth of information regarding the MBA material culture in Chalkidiki.[473] In an excavated area of 850 m², four successive architectural phases, attributed to the Middle Bronze Age on general ceramic affinities, have been identified. The earliest phase comprises three partly excavated, elongated, and freestanding post-framed houses with similar orientation, lying next to one other. The houses were destroyed in a severe conflagration. Hearths, ovens, benches, and vessels for storage, cooking, eating, and drinking testify to domestic activities inside the houses. Pottery from Ayios Mamas displays affinities with ceramics from the early MBA levels of Kastanas, but also includes a

gray, wheelmade jug, most likely an import. In the second phase, brown- and red-slipped kantharoi are distinctive, and in the third, fine gray Minyan ring-stemmed goblets first occur, continuing into the next phase, along with other MBA burnished wares. The quantity and quality of "Minyanlike" pottery diminish in the subsequent level, which may be considered transitional to the Late Bronze Age. Disturbances from the heavy building activity of the Byzantine period have caused severe damages to the LBA levels. Despite that, levels belonging to this period have been identified. A street with parts of houses reminds one of Toumba Thessalonikis, as does the absence of any severe destruction during the period. On the other hand, ramparts similar to those from Toumba Thessalonikis and Assiros are not reported from Ayios Mamas. As far as Mycenaean pottery is concerned, the site conforms to the usual central Macedonian pattern, with LH IIIA2-style pottery being the earliest stratified material.[474]

Following recent research, the picture regarding the central Macedonian Middle and Late Bronze Age is changing. Organizational differences among the excavated LBA sites have already been touched upon, as well as possible differences in the position and role of each site within regional networks.[475] However, more studies of changing communal relationships within sites are essential for the apprehension of the social strategies employed by different groups participating in these networks. Cultural differences are evident even between areas as close to one another as the Thermaic Gulf area and Chalkidiki.[476] Toumba Thessalonikis and Ayios Mamas offer

[471] E. Elster, "Construction and Use of the Early Bronze Age Burnt House at Sitagroi: Craft and Technology," in R. Laffineur and P.P. Betancourt eds., *TEXNH: Craftsmen, Craftswomen and Craftsmanship in the Aegean Bronze Age* (*Aegaeum* 16, Liège 1997) 19–34.

[472] See supra ns. 286, 332. For recent work, see D.V. Grammenos and S. Kotsos, "Ανασκαφή στον προϊστορικό οικισμό Μεσημεριανή τούμπα Τριλόφου," *AEMT* 10 (1996) 355–68. Chance finds of copper tools from the site have been published together with the well-known hoard of Petralona. All are dated on morphological grounds to the late third millennium B.C. See D.V. Grammenos et al., "Ο θησαυρός των Πετραλώνων της Χαλκιδικής και άλλα χάλκινα εργαλεία της ΠΕΧ από την ευρύτερη περιοχή," *ArchEph* 1994, 75–116.

[473] For recent work, see I. Aslanis and B. Hänsel, "Ανασκαφές για τη Μεσοελλαδική της Μακεδονίας στον Αγιο Μάμα," *ArchMak* 6 (1999) 99–108; and Aslanis and Hänsel, "Αγιος Μάμας: Ο πρώϊμος Μεσοελλαδικός οικισμός," *AEMT* 12 (forthcoming). For a preliminary examination of the possible uses of the several thousand marine mollusks found in the archaeological deposits of the site, see C. Becker,

"Nourriture, cuillères, ornaments . . . Les temoignages d'une exploration varié des mollusques marins à Ayios Mamas (Chalcidique, Grèce)," *Anthropozoologica* 24 (1996) 3–17.

[474] For preliminary information, mostly regarding the Mycenaean pottery from Kastanas, see Jung (supra n. 468); R. Jung, "Η μυκηναϊκή και πρωτογεωμετρική κεραμική της Μακεδονίας και η σημασία της," in *B' Διεθνές Διεπιστημονικό Συμπόσιο* (supra n. 470). A LH II sherd, most likely an import from the Argolid, comes from a disturbed level. Three Mycenaean animal figurines, in addition to one from Heurtley's excavations, are reported by Jung, all from disturbed levels.

[475] Supra ns. 306, 320.

[476] A synthesis of northern Greek prehistory from the Neolithic to the Early Iron Age with particular emphasis on regional cultural aspects appeared almost concurrently with RAP V; see K.A. Wardle, "The Prehistory of Northern Greece: A Geographical Perspective," in *Αφιέρωμα στον N.G.L. Hammond* (Παράρτημα Μακεδονικών 7, Thessaloniki 1997) 81–113.

good examples. During the Middle Bronze Age variation exists both in material culture and in settlement organization: neither "Minyan" pottery nor post-frame architecture appears at Toumba. It is equally important to know whether this pattern of cultural differences persists into the Late Bronze Age or has a long ancestry going back to the Neolithic.

The understanding of the patterns of production, circulation, and consumption of Mycenaean-style pottery in central Macedonia has been improved by recent work at the sites of Kastanas, Ayios Mamas, and Toumba Thessalonikis.[477] Chemical analysis of pottery from Kastanas indicates the presence of southern imports, but analytical and macroscopic work at Kastanas, Assiros, and Toumba suggests that most of the pottery was made in Macedonia, beginning as early as LH IIIB. While pottery found at Kastanas, Ayios Mamas, and Toumba Thessalonikis displays notable similarities, the differences in the Mycenaean assemblages of the three sites are marked, suggesting distinct production centers and circulation networks supplying each site.[478] Despite adherence to the canonical repertoire of shapes and motifs, there are divergences and local peculiarities.[479] Technological variability at Kastanas and Toumba may suggest a different provenance for the ceramics, different potters, or varying conditions of production. The development of a regional Macedonian style is most likely to respond to the specific needs and tastes of the local consumers. There is a strong preference evident for painted Mycenaean pottery and a predilection for particular shapes (mainly drinking vessels and other containers for liquids and aromatics). These preferences demonstrate the selective principles formed within a specific cultural context in which Mycenaean-style pottery was consumed. In view of the evidence from recent studies, the traditional interpretations, whereby the presence of Mycenaean-style pottery in central Macedonia is perceived as a sign of Mycenaean settlers or "emporia," seem less compelling.[480] Instead, the gradual adoption of Mycenaean ware may be perceived as part of a long-term process related to the gradual elaboration of material cultural values in the context of specific social practices of members of LBA Macedonian communities. The process probably started, as far as pottery is concerned, with the production and use of matt-painted and incised pottery at the transition between the Middle and Late Bronze Age.[481]

EASTERN MACEDONIA AND THRACE

Dikili Tash (fig. 2:35). The work carried out at Dikili Tash during the last 10 years is summarized in a recent paper published in *AEMT*.[482] Excavations at the site focused on two sectors, one at the foot of the tell, where early LN deposits reaching a depth of 5 m were examined, and another higher up on the mound, where material from the end of the LN period was investigated. In the lower sector, a series of

---

[477] For our previous discussion of Mycenaean pottery in central Macedonia, see supra ns. 303, 319, 330, 342, 343. For Kastanas and Ayios Mamas, see Jung (supra ns. 468, 474); for Toumba Thessalonikis, see Andreou (supra n. 470).

[478] For analytical work from Kastanas, see H. Momsen et al., "Classification of Mycenaean Pottery from Kastanas by Neutron Activation Analysis," in Y. Maniatis ed., *Archaeometry. Proceedings of the 25th International Symposium, Athens, 19–23 May 1986* (Amsterdam 1989) 515–23. Few early sherds were attributed to the Mycenae-Berbati composition group; see Jung (supra n. 468). For petrographic analyses from Thessaloniki, see Kiriatzi (supra n. 470) and Andreou (supra n. 470).

[479] Jung (supra n. 474).

[480] Jung (supra n. 474), in his preliminary discussion of the Ayios Mamas material, argues against the usual interpretation of this particular site as a Mycenaean "emporion." Nor does the evidence from Toumba Thessalonikis, another likely spot for a trading station, seem to offer any support for such an interpretation. See Andreou and Kotsakis (supra n. 306), in *A΄ Διεθνές Διεπιστημονικό Συμπόσιο: "Η περιφέρεια του Μυκηναϊκού κόσμου," Λαμία, 25–29 Σεπτεμβρίου 1994. Πρακτικά* (Lamia 1999) 107–16, where references to discussions of emporia and settlers in Macedonia are given.

[481] See Andreou (supra n. 470). It is suggested that Mycenaean pottery was used in periodic occasions of feasting or body cleansing involving ceremonial consumption of alcohol and aromatic substances during which decorated pottery was displayed. These ceremonial occasions fostered the growth, stability, and cohesion of social groups in the various tell communities of central Macedonia. For some possible indications of this social practice and strategy, see the above section on Kastanas. For a preliminary date for the appearance of matt-painted and incised pottery in central Macedonia, see supra n. 326. For recent opinions about the mechanisms of trade between the Mycenaean mainland and northern Greece, see N. Wardle, "The Impact of Mycenaean on Peripheral Communities," in *Β΄ Διεθνές Διεπιστημονικό Συμπόσιο* (supra n. 470) and H.A. Bankoff, N. Meyer, and M. Stefanovich, "Handmade Burnished Ware and the Late Bronze Age of the Balkans," *JMA* 9 (1996) 193–209. For an evaluation of figurines and burial customs as evidence for Mycenaean contacts with Macedonia, see A. Pilali-Papasteriou, "Η μυκηναϊκή παρουσία στη Μακεδονία: Προβλήματα και επανεκτιμήσεις," in *Η περιφέρεια* (supra n. 480) 103–106.

[482] C. Koukouli-Chrysanthaki, R. Treuil, and D. Malamidou, "Προϊστορικός οικισμός Φιλίππων 'Ντικιλί Τας': Δέκα χρόνια ανασκαφικής έρευνας," *AEMT* 10 (1996) 681–704.

postholes is all that survives from the layout of houses; they seem to run in a northwest–southeast direction. Of particular interest is the conclusion reached from a combination of archaeological macroscopic examination and laboratory analysis that the clays used for different domestic constructions such as walls, floors, benches, roofs, and ovens were deliberately selected for their properties. A large number of ovens were excavated, of which two preserved part of their domed construction, formed with superimposed coils. Ovens, together with adjacent platforms, represent the most tangible remains of the houses. An isolated find related to these houses is intriguing: a bucranium modeled in clay was probably attached to the interior surface of a wall. In the upper sector, the excavation of a complex of four houses dated to the end of the Late Neolithic was continued.[483] Among the structures, house 4 was special in that it was divided into three separate rooms. Each room was equipped with an oven, a bench and/or clay basin, a large number of pots for food preparation and consumption, querns, and other domestic equipment, but no figurines.[484] Sizable vessels of unbaked clay, occasionally with incised decoration, as well as large pithoi testify to the significance of storage inside houses, but also to the control of storage and consumption at the household level. This picture is compatible with the intense use of settlement space seen also at sites of the Balkan Chalcolithic, in which densely packed houses have little or no empty spaces between them. Finally, a series of new ^{14}C dates place this complex of houses in the time span of 4230–4043 B.C.[485]

Promachonas-Topolniča (fig. 2:27). A joint Greek-Bulgarian excavation program was inaugurated at this site, which is bisected by the border between Greece and Bulgaria.[486] The Bulgarian part has been excavated from 1980 to 1990 and three phases were defined, verified subsequently on the Greek side. The lower two phases preserved post-framed architecture dated on the basis of four ^{14}C samples to the beginning of the fifth millennium. Although the site is roughly contemporary with Dikili Tash I, the pattern of settlement organization is completely different, with Promachonas exhibiting scattered habitation.

Makri (fig. 2:42). A recent report on excavations at the Neolithic site of Makri in Thrace gives firmer information on stratigraphy, sedimentology, ceramic sequence, stone industries, and animal and plant remains, as well as charcoal and phytoliths.[487] Makri grew from a small camp to an extensive settlement, although some episodes of abandonment seem to have intervened.

DEPARTMENT OF ARCHAEOLOGY
ARISTOTLE UNIVERSITY OF THESSALONIKI
THESSALONIKI 540 06
GREECE
ANDREST@HIST.AUTH.GR

DEPARTMENT OF HISTORY AND ARCHAEOLOGY
UNIVERSITY OF IOANNINA
DOUROUTI, IOANNINA 451 10
GREECE

DEPARTMENT OF ARCHAEOLOGY
ARISTOTLE UNIVERSITY OF THESSALONIKI
THESSALONIKI 540 06
GREECE
KOTSAKIS@HIST.AUTH.GR

---

[483] Supra n. 365. See also R. Treuil and P. Darcque, "Un 'bucrane' néolithique à Dikili Tash (Macédoine orientale): Parallèles et perspectives d'interprétation," *BCH* 122 (1998) 1–25.

[484] Koukouli-Chrysanthaki et al. (supra n. 482) 693.

[485] Koukouli-Chrysanthaki et al. (supra n. 482) 693–94.

[486] C. Koukouli-Chrysanthaki, H. Todorova, I. Aslanis,

J. Bojadziev, F. Konstantopoulou, I. Vajsov, and M. Valla, "Προμαχώνας-Topolniča: Νεολιθικός οικισμός Ελληνοβουλγαρικών συνόρων," *AEMT* 10 (1996) 745–67.

[487] N. Efstratiou et al., "Excavations at the Neolithic Settlement of Makri, Thrace, Greece (1988–1996): A Preliminary Report," *Saguntum* 31 (1998) 11–62.

Review of Aegean Prehistory VI:
The Palatial Bronze Age of the
Southern and Central Greek Mainland

CYNTHIA W. SHELMERDINE

Dedicated to John Chadwick and William A. McDonald

INTRODUCTION

This review of Aegean prehistory focuses on the Late Bronze Age in southern and central Greece, with emphasis on current scholarly views about Mycenaean culture in the palatial age.* Much of the evidence on which these views depend has emerged or been reassessed during the last two decades. In

* My thanks to Fred Kleiner and Tracey Cullen for inviting me to contribute to this series in *AJA*, and for their editorial help. I owe a particular debt to J.L. Davis, who set the standard and showed the way in the first review of this series (*AJA* 96 [1992] 699–756), and to J.B. Rutter for his coverage of the prepalatial Greek mainland (*AJA* 97 [1993] 745–97). This review is dedicated to two pioneers with whom I was privileged to work: John Chadwick in textual matters, and William A. McDonald on the archaeological side.

Many colleagues have been generous in their response to pleas for information, permissions, and/or advice: Vassilis Aravantinos, Paul Åström, John Bennet, Emmett Bennett, Pierre Carlier, Eric Cline, Fred Cooper, Michael Cosmopoulos, Jack Davis, Peter Day, Katie Demakopoulou, Oliver Dickinson, Elizabeth French, Robin Hägg, Halford Haskell, Spiros Iakovides, John Killen, Eleni Konsolaki-Yannopoulou, Peter Kuniholm, Albert Leonard, Christopher Mee, José Melena, Penelope Mountjoy, Mike Nelson, Jean-Pierre Olivier, Ruth Palmer, Ingo Pini, Cemal Pulak, David Reese, Curtis Runnels, Jerry Rutter, Kim Shelton, Carol Thomas, Gisela Walberg, Peter Warren, Berit Wells, Malcolm Wiener, Jim Wright, and Eberhard Zangger. I am also grateful to those who provided technical and editorial help and general encouragement: John Bennet, Kate Bracher, Jack Davis, Elaine Godwin, Sebastian Heath, Jan Jackson, Jane Okrasinski, Pamela Russell, Jerry Rutter, Susan Shelmerdine, and Chris Williams. Despite the best efforts of all these people, this review does not claim to be a comprehensive treatment of all aspects of LH III Greece. As usual in such cases, the choice of topics included is idiosyncratic, but I hope others too will find them important and interesting.

The following abbreviations are used in this review:

"Chronique"	"Chronique des fouilles," *BCH*.
Davis	J.L. Davis, "Review of Aegean Prehistory I: The Islands of the Aegean," *AJA* 96 (1992) 699–756.
Documents[2]	M. Ventris and J. Chadwick, *Documents in Mycenaean Greek*[2] (Cambridge 1973).
French and Wardle	E.B. French and K.A. Wardle eds., *Problems in Greek Prehistory* (Bristol 1988).
Gazetteer	R. Hope Simpson and O.T.P.K. Dickinson, *A Gazetteer of Aegean Civilisation in the Bronze Age* 1: *The Mainland and Islands* (*SIMA* 52, Göteborg 1979).
Hägg and Marinatos	R. Hägg and N. Marinatos eds., *Sanctuaries and Cults in the Aegean Bronze Age* (Stockholm 1981).
Hägg and Nordquist	R. Hägg and G.C. Nordquist eds., *Celebrations of Death and Divinity in the Bronze Age Argolid* (Stockholm 1990).
Kardulias	P.N. Kardulias ed., *Beyond the Site: Regional Studies in the Aegean Area* (London 1994).
Killen	J.T. Killen, "The Linear B Tablets and the Mycenaean Economy," in A. Morpurgo Davies and Y. Duhoux eds., *Linear B: A 1984 Survey* (Bibliothèque des Cahiers de l'Institut de Linguistique de Louvain 26, Louvain 1985) 241–305.
Mykenaïka	J.-P. Olivier ed., *Mykenaïka: Actes du IXᵉ Colloque international sur les textes mycéniens et égéens, Athènes, 2–6 octobre 1990* (*BCH* Suppl. 25, Paris 1992).
Politeia	R. Laffineur and W.-D. Niemeier eds., *Politeia: Society and State in the Aegean Bronze Age* (Aegaeum 12, Liège 1995).
Rehak	P. Rehak ed., *The Role of the Ruler in the Prehistoric Aegean* (Aegaeum 11, Liège 1995).
Rutter	J.B. Rutter, "Review of Aegean Prehistory II: The Prepalatial Bronze Age of the Southern and Central Greek Mainland," *AJA* 97 (1993) 745–97.
Studies Bennett	J.-P. Olivier and T.G. Palaima eds., *Texts, Tablets and Scribes: Studies in Mycenaean Epigraphy and Economy Offered to Emmett L. Bennett, Jr.* (*Minos* Suppl. 10, Salamanca 1988).
Studies Chadwick	J.T. Killen, J.L. Melena, and J.-P. Olivier eds., *Studies in Mycenaean and Classical Greek Presented to John Chadwick* (*Minos* 20–22, Salamanca 1987).

Originally published in *AJA* 101 (1997) 537–85.

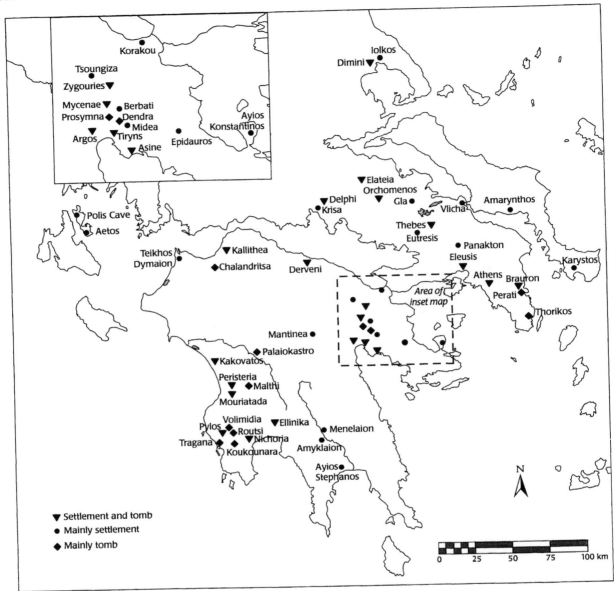

Fig. 1. Map of archaeological sites in Greece mentioned in the text. (C.W. Shelmerdine and C. Williams)

addition to new discoveries, new interpretations have been inspired by advances in technology and by changes in our own cultural attitudes, which influence the way we look at the past.

The geographical scope (fig. 1) coincides with that of Rutter's review in *AJA* on the prepalatial Bronze Age.[1] The northern limit of coverage extends from the Gulf of Arta in the west to the mouth of the Spercheios River in the east. Below this line the entire mainland is included, and the immediately surround-

ing islands except for Euboea. The chronological focus is the high point of Mycenaean culture during the 14th and 13th centuries B.C., defined in ceramic terms as the Late Helladic (LH) IIIA and LH IIIB periods. Any analysis of the Mycenaean states would be incomplete, however, without consideration of their rise and fall. Recent debate on the emergence of statehood has included essential developments during the Early Mycenaean period, LH I–II. Similarly, discussion of the destructions that ended the

---

[1] Rutter 746.

Mycenaean palatial era ca. 1200 B.C. also requires consideration of their consequences for the following LH IIIC period.

Even with some flexibility in its chronological limits, this review covers a shorter time period than most of the others in this series. By way of compensation, an extra dimension is highlighted: the use of textual evidence. Our ability to read Mycenaean Greek increases the range of questions we can ask about the period, and the Linear B tablets raise special problems of their own. In combination with archaeological discoveries, these texts also contribute to research on a variety of cultural issues such as religion and economic administration. The material to be addressed is thus quite diverse, and is better suited to a thematic approach than to a strict chronological or geographical organization. This review is therefore arranged under the following headings: chronology, work at palatial centers and other sites, regional surveys and settlement patterns, technological advances, ceramic studies, development of Mycenaean states, new inscriptions, economic and political administration, religion, and destructions.

The publication of Hope Simpson and Dickinson's *Gazetteer* in 1979 is the starting point for the review of fieldwork.[2] Since then it has been possible to keep abreast of archaeological activity in Greece through the invaluable yearly reviews in *Archaeological Reports* and the "Chronique des fouilles" in the *Bulletin de correspondance hellénique*. Bibliographical access to developments in Linear B studies has been more difficult during the same period. The listings of books, articles, and reviews in *Nestor* include textual as well as archaeological contributions,[3] but the summary publication *Studies in Mycenaean Inscriptions and Dialect* was in hiatus from 1978 until its resurrection in 1995.[4] Until very recently, new work on the Bronze Age has not been much summarized, assessed, or synthesized.[5] A welcome change is now evident, with the appearance of comprehensive studies of Bronze Age Crete and mainland Greece as well as analytical bibliographies of Mycenaean society.[6] These publications, and the "Review of Aegean Prehistory" series itself, document how much has happened in this field in two decades.

CHRONOLOGY

Late Helladic IIIA–B chronology, both relative and absolute, is more straightforward than that of preceding phases of the Bronze Age. Nonetheless, it is affected by several recent developments, and some points remain in dispute. The alternative chronologies of the Late Bronze Age are given in table 1.[7] Ceramic synchronisms still play a role in the debate

---

[2] *Gazetteer*, with information through 1977. Davis 700 and Rutter 747 also acknowledge this publication as a terminus post quem for their reviews.

[3] *Nestor*, published monthly September through May by the Department of Classics, University of Cincinnati, and also available on computer diskette or by FTP (information and searchable database available on the World Wide Web at http://ucaswww.mcm.uc.edu/classics/nestor/nestor.html [22 May 1997]).

[4] The last compilation published was L. Baumbach, *Studies in Mycenaean Inscriptions and Dialect, 1965–1978* (Incunabula graeca 86, Rome 1986). Publication has now been resumed under the auspices of the Program in Aegean Scripts and Prehistory and the Department of Classics, University of Texas at Austin. The first volume to appear under this rubric is E. Sikkenga ed., *Studies in Mycenaean Inscriptions and Dialect, 1979* (Austin 1995). Future volumes are planned to fill the gap from 1980 to 1995, as well as current years.

[5] K. Kilian, "Mycenaeans Up to Date, Trends and Changes in Recent Research," in French and Wardle 115–52 is an admirable exception, characteristically ahead of its time.

[6] R. Treuil et al., *Les civilisations égéennes du Néolithique et de l'Âge du Bronze* (Paris 1989) is a fine textbook survey of Crete and mainland Greece. O.T.P.K. Dickinson, *The Aegean Bronze Age* (Cambridge 1994) is impressive as one man's synoptic overview, organized thematically. *Les mycéniens: Les grecs du IIe millénaire* (DossPar 195, Paris 1994) addresses

a general audience. B. Eder, *Staat, Herrschaft, Gesellschaft in frühgriechischer Zeit. Eine Bibliographie 1978–1991/92* (Anz-Wien 611, Vienna 1994) is part of a handbook project on State and Society of Early Greece by the Mykenische Kommission of the Austrian Academy of Sciences, under the editorship of S. Deger-Jalkotzy. It includes the Dark Ages and Homer as well as the Late Bronze Age. Its coverage of textual matters is quite broad; archaeological studies are included if they pertain to society and kingship. B. Feuer, *Mycenaean Civilization: A Research Guide* (Research Guides to Ancient Civilizations 5, New York 1996) offers a brief introduction to Mycenaean civilization and an annotated bibliography organized by topic. Other bibliographical resources include *Studies in Mycenaean Inscriptions and Dialect* (supra n. 4) and *Nestor* (supra n. 3).

[7] High chronology dates are taken from S.W. Manning, *The Absolute Chronology of the Aegean Early Bronze Age. Archaeology, Radiocarbon and History* (Sheffield 1995) 217–29; and S.W. Manning and B. Weninger, "A Light in the Dark: Archaeological Wiggle Matching and the Absolute Chronology of the Close of the Aegean Late Bronze Age," *Antiquity* 66 (1992) 636–63. Manning and Weninger report the end of LH IIIC as 1125/1065/1060, but the reasoning behind the earliest figure, derived from A. Snodgrass, *The Dark Age of Greece: An Archaeological Survey of the Eleventh to the Eighth Centuries B.C.* (Edinburgh 1971) 122–23, is not now considered feasible.

Low chronology dates are taken from P. Warren and V. Hankey, *Aegean Bronze Age Chronology* (Bristol 1989) 137–69.

Table 1. Late Bronze Age Chronologies

	High	Low	Modified
LH I	ca. 1680–1600/1580	1600–1510/1500	
LH IIA	1600/1580–1520/1480	1510/1500–1440	
LH IIB	1520/1480–1425/1390	1440–1390+	
LH IIIA1	1425/1390–1390/1370	1390+–1370/1360	1390+–ca. 1370
LH IIIA2	1390/1370–1340/1330	1370/1360–1340/1330	1370–1310/1300
LH IIIB	1340/1330–1190/1180	1340/1330–1185/1180	1310/1300–1190/1180
LH IIIC	1190/1180–1065/1060	1185/1180–1065	1190/1180–1065

over absolute chronology. In the last decade, however, the focus has been on radiocarbon and dendrochronological data, both of which have been refined in accuracy and augmented by new samples. An important recent discovery is a dramatic growth anomaly in Anatolian trees, which may bear on the much-debated absolute date of the Minoan eruption of the island of Thera.[8] That debate is crucial for our understanding of the Early Mycenaean period, but it has only indirect consequences for LH III.[9] The point of transition between LH II and LH IIIA1 will of course depend on which chronology is followed, but the two necessarily converge in LH IIIA.

The dates listed above do need one modification, in the length of LH IIIA2. There is widespread agreement that this period lasted longer than 30–40 years.[10] The traditional cutoff date of ca. 1340/1330 accommodated the view that Mycenaean pottery from Tell el-Amarna in Egypt includes two stirrup jar fragments with LH IIIB features. The Egyptian court abandoned Amarna in year 3 of Tutankhamun, who according to the currently favored middle chronology reigned from 1336 to 1327 B.C. A case has been made, however, that both jars can be dated to LH IIIA2.[11] Support for an even later end to LH IIIA2 comes from the shipwreck being excavated off the coast of Turkey at Uluburun. A small log from the wreck that was firewood or dunnage, and was cut not long before the ship sank, has a last ring of 1316 B.C.[12] The Mycenaean pottery on board is all compatible with a date in LH IIIA2 except for one jug, still being restored and studied, that may

The proposed modifications for LH IIIA–IIIB are explained infra. Warren and Hankey provide a good summary of the ceramic and ^{14}C data as of 1988. Proponents of a low or short Aegean chronology rely chiefly on proposed synchronisms between the Aegean and Egypt in dating the eruption on Thera to the later 16th century B.C. The high or long chronology rests primarily on scientific evidence (tree-rings, ice cores, and ^{14}C dates) that documents a "frost event" in 1628 B.C. Supporters draw the inference that the eruption of Thera caused this event.

[8] P.I. Kuniholm et al., "Anatolian Tree Rings and the Absolute Chronology of the Eastern Mediterranean, 2220–718 B.C.," *Nature* 381 (27 June 1996) 780–83; an update on the number of trees observed is reported by Kuniholm, "Aegean Dendrochronology Project December 1996 Progress Report" (unpublished), a newsletter circulated by the project director. The growth spike occurs at and just following relative ring/year 854 of 54 trees from the site of Porsuk in south-central Anatolia. The radiocarbon date range is compatible with linking this event to the 1628/1627 B.C. event observed in dendrochronologies of Europe and the United States. A second event 470 years later also links up plausibly with an anomaly seen in Europe; together the two would anchor a formerly floating 1,503-year dendrochronological sequence from Anatolia. The Aegean chronology is tied in by the further inference that the Minoan eruption of Thera caused the growth event of 1628 B.C.

[9] Davis 736 with n. 160; Manning (supra n. 7) 30–31, 200–29; M. Wiener, *The Chronology of Late Bronze Age Egypt and the Aegean: Science, Texts, Interconnections* (unpublished manuscript). I thank Malcolm Wiener for allowing me to

cite his work.

[10] Manning (supra n. 7) 228; Wiener (supra n. 9). At Nichoria, for example, it accommodates three phases of ceramic development, which occur in a stratified sequence in area IV: C.W. Shelmerdine, "Mycenaean Pottery from the Settlement, Part III: Late Helladic IIIA2–IIIB2 Pottery," in W.A. McDonald and N. Wilkie eds., *Excavations at Nichoria II: The Bronze Age Occupation* (Minneapolis 1992) 495.

[11] In favor of a LH IIIB date: V. Hankey, "Stirrup Jars at El-Amarna," in W.V. Davies and L. Schofield eds., *Egypt, the Aegean and the Levant. Interconnections in the Second Millennium BC* (London 1995) 116–24, nos. 6, 8; cf. Warren and Hankey (supra n. 7) 149–51, 150 figs. 8–9. In favor of a LH IIIA2 date: Elizabeth French, personal communication, also cited by Wiener (supra n. 9). Hankey no. 6 is FS 171 (LH IIIA2–C1) or FS 173 (LH IIIB). The distinction rests on the relationship between height and diameter, which cannot be determined in this case from the amount preserved. The lozenge FM 73 is primarily a LH IIIB motif, which appears in LH IIIA2 chiefly as an accessory: E.B. French, "Late Helladic IIIA 2 Pottery from Mycenae," *BSA* 60 (1965) 181, 190. As for Hankey no. 8, French (personal communication) reports Mountjoy's view that it may be FS 166 (LH IIIA2–IIIB) rather than FS 182 (LH IIIB).

[12] Kuniholm et al. (supra n. 8) 782; C. Pulak, "The Uluburun Shipwreck," in R. Hohlfelder and S. Swiny eds., *Res Maritima 1994: Cyprus and the Eastern Mediterranean, Prehistory through the Roman Period* (BASOR Archaeological Reports 4, Atlanta 1997). I thank Peter Kuniholm and Cemal Pulak for discussing the matter with me and providing this definitive date.

be early LH IIIB.[13] With an absolute date for the shipwreck in or shortly after 1316 B.C., it would appear that LH IIIA2 must continue almost to the end of the 14th century B.C. Furthermore, if one vessel really belongs to the following phase, the transition to LH IIIB (a process, after all, not a moment) is beginning at about that time.

One other chronological issue needs only brief mention. A recent attempt to lower the dates of the Dark Ages would bring the conventional second-millennium chronology down by 250 years, with the Egyptian 18th Dynasty beginning just after 1300 B.C. and ending just after 1050 B.C.[14] This radical redating draws attention to some valid difficulties with the conventional chronology for the Dark Ages. As far as the Late Bronze Age is concerned, though, the attempt flies in the face of sound scientific evidence and has met with significant criticism.[15] The present framework for continued refinement and debate on Aegean chronology is still confined to the alternatives presented in table 1.

WORK AT PALATIAL CENTERS AND OTHER SITES

Palaces and Citadels

In the past 20 years exploration has been renewed or continued at most of the known Mycenaean palatial centers and citadels.[16] The result is a better understanding of the nature of such sites and of their history, especially during LH IIIB. Many cemeteries and isolated tombs have also been excavated, but much less attention has been paid to smaller settlements. This section summarizes recent work at palatial and other settlements, but discoveries at many of the sites receive further attention below in the relevant thematic sections.

Mycenae. The site of Mycenae is now under the general supervision of George Mylonas's successor, Spyros Iakovides, who has conducted some explorations inside the citadel, in the vicinity of the Lion Gate and in the northwest corner of the acropolis.[17] There is still an active British presence here as well, directed by Elizabeth French. Activity during the 1980s and 1990s at this well-explored site has chiefly involved study and publication, rather than new excavations. The latest joint Greek-British effort is a survey project that began in 1991, and will soon be published by the Archaeological Society of Athens.[18] This is not a regional survey, and no systematic collection of material was attempted. Rather, like the earlier Knossos survey,[19] it was designed to locate, identify, and map all visible remains throughout the settlement of Mycenae—an area of about 32 ha—after more than a century of exploration. The effort is especially valuable in the case of structures whose location or identity had been forgotten over time, as for a number of chamber tombs excavated in the 1880s and 1890s by Tsountas. Most of Tsountas's tomb groups have now been reidentified, and over half of the individual tombs have been matched to their old excavation numbers.[20] The project has also retraced the network of roads

---

[13] Rutter has retracted the statement cited by Kuniholm et al. (supra n. 8) 782 that the wreck certainly contains LH IIIB pottery, but the possibility remains for the jug mentioned here: C. Pulak, personal communication, and Pulak (supra n. 12).

There is nothing inconsistent with a late 14th-century end to LH IIIA2 in the unpublished report by Kuniholm (supra n. 8) of a date of 1353 B.C. for wood (without bark) in the upper Hittite level at Maşat Höyük. The wood is from a building that contains a Mycenaean stirrup jar and flask, both of which appear to date to the transition between LH IIIA and IIIB (personal communication, Elizabeth French). The wood dates construction of the building to soon after 1353 B.C., while the pots belong to the time of its destruction.

[14] P. James et al., *Centuries of Darkness* (London 1991).

[15] *Cambridge Archaeological Journal* 1 (1991) 227–53; Manning and Weninger (supra n. 7); Manning (supra n. 7) 23–24.

[16] The regional sequence in the *Gazetteer* is adopted here throughout in discussion of sites and surveys. A possible change in the list of palatial centers is worth mentioning, though it falls outside of the review area. The Kastro site at Volos (*Gazetteer* H1) had previously been identified as Iolkos, on the strength of two successive large buildings. Recent excavation has revealed an extensive Mycenaean settlement at Dimini: *AR* 1991–1992, 39; *AR*

1992–1993, 47; *AR* 1994–1995, 35–36. Though to date only a street and private houses have been found, the excavators have proposed that Dimini is a better candidate for Iolkos. Presumably future work will strengthen or weaken this possibility.

[17] Above and east of the Lion Gate, building N and rooms I–IX: G.E. Mylonas and S. Iakovides, "Ἀνασκαφή Μυκηνῶν," *Prakt* 1984, 233–40; *AR* 1985–1986, 27. Northeast of the Lion Gate: Iakovides, "Ἀνασκαφή Μυκηνῶν," *Prakt* 1989, 38–43; *AR* 1992–1993, 18. Northwest corner of the acropolis: *AR* 1986–1987, 17. Southwest corner of the site: *Ergon* 1989, 8–12; *AR* 1989–1990, 15. For overviews, see also Mylonas, *Mycenae, Rich in Gold* (Athens 1983); and Iakovides, "Ἡ Ἀρχαιολογική Ἑταιρεία στις Μυκήνες," *ArchEph* 1987, 339–59.

[18] S. Iakovides and E.B. French, *Archaeological Atlas of Mycenae* (Athens, forthcoming); cf. *AR* 1991–1992, 16–17; *AR* 1992–1993, 18. I thank Elizabeth French for allowing me to see a preliminary draft of the publication text.

[19] M.S.F. Hood and D. Smyth, *Archaeological Survey of the Knossos Area* (London 1981).

[20] K.S. Shelton, "Tsountas' Chamber Tombs at Mycenae," *ArchEph* 1993, 187–210. The known tombs and their finds had already been restudied, and the problems of identification noted, by A. Xenaki-Sakellariou, *Οι θαλαμωτοί τάφοι των Μυκηνών* (Paris 1985).

Fig. 2. Panoramic view southwest from citadel. From left to right, Treasury of Atreus (dromos into hillside visible), Panayia Houses on ridge just to the north, and the House of the Oil Merchant group (lower right of figure, east of road).

in the Mycenae area, and established that the location of cemeteries is related to it.[21]

Two groups of houses outside the citadel walls have now been fully published, the Panayia Houses north of the Treasury of Atreus, and the Oil Merchant group some 200 m further north and across the modern road (fig. 2). The first group consists of three LH IIIB houses, of modest domestic character.[22] Panayia House I, built first, was destroyed shortly before the end of LH IIIB1. The cause was apparently an earthquake: a woman's body was found in a doorway, her skull crushed, buried by the destruction debris. The same earthquake damaged House II, a somewhat later construction with a more elaborate plan. It was then partially repaired and reoccupied for a time before succumbing to a fire. House III, a small building belatedly squeezed between Houses I and II, continued in use well after House I, at least, was abandoned.

The Oil Merchant group of houses has a very different character. These four houses were constructed early in LH IIIB (first the West House, then in sequence the House of Shields, the House of the Oil Merchant, and the House of Sphinxes), and all were destroyed by fire near the middle of the period. Tournavitou provides a full account of the houses themselves and the materials found in them.[23] Whatever other purposes these houses may have served, they were at least repositories for oil and worked ivories, and probably for perishable commodities as well. This is suggested by the presence of Linear B tablets, which deal, among other issues, with the collection of spices (Ge series), disbursements of wool (Oe), and maintenance of male and female personnel (Au).[24] These topics are characteristic of palatial concerns elsewhere, and Tournavitou is right, in my view, to regard these buildings as an integral part of the palace administration.

Excavations of the South House and Cult Center (Citadel House area) during the 1960s are being presented in a series of fascicles, the first of which summarizes the work year by year and briefly describes the LH IIIB2 remains.[25] In addition to these publication projects, a new museum has been constructed below and north of the citadel. The galleries should be ready by the end of 1997; they will house

[21] A. Jansen, *Stations along the Roads in the Area of Mycenae: An Analysis of the Mycenaean Road System and Its Relation to the Mycenaean State* (Diss. Univ. of Pennsylvania 1994); J. Lavery, "Some 'New' Mycenaean Roads at Mycenae: Εὐρυάγυια Μυκήνη," *BICS* 40 (1995) 264–65. The correlation of tomb placement and roads had been doubted by C.B. Mee and W.G. Cavanagh, "Spatial Distribution of Mycenaean Tombs," *BSA* 85 (1990) 228–29.

[22] I.M. Shear, *The Panagia Houses at Mycenae* (University Museum Monograph 68, Philadelphia 1987).

[23] I. Tournavitou, *The 'Ivory Houses' at Mycenae* (BSA Suppl. 24, London 1995).

[24] The tablets receive admirably thorough and professional treatment in C. Varias García, *Los documentos en Lineal B de Micenas: Ensayo de interpretación global* (Diss. Univ. of Barcelona 1993).

[25] W.D. Taylour, *Well Built Mycenae: The Helleno-British Excavations within the Citadel at Mycenae, 1959–1969* 1: *The Excavations* (Warminster 1981).

all finds from the site, except those on display in the National Museum at Athens.

Tiryns. The history of Tiryns has been greatly clarified, in large part through the work of the late Klaus Kilian.[26] The LH IIIA and earlier remains are discussed below. LH IIIB1 saw rebuilding on the upper citadel, and walls of mudbrick on stone foundations were added around the Lower Citadel (Unterburg). A conflagration at the end of LH IIIB1 necessitated another rebuilding in LH IIIB2. At this point Cyclopean stone fortifications were extended around the entire citadel. At the end of LH IIIB2 the site was destroyed, according to Kilian, by an earthquake.[27] The Lower Citadel was rebuilt and occupied into the Submycenaean period, ca. 1065/1060–1020/1000 B.C.[28] This area was a longstanding part of the Tiryns settlement, consisting of domestic buildings and some cult structures as well, of both LH IIIB2 and LH IIIC date. In addition, a series of casements (38 at present count) provided additional space for storage and offerings. Both the west and east sides have been partially excavated. Meticulous attention to stratigraphy in the Lower Citadel has also led to the refinement of ceramic phases from LH IIIA2 Late through LH IIIC (see below).

Around the hill lay a Lower Town that was inhabited from the Early Helladic period through LH IIIC Late. It expanded greatly in LH IIIB or IIIC; in LH IIIC Early–Middle (the 12th and early 11th centuries B.C.) it covered 24.5 ha.[29] Kilian thought that the town was smaller in LH IIIB. Recent geophysical and soil studies, however, suggest a different view.[30] It is now clear that the Manessi River near the site changed its course in late LH IIIB–early IIIC. A natural shift from the south to the north side of the citadel deposited as much as 4 m of alluvium, burying much of the Lower Town east and north of the citadel under flash flood deposits. The inhabitants subsequently diverted the river well to the south by constructing a dam and canal, so that houses could be built in the former streambed. It is likely that the Lower Town was at least as large in LH IIIB as in LH IIIC, even though much of it is obscured by sediment.[31] The same investigations also show that the coastline was only about 300 m southwest of Tiryns in the Early Bronze Age, ca. 2500 B.C., but receded to ca. 1 km from the citadel during EH II, where it remained throughout the Bronze Age.[32]

Midea. Work at the citadel of Midea in the Argolid resumed as a Greek-Swedish project in 1983, under the direction of K. Demakopoulou with the collaboration of P. Åström.[33] The Swedish team has been working in the area of the East Gate and on the lower terraces, and the Greek team in the area of the West Gate. All three areas suffered a burning destruction late in LH IIIB2, and large fallen blocks and collapsed walls suggest that the cause was an earthquake. Foundation trenches for the citadel wall near the East Gate and on a lower terrace contained LH IIIB2 pottery, showing that at least some sections of the wall were constructed during that phase. A

[26] S. Iakovides, "Das Werk Klaus Kilians," *AM* 108 (1993) 9–27 provides a good summary of Kilian's work at the site. Reports by K. Kilian of the 1976–1983 seasons appear in *AA* 1978, 449–70; *AA* 1979, 379–411; *AA* 1981, 149–94; *AA* 1982, 393–430; *AA* 1983, 277–328; and *AA* 1988, 105–51. They are accompanied by accounts of LH III ceramics by C. Podzuweit in *AA* 1978, 471–98; *AA* 1979, 412–40; *AA* 1981, 194–220; *AA* 1983, 359–402; and *AA* 1988, 213–25; G. Hiesel in *AA* 1982, 431–39; and G. Schönfeld in *AA* 1988, 153–211. The 1984 and 1985 seasons are reported in "Chronique" 1985, 776–78; "Chronique" 1986, 689–91; *AR* 1984–1985, 20–21; and *AR* 1985–1986, 26–27.

[27] Kilian 1981 (supra n. 26) 192; Kilian 1983 (supra n. 26) 277; E. Zangger, "Landscape Changes around Tiryns during the Bronze Age," *AJA* 98 (1994) 207–10.

[28] The most recent statement on Tiryns chronology is by P.A. Mountjoy, *Mycenaean Pottery: An Introduction* (Oxford 1993) 160.

[29] Zangger (supra n. 27) 197, fig. 8.

[30] Zangger (supra n. 27) 189–212; J.M. Balcer, "The Mycenaean Dam at Tiryns," *AJA* 78 (1974) 141–49.

[31] Zangger (supra n. 27) 211–12, with reference to Kilian 1978 (supra n. 26) 470.

[32] Zangger (supra n. 27) 194–98, fig. 4.

[33] *ArchDelt* 38 (1983) Chron. 76–78; P. Åström and K. Demakopoulou, "New Excavations in the Citadel of Midea 1983–1984," *OpAth* 16 (1986) 19–25; Åström, Demakopoulou, and G. Walberg, "Excavations in Midea, 1985," *OpAth* 17 (1988) 7–11; Åström et al., "Excavations in Midea, 1987," *OpAth* 18 (1990) 9–22; Åström et al., "Excavations in Midea, 1989–1990," *OpAth* 19 (1992) 11–22; Walberg, "Excavations on the Lower Terraces at Midea," *OpAth* 19 (1992) 23–39; Demakopoulou, N. Divari-Valakou, and Walberg, "Excavations and Restoration Work in Midea 1990–1992," *OpAth* 20 (1994) 19–41; Demakopoulou, "Mycenaean Citadels: Recent Excavations on the Acropolis of Midea in the Argolid," *BICS* 1995, 151–61; Åström, "The Mycenaean Citadel of Midea," *Journal of Prehistoric Religion* 8 (1994) 5–6; and Walberg, "The 1995 Excavation of the Megaron at Midea," World Wide Web at http://ucaswww.mcm.uc.edu/classics/midea.html (23 May 1997). My thanks to Katie Demakopoulou and Gisela Walberg for letting me see the following progress reports on the excavations in advance of publication: Demakopoulou, "Excavations in Midea 1994," *OpAth* (forthcoming); Demakopoulou, "Excavations in Midea 1995," (unpublished report submitted to the Institute for Aegean Prehistory); and Walberg, "The Excavation of the Megaron at Midea" (unpublished report).

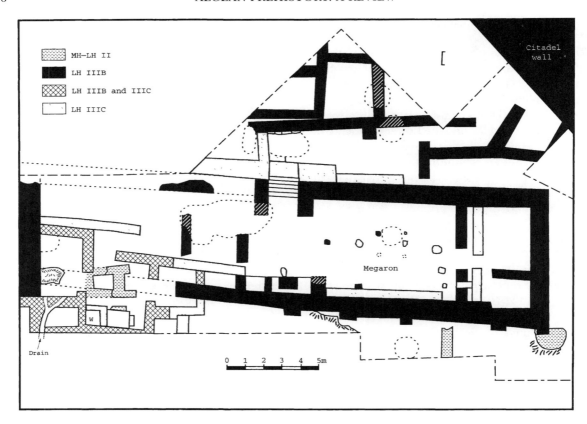

Fig. 3. Midea. Plan of the lower terraces. (C.W. Shelmerdine and C. Williams, after plan courtesy G. Walberg)

section near the West Gate was apparently built in LH IIIB1, however, since no later pottery was found in the foundation trench explored there.

A complex of six rooms abutting the citadel wall inside the West Gate served as workshops and store-rooms. Among the finds were remains of foodstuffs such as figs, olive stones, shellfish, small animal bones, and grain. Evidence of workshop activity includes grinding stones and pestles, a steatite jewelry mold, pieces of fluorite and mother-of-pearl, and a bronze knife of leather-working type.[34] Pottery in the de-struction level is generally of typical LH IIIB2 vari-eties, with good parallels from Mycenae and Tiryns, but with a few features conventionally assigned to early LH IIIC. This mixture defines a transitional LH IIIB2/IIIC Early phase recently identified by Mountjoy (see below).[35]

The lower terraces of the citadel have also been the focus of attention, especially in areas M and N.

Both produced stratified deposits of LH IIIB and LH IIIC below Roman occupation layers, as well as earlier material. Sherds in a foundation trench for the citadel wall in area M confirm a LH IIIB2 con-struction date for that section, matching findings from the upper gate areas. A large (14 × 7.5 m) mega-ron complex is emerging in area N (fig. 3), but few details have yet been published.[36] It had long been assumed that a megaron had stood on the summit of the hill, as at other Mycenaean palaces, although no architectural traces of such a building were ever found. The off-center and less prominent position of the newly discovered structure is thus of interest. The megaron at Midea has two LH IIIB floor levels. Five buttresses against the south wall are an unusual feature, with a parallel in the LH IIIB2 "mansion" at the Menelaion.[37] The excavator suggests that they may have been intended to protect against earth-quakes. In this they were unsuccessful, for a tilted

---

[34] Demakopoulou et al. 1994 (supra n. 33) fig. 36 (fluo-rite), fig. 37 (jewelry mold).

[35] Demakopoulou 1995 (supra n. 33) 155; Demakopou-lou, forthcoming (supra n. 33).

[36] Demakopoulou et al. 1994 (supra n. 33) 41, fig. 65;

Walberg, World Wide Web (supra n. 33). The following ac-count is based chiefly on Walberg, unpublished (supra n. 33).

[37] H.W. Catling, "Excavations at the Menelaion, Sparta, 1973–76," AR 1976–1977, 29, fig. 2.

wall and fallen stones agree with evidence from the upper gate areas that an earthquake severely damaged the site at the end of LH IIIB.[38] The debris includes pottery of the transitional types found in the West Gate area.[39] The building was subsequently repaired and remodeled: in this LH IIIC reuse a row of three column bases bisected the main room, replacing the hearth and four column bases of the LH IIIB phase. Among the finds of interest from the LH IIIB2 floor levels of the lower terraces are a large lead vessel and a stirrup jar decorated with a body zone of double axes and horns of consecration.[40] Linear B inscriptions have been found on both upper and lower terraces (see below).

Pylos. In 1990, members of the project Minnesota Archaeological Researches in the Western Peloponnese (MARWP) began work at the palatial site of Ano Englianos under the direction of F.A. Cooper, with M.C. Nelson as field director.[41] With a view to preparing a complete site plan of the architectural remains, the project members are removing backfill, clearing walls and floors down to the lowest course of stone or the lowest level reached by the original excavators. A state plan of the Main Building is in progress (fig. 4). Remains uncovered to date reveal some discrepancies from the older published plans in a number of areas. For example, the excavator of Pylos, Carl Blegen, restored a door between outer propylon 1 and room 7 of the Archive Complex, in a wall that had been destroyed by post-Mycenaean robbing. Recently it has been suggested that access to the Archive Complex was more likely to have been from the interior of the palace, from inner propylon 2 to room 8.[42] Work in this area during 1995 has brought to light some confirmation of this suggestion: a stone found under the plaster floor of inner

propylon 2 is in a suitable place to have been a footer under the threshold of such a door.[43]

Stratigraphical investigations by the Minnesota team also indicate a more complex relative chronology for the site. The sequence of construction is now clear for the northeastern side of the palace. Five building phases, beginning in the MH period, predate construction of the Main Building and the Wine Magazine, which Blegen dated to the beginning of LH IIIB. Subsequently (phase 7), courts 42 and 47 were created by the construction of a rubble wall. A branch of the water channel to the east was diverted to run parallel to the northeast wall of court 47, and the corridor between the two (ramp 91) was then paved with plaster. The Northeast Workshop is a still later construction (phase 8), for its southwest wall rests on the edge of the water channel. Phase 9 represents post-Mycenaean (Dark Age) habitation of the site, for which there is increasing evidence.[44]

In addition to this work on the site itself, the vicinity of the palace was intensively surveyed by members of the Pylos Regional Archaeological Project in order to determine the size of the settlement. Artifact densities indicate that habitation extended for about 1 km along the Englianos Ridge and covered its full width (ca. 200–300 m), so that the area of the town was between 20 and 30 ha.[45] Geophysical exploration by the project has also produced some welcome surprises. Chief among them is a substantial subsurface lineament, detected by magnetometry and electric resistivity, on the steep northwestern side of the Epano Englianos ridge. In computer models the upper boundary of the source causing the anomaly has been determined to be 1.0–1.5 m below the surface. The lineament is 60 m in length and 2.0–2.7 m wide. Since it runs parallel to the contours of

[38] Walberg 1992 (supra n. 33) 31, 38; Walberg, unpublished (supra n. 33); Demakopoulou et al. 1994 (supra n. 33) 39.

[39] Demakopoulou et al. 1994 (supra n. 33) 35.

[40] Demakopoulou et al. 1994 (supra n. 33) 36, fig. 48 (lead vessel), 36–37, fig. 53 (stirrup jar).

[41] *AR* 1991–1992, 27–28; *AR* 1992–1993, 32–34; *AR* 1993–1994, 29–30; "Chronique" 1993, 796; "Chronique" 1994, 717; M.C. Nelson and F.A. Cooper, "Excavations of the Bronze Age Palace of Nestor, Pylos," *AJA* 96 (1992) 362 (abstract); F.A. Cooper and E. Swain, "Minnesota Archaeological Researches at Pylos, 1991–1993 Seasons," *AJA* 98 (1994) 288 (abstract; text of paper on the World Wide Web at http://marwp.cla.umn.edu/PYLOS/aia1993.html [6 June 1997]); and F.A. Cooper, "Minnesota Archaeological Researches at Pylos, 1994–1995 Seasons," *AJA* 100 (1996) 388 (abstract; text of paper on the World Wide Web at http://marwp.cla.umn.edu/PYLOS/aia1995.html [6 June 1997]).

[42] T.G. Palaima and J.C. Wright, "Ins and Outs of the Ar-

chives Rooms at Pylos: Form and Function in a Mycenaean Palace," *AJA* 89 (1985) 251–62.

[43] Cooper (supra n. 41); and F.A. Cooper, "Preliminary Report: 1995 Season," unpublished report to the Greek Archaeological Service, 6th Classical Ephoreia. My thanks to Fred Cooper for giving me a copy of this report.

[44] C. Griebel and M.C. Nelson, "Post-Mycenaean Occupation at the Palace of Nestor," *AJA* 97 (1993) 331 (abstract; text of paper on the World Wide Web at http://marwp.cla.umn.edu/PYLOS/aia1992.html [6 June 1997]). See also P. Càssola Guida, "Considerazioni sulla crisi della civiltà micenea: Il palazzo di Pilo," in E. De Miro, L. Godart, and A. Sacconi eds., *Atti e memorie del secondo congresso internazionale di micenologia* 2 (Incunabula graeca 98.2, Rome 1996) 693–700.

[45] J.L. Davis et al., "The Pylos Regional Archaeological Project, Part I: Overview and the Archaeological Survey," *Hesperia* (forthcoming).

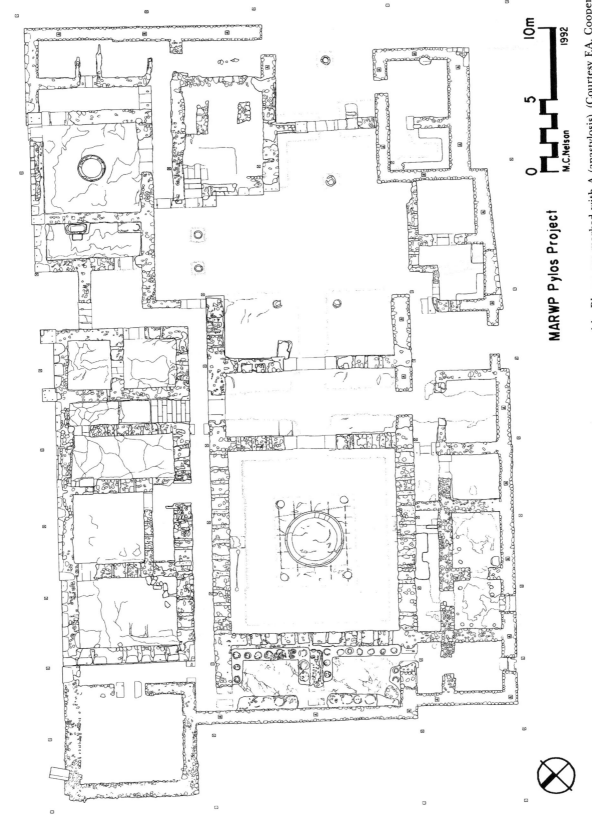

MARWP Pylos Project

M.C.Nelson

1992

Fig. 4. Pylos. State plan of Main Building; draft in progress by M.C. Nelson. Walls reconstructed by Blegen are marked with A (anastylosis). (Courtesy F.A. Cooper and M.C. Nelson)

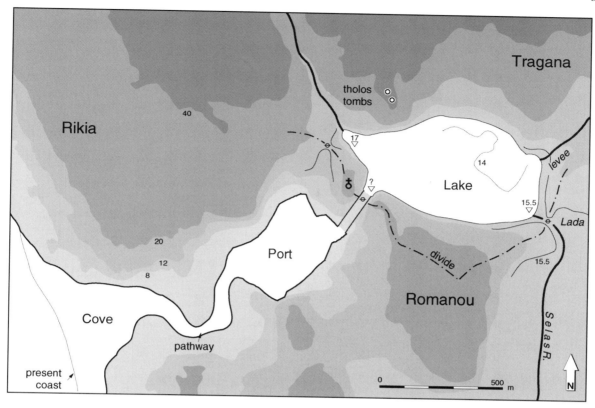

Fig. 5. Port basin southwest of the palace at Pylos. (Courtesy E. Zangger)

the hill, it is conjectured to be a substantial terrace or fortification wall, perhaps marking the limit of the Late Bronze Age settlement in this direction.[46] If confirmed, this discovery would solve the long-standing puzzle of why Pylos, alone among Late Bronze Age palatial centers, seemed to be unwalled. Blegen failed to find traces of such a wall despite extensive test excavations, but he looked only in the immediate vicinity of the palace, while the distance between the westernmost corner of the palace and this anomaly is between 50 and 110 m.

Landscape and soil analysis in the Pylos area has also resulted in the identification, just inland from the west coast near Romanou, of a man-made rectangular basin that is interpreted as a protected port for the Palace of Nestor (fig. 5).[47] The sediments in cores taken from the basin contained marine organisms, showing that it was once linked to the sea. Inland of the basin, and separated from it by a bedrock knoll, was a lake also apparently constructed

by Mycenaean engineers. They diverted the Selas River from its natural course southward to the Osmanaga Lagoon, cutting a channel through the bedrock knoll so that the river would flow through the basin and prevent its outlet to the sea from clogging with sand. Most of the sediment carried by the river would be trapped in the lake. Thus, a relatively clear stream was directed through the basin, and the remainder kept its original course to the lagoon. Cores from the lagoon, dated by radiocarbon, show that the deposition rate of riverine sediment there diminished ca. 1400 B.C., confirming the date at which the diversion was effected. It was reduced even further ca. 1200 B.C. The best explanation is that when the Mycenaean palace was destroyed and careful control of the area ceased, all of the current simply took the shorter route to the sea through the basin — a course it has followed ever since.

Athens. No new excavation of Mycenaean levels has taken place on the Acropolis since 1978, but a re-

---

[46] E. Zangger et al., "The Pylos Regional Archaeological Project, Part II: Landscape Evolution and Site Preservation in the Pylos Region," *Hesperia* (forthcoming). The

source of the anomaly and its date have not yet been verified by excavation.

[47] Zangger et al., forthcoming (supra n. 46).

study of the entrance system of the citadel clarifies many elements and offers a new and convincing reconstruction.[48] It supports the idea of an oblique entrance similar to the Lion Gate at Mycenae: visitors would first head westward, with the bastion on their right and a terrace on their left, and then turn north to pass through the gate.

Thebes. The considerable obstacle of a thriving modern town obscures the full plan of Mycenaean Thebes, but limited probes in various locations continue to show that the site was an important center during LH III.[49] The old debate over the existence of one or two palaces seems to have been resolved in favor of two successive structures on the acropolis, and the site was fortified at least from LH IIIA. Several important groups of Mycenaean remains have been excavated since the publication of the *Gazetteer.* An ivory workshop was found on the M. Loukos plot across Pelopidou Street from the so-called Arsenal, destroyed at the end of LH IIIB1.[50] Two more excavations have unearthed important groups of inscribed Linear B documents (discussed infra).

Gla. Spyros Iakovides has summarized the present state of research at Gla in several recent and forthcoming publications.[51] The huge acropolis was constructed at the end of LH IIIA2, and occupied into LH IIIB2.[52] Its 3-km circuit of fortification walls surrounded an area of 20 ha, but architectural remains are confined to a 2-ha enclosure on the highest part of the site. The northern building consists of two wings, of similar size and construction. They are two-storied, and are made up mostly of two- and three-room units bordered by corridors. The building is sometimes referred to as palatial, and the large units at each free corner as megaron-like. Neither unit shows traces of a hearth or columns, however, and the one in the northwest corner has an uncanonical polythyron between rooms 2 and 3. The southern building complex includes long, narrow storerooms oriented north–south, with a total area of 2,500 m². Finds include storage jars and a quantity of grain. Iakovides estimates the storage capacity of these rooms to be at least 2,000 tons.[53] It appears that the construction of Gla was connected with the Mycenaean system of dikes and canals that controlled drainage of the Copaic Basin, and made up 20,000 ha available for cultivation.[54] As Iakovides suggests, the site may have housed overseers for the area, and also provided storage space for the resulting crops.[55]

Other Settlements

Only the more important settlement work receives attention here.[56] On the hill of *Tsoungiza* at Nemea

[48] J.C. Wright, "The Mycenaean Entrance System at the West End of the Akropolis of Athens," *Hesperia* 63 (1994) 323–60. P.A. Mountjoy, *Mycenaean Athens (SIMA-PB* 127, Jonsered 1995) offers a summary of what is known of Mycenaean Athens generally, with special emphasis on pottery.

[49] S. Symeonoglou, *The Topography of Thebes from the Bronze Age to Modern Times* (Princeton 1985) 26–63; V. Aravantinos, "Old and New Evidence for the Palatial Society of Mycenaean Thebes: An Outline," in *Politeia* 613–22. I have not seen the more recent reports by K. Demakopoulou, C. Piteros, and V. Aravantinos in A.P. Bekiaris ed., *Επετηρίς της Εταιρείας Βοιωτικών Μελετών* 1 (1988) 75–136. A good summary of the various Mycenaean remains has been provided by Demakopoulou, "Palatial and Domestic Architecture in Mycenaean Thebes," in P. Darcque and R. Treuil eds., *L'habitat égéen préhistorique. Actes de la table ronde internationale, Athènes, 23–25 juin 1987 (BCH* Suppl. 19, Paris 1990) 307–17.

[50] Demakopoulou (supra n. 49) 314, site 13; A. Sampson, "La destruction d'un atelier palatial mycénien à Thèbes," *BCH* 109 (1985) 21–29.

[51] S. Iakovides, *Γλάς* I (Athens 1989); Iakovides, *Γλάς* II (Athens, forthcoming); Iakovides, "The Mycenaean Fortress of Gla," in *Mykenaïka* 607–15; and Iakovides, "Γλάς και Ορχομενός," *Επετηρίς της Εταιρείας Βοιωτικών Μελετών* 2 (Athens 1995) 69–81. For the 1990 work (northern building of east wing of central structure = building M): *AR* 1990–1991, 34; *Ergon* 1990, 10–11. For the 1991 work (building K): *AR* 1991–1992, 29; *Ergon* 1991, 8–11.

[52] Size: Iakovides 1995 (supra n. 51) 69. Date range: Iakovides 1989 (supra n. 51) 258, 321.

[53] Iakovides 1989 (supra n. 51) 220–23, 306–307; Iako-

vides 1995 (supra n. 51) 76.

[54] J. Knauss, B. Heinrich, and H. Kalcyk, *Die Wasserbauten der Minyer in der Kopais: Die älteste Flussregulierung Europas* (Munich 1984); J. Knauss, "Die Wasserbau-Kultur der Minyer in der Kopais (ein Rekonstruktionversuch)," in H. Beister and J. Buckler eds., *Boiotika, Vorträge vom 5. internationalen Böotien-Kolloquium zu Ehren von Professor Dr. Siegfried Lauffer* (Munich 1989) 269–74 on the Mycenaean period, with further references.

[55] Iakovides 1995 (supra n. 51) 76.

[56] Notices of work at other settlements include the following: Aetos on Ithaca: S. Symeonoglou, "The Third Season at Aetos: A Summary of the Results," *The Siren: Newsletter of the Odyssey Project* 3 (1986); and S. Symeonoglou and N. Symeonoglou, "The Excavation of 1992 (Aetos, Ithaca)," *Siren* 8 (1992–1993). A fortified Mycenaean acropolis at Mantinea: *AR* 1993–1994, 17; T. Karayiorya-Stathakopoulou, "Η μαντινική πτόλις," in *Πρακτικά του 4 Διεθνούς Συνεδρίου Πελοποννησιακών Σπουδών* 2, 97–115, esp. 98–101 on prehistoric remains.

A number of Mycenaean tombs have also come to light during the years under review. They are numerous and not as distinctive as settlements, and since most have an Early Mycenaean component they appear in Rutter 788–89; thus I do not attempt to chronicle them here. New finds are regularly reported in *AR*, and a comprehensive study of Bronze Age burials and burial customs is in progress: W.G. Cavanagh and C.B. Mee, *Death in Prehistoric Greece* (SIMA, Jonsered, forthcoming). I thank Christopher Mee for letting me see an advance copy of the chapter on LH IIIA–B.

Fig. 6. View from Nichoria across the Messenian valley. (Photo C.W. Shelmerdine)

is a settlement occupied in the Neolithic–Early Bronze Age and again from Late MH through LH IIIB.[57] An early LH IIIA2 deposit with religious significance is interesting (see below), but the settlement is most extensive during LH IIIB, when it reaches 7.5 ha and houses are packed closely together on the sides of the hill.[58] They are purely domestic in character, like the Panayia Houses at Mycenae, and thus give a good picture of an ordinary Mycenaean settlement. Methana is another area with Mycenaean settlement remains, but the only details so far published concern a Mycenaean sanctuary at *Ayios Konstantinos* (see below). The ridgetop settlement of *Nichoria* sported a megaron in LH IIIA1, and it may therefore have been an independent center of power at that time. During LH IIIA2–IIIB it is an

ordinary town, like Tsoungiza the largest in its area.[59] Simple houses are the norm, some lined up along a street in area III. A new tholos was constructed at the site in LH IIIA2, with prestigious grave goods like jewelry, sealstones, and a matched set of bronze vessels. These signs of wealth and some shared vessel types of unusual form show that Nichoria profited from its association with Pylos. Furthermore, its geographical position above the southwest corner of the Messenian valley (fig. 6), along a natural route across the peninsula, fits the profile of one particular lookout site mentioned in the Pylos tablets. Additional points of similarity are the bronze-working establishment that operated here in LH IIIB and the suitability of the site's location for flax production. Nichoria can thus be identified with some confidence

[57] J.C. Wright et al., "The Nemea Valley Archaeological Project: A Preliminary Report," *Hesperia* 59 (1990) 579–659; "The Nemea Valley Archaeological Project, Archaeological Survey: Internet Edition," on the World Wide Web at http://classics.lsa.umich.edu/NVAP.html (23 May 1997), with complete bibliography. On the Early Mycenaean period, see Wright, "An Early Mycenaean Hamlet on Tsoungiza at Ancient Nemea," in Darcque and Treuil (supra n. 49) 347–57. Some activity in LH IIIC is suggested by a few sherds not from architectural contexts.

[58] The size estimate I owe to J.L. Davis (personal communication). Other sites found by the project are smaller

than 2 ha. On the site in this period, see M.K. Dabney, "Craft Product Consumption as an Economic Indicator of Site Status in Regional Studies," in P. Betancourt and R. Laffineur eds., *Τέχνη: Craftsmen, Craftswomen and Craftsmanship in the Aegean Bronze Age* (*Aegaeum* 16, Liège 1997). In addition to architecture, a large deposit (over 20,000 sherds) of early LH IIIB1 pottery was found in a rubbish pit near a building of the same date. P. Thomas, "A Deposit of Late Helladic IIIB:1 Pottery from Tsoungiza," *Hesperia* (forthcoming).

[59] McDonald and Wilkie (supra n. 10).

as the site of *ti-mi-to-a-ke-e*, one of the seven main economic centers of the further province in the Pylos kingdom.[60]

Current investigations of the prehistoric remains at *Eleusis* have established two Late Helladic phases on the southwest side of the hill, LH IIIA1 with some LH I–IIA admixture, and LH IIIA1–IIIB1; no architecture is associated with the finds.[61] *Glipha (Vlicha)* on the eastern Boeotian coast near Chalkis was inhabited from EH to LH IIIC; the LH III remains include a fortification wall and cist graves. The suggestion has been made that it was a local capital and the port for Thebes, perhaps even the Mycenaean Aulis.[62] An excellent summary of the Mycenaean remains at *Delphi* is now available, along with comments on the region, and on cult remains.[63] The site itself has traces of occupation from LH I, and the LH IIIB–early IIIC periods are especially well represented ceramically. The only Mycenaean architectural feature uncovered since 1978 is a terrace wall under the cella of the Temple of Apollo, which may have served also as a fortification wall.[64]

REGIONAL SURVEYS AND SETTLEMENT PATTERNS

Over the last quarter-century, there has been a substantial change in the study of Mycenaean settlement. As is clear from the preceding section, this change is not much reflected in excavations, which have continued to concentrate mainly on palaces and tombs. The Nemea Valley Archaeological Project is one of the few projects to follow the model of the Minnesota Messenia Project at Nichoria in exploring an ordinary habitation site (Tsoungiza) and its environs. The real innovation is a broadening of perspective from single sites to regional settlement patterns. Closely tied to this change is the coming of age of intensive survey as a productive archaeological tactic. It is a tribute to Carl Blegen, one of the great pioneers of Mycenaean archaeology, that he

realized the need for survey work of this kind as early as 1941.[65]

The seed Blegen planted took some time to flourish: the broadening of interest from the Mycenaean king to his subjects, and from the center to its surroundings, did not occur until the 1960s and 1970s, beginning with the pioneering extensive survey project known as the Minnesota Messenia Expedition.[66] The broad-brush approach of extensive survey has been overshadowed by intensive survey, where selected areas are covered at a level of detail designed to insure that no significant archaeological material goes unnoticed. Rutter has provided a thorough review of the way in which intensive survey has developed during the last two decades, with references to a number of recent and current projects.[67] Comments here are therefore restricted to an update on recent results and their particular relevance to the political geography of the Late Bronze Age. It is appropriate to keep in mind recent warnings about the variability of goals and methods in different survey projects, and the difficulties inherent in interpreting ceramic and other data.[68] Nevertheless, the final reports so far published explain clearly their approach to such issues as site definition, functional types, and settlement hierarchy.

Survey data can be especially useful for comparing site densities in different regions. Table 2 shows the numbers of Early, Middle, and Late Bronze Age sites found by nine recent intensive survey projects, and densities per 10 km² to facilitate comparisons among the different project areas and periods.[69] In the following discussion the emphasis is on the Late Helladic settlement patterns, with some comparison to the Middle Helladic period.

The fluctuation of the number of sites in different regions from the Early to the Late Helladic period has interesting historical implications. Particularly noticeable is a striking increase from MH Early–

[60] C.W. Shelmerdine, "Nichoria in Context: A Major Town in the Pylos Kingdom," *AJA* 85 (1981) 319–25.

[61] M.B. Cosmopoulos, "Recherches sur la stratigraphie préhistorique d'Eleusis: Travaux 1995," *EchCl* 40, n.s. 15 (1996) 1–26; a report will also appear in *Prakt* 1995. I thank Michael Cosmopoulos for information on the dates of the two phases.

[62] *AR* 1985–1986, 40; E. Sapouna-Sakellaraki, "Γλύφα η Βλύχα Βοιωτίας: Η μυκηναϊκή Αυλίδα?" *AAA* 20 (1987) 191–210.

[63] S. Müller, "Delphes et sa région à l'époque mycénienne," *BCH* 116 (1992) 445–96.

[64] "Chronique" 1991, 688–90; Müller (supra n. 63) 457–58.

[65] C.W. Blegen, "Preclassical Greece," in *Studies in the Arts and Architecture* (Philadelphia 1941) 1–14, a volume cele-

brating the bicentennial of the University of Pennsylvania, called for "a systematic comprehensive survey of the districts of Greece," after which "we shall know infinitely more than we now do regarding the extent of occupation and the movements and distribution of population from period to period" (pp. 12–13).

[66] W.A. McDonald and G.R. Rapp, Jr., eds., *The Minnesota Messenia Expedition: Reconstructing a Bronze Age Regional Environment* (Minneapolis 1972).

[67] Rutter 747–58.

[68] Rutter 752–58; J.F. Cherry, "Regional Survey in the Aegean: The 'New Wave' (and After)," in Kardulias 91–112.

[69] Bibliography up to 1992 is provided by Rutter 748–49. Subsequent publications are noted in relevant footnotes infra.

Table 2. Comparative Settlement Patterns from Survey Results

Project	Area Surveyed (km²)	Sites (EH/MH/LH)	Site Density per 10 km² (EH/MH/LH)
Berbati-Limnes Archaeological Survey	25	13/—/19	05.20/ — /07.60
Cambridge/Bradford Boeotian Expedition	45	19/16/16	04.22/03.56/03.56
Laconia Survey	70	29/11/10	04.14/01.57/01.43
Methana Survey	10	21/01/05	21.00/01.00/05.00
Nemea Valley Archaeological Project	50	21/02/10	04.20/00.40/02.00
Oropos Survey	22	10/01/02	04.55/00.45/00.91
Pylos Regional Archaeological Project	40	06/11/14	01.50/02.75/03.50
Southern Argolid Exploration Project	44	37/05/27	08.41/01.14/06.14
Stanford Skourta Plain Project	32	15/03/14	04.69/00.94/04.38

Data are taken from Rutter 748, table 1 except for the following; in all cases minimum rather than maximum possible figures are used: Cambridge/Bradford Boeotian Expedition: Information from Oliver Dickinson. Laconia Survey: W.G. Cavanagh et al., *The Laconia Survey* II: *Continuity and Change in a Greek Rural Landscape: Archaeological Data* (BSA Suppl. 27, London 1996) 315–438. Figures reflect securely dated sites within the survey area. R291 should be added to the list of 10 MH sites listed by Cavanagh in *Politeia* 84; cf. 85, and Cavanagh et al. 1996, 413. Nemea Valley Archaeological Project: LH figure raised from 8 to 10 according to information from J.L. Davis. Oropos Survey: M. Cosmopoulos, "Archäologische Forschungen im Gebiet von Oropos: Die vorgeschichtliche Besiedlung," *PZ* (in press). Pylos Regional Archaeological Project: personal information. Figures include revisited sites outside the 40-km² area intensively surveyed. Southern Argolid Exploration Project: M.H. Jameson, C.N. Runnels, and T.H. van Andel, *A Greek Countryside: The Southern Argolid from Prehistory to the Present Day* (Stanford 1994) 415–526.

Middle to MH Late and LH in the northeastern Peloponnese and Boeotia, in contrast to Messenia and Laconia. For useful comparison among regions it is necessary to go beyond numbers of dots on a map, and to consider several other factors. When within the LH period are sites founded or abandoned? Where are the new sites in relation to earlier ones? Are they habitations or other types? Do sites that continue from MH to LH grow or decline in size, or do they continue unchanged? How do such changes relate to developments in the political landscape? A thorough inquiry goes beyond the scope of this review, but some observations can be made for survey areas for which sufficient information is available.

The northeastern Peloponnese has been the focus of a number of recent studies.[70] Members of the Southern Argolid Exploration Project surveyed the southern end of the Akte peninsula, south of the Ad-

heres mountain range.[71] The 44-km² area intensively surveyed shows a dramatic increase from five MH habitation sites to 27 in the LH period. All of the LH sites are habitations except C1 and C3 (quarries; possible habitations).[72] LH III remains are most abundant, but the growth begins in the Shaft Grave period (MH III–LH I).[73] Increased population and intensified land use correlate with a wide dispersal of sites across the landscape and a settlement hierarchy of "villages and smaller satellites."[74]

The same pattern of development was observed in the Nemea Valley area, where the number of sites increases substantially, beginning in the Shaft Grave period. This trend continues through the Early Mycenaean period to LH IIIA1.[75] These new sites tend to be fairly large, and are evenly distributed throughout the study area. The onset of this period of growth coincides with the new prosperity of Mycenae in LH I. Perhaps more interesting in terms of the re-

[70] Information comparable to that discussed here is now available for the Berbati-Limnes project: B. Wells ed., *The Berbati-Limnes Archaeological Survey 1988–1990* (SkrAth 4°, 44, Jonsered 1996).

[71] M.H. Jameson, C.N. Runnels, and T.H. van Andel, *A Greek Countryside: The Southern Argolid from Prehistory to the Present Day* (Stanford 1994); and C.N. Runnels, D.J. Pullen, and S. Langdon, *Artifact and Assemblage: The Finds from a Regional Survey of the Southern Argolid, Greece* 1: *The Prehistoric and Early Iron Age Pottery and the Lithic Artifacts* (Stanford 1995).

[72] MH sites: A6, E9, E13, E76, F5. LH sites: A6, B2, B5, B9, B21, B24, B25, B38, B41, B89, B97, B98, C1, C3, C11, C24, E5, E9, E13, E74, F4, F5, F21, F29, F32, G13, G23.

[73] C.N. Runnels and T.H. van Andel, "The Evolution of Settlement in the Southern Argolid, Greece: An Economic Explanation," *Hesperia* 56 (1987) 315.

[74] Runnels and van Andel (supra n. 73) 323, who also note (328) that the reverse pattern applies in Melos, where nucleation occurs in periods of growth and prosperity.

[75] J.L. Davis, "If There's a Room at the Top What's at the Bottom: Settlement and Hierarchy in Early Mycenaean Greece," unpublished paper presented to the Institute for Aegean Prehistory, 6 April 1988; the summary of an earlier version appears under the same title in *BICS* 35 (1988) 164–65. My thanks to the author for allowing me to cite this paper. Updated data available on the Nemea Valley Archaeological Project World Wide Web site (supra n. 57).

lationship between the two areas, though, is the situation in LH IIIB. As is well known, there is an embarrassment of important Mycenaean citadels in the Argolid, especially during LH IIIB when Midea joins Mycenae and Tiryns as a fortified acropolis with a megaron complex.[76] In the Nemea Valley, Tsoungiza is the only site to exhibit substantial growth at this time. A recent study by Dabney also suggests that its expansion was due to the economic development stimulated by Mycenae, and that its ability to acquire finely decorated pottery depended on its integration into the kingdom of Mycenae.[77] Indeed, with more than one center perhaps competing for dominance of the Argive plain, Mycenae may have been able to increase its power by reaching north into the Nemea Valley.[78] It still remains unclear, however, whether Mycenae, Tiryns, and Midea each controlled a separate state. The status of Midea is especially uncertain; the megaron complex is suggestive of power, but to date no tablets have been found there. A few inscribed nodules attest to an administrative presence (see below), but if the inhabitants of the site did not generate their own tablets, Midea could have been a literate outpost of one of the other two centers.

The Methana peninsula also exhibits growth but to a lesser extent.[79] Of four possible MH habitations only MS10 is certain, and it is sizeable, covering 1.1 ha. All continue into LH, with a particular increase in site size in LH III, when both MS67 and MS124 grow to over 1 ha. Only one new site is founded in LH IIIA, albeit an important one: excavations at Ayios Konstantinos (MS13) have revealed a shrine complex as well as part of the settlement.[80] All of these sites are on or near the coast, and two (MS10, MS67) are described as typical Mycenaean acropolis sites. The picture corresponds to that in the southern Argo-

lid, with growth in both size and numbers of sites in the Early Mycenaean period, and the strongest presence in LH III.

In other areas settlement patterns do not follow the trend just described. The Laconia Survey has located a large number of chiefly small rural sites in central Laconia, in a 70-km² area extending from the Eurotas River on the west to the village of Chrysapha on the east, and from the Menelaion northward to the site of Palaiogoulas.[81] The few that show signs of Middle and Late Bronze Age occupation are located in the southern part of the survey area. The Middle Bronze Age is much better represented there, with 11 inhabited sites. Of these, four were abandoned by the end of that period, and one by the end of LH II. Six MH sites were inhabited into LH IIIB, although two of them (R291, S478) seem diminished in LH III from their earlier extent.[82] Only three LH III sites surveyed have no MH–LH II remains. The small hamlet of Melathria is one of these, inhabited from LH IIIA1 to IIIB2.[83] This general stability over time is interesting, given an apparent break in occupation of the Menelaion itself during LH IIIA2–B1.[84] Monumental buildings exist at the Menelaion in the Early Mycenaean period, and again in LH IIIB2, making it the likeliest candidate yet known in Laconia to have been a center of power. The LH IIIA2–B1 hiatus is rather surprising, as is the fact that it had no apparent effect on settlement in the surrounding area.

Exploration in the survey area continues in the form of the Laconia Rural Sites Project.[85] Twenty single-period sites of different periods were investigated in 1993–1994 to determine their form and function. The project includes geophysical prospection and soil studies, as well as analysis of artifacts

---

[76] A building "sur plan de mégaron" has also been reported on the east side of the Aspis at Argos by G. Touchais: "Chronique" 1978, 664. Only preliminary reports are available for the proposed megaron at Midea, which is not yet fully excavated: Demakopoulou et al. 1994 (supra n. 33) 41, fig. 65; Walberg, World Wide Web (supra n. 33).

[77] Dabney (supra n. 58).

[78] Wright et al. (supra n. 57) 637–38, 641–42; Davis, unpublished (supra n. 75); cf. O.T.P.K. Dickinson, "Parallels and Contrasts in the Bronze Age of the Peloponnese," *OJA* 1 (1982) 134; cf. E. Vermeule, "Baby Aigisthos and the Bronze Age," *PCPS* 213 (1987) 133.

[79] C.B. Mee et al., *A Rough and Rocky Place: The Landscape and Settlement History of the Methana Peninsula, Greece* (Liverpool, forthcoming). I thank Christopher Mee for allowing me to use a draft of the chapter on prehistory.

[80] MH sites: MS10 is certain; MS67, MS103, and MS124 are possible. LH sites: MS10, MS13, MS67, MS103, and MS124 are certain; MS14, MS106, and MS108 are possible.

[81] W.G. Cavanagh, "Development of the Mycenaean State in Laconia: Evidence from the Laconia Survey," in *Politeia* 81–87; Cavanagh et al., *The Laconia Survey* II: *Continuity and Change in a Greek Rural Landscape: Archaeological Data* (BSA Suppl. 27, London 1996); and Cavanagh et al., *The Laconia Survey* I (London, forthcoming).

[82] MH sites: M322, N191, R292, R457 (abandoned after MH); N413 (abandoned after LH II); M349, Q360—the Menelaion site, R291, S434, S478, U514 (continuing into LH IIIB). New LH III sites: H45, R424, U490.

[83] W.G. Cavanagh and J.H. Crouwel, "Melathria: A Small Mycenaean Rural Settlement in Laconia," in J.M. Sanders ed., Φιλολάκων: *Lakonian Studies in Honour of Hector Catling* (London 1992) 77–86; for the cemetery, see *Gazetteer* C5, and K. Demakopoulou, "Μυκηναϊκόν νεκροταφείον Μελαθριάς Λακωνίας," *ArchEph* 1977, 29–60.

[84] Catling (supra n. 37) 24–42, esp. 32–33.

[85] *AR* 1993–1994, 19; *AR* 1994–1995, 14–15.

and their distribution. This multifaceted approach is exemplary, and the concentration on rural sites addresses a gap in current knowledge.[86]

Work by the Pylos Regional Archaeological Project reveals yet another pattern of settlement in western Messenia.[87] Intensive field-walking covered approximately 40 km² within a larger area extending from just north of modern Koryphasion northward to just beyond Gargaliani, and from the coast eastward across the Aigaleon mountain range to the modern village of Maryeli. Eleven sites showed signs of MH occupation. Eight of these were inhabited into LH IIIB, while three were apparently abandoned after LH II/early IIIA.[88] It may be that no new sites were founded in LH, though at three places earlier (MH) occupation is uncertain. Analysis of the data is still in progress, but some points are already clear. The MH period is better represented in Messenia than elsewhere, and there is no upsurge in the number of sites in the Early Mycenaean period. The time of greatest change in the region is not the Shaft Grave period, but the beginning of LH III, which is marked, not by the founding of new sites as in the Argolid and the Nemea Valley, but by the abandonment of earlier ones. It is hard to avoid the inference that this trend is connected with the rising power of the Pylian center. Furthermore, two of the abandoned sites (A2 and L1) lie in valleys just east of the Aigaleon range, which probably formed the provincial boundary of the Pylos kingdom.[89] Border zones tend to be more heavily occupied during periods when there is no strong central power. When the center is strong, people leave the liminal zones, and

it may be that people moved out of these remote valleys and closer to the center of power in LH IIIA (probably LH IIIA2), as Pylos annexed the area beyond Aigaleon.[90]

Several other observations support this inference. Tholos tombs proliferate in Messenia during the Early Mycenaean period, suggesting the presence of rival elites, but fewer tholoi are in use in LH IIIA2–IIIB, when they are limited to Pylos itself and to sites with probable administrative links to the center, like Nichoria.[91] The megaron there goes out of use after LH IIIA1, and a tholos is constructed in LH IIIA2; both developments may indicate the time when local autonomy ended and Nichoria became part of the Pylos kingdom, as the power of the latter expanded to include the Messenian valley.[92]

It is not yet possible to make definitive statements about the Cambridge/Bradford project in southern Boeotia. Analysis to date, however, indicates no major drop in settlement during the MH period and no major expansion thereafter. At most sites all three phases of the Bronze Age are represented.[93] It is to be hoped that when all the results are in, survey data from this area will contribute to the analysis of political history as they have done in the northeastern Peloponnese and Messenia. For the moment, the boundaries of the Theban kingdom are still unclear in most directions, though the appearance of the place-names Karystos, Amarynthos, and now Eleon on tablets from Thebes suggests that it controlled the southern half of Euboea—and therefore presumably the intervening territory of southeastern Boeotia.[94] Worth noting in this connection is the set-

---

[86] Cherry (supra n. 68) 97.

[87] "Chronique" 1993, 795–96; "Chronique" 1994, 715–17; *AR* 1992–1993, 31–32; *AR* 1993–1994, 30; *AR* 1994–1995, 25; J.L. Davis et al., "The Pylos Regional Archaeological Project: Preliminary Report on the 1992 Season," *AJA* 97 (1993) 330–31 (abstract); Davis et al., "The Pylos Regional Archaeological Project: Preliminary Report on the 1993 Season," *AJA* 98 (1994) 287–88 (abstract); Davis et al., "The Pylos Regional Archaeological Project: Preliminary Report on the 1994 Season," *AJA* 99 (1995) 341–42 (abstract); Davis et al. (supra n. 45); Zangger et al. (supra n. 46); and Davis et al., "The Pylos Regional Archaeological Project: Internet Edition," on the World Wide Web at http://classics.lsa.umich.edu/PRAP/html/PRAP.html (23 May 1997).

[88] MH sites: A2, B7 = Palace of Nestor, C3, D1, D2, I1, I3, K1, K2, K3, L1; there is also a possible MH presence at G3, I4, and I21. Of the certain MH sites, A2, C3, and L1 are abandoned after LH II/early IIIA; the rest continue through LH IIIB, and the three possible MH sites are occupied during LH as well.

[89] On the geography of the Pylos kingdom, see J. Chadwick, "The Mycenaean Documents," in McDonald and Rapp

(supra n. 66) 100–16; Chadwick, *The Mycenaean World* (Cambridge 1976) 36–40; and J. Bintliff ed., *Mycenaean Geography* (Cambridge 1977) 55–62.

[90] D.J.L. Bennet, "Space through Time: Diachronic Perspectives on the Spatial Organization of the Pylian State," in *Politeia* 600.

[91] The megaron (unit IV-4A): S. Aschenbrenner, "Late Helladic Settlement: Stratigraphy and Architecture: Unit IV-4a. The Megaron Complex," in McDonald and Wilkie (supra n. 10) 433–39, figs. 7-58 and 7-59, pl. 7-119. The tholos: N.C. Wilkie, "The MME Tholos Tomb," in McDonald and Wilkie 231–60.

[92] Bennet (supra n. 90) 601.

[93] O.T.P.K. Dickinson, personal communication.

[94] Karystos: Wu 55.β; Amarynthos: Of 25, Wu 58.γ; Eleon: new tablet 149. V. Aravantinos, "Mycenaean Place-Names from Thebes: The New Evidence," in *Studies Chadwick* 33–40 also finds evidence for Theban interest on the island of Aegina and in the vicinity of Thespiae; see also Aravantinos, in *Politeia* (supra n. 49) 616–17. See also S. Hiller, "Die Stellung Böotiens im mykenischen Staatenverband," in Beister and Buckler (supra n. 54) 51–64. Thebes

tlement of Glipha/Vlicha, on the mainland across from Chalkis, which may have served Thebes as a port.

Some recent assessments make extravagant claims about survey work: one commentator perceives a threat that practicalities will force a shift from excavation to survey, while another goes so far as to call the development of regional studies a Kuhnian paradigm shift.[95] However, the detailed results now appearing in survey publications indicate the advantages and limitations of this technique more fairly than either its most enthusiastic supporters or its strongest detractors. Surface survey is not a substitute for excavation, but it offers a regional perspective that excavation cannot give. The preceding analysis illustrates how diachronic survey data can clarify the history of an area, and how regional comparison, even at a fairly basic level, can reveal meaningful synchronic variations.[96]

TECHNOLOGICAL ADVANCES

In 1941, when Blegen discussed the value of survey archaeology, he also predicted quite correctly that "we shall come more and more to rely on pure science for help in solving many of the problems that face us."[97] Scientific contributions to archaeological projects have indeed become essential both in fieldwork and in the subsequent analysis of data. Some new kinds of tools and techniques are listed here, and examples of their impact on Late Bronze

Age studies are discussed in the relevant sections of this review. Among new hardware, the Global Positioning System (GPS), developed for military use, has been enthusiastically adopted by some as a means of pinpointing sites and other features. On the ground, advances in surveying equipment like total stations greatly ease the process of mapping sites and surveying architectural remains.[98] Geophysical prospection is also a valuable complement to surface exploration, whether or not excavation is to follow (as we have seen in the detection of the probable wall at Pylos). Landscape and soil studies have also proven invaluable,[99] and have contributed greatly to our understanding of Mycenaean engineering: two Late Bronze Age examples are described above, pertaining to Tiryns and Pylos. Ceramic study of the Late Bronze Age too has been greatly enhanced by advances in provenience analysis, combining petrography and chemical spectrography, and in the analysis of organic residue (see below).

Finally, a word should be said about computer applications in archaeology. Computer Aided Drafting/Design (CAD) software transforms the coordinates of surveyed points into a three-dimensional reconstruction of a structure or a topographical site map.[100] An even more powerful tool for expressing data in terms of spatial relationships is the Geographical Information System (GIS), which allows spatial data to be stored, manipulated, mapped, and visualized on a computer in two or three dimen-

---

has a potential rival to the northwest in Orchomenos, where a complex of three alleged "megaron units" has a LH IIIA2 and a LH IIIB stage: *Gazetteer* G 1; *AR* 1984–1985, 31; and T. Spyropoulos, "Το Ανάκτορο του Μινύου εις τον Βοιωτικόν Ορχομενόν," *AAA* 7 (1974) 313–25. Each unit has elements labeled as vestibule, porch, and megaron, but no column bases survive and only in one "megaron" was a hearth found.

[95] Survey as a threat: M. Popham, "Reflections on 'An Archaeology of Greece': Surveys and Excavations," *OJA* 9 (1990) 29–35. Popham is reacting to A. Snodgrass, *An Archaeology of Greece: The Present State and Future Scope of a Discipline* (Sather Classical Lectures 53, Berkeley 1987), esp. 96–131; Snodgrass in fact never makes such an extreme claim as Popham attributes to him, though he does extol the virtues of survey archaeology. Survey as a paradigm shift: P.N. Kardulias, "Paradigms of the Past in Greek Archaeology," in Kardulias 1–24.

[96] D.J.L. Bennet and M. Galaty, "Classical Archaeology: Recent Developments in the Archaeology of the Prehistoric Aegean and Regional Studies," *Journal of Archaeological Research* 5 (1997) 76–120.

[97] Blegen (supra n. 65) 13. P.E. McGovern, "Science in Archaeology: A Review," *AJA* 99 (1995) 79–142, while not directed specifically at the Bronze Age, surveys a range of scientific approaches and their application to archaeological research.

[98] GPS: Cherry (supra n. 68) 98; *AR* 1991–1992, 27–28 (Minnesota Archaeological Researches in the Western Peloponnese). Total Station: P.M. Fischer, "The Cyclopean Built Wall of the Mycenaean Citadel of Midea: A Survey Using Electronic Distance Measuring Equipment," *JFA* 13 (1986) 499–503; Davis et al. (supra n. 45).

[99] The bibliography in these fields has grown too fast to do it full justice here. Good starting points with further references include E. Zangger, *The Geoarchaeology of the Argolid* (Argolis 2, Berlin 1993); T.H. van Andel, E. Zangger, and A. Demitrack, "Land Use and Soil Erosion in Prehistoric and Historical Greece," *JFA* 17 (1990) 379–96; and Zangger, "Neolithic to Present Soil Erosion in Greece," in M. Bell and J. Boardman eds., *Past and Present Soil Erosion: Archaeological and Geographical Perspectives* (Oxford 1992) 133–47. Recent discussions of the results of geophysical prospection and soil studies: Cavanagh et al. 1996 (supra n. 81) 235–61; Jameson et al. (supra n. 71) passim. These and other scientific topics are covered by several papers in N.C. Wilkie and W.D. Coulson eds., *Contributions to Aegean Archaeology: Studies in Honor of William A. McDonald* (Minneapolis 1985).

[100] M.G. Stys, "The Site within the Region: Architectural Reconstruction Using Computer Technology," in Kardulias 265–87.

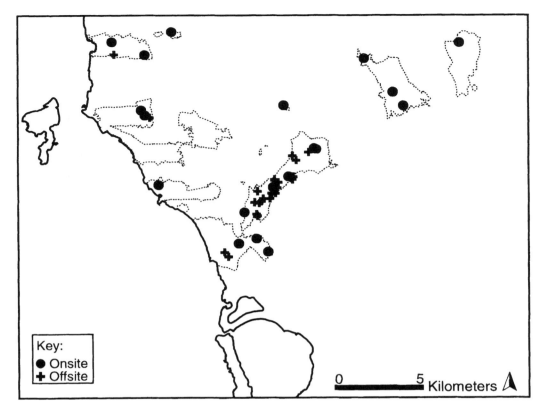

Fig. 7. Pylos Regional Archaeological Project. Distribution of LH III finds. (Courtesy Pylos Regional Archaeological Project)

sions.[101] Sites or artifact types can thus be plotted in relation to general topography, including elevation, slope angle, drainage, water resources, and other geographical information. Projects with a Greek Bronze Age component are just beginning to take advantage of these resources, and they will become more visible as projects present themselves on computer through the Internet and on compact discs, as well as or instead of in printed publications. To date, the most extensive use of GIS technology for Bronze Age data has been by the Pylos Regional Archaeological Project.[102] As a simple example, the distribution of LH III finds can be plotted on a two- or three-dimensional map of the survey area (fig. 7). More complicated plots can include not only the spatial information listed above, but also factors such as traveling distance from one site to its nearest neighbor, factoring in the ruggedness of the intervening terrain.

CERAMIC STUDIES

As noted above, ceramic studies have benefited greatly from scientific applications. Notable in Late Bronze Age studies is an ongoing project under the overall direction of Halford Haskell.[103] One aspect of the investigation is an interdisciplinary study of transport stirrup jars from eastern Mediterranean

[101] V. Gaffney and Z. Stančič, *GIS Approaches to Regional Analysis: A Case Study of the Island of Hvar* (Ljubljana 1991), enthusiastically reviewed by J.L. Davis in *AJA* 97 (1993) 799–800; M.A. Dann and R.W. Yerkes, "Use of Geographic Information Systems for the Spatial Analysis of Frankish Settlements in the Korinthia, Greece," in Kardulias 289–311, with further references. Useful sites on the World Wide Web are "Global Positioning System Overview," at http://www.utexas.edu/depts/grg/gcraft/notes/gps/gps.html (23 May 1997); and "Internet Resources for Geography and GIS," at http://perseus.holycross.edu/PAP/General/Resources-GIS.html (9 June 1997).

[102] Davis et al. (supra n. 45); and Davis et al., World Wide Web (supra n. 87). See also the Nemea Valley Archaeological Project site on the World Wide Web (supra n. 57); and J. Wiseman and A. Dousougli-Zachos, "The Nikopolis Project 1991–1993: Overview of the Multidisciplinary Study of Southern Epirus," *AJA* 98 (1994) 315 (abstract).

[103] H.W. Haskell et al., *Transport Stirrup Jars of the Bronze Age Aegean and East Mediterranean* (Fitch Laboratory Occasional Papers 5, Athens, forthcoming). What follows is based on information kindly provided by Halford Haskell and Peter Day.

contexts, using a combination of typological, petro-graphical, and chemical analyses to determine provenience. This work has important consequences for the study of intra- and extra-Aegean trade. For example, Cretan stirrup jars at mainland sites are a well-known phenomenon.[104] Haskell's study, however, adds several refinements. Petrographic analysis of stirrup jars from Thebes and Mycenae has shown that, in addition to west Cretan vessels, some jars previously thought to have been produced locally originated in central Crete.[105] Most, indeed, are in a south-central Cretan fabric, newly distinguished by petrographic analysis and also prevalent at Knossos. Both sites contain examples of fabrics that were previously considered Knossian, occurring in quantity at Knossos and other sites in the Aegean and beyond. But these same fabrics also appear at other Cretan sites such as Malia,[106] and further recent work on Crete has shown that at least some of these fabrics have their origin in the south-central part of the island. Among the project's future plans is analysis of the organic residue preserved on the clay of such stirrup jars. These jars are known to be containers for olive oil, but the further investigation should confirm whether this oil came in different grades, whether it was plain or perfumed, and whether the jars carried any other commodities.

Other ongoing efforts also pertain to the movement of pottery in international trade. One contribution is the cataloguing of corpora of Aegean pottery found outside Greece; the most recent study covers Syria-Palestine.[107] Another is the study by Nicolle Hirschfeld of Aegean and Canaanite vessels with incised and painted signs.[108] The majority of marked Mycenaean vessels are LH IIIA–B stirrup and piriform jars, with the signs incised after firing. The markings are in the Cypriot system, and such vessels from the Argolid may have been marked there but intended for export.

Traditional pottery studies have not been entirely displaced, and they continue to prove valuable in their own right.[109] P. Mountjoy has provided an update of Furumark's monumental classification for decorated pottery, as well as a more general introduction to Mycenaean pottery.[110] The stratigraphy at Tiryns has led to an extensive refinement of phases there from LH IIIA2 Late through LH IIIC. Early, Middle, Developed, and Late phases have been distinguished within LH IIIB, and Early, Developed, Advanced, and Late phases for LH IIIC.[111] The LH IIIB phases have been described and correlated with standard definitions of LH IIIB1 and LH IIIB2, and with the pottery groups from Mycenae on which these are traditionally based. Within each phase, variants of shapes and motifs are further labeled Fading, Floruit, or Innovative, based on their percentages within each LH IIIA and IIIB phase. It remains to be seen how far such fine distinctions can be applied elsewhere, but the phases themselves do have parallels at other sites. LH IIIB1 Early includes features of both LH IIIA2 and LH IIIB1 as those phases are conventionally defined. Such a transitional phase has also been recognized at other sites (e.g., Nichoria and Korakou),[112] and correlated with the latest LH

[104] E. Hallager, "The Inscribed Stirrup Jars: Implications for Late Minoan IIIB Crete," *AJA* 91 (1987) 171–90; H.W. Catling et al., "The Linear B Inscribed Stirrup Jars and West Crete," *BSA* 75 (1980) 49–114; R.E. Jones, *Greek and Cypriot Pottery: A Review of Scientific Studies* (Athens 1986) 477–93.

[105] Mycenae: appendices by P.M. Day, R.E. Jones, and J. Tomlinson in Tournavitou (supra n. 23) 301–20. Thebes: P.M. Day and H.W. Haskell, "Transport Stirrup Jars as Evidence for Trade in Late Bronze Age Greece," in C. Gillis, C. Risberg, and B. Sjoberg eds., *Trade and Production in Premonetary Greece: Aspects of Trade* (SIMA-PB 134, Jonsered 1995) 87–109.

[106] Appendix by P.M. Day and R.E. Jones in A. Farnoux and J. Driessen, "Inscriptions peintes en Linéaire B à Malia," *BCH* 115 (1991) 94–97.

[107] A. Leonard, Jr., *An Index to the Late Bronze Age Aegean Pottery from Syria-Palestine* (SIMA 114, Jonsered 1994); references to other corpora of Aegean pottery outside Greece are collected on p. 1, n. 4. Leonard also maintains a regularly updated computer database.

[108] N. Hirschfeld, "Cypriot Marks on Mycenaean Pottery," in *Mykenaïka* 315–19. Hirschfeld expands this study in her dissertation (Univ. of Texas at Austin, in progress) to include painted and incised marks on both Aegean and

Canaanite vessels of the Late Bronze Age.

[109] Groups of material published or restudied include the following: P.A. Mountjoy, *Orchomenos V: Mycenaean Pottery from Orchomenos, Eutresis and Other Boeotian Sites* (Bayerische Akademie der Wissenschaft, Philosophisch-historische Klasse, N.F. 89, Munich 1983); Å. Åkerström, *Berbati* II: *The Pictorial Pottery* (Stockholm 1987); B. Santillo Frizell, *Asine* II: *Results of the Excavations East of the Acropolis, 1970–1974* 2: *The Late and Final Mycenaean Periods* (Stockholm 1986); K.S. Shelton, *The Late Helladic Pottery from Prosymna* (Jonsered 1996). Another valuable compilation is E. Vermeule and V. Karageorghis, *Mycenaean Pictorial Vase Painting* (Cambridge, Mass. 1982).

[110] P.A. Mountjoy, *Mycenaean Decorated Pottery: A Guide to Identification* (SIMA 73, Göteborg 1986); Mountjoy, *Mycenaean Pottery: An Introduction* (Oxford 1993).

[111] Cf. Kilian 1988 (supra n. 26) fig. 27; Kilian in French and Wardle (supra n. 5) 117–18, fig. 3. LH IIIA2 Late–IIIB Middle: Schönfeld (supra n. 26). LH IIIB Late: Podzuweit 1981 (supra n. 26). LH IIIC phases: Podzuweit (supra n. 26) all entries.

[112] Nichoria, the LH IIIA2/B1 phase: Shelmerdine (supra n. 10) 503–508. Korakou, the East Alley Deposit: J.B. Rutter, *The Late Helladic IIIB and IIIC Periods at Korakou and Gonia in the Corinthia* (Diss. Univ. of Pennsylvania 1974).

IIIA2 groups at Mycenae, from the terrace on the Atreus Ridge and the terrace below the House of Shields.[113] LH IIIB Middle corresponds to LH IIIB1 groups at Mycenae, and the Developed phase to canonical LH IIIB2.[114] The Late phase at Tiryns is part of a transitional LH IIIB2/LH IIIC Early phase that Mountjoy has recently identified.[115] It is characterized by features that are assigned conventionally to LH IIIC in the Argolid, like coated deep bowls, Group A deep bowls with monochrome interiors, and medium-band deep bowls, but that appear at other sites in contexts dated to LH IIIB2.

Another trend in ceramic studies has been the increasing awareness of variations from site to site and region to region in the palatial period.[116] For example, some LH IIIB2 features like Group B deep bowls are much less common in Messenia and Laconia than in the Argolid. The LH IIIB2 and early LH IIIC periods are well represented at Delphi, and exhibit some typical Argolid features, but again with local peculiarities.[117]

DEVELOPMENT OF MYCENAEAN STATES

One of the important questions occupying scholars of Mycenaean Greece in the last decade concerns the transformation of scattered enclaves of power, characteristic of the Middle Helladic period, into the centralized states of LH IIIA–B.[118] The political

entities of the Early Mycenaean period are best classified as chiefdoms, wherein chiefs wielding inherited power coordinated economic, social, and religious activities, and maintained authority through ritual and the display of prestige goods and symbols of power.[119] The later states exhibit a much higher degree of political and social complexity. The tablets suggest a fairly elaborate official hierarchy, and demonstrate the high degree to which economic control is essential to political power (see below). As Wright notes, the essential difference between a chiefdom and a state is that in the latter offices are "abstracted, formally defined and independent of the individual who fills them."[120] It is widely believed that it took the Mycenaeans all of LH I–II to achieve this level of social, economic, and political development. Conventional measures of statehood include the definition of an administrative center through the construction of a palatial building complex, the development of writing, and the establishment of state institutions such as a state religion. Additional criteria such as complexity of social ranking — best reflected archaeologically in burials — and trade in prestige goods can characterize chiefdoms as well as states, but they too are useful indicators of the development that took place in Greece from Early Mycenaean times to LH III. A comparison of the Early Mycenaean situation with that in LH IIIA–B in these various areas

---

[113] Schönfeld (supra n. 26) 163, table 4; French (supra n. 11) 174–84, 185–92.

[114] LH IIIB1 Middle, first half: E.B. French, "A Group of Late Helladic IIIB 1 Pottery from Mycenae," *BSA* 61 (1966) 216–38; French, "Pottery from Late Helladic IIIB 1 Destruction Contexts at Mycenae," *BSA* 62 (1967) 149–93. LH IIIB1 Middle, second half: P.A. Mountjoy, "Late Helladic IIIB 1 Pottery Dating the Construction of the South House at Mycenae," *BSA* 71 (1976) 77–111; K. Wardle, "A Group of LH IIIB 1 Pottery from within the Citadel at Mycenae," *BSA* 64 (1969) 261–97. Canonical LH IIIB2 at Mycenae is represented by the Causeway Deposit and that from the Perseia West Trench L: Wardle, "A Group of LH IIIB 2 Pottery from within the Citadel at Mycenae: 'The Causeway Deposit,'" *BSA* 68 (1973) 297–348; French, "A Group of LH IIIB 2 Pottery from Mycenae," *BSA* 64 (1969) 71–93.

[115] P.A. Mountjoy, *Regional Mycenaean Decorated Pottery* (Berlin, forthcoming); Mountjoy, "Thorikos Mine No. 3: The Mycenaean Pottery," *BSA* 90 (1995) 195–212. In addition to the sites mentioned in this article (Thorikos, Iria, Korakou, and the North Slope houses at Athens), Mountjoy confirms that the transitional phase existed at Tiryns, Midea, and Nichoria (personal communication). French has now recognized this phase at Mycenae also, in the latest material in the destruction level of the Citadel House area (personal communication).

[116] E.S. Sherratt, "Regional Variation in the Pottery of Late Helladic IIIB," *BSA* 75 (1980) 175–202; P.A. Mountjoy, "Regional Mycenaean Pottery," *BSA* 85 (1990) 245–70; Mount-

joy, forthcoming (supra n. 115).

[117] Müller (supra n. 63) 461, n. 42, 463–65.

[118] K. Kilian, "The Emergence of *Wanax* Ideology in the Mycenaean Palaces," *OJA* 7 (1988) 291–302; M.K. Dabney and J.C. Wright, "Mortuary Customs, Palatial Society and State Formation in the Aegean Area: A Comparative Study," in Hägg and Nordquist 45–53; and the recent volumes *Politeia* and Rehak. Wright, "From Chief to King in Mycenaean Society," in Rehak 63–82 provides a particularly thoughtful theoretical framework for discussion.

[119] Wright (supra n. 118), esp. 69 with references; C.W. Shelmerdine, "A Comparative Look at Mycenaean Administration(s)," in S. Hiller, S. Jalkotzy, and O. Panagl eds., *Floreant Studia Mycenaea. Proceedings of the 10th Mycenaean Colloquium, Salzburg, May 1995* (Salzburg, forthcoming). A few would put the development of kingship, at least, much earlier: for the idea that the *wanax* ideology was formed by the end of the Shaft Grave period, see I. Kilian-Dirlmeier, "Beobachtungen zu den Schachtgräbern von Mykenai und zu den Schmuckbeigaben mykenischer Männergräber: Untersuchungen zur Sozialstruktur in späthelladischer Zeit," *JRGZM* 33 (1986) 159–98; Kilian (supra n. 5) 292–94; T.G. Palaima, "The Nature of the Mycenaean *Wanax*," in Rehak 126; and Palaima, "The Origin and Ideology of Mycenaean Kingship: Homeric, Indo-European and Minoan Priest-King Models," in Palaima ed., *Kingship and the Organization of Power in Greek Society* (Austin, forthcoming).

[120] Wright (supra n. 118) 66.

may be a useful way to organize information and to indicate current thinking on Mycenaean states and their development.

Construction of an Administrative Building Complex

The strict architectural definition of a Mycenaean palace is a large ashlar construction centered on a megaron unit: a rectangular room with four columns surrounding a hearth, its long walls extending to form a porch and a vestibule.[121] Extant traces show that such building complexes existed from LH IIIA at most of the centers that are important in LH IIIB: Mycenae, Tiryns, Pylos, and perhaps Thebes.[122] Suggestions of still earlier palaces at these sites remain unproven, mainly because later construction has obliterated all or most of the architecture that might have existed. Wace demonstrated the existence of a structure on the Mycenae hilltop in LH I-II, adapted to the contours of the terrain, but there is nothing to show whether it included a megaron.[123] The earliest identifiable megaron unit at Tiryns, situated under the later main megaron (rooms V-VII), dates to LH IIIA1.[124] The subsidiary megaron (rooms XXI-XXII) also had a predecessor in early LH IIIA, and the first fortifications also appear in this phase, at the south end of the acropolis. At Py-

los, several phases of walls and stucco flooring underlie the extant LH IIIB palace (notably in rooms 7, 55-57), with similar orientation and poros facade. These are probably part of an earlier palace presumed to date to LH IIIA, although there is little or no ceramic evidence.[125] There is as yet no confirmation that still earlier structures at the site were palatial.[126] The chronology of Thebes is especially difficult, and the architectural remnants sparse. No canonical megaron unit is yet attested, but there do seem to have been two successive structures on the acropolis. The earlier palace, the House of Kadmos, may go back to LH II.[127] If so, and if it were truly a megaron, it would stand out as the earliest example on the mainland. The site was fortified at least from LH IIIA.[128]

As just noted, the nature of Early Mycenaean structures at later palace sites is not clear from the existing architectural traces. Some possibilities are suggested, however, by evidence from contemporary nonpalatial sites whose architecture was not obscured by later construction.[129] After all, the Early Mycenaean chiefs who occupied the known palatial centers were the winners in the competition among local powers to extend their authority over a wider area. At other sites, less successful rivals also left be-

---

[121] The word megaron—with or without mitigating quotation marks—is variously and loosely applied to rectangular buildings of many different places and periods. It would be better to restrict it to the definition given here, if it is to be used at all: cf. P. Darcque, "Pour l'abandon du terme 'mégaron'," in Darcque and Treuil (supra n. 49) 21-31.

[122] R.L.N. Barber, "The Origins of the Mycenaean Palace," in Sanders (supra n. 83) 11-23; this section is a summary of the relevant portion of Shelmerdine (supra n. 119).

[123] A.J.B. Wace, *Mycenae: An Archaeological History and Guide* (Princeton 1949) 87; G.E. Mylonas, *Mycenae and the Mycenaean Age* (Princeton 1966) 59, fig. 14 assumes that this building would have had a megaron unit.

[124] LH IIIA palace: *AR* 1984-1985, 20-21; *AR* 1985-1986, 26-27; K. Kilian, "L'architecture des résidences mycéniennes: Origine et extension d'une structure du pouvoir politique pendant l'Age de Bronze," in E. Lévy ed., *Le système palatial en Orient, en Grèce et à Rome. Actes du Colloque de Strasbourg 19-22 juin 1985* (Strasbourg 1987) 209, figs. 6-7. There was a throne installation at this early stage also: Kilian, "Die 'Thronfolge' in Tiryns," *AM* 103 (1988) 1-9; T. Schulz, "Die Rekonstruktion des Thronpodestes im ersten grossen Megaron von Tiryns," *AM* 103 (1988) 11-23. Claims of a MH palace rest on fresco fragments allegedly associated with MH II-III levels: K. Müller, *Tiryns III: Die Architektur der Burg und des Palastes* (Mainz 1930) 78; Kilian 1987 (supra) 213. Fortifications: Kilian (supra n. 5) 134, fig. 9.

[125] C.W. Blegen and M. Rawson, *The Palace of Nestor at Pylos in Western Messenia* I: *The Buildings and Their Contents* (Princeton 1966) 44, 94, 226-27; C.W. Blegen et al., *The Palace of Nestor at Pylos in Western Messenia* III: *Acropolis and Lower*

Town; Tholoi, Grave Circle, and Chamber Tombs; Discoveries outside the Citadel (Princeton 1973) 34-36; Kilian 1987 (supra n. 124) 209. LH IIIA pottery predominates in debris covering the earlier wall in room 7, though there are a few possibly earlier pieces, and some sherds of LH IIIB. About the material from under rooms 55-57, which had been badly disturbed before excavation, Blegen et al. 36 could report only that "we felt that we were dealing with wares of Mycenaean III A."

[126] The Minnesota Pylos Project has reported walls forming "a megaron-like plan" beside the Wine Magazine (rooms 104-105): *AR* 1992-1993, 33, phase 3; Cooper and Swain (supra n. 41). These walls predate the extant palace by several phases, but no date has yet been assigned to them. There is nothing to recommend the theory of Kilian 1987 (supra n. 124) 213-17, figs. 5, 12a that a Minoan-style palace stood on the hilltop in LH I; doubts are also expressed by O.T.P.K. Dickinson, "'The Origins of Mycenaean Civilisation' Revisited," in R. Laffineur ed., *Transition: Le monde égéen du Bronze moyen au Bronze récent* (Aegaeum 3, Liège 1989) 131, and by Rutter 796, n. 213.

[127] Symeonoglou (supra n. 49) 40-50, table 2.3, figs. 9-10 (reconstructed "megaron" of the first palace); see also discussion by Demakopoulou (supra n. 49) 316-17.

[128] *AR* 1984-1985, 30; I have not seen the reports by V. Aravantinos, "Η μυκηναϊκή οχύρωση της Καδμείας," in Bekiaris (supra n. 49) 113-36; and Aravantinos, "La fortificazione micenea di Tebe. I risultati degli scavi recenti sulla Cadmeia," *Colloqui del Sodalizio tra studiosi dell'arte* 9-11 (Rome 1991) 89-104.

[129] Barber (supra n. 122) 19-21.

hind residential architecture, and it is unlikely that Early Mycenaean buildings obscured by the later complexes at palatial centers were much different from these better-preserved examples. In many cases there are features that prefigure those of the canonical Mycenaean megaron complex, but none meets the strict definition. The earliest example is a likely MH prototype of the megaron unit in house D at Asine, which had a rectangular room and porch, but no hearth or column bases.[130] Several prominent Early Mycenaean buildings also have rooms that approximate megaron units. The LH II mansion I at the Menelaion in Laconia is usually the first building to be suggested in such a context.[131] Building F at Krisa in Phocis is earlier, however, constructed in LH I.[132] At Kakovatos in Elis a LH II building includes a large room with two preserved column bases.[133] None of these structures achieves the canonical form of the later palaces. Even unit IV-4A at Nichoria, which is confined in date to LH IIIA1 and thus contemporary with the earliest true megaron at Tiryns, has only one anteroom (not a true porch and vestibule) and only two column bases at either end of a hearth.[134] The true Mycenaean palace, then, is a product of long evolution, as may also be true of its Minoan counterpart.[135] Though we can identify early megaron complexes and their predecessors, the point at which such a structure begins to represent palatial authority remains a different and challenging question.

Development of Writing

A process of selection and adaptation is visible in the derivation of the Linear B script from Minoan Linear A.[136] There is a considerable overlap in the sign repertories of the two scripts: only about 16 of the 89 Linear B syllabograms have no Linear A predecessor. However, the syllabograms are generally simplified and regularized, many new ideograms were added and most of the Minoan ones abandoned, and a different fractional system was adopted. The Mycenaean tendency to impose their own style on what they borrowed is as clear in their writing system as it is in their art. Palaima has recently argued on palaeographical grounds that LH IIA/LM IB was the most likely time for the adaptation, but a stone with incised Linear B syllabograms has been reported from a late MH context at Kafkania, 7 km north of Olympia.[137] No numbers or logograms appear on this isolated find, however, and it shows at best an early stage of Mycenaean writing, not the kind of written administration seen later. Like the altered syllabary, restriction of writing to administrative use in the Mycenaean palatial era is another change from Minoan practice. Minoan inscriptions appear on a variety of artifacts of different materials, and in a variety of contexts. At the same time, their administrative uses appear to be limited. By contrast, Linear B inscriptions are found only on clay, either painted on transport jars or incised on tablets, labels, and sealings at major centers, but the range of their uses within the administrative sphere is extensive.

As far as is known, the first clear use of Linear B writing for administrative purposes was on Crete. The Room of the Chariot Tablets at Knossos, containing a cache of Linear B tablets, is currently understood to date to LM II.[138] The Mycenaean administration that these early documents reveal is not much different from that seen in the later Knossian documents. We know nothing comparable on the mainland until the end of LH IIIB1, in the Ug tablets and the Wu nodules from Thebes, and the tablets from

[130] Barber (supra n. 122) 20–21, fig. 10; O. Frödin and A.W. Persson, *Asine: Results of the Swedish Excavations, 1922–1930* (1938) 72–73, 102–103, fig. 49.

[131] Rutter 796. Barber (supra n. 122) 11–12, fig. 8 offers the suggestion that it had a hearth and column bases, though this is not certain.

[132] *Gazetteer* G 56; J. Jannoray and H. van Effenterre, "Fouilles de Krisa," *BCH* 61 (1937) 318–22, fig. 16. Here there is no porch, but two flat stones are likely to have served as column bases. I omit from consideration two successive LH I buildings from Tsoungiza, each with a hearth and a stone support for a central post in one rectangular room. These are called "megara" by Rutter 788, n. 176, but not by the excavator: Wright et al. (supra n. 57) 631–32, fig. 19.

[133] *Gazetteer* B 94; K. Kilian, "Zur Funktion der mykenischen Residenzen auf dem griechischen Festland," in R. Hägg and N. Marinatos eds., *The Function of the Minoan Palaces* (Stockholm 1987) 33, fig. 9.

[134] *Gazetteer* D 100; Aschenbrenner (supra n. 91) 433–39,

figs. 7-58 and 7-59, pl. 7-119.

[135] L.V. Watrous, "Review of Aegean Prehistory III: Crete from Earliest Prehistory through the Protopalatial Period," *AJA* 98 (1994) 741–42 gives a brief summary of alternative views on the development of Minoan palaces.

[136] The most recent study is by T.G. Palaima, "The Development of the Mycenaean Writing System," in *Studies Bennett* 269–342.

[137] Palaima (supra n. 136); L. Godart, "Una iscrizione in Lineare B del XVII secolo a.c. ad Olimpia," *RendLinc* ser. 9, 6.3 (1995) 445–47; P. Arapoyianni, J. Rambach, and L. Godart, "Η μυκηναϊκή επιγραφή της Καυκανιάς," *PraktAkAth* 70 (1995) 251–54; and Godart, "L'inscription de Kafkania-Olympie," *AA* 1995 (forthcoming).

[138] J. Driessen, *An Early Destruction in the Mycenaean Palace at Knossos: A New Interpretation of the Excavation Field-Notes of the South-East Area of the West Wing* (ActaArchLov Monograph 2, Louvain 1990).

the Oil Merchant group of houses at Mycenae. The only tablets that could be dated earlier are five discarded fragments found at Pylos, below the southwestern edge of the hill. These certainly predate the main archive of late LH IIIB, and their distinctive palaeography suggests that they may belong to LH IIIA.[139]

Complexity of Social Ranking

Tomb types, grave goods, and tomb placement can all differentiate elite from nonelite members of a society. For the Early Mycenaean period, tombs are much better attested than settlement material. Excavation priorities are part of the reason, but it is also true that elite burials are often highly visible in the archaeological landscape, and in LH I–II there are many of these. The prime example is the tholos tomb. It used to be tempting to assume that these must be "royal" graves, but their early proliferation and their tendency to occur in pairs or triplets militate against this view. At Mycenae itself they first appear only in LH IIA, but in Messenia the earliest are contemporary with the Mycenae Shaft Graves in MH III–LH I.[140] The Early Mycenaean tholos is now understood to be a symbol of elite status, and thus certainly a precursor to statehood, but not an indicator that it begins this early.[141] The nature of the power wielded by the elite members of Early Mycenaean societies is impossible to discern, but wealthy burials are sufficiently numerous and widely dispersed to suggest that the reach of each center

was quite limited. Another notable feature during this period is the diversity of tomb types and burial customs. Cists and pits coexist with chamber tombs and even at times with tholoi, and Dickinson has warned against the equation of cist tombs with a poorer element of society.[142] On a regional basis the tholoi themselves are common in Messenia but virtually unknown in Boeotia, while for chamber tombs the reverse is true.

In LH IIIA2–IIIB, by contrast, some standardization of tomb types can be seen, and the number of large tholoi in use drops significantly. They are concentrated at palatial centers, chiefly in Messenia and the Argolid, though small ones are built on a regional basis, especially in peripheral areas.[143] These phenomena can very plausibly be linked with the rise in power of the Mycenaean states.[144] The general decline in large tholoi coincides with increasingly elaborate architecture in the form of palatial complexes, suggesting a shift in how the elite chose to invest their human and material resources.[145] At the same time, the distribution of these large tombs suggests that the ruling class annexed the tholos tomb as a symbol of power. This does not mean simply that tholoi may at last have become truly royal tombs. The construction of a tholos at Nichoria in LH IIIA2, for example, could be directly associated with its assimilation into the Pylian state. As the site lost its position as an independent center, the status of its leaders may have risen by virtue of their relationship to the central administration, and a tholos may

[139] Thebes Ug series: J. Chadwick, "Linear B Tablets from Thebes," *Minos* 10 (1970) 116 reported a preliminary date of LH IIIA2, but this has been corrected by Symeonoglou (supra n. 49) 40, 231, site 3 and by Demakopoulou (supra n. 49) 312–13, site 4. Thebes Wu series: C. Piteros, J.L. Melena, and J.-P. Olivier, "Les inscriptions en Linéaire B des nodules de Thèbes (1982): La fouille, les documents, les possibilités d'interprétation," *BCH* 114 (1990) 104–105. Mycenae: Tournavitou (supra n. 23) with references. Pylos: T.G. Palaima, "Evidence for the Influence of the Knossian Graphic Tradition at Pylos," in P. Oliva and A. Frolikova eds., *Concilium Eirene* 16 (Prague 1983) 80–84; and Palaima, *The Scribes of Pylos* (Incunabula graeca 87, Rome 1988) 111–13 (Hand 91), 133 (Class iv).

[140] On the LH II date of the first six Mycenae tholoi, see O.T.P.K. Dickinson, *The Origins of Mycenaean Civilisation* (*SIMA* 49, Göteborg 1977) 63. The earliest canonical tholos is the MH III example at ancient Koryphasion *Haratsari* (also referred to as Osmanaga) *Gazetteer* D5; Y. Lolos, "The Tholos Tomb at Koryphasion: Evidence for the Transition from Middle to Late Helladic in Messenia," in Laffineur (supra n. 125) 171–75. On Messenian tombs and their nonroyal status, see O. Pelon, *Tholoi, tumuli, et cercles funéraires: Recherches sur les monuments funéraires de plan circulaire dans l'Égée de l'Âge du Bronze (IIIᵉ et IIᵉ millénaires av. J.-C.)* (Paris

1976) 392–403.

[141] P. Darcque, "Les tholoi et l'organisation sociopolitique du monde mycénien," in R. Laffineur ed., *Thanatos. Les coutûmes funéraires en Égée à l'Âge du Bronze* (*Aegaeum* 1, Liège 1987) 185–205; W.G. Cavanagh and C.B. Mee, "Mycenaean Tombs as Evidence for Social and Political Organisation," *OJA* 3:3 (1984) 45–64; Cavanagh and Mee, "The Location of Mycenaean Chamber Tombs in the Argolid," in Hägg and Nordquist 55–64; J.C. Wright, "Death and Power at Mycenae: Changing Symbols in Mortuary Practice," in Laffineur 1987 (supra) 171–84; and Cavanagh and Mee (supra n. 56).

[142] Dickinson (supra n. 6) 228; cf. O.T.P.K. Dickinson, "Cist Graves and Chamber Tombs," *BSA* 78 (1983) 55–67.

[143] Cavanagh and Mee 1984 (supra n. 141) 51; Darcque (supra n. 141) 200–205; Pelon (supra n. 140) 392–423.

[144] S. Voutsaki, "Social and Political Processes in the Mycenaean Argolid," in *Politeia* 62; G. Kopcke, "The Argolid in 1400—What Happened?" in *Politeia* 89; Bennet (supra n. 90) 596–98; Wright (supra n. 118) 73.

[145] An analogous shift in priorities may have taken place in Neopalatial Crete: the rich tombs of LM II–IIIA1 mark a distinct change from the heyday of the Minoan palaces in LM IA–IB, when funerary architecture is very poorly documented.

have been a status symbol — tangible proof of a new kind of power and of the leaders' ties to Pylos.[146]

Trade in Prestige Goods

Trade in prestige goods implies a market among a society's elite for goods indicative of status as well as wealth. It further means that the society is organized enough to control mechanisms for acquiring such goods, and producing objects to offer in exchange. The imported riches in the Shaft Graves at Mycenae are the first signs of such items reaching Mycenaean Greece, but it is likely that at this stage Minoans, not Mycenaeans, were responsible for Aegean access to them. Throughout the Early Mycenaean period very few Aegean objects found abroad are demonstrably mainland products. Crete had the dominant Aegean role in foreign trade, and for mainland Greece itself the Minoan connection was clearly the most significant. Relevant here is the model of secondary state formation, in which a less highly organized society is stimulated to further development by contact with a more advanced state. In particular, a chief's special access to external prestige goods demonstrates and thereby reinforces his superiority to, and authority over, those whom he rules. Wright shows that this model applies well to the contact between mainland Greece and Crete, which is demonstrated by the contents of the Shaft Graves.[147] A special link has been posited between

Mycenae and the Cretan palace sites, particularly Knossos, but funerary wealth and Cretan contact go hand in hand in Messenia at the same time.[148] In any case, Minoan artistic influence is clear, and for much of the Early Mycenaean period it is difficult to distinguish Minoan from Mycenaean work. Nevertheless, for assessing the impact of this relationship on emerging Mycenaean states, this long-standing difficulty is not crucial: the fact of close contact is the point.[149] In LH IIB/LM II, however, recognizable Mycenaean artifacts and styles are seen in Crete, mainland burial practices are adopted in the Cretan "Warrior Graves," especially in the Knossos area, and Mycenaean administrators are keeping records in Greek at the Palace of Minos itself.[150]

There is a marked difference between this continuum of growth in external contacts, chiefly with Crete, and what we know of Aegean trade in LH IIIA2–LH IIIB. Bronze Age exchange systems have recently received much attention. They took a variety of forms, and only aspects directly relevant to Mycenaean Greek states are summarized here.[151] The Mycenaean presence abroad becomes far more extensive than before, by the measures of pottery traded and actual outposts, and signs of Minoan presence simultaneously diminish. Imports from the East show the same shift in the balance of Aegean power: they are much more common in Crete than mainland Greece until LH IIIA2, at which time the situation

---

[146] This discussion does not include burial rituals, which are much the same in different kinds of tombs: Dickinson (supra n. 6) 228. Discussions of such rituals usually focus on the Early Mycenaean period when the funerary material is most abundant: several papers in Hägg and Nordquist; M.J. Boyd, "Mortuary Archaeology: Performance, Architecture, Time, Memory," *Archaeo* 2 (1994) 83–94.

[147] Wright (supra n. 118).

[148] Crete and Mycenae: Wright (supra n. 118) 70; Dickinson (supra n. 140) 54–55; Dickinson (supra n. 126) 136. Crete and Messenia: G. Korres, "The Relations between Crete and Messenia in the Late Middle Helladic and Early Late Helladic Period," in R. Hägg and N. Marinatos eds., *The Minoan Thalassocracy: Myth and Reality* (Stockholm 1984) 141–52; Hägg, "On the Nature of the Minoan Influence in Early Mycenaean Messenia," *OpAth* 14 (1982) 27–37.

[149] Rutter 791 with n. 194. On artistic contact, see E. Davis, "The Vapheio Cups: One Minoan and One Mycenaean?" *ArtB* 56 (1974) 472–87; J. Hurwit, "The Dendra Octopus Cup and the Problem of Style in the Fifteenth Century Aegean," *AJA* 83 (1979) 413–26; and several papers in Hägg and Marinatos (supra n. 148).

[150] "Warrior Graves": H. Matthäus, "Minoische Kriegergräber," in O. Krzyszkowska and L. Nixon eds., *Minoan Society* (Bristol 1983) 203–15; I. Kilian-Dirlmeier, "Noch einmal zu den 'Kriegergräber' von Knossos," *JRGZM* 32 (1985) 196–214; Kilian-Dirlmeier, "Jewellery in Mycenaean and Minoan 'Warrior Graves,'" in French and Wardle 161–71;

and D. Doxey, "Causes and Effects of the Fall of Knossos in 1375 B.C.," *OJA* 6 (1987) 301–24. Greek administration at Knossos: Driessen (supra n. 138).

[151] In general and for further references, see N.H. Gale ed., *Bronze Age Trade in the Mediterranean* (SIMA 90, Jonsered 1991); A.B. Knapp and J.F. Cherry, *Provenance Studies and Bronze Age Cyprus: Production, Exchange, and Politico-Economic Change* (Madison 1994); R. Laffineur and L. Basch eds., *Thalassa: L'Égée préhistorique et la mer* (Aegaeum 7, Liège 1990). On Mycenaean pottery abroad, see Leonard (supra n. 107). A handy summary of Mycenaean foreign contact, with further references, may be found in Dickinson (supra n. 6) 250–56. An intriguing addition to the evidence for Egyptian contact is a papyrus from Amarna depicting warriors, some of whom wear Mycenaean-looking clothing and boar's tooth helmets: L. Schofield and R. Parkinson, "Of Helmets and Heretics: A Possible Egyptian Representation of Mycenaean Warriors on a Papyrus from El-Amarna," *BSA* 89 (1994) 157–70. Two different views of Mycenaean relations with Europe are presented by J. Bouzek, *The Aegean, Anatolia and Europe: Cultural Interrelations in the Second Millennium B.C.* (Prague 1985), who believes the Mycenaeans relied on northern sources for such raw materials as amber, and by A.F. Harding, *The Mycenaeans and Europe* (London 1984), who argues that direct contact was minimal; see also B.P. Hallager, "Crete and Italy in the Late Bronze Age III Period," *AJA* 89 (1985) 293–305.

is reversed.[152] More important, the foreign goods found in Greece in LH IIIA–B include royal artifacts, suggesting the possibility of exchange between rulers. Nine of the 14 objects from the Aegean inscribed with the cartouche of Amenhotep III or his wife Queen Tiy were found at Mycenae.[153] Most are heirlooms in LH IIIB contexts, but this pharaoh's reign overlaps with LH IIIA1–2, and the presence of artifacts with the royal cartouche may suggest contact with Mycenae at the highest diplomatic level. Similarly, the cache of lapis lazuli cylinder seals discovered in a LH IIIB context in Thebes has been interpreted by one scholar as a gift from the king Tukulti-Ninurta I of Assyria.[154]

The Linear B tablets occasionally refer to textiles (Knossos) and perfumed oil (Pylos) as *ke-se-nu-wi-ja* /*xenwia*/. The root suggests a connection with the Classical Greek ξένος, "host, guest, stranger," and thus with the world of hospitality and formal gift exchange.[155] The term seems to characterize a type or quality of the product; the oil in question (Fr 1231) is actually designated for a goddess. Nor do the tablets contain any direct evidence for extra-kingdom trade, an omission that continues to surprise and to attract various explanations. They do, however, contain hints of foreign contacts.[156] Mainland states may not have controlled all of Mycenaean trade with Canaanites, Egyptians, and others, but they did organize the production of goods for export, not all of them visible in the archaeological record. They also retained the Semitic names of the spices, gold, and ivory they received, among other commodities, in return. A number of ethnics in the tablets also reflect associations with other lands. Sometimes these appear to be men's names: *mi-sa-ra-jo* /*Misraios*/ (Knossos), "Egyptian"; *ai-ku-pi-ti-jo* /*Aiguptios*/ (Knossos), "Memphite"; *ku-pi-ri-jo* /*Kuprios*/ (Knossos, Pylos; also adjectival), and possibly *a-ra-si-jo* /*Alašios*/ (Knossos, Mycenae), "Cypriot." Some of the dependent textile workers at Pylos (A-series) are groups of women designated by foreign ethnics: *a-si-wi-ja* / *a-*64-ja* /*Aswiai*/, "Asians," *ki-ni-di-ja* /*Knidiai*/, "Knidians," *mi-ra-ti-ja* /*Milātiai*/, "Milesians," and *ze-pu₂-ra₃* /*Zephyrai*/, "Halikarnassians" (cf. Strabo 14.2.16). These references raise the interesting possibility that Pylos was able to conscript groups of foreigners into full-time service.[157] Apart from these few textual points, however, the chief evidence for a Mycenaean role in Aegean trade remains the Mycenaean pottery found abroad, especially in Cyprus, Syria-Palestine, Egypt, and Italy.[158]

---

[152] E.H. Cline, *Sailing the Wine-Dark Sea: International Trade and the Late Bronze Age Aegean* (*BAR-IS* 591, Oxford 1994) 9–10. Cline generally contrasts LH IIIA with LH IIIB, but on pp. xvii, 10–11, and in personal communication he acknowledges his belief that the shift takes place in LH IIIA2.

[153] E.H. Cline, "Amenhotep III and the Aegean: A Reassessment of Egypto-Aegean Relations in the 14th Century B.C.," *Orientalia* 56 (1987) 1–36; Cline, "An Unpublished Amenhotep III Faience Plaque from Mycenae," *JAOS* 110 (1990) 200–12; Cline (supra n. 152) 39 (further references in catalogue); and Cline, "Contact and Trade or Colonization: Egypt and the Aegean in the 14th–13th Centuries B.C.," *Minos* 25–26 (1990–1991) 7–36. Also important in assessing the relations of this pharaoh with the Aegean is the list of place-names on a statue base from Kom el-Hetan: Cline (supra n. 152) 38–39 (further references in catalogue).

[154] E. Porada, "The Cylinder Seals Found at Thebes in Boeotia," *AfO* 28 (1981) 1–70, 77, esp. 68–70, 77. Others dispute this claim; discussion in Cline (supra n. 152) 25–26 (further references in catalogue). Our appreciation of the way in which Mycenaean Greece was regarded by other political leaders is greatly affected by whether it or any part of it was the entity known as Ahhijawa. On this issue, which falls outside the scope of the present review, see W.-D. Niemeier's forthcoming "Review of Aegean Prehistory VIII" in *AJA* on the Mycenaeans in Anatolia.

[155] The only two certain imports among pottery in the Pylos palace are small stirrup jars, from the perfumed oil storeroom room 32, which appear similar in fabric and quality of decoration to Argolid pottery: Blegen and Rawson (supra n. 125) 407–408 nos. 411–12, with the explicit suggestion that no. 411 is an Argolid import.

[156] Cline (supra n. 152) 128–31 offers a list of "Linear B references to Egypt and the Near East." This heading is misleading; it is actually a list of words in the tablets for which a specific foreign origin can be suggested. Not all the suggestions are equally attractive to a Linear B scholar, and not all imply direct or indirect contact with the place in question.

[157] On the status of the female textile workers, see J. Chadwick, "The Women of Pylos," in *Studies Bennett* 43–95; also among those listed are women from Lemnos (*ra-mi-ni-ja*), and possibly Khios (*ki-si-wi-ja*). The masculine forms of "Asian" and "Halikarnassian" also appear: *ze-pu₂-ro* is the name of a Pylian tailor who holds land on Ea 56, while the name *a-si-wi-jo/a-*64-jo*, "Aswios," recurs more than once each at Pylos, Knossos, and Mycenae.

[158] Also of critical importance to an understanding of Aegean trade are the excavated shipwrecks. That off Point Iria in the Argolid dates to the end of the LH IIIB period, with Cypriot (LC II/IIIA), Minoan (LM IIIB), and Mycenaean (LH IIIB2) pottery: C. Pennas, Y. Vichos, and Y. Lolos, "Point Iria Wreck 1992," *Enalia* Annual 1992:4 (1996) 4–5; Pennas, Vichos, and Lolos, "Point Iria Wreck 1993," *Enalia* Annual 1992: 4 (1996) 6–31. On the earlier Uluburun wreck in southern Turkey, see G. Bass, "Evidence of Trade from Bronze Age Shipwrecks," in Gale (supra n. 151) 69–82, and Pulak (supra n. 12), with further bibliography. It appears to have sunk while traveling westward, yet it contains some Mycenaean pottery and swords in addition to large quantities of Cypriot pottery and metal ingots, and Syro-Palestinian amphoras. The combination suggests a generally circular trade route in the eastern Mediterranean, showing equal favor to a number of clients.

Religion and Other State Institutions

Relations between Crete and mainland Greece in LH I–II have already been mentioned in the sections above on trade and the development of writing. Several scholars have suggested that the Mycenaeans were equally receptive to Minoan ideas and beliefs. Many institutions of the later states—written administration, religious rituals, perhaps even the Mycenaean form of kingship itself—may reflect the influence of Minoan concepts and practices. However, there is no reason to think in terms of wholesale adoption. The process of reasoned selection and adaptation already observed applies equally well to the world of ideas, and the transformation of Middle Helladic chiefdoms into Late Mycenaean polities resulted in a new and distinctive culture. Religion has been the most productive area of scrutiny, because Minoan influence there takes a tangible form in iconography (see below).[159] Social institutions are harder to discern, but Wright has proposed that a wine-drinking ritual was adapted from Crete by the Mycenaeans.[160] The ceremony is most clearly depicted in the LM IIIA Campstool Fresco from Knossos, where one man holds a Mycenaean goblet and another a stem restored as a Minoan chalice.[161] These are two of the three gold vessel shapes offered to deities on the later Pylos tablet Tn 316, and the fresco itself is similar to the banquet scene depicted in the Pylos megaron. It should be noted, though, that all of the evidence for this ritual belongs to the Mycenaean period,[162] so its Minoan origin is still speculation. The chalice itself is a Minoan shape in stone, and its presence in the Shaft Graves demonstrates the Mycenaeans' early interest in it, but there is no evidence from the Cretan Neopalatial period concerning the way in which it was used.[163]

Recent discussions of Minoan influence on mainland religion are also relevant to the institution of kingship, since the Mycenaean king played an important role in religious affairs (see below). Palaima has offered the idea that the later Greek skēptron, or staff of office, goes back to Mycenaean times, and is derived from Crete along with the ideology of the wanax, or king.[164] So little evidence exists about Minoan rulers that this idea is difficult to evaluate, especially since what we know of later mainland kings presumably represents a substantial transformation into Mycenaean form.[165] It does seem likely, as Wright observes, that Minoan influence on evolving Mycenaean institutions and ideology set the Mycenaean elites apart from the rest of their society.[166] The process of development, however, served equally to distinguish them from their Cretan neighbors.

NEW INSCRIPTIONS

Recent work at palatial centers has brought to light a number of inscriptions. Those from Tiryns, Thebes (except those from Pelopidou Street), and Mycenae are now conveniently brought together in a single publication, and so do not need a full description here.[167] The 24 examples from Tiryns are extremely fragmentary, but the topics are familiar: lists of men, wheels and armor, animals, and land. A number of these come from a LH IIIB2 context in a building with religious significance in the Lower Citadel, but their contents are routinely administrative. Ef 2 and Ef 3, from the southeastern part of the Upper Citadel, are land-tenure tablets: one refers to ke-ke-me[-na land, a class of landholding also known at Pylos, and the other gives an amount of land in terms of the amount of seed-grain that would be needed to sow it, a convention also known at Py-

[159] Rutter 793; C. Renfrew et al., *The Archaeology of Cult: The Sanctuary at Phylakopi* (BSA Suppl. 18, Oxford 1985) 393–94; R. Hägg, "Mycenaean Religion: The Helladic and the Minoan Components," in A. Morpurgo Davies and Y. Duhoux eds., *Linear B: A 1984 Survey* (Bibliothèque des Cahiers de l'Institut de Linguistique de Louvain 26, Louvain 1985) 203–25; J.C. Wright, "The Archaeological Correlates of Religion: Case Studies in the Aegean," in *Politeia* 341–48; Wright (supra n. 118), esp. 70–72, 74; Palaima, in Rehak (supra n. 119), esp. 127; Palaima, forthcoming (supra n. 119).

[160] J.C. Wright, "Empty Cups and Empty Jugs: The Social Role of Wine in Minoan and Mycenaean Societies," in P.E. McGovern, S.J. Fleming, and S.H. Katz eds., *The Origins and Ancient History of Wine* (Philadelphia 1995) 287–309.

[161] M.A.S. Cameron, "An Addition to La Parisienne," *CretChron* 1964, 38–53, esp. 51–52; Cameron, "The 'Palatial' Thematic System in the Knossos Murals: Last Notes on Knossos Frescoes," in Hägg and Marinatos (supra n. 133)

324–25, fig. 2.

[162] Or later, from the sanctuary at Kato Syme: Wright (supra n. 160) 289, with references.

[163] S. Hiller, "Levanto-Mykenische Kelche—Zur Herkunft der Gefässform," *RDAC* 1978, 91–102.

[164] Palaima, in Rehak (supra n. 119); Palaima, forthcoming (supra n. 119). On the staff of office Palaima is supported by Wright (supra n. 159) 345; a cautionary note is sounded in C.W. Shelmerdine, review of Rehak, *Minos* (forthcoming).

[165] Kilian (supra n. 118); on Minoan rulers see Rehak passim.

[166] Wright (supra n. 118) 72.

[167] J.L. Melena and J.-P. Olivier, *TITHEMY: The Tablets and Nodules in Linear B from Tiryns, Thebes and Mycenae* (*Minos* Suppl. 12, Salamanca 1991). A sequel, *TITHEMY + MIKHA*, is in progress; it will include tablets and nodules from Midea and Khania.

Fig. 8. Thebes. Excavation on Pelopidou Street. (Photo E. Godwin)

los. This discovery suggests that administrative systems operated in generally similar ways from kingdom to kingdom, though differences in details can be observed as well.[168]

Published in the same volume is an important cache of 56 sealings at Thebes that comes from a small room in a house on Oidipodos Street.[169] The sealings belong to the earlier of two destruction levels, with a reported ceramic date near the end of LH IIIB1. The subject of the inscriptions is a variety of animals and other foodstuffs sent to the palace from outlying areas, probably for a state banquet. Still more recently, excavations from 1993 to 1996 under Pelopidou Street have unearthed some 250 tablets, dramatically increasing the number of texts from Thebes.[170] The new location, approximately 200 m² in area, is very near the "Arsenal" site where the Ug tablets had previously been found (fig. 8). The tablets are not in situ, but they are associated with a pavement, in a destruction level reported to date to the second half of the 13th century B.C. The texts deal chiefly with rations, especially wine, figs, and grain. These are given to both men and women,

but divine offerings are also attested. The tablets are still undergoing restoration and study, but preliminary reports show that they have the capacity to advance our knowledge in several ways, from further attestation and better transliteration of rare syllabograms, to some possible new theonyms and occupational terms. Especially interesting for geographical relations is the term *ra-ke-da-mo-ni-jo-u-jo* /Lakedaimonios huios/, "son of Lakedaimon," along with three attestations of the ethnic *ra-ke-da-mi-ni-jo*. A Lakedaimonian connection, even if confined to the presence at Thebes of individuals from that area, raises the issue of interstate relations in an interesting way. Two more tablets were found in 1994 during further exploration of the Arsenal area. The longer document, TH 149, lists quantities of grain and olives against various names. At least two of these are place-names in the dative-locative: Thebes itself, and *e-re-o-ni*, thought to represent Eleon, a Boeotian place-name attested in Homer and later authors.

Three inscribed sealings now confirm the status of Midea as an administrative center of some kind, though no tablets have yet been found there. One

[168] A brief account of some representative differences, with further bibliography, is provided by Shelmerdine (supra n. 119).

[169] V. Aravantinos, "The Mycenaean Inscribed Sealings from Thebes: Problems of Content and Function," in T.G. Palaima ed., *Aegean Seals, Sealings and Administration* (*Aegaeum* 5, Liège 1990) 149–74; Piteros et al. (supra n. 139) 103–84.

[170] Aravantinos (supra n. 49) 619, 621; V. Aravantinos,

L. Godart, and A. Sacconi, "Sui nuovi testi del palazzo di Cadmo a Tebe: Noti preliminari," *RendLinc* ser. 9, 6.4 (1995) 809–45; Godart and Sacconi, "La triade tebana nei documenti in Lineare B del Palazzo di Cadmo," *RendLinc* ser. 9, 7.2 (1996) 283–85; and Aravantinos, "New Linear B Tablets from Thebes: Texts and Contexts," in Hiller et al. (supra n. 119). I thank Vassilis Aravantinos for letting me examine the new tablets in 1994 and 1996.

nodule (Wv 3), with the ideogram GRA(num), comes from room VI in the West Gate area; the other two finds are from a room north of the megaron complex in area N of the lower terraces.[171] Face .α of the nodule Wv 1 bears the ideogram CYP(erus), and facet .β the syllabograms *ro* and *zo*, while the newly discovered sealing Wv 5 is reportedly inscribed .α OLE(um) and .β *pa-zo-we*. All three inscriptions date to LH IIIB2.

At Pylos, three tablet fragments have been found in the course of clearing backfill and reexcavating Blegen's dump near the south corner of the site. An inscribed nodule (Wr 1480) was also recovered from the site by a guard.[172] The nodule refers to javelin handles. Only personal names are preserved on Xn 1481 (fig. 9), while Un 1482 lists beds and baskets, both items familiar from other Pylos texts. The third fragment, which includes ideograms for honey and unguent, probably goes with previously known Un fragments to comprise a tablet listing banquet supplies. Such documents are understood to have special political and religious importance, so it is especially interesting that the word *wanax* appears here in the dative (for further discussion, see below).

The painted signs and sign groups occasionally found on pottery—usually coarse stirrup jars—belong in a different category from these administrative documents. Ceramic fragments with painted signs are known from Tiryns, Mycenae, Eleusis, Thebes, Gla, and now Midea.[173] This new find, MI Z 4, is one of many storage stirrup jars from the LH IIIB2 floor level of room VI in the West Gate area. It is inscribed with the name *wi-na-jo*, which also appears on a locally made stirrup jar from Knossos

Fig. 9. Pylos. Tablet Xn 1481. (Photo T. McKern, courtesy Pylos Regional Archaeological Project)

(KN Z 1716), and on the inscribed stirrup jar from Armenoi.[174] All three inscriptions appear to be in the same hand.

---

[171] West Gate area: K. Demakopoulou and N. Divari-Valakou, "New Finds with Linear B Inscriptions from Midea (MI Z 2, Wv 3, Z 4)," *Minos* 29–30 (1994–1995 [forthcoming]). Lower Terraces: Demakopoulou et al. (supra n. 33) 39, figs. 58–60; G. Walberg, "A Linear B Inscription from Midea," *Kadmos* 31 (1992) 93. GRA is traditionally understood to represent "wheat," though R. Palmer, "Wheat and Barley in Mycenaean Society," in *Mykenaïka* 475–97 prefers "barley."

[172] Wr 1480 and Xn 1481 are published by C.W. Shelmerdine and D.J.L. Bennet, "Two New Linear B Documents from Bronze Age Pylos," *Kadmos* 34 (1995) 123–36. Study of the other tablets is in progress by John Bennet, Emmett Bennett, and Cynthia Shelmerdine. The proposed join of one new fragment is José Melena's suggestion; the pieces have not yet been brought together to confirm the joins. In addition to these new discoveries, the definitive study of scribal hands at Pylos has appeared, Palaima 1988 (supra n. 139).

[173] A. Sacconi, *Corpus delle iscrizioni vascolari in Lineare B* (Incunabula graeca 57, Rome 1974). For subsequent finds,

see H. Döhl, "Bronzezeitliche Graffiti und Dipinti aus Tiryns," *Kadmos* 18 (1979) 67–69; J.-P. Olivier, "Tirynthian Graffiti," *AA* 1988, 262; S. Iakovides, "Ενεπιγραφός ψευδόστομος από τον Γλά," in *Αριαδνή. Αφιέρωμα στον Στυλιανό Αλεξίου* (Athens 1989) 39–43; and Demakopoulou and Divari-Valakou (supra n. 171). In the last mentioned article, the authors also publish a join showing that the stirrup jar previously published as MI Z 2 (K. Demakopoulou and N. Divari-Valakou, "A Linear B Inscribed Stirrup Jar from Midea (MI Z 2)," *Minos* 27–28 [1992–1993] 303–305) is not inscribed after all. Three new fragments from Thebes are mentioned by Piteros et al. (supra n. 139) 107, n. 18. A summary of all painted inscriptions then known is provided by Farnoux and Driessen (supra n. 106) 87–88.

[174] Hallager (supra n. 104) 187; photographs in K. Demakopoulou ed., *The Mycenaean World: Five Centuries of Early Greek Culture 1600–1100 B.C.* (Athens 1988) 208–209, nos. 186, 187. The Knossos jar is published by M. Popham, "An LM III B Inscription from Knossos," *Kadmos* 8 (1969) 43–45, and by Sacconi (supra n. 173) 59–60, 178. Its Knossian provenience is certified by Catling et al. (supra n. 104) 83.

ECONOMIC AND POLITICAL ADMINISTRATION

Much can be inferred about economic and political matters from the Linear B tablets, but it is necessary to remember that these are concerned exclusively with palatial affairs. The tablets existed as an aide-mémoire for the central administration, and they say nothing explicit about any activities not under its control. A further limiting factor is that the tablets we possess refer to a single year—the last before the destruction that baked and preserved them. Scholars must generalize from these tablets to develop any picture of Mycenaean economy in LH IIIB, without clear knowledge of how representative they are of the 13th century B.C. as a whole.

Political Organization

The Linear B tablets contain a number of titles with clear political significance. The relative hierarchical position of a few officials has been known since before the publication of the second edition of Ventris and Chadwick's *Documents in Mycenaean Greek*, but the status of others remains uncertain. As usual, most of our information from the mainland comes from the Pylos archive, but we have nothing to suggest that other kingdoms were organized differently. The paramount figure is the *wanax*, and second in importance is the *ra-wa-ke-ta* /lāwāgetās/, "leader of the people." Among the figures at a lower level are the *qa-si-re-u* /gʷasileus/ (see below), the *e-qe-ta* /hekʷetās/, "companion" (presumably of the king), the *te-re-ta* /telestās/, "officials," and the *ko-re-te* /koretēr/ and *po-ro-ko-re-te* /prokoretēr/, "mayor" and "vice-mayor" of the 16 major economic districts of the kingdom. Beyond this much remains uncertain. In particular, despite much fruitful debate over the last 20 years, there is not a single official about whose functions all are in complete agreement. Discussion has focused principally on the first three figures listed above.

The *wanax* presents less difficulty than the others, yet the extent even of his responsibilities is not fully understood: we cannot with certainty demonstrate for him a judicial or a military role, or that of an international statesman.[175] He seems, however, to have had a presiding role in religious affairs (infra), and the designation of certain craftsmen as "royal" suggests either that they served his personal or professional requirements, or that he had particularly direct authority over one branch of the palatial workforce.[176] In addition, he makes an official appointment on Pylos tablet Ta 711, and few would deny that he has secular as well as religious authority.[177]

Debate on the status and responsibilities of other officials is still less conclusive, even when the title is transparently Greek, like *qa-si-re-u* /gʷasileus/ (cf. Classical Greek βασιλεύς) or *ra-wa-ke-ta* /lāwāgetās/ (cf. Classical Greek λαγέτας, from λαός + ἄγω). On the Pylos Jn tablets three *gʷasileis* act as overseers of working groups of bronzesmiths. Most of the groups in this series do not have an overseer, and it is not clear why only three are thus provided.[178] More frequently attested is the derivative *qa-si-re-wi-ja* /gʷasileia/. Three such groups, designated by the name of the man responsible for them, receive rations on Pylos tablet Fn 50 (cf. also Fn 867.3). For Carlier, the presence of religious personnel on both tablets is significant, suggesting that *gʷasileis* played a role in religious affairs.[179] Nonreligious recipients are listed as well, however, so the inference seems unwarranted. As for the *lawagetas*, it has been traditional to view him as second in power to the king, and a military leader. The first point has not been challenged, but some scholars have recently pointed out, rightly I believe, that there is no necessary connection of this official to military matters.[180]

The larger political questions of importance are what kind of polity the Mycenaean state was, and how directly it was controlled by the king and his palace officials. In this context "political" control is hardly separable from economic control, and one must turn to the realm of economic administration for the partial answers reached to date. In general,

[175] For an even more pessimistic view of our ability to interpret this and other titles, see J.T. Hooker, "Titles and Functions in the Pylian State," in *Studies Chadwick* 257–67. On the *wanax*, see P. Carlier, *La royauté en Grèce avant Alexandre* (Strasbourg 1984) pt. 1, esp. 44–101; several papers in Palaima, forthcoming (supra n. 119) and in Rehak.

[176] Carlier (supra n. 175) 63–72 prefers the first alternative.

[177] As Hooker (supra n. 175) 258–59 and others have noted, it is not possible to prove that the term *wanax* always refers to a single individual, or even that it always refers to a human rather than a divine lord. Each student of the tablets must develop a personal view; my own is that *wanax*

always does signify the king. Another question is whether or not the man *e-ke-ra₂-wo* /Enkheliāwōn/ is the *wanax* of Pylos at the time of the tablets. For a recent argument in support of this view, see Palaima, in Rehak (supra n. 119) 129–35, passim.

[178] P. Carlier, "*Qa-si-re-u* et *qa-si-re-wi-ja*," in *Politeia* 355–64; Carlier (supra n. 175) 108–16.

[179] Carlier (supra n. 178) 359, 360–61, 364; Carlier does bring other evidence to bear also, but none of it seems conclusive.

[180] Carlier (supra n. 175) 106–107; Hooker (supra n. 175) 262.

there is a growing trend toward acknowledging that the authority of state officials is not absolute, and that considerable activity went on, at least in the Pylos kingdom where records are most plentiful, independent of palatial control.[181]

Economic Administration

The economic themes reflected in the tablets are, generally speaking, limited to agricultural production, taxation, industries (the manufacture and distribution of goods, chiefly goods of high economic status), and personnel. To a greater or lesser degree, all these topics are better understood today than they were 20 years ago, and together they form a fairly coherent picture of Mycenaean administration. There is widespread agreement that the Mycenaean palatial sites were redistributive centers, taking in a variety of commodities from their dependencies, storing them centrally, and allocating them (or products made from them) again within the kingdom. The tablets document each stage: the collection of goods, the allocation of resources to dependent workers, and the distribution of a variety of commodities. Redistributive economies may be primarily altruistic, pooling needed or desirable goods and services to ensure widespread access to them, or the motive may be rather to mobilize such resources upward to the elite. In the case of the Mycenaeans both impulses may have been at work, though the Linear B evidence is slanted toward concerns of the central elite, so that we observe only the economic activity that it dominates.[182] The complex, even inconsistent, details hinted at in the texts are a further deterrent to understanding. A redistributive economy is normally viewed as an alternative to a market economy, in which the relative values of different commodities make market exchange possible. Yet the Mycenaean equivalent of Classical Greek πρίασθαι, "buy," is used at Knossos with reference to human

beings.[183] There are also a few cases where the value of one commodity is expressed in terms of others in what appear to be payment records: cloth is valued in terms of wheat and figs (Pylos Un 1322), and alum in terms of several commodities (Pylos An 35, Un 443.1).[184] Thus, it does not appear that staples and prestige goods were handled in completely separate exchange systems, as happens in some cultures.[185] Nevertheless, the overall picture is clear: the palace was the focal point of a redistributive system, mobilizing both goods and services. It exercised minimal control over the production of staple goods, though it acquired these selectively for such uses as ration payments to workers and suppliers. By contrast, it did directly oversee the production of particular agricultural resources, such as flax for the linen industry, and over the industrial processes themselves.

Animal husbandry and agricultural production. Records of livestock indicate that the palace controlled large flocks and herds. The prominence of records pertaining to sheep at Knossos is due to the importance of the wool industry there, and listings of thousands of animals (more than 19,200 on Dn 1088 alone) are without parallel on the mainland. The Pylos archive also records extensive holdings of sheep and goats, and refers as well to other important animals like oxen.[186] Much of the direct written evidence for agricultural production concerns grapevines, figs, olives, and grain, particularly one variety of wheat.[187] A recent study by Palmer has clarified both the place of wine in the economy, and documents relating to the assessment of vines and the collection and distribution of the finished product.[188] The bulk of our information comes from Pylos, but the meager evidence from Knossos and Mycenae is consistent with it. Palmer shows that wine was a high-status item, stored perhaps at outlying centers as well as in the Wine Magazine (rooms 104–

---

[181] For good discussions of the issue, with further references, see J. Chadwick, "L'économie palatiale dans la Grèce mycénienne," in Lévy (supra n. 124) 283–90; S. Deger-Jalkotzy, "'Near Eastern Economies' versus 'Feudal Society': Zum mykenischen Palaststaat," in *Studies Chadwick* 137–50; P. Halstead, "Agriculture in the Bronze Age Aegean: Towards a Model of Palatial Economy," in B. Wells ed., *Agriculture in Ancient Greece* (Stockholm 1992) 105–17; Halstead, "The Mycenaean Palatial Economy: Making the Most of the Gaps in the Evidence," *PCPS* 38 (1992) 57–86; and Killen.

[182] Cf. Halstead, in Wells (supra n. 181) 57.

[183] J.-P. Olivier, "Des extraits de contrats de vente d'esclaves dans les tablettes de Knossos," in *Studies Chadwick* 479–98; Killen 284–85, n. 39.

[184] See now J.T. Killen, "Some Further Thoughts on Col-

lectors," in *Politeia* 217–19.

[185] Halstead, in *PCPS* (supra n. 181) 57–58.

[186] T.G. Palaima, "Perspectives on the Pylos Oxen Tablets: Textual (and Archaeological) Evidence for the Use and Management of Oxen in Late Bronze Age Messenia (and Crete)," in Palaima, C.W. Shelmerdine, and P.H. Ilievski eds., *Studia Mycenaea (1988)* (*ŽivaAnt* Monograph 7, Skopje 1989) 85–124.

[187] Halstead, in Wells (supra n. 181); Halstead, in *PCPS* (supra n. 181) 60–61, 64. As Halstead notes, the archaeological record is more diverse, suggesting that other staples reached the center from the nonpalatial sector of the economy.

[188] R. Palmer, *Wine in the Mycenaean Palace Economy* (*Aegaeum* 10, Liège 1994).

105) at Pylos itself. Even if only some of the storage jars in room 105 contained wine, the sealings found in the building (four of 50 inscribed with the wine ideogram) mark deliveries by those who owned the seals. Wine also figures along with other high-status commodities like meat and honey in lists of elite banqueting supplies and offerings to the gods. Among documents related to agriculture, landholding records are particularly numerous at Pylos (E- series), and they indicate a close reciprocal relationship between land tenure and obligations on the part of the holders to provide agricultural produce or services. So much is clear, but debate continues on the precise nature of the various kinds of plots themselves, and of the obligations associated with them.[189]

Taxation. The tablets record the flow of selected staple goods into the palace through taxes on the production of various commodities. The bulk of our information comes from Pylos, where the Ma series records assessments, collections and deficits of hides, honey, locally made cloth, and other goods not securely identified. A consensus has emerged that these collections were organized from the top down: that is, an overall assessment was levied on each of the two provinces into which the kingdom was divided, and the tax burden then distributed among regional subsections of these provinces.[190] Halstead stresses the decentralized nature of this system, and the disinterest of the administration in the production of the commodities taxed.[191] He includes in this characterization the assessment records of flax (N- series), but here the level of detail is much greater than in the regular tax records of the Ma series. The forecasts of flax contributions in the Na records refer to individual towns, not whole districts, and Nn 831 goes into detail about the obligations of specific in-

dividuals in one such town.[192] This greater degree of interest is at variance with the Ma series, and it is appropriate for an industry under direct palatial control.

Industries. Several recent studies have clarified the industrial activities supervised by the central administration. These chiefly involved bronze-working and the production of prestige goods like perfumed oil and fine textiles. The control of most industries appears highly centralized, and most operate in a redistributive fashion referred to as the *ta-ra-si-ja /talasia/*, or "allotment" system (cf. Classical Greek ταλασία, "an amount [of wool] weighed out and allocated for processing"). Under this system the palace brought in the necessary raw materials for an industry and allocated them to craftsmen. The term *ta-ra-si-ja* appears at Pylos in the Jn series, which lists bronzesmiths with and without an allotment of bronze, and at other sites in records of textiles (Knossos, Mycenae) and chariot wheels (Knossos).[193] The only extant bronze collection record (Jn 829) seems to be a tax document, recording contributions of bronze from almost the same districts named in the Ma series. Archaeological evidence that the palace redistributed lump bronze to smiths around the kingdom comes from Nichoria. If the identification with *ti-mi-to-a-ke-e* is correct, Nichoria is one of the places with palatial smiths in residence. A LH IIIB2 smithy there, contemporary with the Pylos tablets, shows evidence of remelting and reworking of bronze, rather than the smelting of copper and its alloying with tin.[194]

In the oil industry raw materials are similarly distributed to perfumers on several tablets from the Archives Complex at Pylos.[195] These tablets shed some light on the manufacturing process, which resembles that described in later Greek recipes. The

---

[189] Killen 243–50; S. Deger-Jalkotzy, "Zum Charakter und zur Herausbildung der mykenischen Sozialstruktur," in A. Heubeck and G. Neumann eds., *Res Mycenaeae: Akten des VII. internationalen mykenologischen Colloquiums* (Göttingen 1983) 89–111. Recent discussions of some landholding tablets, with further bibliography, are Deger-Jalkotzy, "Noch Einmal zur Ea-Serie von Pylos," in *Studies Bennett* 97–122; and M. Carpenter, "*ki-ti-me-na* and *ke-ke-me-na*," *Minos* 18 (1983) 81–88.

[190] P. de Fidio, "Fiscalità, redistribuzione, equivalenze: Per una discussione sull'economia micenea," *SMEA* 23 (1982) 83–136 suggested a kingdom-wide assessment of 200 units of each commodity. In a response, C.W. Shelmerdine, "Mycenaean Taxation," in Palaima et al. (supra n. 186) 125–48 proposed a modification to 100 units, but de Fidio's figure now seems preferable: J.T. Killen, "Administering a Mycenaean Kingdom: Some Taxing Problems," *BICS* (forthcoming). I thank John Killen for discussing this paper with me and providing a copy of the abstract.

[191] Halstead, in *PCPS* (supra n. 181) 59.

[192] Killen 247–49; Shelmerdine (supra n. 190) 139–41.

[193] On the Jn series, see now J. Smith, "The Pylos Jn Series," *Minos* 27–28 (1992–1993) 167–260.

[194] G.R. Rapp, Jr., et al., "Analysis of the Metal Artifacts," in G.R. Rapp, Jr., and S.E. Aschenbrenner eds., *Excavations at Nichoria in Southwest Greece* I: *Site, Environs, and Techniques* (Minneapolis 1978) 178–80.

[195] The account that follows is based on C.W. Shelmerdine, *The Perfume Industry of Mycenaean Pylos* (*SIMA-PB* 34, Göteborg 1985); see also I. Érard-Cerceau, "Végétaux, parfums et parfumeurs à l'époque mycénienne," *SMEA* 28 (1990) 252–85. Collection records are not attested at Pylos, but they are known from Knossos and Mycenae: E. Foster, "An Administrative Department at Knossos Concerned with Perfumery and Offerings," *Minos* 16 (1977) 19–51; and J.T. Killen, "On the Mycenae Ge Tablets," in Heubeck and Neumann (supra n. 189) 216–33.

Fr tablets, records of finished products, are found elsewhere in the palace, in specialized storage contexts. These tablets describe the oil both by variants of the oil ideogram and by adjectives like *pa-ko-we* /sphakowen/, "sage-scented"; *wo-do-we* /wordowen/, "rose-scented"; and *e-ti-we* /ertiwen/, "henna-dyed." The majority were found in room 23, one of two oil storerooms behind the megaron. Large storage jars set into benches along the walls contained oil, as is clear from residue found in and around them and from the intensity of the fire in this area at the time of the destruction.[196] Twelve twists of clay also preserved by the fire show that tablets were actually fashioned and written here.[197] Other perfume tablets come from room 32, a well-finished storeroom, and from a location upstairs, above room 38. The Fr tablets together constitute a scribal department concerned with the perfumed oil industry.[198] Many of the entries are allocations, most of a religious character, but there are also disbursements to "attendants" who may well be secular, while still other tablets are inventory records. Several scribes wrote the tablets concerned; each handled a specific variant of the oil ideogram, and for the most part each is represented in only one room. The notable exception is Hand 2, who has a greater range of responsibilities, and whose tablets appear in all three storerooms. He also wrote a transaction of oil within the department, Fr 1184, which was found in the Archives Complex. Thus, he seems to have been the head of this administrative department, in which other scribes had very specific assignments, so that each could be readily held accountable for the oil on which he reported.

The textile industry is equally central to the Mycenaean economy, and tablets referring to it were found at Thebes and Mycenae as well as Knossos and Pylos. The Cretan sheep and wool texts have received the most attention, particularly from John Killen, who has also made some comparative observations about the Pylian industry.[199] It is interesting that production is centralized here to a greater degree than at Knossos. Specialized personnel are located at a small number of places, chiefly Pylos itself, and there are small outlying groups of less-specialized workers, one of them at the probable capital of the Further Province, Leuktron. The textile records from Thebes and most of those from Mycenae concern wool that has been delivered to the center, and is being disbursed for further treatment.[200] At each site the relevant tablets were found in buildings that apparently served as clearinghouses for wool. Like the Wine Magazine at Pylos, these central collection and storage points complement the ample textual evidence for the redistributive system at work.

What happened to the goods produced by these industries? In Halstead's view, the tablets are much less informative about the disbursement of finished products than about the previous stages of the industries,[201] but actually, plenty of textual evidence exists for the use of these products within the kingdom. The Pylos Fr records of the disbursement of perfumed oil have already been mentioned, and Jn 829 earmarks collected bronze for the manufacture of spearpoints and arrowheads. These weapons are presumably for local use, like the chariots being manufactured and repaired in the Northeast Workshop.[202] On three texts associated with this workshop, the term *e-qe-si-jo-ja* is applied to wheels (as it is elsewhere to cloth). The adjective derives from the term *e-qe-ta* /hek^{w}etās/, "companion (of the king)," and may designate elite goods of a kind belonging to or suitable for such officials.

Halstead is correct, however, in that there is almost no textual evidence for the deployment of such prestige goods outside the kingdom.[203] Yet perfume

---

[196] Blegen and Rawson (supra n. 125) 135–36.

[197] Blegen and Rawson (supra n. 125) 137, fig. 267 nos. 1–7.

[198] The term was introduced by J.-P. Olivier, *Les scribes de Cnossos* (Incunabula graeca 17, Rome 1967) 8, 125, to characterize a group of tablets linked by findspot, scribal hand, and content to form an office; a department is a group of related offices.

[199] J.T. Killen, "The Textile Industries at Pylos and Knossos," in C.W. Shelmerdine and T.G. Palaima eds., *Pylos Comes Alive: Industry + Administration in a Mycenaean Palace* (New York 1984) 53–61.

[200] T. Spyropoulos and J. Chadwick, *The Thebes Tablets* II (*Minos* Suppl. 4, Salamanca 1975) published the Theban records; two recent studies that include the Mycenae material are Varias García (supra n. 24) and Tournavitou (supra n. 23). C.W. Shelmerdine, "Workshops and Record Keeping in the Mycenaean World," in Betancourt and Laffineur

(supra n. 58) considers the material from each site in relation to its archaeological context, which in each case is interpreted as a clearinghouse rather than a workshop. On the general topic of prehistoric textiles, E.J.W. Barber, *Prehistoric Textiles: The Development of Cloth in the Neolithic and Bronze Ages, with Special Reference to the Aegean* (Princeton 1991) is an invaluable resource for future studies.

[201] Halstead, in *PCPS* (supra n. 181) 62.

[202] The most recent study of the Northeast Workshop, with references to earlier works, is R. Schon, "Chariot Manufacture and the Organization of Industry at Pylos," in Betancourt and Laffineur (supra n. 58).

[203] The Mycenaeans' own written evidence is discussed briefly above. Foreign textual evidence, apart from the Kom el-Hetan statue base (supra n. 153), depends largely on the equation of Mycenaean Greece with Ahhijawa (supra n. 154). Killen 264 outlines the few possible tablet references to external transactions.

was clearly an important trade item: the stirrup jars that functioned as oil containers are tangible signs of this commodity, and they are heavily represented among Mycenaean pottery found abroad. It is assumed that textiles too were offered in trade, in return for the metals, spices, ivory, and other raw materials that the Mycenaeans were interested in importing.[204] Indeed, the reticence of the tablets is so much at variance with the archaeological evidence that it has tempted some to assume that records of foreign exchange were kept on leather or some other material that perished in the very fires that preserved the tablets.[205] It is worth noting that the largest extant archive—that from Pylos—dates to the very end of LH IIIB when trade was dramatically reduced from its heyday of LH IIIA2–B1. Even under this circumstance, however, the production of elite goods remained, on present archival evidence, a high priority.

Most of the people who worked in these industries were fully dependent on the palace for their upkeep.[206] In some cases the records of their support are extant: for instance, the Pylos Ab series records food rations allocated to textile workers and their children, and the Pylos Fn series lists rations given to other personnel. The tablets also provide a few hints, however, that some work may have been done by more independent workers, who received goods in return for their services.[207] Such indications support a growing awareness that, although our written evidence is limited to palace business, a wider economic sphere existed in the Mycenaean world that the palaces did not control.[208]

RELIGION

A fair amount of textual, iconographical, and artifactual evidence can be cited for Mycenaean reli-

gion, but it has always been difficult to interpret,[209] in part because the various sources point in different directions. Linear B texts link the Late Bronze Age to later Greek religion, recording a similar pantheon and range of offerings. Iconography, on the other hand, particularly in Early Mycenaean glyptic art, echoes the symbols of Minoan religion—without, however, indicating whether the beliefs behind them were also adopted on the mainland. Until recently, little attention was paid to the third source of evidence: archaeological remains of cult sites and artifacts. New finds and new interpretations have improved this situation in the 1980s and 1990s, so that more can now be said about where the Mycenaeans worshipped, and a little about the forms their rituals may have taken. These topics are addressed here; for information about the gods themselves, older bibliographical sources are still valid.[210]

Cult Places

Cult environments range from separate shrines at palatial and other urban sites to simple open-air settings, and it has been proposed that rituals also took place in the megaron itself. Some see in this diversity a distinction between official and popular, or urban and rural, religion; others interpret it as a continuum from the humblest expressions of piety up to elaborate celebrations at the center of state power. We begin with public or urban shrines at palatial and other sites, where it is easiest to identify the trappings of cult.[211] The two shrine complexes most often discussed are the cult center at Mycenae and the sanctuary at Phylakopi on Melos. Though the latter site lies outside mainland Greece, it is useful for purposes of analogy since the installation and its contents conform closely to those on the mainland.[212]

[204] Halstead, in *PCPS* (supra n. 181) 63 on exports.

[205] Shelmerdine (supra n. 195) 139–41. For other possible explanations, see Killen 265–70. Traces of leather or parchment have been noticed on the back of a single (uninscribed) sealing from the House of Kadmos at Thebes: Aravantinos (supra n. 169) 151, n. 10, pl. 24a. However, the claim by Aravantinos (supra n. 49) 619 that this sealing is certain evidence for perishable texts "of non-economic character or . . . correspondence" is wholly speculative.

[206] S. Hiller, "Dependent Personnel in Mycenaean Texts," in M. Heltzer and E. Lipinski eds., *Society and Economy in the Eastern Mediterranean (c. 1500–1000 B.C.)* (*Orientalia Lovaniensia Analecta* 23, Louvain 1988) 53–68; Killen 252–53, 272–73; Chadwick (supra n. 157) 43–95.

[207] Y. Duhoux, *Aspects du vocabulaire économique mycénien* (Amsterdam 1976), esp. 147–49; J.L. Melena, "Further Thoughts on Mycenaean *o-pa*," in Heubeck and Neumann (supra n. 189) 258–86; C.W. Shelmerdine, "Industrial Activity at Pylos," in P.H. Ilievski and L. Crepajac eds., *Tractata Mycenaea: Proceedings of the 8th International Colloquium on Mycenean Studies, Held in Ohrid, 15–20 September 1985*

(Skopje 1987) 333–42; Killen (supra n. 184) 219.

[208] Halstead, in *PCPS* (supra n. 181) 64.

[209] Renfrew et al. (supra n. 159) 11–26 provides a good methodological framework for the investigation of Bronze Age religion.

[210] *Documents*²; M. Gérard-Rousseau, *Les mentions religieuses dans les tablettes mycéniennes* (Incunabula graeca 29, Rome 1986); L. Baumbach, "The Mycenaean Contribution to the Study of Greek Religion," *SMEA* 20 (1979) 143–60; E. Vermeule, *Götterkult* (*ArchHom* 3V, Göttingen 1974); and J. Chadwick, "What Do We Know about Mycenaean Religion?" in Morpurgo Davies and Duhoux (supra n. 159) 191–202.

[211] G. Albers, *Spätmykenische Stadtheiligtümer: Systematische Analyse und vergleichende Auswertung der archäologischen Befunde* (*BAR-IS* 596, Oxford 1994) brings together the evidence for such shrines at Mycenae, Phylakopi, Tiryns (Lower Citadel), Asine, and Ayia Irini. I owe this reference to Robin Hägg.

[212] Renfrew et al. (supra n. 159) 407–11 offers concise comparisons to the installations at Mycenae, the Tiryns Lower Citadel, and Asine.

Fig. 10. Mycenae. Cult center. (Photo C.W. Shelmerdine)

Mycenae. Most of the complex at Mycenae was built and used only in LH IIIB.[213] Though the Tsountas House shrine may have been built in LH IIIA2, the Temple, the Room with the Fresco, and the Megaron all postdate the construction of the South House in mature LH IIIB1.[214] Some alterations were made to the area in LH IIIB2, perhaps after an earthquake, and a final destruction took place at the end of that period. A brief summary of the most significant remains may serve to introduce most of the tangible elements of Mycenaean cult.

The Tsountas House shrine lies on the upper of three terraces (fig. 10).[215] A bolster-shaped altar in front of a bench belongs to the first of two phases. The altar has a hollow extension on the western side; a runnel leads from it to a jar in the floor, suggesting that it was used for libations.[216] A miniature kylix and a flat dish (FS 322) also belong to this phase.

The Temple lies in the center of the complex, and is entered from the south. A low dais occupies the middle of the main room, and at the back is a series of stepped benches or platforms. These apparently served as altars, in the sense of offering places, for a clay tripod offering table was found at the northeast corner of the bench, next to a large female idol embedded in the bench. These were the only finds from the room, but a cache of large clay human and snake figurines was found in a small sealed room up a flight of stairs, and joining fragments came from a triangular area behind the main room. Drinking vessels and bowls were also found in the building.

The building containing the Room with the Fresco lies west of the Temple. The fresco in question decorated the southern part of the east wall of the room (fig. 11). In front of it was a platform of clay and rubble; a Minoan-style painting of horns of consecration above a row of circles decorates the top of its north face. The upper surface of the platform at the west end forms a ledge shaped into three shal-

[213] W.D. Taylour, "Mycenae 1968," *Antiquity* 43 (1969) 91–97; Taylour, "New Light on Mycenaean Religion," *Antiquity* 44 (1970) 270–80; G.E. Mylonas, *Το Θρησκευτικόν Κέντρον των Μυκηνών/The Cult Center of Mycenae* (Πραγματείαι της Ακαδημίας Αθηνών 33, Athens 1972); Mylonas, "The Cult Center of Mycenae," *Proceedings of the British Academy* 67 (1981) 307–20; and E.B. French, "Cult Places at Mycenae," in Hägg and Marinatos 41–48.

[214] French (supra n. 213) 43; Taylour (supra n. 25) 8–9. The date of the Tsountas House shrine is based on information from Elizabeth French.

[215] French (supra n. 213) 44–45.

[216] A.J.B. Wace, "Mycenae 1950," *JHS* 71 (1951) 254; R. Hägg, "The Role of Libations in Mycenaean Ceremony and Cult," in Hägg and Nordquist 178.

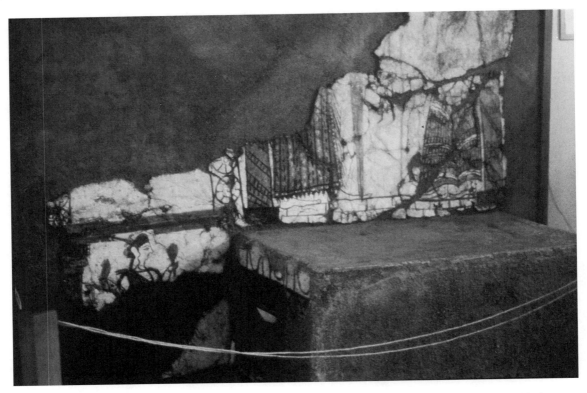

Fig. 11. Mycenae. Fresco and platform from the Room with the Fresco. (Photo C.W. Shelmerdine)

low discs. Ash in the discs suggests that this platform too functioned as an altar.[217] The lower register of the fresco beside this altar depicts a female, probably divine, and an animal restored as a griffin. Above the altar the upper register depicts two females, also thought to represent deities, in an architectural setting. They wear long robes of different types; one holds a sword and the other a staff, and between them hover two small human silhouettes.[218] In the center of the room is a large elliptical hearth, and a bench runs along the south side. A number of objects were found in the fill of the bench, including kylikes, cups and cooking pots, worked ivories, and a faience plaque of Amenophis III. The adjacent room 32 may have been a shrine or a related storage area.[219] The former interpretation is supported by the discovery of a terracotta figurine, probably a divine image, on

a dais in the southwestern corner. In front of it was a pile of glass paste beads. However, the room also contained storage debris such as worked and unworked ivory fragments, and a variety of pottery.

The variety in orientation and contents of these three buildings suggests that they served different deities, but there is a certain consistency in the cult installations themselves. The main rooms all contain a low central raised area. That in the Room with the Fresco was a hearth, while the dais in the Temple and the altar in the Tsountas House shrine show no trace of burning, and both have been tied to libations.[220] Another common feature is one or more benches or platforms, where offerings were placed. Large figures and small figurines are the most common offerings found in religious locales.[221] The examples from Mycenae are all large enough to be

[217] Taylour 1969 (supra n. 213) 94; P. Rehak, "New Observations on the Mycenaean 'Warrior Goddess'," AA 1984, 539; and R. Hägg, "Ritual in Mycenaean Greece," in F. Graf ed., Ansichten griechischer Rituale: Geburtstags-Symposium für Walter Burkert (Stuttgart, forthcoming). I thank the author for sending me a draft of this paper.

[218] N. Marinatos, "The Fresco from Room 31 at Mycenae: Problems of Method and Interpretation," in French and Wardle 245–51; P. Rehak, "Tradition and Innovation in the Fresco from Room 31 in the 'Cult Center' at Myce-

nae," in R. Laffineur and J.L. Crowley eds., Εικών: Aegean Bronze Age Iconography: Shaping a Methodology (Aegaeum 8, Liège 1992) 39–62.

[219] French (supra n. 213) 45.

[220] Temple: Taylour (supra n. 25) 18; Tsountas House shrine: references supra n. 216.

[221] For the distinction between figures and figurines, see E.B. French, "Mycenaean Figures and Figurines, Their Typology and Function," in Hägg and Marinatos 173–77.

called figures, though there are two sizes. The large (50–60 cm tall) "grotesques," hollow human figures of both female and ambiguous gender, probably depict celebrants rather than deities.[222] Two smaller (ca. 30 cm tall) female figurines found with them are carefully shaped and finely painted. These figurines and the similar example from room 32 could represent goddesses. The third type found at Mycenae consists of the snake figures from the Temple.

Tiryns. Several cult areas were identified at Tiryns in addition to the megaron: the earliest date to LH IIIB2.[223] Three deposits in the Upper Citadel are little more than concentrations of figurines. At the north end of the colonnaded court above the eastern galleries, human and animal figurines were found with a few other artifacts.[224] More diverse is a group of material thought to come from pits 10 and 17 of the Geometric bothros, south of court XXX.[225] In addition to Psi-figurines, this cache contains two animal rhyta, a miniature throne, and a figurine perhaps depicting a person on a bed. Most extensive is a deposit from the so-called *epichosis*-complex, in the southern part of the palace quarters. This material included several rhyta, five models of thrones, 56 female figurines, and 126 miniature vessels.[226]

The installations in the Lower Citadel are better preserved. Casement room 7 in the fortification wall was a LH IIIB2 cult room, as is clear from debris accumulated outside in the courtyard—more than 239 Psi-figurines, two larger figures (30 + cm), several representations of thrones and chariots, and two animal rhyta.[227] Building VI nearby seems to date from the same period. It contained an altar and animal rhyta in room 123, and Kilian therefore interpreted it as the house of the priestess of the cult practiced in room 7. However, Linear B tablets were found in a pit at the end of the corridor in building VI; they are thought to have fallen from a room above room 130, which connects to building VI on the

east.[228] Among the subjects are lists of personnel and chariot wheels, and the complex is clearly part of the palace administration. A cult building also stood in the Lower Citadel during the post-palatial era. R 117 was a small one-room structure built in LH IIIC Early against the interior of the fortification wall. This simple building had a bench at the rear and a column in the center of the room, as well as three columns outside the entrance. R 110 was subsequently built, without columns, directly above the ruins of R 117 in LH IIIC Developed; the two-room structure R 110a in turn replaced R 110. At this point a hearth occupied the center of the main room. In each phase the building had a bench at the back, on which clay figures were found. These portray a known type of female deity with upraised arms; headdresses are preserved in some cases, as well as applied and painted jewelry and other painted decoration. Other cult paraphernalia include rhyta, miniature and regular-sized vessels, and animal bones in ash layers.

Pylos. The small room 93 northeast of the Main Building at Pylos has been interpreted as a shrine.[229] Plowing had obliterated the floor level and only a few artifacts were found in the room. Among the chance finds is a miniature kylix. Essential to the identification of this room as a shrine is a stuccoed block a few meters to the southeast in court 92, which the excavators thought was an altar.[230]

Phylakopi. The sanctuary at Phylakopi also consists of more than one building; the West Shrine was built during LH IIIA2, and the small East Shrine was added in LH IIIB.[231] The sanctuary continued as before in LH IIIC. Bench altars in both shrines hold small human and animal figurines and chariot groups, as well as large wheelmade bovids and human figures. Of the human figures, the elaborately shaped and decorated "Lady of Phylakopi" is unique at this site.[232] Other figures are clearly delineated as male or female, down to their genitalia. There

[222] A. Moore, "The Large Monochrome Terracotta Figures from Mycenae: The Problem of Interpretation," in French and Wardle 219–28.

[223] K. Kilian, "Zeugnisse mykenischer Kultausübung in Tiryns," in Hägg and Marinatos 49–58; Kilian, "Patterns in the Cult Activity in the Mycenaean Argolid: Haghia Triada (Klenies), the Profitis Elias Cave (Haghios Hadrianos) and the Citadel of Tiryns," in Hägg and Nordquist 193–96.

[224] Müller (supra n. 124) 210; Kilian, in Hägg and Nordquist (supra n. 223) 193.

[225] Kilian, in Hägg and Nordquist (supra n. 223) 193. Some uncertainty about the findspot arises from ambiguous labeling of boxes in the storeroom.

[226] Kilian, in Hägg and Nordquist (supra n. 223) 195;

W. Voigtländer, "Epichosis," in *Tiryns* X (Mainz, forthcoming); Müller (supra n. 124) 45.

[227] Kilian, in Hägg and Marinatos (supra n. 223) 53; Kilian 1981 (supra n. 26) 170–71; Kilian 1988 (supra n. 26) 142–45.

[228] L. Godart, J.T. Killen, and J.-P. Olivier, "Eighteen More Fragments of Linear B Tablets from Tiryns," *AA* 1983, 413–26 (fragments 7–24); 413 on the findspot.

[229] Blegen and Rawson (supra n. 125) 303–305, fig. 223.

[230] Blegen and Rawson (supra n. 125) 301–302, figs. 227–28.

[231] Davis 729–30, with references.

[232] Renfrew et al. (supra n. 159) 215–16, SF 2660, fig. 6.4, pl. 31.

Fig. 12. Methana. Cult rooms A, B, and Γ at Ayios Konstantinos, from the south. (Courtesy E. Konsolaki)

is some duplication of types in the two shrines, but within the West Shrine the genders are separated: male figures are associated with the northwest altar, and female figures with those in the northeast and southwest corners. The range of figures and figurines is closer to that at Tiryns than to the assemblage from Mycenae. The Lady of Phylakopi, though rather large (45 cm tall), resembles the three finer figurines from Mycenae and their counterparts from Tiryns, but no parallels exist here for the "grotesques" from Mycenae. Phylakopi is unique in having clearly male idols, but some figurines from the newly discovered shrine at Ayios Konstantinos on Methana are interpreted as male (see below).

Other indoor cult areas. A few other sites have cult places, all with features similar to those just described. House shrines are reported at both Asine and Berbati. The shrine in Asine House G dates to LH IIIC. Pottery, female figurines, and a larger head (the "Lord of Asine," now understood as female) were found near a bench in the corner near the entrance at the north end of the room, which also contained two centrally placed column bases. A thick layer of ash and bones extended from near the bench along the east long wall.[233] A deliberately broken jug was fixed upside down at the east end of the bench, suggesting that libations were offered there. Two rooms in the Potter's Quarter at Berbati also had bench altars in LH IIIB.[234] In room A, a broken amphora and a clay spoon were found on the bench, and a Psi-figurine in the fill above. Room B, a subsequent construction, has the more interesting installation: a channel formed by two rows of stones, with part of a large kylix wedged under smaller blocking stones at one end. In addition, a separate room to the north (room C) features a pictorial krater fixed in the floor, its bottom pierced.

The work at Ayios Konstantinos on Methana is too recent to have been much discussed in print yet, and I only highlight here a few salient features of the shrine (fig. 12).[235] All of the finds in this building complex date to LH IIIA–B; the pottery includes

---

[233] R. Hägg, "The House Sanctuary at Asine Revisited," in Hägg and Marinatos 91–94, with references. Hägg observes (94) that the bench may have differed in appearance and use from those at Mycenae and Tiryns.

[234] Å. Åkerström, "Cultic Installations in Mycenaean Rooms and Tombs," in French and Wardle 201–202.

[235] *AR* 1993–1994, 13; *ArchDelt* 46 (1991) Chron. 71–74;

E. Konsolaki, "The Mycenaean Sanctuary on Methana," *BICS* 1995, 242; Konsolaki, "A Mycenaean Sanctuary on Methana," in R. Hägg ed., *Peloponnesian Sanctuaries and Cults* (Stockholm, forthcoming). I thank Eleni Konsolaki-Yannopoulou for providing information and abstracts of her forthcoming publications.

Fig. 13. Methana. Figurines, triton shell, and pottery on bench in room A at Ayios Konstantinos. (Courtesy E. Konsolaki)

rhyta, kylikes, and tripod pots. The main room A, oriented east–west, features a stepped bench in the northwest corner, a platform along the south wall, and a hearth in the southeast corner. Near the south-west corner a broken jar neck on the floor may have been a receptacle for libations; a rhyton, cup, and dipper were found with it. About 150 figurines were associated with the bench in the northwest part of the room. Many are bovids, but a number of rare types are also present, including chariot groups, hel-meted riders on horseback, and people driving and riding oxen (fig. 13). The human figures are pre-sumed from their activities to be male. The absence of female figurines, apart from one Psi-type with a hollow stem, is notable.

Finally, a LH IIIA2 Early deposit at Tsoungiza may be mentioned here (fig. 14).[236] It is a dump below

the crown of the hill, with which no architectural remains are associated, but the contents are thought to have come from a structure higher up. The lower half of a figure was found here, along with numer-ous human and animal figurines, including two rep-resentations of breadmakers. Additional finds in-clude a limited range of pottery, chiefly kylikes and bowls, and animal bones.

Outdoor cult areas. Traces occasionally remain of ritual activity conducted in the open air. The only certain Mycenaean cult installations predating LH III are those at the later site of the sanctuary of Apollo Maleatas at Epidauros.[237] The Early Mycenaean re-mains have been described by Rutter.[238] In LH IIIA–B the large Early Mycenaean open-air altar ter-race on the hilltop continues in use, with an exten-sion to the east. A deep deposit of ash, animal bones

[236] Wright et al. (supra n. 57) 635–37; J.C. Wright, "The Spatial Configuration of Belief: The Archaeology of Myce-naean Religion," in S. Alcock and R. Osborne eds., *Placing the Gods: The Landscape of Greek Sanctuaries* (Oxford 1994) 69–70.

[237] V. Lambrinoudakis, "Remains of the Mycenaean Period in the Sanctuary of Apollon Maleatas," in Hägg and Marinatos 59–65; R. Hägg, "Open Cult Places in the Bronze Age Aegean," in A. Biran and J. Aviram eds., *Biblical Archaeol-*

ogy Today, 1990: Proceedings of the Second International Con-gress on Biblical Archaeology, Jerusalem, June–July 1990 (Jeru-salem 1993) 191–92.

[238] Rutter 794. Rutter notes a complete absence of MH cult remains, but Hägg (supra n. 237) 191 mentions a possible MH altar site at Nisakouli with sherds and animal bones near Methoni, published by A. Choremis, "M.E. Βωμός εις 'Νησακούλι' Μεθώνης," *AAA* 2 (1969) 10–14.

Fig. 14. Tsoungiza. Figure and figurines, LH IIIA2 Early. (Courtesy J.C. Wright)

(chiefly bull and goat), and pottery accumulated on the hillside under the terrace. Among the other LH III offerings were large and small bovid figures, Psi- and Phi-figurines, and small horse figurines, including one from a chariot group. Only a few meters away from the altar terrace is a settlement with three layers of Mycenaean habitation (above two of EH date). Thus, despite its lofty location on Mt. Kynortion, this installation is not a remote peak sanctuary of Minoan type.

Two more open-air cult places of the palatial period are known, both in the vicinity of Tiryns. One site is a surface deposit found near a chapel of Ayia Triada near Klenies, and the other is a cave on Profitis Elias near Ayios Adrianos.[239] The Klenies deposit comprises 123 Phi-figurines of middle LH IIIB style,

three animal figurines, an animal rhyton, and pottery, including some deliberately broken drinking vessels. A naked male figurine was originally reported, but is now lost. The Profitis Elias cave lies near a LH IIIB building on the hilltop. No figurines were found there, but cookpots, a cup, and kylikes (some broken) lay on the floor and on a natural rock bench. A more elaborate outdoor cult area is also attested in the late LH IIIB or IIIC period at Amyklai, with finds similar to those from earlier indoor shrines and from Epidauros, including many female and animal figurines and some figures.[240]

The LH III iconographical evidence for the appearance of cult areas consists of a number of fresco fragments depicting shrine facades.[241] Several elements recalling Minoan shrine features appear on

[239] Kilian, in Hägg and Nordquist (supra n. 223) 185–93, with references. Finds of figurines and rhyta at Delphi suggest the existence of a cult place, probably of the outdoor type, but none has been located: Müller (supra n. 63) 475–86. Nor is there any demonstrable ritual content to the Mycenaean remains under the Telesterion at Eleusis: P. Darcque, "Les vestiges mycéniens découverts sous le Télestérion

d'Eleusis," *BCH* 105 (1981) 593–605.

[240] K. Demakopoulou, *Το μυκηναϊκό ιερό στο Αμυκλαίο και η ΥΕ ΙΙΙΓ περίοδος στη Λακωνία* (Diss. Univ. of Athens 1982); Wright (supra n. 236) 65.

[241] Pylos: M. Lang, *The Palace of Nestor at Pylos in Western Messenia* II: *The Frescoes* (Princeton 1969) 131–40. Tiryns: G. Rodenwaldt, *Tiryns* II: *Die Fresken des Palastes* (Mainz 1912)

one or more of these: antas, central column, half-rosettes, beam ends, and horns of consecration. The last two designs recur on the side of the bench by the fresco in room 31 at Mycenae (see above, fig. 11). Two of the Pylos facades are crowned by pairs of animals, 1 A 2 by sphinxes and 2 A 2 by lions. The Linear B tablets use several words for shrine, and make reference to particular cult places in the Pylos area, but no information is offered about their layout or contents.[242]

Cult Practices

Certain ritual practices can be deduced from the layout and contents of cult places: the offering of figurines/figures and other objects, libations, and animal sacrifices. Frescoes and Linear B texts reinforce the archaeological evidence, and extend the range of information beyond it, particularly on ritual processions and ritual feasting. The most widely attested practice is the offering of various objects, particularly animal and human figures and figurines. Not all of the large anthropomorphic figures represent deities. To date, the "grotesques" from Mycenae are unique, and seem to represent worshippers. The hands, in various positions, are thought to have held either actual offerings, such as jewelry, or clay replicas of them.[243] Some of the other figures from various sites, more finely shaped and decorated, may also stand for human celebrants. One type, however, certainly depicts the goddess with upraised arms, and it is easy enough to picture such an image draped with or holding offerings.

These figures clearly overlap in function with the more common small figurines, which were sometimes placed on benches in the same way, often in the same shrines. Comparison of their distributions, however, shows that the figurines had a wider range of uses.[244] Figurines (human and animal) appear in tombs as funerary offerings, and were also deposited near hearths and doorways, where they perhaps served an apotropaic function.[245] They are the only offerings, apart from cookpots and drinking vessels, in the simplest cult places like Berbati, Klenies, and the Profitis Elias cave. It has been argued that this restricted ritual assemblage represents a popular level of cult, as opposed to official cult places where figures and figurines appear together, along with animal figures and figurines, small clay models of furniture, rhyta, and miniature and full-sized vessels.[246] If the range of offerings is the basis for such a distinction, location is not: official cult attributes occur both at palatial sites (Mycenae, Tiryns) and elsewhere (Phylakopi, Asine),[247] both indoors and outdoors (Epidauros), both during the palatial period and afterward (Tiryns, Phylakopi, Amyklai).

Some frescoes show offerings of various kinds being carried in procession. Objects depicted include flowers (Thebes, Pylos), vessels of metal, stone, and clay (Mycenae, Tiryns, Thebes), boxes or pyxides (Mycenae, Tiryns), trays (Pylos), a necklace (Mycenae), and a frame or table (Pylos).[248] Figures or figurines have also recently been identified in procession frescoes from Mycenae and Tiryns. After the procession, such offerings might have been placed on a bench in a shrine, though the figurine of a celebrant actually embedded in a bench in the Temple

---

18–19 no. 24, pl. I.1; 137–38 no. 194, pl. XI.9; 137–38 no. 195, pl. XVI.5 (with beam ends); 137–38 no. 196, fig. 58 (with half-rosette?).

[242] S. Hiller, "Mykenische Heiligtümer: Das Zeugnis der Linear B-Texte," in Hägg and Marinatos 95–126; see also P. Carlier, "Palais et sanctuaire dans le monde mycénien," in Lévy (supra n. 124) 255–82. The range of terms is striking: *i-je-ro* /hieron/, "temple" (Knossos, Pylos); *wo-(i-)ko* /woikos/ and *do* /*dō(n)/, "house" (Knossos, Pylos, Thebes); *e-do* /hedos/, "seat" (Pylos).

[243] One of the figures from Mycenae is shown actually holding an ax-hammer, and French long ago suggested that others may have held necklaces: Taylour 1970 (supra n. 213) 277; French (supra n. 221) 173; Moore (supra n. 222); and Hägg (supra n. 217).

[244] In my view, French (supra n. 221) 173 is right to insist that figurines take their function from their context, not the other way around. On figurines, see also E.B. French, "The Development of Mycenaean Figurines," *BSA* 66 (1971) 101–87.

[245] Kilian (supra n. 5) 148, fig. 16.

[246] On official and popular cults, see R. Hägg, "Official

and Popular Cults in Mycenaean Greece," in Hägg and Marinatos 35–39; Hägg, "State and Religion in Mycenaean Greece," in *Politeia* 387–91; and K. Kilian, "Mykenische Heiligtümer der Peloponnes," in H. Froning, T. Hölscher, and H. Mielsch eds., *Kotinos: Festschrift für Erika Simon* (Mainz 1992) 10–25. Wright (supra n. 236) 72–73 prefers to view the various manifestations of Mycenaean religion as a continuum rather than a series of levels.

[247] In addition to the sites discussed here, there is a head from Nichoria, probably to be associated with a LH IIIB2 building: H. Hughes-Brock, "The Metal Objects and Miscellaneous Small Finds, Part II: Terracotta and Miscellaneous Small Finds," in McDonald and Wilkie (supra n. 10) 631, 655 no. 2064, fig. 10-8, pl. 10-76.

[248] Procession frescoes are attested from all the major palace sites. They are discussed, with references, by Lang (supra n. 241) 38–40, 51–62; and Hägg (supra n. 217). Vessels in processions and other frescoes are discussed by E. Mantzourani, "Vases and Vessels in Aegean Wall Painting," in C. Morris ed., *Klados: Essays in Honour of J.N. Coldstream* (*BICS* Suppl. 63, London 1995) 123–41.

at Mycenae shows that not all idols were carried in processions.[249] Among the vessels carried in the frescoes are two that from their yellow color appear to be made of gold.[250] Highly relevant, therefore, is Pylos tablet Tn 316, which itemizes donations of a gold vessel and a man to several gods, and a gold vessel and a woman to goddesses. It was once suggested, well before the cumulative archaeological and iconographical evidence for the offering of figures and figurines was as substantial as it is now, that the "people" were actually figurines.[251] The verb used, however, is ἄγω, not φέρω, so they should be led and not carried as figurines would be. The conventional view is preferable, that the men and women referred to are real people, marked for sacrifice or for a life of service to a deity, or simply detailed to carry the vessels. Another notable offering mentioned in the tablets is perfumed oil. The majority of Fr tablets from Pylos list disbursements of perfume to deities and sanctuaries, and for two festivals, one of which takes place at pa-ki-ja-na and is associated with Poseidon.[252] In only one case (Fr 1225) is the purpose of the oil stated: it was to serve as ointment for clothing.[253]

The procession frescoes and the tablets bring us into the Mycenaean palace proper, and to the highest level of official cult—that associated with the palatial elite, and in particular the wanax. Indeed, the presentation of offerings has been directly linked

to the megaron itself, and so have the two other rituals detectable in the archaeological record, libation and animal sacrifice. In addition to the rhyta discovered at a number of cult places, permanent installations discussed above at Mycenae (Tsountas House shrine), Asine, and Berbati clearly point to the pouring of libations.[254] In the porch of the megaron at Mycenae an alabaster slab beside a low rounded altar has a shallow oval depression that Hägg suggests may also have been for this purpose.[255] This evidence gives a meaningful context to the two round depressions, joined by a channel, in the floor next to the cutting for a throne in the Pylos megaron. This arrangement has long been tied to libations, and the relevance of a painting of a stone jug on the dado immediately above has recently been observed.[256] Hägg believes that tripod offering tables may have been receptacles for libations, and that kylikes, like rhyta, were used as libation vessels.[257] Significant for his argument is a pair of miniature kylikes found lying on an offering table in the Pylos megaron.[258] Both miniature and standard kylikes are common in cult contexts; indeed, drinking vessels and bowls are the only offerings besides figurines found in the humblest shrines. Hägg also associates libations with animal sacrifice, which is clearly attested by the accumulation of animal bones in ash layers at Asine, Phylakopi, and Epidauros.[259]

While the slaughtering of animals may represent

---

[249] Kilian, in Hägg and Marinatos (supra n. 223) 49. On the Tiryns example, see Rodenwaldt (supra n. 241) 87 no. 103, pl. X.7; C. Boulotis, "Zur Deutung des Freskofragmentes Nr. 103 aus der Tirynther Frauenprozession," Arch-KorrBl 9 (1979) 59–67, fig. 1; S.A. Immerwahr, Aegean Painting in the Bronze Age (University Park 1990) 114, 202 TI no. 4, fig. 33b. Mycenae: Mylonas 1972 (supra n. 213) pl. XIV; I. Kritseli-Providi, Τοιχογραφίες του Θρησκευτικού Κέντρου των Μυκηνών (Athens 1982) 41–42, pl. 6a. Some think this image resembles a naturalistic doll rather than a figure: Immerwahr (supra) 119. A sarcophagus from Tanagra depicts mourning women approaching a male holding a figure: "Chronique" 1975, 642, fig. 118.

[250] Rodenwaldt (supra n. 241) 86–87 nos. 101–102, pl. X.2 (no. 101); Immerwahr (supra n. 249) 114, 202 TI no. 4, fig. 32g; Mantzourani (supra n. 248) 133 nos. 41–42, 137.

[251] Discussion in Documents² 284–89, 458–62. S. Hiller, "Te-o-po-ri-ja," in C. Nicolet ed., Aux origines de l'hellénisme: La Crète et la Grèce. Hommage à Henri van Effenterre (Paris 1984) 139–50 has connected this practice with a term on two Knossos tablets, te-o-po-ri-ja /theophorial, "carrying of gods."

[252] Neither festival name is securely interpreted: F. Aura Jorro, Diccionario micénico II (Madrid 1993) 237–38, s.v. re-ke-(e-)to-ro-te-ri-jo, 362, s.v. to-no-e-ke-te-ri-jo. On the Fr tablets see Shelmerdine (supra n. 195).

[253] On this practice in the Mycenaean world and Homeric epic, see C.W. Shelmerdine, "Shining and Fragrant Cloth in Homer," in S. Morris and J. Carter eds., The Ages of Homer: A Tribute to Emily T. Vermeule (Austin 1995) 99–107.

[254] The archaeological evidence is well laid out by Hägg (supra n. 216) 177–84.

[255] Hägg (supra n. 216) 180; I. Papadimitriou, "Ἀνασκαφαὶ εν Μυκηναίς," Prakt 1955, 230–31, fig. 7, pls. 77–79; K. Kilian, "Der Hauptpalast von Mykenai," AM 103 (1987) 99–113.

[256] The channel: Blegen and Rawson (supra n. 125) 85–88, fig. 70. Fresco fragment depicting a stone jug: Lang (supra n. 241) 178–79 no. 2 M 6, pls. 108, 141; Mantzourani (supra n. 248) 132 no. 37; P. Rehak, "Enthroned Figures in Aegean Art and the Function of the Mycenaean Megaron," in Rehak 111. A similar stone jug is carried in the Tiryns procession fresco: H. Reusch, Die zeichnerische Rekonstruktion des Frauenfrieses im böotischen Theben (AbhBerl 1955.1, Berlin 1956) 10 no. 29, 25–28, fig. 16, pl. 10; Immerwahr (supra n. 249) 115, 200–201 Th. no. 1, fig. 32f; Mantzourani (supra n. 248) 130 no. 33, fig. 9. The other parallels adduced by Rehak are rather different; there is no variegated pattern indicating stone, and both have vertical handles from a rim or a false neck rather than a jug neck. One is from Mycenae: Kritseli-Providi (supra n. 249) 51 no. B-25, pl. 7b; Mantzourani (supra n. 248) 132 no. 54. The other is from Tiryns: Rodenwaldt no. 101 (references supra n. 250).

[257] Hägg (supra n. 216) 183.

[258] Blegen and Rawson (supra n. 125) 89, fig. 68. Hägg (supra n. 216) 183 notes that rhyta are similarly associated with offering tables at Akrotiri on Thera and on a seal from Naxos.

[259] Hägg (supra n. 217).

sacrifice in certain circumstances, it is also a necessary part of food preparation. Similarly, the kylix may be used for libations, but it is also the Mycenaean drinking vessel par excellence. A growing body of evidence suggests that communal feasting was an important feature of Mycenaean culture, and it may thus be only a question of terminology whether one views animal bones in ash layers, and kylikes in cult settings, as evidence for sacrifice and libations or for ritual meals.[260] In addition to the accumulations of animal bones already mentioned, others have been directly tied to such feasts. One example comes from LH IIIC levels of the Tiryns Lower Citadel, where animal bones were found in the courtyard outside the cult building.[261] Another is the LH IIIA2 deposit at Tsoungiza, where the discard pattern of animal bones is consistent with feasting.[262]

This archaeological evidence is significantly augmented by references to banquet supplies in the Linear B texts. The liquid component of the banquet may be discernible in the gold vessels brought to deities on Tn 316, the Pylos tablet mentioned above. The three shapes listed are the conical cup, the goblet or kylix, and the chalice. The last two were associated even in the Early Mycenaean period with ritual drinking, and appear in the LM IIIA Campstool Fresco from Knossos, which has been interpreted as a ceremonial drinking scene. The 56 inscribed sealings found at Thebes in 1982 document animals (sheep, goats, pigs, and oxen) and two other foodstuffs coming into the palace. It has been demonstrated that the types and numbers of the animals, and some of the terminology, are remarkably similar to those on Pylos tablets Un 2 and Un 138, which list animals and various other edibles.[263] It is very likely that the commodities listed are ingredients for a state banquet: the heading of Un 2 reveals the kind of occasion that would prompt such a feast. It refers to a special ceremony at *pa-ki-ja-na*, which

the king either undergoes or presides over.[264] *Pa-ki-ja-na* is an important Pylian sanctuary, and the proposed interpretation of its name as *Isphagianal*, "place of slaughter," takes on new relevance in the light of evidence for the slaughter and ritual consumption of animals.[265] A recent find from Pylos further links such banquets to the king. A fragment unearthed from Blegen's dump in 1995 has been associated with several fragmentary tablets of the Un series, all previously known. If the joins prove correct, the resulting tablet, while still incomplete, includes the word *wanax* in the dative, above a list of commodities, including wheat and barley, an ox, honey, unguent, and figs. It is hard to see here anything but another list of banquet supplies. Killen has identified similar lists at Knossos, so it appears that ceremonial banquets were a widespread Mycenaean phenomenon.[266] One occasion mentioned in writing is the Pylos ceremony involving the king, and in many societies such meals are mechanisms whereby a chief can assert and enhance his authority by rewarding his dependents. It may have served this purpose in Bronze Age Greece, but the ceremony on Un 2 takes place at a sanctuary, and most of the archaeological evidence comes from nonpalatial and religious sites. It is safe to say that such occasions always had a ritual dimension, even though it is not always possible to distinguish purely religious feasts from those that also served a political purpose.

An illustration of just such a ceremonial feast appears on the northeast wall of the Pylos megaron, the culmination of the procession with a bull in vestibule 5.[267] At the right-hand end of the wall, the famous bard with a lyre entertains at least two pairs of men seated at tables, while nearer the throne is a bull either standing or, in a more recent reconstruction, recumbent and actually trussed for sacrifice. The setting by the throne suggests that the king himself presides over the kind of event depicted, if in-

---

[260] B. Bergquist, "The Archaeology of Sacrifice: Minoan-Mycenaean versus Greek. A Brief Query into Two Sites with Contrary Evidence," in R. Hägg, N. Marinatos, and G.C. Nordquist eds., *Early Greek Cult Practice* (Stockholm 1988) 21–34; Hägg (supra n. 217), with references.

[261] Kilian 1981 (supra n. 26) 150; the debris is characterized as "bone waste from meals" by Kilian (supra n. 5) 148. See also Albers (supra n. 211) 106–10, 132–34.

[262] Wright (supra n. 236) 69.

[263] Piteros et al. (supra n. 139), esp. 171–84; J.T. Killen, "Observations on the Thebes Sealings," in *Mykenaïka* 365–80; and Killen, "Thebes Sealings, Knossos Tablets and Mycenaean State Banquets," *BICS* 1994, 67–84.

[264] The most plausible translation is "at *pa-ki-ja-na*, upon the initiation of the king . . .," though there is some debate about this: *Documents*² 440–41, 562, s.v. *mu-jo-me-no*; Killen 1994 (supra n. 263) 72; F. Aura Jorro, *Diccionario micénico*

I (Madrid 1985) 80–81, s.v. *a-pi-e-ke*; 459–60, s.v. *mu-jo-me-no*.

[265] Hiller (supra n. 242) 107–108; for the suggested translation see Aura Jorro (supra n. 252) 72–74, s.v. *pa-ki-ja-na, pa-ki-ja-ne*. The toponym persists in the Pylos area: Σφαγία is an alternative name for Sphakteria (Strabo 8.4.2), though Mycenaean *pa-ki-ja-na* is not thought to be that small, barren island.

[266] Killen 1994 (supra n. 263), adducing Inka and Classical Greek parallels.

[267] Lang (supra n. 241) 38–40, 192–93, reconstruction pl. 119. In the megaron itself L. McCallum, *Decorative Program in the Mycenaean Palace of Pylos: The Megaron Frescoes* (Diss. Univ. of Pennsylvania 1987) 68–141 reconstructs a trussed bull lying on a table, but only the bull's shoulder actually survives: Lang (supra) 109–10 no. 19 C 6, pls. 53, 125.

deed that was the seat of a king.[268] That the fresco decorates the megaron is no guarantee that the ceremony took place in this room. However, the cumulative testimony of this painting, the miniature kylikes and an offering table near the hearth, and a libation channel beside the throne offers strong support to the view that the megaron was yet another locus of ritual activity.[269] The importance of the bull as a high-status victim is borne out by textual references other than its appearance on banquet lists.[270]

DESTRUCTIONS

The destructions and abandonments that Mycenaean sites suffered at about the end of LH IIIB continue to fascinate. We now possess somewhat more information about these events and their aftermath than was available in 1978, but new data have not much changed the basis for debate. The search for explanations has continued too, but it must be said that the field is not much nearer consensus about either the immediate or the more remote cause(s) responsible for the end of the palaces. The remarks offered here are not an exhaustive review of the problem, but a brief attempt to assess the more recent information and interpretations.

The historical sequence of construction and destruction at palatial centers in LH IIIB–C has already been touched on above. The first signs of widespread damage appear in the middle of LH IIIB, with destructions in the citadel at Tiryns, in the Oil Merchant group and Panayia Houses I and II outside the walls at Mycenae, and at Gla (perhaps in LH IIIB2). The sequence of events at Thebes is not certain, but a destruction at the end of LH IIIB1 is apparent at some locations, with Linear B tablets preserved by fire. Fortification walls are substantially extended at Mycenae and Tiryns in the aftermath of the destructions there. At Midea the wall was built

in sections, and several foundation trenches have now been excavated. Sections examined in the East Gate area and lower terraces were built in LH IIIB2, according to ceramic evidence. A foundation trench in the West Gate area contains LH IIIB1 pottery but no certain LH IIIB2 sherds; the construction date suggested for this section is near the middle of the 13th century B.C., pointing to the latter part of LH IIIB1. The first half of this phase is also reported as the date of the fortification wall at Athens, but Wright has recently argued that the original plan was later modified. Subsequent alterations are made at Mycenae and Athens near the very end of LH IIIB, to ensure access to water from within the walls.[271]

How closely were these redoubled efforts at fortification building connected with the destructions that immediately preceded them? The disasters at Tiryns and Mycenae have been attributed to earthquakes.[272] Yet the building of massive Cyclopean walls is not a useful response to the threat of earthquake: it is a clear indicator that human enemies threatened the palatial centers in the Argolid, and perhaps at Athens. Other signs point in the same direction. Within the citadel at Mycenae further construction efforts include workshops and storage areas, notably the House of Columns and the Artists' Workshop in the east wing of the palace. Most of the cult center, which includes workshops and storage rooms, also postdates the mature LH IIIB1 South House. At Pylos, nothing is yet known of the putative fortification/terrace wall now indicated by geophysical prospection, but a number of alterations to the original plan restricted access to the Main Building and altered its character. The most obvious change was the walling in of courts 42 and 47, preventing entry through gateway 41. Room 27 and corridor 18 were added to the storage facilities, and room 32 was converted to a storeroom. Finally, the Northeast Workshop was a very late addition to the overall

---

[268] Rehak (supra n. 256) 109–12 argues from iconographic associations of seated figures and griffins that the "throne" was in fact the seat of a priestess or queen, not a king.

[269] As often suggested: see Hiller (supra n. 242) 117–19; Kilian (supra n. 246) 17; and Hägg, in *Politeia* (supra n. 246) 389–90.

[270] Palaima (supra n. 186). The bones at Epidauros are mainly from bulls and goats.

[271] Mycenae: S. Iakovides, *Late Helladic Citadels on Mainland Greece* (Leiden 1983) 24–37, 70–72; Shear (supra n. 22). Iakovides, "Destruction Horizons at Late Bronze Age Mycenae," in Φιλία Επη εις Γ.Ε. Μυλωνάν I (Αρχαιολογική Εταιρεία της Αθήνας, Βιβλιοθήκη 103, Athens 1986) 233–60 has pro-

posed that the Oil Merchant houses referred to were destroyed not at the end of LH IIIB1, but in a general disaster in LH IIIB2 that was responsible for all the LH IIIB destructions observed at Mycenae. The ceramic links on which the argument is based, however, do not force this conclusion, and it has not met with universal approval. Tiryns: Iakovides 1983 (supra) 3–13, 19. Thebes: supra n. 139. Midea: Walberg 1992 (supra n. 33) 33 (Lower Terraces); Demakopoulou, forthcoming (supra n. 33) (West Gate area); Åström et al. 1992 (supra n. 33) 11 (East Gate area). Athens: Iakovides 1983 (supra) 79–86, 90; Wright (supra n. 48) 348–49.

[272] Tiryns: Kilian (supra n. 5) 134. Mycenae: Iakovides 1986 (supra n. 271) 259.

plan, postdating the walling-in of the courts.[273] Thus, at both Mycenae and Pylos the latter part of LH IIIB saw an increase of storage and work areas close to the palace; at Mycenae this development was correlated with the abandonment of an administrative complex, the Oil Merchant group of houses, outside the walls. The extramural settlement itself continued in LH IIIB2, as it did at Tiryns, though at both sites houses were also built within the citadel. The real change was directly connected to the central administration. An increased centralization of resources and personnel sends the same message as the building of new and massive fortifications: Mycenaean officials perceived a very human threat, from quarters as yet unknown. The Pylos tablets reflect only the administrative situation at the end of LH IIIB, not its evolution, but they do demonstrate a highly centralized bureaucracy at that time.[274]

It is against this background that the disasters that struck the greater Mycenaean world at the end of LH IIIB must be considered. Most of these were already well documented by 1978.[275] Since then evidence has become clearer for destructions at Midea and Thebes, and the abandonment without destruction of Nichoria and Tsoungiza.[276] The relative date of many of these events is only now emerging as the newly recognized transitional phase LH IIIB2/IIIC Early. The latest pottery in destruction levels at Tiryns, Midea, and in the Citadel House area at Mycenae belongs to this phase, as does the latest Mycenaean material at Nichoria. The destruction date of Pylos is a matter of renewed debate, but there too the LH IIIB/IIIC transition still seems most likely.[277] The impact of these destructions on settlement patterns was not uniform. In Messenia, the dramatic depopulation previously documented is reflected in a dearth of LH IIIC pottery among surface finds of the Pylos Regional Archaeological Project.[278] Many sites in other regions also went out of use, but habitation continued at the citadels of Mycenae, Tiryns, Midea, and Athens, and at other sites like Argos, Korakou, and Chalandritsa and Derveni in Achaea.[279] Cham-

[273] J.C. Wright, "Changes in Form and Function of the Palace at Pylos," in Shelmerdine and Palaima (supra n. 199) 19-29; C.W. Shelmerdine, "Architectural Change and Economic Decline at Pylos," in Studies Chadwick 557-68. The sequence of construction in this area has been confirmed by the Minnesota team. The assemblages in courts 42 and 47—stirrup jars, broken and discarded kylikes, and coarse kitchen ware—indicate that these courts were added to serve mundane purposes, possibly including the manufacture of perfumed oil (Shelmerdine [supra n. 195] 59-62).

[274] Shelmerdine (supra n. 273); P. de Fidio, "Fattori di crisi nella Messenia della tarda Età del Bronzo," in Studies Chadwick 127-36.

[275] Sites destroyed: Argolid: Mycenae, Tiryns, Midea, and Iria; Laconia: Menelaion; Messenia: Pylos; Achaea: Teichos Dymaion; Boeotia and Phocis: Thebes, Orchomenos, and Krisa. Sites abandoned: Argolid and Corinthia: Berbati, Prosymna, Zygouries, and Tsoungiza; Laconia: Ayios Stephanos; Messenia: Nichoria; Attica: Brauron; Boeotia and Phocis: Eutresis. See Gazetteer. Sensible accounts are offered by J.T. Hooker, Mycenaean Greece (London 1976) 140-82; P. Betancourt, "The End of the Greek Bronze Age," Antiquity 50 (1976) 40-47.

[276] Thebes: The insistence of Symeonoglou (supra n. 49) 47-50 on LH IIIB1 as the destruction date for the later palace site requires refutation. Two groups of Linear B tablets, certainly part of the palatial bureaucracy, clearly belong to a LH IIIB2 context. The Of tablets from the corner of Epaminondas and Metaxas Streets were found with LH IIIB2 pottery including coated deep bowls: T. Spyropoulos and J. Chadwick, The Thebes Tablets II (Minos Suppl. 4, Salamanca 1975), contra Symeonoglou (supra n. 49) 48, 291. This is also the date of the new finds under Pelopidou Street: Aravantinos et al. (supra n. 170) 823. Nichoria: McDonald and Wilkie (supra n. 10) 767-68. Tsoungiza: Wright et al. (supra n. 57) 638, 641.

[277] There is proportionally very little decorated pottery from the Pylos palace, most of it anomalous. The motifs on a few vessels, including the five distinctive pithoid jars of shape 53, look early (LH IIIA2-IIIB1), while some deep bowls with debased and sloppy designs would be more at home in LH IIIC than in LH IIIB. On the strength of this handful of pots, M. Popham, "Pylos: Reflections on the Date of Its Destruction and on Its Iron Age Reoccupation," OJA 10 (1991) 315-24 argued for a destruction in LH IIIB1 and a later reoccupation. Unfortunately he takes no account of the other 90+% of the palace pottery, which is unpainted. The high proportion of unpainted shapes, its range of shapes, and its profiles are all entirely typical of LH IIIB2, and militate against an earlier destruction date. Popham's suggestion that the exterior wall of courts 42-47 might be Geometric has now been conclusively disproven, since the wall predates the construction of the Northeast Workshop (supra n. 273). As he and others have suggested, however, a postpalatial reoccupation now seems certain (supra n. 44); future work by the Minnesota project will, it is hoped, clarify its date. A response to Popham's article by P.A. Mountjoy is forthcoming in BSA.

[278] McDonald and Rapp (supra n. 66) 142-43; Davis et al. (supra n. 45).

[279] Information from Gazetteer, unless otherwise noted. Tiryns: further references supra n. 26. K. Kilian, "Zum Ende der mykenischen Epoche in der Argolis," JRGZM 27 (1980) 166-95; and Kilian, "La caduta dei palazzi micenei continentali: Aspetti archeologici," in D. Musti ed., Le origini dei Greci: Dori e mondo egeo (Rome 1985) 73-95 propose that Tiryns was a refuge center in LH IIIC. This idea, however, rests on the assumption that the Lower Town around the citadel reached its greatest size at this time. Zangger (supra n. 27) 189-212 has shown that the LH IIIB town was probably equally large. Midea: supra n. 33. Chalandritsa: ArchDelt 40 (1985) Chron. 136-38; AR 1992-1993, 23. Derveni and Achaea generally: T.J. Papadopoulos, Mycenaean Achaea (SIMA 55, Göteborg 1979).

ber tombs at Thebes are the only evidence so far of a LH IIIC presence there. Only a few other places stand out as more prominent in this period than in LH IIIB: the fortified settlement of Teichos Dymaion in Achaea, Asine in the Argolid, Panakton in Boeotia, Elateia in Phokis, and cemeteries at Perati in Attica, Palaiokastro in Arcadia, and on Kephallenia.[280] At the sites where settlement continues, a considerable degree of continuity is evident: of the new elements associated with LH IIIC, handmade burnished pottery and the Naue II type sword are first attested in LH IIIB before the destructions, while in burial customs the change to cremation and the use of cist graves does not occur until the middle of LH IIIC.[281] The significant change from LH IIIB to LH IIIC is the demise of palatial administration. Though life went on at Mycenae and Tiryns, the megaron units went out of use. At Midea, the megaron itself was remodeled and converted to other uses, while Pylos was abandoned, at least for a while. Fortunately for students of ancient Greek, the end of Mycenaean bureaucracy meant the end of literacy, leaving the Greeks of the mainland free to adapt a more serviceable script in due course.

What caused these events of the LH IIIB/C transition is a question that may never receive a clear answer. The theories proposed have all fallen into one of three categories: foreign attack, internal strife, or natural disaster, and discussion continues along these three lines.[282] Those who favor natural causes now think in terms of earthquake rather than a change of climate.[283] The Greek excavators of Mycenae have favored this explanation for the destructions there, though their British colleagues have not agreed. Kilian not only attributed all the LH IIIB destructions at Tiryns to earthquake, but extended this theory beyond the Argolid to the entire Peloponnese, specifically Pylos and the Menelaion. There is no good evidence to justify including the last two sites, but convincing signs of earthquake damage have been observed at Midea. Even if earthquakes are accepted as the immediate cause of damage at some sites, however, much remains unexplained. Why are their effects noticeable only at palatial centers (and not all of those)? Why, in their wake, were the megaron units at Mycenae and Tiryns not rebuilt, though plenty of construction took place in other parts of those sites? Why did palatial administration

---

[280] Information from *Gazetteer*, unless otherwise noted. Panakton: M.H. Munn, "New Light on Panakton and the Attic-Boeotian Frontier," in Beister and Buckler (supra n. 54) 231–44; M.H. Munn and M.L.Z. Munn, "On the Frontiers of Attica and Boeotia: The Results of the Stanford Skourta Plain Project," in A. Schachter ed., *Essays in the Topography, History, and Culture of Boeotia* (*Teiresias* Suppl. 3, Montreal 1990) 33–40. Elateia: S. Deger-Jalkotzy and P. Dakoronia, "Elateia (Phokis) und die frühe Geschichte der Griechen: Ein österreichisch-griechisches Grabungsprojekt," *AnzWien* 127 (1990 [1991]) 77–86.

[281] Of these new elements, handmade burnished pottery has received the most attention in recent years. It appears in very small quantities at a number of Mycenaean sites, and though locally made it has been thought to come from both Italy and the central Danube region: J.B. Rutter, "Ceramic Evidence for Northern Intruders in Southern Greece at the Beginning of the Late Helladic IIIC Period," *AJA* 79 (1975) 17–32; S. Deger-Jalkotzy, *Fremde Zuwanderer im spätmykenischen Griechenland* (*AnzWien* 326, Vienna 1977). Debate on the significance of this pottery continues: H.A. Bankoff and F.A. Winter, "Northern Intruders in LH IIIC Greece: A View from the North," *JIES* 12 (1984) 1–30; N.K. Sandars, "North and South at the End of the Mycenaean Age: Aspects of an Old Problem," *OJA* 2 (1983) 43–68; Deger-Jalkotzy, "Das Problem der 'Handmade Burnished Ware' von Myk. IIIC," in Deger-Jalkotzy ed., *Griechenland, die Ägäis und die Levante während der "Dark Ages" vom 12. bis zum 9. Jh. v. Chr.* (*AnzWien* 418, Vienna 1983) 161–78; D.B. Small, "'Barbarian Ware' and Prehistoric Aegean Economics: An Argument for Indigenous Appearance," *JMA* 3 (1990) 3–25; Rutter, "Some Comments on Interpreting the Dark-surfaced Handmade Burnished Pottery of the 13th and 12th Cen-

tury B.C. Aegean," *JMA* 3 (1990) 29–49.

[282] Some general bibliography since 1978: Deger-Jalkotzy 1983 (supra n. 281); K. Lewartowski, *The Decline of Mycenaean Civilization: An Archaeological Study of Events in the Greek Mainland* (*Archiwum Filologiczne* 43, Wroclaw 1989); F. Schachermeyr, *Die ägäische Frühzeit* 4: *Griechenland im Zeitalter der Wanderungen: Von Ende der mykenischen Ära bis auf die Dorier* (*AnzWien* 372, Vienna 1980); Schachermeyr, *Die ägäische Frühzeit* 5: *Die Levante im Zeitalter der Wanderungen vom 13. bis zum 11. Jahrhundert v. Chr.* (*AnzWien* 387, Vienna 1982); Schachermeyr, *Griechische Frühgeschichte* (*AnzWien* 425, Vienna 1984); E. Thomas ed., *Forschungen zur ägäischen Vorgeschichte: Das Ende der mykenischen Welt* (Cologne 1987); W.A. Ward and M.S. Joukowsky eds., *The Crisis Years: The 12th Century B.C.* (Dubuque 1992).

[283] In general, with special reference to Tiryns: Kilian 1980 (supra n. 279); Kilian 1985 (supra n. 279); Kilian (supra n. 5) 134, 151, n. 2, fig. 10. Mycenae: S. Iakovides, "The Present State of Research at the Citadel of Mycenae," *BIALond* 1977, 134; Iakovides 1986 (supra n. 271). Midea: Åström et al. 1990 (supra n. 33) 9, 13; Åström et al. 1992 (supra n. 33) 14; Walberg 1992 (supra n. 33) 31, 38; Demakopoulou et al. 1994 (supra n. 33) 34, 39; and P. Åström and K. Demakopoulou, "Signs of an Earthquake at Midea?" in S. Stiros and R.E. Jones eds., *Archaeoseismology* (Fitch Laboratory Occasional Paper 7, Athens 1996) 37–40.

The theory of climatic change, revisited by R.A. Bryson, H.H. Lamb, and D.L. Donley, "Drought and the Decline of Mycenae," *Antiquity* 48 (1974) 46–50, is countered by O.T.P.K. Dickinson, "Drought and the Decline of Mycenae: Some Comments," *Antiquity* 48 (1974) 228–30, and by G. Shrimpton, "Regional Drought and the Economic Decline of Mycenae," *EchCl* 6 (1987) 137–76.

collapse at this point, and not after the earthquake damage postulated for the end of LH IIIB1? Above all, this is not the disaster for which the Mycenaeans had been preparing. However intriguing the mystery of the demise of the Mycenaeans, an equally interesting question is what threat they perceived. The heavy fortifications of LH IIIB2 and protected access to water (Mycenae, Tiryns, Athens), the increasing restrictions on circulation (Pylos), and the addition of workshop and storage areas within the walls (Mycenae, Tiryns) or close to the megaron unit (Pylos) all suggest that an attack was anticipated.

Thus, the theory that Mycenaean Greece succumbed to raids or invasions by foreigners also has its adherents.[284] In addition to citing the archaeological evidence of preparations, some have attempted to discern signs of an imminent attack in the Linear B tablets from Pylos.[285] The arguments put forward focus on activities that may have been prompted by an emergency. Chief among them are the following: 1) the o-ka tablets in the An series detail watchers guarding the coast at various points; 2) bronzesmiths in the Jn series are given small allocations or none at all, while "temple bronze" is collected, suggesting a shortage at the center; 3) various craftsmen are exempted from taxes; and 4) the sloppy execution of Tn 316, recording human offerings to deities, suggests urgent appeasement. In fact there is no reason to view any of these phenomena as extraordinary, or to connect them with the fall of Pylos. The arguments that an immediate crisis can be inferred from the tablets have not convinced those who work with the archive on a regular basis, and several refutations have been offered.[286]

If an assault on the Mycenaean world was a reality, two groups are most often proposed as the culprits. One is the Sea Peoples, a band of mercenaries or pirates who, according to Egyptian sources, caused a great deal of damage in Egypt, the Levant, Cyprus, and Anatolia in the late 13th–early 12th century B.C.[287] There is, however, no archaeological evidence that these pirates attacked the Greek mainland; nor do the Aegean islands suffer destructions at this time.[288] The other candidates are invaders from the north. The old view that these could be equated with the Dorians of Greek tradition has given way to a scenario of raiding, followed by the gradual infiltration of West Greek speakers over the course of a century or more. At issue in recent discussions has been the difficulty of tying new customs and artifact types to the time of the destructions; as noted above, some first appear in LH IIIB, and others not until the middle of LH IIIC.[289]

Another approach to the problem has been to focus on why the Mycenaeans were vulnerable, and why the setbacks of the LH IIIB/C transition had precisely the kind and degree of impact that they did. According to this line of reasoning, Mycenaean administration had been in trouble for a long time. The highly centralized control of industries and resources documented by the tablets, and their preoccupation with detail, along with the construction of workshop and storage areas in the immediate vicinity of the megaron, all reflect a response to economic decline rather than to any immediate threat.[290] A "systems collapse" of this kind could have involved competition for increasingly scarce resources of various kinds, from depleted agricultural supplies to metals and other imported commodities. Some have even attributed attacks on palatial centers to local uprisings or interkingdom warfare resulting from this competition, rather than to foreign incursions. An economic decline does not explain everything that took place during the latter half of LH IIIB, from the building of

[284] R. Drews, *The End of the Bronze Age: Changes in Warfare and the Catastrophe ca. 1200 B.C.* (Princeton 1993), with a review of earlier theories.

[285] L. Baumbach, "An Examination of the Evidence for a State of Emergency at Pylos c. 1200 B.C. from the Linear B Tablets," in Heubeck and Neumann (supra n. 189) 28–40.

[286] J.T. Hooker, "The End of Pylos and the Linear B Evidence," *SMEA* 23 (1982) 209–17; de Fidio (supra n. 274); T.G. Palaima, "The Last Days of the Pylos Polity," in *Politeia* 623–33.

[287] N.K. Sandars, *The Sea Peoples: Warriors of the Ancient Mediterranean* (London 1978); Schachermeyr 1982 (supra n. 282); G.A. Lehmann, *Die mykenisch-frühgriechische Welt und der östliche Mittelmeerraum in der Zeit der "Seevölker"-Invasionen um 1200 v. Chr.* (Opladen 1985).

[288] Davis, passim; D. Schilardi, "Paros and the Cyclades after the Fall of the Mycenaean Palaces," in *Mykenaïka* 621–39, esp. 638.

[289] The most recent proposal attributing the destructions to hostile action has the merit of seeking to explain how it succeeded rather than simply who was responsible. Drews (supra n. 284) argues that raids by the Sea Peoples on the kingdoms of the eastern Mediterranean succeeded because of a new type of warfare, which favored infantry over chariots. Specifically, he sees evidence of this shift in military tactics in the advent of the Naue II slashing sword, and other changes in weaponry and armor, during the 13th and early 12th centuries B.C. His arguments for the change in tactics are well made and interesting, though his general thesis leaves open some essential questions, and is perhaps too monolithic. Early reviews have been mixed: those by D. Haggis in *AJP* 116 (1995) 321–24 and N.V. Sekunda in *CR* 45 (1995) 119–21 are a study in contrasts.

[290] Betancourt (supra n. 275); de Fidio (supra n. 274); Shelmerdine (supra n. 273).

fortifications to the abandonment of most sites in Messenia, nor does this explanation indicate the proximate cause of palatial collapse. Most useful about the notion of systems collapse, however, is that it takes into account the fact that it was the top level of Mycenaean society that suffered most directly. The key elements lost in the disasters were the trappings of those in power: the megaron proper, the enriching contact with other cultures, the elaborate administrative system, and, with nothing to record, the art of writing. Thus, any plausible scenario for the transition to LH IIIC must take into account the architectural modifications following LH IIIB1, the destructions and abandonments at the LH IIIB/C transition itself, the end of palatial administration, and also the continuity of normal Mycenaean life at a lower level, with no immediate change either in material goods such as ceramics or in practices such as religion. It is improbable that all these phenomena, at all sites, could have had a single cause. Indeed, many now agree that a combination of factors must have been at work, and that the collapse of the Mycenaean states required both a process of decline and a precipitating event or events.[291]

A LOOK BACK AND FORWARD

Writing this review has brought an appreciation of the great progress made over the past 20 years in the disciplines that contribute to the study of Late Bronze Age Greece. At the same time, some avenues for future work are emerging. The position of the Mycenaean Greek dialect remains as ambiguous as ever, but Linear B studies have continued to refine our understanding of specific issues like land tenure, taxation, and industrial production, the general outlines of which were in many cases already clear by 1978. A newer development has been an advance in the study of institutions. The *wanax* himself has been one focus of attention, in conjunction with an interest in the formation of Mycenaean states. Another has been the industrial operations of the palaces, and the kinds of activities that took place in specific areas. Here textual and archaeological studies have necessarily gone hand in hand, and this sort of interdisciplinary approach will continue to be of great value. Of all topics that the tablets cover, the greatest progress can be seen in the field of Mycenaean religion. The discovery of new texts has been partly responsible. Most of the strides, however, have come from new archaeological discoveries, and these are only beginning to be integrated with textual in-

formation. A good example is the practice of ceremonial banquets described above. Excavators have reported suggestive caches of pottery and/or bones, while tablet experts have found written evidence for such feasts, but the two kinds of evidence have not yet been thoroughly discussed together.

Further indications of the importance of interdisciplinary research have come from the sciences. In particular, the combination of geophysical exploration and soil studies with intensive survey has already begun to generate new questions that can be asked about the evolution of individual settlements, before or in lieu of excavation. This is an area of great potential for future research, as is the larger issue of regional settlement patterns. In terms of excavation itself, archaeologists interested in the palatial period have continued to concentrate on the major centers, and on cemeteries. New questions have been asked and answered about the palatial sites themselves, regarding the size of the towns and the territories that they controlled. There is still a shortage of knowledge about ordinary settlements, however, which can only be filled by a willingness to forgo material rewards and explore some of the many smaller habitation sites that surveys have identified. In addition to the value of such knowledge for its own sake, it can also shed light on the organization of the Mycenaean states. The cases of Nichoria and Tsoungiza have shown how a combination of survey, excavation, and textual study can clarify the relationship between a satellite and the center. Further work along these lines could greatly improve our understanding of economic geography in Mycenaean Greece, the manner and degree to which different centers controlled their territories, and the consequences of expanding authority (and subsequently the end of that authority) for land use and settlement.

The painstaking analysis of artifacts remains essential to the successful study of these and other thematic problems, notably foreign trade. Categories like shell and bone, metalwork and glyptic art, and even frescoes receive little or no coverage in this review, but all continue to receive scholarly attention, and all must form part of any consideration of Mycenaean culture. Assimilating and organizing the proliferation of published objects will pose an increasing challenge in the future. Rapid advances in computer resources can be of great assistance, making it possible to assemble searchable illustrated databases of all sorts, from grave goods to Mycenaean pottery found abroad to assemblages from

---

[291] Dickinson (supra n. 6) 307–308.

specific excavations and surveys. Those wishing, for instance, to develop arguments about the growth of states based on metal finds in tombs, or about the rise of infantry tactics based on numbers of different weapon types, must have comprehensive and reliable figures on which to depend.[292] So must those who wish to evaluate such arguments. It would be extremely useful if this kind of detailed information were computerized and made widely available. At the same time, students of Late Bronze Age Greece must continue to strike a graceful balance between the analysis of specific artifact types and assemblages and the contemplation of broad theoretical problems. Only in this way will the achievements described above in bringing Mycenaean culture into focus be matched by the gains of the next 20 years.

DEPARTMENT OF CLASSICS
UNIVERSITY OF TEXAS AT AUSTIN
AUSTIN, TEXAS 78712
CWSHELM@MAIL.UTEXAS.EDU

---

[292] Jim Wright's forceful advocacy of databases (personal communication) has prompted me to include the point here. Leonard (supra n. 107) is an example of a useful database now in existence. Argument based on metal finds in tombs: Wright (supra n. 118). Argument based on changes in weapon types: Drews (supra n. 284), esp. 180–208.

Of course computer access is not available to everyone. It is, however, less expensive both to "publish" and to "buy" a computer database than to publish or to buy a book. Furthermore, towns and institutions worldwide that lack both computers and libraries are perhaps more likely in the future to acquire the former.

Addendum: 1997–1999

CYNTHIA W. SHELMERDINE

Two years have passed since the publication of my earlier review of the palatial Bronze Age of the southern and central Greek mainland (RAP VI)—not time for much new work to unfold. The bibliography has nevertheless expanded, as publications noted there as forthcoming have appeared, and as studies have continued on all aspects of Mycenaean material and social culture. In this addendum, I provide an update on several topics covered in the original article.

CHRONOLOGY

The date of the Uluburun shipwreck now appears to be even nearer the end of the 14th century B.C. than previously reported. Twelve more rings have now been found on the dunnage log used for radiocarbon testing, indicating that the log was cut no earlier than 1305 B.C., the date of the latest preserved ring.[293] This refinement has no real effect on the conclusion that LH IIIA2 evolved into LH IIIB1 around the beginning of the 13th century B.C.

WORK AT PALATIAL CENTERS AND OTHER SITES

Study continues of material from both within and outside the citadel at Mycenae.[294] Work also continues at Thebes,[295] and at Midea, where recent publications reinforce the earlier impression of a wealthy citadel that suffered a destruction by earthquake late in LH IIIB.[296] At Pylos, the Minnesota Archaeological Researches in the Western Peloponnese project has finished its review of areas uncovered during Blegen's excavation; interesting findings include the identification of a monumental gateway southwest of the palace, on the same axis as the Northeast Gateway.[297] Members of the Pylos Regional Archaeological Project were able to trace further the subsurface lineament mentioned in RAP VI; it now seems very likely to be part of a circuit fortification wall, though its date is still unknown.[298]

In RAP VI, I did not attempt to cover Mycenaean tombs, which are attested for the palatial period in great numbers and a variety of types, and on which the bibliography is vast. One consideration motivating, and mitigating, this omission was the impending publication by Cavanagh and Mee of a detailed overview of prehistoric Greek burials and burial customs.[299] This volume, now available, provides a period-by-period account of tomb architecture and grave goods, with catalogue and bibliography. The authors also offer an analysis of the ritual acts for which they discern evidence, and discuss the bearing of funerary data on questions of social identity and social structure. Mycenaean studies generally have benefited from a recent expansion of the use of archaeological evidence to illuminate issues of social history, and mortuary evidence is a productive example (see also below, "Ceramics and Other Crafts").[300]

Ordinary habitation sites in Mycenaean studies have received too little attention in the past.[301] It is therefore encouraging to report that new projects

[293] Recent on-line report on the Uluburun ship: http://www.arts.cornell.edu/dendro/97news/97adplet.html.

[294] Cf. AR 1994–1995, 11–12; S. Iakovides, "Mycenae in the Light of Recent Discoveries," in E. De Miro, L. Godart, and A. Sacconi eds., Atti e memorie del secondo Congresso internazionale di micenologia, Roma–Napoli, 14–20 ottobre 1991, 3: Archeologia (Incunabula Graeca 98, Rome 1996) 1039–49.

[295] V. Aravantinos, "New Archaeological and Archival Discoveries at Mycenaean Thebes," BICS 41 (1996) 135–36; Aravantinos, ArchDelt 48 (1993) [1998] Chronika 170–73. See also A. Dakouri, "New Light on the Stratigraphy and Dating of the House of Kadmos in Mycenaean Thebes: Assessing the Impact on Theban Chronology," Symposium on Mediterranean Archaeology '99 (University of Birmingham, 19–20 February 1999).

[296] Reports in De Miro et al. (supra n. 294) by P. Åström (1133–35), K. Demakopoulou (979–94), and G. Walberg (1333–38); and by Demakopoulou et al. in OpAth 21

(1997) 13–32 have now appeared; cf. also Demakopoulou, "Mycenaean Citadels: Recent Excavations on the Acropolis of Midea in the Argolid," BICS 40 (1995) 151–61. The first book-length report concerns early work on the lower terraces (a separate volume is planned for the megaron-type building excavated in 1994–1997): G. Walberg, Excavations on the Acropolis of Midea 1: The Excavations on the Lower Terraces, 1985–1991 (Stockholm 1996). For the most recent fieldwork see AR 1996–1997, 27–29; 1997–1998, 31–32.

[297] AR 1997–1998, 55–56; earlier reports in AR 1994–1995, 24–25; 1995–1996, 18–19; 1996–1997, 50–51.

[298] See above, RAP VI, 337–39; AR 1997–1998, 52–55.

[299] W. Cavanagh and C. Mee, A Private Place: Death in Prehistoric Greece (SIMA 125, Jonsered 1998).

[300] See also K. Branigan ed., Cemetery and Society in the Aegean Bronze Age (Sheffield Studies in Aegean Archaeology 1, Sheffield 1998).

[301] See above, RAP VI, 333, 376.

are addressing this problem. The Laconia Rural Sites Project has examined 20 sites by grid collection, geophysical prospection, and soil sampling. Among these are two sites belonging to the palatial period: LP 10 (MH–LH IIIB) and LP 20 (LH IIIA–B).[302] At Iklaina in Messenia a team under the direction of M. Cosmopoulos began work during summer 1999; excavation will follow a surface survey of the site. Further reports of work at known sites are also becoming available. These include a long-awaited account of the Mycenaean period at Lerna, where little activity took place during LH IIIA1, but where graves and household deposits characterize a settlement of LH IIIA2–IIIB date.[303] Other settlements that have received recent attention in print include Argos, Asea, Asine, Ayios Stephanos, and Eleusis.[304]

REGIONAL SURVEYS

Survey archaeology continues to receive theoretical attention as a discipline,[305] and also practical attention as a tool of Bronze Age studies. The results of survey projects in the Argolid, Boeotia, the Methana peninsula, Laconia, and Messenia were already outlined in RAP VI. Most of these have received further publication in one form or another, and in some cases study of the data continues.[306] New surveys are also under way in the Asea Valley and the Berbati Valley, while a topographical survey in Achaia by the Greek Archaeological Service and the National Research Foundation has led to the discovery of Mycenaean settlements as well as more examples of the tombs for which the region was already well known.[307]

CERAMICS AND OTHER CRAFTS

Mycenaean crafts have long been the subject of both technical and artistic studies. This topic was not a focus of RAP VI, but the last several years have seen a proliferation of studies of each kind, whose existence should at least be noted. Chemical analysis of stirrup jars at Mycenae has shed further light on their Cretan origin.[308] Clay sealings, both inscribed and uninscribed, from Mycenae, Pylos, and Elateia have recently received thorough publication.[309] Another welcome sign of progress is the compilation of a database of Aegean glyptic at the University of Tasmania.[310]

---

[302] *AR* 1994–1995, 14; 1995–1996, 13.

[303] M.H. Wiencke, "Mycenaean Lerna," *Hesperia* 67 (1998) 125–214.

[304] Argos: G. Touchais, "Argos à l'Âge du Bronze: État présent des recherches," in De Miro et al. (supra n. 294) 1319–26. Asea: J. Forsén, "Prehistoric Asea Revisited," *OpAth* 21 (1997) 41–72. Asine: R. Hägg, G.C. Nordquist, and B. Wells eds., *Asine* III: *Supplementary Studies on the Swedish Excavations, 1922–1930* (*SkrAth* 4°, 45.1, Stockholm 1996); A. Penttinen, "Excavations on the Acropolis of Asine in 1990," *OpAth* 21 (1997) 149–67. Ayios Stephanos: R. Janko, "Ayios Stephanos: A Bronze Age Village in Laconia," *BICS* 41 (1996) 139. Eleusis: M. Cosmopoulos, "Ἀνασκαφή Ἐλευσίνας," *Prakt* 1994, 45–60. Though outside the geographical scope of this chapter, the site of Dimini is relevant for its possible identity as the Mycenaean administrative center of Iolkos (supra n. 16). Work there has been summarized by B. Adrymi Sismani, "Η μυκηναϊκή πόλη στο Διμήνι: Νεότερα δεδομένα για την αρχαία Ιωλκό," in De Miro et al. (supra n. 294) 1295–1309.

[305] G. Barker, "Regional Archaeological Projects: Trends and Traditions in Mediterranean Europe," *Archaeological Dialogues* 3 (1996) 160–75; J. Bintliff, "Regional Survey, Demography, and the Rise of Complex Societies in the Ancient Aegean: Core-Periphery, Neo-Malthusian, and Other Interpretive Models," *JFA* 24 (1997) 1–38.

[306] Cambridge/Bradford Boeotian Expedition: *AR* 1996–1997, 52; 1997–1998, 59. Laconia Rural Sites Project: supra n. 302. Methana Survey: C. Mee and H. Forbes eds., *A Rough and Rocky Place: The Landscape and Settlement History of the Methana Peninsula, Greece* (Liverpool 1997). Pylos Regional Archaeological Project: J.L. Davis et al., "The Pylos Regional Archaeological Project, Part I: Overview and the Archaeological Survey," *Hesperia* 66 (1997) 391–494; E. Zangger et al., "The Pylos Regional Archaeological Project, Part II: Landscape Evolution and Site Preservation," *Hesperia* 66 (1997) 549–641; J.L. Davis, J. Bennet, and C.W. Shelmerdine, "The Pylos Regional Archaeological Project: The Prehistoric Investigations," in P.P. Betancourt et al. eds., *Meletemata: Studies in Aegean Archaeology Presented to Malcolm H. Wiener as He Enters His 65th Year* (*Aegaeum* 20, Liège 1999) 177–84. A general history of activity in the Pylos region, incorporating some of the survey results, is provided by J.L. Davis ed., *Sandy Pylos: An Archaeological History from Nestor to Navarino* (Austin 1998).

[307] Asea Valley: J. Forsén, B. Forsén, and M. Lavento, "The Asea Valley Survey: A Preliminary Report of the 1994 Season," *OpAth* 21 (1997) 73–97. Berbati Valley: B. Wells, G. Ekroth, and K. Holmgren, "The Berbati Valley Project: The 1994 Season," *OpAth* 21 (1997) 189–209. Achaia: *AR* 1996–1997, 40.

[308] J.E. Tomlinson, "Chemical Evidence for a Cretan Origin of Heavy Ware Stirrup Jars Found at Mycenae," in I. Stratis et al. eds., *Proceedings of the 2nd Symposium of the Hellenic Archaeometrical Society (26–28 March 1993): Archaeometrical and Archaeological Research in Macedonia and Thrace* (Thessaloniki 1996) 371–78.

[309] Mycenae: W. Müller et al., "Die Tonplomben aus Mykene," *AA* 1998, 5–55. Pylos: I. Pini et al., *Die Tonplomben aus dem Nestorpalast von Pylos* (Mainz 1997). Elateia: P. Dakoronia et al. eds., *Kleinere griechische Sammlungen: Die Siegel aus der Nekropole von Elatia-Alonaki* (*CMS* V, Suppl. 2, Berlin 1996). See also B. Sergent, "Les petits nodules et la grande Béotie," *REA* 99 (1997) 11–32.

[310] J. Crowley and A. Adams, "Iconaegean and Iconostasis: An Iconographic Classification and a Comprehensive Database for Aegean Glyptik," in W. Müller ed., *Sceaux minoens et mycéniens* (*CMS* Beiheft 5, Berlin 1995) 39–58.

Other authors have concentrated on metalworking of various kinds.[311] Not only small-scale crafts but also Mycenaean architecture and engineering have received systematic technical study.[312] In addition to such specific studies, Mycenaean crafts in general have been the subject of recent conferences and of papers at more general conferences.[313] Many papers explore implications for trade, social hierarchy, and political symbolism, as well as Mycenaean technology. To cite just two representative examples, recent artistic studies of Mycenaean war and hunt scenes also focus on their value as symbols of power of all kinds.[314] Discussion of crafts is now joined to consideration of craftsmen, their status, degree of autonomy vis-à-vis central administrations, and organization.[315] Thus, even as our understanding of Mycenaean technology improves, so does our appreciation of the place of that technology, and its products, in the Mycenaean world.

ECONOMIC AND POLITICAL ADMINISTRATION

As noted above in RAP VI, the bibliographical reports that make it possible to keep up with Mycenaean textual studies were resurrected in 1995, and several volumes have appeared since then.[316] Reports of joins among extant tablet fragments appear from time to time in the journal *Minos*, and the de-

finitive publication of the Pylos tablets nears completion, while further reports have been issued on the new cache of tablets from Thebes.[317] Scholars continue to pursue the topics of interest previously outlined: political hierarchy, taxation, production, and redistribution of agricultural goods and other commodities. A newer trend is an increasing emphasis on the role of nonpalatial production in the Mycenaean economy. A useful result of this emphasis has been that archaeological evidence has been scrutinized for information on sociohistorical topics about which the texts are silent, for example, the status of nonpalatial craftsmen such as potters and stoneworkers. Questions have also been raised about the degree of control that palatial administrators had over the full economic and political spectrum of Mycenaean society.[318]

RELIGION

Little new archaeological material relevant to religion has emerged recently, though a new report has appeared on the sanctuary at Ayios Konstantinos on the Methana peninsula.[319] I offer a correction to my earlier discussion of the Room of the Fresco in the Cult Center at Mycenae: what I described above in RAP VI as a bench running along the south side of the room is in fact a line of slabs used to seal the deposit covered over at the beginning of phase VIII.[320]

---

[311] R. Laffineur, "Polychrysos Mykene: Toward a Definition of Mycenaean Goldwork," in A. Calinescu ed., *Ancient Jewelry and Archaeology* (Bloomington 1996) 89–116; C. Gillis et al., "Aegean Bronze Age Tinned Vessels: Analyses and Social Implications," in P. Vicenzini ed., *The Cultural Ceramic Heritage* (Monographs in Materials and Society 2, Faenza 1995) 251–60; T.J. Papadopoulos, *The Late Bronze Age Daggers of the Aegean* 1: *The Greek Mainland* (Prähistorische Bronzefunde 6.11, Stuttgart 1998). I call attention also to a forthcoming study of decorated finger-rings by I. Pini.

[312] M. Küpper, *Mykenische Architektur: Material, Bearbeitungstechnik, Konstruktion und Erscheinungsbild* (Internationale Archäologie 25, Espelkamp 1996); J. Knauss, "Arkadian and Boiotian Orchomenos, Centres of Mycenaean Hydraulic Engineering," in De Miro et al. eds. (supra n. 294) 1211–19.

[313] C. Gillis, C. Risberg, and B. Sjöberg eds., *Trade and Production in Premonetary Greece: Aspects of Trade. Proceedings of the 3rd International Workshop, Athens 1993* (*SIMA-PB* 134, Jonsered 1995); Gillis et al. eds., *Trade and Production in Premonetary Greece: Production and the Craftsman. Proceedings of the 4th and 5th International Workshops, Athens 1994 and 1995* (*SIMA-PB* 143, Jonsered 1997); Laffineur and Betancourt (supra n. 58). In addition to the general conferences already cited, others relevant here are E.H. Cline and D. Harris-Cline eds., *The Aegean and the Orient in the Second Millennium* (*Aegaeum* 18, Liège 1998) and R. Laffineur ed., *Polemos: Le contexte guerrier en Égée à l'Âge du Bronze* (*Aegaeum*

19, Liège 1999).

[314] For the Mycenaean mainland, see papers by E.F. Bloedow, N.R. Thomas, R. Laffineur, S. Hiller, and L. Kontorli-Papadopoulou in Laffineur (supra n. 313).

[315] See papers by C. Gillis, M.-L. Gregersen, T.G. Palaima, and others in Laffineur and Betancourt (supra n. 58), and by M.-L. Gregersen and I. Tournavitou in Gillis et al. 1997 (supra n. 313).

[316] *Studies in Mycenaean Inscriptions and Dialect* (supra n. 4): volumes for 1979, 1980–1981, 1982–1983, and 1994–1995 have appeared.

[317] Pylos: J.L. Melena et al., *The Palace of Nestor* IV: *The Mycenaean Documents* (in preparation). Thebes (see above, RAP VI, 356 n. 170): Aravantinos (supra n. 295); V. Aravantinos, "Mycenaean Texts and Contexts at Thebes: The Discovery of New Linear B Archives on the Kadmeia," in S. Deger-Jalkotzy, S. Hiller, and O. Panagl eds., *Floreant Studia Mycenaea: Akten des X. Internationalen Mykenologischen Colloquiums in Salzburg vom 1–5 Mai 1995* (Österreichische Akademie der Wissenschaften, Philosophisch-historische Klasse, Denkschriften 274, Vienna 1999) 45–78.

[318] See, e.g., M.L. Galaty and W.A. Parkinson eds., *Rethinking Mycenaean Palaces: New Interpretations of an Old Idea* (Los Angeles 1999).

[319] *ArchDelt* 46 (1991) [1996] Chronika 71–74.

[320] Correction to RAP VI, 364, above; see Taylour (supra n. 25) 10. I thank Lisa French for calling this point to my attention (personal communication, 28 August 1997).

Religious frescoes from the Aegean are brought together in a topical study by Kontorli-Papadopoulou, and Hägg provides a good overview of advances in the study of Mycenaean religion over the last 30 years.[321] In RAP VI, I highlighted some new contributions of textual evidence to religious questions. An edition of tablets bearing on religion is now in preparation by T. Palaima, and discussion is under way about the possible appearance of previously unattested deities in the new group of tablets from Thebes.[322]

DESTRUCTIONS

The most important addition that must be made to RAP VI in this area is the increasing evidence for earthquakes at Mycenaean sites during the course of the 13th century B.C. A collection of papers published by the Fitch Laboratory includes discussions of earthquake evidence at Mycenae, Tiryns, Midea, Thebes, and, for the 12th century B.C., Kynos in central Greece.[323] Debate continues on the number and date of quakes at specific sites; evidence from the Citadel House area at Mycenae suggests that there, as at Tiryns, earthquakes caused destructions at both the LH IIIB1/2 and the LH IIIB/IIIC transitions.[324] It is now clear that earthquakes were a major cause of damage to several Mycenaean centers and probably one factor contributing to their decline. Earthquake damage has not been confirmed at Pylos, but Blegen's date of the LH IIIB/C transition for this destruction receives firm support from Mountjoy's review of the ceramic evidence.[325] Finally, the handmade burnished ware sometimes taken as evidence for intruders at the end of the palatial period continues to be the subject of debate, without conclusive results.[326]

FINAL THOUGHTS

In the concluding section of RAP VI, I expressed a wish that traditional Mycenaean studies of all kinds might continue, but that they might be joined by progress in some new directions: the use of scientific tools for research and study, investigation of nonpalatial settlements, the integration of textual and archaeological study, and the development of databases for various artifacts and assemblages from excavations and surveys. This addendum indicates that even in the short time since RAP VI was published, there have been advances in all these areas. The Laconia Rural Sites Project and the new work at Iklaina are good examples of the attempt to understand the nature of life and settlement at a level below that of the palace elite. The database of Aegean glyptic underway at the University of Tasmania will be a powerful tool for all those interested in iconography, both for artistic purposes and as a window into Mycenaean beliefs. Finally, archaeological study of both agriculture and crafts has gone hand in hand with the evidence of the Linear B tablets as a source of information about Mycenaean economic structures. The result of all this work, along with continued careful attention to excavation and study of material remains, ensures that the field of Mycenaean studies is lively and productive, with a future as durable in the next century as its roots have proved durable in this one.

DEPARTMENT OF CLASSICS
UNIVERSITY OF TEXAS AT AUSTIN
AUSTIN, TEXAS 78712-1181
CWSHELM@MAIL.UTEXAS.EDU

---

[321] L. Kontorli-Papadopoulou, *Aegean Frescoes of Religious Character* (*SIMA* 117, Göteborg 1996); R. Hägg, "The Religion of the Mycenaeans Twenty-four Years after the 1967 Mycenological Congress in Rome," in E. De Miro, L. Godart, and A. Sacconi eds., *Atti e memorie del secondo Congresso internazionale di micenologia* 2: *Storia* (Rome 1996) 599–612.

[322] Godart and Sacconi (supra n. 170); L. Godart and A. Sacconi, "Les dieux thébains dans les archives mycéniennes," *CRAI* 3 (1996) 99–113.

[323] Stiros and Jones (supra n. 283), there mentioned only with reference to Midea.

[324] E.B. French, "The Ups and Downs of Mycenae: 1250–1150 BCE," in S. Gitin, A. Mazar, and E. Stern eds., *Mediterranean Peoples in Transition, Thirteenth to Early Tenth Centuries BCE* (Jerusalem 1998) 2–5; for the alternative of a single destruction horizon in LH IIIB2, see Iakovides 1986 (supra n. 271) and Iakovides (supra n. 294) 1048.

[325] P. Mountjoy, "The Destruction of the Palace at Pylos Reconsidered," *BSA* 92 (1997) 109–37, a sufficient response to the suggestion by Popham (supra n. 277) that

Pylos was destroyed in the middle of LH IIIB rather than at the end. Mountjoy's assessment also obviates the need to postulate a substantial LH IIIC reoccupation (P. Càssola Guida, "Considerazione sulla crisi della civiltà micenea: Il palazzo di Pilo," in De Miro et al. [supra n. 321] 693–700). S. Deger-Jalkotzy, "The Aegean Islands and the Breakdown of the Mycenaean Palaces around 1200 B.C.," in V. Karageorghis and N. Stampolidis eds., *Eastern Mediterranean: Cyprus–Dodecanese–Crete, 16th–6th Cent. B.C.* (Athens 1998) 106 n. 5, offers a more moderate variant of Popham's view, placing the Pylos destruction late in LH IIIB but not at the end of the period.

[326] H.A. Bankoff, N. Meyer, and M. Stefanovich, "Handmade Burnished Ware and the Late Bronze Age of the Balkans," *JMA* 9 (1996) 193–209; H. Genz, "Northern Slaves and the Origin of Handmade Burnished Ware: A Comment on Bankoff et al.," *JMA* 10 (1997) 109–11. A comprehensive study of this ware is provided by D. Pilidou, *Handmade Burnished Wares of the Late Bronze Age in Cyprus* (*SIMA* 105, Göteborg 1994).

Review of Aegean Prehistory VII: Neopalatial, Final Palatial, and Postpalatial Crete

PAUL REHAK AND JOHN G. YOUNGER

Dedicated to our teachers, Machteld J. Mellink and John L. Caskey *

INTRODUCTION

In an earlier article in this series, Watrous reviewed the archaeology of Crete from earliest times to the end of the Protopalatial period (MM II).[1] We continue from where he left off, focusing on Crete from MM III to the end of the Bronze Age (ca. 1700–1100 B.C.). Our main goals are twofold: to summarize critically the present state of the field, concentrating especially on developments of the last 25 years, and to indicate issues, problems, and areas of investigation that need to be addressed in the future.

Some changes have occurred since the earlier review and new sources of information have become available: *Nestor*, a listing of bibliography, has moved from Indiana University to the University of Cincinnati and is published in hard copy and on diskette, and will be responsible for future updates of the *International Directory of Aegean Prehistorians* (*IDAP*). The electronic mail discussion network *AegeaNet* has provided a public forum for a wide range of Aegean topics since 1993. Increasing use is being made of the Internet by archaeologists, and the scholarly acceptance of electronic publication is steadily gain-

* We are grateful to Fred Kleiner and Tracey Cullen for the invitation to write this article and for their editorial assistance. We are also indebted to many individuals who gave freely of their knowledge, especially J. Bennet, H. Blitzer, G. Cadogan, E.H. Cline, L.H. Cole, W. Coulson, C. Davaras, L.P. Day, J. Driessen, T. Eliopoulos, G. Gesell, B.P. Hallager, E. Hallager, B. Hayden, L. Hitchcock, S. Hood, A. Kanta, P. Kienzle, O.H. Krzyszkowska, R. Laffineur, M. Lee, A. Lembesi, C. Lilyquist, L. Little, C.F. Macdonald, J.A. MacGillivray, S.W. Manning, J. Moody, P. Muhly, M. Nikolaïdou, B. Olsen, C. Palyvou, I. Pini, G. Rethemiotakis, J. Rutter, L.H. Sackett, I.A. Sakellarakis, E. Sapouna-Sakellaraki, M. Schmid, C. Shelmerdine, J. Soles, M. Tsipopoulou, A.M.P.A. Van de Moortel, L.V. Watrous, J. Weingarten, and J. Zielinski.

The following abbreviations have been used:

Aegean and Orient	E.H. Cline and D. Harris-Cline eds., *The Aegean and the Orient in the Second Millennium. Proceedings of the 50th Anniversary Symposium, Cincinnati, 18–20 April 1997* (*Aegaeum* 18, forthcoming).
Archanes	I.A. Sakellarakis and E. Sapouna-Sakellaraki, *Archanes* (Athens 1991).
Atlas	J.W. Myers, E.E. Myers, and G. Cadogan eds., *The Aerial Atlas of Ancient Crete* (Berkeley 1992).
Begg	I. Begg, *Minoan Storerooms in the Late Bronze Age* (Diss. Univ. of Toronto 1975).
Cline	E.H. Cline, *Sailing the Wine-Dark Sea. International Trade and the Late Bronze Age Aegean* (*BAR-IS* 591, Oxford 1994).
CM	S. Marinatos and M. Hirmer, *Crete and Mycenae* (New York 1960).
CretCong	Τα Πεπραγμένα του Διεθνούς Κρητολογικού Συνεδρίου.
Doumas	C. Doumas, *The Wall-Paintings of Thera* (Athens 1992).
Eikon	R. Laffineur and J.L. Crowley eds., Εικών: *Aegean Bronze Age Iconography. Shaping a Methodology* (*Aegaeum* 8, Liège 1992).
Ergon	Το Εργον της Αρχαιολογικής Εταιρείας.
Gesell	G. Gesell, *Town, Palace and House Cult in Minoan Crete* (*SIMA* 67, Göteborg 1985).
Hallager	E. Hallager, *The Minoan Roundel and Other Sealed Documents in the Neopalatial Linear A Administration* I–II (*Aegaeum* 14, Liège 1996).
Immerwahr	S. Immerwahr, *Aegean Painting in the Bronze Age* (London 1991).
Jones	R.E. Jones, *Greek and Cypriot Pottery* (*BSA Fitch Laboratory Occasional Paper* 1, London 1986).
Kanta	A. Kanta, *The Late Minoan III Period on Crete: A Survey of Sites, Pottery, and Their Distribution* (*SIMA* 58, Göteborg 1980).
Kommos I	J. Shaw and M. Shaw eds., *Kommos* I: *The Kommos Region and the Houses of the Minoan Town*, pt. 1 (Princeton 1995); pt. 2 (Princeton 1996).
Kommos III	L.V. Watrous, *Kommos* III: *The Late Bronze Age Pottery* (Princeton 1992).
Palaces	R. Hägg and N. Marinatos eds., *The Function of the Minoan Palaces* (Stockholm 1987).
PGC	H.-G. Buchholz and V. Karageorghis, *Prehistoric Greece and Cyprus* (New York 1973).
Politeia	R. Laffineur and W.-D. Niemeier eds., *Politeia: Society and State in the Aegean Bronze Age* (*Aegaeum* 12, Liège 1995).
Sanctuaries	R. Hägg and N. Marinatos eds., *Sanctuaries and Cults in the Aegean Bronze Age* (Stockholm 1981).

Originally published in *AJA* 102 (1998) 91–173.

ing ground.[2] Other important tools include the continuing publication of seals and sealings in the *CMS* and its *Beihefte*, and the compilation of Linear A texts in *GORILA*.

Since 1987, the *Aegaeum* series has provided a timely venue for the publication of conferences and monographs on Aegean subjects, and the latest Cretological Congress took place in Herakleion on 10–13 September 1996. Authoritative publication volumes for a number of important sites are appearing or imminent, including Mallia, Mochlos, Chania, Kavousi, Kommos, Kato Syme, and Pseira. The palace at Knossos, which never received a final report in the modern sense, is now being published by areas.[3] Much important information can be gleaned on individual sites from the photographs and bibliographies in *The Aerial Atlas of Ancient Crete* (*Atlas*). An important archaeological resource, the East Cretan Center, endowed by the Institute for Aegean Prehistory, was inaugurated on 19 July 1997, and will be used by excavations all over the east end of the island primarily for study and the storage of finds.

On Crete, the Late Bronze Age is a long and complex period and presents a variety of problems, beginning with terminology and chronology. There is general agreement that the Neopalatial period began after widespread destruction of the Protopalatial centers at the end of MM II and endured through the pottery phases MM III, LM IA, and LM IB. The beginning of this period and the distinction between MM IIIA and B remain hazy, however.[4] In particular, little agreement exists about the causes of the MM II destructions.

The era following another destruction horizon at the end of the Neopalatial period in LM IB has been called "Postpalatial," based largely on developments observed at Knossos. In recent years, however, it has become clear that palatial administrative activity continued at Knossos until LM IIIA2–B early (discussed below), and certainly into LM IIIB at Chania. It therefore seems misleading to use the term "Postpalatial" for the pottery phases LM II–LM IIIB early, which represent a period of Mycenaean Linear B administration on the island at Knossos and Chania, and perhaps elsewhere; we have abandoned it in favor of the designation "Final Palatial."[5]

Society   O.H. Krzyszkowska and L. Nixon eds., *Minoan Society. Proceedings of the Cambridge Colloquium, 1981* (Bristol 1983).

TAW I–III   C. Doumas ed., *Thera and the Aegean World* I (London 1978); Doumas ed., *Thera and the Aegean World* II (London 1980); D.A. Hardy et al. eds., *Thera and the Aegean World* III.1: *Archaeology*; 2: *Earth Sciences*; 3: *Chronology* (London 1990).

Techne   R. Laffineur and P.P. Betancourt eds., Τέχνη: *Craftsmen, Craftswomen and Craftsmanship in the Aegean Bronze Age* (*Aegaeum* 16, Liège 1997).

Thalassocracy   R. Hägg and N. Marinatos eds., *The Minoan Thalassocracy, Myth and Reality* (Stockholm 1984).

Zakros   N. Platon, *Zakros: The Discovery of a Lost Palace of Ancient Crete* (New York 1971).

[1] L.V. Watrous, "Review of Aegean Prehistory III: Crete from Earliest Prehistory through the Protopalatial Period," *AJA* 98 (1994) 695–753; and relevant papers by J.D. Evans, D. Wilson, J.A. MacGillivray, and G. Cadogan in D. Evely et al. eds., *Knossos: A Labyrinth of History* (Oxford 1994).

[2] J.F. Cherry and J.L. Davis eds., *IDAP*[2] (1995): http://129.137.36.38/nestor/IDAP/isearch.html. URL for "Argos," a search engine for limited areas in the ancient and medieval worlds: http://argos.evansville.edu; "Kapatija," a web site for web sites in Aegean and classical archaeology: http://www.duke.edu/web/jyounger/kapat97.html; and "Abzu," a web site for web sites in Near Eastern archaeology: http://www-oi.uchicago.edu/OI/DEPT/RA/ABZU/ABZU_NEW.HTML.

[3] J. Raison, *Le palais du second millénaire à Knossos* I.1–2: *Le quartier nord* (Paris 1988); II.1–2: *Le front ouest et ses magazins* (Paris 1993); R. Laffineur, "Habitat égéen et reconstructions: Quelques réflexions méthodologiques à propos du quartier nord-est du palais de Cnossos," in P. Darcque and R. Treuil eds., *L'habitat égéen préhistorique* (Paris 1990) 3–19; S. Hood and W. Taylour, *The Bronze Age Palace of Knossos. Plan and Sections* (London 1981); S. Hood and D. Smyth, *Archaeological Survey of the Knossos Area* (London 1981).

[4] P.P. Betancourt, *The History of Minoan Pottery* (Princeton 1985) 103; P.M. Warren and V. Hankey, *The Absolute Chronology of the Aegean Bronze Age* (Bristol 1988) 54–60, 135–37; Warren, "A New Minoan Deposit from Knossos c. 1600 B.C., and Its Wider Relations," *BSA* 86 (1991) 319–40.

[5] "Postpalatial" is used by N. Platon, *Crete* (Cleveland 1966) 206–207. See E. Hallager and B.P. Hallager eds., *Late Minoan III Pottery. Chronology and Terminology* (Athens 1997); E. Hallager, "The History of the Palace at Knossos in the Late Minoan Period," *SMEA* 19 (1978) 17–33; E. Hallager, "Final Palatial Crete. An Essay in Minoan Chronology," in *Studies in Ancient History and Numismatics Presented to Rudi Thomsen* (Aarhus 1988) 11–21; W.-D. Niemeier, "Mycenaean Knossos and the Age of Linear B," *SMEA* 23 (1982) 275–76; Niemeier, "Das mykenische Knossos und das Alter von Linear B," *Beiträge zur ägäischen Bronzezeit* 11 (Marburg 1982) 29–126. The distinction between LM II and IIIA1 rests primarily on the deposits from the Unexplored Mansion (M.R. Popham et al., *The Minoan Unexplored Mansion at Knossos* [London 1984] section 4) and Chamalevri (M. Andreadaki-Vlasaki and E. Papadopoulou, "LM IIIA:1 Pottery from Khamalevri, Rethymnon," in Hallager and Hallager [supra] 111–51); and between LM IIIA1 and A2 on deposits from the Unexplored Mansion and Phaistos-Chalara (Kanta 244).

Here too there is a problem, since it has become increasingly apparent to archaeologists working on Crete that Furumark's phases for Mycenaean pottery, worked out in detail for the Argolid half a century ago, require substantial revision when applied to Crete.[6] While on the mainland there are accepted diagnostic criteria for distinguishing among the major and minor divisions of LH IIIA–C, there is considerable disagreement among scholars about when these phases begin and end on Crete. Thus, few pottery experts on Crete currently employ the terms IIIB1 and 2, or IIIC1 and 2, preferring instead to refer to IIIB early or late, and IIIC early or late. At the same time, there is no evidence for palatial administration after LM IIIB early, and we therefore restrict the term "Postpalatial" to the late phase of IIIB and all of IIIC. Recently, some scholars have focused their attention on the still problematic transition from the Bronze Age to the Iron Age.

Even the nature of archaeological investigation on Crete is changing. Now that Minoan archaeology is nearing its centenary, its historiography has become a subject in its own right with numerous articles and books. Increasingly within the last two decades, the old arrangement of unilateral, single-nationality excavations is being augmented by surveys and joint projects involving Greeks and the foreign archaeological schools (synergasiai). In addition, much material from earlier excavations is being restudied or reevaluated using new methodologies.

The move toward surveys has become particularly vital, as Crete is subjected to the pressures of its own population and, more importantly, the exigencies of tourism and a tourist-based economy. It is difficult to emphasize sufficiently the seriousness of this problem. It is therefore of crucial importance that intensive recent efforts have been made to survey the existing environment and to safeguard areas of potential archaeological interest. Surveys have been conducted all over the island (figs. 1–3), including the regions of Sphakia, the Amari valley, the western Mesara plain, the Ayios Vasileios valley, Vrokastro, Gournia, and Kavousi-Thriphti.[7] The north end of the Isthmus of Ierapetra now represents the most intensively surveyed area of the island.

The expansion of tourist resorts, especially along the north coast, now presents a serious danger to the archaeological heritage of Crete. The area from Herakleion to the palace at Knossos is completely built up along the major road, while to the east the sprawl of Herakleion has enveloped the Minoan port and cemetery areas at Poros, at the mouth of the Kairatos stream. Almost the entire Mallia plain from Chersonissos to the palace site has been subjected to strip building of villas and hotels along the shore. The impending construction of a new hotel at Ayia Varvara just east of Mallia and the construction of a sewer north across the plain from Ayios Nikolaos have prompted a thorough survey of the Mallia region.[8] In East Crete, the most controversial plan concerns the proposed building of an airfield in the Isthmus of Ierapetra near Vasiliki to service that end of the island; as of summer 1997, the project was still being debated.

Two recent trends are the continuing decentralization of the island's museums and the restudy of monuments and sites, particularly those excavated early in this century and inadequately published according to today's standards.[9] A new circulatory pattern is being established to accommodate the approximately 2 million annual visitors to Knossos while protecting the exposed architectural remains. Outside Crete, the Evans Archive has been established at the Ashmolean Museum at Oxford (S. Sherratt, director). Perhaps inevitably and necessarily, reevaluations of work by the early excavators on Crete

LM IIIB can only be distinguished in early and late phases (Kanta 3), and early IIIB pottery seems almost always to be accompanied by IIIA2 creating a transitional phase. LM IIIB seems more or less contemporary with LH IIIB, and LM IIIC with LH IIIC. The character of Subminoan is still sketchy, but Cretan Protogeometric is roughly contemporary with Attic Protogeometric.

[6] A. Furumark, *The Mycenaean Pottery: Analysis and Classification* (Lund 1941).

[7] O. Rackham and J. Moody, *The Making of the Cretan Landscape* (Manchester 1997); J. Bennet and M. Galaty, "Ancient Greece: Recent Developments in Aegean Archaeology and Regional Studies," *Journal of Archaeological Research* 5 (1997) 75–120; D.C. Haggis, "Archaeological Survey at Kavousi, East Crete," *Hesperia* 65 (1996) 373–432; Haggis, *JMA*

6 (1993) 131–74 (Kavousi); B.J. Hayden, J.A. Moody, and O. Rackham, *Hesperia* 61 (1992) 293–353 (Vrokastro); papers in L. Rocchetti ed., *Sybrita. La valle di Amari fra Bronzo e Ferro* (Incunabula Graeca 96, Rome 1994), esp. A. Kanta, 67–74; J. Moody et al., *8th CretCong* (forthcoming; Agios Vasilios); L. Nixon, *8th CretCong* (forthcoming; Sphakia); L.V. Watrous et al., *Hesperia* 62 (1993) 191–248 (western Mesara).

[8] *AR* 36 (1990) 74; *AR* 42 (1996) 43; H. van Effenterre, *Étude du site* (EtCret 13, Paris 1963) 1–53.

[9] E.M. Hatzaki, "Construction, Repairs and Reoccupation in the Knossos Town: The Architectural History of the Little Palace," *8th CretCong* (forthcoming). P. Kienzle of York University is studying the restorations at Knossos.

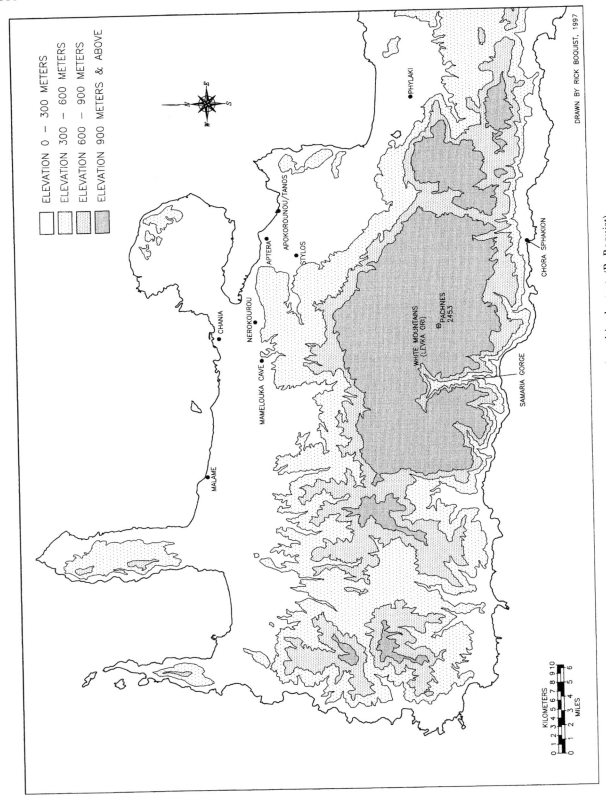

Fig. 1. Map of West Crete with sites mentioned in the text. (R. Boquist)

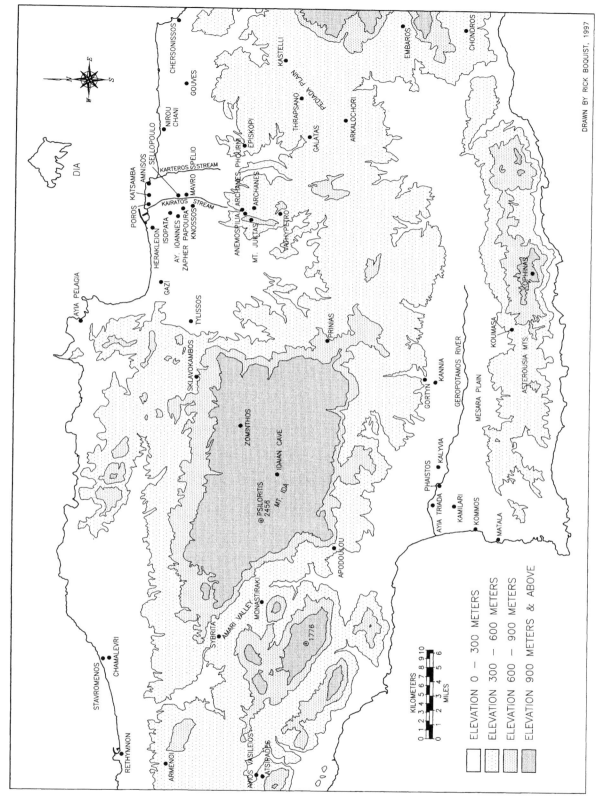

Fig. 2. Map of Central Crete with sites mentioned in the text. (R. Boquist)

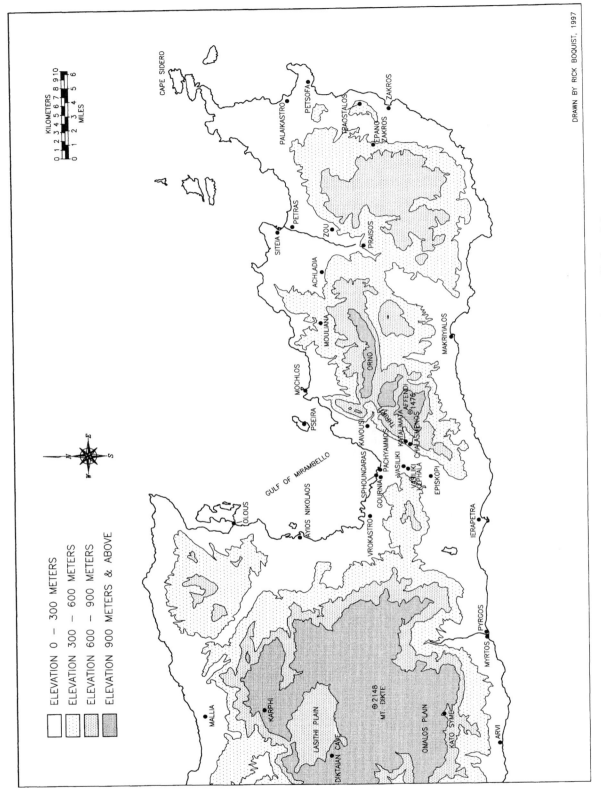

Fig. 3. Map of East Crete with sites mentioned in the text. (R. Boquist)

are challenging traditional interpretations of the evidence.

Recent intellectual developments have also contributed to a reevaluation of archaeology on Crete. The New Archaeology of the 1960s and 1970s has led to the investigation of issues in state formation, administration, and economy. More recently, postprocessual archaeology has encouraged an investigation of gender issues, landscape, and ecology. One source of concern is the failure of Aegean archaeologists to engage in constructive dialogue with advocates of more controversial interpretations of Minoan society, particularly the popularized view of ancient Crete as a matriarchy.[10]

SCIENTIFIC STUDIES

Major advances are taking place in the area of scientific analysis, often fueled by the desire to resolve specific problems (like the origin of the inscribed stirrup jars) or to take advantage of new excavation evidence. Spearheaded by the Fitch Laboratory at the British School and the Wiener Laboratory at the American School of Classical Studies, ceramic and petrographic analyses are beginning to answer questions about the origin and distribution of clays and vessel types. The recent dramatic rise in the number of potter's kilns discovered[11] increases the possibility of constructing archaeomagnetic and palaeointensity sequences, helping to refine thermoluminescence dates and to establish the contemporaneity of separated archaeological assemblages. The question of copper and tin sources, which has been bedeviling metallurgical studies, has spawned its own techniques, notably lead isotope analysis.[12] Forensic work on skeletal material, especially from cemeteries at Armenoi (LM IIIA–B), Mochlos (IIIB), and specific buildings at Anemospilia (MM IIIA) and Knossos (LM IB), helps repopulate the archaeological landscape with images of actual Minoans.[13] An interest in archaeoastronomy is potentially promising, but its value remains to be demonstrated.[14] A new study of early earthquakes promises a discussion of the problems inherent in identifying seismic damage in antiquity.[15]

For the last decade, Late Bronze Age Aegean chronology has been the subject of serious debate, centering around the dates for the earlier part of the period and particularly the date of the eruption of

[10] E.g., G. Gesell, "The Place of the Goddess in Minoan Society," in *Society* 93–99; L. Goodison, *Death, Women and the Sun* (London 1989); L. Meskell, "Goddesses, Gimbutas and 'New Age' Archaeology," *Antiquity* 69 (1995) 74–86; P. Muhly, "The Great Goddess and the Priest King: Minoan Religion in Flux," *Expedition* 32:3 (1990) 54–60; L. Talalay, "A Feminist Boomerang: The Great Goddess of Greek Prehistory," *Gender and History* 6 (1994) 165–83.

[11] Jones 227, 236, 829 gives an overview and bibliography; also see J.A. MacGillivray, "Pottery Workshops and the Old Palaces in Crete," in *Palaces* 273–78. We add the following: late LM IA: Kommos (J.W. Shaw et al., in *Techne* 323–31), Miletos (W.-D. Niemeier, in *Techne* 347–52); LM II–IIIA: Knossos, east of the Monolithic Pillar Basement (Hood and Taylour [supra n. 3] 282); LM IIIB: Achladia (Kanta 178), Chania (*Prakt* 1977, 457, fig. 1, pl. 237), Stylos (C. Davaras, *ArchEph* 1973, 75–80), and Gouves (D. Vallianou, in S. Stiros and R.E. Jones, *Archaeoseismology* [Exeter 1996] 153–67, esp. 161). Horseshoe-shaped kilns with several parallel flues seem to be early, and π-shaped kilns are late. The thermoluminescence dates for the MM IB kiln 3 at Phaistos (late 19th century) and for the LM I kiln at Ayia Triada (ca. 1600) seem appropriate; Y. Liritzis and R. Thomas, "Palaeointensity and Thermoluminescence Measurements on Cretan Kilns from 1300–2000 BC," *Nature* 283 (1980) 54–55.

[12] J.D. Muhly, "Lead Isotope Analysis and the Archaeologist," *JMA* 8 (1995) 54–58; Z.A. Stos-Gale, N.H. Gale, and N. Annetts, "Lead Isotope Data from the Isotrace Laboratory, Oxford: *Archaeometry* Data Base 3, Ores from the Ae-

gean, Part 1," *Archaeometry* 38 (1996) 381–90; Z.A. Stos-Gale and C.F. Macdonald, "Sources of Metals and Trade in the Bronze Age Aegean," in N.H. Gale ed., *Bronze Age Trade in the Mediterranean* (*SIMA* 90, Jonsered 1991) 249–88; M.S. Tite, "In Defence of Lead Isotope Analysis," *Antiquity* 70 (1996) 959–62; N.H. Gale, "The Isotopic Composition of Tin in Some Ancient Metals and the Recycling Problem in Metal Provenancing," *Archaeometry* 39 (1997) 71–82.

[13] J.H. Musgrave et al., "The Priest and Priestess from Archanes-Anemospilia: Reconstructing Minoan Faces," *BSA* 89 (1994) 89–100. In several studies, P.J.P. McGeorge argues for surprisingly low age-of-death rates (35 in EM, 34 in MM, and 30 for the LM period), a condition that she links to the Minoan economy that prized sheep for their wool and stored commodities (oil, wine, grain) high in carbohydrates; see "Νέα στοιχεία για το μέσο όρο ζωής στη μινωϊκή Κρήτη," *Κρητική Εστία* series 4, vol. 1 (1987) 9–15; "Biosocial Evolution in Bronze Age Crete," in *Ειλαπίνη: Τόμος τιμητικός για τον Καθηγητή Νικολάο Πλάτωνα* (Athens 1987) 407–16; and "A Comparative Study of the Mean Life Expectation of the Minoans," *6th CretCong* A1 (1990) 419–28.

[14] M. Blomberg and H. Göran, "*Minos Enneoros*: Archaeoastronomical Light on the Priestly Role of the King in Crete," in P. Hellström and B. Alroth eds., *Religion and Power in the Ancient Greek World* (Uppsala 1996) 27–39; G. Henriksson and M. Blomberg, "Evidence for Minoan Astronomical Observations from the Peak Sanctuaries on Petsofas and Traostalos," *OpAth* 21 (1996) 94–114.

[15] Stiros and Jones (supra n. 11).

the Thera volcano.[16] The subject is too complex to rehearse in its entirety here, but a few of the latest developments should be mentioned. In the field of chronometrics, Kuniholm's Aegean Dendrochronology Project[17] has established a master ring sequence (CORINA, the Cornell Ring Analysis Program) that supports a date of 1628/7 B.C. for the eruption of Thera.

According to the traditional (low) chronology, based largely on cross-dating with the other cultures of the Mediterranean, the Late Bronze Age begins ca. 1600, with a date for the eruption of the Thera volcano late in the LM IA phase ca. 1500 B.C. The earlier date for the Thera eruption shifts the beginning of the Late Bronze Age even earlier, to ca. 1700 B.C. At present, the high dating for the Thera eruption seems marginally more likely to be correct, and in a recent survey of the material, Manning has suggested a "revised high chronology," which is employed here with slight modifications (table 1), in conjunction with the low Egyptian chronology that is now favored by many Egyptologists.[18]

Since LM IA pottery, but no LM IB pottery, was found in eruption deposits on Thera, LM IA must end after 1628/7, let us say ca. 1600 B.C. LM IB now appears to be a longer period than was formerly believed, but its end shortly before the long reign of Tuthmosis III in Egypt is increasingly supported by recent radiocarbon dates.[19] LM II, a transitional pottery style, is of short duration. There are good Aegean-Egyptian synchronisms between Tuthmosis

III and LM IIIA1, and LM IIIA1 pottery was still in use when Amenhotep III came to the throne. The latter's lengthy reign appears to cover much of LM IIIA2. Aegean pottery at Amarna shows that the transition between LH IIIA2 and B1 occurred toward the end of the 14th century B.C. LH IIIB2 is approximately contemporary with some or most of the 19th Dynasty in Egypt, and LH IIIC with the 20th Dynasty.

The Aegean revised high chronology and the traditional low chronology are basically in accord for the latter half of the Late Bronze Age. The primary revision comes at the beginning of the period, with the Neopalatial period contemporary with the late 13th Dynasty in Egypt, the Hyksos period, and the very beginning of the 18th Dynasty, rather than coinciding entirely with the early 18th Dynasty.

The physical effects of the Thera eruption on surrounding areas are being debated as well. Seaborne pumice, if occurring in post-destruction contexts, may indicate industrial, ritual, or other uses; Theran airborne ash and seaborne pumice have been recovered at a number of sites.[20] Ash has been detected at Gournia, Knossos, Mallia, Nirou Chani, Pyrgos, and Vathypetro in Crete, Phylakopi in Melos, Trianda in Rhodes, Cyprus, Anatolia, the Nile valley, and the Near East (Syria and Israel); larger deposits come from LM IA levels at Palaikastro and Pseira, sealed between LM IA and LM IB floors at Mochlos, in the Dodecanese and Anatolia, and even in the Black Sea region.[21] Pumice has been found in a LM IA destruction level at Poros (brought by tsunami?)

[16] For good summaries and bibliography, see J.L. Davis, "Review of Aegean Prehistory I: The Islands of the Aegean," *AJA* 96 (1992) 735–36; C.W. Shelmerdine, "Review of Aegean Prehistory VI: The Palatial Bronze Age of the Southern and Central Greek Mainland," *AJA* 101 (1997) 539–41. See also S.W. Manning, "Dating the Aegean Bronze Age: Without, with, and beyond Radiocarbon," in K. Randsborg ed., *Absolute Chronology: Archaeological Europe* (ActaArch 67, Suppl. 1, Copenhagen 1996) 15–37; K.P. Foster and R.K. Ritner, "Texts, Storms, and the Thera Eruption," *JNES* 55 (1996) 1–14. On the physical dynamics of the eruption, see various authors in *TAW* III.2; and Manning, *The Absolute Chronology of the Aegean Early Bronze Age* (Sheffield 1995) 200–16.

[17] Project reports are available on line: http://www.arts.cornell.edu/dendro/. P.I. Kuniholm et al., "Anatolian Tree Rings and the Absolute Chronology of the Eastern Mediterranean, 2200–718 B.C.," and C. Renfrew, "Rings, Tree Rings and the Old World," *Nature* 381 (1996) 780–83 and 733, respectively; Kuniholm, *AJA* 99 (1995) 99–102; Shelmerdine (supra n. 16) 539–40, n. 8.

[18] Manning 1995 (supra n. 16) 217–29.

[19] S.W. Manning, "From Process to People: Longue Durée to History," in *Aegean and Orient.*

[20] C. Renfrew, "Obsidian and Pumice," in *Acta of the 1st*

International Scientific Congress on the Volcano of Thera (Athens 1971) 430–36; J. Driessen and C.F. Macdonald, *The Troubled Island* (in preparation), sections 5.2 and 7 give the circumstances and bibliographies, including A.L. Wilson, "The Presence in Crete of Volcanic Ash from Thera," *AJA* 80 (1976) 419–20.

[21] Trianda: thick ash layers have been reported in LM IA levels in two different parts of the town: *AR* 38 (1992) 58–59; *AR* 41 (1995) 59. Dodecanese: ash occurs in LM IA levels at Seraglio on Kos: *AR* 41 (1995) 58; and in LM I levels on Karpathos: E.M. Melas, *BICS* 29 (1982) 131. Turkey: D.G. Sullivan, *AJA* 97 (1993) 330 (abstract). Nile valley: D.J. Stanley and H. Sheng, *Nature* 320 (1986) 733–35. Crete: J.A. MacGillivray et al., *BSA* 87 (1992) 121–52, esp. 134; *AR* 41 (1995) 69 (Palaikastro). P.P. Betancourt et al., *TAW* III.3, 96–99; Betancourt and C. Davaras eds., *Pseira* I: *The Minoan Buildings on the West Side of Area A* (Philadelphia 1995) 134–36 (Pseira). J. Soles and Davaras, *TAW* III.3, 89–95; J. Soles, R. Taylor, and C. Vitaliano, *Archaeometry* 37 (1995) 385–93 (Mochlos). Black Sea region: F. Gulchard et al., *Nature* 363 (1993) 610–12. Egypt: Tell el-Dab'a: P. Jànosi, *Atti del 6° Congresso internazionale di egittologia* 1 (1992) 345–49, esp. 348; M. Bietak, *Avaris: The Capital of the Hyksos* (London 1996) 77–78.

Table 1. Modified High Minoan and Low Egyptian Chronology*

```
- 1750 -------------------------------------
    N    neopalatial palaces rise
    E      MM III
    O      1750-1700
- 1700 -------------------------------------        13th Dynasty - 1759-1606

    P
    A      LM IA
    L      1700-1580
    A                                                     ------------------------------
    T.   Thera eruption ca. 1628                         15th (Hyksos) Dynasty
                                          ----------------------   1637-1529
- 1600                                     17th Dynasty (Thebes)
                                           1606-1539

         ------------------------------------

         LM IB
         1580-1490

                                           18th Dynasty - 1539-1296 --------------------
                                            Ahmose I        1539-1514   Hyksos expelled
-1500                                       Amenhotep I     1514-1493   Dab'a frescoes
         ----Cretan destructions ------------- Tuthmosis I  1493-1481
    F      LM II          Mycenaean        Tuthmosis II     1481-1479
    I      1490-1430      presence?        Hatshepsut       1479-1457   |
    N                                      Tuthmosis III    1479-1425   | Keftiu  tomb
    A      ------------------------------              | paintings
    L                     transition       Amenhotep II    1427-1392   |
         LM IIIA1         period
- 1400   1430-1370
                                           Tuthmosis IV     1392-1382
    P    . . . . . . . . . . . . . .       Amenhotep III    1382-1344
    A      LM IIIA2    Knossos destruction
    L      1370-1320                       Akhenaten        1352-1336
    A      -----------------------------   Smenkhkare 1338-36; Tutankhamen 1336-27
    T.                                     Ay               1327-1323
                        Knossos final      Horemheb         1323-1295   Uluburun  wreck
- 1300   early          destruction                                     ca. 1316
         palatial administration ends      19th Dynasty - 1295-1186--------------------
                                            Ramses I 1295-1294; Seti I 1294-1279
    P      LM IIIB                          Ramses II        1279-1213
    O      1320-1200
    S
    T    late                              Merenptah        1213-1203 Libyans attack Delta
                                           Amenmesses       1203-1200
- 1200   ---------------------------------- Seti II, Siptah, Tewosret 1200-1186
                                           20th Dynasty - 1186-1069 --------------------
    P    early                             Setnakht         1186-1184
    A                                      Ramses III       1184-1153   Sea Peoples
    L    LM IIIC   1200-1100
    A                                      Ramses IV - VI   1153-1136
    T.   late                              Ramses VII 1136-29; Ramses VIII 1129-26
                                           Ramses IX        1126-1108
- 1100   ----------------------------------- Ramses X        1108-1099
                                           Ramses XI        1099-1070/69
         Subminoan
         (transition to Iron Age)
         1100-1000/975
         ------------------------------------
```

* Revised Aegean high chronology based on S.W. Manning, *The Absolute Chronology of the Aegean Early Bronze Age* (Sheffield 1995); Egyptian low chronology based on K. Kitchen, "The Basics of Egyptian Chronology in Relation to the Bronze Age Aegean," in P. Aström ed., *High, Middle, or Low? Acts of an International Colloquium on Absolute Chronology Held at the University of Gothenburg 20th–22nd August 1987*, pt. I (Göteborg 1987) 37–55.

and in levels postdating the LM IA destruction at Palaikastro; pumice also comes from mature LM IA deposits at the Amnisos villa, Arkalochori, Chania, Mallia palace (IX: 2) and houses (Zb, Zg, E), Nirou Chani, Palaikastro, and Zakros (palace and House F), and from other deposits throughout the Levant and in Egypt.[22]

The effects of the Theran eruption on Crete have been variously interpreted. Because the prevailing winds carried ash east and southeast, some scholars have thought it likely that East Crete may have been hard hit by ash fall, perhaps enough to cause widespread famine. Others, however, more plausibly minimize the effects, suggesting, at worst, a loud bang and a light coating of pumice on the northeastern part of the island that might even have been beneficial to agriculture.[23]

Since the final stages of the Thera eruption must have been visible from the north coast of Crete, the psychological effects of the disaster may have been more devastating than the physical. Economically, the Thera eruption must have forced an immediate reorganization of trade routes, for Thera no longer could have functioned as a critical staging post or emporion for trade. While it is possible that the eruption marks the beginning of a slow shift in the balance of power from the Minoans to the Mycenaeans even before the end of the Neopalatial period, certainly one consequence would have been to shift the direct communication between Crete and the mainland westward through Kythera and West Crete in the latter half of the Neopalatial period.[24]

NEOPALATIAL CRETE (MM III–LM IB)

Sites and Architecture

The main foundations of Neopalatial Crete were laid in the Protopalatial period (MM II) with the rise of complex society on Crete, the appearance of peak sanctuaries on low mountains, the continuing use of communal tombs, the emergence of the major

palaces with monumental architecture, sealing administration, a push toward urbanization, and evidence for foreign contacts.[25] The causes of the interruption between the Proto- and Neopalatial periods have not been determined satisfactorily, but major MM II destructions, often by fire, have been noted at Knossos, Phaistos, Mallia (especially Quartiers Mu and Nu), Monastiraki, Apodoulou, and Galatas (figs. 1–3).[26] The trend toward centralization represented by the first palaces may not have been accomplished without resistance. Nevertheless, there seems to have been no significant break in Minoan culture, and the rise of the new palaces appears to signal architectural and administrative consolidation at these centers, probably at different rates at different sites.

At many sites, new building and expansion occurs in MM III/LM IA. The Knossos palace underwent extensive rebuilding or remodeling in the MM IIIB/LM I transition, traces of which are particularly apparent in the west wing.[27] Recent studies have shown that this expansion is not limited to palatial centers: at Chania, the MM II settlement, remains of which are extensive, was cut back for the construction of MM III/LM I buildings; at Ayia Triada, the villa was built in two stages over an earlier Protopalatial building; at Kommos, a monumental Protopalatial building, AA, was replaced by a monumental Neopalatial building, T. A general trend observable in LM I, toward fewer but larger sites than in MM II, has been noted in the Mesara and Mallia plains. The MM III–LM I foundations or refoundations at many sites are accompanied by extensive terracing, often using megalithic blocks. For instance, the small plateau at Petras was terraced throughout, with a monumental fortification wall with square towers around the base of the hill.

While it is fair to say that, architecturally, Crete reaches its greatest degree of complexity in the Neopalatial period, it is also clear that our general assessment of developments during this period has been simplistic. Neopalatial Crete is not a monolithic

[22] AR 38 (1992) 68; AR 41 (1995) 69.

[23] Vallianou (supra n. 11); H. Sigurdsson, S. Carey, and J.D. Devine, "Assessment of Mass, Dynamics and Environmental Effects of the Minoan Eruption of the Santorini Volcano," in TAW III.2, 100–12. Some possible effects of the eruption on East Crete are discussed by S. Hood, "The Eruption of Thera and Its Effects in Crete in LM I," 3rd CretCong (1973) 111–18. We are grateful to L.H. Cole for a valuable recent reassessment (personal communication).

[24] E. Schofield, "Plus and Minus Thera: Trade in the Western Aegean in Late Cycladic I–II," TUAS 7 (1982) 9–14.

[25] Watrous (supra n. 1) 735–36, 747–50.

[26] J. Driessen and I. Schoep, "The Architect and the

Scribe: Political Implications of Architectural and Administrative Changes on MM II–LM IIIA Crete," in Politeia 649–64.

[27] See Raison 1993 (supra n. 3); W.-D. Niemeier, "Knossos in the New Palace Period (MM III–LM I B)," in Evely et al. (supra n. 1) 71–88; and AR 42 (1996) 40–41. The Temple Repositories were filled in MM IIIB or LM IA: Hallager I, 54–56; M. Panagiotaki, "The Temple Repositories of Knossos: New Information from the Unpublished Notes of Sir Arthur Evans," BSA 88 (1993) 49–91; I. Pini, "The Hieroglyphic Deposit and the Temple Repositories at Knossos," Aegaeum 5 (1990) 33–60.

entity that rises uniformly in MM III/LM I and falls at the end of LM IB: rather, the period is punctuated by a series of destructions and rebuildings at almost all sites, and these may have occurred at different times in different places, and perhaps for different reasons. For example, two Neopalatial building phases have been recently distinguished at Pyrgos. Significant LM IA destructions have been documented in recent years at a number of sites, many of them attributed to earthquakes. Palatial Building T at Kommos passed out of use before the end of IA and a pottery kiln was constructed in its south stoa. The Galatas palace (discussed below) declined and passed out of use in IA. Vathypetro seems to have been abandoned in LM IA after an earthquake. At Petras, an earthquake in LM IA may have occasioned much remodeling; the small palace was altered and continued in use in reduced circumstances in IB. The town at Palaikastro has evidence of severe earthquake damage in LM IA, followed by deliberate demolition of buildings; some areas of the town were unoccupied at the time of the IB destructions. Two wells at Palaikastro with primary deposits datable to IB also contain material probably from the IA destructions.[28]

Some of the changes on Crete may be attributable to the eruption of the Thera volcano late in LM IA, though as noted above, the degree of severity of the attendant factors is debated. In several cases, Theran pumice appears to have been deposited deliberately following the destruction, perhaps in ritual circumstances. At Petras, some of the pumice was deposited in conical cups set on the steps of a monumental stairway, perhaps as votive offerings.[29] On Pseira, pumice was used as part of the fill under the floor of a LM IB shrine with wall frescoes in relief. Pumice was also deposited under the blocked doorway of a room used as a shrine at Nirou Chani.[30]

In LM IB, it is not entirely clear how extensively the palaces at Knossos and Phaistos were functioning as administrative or habitation centers (they both lack significant deposits of LM IB pottery), but a number of villas show signs of architectural modifications, particularly in increased storage capacity and the restriction of access through areas with pier-and-door partitions (polythyra). The town at Ayia Triada consists mainly of several houses north and east of the villa apparently in two phases, one dating to the end of MM III, the other destroyed in LM IB, though at least one room contained a destruction fill with much LM IA pottery.[31] The town at Zakros is spread over two hills, Ayios Antonios to the west and a long ridge north and northeast of the palace.[32] At least 10 houses on Ayios Antonios and an additional 15 on the northeast ridge have been excavated, revealing a closely packed settlement with large houses, many of which are terraced. At least one house, Hogarth's House A, was destroyed by fire presumably in LM IB, but other houses, like Hogarth's I/J, were destroyed by earthquake, while some of the houses on Ayios Antonios seem to have been abandoned in LM IA.

The situation is similarly uneven in East Crete. The town of Mochlos seems to have been expanding, perhaps under an influx of new settlers.[33] A LM IB industrial area has been identified on the shore of Crete opposite Mochlos, and a farmhouse at Chalinomouri was established nearby at the same time. The town on Pseira reached its greatest size with ap-

---

[28] Pyrgos: *AR* 41 (1995) 68; Kommos, Building T: *AR* 42 (1996) 42–43; Vathypetro: *Atlas* 282–85; J. Driessen and I.A. Sakellarakis, in R. Hägg ed., *The Function of the "Minoan Villa"* (Stockholm 1997) 63–77; Petras: *AR* 41 (1995) 69–70; Palaikastro: *AR* 41 (1995) 69. These wells were used into LM IIIA–B as dumps that included a fragment of a relief rhyton, sandstone horns of consecration, and large bulls' horns.

[29] Personal communication, M. Tsipopoulou.

[30] M.S.F. Hood, "The Destruction of Crete c. 1450 B.C.," *BICS* 20 (1973) 152.

[31] Phaistos: *Atlas* 232–43; F. Carinci, "The 'III fase protopalaziale' at Phaestos," in R. Laffineur ed., *Transition: Le monde égéen du Bronze moyen au Bronze récent* (*Aegaeum* 3, Liège 1989) 73–80; E. Fiandra, "La cretula del vano 10 a Festòs," in Rocchetti (supra n. 7) 15–26; *AR* 41 (1995) 63. Ayia Triada: *Atlas* 70–77; F. Halbherr, E. Stefani, and L. Banti, "Haghia Triada nel periodo tardo palaziale," *ASAtene* 39 (1977) 9–342; L.V. Watrous, "Ayia Triada: A New Perspective on the Minoan Villa," *AJA* 88 (1984) 123–34; and the following articles in Hägg (supra n. 28): V. La Rosa, "La 'Villa Royale'

d'Haghia Triada," 79–89; R. Koehl, "The Villas at Ayia Triada and Nirou Chani and the Origin of the Cretan *Andreion*," 137–49; P. Rehak, "The Role of Religious Painting in the Function of the Minoan Villa: The Case of Ayia Triadha," 163–75. See also *AR* 36 (1990) 70–71; *AR* 37 (1991) 67–68. It is possible that the rebuilding of Phaistos did not go smoothly or quickly, and that administration of the western Mesara moved first to Kommos Building T early in LM IA and subsequently, later in LM IA, to Ayia Triada when the villas there were completed (*Kommos* I.2: 392–96).

[32] Zakros: *Atlas* 292–301; D.G. Hogarth, *BSA* 7 (1900–1901) 121–49; *Zakros*; *Ergon* 1990, 127–32; *AR* 36 (1990) 73; *AR* 37 (1991) 71; *AR* 38 (1992) 64.

[33] Mochlos: *Atlas* 186–93; J.S. Soles and C. Davaras, *Hesperia* 61 (1992) 413–45; Soles and Davaras, *Amaltheia* 94–97 (1993) 45–65; Soles and Davaras, *Hesperia* 63 (1994) 391–436; Soles and Davaras, *Hesperia* 65 (1996) 175–230; Soles, *AJA* 97 (1993) 302 (abstract); Soles, *AJA* 98 (1994) 306 (abstract); *AR* 36 (1990) 75; *AR* 37 (1991) 74–75; *AR* 38 (1992) 67; *AR* 41 (1995) 68.

proximately 60 buildings.[34] Within Mochlos, however, House B2 was modified when an extra column base was inserted between two existing columns, perhaps to provide additional support for a sagging roof. At Petras, much of the LM IA settlement was abandoned, and a decline in the quality of LM IB architecture has been observed. Similarly, as noted above, less of the area of the town of Palaikastro was occupied in IB than in IA.

It is also clear that our terminology for describing some of the main architectural features on Crete during the Neopalatial period is no longer adequate. Within the architectural landscape of Crete, there have been three traditional foci of investigation: the palaces, villas, and towns. As noted earlier, however, attempts have been made in recent years in many parts of the island to understand these in terms of their wider territorial settings.

The archaeological preoccupation with the Minoan palaces is evident in the very title of this review, but the meaning of the term is still being debated even after a symposium was dedicated to the subject in 1984.[35] The term "palace" has traditionally been applied to large court-centered buildings with sophisticated stone architecture that provided for the storage of agricultural produce and its distribution to the surrounding community, housed workshops, and served ritual needs.[36] In Protopalatial Crete, the palaces generally functioned as the heads of agricultural states, whose territories may have been defined by the natural landscape.[37] An important role of the palaces was the systematic manufacture of wine, beginning in the Protopalatial

period and peaking in the Neopalatial era, and of oil, beginning in the Neopalatial period and peaking in Final Palatial times.[38] If we are to think away the usual romantic notions about what constitutes a palace, we might do better to substitute the more neutral term "regional center," especially since there is no evidence that the protopalaces or new palaces were the seats of authority for a king or queen.[39]

Four major Neopalatial palaces with Protopalatial predecessors have been excavated on Crete: Knossos, Phaistos, Mallia, and Zakros. These vary in size. Three of the palaces (Knossos, Mallia, and Phaistos) are also characterized by a sizable west court crossed by raised walkways, like modern sidewalks. A fifth palace recently identified at Galatas in the Pediada plain near Kastelli is still being excavated. A sixth (undiscovered) palace may have existed at Chania in the west, and it would be surprising if there is not a seventh still to be discovered in the Rethymnon area, perhaps at Stavromenos-Chamalevri east of the modern town. Monumental Building T at Kommos consists of four wings arranged around a central court larger than the one at Zakros but smaller than the one at Phaistos; by current definitions, it too could be classed as a palace, perhaps even including its Protopalatial predecessor AA.[40] A sumptuous building at Tourkogeitonia in Archanes near Knossos has architecture that looks palatial, but it has not been excavated in its entirety, and thus it is not clear whether a central court is present.[41]

Some court-centered buildings are much smaller than the main palaces, an example of which is currently being excavated at Petras in northeastern

[34] Pseira: *Atlas* 262–67; P.P. Betancourt, in *Politeia* 163–66; Betancourt and C. Davaras, *Cretan Studies* 1 (1988) 35–37; Betancourt and Davaras, *Hesperia* 57 (1988) 207–25; Betancourt and Davaras (supra n. 21); E.S. Banou, *Pottery Groups from the West Side of Area A at Pseira, Crete* (Diss. Univ. of Pennsylvania 1992); *AR* 36 (1990) 76; *AR* 37 (1991) 75–76; *AR* 42 (1996) 47.

[35] *Palaces* 235–41 (J. Moody); 255–60 (G. Kopcke); 251–53 (S. Alexiou); 261–67 (M. Wiener).

[36] Various authors in *Palaces*. See also K. Branigan, "Social Security and the State in Middle Bronze Age Crete," *Aegaeum* 2 (1988) 11–16; P. Halstead, "On Redistribution and the Origin of the Minoan-Mycenaean Palatial Economies," in E. French and K. Wardle eds., *Problems in Greek Prehistory* (Bristol 1988) 519–30; Halstead, "Agriculture in the Bronze Age Aegean: Towards a Model of Palatial Economy," in B. Wells ed., *Agriculture in Ancient Greece* (Stockholm 1992) 105–17.

[37] J.F. Cherry, "The Emergence of the State in the Prehistoric Aegean," *PCPS* 30 (1984) 18–48; Cherry, "Politics and Palaces. Some Problems in Minoan State Formation," in C. Renfrew and J.F. Cherry eds., *Peer Polity Interaction and Socio-Political Change* (New York 1986) 19–45; K. Bran-

igan, "Social Transformation and the Rise of the State in Crete," in *Politeia* 33–40; M.K. Dabney, "The Later Stages of State Formation in Palatial Crete," in *Politeia* 43–47; S.W. Manning, *Before Daidalos. The Origins of Complex Society and the Genesis of the State on Crete* (Diss. Cambridge Univ. 1995).

[38] Y. Hamilakis, "Wine, Oil and the Dialectics of Power in Bronze Age Crete: A Review of the Evidence," *OJA* 15 (1996) 1–32, esp. 24–25; R. Palmer, *Wine in the Mycenaean Palace Economy* (Aegaeum 10, Liège 1994); K. Kopaka and L. Platon, "Ληνοί μινωϊκοί. Installations minoennes de traitement des produites liquides," *BCH* 117 (1993) 35–101.

[39] Various papers in P. Rehak ed., *The Role of the Ruler in the Prehistoric Aegean* (Aegaeum 11, Liège 1995).

[40] See J.S. Soles, "The Gournia Palace," *AJA* 95 (1991) 72–73 for defining attributes of a palace. Kommos: *Atlas* 148–53; *Kommos* I and III; J.W. Shaw, *AJA* 98 (1994) 305–306 (abstract); Shaw, in *Palaces* 101–10; J.W. Shaw and M.C. Shaw, *Hesperia* 62 (1993) 129–90; *AR* 36 (1990) 71; *AR* 38 (1992) 60; *AR* 41 (1995) 61; *AR* 42 (1996) 43.

[41] Archanes Tourkogeitonia: *Atlas* 59–62; *Archanes* 27–48; E. Sapouna-Sakellaraki, *BCH* 114 (1990) 67–102; I. Sakellarakis and E. Sakellaraki, *ArchEph* 1991, 169–218; *AR* 32 (1986) 85–86; *AR* 36 (1990) 71.

Crete.[42] Makriyialos in southeastern Crete is another example that, despite its court, is an architecturally unsophisticated structure probably only a single story in height.[43] For Gournia, a case has recently been advanced for identifying its main building as a palace in its LM IB phase, although here the court is actually the town's plateia, and the palace encloses it only on the north and west sides, exactly as the villa at Ayia Triada encloses the "cortile superiore."[44] As more and more court-centered buildings are discovered, it is becoming clearer that the presence of a central court alone is not a good indicator of whether a building was a palace. Central courts vary in size from 1,458 m² in the case of Knossos, the largest, to just 78 m² in the case of Petras and Palaikastro Building 6, with a wide range in between.[45] The court in Building T at Kommos is shorter than those in the major palaces, but proportionately much wider.

Thus, not only are there more palaces than we had suspected, but some seem to exist in the immediate territory of another (Archanes is only 8 km from Knossos, and Kommos 7 km from Phaistos and Ayia Triada). Given the wide range of court-centered buildings in Neopalatial Crete, it would be useful if we knew more about how they functioned in relationship to one another and to their communities. Also, now that we are coming to recognize varieties of court-centered buildings across Crete, it is increasingly clear that two structures stand apart from the rest as "superpalaces" in terms of sheer size and architectural sophistication: Knossos and Phaistos.

With the rise of the new palaces in MM III–LM I certain general changes have been noted. These palaces have less space for storage and redistribution, but more areas for ceremonial activity. Access to the palaces from outside becomes more restricted. In most cases, the dimensions of the central court are reduced. This situation contrasts markedly with the more fluid boundaries of the earlier palaces.

Two new court-centered buildings discovered at Galatas and Petras change our fundamental concept of the Minoan palace. Galatas, excavated by G. Re-

themiotakis,[46] crowns a small plateau overlooking the Pediada, with a steep precipice on the west side and gentler slopes to the north, south, and east (fig. 4). Traces of a substantial surrounding community, including a house with floral fresco decoration, have been detected. From its location, this center must have commanded routes northeast to Kastelli, south to Arkalochori, and northwest to Knossos.

A large paved central court oriented north–south is enclosed by wings; that on the east has been almost completely excavated (including a pillar hall with four piers enclosing a large rectangular hearth, a polythyron, and storerooms with pithoi), the west and south wings are poorly preserved, and the north wing remains to be investigated, except for a small stoa bordering on the court. There appears to be no room for a west court on the plateau. At the north end of the central court is an impressive facade of ashlars resting on a substantial euthynteria, and at least 50 ashlar blocks on the site carry deeply carved mason's marks.

The phasing at Galatas appears substantially different from the other palaces: there is occupation in EM I/II and MM IB–II, but apparently no palace in MM II. The east wing, constructed in MM IIIA, has Knossian affinities in architecture, pottery, and scraps of frescoes with pictorial decoration in miniature; the west wing, overlying substantial architectural remains of the MM II period, dates to MM IIIB/LM IA. The main phase of the complex is MM IIIB–LM IA, but it seems to have been in decline before a destruction in IA, since only remodeling, including door blockings, was undertaken during this period. Thus far there are no traces of LM IB or LM III material at all, and at the end of the Neopalatial period Galatas may have been supplanted by Kastelli.

Petras, excavated by M. Tsipopoulou, lies a little to the east of Siteia and almost on the coast, occupying a small plateau overlooking the surrounding territory where the Pandelis River empties into the sea. Here, the central court, oriented north–south, is quite small, with the most extensive wing located to the west. The building is actually larger in its LM IA

[42] Petras: M. Tsipopoulou, *AAA* 20 (1987) 11–30; Tsipopoulou, *Αρχαιολογία* 28 (1988) 46–48; Tsipopoulou, *AJA* 100 (1996) 387 (abstract); *AR* 32 (1986) 94; *AR* 35 (1989) 105–106; *AR* 36 (1990) 76; *AR* 37 (1991) 76; *AR* 41 (1995) 69–70.

[43] Makriyialos: *Atlas* 172–74; C. Davaras, *5th CretCong* (1985) 77–92; Davaras, in Hägg (supra n. 28) 117–35.

[44] Gournia: *Atlas* 104–11; H.A.B. Hawes et al., *Gournia, Vasiliki, and Other Prehistoric Sites on the Isthmus of Hierapetra, Crete* (Philadelphia 1908); J.S. Silverman, *The Gournia Collection in the University Museum* (Diss. Univ. of Pennsylvania

1978); Soles (supra n. 40).

[45] Sizes of courts in court-centered buildings: Knossos 27 × 54 m (1,458 m²); Phaistos 22.5 × 63 m (1,417.5 m²); Mallia 23 × 48 m (1,104 m²); Kommos Building T, 38 × 29 m (1,102 m²); Galatas 16 × 36 m (576 m²); Gournia ca. 17.5 × 25 m (437.5 m²); Zakros 12 × 29 m (348 m²); Palaikastro Building 6, 7.3 × 10.7 m (78.1 m²); Petras, first phase, 6 × 13 m (78 m²).

[46] We are grateful to the excavator for guiding us around the site (June 1996) and for supplying the information given here.

Fig. 4. View of Galatas, northern parts of the east wing and central court. (Courtesy G. Rethemiotakis)

phase; during LM IB, the size of the court was reduced slightly, and a series of storerooms was built at a lower level on the north, using large ashlar blocks with mason's marks, replacing the impressive, wide staircase of the earlier phase. Despite its small size, the commanding location of Petras, its wine press, Hieroglyphic documents, Linear A tablets, and small finds suggest that it was an important administrative center for the region.

In addition to the palaces, smaller freestanding buildings appeared with palatial architectural features but without central courts, which for the sake of convenience we call villas, following Evans.[47] Whether villas originated in the Protopalatial period is debated, but it is clear that the type proliferated in Neopalatial times, and began to disappear after the LM IB destructions, at the same time as many of the palace centers. This indicates that the villas and palaces formed part of the same basic system. The largest concentration of villas is located around Knossos, and the majority of excavated examples have been found in Central and East Crete, but the villa

at Nerokourou near Chania (MM III/LM I) attests to the fact that the type was already established in the west from the beginning of the Neopalatial period.[48]

At the "Minoan Villa" conference in 1992, an attempt was made to define a typology for the various types of villas and their functions, following useful guidelines set down by McEnroe for the analysis and classification of Neopalatial houses. Suburban villas cluster around palaces such as Knossos and Mallia, manorial villas served as centers in small towns, and country villas or country houses stood alone in the landscape. Some villas seem to have consisted of one structure linked to another freestanding structure that was subordinate to it: these subsidiary structures have been called villa annexes.[49]

Unfortunately, almost all of these terms are problematic. The term "villa" itself has romantic 19th-century overtones of the leisure life, and the adjective "manorial" similarly conjures up associations of a rural gentry. Such concepts may have been completely foreign to Minoan society. Moreover, the

[47] Various papers in Hägg (supra n. 28); G. Cadogan, "Was There a Minoan Landed Gentry?" *BICS* 18 (1971) 145–48; J. McEnroe, "A Typology of Minoan Neopalatial Houses," *AJA* 86 (1982) 3–19; S. Hood, "The 'Country House' and Minoan Society," in *Society* 129–35; D. Preziosi, *Minoan Architectural Design: Formation and Signification* (Berlin 1983); G. Walberg, "The Function of the Minoan Villas," *Aegean Archaeology* 1 (1994) 49–53.

[48] Nerokourou: *Atlas* 210–12; *Scavi a Nerokourou, Kydo-*

nias I (Rome 1989), rev. by J.A. MacGillivray, *AJA* 97 (1993) 360–61; S. Chrysoulaki, "Nerokourou Building I and Its Place in Neopalatial Crete," in Hägg (supra n. 28) 27–32; *AR* 37 (1991) 77.

[49] L.A. Hitchcock and D. Preziosi, "The Knossos Unexplored Mansion and the 'Villa-Annex Complex,'" in Hägg (supra n. 28) 51–62; cf. Preziosi and Hitchcock, *AJA* 97 (1993) 349 (abstract).

buildings usually called Minoan villas vary widely in size, architectural complexity, and sophistication of their contents. The villas around the Knossos palace, for example, are generally far more "palatial" in appearance than the houses around some of the smaller palaces like Mallia or Zakros.

It would be useful if we could distinguish between administrative centers and residences, and between urban and rural expressions, and so discard the term "villa" entirely. A wide range of house types, some of them quite sophisticated, have been identified in the excavated towns of Gournia, Chania, Knossos, Mallia, Mochlos, Palaikastro, Pseira, and Zakros.[50] At Kastelli, excavation under the modern town has revealed at least one large Neopalatial building of two phases. The structure is monumental and includes a Minoan hall with polythyron, storerooms with pithoi, and small finds suggestive of feasting or libations.[51]

The lack of excavation around some so-called villas makes it unclear whether they stood alone in the countryside, as they appear to us today, or in the midst of urbanized areas. For example, it seems clear that urban areas of greater or lesser extent surrounded the main structures at Ayia Triada, Archanes Tourkogeitonia, Kannia, Tylissos, Nirou Chani, Vathypetro, Pyrgos, and Nerokourou.[52] More likely to qualify as actual country houses are structures at Zou and Achladia (both inland from Siteia at the east end of Crete), at Epano Zakros, and at Sklavokambos, west of Tylissos and Knossos.[53] These are located in the agricultural hinterland, some distance away from any major palace center, but even so may have been surrounded by outbuildings and associated structures.[54] Achladia and Zou, for example, consisted of clusters of two or three buildings, and further excavation might show that their settlements were even more extensive. Some important buildings do not fit the designation of either palace or villa. At Zominthos, on the Minoan road up to the Idaian Cave, a massive building has been partly excavated that may have served as a *caravanserai*, or a hotel for visitors.[55]

Despite their architectural diversity, many town houses and even country houses imitate palatial architectural features or furnishings, a type of emulation that has been termed the "Versailles effect."[56] Such emulation need not imply control of the villas by the palaces; in fact, the evidence for late architectural modifications that include storage areas for agricultural products as at Nirou Chani and for Linear A documents as at Chania House I may suggest that during LM IB many of the town houses and country houses were taking over some palatial functions. While this apparent decentralization could be read as a sign that palatial control over outlying centers was weakening, it might signal the opposite: that the palaces were extending their control into distant regions.

It is difficult to see how some villas could have operated outside the authority of a nearby palace. Tylissos, for instance, overlooks a fertile agricultural area immediately to the west of Knossos and just 13 km from it. From Tylissos, a direct Minoan route would have led through the gorge on the slopes of the Ida massif up to Sklavokambos and eventually up to Zominthos and the Idaian Cave.

Several suggestions have been made about the

[50] Chania: Y. Tzedakis, *Prakt* 1977, 455–58; Tzedakis and E. Hallager, *AAA* 16 (1983) 3–17; Hallager and Tzedakis, *AAA* 17 (1984) 3–20; Hallager and Tzedakis, *AAA* 21 (1988) 15–55; *AR* 36 (1990) 78. Knossos: N. Roberts, *BSA* 74 (1979) 231–41; E.A. Catling, H.W. Catling, and D. Smyth, *BSA* 74 (1979) 1–80; *Atlas* 124–47. Mallia: *Atlas* 175–85; town expansion and LM IA destruction within the palace, *AR* 37 (1991) 73–74. Palaikastro: *Atlas* 222–31; R.C. Bosanquet and R.M. Dawkins, *The Unpublished Objects from the Palaikastro Excavations, 1902–1906* (BSA Suppl. 1, London 1923); J.A. MacGillivray et al., *BSA* 95 (1991) 121–47; MacGillivray et al. (supra n. 21); MacGillivray and J. Driessen, in Darcque and Treuil (supra n. 3) 395–412; *AR* 38 (1992) 67–68; *AR* 41 (1995) 69.

[51] *AR* 36 (1990) 72; *AR* 37 (1991) 68; *AR* 42 (1996) 39; *ArchDelt* 44 (1989) 428–29.

[52] Kannia: D. Levi, *BdA* 1959, 237–65; *AR* 22 (1976) 17, fig. 25. Tylissos: *Atlas* 272–75; *BCH* 79 (1955) 299–300, figs. 11–12 (later excavation and restorations). Nirou Chani: S. Xanthoudides, *ArchEph* 1922, 1–25; *PM* II.1, 282 fig. 167 (plan), 280–85. Vathypetro: *Atlas* 282–85; Driessen and

Sakellarakis (supra n. 28). Pyrgos: *Atlas* 202–209; G. Cadogan, in *Sanctuaries* 169–71; Cadogan, in Hägg (supra n. 28) 99–103; *AR* 41 (1995) 68.

[53] Zou: *Ergon* 1956, 110–13; *Prakt* 1957, 232–40; *Zakros* 44–45. Achladia: *Atlas* 48–50; Kanta 178; *Ergon* 1959, 142–47; L. Platon, in Hägg (supra n. 28) 187–202; M. Tsipopoulou and L. Vagnetti, *Achladia. Scavi e ricerche della Missione greco-italiana in Creta Orientale (1991–1993)* (Rome 1995); *AR* 38 (1992) 64–65. Epano Zakros: *Zakros* 70–71. Sklavokambos: S. Marinatos, *ArchEph* 1939–1941, 69–96.

[54] L. Nixon, "Neopalatial Outlying Settlements and the Function of the Minoan Palaces," in *Palaces* 95–98.

[55] *Ergon* 1988, 165–72; I.A. Sakellarakis, "Ιδαίο Αντρο: Η μινωϊκή και η ελληνική λατρεία," *CretChron* 29–30 (1988–1989) 22–27.

[56] M.H. Wiener, "Crete and the Cyclades in LM I: The Tale of the Conical Cups," in *Thalassocracy* 17. See also comments by C. Renfrew, "Introduction: Peer Polity Interaction and Socio-Political Change," in Renfrew and Cherry (supra n. 37) 1–18.

identity of the occupants of the town houses and country houses. To some, they were members of a wealthy upper class who were taxed by the palaces and took part in the palatial redistributive system.[57] Others have suggested an agricultural base for at least some of these people, as members of a Minoan landed gentry.[58] A third suggestion is that the villas were the seats of members of a priestly class in a theocratic state.[59] It is quite likely that these regional centers performed several or all of these functions, at least in part.

All of the operating palaces were surrounded by towns, though some towns like Pseira flourished without palaces. The main organizing architectural feature in most towns was the plateia, or town square, which probably served the same centralizing function as the palatial courtyards. Like the palaces, many of the towns seem to have had mixed economies that depended on a combination of agriculture, seafaring, and trade. We do not yet know how to read the architecture of these towns in relation to that of the palatial centers, however, and several types of political structures thus may have coexisted throughout the island.

Most of the excavated towns are concentrated at the east end of the island.[60] Gournia, at the north end of the Isthmus of Ierapetra, was excavated at the beginning of the 20th century by a pioneering pair of women archaeologists, Harriet Boyd and Edith Hall. The architecture of most of the houses there is fairly humble. Along the north coast of Crete east of Gournia are two more extensively excavated towns, Mochlos and Pseira. Mochlos, originally a small peninsula and now an island, had protected harbors and several impressive houses. A small town flourished on the island of Pseira, which had the only south-facing harbor on the north shore of Crete.[61] The larger town of Palaikastro at the east end of Crete is currently being excavated; there are many impressive buildings, but as yet no sign of a palace. New settlements are continuously being identified, like the one near the Achladia tholos in East Crete, and a MM III–LM I settlement at Episkopi Pediados.[62]

These and other examples suggest that Neopalatial Crete may have been far more densely settled than we have suspected.

At the western edge of the Mesara plain stands the major port town of Kommos; it undoubtedly had an important relationship with the nearby palace at Phaistos and villa at Ayia Triada. At Zakros, there is evidence for a substantial Protopalatial and Neopalatial town occupying the hills around the palace. A major town existed at the west end of the island, at Chania, under the modern city.

One of the salient features of Neopalatial Crete, which separates it from the cultures of the Cyclades and the mainland at this time, was the degree to which it was urbanized. No single site has yet been excavated in its entirety, excepting Neopalatial Pseira, and thus we do not know the exact size of any Neopalatial center on Crete itself; nonetheless the size of some Neopalatial urban areas can be estimated. The tight spacing of the houses at Chania, Zakros, and Palaikastro implies that some of the major Cretan centers might have compared favorably in extent with the highly urbanized centers in the eastern Mediterranean.

At Knossos, the eastern limit of occupation is bordered by the lower slopes of the Ailias ridge across the Kairatos stream, while the higher slopes behind the Stratigraphic Museum should curtail the settlement to the west; the Vlychia stream with the Gypsades cemeteries beyond should bound the settlement on the south, while the Zapher Papoura cemetery should be beyond the settlement to the north. With the palace itself at slightly under 1.5 ha, we can estimate the area of urban Knossos around it as a rough rectangle slightly over 0.5 km wide and slightly under 1 km long, or about 50 ha in extent, almost exactly the size of Venetian Candia (Herakleion). If the populations were also roughly equivalent, urban Knossos might have had an approximate population of 17,000.[63] Knossos is unique in Crete not only in its estimated size, but also in the complexity and variety of its architectural forms.

Many of the houses at sites that have been exca-

[57] Watrous (supra n. 31).

[58] G. Cadogan, in Hägg (supra n. 28) and Cadogan (supra n. 47).

[59] S. Hood, "The Magico-Religious Background of the Minoan 'Villa,'" in Hägg (supra n. 28) 105–16.

[60] S.D. Indelicato, "Minoan Town Planning—A New Approach," BICS 33 (1986) 138–39; J. Driessen and J.A. MacGillivray, "The Neopalatial Period in East Crete," in Laffineur (supra n. 31) 99–111.

[61] Betancourt (supra n. 34).

[62] AR 36 (1990) 71.

[63] M.H. Wiener, "The Isles of Crete," TAW III.1, 129–33 gives formulas for size and population. Candia's Venetian population of 17,000 on the eve of the Turkish conquest in 1669 (C. Davaras, Guide to Cretan Antiquities [Park Ridge 1976] 140) yields the reasonable ratio of 340 people per hectare. Hood and Smyth (supra n. 3) 10 estimate a population of 12,000 on 40 densely settled hectares; cf. the similar estimate by T.M. Whitelaw, in Society 339–40, fig. 73. Cf. estimates for Troy: M. Korfmann, in Politeia 179–80, pl. XXX.

vated so far are quite large, seldom under 100 m² on the ground floor, and most are equipped with at least one upper floor as well. Despite the large size of most houses, however, there are few features that allow us to determine the function of various rooms. There are few fixed hearths or kitchen areas, for example, nor has it been possible to identify bedrooms with any degree of certainty.[64] On the other hand, baths with cement floors and drains and toilets with drains are common.

Despite the diversity of building types, Minoan architects shared several basic techniques in constructing buildings. Extensive terracing with megalithic limestone boulders was necessary to support many buildings,[65] and the techniques used in terracing were also applied to the creation of small dams on the island of Pseira and probably elsewhere. Some roads were paved, and occasional watchtowers or strong buildings overlooked strategic points.[66] Architects tended to employ materials found nearby, probably for reasons of economy, and they may have used a standard foot of approximately 33 cm.[67]

The broad range of Minoan building types is also reflected in the Neopalatial choice of materials. Poros, a soft, creamy yellow limestone, is common on the island. Gypsum, a calcium silicate, is found in several areas, notably near Knossos, Ayia Triada, and Pyrgos; it forms in crystals or sheets, and is translucent. When it is burnt (as it often was in destructions), it turns opaque white. Sandstone (*ammouda*) is found at Mallia and other sites throughout the island.[68]

Two fancifully named buildings at Knossos were constructed almost entirely of gypsum, the Royal Villa, located north of the palace, and the Temple Tomb to the south.[69] At Pyrgos, architects found a convenient outcrop of poros a short distance to the

west of the site and a gypsum source to the east, permitting the use of both materials in the local villa. The sandstone used in the Gournia "palace" was probably quarried at Mochlos to the east. At Pyrgos, Gournia, and other sites near the coast, it was probably easier to ship these materials by sea rather than transport them over land.

A very hard, close-grained blue limestone (*sideropetra*), found on Cape Sidero, was used in East Cretan architecture, especially for thresholds and column bases. A less fine blue limestone is the basic bedrock of Crete and mainland Greece, and unworked or hammer-dressed boulders of this stone were piled up into irregular courses for terrace walls and the lower walls of major buildings. These walls of megalithic rubble on Crete are basically the same as cyclopean masonry on the Greek mainland.[70] On Crete, these same blue limestone blocks were also trimmed for thresholds and column bases, sometimes leaving a rough, unworked part below ground or floor level where it would not be visible. Green, blue, or maroon schist, mottled green serpentine, and pink limestone were also used for pavers for exposed floors and for architectural accents, and all of these materials might be used as regular interior floor paving or for a patchwork effect of irregular pieces, separated by thin bands of plaster painted a contrasting color, often red. Waterproofed floors for bathrooms were paved with *tarazza*, pebbles set in a plaster mortar.

The Minoan love of architectural polychromy goes back at least into MM II, when a house at Mallia was given a floor of red plaster panels separated by strips of white plaster.[71] Neopalatial architectural polychromy is extravagant. At Pseira, red plaster, sometimes with white borders, was laid in strips, perhaps between wooden frames. Although Building 6 at Pa-

[64] K. Kopaka, "Des pièces de repos dans l'habitat minoen du IIᵉ millénaire avant J.-C.?" in Darcque and Treuil (supra n. 3) 217–30.

[65] V. Fotou, "L'implantation des bâtiments en Crète à l'époque néopalatiale: Aménagement du terrain et mode d'occupation du sol," in Darcque and Treuil (supra n. 3) 45–73.

[66] Y. Tzedakis et al., "Les routes minoennes: Rapport préliminaire. Défense de la circulation ou circulation de la défense?" BCH 113 (1989) 43–75; Tzedakis, "Ο δρόμος στη μινωϊκή Κρήτη," 6th CretCong A2 (1990) 403–14; Tzedakis, "Les routes minoennes: Le poste de Hiromandres et le controle des communications," BCH 114 (1990) 43–62; S. Chrysoulaki and L. Vocotopoulos, "Το αρχαιολογικό τοπίο ενός ανακτόρου. Η έρευνα επιφανείας στην περιοχή του μινωϊκού ανακτόρου Ζάκρου Σητείας," Αρχαιολογία 49 (1993) 70–78.

[67] J.W. Graham, "Further Notes on the Minoan Foot," 2nd

CretCong (1968) 157–65; M.L. Lang, The Palace of Nestor at Pylos in Western Messenia II: The Frescoes (Princeton 1969) 225.

[68] J.W. Shaw, "Minoan Architecture: Materials and Techniques," ASAtene 49 (1971) 1–256. For gypsum, see P.M. Warren, Minoan Stone Vases (Cambridge 1969) 132; N.H. Gale et al., JAS 15 (1988) 57–72. For sandstone, see M.J. Becker, ArchDelt 30 A (1975) 44–85; Becker, JFA 3 (1976) 361–74; J.S. Soles, JFA 10 (1983) 33–46.

[69] Royal Villa: PM II, 396–413. At the back of the Minoan hall there is even gypsum veneer over a wall of gypsum blocks. Temple Tomb: PM IV.2, 962–1018; for illustrations, see CM pls. 46–47. The Temple Tomb is the subject of a forthcoming study by E. Hatzaki.

[70] J. Zielinski is currently writing a dissertation on the use of cyclopean architecture in the sociopolitical organization of Minoan regional territories.

[71] AR 11 (1965) 29, fig. 36.

laikastro was demolished before the end of the Neopalatial period, surviving traces show that it had floors of maroon schist, green schist, and creamy limestone, blue limestone column bases, and piers of mottled green serpentine. At Archanes, blue limestone column bases are set in a creamy poros threshold. In the South Propylaeum at Knossos, blue-green schist slabs were used as pavers around a cemented pebble floor.[72] Ornamental stone is also suggested in wall paintings, and patterns imitating veined marble were painted on the walls of a lustral basin at Chania and in the Knossos palace.[73]

Several distinctive masonry styles are known. Neopalatial Crete only rarely had fortification walls, but these were of the same megalithic blocks and boulders used in other buildings.[74] Dry masonry constitutes entire walls at Zominthos. Megalithic rubble is used to great effect in the west facade of the Zakros palace, where it creates an impression of strength, and, in the town on the hill above, House G commands attention not only by its location but also for its extensive use of these rough limestone boulders. Ashlar masonry of various types can be found on Crete as early as the Protopalatial period, but its use expands greatly in the Neopalatial era.[75] Because shaping ashlar was time-consuming, and therefore expensive, it is not uncommon to find ashlar used sparingly, around doorways, and as quoin and anta blocks. Occasionally immense blocks are employed: one at Kommos is more than 3 m in length. Even in the palaces, ashlar was often used judiciously (the west facade at Mallia, and the west side of the central court at Zakros). Long stretches of ashlar are an impressive sight, though such facades were usually constructed of pseudo-ashlar blocks (rectangular in exterior elevation, roughly trapezoidal on the interior of walls) or orthostats set atop a footing course.

Orthostats are thought to be an architectural feature mainly of the Protopalatial palaces, and they appear only rarely in Neopalatial structures like the Little Palace at Knossos and Building T at Kommos.[76] The gypsum orthostats resting on a euthynteria course visible in the west facade of the Knossos palace are probably remnants of the Protopalatial phase; above them, and on top of a horizontal timber, the walls were constructed of rubble, not the ashlar blocks that appear in many reconstructions.[77]

Enigmatic mason's marks were sometimes incised on ashlars of poros, sandstone, or gypsum, not always on the exposed outer wall surface.[78] Designs include the double ax, trident, stars, branches, and other motifs, several of which appear as signs in Linear A. As a general rule, deeply cut mason's marks are early (Protopalatial), and shallower ones late (Neopalatial). In the central courts at Phaistos and Galatas, blocks with mason's marks were reused as pavers in the Neopalatial era.

Walls meant to support a second story are thick and have an inner and outer face flanking a rubble core or fill. Half-timber construction, also used for upper courses of walls, employed wooden beams in a variety of ways. Horizontal beams laid on and doweled into ashlar supported wooden frames filled with rubble, and tie beams laid through the rubble wall core were mortised into ashlar faces by swallowtail clamps. Such wooden constructions added elasticity to the wall in case of an earthquake.[79]

The floors in upper story rooms were sometimes paved with thin, square slabs of stone with beveled edges so that they would rest securely on the roofing beams of the rooms below. These slabs are generally of schist, but elegant gypsum pavers were used at Pyrgos. Although Neopalatial red painted floors are common, the MM III Zebra Fresco, painted in black and white stripes in a building outside the Knossos palace, shows that interesting variations did exist.[80]

Stone was often used more sparingly in upper stories, and the Minoans made considerable use of mudbrick for these and other walls and for internal partitions.[81] In some buildings, closets were constructed of mudbrick, as in the Zakros palace and town, where

[72] *PM* II.2, 691, fig. 434.

[73] A Knossos fresco depicts a facade resembling Giali obsidian: *PM* I, 446 fig. 321. Chania: M. Andreadaki-Vlasaki, *AAA* 21 (1988) 56–76. Knossos: Immerwahr 178 Kn no. 41: from the east wing of the palace, MM III.

[74] Gournia and Petras may be two examples: Driessen and Schoep (supra n. 26). The Zakros wall encircling the south side of the palace is not a fortification wall.

[75] J.W. Shaw, "The Development of Minoan Orthostates," *AJA* 87 (1983) 213–16.

[76] *AR* 38 (1992) 62.

[77] Shaw (supra n. 68) 88–91; R. Hägg, "On the Reconstruction of the West Facade of the Palace at Knossos," in

Palaces 129–33.

[78] Shaw (supra n. 68) 109–11; S. Hood, "Mason's Marks in the Palaces," in *Palaces* 205–10; we are grateful to S. Hood for supplying us with new information.

[79] J. Driessen, "Earthquake-Resistant Construction and the Wrath of the 'Earth-Shaker,'" *JSAH* 46 (1987) 171–78.

[80] M.A.S. Cameron, "New Restorations of Minoan Frescoes from Knossos," *BICS* 17 (1970) 163–66, esp. 166; E.S. Hirsch, *Painted Decoration on the Floors of Bronze Age Structures on Crete and the Greek Mainland* (*SIMA* 53, Göteborg 1977) 7–22.

[81] Shaw (supra n. 68) 187–205.

mudbrick chests or cists at floor level were used for the storage of goods.

Both ground floor rooms and upper stories could have porches with one or two wooden columns resting on stone bases. Longer stoas used columns and/or piers (sometimes alternating, as at Mallia and Pyrgos), a building form that anticipates the architecture of Archaic and Classical Greece. A pair of impressive stoas, not identical in their arrangement, face each other across the central court of the palatial Building T at Kommos.

Columns were generally of wood resting on circular stone bases and surmounted by square abaci; most of the latter have not survived and so were probably made of wood as well.[82] The bases were often of blue limestone, though red was available at Pyrgos. Breccia, an ornamental stone also used for vases, was employed for column bases in the Knossos palace, along with gypsum bases that were sometimes colossal. Columns represented in frescoes are often painted red, sometimes black, and usually taper significantly from top to bottom. In the Little Palace at Knossos, impressions of fluted columns have been preserved, and a cruciform base at Ayia Triada suggests another type of shaped column.

Windows are found throughout Neopalatial buildings, looking out of ground floor rooms to exterior spaces (e.g., Zominthos, Ayia Triada, Mochlos, Nirou Chani, and Zou) and communicating between interior spaces (e.g., Nirou Chani, Ayia Triada, Tylissos House A). Large windows also appear on the upper floors of buildings; offset sections in the walls of some buildings mark the probable location of such windows, as in the west facade of the Knossos palace.[83]

Several architectural components of buildings are characteristic of Neopalatial Crete but are found only rarely in the Cyclades and not at all on the mainland. These include polythyra, which made it possible to subdivide rooms on specific occasions,[84] light wells to illuminate interior rooms without admitting wind and dust, pillar rooms with one, two, or four massive rectangular piers, sunken pits or lustral basins (discussed below; we do not know their exact function, but they were probably not bathrooms as

some have suggested), and a large rectangular reception room that we label the Minoan hall.[85] These modular elements were capable of almost infinite placement: no two Neopalatial buildings have the same plan.

The stone piers for pier-and-door partitions have several different shapes, most commonly resembling the capital Greek letter iota or gamma, and less often the letter tau. These piers are often made of poros or gypsum. Usually only the lowermost pier block was of stone, with mudbrick, timber, or rubble employed above. The general lack of pivot holes in the sills between piers indicates that wooden doors were rare, and curtains may have been used instead.

Pillar rooms (sometimes misleadingly called pillar crypts) are a feature of palaces and villas: these are usually square or rectangular rooms with thick walls that supported a room on the upper story. Inside are square piers, sometimes monolithic, of poros, sandstone, or even gypsum in the case of the Royal Villa at Knossos. Pillar rooms are often considered to have a cultic function, but many have been found to contain large storage pithoi, and they may simply be storage areas.[86] One pair of basement pillar rooms in Building B-2 at Mochlos has a large window looking onto a street outside the building.[87]

A small stone-lined cist or impluvium is a feature of some houses, mainly at Knossos and in East Crete. In the Royal Villa and Little Palace at Knossos, such sunken cists are a feature of the pillar rooms, perhaps intended for drainage since they may be connected to channels. An example lined with pink limestone to match the rest of the floor appears in the light well of the Pyrgos villa, and another, drained by a covered channel, exists in Building B-2 at Mochlos. On Pseira, an impluvium with a drain has been identified as part of a bathroom, and another was excavated at Palaikastro. One example in the east wing of the palace at Galatas is enigmatic; since it contained burnt material, the excavator has considered it a hearth.

A number of palaces and villas also have low stone benches of similar design. They occur around the walls of the Knossos throne room and its anteroom.

[82] Shaw (supra n. 68) 111–25; B. Wesenberg, *Kapitelle und Basen* (Düsseldorf 1971); cf. H. Plommer, "A Carved Block from the Megaron of Mycenae," *BSA* 60 (1965) 207–11.

[83] J.W. Graham, *The Palaces of Crete* (Princeton 1972) 162–64; Hägg (supra n. 77).

[84] J.M. Driessen, "The Minoan Hall in Domestic Architecture on Crete: To Be in Vogue in Late Minoan IA?" *Acta-ArchLov* 21 (1982) 27–92; N. Marinatos and R. Hägg, "On the Ceremonial Function of the Minoan Polythyron," *OpAth*

16 (1986) 57–73.

[85] J.W. Graham, "The Residential Quarter of the Minoan Palace," *AJA* 63 (1959) 47–52; Driessen (supra n. 84); L. Hitchcock, "The Minoan Hall System: Writing the Present Out of the Past," in M. Locock ed., *Meaningful Architecture* (Avebury 1994) 14–43.

[86] Gesell 26–29, for a discussion of the evidence; Begg 29–32.

[87] Soles and Davaras 1994 (supra n. 33) 410.

At both Ayia Triada and Archanes Tourkogeitonia, benches lined three sides of rooms that opened onto courtyards, suggesting that the benches may have served for special gatherings.[88] In the villas at Pyrgos and Nirou Chani, gypsum benches are situated to provide a view of the interior of the light well.

Despite the richness and variety of Minoan Neopalatial architecture, much of its meaning still eludes us.[89] Almost certainly, different architectural styles conveyed different messages to the Minoans, with megalithic rubble signaling low-level (local) administration, poros ashlar a higher level (provincial or national), and gypsum (where available) denoting structures that included administrative and religious functions. These visual distinctions among different masonry styles may have been especially important as clues for a largely nonliterate population. The importance of architecture on Neopalatial Crete is underscored by its frequent representation in a variety of media.[90] The architecture of palace and peak is shown on sealstones and metal rings, as terracotta models, and on stone relief vessels.

Tombs and Burials

In contrast to the rich and varied architecture of the Neopalatial period, there is a relative dearth of evidence for tombs, though even this situation has changed slightly in recent years. Of the cemeteries close to the Knossos palace, only Mavro Spelio seems to have had extensive Neopalatial use.[91] On the Kephala ridge north of the Knossos palace, a MM III–LM I tholos tomb was constructed of limestone and gypsum ashlar blocks.[92] The Temple Tomb south of Knossos on the road to Archanes was used for burials in the Final Palatial period, but its orig-

inal Neopalatial use is unknown, and it may not have been planned originally as a tomb.[93]

At Poros, one of the harbor towns of Knossos, cave-tombs of several chambers were hollowed out of the soft *kouskouras* during MM II–LM IB and served as ossuaries for hundreds of burials, and similar tombs have been excavated at the Minoanized site of Kastri on Kythera.[94] One tomb at Poros, excavated in 1967, has already been published, and a second, excavated in 1986–1987, was in use in MM III–LM I, with rich and unusual finds.[95] A few Neopalatial chamber tombs have been identified at Rethymnon, and some MM III pithos burials at Pachyammos and Sphoungaras.[96] The large funerary complex at Archanes Phourni was apparently in continuous use from MM II onward, but again there is little evidence for Neopalatial burials.

The relative dearth of identifiable Neopalatial tombs contrasts starkly with the large role of tomb cult in Minoan society in the Pre- and Protopalatial periods and in Final and Postpalatial times. Before the Neopalatial era, built tombs of several forms were used as ossuaries for communal burials, and many tombs were equipped to allow the living to gather, perhaps on ceremonial occasions as well as at the time of burial. From this evidence, Branigan and Soles have hypothesized a widespread veneration of the dead ("cult of the dead"), with the tombs serving as focal points for rituals enacted by the surrounding community.[97] N. Marinatos has made this earlier cult a centerpiece for her reconstruction of later Minoan religion.[98]

While it is remotely possible that accidents of excavation have caused Neopalatial tombs to be missed, it is reasonable to assume that if tombs had been

---

[88] Koehl (supra n. 31) suggests that some of these may have been used by men for drinking ceremonies, anticipating the later Greek *andreion*.

[89] J. Driessen, "The Proliferation of Minoan Palatial Architectural Style, I: Crete," *ActaArchLov* 28–29 (1989–1990) 3–23; J. McEnroe, "The Significance of Local Styles in Minoan Vernacular Architecture," in Darcque and Treuil (supra n. 3) 195–202.

[90] K. Krattenmaker, *AJA* 95 (1991) 291 (abstract); Krattenmaker, *Minoan Architectural Representation* (Diss. Bryn Mawr College 1991); Krattenmaker, in Rehak (supra n. 39) 49–59; Krattenmaker, in *CMS* Beiheft 5 (Berlin 1995) 117–33.

[91] Hood and Smyth (supra n. 3) 12, 53, no. 251.

[92] R.W. Hutchinson, "A Tholos Tomb on the Kephala," *BSA* 51 (1956) 74–80.

[93] M.R. Popham, *The Destruction of the Palace at Knossos. Pottery of the Late Minoan IIIA Period* (*SIMA* 12, Göteborg

1970) 74.

[94] *AR* 10 (1964) 25.

[95] A. Lembesi, *Prakt* 1967, 195–209; P. Metaxa-Muhly, Μινωϊκός λαξευτός τάφος στον Πόρο Ηρακλείου (Athens 1992). N. Dimopoulou-Rethemiotaki, *ArchDelt* 42 B2, Chronika (1987) 528–29; *AR* 33 (1987) 53; *AR* 36 (1990) 72.

[96] M.A. Vlasaki, "Ομάδα νεοανακτορικών αγγείων από τον Σταυρομένο Ρεθύμνης," in Ειλαπίνη (supra n. 13) 55–68; R. Seager, *The Cemetery of Pachyammos, Crete* (Philadelphia 1916); E.H. Hall, *Excavations in Eastern Crete: Sphoungaras* (Philadelphia 1912) 58–73.

[97] J.S. Soles, *The Gournia House Tombs* (Diss. Univ. of Pennsylvania 1973); K. Branigan, *Dancing with Death* (Las Palmas 1992). See also N. Marinatos, *Minoan Religion* (Columbia 1993) 13–37.

[98] Marinatos (supra n. 97) 87–98 connects Neopalatial pillar basements, presence of lamps, baetylic cults, etc., with the earlier cult of the dead.

constructed in quantity, we would have found more of them. Two recent findings give us pause: the cave-tombs at Poros, and the complete lack of Neopalatial tombs on Pseira though the entire island has been investigated. Both suggest that burials were carried out in ways that make detection difficult. One possibility that should be considered is burial at sea. It is possible that, as the Neopalatial palaces centralized societal functions and ceremonies, family and clan groups may have devised more private ways of burying and commemorating their dead.

Art

Virtually all the craft forms that flourished in the Neopalatial era originated in Protopalatial times or even earlier. The MM II workshops of Quartier Mu at Mallia, for example, provide evidence for the production of seals, decorated weapons, utilitarian metal vessels, faience, carved ivory, stone vases, and terracotta relief.[99]

The hallmarks of Minoan Neopalatial art include its tendency toward miniature scale, use of precious materials, often imported, in combination for color contrast and enhanced value, and its sharing of artistic techniques and iconographic motifs among several media.[100] Most Neopalatial workshops and their products are connected with the palaces and major villas; art can therefore be considered a form of elite expression and self-definition.

Stoneworking was the Minoan craft at which artisans excelled from early times through the Neopalatial period. The commonest types of stone in all periods were the local soft stones (2.5–4 on the Mohs scale), steatite, serpentine, sandstone, and limestone.[101] In the Neopalatial period, harder stones (up to 7+ on the Mohs scale) could be worked: the conglomerate breccia and the porphyritic lapis

lacedaemonius; minerals like lapis lazuli, hematite, and red and green marbles (often called jaspers, or antico verde and antico rosso); and especially the silicates: translucent brown agate, light blue chalcedony, red sard, transparent red cornelian, purple amethyst, and clear rock crystal. These new materials allow fine and sharp engraving that can take on sculptural nuances of great variety, color, and depth.

Most of the harder stones were imported, although their source is not always certain: rich brown agate from Egypt or even Idar-Oberstein in central Germany; breccia and amethyst should come from Egypt, cornelian from the Sinai or Mesopotamia, hematite from Mesopotamia, a light brown agate from Cambay in western India, and lapis lazuli from Afghanistan. It is possible that some rock crystal may have been local to Crete, but it was also available from Mesopotamia.[102] Only lapis lacedaemonius from Krokeai south of Sparta and both antico verde and antico rosso from Cape Tainaron are certain to be local to the Aegean, and these three stones were probably imported to Crete via Kythera.[103]

Sealstones. At the heart of most of the artistic developments of the Neopalatial period is the "glyptic revolution" (late MM II–early MM III): the introduction of the horizontal bow-lathe in sealstone engraving, which allowed the cutting of hard stones and a greater subtlety in modeling.[104] Moving the seal against the drill demanded convex surfaces to allow the artist to see clearly the point of contact; thus new shapes were developed. By the end of MM III, biconvex forms—lentoids, amygdaloids, and cushions—dominate the repertory.

The new technique, coupled with the Minoan ability to visualize sculpture in terms of both negative (intaglio) and positive (relief) space, affected a wide range of Minoan crafts: carving in ivory and wood,

[99] B. Detournay, J.-C. Poursat, and F. Vandenabeele, *Les fouilles exécutées à Mallia: Le Quartier Mu* (Paris 1980).

[100] K. Branigan, "Craft Specialization in Minoan Crete," in *Society* 23–33; G. Clarke, *Symbols of Excellence* (Cambridge 1986); M. Helms, *Ulysses's Sail* (Princeton 1988); Helms, *Craft and the Kingly Ideal* (Austin 1993); F. Matz, "The Maturity of Minoan Civilization," *CAH²* II.1 (1973) 156–59 argues that Minoan art developed first on a small scale, largely due to developments on seals.

[101] Serpentine is used here as a general term for a soft (Mohs 2–3), dull, dark (gray, gray-green) stone that is common in Crete; steatite is slightly softer (a variety of talc), greasy, shiny, and bright, with a wider color range from white to black; sandstone was used primarily in architecture: Shaw (supra n. 68) 23–24; Becker (supra n. 68); Soles

(supra n. 68).

[102] J.G. Younger, "Semi-Precious Stones to the Aegean," *ArchNews* 8:2–3 (1979) 40–44. Agate: P. Yule and K. Schürmann Yule, *CMS* Beiheft 1 (Berlin 1981) 273–82; and G.L. Possehl, *Expedition* 23:4 (1981) 39–46. Lapis lazuli: L. von Rosen, *Lapis Lazuli in Geological Contexts and in Ancient Written Sources* (*SIMA-PB* 65, Partille 1988). Rock crystal: S. Marinatos, *ArchEph* 1931, 158–60.

[103] *Archanes* 35; P. Warren, "Lapis Lacedaemonius," in J.M. Sandars ed., Φιλολάκων: *Lakonian Studies in Honour of Hector Catling* (Exeter 1992) 285–96.

[104] J.G. Younger, *Bronze Age Aegean Seals in Their Middle Phase (ca. 1700–1550 B.C.)* (*SIMA* 102, Jonsered 1993) 179–84, charts V–VIII; P.R.S. Moorey, *Ancient Mesopotamian Materials and Industries* (Oxford 1994) 74–103.

sculpted stone relief vases, relief decoration of metal vessels (both cast and repoussé), the use of intaglio molds to produce faience, glass, and metal objects, including jewelry, and the molding of ceramic relief on pottery[105] and painted plaster relief.

Technical and stylistic analyses of MBA and LBA seals have produced a fairly reliable stylistic chronology (fig. 5).[106] Sealstone engravers, continuing the figural and narrative compositions developed first in the MM II Mallia Workshop, began immediately to experiment with the finer sculpting qualities that the hard stones presented. By the end of MM III the richly modeled seals in the Chanting Priest group present impressive studies of the human figure.

In LM I two stylistic groups dominate: in the hard stones, the Mycenae-Vapheio Lion group, and in soft stones, the Cretan Popular group. The Mycenae-Vapheio Lion group exhibits a monumental style: the lions and bulls have powerful muscles and pronounced saphenous veins, while the lions also have flame-lock manes whose edges are articulated like fish gills. The seals are fairly common on the Greek mainland (e.g., the Shaft Graves at Mycenae and the Vapheio tholos) and rare in Crete. The Cretan Popular group consists of serpentine seals often depicting simple animals, monsters (e.g., the common bird-woman), and people in cult scenes. Contemporary with these seals are those used to impress the sealings in House A at Zakros.[107]

The monumental style of the Mycenae-Vapheio Lion group continues into the LM IB period in a series of groups collectively termed Almond-Eyes; typical seals show sleekly modeled bulls. Starting just before the end of the Neopalatial period and continuing into LM II, the so-called Dot-Eyes seals depict bulls whose modeling is dry and plain. Almost all these seals are made of hard stones; there is virtually no soft stone group of seals after the Cretan

Popular group until the Mycenaean Mainland Popular group datable to LH IIIA2–B1. Further developments in Minoan seals are discussed below in the section on Final Palatial art.

It is likely that seals were considered personal possessions and that a person could own, in some fashion, several. The large numbers of seals in the soft stone classes, the Mallia Workshop group in the Protopalatial period and the Cretan Popular group in Neopalatial times, found throughout settlement areas and in domestic contexts make it certain that the practice of owning and wearing seals was not restricted to the upper classes.[108] Since steatite and serpentine are commonly available in Crete, the manufacture and distribution of soft stone seals might not have been under administrative control, although a few seals in the Cretan Popular group were used to impress nodules found at Knossos and elsewhere.[109] Since the hard stone seals were made from imported material, it is likely that the regional centers commissioned artists to make them; if so, administrators may have dispensed these seals, perhaps at formal occasions. Among the many representations of people wearing jewelry and strung beads, a few depict women and men wearing a single circular bead, probably a lentoid seal, on a bracelet at their wrist.[110]

In addition to their administrative uses, seals probably also functioned as amulets,[111] and markers of status. The relationship between a seal's iconography and its owner's administrative function has not been much studied,[112] although it is assumed that gold rings with cult scenes, discussed below, probably belonged to elite members of Minoan society. It is likely, too, that seals functioned politically, with a sealstone iconography or style more popular or appropriate in one region than in another. Thus, during LM I the odd monsters by the Zakros Master would have

[105] K.P. Foster, *Minoan Ceramic Relief* (*SIMA* 54, Göteborg 1982).

[106] J.H. Betts and J.G. Younger, "Aegean Seals of the Late Bronze Age: Masters and Workshops, I: Introduction," *Kadmos* 21 (1982) 104–21; Younger, "Aegean Seals of the Late Bronze Age: Stylistic Groups," a series in *Kadmos*: 22 (1983) 109–36; 23 (1984) 38–64; 24 (1985) 34–73; 25 (1986) 119–40; 26 (1987) 44–73; 28 (1989) 101–36; Younger, *The Iconography of Late Minoan-Mycenaean Sealstones and Finger Rings* (Bristol 1988).

[107] J. Weingarten, *The Zakro Master and His Place in Prehistory* (*SIMA-PB* 26, Göteborg 1983). One sealstone from this group has survived, *CMS* XI, no. 164.

[108] J.H. Betts, in Popham et al. (supra n. 5) 192–93.

[109] Younger 1983 (supra n. 106) 124–25.

[110] P. Rehak, "The Aegean 'Priest' on *CMS* I 223," *Kadmos* 23 (1994) 76–84; J.G. Younger, "Representations of Minoan-Mycenaean Jewelry," in *Eikon* 257–93, esp. 266–68.

[111] C. Bonner, *Studies in Magical Amulets* (Ann Arbor 1950); E.A. Wallis Budge, *Amulets and Superstitions* (London 1930) 12, 306–30; J.G. Younger, "Non-Sphragistic Uses of Minoan-Mycenaean Sealstones and Rings," *Kadmos* 16 (1977) 141–59.

[112] Some scholars assume a direct relationship: I. Kilian-Dirlmeier, "Das Kuppelgrab von Vapheio," *JRGZM* 34 (1987) 197–212; H. Wingerath, *Studien zur Darstellung des Menschen in der minoischen Kunst der älteren und jüngeren Palastzeit* (Marburg 1995) 147–48. For a summary of more complex views, see J.G. Younger, "Seals and Sealing Practices: The Ancient Near East and Bronze Age Aegean," *AJA* 100 (1996) 161–65.

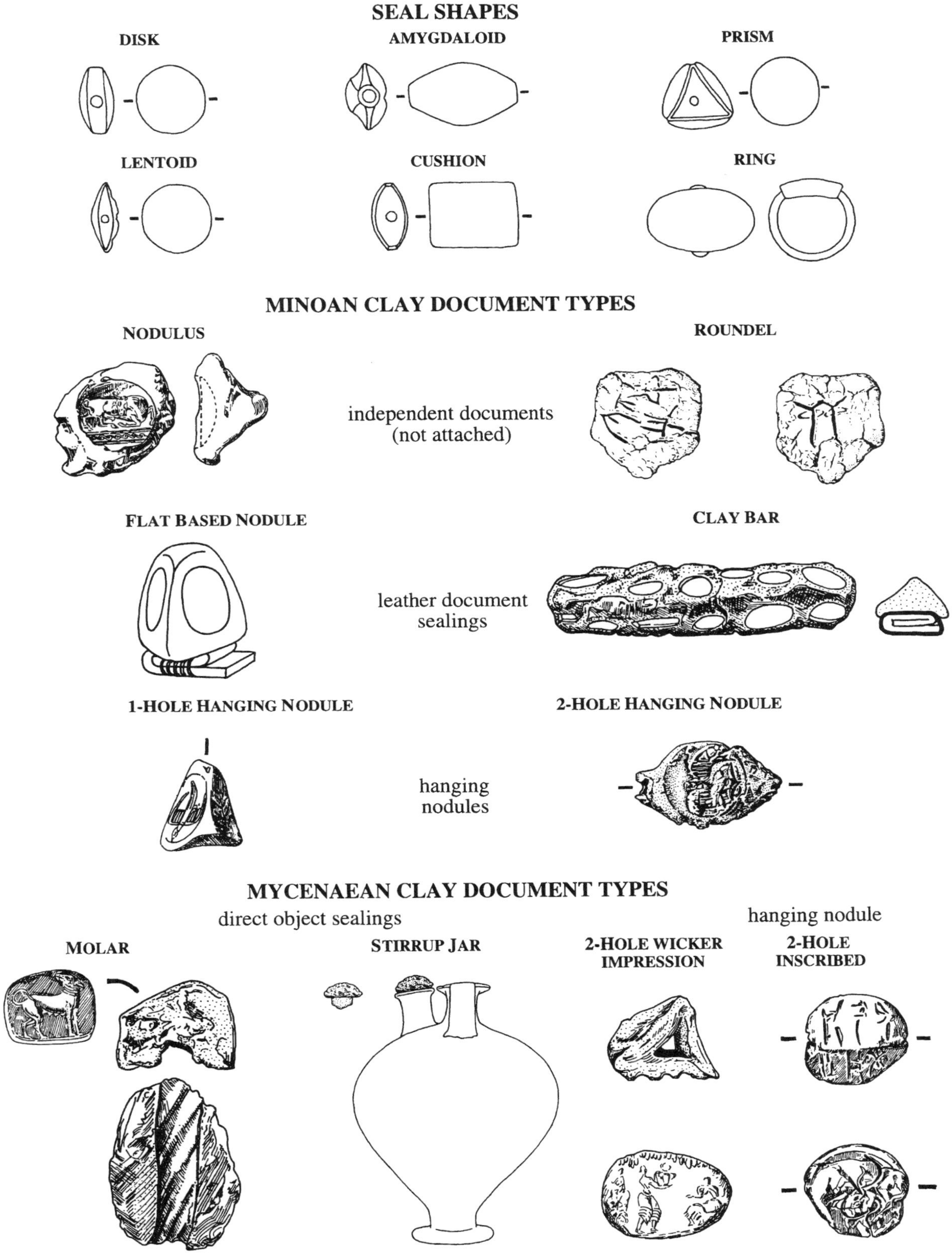

SEAL SHAPES

DISK

AMYGDALOID

PRISM

LENTOID

CUSHION

RING

MINOAN CLAY DOCUMENT TYPES

NODULUS

ROUNDEL

independent documents
(not attached)

FLAT BASED NODULE

CLAY BAR

leather document
sealings

1-HOLE HANGING NODULE

2-HOLE HANGING NODULE

hanging
nodules

MYCENAEAN CLAY DOCUMENT TYPES

direct object sealings

hanging nodule

MOLAR

STIRRUP JAR

**2-HOLE WICKER
IMPRESSION**

**2-HOLE
INSCRIBED**

Fig. 5. Diagram of seals, sealings, and clay documents. (P. Rehak and J.G. Younger; drawn by P. Rehak)

identified Zakros, and different types of bulls might have distinguished Chania from Knossos.[113]

Reliefs. Seals represent art on a miniature scale, but the technological and conceptual advances that began there soon spread to other media. Stone-workers also carved large-scale figural reliefs, though only two have survived, the pair of gypsum plaques removed from Mycenae by Lord Elgin.[114] They prob-ably had been exported from Knossos as spolia to decorate the facade of the Treasury of Atreus (LH IIIA1–2), long after their original manufacture.[115] The two reliefs are less than half life-size and depict a bovine standing to left and a bovine running to right.

Most other sculpted plaques, however, are decora-tive architectural friezes, limited to the Knossos area and difficult to date. Several segments of limestone and colored marble carved with a triglyph-half ro-sette pattern, rosettes, running spirals with dot cen-ters, or plain dado slabs with moldings along their edges once decorated the palace.[116] Fragments of column capitals carved in relief with floral petals were found in the central court: these have flat backs and mortices and so must have been nonsupporting revetments attached to a flat wall surface. Some Neo-palatial frescoes and relief frescoes show the triglyph-half rosette motif as part of the facade of palaces or shrines,[117] and it is reasonable to assume that stone and wooden friezes with these designs existed contemporaneously.

Stone vessels and other objects. Stone vases come in many shapes ranging from the purely utilitarian cups, bowls, and buckets to the more decorative blos-som bowls and relief rhyta. Because of their dura-

bility some vessels survived for centuries, and when broken they were frequently repaired or their frag-ments sometimes saved.[118] While serpentine and steatite were most common, artisans employed a range of harder ornamental stones, including banded limestone from Kakon Oros ("banded tufa"), east of Amnisos, lapis lacedaemonius and antico rosso from Laconia, and the white-spotted obsidian from the island of Giali off the coast of Asia Minor.[119] Un-worked lumps of antico rosso have been found at the peak sanctuary on Kythera and at Archanes Tourkogeitonia.[120] Although amethyst and rock crys-tal were more commonly used for beads, jewelry, seals, and inlays,[121] these materials were occasion-ally also used for special vases. Amethyst was used for two triton fragments from Mycenae and Midea, probably of Neopalatial origin though found in later contexts, and rock crystal was used for a variety of vessels, including a rhyton from Zakros.[122]

Elaborately shaped vessels were pieced together from several pieces of stone. Attached handles are common, but several vessels also have attached necks and spouts. One globular jug from the Zakros pal-ace is of veined limestone with a separately added neck and two curving handles attached to the body with bronze wires; similar vases are represented on sealstones.[123] A distinctive shape of stone vessel is the large, footed drinking cup or chalice.[124] The most spectacular surviving example, of spotted Giali obsidian, was found in the west wing of the Zakros palace. These may be palatial versions of the sim-ilarly shaped terracotta chalices, some with applied surface decoration, that have been found in large numbers at the Kato Syme sanctuary.[125] From Thera

[113] B.P. Hallager and E. Hallager, "The Knossian Bull—Political Propaganda in Neo-Palatial Crete?" in *Politeia* 547–56.

[114] J.G. Younger, "The Elgin Plaques from the Treasury of Atreus," in W. Schiering ed., *Kolloquium zur ägäischen Vor-geschichte* (Mannheim 1987) 138–50.

[115] E.B. French, "'Dynamis' in the Archaeological Record at Mycenae," in M.M. Mackenzie and C. Roueché eds., *Images of Authority* (Cambridge 1989) 122–30, esp. 124–25.

[116] *PM* II.1, figs. 83–84; II.2, figs. 368, 372, and 436; IV.1, figs. 172, 174, 175, and 191a–b; *AR* 3 (1957) 21, figs. 18–19.

[117] E.g., *PM* II.2, 597 fig. 371 and 604 fig. 377; III col. pl. XVI.

[118] Warren (supra n. 68), rev. by E.T. Vermeule, *CJ* 69 (1973–1974) 177–80. For repairs, see, e.g., a spouted ser-pentine bowl found at Knossos: Catling et al. (supra n. 50) 56, 58 fig. 41.2, 59 no. S2, pl. 13.

[119] P.P. Betancourt, "The Trade Route for Ghyali Obsid-ian," in *Techne* 171–75; C. Renfrew, J.R. Cann, and J.E. Dixon, "Obsidian in the Aegean," *BSA* 60 (1965) 50–72.

[120] P. Warren, "Κνωσός και Αρχάνες," Αρχαιολογία 53 (1994) 57–67, 67 col. fig.

[121] E.g., inlays for the gaming-board from Knossos, the

[122] K. Demakopoulou, N. Divari-Valakou, and G. Wal-berg, *OpAth* 20 (1994) 32, 34, fig. 45; Demakopoulou, in *Ae-gean and Orient; PM* III, 410 fig. 272a–b (crystal from Knos-sos); *Zakros* 139 col. fig. (upper right). The lower half of a crystal cup from Palaikastro is on display in Herakleion.

[123] *Zakros* 10 col. fig.; cf. the rhyton of white marble from Mycenae SG IV. For sealstones, see Metaxa-Muhly (supra n. 95) 100, pl. 32 no. 302, pl. 33 no. 303.

[124] Zakros: *PGC* 92–93, nos. 1152 and 1155; Thera: *PGC* 92–93, nos. 1153 and 1154; Mycenae SG IV and V: Karo nos. 600, 854; Pseira: HM 1123; Knossos: *PM* II.1, 127 fig. 62a; and Makriyialos: C. Davaras, *Hagios Nikolaos Museum* (Athens n.d.) col. fig. 48.

[125] A. Lembesi and P. Muhly, "Aspects of Minoan Cult: Sacred Enclosures. The Evidence from the Syme Sanctu-ary (Crete)," *AA* 1990, 315–36, esp. 325, figs. 10–11.

Temple Repositories (*PM* I, 470–81), and for the eyes of the bull's head rhyton from the Little Palace. A rectangu-lar plaque from Knossos is painted on the back with a bull-leaping scene (*PM* III, 108–11, col. pl. XIX). See now D. Plantzos, "Crystals and Lenses in the Graeco-Roman World," *AJA* 101 (1997) 451–64.

and the mainland come chalices that are shorter and of calcite ("alabaster"). Another special class of stone vessel consists of stone imitations of shells, especially triton shells.[126] One such probable trumpet is the dark steatite triton from Mallia displaying marine rockwork and a low relief composition of two genii.[127]

Imported baggy and ovoid alabastra of veined calcite were occasionally modified by Minoan artisans once the vessels had reached Crete, and are thus a sign of trade and intercultural contacts as well as of Minoan aesthetics. These have usually been considered Egyptian, but recently Lilyquist has suggested that some may be Syrian, and similar vessels were exchanged as prestige objects throughout the Near East.[128] One predynastic vase from the Zakros palace had been "Minoanized" through the addition of a typical Cretan beaked spout.[129] Another vessel, an alabastron, had been inverted in Crete, its original mouth plugged for a foot and its body outfitted with new handles and a spout; so modified, it was then sent on to Mycenae where it was deposited in Shaft Grave V.[130]

Black or green steatite, green chlorite, and white or colored limestones were often used to make rhyta in several shapes that imitate pottery funnels: globular, ovoid, piriform, and conical. Rhyta and other stone vessels are common finds in the palaces and major villas, even occurring in sets like those from the Sanctuary Hall deposit at the Knossos palace, Ayia Triada,[131] and the Zakros palace, where they may have been paired with chalices of similar stone.

A special class of rhyta takes the form of the heads of bovines or lions.[132] These heads were often inlaid with other materials for color contrast and to enhance their value. Since the Little Palace bull's head was found built into a wall it may have been part of a deliberate foundation deposit. Fragmentary lion-

and lioness-head rhyta of white limestone were found in the Knossos palace; a piece of the muzzle of a third was discovered under the Temple of Apollo at Delphi.

Some stone rhyta have pictorial compositions carved in low relief on their outer surface.[133] Only a few themes are represented: marine motifs, bull sports, combats and warfare, cult scenes in architectural settings suggesting palaces or peak sanctuaries, and possibly hunting scenes. The most discussed of these vessels is the Sanctuary Rhyton from Zakros.[134] A recent addition to the corpus is a fragment with dolphins from a well at Palaikastro (fig. 6). Some of these themes are also found in gold and silver plate, like the silver Siege Rhyton from Mycenae and the gold cups from the Vapheio tholos.[135] The most unusual aspect of these stone relief rhyta is that when human figures are included only men are shown, perhaps indicating that only men made and used them. The presence of some warlike elements also indicates clearly that militarism was a Minoan, and not just a Mycenaean, feature early in the Late Bronze Age. Koehl has suggested that one vessel, the Chieftain Cup from Ayia Triada, played a specific role in a male initiation rite.[136]

Relief rhyta are often discussed mainly for their artistic and iconographic value; their use remains problematic. Liquids poured in at the top would drain out at the bottom, unless a fingertip was held over the lower opening. It is usually assumed that rhyta served as wine vessels: the larger ones could have provided up to 30 servings in small conical drinking cups, but they would also have been extraordinarily heavy.[137]

Almost all relief rhyta and bovine-head rhyta, however, are found in fragments, in contrast to the many complete plain stone rhyta. It has therefore been suggested that the relief vessels may have been de-

---

[126] J.G. Younger, *Aegean Music* (*SIMA-PB* 144, in preparation); for examples, see *CM* pl. 115 (below), and Halbherr et al. (supra n. 31) 90 fig. 57.

[127] C. Baurain and P. Darcque, *BCH* 107 (1983) 3–73.

[128] P. Warren, "The Lapidary Art—Minoan Adaptations of Egyptian Stone Vessels," in *Techne* 209–23; cf. C. Lilyquist's response: *Techne* 225–28.

[129] *Zakros* 138 col. fig. (top); cf. *PM* IV.2, 976, Suppl. pl. LXVIa from the Temple Tomb at Knossos.

[130] Karo 147 no. 829, pl. CXXXVII. Cline 5–6 calls it an 18th Dynasty vessel, but Manning 1995 (supra n. 16) 229 notes that V. Hankey has identified it as a Middle Kingdom "drop vase." At the *Techne* conference in 1996, P. Warren mentioned that the plug was not cemented in place: the vessel could not have been used to contain a liquid.

[131] E.g., Halbherr et al. (supra n. 31) 60 fig. 28; 66 fig. 32; 84, 86 fig. 53.

[132] Bovines: P. Rehak, "The Use and Destruction of Mi-

noan Stone Bull's Head Rhyta," in *Politeia* 435–60. For the fragment from Zakros with gilded nostrils, add *Prakt* 1972, 180, pl. 169α–β. Lions: *PM* II.2, 827–34, 828 figs. 542a–b, 549; *CM* pl. 99; S. Marinatos and M. Hirmer, *Kreta, Thera und das mykenische Hellas* (Munich 1976) pl. 99; *PGC* 102 no. 1237, pl. 1237; Warren (supra n. 68) 90 (type E).

[133] B. Kaiser, *Untersuchungen zum minoischen Relief* (Bonn 1976), with updates: P. Rehak, "The Ritual Destruction of Minoan Art?" *ArchNews* 19 (1994) 1–6.

[134] J.W. Shaw, "Evidence for the Minoan Tripartite Shrine," *AJA* 82 (1978) 429–48; P. Rehak and J.G. Younger, *AJA* 98 (1994) 306–307 (abstract).

[135] E. Davis, *The Vapheio Cups and Aegean Gold and Silver Ware* (New York 1977) nos. 87, 103, and 104.

[136] R.B. Koehl, "The Chieftain Cup and a Minoan Rite of Passage," *JHS* 106 (1986) 99–110.

[137] The Boxer Rhyton: D. 17 cm; H. 45.5 cm, weighing ca. 1 kg empty and 3 kg full.

Fig. 6. Rhyton fragment from Palaikastro. (Courtesy L.H. Sackett and J.A. MacGillivray)

liberately destroyed after use as part of a social or religious ceremony and the fragments taken as tokens by the participants,[138] though the new Palaikastro fragment was found discarded in a well. Several of the surviving fragments are from LM IA contexts, indicating that at least some of the relief rhyta had been reduced to pieces before the end of the Neopalatial period.

Steatite or serpentine was also used for offering tables in a variety of shapes. A small percentage of these are inscribed in Linear A, and both inscribed and uninscribed offering tables are often found in peak sanctuaries and caves, less often at habitation sites.[139] An incurved example with a circular depression in the top was found in a house shrine at Knossos; the hollowed upper surface may have served as a kernos. Miniature versions of such kernoi have been found in the peak sanctuary on Mt. Juktas. Some kernoi have multiple depressions, presumably for pinches of different kinds of grain or spice, while others have small cupules that communicate with a larger, central depression, suggesting liquid offerings. Only a few examples of offering tables have been found on the mainland, all of them probably imported from Crete.[140] Some offering tables are parts of composite offering stands, like a serpentine example found at Kato Syme: the table fits atop another block with moldings and a dowel in its upper and lower surfaces, and this fits atop a serpentine pier.[141]

Another type of offering vessel, rounded at one end, tapering to a pointed tip at the other, has been called a "ladle," and is sometimes inscribed in Linear A.[142] Although some have been found in habitation sites, like the offering tables they seem to have been meant for use at peak sanctuaries, and many miniature ladles, perhaps votives, were found on Mt. Juktas. One relief rhyton fragment shows two men in procession carrying ladles toward a shrine at a higher level.[143] The suggestion has been made that ladles were used to pour liquid offerings, perhaps oil or wine, into the offering tables or kernoi.[144] If the ladles and offering tables, as well as relief rhyta, were used exclusively by men, we have an important example of the gendered use of certain types of ritual vessel.

Also distinctive are Neopalatial stone, hammer-shaped "mace-heads" found on Crete and at a few

[138] Rehak (supra ns. 132–33). Cf. R. Bradley, "The Destruction of Wealth in Later Prehistory," *Man* 17 (1982) 108–22.

[139] P. Muhly, *Minoan Libation Tables* (Diss. Bryn Mawr College 1981); I. Schoep, "Ritual, Politics and Script on Minoan Crete," *Aegean Archaeology* 1 (1994) 7–25. Kato Syme: *AR* 36 (1990) 72; Lembesi and Muhly (supra n. 125) 342 fig. 12. Juktas: *Prakt* 1975, pl. 264ς'. Psychro: *ArchDelt* 37 B1 (1982) pl. 276γ. Knossos: *AR* 3 (1957) 22–23, fig. 7.

[140] E.g., B. Kaiser, "Mykenische Steingefässe und verwandtes im Magazin zu Nauplia," *AM* 95 (1980) 1–19.

[141] L.N. Platon and Y. Pararas, *Pedestalled Offering Tables in the Aegean World* (*SIMA-PB* 106, Göteborg 1991). From Kato Syme: Lembesi and Muhly (supra n. 125) 330–31, figs.

19–22.

[142] Stone ladle from Knossos: *PM* II.2, 439 fig. 256c; and from Juktas: *Prakt* 1975, pl. 265β, and on display in the Herakleion Museum. Clay ladle from Knossos palace: *PM* I, 624 fig. 460. Inscribed examples: Archanes: *GORILA* 4, TL Zc 1; *PM* I, 625 fig. 462; *Archanes* 52 col. fig. 30. Juktas: *PM* I, 624 fig. 461 (the inscription A-JE-SA looks like a botched attempt to start JA-SA-SA-RA). Kythera: *GORILA* 4, KY Zc 2; I.A. Sakellarakis and J.-P. Olivier, *BCH* 118 (1994) 343–51.

[143] *PM* III, 65 fig. 37.

[144] K. Nikolidaki and G. Owens, "The Minoan Libation Formula," *Cretan Studies* 4 (1994) 149–55, esp. 152–53.

other Aegean sites.[145] A sealstone from Mallia shows a robed figure apparently holding such a mace, which may be a sign of status or insigne of office, as similar objects were in Syria and Egypt.[146] The shape also inspired a terracotta rhyton.[147] Only one of the Cretan examples comes from a context later than LM IB, and its form is spherical.[148]

Lamps come in a variety of stones and shapes; beginning in MM II, they become more elaborate in the Neopalatial period.[149] Most lamps have a shallow bowl for oil and have one to four depressions on the lip for the wick. Some lamps have short pedestals, while others were attached to columnar supports, the surface of which was occasionally carved in relief. A few lamps have been found outside Crete, especially at Mycenae, though one elaborate lamp comes from the palace at Alalakh. In Crete elaborate stone lamps come from Minoan halls, pillar basements, and other specialized rooms where they may have had a ritual function.

Limestone and gypsum stands or bases are usually trapezoidal in section with a hole in the top; double axes could, on analogy with the depiction on the later Ayia Triada sarcophagus, be inserted in the base. Bases with incurved sides have been found at a few sites.[150] In a few frescoes incurved

bases could also serve an architectural function,[151] primarily as supports for platforms upon which a goddess may sit or griffins may recline or for a column flanked by lions as on the Lion Gate relief from Mycenae. A unique large, pierced, porphyry pyramid from Knossos is probably a talent-weight.[152] It is carved with an octopus on one side, its tentacles embracing the other sides.

Ivories. Elephant and especially hippopotamus ivory had been imported from Syria or perhaps Egypt in the Early Bronze Age through a system of long-distance trade networks with the eastern Mediterranean.[153] Though evidence for Protopalatial ivory carving is scanty, in the Neopalatial period the carving of ivory is conducted on a large scale. A carved ivory disk found at Palaikastro, but possibly Cypriot in manufacture, and several uncarved elephant tusks from the Zakros palace attest to trade, and several workshops at the palaces handled ivory and other exotic materials.[154] Ivory was most often used for furniture inlays and cosmetic objects (especially jewelry boxes and mirror handles), as well as for a small group of figurines.

There is little evidence for the creation of large pieces of ivory furniture like beds and chairs,[155] but a small ivory footstool volute has been found at

[145] From Crete: N. Mante-Platonos, *ArchEph* 1981, 74–83. From Aegina: C. Reinhold, *ArchKorrBlatt* 22 (1992) 57–62. In the Nauplion Museum: Kaiser (supra n. 140) esp. 16 no. M69:40, 17 fig. 4, pl. 7.4. For a different stone hammer-ax from a chamber tomb at Poros Herakleion, see Metaxa-Muhly (supra n. 95) 96 no. 284, pl. 31 no. 284.

[146] *CMS* II.3, no. 147. Two maces were found in the Tomb of the "Lord of the Goats" at Ebla: M.G. Scandone, *Studi Eblaiti* 1 (1979) 119–28; Scandone, in *Studies in the History and Archaeology of Palestine* 2 (Aleppo 1986) 49–55. C. Lilyquist informs us (personal communication) that the mace may be a Syrian imitation of an Egyptian object.

[147] W. Schiering, "Ein minoisches Tonrhyton in Hammerform," *CretChron* 24 (1972) 476–86.

[148] Tomb of the Mace Bearer at Knossos (LM II–IIIA): A.J. Evans, "The Tomb of the Double Axes," *Archaeologia* 65 (1914) 18 fig. 25; *PM* IV.1, 356 fig. 299. A similar lapis lacedaemonius mace-head, apparently from the Zakros palace, was on display in the Siteia Museum in 1996.

[149] MM II: Detournay et al. (supra n. 99) 59–60 no. 95, 60 fig. 79. MM III: *PM* II.1, 298 fig. 174. A. Blasingham, *AJA* 99 (1995) 334 and *AJA* 100 (1996) 366 (abstracts); Blasingham, "Minoan Lamps in Domestic Contexts," *8th CretCong* (forthcoming). Elaborate lamps do not long survive LM IB, if at all. Archanes Tourkogeitonia: *Archanes* 35 col. fig. 18; and *Ergon* 1989, 144 fig. 135 (in situ); Ayia Triada: *CM* pl. 115 (above); Halbherr et al. (supra n. 31) 71 fig. 41, 75 fig. 46, 167 fig. 105. Zakros: *Zakros* 139 col. fig. (below), 149 fig. (above). Knossos: *PM* II.1, 124 fig. 59; II.2, 481 fig. 288a. Juktas: *AR* 36 (1990) 71. Mainland: Vapheio tholos on display in the National Museum; Mycenae Lion tholos (R. Hampe and E. Simon, *The Birth of Greek Art* [Oxford 1981]

fig. 201); Nauplion Museum: Kaiser (supra n. 140). Alalakh: L. Woolley, *Alalakh* (Oxford 1955) 294–95, pl. LXXIX.

[150] Archanes: *Archanes* 32 fig. 16. Knossos: *PM* IV.1, 209 and fig. 160a.

[151] M.C. Shaw, "The Lion Gate Relief of Mycenae Reconsidered," in *Φίλια έπη εις Γεώργιον Ε. Μυλωνάν* 1 (Athens 1986) 108–23; *PM* III, 207 fig. 141; Doumas pl. 122; *CMS* I, no. 282.

[152] H. 42 cm; W. 27 cm; Th. 13 cm; Wt. 28.6 kg. Cf. K. Petruso, *Keos* VIII: *Ayia Irini: The Balance Weights* (Mainz 1992) 38 no. 73.

[153] P. Rehak and J.G. Younger, "International Styles in Ivory Carving in the Bronze Age: The Aegean and the East," in *Aegean and Orient*; J.-C. Poursat, *Catalogue des ivoires mycéniens du Musée National d'Athènes* (Paris 1977); Poursat, *Les ivoires mycéniens* (Paris 1977); Poursat, "Ivory Carving in Minoan Crete (2000–1450 B.C.)," in J.L. Fitton ed., *Ivory in Greece and the Eastern Mediterranean from the Bronze Age to the Hellenistic Period* (London 1992) 3–5. O.H. Krzyszkowska, "Ivory in the Aegean Bronze Age: Elephant Tusk or Hippopotamus Ivory?" *BSA* 83 (1988) 209–34; Krzyszkowska, *Ivory and Related Materials* (London 1990).

[154] Palaikastro: J.A. MacGillivray et al., *BSA* 84 (1989) 426 n. 8; D. Evely, "Seeing Is Believing?" in *Techne* 463–65; Zakros: *Zakros* 210–21. Knossos: *AR* 4 (1958) 21–22; *AR* 5 (1959) 20; *AR* 6 (1960) 24; *AR* 7 (1961) 26–27. Archanes: *ArchEph* 1991, 214 fig. 44: arm and hand, 217 fig. 46: leg and foot; *Archanes* 46 col. fig. 24, 47 col. fig. 25.

[155] O.H. Krzyszkowska, "Furniture in the Aegean Bronze Age," in G. Herrmann ed., *The Furniture of Western Asia* (Mainz 1996) 85–103.

Zakros, the earliest example of a type that is better attested in LM/LH II–IIIA contexts. While the carving of furniture relief plaques goes back to MM II Quartier Mu at Mallia,[156] Neopalatial plaques and cutouts were used to decorate boxes, small chests, and other objects: butterflies, double axes (some combined with "sacral knots"), a house facade reminiscent of the faience Town Mosaic, and other plain or ornamented strips such as those that decorated the Knossos "game-board."[157]

Cosmetic objects were also made of ivory, as they were in Syria and Egypt. Cylindrical pyxides, cut from a section of elephant tusk, carry decoration on their sides and sometimes the lid; the decoration is often figural (e.g., an incised cult scene with young girls on an ivory pyxis from Ayia Triada, a bull-hunt modeled in low relief from Katsamba) but also purely decorative (e.g., spirals from Kea).[158] Other Neopalatial toilet articles are combs and mirror handles.[159] Though many of these are found in later contexts and have been considered Mycenaean works, we suggest that most are Neopalatial instead. Three mirror handles from late contexts at Mycenae present pairs of young girls in short skirts and short coiffures holding flowers or ducks; their hairstyles and costumes resemble those of the girls on the Ayia Triada pyxis and the girls in the Thera frescoes.[160] If these mirror handles are Neopalatial works, so is the technique of using rivets ornamented with lapis lazuli or blue glass disks surrounded by gold granulation to attach the handles.

The most intriguing and problematic ivories are the figurines carved in the round and usually pieced together from several pieces of hippopotamus incisor; these figures may have formed vignettes, sometimes of bull-leapers.[161] Examples have been found in the Knossos palace, along the Royal Road, at Archanes, Mallia (Chrysolakkos), and Palaikastro. The recently discovered Palaikastro ivory youth (fig. 7) had ivory flesh (one arm at least was overlaid with gold), inlaid nipples, crystal eyes, gold clothing, and an incised "wig" of black steatite.[162] The ivory figure's pose with elbows bent and hands clenched below the pectorals mimics that of MM II terracotta figurines from nearby Petsofa; it recurs rarely.[163] The shaved head with a single thick lock of hair braided down the middle characterizes the youth as adolescent rather than adult.[164] Since ivories and relief frescoes from Knossos usually depict fingernails, veins, and an elongated thumb, the occurrence of these traits on the Palaikastro youth suggests that he was commissioned from there.[165] One serious problem with the youth, however, is that at present it consists of two nonjoining halves with the tenon at the bottom of the torso having no corresponding mortise in the upper surface of the hip. Since no satisfactory reconstruction of the costume has been published for the intervening gap, the restoration of the figure, as well as its proportions, remains problematic.

None of the Neopalatial figurines from archaeological contexts is immediately identifiable as female, and it is likely that all of the ivory "goddesses" on the art market early in the 20th century are fakes.[166] A probable Neopalatial work that does depict women, however, is the Ivory Triad that comes

---

[156] Poursat 1992 (supra n. 153) 3–5, pl. 1.

[157] Zakros: E. Platon, in Ειλαπίνη (supra n. 13) 209–26, figs. 1–9. S. Hood, *The Arts in Prehistoric Greece* (Harmondsworth 1978) 121 fig. 109 (heron); *Zakros* 131 and fig. (axes), 148 fig. (butterfly); Gesell 192 fig. 89 (sacral knot).

[158] Ayia Triada: Halbherr et al. (supra n. 31) 97–98, figs. 64–65. Katsamba (LM II–IIIA): Poursat, *Les ivoires* (supra n. 153) pl. X.3 and 4; S. Alexiou, Υστερομινωικοί τάφοι λιμένος Κνωσού (Κατσαμπά) (Athens 1967) col. frontispiece, pls. 30–33; J.-C. Poursat, "Les ivoires mycéniens," *DossPar* 195 (1994) 90 col. fig. Kea: W.W. Cummer and E. Schofield, *Keos* III: *Ayia Irini: House A* (Mainz 1984) 95 no. 1083, pl. 41.

[159] A. Papaefthimiou-Papanthimou, Σκεύη και σύνεργα του καλλωπισμού στον κρητομυκηναϊκό χόρο (Salonika 1979); A.P. Iliaki, *Mycenaean Ivories* (Diss. Bryn Mawr College 1976). An ivory comb from Knossos, Royal Road (LM IB): *AR* 7 (1961) 27.

[160] Poursat, *Catalogue* (supra n. 153) no. 300 from Mycenae chamber tomb 55, and nos. 331 and 332 from Clytemnestra Tholos dromos; E.N. Davis, "Youth and Age in the Thera Frescoes," *AJA* 90 (1986) 399–406; D. Withee, *AJA* 96 (1992) 336 (abstract); Younger (supra n. 110) 288–89.

[161] *PM* III, 428–30 and II.2, 727 fig. 455; *AR* 7 (1961) 29

fig. 40.

[162] L.H. Sackett and J.A. MacGillivray, *Archaeology* 42.5 (1989) 26–31; MacGillivray et al. (supra n. 154) 426–27, 427 fig. 7 (left foot), 428 fig. 8 (drawing of upper body), pls. 62–63; MacGillivray et al. 1991 (supra n. 50) 141–44; L.H. Sackett, *AJA* 95 (1991) 293 (abstract); *AR* 37 (1991) 74–75 fig. 72 (figure completed with legs); J.H. Musgrave, in Fitton (supra n. 153) 17–23 (with clear details); J. Weingarten, in *Politeia* 249–61. For steatite hair, cf. H. Weiss ed., *Ebla to Damascus* (Washington, D.C. 1985) 166–67 nos. 73–74.

[163] Ivory statuette: Poursat, *Catalogue* (supra n. 153) 87 no. 286, pl. XXVI (cf. 116 no. 359, pl. XXXVIII); bronze statuette: Lembesi and Muhly (supra n. 125) 326 fig. 14; sealstone: *CMS* V, no. 201. Petsofa: B. Rutkowski, *Petsophas* (Warsaw 1991) 22–29, pls. A–B, 3–18, and 20–22.

[164] Davis (supra n. 160); cf. the youth in a LM IA fresco from Xeste 3, Akrotiri: Doumas pls. 109, 113.

[165] Ivories from Knossos, the palace: *PM* III, 428–35; Royal Road: *AR* 7 (1961) 25–29; cf. the Priest King's elongated thumb: *PM* II.2, 780 fig. 508.

[166] K. Lapatin, "Minoan and 'Minoan' Chryselephantine Statuary," an unpublished paper given at the *Techne* conference, Philadelphia, 18 April 1996.

Fig. 7. Ivory youth from Palaikastro. H. total figure as reconstructed, without tenons 49.9 cm. (Courtesy L.H. Sackett and J.A. MacGillivray)

from a later context from the palace at Mycenae; it represents two women and a child.[167] The Minoan court costumes that the two women wear are well understood by the artist and the patterns, including a scale motif and a net pattern, suggest a date in LM

IA, certainly no later than LM II.[168] The child, moreover, is probably a girl since it wears a robe, whereas small boys in Aegean art are usually shown nude.[169]

Frescoes. Simple painted plaster was in use already in EM II, and wall and floor paintings with abstract patterns were produced in MM times. It is not until the Neopalatial period, however, that we have our first evidence for figural frescoes, a development in which Knossos again took the lead.[170] Wall surfaces were painted in three main areas: major panels flanked by a frieze at the top of the wall and by a dado at the bottom painted solid or with ornamental patterns (often veining); ceilings and floors also afforded areas for decoration.[171]

At Knossos, the palace gives evidence for several Neopalatial phases of figural wall painting.[172] Early Neopalatial compositions include the earliest figural fresco, the Saffron Gatherer, and the Ladies in Blue and the Lady in Red. Later Neopalatial frescoes include (in LM IA) the Grandstand and Sacred Grove and Dance. If these frescoes have been correctly restored by Cameron as the decoration of a single room in the palace, we seem to have depictions of ceremonies taking place in the central and west courts,

[167] Poursat, *Catalogue* (supra n. 153) 20–21 no. 49, pl. IV. Hood (supra n. 157) 124–26, 125 fig. 114: "probably LH III A," but Hood notes (124) that the Triad shows "all the grace and attention to detail characteristic of Cretan figurines of the best period before ca. 1450" (i.e., before the end of LM IB).

[168] E. Barber has informed us (personal communication) that on the basis of dress patterns she thinks the Triad is unlikely to be later than LH II. Scale patterns on costumes in Neopalatial frescoes from Knossos (*PM* I, 545 fig. 397; II.2, 731 fig. 457; III, 297 fig. 194), and on a ship cabin fresco (LM IA) from the West House at Akrotiri: Doumas pls. 55, 58. Net pattern on costumes in the Priestess fresco from West House room 4 at Akrotiri: Immerwahr pl. 21; Doumas pls. 24–25; cf. the acrobat on the MM II gold repoussé sword guard from Mallia, in P. Darcque and J.-C. Poursat eds., *L'iconographie minoenne* (Paris 1985) 36 fig. 1.

[169] Ivory figurines from Palaikastro: *PM* III, 446 fig. 310a–b. Attendants in the fresco from Xeste 3, Akrotiri: Doumas pls. 109, 111.

[170] M. Cameron, *A General Study of Minoan Frescoes with Particular Reference to Unpublished Wall Paintings from Knossos* (Diss. Newcastle-upon-Tyne 1974), in preparation for publication by L. Morgan. New material: patterned fresco fragments from Mallia (LM IA; *AR* 37 [1991] 73), spiral relief fragments from Zakros, House Δα (*AR* 36 [1990] 73).

[171] Ceilings: Immerwahr Kn no. 38. Floors: Hirsch (supra n. 80).

[172] We follow primarily Immerwahr; C.F. Hawke-Smith, "The Knossos Frescoes: A Revised Chronology," *BSA* 71 (1976) 65–76 gives an alternative and detailed chronology.

respectively.[173] Unusually for Minoan art, these scenes include both men and women, though in each case some women are singled out as more important than the other figures in terms of their size, costume, hairstyle, and placement within the scene. These paintings thus are important evidence for the exceptional role of women in Minoan society. Outside the palace, nature scenes involving blue monkeys and other animals decorated the walls of the House of the Frescoes (LM IA). In the area of the Stratigraphic Museum, a fresco with a repeating frieze of floral garlands may date to LM IB.[174] In general, Neopalatial frescoes tended toward figures in lithe and supple movements in miniature, busy scenes, painted with a polychrome palette.

The "glyptic revolution" in sealstones may have influenced the creation of relief fresco as well, and developments in media like terracotta appliqués and molded faience plaques (for both, see below) may have played a role; the creators of relief frescoes substituted plaster for clay, expanded the scale, and added paint. The earliest-known relief fresco fragment, of MM II date from Knossos, lacks human figures,[175] but by LM I, humans, animals, and vegetation were being attempted, along with geometric motifs.

Relief frescoes emphasize the anatomy of the human body,[176] with muscles, veins, and tendons all stretched and active (cf. fig. 7). Faces, by contrast, are painted flat. Men are wasp-waisted and muscular; they wear breechcloths with codpieces but are otherwise nude. Women are usually clothed in brightly colored and patterned robes with aprons tied around the waist, but their costume exposes the breasts, which were sometimes built up on conical cups embedded in the wall (the same technique used in the contemporary large terracotta figurines from Kea).[177]

The Egyptian and Near Eastern convention of painting females white and males red is also seen in Minoan fresco; white-painted females leapt bulls as did red-painted males, and they even wore the same costume, high shoes, and wristbands. Some scholars dispute that the color convention holds in this case,[178] although this seems to be needlessly creating a problem: there is no reason why athletic young women could not have engaged in bull-leaping. The well-known and frequently reproduced Priest-King from the south entrance corridor at Knossos is problematic in its iconography and skin color, because it was reconstructed from the fragments of several figures that may not belong together.[179] The cap with floral ornaments and plume, for example, should belong to a sphinx or a woman dressed like the small faience Snake Handler.

Among the Cretan palaces, relief frescoes with human figures are a hallmark of Knossos alone. Images of bulls and male and female bull-leapers in relief dominated both sides of the north entrance passage.[180] Sophisticated relief frescoes adorned the Great East Hall located on the edge of the central court opposite the throne room.[181] Here, the relief decoration was probably renewed several times during the Neopalatial era. These phases are now difficult to distinguish, but the pictorial programs included bulls, athletic youths (bull-leapers or combatants), and important women. There are also leashed griffins, but these were probably not tied

---

[173] Immerwahr 173 Kn nos. 15–16, pls. 23–24; E. Davis, "The Knossos Miniature Frescoes and the Function of the Central Courts," in Palaces 157–61; cf. N. Marinatos, "Public Festivals in the West Courts of the Palaces," in Palaces 135–42. For a reconstruction of the room, see M.A.S. Cameron, "The 'Palatial' Thematic System in the Knossos Murals," in Palaces 321–25, 327 fig. 11; R. Hägg, "Pictorial Programmes in Minoan Palaces and Villas," in Darcque and Poursat (supra n. 168) 209–17.

[174] M.A.S. Cameron, "Unpublished Paintings from the 'House of the Frescoes' at Knossos," BSA 63 (1968) 1–31. P. Warren, "The Fresco of the Garlands from Knossos," in Darcque and Poursat (supra n. 168) 187–207; for additions, see Warren, Minoan Religion as Ritual Action (Göteborg 1988) 24–27.

[175] Kaiser (supra n. 133) 286.

[176] J. Coulomb, "À propos de l'art plastique minoen: Données anatomiques et iconométriques," RA 1978, 205–26.

[177] M.E. Caskey, Keos II: The Temple at Ayia Irini, Pt. I: The Statues (Princeton 1986); Caskey, in Sanctuaries 127–35.

[178] S.D. Indelicato, "Were Cretan Girls Playing at Bull-Leaping?" Cretan Studies 1 (1988) 39–47; N. Marinatos, "The Bull as an Adversary: Some Observations on Bull-Hunting and Bull-Leaping," Κρητική Εστία 5 (1989) 23–32; Marinatos, "Formalism and Gender Roles: A Comparison of Minoan and Egyptian Art," in Politeia 577–85.

[179] PM II.2, col. frontispiece pl. XIV, 780 fig. 508 (torso), 773 fig. 504a (plume), 776 fig. 504b (headdress), 782 fig. 510 (lower leg), 784 fig. 511 (upper thigh and backflap), 774–86; J. Coulomb, "Le 'Prince aux Lis' de Knossos reconsideré," BCH 103 (1979) 29–50; W.-D. Niemeier, "The 'Priest King' Fresco from Knossos: A New Reconstruction and Interpretation," in French and Wardle (supra n. 36) 235–44; E. Davis, "Art and Politics in the Aegean: The Missing Ruler," in Rehak (supra n. 39) 11–21; M.C. Shaw, "The 'Priest-King' from Knossos: Man, Woman, King, or Someone Else?" 8th CretCong (forthcoming).

[180] PM III, 158–77; PM IV.1, 11–18; L. Palmer, "Knossos: The High Relief Frescoes," in Forschungen und Funde (Innsbruck 1980) 325–34.

[181] PM III, 497–518; Kaiser (supra n. 133) 277–82.

to columns, as Evans thought. Another fragment, identified by Kaiser, shows a figure wearing a "hide skirt," the same garment that appears in the Final Palatial Procession Fresco from the west entrance passage, discussed below. If this identification is correct, we may have links between the Procession Fresco and the procession's ultimate destination in the Great East Hall. The hall also included flat frescoes of life-sized women in elaborate costumes and jewelry, the Ladies in Blue and Lady in Red.[182]

Toward the end of the Neopalatial period, some nonpalatial buildings were decorated with relief frescoes of elaborately dressed women. At Pseira, a small house or town shrine was decorated with two women in relief. Fragments of another relief depicting a woman were found at Palaikastro, her clothing decorated with crocuses like the Thera goddess and the faience robes from the Knossos Temple Repositories. Other relief frescoes without human figures have been identified at Ayia Triada, Zakros (the palace and Houses Δα and N), and several other sites, including at least one in the Argolid.[183]

Plaster or terracotta offering tables, circular in shape and resting on three stubby feet, were often painted in the fresco technique, and since they show no signs of burning they were evidently not portable hearths.[184] Some 40–50 of these tables were stockpiled in the villa at Nirou Chani; approximately 30 others were stored in the palatial building at Archanes Tourkogeitonia. The painting is often impressive; one found recently at Palaikastro is decorated with narcissus flowers. In this context, it may be convenient to add the large stucco horns of consecration: two come from Archanes Tourkogeitonia, and two more were found in the Knossos palace, one near the Great East Hall, and the other at the northwest corner of the central court, near the throne room complex.[185]

Ceramics. Our knowledge of painted pottery at the beginning of the Neopalatial period is uneven. Developments in West Crete are largely unknown,

while in East Crete the earlier light-on-dark style continues until LM I styles supersede it.[186] In Central Crete, a simpler, less colorful style supplants the earlier Kamares ware. On the best pottery, polychrome motifs on a dark background are repeated in zones, and the standardized high quality of the ware probably means that only a few workshops are producing it, though in large enough amounts to be exported to the Cyclades. Utilitarian pottery, instead, was produced in fewer but more specialized shapes than before. A new ware, with a lustrous dark paint on a light background, is found mainly at Knossos. Patterns include tortoise-shell ripple and thick retorted spirals. Unpainted conical cups, the drinking vessel of the period, are ubiquitous.

Although light-on-dark painted pottery continues strongly into LM I, the beginning of the LM period is heralded by the widespread appearance of new dark-on-light wares. Some vases combine the two painting schemes, like a conical rhyton from Gournia decorated with a band of antithetic quirks in light-on-dark and spirals in dark-on-light.[187] Better kilns and firing techniques produced fine, hard wares. A Floral Style and fabrics painted with finer tortoise-shell ripples appear to come from Knossos, though toward the end of LM IA local workshops elsewhere imitate these. At Kommos, for instance, light-on-dark pottery and high-quality utilitarian ware are made in the kiln associated with Building T. By the end of LM IA, tortoise-shell ripple has virtually disappeared and dark-on-light pottery has increased in importance. The shape and size of conical cups throughout Central Crete become standardized, suggesting a conventional capacity of about 61 g.

LM IB pottery is complicated. Two main classes have been distinguished: the Standard Tradition and the Special Palatial Tradition. The former represents a continuity from LM IA and a slow development. Motifs are often simplified and rendered quickly. Two major classes have been distinguished, the plain style and the polychrome style with added red and

---

[182] Kaiser (supra n. 133) 281–82, pl. 50; M.A.S. Cameron, "The Lady in Red," *Archaeology* 24 (1971) 35–43.

[183] Pseira: M.C. Shaw, "Aegean Sponsors and Artists," in *Techne* 481–504; Betancourt and Davaras, in *Hesperia* (supra n. 34) 215–19. Palaikastro: Bosanquet and Dawkins (supra n. 50) 148 and fig. 130. Ayia Triada: Halbherr et al. (supra n. 31) 89 fig. 55; Kaiser (supra n. 133) 304; Cameron (supra n. 170) 474. Zakros: *AR* 22 (1976) 31; *AR* 38 (1992) 64. Prassa: Cameron (supra n. 170) 402. The Argolid (Mycenae or Tiryns): 1) (now lost?) Immerwahr 194, MY additional no. 1; *AA* 1923, fig. 3; 2) (a second piece) Kaiser (supra n. 133) 306, fig. 473, pl. 26; U. Jantzen, *Führer durch Tiryns* (Athens 1975) figs. 35–36.

[184] Knossos: *PM* II.1, 302 fig. 175; IV.1, 180 fig. 142. Archanes: *Archanes* 38, col. fig. 21. Palaikastro: *AR* 37 (1991) 75. Nirou Chani: Xanthoudides (supra n. 52). Cf. N. Polychronakou-Sgouritsa, *ArchEph* 1982, 21–33.

[185] Archanes: *Archanes* 38, 40 col. fig. 21. Knossos: *PM* III, 19 fig. 9: plan, and 524 fig. 367.

[186] Betancourt (supra n. 4). A.M.P.A. Van de Moortel, *The Transition from the Protopalatial to the Neopalatial Society in South-Central Crete: A Ceramic Perspective* (Diss. Bryn Mawr College 1997). We are grateful to the author for the opportunity to read and cite sections of her dissertation.

[187] Betancourt (supra n. 4) fig. 100 B.

white. The Special Palatial Tradition comprises a relatively small class but its preference for unusual shapes and elaborate decoration has given it great weight in the literature. The Special Palatial Tradition has been subdivided into a Plant Style related to the earlier Floral, an Abstract/Geometric Style, the famous Marine Style, and, by the end of LM IB, the Alternating Style. Since several of these styles may coexist on a single vase,[188] it is likely that these elite wares were made in a limited number of workshops and by a few artisans.[189] Because the distribution of these wares is uniform throughout the island, it is likely that the center of production was at Knossos, though there are local varieties in the south, some apparently coming from the kiln at Ayia Triada. By the end of LM IB even utilitarian wares are emulating the high quality of elite wares.

Many of the motifs popular in LM IB pottery imitate designs that were already popular in other media in LM IA or even earlier, suggesting that even the Special Palatial Tradition is following, rather than leading, artistic developments. For example, the running spiral and lozenge pattern occurs on silverware and as a textile pattern on the large faience Snake Handler (see below) before it appears on LM IB pottery; strings of crocus buds in garlands or as necklace pendants in frescoes predate their representation on Floral Style vases.

Because of its modern aesthetic appeal, Marine Style pottery is often reproduced and discussed to the point of obscuring its highly specialized production and limited distribution.[190] Mountjoy has suggested that vases in this style may have been produced primarily at Knossos and that they had a specialized use as ritual vessels on Crete. Scientific analyses of Marine Style pottery from outside Crete, however, show that much of it represents local Cycladic or mainland imitations.[191] Thus, pot painters may be traveling more often than their wares, influencing the development of LH I mainland Mycenaean pottery.[192]

The influence of other media is apparent on much of the pottery. Some vases take their inspiration from fresco: the polychrome dolphins, rockwork, and seaweed on a LM IA painted tripod-stand in Minoan style from Akrotiri,[193] and the same elements on LM IB Marine Style vases compare favorably with fresco representations; and the garlands on LM IB pots resemble those suspended from the posts of ship cabins in the LM IA fresco from the West House at Akrotiri.[194] Some vases reflect the influence of metalwork: the spiral and arcade pattern on LM IA metalware recurs as a painted pattern on LM IB pottery.[195] Building Z at Zakros contained a pithos with a frieze of double axes in relief.[196] Other vases imitate stonework: a pithos from Pseira has a segmented collar shaped like that encircling the neck and body of some stone rhyta, and at Kythera clay imitations of stone blossom bowls were made.[197] We should consider the possibility that artists were trained and worked in more than one medium with equal versatility. Another important aspect of the painted fine wares of the Neopalatial period is that pottery was often made in pairs or sets, like some of the stone vases discussed above. This seems to be particularly true of cup rhyta and conical and ovoid rhyta.

Archaeologists tend to focus on fine, decorated wares, but plain pottery was always the most abundant. Two common Minoan shapes in domestic pottery are the small conical cups, which were produced in the tens of thousands annually, and large storage pithoi.[198] Because of their size and shape, conical cups were easy to make and served a multitude of

---

[188] E.g., Betancourt (supra n. 4) pl. 23 H.

[189] C. Floyd, "The Alternating Floral Style as Evidence for Pottery Workshops in East Crete during the Protopalatial Period," in *Techne* 313–16. Olive Spray Group: M.R. Popham, "Late Minoan Pottery," *BSA* 62 (1967) 337–51, esp. 341; Banou (supra n. 34) 157–58. The Reed Painter, Arcading Group: Betancourt (supra n. 4) 145–46, pl. 21 A–C, fig. 22 E; J.N. Coldstream and G.L. Huxley, *Kythera* (London 1972) pl. 33; Banou (supra n. 34) 159. Attempts to recognize individual artists in other media have been criticized: J.F. Cherry, "Beazley in the Bronze Age? Reflections on Attribution Studies in Aegean Prehistory," in *Eikon* 123–44, and comments, 339–44.

[190] The LM IB Marine Style was apparently very special; at Pseira it was found in only one building, BQ: Banou (supra n. 34) 145. See P.P. Betancourt, *Archaeology* 30 (1977) 38–43; Betancourt, *AJA* 81 (1977) 561; P.-A. Mountjoy, *BSA* 69 (1974) 173–75; Mountjoy, *BSA* 69 (1974) 177–78; Mountjoy, *AAA* 9 (1976) 83–86; Mountjoy, *AJA* 81 (1977) 557–60; Mountjoy, *BSA* 79 (1984) 161–219; Mountjoy, in Darcque

and Poursat (supra n. 168) 231–42. See also P.-A. Mountjoy et al., *BSA* 73 (1978) 143–72; and T. Marketou, *BSA* 82 (1987) 165–70.

[191] Jones 444.

[192] R.E. Jones and J.B. Rutter, "Resident Minoan Potters on the Greek Mainland?" *Archaeometry* 19 (1977) 211–19.

[193] Doumas pls. 181–83.

[194] Cf. a handled jar from Pseira (*CM* pl. 84, lower left) with the ship cabin fresco from Akrotiri, West House: Doumas pls. 49–62.

[195] Cf. a silver ewer from SG IV at Mycenae (Davis [supra n. 135] 149–55 no. 43, fig. 120) with cups from Archanes (*Archanes* 55 col. fig. 32).

[196] *AR* 38 (1992) 64; *Prakt* 1991, pl. 222α.

[197] Pithos from Pseira: Banou (supra n. 34) 68, 230 fig. 15 (drawing); Betancourt (supra n. 4) pl. 8 H. Clay bowls from Kythera: *AR* 10 (1964) 25 and fig. 30.

[198] C. Gillis, *Minoan Conical Cups* (*SIMA* 89, Göteborg 1990), rev. by P. Warren, *JHS* 113 (1993) 219–20; M.H. Wiener, "Crete and the Cyclades in LM I: The Tale of the Conical

purposes. In a house at Knossos, dozens of conical cups were inverted for stability and to keep the dust out, and placed on the floor of a pillar basement, while at Mochlos they were used as lamps in another basement pillar room.[199]

Pithoi were equally important and were made in quantity. These were probably built up with coils of clay on a thick disk base. Despite their large size, they were transported considerable distances; Cretan pithoi have been found in Cyprus and Sardinia.[200] Similar pithoi are still being manufactured today in the Cretan village of Thrapsano, affording the archaeologist modern parallels for manufacture and distribution. Since several of the ancient examples were inscribed in Linear A before they were fired (see below), some potters may have been literate or scribes intervened in the potting process.

Textiles. Textiles have not survived well, and their study is made more difficult by their scant mention in the Linear A texts.[201] The discovery of spindle whorls and loomweights at many sites, however, and the depiction of textiles in paintings make it possible to reconstruct some aspects of the craft. The Minoans made use of the warp-weighted loom, and were ex-pert weavers of dyed wool and probably of linen.[202] Fresco scraps with textile patterns from the Northwest Fresco Heap at Knossos augment details of costume in the other frescoes, as do the faience votive dresses and three-dimensional figurines from the Temple Repositories. Based on frescoes, there have been several convincing attempts at reconstructing costume.[203]

Metalwork. Crete is relatively poor in metals, and most of its needs must have been supplied from outside the island.[204] Well before the Neopalatial period, Crete was obtaining silver and lead from Cycladic sources, and gold may have been supplied in small quantities from Egypt or Syria. Bulk shipments of raw copper did not begin until the Late Bronze Age, and all signs indicate that Crete took an early and important lead in this trade.[205] Copper oxhide ingots first appear on Crete in LM I at Tylissos, Ayia Triada, Zakros, Gournia, Kato Syme, and possibly Kommos;[206] their weights center on 29 kg, a Minoan talent. Later, in the 15th century, Egyptian tombs from the time of Hatshepsut and Tuthmosis III show men carrying oxhide ingots. The manufacture of bronze, however, demanded tin as well as copper,

Cups," in *Thalassocracy* 17–26. Pithoi: Begg passim, esp. 91–93; C. Doumas and A.G. Constantinides, "Pithoi, Size and Symbols," *TAW* III.1, 41–44; Jones 844–47; H. Blitzer, "Κορωνεϊκά: Storage Jar Production and Trade in the Traditional Aegean," *Hesperia* 59 (1990) 675–711.

[199] *PM* II.2, 548 fig. 348; Begg 178; Soles and Davaras 1996 (supra n. 33) 190.

[200] R.E. Jones and P. Day, "Aegean-type Pottery on Sardinia," in M.S. Balmuth ed., *Studies in Sardinian Archaeology* III (Oxford 1987) 263.

[201] Studies by E.J.W. Barber include *Prehistoric Textiles* (Princeton 1991); "The Peplos of Athena," in J. Neils ed., *Goddess and Polis* (Princeton 1992) 103–17; *Women's Work* (London 1994); *AJA* 99 (1995) 303 (abstract); and "Minoan Women and the Challenges of Weaving for Home, Trade, and Shrine," in *Techne* 515–19.

AB sign 54, presumably the Linear A equivalent to B *159 TELA, functions as an ideogram on only three tablets: HT 16, 20, 27 (*GORILA* 1, 32–33, 36–37, 50–51).

[202] Little is known about the dyes, except purple: D. Reese, "Palaikastro Shells and Bronze Age Purple-Dye Production in the Mediterranean Basin," *BSA* 82 (1987) 201–206. See also J.L. Davis, "Cultural Innovation and the Minoan Thalassocracy at Ayia Irini," in *Thalassocracy* 159–65, esp. 161–63 on technology.

[203] E. Sapouna-Sakellaraki, Μινωϊκόν ζώμα (Athens 1971); G. Lyberopoulou, *Le costume égéen* (Diss. Université de Paris I 1978); C. Televantou, "Η απόδοση της ανθρωπινής μορφής στις Θηραϊκές τοιχογραφίες," *ArchEph* 1991, 135–66; P. Rehak, "Aegean Breechcloths, Kilts, and the Keftiu Paintings," *AJA* 100 (1996) 35–51.

[204] N.H. Gale, "Lead and Silver Sources for Bronze Age Crete," *5th CretCong* (1985) 365–72; Gale, "The Provenance for Metals for Early Bronze Age Crete," *6th CretCong* A1 (1990) 299–316; H.S. Georgiou, *The Late Minoan I Destruc-tion of Crete* (Los Angeles 1979).

[205] J.D. Muhly, R. Maddin, and T. Stech, "Cyprus, Crete and Sardinia: Copper Ox-Hide Ingots and the Bronze Age Metals Trade," *RDAC* 1988, 281–98; M.H. Wiener, "The Nature and Control of Minoan Foreign Trade," in Gale 1991 (supra n. 12) 325–50.

[206] H.G. Buchholz, "Keftiubaren und Erzhandel im zweiten vorchristlichen Jahrtausend," *PZ* 37 (1959) 1–40; Muhly et al. (supra n. 205); J.D. Muhly, "The Crisis Years in the Mediterranean World," in W.A. Ward and M.S. Joukowsky, *The Crisis Years* (Dubuque 1992) 10–26, esp. 18: the *ka-ko-na-wi-jo* of Pylos tablet Jn 829 is "ship copper," i.e., "ingots." Copper ingots from Neopalatial (LM IB) sites (Georgiou [supra n. 204] gives inventory numbers, sizes, weights, and inscribed marks): 1 ingot from Tylissos (J. Hazzidakis, *ArchEph* 1912, 220–22, fig. 31; weight 26.5 kg); 19 ingots in Building A at Ayia Triada (Halbherr et al. [supra n. 31] 123 fig. 85); 1 ingot fragment from Kato Syme; 4 ingot fragments from Gournia (P.P. Betancourt et al., *MASCAJ* 1 [1978] 7–8); 6 ingots from Zakros (N. Platon, in V. Karageorghis ed., *Acts of the International Archaeological Symposium "The Relations between Cyprus and Crete, ca. 2000–500 B.C."* [Nicosia 1979] 101–10; *Zakros* 116–20, fig. 117; weights 29–30 kg); and 2 Cypriot copper ingots from Kommos, "almost certainly LM I in date" (L.V. Watrous, *Kommos* III, 172; the ingots: H. Blitzer in *Kommos* I.1, 501 nos. M2–M3), though Shaw (*Kommos* I.2, 398–99, n. 6) infers a LM III date from their findspot. Whole or fragmentary ingots have also been found at Chania, Palaikastro, Juktas, and Kophinas (*BCH* 118 [1994] 822). Four other ingot fragments from Kommos may date as late as LM IIIA2 (Blitzer, in *Kommos* I, 501 nos. M1 and M4–6); these are also metallurgically consistent with a Cypriot origin (Muhly et al. [supra n. 205] 283–84).

in ratios of approximately 1:10, and a variety of sources for both metals have been postulated and are still being debated. Some of the copper from Crete has been tested but only the ingots from Kommos are of Cypriot copper and most of these, if not all, are Final Palatial. Other, Neopalatial ingots from Crete that have been tested are not Cypriot, though Cyprus was a major producer of this metal then and later in the Late Bronze Age. The sources for tin are probably located farther east.[207]

Since bronze was inherently valuable, it was continually melted down and reworked.[208] At Mochlos, several foundry hoards included ingots, ingot fragments, and broken tools that could represent scrap metal.[209] A large amount of scrap bronze was stored in the Arkalochori Cave, perhaps under religious auspices since the cave was used to house dedications such as bronze swords, along with bronze, gold, and silver double axes. The bronzes from the cave probably constitute the largest deposit of metal found anywhere in the Mediterranean.[210] Smaller amounts of bronze have been found at the sanctuaries at Kato Syme and on Juktas and Kophinas.

Lead and bronze were used for manufacturing small figurines depicting men, women, at least one child, and several agrimia.[211] Many of the anthropomorphic figurines are identifiable as men or women on the basis of anatomy, but a large number are of indeterminate sex. Of the male figurines, many wear the breechcloth with rigid codpiece and have long hair like the individuals on stone relief rhyta; females usually wear a flounced skirt and have long hair. Some figurine poses are gender-specific. Male figures often stand with one fist clenched at the forehead, the other arm held straight at the side, while women almost never assume this pose.[212]

Metal figurines were often dedicated at peak sanctuaries or in caves, presumably as votive offerings. A large number have been reported from the Minoan peak sanctuary on Kythera.[213] A group of miniature bronze "wigs" found at Knossos may have been used to complete figurines in another material.[214] A bull and leaper group said to be from Rethymnon, currently in the British Museum, is unique.[215]

Bronze was also used for weapons.[216] Type A Minoan swords were the finest in the Aegean, and they probably served as the ancestors to the subsequent sword types. Type A swords have been found in the palaces of Mallia and Zakros, and several fine blades were dedicated in the cave at Arkalochori. Before the end of the Neopalatial period, type B swords had been introduced on the mainland, though opinions differ over whether these were produced at Knossos or at Mycenae under Minoan influence.[217] Ornamented weapons first appear in the Protopalatial

---

[207] The ingots from Ayia Triada, Gournia, and Kato Syme are metallurgically similar and are not of Cypriot copper: N.H. Gale and Z.A. Stos-Gale, "Oxhide Copper Ingots in Crete and Cyprus and the Bronze Age Metals Trade," *BSA* 81 (1986) 81–100; Gale and Stos-Gale, "Recent Evidence for a Possible Bronze Age Metal Trade between Sardinia and the Aegean," in French and Wardle (supra n. 36) 349–84. The copper ingots from Ayia Irini, Kea (LM I context) are consistent with a Cypriot source, as are the ingots from the Cape Gelidonya wreck (early 13th century): A.B. Knapp, "Cyprus, Crete and Copper: A Comment on Catling's Paradox," *RDAC* 1990, 55–63, esp. 58. See too P. Budd et al., "Lead Isotope Analysis and Oxhide Ingots," *JMA* 8 (1995) 70–75; Muhly (supra n. 12); E. Pernicka, "Crisis and Catharsis in Lead Isotope Analysis?" *JMA* 8 (1995) 59–64. The mid-14th century Amarna tablets mention that the King of Alashiya was sending copper (presumably Cypriot if Alashiya is Cyprus) to Egypt. T.S. Wheeler, "The Ancient Tin Trade in the Eastern Mediterranean and Near East," *TUAS* 2 (1977) 23–26; E. Pernicka et al., *JMA* 5 (1992) 91–98; K.A. Yener and P.B. Vandiver, "Tin Processing at Göltepe," *AJA* 97 (1993) 207–38; J.D. Muhly, "Early Bronze Age Tin and the Taurus," *AJA* 97 (1993) 239–53; and Yener and Vandiver, *AJA* 97 (1993) 255–64 (reply); W.E. Sharp and S.K. Mittwede, *Geoarchaeology* 10 (1995) 139–42; E. Kaptan, "Tin and Ancient Tin Mining in Turkey," *Anatolica* 21 (1995) 197–203.

[208] P. Budd et al., "Oxhide Ingots, Recycling and the Mediterranean Metals Trade," *JMA* 8 (1995) 1–32, with com-

ments by N.H. Gale and Z.A. Stos-Gale (33–41), M. Hall (42–44), and E.V. Sayre, K.A. Yener, and E.C. Joel (45–53).

[209] Soles and Davaras 1996 (supra n. 33).

[210] E.P. Blegen, *AJA* 39 (1935) 134–36; S. Marinatos, *Prakt* 1935, 212–20; A.B. Knapp, J.D. Muhly, and P. Muhly, "To Hoard Is Human," *RDAC* 1988, 251.

[211] E. Sapouna-Sakellaraki, *Die bronzenen Menschenfiguren auf Kreta und in der Ägäis* (Stuttgart 1995); C. Verlinden, *Les statuettes anthropomorphes crétoises* (Providence 1984); Verlinden, "Réflexions sur la fonction et la production des figurines anthropomorphes minoens en bronze," *OpAth* 17 (1988) 183–90. Agrimia from Ayia Triada: Halbherr et al. (supra n. 31) 126 fig. 87.

[212] M. Lee, *AJA* 100 (1996) 366 (abstract).

[213] I.A. Sakellarakis, "Minoan Religious Influence in the Aegean," *BSA* 91 (1996) 81–99.

[214] R. Hägg, "The Bronze Hair Locks from Knossos," *AA* 1983, 543–49.

[215] *PM* II.2, 651 fig. 416; J.G. Younger, "Bronze Age Representations of Aegean Bull-Leaping," *AJA* 80 (1976) 125–37, esp. 127–28, no. I.6, pl. 20.3.

[216] N.K. Sandars, "The First Aegean Swords and Their Ancestry," *AJA* 65 (1961) 17–29; Sandars, "Later Aegean Bronze Swords," *AJA* 67 (1963) 117–53; O. Höckmann, "Lanze und Speer in spätminoischen und mykenischen Griechenland," *JRGZM* 27 (1980) 13–158.

[217] S. Hood, "Shaft Grave Swords: Mycenaean or Minoan?" *4th CretCong*, 233–42.

period,[218] perhaps under influence from Syria and Egypt. In the Neopalatial period, Minoan smiths may have been responsible for the decorated weapons found mostly on the mainland.

Examples of practical metal tools also survive: double axes, saws, chisels, and hammers.[219] A small number of double axes are decorated with incised motifs: a plumed helmet on each side, a frontal bucranium, and a butterfly.[220] The most elaborate example, an ax from Vorou, has a figure-eight shield flanked by sacral knots on one side, and on the other a single "sacral robe" flanked possibly by quivers;[221] all these emblems have suspension loops at the top. Shields with similar suspension loops are sometimes painted as a repeating frieze on LM IB pottery, and these may be ancestral to the frescoed shield friezes of LM/LH III date found at several Aegean sites. A bronze spearhead from Anemospilia, dating to the beginning of the Neopalatial period, is engraved with a frontal boar's head.[222] Similar lanceheads and spearheads come from later tombs in the New Hospital and Ayios Ioannes cemeteries.

Sheets of gold, silver, and bronze were also used for nonfunctional double axes, some of which have elaborate surface decoration: two from the Arkalochori Cave are inscribed, and several huge bronze examples were found in the villa at Nirou Chani.[223] Two elaborately engraved, sheet bronze double axes with traces of gilding come from the Zakros palace. A few Neopalatial representations show these axes

being carried in processions or associated with bucrania,[224] but no scene of sacrifice where the victim is trussed on the table includes a double ax.

Metalsmiths also made a variety of copper and sheet bronze vessels beginning in MM II. Their manufacture continued on into the Neopalatial period, when the complexity of shape and decoration increased.[225] Some of these are strictly utilitarian, and were probably manufactured in large numbers. Many of the clay roundels found at Chania are incised with tripod cauldrons.[226] A hoard of enormous bronze cauldrons was discovered at Tylissos,[227] and the bronze handle of an even larger cauldron was found in the Zakros palace. Other sheet metal vessels are more elaborate, with handles and rims decorated in relief with shells, abstract designs, and even friezes of double axes.[228] Many of these relief patterns are cast, and thus are more durable versions of the terracotta appliqués on pottery. Low open bowls or lavers with upswung handle were made of silver or bronze, often with relief decoration along the rim. Sometimes these and other metal vessels were manufactured to function together as pairs or sets, like examples found at Knossos and Mochlos.[229]

Apart from bronze, vessels were also made of gold and silver from early on, though very few pieces have survived from the Protopalatial period.[230] Most precious metal vessels were "raised" by hammering a single sheet of malleable gold or silver to a desired shape and thinness. Since Crete is poor in silver and

---

[218] Mallia: dagger from Quartier Mu (Detournay et al. [supra n. 99] col. frontispiece, 147–49 no. 219, figs. 219–20); and three swords from the west wing, including one decorated with the figure of an acrobat (O. Pelon, in Darcque and Poursat [supra n. 168] 35–39, 36 fig. 1). Cf. the Mitsotakis dagger: A. Xenaki-Sakellariou, *RA* 1986, 235–44.

[219] Shaw (supra n. 68) 44–74; R.D.G. Evely, *Minoan Crafts* 1 (*SIMA* 92.1, Göteborg 1993) 2–141. Hammers: Mante-Platonos (supra n. 145). Saws: B.H. Wells, *Expedition* 16:4 (1974) 2–8.

[220] P. Cassola Guida, *Le armi difensive micenei nella figurazione* (Rome 1973) 163 no. 152, pl. XXVIII.3. Axes: H.G. Buchholz, *Zur Herkunft der kretischen Doppelaxt* (Munich 1959) 40, pl. VIIa.

[221] C. Verlinden, "Nouvelle interprétation du décor incisé sur une double hache en bronze supposée provenir de Voros," in Darcque and Poursat (supra n. 168) 139–49; N. Marinatos, *Minoan Sacrificial Ritual* (Stockholm 1986) 56 and fig. 46; I. Kilian-Dirlmeier, "Remarks on the Non-Military Function of Swords in the Mycenaean Argolid," in R. Hägg and G.C. Nordquist eds., *Celebrations of Death and Divinity in the Bronze Age Argolid* (Stockholm 1990) 160 and fig. 3b (drawing).

[222] *Archanes* 151 col. fig. 130.

[223] From Pinakiano, also in Linear A: *PGC* 59 no. 720. Chania: *BCH* 110 (1986) 755 fig. 162. Arkalochori, one in Linear A: M. Pope, *BSA* 51 (1956) 132–35; *ArchEph* 1953–1954, 64; one near the "Phaistos" syllabary: L. Godart, *Il disco di Festos* (Florence 1993). Nirou Chani: Xanthoudides (supra n. 52). Zakros: *Zakros* 146 and reconstruction; *PGC* 59 no. 722.

[224] *CMS* II.3, nos. 8 and 11.

[225] H. Matthäus, *Die Bronzegefässe der kretisch-mykenischen Kultur* (Munich 1980); Detournay et al. (supra n. 99) 71–88.

[226] Hallager II, roundels KH Wc 2008–25, incised with Linear A *409[VAS] (no handles) and *411[VAS] (horizontal handles).

[227] Hazzidakis (supra n. 206) 220, fig. 29; *PM* II.2, 569 fig. 355. Hazzidakis also gives the weights for the cauldrons: 52.564, 24.360, 15.700, and 12.500 kg.

[228] E.g., *Zakros* 147 fig.

[229] E.g., *PM* II.2, 637–44, figs. 402, 403, 407, 409a–b; Soles and Davaras 1996 (supra n. 33).

[230] E.g., deposit of silver vessels from the South House at Knossos: *PM* II.1, 387 and fig. 221. Part of a fluted clay vessel from a MM II context in Quartier Mu at Mallia may imitate metal: Detournay et al. (supra n. 99) 89 no. 120, 88 fig. 119.

gold sources, the metals, and initially the techniques for creating plate, were probably imported from Syria. Few pieces of Neopalatial plate have been found on Crete, although those that come from early Final Palatial contexts are probably heirlooms, and many of those found on the mainland were probably made in Crete.[231] A characteristic aspect of the silver vessels is that they use gold sparingly, often for accents. Some Minoan stone relief vessels, such as the Zakros Sanctuary Rhyton, however, seem to have been covered with gold foil originally.

Jewelry. Jewelry is beginning to receive the attention it deserves.[232] Although many types of jewelry are depicted in fresco, few actual pieces have survived, yet these seem more individualized than Final Palatial and mainland Mycenaean jewelry, which used a more restricted range of materials and was mostly mass-produced. Neopalatial jewelry builds on trends already established in earlier periods.[233] In the Protopalatial and early Neopalatial periods, jewelry and other objects are imported from Syria or Egypt that employ new techniques (cloisonné, granulation, repoussé, and combinations of precious and semiprecious materials).[234] Aegean artists may not have adopted these techniques immediately. The earliest demonstrably Minoan example of granulation occurs on a gold band that encloses a sard prism seal from the Poros Herakleion chamber tomb,[235] while the gold amygdaloid jewel from Pylos (*CMS*

I, no. 293) may be the earliest Aegean piece to employ cloisonné. Two rings from Sellopoulo tomb 4 (LM IIIA1) and a tomb at Kalyvia (LM IIIA1–2) carry a cloisonné bezel surrounded by granulation.[236]

While most Neopalatial gold jewelry takes simple shapes,[237] especially lentoid, amygdaloid, teardrop, granular, and spherical beads, some items are figural. The early Neopalatial relief Jewel Fresco from Knossos depicts a man's hand holding one end of a necklace composed of beads in the shape of frontal male heads with pendant triple earrings.[238] The Poros Herakleion tomb included a pair of moldmade gold foil ornaments with ducks against a backdrop of lily flowers, as well as beads in the shape of figure-eight shields. A gold fish-bead comes from the drain shaft in the east wing of the Knossos palace.[239]

Women's gold hair rings survive from Archanes Tholos A and the Mafeze tomb at Amnisos. Hairpins, however, have also been found and these tend to be highly individualized.[240] One pin found at Mavro Spelio was engraved with crocus blossoms on one side and a Linear A inscription on the other. A silver pin with a Linear A inscription was found in Tholos B at Archanes. Another silver pin found near the Royal Road has a gold finial in the shape of a human eye, a device that occurs as a floating element on some gold cult rings.[241] A fresco from Akrotiri shows a woman wearing two hairpins, one like a myrtle or olive twig, the other with an iris finial.

---

[231] Neopalatial Crete: Davis (supra n. 135) 102–109; Final Palatial Crete: Davis (supra n. 135) 109–17. Davis attributes the "quiet" Vapheio cup to a Minoan workshop, the "active" cup to a Mycenaean workshop; also see her "The Vapheio Cups: One Minoan and One Mycenaean?" *ArtB* 56 (1974) 472–87; cf. J. Hurwit, "The Dendra Octopus Cup and the Problem of Style in the Fifteenth Century Aegean," *AJA* 83 (1979) 413–26.

[232] M. Effinger, *Minoischer Schmuck* (Oxford 1996); R. Higgins, *Greek and Roman Jewellery*[2] (Berkeley 1980); Younger (supra n. 110). A. Xenaki-Sakellariou, Οι θαλαμωτοί τάφοι των Μυκηνών (Paris 1985) 292–312 provides a detailed typology of beads from Mycenae.

[233] A.S. Vasilakis, "Χρυσά και άργυρα τεχνουργήματα στην πρωτοανακτορική Κρήτη," *CretChron* 30 (1990) 35–50; I. Pini, "Minoan and Mycenaean Decorated Gold Finger-Rings," in *Techne* 199 (abstract); Higgins (supra n. 232) 20–24.

[234] From the Poros Herakleion chamber tomb comes a ring with a circular cloisonné bezel (Metaxa-Muhly [supra n. 95] 90 no. 240, pl. 26), and two early pieces of jewelry carry granulation: a gold lion from Koumasa Tholos B (S. Xanthoudides, *Vaulted Tombs of Mesara* [London 1924] 29, pl. IV no. 386), and the "wasp" pendant from Mallia (*PGC* 108–109 no. 1296; E.F. Bloedow and C. Björk, "The Mallia Pendant," *SMEA* 27 [1989] 9–68). These three early pieces may not be Minoan in manufacture but Syrian, along with the pieces from the Aegina Treasure: C. Gates, "Iconography at the Crossroads: The Aegina Treasure," in Laffineur

(supra n. 31) 215–25. J. Weingarten, *The Transformation of Egyptian Taweret into the Minoan Genius* (*SIMA* 88, Partille 1991); Rehak and Younger (supra n. 153).

[235] Metaxa-Muhly (supra n. 95) 100 pl. 32 no. 302. The granulated bucrania earrings from the same tomb (pl. 26 nos. 238–39) are probably Cypriot: R. Laffineur, "Les pendants d'oreilles minoens en forme de bucrâne," *4th Cret-Cong* I (1980) 281–96.

[236] Sellopoulo: M.R. Popham and H.W. Catling, *BSA* 69 (1974) 195–257, esp. 219 fig. 14H, pl. 37g. Kalyvia: L. Savignoni, *MonAnt* 14 (1904) 500–666, esp. 546 fig. 53.

[237] Cf. necklaces from Ayia Triada (S. Alexiou, *Guide to the Archaeological Museum in Herakleion* [Herakleion 1969] 70) and Archanes Tholos A (*Archanes* 80–81, figs. 56–58).

[238] *PM* I, 525–27, 526 fig. 383; Immerwahr 172 Kn no. 29. Cf. the frontal head of the "Master" on the pendant from the Aegina Treasure: Gates (supra n. 234) pl. XLIX.

[239] Metaxa-Muhly (supra n. 95) 90–91 nos. 241–45, pls. 27–28; *PM* III, 405, fig. 274.

[240] Younger (supra n. 110) 260. Mavrospelio: S. Alexiou, *AAA* 8 (1975) 133–38; *GORILA* 4, KN Zf 31. Katsamba: Alexiou (supra n. 158) pl. 128. Archanes: *Archanes* 95, ARKH Zf 9 unpublished, and 131 fig. 109. Knossos: *AR* 3 (1957) 20; A.J. Evans, "The Prehistoric Tombs of Knossos," *Archaeologia* 59 (1905) 541 fig. 129, also published separately (London 1906) 151 fig. 129. Thera: Doumas pls. 100, 105, 106.

[241] E.g., the Isopata ring, *CMS* II.3, no. 51.

Metal rings first appeared in MM II, reaching a high level of excellence in the Neopalatial era. These rings have been typed into seven classes with both elliptical and circular bezels (MM II).[242] Their hoops are too small for them to have been worn on the fingers; instead, evidence from burials indicates they were probably suspended from necklaces or bracelets.[243] Gold rings with oval bezels are well known for their cult scenes.[244] They probably were first made in late MM III since their human figures display a well-modeled anatomy, and continued at least into LM I. How much later these cult rings continued is debated. Certainly the main type belongs primarily to LM I, but the number of them found in later contexts and reflected in Knossos sealings has led a few scholars to date them as late as LM IIIA1.

The religious scenes on rings consist of a few topoi: a frieze of sacred knots and/or figure-eight shields, griffins and sphinxes, women and griffins, and women at altars.[245] The more elaborate rings, however, depict rituals involving one or more of the following elements: a man or woman at a baetyl; a man or woman touching, tugging, or plucking a tree; and a central woman apparently in movement.[246]

Glass for jewelry was introduced in the Neopalatial period.[247] From a Poros Herakleion tomb (LM I) come ladle-shaped glass beads, a glass seal, and a cloisonné ring that had glass inserts.[248] A fragment of a steatite mold for casting glass or gold jewelry comes from the Kephala tholos at Knossos; its matrices produced beads or plaques in the shape of a crocus bud and a "sacral ivy" leaf, both of which

were apparently popular forms of jewelry for women depicted in fresco[249] and common motifs on LM IA–B pottery.

Faience. Related to glass is faience production, a technique imported from Syria or Egypt during MM II that demands a high level of technical expertise and a skillful control of firing temperatures to create quartz-glazed objects in subtle colors. Inlays and plaques are common, along with vessels, seashells, and three-dimensional figurines.[250] Molds and unworked material from the Northwest Building at Knossos, and the south wing workshops in the Zakros palace, indicate that faience was probably made at just a few palatial sites.

Moldmade plaques of faience, probably for inlays, include a wide range of shapes at Knossos: house facades combined to create the Town Mosaic, depictions of animals suckling their young, models of women's dresses, some patterned with rockwork and crocus plants, and abstract and geometric inlays.

The faience figurines of women are well known. There are parts of at least three Snake Handlers from the Knossos Temple Repositories, not only the two usually illustrated.[251] The skirt and hand of another faience figurine were found in the Zakros palace, and the breast of another woman came to light in the Royal Road South excavations at Knossos. Since this type of female figurine is unique, it is difficult to tell what they represent, although most scholars call them goddesses, priestesses, or votaries, and their snakes symbols of domestic or chthonic cult.[252] Handling of snakes should be an attribute of the Pot-

---

[242] J.G. Younger, "Seven Types of Ring Construction in the Greek Late Bronze Age," in *Aux origines de l'Hellénisme* (Paris 1984) 84–90; and the same seven types: A. Xenaki-Sakellariou, "Techniques et évolution de la bague-cachet dans l'art crétomycénien," *CMS* Beiheft 3 (Berlin 1989) 323–38; Xenaki-Sakellariou, "Το δαχτυλίδι-σφραγίδα στην κρητομυκηναϊκή σφραγιδογλυφία," *Κρητική Εστία* 5 (1989) 11–16; Younger (supra n. 104) 181–82. Early rings and ring impressions: P. Yule, *Early Cretan Seals* (Mainz 1981) 77, class 28d; I.A. Sakellarakis, "Matrizen zur Herstellung kretisch-mykenischer Siegelringe," *CMS* Beiheft 1 (Berlin 1981) 167–80; *CMS* II.3, no. 38; II.5, nos. 201, 202, 270, 304; V Suppl. 1A, nos. 45–46; VII, no. 68.

[243] Younger (supra n. 111) 149–52.

[244] Most discussions of religion include the representations on rings; few studies, however, center on rings and their iconography: W.-D. Niemeier, "Zur Ikonographie von Gottheiten und Adoranten in den Kultszenen auf minoischen und mykenischen Siegeln," *CMS* Beiheft 3 (Berlin 1989) 163–86; M. Wedde, "Pictorial Architecture," in *Eikon* 181–203.

[245] E.g., *CMS* I, nos. 127, 128, 191, 218, and 410; II.3, nos. 15, 39, 56, 113; and V, no. 728; *Archanes* 93 fig. 68; *ILN* 26 March 1966, 32–33 fig. 8.

[246] E.g., *CMS* I, no. 126; and II.3, no. 114; Popham and

Catling (supra n. 236) 217–19, fig. 14D and pl. 37a–b; and *Archanes* 79 fig. 54.

[247] T.E. Haevernick, "Mykenisches Glas," *JRGZM* 7 (1960) 36–58, and "Mycenaean Glass," *Archaeology* 16 (1963) 190–93; I. Pini, "Spätbronzezeitliche ägäische Glassiegel," *JRGZM* 28 (1981) 48–81.

[248] Poros: Metaxa-Muhly (supra n. 95) 90 no. 240 and pl. 26, 91 no. 248 and fig. 22, 100 no. 304 and pl. 33, 188–89. Knossos: Hutchinson (supra n. 92) 79–80 no. 17, pl. 12f; *PM* IV.2, 963–64, col. pl. XXXIV.

[249] Immerwahr 172 Kn no. 11; *PM* II.2, 679–82, fig. 430a.

[250] K.P. Foster, *Aegean Faience of the Bronze Age* (New Haven 1979); Foster, "Reconstructing Minoan Palatial Faience Workshops," in *Palaces* 287–92, and discussion 292; H. Waterhouse, "The Knossos 'Town Mosaic' Reconsidered," *Cretan Studies* 4 (1994) 165–74; M. Panagiotaki, "Preliminary Technical Observations on Knossian Faience," *OJA* 14 (1995) 137–49. Mallia Quartier Mu (MM II): Detournay et al. (supra n. 99) 133 no. 183, 135 fig. 186. Knossos: *PM* I, 301–11, 471–90, 497 fig. 349, 506 and fig. 364, 510–12; *CM* pl. 71. Archanes Tourkogeitonia: *AR* 36 (1990) 71.

[251] Knossos: *PM* I, figs. 360–62, 503, 523 fig. 382; Foster 1979 (supra n. 250) 70–76, pls. 7–11; *CM* pls. XXIV–XXV; the Royal Road fragment is unpublished. Zakros: *Zakros* 218.

[252] *MMR*² 311–16.

nia Theron; in later Greek vase painting, however, women who handle snakes are maenads. The small Knossos Snake Handler with the flat cap also has a spotted feline mounted on it, probably a leopard, an animal that also has parallels in the depictions of later maenads.

Terracottas. Anthropomorphic and zoomorphic figurines of terracotta were already being made in EM times, and in the MM period they were commonly dedicated at peak sanctuaries. At most sites, male figures outnumber female, and bovids are also common. Some male figurines half a meter in height from Kophinas approach the size of small statues.[253] A few Prepalatial and Protopalatial figurines may allude to the origin of bull sports. In the Neopalatial era, terracotta bull rhyta, some of them mold-made, were produced at several sites; occasionally the backs of the animals are painted with net patterns.[254] One bull rhyton from Pseira has deliberately truncated horns, as if they had been sawn down.

Clay relief appliqués, presumably fashioned in molds, were also applied to vessels of clay beginning late in the Protopalatial period and continuing into the Neopalatial period.[255] In the Protopalatial period such appliqués often took the form of marine shells and rockwork, but some figural appliqués exist as well, notably cups from Mallia with entire landscapes depicted, including palms and cats. The relief bull on a jar from Anemospilia (MM IIIA) foreshadows the relief bulls on the walls of the Knossos palace. Finally, terracotta versions of triton shells and bull's-head rhyta form counterparts to more elaborate examples in stone and faience.[256] Other specialized terracottas such as architectural models, stands, and human feet are considered below under "Religion."

Furniture. Although very few pieces of actual furniture have survived, we assume that the Minoans were competent woodworkers.[257] From Akrotiri

come the plaster casts of several items, including beds, chests, and baskets;[258] and a tomb at Poros Herakleion contained the remains of two cedar beds, the components of which had been secured by bronze staples. Wooden coffins[259] are known as early as the Shaft Grave period on the mainland, though the earliest Minoan wooden coffins may date to LM II and other examples are known from LM IIIA graves. Stone furniture that may reflect wooden prototypes provides more evidence.[260] The gypsum seat from the Knossos throne room includes a number of details in relief that derive from woodwork: the crockets on the legs, the curved strut at the front, the contoured seat, and the undulating profile of the back. Three less elaborate but related stone seats were found in the Knossos area: a low limestone seat from the service section of the throne room complex, a similar seat from Myristis near Anemospilia, and a backless stone seat from Katsamba. The gypsum or limestone benches with "triglyph" panels, found in many palaces and villas, may also imitate wooden examples.

The Palatial Prestige System and the Role of Knossos

In Neopalatial Crete, local and imported raw materials, artisans and their labor, and finished products apparently were all controlled by the major palaces and villas. In these centers the objects would be manufactured and then distributed elsewhere, perhaps in exchange for other goods and services or as gifts and markers of status.[261] Neopalatial art must have therefore reflected the contemporary value system of these centers, providing images which the elite in power used to promote itself.[262]

As in the Near East and Egypt, these display items consisted mostly of rich, miniature, and portable art objects. Many of these were stored and brought out when needed.[263] In the west wing at Zakros, rooms

---

[253] *BCH* 118 (1994) 822; *AR* 42 (1996) 45; and *ArchDelt* 45 (1990) 429–30.

[254] J.G. Younger, "Bronze Age Representations of Aegean Bull-Games, III," in *Politeia* 507–45, esp. the terracotta rhyta nos. 7–9 and 14–18. Net patterns: e.g., *PGC* 101 nos. 1220–22; *PM* II.1, 259 fig. 154b.

[255] Foster (supra n. 105); Detournay et al. (supra n. 99) 116–32; *PM* IV.1, 116–20 for discussion of relief shells on vases.

[256] J.L. Lloyd, "A Clay Triton Shell," *OpAth* 20 (1994) 75–88.

[257] J.G. Younger, "The Iconography of Rulership: A Conspectus," in Rehak (supra n. 39) 151–211, esp. 188–93; Krzyszkowska (supra n. 155).

[258] Beds: *Thera* IV, pls. 104–105; Metaxa-Muhly (supra n. 95) 149–64. Baskets, etc.: *AR* 41 (1995) 57. Stool: *Thera*

IV, pls. 102–103.

[259] P. Muhly, "Furniture from the Shaft Graves," *BSA* 91 (1996) 197–211; R. Hägg and F. Sieurin, "On the Origin of the Wooden Coffin in Late Bronze Age Crete," *BSA* 77 (1982) 177–86.

[260] Younger (supra n. 257) 188–93.

[261] Kopcke (supra n. 35); Alexiou (supra n. 35); Wiener (supra n. 35); Clarke (supra n. 100). Cf. M. Mauss, *The Gift: Forms and Functions of Exchange in Archaic Societies* (London 1966); S.M. Pollock, *The Symbolism of Prestige: An Archaeological Example from the Royal Cemetery of Ur* (Diss. Univ. of Michigan 1983).

[262] Moody (supra n. 35).

[263] Storage areas could be small rooms, partitioned areas, mudbrick closets, built chests, and cists below floors. See Begg, passim.

with clay storage cists existed in close proximity to the workshops where some of the objects stored must have been manufactured;[264] both work and storage rooms, however, do not communicate with the supposed "shrine" nearby, but rather with the banqueting halls where the stone maces, rhyta, and chalices may actually have been displayed and used. In addition to a stone relief rhyton fragment showing men carrying stone ladles, ring impressions depict women and men carrying poles, double axes, fabrics, and vessels in procession. It is significant that, outside the peak sanctuaries, very few fixed areas for social or religious ritual have been identified for the Neopalatial era. Presumably, these portable objects were displayed in other formal settings, like courts and in processions.

These prestige objects are widely distributed. For instance, an ornamental stone mace, a stone rhyton, palatial pottery, and sealed documents impressed by gold look-alike rings (see below) were sent to the country house at Sklavokambos on the main route leading from Knossos to Mt. Ida; the villa at Pyrgos received imported Egyptian stone vases and a mold-made triton shell of pink faience; the court-centered building at Makriyialos obtained a stone chalice and Marine Style pottery; and, on stylistic grounds, Palaikastro may have received its ivory youth and the Zakros palace its Sanctuary Rhyton from workshops at Knossos. Ayia Triada is particularly rich in prestige objects probably manufactured at Knossos: the Boxer Rhyton has scenes of bull sports and sinewy human figures that seem particularly Knossian.

These objects found scattered across the island suggest a system of exchange by which these centers are tied into a palatial prestige system that reflects a network not just of political ties to Knossos, but also of artistic techniques, iconography, and religious beliefs and symbolic practices, most of which seem to emanate from Knossos.

As a leader and innovator in artistic production, Knossos was surely the most important Neopalatial center in Crete. The central court and west court of the palace are the largest on Crete, and would have provided gathering spaces for hundreds of individuals at a single time. The west wing, with its long storage magazines lined with large pithoi, was the main supply center for the palace.[265] The remainder of the west wing housed ceremonial rooms including the only undisputed throne room on Crete, pillar basements, and the so-called Temple Repositories. Over all these, an upper floor that Evans called the "piano nobile" has been reconstructed, the rooms of which were decorated with frescoes. Extensive terracing on the east side of the palace supported the Great East Hall at the level of the central court, and south of it the Grand Staircase led to the "Domestic Quarter," a misnomer since its stone drains and polythyra indicate ceremonial rather than living areas.[266]

Recently, several scholars have suggested that Neopalatial Knossos may have been most important as a ritual center.[267] In support of this hypothesis are the lack of identifiable deposits of domestic pottery of Neopalatial date (although these are common in many of the houses outside the palace) and the presence of LM IA pottery choking the drains of the east wing. The Phaistos palace similarly shows few signs of actual human occupation in the final phase of the Neopalatial period.

Knossos is the only palace with both large-scale and miniature frescoes depicting the human form; the large-scale figures are sometimes executed in relief. As noted earlier, these frescoes emphasize important women, gatherings of women and men, physical combat among athletic youths, bull-leaping with adolescent youths and maidens as participants, and the architecture of palatial buildings and peak sanctuaries. Several of these topoi were also carved on gold rings carried by top administrators and on stone relief rhyta. The repetition of a few select images in a variety of media suggests that the Neopalatial elite wanted to project these images to the rest of the population. The pictorial programs of the major entrances to the palace deserve emphasis, since here stood bull and procession scenes that confronted all visitors to the complex.

These pictorial themes suggest that the palace had three important functions. First, it was a setting for ritual activities involving women and men, perhaps on a seasonal basis or according to a religious calendar. Second, the depiction of supernatural creatures like griffins or sphinxes may indicate that the palace was considered a liminal zone where the real and supernatural worlds intersected. Third,

---

[264] *Zakros* 217–18, 218 fig. Stoneworking areas were located in rooms II upper floor, XIII upper floor, XXVI, and XLIII.

[265] I. Begg, "Continuity in the West Wing at Knossos," in *Palaces* 179–84.

[266] J. Driessen and C. Macdonald, "The Drainage System in the Palace of Knossos," *BSA* 83 (1988) 235–58; Macdonald and Driessen, "The Storm Drains of the East Wing at Knossos," in Darcque and Treuil (supra n. 3) 141–46. There is no evidence for the flush toilets sometimes claimed to exist.

[267] E.g., J. Soles, "The Functions of a Cosmological Center: Knossos in Palatial Crete," in *Politeia* 404–14.

Knossos seems to have been a major center on Crete for the performance of bull-leaping and related activities, and these events may have been central to the identity of the palace.[268] The dissemination of Knossian iconography and artistic techniques to other Minoan sites, especially toward the end of the Neopalatial period, appears to be part of a deliberate scheme.

Writing and Administration

Sealing administration began in the Near East in the sixth millennium B.C. followed by writing ca. 3100, but it is unlikely that Crete had administrative systems before the beginning of the MM period. An administration at Knossos may have been using sealings in the Prepalatial period, in MM I, but the practice becomes widespread in Crete only in MM II.[269]

Cretan Hieroglyphic writing makes a first appearance in MM IA, shortly before the rise of the first palaces.[270] Although the Hieroglyphic script dies out at the beginning of the Neopalatial period,[271] its genesis is important because it is the first Aegean

linear script and with it we see the beginning of administrative practices that will remain fairly constant throughout the Neo- and Final Palatial periods.

Linear A develops in MM IIA and is the major writing system on Crete throughout the Neopalatial period; it does not survive this period long, if at all.[272] Because Hieroglyphic and Linear A seem to share some signs, it is probable that Linear A derives in part from Hieroglyphic, though that does not necessarily imply that they represent the same language. Nevertheless, a number of sites use both Hieroglyphic and Linear A (Phaistos, Knossos, Mallia, Petras), and in MM II–IIIA Knossos was apparently using both contemporaneously. The development of Linear B out of A is probable and may have occurred at Knossos prior to the end of the Neopalatial period or soon after.[273] As a script and administrative tool, Linear B is considered below under "Final Palatial Administration." Cypro-Minoan, which lies outside the scope of this review, seems to have developed in large measure from Linear A as well.[274]

---

[268] Younger (supra n. 254); Hallager and Hallager (supra n. 113); Rehak (supra ns. 132–33).

[269] Hallager I, 21–25; J. Weingarten, "The Sealing Structures of Minoan Crete," OJA 5 (1986) 279–98, and OJA 7 (1988) 1–25; Weingarten, "Three Upheavals in Minoan Sealing Administration," Aegaeum 5 (1990) 105–20; Weingarten, "The Sealing Studies in the Middle Bronze Age, I: Karahöyük, II: Phaistos," in P. Ferioli et al. eds., Archives before Writing (Rome 1994) 261–96; Weingarten, "Sealings and Sealed Documents at Bronze Age Knossos," in Evely et al. (supra n. 1) 171–88.

[270] J.-P. Olivier and L. Godart, Corpus hieroglyphicarum inscriptionum Cretae (Paris 1996) (=CHIC) presents the primary evidence; add A. Lembesi, P. Muhly, and J.-P. Olivier, "An Inscription in the Hieroglyphic Script from the Syme Sanctuary, Crete (SY Hf 01)," Kadmos 34 (1995) 63–77. Hieroglyphic uses 96 syllabograms, 34 logograms, nine fractions, and a few other signs as adjuncts and punctuations. CHIC catalogues a corpus of 331 Hieroglyphic inscriptions, the majority of which are seals or seal impressions. The script is basically pictographic (CHIC 19). Within the Protopalatial period, there is at least one other script, that which appears on the Phaistos Disc; the inscription on the Arkalochori ax is similar, but perhaps distinct: Godart (supra n. 223); J.-P. Olivier, "Le Disque de Phaistos," BCH 99 (1975) 35–44. MM IA examples: CMS II.1, no. 391 (CHIC 315), no. 393 (CHIC 252), and no. 394 (CHIC 202).

[271] No inscribed Hieroglyphic material comes from a Late Bronze Age context. Material from late contexts includes either Hieroglyphic sealstones (e.g., CMS V, Suppl. 1B, no. 337, CHIC [supra n. 270] 289, and CMS II.2, no. 256, CHIC 293) or nodules impressed by Hieroglyphic sealstones (e.g., CHIC 138, 152, 153, and 155). See also the jar stopper AM 1938.1153b: I. Pini, "Eine Tonplombe aus Knossos im Ashmolean Museum," Kadmos 21 (1982) 1–4.

[272] For a basic introduction to Linear A and B, with bibliography, see J.T. Hooker, Linear B: An Introduction (Bristol 1980) 11–18. GORILA presents the inscriptions. From Knossos, a tablet and one or two nodules/noduli from below

the South West House (MM IIA): AR 39 (1993) 68; Hallager I, 57. From Final Palatial contexts come three incised roundels from Chania (LM IIIA1 context): KH Wc 2005, 2117, and 2118 (Hallager I, 52–53); a pithos from Knossos, the Unexplored Mansion (LM II context): GORILA 4, KN Zb 40 (M.R. Popham, Kadmos 15 [1976] 102–107); and a LM II–IIIA terracotta figurine from Poros Herakleion with a Linear A inscription: N. Dimopoulou, J.-P. Olivier, and G. Rethemiotakis, BCH 117 (1993) 501–21; Rethemiotakis, in Techne 117–21.

[273] J.T. Hooker, The Origin of the Linear B Script (Salamanca 1979) 16–73; Hooker, "The Varieties of Minoan Writing," Cretan Studies 1 (1988) 169–89; Shelmerdine (supra n. 16) 559. Linear B at Chania seems so dependent on developments at Knossos (E. Hallager, M. Vlasakis, and B.P. Hallager, "New Linear B Tablets from Khania," Kadmos 31 [1992] 61–87) that J.-P. Olivier, "KN 115 = KH 115," BCH 117 (1993) 19–33 suggested that a Knossos scribe wrote tablet KH Ar 4; T.G. Palaima, "Ten Reasons Why KH 115 ≠ KN 115," Minos 27–28 (1992–1993) 261–81 argued against the identification, and Olivier graciously withdrew his suggestion at the Politeia conference in 1996. Early tablets at Pylos also exhibit a close relationship with Knossian palaeography: Palaima, "Evidence for the Influence of the Knossian Graphic Tradition at Pylos," in P. Oliva and A. Frolikova eds., Concilium Eirene 16.3, section 4: Mycenaeological Colloquium (Prague 1982) 80–84.

[274] Hooker (supra n. 272) 15–16, 18; J. Chadwick, "The Minoan Origin of the Classical Cypriote Script," in Karageorghis (supra n. 206) 139–43; T.G. Palaima, "Cypro-Minoan Scripts: Problems of Historical Context," in Y. Duhoux, T.G. Palaima, and J. Bennet eds., Problems in Decipherment (Louvain-la-Neuve 1989) 121–67; Palaima, "Ideograms and Supplementals and Regional Interaction among Aegean and Cypriot Scripts," Minos 24 (1989) 29–54. Only two documents, both from Enkomi, are apparently contemporary with the major use of Linear A: L. Godart and A. Sacconi, "La plus ancienne tablette d'Enkomi et le Linéaire A," in Karageorghis (supra n. 206) 128–33.

As a script, Linear A is complex, and its corpus is also greatly varied.[275] In stark contrast to the Hieroglyphic corpus, no sealstone carries a Linear A inscription, while the many kinds of objects that carry Linear A are restricted almost exclusively to clay tablets, nodules, and stirrup jars for Linear B. The bulk of Linear A documents comes from MM III and LM I contexts.[276] The three Linear A documents from Phaistos that may also date to the Neopalatial period may imply that Phaistos was operating administratively at that time.[277]

There are four types of Linear A clay documents (fig. 5): tablets, roundels, nodules, and *noduli*. A distinction is usually made between inscribed (written) documents and those that are impressed by seals. Tablets are never impressed, while nodules may, or may not, be impressed and/or inscribed. Most Linear A tablets are page-shaped with the inscription ranked in rows, and all carry lists of commodities and personnel.[278]

Two types of monumental or conventional formulae are known, the "Libation Formula" and apparent gibberish, and these do not occur on tablets. The gibberish consists of several long inscriptions, usually not separated into word groups, on three gold hairpins, a bronze bowl, and a gold finger-ring; for the most part, except for the "JA-SA-SA-RA" on PL Zf 1, they are hapax legomena.[279] In full, the Libation Formula consists of a phrase or sentence of eight words inscribed on a wide variety of objects, stone libation tables, cups, ladles and altars, inked terracotta cups, and a silver pin, most of which were dedicated at peak sanctuaries.[280] In its full form, and

in Linear B values, the Libation Formula is as follows: 1) T/A-TA-I-*301-; 2) word; 3) word; 4) J/A-SA-SA-RA; 5) U-NA-KA-NA-SI; 6) I-PI-NA-MA; 7) SI-RU-TE; and 8) I-NA-JA-PA-QA.

The word J/A-SA-SA-RA has usually been assumed to be the name of a goddess allied with the Semitic Astarte/Asshra.[281] The final four words from U-NA-KA-NA-SI to I-NA-JA-PA-QA do not change. The first word T/A-TA-I-*301- appears in many variations that are difficult to resolve. Word 3 is always different, perhaps the name of the dedicant. The second word is often A-DI-KI-TE (or some variant) or I-DA (or some variant); six other words appear in this slot, including TU-RU-SA and SE-TO-I-JA. Since the last two are toponyms representing Tylissos and perhaps either Mallia or Archanes,[282] and since A-DI-KI-TE and I-DA look like the mountains Dikte and Ida, this slot in the Libation Formula appears reserved for a toponym.

Clay documents other than tablets can also be impressed and come in a wide range of shapes: documents that were not attached to anything (independent documents), documents that were pressed against something (direct-object sealings), and documents that hung from a cord (nodules or hanging nodules).

The Linear A roundel is a clay, disk-shaped independent document that could be written on one or both faces and/or impressed along the rim. As receipts for objects leaving the administrative centers, they record a word on one side, the ideogram for the commodity on the other, and on the rim a number of impressions of seals, presumably be-

---

[275] Linear A and B share 80 signs, both syllabograms and logograms, with four signs as variants unique to Linear A. In addition, like Linear B, Linear A has a long list of unique signs that appear rarely, only in conjunction with some other sign, or only as hapax legomena; 18 signs function as ideograms for vases; 154 ligatures serve as shorthand notations of commodities; and 13 simple and 30 complex fractions attest to a still baffling but precise measuring system. *GORILA* catalogues 1,487 inscriptions, almost all inscribed: 323 tablets, 887 nodules, 7 noduli, 178 roundels, 34 inscribed vessels, 3 graffito inscriptions in plaster, 2 inscriptions on architectural blocks, 8 inscriptions on metal objects (including a bowl, hairpins, and a gold ring), and 5 inscriptions on miscellaneous objects; 37 inscriptions were painted on vessels.

[276] Site summaries in Hallager I, 39–77; add Thera: *AR* 40 (1994) 69; *Ergon* 41 (1994) 56–62. MM IIIB: Knossos, Corridor of the Loomweights (southeast insula). MM III/LM IA: Knossos, East Temple Repository. LM IA: Gournia House Cf, Palaikastro Block B13, Akrotiri, Thera, Δ8 and the House of the Ladies. LM IB: Ayia Triada, Gournia House Fg and palace, Chania Kastelli House I and Odos Katre no. 10, Zakros House A and palace, Knossos Stepped Portico, Palaikastro Building V, Pyrgos, Sklavokambos, and Tylissos.

[277] Two tablets, PH 1 (W.C. Brice, *Inscriptions in the Mi-*

noan Linear Script of Class A, 4 [Oxford 1961] 13; *GORILA* 1, 286–87) from the same repository 8 that produced the Phaistos Disk and MM IIIB pottery, and PH 3 (*GORILA* 1, 290–91) from a window sill in vano XLIV/38 (the lustral basin in the west magazines), and the inscribed nodule Wa 32 from vano 10 (*GORILA* 2, vii and 90). See also Fiandra (supra n. 31).

[278] A few tablets anticipate the later (and rarer) Linear B palm leaf-shaped tablet, a couple resemble Hieroglyphic labels, while a few are unique, roughly square. R. Palmer, "Linear A Commodities," in *Politeia* 133–55; D.W. Packard, *Minoan Linear A* (Berkeley 1974) 38–53.

[279] *GORILA* 4: Cr (?) Zf 1, KN Zf 13, KN Zf 31, KO (?) Zf 2, PL Zf 1. T.G. Palaima, "Comments on Mycenaean Literacy," *Minos* 20–22 (1987) 499–510.

[280] Schoep (supra n. 139); G.A. Owens, "Evidence for the Minoan Language: The Minoan Libation Formula," *Cretan Studies* 5 (1996) 163–208.

[281] G.A. Owens, "Astarte/Ishtar/Ishassaras/Asasarame: The Great Mother Goddess of Minoan Crete and the Eastern Mediterranean," *Cretan Studies* 5 (1996) 209–18; G. Huxley, "Cretan *Paiawones*," *GRBS* 16 (1975) 118–19.

[282] G.A. Owens, "Minoan DI-KA-TA," *Kadmos* 32 (1993) 22–28; Owens, "Was se-to-i-ja at Archanes?" *Kadmos* 33 (1994) 156–61.

longing to the parties involved, that correspond to the number or amount of the commodities dispensed.[283] Another independent document, the *nodulus*, is a lump of clay impressed by a seal and only rarely also inscribed; noduli may have served as dockets, "obligations to pay workers."[284]

Other classes of small, lumpy clay documents were perforated, written on, and/or impressed. Most scholars give them the generic term "sealings" or "nodules." Sealings, as the term implies, however, seal objects directly—chests, boxes, jars, pegs (chest doors, storeroom doors?), and leather documents.[285] Nodules secure the ends of string and hang from objects; they come in two forms, those into which the string entered at only one end (one-hole nodules) and those into which string entered at both ends (two-hole nodules). One-hole nodules are thought to have occurred in pairs, each securing one of the two ends of a single piece of string that perhaps tied up papyrus documents.[286] Two-hole nodules sealed the knot that ties together the two ends of one string, which was probably looped about an object.

The Protopalatial use of direct-object sealings (pegs and jars) continues selectively into the Neopalatial period. In the late Protopalatial period, however, an entirely new set of clay documents is introduced for both Hieroglyphic and Linear A: tablets and noduli, one-hole and two-hole hanging nodules, and document sealings.[287]

Briefly, an administration uses a sealing system to monitor the reception, storage, distribution, and inventory of goods.[288] Tokens may represent the entry of goods into the storerooms. The goods may be placed in containers sealed with an impressed sealing, have an impressed nodule hanging from them, or simply be left in a magazine whose door is tied closed with string and sealed with an impressed sealing. The clay sealings on the containers or on the doors constitute a "living archive."

Withdrawals should be of a standardized quantity, represented by the broken sealing or detached nodule that is reserved; the reserved nodules and sealings comprise a "temporary archive." At the end of the accounting period, the reserved nodules are brought together as a "final archive," like that at Pylos, and are counted and subtracted from the original amount. The total is then matched against the remaining amount of the commodity. Audited sealings are then discarded (a "discard archive") where they cannot be reinserted into the next administrative period to falsify later accounts. Favorite places for discarding sealings in the Neopalatial period are in closets under stairs; they are also used as fill in abandoned rooms or spaces, and in blocking walls. To be preserved, all clay documents need to be baked in a fire; since there is no evidence for any deliberate firing of documents, as exists in the Near East, all documents from Crete were fired in conflagrations, whether accidental or deliberate.

Living archives from Neopalatial Crete are rare, but several temporary archives have been excavated (e.g., the sealings in House A, Zakros), and one final archive of Linear A documents may survive from Chania, Odos Katre.[289] Most impressed sealings,

---

[283] Hallager; P. Rehak and J.G. Younger, "A Minoan Roundel from Pyrgos, Southeastern Crete," *Kadmos* 34 (1995) 81–102.

[284] J. Weingarten, "Some Unusual Minoan Clay Nodules," *Kadmos* 25 (1986) 1–21; Hallager I, 121–33.

[285] Chests: N. Platon and W. Brice, Ἐνεπίγραφαι πινακίδες καὶ πίθοι γραμμικοῦ συστήματος Α ἐκ Ζάκρου (Athens 1975); cf. Hallager I, 74–77. Jars: e.g., *CMS* V, Suppl. 1A, no. 149 from Chania; sealings from Knossos, Room of the Olive Press (Weingarten 1988 [supra n. 269] 2). Pegs (doors?): the majority of sealings from Lerna and Phaistos: P. Ferioli and E. Fiandra, "The Use of Clay Sealings in Administrative Functions from the 5th to 1st Millennium B.C.," *Aegaeum* 5 (1990) 221–32; Ferioli and Fiandra, "Change in the Juridical Significance of the Clay Sealing between the MM and LM in Crete and in the East," in M. Perna ed., *Administrative Documents in the Aegean and Their Near Eastern Counterparts* (Naples, forthcoming); J. Aruz, "Seal Imagery and Sealing Practices in the Early Aegean World," in Ferioli et al. (supra n. 269) 211–35; Weingarten 1994 (supra n. 269). One peg sealing is known from Knossos: Hallager II, 290 (KSPI L44). Documents: Hallager I, 135–58.

[286] E. Hallager, "The Hanging Nodules and Their Inscriptions," and M. Marazzi, "Sigilli e tavolette di legno," both forthcoming in Perna (supra n. 285).

[287] Hallager I, 31–38; II, 291. The Hieroglyphic crescent

[288] Younger (supra n. 112); T.G. Palaima, "Sealings as Links in an Administrative Chain," in P. Ferioli, E. Fiandra, and G.G. Fissore, *Administration in Ancient Societies* (Torino 1996) 37–66.

[289] Living archives: Hallager I, 39–77: Tylissos House A, the Knossos west magazines (G-series), and the unidentified sealings that secured a gypsum chest containing tablets from the Room of the Column Bases, and perhaps from the "archives room" at Zakros: Platon and Brice (supra n. 285). J. Weingarten, "Late Bronze Age Trade within Crete," in Gale 1991 (supra n. 12) 305. Temporary archives: Hallager I, 73–74; Weingarten (supra n. 107). A personal visit to Zakros House A convinced us that the collapsed upper courses of the brick partition wall in room 7 had been misidentified in the original report as remains of a "brick chest." Other temporary archives (Hallager I, 39–77) include the sealings in the cupboard in room D, House 1, in Chania, and the sealings from the cupboard in the blocked-up doorway at Sklavokambos. Final archive: Hallager I, 50–51. The deposit held 82 tablets, 112 roundels, 26 hanging nodules, 57 document sealings, and one nodulus found together in an ashy layer, perhaps having been tossed out in the cleanup after the fire destruction that burned the audit while still in progress.

and medallion may be related to the Linear A two-hole nodule and roundel, respectively.

however, come from discard archives. In fact, the scatter of Linear A and B documents throughout the Knossos palace and the lack of any identifiable central archive strongly suggest that many of these deposits represent discard archives. This hypothesis has considerable consequences for the interpretation of the final destruction of Knossos, considered below under "Final Palatial Administration."

There are two major ways to analyze the patterns of seal use on impressed documents. One is to determine the frequency or "intensity" of a single seal's use within a deposit. When seals are used only a few times each to impress documents, it may imply, for instance, that members of the rural populace were sending their individual contracts or contributions to the central administration. When a few seals are used many times to impress documents, it may reflect an internal administration with a limited number of palace bureaucrats sealing and unsealing commodities and storerooms many times over the course of an administrative period. A document can be impressed several times by one seal (Weingarten's Single Seal System, or SSS) or by two or more seals in combination (the Multiple Seal System, or MSS).[290] The SSS presumably involves a single person responsible for impressing a document, while the MSS requires two or more people to authenticate or administer a document together. The two systems can be found at the same site.[291] Such analyses allow us to envision in some detail a Neopalatial administration's concern with incoming goods from the outlying areas and with the internal management of these goods. In the debate over whether these Neopalatial sites, including Knossos, were palatial or domanial in character, deposits like those at Zakros, where the

MSS dominates, seem to reflect the management of an estate rather than a state-management.[292]

While some classes of impressed documents appear in virtually every sealing deposit in Crete, others appear to be restricted to individual sites: one-hole hanging nodules, for instance, are so characteristic of Ayia Triada that the few found at Zakros may imply some communication, perhaps written on papyrus, from Ayia Triada.[293]

Numerous seals carry almost identical scenes and can be distinguished from each other only with difficulty; they may have belonged to administrators who functioned similarly.[294] Several of these "look-alikes" were gold rings with bull-leaping scenes, used to impress documents found at numerous sites. For example, one of these rings impressed three leather document sealings found at Ayia Triada, two document sealings from Sklavokambos, and two noduli, one from Gournia and one from the Zakros palace. It may be that the administrators traveled, or, more likely, impressed the documents at one regional center and sent them out to others. If the gold rings belonged to an elite administration at Knossos, the leather documents may have concerned sociopolitical and ceremonial (perhaps ritual or religious) issues.[295]

It is usually assumed that the pre-Classical language of Crete was not Greek. Ancient writers describe the Cretans as *sui generis*. Eteo-Cretans and Pelasgikoi lived in eastern Crete in Classical times; and, as if to confirm the presence of non-Greek speakers, Classical and Hellenistic inscriptions have been recovered from East Crete, written with Greek letters but reflecting a non-Greek language.[296]

It is a common practice, called "normalizing," to

[290] Weingarten (supra n. 107) and Weingarten 1988 (supra n. 269). Some caution needs to be exercised when translating seal use into personnel, however. Tomb evidence demonstrates that a single individual could own more than one seal (I. Pini, *CMS* V, Suppl. 1A, xviii), and it can be shown that the several faces of a single multifacial seal could impress a single document (e.g., Knossos Wc 41, Hallager II, 166–67; Samothrace Wc 2, Hallager II, 200–201). Thus, not all MSS documents need to have been impressed by two or more people.

[291] Of the approximately 525 nodules in House A at Zakros, 360 (69%) were MSS documents impressed by two or three seal faces, while 165 (31%) were SSS documents impressed by one seal face only. The SSS seals belonged to the Cretan Popular group, common throughout the island, and perhaps reflecting a rural population; the MSS seals, however, belonged to the so-called "Zakro Master" group, distinctive of Zakros, perhaps belonging to members of the administration; Weingarten 1988 (supra n. 269) 46.

[292] Weingarten 1988 (supra n. 269) 16 n. 15, citing J. Bennet, "The Structure of the Linear B Administration at Knossos," *AJA* 89 (1985) 247 and n. 76. T.G. Palaima, "Seal-Users

and Script-Users: Nodules and Tablets at LM IB Hagia Triada," in Ferioli et al. (supra n. 269) 307–30 argues for a greater administrative purview; he estimates Ayia Triada's agricultural territory as about 830 ha. This amount of land would fit comfortably in the immediate area, between the Geropotamos River and the western foothills of the Asterousia Mountains, and would resemble the territories of other and similar regional centers: P. Rehak and J.G. Younger, "Minoan and Mycenaean Administration in the Early Late Bronze Age: An Overview," forthcoming in Perna (supra n. 285).

[293] Weingarten (supra n. 289) 305.

[294] Hallager I, 205–24; J.H. Betts, "New Light on Minoan Bureaucracy," *Kadmos* 6 (1967) 15–40.

[295] Hallager and Hallager (supra n. 113); Younger (supra n. 254); Rehak (supra ns. 132–33); Rehak and Younger (supra n. 292).

[296] Hom. *Od.* 19.177; Hdt. 7.171. M. Guarducci ed., *Inscriptiones Creticae* (Rome 1942) III, "Tituli Cretae Orientalis," VI, nos. 1–6 from Praisos; add *RPhil* 20 (1946) 131–38. For Eteo-Cretan: Y. Duhoux, *L'Étéocrétois: Les textes, la langue* (Amsterdam 1982); and H. van Effenterre, "De l'Étéocrétois à la selle d'agneau," *BCH* 113 (1989) 447–49.

assign Linear B phonetic values to similar-looking Linear A signs for convenience.[297] When normalized, Linear A reveals some similarities to Linear B: a few Linear A words can be recognized in Linear B, including toponyms, and many of the ideograms seem the same. It is also likely that the unit of capacity in Linear A was the same as that in Linear B, 28.8 liters.[298] Linear A, however, exhibits a significantly reduced o-series (in Linear A, no DO, JO, MO, NO, QO, SO) and the apparent tendency to use a final -u where Linear B uses final -o.

There are too few Linear A documents to give any complete sense of grammar, but the repetitions of word stems with varied endings within the Libation Formula suggest some inflections.[299] As for vocabulary, it is certain from their context that KU-RO means "total" and PO-TO-KU-RO means "grand total"; KI-KI-NA might mean "fig(s)," and TA-RA should mean "five."[300] In addition to the identification of the AB ideograms, special Linear A ideogram *A302 may signify olive oil and *A303 grain.

Several languages have been proposed for Linear A based on resemblances in vocabulary: Semitic, especially East Semitic, and some Indo-European languages like Greek, Luvian (a southwestern Anatolian dialect of Hittite), and Lycian.[301] Of these proposals, Semitic and Luvian are attractive for historical reasons: Semitic because of the evidence of trade con-

nections between Crete and the eastern Mediterranean, and Luvian because of the close ceramic connections between southwestern Anatolia and Crete, especially in the Neolithic and Early Bronze Age. It should be remembered, however, that lexical resemblances do not specify a language; grammar and syntax do, and too little of either is known securely for Linear A.

Trade and Interconnections

Closely tied to issues of production, exchange, and administration within Crete during the Neopalatial period are questions concerning the nature of Minoan trade and interconnections with other cultures of the Aegean and the eastern Mediterranean. Much work has been done in this area, with several international conferences in the last 15 years devoted entirely to aspects of the subject.[302] Although the most attention continues to be paid to pottery (both imported and exported)[303] and to metals, especially copper and tin, recent interest has concentrated on Neopalatial Crete's contacts with all surrounding areas, both within and outside the Aegean, and on the cultural correlates that accompany such contact.

The origins of Neopalatial trade must be sought in the Protopalatial period.[304] MM II pottery has been found at many sites in the Cyclades, and especially the island of Aegina, Cyprus and the eastern

[297] In only a few cases can it be demonstrated that the same word or its derivative appears in both Linear A and B, and from these only 12–15 Linear A signs can be assigned Linear B phonetic values with any confidence (DA, I, JA, KI, PA, PI, RO, RI, SE, SU, TA, O, and possibly TE, A, KO): L. Godart, "Du Linéaire A au Linéaire B," in *Aux origines de l'Hellénisme* (supra n. 242) 121–28.

[298] A pithos from Epano Zakros carries an inscription (*GORILA* 4, 112: ZA Zb3) that begins with "VIN 32," probably recording the volume, 32 units; if Mycenaean units, the volume would have been 921.6 l. Since the pithos stands about 170 cm high, the vase-capacity program ("Vase" by Gregory Christiana, copyright 1994) calculates its maximum volume from its profile as slightly over 1000 l. If this is correct, both Palmer (supra n. 38) 37 and Palaima (supra n. 292) 327–28 n. 62 underestimate the size of the pithos.

[299] E.g., JA-SA-SA-RA, JA-SA-SA-RA-MA-NA resembles I-PI-NA-MA, I-PI-NA-MI-NA; U-NA-KA-NA-SI resembles U-NA-RU-KA[ ]JA-SI and DI-DI-KA-SE; and U-NA-RE-KA-NA-TI resembles DI-DI-KA-TI. Packard (supra n. 278) 75–80.

[300] J.-P. Olivier, "'Cinq' en Linéaire A?" in B. Brogyanyi and R. Lipp eds., *Historical Philology: Greek, Latin, and Romance* (Amsterdam 1992) 135–36.

[301] J.T. Hooker, "Problems and Methods in the Decipherment of Linear A," *Journal of the Royal Asiatic Society* 1975, 164–72. J.-P. Olivier, "'Lire' le Linéaire A?" in *Le Monde grec, pensée, littérature, histoire, documents: Hommages à Claire Préaux* (Brussels 1975) 441–49. East Semitic: C.H. Gordon, *Evidence for the Minoan Language* (Princeton 1966); Gordon, "The Semitic Language of Minoan Crete," in Y.L. Arbeitman and

A.R. Bomhard eds., *Bono homini donum* (Amsterdam 1981) 761–82. For arguments against this identification, see Hooker 1988 (supra n. 273). Greek: G. Nagy, "Greek-like Elements in Linear A," *GRBS* 4 (1963) 181–211. Luvian: E.L. Brown, "The Linear A Signary: Tokens of Luvian Dialect in Bronze Age Crete," *Minos* 27–28 (1992–1993) 25–54; Brown, "Minoan Linear A: The Luvian Thesis Revisited," *American Philological Association Abstracts of the 126th Annual Meeting* 147. Lycian: M. Finkelberg, "Minoan Inscriptions on Libation Vessels," *Minos* 25–26 (1990–1991) 43–85.

[302] Papers in *Thalassocracy*, Gale (supra n. 12), C.W. Zerner and P.Z. Zerner eds., *Wace and Blegen: Pottery as Evidence for Trade in the Aegean Bronze Age, 1939–1989* (Amsterdam 1993), and *Aegean and Orient*. See also J.N. Coldstream, "Kythera and the Southern Peloponnese in the LM I Period," *TAW* I, 389–401; J.L. Davis, "Minos and Dexithea: Crete and the Cyclades in the Late Bronze Age," in J.L. Davis and J.F. Cherry eds., *Papers in Cycladic Prehistory* (Los Angeles 1979) 143–57.

[303] B.J. Kemp and R.S. Merrillees, *Minoan Pottery in Second Millennium Egypt* (Mainz 1980); V. Hankey, "Pottery as Evidence for Trade," in Zerner and Zerner (supra n. 302) 109–16; Hankey and A. Leonard, "Aegean LB I and II Pottery in the East," in *Aegean and Orient*. Kommos III, 156–83 gives a summary of Minoan pottery found abroad and of foreign pottery found in Crete.

[304] Watrous (supra n. 1) 711–12, 734–35, 747–50. In *Aegean and Orient*: P.P. Betancourt, "Middle Minoan Objects in the Near East"; and L.V. Watrous, "Egypt and Crete in the Early Middle Bronze Age."

Mediterranean, and Egypt; and close ties existed between Crete and Kastri on Kythera, and perhaps Samothrace.[305] Minoan contacts with northern and southern Syria were apparently well established, and much of the Egyptian influence on Crete at this time may have come through port towns like Byblos.[306] Ugaritic texts relate how the goddess Anat sent her messenger, Quadesh wa-Amrur, by way of Byblos to the land of Kaphtor, probably Crete,[307] from where he was to return with the god of crafts, Kothar wa-Hasis, to build and embellish a palace for Anat. But the primary focus of Minoan interest in Anatolia and Syria in both the Protopalatial and Neopalatial periods is likely to have centered on the metals trade, particularly tin.[308] If so, the evidence for Protopalatial contact with Cyprus, and Cypriot copper, seems slight, while Middle Cypriot II sherds have been found at Zakros and Mallia in early Neopalatial levels, and some White-Painted Cross Line pottery occurs at Kommos.[309]

In LM I, however, there is a veritable wave of imported pottery. Much Cycladic pottery, especially from Thera, is imported into East Crete and to Kommos, which also receives some imported Mycenaean wares, while Central Cretan pots are exported to Thera. LM I also sees the most contact between Crete and Cyprus: Cypriot pottery is imported in some quantity, and much LM IA and B pottery is exported

to Cyprus. Contact between the Levant and Crete intensifies in LM I.[310] Although there is a minimum of Anatolian and Egyptian wares in Crete, a number of Canaanite amphoras attest to contact with the Levant, and LM I pottery is found throughout the Near East.[311]

In this regard it is difficult to know how to assess the evidence from pottery. We cannot assume, for instance, that the presence of a pot implies the presence of the people that produced it.[312] Recent scientific analysis has shown that much of the pottery considered Minoan was actually locally produced. Raw bulk goods such as metal ingots can also be difficult to trace because, as already smelted copper, they were redistributed and reworked, and perishable goods like foods and textiles have left few traces in Aegean contexts. The durable materials may simply be the surviving visible markers of a much more extensive trade in other goods.[313] The wide range of the preserved contents of the Uluburun shipwreck has completely changed the way we imagine ancient trade.[314]

In 1980, Catling formulated his well-known paradox: in the Neopalatial period, there is much bronze in the Aegean, but little evidence for contact between the Aegean and Cyprus; in the Final Palatial period, the situation is reversed, with little Cypriot copper in the Aegean, but much Aegean pottery in Cy-

305 Kythera: Sakellarakis (supra n. 213); Coldstream and Huxley (supra n. 189); I. Tournavitou, "Μινωϊκό ιερό κορυφής στα Κύθηρα: Η κεραμεική," 8th CretCong (forthcoming). Aegina: W.-D. Niemeier, in Politeia 73–78. Samothrace: D. Matsas, in Politeia 235–47.

306 O. Tufnell and W.A. Ward, "Relations between Byblos, Egypt and Mesopotamia at the End of the Third Millennium B.C.," Syria 43 (1966) 165–241; M. Saghieh, Byblos in the Third Millennium B.C. (Warminster 1984).

307 N.H. Walls, The Goddess Anat in Ugaritic Myth (Atlanta 1992). G.A. Wainwright, "Asiatic Keftiu," AJA 56 (1952) 196–212 attempts to locate the Keftiu in northwestern Syria or southeastern Anatolia.

308 G. Dossin, "La route d'étain en Mésopotamie au temps de Zimri-Lim," RAssyr 64 (1970) 97–106; A. Malamat, "Syro-Palestinian Destinations in a Mari Tin Inventory," IEJ 21 (1971) 31–38.

309 L.V. Watrous, "Late Bronze Age Kommos," Scripta Mediterranea 6 (1985) 7–11, esp. 7. Banou (supra n. 34) 174; Knapp (supra n. 207).

310 Cycladic pottery: Banou (supra n. 34) 171–72; Kommos III, 154–55; Jones 427. Interaction between Crete and Cyprus: Banou (supra n. 34) 171–74; G. Cadogan, "Cypriot Objects in the Bronze Age Aegean and Their Importance," in V. Karageorghis, Acts of the First International Congress of Cypriot Studies (Nicosia 1972) 5–13; Cadogan, "Crete and Cyprus, c. 2000–1400 B.C.," in Karageorghis (supra n. 206) 63–68; C. Lambrou-Phillipson, "Cypriot and Levantine Pottery from House AD Center at Pseira," JAOS 110 (1990) 1–10;

R.S. Merrillees, Trade and Transcendence in the Bronze Age Levant (SIMA 39, Göteborg 1974); Y. Tzedakis, "Κυπριακή κεραμεική στη Δυτική Κρήτη," in Karageorghis 1972 (supra) 163–66; E.T. Vermeule, "Minoan Relations with Cyprus," TUAS 5 (1980) 22–24. A pithos from Pyla-Kokkinokremos may have been made at Chania: Jones and Day (supra n. 200) 263. Interaction between Crete and the Near East: a flask perhaps from Beycesultan and an Egyptian jug and jar come from LM IB levels at Kommos: Kommos III, 156, 162.

311 Banou (supra n. 34) 182–83; Lambrou-Phillipson (supra n. 310) 5–6; Zakros 341; AR 36 (1990) 73. A Canaanite amphora from Thera Δ9 (Thera VII, 30 pl. 96) contained East Cretan pots, implying a trade route. V. Hankey, "Late Minoan Finds in the South-Eastern Mediterranean," 3rd CretCong (1973) 104–10, esp. 104–108.

312 The "Harvey Thesis": Muhly (supra n. 206) 13.

313 Muhly et al. (supra n. 205) 288 cite the following trade cycle: Assyrian merchants in Assur used silver to buy tin from Afghanistan and textiles from Babylonia, exported them to their colony in the karum at Kaniš (modern Kültepe), where they traded them for twice the amount of silver, which they then brought, undoubtedly with Hittite textiles, back to Assur.

314 C. Pulak, seasonal reports in INA Newsletter, also on line: http://nautarch.tamu.edu/. G.F. Bass, "Prolegomena to a Study of Maritime Traffic in Raw Materials to the Aegean during the Fourteenth and Thirteenth Centuries B.C.," in Techne 153–70; Bass, "Sailing between the Aegean and the Orient in the Second Millennium B.C.," in Aegean and Orient.

prus.[315] Although more LM I pottery is now known from Cyprus, the copper at most Neopalatial sites still cannot be shown to come from Cypriot sources, and may instead be from Lavrion.[316] The puzzle remains: if Minoans were not importing Cypriot copper to Crete in the Neopalatial period, why is their pottery found on Cyprus?[317]

In the Neopalatial period, there were at least three major Minoan trade routes within the Aegean: from Crete to Kythera, Laconia, and southwestern Messenia; the "Western String" of the Cyclades through Thera, Melos, and Kea, to the copper and silver mines at Lavrion; and the "Eastern String" through the Dodecanese to Anatolia and beyond.[318] Crete was connected to the central and eastern Mediterranean largely through a single latitudinal route that connected the two regions but which ran along the north coast of Crete going east and along the south coast going west.[319] From the east, the route proceeded counterclockwise up the Levantine coast, past Cyprus and the coast of Anatolia, through the straits of Rhodes to Karpathos, and south to Crete's Cape Sidero. Ships might then travel west along the north coast to enter the Gulf of Mirambello, but apparently the major route called for them to turn south to Zakros and Kommos, from where they could continue west or, taking advantage of prevailing winds and currents, head south across the Libyan Sea. The route from the west would have reached Crete at Chania, continuing along the north coast to Knossos.

According to these models for the principal trade routes, Minoans would have come into contact with the peoples of the western and eastern Mediterranean primarily in the various harbors and emporia along the routes themselves, and with the Mycenaeans directly in the southern Peloponnese and indirectly in the Cyclades, primarily on Thera and

Melos.[320] It is unlikely, however, that Minoan trade and contact with all these areas remained unchanging throughout the Neopalatial period. While trade with Cyprus apparently remains relatively steady from MM into Postpalatial times, contact with Syria seems to quicken in LM I and with Italy and Sardinia at the end of the Final Palatial period.

Trade, which may originate in part from a desire of local elites to obtain certain goods, can be considered from a number of different viewpoints: society, politics, technology, and distance.[321] Four models seem particularly useful in assessing the multiple functions of trade: centralized control, localized control, independent or entrepreneurial trade, and ceremonial or gift exchange.[322] The first assumes that trade was organized by a central authority, like the legendary thalassocracy of King Minos, for which there is very little concrete evidence. A model of localized control assumes the existence of "gateway" communities as a conduit for the transfer of commodities (especially metals) and finished products to subsidiary centers.[323] Independent or entrepreneurial trade models assume that some traders coexisted alongside merchants controlled or administered by the state. Finally, ceremonial or gift exchange may involve aspects of the other models, since its principal aim is not to gain a material advantage but rather to create stable relations and establish social ranking. This last function is a particularly important aspect of chiefdoms.[324]

The nature of the relationship between Crete and the Aegean islands in the Neopalatial period demands some explanation and characterization. Crete may have been primarily interested in the copper and silver deposits at Lavrion. By LM IB, both Minoans and Mycenaeans were present at Ayia Irini in Kea, where much of the working of the Lavrion

[315] Knapp (supra n. 207).

[316] Knapp (supra n. 207) 57. Gale 1985 (supra n. 204).

[317] J.D. Muhly, "The Development of Copper Metallurgy in Late Bronze Age Cyprus," in Gale 1991 (supra n. 12) 187.

[318] J.L. Davis, "The Earliest Minoans in the South-East Aegean," AnatSt 32 (1982) 33–41; Davis (supra n. 16) 706; Sakellarakis (supra n. 213); G.S. Korres, "Messenia and Its Commercial Connections in the Bronze Age," in Zerner and Zerner (supra n. 302) 231–48 argues against Minoan influence on Messenian tholoi.

[319] Kommos III, 180 and fig. 10; G.W. Harrison, "Background to the First Century of Roman Rule in Crete," Cretan Studies 1 (1988) 145, citing these trade routes to explain the ideal situation of Gortyn as the Roman capital of the province Crete-Cyrene.

[320] J.F. Cherry and J.L. Davis, "The Cyclades and the Greek Mainland in LC I: The Evidence of Pottery," AJA 86 (1982) 333–41; C. Gillis, "Akrotiri and Its Neighbors to the South: Conical Cups Again," TAW III.1, 98–116; M. Mar-

thari, T. Marketou, and R.E. Jones, "LB I Ceramic Connections between Thera and Kos," TAW III.1, 171–84; J.-C. Poursat, "Craftsmen and Traders at Thera: A View from Crete," TAW III.1, 124–27; J.A. MacGillivray, "Priest-Kings and Keftiu: Knossos and Thebes in the Eighteenth Dynasty," in Aegean and Orient, reports that the Lisht jug was locally made.

[321] A.B. Knapp, "Mediterranean Bronze Age Trade: Distance, Power and Place," in Aegean and Orient.

[322] A.B. Knapp and J.F. Cherry, Provenience Studies and Bronze Age Cyprus (Madison 1994) esp. ch. 4. See also E. Brumfiel and T.K. Earle eds., Specialization, Exchange, and Complex Societies (New York 1987); F.A. Gunder, "Bronze Age World System Cycles," CurrAnthr 34 (1993) 383–429.

[323] These categories are paraphrased from N.P. Kardulias, review of Knapp and Cherry (supra n. 322), JFA 23 (1996) 118–21, esp. 120.

[324] T.K. Earle ed., Chiefdoms: Power, Economy, and Ideology (New York 1991).

ores was taking place. For the making of bronze, however, Crete may have been the sole possessor of tin, receiving it from the east. Such a monopoly might have created tensions. If Akrotiri was the mutual emporion for both Cretan and mainland trade,[325] the eruption of the island might have caused a significant disruption in Crete's access to Lavrion and the mainland's access to Minoan bronze.

Since we do not know who the rulers in Neopalatial Crete were, we do not know how centralized the Minoan trade with the Cyclades was.[326] Proponents of a thalassocracy ruled by Minos have based their argument on anachronistic sources like Thucydides, who was attempting to justify the Athenian imperialism of his own day, or on the distribution of Aegean sites named Minoa and the mythological stories that record the conquests of Minos.[327]

A natural corollary to the notion of a Minoan thalassocracy is the suggestion by Diodorus Siculus (5.54.4) that the Cretans established colonies on several Aegean islands.[328] Evans had even postulated that Minoan settlers on the mainland were responsible for the rise of Mycenaean civilization, a theory that is now largely discounted.[329] Since there are many types of colonies in addition to the Classical Greek model,[330] including trading and agricultural colonies, scholars need to make their definitions clear. Another important aspect to be considered

is that colonization always involves the development of ethnic identities that both the motherland and the colony share yet make distinct.

Several Aegean sites have been proposed as Minoan colonies because they exhibit Minoan domestic pottery (imported and locally made), evidence for Minoan cult, the use of Minoan burial customs, and Minoan architectural and decorative styles: Kythera, Ialysos and Trianda on Rhodes, Seraglio on Kos, and Miletos.[331] It should be stressed, however, that these excavations are quite small, sometimes not much more than a few trenches, and generalizations should be offered cautiously. By contrast, the extensively excavated and heavily Minoanized sites of Phylakopi, Akrotiri, and Ayia Irini are generally not considered colonies.

Sometimes included in discussions of a possible Cretan thalassocracy is the imitation outside Crete of Minoan building styles, pottery, and art without imputing Minoan political and military control, called the "Versailles effect" after the tendency to imitate court styles at Versailles in areas of Europe outside French political control.[332] Similarly, Linear A may have served as a common script for business purposes outside Crete without indicating political domination by the Minoans, just as English and German are widely used in international business transactions today.[333]

---

[325] The relatively higher incidence of Cycladic, as opposed to Minoan, pottery in the Mycenae Shaft Graves (J. Rutter, *AJA* 97 [1993] 791–93) suggests that until the end of LM IA, much trade with the mainland may have been in the hands of Cycladic islanders. M. Marthari, "The Ceramic Evidence for Contacts between Thera and the Greek Mainland," in Zerner and Zerner (supra n. 302) 249–56 notes that of the pottery at Thera, 85% is local and 15% imported, of which less than 2% is from the mainland. Z.A. Stos-Gale and N.H. Gale, "The Role of Thera in the Bronze Age Trade in Metals," *TAW* III.1, 72–90. There are also relatively few pieces of Early Mycenaean pottery from Crete (e.g., a LH IIA spouted jug found at Palaikastro, *PM* II.2, 490 fig. 296a), but examples are increasing.

[326] C. Mee, review of Rehak (supra n. 39), *CR* 46 (1996) 380–81; A. Farnoux, "La fondation de la royauté minoenne," in *Politeia* 323–33.

[327] Thuc. 1.4. S. Morris, "Prehistoric Iconography and Historical Sources," in *Eikon* 205–11; C.G. Starr, "The Myth of the Minoan Thalassocracy," *Historia* 3 (1953) 282–86. See also various authors in *Thalassocracy*; M. Wiener, "The Isles of Crete? The Minoan Thalassocracy Revisited," *TAW* III.1, 128–60; Wiener (supra n. 205) 325–30; M. van Effenterre and H. van Effenterre, "Menaces sur la thalassocratie," in R. Laffineur ed., *Thalassa* (*Aegaeum* 7, Liège 1991) 267–70; and G. Huxley, *Minoans in Greek Sources* (Belfast 1968).

[328] J. Shaw, "Consideration of the Site of Akrotiri as a Minoan Settlement," *TAW* I, 429–36.

[329] O.T.P.K. Dickinson, "Cretan Contacts with the Mainland during the Period of the Shaft Graves," in *Thalassoc-*

racy 115–17.

[330] R. Hägg and N. Marinatos, in *Thalassocracy* 222.

[331] Kythera (supra n. 305). Ialysos: T. Marketou, *BICS* 41 (1996) 133–34; *AR* 41 (1995) 58. Trianda: *AR* 38 (1992) 58–59. Seraglio in Kos town, MM-LM IIIC: *AR* 36 (1990) 70. Miletos: W.-D. Niemeier, "New Excavations in Bronze Age Miletus, 1994," *BICS* 40, n.s. 2 (1995) 258–61; Niemeier (supra n. 11); Niemeier, "Recent Excavations at Miletus," in *Aegean and Orient*.

[332] The militarism of the early Late Bronze Age, which has been considered a sign of both Minoan and Mycenaean influence, is now seen as a general characteristic of the entire Aegean in this period: S.W. Manning, "The Military Function in Late Minoan I Crete," *WorldArch* 18 (1986) 284–88. The file of warriors in the Miniature Fresco from the West House at Akrotiri (Doumas pl. 28) could represent Mycenaeans, Minoans, or, more simply, Cycladic islanders; cf. the stele from Kea: J.L. Caskey, *Hesperia* 35 (1966) 363–76, esp. 175, pl. 90b. "Versailles effect": Wiener (supra n. 56).

[333] Accepted Linear A inscriptions from Mycenae SG IV (*PGC*, no. 1411); Ayios Stephanos in Laconia (*GORILA* 5, HS Zg 1); Kea (*GORILA* 1, KE 1; 2: 80, Wc 2; 4, Zb 3–5); Melos (*GORILA* 4, MI Zb 1; 5, MI 2); Kythera (*GORILA* 4, KY Zg 1); Thera (*GORILA* 4, THE Zb 1–4; fragments of tablets and one more inscribed pithos: *AR* 40 [1994] 69; *Ergon* 41 [1994] 56–62; *BCH* 118 [1994] 791); Samothrace (*CMS* V, Suppl. 1 B, no. 327); Miletos (Niemeier [supra n. 331]).

We can see clear architectural indications of the Versailles effect: polythyra at Akrotiri and Trianda; a lustral basin, light well, and ashlar architecture at Akrotiri; a pillar basement at Phylakopi; and a Minoan-style "parlor" in House A at Ayia Irini. On the mainland, one tholos at Peristeria has an ashlar facade with Minoan-style mason's marks, and similar blocks have been found reused at Pylos, Mycenae, and Colonna on Aegina.[334]

Another model to account for the spread of Minoan Neopalatial culture in the Aegean is the suggestion that it had a religious underpinning.[335] Later history provides well-documented examples for religion-based models of exchange, especially in "contact periods," where technological exchanges were tied (often unsuccessfully) to the adoption of religious beliefs (e.g., European contacts with Native American populations or with the Aborigines in Australia); a careful reading of such examples for the Aegean might give the necessary grounding for a systematic argument for a Minoan "threskeiocracy."[336]

Certainly the physical evidence exists for a persuasive prima facie argument. Peak and cave sanctuaries of Minoan type can be postulated for Thera, Kea, the Vathy Cave on Kalymnos, and Apollo Maleatas at Epidauros, while an actual example of a Minoan peak sanctuary has now been excavated on Kythera.[337] From the peak on Kythera, it is possible to see the peak of Mt. Ida on Crete, and other line-of-sight networks may have existed from Kea to Thera, and from there to Crete. Minoan religious themes appear in frescoes outside Crete, and Minoan-inspired terracotta statues were excavated at the temple at Ayia Irini on Kea. Many sites outside Crete have yielded Minoan cult equipment, including horns of consecration and offering tables, as well as prestige items like bull's head rhyta, maces, real or imitation tritons, and "game-boards."[338] Exported stone chalices reflect Minoan wine-drinking rituals;[339] compare the Tiryns ring (CMS I, no. 179) that depicts the enthroned goddess holding a chalice and attended by a file of genii with pitchers. Moreover,

---

[334] Pylos: a double ax on a block at Pylos (PN I, 94, figs. 15-16). Mycenae: AB 58 on a stele fragment from Grave Circle A (E. Protonotariou-Deilaki, in Hägg and Nordquist [supra n. 221] 69-83, fig. 27); on blocks (PPS 97 [1953] 437) near the South House (trident), near the Acropolis Wall (a "chariot wheel": REG 18 [1905] 78), and on two reused poros blocks in the blocking wall of the Atreus dromos (a branch on both: ILN 23 Dec. 1939, 942; A.J.B. Wace, BSA 51 [1956] 119, pl. 25). Aegina: a double ax (Niemeier [supra n. 305] 78, pl. XV). Peristeria tholos 1: a double ax and a branch (AR 7 [1961] 13 fig. 11; Prakt 1960, pls. 158β and 159α). O.T.P.K. Dickinson, The Origins of Mycenaean Civilisation (SIMA 49, Göteborg 1977) 93 interprets the mason's marks on the Peristeria tholos to mean that it was planned by a Minoan.

[335] N. Marinatos, "Minoan Threskeiocracy on Thera," in Thalassocracy 167-78; Marinatos, "Minoan-Cycladic Syncretism," TAW III.1, 370-76; Marinatos, "The West House at Akrotiri as a Cult Center," AM 98 (1983) 1-19; W.-D. Niemeier, "Iconography and Context: The Thera Frescoes," in Eikon 94-107. Cf. M.A.S. Cameron, "Theoretical Interrelations among Theran, Cretan, and Mainland Frescoes," TAW II, 579-92.

[336] For recent studies of the motives and machinery for Classical Greek colonization, see I. Malkin, Religion and Colonization in Ancient Greece (Leiden 1987); and C. Dougherty, The Poetics of Colonization (Oxford 1993).

[337] Thera: B. Rutkowski, "Religious Elements in the Theran Frescoes," TAW I, 661-64. From Troullos above Ayia Irini on Kea come a stone ladle, offering table, and a bronze figurine: J.L. Caskey, Hesperia 40 (1971) 392-95; Davis (supra n. 202) 164-65, n. 24. From the Vathy Cave come an imported conical rhyton and a stone ladle: M. Benzi, in Zerner and Zerner (supra n. 302) 275-88, pl. 36c (ladle). Apollo Maleatas: V. Lambrinoudakis, in Sanctuaries 59-65; for the sanctuary's terracotta figurines, see E. Peppa-Papaioannou, Πήλινα ειδώλια από το ιερό του Απόλλωνος Μαλεάτα

Επιδαυρίας (Diss. Univ. of Athens 1985). Kythera: Sakellarakis (supra n. 213); I.A. Sakellarakis, in Λοιβή. Εις μνήμην Ανδρέα Γ. Καλοκαιρινού (Herakleion 1994) 195-203; Sakellarakis and Olivier (supra n. 142).

[338] Frescoes: L. Morgan, "Island Iconography: Thera, Kea, Milos," TAW III.1, 252-66, esp. 259-60, fig. 8. Akrotiri: Immerwahr 185-88; Doumas. Ayia Irini: Immerwahr 188-89; Davis (supra n. 16) figs. 4-5. Phylakopi: Immerwahr 189-90; Davis (supra n. 16) fig. 13; recent excavations by the British School uncovered more fragments of the dolphin fresco and of another fresco with white lilies on a red background. Trianda: Immerwahr 190. Ramp House at Mycenae: Immerwahr 190-91; M.C. Shaw, BSA 91 (1996) 167-90. Argolid relief fresco (supra n. 183). Miletos (griffin): W.-D. Niemeier, "Minoan Frescoes in the Eastern Mediterranean," in Aegean and Orient. Horns of consecration: Akrotiri (Thera VI, 34 pl. 83a) and Trianda (AR 38 [1992] 58). From the mainland: S. Hood, "A Mycenaean Horns of Consecration," in Φίλια έπη (supra n. 151) 149. Cyprus: M. Loulloupis, "Mycenaean 'Horns of Consecration' in Cyprus," in V. Karageorghis ed., Acts of the International Archaeological Symposium "The Mycenaeans in the Eastern Mediterranean" (Nicosia 1973) 225-44. Offering tables: Phylakopi: AR 22 (1976) 26 and fig. 33. Thera: Prakt 1990, pl. 140α. Rhyta: Rehak (supra n. 132). Maces from Aegina and the Argolid: Kaiser (supra n. 140) 16, 17 fig. 4.40, pl. 7.4. Triton in blue faience from SG III at Mycenae: Karo 64-65 no. 166, pl. CXLVIII. Game-boards from Kakovatos and Mycenae: Foster 1979 (supra n. 250) 142-43.

[339] Chalices: Akrotiri: Thera V, pls. 61, 67, 68; Prakt 1971, pls. 282-83; AR 41 (1995) 57. Ayia Irini: Cummer and Schofield (supra n. 158) 122 nos. 1499-1500, pl. 42. Mycenae: SG IV (NMA 600) and V (NMA 854). Miletos: Niemeier 1995 (supra n. 331) 261. Zakros: Zakros 144. Makriyialos: Davaras 1985 (supra n. 43) fig. 48. On drinking rituals, see Hamilakis (supra n. 38) 1-32.

sealings impressed by Minoan seals and gold rings, the latter at least possibly used by religious personnel, have been found in the islands from Samothrace to Thera.[340]

The extent to which these religious paraphernalia abroad reflect how deeply the people of the Cyclades and the mainland were affected by Minoan religious beliefs is unclear. Most of these objects in the Cyclades are found in habitation sites, however, while most of those on the mainland have been found in tombs. It is possible, therefore, that the Mycenaeans regarded Minoan religious items merely as prestige goods, and their possession as an indicator of status.

The second model, that of localized control, posits the existence of gateway communities from which raw materials and finished goods were sent on to subsidiary centers. Zakros is an obvious gateway with its hoard of unworked elephant tusks and metal ingots; in the Final Palatial period, Kommos seems to have fulfilled a similar function. Port towns such as Kythera, Akrotiri, and Poros Herakleion are likely places for different ethnic groups to have mixed. The contents of the rich tombs at Poros suggest that they served individuals with international connections. Thus, it is not impossible that some Mycenaeans were already present on Crete in LM IA. If so, were they sightseers, businessmen, mercenaries, or envoys? It also might be useful to coin a new term for some of these individuals, perhaps "warrior trader" or "merchant prince."[341]

A third model of independent or entrepreneurial trade has been used to suggest that private merchants existed alongside royal merchants. This may be assumed for Crete, if only because it can be documented even for the strongly centralized royal authorities of the eastern Mediterranean.[342]

The fourth model, ceremonial or gift exchange among rulers, is implied by some objects. For example, at least 25 statuettes of Middle Kingdom Egyptian envoys of the pharaohs are attested from Anatolia to Nubia; the stone figure of User found at Knossos in a chronologically problematic context must be one such figure.[343] The reciprocal nature of such exchanges is indicated by the Levantine-Aegean silver cups deposited at Tôd in southern Egypt.[344] The stone lid inscribed with the name of the Hyksos pharaoh Khyan, again from a controversial context at Knossos, also fits into this pattern, for other objects inscribed by this ruler have been found in Syria, Anatolia, and Mesopotamia.[345] Another possible example of gift exchange is the presence of African blue monkeys or vervets (*cercopithecus aethiops aethiops*) in Knossian wall paintings, where they appear in ritual scenes; their importance must have been enhanced by their exotic quality. From Knossos, some of these monkeys may then have been shipped to Minoanized sites such as Akrotiri and Phylakopi, where they again appear in wall paintings.[346]

A variant of the "gift exchange" model is the Minoan or Minoanizing artistic koiné in the Aegean, elements of which we recounted above. This koiné consisted of geographically widespread similarities in special objects, techniques, iconography, and style, often so uniform that it is sometimes extremely difficult to separate Minoan from Mycenaean from Cycladic art; to some extent this Aegean koiné is part of a larger common culture within the eastern Med-

---

[340] Late Protopalatial sealings: a peg sealing from Ayia Irini in Kea (*CMS* V, no. 479); and two cord sealings, two impressed noduli (one inscribed with NA-TA), and an impressed roundel from Samothrace (*CMS* V, Suppl. 1B, nos. 320–28). Neopalatial document sealings are now reported from Thera (*Ergon* 42 [1995] 52–54, figs. 37–38) impressed by rings depicting bull-leaping and a chariot, the latter duplicated on similar sealings from Ayia Triada (HMs 516; *PM* IV, fig. 808) and Sklavokambos (HMs 632–35).

[341] The later Lefkandi burial resembles both the Poros burials and the Vapheio prince: M.R. Popham and I. Lemos, "A Euboean Warrior Trader," *OJA* 14 (1995) 151–57.

[342] A. Archi ed., *Circulation of Goods in Non-Palatial Contexts in the Ancient Near East* (Rome 1984).

[343] *PM* I, 286–90, 288 fig. 220. E. Uphill, "User and His Place in Egypto-Minoan History," *BICS* 31 (1984) 213; cf. W. Ward, "Remarks on Some Middle Kingdom Statuary Found at Ugarit," *UgaritF* 11 (1979) 799–806. See also H.P. Wotzka, "The Abuse of User," *BSA* 85 (1990) 449–53.

[344] The deposit dates to the 12th Dynasty, reign of Amenemhat II. R. Laffineur, "Réflexions sur le trésor de Tôd," *Aegaeum* 2 (1988) 17–30; C. Lilyquist, "Granulation and Glass," *BASOR* 290–91 (1993) 35–36; K.R. Maxwell-Hyslop, "A Note on the Anatolian Connections of the Tôd Treasure," *AnatSt* 45 (1995) 243–50.

[345] *PM* I, 416–22, 419 fig. 304b; *PGC* 92 no. 1142, pl. 1142; M.J. Mellink, "New Perspectives and Initiatives in the Hyksos Period," *Ägypten und Levante* 5 (1995) 85–89. See also M. Liverani, "Dono, tributo, commercio," *AIIN* 26 (1979) 9–28.

[346] Helms 1988 and 1993 (supra n. 100). P.J. Parker, *AJA* 101 (1997) 348 (abstract); T.F. Strasser, *AJA* 101 (1997) 348 (abstract). We are particularly grateful to Parker for allowing us to read her unpublished M.A. thesis, *Monkeys and Their Role in the Aegean Bronze Age, MM III–LM I* (Univ. of Texas at Austin 1996). Depictions in wall paintings on Thera and Melos: Akrotiri, Xeste 3, rooms 3a and 4, and sector A: Doumas pls. 95, 122, 147. Phylakopi, the Pillar Crypt area: Morgan (supra n. 338) 256 fig. 7, 260.

iterranean.[347] Three technological innovations in the Aegean are probably the result of Syrian influence: cloisonné, granulation, and the niello technique of inlaying different colors of metal against a black background. The ceremonial ax of the Egyptian queen Aahotep employs the niello technique and includes the representation of a distinctively Aegean crested griffin.[348] At the Syrian site of Kabri, floor and wall paintings in Minoan fresco technique have been uncovered, and other fresco fragments with Minoan elements have been identified in the decoration of the palace of Yarim Lin at Alalakh (level VII), well inland from Ugarit, and in the palace of Zimri Lim at Mari on the Upper Euphrates.[349] The recent discovery at Tell el-Dab'a in the Nile Delta of paintings in Minoan fresco technique and employing a strongly Minoanizing iconography has been much discussed.[350] Whether these paintings are to be dated to late in the Hyksos period or to the early 18th Dynasty (as now seems more likely), they should be contemporary with the end of the Neopalatial period (LM IB). The scenes published thus far are strongly suggestive of Knossian influence: the technique of fresco, the use of colored backgrounds, the iconography of bull-leaping, and bulls, griffins, and a leopard in flying gallop. Nonetheless, some aspects suggest an unfamiliarity with the details of Minoan iconography.[351] So far, there have been many interpretations of the meaning of these frescoes, but more likely than not they are simply symptomatic of an international cultural sophistication in the larger eastern Mediterranean. Like African blue monkeys in the Aegean, Minoan frescoes in the Levant and Egypt may have been of interest primarily because they were exotic.

While most studies of trade have concentrated on items that originate in one place and are found in another, we wish to point out one unusual pattern in Neopalatial trade: three items not found in Crete. One of the most obvious is the object decorated in niello. Virtually all Aegean niello work has been found in early and rich Mycenaean tombs on the mainland, but the iconography of these objects is strongly Minoan. Nonetheless, articles also in this technique come from Syria-Palestine and Egypt, and it seems likely that the technique originates in Syria. While it is difficult to imagine any Aegean workshop outside Knossos capable of producing them, Laffineur has intriguingly proposed a workshop at Mycenae staffed by Syrian craftsmen.[352]

Two materials are also found almost exclusively on the mainland: amber and amethyst. Most of the amber in the Aegean is of Baltic origin, and large quantities of it have been found in mainland contexts in LH I–IIA, but almost none is found from that period in the Cyclades or on Crete.[353] Thereafter, the amounts declined markedly, as if little more was coming into the Aegean, and the existing supply was simply being redistributed; even then, little reached Crete. Amethyst, on the other hand, probably came from Egypt and into the Aegean via the eastern Mediterranean, perhaps in exchange for silver from Lavrion. Like amber, amethyst is found in quantity in early LBA funerary contexts on the mainland. Only a few amethyst beads and seals occur in Neopalatial Cretan contexts, however, and from LH/LM IIIA1 on, little amethyst is recorded anywhere in the Aegean.[354]

These items possibly point to three peculiarities in Aegean trade networks: a set of foreign craftsmen

347 E.g., R. Laffineur, "Craftsmen and Craftsmanship in Mycenaean Greece," in *Politeia* 189–99. Wall painting: W.S. Smith, *Interconnections in the Ancient Near East* (New Haven 1965) figs. 126–28, 129b–c, 130, 134–37; *CAH* plates to vols. I–II (1977) pl. 66. Seals: B. Teissier, *Egyptian Iconography on Syro-Palestinian Cylinder Seals of the Middle Bronze Age* (Fribourg 1996); J. Aruz, "Syrian Seals and the Evidence of Cultural Interaction," *CMS* Beiheft 5 (Berlin 1995) 1–21.
348 *PM* I, 551 fig. 402: detail of griffin; cf. the wing of the griffin from Xeste 3 at Akrotiri: Doumas pl. 128.
349 W.-D. Niemeier, "Minoans and Hyksos: Aegean Frescoes in the Levant," *BICS* 40 (1995) 258–60; Niemeier (supra n. 338).
350 E. Cline, "Rich beyond the Dreams of Avaris," *BSA* 92 (forthcoming); M. Bietak and C. Palyvou, "A Large Griffin from a Royal Citadel of the Early 18th Dynasty at Tell el-Dab'a," *8th CretCong* (forthcoming); P. Rehak, "Interconnections between the Aegean and the Orient in the Second Millennium B.C.," *AJA* 101 (1997) 398–402.
351 The triglyph-half rosette is different from all Aegean examples, and bull-leapers are shown in anomalous positions, their costumes having been misunderstood: one bull-

leaper wears a cushion seal while only lentoids are depicted in the Aegean, and some bulls have been set against the backdrop of a textile pattern (often misleadingly referred to as a "maze" or "labyrinth"), a treatment without parallel in the Aegean but at home in Syria.
352 R. Laffineur, "From West to East," in *Aegean and Orient*. See also A. Xenaki-Sakellariou and C. Chatzilou, *"Peinture" en metal à l'époque mycénienne* (Athens 1989); M. Boss and R. Laffineur, "Mycenaean Metal Inlay," in *Techne* 191–97.
353 H. Hughes-Brock, "Amber in the Aegean in the Late Bronze Age," in C.W. Beck, J. Bouzek, and D. Dreslerová eds., *Amber in Archaeology* (Prague 1993) 219–29.
354 I. Shaw and R. Jameson, "Amethyst Mining in the Eastern Desert," *JEA* 79 (1993) 81–97; Higgins (supra n. 232) 36; C.A.R. Andrews, *Catalogue of Egyptian Antiquities in the British Museum* VI: *Jewellery* I (London 1981) 95–96. N. Gale and Z. Stos-Gale, "Ancient Egyptian Silver," *JEA* 67 (1981) 103–15. Amethyst in funerary contexts: Argos: D. Kaza-Papageorgiou, *AM* 100 (1985) 19–20, pl. 3.7; Mycenae: A.J.B. Wace, *Archaeologia* 82 (1932) 208–209. Neopalatial amethyst beads: Poros Herakleion chamber tomb (Metaxa-Muhly [supra n. 95] 92 no. 258, pl. 27); Archanes Phourni, Tholos

working on the mainland producing highly sophisticated niello objects in Minoan style for Mycenaean patrons; an imported material from the north, amber, that arrives in mainland Greece and is not shipped to Crete; and another imported material, amethyst from the east, which may be worked in Crete but, if so, is almost exclusively reserved for exportation to the mainland. In these three instances, Crete is a "present absence" that demands an explanation.

Religion

We know a great deal about Minoan cult locations and equipment, and practically nothing about belief systems for the Neopalatial period.[355] Since Linear B makes available religious documents pertaining to the Final Palatial period, it is possible that a decipherment of Linear A or Hieroglyphic might provide some help, but the obviously religious texts are few and conventional, as noted above.[356] The groundwork for the study of Minoan religion was laid at the beginning of the 20th century by Evans; his influence has been enormous and his views are still too often accepted uncritically, particularly his belief in a Great Mother Goddess and her Young Male Consort. Nearly half a century ago, Nilsson was unable to distinguish between Minoan and Mycenaean religion.[357] Efforts in the last two decades have concentrated on identifying and separating the contributions of the two cultures. Nevertheless, much work remains to be done.

As in so many other areas, the origins of Neopalatial religion must be sought in the Protopalatial period. Even before the rise of the first palaces, the Minoans were making offerings, perhaps on a seasonal basis, at caves throughout the island and at sanctuaries on mountain peaks and mountainsides, such as Juktas near Knossos and Kato Syme on the south coast. Monumental architecture, as well as Hieroglyphic script for religious administration, appears at some of these locations prior to the appearance of the first palaces. Equally early are the communal tholos tombs, especially in the Mesara, which were used by extended families or communities for burials and for the veneration of their ancestors. Finally, with the appearance of the first palaces, small ritual rooms with equipment for the preparation of drink and food can be identified at habitation sites, along with other possible cult paraphernalia. It is not clear, however, that there was a unified set of cult practices or beliefs across Crete even in Protopalatial times, though the sporadic appearance of images of women has led some to hypothesize the existence of a major Minoan goddess.[358] The figurines at peak sanctuaries, however, include both men and women, with the former outnumbering the latter.

At the beginning of the Neopalatial period, fewer peak and mountain sanctuaries remain in use but some now receive palatial dedications.[359] Evidence for burial ritual and the burials themselves virtually ceases, while at the palaces and major centers cult equipment becomes much richer and more complex, and Linear A supersedes Hieroglyphic. These fac-

---

E (*Archanes* 127 fig. 104), MM IA, a date too early for local work. Seals: *CMS* V, Suppl. 1A, no. 387, and B, no. 331 (color fig. on 467, h). Later contexts: a single bead comes from the West Shrine at Phylakopi (LH I–IIIA1 context): C. Renfrew et al., *The Archaeology of Cult: The Shrine at Phylakopi* (London 1985) 64, 97, 319. Six globular beads from the Nichoria tholos (LH IIIA2–B1 context): W.A. McDonald and N.C. Wilkie eds., *Nichoria* II: *The Bronze Age Occupation* (Minneapolis 1992) 281 and n. 22.

[355] D. Crawford, "Re-evaluating Material Culture," in *Society* 48–53; O.T.P.K. Dickinson, "Comments on a Popular Model of Minoan Religion," *OJA* 13 (1994) 173–84; Gesell *passim*; N. Marinatos, "Divine Kingship in Minoan Crete," in Rehak (supra n. 39) 37–47; Marinatos (supra ns. 97, 221); J. Wright, review of Marinatos (supra n. 97) in *Bryn Mawr Classical Review* (gopher:llgopher.lib.Virginia.EDU:70/11/ alpha/bmcr) 95.3.17, and Marinatos's reply, 95.8.11; F. Matz, *Göttererscheinung und Kultbild im minoischen Kreta* (Mainz 1958); B. Rutkowski, *The Cult Places of the Aegean* (New Haven 1986); I.M. Ruud, *Minoan Religion: A Bibliography* (*SIMA-PB* 141, Göteborg 1996); P. Warren, "The Beginnings of Minoan Religion," *AntCr* 1 (1973) 137–47; Warren 1988 (supra n. 174); L.V. Watrous, *The Cave Sanctuary of Zeus at Psychro* (*Aegaeum* 15, Liège 1996).

[356] A. Furumark, "Linear A and Minoan Religion," *OpAth* 17 (1988) 51–90.

[357] *MMR*²; A.J. Evans, *The Mycenaean Tree and Pillar Cult and Its Mediterranean Relations* (London 1901 = *JHS* 21 [1901] 99–204). Also see Davis (supra n. 179); H. Waterhouse, "Priest Kings?" *BICS* 21 (1974) 153–54.

[358] There is a chronological gap between the EM II "goddess" figurines from Myrtos and elsewhere (E. Fowden, "The Early Minoan Goddess," *Journal of Prehistoric Religion* 3–4 [1990] 15–18) and the first female terracotta figurines at peak sanctuaries. P. DuBois, *Sowing the Body* (London 1988) 47–49 and 132–36 refers to "feminiform" vases as signaling the common concept of woman as vessel.

[359] A. Peatfield, "The Topography of Minoan Peak Sanctuaries," *BSA* 78 (1983) 273–80; Peatfield, "Minoan Peak Sanctuaries," *OpAth* 17 (1990) 117–31; Peatfield, "Palace and Peak," in *Palaces* 89–93; Peatfield, "Rural Ritual in Bronze Age Crete: The Peak Sanctuary at Atsipades," *CAJ* 2 (1992) 59–87; L.V. Watrous, "Some Observations on Minoan Peak Sanctuaries," in *Politeia* 393–404; Rutkowski (supra n. 163); B. Rutkowski, "Minoan Peak Sanctuaries," *Aegaeum* 2 (1988) 71–98; N. Schlager, "Korakomouri," *ÖJh* 64 (1995) 1–24; K. Nowicki, "Some Remarks on the Pre- and Protopalatial Peak Sanctuaries in Crete," *Aegean Archaeology* 1 (1994) 31–48; I. Loucas and E. Loucas, "Sur le déclin des sanctuaires de sommet au minoen récent," in Laffineur (supra n. 31) 35–38. The decline of smaller peak sanctuaries has been read as part of a process of consolidation at a few large ones.

tors suggest that the new palaces may have engaged deliberately in reorganizing and reforming Minoan religion along official lines. With the LM IB destructions that signal the end of the Neopalatial period, many forms of cult equipment connected with the palaces and major centers disappear, along with Linear A, and tombs reemerge as focal points for funerary cult, indicating that in some way the destructions mark a rejection of the Neopalatial religious system and a reemergence of long-held beliefs and customs. Historical parallels suggest that throughout the Neopalatial period, popular cults probably existed outside of palatial control alongside official cults.

The peak sanctuary on Juktas, in use in Protopalatial times, had its first major building program in MM II–III when megalithic terraces I and II were established around an altar used for burning, adjacent to a natural cleft into which debris was swept.[360] Several offering tables or kernoi have been found built into the altar and set alongside the area of burning. A series of small subsidiary rooms was built against the slope on the east. After a MM III destruction, the sanctuary was reorganized and blocking walls subdivided the subsidiary rooms I–V, reusing poros blocks and a column base from the earlier phase. Neopalatial finds included stone offering tables and vessels, a fragment of a painted terracotta house model, anthropomorphic figurines, sheet bronze votive tools, scraps of gold foil, and sealstones. The open terraced areas and their formal approach ramp should be considered an example of a "sacred enclosure," not a temple or a tripartite shrine. A megalithic circuit wall enclosing the peak might be as early as MM III/LM I or as late as LM III.

Juktas was approached by at least one Minoan road from Knossos to the north. Along this route, just below the peak and outside the circuit wall, lay Building B, begun late in Protopalatial times (MM IIB–MM IIIA) and rebuilt along more impressive lines at the beginning of Neopalatial times (MM IIIA–B). Each phase ended in a destruction by fire. Because many of the finds are of a practical nature (e.g., a stone

water channel, a pottery workshop), this building may have served the sanctuary as a way station and manufactory for votive items.

Lower still and farther north along this route is the shrine building at Anemospilia,[361] perhaps another station on the road up to Juktas. This building collapsed in an earthquake in MM IIIA, followed by fire, entombing four individuals; forensic reconstruction of their faces provides important new evidence about Minoan physiognomy. There is no real evidence that human sacrifice was taking place here, although the recently discovered children's bones at Knossos in a LM IB context have been interpreted as evidence for ritual cannibalism.[362]

A mountainside (but not peak) sanctuary at Kato Syme forms an important comparison to Juktas, but unlike it, Syme seems to have existed outside any one direct palatial authority and to have served more than one geographic region.[363] Located at an elevation of 1,200 masl in a natural concavity at the foot of a cliff on the south slope of Mt. Dikte, Syme's setting is reminiscent of that of Delphi. Integral features of the site were a perennial gushing spring of ice-cold water and a waterfall, both of which probably attracted the attention of the Minoans. Because of its relative inaccessibility, Syme can only have been used on a seasonal basis, and even now the site is inaccessible in winter. Minoan visitors from Central Crete probably took an overland "pilgrimage" route from the Mesara and Pediada up to modern Embaros on the southwest slope of Dikte; from there, one fork ascends east up to Omalos and over to Syme, and another fork leads north to Lasithi and the Diktaian Cave at Psychro.

Despite Kato Syme's complicated stratigraphy, two Protopalatial phases with impressive serpentine architectural elements have been identified. The center of the sanctuary was an open area where stone libation tables were set at the edges of small fires, recalling the arrangement at Juktas. Following a break after MM IIB, a reorganization of the peribolos took place with three recognizable Neopalatial phases. After the first of these, a paved road was constructed

[360] A. Karetsou, "The Peak Sanctuary of Mt. Juktas," in *Sanctuaries* 137–53; Karetsou, *Prakt* 1975, 330–42, esp. pl. 268α–β; *Ergon* 1975, 176–77; *Ergon* 1985, 83–87; *Ergon* 1988, 160–65; *AR* 33 (1987) 55; *AR* 35 (1989) 99; *AR* 36 (1990) 71; *AR* 41 (1995) 60; *Archanes* 10–22.

[361] *Atlas* 51–53; *Archanes* 137–56; Vallianou (supra n. 11) 153–67; Musgrave et al. (supra n. 13).

[362] D. Hughes, *Human Sacrifice in Ancient Greece* (London 1991); P.M. Warren, *AR* 29 (1983) 63–87; S. Wall et al., "Human Bones from a Late Minoan IB House at Knossos," *BSA*

81 (1986) 333–38.

[363] We are grateful to A. Lembesi and P. Muhly for showing us the site in June 1996. *Atlas* 268–71; A. Lembesi, *Prakt* 1992, 211–30; Lembesi and Muhly (supra n. 125); A. Kanta, "Cult, Continuity and the Evidence of Pottery at the Sanctuary of Syme Viannou, Crete," in D. Musti et al. eds., *La transizione dal miceneo all'alto arcaismo: Dal palazzo alla città* (Rome 1991) 479–505; *AR* 36 (1990) 70; *AR* 37 (1991) 68; *AR* 38 (1992) 59.

over a series of small subsidiary rooms, leading up to an enclosure that contained a large, well-built megalithic platform. Between the peribolos wall and interior platform were traces of burning, fragments of stone offering tables (a few inscribed in Linear A), and other equipment: tubular stands, chalices with plain surfaces or relief decoration, figurines, huge numbers of conical cups, cooking pots, and jars, and the burnt and cooked bones of animals (sheep, goats, deer) suggesting ritual dining but not holocausts.[364] Later in the Neopalatial period, the construction of Building 5 covered part of the approach ramp. Although some fine bronze figurines have been found, the lack of "palatial" dedications is noteworthy in contrast to Juktas, and the most common finds are pottery—often specialized cooking shapes and drinking vessels. Other sacred enclosures with terraces existed elsewhere on Crete, at the peak sanctuary at Kophinas on the south coast[365] and at Petsofa above Palaikastro.

Caves were also important, and a number of them show continuing use from MM II into LM I.[366] There are Neopalatial deposits in the Diktaian Cave at Psychro on the north side of Mt. Dikte overlooking the Lasithi plain, the Arkalochori Cave in the Pediada plain, the Idaian Cave on Mt. Ida, and the cave of Eileithyia south of Amnisos at Episkopi. In all these locations, the finds include terracottas, along with bronze double axes and figurines. Much of the material deposited in caves is indistinguishable from the material dedicated at peak sanctuaries, and none of the locations can be distinguished from others on the basis of its finds, except for Arkalochori with its rich deposits of bronzes and precious metal double axes. This might mean that the same divinity was worshipped at each, or that offerings for one divinity were appropriate for another. Later Greek myth connects other caves with birthplaces and the cults of goddesses: Dikte and Ida, for example, are associated with the worship of the mother goddess, Rhea, and the birthplace of her son, Zeus,[367] but it is not possible to push these last identifications convincingly back into the Bronze Age.

The origin of the horns of consecration is uncertain, but they do not at all resemble bulls' horns: an early (MM II) plaster model of composite horns found at Petsofa suggests that they had a longstanding connection with peak sanctuaries, and perhaps their resemblance to the Egyptian horizon sign is not accidental.[368] Horns, when attached to architecture, thus seem to signpost buildings or areas where ritual could take place. Large stone horns were set up in the courtyard at Nirou Chani and near the north and south entrances to the palace at Knossos; half of an immense pair of gypsum horns is now located at the north end of the west court at Knossos near the Theatral Area.[369] In some representations, however, buildings are crowned by horns or by small conical projections that cannot be equated with horns of consecration.

At habitation sites, possible locations for ritual activity include paved courtyards, especially the central and west courts of the palaces, stepped "theatral areas," and in the interiors of buildings in or at lustral basins, pillar basements, and polythyra.[370] Raised walkways suitable for processions or dances have been noted in courts at Knossos, Phaistos, Nirou Chani, Archanes Tourkogeitonia, and Pyrgos.[371] The Knossos Sacred Grove and Dance Fresco shows gesticulating women in such a location, observed by male and female spectators. The Grandstand Fresco has been interpreted as showing a rit-

[364] Lembesi and Muhly pointed out to us that there is no evidence for holocausts (as in later Greek religion), but they noted that the heads of some animals may have been placed at the edges of the fires.

[365] AR 42 (1996) 45: the main period of use is MM III–LM I.

[366] P. Faure, "Cavernes sacrées de la Crète antique," Cretan Studies 4 (1994) 77–83; B. Rutkowski and K. Nowicki, The Psychro Cave and Other Sacred Grottoes in Crete (Warsaw 1996); Watrous (supra n. 355); I.A. Sakellarakis, "The Idaean Cave," Kernos 1 (1988) 207–14; E.L. Tyree, Cretan Sacred Caves (Diss. Univ. of Missouri–Columbia 1974). Individual caves: Mamelouka (Kanta 228–29; Tzedakis [supra n. 310]); Melidone cave, West Crete (AR 36 [1990] 80]); Skales near Praisos (AR 37 [1991] 76]); Diktaian Cave (J. Boardman, The Cretan Collection in Oxford [Oxford 1961]); Arkalochori (S. Marinatos [supra n. 210]); Idaian Cave (I.A. Sakellarakis, Αρχαιολογία 15 [1985] 14–22; Sakellarakis,

ArchEph 1987, 237–63; Sakellarakis 1988 [supra]).

[367] Archanes 18–20. A.H. Griffiths, "Six Passages in Callimachus and the Anthology," BICS 17 (1970) 32–43, esp. 32–33; S. MacVeagh Thorne and A. Prent, "The Sanctuary of Diktaian Zeus at Palaikastro," 8th CretCong (forthcoming); G.A. Owens, "New Evidence for Minoan 'Demeter'," Kadmos 35 (1996) 172–75.

[368] A.L. D'Agata, "Late Minoan Crete and Horns of Consecration," in Eikon 247–56; Davaras (supra n. 124) fig. 31; Gesell passim, figs. 71–79; T.F. Strasser, "Horns of Consecration or Rooftop Granaries?" in Techne 201–206; E. Giannouli, "Μινωϊκά κέρατα καθοσιώσεως," 8th CretCong (forthcoming); A.J. Evans, Scripta Minoa (Oxford 1909) 223–24, sign 114 = CHIC (supra n. 270) sign 34.

[369] PM II.2, 589 fig. 367; cf. the limestone horns now set up on the south side of the palace (PM II.1, 159 fig. 81, 160).

[370] Gesell passim, esp. 30.

[371] Davis (supra n. 173); Marinatos (supra n. 173).

ual activity in the central court of the Knossos palace. The size and shape of the courtyards and theatral areas, and the large numbers of spectators of both genders in the Knossos frescoes, once again stress communal, not individual, activities. Small constructions in the west court at Knossos and in the central courts at Zakros, Mallia, and Galatas may have had a ritual function. Those in the central courts would have presented obstacles if the central courts really were used for the sport of bull-leaping.

The importance attached to architectural representation is reflected in the use of terracotta architectural models attested at a number of Protopalatial sites, including peak sanctuaries. Important examples date from the beginning of the Neopalatial period, like the models from the Loomweight Basement of the Knossos palace (traditionally MM II, but probably MM III), and funerary and domestic models from Kamilari.[372] The house model from Archanes (MM IIIA context) is two-storied. The ground floor plan resembles that of Zakros House G; upstairs, three steps lead up to a small projecting balcony on the roof on which are preserved the feet of a terracotta figurine. A similar scene appears on the Miniature Fresco from the West House at Akrotiri where a woman stands at a balcony on the roof of a building.[373] Another Neopalatial terracotta model (a house or a shrine?) was found at the peak sanctuary on Mt. Juktas.

The interior constructions identified as ritual areas are all, in some way, problematic. Lustral basins, small sunken chambers approached by a short flight of stairs, are first attested at Mallia in MM II with an example that is truly subterranean.[374] Shallower examples proliferated early in the Neopalatial period and have been found at most of the palaces

and many, but not all, of the villas. Since they have no drainage, they are clearly not baths, and many of them are provided with low balustrades over which spectators could view activities in the interior. The figural fresco decorating a lustral basin on Thera depicts young women associated with crocuses and blood; if these paintings relate to the use of the Thera basin and if the basin was used in the same way as the Cretan examples, they should all have some connection with female rites of passage. If this identification is correct, lustral basins shed important light on the function of Neopalatial palaces and villas and again underscore the importance of women in Minoan society. Some lustral basins, including one at Chania painted with marbled decoration, had passed out of use before the end of the Neopalatial period, suggesting that the societal need for these rooms was changing. After the LM IB destructions, no more are built and existing ones are filled in.

Pillar basements are another regular feature of Neopalatial villas and palaces, where they are often located in the west wings.[375] Although ritual objects often fell into pillar basements from upper floor rooms when the buildings were destroyed,[376] the discovery of pithoi and drainage channels in many of the basements indicates clearly that they are primarily storerooms. Similarly, polythyra with pier-and-door partitions are a regular feature of Neopalatial palaces and villas.[377] The many openings permitted free flow of traffic, and the openings could be closed selectively to create privacy, but their ritual use is unproven and very little specialized equipment has ever been found in them. During LM IB, the openings between piers at many sites were closed off by partitions and built cupboards, sometimes for the storage of documents, suggesting that

---

[372] Krattenmaker 1991 (supra n. 90); R. Hägg, "The Cretan Hut-Models," *OpAth* 18 (1990) 95–108; R. Mersereau, "Cretan Cylindrical Models," *AJA* 97 (1993) 1–47; Mersereau, *AJA* 96 (1992) 334 (abstract); I. Schoep, "'Home Sweet Home.' Some Comments on the So-Called House Models from the Prehellenic Aegean," *OpAth* 20 (1994) 189–210. Models from Knossos: *PM* I, 220 fig. 166. Kamilari: *PGC* 101 no. 1223, pl. 1223; Marinatos (supra n. 97) figs. 21–23. Archanes: A. Lembesi, *ArchEph* 1976, 12–43 (dimensions: 31.3 × 28.7 × 23.5 cm); C. Palyvou, Ακροτίρι Θήρας. Οικο-δομική τέχνη και μορφολογικά στοιχεία στην υστεροκυκλα-δική αρχιτεχτονική (Diss. National Metsobio Polytechnic Univ. 1988) pl. 89; *Archanes* 61 fig. 36 (color). Juktas: *AR* 23 (1977) 63 fig. 100.

[373] Doumas pl. 48.

[374] We thank M. Schmid, architect at Mallia, who gave us a tour of Quartier Mu and the lustral basin, June 1996. For lustral basins in general, see A. Nordfeldt, "Residential

Quarters and Lustral Basins," in *Palaces* 187–93. Gesell 22–26, for discussion and catalogue. For more recent work: N. Mante-Platanos, "Νέες ενδείξεις για το πρόβλημα των καθαρτηριών δεξαμενών και των λουτρών στο μινωϊκό κόσμο," *6th CretCong* A2 (1990) 141–55; M. Andreadaki-Vlasaki (supra n. 73); W.-D. Niemeier, "On the Function of the 'Throne Room' in the Palace at Knossos," in *Palaces* 163–68, esp. 163–64 on various interpretations: bathrooms (Nordfeldt), imitations of cult caves (S. Marinatos), or as special rooms or adyta for sacrifices and offerings (N. Marinatos); L. Hitchcock, "The Best Laid Plans Go Astray: Modular (Ir)regularities in the 'Residential Quarters' at Phaistos," in *Techne* 243–50.

[375] Gesell 26–29; E. Hallager, "A 'Harvest Festival Room' in the Minoan Palaces?" in *Palaces* 169–77; Begg 29–32.

[376] Cf. Soles and Davaras 1994 (supra n. 33) 408–10.

[377] Marinatos and Hägg (supra n. 84); Graham (supra n. 85); Driessen (supra n. 84); Hitchcock (supra n. 85).

the use of the polythyron was also changing before the end of the Neopalatial period. It too disappears rapidly after the LM IB destructions.

Several types of architectural construction represented in frescoes, glyptic, and on stone vases are poorly represented in the archaeological record, notably the tripartite shrine (only surely attested in the west wing at Knossos), and constructions enclosing or adjoining "sacred trees," which seem to be portable since two are represented on ships.[378] Four stone incurved bases found at Archanes Tourkogeitonia may have been used as supports for a temporary platform like those shown in paintings and on seals. Some representations of shrines have slender columns with floral heads, suggesting that such architecture could be set up quickly for specific events and then taken down.[379] The portable nature of much other cult equipment may help explain why so little cult architecture has been found and reinforces the notion that there were relatively few fixed locations for ritual.

There is evidence for a small house shrine at a number of sites, though the equipment differs in each. A possible shrine on the Royal Road at Knossos[380] included two tables of offerings, a small limestone horns of consecration, a fragment of an animal-head rhyton, and Special Palatial Tradition pottery. The shrine identified in the west wing of the Zakros palace is a figment: there is no direct connection between the room (which was devoid of special contents) and the workshops and storerooms with ritual equipment; as noted above, the latter rooms communicated instead with the large banqueting hall of the palace. At Knossos, several upper floor rooms have been identified as shrines on the basis of the frescoes that once adorned them, but proof of their ritual use is again lacking.

Special rocks, or baetyls, depicted on gold rings have been suggested as the seats of divinities or divine forces.[381] In most of these representations, a man or a woman kneels at the stone, sometimes gesturing. It is possible that these stones were located in sanctuaries like the possible omphalos at Phylakopi.

Many art objects have been identified as cultic or ritual equipment, not always on very solid grounds. Probable cult equipment includes stone kernoi (portable and fixed) and offering tables, stone ladles, clay and stone rhyta of specialized shapes and decoration, plastered and painted tripod tables, sea shells (real and of faience, or stone rhyta carved in the shape of tritons), and nonfunctional double axes, often elaborately engraved, which may have been used as votives or emblems. The recurring emphasis on sea imagery, particularly on Marine Style pottery, could mean that important activities took place at the shore or even in the water (cf. the Mochlos ring).

The various rhyton shapes made of stone, terracotta, and perhaps metal, along with conical cups, suggest that wine-drinking played an important role in cult activities. The distribution patterns of rhyta imply that most were manufactured at Knossos and perhaps disseminated from there to other sites. The possibly deliberate breakage of these objects has been discussed above. Tubular stands, the ancestors of the Final and Postpalatial "snake tubes," were meant to support open bowls, perhaps for offerings.[382] Anthropomorphic and zoomorphic figurines were made of terracotta, bronze, or lead, presumably for use as votive objects.

Although bucrania are often represented in association with double axes, there is no certain evidence that animals were sacrificed before the Final Palatial period. There may therefore be an aspect to the association of the bucranium and ax that we do not yet understand.[383] The double ax is combined with a loop-fillet, a frequent device on LM IB Alternating Style pottery. "Sacral knots" with fringed ends were sometimes manufactured in faience, painted on a wall at Nirou Chani, or carved of ivory.[384]

---

[378] Tripartite shrine: Shaw (supra n. 134). "Sacred trees": B. Rutkowski, "Der Baumkult in der Ägäis," *Visible Religion* 3 (1985) 159–71. C. Sourvinou-Inwood, "Boat, Tree and Shrine: The Mochlos Ring and the Makrygialos Seal," *Kadmos* 28 (1989) 97–101, on *CMS* II.3, no. 252, and *CMS* V, Suppl. 1A, no. 55, both from LM I contexts.

[379] E.g., on the Ayia Triada ivory pyxis, Halbherr et al. (supra n. 158); cf. the shrine on a fresco from Thera: Doumas pl. 147.

[380] Gesell 101, no. 64.

[381] P. Warren, "Of Baetyls," *OpAth* 18 (1990) 193–206; Younger 1988 (supra n. 106) 282–83; Renfrew et al. (supra n. 354) 430–31.

[382] G.C. Gesell, "The Minoan Snake Tube," *AJA* 80 (1976)

247–59.

[383] E.g., a cushion seal from Knossos (*CMS* II.3, no. 11); a LM IB amphora from Pseira (Betancourt and Davaras [supra n. 21] 35–36, figs. 16 and 38, pl. 13). See I.A. Sakellarakis, "Das Kuppelgrab A von Archanes und das kretischmykenische Tieropferritual," *PZ* 45 (1970) 135–219.

[384] Pottery: e.g., *CM* pls. 82 left, 83 lower right; *Archanes* 55 col. fig. 32; Cummer and Schofeld (supra n. 158) no. 1553, pl. 85; K. Demakopoulou ed., *The Mycenaean World* (Athens 1988) 105 no. 36 and col. fig. The Vapheio ring: *CMS* I, no. 219. Nirou Chani fresco: *PM* II.1, 284 fig. 168; Gesell 192 fig. 90. Ivory from Knossos: *PM* I, 427 fig. 308; Gesell 192 fig. 87.

Another possible religious symbol is the figure-eight shield.[385] Both the figure-eight and the tower shield had a functional use as body armor. But unlike the tower shield, the figure-eight shield appears in ways that suggest that it had a ritual symbolism as well. Repeating friezes of figure-eight shields appear on pots as early as LM IA, and in LM IB this shield is a regular element on Alternating Style pottery, including an unusual piece from the Cult Basement at Knossos, which contained the bones of children. The shield also appears as a jewelry pendant, and a Minoan silver rhyton in the shape of a figure-eight shield comes from Mycenae Shaft Grave IV. The shield also appears on the LM I Vapheio ring (*CMS* I, no. 219).

The principal Minoan cult symbol, the double ax, occurs as a motif in a variety of media.[386] While double axes can exist as functional tools, many examples survive made of thin bronze or precious metal, which could not possibly have been used for practical purposes. A fresco fragment from Knossos shows double axes attached to or embedded in columns that alternate with horns of consecration. Since the axes are portable, they could have been carried to the locations where they were needed, set in stone bases, and then removed after use. Since we never see the double ax being used as a sacrificial tool, the main function of the decorative examples may have been to demarcate the locations where ritual activities were to be performed.

Attempts to identify divinities or their representations are generally problematic. Most convincing is one iconographic topos: a large woman seated facing left on an architectural platform attended by women and/or animals.[387] This topos appears on several seals and gold rings, and in fresco, especially in the large-scale fresco from Xeste 3 at Akrotiri. A frontal Mistress of Animals appears on some Neopalatial sealstones, wearing the "Snake Frame" headdress and flanked by antithetic griffins or lions.[388] The presence of antithetic griffins flanking the throne in a Final Palatial renovation of the Knossos throne room has been used to support the hypothesis that during the Neopalatial era a ruler or priestess occupied the throne in an epiphanic ritual.[389] Recent discussion of the Final Palatial evidence for the throne room tends to obscure the fact that in the Neopalatial period the area combined a polythyron with a lustral basin. The three faience figurines from the Temple Repositories are sometimes claimed as snake goddesses, but a wide chronological gulf separates them from the Postpalatial terracotta figurines holding snakes.

Figures of women and men who hold one arm outstretched and grasp a staff or spear in the "commanding gesture" have been called rulers or gods.[390] The most likely to represent divinities are the small descending youth in this pose on a gold ring in the Ashmolean Museum and the woman in restored sealings from the area of a shrine on the west side of the central court at Knossos.[391] In the Knossos sealings, the woman with the commanding gesture stands atop a mountain peak flanked by antithetic rampant lions; to one side is an architectural representation with horns of consecration, and on the other side is a standing male who salutes her. Despite the small size of the elevated figures, their identification as divinities is strengthened by the presence of a woman on the ring and a man on the sealings, both of whom bow their heads and hold a clenched fist at the brow, a pose known from bronze statuettes of figures presumed to be votaries. Opinion is divided over the man performing the commanding gesture on the Master Impression from Chania who stands atop a cityscape: he could be a ruler or a god.[392] Many other proposed divinities are ambiguous or doubtful. It is difficult to identify gods and rulers because no text labels them and no trait distinguishes one

[385] P. Rehak, "Minoan Vessels with Figure-Eight Shields," *OpAth* 19 (1992) 115–24. Add a vessel from Pseira: *AR* 38 (1992) 69.

[386] E.g., a basket-vase from Pseira (Betancourt and Davaras [supra n. 21] 12, fig. 9); in relief on a pithos from Zakros (*Prakt* 1994, pl. 222α); ivories from Zakros (*Zakros* 131 fig.); a fresco from Knossos (M.A.S. Cameron and S. Hood, *Sir Arthur Evans' Knossos Fresco Atlas* [London 1967] pl. 5.1).

[387] Younger (supra n. 257) 171–77, pls. LXIc, LXII (all), LXIIIa–c, LXIVa–b, LXVc–f, LXVIa–f.

[388] Younger (supra n. 257) 182–83; R. Hägg and Y. Lindau, "The Minoan 'Snake Frame' Reconsidered," *OpAth* 15 (1984) 67–77; M.A.V. Gill, "The Minoan 'Frame' on an Egyptian Relief," *Kadmos* 8 (1969) 85–102.

[389] S. Mirié, *Das Thronraumareal des Palastes von Knossos* (Bonn 1979); R. Hägg, "Epiphany in Minoan Ritual," *BICS* 30 (1983) 184–85; Hägg, "Die göttliche Epiphanie im minoischen Ritual," *AM* 101 (1986) 41–62; W.-D. Niemeier, "Zur Deutung des 'Thronraumes' im Palast von Knossos," *AM* 101 (1986) 63–95; Niemeier (supra ns. 244, 374).

[390] Younger (supra n. 257) 156–62; T. Corsten, "Zu den sogenannten Schwebenden Gottheiten," in E. Thomas ed., *Forschungen zur ägäischen Vorgeschichte: Das Ende der mykenischen Welt* (Cologne 1987) 193–200.

[391] M.R. Popham and M.A.V. Gill, *The Latest Sealings from the Palace and Houses at Knossos* (Oxford 1995) 41, pls. 5 and 27 (KSPI M1–5).

[392] E. Hallager, *The Master Impression* (*SIMA* 69, Göteborg 1985), on *CMS* V, Suppl. 1A, no. 142.

from the other. This ambivalence underscores a fundamental difference between Neopalatial Crete and its neighboring civilizations of the eastern Mediterranean. In almost every culture, even those with documentary texts, the precise nature of the relation between god and ruler is problematic.[393] Typically, rulers have claimed divinity in three ways—directly, rhetorically, or only on special occasions. If the seal that impressed the Master Impression was not a commemorative piece, it may reflect one of the first two relationships.

The evidence for cult statues is controversial.[394] Although terracotta feet with pointed, upturned toes have sometimes been identified as the feet of statues, like the separate feet inserted into the skirts of terracotta figurines in LM III, they have been found more often singly than in pairs, starting in the Protopalatial period.[395]

The scholarly investigation of gender in Minoan religion and society has gotten off to a slow start,[396] despite much popular discussion about the role of women on Crete. The deposition of male and female figurines at peak sanctuaries suggests that these locations were used by men and women, though perhaps at different times. Only two Neopalatial frescoes (the Grandstand and the Sacred Grove and Dance frescoes, both from Knossos) show men and women together, but the women are larger and more elaborately dressed. In contrast to stone relief vases, where only men appear, women and animals like agrimia and blue monkeys are shown in nature scenes in frescoes and in glyptic, and there are repeated references to flowering plants like crocuses and lilies, which have medicinal properties. These gendered scenes suggest a culture/nature dichotomy

rather than an innate interest in nature on the part of the Minoans.[397] The only ritual activity that seems to include both women and men as participants is bull-leaping.

The use of wine seems to have played an important part in religious activities, including feasting, drinking ceremonies, and exchange systems among the palatial elite. One of the calcite Thera chalices was found with a miniature Minoan wine vat of the same material, suggesting a connection; the Vapheio ring depicts a large pithos at one side of the cult scene; and the wine pithos found in a country house at Epano Zakros has a Linear A inscription around its rim recording a huge quantity of wine, 32 units (921.6 l). Several installations for producing wine have been found in buildings with palatial features and fresco decoration. Finally, a number of rhyta and other vessels may have been used in drinking, along with the stone chalices found at various sites, the clay chalices from Kato Syme, and the ubiquitous conical cups. The archaeological evidence for the Minoan use of wine, and the depiction in fresco and glyptic of figures in exaggerated movement have led some scholars to postulate the existence of ecstatic religion.[398]

In summary, during the Neopalatial period religion seems to have been used by the palaces and villas to support a political system in which the ruling class may also have been religious officials. The lack of identifiable cult buildings, the creation of open areas that could accommodate gatherings of people, and the portable nature of most Minoan cult equipment suggest that an essential aspect of Neopalatial religion was its theatrical or performative nature. Minoan social and perhaps political organi-

---

[393] H. Frankfort, *Kingship and the Gods* (Chicago 1948); J. Baines, "Kingship, Definition of Culture, and Legitimation," in D. O'Connor and D.P. Silverman eds., *Ancient Egyptian Kingship* (Leiden 1995) 3–47; D. Cannadine, in D. Cannadine and S. Price eds., *Rituals of Royalty* (Cambridge 1987) 1–19; D.A. Freidel and L. Schele, "Kingship in the Late Preclassic Maya Lowlands," *American Anthropologist* 90 (1988) 547–67; R. Garland, "Priests and Power in Classical Athens," in M. Beard and J. North eds., *Pagan Priests* (London 1990) 75–91; S. Houston and D. Stuart, "Of Gods, Glyphs, and Kings," *Antiquity* 70 (1996) 289–312, esp. 290; D. Kertzer, *Ritual, Politics, and Power* (New Haven 1988); C. Geertz, "Centers, Kings and Charisma," in J. Ben-David and T.N. Clark eds., *Culture and Its Creators* (Chicago 1977) 150–71.

[394] N. Marinatos and R. Hägg, "Anthropomorphic Cult Images in Minoan Crete?" in *Society* 185–201; I.B. Romano, "Early Greek Cult Images and Cult Practices," in R. Hägg, N. Marinatos, and G.C. Nordquist eds., *Early Greek Cult Practice* (Stockholm 1988) 127–34.

[395] B. Forsén and J. Forsén, "A Prehistoric Foot from Ar-

golis," *Journal of Prehistoric Religion* 6 (1992) 24–29. Single feet: Gournia, Sklavokambos, Phaistos; add Chania (Tzedakis and Hallager [supra n. 50] 15 fig. 14) and Mochlos (Soles and Davaras 1994 [supra n. 33] 419, 420 fig. 16). Pairs of feet: Mallia (Protopalatial) and Anemospilia (early Neopalatial). Five different single feet come from Ayia Irini: Caskey, in *Sanctuaries* 134 fig. 10, and discussion, 136.

[396] T. Cullen, "Contributions to Feminism in Archaeology," *AJA* 100 (1996) 409–14; D. Kokkinidou and M. Nikolaïdou, Η αρχαιολογία και η κοινωνική ταυτότητα του φύλου (Salonika 1993); S. Brown, "Feminist Research in Archaeology," in N.S. Rabinowitz and A. Richelin eds., *Feminist Theory and the Classics* (New York 1993) 238–71.

[397] S.B. Ortner, "Is Female to Male as Nature Is to Culture?" *Feminist Studies* 1 (1972) 5–21. P. Rehak and R.R. Snihurowych, "Medicine, Myth and Matriarchy in the Thera Frescoes," forthcoming in *American Philological Association Abstracts of the 129th Annual Meeting* (New York 1997).

[398] P. Warren, "Minoan Crete and Ecstatic Religion," in *Sanctuaries* 155–66.

zation may thus have been based on public action that merged religion and ceremony. If so, the Minoans were in good company, since this type of performative religion as an aspect of politics was well established in Egypt and the Near East, and examples continue in some parts of the world today.[399]

LM IB Destructions

Toward the end of the LM IB period, there is evidence for significant disruptions at a number of Minoan sites throughout Crete and at heavily Minoanized sites in the Cyclades. At many locations, abandonment follows burning, and in many cases there is little sign of resettlement until LM IIIA1-2. The destructions thus mark a much more significant interruption of Minoan culture than those in MM II that signaled the end of the Protopalatial period. Major destructions are recorded at Chania and Nerokourou in the west; Phaistos and Ayia Triada in the south; Mochlos, Gournia, Pseira, Pyrgos, Makriyialos, Petras, Palaikastro, and Zakros in the east; and Zominthos, Sklavokambos, Tylissos, the Knossos area, Archanes Tourkogeitonia, Amnisos, Nirou Chani, and Mallia in Central Crete. At Knossos, the palace is unique in having no identifiable LM IB destruction deposits, but several buildings in the surrounding community were damaged or destroyed: the Stratigraphic Museum area (including the so-called Cult Basement) and structures along the Royal Road.[400]

These destructions appear selective and carefully planned to destroy as many administrative centers as possible. Settlements, and specific buildings that housed Linear A administrations, are particularly badly hit, so much so that they seem occasionally to have been deliberate targets: at Pyrgos, the villa was burned, but not the surrounding town; at Mochlos, ashlar Building B2 was destroyed, but not the artisans quarter, which continued into LM II;[401] and Kommos escaped a major destruction, though House X yielded limited evidence of LM IB burning.

The causes of the Cretan and Cycladic destructions have not been determined to the satisfaction of all scholars, although three main interpretations have been advanced: natural causes such as earthquakes followed by fire, invasion by mainland Mycenaeans, or a Knossian takeover of the rest of the island.[402] Several earlier attempts had been made to link the LM IB Cretan destructions with the IA Thera eruption; this position has now been abandoned by virtually all scholars. In any case, the conflagrations on Crete were so widespread that it is hard to attribute them to a single natural occurrence like earthquakes.

If the destructions are the work of Mycenaean invaders from the mainland, Knossos must have been spared, perhaps to serve as a base of operations against the other Minoan palaces and administrative centers, with the exception of a few key places like Kommos. Such a Mycenaean military intervention might explain the deliberately buried hoards of bronzes at Knossos and Mochlos and the signs of violent death (unburied bodies at Mochlos and defleshed children's bones at Knossos, possibly from siege conditions) and looting.[403] Following the destructions, during LM II–IIIA1, new features appear on Crete that are similar to contemporary developments on the mainland, though it is doubtful that there was an active Mycenaean colonization of Crete at this time.[404] The military hypothesis also best explains the concentration of new features in and around Knossos. Perhaps the Mycenaeans collaborated with the Knossians or even were invited into Crete by them. If LM IB Knossos was primarily a religious center, it may have been spared on those grounds. Alternatively, the wealth of Knossos and the presence of so many important workshops there may have made it too valuable to be destroyed.

An alternative hypothesis of interstate warfare on Crete, without a Mycenaean component, could account equally well for many of the arguments listed above. The introduction of Mycenaean features could have taken place without a military conquest, and

[399] C. Geertz, *Negara* (Princeton 1980) 98–120. We thank M. Nikolaïdou for mentioning this work on *AegeaNet*, 12 March 1996 (*AegeaNet* archive no. 960312.06).

[400] The Stratigraphic Museum area: P. Warren, *AR* 27 (1981) 73–92; and *AR* 29 (1983) 63–87. The Royal Road: *AR* 7 (1961) 26–27; *AR* 8 (1962) 25–27.

[401] J.S. Soles, "A Community of Craft Specialists at Mochlos," in *Techne* 425–31.

[402] S. Hood, "Warlike Destruction in Crete c. 1450 B.C.," *5th CretCong* (1985) 170–78; Hood (supra n. 30); Popham and Catling (supra n. 236) 252–57.

[403] Fragments of the Palaikastro ivory youth were found strewn within and outside Building 5. At Ayia Triada, six fragments of the Boxer Rhyton were found at ground level in the courtyard of Villa A, while nine other fragments

were found higher up in the Cortile Superiore. The fragments of the Zakros Sanctuary Rhyton were found widely scattered throughout the palace. House AF N at Pseira showed signs of looting: *AR* 38 (1992) 68.

[404] M.R. Popham, "Mycenaean-Minoan Relations between 1450 and 1400 B.C.," *BICS* 23 (1976) 119–21 lists "intrusive mainland" features: chamber tombs with long "keyhole" dromoi, tholos tombs, "warrior burials" and "burials with bronzes," certain types of bronze vessels, utensils, tools, weapons and armor, specific types of jewelry, and specific ceramic shapes and decoration. Popham also notes changes in frescoes, stone vases, religion, architecture, writing, larnakes, and ivories. For a skeptical view of Mycenaean colonization, see H.W. Catling, *Some Problems in Aegean Prehistory c. 1450–1380 BC* (Oxford 1989).

the militarism often imputed to the mainlanders is part of a general trend in the Aegean in the early part of the Late Bronze Age; it does not appear suddenly with the LM IB destructions and their aftermath. In searching for an agent of destruction, the obvious question is "cui bono"? Since the Knossos area survives relatively unscathed, some scholars have suggested that the destructions mark a Knossian takeover of the rest of the island centers.[405] But it is hard then to explain the destructions at nearby Archanes, Tylissos, and Sklavokambos, all of which were presumably within the Knossian orbit at the time they were destroyed. Moreover, sites that were receiving leather documents sealed and impressed by Knossian look-alike gold rings are also destroyed: Chania, Sklavokambos, Ayia Triada, Gournia, and Zakros.

The destruction of administrative sites and elite objects could even be read in Marxist terms as a rejection by an underclass of a ruling elite and its trappings. The eruption of Thera could have caused crop failure in East Crete, which could have destabilized the economy of the island and led to a dissatisfaction with the existing palatial system. It is also possible to imagine a combination of factors, such as a Knossian takeover of the rest of the island with the help of Mycenaeans, some of whom stayed on the island and introduced new features.

All assessments of the nature and intensity of the LM IB destructions on Crete, however, have been modified in recent years by the recognition that many sites show evidence of destructions throughout the Neopalatial period, including LM IA. In addition, there is some disagreement whether the Cretan LM IB destructions are all contemporary or not: perhaps what looks to us like a single horizon may actually have taken place over years or decades.

Whatever their causes, the destructions unquestionably signal a major disruption in Minoan culture and a rejection of many of the features we think of as characteristic of Neopalatial society and its symbolic language. With the losses come new features, some of which we characterize as Mycenaean, leading us to prefer a scenario that includes some Mycenaean involvement. Some crafts survive, but we can document an immediate loss of decorative detail and a gradual decline in quality in the manufacture of decorated weapons, sheet bronze vessels, gold and silver plate, ivory carving for furniture and toilet implements, and stone vases. In hard stone seals, the decline occurs gradually over several generations.

The losses in art and culture, however, are immense, and even a partial catalogue is staggering: Linear A, court-centered buildings, lustral basins, polythyra, stone relief rhyta, stone lion's and bull's head rhyta, stone chalices and maces, niello daggers, relief frescoes, and three-dimensional figures in faience and ivory.[406] There is an end to experimentation in rendering the human figure, an end to work in exotic materials, a divorce between writing and art, and the disappearance of major iconographic themes such as marine motifs, enthroned women, and landscapes with women and animals. This last loss we feel is significant. The gendered dichotomy between the scenes involving men in fairly restricted activities and the natural landscapes that include animals and women is replaced in Final Palatial art with recurrent scenes of men, processions of men and women, and the constructed world.

The losses in Neopalatial art and culture must reflect the subsequent preferences in the Final Palatial period. For example, Mycenaean religion apparently made little use of peak sanctuaries or caves, and so there was no need for the types of objects that portrayed them or had been dedicated there. Instead, the succeeding art forms—terracotta figurines, pictorial pottery, mass-produced jewelry, flat wall painting—and the prevalence of tholoi all express different cultural values and constructions of political power. The Neopalatial period on Crete represented a high point in Aegean culture that would not be reached again.

FINAL PALATIAL CRETE (LM II–IIIB EARLY)

As we stressed at the beginning of this review, the designation "Postpalatial" for the period on Crete following the LM IB destructions is no longer adequate, for it is clear that the Knossos palace survived and continued to function as an administrative center well after LM IB, and that Linear B was in use early in LM IIIB at Chania, and probably at Knossos too. With Linear B tablets being written at least at two major sites after LM IB, "monopalatial" does not accurately describe the period either.[407] After LM IIIB early there is no evidence for writing in Crete or for any centralized administration; the period LM II–IIIB early, therefore, may be termed Final Palatial. Thus Crete contrasts with the mainland, where we know that some palatial administrations continued to exist until the IIIB/C transition.

LM II represents the immediate aftermath of the

[405] W.-D. Niemeier, "The Character of the Knossian Palace Society in the Second Half of the Fifteenth Century B.C.: Mycenaean or Minoan?" in *Society* 217–36.

[406] P. Rehak, "Aegean Art before and after the LM IB Cretan Destructions," in *Techne* 51–66.

[407] For important studies of this period, see Kanta; M.R. Popham, "Late Minoan II to the End of the Bronze Age," in Evely et al. (supra n. 1) 89–102; Niemeier (supra n. 405) with a useful summary of opinions; Catling (supra n. 404); and Bennet (supra n. 292).

Cretan destructions, and is a time of severe disruption at most centers: some sites were abandoned, others depopulated, and only Knossos shows sure signs of operating on a large scale, including the continued creation of a number of specialized products. LM II may have seen a Knossian reestablishment of its control at other sites and may have been the first period of Mycenaeanization of the island.[408] On the mainland, palaces seem to have begun emerging at this time, notably the Menelaion near Sparta.[409]

In LM IIIA, signs of recovery and reoccupation are seen at many sites on Crete, though most settlements are smaller and less urbanized than their Neopalatial predecessors. New types of burials are introduced and there is a noticeable change in material culture. At Knossos, a destruction is documented at the transition from LM IIIA1 to 2 that is not mirrored at most other sites, where recovery continues relatively smoothly into LM IIIB early. In pottery, the distinguished Chania workshop[410] begins production in LM IIIA and by LM IIIA2 local pottery centers are known at Palaikastro and perhaps Episkopi. There is no discernible break between LM IIIA1 and 2 pottery, and existing trends continue on into IIIB early. While LM IIIA pottery is found abroad, especially in Cyprus, it is overshadowed by Mycenaean pottery exported in bulk. Nonetheless, Crete is not at all out of contact with the Near East.

The IIIA1–2 interruption at Knossos is fraught with problems of interpretation; we give a summary here of opinions presented in more detail below. Several scholars who think that the Mycenaeans arrived at the time of the LM IB destructions believe that the Knossos palace no longer functioned after the IIIA1–2 break; they would date the Linear B tablets at the site to this horizon. Others have argued instead that the IIIA1–2 transition marks the first major arrival of Mycenaeans on Crete, and would date

the Knossos tablets to the last phase of Final Palatial at the site (IIIA2–IIIB early). We follow a mix of these two scenarios: Linear B was probably being written at Knossos in IIIA1 but the final administrative activity probably belongs to IIIA2–B early. Whatever its causes, however, the IIIA1–2 transition is significant because it ends Knossos's longstanding role as premier administrative and artistic center in the Aegean, and marks the dissolution and scattering of its workshops and workshop personnel. In this last phase of Final Palatial we can see evidence of a permanent change in Minoan art, the culmination of forces that had been in operation since the LM IB destructions. The following period, LM IIIA2–B early, is marked by the Linear B tablets at Chania and the inscribed stirrup jars (ISJs) at many sites. The Final Palatial period ends with another destruction at Knossos and perhaps at Chania. Thus, the Final Palatial, like the Neopalatial period, cannot be regarded as a single monolithic entity.

Sites and Architecture

A few sites have uninterrupted occupation from LM IB to LM II; while most are destroyed and abandoned in LM IB, some are reoccupied in LM IIIA1, others in IIIA2.[411] The overall population appears to have declined significantly by LM IIIB, especially in East Crete, although this trend toward depopulation had already begun in some places in LM IB. In the west, Chania was hard hit but began to recover immediately: squatters cleared some of the settlement in LM II.[412] After a destruction by fire at the end of LM IIIA1, there was a short abandonment. In LM IIIA2–B early, reoccupation resulted in two building complexes, Houses I and II, making use of the orientation of some earlier walls. New features, however, suggest the presence of Mycenaeans: poorly constructed rubble walls, single-story buildings (no stairs and no material fallen from above), circular

---

[408] LM II pottery has been found across the island. Bennet (supra n. 292) 244: the sites with LM II "may reflect the initial stages of the Knossian administrative system after the LM IB disturbances," i.e., as second-order [palace] sites within a "new administrative system."

[409] Watrous (supra n. 1) 796; Shelmerdine (supra n. 16) 559.

[410] Y. Tzedakis, "L'atelier de céramique post-palatiale à Kydonia," BCH 93 (1969) 296–418; Demakopoulou (supra n. 384) 147, no. 103 (color illustration).

[411] Praisos, Achladia, and Piskokephalo are reoccupied in LM IIIA2: J. Bennet, "The Wild Country East of Dikte," Minos 20–22 (1987) 77–88, esp. 85. Pseira (Betancourt and Davaras 1995 [supra n. 21] 69; and in Cretan Studies [supra n. 34] 35) and Zakros (Kanta 195) show slight reoccupation

in LM IIIA2. Kastelli Pediados may be occupied at the very end of the Final Palatial period and continue into Postpalatial (AR 36 [1990] 72). Along with these later sites are later cemeteries that continue into the Postpalatial period.

[412] B.P. Hallager, "Some LM IIIB:1 Floor Deposits at Khania (summary)," in Schiering (supra n. 114) 89; B.P. Hallager, "Mycenaean Pottery in LM IIIA1 Deposits at Khania," in French and Wardle (supra n. 36) 173–83; B.P. Hallager, "LM II and Khania," 6th CretCong A2 (1990) 77–83; E. Hallager, "The Late Minoan III A2 and III B Periods in Khania," in Schiering (supra n. 114) 88; E. Hallager, "Khania and Crete ca. 1375–1200 B.C.," Cretan Studies 1 (1988) 115–24; Y. Tzedakis, "The Late Minoan III Settlement of Kydonia," BICS 20 (1973) 154–56.

hearths fixed in the center of major rooms, and local and imported figurines of types known in the Argolid, many placed near the hearth.

In the south, the Mesara plain continued to be an important area.[413] At Ayia Triada, in LM IIIA1 the impressive Megaron is erected, and in LM IIIA2 there is much building activity. The Megaron has enormous cyclopean foundations sunk several meters deep through the remains of the Neopalatial villa, and stone drainage channels were cut to draw runoff water away from the building.[414] Although the Megaron's superstructure has not survived, the dimensions of the foundations indicate a building larger than any of the surviving mainland megara. Adjacent to this building to the east was a small stoa, with a large and impressive second stoa to the northeast, the so-called Agora. Building W, of IIIA2 date, delimits another side of the Agora, along with buildings on the slope to the west. There is evidence for two shrines, one west of the Agora and one to the southeast of the Megaron. Judging by architectural remains alone, Ayia Triada was a major administrative center, even though no Linear B tablets have been recovered there.

With much imported pottery from the Near East and Italy, the port at Kommos flourished from the Neopalatial period through LM II into IIIA, but was almost completely abandoned at the end of IIIB early. In IIIA2, a series of shipsheds (Building P) was constructed over the east wing of Neopalatial Building T. The masonry of this building reused Neopalatial ashlar blocks, but they were set in a new way with small stones in the horizontal and vertical joints, a style of Final Palatial architecture seen at many other sites on Crete.

At Gournia, the ruined LM IB "palace" seems to have remained deserted, but in LM IIIA a megaron-like structure was inserted into the community at the south end of the plateia, on a different orientation from the Neopalatial structures.[415] At Mochlos, a few new structures were built in LM IIIA2 making use of the earlier Neopalatial buildings; remodeled, they continued in use into IIIB. At the east end of the site, a LM III cobbled road has been traced. Palaikastro had extensive IIIA1 reoccupation, and two wells dug through the earlier Building 7 were in use the entire IIIA period.

North-central Crete follows, in general, much the same pattern as elsewhere. Tylissos, mentioned in the Knossos tablets, must have been an important Final Palatial center though the excavated LM IIIA architecture is scrappy.[416] Simple house plans, a short stoa, and a circular cistern, like those at Archanes, Amnisos, and Zakros, are among the innovations. Recent excavations at Quartier Nu at Mallia have revealed new features: a megaron with a fixed hearth flanked by two columns, a room with a rare pebble mosaic, and stirrup jars inscribed in Linear B.[417] At Archanes Tourkogeitonia, much of the Neopalatial building lay in ruins, but foundation walls associated with LM IIIA–B pottery were dug deeply into the west side of the building.

As noted above, the only Minoan site that seems to have flourished uninterruptedly and on a large scale is Knossos.[418] Both the palace and its dependencies, the Little Palace, Unexplored Mansion, and Royal Villa, show continuous occupation into LM IIIB. Another important sign of continuity is the erection of a LM II house (not yet published) south of the palace that uses gypsum and includes a polythyron, an important indicator that the LM IB destructions did not mark a complete break with earlier building practices. A megaron-type structure may also have been inserted into the palace at the south end of the west wing, but so little evidence has survived that its existence is largely conjectural.[419] The size of the community, however, may have shrunk since no other buildings occur on the hillside west

---

[413] Phaistos exhibits limited reoccupation, mostly houses (Kanta 96–101). The stepped construction in the northwest corner of the central court could be Final Palatial as well as the pithoi there (*Atlas* 235).

[414] V. La Rosa, "Haghia Triadha in età micenea," in J.-P. Olivier ed., *Mykenaïka* (Paris 1992) 617–20; La Rosa, "Osservazioni sul centro di Aghia Triadha in età TM IIIB–C," in Rocchetti (supra n. 7) 75–80; B.J. Hayden, "Crete in Transition: LM IIIA–IIIB Architecture," *SMEA* 26 (1987) 199–234; D. Preziosi, "Mainland-Type Megara in Crete and the Cyclades during LM III," *AJA* 74 (1970) 201; Preziosi (supra n. 47) 175–93; K. Schaar, "Aegean House Form," in Darcque and Treuil (supra n. 3) 173–82; *AR* 36 (1990) 70–71; *AR* 38 (1992) 59. See also Niemeier, in *SMEA* (supra n. 5) n. 430, based on La Rosa, "Nuovi indagini ad Haghia Tri-

ada," *5th CretCong* (1985) 190–98.

[415] F. Oelmann, "Ein archäisches Herrenhaus auf Kreta," *JdI* 27 (1912) 38–51.

[416] B. Hayden, *The Development of Cretan Architecture from the LM IIIA through the Geometric Periods* (Diss. Univ. of Pennsylvania 1981); and Hayden, "Late Bronze Age Tylissos," *Expedition* 26:3 (1984) 37–46.

[417] *AR* 36 (1990) 74–75; *AR* 37 (1991) 73–74; *AR* 38 (1992) 64–65; J. Driessen, "La Crète mycénienne," *DossPar* 195 (1994) 70–78. Cf. the pebble mosaic from Tiryns (LH IIIA): O. Pelon, in *BCH* 109 (1985) 776: "une mosaïque de galets à décor spiraloïde découvert dans la pièce XXII."

[418] D. Doxey, "Causes and Effects of the Fall of Knossos in 1375 B.C.," *OJA* 6 (1987) 301–24.

[419] *PM* II.2, 6–7.

of the palace, except for the two stone-bordered circular "dancing" platforms constructed in LM II–IIIA and excavated near the Stratigraphical Museum.[420]

In recent years, a restudy of the Little Palace and the excavation of its "villa annex," the Unexplored Mansion, have shed important new light on Knossos in LM II–IIIA.[421] Both are Neopalatial buildings, but the latter may not have been completed at the time of the IB destructions, since the floor of its pillar basement had not been laid. The building was occupied in LM II, although after one of several destructions in this period the south half of the structure was filled with debris and went unused while the north half continued to be occupied into LM IIIA and early B. At the same time there were modifications in the Little Palace, including blocking up the polythyron.

Within the palace there is evidence for continuous use and architectural modification through LM IIIA and into IIIB. While the east wing underwent some modifications, including blocked walls, and was eventually destroyed at least in part by fire, the west wing, which also was rebuilt, eventually collapsed.[422] Especially important are the architectural modifications datable to LM IIIA2–B early.[423] These include new paving in the central court, the final arrangement of the throne room, and rearrangements in the west magazines. In the area of the South Basements, pits of plaster may attest to the same general construction efforts.[424]

Tombs and Burials

In the period after the LM IB destructions new cemeteries with new types of burials are established in different parts of the island. Among these are Warrior Graves at Knossos, Archanes, Phaistos, and Chania, similar in form and contents to contemporary Warrior Graves on the mainland;[425] chamber tombs, approached by a short dromos; "shaft graves" slightly different in form from those of earlier date at Mycenae; pit caves; and tholoi whose keyhole-shaped dromoi incline at the top.

Near Knossos, several cemeteries were in use in the Final Palatial period on the hills flanking the Kairatos stream north of the palace. The Mavro Spelio cemetery on Ailias, east of the palace, was already in use in Neopalatial times. Farther north, on the west, is the Zapher Papoura cemetery established in LM II–IIIA1 and the contemporary scatter of tombs toward Ayios Ioannes and the New Hospital. Continuing up the Kairatos is first the small group of five LM IIIA1–2 tombs at Sellopoulo, and finally the Isopata cemetery with a number of graves including the Royal Tomb. Near the mouth of the Kairatos at Katsamba on the coast is a series of rich tombs that began to be used in LM II.[426]

It is generally assumed that the Katsamba, Zapher Papoura, and Sellopoulo tombs belonged to Mycenaean communities established at this time. Although it is difficult to determine ethnicity from grave goods or grave forms, many of the Katsamba tombs included Palace Style jars, just as many mainland tholoi had during LH IIA. Some graves in these and other cemeteries exhibit what seem to be other Mycenaean features: the practice of burying select individuals with important sets of bronze vessels;[427] and burials on biers or beds or in wooden coffins painted blue, yellow, or red.

---

[420] Warren 1983 (supra n. 400) 69. Some of the blocks of the surrounds have mason's marks, making them some of the latest examples, if they are not reused; see Driessen (supra n. 417) 75 for col. ill.

[421] Popham et al. (supra n. 5); Hitchcock and Preziosi (supra n. 49).

[422] Begg 201. We are grateful to P. Kienzle for allowing us to cite his message on *AegeaNet*, 15 February 1997 (*AegeaNet* archive no. 970215.06): "The Magazines are destroyed by fire" with fill equal to two stories. "In the Domestic Quarter there are no burn marks" with fill equal to six stories.

[423] LM IIIA2 pottery has been found beneath the central court pavers and the throne room floor: Cameron (supra n. 182); Niemeier (supra n. 374) esp. 163, 167. Begg 167–75: in the west wing, after a fire in IIIA2 that ignited oil in magazine 12 and blackened the gypsum revetments added throughout the west magazines, there is major architectural remodeling; early IIIA2 sherds were found and fragments of a LM IIIA cup from magazine 13, cist 7, joined sherds from cist B4 in the Long Gallery; at the South Propylaeum, the remodeling of the west pier incorporated IIIA2 and B material, the IIIA2 sherds joining sherds from magazines 8 and 18.

[424] N. Momigliano and S. Hood, *BSA* 89 (1994) 103–50.

[425] Evans (supra ns. 148, 240); Alexiou (supra n. 158); M.S.F. Hood, "Another Warrior Grave at Ayios Ioannis near Knossos," *BSA* 51 (1956) 81–103; Hood, "A Minoan Shaft-Grave on the Slopes opposite the Temple Tomb," *BSA* 53–54 (1958–1959) 281–82; Hood, "A Minoan Shaft-Grave in the Bank with Hogarth's Tombs," *BSA* 53–54 (1958–1959) 283–84; Hood and P. De Jong, "Late Minoan Warrior Graves from Ayios Ioannis," *BSA* 47 (1952) 243–77; S. Hood, G. Huxley, and N. Sandars, "A Minoan Cemetery on Upper Gypsades," *BSA* 53–54 (1958–1959) 194–262; Popham and Catling (supra n. 236). For Sellopoulo tombs 1 and 2, see *AR* 3 (1957) 24–25.

[426] Alexiou (supra n. 158); *BCH* 79 (1955) 295–96, fig. 6.

[427] The practice occurs first in the Shaft Graves of Mycenae Circle A, especially SG IV. See A.B. Knapp, "Hoards d'Oeuvres: Of Metals and Men on Bronze Age Cyprus," *OJA* 7 (1988) 149–50; Knapp et al. (supra n. 210); Matthäus (supra n. 225). Other burials with bronzes in Crete: Archanes Phourni, Tholos A and Grave Enclosure, shaft 4; Chania, tomb near the Law Courts (E. Karantzali, *BCH* 110 [1986] 53–87); Kalyvia, Tombe dei Nobili no. 8 (*MonAnt* 14 [1904] 533–34); Phylaki Apokoronou tholos (Y. Tzedakis, *ArchDelt*

At Archanes Phourni, to the north and south of the Protopalatial and Neopalatial cemetery, new tombs are constructed: to the north, a group of Warrior Graves in a rectangular enclosure with plain stelae and the small tholos A are added in LM IIIA1–2; to the south, another small tholos, D, was inserted at the beginning of IIIA2.[428] Burials, however, continued to be made in the funerary building 3, whose earliest contents date to the Protopalatial period.

An untouched LM IIIA2 larnax burial, a rich woman of high status, was found in the side chamber of Tholos A. Her jewelry includes four gold signet rings with religious iconography, one a Neopalatial heirloom. Of the three smaller gold cult rings, two feature friezes of figure-eight shields, while the third carries a double frieze of shields alternating with sacral knots. On the chamber floor were various offerings, including a necklace of blue glass beads and two gold rings, and, in front of the larnax, an ivory footstool decorated with images of warrior's heads and figure-eight shields. In a corner of the chamber was a full set of bronze vessels like those found in contemporary male Warrior Graves. The entrance to the chamber had been walled up, but in the fill was a hornless bull's skull, and just outside the doorway, on the floor of the tholos, was the carefully piled heap of a butchered horse. The deceased may have had both administrative and religious functions, possibly connected with the Juktas peak sanctuary nearby.

Sites in western Crete are also rich in the number and quality of burials. At Armenoi, on the upland plain immediately south of Rethymnon, a large new cemetery was established in LM II.[429] The earliest tomb is underground and corbeled like a tholos. More than 200 rock-cut chamber tombs date to LM IIIA1–B, and several were marked by stone stelae,

a Mycenaean practice. Other rich Final Palatial tombs have been excavated around Chania.[430]

In recent years, a number of large and important LM III tholos tombs have been excavated in western and eastern Crete. Three of these share the unusual feature of a rectangular chamber, two in the Chania area (Malame and Phylaki),[431] and one south of Siteia at the edge of the settlement site at Achladia. Another architectural peculiarity further links the Malame and Phylaki tholoi: the lintel slab over the front facade, facing the dromos, is set vertically on end, to create a rectangular "plaque" over the doorway.

Art

Ceramics. LM II undecorated as well as decorated pottery has been recognized at an increasing number of sites. It used to be thought that the chronological phase LM II was virtually confined to Knossos, a situation we now know is not the case.[432] LM II pottery shows an increasing trend toward simplifying and fossilizing motifs, which some have attributed to increasing mainland influence, although the trend was already apparent in LM IB and need not reflect either mainland influence or conquest. These general trends continue into LM IIIA and B in a clear evolutionary development with few interruptions.[433]

Three shapes have been considered typical of LM II: flat alabastra, Ephyraean goblets, and Palace Style jars. The flat alabastron is a shape that occurred in LM IB and on the mainland but became popular on Crete in LM II, both in pottery and in stone, the latter examples probably produced only at Knossos. During LM II/LH IIB, another mainland shape, the Ephyraean goblet, is also produced on Crete and in nearly identical forms.[434] Contrasting sharply with the earlier semiglobular cup and the Vapheio cup, the Cretan goblets tend to be decorated with a rel-

36 B2, Chronika [1981] 398–99; *BCH* 106 [1982] 628–30; L. Godart and Y. Tzedakis, *Témoignages archéologiques et épigraphiques en Crète occidentale du Néolithique au Minoen Récent III B* [Rome 1992] 59–60, pls. LIV–LVII; *AR* 28 [1982] 58); Sellopoulo tomb 4 (Popham and Catling [supra n. 236]).

[428] Archanes Phourni: *Atlas* 54–58; Sakellarakis and Sakellaraki (supra n. 41); *Archanes* 66–135.

[429] Armenoi: *Atlas* 63–65; E. Banou, "Το οδοντοφρακτό κράνος από το ΥΜ III νεκροταφείο στους Αρμένους Ρεθύμνης," *6th CretCong* A2 (1990) 39–47, pls. 3–4; E. Papadopoulou, "Mycenaean Burial Customs in Minoan Culture," in *Atti IIº Congresso internazionale di micenologia* (Rome, forthcoming); Papadopoulou, "The Tholos Tomb of the Late Minoan Cemetery at Armenoi of Rethymnon," *7th CretCong* (forthcoming); M. Papathanassiou, M. Hoskin, and H. Papadopoulou, "Orientations of Tombs in the Late-Minoan Cemetery at Armenoi, Crete," *Archaeoastronomy* 17 (1992) 543–55; *BCH* 113 (1989) 692; *BCH* 118 (1994) 834; *AR* 36 (1990) 77.

[430] B.P. Hallager and P. McGeorge, *Late Minoan III Burials at Khania* (*SIMA* 93, Göteborg 1992); Karantzali (supra n. 427); *AR* 38 (1992) 70; *AR* 40 (1994) 84; *BCH* 118 (1994) 835–36.

[431] Malame: *Prakt* 1966, 185–88; *Ergon* 1966, 144–47. Phylaki: supra n. 427.

[432] Supra n. 408. S. Hiller, "Der SM II-Palaststil," in *Politeia* 561–73; M.R. Popham, "LM II Crete," *AJA* 79 (1975) 372–74; and Popham, "Cretan Sites Occupied between ca. 1450 and 1400 B.C.," *BSA* 75 (1980) 163–67; W.-D. Niemeier, "Towards a New Definition of LM II," *AJA* 83 (1979) 212–14; L.V. Watrous, "The Relationship of Late Minoan II to Late Minoan III A:1," *AJA* 85 (1981) 75–77; B.P. Hallager, in *6th CretCong* (supra n. 412); Hallager and Tzedakis 1984 (supra n. 50) 11–12.

[433] Popham (supra n. 189); M.R. Popham, "Late Minoan III B Pottery from Knossos," *BSA* 65 (1970) 195–202.

[434] P. Mountjoy, "The Ephyrean Goblet Revisited," *BSA* 78 (1983) 265–71.

atively small number of motifs, usually the same on each side of the vessel: a stylized argonaut, a rosette, a lily, a palm tree, and a few other designs; a few examples are decorated in the Marine Style. The Palace Style jar is another characteristic LM II shape that descends from the large LM IB jar. These jars are imitated extensively on the mainland in LH IIA; in LM II Crete their decoration becomes increasingly schematic and simplified.[435]

Another important development in LM II is the increasing appearance of pictorial pottery on Crete, especially pieces depicting the human figure or birds.[436] Two early examples come from the Unexplored Mansion, a jug depicting a hunter with a spear and a pyxis with birds; both scenes recur on larnakes.

The development of LM IIIA pottery closely follows that of Mycenaean IIIA.[437] The decorations include animals, birds, and exotic plant life, as well as abstract patterns. All are rendered with confidence in an even style throughout the island that probably reflects close contacts. The cup with an everted or ledge-like rim appears first in IIIA1 and is paralleled by the kylix, a development of the Ephyraean goblet toward a shallower body and taller stem. Earlier shapes, like the krater and the stirrup jar,[438] now become common, while the conical cup finally declines in popularity. At the beginning of LM IIIA2, the one-handled goblet or champagne cup with a low stem makes its appearance and these begin to replace the ledge-rimmed cup; in contrast, the kylix becomes

less popular as its stem becomes even taller. What few naturalistic motifs remain are gradually replaced by more abstract patterns.

In LM IIIA a new workshop at Chania begins producing a distinctive pottery whose fabric is pale gray with a yellow or pale orange slip and whose biscuit turns sugary white when scratched. The workshop flourishes in LM IIIA2, dramatically so in LM IIIB, before tapering off in LM IIIC.[439] Its pottery is exported not only throughout the island, but also to Cyprus, Sardinia, and the Greek mainland.

Larnakes. Clay larnakes, in use throughout the Proto- and Neopalatial periods as coffins, and occasionally as storage containers in the Neopalatial and Final Palatial periods, come in two shapes, the chest larnax and the tub larnax, both perhaps inspired by wooden prototypes.[440] The gabled lids are separate, and usually fit tightly atop the clay chest. The box shape of the chest larnax created four rectangular side panels for painted decoration, six in the case of larnakes that have an extra set of legs in the middle of their long sides. These rectangular or square side panels are reminiscent of wall surfaces in buildings, and invited the type of decoration found in wall frescoes or in woven textiles.

As coffins they become popular in the Final Palatial period, and their decoration is often elaborate. They are thus an important source of information about Late Minoan iconography and beliefs. Running spirals, circles, and wavy bands are common

---

[435] Marine Style: Popham et al. (supra n. 5) pl. 124b. Palace Style jar: W.-D. Niemeier, *Die Palaststilkeramik von Knossos: Stil, Chronologie und historischer Kontext* (Berlin 1985).

[436] There is some pictorial pottery before the Cretan destructions: e.g., *BCH* 107 (1983) 830–31, fig. 155. J.H. Crouwel and C.E. Morris, *BSA* 90 (1995) 157–82; M.R. Popham, in Evely et al. (supra n. 1) 98–101; Popham et al. (supra n. 5) pls. 62a–b and 153.6–7, and 65b and 155.1.

[437] Betancourt (supra n. 4) 163–72.

[438] H. Haskell, "From Palace to Town Administration," in *Society* 121–28; Haskell, *The Coarse Ware Stirrup Jars of Crete and the Cyclades* (Diss. Univ. of North Carolina 1981); A. Leonard et al., "The Making of Aegean Stirrup Jars," *BSA* 88 (1994) 105–23.

[439] Tzedakis (supra n. 410); Karantzali (supra n. 427); *Kommos* III, 152, 182.

[440] Begg 109–10 lists storage larnakes from Neopalatial Thera A2, Zakros Strong Building fallen from above and House A, Vathypetro from above room 4 and the southeast wing, and Phaistos; and from Final Palatial Gournia Ej.58 or 59, and Knossos Little Palace; the larnax in the South Entrance System of Knossos should also be a storage chest. General studies: B. Rutkowski, *Larnaksy Egejskie* (Warsaw 1966); Rutkowski, "The Origin of the Minoan Coffin," *BSA* 63 (1968) 219–27; Hägg and Sieurin (supra n. 259); and L.V. Watrous, "The Origin and Iconography

of the Late Minoan Painted Larnax," *Hesperia* 60 (1991) 285–307. Regional studies: K. Mavriyannaki, *Recherches sur les larnakes minoennes de la Crète occidentale* (Rome 1972); Mavriyannaki, "Το πρόβλημα της σπανιότητος ταφικών μινωϊκών λαρνάκων εις το νόμον Χανιών," *3rd CretCong* (1973) 191–94; G. Rethemiotakis, "Λάρνακες και αγγεία από Καβροχόρι Ηρακλείου," *ArchDelt* 34 (1979) 228–59; Y. Tzedakis, "Οι λάρνακες του υστερομινωϊκού νεκροταφείου των Αρμένων του Ρεθύμνου," *AAA* 4 (1971) 216–22. Specific studies: K. Baxevani-Kouxioni, "Η τεχνική κατασκευής των μινωϊκών λαρνακών," *8th CretCong* (forthcoming); Mavriyannaki, "Une larnax inscrite provenant de Chouméri Mylopotamou," *Kadmos* 24 (1985) 13–22; L. Morgan, "A Minoan Larnax from Knossos," *BSA* 82 (1987) 171–200; M. Poloyiory, "Παρατηρήσεις στην παράσταση μορφή με υψωμένα χέρια σε υστερομινωϊκή λάρνακα από το Αποδούλου, επαρχίας Αμαριού," *6th CretCong* A2 (1990) 207–32; K. Baxevani, "A Minoan Larnax from Pigi Rethymnou," in C. Morris ed., *Klados* (London 1995) 15–33. Attribution studies: C. Morris, "Fishy Tales from Knossos," in *Klados* 185–93; and M. Tsipopoulou and L. Vagnetti, "Workshop Attributions for Some Late Minoan III East Cretan Larnakes," in *Techne* 473–79. Specific examples illustrated: Demakopoulou (supra n. 384) 76–77, no. 6; Godart and Tzedakis (supra n. 427) pls. CIX.1–2, CX.1, CXIV.3, CXIX.1–2, CXX–CXVI, CXXVII.1, CLVI; cf. I. Papapostolou, *Prakt* 1974, 247–56, pls. 185–91.

decorations on the legs and horizontal raised bands at the top and bottom. The side panels often include argonauts and octopi, fish, plants, birds, and animals, of which bulls, deer, and agrimia are the most frequent. The landscapes that had ceased to appear in fresco at the end of the Neopalatial period now appear in abbreviated forms on larnakes, but fish and fowl are sometimes mingled. A cult symbol that appears frequently is the horns of consecration; one larnax in Rethymnon shows horns set atop an incurved base.

Human figures, mostly men, appear infrequently. One panel of a sarcophagus from Armenoi depicts a landscape with rockwork where a hunter armed with sword and spear lets fly at an outsized deer while he holds a dog on a tether in his free hand. On the end of the gabled lid of another larnax from Armenoi a mourning figure stands beside the deceased individual who is stretched out on a bier, perhaps a wooden one like those found in contemporary tombs. This may be our earliest prothesis scene, well known in Geometric art.

From a tomb northeast of the villa at Ayia Triada comes a unique, frescoed limestone sarcophagus.[441] The legs of the Ayia Triada sarcophagus and the roughly contemporary larnax from Archanes Tholos A are painted similarly with vertical bands of running spirals. One long side of the sarcophagus shows the sacrifice of a bull and an offering at an altar in front of a small built shrine. All of the figures here are women, except for a male aulete. The other long side depicts the pouring of liquid offerings and a procession of three men holding small bulls (rhyta?) and a boat model moving toward an armless male figure standing before a building who may represent the deceased before his tomb.[442] The end panels also show important scenes. One shows two women riding in a dual chariot drawn by agrimia altered from horses, the other a pair of women in a chariot drawn by griffins. Over the backs of the griffins ca-

vorts a small, birdlike creature, probably a baby griffin since it shares the blue, white, and yellow colors of the adults.

Frescoes. Only two sites have produced significant evidence of fresco painting after LM IB: Knossos and Ayia Triada, though at the former some Neopalatial compositions remained on the walls. Almost no Cretan frescoes can be dated to LM IIIA2–B, with the possible exception of the frescoes in the Knossos throne room complex, the final architectural modification of which has been dated to LM IIIA2. On the walls flanking the stone throne are a pair of palm trees and recumbent antithetic wingless griffins (the papyrus blossoms included in Evans's reconstruction and often reproduced are a mistake).[443] This scheme, like the throne, probably repeats a Neopalatial arrangement. In the east wing at Knossos, a fresco of dolphins has been attributed to a floor.[444]

The wall frescoes at Knossos assigned to the Final Palatial period on stylistic grounds show that some Minoan customs may have continued on Crete, particularly those connected with the high status of women and the social importance of ritual activity. These paintings include the Toreador Panels with female, as well as male, bull-leapers, and a possible administrator or ruler in a dual chariot who wears the diagonally banded robe of men on some Neopalatial sealstones, along with a sword baldric slung around his neck.[445]

Both sides of the west entrance corridor of the palace were lined with life-sized processional figures of at least two women and approximately 20 men, some carrying metal and stone vases.[446] Both old and new elements can be seen. Although processions of men occurred on the Neopalatial Harvester Vase and in a fresco from Xeste 4 at Akrotiri, they now become standard in Mycenaean painting. Both women wear the Neopalatial Minoan robe and apron, garments now highly stylized, and perhaps worn only on special ritual occasions. The central figure in the

[441] C. Long, *The Ayia Triada Sarcophagus* (*SIMA* 41, Göteborg 1974); Hood (supra n. 157) 70–71, figs. 53–54; *CM* pls. XXVII–XXX.

[442] Cf. the large (45 cm long) terracotta boat model from a tomb on Cyprus: *AR* 12 (1966) 29–30, fig. 3a–b, and the Neopalatial alabaster boat found at Ayia Triada: Halbherr et al. (supra n. 31) 90 fig. 56. E. French suggests that the man might represent a large terracotta figurine: "Mycenaean Figures and Figurines," in *Sanctuaries* 174. For other interpretations, see, e.g., R. Laffineur, "À propos du sarcophage d'Aghia Triadha," *Kernos* 4 (1991) 277–85. The painted facade of the tomb recalls Mycenaean practices: K. Demakopoulou, "The Burial Ritual in the Tholos Tomb at Kokla, Argolis," in Hägg and Nordquist (supra n. 221) 113, 116

fig. 4; K. Müller, "Das Kuppelgrab von Tiryns," *Tiryns* VII (Mainz 1975) 2; O. Pelon, *Tholoi, tumuli et cercles funéraires* (Athens 1976) 181, 319; C. Blegen, *Prosymna* (Cambridge 1937) pl. 39.

[443] M. Shaw, "The Aegean Garden," *AJA* 97 (1993) 677, fig. 16 for a recent, correct restoration.

[444] R.B. Koehl, "A Marinescape Floor from the Palace at Knossos," *AJA* 90 (1986) 407–17.

[445] Fragments are divided between the Ashmolean Museum and the Herakleion Museum: Immerwahr 175–76 Kn nos. 23 and 25; S. Alexiou, "Neue Wagendarstellungen aus Kreta," *AA* 1964, 785–804; cf. the similar composition on *CMS* I, no. 229.

[446] *PM* II.2, 679–85; Immerwahr 174–75 Kn no. 22.

procession is a woman, separated in space from the files approaching from either side. She wears a dress patterned with beam ends and triglyph-half rosette designs,[447] architectural elements that had been important in the iconography of the Neopalatial palaces and their peak sanctuaries. Several men wear costumes whose detailed patterns and surface treatments recall those in Neopalatial paintings, and at least two individuals wear the early hide skirts, but others in the procession wear a new garment, the long tunic, a "unisex" robe increasingly evident in Mycenaean representations. The breechcloth and codpiece, which had been so prominent in Neopalatial art, are apparently missing from the Procession Fresco and are now confined to scenes of bull-leaping, even on the mainland.[448] Even the undulating, horizontal background bands, alternately red and white, recall similar backgrounds from the earlier House of the Frescoes, but here they are static and repetitious as in subsequent Mycenaean painting.

The multiple registers of the Campstool Fresco present intriguing problems of reconstruction and interpretation. Men sitting on campstools wear diagonally banded robes and toast each other with LM IIIA stemmed kylikes in the presence of at least two women.[449] One of the women, facing left against a yellow background, is at the same small scale as the men. The other woman, facing right against a blue background, is larger. Dubbed "La Parisienne" by Evans, she is armless like the presumed deceased on the Ayia Triada sarcophagus and wears an unusual garment with a sacral knot attached to the collar at the back. As in the Procession Fresco, men are more numerous than women, reversing the gender imbalance of Neopalatial art, and their red sword baldrics and campstools with distinctive red tassels may allude to their high status.

Sealstones. Knossian workshops were still producing seals in the Final Palatial period, but it now becomes difficult to distinguish between Cretan and mainland products, as if the gem engravers or even entire workshops were moving around and finding new homes. Sealstones whose animals have distinctively rendered "spectacle eyes" were produced at Knossos in IIIA1, but the location of the IIIA2–B early Island Sanctuaries workshop that made seals with smoothly modeled animals cannot be determined precisely.[450] In the Postpalatial period, hard stone seals were no longer produced in the Aegean (see below), although heirloom seals continued in circulation and were used on the mainland for administrative purposes.

Some Neopalatial gold cult rings evidently survived to be buried in Final Palatial tombs; other cult rings are more vigorous in style and these could date later, to LM II–IIIA. Similarly late could be a few flimsy rings of thin gold plate over a flat bronze core.[451]

Burials with bronzes are sometimes accompanied by large lentoids of a dark, rich red-brown agate, carved with bulls in recumbent poses.[452] If this motif is an insigne, it would be tempting to link it with a high official.

Stone vessels. Following the LM IB destructions, there is a noticeable decline in the quality, variety of shapes, and volume of production of stone vases. Knossos housed a couple of stone workshops in LM

---

[447] *PM* II.2, 719–36, Suppl. pl. XXV fig. 7; C. Boulotis, "Nochmals zum Prozessionsfresko von Knossos," in *Palaces* 145–55. Cf. the bodice of the Thera goddess from Xeste 3: Doumas pl. 125.

[448] The only possible processional figure wearing a breechcloth occurs on a fresco fragment (*PM* II.2, 751 fig. 485) that Evans found just south of the Procession Corridor. Cameron (supra n. 335) 587, pl. 4, dates it to Neopalatial and moves it to the east wing to accompany the Grand Staircase, though the relative difference in height of the figures cannot match the changes in height of the staircase's risers.

[449] *PM* IV.2, 379–90, pl. XXX B; Immerwahr 95, 176 Kn no. 26, pl. 44; M.A.S. Cameron, "An Addition to 'La Parisienne,'" *CretChron* 18 (1964) 38–53. Two fragments (*PM* IV, pl. XXXI A and G) present the kylix, one the bowl, the other the tall stem; if pottery, the kylix could be as late as LM IIIA2. J. Wright, "Empty Cups and Empty Jugs," in P.E. McGovern, S.J. Fleming, and S.H. Katz eds., *The Origins and Ancient History of Wine* (Philadelphia 1995) suggests there are two cups, a chalice for Minoans and a gob-

let for Mycenaeans.

[450] Most, but not all, of the latest impressions at Knossos were made by seals belonging to the Spectacle Eyes group (Younger 1986 [supra n. 106] 121–38). Island Sanctuaries workshop: J.G. Younger, "The Island Sanctuaries Group," *CMS* Beiheft 1 (Berlin 1981) 263–72; Younger 1987 (supra n. 106) 61–64; I. Pini, "Minoan Glyptic after the Assumed Fall of the Palace at Knossos," *BICS* 29 (1982) 132.

[451] Grave goods: Younger 1983 (supra n. 106) 134–35; Sellopoulo tomb 4 ring: Popham and Catling (supra n. 236) no. J8. Archanes ring: *Archanes* 79 fig. 53. Cultic rings: *CMS* I, nos. 126–29. Younger 1984 (supra n. 106) attributes these rings to the Group of the Buxom Women, none of whose members comes from a dated context earlier than LH II. Bronze core rings: Younger (supra n. 242) 87: ring type VI. Archanes rings: *Archanes* 62 fig. 37 (the pair at upper left and one at lower right). Kalyvia tomb 9: *CMS* II.3, no. 39. Sellopoulo tomb 4: Popham and Catling (supra n. 236) no. J7.

[452] Younger 1988 (supra n. 106) 79–80 lists 26 examples; add *CMS* I, Suppl. 1A, no. 69 from Koukaki.

II–IIIA, from which unworked or unfinished pieces exist, including a stock of unworked lapis lacedaemonius and unfinished gypsum vase fragments identified among debris swept into the cists of west magazine 13.[453] Finished products of this gypsum vase workshop were found in the palace at Knossos and a few other sites. These include approximately a dozen baggy gypsum alabastra from the throne room complex, some with lids and most with rim decoration of compass-drawn running spirals with dotted centers and handles shaped like figure-eight shields.[454] While the alabastron resembles a Mycenaean pottery shape, the dotted spirals and figure-eight shield handles are Minoan. These gypsum vases were apparently in use at the time the palace was destroyed, though their exact purpose is unclear. They are too heavy to have been moved easily, and their contents (scented oil?) must have been taken out by dipper, not poured.

Stone vessels, many of which were deposited in tombs, continued to be imported from Syria or Egypt. One important vase inscribed with the name of Tuthmosis III found at Katsamba probably dates to this period but may be a Syrian imitation of an Egyptian vase. The Royal Tomb at Isopata, in use in LM II, contained a large number of imported stone vessels, including a shallow footed bowl with carinated sides. Similar examples have been found in Cyprus, Syria-Palestine, and Egypt, indicating that Crete was still part of an international network of trade.[455]

Metalwork. During the Final Palatial period, Knossos was still a center for the production of bronze tools and weapons. Of particular importance is the bronze workshop at the Unexplored Mansion in LM II. Analysis of these bronzes and bronze scrap shows that they contain lead from Lavrion, as do late bronzes from Ayia Irini in Kea, although that does not necessarily indicate where their copper came from. The metal vessels found in Warrior Graves on both Crete and the mainland at this time are virtually certain to have been produced at Knossos.[456]

Three new sword forms belong to LM II–IIIA and are made only during this time: types Ci, Di, and G, all of which are found in Warrior Graves on Crete and in the Argolid.[457] Type C swords are characterized by "horned" hand-guards, type D by cross-shaped hand-guards. Type Gi swords represent a variant of type C swords and have a "dropped horn" hand-guard. Continuing the earlier tradition of decorated blades, though less elaborately, these three types of swords may have decorated hilts and a midrib with incised decoration, while some spear points are similarly decorated.[458] After LM/LH IIIA, however, decorated weapons are no longer manufactured in the Aegean.

An elaborate cruciform (Di) sword from the Chieftain Grave at Zapher Papoura has a midrib and tang engraved with spirals, a gold foil hilt, and an agate pommel. Incised on the gold hilt are an antithetic addorsed lion and an agrimi; the same animals appear in a chase scene on the hand grip. The design is important because of its pictorial style, recalling Neopalatial frescoes and the landscapes with pendant rockwork, as on the gold Vapheio cups. On the sword hilt there is even an attempt to render foliage, a single crocus flower blooming among the rocks. Also manufactured about this time are a spearhead

[453] P. Warren, "Two Palatial Stone Vases from Knossos," *BSA* 60 (1965) 154–55; Evely (supra n. 154); Begg 77, 204 ns. 650–51.

[454] *PM* IV.2, 937–39 fig. 910; H. von Arbin, "The Alabastron-Shaped Vases Found in the Throne Room at Knossos," *OpAth* 15 (1984) 7–11; P. Magrill, "A Minoan Alabastron in Dublin," *BSA* 82 (1987) 155–64; R. Hägg, "The Last Ceremony in the Throne Room at Knossos," *OpAth* 17 (1988) 99–106; H. Waterhouse, "The Flat Alabastron and the Last Ritual in the Knossos Throne Room," *OJA* 7 (1988) 361–67; H. Busing, "Zum Spiralschmuck der steineren Alabastra aus dem Thronsaal von Knossos," *JRGZM* 40 (1993) 317–31, pl. 32; Rehak (supra n. 385). For the decoration, cf. a probable MM III fresco from the east wing at Knossos (*PM* I, 371 fig. 269; III, 30–31, pl. XV; Immerwahr 178 Kn no. 38) and a relief fresco from Zakros (*Zakros* 172–73; Immerwahr 184 Za no. 1).

[455] Katsamba tomb beta: Alexiou (supra n. 158) pl. 10; Cline 189 no. 491. Lilyquist (supra n. 128) now thinks that the vessel may not be Egyptian. The inscribed vase is one of two imported stone vessels from the tomb, the other being an Egyptian diorite bowl: Cline 190 no. 496. Stone vessels from the Royal Tomb include two alabaster bowls, a diorite bowl, a porphyrite bowl, and an alabaster jug (Cline 189 nos. 489–90, 495, 504, 629, respectively). For an example of a footed bowl in Cyprus, see I. Todd et al., "Kalavasos-Mangia," *RDAC* 1988, 218.

[456] C. Macdonald, "A Knossian Weapon Workshop in Late Minoan II and III A," in *Palaces* 293–95. Unexplored Mansion: H.W. Catling and E.W. Catling, "The Bronzes and Metalworking Equipment," in Popham et al. (supra n. 5) 203–22. Knapp et al. (supra n. 210) 57–58, 258: the metallurgical evidence in the Minoan Unexplored Mansion is for vessel production, not smelting. Warrior Graves: Popham and Catling (supra n. 236) 203–22; H. Matthäus, "Representations of Keftiu in Egyptian Tombs," *BICS* 40 (1995) 177–94.

[457] J. Driessen and C. Macdonald, "Some Military Aspects of the Aegean in the Late Fifteenth and Early Fourteenth Centuries B.C., Part II: Aegean Swords and Warrior Graves," *BSA* 79 (1984) 72–74 (catalogue); Macdonald (supra n. 456).

[458] Höckmann (supra n. 216); for an example decorated with spirals from Archanes, see *Archanes* 110.

from a tomb at Archanes, decorated with running spirals, and the Lasithi dagger with incised decoration showing a man hunting a boar on one side and two bulls fighting on the other, a lineal descendant of the much more elaborately rendered scenes on the Neopalatial niello daggers.[459]

Precious metals continue to be used for jewelry and other ornaments, but many of these are of thin foil, often mass-produced in molds. At Archanes Phourni, funerary building 3 contained a large gold-foil cutout of a figure-eight shield that may have decorated a wooden box or piece of furniture, and the LM IIIA burials in Tholoi A and D included gold rosette necklaces or dress beads and a series of double argonaut beads that were evidently worn around the head as a diadem.[460]

With the LM IIIA1–2 disruption at Knossos, the relative homogeneity of Aegean metalwork breaks down, suggesting that there was no longer a single major palatial workshop on Crete. There is less evidence for the manufacture of large bronze vessels, decorated swords virtually disappear, and precious metal jewelry becomes increasingly scarce in habitation and funerary contexts.

Important recent evidence for bronzeworking in the first half of LM IIIB comes from Palaikastro, where a pit was found in 1991 containing metal debris, tuyères, crucibles, and molds for a double ax and a tripod stand of the type more familiar from Late Cypriot IIIA contexts in Cyprus. The Cretan example is important because it predates the earliest Late Cypriot IIC example found at Kaloriziki tomb 40 and is larger than the ones often used in tombs.[461]

Ivories. Despite the fact that three-dimensional ivory figurines were no longer carved by the end of LM IB, a group of surviving Neopalatial ivories, prob-ably heirlooms, was found along the Royal Road in a LM IIIA context.[462] Other ivory products, stylistically datable slightly before or after the Cretan destructions, may also have been produced at Knossos. Among these is an ivory comb from the Mycenaean grave enclosure at Archanes Phourni and, from funerary building 3 there, several plaques that probably decorated a wooden box or piece of furniture. Four horizontal plaques, carved with almost identical lions in a flying gallop, recall the gilded hexagonal wooden box from Circle A at Mycenae; both these lions and the agrimi on the large plaque have almond-shaped eyes, a shape that is popular on sealstones in LM IB–II.[463] A Knossian workshop may also have been responsible for producing what is apparently a new type of status symbol: a footstool inlaid with ivory figure-eight shields and warrior's heads. These have been found in tholos tombs at Archanes and at Phylaki Apokoronou, as well as on the mainland.[464]

The ivories from the tholos at Phylaki are important because they expand the Cretan artistic repertory in this medium. One plaque, carved front and back, has a tenon at the bottom, perhaps for insertion into a piece of furniture or a scepter. Two antithetic kneeling male figures are shown embracing, in a pose somewhat reminiscent of the women on the Mycenae ivory triad. Parts of three more male figures, carved in the round, were also found, along with crudely carved ivory plaques with standing sphinxes. A trait shared by all the faces of the Phylaki ivories, including the warriors' heads on the footstool, is the carving of the eye in relief as an almond shape, with no indication of a pupil; compare the similar eye of a sphinx on an ivory pyxis from a chamber tomb at Thebes.[465]

Faience. Cretan faience manufacture lingered into

[459] Zapher Papoura: Evans (supra n. 148) 55–58. A lapis lacedaemonius pommel with a gold foil ferrule found at Nichoria on the mainland probably came from a Knossos workshop as well (McDonald and Wilkie [supra n. 354] 262 no. 1008, 325 fig. 5-27, 845 pl. 5-52). Cf. the Zapher Papoura hilt foliage with the single clump of blooming crocus on the Zakros Sanctuary Rhyton (Shaw [supra n. 134] 434 figs. 7–8). Archanes spearhead: *BCH* 91 (1967) 792 fig. 19. See also C. Long, "The Lasithi Dagger," *AJA* 82 (1978) 35–46.

[460] *Archanes* 110, 130 fig. 108, 132 fig. 110.

[461] S.A. Hemingway, "Minoan Metalworking in the Postpalatial Period," *BSA* 91 (1996) 213–52. *PGC* no. 1687. Cf. T.M. Cross, *Bronze Tripods and Related Stands in the Eastern Mediterranean from the 12th through the 7th Centuries B.C.* (Diss. Univ. of North Carolina 1974).

[462] *AR* 4 (1958) 22, pl. 2a; and *AR* 5 (1959) 20 and fig. 33: ivory foot.

[463] *Archanes* 71 col. fig. 45, 108 fig. 83, 109 fig. 84; Pour-

sat, *Les ivoires* (supra n. 153) pls. VI.1–2, VII.1–2. Cf. the comb from Katsamba tomb eta: Alexiou (supra n. 158) pls. 34–35. Almond-eyes on sealstones: J.G. Younger, "A Large Stylistic Group of the Late XVth Century," *CMS* Beiheft 3 (Berlin 1989) 339–53; Younger 1985 (supra n. 106) 53–62.

[464] I.A. Sakellarakis, "Mycenaean Footstools," in Herrmann (supra n. 155) 105–10. Illustrations of examples include *Archanes* 82 fig. 59, 83 fig. 60 from Archanes; Poursat, *Les ivoires* (supra n. 153) pls. IV.1 (Mycenae), IV.3 (Thebes), VII.3 (Archanes), XIV.4 (Delos); and, from Phylaki, *BCH* 106 (1982) 630 fig. 182 (head only); Godart and Tzedakis (supra n. 427) pls. LVII.1–2 (heads), and LV.1–2 and LVII.3 (shields).

[465] Phylaki: Godart and Tzedakis (supra n. 427) pls. LVI.3–4, LXV.1–2. Cf. the ivory pyxis from Thebes: Poursat, *Les ivoires* (supra n. 153) pl. V.6. For color illustrations: Poursat 1994 (supra n. 158) 88 col. fig.; and Demakopoulou (supra n. 384) 72, no. 3.

LM II–IIIA; for instance, Mycenae chamber tomb 102 produced a faience hilt for a Knossian type D sword, clearly a prestige item, and from Tholos D at Archanes Phourni (LM IIIA2 context) come a variety of simple faience beads.[466] There is no good evidence for faience manufacture on Crete after the beginning of IIIB.

Writing and Administration

The relationship of Linear B to Linear A has been analyzed extensively. It is often and wrongly assumed that Linear A developed into Linear B, that the two scripts are mutually exclusive, and that, since Linear B was used to write Greek, Linear A reflects a non-Greek language. While Linear B inherited numerous features from Linear A, including most of its syllabary, some interesting changes also occur. Linear B's writing style is more cursive, perhaps revealing a candid response to the papyrus and leather texts that the Neopalatial one-hole hanging nodules imply. Furthermore, Linear B often uses a format that strives for redundant clarity in its statements.[467]

From Knossos come over 3,000 inscribed Linear B tablets (fewer than 2,400 with provenience known) and 69 inscribed (19 with provenience known) and approximately 400 impressed nodules whose LM III date is presumed. From Chania come three or possibly five tablets but no inscribed nodules; and from various places in Crete come 29 inscribed stirrup jars or their fragments.[468] While the amount of administrative material from Knossos is thus large, its incomplete publication makes working with the material difficult.[469] Chania provides the only ceramically dated contexts for Linear B documents. Three Linear B tablets were found on the floor of House I, room E, destroyed by fire early in LM IIIB, while another comes from pit H (primarily LM IIIA2 and B early pottery).[470]

No central or "final" archives deposit has been securely identified at Knossos. Instead, throughout the palace there are concentrations of tablets whose specific subjects suggest scattered bureaus, stores, or workshops.[471] The few inscribed and impressed nodules with known findspots also support the identification of "living" and "temporary" archives in storage and work areas rather than a "final" archives. Until relatively recently, it had been presumed that all the clay Linear B texts at Knossos belonged to a single administrative period, and had been fired hard in a single and final conflagration that also destroyed the palace. There are indications, however, that this "unity of the archives"[472] did not exist.

---

[466] Mycenae: Wace (supra n. 354) 281 no. 4910, pl. 137. Archanes: *Archanes* 131 fig. 109.

[467] Linear B uses far fewer ligatures than Linear A. Whereas Linear A either uses the word or the ideogram for a commodity, rarely both (HT 88.2: FICus KI·KI·NA 7), Linear B usually uses both.

[468] Knossos: Palaima (supra n. 279) 504 gives the numbers of documents; J.-P. Olivier, *Les scribes de Cnossos* (Rome 1967) gives the findspots at Knossos where known, although J.T. Killen and J.-P. Olivier, *The Knossos Tablets*[5] (Salamanca 1989) [*KT*[5]] xiv, emphasize caution. LM III date: Popham and Gill (supra n. 391) 56. Chania: L. Godart and Y. Tzedakis, "La storia della Lineare B e le scoperte di Armenoi e la Canea," *RivFil* 117 (1989) 385–409; Godart and Tzedakis, "Les nouveaux textes en Linéaire B de la Canée," *RivFil* 119 (1991) 129–45; E. Hallager, M. Vlasakis, and B.P. Hallager, "The First Linear B Tablet(s) from Khania," *Kadmos* 29 (1990) 24–34; Hallager et al. (supra n. 273).

ISJs: Jones 477–94 gives a summary and basic bibliography; add Shelmerdine (supra n. 16) 556 and 565. ISJ Cretan proveniences: singletons from a provenience unknown, the Mamelouka Cave near Chania, Armenoi, and Knossos; 3 from Mallia; and 23 from Chania. Minoan context dates range from LM IIIA2 (Chania Z27) to LM IIIB2 (Mallia: J.M. Driessen and A. Farnoux, "Mycenaeans at Mallia?" *Aegean Archaeology* 1 [1994] 54–64; cf. *AR* 38 [1993] 65–66, fig. 56). While most Minoan ISJs were made from West Cretan clays (e.g., Chania Z27), two from Crete were made from Mid-Central Cretan clay (Armenoi and Knossos Z1716). From Knossos tablet K778, we know the Mycenaean name and ideogram for stirrup jars: *ka-ra-re-u* and *210*[vas].

[469] Evans's notebooks and Mackenzie's daybooks, the diaries of the excavations, have not yet been fully published; for some citations: L.R. Palmer and J. Boardman, *On the Knossos Tablets* (Oxford 1963). For the two latest corpora of tablets, see *KT*[5] (supra n. 468); and J. Chadwick et al., *Corpus of Mycenaean Inscriptions from Knossos* I (1–1063) (Cambridge 1986), and II (1064–4495) (Cambridge 1990). The impressed nodules will soon be published in *CMS*; also see M.A.V. Gill, "The Knossos Sealings," *BSA* 60 (1965) 58–98, updated by Popham and Gill (supra n. 391); for stylistic dates of the seals that impressed the nodules, see Younger, the *Kadmos* series (supra n. 106); for some of the classes, shapes, and types of nodules, see Hallager, and Weingarten 1988 (supra n. 269).

[470] We are grateful to E. Hallager and B.P. Hallager for showing us the inscribed material. For practical reasons, that portion of the floor on which tablets KH Ar 4, Gq 5, and X 6 lay was excised for removal to the Chania Museum, where it is still stored and where we saw it: the floor is neatly strewn with pebbles and we could easily see where the tablets had lain since they had slightly depressed the pebbles. Hallager et al. (supra n. 468).

[471] The D series concerning sheep comes from the east–west corridor in the east wing; the As/Ak and L series concerning personnel and cloth come from magazine XV; and the S series concerning arms and armor comes from both the Corridor of the Sword Tablets and the Arsenal: S. Hiller, "The 'Corridor of the Sword Tablets' and the 'Arsenal'," in Olivier ed. (supra n. 414) 303–14.

[472] L.R. Palmer, "The Find-Places of the Knossos Tablets," in Palmer and Boardman (supra n. 469) 170–72.

Evans himself had selected the so-called Hieroglyphic Deposit from among scattered Linear B tablets and late impressed nodules.[473] Driessen has established that the tablets from the Room of the Chariot Tablets were fired probably in LM II or early IIIA.[474]

The mix of Hieroglyphic and Linear B material in the west wing suggests the presence of "discard" archives. In fact, the lack of an identifiable main archive at Knossos may imply at least that other deposits of documents belong to "discard" archives.[475] If so, their firing, whether by one burning or several (e.g., by fires in LM IIIA2 early as well as in IIIB early), could have occurred long after the documents were inscribed and the nodules impressed. This more haphazard survival of the documents may account for the often noted incompleteness of several series.[476]

The controversy over the "final destruction" at Knossos has spanned four decades.[477] In 1958 Blegen noted that Linear B at Pylos (dated LH IIIB2–C1) was too much like Linear B at Knossos to warrant a long chronological gap between them. Four years later, Palmer and Boardman published their debate over the stratigraphy at Knossos, with the eventual result that Evans's LM II date for the "final destruction" of the palace was revised downward at least to LM IIIA early. Palmer later adduced strong reasons for proposing a LM IIIB date. Popham conducted two thorough reexaminations of the pottery and came to the conclusion that, though there was a destruction by fire at Knossos in IIIB early, the major destruction responsible for burning the Linear B tablets occurred in IIIA late, which he eventually refined

to IIIA2 early. In the late 1970s Hallager came forward as one of the first to support Palmer's case for the IIIB destruction, and Niemeier soon added more arguments. In order to resolve Blegen's problem, Popham has recently suggested raising Pylos's destruction to very early LH IIIB. As noted in our introduction, we favor the early LM IIIB date for the end of palatial administration at Knossos.

In addition to the difficult problems in reconstructing the original stratigraphy and refining Minoan ceramic phases, the phrase "final destruction" implies assumptions concerning the importance of the palace as capital of the island or simply as regional center, the finality of its destruction (obliteration or one of a series of setbacks?), and, most important, its "Minoan" or "Mycenaean" cultural and ethnic character. The difference between a "final" destruction in LM IIIA2 early and IIIB early is not great in terms of years, perhaps two generations, but the conventional cultural characterizations of these two periods are important: was a Minoan Knossos eradicated in IIIA to facilitate the growth of a Mycenaean empire that reached its zenith in IIIB, or was its destruction one of the earliest symptoms of the destabilization of that empire? The bias against locating Minoan culture beyond the boundaries of the Neopalatial period has produced severe dissonance in discussions of the island's later periods, especially LM IIIB–C, the period that has been, from the earliest scholarship, often characterized pejoratively ("squatters," "backwater"), whereas, as far as we can see, the Final Palatial period is just as distinctive as the Neopala-

---

[473] Hieroglyphic tablets and labels were found in the Area of the Pictographic Tablets (the sottoscala at the north end of the west wing's north–south corridor), in magazines 4, 5, 6, 12, and 13, in the Room of the Lady's Seat, and in the Room West of the Stone Drum; they were found with Linear B tablets in magazines 4, 12, and 13. Begg 190–91: "The conclusion is inescapable that the scattering of the Hieroglyphic tablets in the West Wing at Knossos was contemporary with the scattering of the Linear B tablets."

[474] J.M. Driessen, *An Early Destruction in the Mycenaean Palace at Knossos* (Louvain 1990). For reviews, see J. Bennet, *AJA* 97 (1993) 172–74, and M.R. Popham, *JHS* 113 (1993) 174–78. Cf. Driessen, "The Scribes of the 'Room of the Chariot Tablets,'" *Minos* Suppl. 10 (Salamanca 1988) 123–65; Driessen, *The Room of the Chariot Tablets at Knossos* (Diss. Katholieke Universiteit Leuven 1989); Driessen, "The Room of the Chariot Tablets Reconsidered," *6th CretCong* A2 (1990) 267–75; G. Owens, "The Date of the Linear B Archive from the 'Room of the Chariot Tablets' at Knossos," *Talanta* 26–27 (1995) 29–48; C.W. Shelmerdine, "Historical and Economic Considerations in Interpreting Mycenaean Texts," in Olivier (supra n. 414) 569–90, esp. 571 and 585.

[475] Tablets and impressed nodules were found under a blocked doorway in the east wing: J.T. Hooker, "The 'Unity of the Archives' at Knossos," *Kadmos* 4 (1965) 114–21.

[476] The Da-Dg series, for instance, records only partly

the maintenance of flocks of sheep: P. Halstead, "Lost Sheep? On the Linear B Evidence for Breeding Flocks at Knossos and Pylos," *Minos* 25–26 (1990–1991) 343–65.

[477] C.W. Blegen, "A Chronological Problem," in E. Grumach ed., *Minoica* (Berlin 1958) 61–66; Palmer and Boardman (supra n. 469); L.R. Palmer, *The Penultimate Palace of Knossos* (Rome 1969); Popham (supra n. 93); M.R. Popham, *The Last Days of the Palace at Knossos. Complete Vases of the Late Minoan III B Period* (SIMA 5, Göteborg 1964); Popham, "Connections between Crete and Cyprus 1300–1100 B.C.," in Karageorghis (supra n. 206) 178–91; E. Hallager, *The Mycenaean Palace at Knossos* (Stockholm 1977); Hallager, "The History of the Palace at Knossos in the Late Minoan Period," *SMEA* 19 (1978) 17–33; Niemeier (supra n. 5); Popham, "The Historical Implication of the Linear B Archive at Knossos Dating Either c. 1400 or 1200 B.C.," *Cretan Studies* 1 (1988) 217–27; Popham, "Pylos: Reflections on the Date of Its Destruction and Its Iron Age Reoccupation," *OJA* 10 (1991) 315–24. In this controversy it is usually assumed that the "final destruction" is of the main palace; the Little Palace and Arsenal were also destroyed by fire but the Arsenal's destruction may have been earlier while the Little Palace's may have been later (J. Boardman, "The Date of the Knossos Tablets," in Palmer and Boardman [supra n. 469] 66 and 69).

tial. The Postpalatial period was probably one of Crete's most prosperous and peaceful until recent modernity.

In addition to stratigraphic and ceramic studies, there has been a major focus on the character and history of administration. Bennet and Shelmerdine have studied the political nature of Crete as a whole, and several scholars have concentrated on the clay nodules and their impressions.[478] It seems logical that, when taking over the administration at Knossos, the Mycenaeans would have adapted the administrative procedures already in place and dating back, relatively unchanged, to the Neopalatial period.[479] On the mainland, where one can analyze Mycenaean sealing practices more or less clearly, there are no leather document sealings characteristic of the Neopalatial period. Instead, the Mycenaeans seem to have resuscitated the use of jar-stoppers and to have used two-hole hanging nodules exclusively as the nodule adjunct to their written documents (fig. 5).[480] Knossos, according to the nodules from the presumably pure Mycenaean deposits in the east wing, followed

these Mycenaean practices, with the addition that the two-hole hanging nodules were also pressed against containers. Contemporary nodules at Mallia and Chania are similar.[481]

At Knossos few seals were used to impress more than one nodule, reflecting a SSS system with a low-intensive, nonelite pattern of seal use. It would therefore seem that nonresident seal owners were contributing commodities to the palace and sending them, perhaps as taxes, along with an impressed nodule.[482] Evidence for the internal administration of the palace is slight.

There has been much speculation concerning the role of Knossos within the island in LM III. The arrangement of toponyms in the tablets clearly reveals that the palace recognized at least four separate geographical areas. A fifth grouping links *a-mi-ni-so* (Amnisos), *ko-no-so* (Knossos), and *se-to-i-ja* (Archanes/ Juktas?), perhaps because they were the main sanctuary sites. There must have been written communication not only from Knossos to these sites but also from these areas to Knossos.[483]

---

[478] See J. Bennet, "Knossos in Context," *AJA* 94 (1990) 193–211; Shelmerdine (supra n. 474); P. Warren, "The Destruction of the Palace of Knossos," in V. Karageorghis ed., *The Civilizations of the Aegean and Their Diffusion in Cyprus and the Eastern Mediterranean, 2000–600 B.C.* (Nicosia 1991) 32–37; Warren, "The Palace at Knossos and Its Administration during LM II–III A," *BICS* 40 (1995) 244–46. See Popham and Gill (supra n. 391) for a photographic dossier of the latest nodules; Weingarten 1988 (supra n. 269) for the identification of Mycenaean class XIIB "molar." For LM IIIA2–B early seals that impressed nodules, see Younger 1987 (supra n. 106) 61–64, especially the nodule HMs 259, for which also see I. Pini, "Ein Siegelabdruck im Archäologischen Museum Iraklion," *3rd CretCong* (1973) 221–30; and Pini, "Nochmals zu einem tönernen Siegelabdruck des Museums Iraklion," *Φίλια ἔπη* (supra n. 151) 300–303.

[479] J. Bennet, *Aspects of the Administrative Organisation of LM II–III B Crete* (Diss. Cambridge Univ. 1986); Bennet (supra n. 292); articles in Olivier (supra n. 414). Mycenaeans may have exerted a more rigid control over administrative concerns and a greater reliance on writing to express them. We also see a slightly different filing system: many Linear A tablets record several commodities each and specify them by ideogram, but most Linear B tablets concern just one kind of commodity each. This procedure may reflect differences in the physical layout of some of the mainland palaces. Pylos had one storage area for oil and another for wine; the Knossos magazines, whose pithoi were of various shapes and sizes, may have been filled with an assortment of commodities. The items recorded on the tablets that fell into the magazines from rooms above may have had no connection with the objects stored in the magazines (*pace* Begg 55–56, and Popham, in Popham and Gill [supra n. 391] 57).

[480] Weingarten 1988 (supra n. 269) 13: "All Pylian sealings are hanging nodules (most akin to Knossos Class VI/A)"; cf. Demakopoulou (supra n. 384) 210, no. 189.

[481] Mallia (Driessen and Farnoux [supra n. 468] 61–62): two stirrup jar stoppers from Quartier Epsilon (LM IIIA; HMs 1049, O. Pelon, *Malia. Maisons* III [Paris 1970] 130–35, no. 265, pl. XXVI.4–6) and Quartier Nu (HMs 1042, *BCH* 81 [1957] 693; *BCH* 102 [1978] 831–36), and a class XIIA nodule from Quartier Nu room X7 (Driessen and Farnoux [supra n. 468] 62, pl. IV.3). Chania (Hallager et al. [supra n. 273] 70–72): KH 1558 (LM IIIA1), a class XII nodule (Weingarten 1988 [supra n. 269] 7 n. 5); and the direct-object sealing KH 1568 (early LM IIIB).

[482] Weingarten 1988 (supra n. 269) 14.

[483] Halstead (supra n. 476); Shelmerdine (supra n. 474) 573 and 578. Few of the 100 or so secure place-names can be equated with known sites (Bennet [supra n. 292] 236–38): *ko-no-so* "Knossos," *a-mi-ni-so* "Amnisos," *tu-ri-so* "Tylissos," *pa-i-to* "Phaistos," *ku-do-ni-ja* "Kydonia" or "Chania," *a-pa-ta-wa* "Aptera" from the archaic form Aptarwa. E. Scafa, "SU-KI-RI-TA / Σύβριτα," in Rocchetti (supra n. 7) 165–200: *su-ki-ri-ta* "Sybrita." A.L. Wilson, "The Place-Names in the Linear B Tablets from Knossos," *Minos* 16 (1977) 67–125 presents the geographical groups: group I, from Rethymnon/ Stavromenos (*ku-ta-to*?) down through the Amari valley to Phaistos (*pa-i-to*): *da-wo, da-*22-to, e-ko-so, e-ra, pa-i-to* (Phaistos), *ku-ta-to*; group II, the area east of the Pediada, perhaps even mentioning the Lasithi plain (*ra-su-to*): *pu-na-so, ra-ja, ra-su-to, ra-to, ri-jo-no, tu-ni-ja, do-ti-ja*; group III, the north central plain itself containing Tylissos (*tu-ri-so*): *a-ka, pu-so, qa-mo, qa-ra, ru-ki-to, su-ri-mo, ti-ri-to, tu-ri-so* (Tylissos), *u-ta-no*; and group IV, a far west group mentions *wa-to* (Lato): *o-du-ru-wo, *56-ko-we, si-ra-ro, wa-to* (Lato). Add the ethnics *pu-na-si-jo* and *wa-ti-jo* on KH Ar4: Hallager et al. (supra n. 468). For *se-to-i-ja*, Bennet (supra n. 292) 241, 243 suggests either Mallia or, less likely, Archanes; Owens 1994 (supra n. 282) prefers Archanes. Bennet (supra n. 292) 231 n. 4: "*ko-no-so-de*," "to Knossos" appears on KN C5753, which may have been written at a western site and brought to Knossos for tallying since its scribe, 107, deals only with western matters.

Since Knossos was interested in separate districts from the far west to perhaps the western borders of Lasithi,[484] it seems logical to assume that Knossos had some kind of centralizing control over the island, especially since some places mentioned in the tablets (e.g., Phaistos) do not appear archaeologically to have been able to function administratively on their own. On the other hand, the Neopalatial distribution of palaces and villas suggests at least a partial decentralization, which may have continued in the form of secondary regional centers surrounded by small settlements.

The Knossos tablets mention most of the conventional officials known in somewhat more detail on the mainland. The surprisingly small number of references, however, may reflect the tablets' focus on external administration.[485] Much discussion has centered around the identity of those whose name in the genitive heads lists of workers; scholars refer to them as "collectors" or "supervisors."[486] One oddity is that the names of several collectors recur at various places in the Mycenaean world.

The interest of Knossos in the outlying areas centers mainly around the textile industry and the manufacture of four kinds of wool cloth,[487] ranked according to thickness. Linen cloth is not fully recorded at Knossos, but may appear on one tablet as the material for the special garment *146 (a tunic?). Borders (o-nu-ke), fringes, and tassels (ko-ro-ta₂) are listed separately. Some male workers are recorded in the textile industry as fullers (ka-na-pe-we), who may also be finishers and decorators, and as weavers. Women, however, outnumber men 2 or 3 to 1, and these, along with their children and TA and DA supervisors, received allocations of raw material from the central authorities from which to make cloth. Tablets record production targets and the receipt of the final products in the palace. Female decorators (a-zelke-ti-ri-ja) are specialists, stationed outside Knossos, where special cloth is produced from which they make fancy borders. Other female cloth workers include weavers and spinners, women who make special kinds of cloth (ne-ki-ri-de workers, ko-u-ra cloth), "old women" (ka-ra-we, γραῦες), and possibly "apprentices" (di[-da-ka-re]).

Related to the textiles is the interest in maintaining large flocks of sheep, especially wethers (castrated adult males) that produce the better wool.[488] The flocks in areas far away were apparently administered by the collectors, while the flocks in nearer areas are grouped according to assembly places (a-ko-ra-ja, related to ἀγορά?). Since the nearer sheep number twice as many as the farther sheep, and since the approximately 100,000 sheep listed in the Knossos tablets needed well over 100,000 ha of grazing land, it is likely that the main area of concern was Central Crete.[489]

Another region that figures prominently is Da-wo, a place closely linked to Phaistos. Knossos tablet F(2) 852 records 10,000+ units of grain there, or approximately 960,000 l.[490] Da-wo must be somewhere in the Mesara, which makes it certain that that plain functioned as a "breadbasket" as much in the Final Palatial period as it did in the Neopalatial.

Trade and Interconnections

It is difficult to assess Crete's contacts with the eastern Mediterranean in the Final Palatial period. LM pottery continues to be exported to Cyprus. On the basis of early LM IIIA2 pottery from the cemetery at Kition and because of the presence of horns of consecration at Kition, Myrtou-Pigadakia, and Pa-

---

[484] Ra-su-to in group II may be "Lasithi," although that name cannot be traced earlier than the Byzantine period: Bennet (supra n. 292) 240; C.B. Kritzas, "Νέα επιγραφικά στοιχεία για την ετυμολογία του Λασυθίου," 8th CretCong (forthcoming).

[485] The wanax is associated with spice, and his bureaus are concerned with cloth and perhaps with purple dying (T.G. Palaima, "Maritime Matters in the Linear B Tablets," Aegaeum 7 [1991] 273–310); the bureau of the ra-wa-ke-ta is responsible for grain; Anutos, the qa-si-re-u at Knossos, and Sukereos, the qa-si-re-u at Setoija, are responsible for men; some te-re-ta hold plots of land in the central region, and a te-re-ta of Aptera is responsible for 45 men; the e-qe-ta Pisawatas is at Knossos, and an e-qe-si-ja bureau is responsible for fine cloth borders; a mayor (ko-re-te) in the west supplies an ox; and there is a vice-mayor (po-ro-ko-re-te) at Qa-ra, and an unknown functionary, the a-ke-re-mo-no.

[486] In Olivier (supra n. 414), see the following: J. Bennet, "'Collectors' or 'Owners'?" 65–101; J. Driessen, "'Collectors' Items,'" 197–214; L. Godart, "Les collecteurs dans le

monde égéen," 257–83. See also J.T. Killen, "The Knossos Ld(1) Tablets," in E. Risch and H. Mühlestein eds., Colloquium Mycenaeum (Geneva 1979) 152–81, esp. 176–77.

[487] Killen (supra n. 486); J.T. Killen, "The Textile Industries at Pylos and Knossos," in C.W. Shelmerdine and T.G. Palaima eds., Pylos Comes Alive (New York 1984) 49–63: the thin pa-we-a ko-u-ra (1 unit wool: 1.7 units cloth), tu-na-no (3:1), TELA + TE (7:1), and the thick pe-ko-to (10:1).

[488] P. Halstead, "Counting Sheep in Neolithic and Bronze Age Greece," in I. Hodder, G. Isaac, and N. Hammond eds., Patterns in the Past (Cambridge 1981) 307–39.

[489] The modern nome of Herakleion occupies approximately 2,800 km² or 280,000 ha.

[490] M. Ventris and J. Chadwick, Documents in Mycenaean Greek (Cambridge 1959) 157–58, 170, 412 calculate this amount of GRA into rations (one unit equals 10 T, and 2 T equals a monthly ration for a woman worker), approximately a month's ration for 50,000 women workers or a year's ration for 4,166 women workers. See L. Foxhall and H.A. Forbes, "Σιτομετρεία," Chiron 12 (1982) 44 and 65–68.

phos, Karageorghis identifies possible Minoan settlements and sanctuaries in the area of Kokkinokremos. Popham, however, postulates a suspension of trade between the two islands.[491] The bulk of Aegean pottery found in Cyprus and the Near East is said to be Mycenaean, although this has not been scientifically tested.[492] Minoan pottery, however, is found in the Near East and surprising amounts of Canaanite pottery come from Kommos, along with Egyptian pottery and Canaanite anchor stones.[493]

In the Final Palatial period, pottery workshops at Chania were producing wares that were exported elsewhere in Crete, to the Greek mainland and the Cyclades, east to Cyprus, and west to Italy and Sardinia.[494] Chania was also producing stirrup jars for trade, some with painted inscriptions that were being exported to the mainland.

There are signs of growing contact with the west.[495] Handmade burnished ware in typical sub-Apennine shapes has been found at Kommos in IIIA1 levels and at Chania starting in IIIB early and continuing into IIIC; although the pottery looks Italian, analysis of some pieces shows it to be local. Presumably, then, some pots at least were made by resident Italians for their own use, rather than imported from Italy. The same contexts at Chania have yielded wheel-made Gray ware cups and kylikes, some with high-swung handles. The source of this ware has not been determined, but it may not be Italy; similar pieces have been found in Anatolia in chamber tombs at Müskebi near Halikarnassos.

The LM II–IIIA period also marks significant changes in Egypt's relations with its neighbors, in which the inhabitants of the Aegean clearly played a part. Following the expulsion of the Hyksos, the Egyptians had embarked on the creation of an empire in Syria-Palestine that eventually stretched to the upper Euphrates. By the mid-15th century, Aegean merchants would have been trading at Syrian ports, some of them under Egyptian control. It is not surprising, therefore, that we find Aegean natives, occasionally labeled Keftiu, represented in Egyptian tombs at Thebes, along with Syrians and other foreigners.[496]

Although the Keftiu had vanished from Egyptian paintings by the time of Tuthmosis IV, a trade in textiles from the Aegean seems to have continued to influence decorative patterns, which often survive painted on the ceilings and walls of tombs and palaces. Ceilings in the tomb of Senenmut included meander patterns or interlocking running spirals with dotted centers, alternating with rosettes, all of which find close parallels in Minoan decorative patterns.[497] These continue until at least the end of the 18th Dynasty. A well-known ceiling from the palace of Amenhotep III at Malkata (West Thebes) includes running spirals with dotted centers alternating with bucrania supporting rosettes.

The long reign of Amenhotep III overlaps with much of LM IIIA1–2, during which Crete, not the mainland, receives the lion's share of Egyptian imports.[498] The discovery of LH IIIA2 pottery and a few incipient IIIB sherds at Akhenaten's short-lived capital of Amarna fits what we know of the reigns

---

[491] *Kommos* III, 157 lists Cypriot pottery in IIIA levels at Kommos: 22 White Slip milkbowls, two Base Ring juglets and a bowl, a White Shaved juglet, two Plain White Wheelmade pithoi, and an amphora. V. Karageorghis, "Some Reflections on the Relations between Cyprus and Crete during the Late Minoan III B Period," in Karageorghis (supra n. 206) 199. Popham, in Karageorghis (supra n. 477) 183.

[492] H. Catling, quoted in Jones 589, 593; G. Cadogan, "Cyprus, Minoan Pottery, Trade and Colonization," in Zerner and Zerner (supra n. 302) 91–99, esp. 93; J.H. Crouwel, "Mycenaean Pictorial Pottery from Cyprus in Oxford," *OJA* 10 (1991) 45–53; Hankey (supra n. 303) 101–10.

[493] V. Hankey, "Crete, Cyprus, and the South-East Mediterranean, 1400–1200 B.C.," in Karageorghis (supra n. 206) 144–57 lists LM IIIA from Akko tomb 3, Tell Abu Hawam, Khirbet Judur, and Minet el Beida; and IIIA1 from Gurob and Minet el Beida. The only Canaanite from East Crete in LM IIIA is a flask and some sherds from Pseira, House DA (Betancourt and Davaras, in *Cretan Studies* [supra n. 34]). Kommos, however, has yielded much more in IIIA levels; *Kommos* III, 160–61 lists 14 South and 6 North Canaanite jars, and four Egyptian jars, five storage jars, two flasks, and two closed vessels. J. Shaw, "Two Three-Holed

Stone Anchors from Kommos, Crete," *IJNA* 24 (1995) 279–91.

[494] Mochlos: *AR* 40 (1994) 81. Mallia, Quartier Nu: *AR* 39 (1993) 76. Ayios Stephanos: Jones 424. Cyprus: Jones and Day (supra n. 200) 263; Karageorghis (supra n. 491); Popham, in Karageorghis (supra n. 477) 187; E. Hallager 1988 (supra n. 412) fig. 3, caption. Italy: L. Vagnetti, "Ceramiche del Tardo Minoico III rinvenute in Italia," in M. Liverani, A. Palmieri, and R. Peroni eds., *Studi di palentologia in onore di Salvatore M. Puglisi* (Rome 1985) 825–32. Sardinia: M.L.F. Ceruti, L. Vagnetti, and F. Lo Schiavo, "Minoici, Micenei e Ciprioti in Sardegna nella seconda meta del II millennio a.C.," in Balmuth (supra n. 200) 7–38, esp. 17; B.P. Hallager, "Crete and Italy in the Late Bronze III Period," *AJA* 89 (1985) 293–305; and Jones and Day (supra n. 200).

[495] Kommos: *Kommos* III, 164–68; Chania: B.P. Hallager (supra n. 494) and personal communication.

[496] Rehak (supra n. 203); P. Rehak, "Aegean Natives in the Theban Tomb Paintings," in *Aegean and Orient*; Matthäus (supra n. 456).

[497] P.F. Dorman, *The Tombs of Senenmut* (New York 1991) col. pls. 20b, 27b–c, 28, 60 fig. 13.

[498] Cline, passim.

of the immediate successors of Amenhotep III; Amarna was probably abandoned during the reign of Tutankhamen. Inscribed objects dating to the reign of Amenhotep III have been found both on Crete and the mainland, and the "Aegean itinerary" on a statue base in Amenhotep's funerary complex at Kom el-Hetan and faience plaques at Mycenae support the notion that Egypt was acknowledging the increasing importance of the mainland centers.

Religion

During the Final Palatial period, marked changes in Minoan religion take place, following what appears to be a massive rejection of the Neopalatial religious-political system at the end of LM IB. While there is evidence for both continuity and change, the following five main developments may be noted in particular. First, as noted above, the production of certain types of palatial prestige ritual objects ceases after the LM IB destructions. Some of these objects are now appropriated for tombs. Tripod offering tables of stucco or clay continue, including painted examples, but these are also sometimes found in tombs.[499] Second, certain Neopalatial symbols of possible religious significance become uncommon or disappear: inscribed stone offering tables are no longer produced (though some are reused), stepped stands for double axes and the sacral knot seem to vanish, and stone and stucco horns of consecration are replaced by painted examples on pottery and terracotta larnakes.

Third, cult equipment on Crete is increasingly manufactured of terracotta, a trend that continues to the end of the Bronze Age. The house or sanctuary models of the Proto- and Neopalatial periods are superseded by "hut models." Plastic horns of consecration are modeled on some stands.[500] Tubular stands, which may have had a cultic use in the Neopalatial period, now become larger and more elaborate. With the addition of plastic surface decoration resembling snakes, these are now referred to as snake tubes, though they may have no connection with these animals. There is also a resurgence in the use of terracotta for zoomorphic and anthropomorphic (especially female) figurines, and these are now found in several locations, including shrines connected with habitation areas. It has not been established whether these figurines represent goddesses or votaries, but they have an important role in the small shrines, where they are often set on stands or benches facing the doorway to the room. Many of the female figurines have upraised arms, a gesture of uncertain meaning. A seminal study by Alexiou labeled this type the "Minoan Goddess with Upraised Arms" (MGUA).[501] Although these are especially characteristic of the Postpalatial period (see below), they originate in the Final Palatial period or earlier. Their gestures may derive from the upraised arms of Neopalatial faience figurines or of the women on sealstones who wear the "snake frame" headdress.

The mainland class of psi, phi, and tau figurines is introduced into Crete in LM IIIA2, a sign of Mycenaean presence.[502] The IIIA2–B period also sees the introduction of large wheelmade bovid figurines. Moldmade bovid rhyta had existed in the Neopalatial period, but these seem to die out after the end of LM IB. The concept of the bull rhyton is revived, perhaps under Mycenaean influence, but the rhyton is now much less naturalistic in form.

Fourth, new types of cult practice become visible, particularly in the area of funerary cult. As we have seen, painted terracotta larnakes introduce a new iconography, and the painted sarcophagus from Ayia Triada provides one of the most important, if de-

---

[499] The ears and inlays from a bull's head rhyton in the Tomb of the Double Axes at Knossos: Evans (supra n. 148) 52 fig. 70. A trapezoidal base (for a double ax?) was deposited in a shaft grave at Knossos: Hood 1958–1959 (supra n. 425). A marble triton comes from a Warrior Grave at Kalyvia: *CM* pl. 115 (below). Tripod offering tables: *BCH* 102 (1978) 836 fig. 8, from Mallia. Katsamba tombs: Alexiou (supra n. 158) pl. 12α–β, pl. 26β.

[500] J.-C. Poursat, "Malia au MR III," *6th CretCong* A2 (1990) 160, pl. 28d.

[501] Zoomorphic and anthropomorphic figurines: Rethemiotakis (supra n. 272). From habitation sites come others, like the elaborately painted figurines of LM II date from the Unexplored Mansion at Knossos (Popham et al. [supra n. 5] pl. 159.5), the figurine of LM II–IIIA date from Poros painted with a Linear A inscription, the LM IIIA2 figurine of a kourotrophos who holds her child aloft, and the upper half of a naturalistic female figurine from Quartier Nu at Mallia (Driessen and Farnoux [supra n. 468] pl. V.3). The so-called Shrine of the Double Axes in the Knossos palace, Gesell 90–92, was dated by Evans to LM IIIB, but its female figurines may be of LM IIIA date. Other female terracotta figurines were found in the Little Palace (Gesell 93–94), in a domestic shrine at Kannia near Phaistos (Levi [supra n. 52] 253–64). Part of the head of a terracotta figurine, from a figure originally more than 1 m tall, was found on Mt. Juktas (*Prakt* 1975, pl. 267α). MGUAs: S. Alexiou, Η μινωϊκή θεά μεθ' υψομενών χειρών (Diss. Univ. of Athens 1958), and published separately in *CretChron* 12 (1958) 179–299. Photographs: *CM* pls. 128–31 (Gazi), 135–37 (Karphi).

[502] E. French, "The Development of Mycenaean Terracotta Figurines," *BSA* 66 (1971) 101–87; French (supra n. 442).

bated, glimpses into the Minoan view of the afterlife during this period. A major development of the Final Palatial period is the evidence for bull sacrifice; it is possible that the killing of the animal now becomes the final feature of the Minoan bull-games, perhaps under Mycenaean influence. It may be significant too that the bull sacrifice is attested at exactly the moment when the new iconographic topos of the Minotaur appears on seals. If the minotaurs represent men in masks, they may be appropriating some of the powers associated with the bull for symbolic, even shamanistic, purposes.[503] Women still played an important role in religion, however, as the Knossos Procession Fresco, Ayia Triada sarcophagus, and Archanes Tholos A all demonstrate.

Fifth, it is hardly surprising that there is slight evidence for a general reuse of peak sanctuaries in LM II–III,[504] generally at peaks that are close to habitation sites. Continuity of cult activity occurs at Juktas and Kato Syme, and although prestige dedications decline, they are nevertheless still present,[505] and sherd material indicates that cave cult continues as well. A new feature is the emphasis on small "house shrines" or "town shrines." Some of these replace Neopalatial ritual areas, like the "fetish shrine" in the Little Palace from a remodeled lustral basin, while others appear to be new creations (the Shrine of the Double Axes in the Knossos palace; the freestanding town shrine at Ayia Triada; and the Gournia town shrine). The use of piers in the Shrine of the Double Axes and the piers and floor fresco at Ayia Triada may be deliberate attempts to recall Neopalatial forms.[506] A LM IIIA2–B house shrine in Building 7

at Palaikastro included pithoi, a terracotta bull's head rhyton, triton shells, cylindrical stands, stalactites, and benches. A distinctive feature of the new small shrines is the bench at the back of the room, used to support MGUAs, along with other figurines and offerings.

Finally, the Linear B texts shed light on the religious concerns of the major administrative centers. Most of the Linear B religious texts from Knossos concern amounts of oil or honey going to various divinities: Ares, Diktaian Zeus, Enyalios, Eileithyia, Erinyes, Pan (?), Paian, and Poseidon. The Pantheon (pa-si-te-o-i, in the dative) is frequently mentioned, at Amnisos, at Au-ri-mo, and at a locality not specified and probably therefore Knossos. At Chania there is mention of a shrine of Zeus as well as the god Dionysos for the first time.[507]

At least one sanctuary and possibly more existed at Amnisos. The divinities mentioned there are Eileithyia, Ares, probably Poseidon, and frequently the Pantheon. Of the religious administration, there is mention of a couple of shrines, the da-da-re-jo (the Daidaleion), the da-pu₂-ri-to (Labyrinth), and the shrine to Diktaian Zeus. There is a qe-ra-si-ja (Gerousia?) at a locality not mentioned (probably Knossos), as well as at Amnisos and at Au-ri-mo; but only one type of priestess is listed, the Priestess of the Winds located at three sites, *47-da, Au-ri-mo, and U-ta-no (Fp 1 and 13), and only one priest is mentioned, that at da-*83-ja (Fp 363).[508]

More controversial have been the mentions of a da-pu₂-ri-to-jo po-ti-ni-ja and a-ta-na-po-ti-ni-ja. Many scholars have assumed po-ti-ni-ja is the goddess Pot-

---

[503] Sakellarakis (supra n. 383); Younger (supra n. 254) 518–21. N. Schlager, "Minotauros in der ägäischen Glyptik?" CMS Beiheft 3 (Berlin 1989) 225–37. A LM IIIA larnax found at Mochlos is painted on the interior with two standing figures, one seemingly wearing a mask with pointed ears: Soles and Davaras 1996 (supra n. 33). For a new seal depicting the Minotaur, found at Midea on the mainland, see Demakopoulou et al. 1994 (supra n. 122) 32–33 figs. 43–44. For masks, cf. C.F. Klein, "Masking Empire," Art History 9 (1986) 135–67.

[504] J.F. Cherry, "Generalisation and the Archaeology of the State," in D. Green, C. Haselgrove, and M. Spriggs eds., Social Organisation and Settlement (Oxford 1978) 429, fig. 1; Peatfield (supra n. 359).

[505] Sapouna-Sakellaraki (supra n. 41) 72–73 figs. 6–7; AR 36 (1990) 71. Finds include wheelmade bovids. Juktas: AR 36 (1990) 71; Kato Syme: AR 36 (1990) 72. LM II pottery has been discovered at Juktas, and a type Gi sword decorated with spirals and semicircles was dedicated at Kato Syme: A. Lembesi, ArchEph 1981, 1–24, esp. 15, pl. 2.

[506] The Ayia Triada shrine has a vivid but crude floor fresco with marine motifs that include dolphins, rockwork,

and a bold red octopus: Immerwahr 102 and n. 14. Hood's date of LM I is too early: Hood (supra n. 157) 71, 249, n. 134; Hirsch (supra n. 80) 10–11, pl. I; E.S. Hirsch, "Another Look at Minoan and Mycenaean Interrelationships in Floor Decoration," AJA 84 (1980) 459–61.

[507] J.T. Killen, "Piety Begins at Home," in P. Ilievski and Ljiljana Crepajac eds., Tractata Mycenaea (Skopje 1987) 163–78, esp. 164. Respectively, a-re (KN Fp 140); di-ka-ta-jo di-we (Fp 1, 7?); e-nu-wa-ri-jo (V 53); e-re-u-ti-ja (Gg 705); e-ri-nu-we (Fp 1; V 53); pa-de (Fp 1; Ga 953); pa-ja-wo-ne (Fp 354; V 53); and po-si-da-o-ne (Gg 705?, 717; V 53); the Pantheon (pa-si-te-o-i: Fp 1, 5, 6, 13, 14, 16; Ga 953). Chania: KH Gq 5. Hallager et al. (supra n. 468). M.S. Ruiperez, "The Mycenaean Name of Dionysos," in A. Heubeck and G. Neumann eds., Res Mycenaeae (Göttingen 1983) 408–12.

[508] S. Hiller, "The Administration of Minoan Sanctuaries by the Mycenaean Palace at Knossos," in A. Farnoux and J. Driessen eds., La Crète mycénienne (forthcoming). Killen (supra n. 486) 173: a shrine to Diktaian Zeus in central Crete and near Knossos accords well with Strabo's quote from Aratus (ὄρεος σχεδὸν Ἰδαίοιο). qe-ra-si-ja: Fp 5, 6, 13, 16, 48. S. Hiller, "Minoan qe-ra-si-ja," TAW I, 675–79.

nia, but at Pylos she is occasionally mentioned in connection with other places (e.g., Elis? in PY Fr 1228) and is occasionally paired with the *wanax* of Pylos himself (e.g., Fr 1235), the two forming the *wa-na-so-i*.[509] If Atana is the Minoan version of Utano, a place-name in the Tylissos group, located in northwestern Crete and connected with ancient Tanos,[510] then *po-ti-ni-ja* may simply be a "chief priestess" there as well as at the Labyrinth. Two Knossos tablets (KN Ga 1058 and Od 696) mention a festival, the *te-o-po-ri-jo* (θεοφορία), or "carrying of the deity."

POSTPALATIAL CRETE (LM IIIB LATE–SUBMINOAN)

Sites and Architecture

Both the beginning and the end of the Postpalatial period have proved difficult to define, except by the apparent loss of literacy on Crete.[511] On present evidence, there were no palatial administrations anywhere on Crete from LM IIIB late through the end of the Bronze Age. Some inscribed stirrup jars in late IIIB contexts at Quartier Nu, Mallia, could simply be holdovers. Similarly, scholars have debated over how to define the end of the Bronze Age on Crete. Is it marked by the latest IIIC pottery, or does a Subminoan phase exist as an independent period transitional to the Protogeometric/Early Iron Age?[512]

Despite the nebulous boundaries to this period, there is general agreement that the picture of Postpalatial Crete is vastly different from the scenario envisioned earlier by Evans and Pendlebury of depressed refugee populations hiding in the mountains.[513] Nevertheless, it is clear that the disappearance of palatial administration after LM IIIB early marks a watershed on Crete. Up to this point, there had been evidence across the island from both habitation and burial sites. The most common Postpalatial site, however, is the tomb, with few habitation sites known for the latter part of LM IIIB and C. While some tholoi appear fairly canonical, most in the Postpalatial period are small, with diameters and heights of about 1 m.[514] They contain only a few burials, sometimes in larnakes.

The diminishing number of settlements from LM IIIB late seems to indicate a shrinking of population. In IIIC, a progressive movement away from the shore may have occurred, though what this means precisely is still being debated. Sites toward the eastern end of the island, like Kavousi Vronda and Kastro, Vrokastro, and Vasiliki Kephala, however, are near the coast and have good views of the sea, as does Karphi. It may be, as Watrous suggests, that piracy forced the move inland and to higher elevations, as well as

[509] *da-pu₂-ri-to-jo po-ti-ni-ja*: Gg 702. L. Godart, "Il labirinto e la potnia nei testi micenei," *RendNap* 50 (1975) 141–52. *a-ta-na-po-ti-ni-ja*: V 53. C. Milani, "Atena e la Potnia micenea," in M. Sordi ed., *Politica e religione nel primo scontro tra Roma e l'Oriente* (Milan 1982) 29–42. *po-ti-ni-ja*: for a recent study, see D. Danielidou, "Η Σιτοποτίνια των Μυκηνών και η μυκηναϊκή Πότνια," in *Φίλια έπη* (supra n. 151) 323–42; C.J. Ruijgh, "À propos de mycénien po-ti-ni-ja-we-jo," *SMEA* 4 (1967) 40–52; M.G. Rousseau, *Les mentions religieuses dans les tablettes mycéniennes* (Rome 1968) 189; S. Hiller, "Wanasoi tonoeketerijo," *Minos* 10 (1969) 78–92; J.C. van Leuven, "Mycenaean Goddesses Called 'Potnia,'" *Kadmos* 18 (1979) 112–29; J.T. Hooker, *Mycenaean Greece* (London 1976) 208; S. Hiller, "Mykenische Heiligtümer," in *Sanctuaries* 122–24; M. Del Freo, "Pa-sa-ro, wa-na-so-i e il valore dei sillabogrammi [s-] e [z-] in miceneo," *SMEA* 26 (1987) 151–90; F.A. Jorro ed., *Diccionario micenico* II (1993) s.v. *po-ti-ni-ja*.

[510] K.T. Witczak, "Notes on Cretan Place-Names in the Linear B Tablets," *Kadmos* 31 (1992) 161–62. C. Buondelmonti (travels A.D. 1415; included in Cornelius, *Creta Sacra* I.123 [1755]; and quoted by S.G. Spanakis, Κρήτη B [Herakleion n.d.] 371, s.n. Τάνος) gives the name as an alternative for Apokoronou, the fort on the Bamos peninsula.

[511] Basic bibliography on this period includes S. Deger-Jalkotzy, "The Post-Palatial Period of Greece," in V. Karageorghis ed., *Cyprus in the 11th Century B.C.* (Nicosia 1994) 11–29; K. Nowicki, "Topography of Refuge Settlement in Crete," *JRGZM* 34 (1987) 213–34; Nowicki, "The History and Setting of the Town at Karphi," *SMEA* 26 (1987) 235–50;

B.J. Hayden, "Fortifications of Postpalatial and Early Iron Age Crete," *AA* 1988, 1–21; L. Godart and Y. Tzedakis, "La Crète du Minoen Récent III B à l'époque géométrique," in Musti et al. (supra n. 363) 187–95; H. van Effenterre, "Développements territoriaux dans la Crète postminoenne," in Musti et al. (supra n. 363) 197–206; G. Rizza, "Priniás in età micenea," in *Atti* (supra n. 429).

[512] For discussions of Subminoan pottery, see M. Tsipopoulou, "Ceramica dei periodi subminoico geometrico ed orientalizzante," in M. Rocchi and L. Vagnetti eds., *Seminari, anno 1990* (Rome 1991) 137–64; M. Popham, "The Subminoan Pottery," in L.H. Sackett ed., *Knossos: From Greek City to Roman Colony* II.1 (*BSA* Suppl. 21, Athens 1992) 59–66. A related problem is whether "Submycenaean" exists: J.B. Rutter, "A Plea for the Abandonment of the Term 'Submycenaean,'" *TUAS* 3 (1978) 58–65.

[513] J.D.S. Pendlebury, *The Archaeology of Crete* (London 1939) 303: "We seem to be back in the Neolithic Period with its life of terror."

[514] Kanta 322: large, regular tholoi include Stylos Apokoronou (Kanta 235). Large tholoi with rectangular chambers: Malame, Phylaki, Achladia (supra n. 431). Small tholoi: Kanta 322: Panayia Pediadas (Kanta 74–75), Erganos Pediadas (75–76), Dhamania Monophatsiou (79), Karphi Lasithiou (121), Vasiliki in Ierapetra (146), Khamaizi Siteias (176), Praisos Siteias (179); G.C. Gesell, L.P. Day, and W.D.E. Coulson, "Tombs and Burial Practices in Early Iron Age Crete," *Expedition* 32:3 (1990) 22–30.

provided the various imports one sees at such sites as Karphi (Cypriot pottery and bronzes and Italian pins).[515]

Some sites look prosperous. At Chania new houses are built and the Mycenaean settlement is extended farther up the Kastelli hill.[516] At least one import from Cyprus and local imitations of Italian hand-made burnished ware are known. After a heavy fire destruction at the end of LM IIIB, some reoccupation took place in LM IIIC, with reuse of rooms and new construction. Though there are few finds, local imitations of Gray wares are among them. No major destruction occurs at Chania in LM IIIC and the site is quietly abandoned before reoccupation in the Late Geometric. Excavations conducted by a Greek-Italian team in western Crete in 1989 and 1990 have revealed a new LM IIIC settlement site at Sybrita, with pits containing bones, traces of burned material, and pottery (coarse and fine wares).[517]

Quartier Nu and several other areas at Mallia experience a destruction by fire in LM IIIB early, followed by an orderly cleanup and reoccupation. A destructive fire at the end of IIIB and scanty occupation in IIIC follow, with an abandonment before the end of the period. Gournia's Mycenaean buildings west beyond the ravine may date to LM IIIB; at least one Mycenaean burial took place in the earlier town. Along the coast east of Herakleion thriving settlements existed, with houses at Katsamba, Poros, and Gouves.

Some sites, however, disappear in LM IIIB: Pseira is abandoned early, Chondros is destroyed by fire and abandoned, and Kommos is virtually deserted toward the end of IIIB early though small amounts of late IIIB and C pottery have been found at the site.[518] Ayia Triada has LM IIIB pottery but not, apparently, LM IIIC. The South-West houses at Knossos are abandoned, and LM IIIC Knossos is known primarily from tombs.

While a few sites are abandoned in LM IIIC (e.g., Stavromenos-Chamalevri), some new sites are also founded. Those at high elevations are well known: Karphi and Kavousi Vronda are first settled early in the period, Prinias and Chalasmenos are settled by the end of the period, and Arvi and Katalimata sometime in IIIC. Some sites lower down, however, also thrive: a house in Katsamba contained iron in its second phase and Phaistos is well settled into the Subminoan period. A couple of sites seem to move their populations late in LM IIIB or in LM IIIC: Ayia Pelagia may move to Kastrokephala, which is surrounded by a fortification wall, late in IIIB; Zakros has little if any LM IIIB pottery, but the Lenika peak in the adjacent Gorge of the Dead is inhabited in LM IIIC. Palaikastro suffers a fire late in LM IIIB and the population apparently moves to the acropolis Kastri, overlooking the sea for LM IIIC.

In recent years, intensive excavation and survey work by several teams in the Gulf of Mirambello and Isthmus of Ierapetra have revealed important evidence for the final phases of Bronze Age Crete: Kavousi (Vronda and Kastro), Vrokastro, Chalasmenos and Katalimata, and, at the edge of Lasithi, Karphi. Another large IIIC habitation site has been identified by survey at the peak of Profitis Elias south of Episkopi.[519] Importantly, many of these late commu-

[515] A summary of the settlement history in the Lasithi plain makes the trend toward a shrinking population clear (L.V. Watrous, *An Archaeological Survey of the Lasithi Plain in Crete from the Neolithic to the Late Roman Period* [Diss. Univ. of Pennsylvania 1975]): in the Neolithic period, 15 open-air sites and caves; in EM II, six or seven hamlets with cemeteries; in MM I, the previous hamlets plus three or four new sites; in MM III, 11 large settlements altogether; in LM I, nine settlements; in LM IIIA–B, only three of the previous sites continue plus two more; in LM IIIB late, only Karphi is a major settlement, plus six smaller sites; at the end of the Bronze Age, only Papoura. For a shift away from the shore, see V.R.d'A. Desborough, "Crete in the First Half of the Twelfth Century B.C.," *3rd CretCong* (1973) 62–69. Piracy: Watrous (supra) 326.

[516] E. Hallager 1988 (supra n. 412); *AR* 42 (1996) 47.

[517] N. Metaxa Prokopiou, "Sybrita Amariou," in Musti et al. (supra n. 363) 373–401; Metaxa Prokopiou, "Η μετάβαση από το τέλος της εποχής του χαλκού στην πρώιμη εποχή του σιδέρου," in Rocchetti (supra n. 7) 249–54; Metaxa Prokopiou, "Σύβριτος/Θρόνος Αμαρίου," *8th CretCong* (forthcoming); L. Rocchetti, "Sybrita," in *Atti* (supra n. 429).

[518] *Kommos* III, 146–47.

[519] Kavousi: *Atlas* 120–24; W.D.E. Coulson et al., "Excavations on the Kastro at Kavousi," *Hesperia* 66 (1997) 315–90; Day, "Early Iron Age Architecture at Kavousi," in *6th CretCong* A2 (1990) 173–84; *AR* 36 (1990) 73–74; *AR* 37 (1991) 71–72; *AR* 38 (1992) 64; *AR* 41 (1995) 65–67; *AR* 42 (1996) 46. Vrokastro: *Atlas* 286–91; B.J. Hayden, "Terracotta Figures, Figurines, and Vase Attachments from Vrokastro, Crete," *Hesperia* 60 (1991) 101–44; Hayden et al. (supra n. 7); *AR* 38 (1992) 67–68. Chalasmenos and Katalimata: D.C. Haggis and K. Nowicki, *Hesperia* 62 (1993) 303–37; Coulson and M. Tsipopoulou, "Preliminary Investigations at Halasmenos, Crete, 1992–93," *Aegean Archaeology* 1 (1994) 65–97; Nowicki, "Kataleimata," in Coulson and Tsipopoulou (supra) 94–97; *AR* 41 (1995) 65; *AR* 42 (1996) 45. Karphi: *Atlas* 117–19; Nowicki, "History, Topography and Economy of Karphi," in Thomas (supra n. 390) 25–32; Nowicki (supra n. 359) 43–46; Day, *AJA* 101 (1997) 348 (abstract). A small Subminoan-Protogeometric cemetery at Karphi Pediados-Mnemata: *AR* 37 (1991) 71; *AR* 42 (1996) 46. Profitis Elias near Episkopi: *AR* 41 (1995) 65.

nities are preceded by evidence of early habitation, generally Neolithic, EM II, and MM II. The late settlements thus are not new foundations, but rather reestablishments of previously existing sites.

Kavousi actually consists of two settlement sites initially explored in 1900, a lower one at Vronda (380 masl) and the upper one at the Kastro (700 masl), separated by a short walk. Like many sites in this area, Vronda had Neolithic and Early Minoan remains (EM IIB–III) and extensive MM II habitation. In LM IIIC the area was reoccupied, and at least one building (E) was probably abandoned at the end of IIIC. Room 1 in Building E contained pithoi in different shapes and decoration. A Late Geometric cemetery is at Vronda. At Kavousi Kastro nearby, three main phases have been identified: I (transitional from IIIB–C), II (mid-IIIC), and III (late IIIC, contemporary with Vronda). Kastro thus is important because it appears to give a complete habitation sequence through LM IIIC. Phase V represents a transition from LM IIIC to Protogeometric.

Watrous has argued persuasively for paired villages, one below the elevation limit for olive trees (600–800 masl) and one above in the mountainous regions suitable for herding; such paired sites would include Kavousi Vronda and Kastro. In addition, Nowicki's indefatigable mountain surveys across the island have revealed a more horizontal dimension; sites at high altitudes often work together to guard passes and oversee approaches to the upland valleys.[520] Habitation at these sites is not limited to the Postpalatial period, but recurs throughout Crete's history.

The new excavation of Vasiliki Kephala under the direction of Eliopoulos is also changing our perceptions of this period.[521] A small tholos tomb had been excavated by Seager south of the site in 1906. Although naturally defensible, Kephala occupies a relatively low-lying site (213 masl) on the flat-topped ridge just above Vasiliki, far lower and more accessible than some of the other Isthmus sites. More importantly, the location of Kephala gives it direct control over trade and movement of people north and south over the Isthmus, and a direct line of sight to contemporary sites like Kavousi Kastro and Vronda, and Chalasmenos. Excavations since 1994

have already revealed a substantial settlement, LM IIIC to Protogeometric. The Dark Age settlement was large, occupying the whole flat top (ca. 230 m, north–south) of Kephala hill. Parts of 10 buildings, in varying degrees of preservation, have been located. One, Epsilon, has been completely excavated and seems to be unique for the period; a temple complex (17 × 25 m), it consists of eight rooms grouped in three wings, each of which may have served a specific cult function. In the south wing, cult figures and equipment were found in situ on benches. Parts of at least five MGUAs have been recognized, one of them enthroned (H. 44 cm), as well as snake tubes, fenestrated stands, and votive backing plaques. In the main room of the central wing two axial wooden columns rested on stone slab bases framing a central hearth. In an attached magazine an heirloom seal with a cow suckling a calf was found. The northern wing consists of large rooms, one of which (E3) may have seen important cult activity (fig. 8). It has low benches around the walls and in the middle a low stone platform incorporating an upright unworked stone, possibly an altar with baetyl.

At Chalasmenos, traces of a small settlement have been excavated since 1993 by a joint Greek-American team. On either side of a rocky outcrop some preserved house walls incorporate the natural bedrock, and individual stones about 0.5 m in diameter present worked interior and exterior faces. Rooms are small, with doors generally at the ends of their short sides. Roofs consisted of wooden beams covered by hard-packed waterproof orange-yellow clay, with floors of hard-packed earth. In some rooms, flat stones on the floor served as vessel stands and hearths consisted of small stones. A small tholos, A, is located nearby, built of medium and large blocks in seven courses. It held the bodies of five individuals, four adults and one adolescent.[522] Though short by today's standards (H. men ca. 168.5 cm, H. women 145.6 cm), they were muscular and robust. A kalathos from Tholos A has a nearly exact parallel from the settlement, and both may have been made by the same local potter.

Some architecture survives from the LM IIIB late and IIIC periods.[523] Where the terrain permits, square house plans seem to be common: Chania in

[520] Watrous (supra n. 515) 322–27. E.g., K. Nowicki, "Settlements of Refuge in Crete," in Schiering (supra n. 114) 83–87; Nowicki, "Investigations in the Cretan Mountains," *ArcheologiaWar* 39 (1988) 189–98; Nowicki, *ArcheologiaWar* 44 (1993) 95–101.

[521] We are grateful to the excavator, Theodoros Eliopoulos, for graciously giving us a tour of the site in June 1996, and for providing the following information.

[522] L. Little, "The Burials in Tomb A at Halasmenos," in Coulson and Tsipopoulou (supra n. 519) 87–91. Dimensions of the tholos: D. 1.60 m; H. 1.40 m; entrance W. 0.90 m.

[523] B.J. Hayden, "Aspects of Village Architecture in the Cretan Postpalatial Period," *Aegaeum* 6 (1990) 203–13; Hayden (supra ns. 414, 416); and M.S. Mook, *The Northwest Building: Houses of the Late Bronze and Early Iron Ages on the Kastro at Kavousi, East Crete* (Diss. Univ. of Minnesota 1993).

Fig. 8. View of Vasiliki Kephala, room E3. (Courtesy T. Eliopoulos)

IIIB; and Kavousi Vronda, Karphi, and Chalasmenos (as far as can be judged) in IIIC. Where the steep terrain limits the accessible area, as at Kavousi Kastro, Vrokastro, Karphi, and Katalimata, long rectangular houses with rooms in rank occupy narrow terraces. Chania, Karphi, and Kavousi Vronda provide some idea of a village plan: units clustered closely together, in no rigidly maintained alignment, separated by dog-leg alleys. An occasional plateia breaks the claustrophobia, allowing for outside work areas and gatherings. The result is not unlike modern Cretan traditional villages. Walls at Chalasmenos were preserved up to 1 m in height and consisted of carefully laid limestone blocks held together with a mortar of mud, as at Vronda. One oddity, the absence of an apparent doorway, has commonly led to the assumption that these rooms are basement rooms, but in early modern villages in Crete doorways are often raised above the level of the exterior road or alley and approached by a short flight of steps that hugs the exterior wall.

Important buildings may be isolated and rectangular with a central rectangular hearth flanked by two wooden columns on bases (Chania, Vasiliki Kephala). This form later becomes the Archaic Cretan temple like those found at Kommos and Prinias. The LM IIIB and C temple, however, seems to consist of a building that is rectangular (Kavousi Vronda) or square (Vasiliki Kephala) with one or more benches on which to set MGUAs, and a storage room at one end.

A special type of site is the so-called refuge settlement, placed high atop a mountain and surrounded by a cyclopean fortification wall.[524] These sites, however, are not limited to this period only; as noted above, the "refuge" fortification wall on Juktas may be Neopalatial.

Art

A significant, and as yet unresolved, problem is the ceramic chronology and phasing of LM IIIB–C.[525] Nevertheless, excavators on Crete are in general agreement on two points: IIIB–C pottery shows innovations that indicate that it is not simply trailing behind developments on the mainland, and the stylistic sequences worked out for the mainland by Furumark and others do not hold for Crete. Current research is directed to establishing these later sequences. Groundbreaking work in the former area took place at the conference on LM III pottery held at the Danish Institute in Athens in 1994.[526]

The most common IIIC shapes are stirrup jars, kraters, and bowls, continuing the trend toward fewer shapes in use. Painted decoration becomes sim-

[524] Hayden (supra n. 511); K. Nowicki, "A Dark Age Refuge Centre near Pefki, East Crete," *BSA* 89 (1994) 235–68; Nowicki, "Arvi Fortetsa and Loutraki Kandilioro," *BSA* 91 (1996) 253–85.

[525] For a survey of Final Palatial and Postpalatial pottery, see Popham, in Evely et al. (supra n. 1) 89–103. See also M.C. Shaw, "Two Cups with Incised Decoration from Kom-

mos, Crete," *AJA* 87 (1983) 443–52; and P. Sotirakopoulou, "The Chronology of the 'Kastri Group' Reconsidered," *BSA* 88 (1993) 5–20.

[526] Hallager and Hallager (supra n. 5); we are grateful to the editors for allowing us to read the manuscript before publication.

plified and does not fill the entire surface of the pot. Close Style pottery is present on Crete throughout IIIC; it does not develop within it. A diagnostic feature of IIIC stirrup jars is a bump atop the "spool" of the handle, with the "spool" itself added separately, not pinched out of the clay of the vessel. One unusual IIIC shape is the lid, which often has piecrust decoration and burning on the underside. These may be fire-dampers. Pictorial vase painting, which continues into the Early Iron Age (see below), has attracted attention, although major studies have been conducted so far only on pictorial larnakes. Coarse ware pottery is also finally receiving serious consideration.[527]

After LM IIIB early, many art forms become defunct. No frescoes, hard stone seals, or stone vases seem to be manufactured in this period or later, and it is doubtful that faience or ivory is being worked anywhere in the Aegean. Instead, many objects manufactured earlier are now deposited deliberately as heirlooms. For example, the surviving examples of seals are now offered as votives in tombs and shrines; a few come from late contexts in domestic areas.[528]

Trade and Interconnections

In Crete, Mycenaean pottery continues to be imported, while Chania Workshop pottery is exported to Boeotia, Euboea, the Cyclades, and Cyprus.[529] Chaniot pottery continues to be found in Italy and at Antigori, Sardinia, while Gray wares and locally made Italian wares have been identified in late levels at Kommos and Chania. Contemporary Gray wares look like Minyan ware, though dull; they are not very well fired, come in local shapes, and are wheelmade. Similar wares come from Karphi and East Crete.[530] Cypriot pottery, especially White Slip II milkbowls, is found at several sites—Knossos, Kommos, Zakros, and especially Chania—and Canaanite jars appear at no fewer than 12 sites, produced in both northern and southern Syro-Palestinian and occasionally local Cretan fabrics.[531]

Little Minoan pottery, however, was exported farther eastward, especially east or south of Cyprus.[532] It is possible, as Banou notes, that the earlier "commercial line that had been established in LM I between several sites of E. Crete (Pseira, Zakros and possibly Gournia and Mochlos) and the E. Mediterranean was no longer a vital vein of commerce."[533] Texts that date to the reign of Ramses III refer to the 12th-century invasions of the Sea Peoples,[534] some of whom have been thought to be Minoan, but there is no explicit proof of this.

Religion

With the disappearance of the Cretan palaces early in IIIB, the exercise of any palatial control over religion vanishes. In the succeeding period, three main types of cult area can be identified: 1) at the borders of ruined centers, where vestiges of structures were still standing (e.g., Kannia, the Shrine of the Double Axes in the east wing at Knossos, the nearby Cara-

---

[527] D.C. Haggis and M.S. Mook, "The Kavousi Coarse Wares," *AJA* 97 (1993) 265–93.

[528] From tombs come, e.g., *CMS* II.3, nos. 133–36 and 276, and V, Suppl. 1A, no. 50. From the shrine at Karphi comes the Protopalatial seal *CMS* II.2, no. 199. Domestic contexts: *CMS* V, Suppl. 1A, nos. 123 and 397; and Nowicki, in Coulson and Tsipopoulou (supra n. 519) pl. XV.6–7.

[529] F. Schachermeyr, "Mykenisch IIIC auf dem griechischen Festland und auf Kreta," *4th CretCong* I (1980) 539–43. Chania Workshop pottery: Popham, in Karageorghis (supra n. 477) 178–91, esp. 187; E. Hallager 1988 (supra n. 412) fig. 3, caption.

[530] *Kommos* III, 165–68. M. Tsipopoulou and L. Vagnetti, "A Late Minoan III Grey Wheel-made Piriform Jar from Eastern Crete," *SMEA* 34 (1994) 43–50.

[531] Cypriot pottery: J.A. Barlow, D.L. Bolger, and B. Kling eds., *Cypriot Ceramics* (Philadelphia 1991); *Kommos* III, 182–83. For special studies, see F. Schachermeyr, "The Pleonastic Pottery Style of Cretan Middle III C and Its Cypriote Relations," in Karageorghis (supra n. 206) 204–14; E. Hallager 1988 (supra n. 412) 119; Lambrou-Phillipson (supra n. 310). Canaanite jars: *Kommos* III, 157–61, 182–83; O. Negbi and M. Negbi, "Stirrup Jars versus Canaanite Jars," in Zerner and Zerner (supra n. 302) 319–29. The only Canaanite ware

from East Crete is a flask and some sherds from Pseira, House AD: Betancourt and Davaras, in *Cretan Studies* (supra n. 34); Banou (supra n. 34) 185.

[532] Two LM IIIB coarse-ware stirrup jars, one of which is inscribed, and a LM IIIC deep bowl come from Athienou in Cyprus: T. Dothan, "Minoan Elements and Influence at Athienou, Cyprus," in Karageorghis (supra n. 206) 175 (from stratum III). Hankey (supra n. 493) lists LM IIIB pottery from Amman, Tell Abu Hawam, and Lachish, and coarse-ware stirrup jars from Beirut, Tell Abu Hawam, and Minet el Beida tomb 3, two of which are inscribed with potter's marks. S. Hiller, "Levanto-Helladic Kelche," *RDAC* 1978, 91–102 cites LM IIIC from Enkomi. Some Cypriot White Slip II is found in LM IIIB levels at Chania (E. Hallager 1988 [supra n. 412] 119). *Kommos* III, 162–63 lists a single Egyptian jar in LM IIIB levels at Kommos. None of this material has been scientifically tested.

[533] Banou (supra n. 34) 187. There are no "fine, large decorated kraters" of early IIIB found east or south of Cyprus (Hankey [supra n. 493] 153) and no foreign pottery, for instance, in the LM IIIA and B levels at Zakros or Palaikastro: Banou (supra n. 34) 191, n. 19.

[534] Cline 116–20; T. Dothan, "Tel Miqne-Ekron," in S. Gitin ed., *Recent Excavations in Israel* (Dubuque 1995) 41–59.

vanserai Spring Chamber, and presumably at Gazi); 2) local shrines in settlements and individual houses (e.g., Ayia Triada, Prinias, Karphi, Kavousi Vronda); and 3) at peak and cave sanctuaries (e.g., Koumasa) and earlier tholoi, as at Stylos. All these are now evidently under local control.[535]

The changes in cult equipment that began in the Final Palatial period become even more pronounced in the later stages of IIIB and C: MGUAs remain the dominant religious statuette, often occurring in multiple examples associated with snakes, horns of consecration, and the double ax. The MGUA may have replaced, subsumed, or supplemented the deities mentioned in the earlier Linear B texts at Knossos and Chania. At Kavousi Vronda, these figures were made apparently in sets with a backing plaque and a snake tube. The terracotta statues themselves, some approaching 80 cm in height, come from Gazi, west of Herakleion; Kannia in the Mesara; and Karphi and Kavousi, toward the eastern end of the island. The goddess often wears an elaborate tiara with various combinations of elements: poppy seedpods, horns of consecration, or birds.

The third locus of cult activity, peaks and caves, shows a resurgence and revival after the Final Palatial period, continuing on into the Early Iron Age. The peak sanctuary on Mt. Juktas continued to be used, as well as the open-air sanctuary of Kato Syme. The latter is one of the few places in the Aegean where continuity of cult can be demonstrated between the prehistoric and Archaic periods. After an apparent gap between LM IB and IIIB, the Kophinas peak was reused in IIIC, and a small IIIC settlement was established just outside the sanctuary.

It is surely significant that, in IIIC, Crete and the mainland share several religious features: Mycenaean figurines of the phi type[536] found around hearths and doorways as at Chania, and the small community bench shrine with terracotta female figurines. But the differences are equally important. The mainland assemblages do not include the snake tubes and backing plaques found on Crete, and the terracotta cylindrical model seems purely Cretan. While the figurines in both locations lift their arms, only the Cretan ones have detailed renderings of the thumbs, and only the Cretan figures wear elaborate tiaras, in contrast to the simple *poloi* of the mainland figures. The headgear suggests that these are divine, not human, figures, but it is not clear whether they represent different goddesses or aspects of a single goddess.[537]

Recent experiments with re-creating some of the Kavousi figurines demonstrate that each large terracotta statuette is built of two pot shapes, a jug for the body and a smaller, inverted jug for the head, with facial features, breasts, and arms modeled separately. These figures took at least a day, and probably several, to make. Their technique strongly suggests that they were made not by sculptors but rather by local potters, who used the same fabrics in making local cooking pots and pithoi (the two fabrics required different firing temperatures); perhaps the cult equipment was ordered in sets by individuals or families.[538]

END OF THE BRONZE AGE IN CRETE

The transition from the Late Bronze Age in Crete to Cretan Protogeometric seems to have been effected relatively peacefully: sites continue or are abandoned without major destructions.[539] Often termed Subminoan, material from this period, roughly 1100–1000/975 B.C., comes mainly from Karphi, Kavousi Vronda, and Vrokastro. Some Subminoan material

[535] Gesell 61; Kanta; B. Rutkowski, "Tradition und neue Formen in den spätminoischen Heiligtümern," in Thomas (supra n. 390) 13–24; A. Peatfield, "After the 'Big Bang'— What?" in S.E. Alcock and R. Osborne eds., *Placing the Gods* (Cambridge 1994) 19–36; A. Konecny, *Gebaute minoische und mykenische Siedlungsheiligtümer der ägäischen Spätbronzezeit III* (Diss. Univ. of Vienna 1988). Ayia Triada: F. Carcini and A.L. D'Agata, "Aspetti dell'attività cultuale a Creta nel III e nel II millennio a.C.," in *Scienze dell'antichità. Storia archeologia antropologia* 3–4 (1989–1990) 238–42; D'Agata, "I santuari sul 'Piazzale dei Sacelli' ad Haghia Triada (Creta)," in *Atti* (supra n. 429). Prinias: G. Rizza, "Nuove scoperte a Priniás," *3rd CretCong* (1973) 286–89; Rizza, "Ceramiche figurate da Priniás," *AntCr* 2 (1974) 153–60; Rizza (supra n. 511). Karphi: B. Rutkowski, "The Temple at Karphi," *SMEA*

26 (1987) 257–65. Kavousi: G. Gesell, "The Goddess with Up-raised Hands from Kavousi, Ierapetras," in *Atti VII° Congresso internazionale di studi cretesi, Rethymnon 1991* (in press). Stylos Apokoronou: C. Davaras, *AAA* 4 (1971) 42–44.

[536] E. Mavriyannaki, "Ιδόλια τύπου Φ εκ της επαρχίας Ρεθήμνης," *ArchEph* 1974–1975, 16–18.

[537] J.N. Coldstream, *Deities in Aegean Art before and after the Dark Age* (Bedford College Inaugural Lectures, London 1977); G.C. Gesell, *AJA* 100 (1996) 404 (abstract).

[538] G.C. Gesell and T.C. Saupe, "Methods Used in the Construction of Ceramic Objects from the Shrine of the Goddess with Up-raised Hands at Kavousi," in *Techne* 123–26.

[539] For two general studies: F. Schachermeyr, *Kreta zur Zeit der Wanderungen* (Vienna 1979); and D.G. Gondicas, *Recherches sur la Crète occidentale* (Las Palmas 1987).

is known from Knossos, especially the Spring Chamber and from the nearby cemeteries at Zapher Papoura, Ayios Ioannes, and Fortetsa.[540] Several features characterize the transition to the Early Iron Age: the slow appearance of iron for tools and weapons, the increasing frequency of cremation burials and small tholos tombs from early in LM IIIC on, including the reuse of tombs, and the eventual disappearance of MGUAs.[541]

Among the many survivals and revivals, some social customs may have been retained, including aspects of law, land tenure, herding, and possibly rites of male passage.[542] Two examples of continuity are impressive: pictorial vase painting[543] and the inscriptions from East Crete using Greek letters to write "Eteo-Cretan."

DIRECTIONS FOR FURTHER WORK

It should be clear from this survey that the archaeology of Late Bronze Age Crete has changed enormously since its inception just over a century ago. Excavation has far outpaced publication, and a major priority for at least the next decade should be the publication of sites and material. The concentration on excavating elite architecture needs to be balanced with a more comprehensive presentation of domestic and nonelite architecture, especially for the Final and Postpalatial periods where much

of our evidence has come from funerary contexts. For all periods, future excavation should be directed toward establishing the actual limits of a settlement; the precise size of most sites is unknown.

A few specific concerns follow. Jewelry must be analyzed in terms of typology, context, technique, and representations before it can be incorporated into analyses of Minoan society and be appreciated as a social artifact. Important advances are taking place in the study of Minoan pottery, particularly for the Final and Postpalatial periods, but for all periods the study of pottery needs to be integrated more thoroughly with analyses of architectural and demographic change. The groundwork for the study of Minoan seals and sealings has been laid, but nonspecialist scholars generally have not made use of these artifacts as yet. A new book on Minoan architecture is needed, integrating the architectural evidence—materials, techniques, and the buildings themselves—with theoretical models for building a cognitive plan of Minoan space. Despite several surveys of Minoan larnakes, the painted larnakes are today largely unstudied; a comprehensive catalogue of these could greatly increase our understanding of Late Minoan society.

Finally, life on Crete has been revolutionized, for better or for worse, in just the last three generations. Not only will the archaeological heritage of Crete

[540] J.N. Coldstream, "Knossos: An Urban Nucleus in the Dark Age?" in Musti et al. (supra n. 363) 287–99, esp. 290; AR 25 (1979) 46, figs. 8–11; Sackett (supra n. 512) 60–65; J.K. Brock, Fortetsa (Cambridge 1957).

[541] R. Maddin, J.D. Muhly, and T.S. Wheeler, "How the Iron Age Began," Scientific American 237:4 (1977) 122–31; S. Sherratt, "Commerce, Iron, and Ideology," in Karageorghis (supra n. 511) 88–91; A.M. Snodgrass, "The Coming of Iron in Greece," in M.L.S. Sorensen and R. Thomas eds., The Bronze Age–Iron Age Transition in Europe (Oxford 1989) 22–35; and J.C. Waldbaum, "Copper, Iron, Tin, Wood," Archaeomaterials 3 (1989) 111–22. Early iron from Crete: Vrokastro (late LM IIIC: Coulson and Tsipopoulou [supra n. 519] 84), Karphi (LM IIIC: Watrous [supra n. 515] 325, tools), Katsamba house, phase II (LM IIIC: Kanta 27, a piece), Mouliana Tholos B (LM IIIC: Kanta 176, a piece).
The earliest cremation burials date to LM IIIA2, in the Olous cemetery (Kanta 129; cf. the possible cremation burial in Kalyvia tomb 8, LM IIIA1–2; Kanta 99). Also see C. Davaras, "Cremations in Minoan and Sub-Minoan Crete," AntCr 1 (1973) 158–67. For Early Iron Age tombs, see M. Tsipopoulou, "Τάφοι της πρώϊμής εποχής του Σιδήρου στην Ανατολική Κρήτη," in Ειλαπίνη (supra n. 13) 253–69. For reuse of tombs, see H. Catling, "Heroes Returned? Subminoan Burials from Crete," in J.B. Carter and S.P. Morris eds., The Ages of Homer (Austin 1995) 123–36; Kanta (supra

n. 363). MGUAs: R. Hägg, "Sacred Horns and Naiskoi," in V. Karageorghis ed., Proceedings of an International Symposium: "The Civilizations of the Aegean and Their Diffusion in Cyprus and the Eastern Mediterranean, 2000–600 B.C." (Nicosia 1991) 79–83.

[542] G. Korres, "Μινωϊκαί επιβιώσεις και αναβιώσεις Α'," 3rd CretCong (1973) 411–76. L. Foxhall, "Bronze to Iron," BSA 90 (1995) 239–50; J. Whitley, "Social Diversity in Dark Age Crete," BSA 86 (1991) 341–65; R.F. Willetts, "Cretan Law and Early Greek Society," AntCr 2 (1974) 22–31; Willetts, "Neoi and neotas," 4th CretCong I (1980) 643–53; Willetts, "Economy and Society," Cretan Studies 1 (1988) 257–68; and Willetts, "Aspects of Land Tenure in Dorian Crete," in Musti et al. (supra n. 363) 209–14. Koehl (supra ns. 31, 136); A. Lembesi, "Οι γραπτές πηγές και τα αρχαιολογικά δεδομένα για την αγωγή των Κρητών," 8th CretCong (forthcoming).

[543] J.N. Coldstream, "Sphinxes and Griffins from Geometric Crete," AntCr 2 (1974) 161–64; Coldstream, "The Meaning of the Regional Styles in the Eighth Century B.C.," in R. Hägg ed., The Greek Renaissance of the Eighth Century B.C. (Stockholm 1983) 17–25; N.B. Reed, "Griffins in Post-Minoan Cretan Art," Hesperia 45 (1976) 365–79; and L. Rocchetti, "La necropoli di Curtes," 5th CretCong A2 (1990) 261–65.

need vigorous, concerted efforts and judicious choices to preserve it, but, as Blitzer has passionately pointed out to us, within just a few years, direct, personal experience of the self-sufficient life will become a memory to all but the oldest inhabitants of the island. Careful efforts must be made now not only to record it but also to retrieve it through academic studies of daily living: animal and plant husbandry, pharmacopiae, customs, and traditions. Much attention has been devoted in recent decades to major theoretical constructs of politics, state theory, and the state of the profession. One of the consequences

is that the lived life of individuals has all but been neglected.[544] We should want to know more about the Minoans themselves, for if ever there was a goal of archaeology, it is the study of people, especially at the commonest level.

DEPARTMENT OF CLASSICAL STUDIES
DUKE UNIVERSITY
P.O. BOX 90103
DURHAM, NORTH CAROLINA 27708-0103
PREHAK@ACPUB.DUKE.EDU
JYOUNGER@ACPUB.DUKE.EDU

---

[544] A major theme of the Eighth Cretological Congress, 10–13 September 1996, concerned the domestic aspects of Cretan archaeology.

Addendum: 1998–1999

PAUL REHAK AND JOHN G. YOUNGER

Little more than a year has elapsed since the original publication of our review of Neopalatial, Final Palatial, and Postpalatial Crete (RAP VII), and while there have been no major upheavals in our overview of Minoan archaeology, many new studies have appeared, including some that were listed earlier as forthcoming.[545] This update, therefore, concentrates primarily on bibliographical additions and follows the basic outline of information presented above in RAP VII.

INTRODUCTION

As we reported earlier, the era of large-scale excavations on Crete by foreign schools seems to be drawing to a close as survey work increases. Many excavation projects are now in study session (e.g., Galatas, the Gournia Survey, Kavousi, Kommos, Palaikastro, Petras, Pseira, Syme Viannou, Vasilike Ierapetras), while several surveys have been completed in remote regions: in Ziros in southeast Crete, the Ayios Vasileios valley west of Amari, the southern island of Gavdos, and in the region around Sphakia.[546]

Publications of major sites are appearing with reassuring regularity, including new volumes in the *Kommos*, *Khania*, and *Pseira* series. A lavish two-volume publication, available in Greek and English, presents the sites at Archanes (Phourni, Tourkogeitonia, and Anemospilia); the format, a series of essays, will remind readers of Evans's *Palace of Minos*, but the lack of indices, inventory numbers, dimensions, and scientific data will limit the books' usefulness.[547] The *CMS* has published new volumes of seals and sealings, and is planning its fifth septennial conference in September 1999 in Marburg, Germany. Although not yet published, the 8th Cretological Congress (September 1996) focused on Minoan domestic life, no doubt influenced by the shift in archaeology as a whole toward analyzing all levels of soci-

---

[545] Many of our new observations in this addendum follow a visit to Crete in January 1999. In addition to the abbreviations used in RAP VII, the following are found below:

Aegean and Orient   E.H. Cline and D. Harris-Cline eds., *The Aegean and the Orient in the Second Millennium* (*Aegaeum* 18, Liège 1998).

Crète mycénienne   J. Driessen and A. Farnoux eds., *La Crète mycénienne* (*BCH* Suppl. 30, Paris 1997).

LM III Pottery   E. Hallager and B.P. Hallager eds., *Late Minoan III Pottery: Chronology and Terminology* (Monographs of the Danish Institute at Athens 1, Athens 1997).

Urbanism   W.E. Aufrecht, N.A. Mirau, and S.W. Gauley eds., *Urbanism in Antiquity* (*Journal for the Study of the Old Testament* Suppl. 244, Sheffield 1997).

The following studies listed in RAP VII as forthcoming have since appeared: *Aegean and Orient*; n. 69: E.M. Hatzaki, "Was the Little Palace at Knossos the 'Little Palace' of Knossos?" in D. Evely, I.S. Lemos, and S. Sherratt eds., *Minotaur and Centaur* (*BAR-IS* 638, Oxford 1996) 34–45; n. 186: A. Van de Moortel's dissertation is now available from University Microfilms, Ann Arbor, Michigan, no. 9806356; n. 350: E.H. Cline, "Rich beyond the Dreams of Avaris," *BSA* 93 (1998) 199–219; n. 397: P. Rehak and R.R. Snihurowych, "'Is Female to Male as Nature Is to Culture?'" in *American Philological Association Abstracts of the 129th Annual Meeting* (New York 1997) 108; and n. 508: *Crète mycénienne*.

[546] Ziros: K. Branigan et al., "Prehistoric and Early Historic Settlement in the Ziros Region, Eastern Crete," *BSA* 93 (1998) 23–90. Ayios Vasileios valley: *AR* 1997–1998, 120–21. Gavdos: A. Kopaka, "Αρχαιολογική επιφανειακή έρευνα στην Γαύδο," *8th CretCong* (forthcoming). Sphakia: J. Moody, L. Nixon, S. Price, and O. Rackham, "Surveying Poleis and Larger Sites in Sphakia," in W.G. Cavanagh et al. eds., *Post-Minoan Crete* (London 1998) 87–95. See also L. Nixon, S. Price, W. Morris, and J. Moody, "Computers and Mapmaking," *Archeologia e calcolatori* 6 (1995) 159–72; and L. Nixon and S. Price, "The Sphakia Survey (Greece)," a video produced in 1995 by Education Technology Resources Centre (37 Wellington Square, Oxford OX1 2JF, United Kingdom; e-mail: etrc@etrc.ox.ac.uk).

[547] Petras: a stone-by-stone phase plan: *Κρητική Εστία* 5 (1994–1996) [1997] 344–58. Palaikastro: J.A. MacGillivray, L.H. Sackett, and J.M. Driessen, "Excavations at Palaikastro, 1994 and 1996," *BSA* 93 (1998) 221–68; MacGillivray, Driessen, and Sackett eds., *Palaikastro Kouros: A Minoan Chryselephantine Statuette and Its Aegean Bronze Age Context* (*BSA* Studies 6, forthcoming). Pseira: P.P. Betancourt and C. Davaras eds., *Pseira* II: *Building AC (the "Shrine") and Other Buildings in Area A* (Philadelphia 1998). Vasilike: five volumes and over 20 CD-ROMs in preparation (*AR* 1997–1998, 115–19). Kommos: at least two more volumes, *The Greek Sanctuaries* and *The Minoan Civic Center*, in preparation. Mochlos: vol. II.1, *Period III: The Neopalatial Settlement on the Coast*, and vol. III, *Period IV: The Mycenaean Settlement and Cemetery*, in preparation. Archanes: Y. Sakellarakis and E. Sapouna-Sakellarakis, *Archanes* (Athens 1997).

ety.[548] The *Aegaeum* series continues to publish conference proceedings and specialized studies; one recent volume presents the conference on the Aegean and Orient that took place in Cincinnati (April 1997). In Athens, as of May 1999, Mark Cameron's studies and reconstructions of the Knossos frescoes are being exhibited at the Goulandris Museum.

In preparation for "Knossos 2000," the centenary celebration of Evans's excavations, the palace has been given a new circulation pattern (director A. Karetsou, architect C. Palyvou), including wooden walkways to protect the pavements.[549] Plans are under way at several other sites to accommodate tourists: at Kommos viewing platforms will keep the visitor from areas threatened by sand, and an extensive roof will protect the temple area.

The problems with Minoan chronology for the Neopalatial period are not yet resolved.[550] While more Aegean scholars seem to accept the low Aegean chronology, supported by colleagues in Egyptian archaeology, we continue to favor the high chronology, as does Manning.[551] The date of the LM IA Thera eruption is still a linchpin in this debate. It is now clear that the volcanic tephra samples dated to 1628 cannot belong to the LM IA Thera eruption, but neither have samples been found that match the 1520/1500 date argued by supporters of the low chronology. A series of radiocarbon dates for LM IB destructions on Crete at sites like Mochlos cluster convincingly around 1490, implying a higher chronology for LM IA. For the Uluburun shipwreck, however, the last existing ring on a log of firewood or dunnage gives a terminus ante quem non of 1305.[552]

The controversy over the source(s) of tin used in the Aegean continues, but an extended trade route from the east now seems likely. Gale and others have noted that texts from Mari of the time of Zimri-Lim (early 18th century) mention tin being sent on westward "to Qatna, to Ugarit, to Laish/Dan, to Hazor and to a Caphtorite," the last probably a Minoan. The tin may have been coming to Mari from deposits in the east, perhaps "by donkey caravan from Susa (Susiana) and Anshan (Elam) through Eshnunna (Tell Asmar)," which may also have conveyed lapis lazuli and other precious stones like carnelian and Cambay agate.[553]

NEOPALATIAL CRETE (MM III – LM IB)

Our conviction remains unchanged that the roots of many Neopalatial developments must be sought in the Protopalatial period, whose social complexity can be seen reflected in burial practices and at peak sanctuaries. At Atsipades, for instance, there is evidence for different, perhaps gendered, ritual activities in the separate areas of the sanctuary: in trench area B female figurines were concentrated in the center and male at the periphery, and all employed the arms-to-chest gesture, while those from trench areas C and D preferred the upraised-arms gesture.[554]

New discoveries at individual sites help expand our picture of Neopalatial architecture and the landscape of communities. For example, at Knossos, near the Stratigraphic Museum, a paved LM I road has been found, apparently continuing the line of the Royal Road, and there are new studies of various areas in and about the palace. In the Splantzia neighborhood of Chania the LM I building with the frescoed lustral basin is part of a large (320 m²) architectural complex that reflects the extent and orientation of the Neopalatial city toward the sea. At Petras, work continues on the settlement surrounding the MM–LM I court-centered building, now almost completely

[548] In *8th CretCong* (forthcoming), see, e.g., G. Cadogan, "Domestic Life at Minoan Myrtos-Pyrgos"; H. Deligianni Evfrosini, "Το Κρασί στη μινωϊκή Κρήτη"; L.A. Hitchcock, "Of Barstools and Beehives"; J.P. Olivier, "Quelques reflets de la vie privée dans les écritures crétoises du Iᵉʳ millénaire?"; A. Papaevthymiou-Papanthimou, "Πρακτικές τελετουργικού καλλωπισμού στο προϊστορικό Αιγαίο"; E. Scafa, "Alcuni aspetti della vita privata in Creta micenea"; L.V. Watrous, "Daily Life in the Gournia Region of Crete: Economy and Society"; and P. Militello, "Organizzazione dello spazio e vita quotidiana nelle case TM I di Haghia Triada."

[549] *AR* 1997–1998, 111; S.P.M. Harrington, "Saving Knossos," *Archaeology* 52 (1999) 30–40.

[550] We thank P. Betancourt, M. Wiener, and S. Manning for their personal communications on the subject in April 1999.

[551] J. Phillips, "The 'New' Aegean Chronology: An Egyptian Perspective," *BICS* 42 (1997–1998) 219–20; G. Walberg, "The Date and Origin of the Kamares Cup from Tell el-Dab'a," *Ägypten und Levante* 8 (1998) 107–108; and Manning (supra n. 19) 311–27.

[552] Date given in an on-line dendrochronology report: http://www.arts.cornell.edu/dendro/97news/97adplet.html; cf. Bass, in *Aegean and Orient* (supra n. 314) 184, and M. Wiener, "Discussion," in *Aegean and Orient* 190.

[553] N. Gale, message sent to the e-mail discussion list "Arch-Metals" on 25 March 1999 (no. 6FA1986.4C9@ ph.ox.ac.uk); G. Dossin, "La route de l'étain en Mésopotamie au temps de Zimri-Lim," *RAssyr* 64 (1970) 97–106; and P. Villard, "Comptes d'étain et d'argent," in G. Bardet et al., *Archives administratives de Mari* I (Archives royales de Mari 23, Paris 1984) 527–36.

[554] Burials: K. Branigan ed., *Cemetery and Society in the Aegean Bronze Age* (Sheffield 1998). Atsipades: *AR* 1997–1998, 122–23.

uncovered, and its relations with other communities in the area.[555]

Some of the changes in late Neopalatial Crete may be attributable to the Thera eruption. For instance, the habitation sequence at Kavousi-Charkia, Rousses, is long (EM, MM II, MM III–LM IA, and LM IIIA/B), but evidence for LM IB and II is missing; at Galatas the palace was destroyed by an earthquake "about the time of the eruption of Santorini."[556]

Continuing excavation shows that the complex at Galatas covers at least 4 stremmata (ca. 0.4 ha) with four wings surrounding a well-paved central court (16 × 37 m) with an impressive north facade: large ashlar orthostats occur in a tripartite arrangement (cf. Phaistos) with a pillared stoa at the northwest entrance. The east wing was built and destroyed by fire within MM IIIA, then rebuilt at the MM IIIB/LM IA transition; from the earlier phase come the earliest Neopalatial fresco fragments that can be dated stratigraphically. In the last phase, LM IA, squatters blocked doorways and constructed rough installations in several rooms and hallways, including a large fireplace in the pillar room.

The urbanization of Neopalatial Crete continues to be documented, with individual building complexes— the palaces and villas—still receiving most of the attention. The publication of the 1992 conference "The Function of the Minoan Villa" includes papers that discuss specific modular units like the Minoan "Hall," while many others grapple with villa terminology without reaching consensus.[557] In the broader urban landscape, however, an impressive series of roads connects the rural farms to towns and cities in what is beginning to resemble the expected nucleated pattern. In eastern Crete a cluster of "villas" in the Zakros region is connected by a system of roads, towers, and industrial installations.[558] Within this urban environment, documented to some extent for all but southwestern Crete, we should expect to see some aspects of architecture that are pan-Cretan and others that are regional; for instance, some mason's marks, like the double ax and the branch, appear at all palatial sites, while others, like the trident at Phaistos, occur only at specific sites.[559] Now that much is known about Minoan architecture and its tendency toward an urban landscape dotted with building complexes, scholars are once again investigating comparisons with the eastern Mediterranean and Near East.[560]

An extremely important contribution to the discussion of Neopalatial Crete is the publication by Driessen and Macdonald of *The Troubled Island*.[561] Contrary to established opinion, the authors argue that the LM IA period, rather than LM IB, marks the acme of the Neopalatial period. A detailed gazetteer of sites assembles an impressive list of architectural modifications at many sites between LM IA and IB, which according to the authors reflect societal change and political insecurity in the aftermath of the Thera eruption. The appearance of palatial elements in LM IB pottery, for instance, is read as an index of decline in other artistic media. The picture from the evidence is, however, extremely complex and susceptible to alternate interpretations. As we noted earlier, architectural changes can be seen throughout the island during the entire Neopalatial period. The borrowing of palatial elements by LM IB pottery could be interpreted as a trickle-down process through which these motifs were actually disseminated to a wider audience. Nevertheless, *The Troubled Island* is likely to engage the attention of Aegeanists for some time to come.

In our earlier report (RAP VII) we concentrated on providing a survey of major Neopalatial art forms

[555] Knossos: *AR* 1997–1998, 114. See also V. Fotou, "The Arsenal and Other Unpublished Buildings from Evans's Excavations at Knossos," and M. Panagiotaki, "Knossos: Recent Work in the Central Palace Sanctuary Area," both in *8th CretCong* (forthcoming). Chania: *AR* 1997–1998, 123–24. Petras: M. Tsipopoulou, "Palace-centered Polities in Eastern Crete," in *Urbanism* 263–77.

[556] In *AR* 1997–1998: Kavousi-Charkia, 126; and Galatas, 112.

[557] See Hägg (supra n. 28): on the Minoan "Hall," M.K. Pedersen, "Minoan Halls in Neopalatial Buildings," 177; and A.C. Nordfeldt, "On Possible Minoan Halls in Art," 179–84; and on terminology, C. Palyvou, "Session on the Functional Analysis of Architecture," 155–56; W.-D. Niemeier, "The Origins of the Minoan 'Villa' System," 15–19; V. Fotou, "Éléments d'analyse architecturale," 33–50; P.P. Betancourt and N. Marinatos, "The Minoan Villa," 91–98; and H. van Effenterre and M. van Effenterre, "Towards a

Study of Neopalatial 'Villas,'" 9–13.

[558] M. Tsipopoulou and A. Papacostopoulou, "'Villas' and Villages in the Hinterland of Petras, Siteia," in Hägg (supra n. 28) 203–14; Tsipopoulou (supra n. 555); and P.P. Betancourt, "Village Life in Minoan Crete," *8th CretCong* (forthcoming). For mention of the Minoan Roads Research Programme, see *AR* 1997–1998, 120.

[559] I. Begg, "An Archaeology of Palatial Mason's Marks," in *Festschrift S.A. Immerwahr* (in preparation); we are grateful to the author for permission to read this study in advance of publication.

[560] See, e.g., E. Fiandra, "Similarities and Differences in the Architectural Structures of the Palaces in Crete and Ugarit," *SMEA* 39 (1997) 49–73.

[561] J. Driessen and C.F. Macdonald, *The Troubled Island: Minoan Crete before and after the Santorini Eruption* (*Aegaeum* 17, Liège 1997); see also J. Driessen, "An Archaeology of Crisis," *BICS* 42 (1997–1998) 207–208.

and materials, but more work remains to be done on tools, techniques, and the organization and outfitting of workshops; a newly excavated workshop in the Poros area of Herakleion provides valuable evidence for the production of sealstones, beads, and other objects.[562] Other, specialized, forms of production have received attention including the objects deposited at specific types of sites like peak sanctuaries.[563] In the area of pottery production, general studies are balanced by work on specialized fabrics and style, and on trade networks within Crete and the Aegean.[564] Cloth production, exchange, and the codification of social values in clothing are the subjects of dissertations now in preparation or recently completed.[565] Two important studies of bronze animal figurines include catalogues of those from throughout the island and those from Syme in particular. The human figurines, both in bronze and terracotta, yield information concerning gender.[566]

The number of gender studies has finally begun to increase noticeably; while some are synoptic, adhering to the broader issues of archaeological theory, others document more specific aspects. Some crafts, for instance, once thought to be the exclusive domain of men, like pottery production, were surely also practiced by women.[567]

The publication of CHIC has prompted further studies on Cretan Hieroglyphic, including a review that attempts to set out what is now known.[568] The CMS series on Minoan sealings now includes CMS II.7: Die Siegelabdrücke von Kato Zakros (Berlin 1998), and two further volumes, on sealings from Ayia Triada and elsewhere in the island and the Knossos sealings, are scheduled to appear shortly.

Linear A studies have moved in two new directions: the probable participation of Linear A in the development of linear scripts in the eastern Mediterranean has been explored, as has its evidence for the Minoan language. While new Linear A inscriptions have been excavated at Akrotiri in Thera and at Miletos and have been claimed at Troy and elsewhere in Turkey, other linear inscriptions that bear distinct similarities to Linear A have been found in Israel: an inscribed stone bowl fragment from Lachish (dated

---

[562] To the discussion of ivory, add Rehak and Younger (supra n. 153) 229–56. On frescoes, add F. Blakolmer, "Minoan Wall-painting," in Techne 95–105; and A.-L. Schalling, "The Wall-paintings and Plaster from the Greek-Swedish Excavations at Khania," 8th CretCong (forthcoming). Poros: N. Dimopoulou, "Workshops and Craftsmen in the Harbour-Town of Knossos at Poros-Katsambas," in Techne 433–38.

[563] A. Banou, "Τα λίθινα αντικείμενα από το μινωϊκό ιερό κορυφής στον Αη–Γειώργη στο Βουνό Κυθήρων," 8th Cret-Cong (forthcoming).

[564] General: Van de Moortel (supra n. 545); and R. Hampe and A. Winter, Bei Töpfern und Töpferinnen in Kreta, Messenien und Zypern (Mainz 1976). Fabrics: N. Cucuzza, "Una nota sul problema dell'identificazione delle officine ceramiche minoiche di età neopalaziale a Creta," SMEA 39 (1997) 163–76; and, in 8th CretCong (forthcoming): D.C. Haggis, "The Cultural and Economic Implications of Coarse Ware Ceramic Distribution in the North Isthmus of Ierapetra in the Bronze Age"; and J. Moody, "Dust to Dust and Rock to Rock." Style: W. Müller, Kretische Tongefässe mit Meeresdekor (AF 19, Berlin 1997); and Müller, "An Unbroken LM IB Rhyton with Marine Decoration in the Giamalakis Collection at Heraklion," 8th CretCong (forthcoming). Exchange: P.M. Day, "Ceramic Exchange between Towns and Outlying Settlements in Neopalatial East Crete," in Hägg (supra n. 28) 219–28.

[565] E.J.W. Barber, "Minoan Women and the Challenges of Weaving for Home, Trade, and Shrine," in Techne 515–19; and B.R. Jones, Minoan Women's Clothes (Diss. Institute of Fine Arts, New York Univ. 1998).

[566] W. Schurmann, Das Heiligtum des Hermes und der Aphrodite in Syme Viannou II (Athens 1996); and A. Pilali-Papasteriou, Die bronzenen Tierfiguren aus Kreta (Prähistorische Bronzefunde 1.3, Munich 1985). In J. Moore and E. Scott eds., Invisible People and Processes (London 1997): D. Kokkinidou and M. Nikolaidou, "Body Imagery in the Aegean Neolithic," 88–112; and L.A. Hitchcock, "Engendering Domination," 113–30. See also A. Pilali-Papasteriou, Μινωϊκά πήλινα ανθρωπόμορφα ειδώλια της συλλογής Μεταξά (Thessaloniki 1992); and Pilali-Papasteriou, "Social Evidence from the Interpretation of Middle Minoan Figurines," in I. Hodder ed., The Meanings of Things (London 1989) 97–102.

[567] Theory: the first three "Australian Women in Archaeology Conferences" are now available as a set: vol. I: H. du Cros and L. Smith eds., Women in Archaeology (Canberra 1993), see esp. L. Zarmotti, "Popular Archaeology and the Archaeologist as Hero," 43–47 on Harriet Boyd; II: J. Balme and W. Beck eds., Gendered Archaeology (Canberra 1995); and III: M. Casey, D. Donlon, J. Hope, and S. Wellfare eds., Redefining Archaeology (Canberra 1998), see esp. P. Rehak, "The Construction of Gender in Late Bronze Age Aegean Art," 191–98; and L. Meskell, "That's Capital M, Capital G," 147–53 on the Minoan "Mother Goddess." Social aspects: B. Olsen, "Women, Children and the Family in the Late Aegean Bronze Age," WorldArch 29 (1998) 380–92; cf. A.M.G. Capomacchia, "Le donne di Creta: Una tradizione emarginante," 8th CretCong (forthcoming). Pottery production: Hampe and Winter (supra n. 564); and, in Techne, see A. Kalogirou, "Pottery Production and Craft Specialization in Neolithic Greece," 11–18; E.S. Elster, "Construction and Use of the Early Bronze Age Burnt House at Sitagroi," 19–36; J.K. Papadopoulos, "Innovations, Imitations and Ceramic Style," 449–62; Barber (supra n. 565); K. Kopaka, "'Women's Arts—Men's Crafts?'" 521–32; and G. Nordquist, "Male Craft and Female Industry," 533–38.

[568] CHIC (supra n. 270). Inscriptions: G. Owens, "A Possible 'Cretan Hieroglyphic' Inscription from Mount Ida (IDA Ya 332)," Kadmos 36 (1997) 171. Signs: F.C. Woudhuizen, "The Bee-Sign (Evans No. 86)," Kadmos 36 (1997) 97–110. Review by J.G. Younger, Minos 31–32 (1996–1997) 379–400.

by context to ca. 1200) and an incised LBA potsherd from Tel Haror.[569] These finds suggest that linear inscriptions in the Late Bronze Age may be more widespread than previously thought and that Linear A is probably involved in their development.

Renfrew has laid out a strong case for identifying the Minoan language as a development of Indo-Hittite.[570] If the Cretan people came from southwest Anatolia, he argues, then their language should derive from southwest Anatolian languages and be related to Luvian or perhaps Carian,[571] deriving ultimately from Indo-Hittite, which had branched off from a greater language system, the rest of which "moved on" (as it were) west to develop into the Indo-European languages, including Greek. Such a reconstruction suggests that a decipherment of Minoan is inevitable, but since several different writing systems were in use in MM Crete at more or less the same time (Hieroglyphic, Linear A, and the inscription on the Phaistos Disc to which that on the Arkalochori ax seems to be partially related), there may have been several separate languages or dialects.[572]

Renfrew also suggests that many words identified as non- or pre-Greek, many of which occur in Linear B, were adopted from Minoan into early Greek during its development; two words for high male officials in Mycenaean Greek, *wa-na-ka* and *qa-si-re-u* (the later Greek words for lord and king, "wanax" and "basileus"), are prime candidates, but they have not yet been identified in Linear A, nor can similarly high-ranking male officials be identified in Minoan art. By contrast, high-ranking Minoan women and goddesses can be identified in Minoan art, yet the relevant Mycenaean word, *po-ti-ni-ja*, is transparently Greek ("powerful female"); no masculine form of the word is attested in Mycenaean or classical Greek.

The excavations at Tell el-Dab'a, and studies of specific imports and exports, all document a fusion of cultures in the eastern Mediterranean, of which the later Uluburun shipwreck provides a freeze-frame picture.[573] To explain how this fusion works Aegeanists have begun assembling theoretical models: two workshops at the Swedish School in Athens in 1994 and 1995 concentrated on the economic engines that drove this cultural mingling, and the "Aegean and Orient" conference in Cincinnati in 1997 presented a lively series of papers on a variety of cultural issues.[574]

Current trends in Neopalatial religion include the study or restudy of specific buildings or deposits of material, individual objects or types of artifact, and the social aspects of religion and ritual on the common as well as elite level.[575]

[569] Akrotiri: A. Michailidou, "'Ostrakon' with Linear A Script from Akrotiri (Thera)," *Minos* 27–28 (1992–1993) 7–24; and G. Owens, "Further Comments on the Linear A Inscriptions from Thera," *Kadmos* 36 (1997) 172–73. Miletos: W.-D. Niemeier, "A Linear A Inscription from Miletus (MIL Zb1)," *Kadmos* 35 (1996) 87–99. Other sites: an incised pot from Amisos and a terracotta ram from Samsun, both in Turkey (*PM* IV.2, 768–69, figs. 759–60; H.T. Bössert, *Altanatolien* [Berlin 1942] 3, pl. 3.6); and on spindle whorls from Troy, L. Godart, "La scrittura di Troia," *RendLinc* 5 (1994) 457–60; and E.L. Brown, "Linear A on Trojan Spindlewhorls," in G. Schmeling and J.D. Mikalson eds., *Qui miscuit utile dulci: Festschrift Essays for Paul Lachlan MacKendrick* (Wauconda 1998) 51–68. Israel: M. Finkelberg, "Bronze Age Writing," in *Aegean and Orient* 265–72. Tel Haror: E.D. Oren, "Minoan Graffito from Tel Haror (Negev, Israel)," *Cretan Studies* 5 (1996) 91–118.

[570] C. Renfrew, "Word of Minos," *BICS* 42 (1997–1998) 225, and "Word of Minos: The Minoan Contribution to Mycenaean Greek and the Linguistic Geography of the Bronze Age Aegean," *CAJ* 8 (1998) 239–64; cf. M. Finkelberg, "Anatolian Languages and Indo-European Migrations to Greece," *CW* 91 (1997) 3–20.

[571] W. Blümel, P. Frei, and C. Marek eds., "Colloquium Caricum," *Kadmos* 37 (1998), entire volume.

[572] Y. Duhoux, "Pre-Hellenic Language(s) of Crete," *JIES* 26 (1998) 1–39.

[573] Tell el-Dab'a: Cline (supra n. 545); and N. Marinatos, "The Tell el-Dab'a Paintings," *Ägypten und Levante* 8 (1998) 83–99. Uluburun: C. Pulak, "The Uluburun Shipwreck," *IJNA* 27 (1998) 188–224; and P.T. Nicholson, C.M. Jackson, and K.M. Trott, "The Ulu Burun Glass Ingots,"

JEA 83 (1997) 143–53.

[574] C. Gillis, C. Risberg, and B. Sjöberg eds., *Trade and Production in Premonetary Greece: Production and the Craftsman* (*SIMA-PB* 143, Jonsered 1997). In *Aegean and Orient*: Manning (supra n. 19) 311–27; Rehak and Younger (supra n. 153) 229–56; Hankey and Leonard (supra n. 303) 29–37; Betancourt (supra n. 304) 5–11; Bass (supra n. 314) 183–91; Knapp (supra n. 321) 193–207; W.-D. Niemeier and B. Niemeier (supra n. 338) 69–97; Laffineur (supra n. 352) 53–67; Rehak (supra n. 496) 39–51; and E.J.W. Barber, "Aegean Ornaments and Designs in Egypt," 13–17; R.S. Merrillees, "Egypt and the Aegean," 49–58; A. Caubet, "'International Style' in the Aegean and the Levant," 105–13; J.L. Crowley, "Iconography and Interconnections," 171–81; C. Mee, "Anatolia and the Aegean in the Late Bronze Age," 137–48; S.P. Morris, "Daidalos and Kothar," 281–89; and A. Sherratt and S. Sherratt, "Small Worlds," 329–43.

[575] K.D.S. Lapatin, "Mysteries of the Snake Goddess," *BICS* 42 (1997–1998) 244–45; M. Panagiotaki, "Dating the Temple Repositories' Vases," *BSA* 93 (1998) 185–98; and the following by A. Pilali-Papasteriou: "Ιερά και αποθήκες στην ανακτορική Κρήτη," in *Ειλαπίνη* (supra n. 13) 179–96; "Το θρανίο στα μινωϊκά ιερά," *Ανθρωπολογικά* (Thessaloniki) 6 (1984) 15–29; and "Ανακτορικά ιερά της μινωϊκής Κρήτης," in *Αμιτος* (*Festschrift M. Andronikos*, Thessaloniki 1986) 665–79. In *8th CretCong* (forthcoming): J. Ernston, "The 'Temple Repositories' at Knossos"; R. Hägg, "Personal Religion in Minoan Crete"; S. Hood, "Religion in Bronze Age Crete"; V. La Rosa, "Preghiere fatte in casa: Altari mobili da un edificio di H. Triada"; A. Peatfield, "Minoan Religion for Ordinary People"; and P. Warren, "Shield and Goddess in Minoan Crete and the Aegean."

FINAL PALATIAL CRETE (LM II–IIIB EARLY)

In 1991 a conference on the mycenaeanization of Crete focused on several major issues: the process of mycenaeanization; the conditions in LM I–II that preceded the takeover; the subsequent differences in art and craft production and in religious expression; and the relative positions of Knossos and the rest of the island, including the patterns of destruction at Knossos itself.[576] The conference also featured some synoptic reports on Mycenaean activity at specific sites, including Archanes, Chania, Kommos, and Mallia. At Knossos recent excavations have confirmed not only that outlying buildings were destroyed in LM II, but that the LM IIIA1/2 destruction of the palace finds another parallel at Chamalevri, Rethymnon. At Ayia Triada, Mycenaean building began at this time, early in LM IIIA2, and included the "Casa delle camere decapitate" and the famous "Tomb of the Painted Sarcophagus." Chrysokamino exhibits several phases of activity in LM IIIA, with a final phase in LM IIIA2 late/IIIB, contemporary with the final phase of palatial activity at Knossos. Farms in megalithic masonry, a hallmark of the Neopalatial period, continue into the Final Palatial period.[577]

Minoan art in the Final Palatial period has yet to receive its own synoptic study, but specialized studies continue. The "LM III Pottery" conference held at the Danish Institute in Athens in 1994 presented papers that addressed the preceding LM II style, and pottery of LM IIIA–C in all aspects—terminology, shapes, fabrics, regional styles, and centers of production; further studies of stirrup jars detail their fabrics and places of manufacture; and some Linear B studies focus on crafts in the texts.[578]

While some attention continues to be paid to tholoi and, to a certain extent, to the more humble pithos burials,[579] the study of painted larnakes is picking up pace with the increasing display of examples in the Chania, Rethymnon, and Ayios Nikolaos museums, and with the ongoing publication of individual examples.[580] These studies lay the groundwork for a reinvestigation of the relationship between the Cretan and Tanagra larnakes and of the possible influence of painted larnakes on the rebirth of figural art in Crete following the Dark Age.

---

[576] See the following in *Crète mycénienne*: Process: E. Banou and G. Rethemiotakis, "Centre and Periphery," 23–57. Preconditions: C.F. Macdonald, "The Prelude to Mycenaean Crete," 267–73. Art, craft, religion: R. Hägg, "Religious Syncretism at Knossos and in Post-palatial Crete?" 163–68; S. Hiller, "Cretan Sanctuaries and Mycenaean Palatial Administration at Knossos," 205–12; W.-D. Niemeier, "Cretan Glyptic Arts in LM I–III," 297–311; J.-C. Poursat, "La fin des arts 'palatiaux' dans la Crète mycénienne," 387–90; V. Stürmer, "Culture minoenne versus pouvoir mycénien," 435–43; and I. Tournavitou, "Arts and Crafts," 445–54 (see also A. Karetsou and N. Kourou, "Terracotta Wheelmade Bull Figurines from Central Crete," in *Techne* 107–16; and H. Whittaker, *Mycenaean Cult Buildings*, Bergen 1997). Knossos and Crete: J. Driessen, "Le palais de Cnossos au MR II–III," 113–34; L. Godart and Y. Tzedakis, "Les royaumes mycéniens de Crète," 153–61; H.W. Haskell, "Mycenaeans at Knossos," 187–93; and J.A. MacGillivray, "The Re-Occupation of Eastern Crete in the Late Minoan II–IIIA1/2 Periods," 275–79.

[577] In *Crète mycénienne*: A. Farnoux, "Malia au Minoen récent II–IIIA1," 135–47; E. Hallager, "Architecture of the LM II/III Settlement in Khania," 175–85; H. Kallitsaki, "The Mycenaean Burial Evidence in Phourni, Archanes," 213–27; J.W. Shaw and M.C. Shaw, "Mycenaean Kommos," 423–34; and M. Andréadaki-Vlasaki, "La nécropole du Minoen récent III de la ville de La Canée," 487–509. Chamalevri: *AR* 1997–1998, 114 and 123. Ayia Triada, in *Crète mycénienne*: N. Cucuzza, "The North Sector Buildings of Haghia Triada," 73–84; and V. La Rosa, "Haghia Triada à l'époque mycénienne," 249–66; and *AR* 1997–1998, 111. Chrysokamino: *AR* 1997–1998, 117. Farms: B. Hayden, "Evidence for 'Megalithic Farmsteads' of Late Minoan III through Early Iron Age Date," in *Crète mycénienne*, 195–204.

[578] LM II: in *LM III Pottery*, J.A. MacGillivray, "Late Minoan II and III Pottery and Chronology at Palaikastro," 193–202; and N.M. Prokopiou, "LM II Pottery from the Greek-Italian Excavations at Sybritos Amariou," 371–94; see also E.B. French, "Ephyrean Goblets at Knossos," in *Crète mycénienne* 149–52. LM III: in *LM III Pottery*, B.P. Hallager, "Terminology—The Late Minoan Goblet, Kylix and Footed Cup," 15–47; and Hallager, "LM III Pottery Shapes and Their Nomenclature," 407–17; P.P. Betancourt, E.S. Banou, and C.R. Floyd, "Provincial LM III at Pseira, Crete," 57–76; P.M. Warren, "Late Minoan III Pottery from the City of Knossos," 157–84; M. Tsipopoulou, "Late Minoan III Reoccupation in the Area of the Palatial Building at Petras, Siteia," 209–52; A. Farnoux, "Quartier Gamma at Malia Reconsidered," 259–72; E. Borgna, "Some Observations on Deep Bowls and Kraters from the 'Acropoli mediana' at Phaistos," 273–98; and G. Rethemiotakis, "Late Minoan III Pottery from Kastelli Pediada," 305–26. See also D. Vallianou, "The Potters' Quarter in LM III Gouves," in *Techne* 333–44. Stirrup jars: P. Day, "Coarseware Stirrup Jars and Central Crete," *BICS* 42 (1997–1998) 209. Linear B: M.-L.B. Gregersen, "Craftsmen in the Linear B Archives," in Gillis et al. (supra n. 574) 43–55; and M.S. Speciale, "Designazioni e ideogrammi di mobili in lineare B," *8th CretCong* (forthcoming).

[579] Pithos burials: I. Georgiou, "Παρατηρήσεις στο έθιμο της ταφής σε πίθους στη μινωϊκή Κρήτη," *8th CretCong* (forthcoming). Tholoi: P. Belli, "Architecture as Craftsmanship," in *Techne* 251–56; and A. Kanta, "Late Bronze Age Tholos Tombs: Origin and Evolution," in *Crète mycénienne* 229–47.

[580] N. Marinatos, "Minoan and Mycenaean Larnakes," in *Crète mycénienne* 281–92; and G. Rethemiotakis, "Μινωϊκή λάρνακα από το Κλήμα Μεσαράς," *ArchEph* 1995, 163–83.

For Linear B, bibliographies and studies continue to appear, presenting new tablets from Chania, joins among the Knossos tablets, and a broader diachronic understanding of the textile industry.[581] The archaeological background of the Knossos tablets and the "final" destruction of the palace both still receive emphasis, but a new study by Weingarten not only discusses how Knossian administrators used seals in general but how one administrator, *A-nu-wi-ko*, possibly a *ra-wa-ke-ta*, used his own seal (KSPI K4, a lentoid depicting a "collared bitch").[582]

Several papers presented at the "Aegean and Orient" and "Crète mycénienne" conferences focused on economic activity in the Final Palatial period, ranging from intra-Aegean trade to trade between the Aegean, the Levant, and Egypt.[583]

POSTPALATIAL CRETE (LM IIIB LATE–SUBMINOAN)

Work on Postpalatial Crete occurs in disparate areas. Individual village sites such as Chamalevri,

Chondros, Kavousi, Mallia, Phaistos, Praisos with its distinctive fabrics, Prinias, Sybritos, and especially the LM IIIC–Subminoan site at Kephala in the Isthmus of Ierapetra continue to shed important light on the architecture, society, and religious practices of this transitional period.[584] In addition to papers given at the "LM III Pottery" conference, other studies have also focused on the ceramic chronology of LM IIIB–C.[585] Religion continues to be another major area of concern, with articles appearing on ritual dining and the character of Postpalatial shrines.[586] While MGUAs remain the dominant religious statuette on Crete at the end of the Bronze Age, what they represent, person or divinity, is not clear; some Archaic wheelmade MGUAs from Cyprus, if they continue the Bronze Age tradition, may shed some light on this problem since they wear signet rings on necklaces, implying persons, not divinities.[587]

Although general surveys of the transitional period between the Bronze Age and Iron Age are still lacking,[588] some work continues at specific sites, especially Kavousi;[589] a 1995 conference in

[581] "Session on Administration and Bureaucracy," in Hägg (supra n. 28) 215–17; E. Sikkenga ed., *Studies in Mycenaean Inscriptions and Dialect 1980–81* (Austin 1997); J. Chadwick et al., *Corpus of Mycenaean Inscriptions from Knossos* III–IV (Cambridge 1997, 1998); G. Bandini, "Proposta di raccordi fra tavolette della seria Ra di Cnosso," *SMEA* 39 (1997) 267–69; E. Hallager and M. Vlasaki, "New Linear B Tablets from Khania," in *Crète mycénienne* 169–74; and, in *Techne*, C.W. Shelmerdine, "Workshops and Record Keeping in the Mycenaean World," 387–95; and B. Burke, "The Organization of Textile Production on Bronze Age Crete," 413–22.

[582] In *Crète mycénienne*: M.R. Popham, "The Final Destruction of the Palace at Knossos," 378–85; L.V. Watrous and H. Blitzer, "Central Crete in LM II–IIIB1," 511–16; and J. Weingarten, "The Sealing Bureaucracy of Mycenaean Knossos," 517–35.

[583] In *Aegean and Orient*: A. Leonard, Jr., "Trade during the Late Helladic III Period," 99–104; and A.E. Killebrew, "Aegean and Aegean-style Material Culture in Canaan during the 14th–12th Centuries B.C.," 159–69. See also K. Demakopoulou, "Crete and the Argolid in the LM II/LH IIB to IIIA1 Periods," in *Crète mycénienne* 101–12; and E.H. Cline, "Amenhotep III, the Aegean, and Anatolia," in D. O'Connor and E.H. Cline eds., *Studies in the Reign of Amenhotep III* (Ann Arbor 1998).

[584] Chamalevri: *AR* 1997–1998, 123. Chondros: L. Platon, "Caractère, morphologie et datation de la bourgade postpalatiale de Képhali Chondrou Viannou," in *Crète mycénienne* 357–73. Kavousi: in *Crète mycénienne*, W.D.E. Coulson, "The Late Minoan IIIC Period on the Kastro at Kavousi," 59–72, and L. Preston Day, "Vronda," 391–406. Mallia: O. Pelon, "Le palais post-palatial à Malia," in *Crète mycénienne* 341–55. Phaistos: E. Fiandra, "Private Houses on the Slope South of the Palace of Phaistos," *8th CretCong* (forthcoming). Praisos: *AR* 1997–1998, 119. In *8th CretCong* (forthcoming): Prinias: R. Giovanni, "Scavi e ricerche a Priniás dal 1992 al 1996." Sybritos: L. Rocchetti, "Σύβριτος/Θρόνος." T. Eliopoulos, "A Preliminary Report

on the Discovery of a Temple Complex of the Dark Ages at Kephala Vasilikis," in V. Karageorghis and N. Stampolidis eds., *Eastern Mediterranean: Cyprus–Dodecanese–Crete, 16th–6th Cent. B.C.* (Athens 1998) 301–13.

[585] In *LM III Pottery*: A. Kanta, "LM IIIB and LM IIIC Pottery Phases," 83–101; and M.S. Mook and W.D.E. Coulson, "The Late Minoan IIIC Pottery from the Kastro at Kavousi," 337–65; and G. Rethemiotakis, "A Chest-shaped Vessel and Other LM IIIC Pottery from Kastelli Pediada," *Crète mycénienne* 407–21; E. Borgna, "Kitchen-ware from LM IIIC Phaistos," *SMEA* 39 (1997) 189–217; and J.B. Rutter, "The Short-Necked Amphora of the Post-palatial Messara," and D. Chatzi-Vallianou and O. Evthymiou, "Κεραμεική από την ακρόπολη Σμαριού," both in *8th CretCong* (forthcoming).

[586] E. Borna, "Food Preparation and Ritual Activity in LM IIIC Crete," and L.P. Day, K.T. Glowacki, and N.L. Klein, "Cooking and Dining in LM IIIC Vronda, Kavousi," both in *8th CretCong* (forthcoming); and A.-L. D'Agata, "The Shrines on the Piazzale dei Sacelli at Ayia Triadha," in *Crète mycénienne* 85–100; and D'Agata, "Changing Patterns in a Minoan and Post-Minoan Sanctuary," in Cavanagh et al. (supra n. 546) 19–26.

[587] V. Karageorghis, *The Coroplastic Art of Ancient Cyprus* 5 (Nicosia 1998) nos. 3–5.

[588] See, however, S. Deger-Jalkotzy, "The Last Mycenaeans and Their Successors Updated," in S. Gitin, A. Mazar, and E. Stern eds., *Mediterranean Peoples in Transition* (*Festschrift T. Dothan*, Jerusalem 1998) 114–23.

[589] Kavousi, in Cavanagh et al. (supra n. 546): W.D.E. Coulson, "The Early Iron Age on the Kastro at Kavousi in East Crete," 40–44; and M. Mook, "Early Iron Age Domestic Architecture," 45–57. Other sites, in *8th CretCong* (forthcoming): N. Cucuzza, "Funzione dei vani nel quartiere geometrico di Festòs"; E. Tsoukala and D. Chatzi-Vallianou, "Πανίδα και διατροφικές συνήθειες στην ακρόπολη Σμαριού"; and A.S. Vasilakis, "Ανασκαφή πρωτογεωμετρικού οικισμού στη Γριά Βίγλα Πηγαϊδακίων–Πόμπιας Καινουργίου."

London focused on post-Minoan (i.e., post-Bronze Age) Crete.[590]

CONCLUSION

It is clear that current research on Neopalatial, Final Palatial, and Postpalatial Crete is not static; important questions are being asked of the evidence, for which the answers are forthcoming—some quickly, and some slowly. If Cretan archaeology of the century now ending has taught us anything, it is that surprising developments are still in store for us.

DEPARTMENT OF CLASSICAL STUDIES
DUKE UNIVERSITY
P.O. BOX 90103
DURHAM, NORTH CAROLINA 27708-0103
PREHAK@DUKE.EDU
JYOUNGER@DUKE.EDU

---

[590] Cavanagh et al. (supra n. 546) passim, and esp. J. Whitley, "From Minoans to Eteocretans," 27–39.

Index

Page numbers in italics refer to illustrations.